PEARSON

COMMON CORE

Literature

GRADE 8

PEARSON

HOBOKEN, NEW JERSEY • BOSTON, MASSACHUSETTS
CHANDLER, ARIZONA • GLENVIEW, ILLINOIS

ISBN-13:   978-0-13-326819-5
ISBN-10:   0-13-326819-5
6 7 8 9 10 11 12 V057 18 17 16 15 14

PEARSON

COMMON CORE

Literature

GRADE 8

PEARSON

HOBOKEN, NEW JERSEY • BOSTON, MASSACHUSETTS
CHANDLER, ARIZONA • GLENVIEW, ILLINOIS

The contributing authors guided the direction and philosophy of Pearson Common Core Literature. They helped to build the pedagogical integrity of the program by contributing content expertise, knowledge of the Common Core State Standards, and support for the shifts in instruction the Common Core will bring. Their knowledge, combined with classroom and professional experience, ensures Pearson Common Core Literature is relevant for both teachers and students.

 **William G. Brozo, Ph.D.,** is a Professor of Literacy in the Graduate School of Education at George Mason University in Fairfax, Virginia. He earned his bachelor's degree from the University of North Carolina and his master's and doctorate from the University of South Carolina. He has taught reading and language arts in the Carolinas and is the author of numerous articles on literacy development for children and young adults. His books include *To Be a Boy, To Be a Reader: Engaging Teen and Preteen Boys in Active Literacy; Readers, Teachers, Learners: Expanding Literacy Across the Content Areas; Content Literacy for Today's Adolescents: Honoring Diversity and Building Competence; Supporting Content Area Literacy with Technology* (Pearson); and *Setting the Pace: A Speed, Comprehension, and Study Skills Program*. His newest book is *RTI and the Adolescent Reader: Responsive Literacy Instruction in Secondary Schools*. As an international consultant, Dr. Brozo has provided technical support to teachers from the Balkans to the Middle East, and he is currently a member of a European Union research grant team developing curriculum and providing adolescent literacy professional development for teachers across Europe.

 **Diane Fettrow** spent the majority of her teaching career in Broward County, Florida, teaching high school English courses and serving as department chair. She also worked as an adjunct instructor at Broward College, Nova Southeastern University, and Florida Atlantic University. After she left the classroom, she served as Secondary Language Arts Curriculum Supervisor for several years, working with more than 50 of the district's high schools, centers, and charter schools. During her time as curriculum supervisor, she served on numerous local and state committees; she also served as Florida's K–12 ELA content representative to the PARCC Model Content Frameworks Rapid Response Feedback Group and the PARCC K–12 and Upper Education Engagement Group. Currently she presents workshops on the Common Core State Standards and is working with Pearson on aligning materials to the CCSS.

 Kelly Gallagher is a full-time English teacher at Magnolia High School in Anaheim, California, where he has taught for twenty-seven years. He is the former co-director of the South Basin Writing Project at California State University, Long Beach, and the author of *Reading Reasons: Motivational Mini-Lessons for Middle and High School; Deeper Reading: Comprehending Challenging Texts, 4–12; Teaching Adolescent Writers;* and *Readicide: How Schools Are Killing Reading and What You Can Do About It*. He is also a principal author of *Prentice Hall Writing Coach* (Pearson, 2012). Kelly's latest book is *Write Like This* (Stenhouse). Follow Kelly on Twitter @KellyGToGo, and visit him at www.kellygallagher.org.

 **Elfrieda "Freddy' Hiebert, Ph.D.,** is President and CEO of TextProject, a nonprofit organization that provides resources to support higher reading levels. She is also a research associate at the University of California, Santa Cruz. Dr. Hiebert received her Ph.D. in Educational Psychology from the University of Wisconsin-Madison. She has worked in the field of early reading acquisition for 45 years, first as a teacher's aide and teacher of primary-level students in California and, subsequently, as a teacher educator and researcher at the universities of Kentucky, Colorado-Boulder, Michigan, and California-Berkeley. Her research addresses how fluency, vocabulary,

and knowledge can be fostered through appropriate texts. Professor Hiebert's research has been published in numerous scholarly journals, and she has authored or edited nine books. Professor Hiebert's model of accessible texts for beginning and struggling readers—TExT—has been used to develop numerous reading programs that are widely used in schools. Dr. Hiebert is the 2008 recipient of the William S. Gray Citation of Merit, awarded by the International Reading Association; is a member of the Reading Hall of Fame; and has chaired a group of early childhood literacy experts who served in an advisory capacity to the CCSS writers.

 Donald J. Leu, Ph.D., is the John and Maria Neag Endowed Chair in Literacy and Technology and holds a joint appointment in Curriculum and Instruction and Educational Psychology in the Neag School of Education at the University of Connecticut. Don is an international authority on literacy education, especially the new skills and strategies required to read, write, and learn with Internet technologies and the best instructional practices that prepare students for these new literacies. He is a member of the Reading Hall of Fame, a Past President of the National Reading Conference, and a former member of the Board of Directors of the International Reading Association. Don is a Principal Investigator on a number of federal research grants, and his work has been funded by the U.S. Department of Education, the National Science Foundation, and the Bill and Melinda Gates Foundation, among others. He recently edited the *Handbook of Research on New Literacies* (Erlbaum, 2008).

 **Ernest Morrell, Ph.D.,** is a professor of English Education at Teachers College, Columbia University, and the president-elect of the National Council of Teachers of English (NCTE). He is also the Director of Teachers College's Harlem-based Institute for Urban and Minority Education (IUME). Dr. Morrell was an award-winning high school English teacher in California, and he now works with teachers and schools across the country to infuse multicultural literature, youth popular culture, and media production into standards-based literacy curricula and after-school programs. He is the author of nearly 100 articles and book chapters as well as five books, including *Critical Media Pedagogy: Achievement, Production, and Justice in City Schools* and *Linking Literacy and Popular Culture*. In his spare time he coaches youth sports and writes poems and plays.

 Karen Wixson, Ph.D., is Dean of the School of Education at the University of North Carolina, Greensboro. She has published widely in the areas of literacy curriculum, instruction, and assessment. Dr. Wixson has been an advisor to the National Research Council and helped develop the National Assessment of Educational Progress (NAEP) reading tests. She is a former member of the IRA Board of Directors and co-chair of the IRA Commission on RTI. Recently, Dr. Wixson served on the English Language Arts Work Team that was part of the Common Core State Standards Initiative.

 Grant Wiggins, Ed.D., is the President of Authentic Education in Hopewell, New Jersey. He earned his Ed.D. from Harvard University and his B.A. from St. John's College in Annapolis. Grant consults with schools, districts, and state education departments on a variety of reform matters; organizes conferences and workshops; and develops print materials and Web resources on curricular change. He is perhaps best known for being the co-author, with Jay McTighe, of *Understanding by Design* and *The Understanding by Design Handbook,* the award-winning and highly successful materials on curriculum published by ASCD.

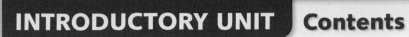

COMMON CORE FOUNDATIONS

COMMON CORE STATE STANDARDS

The following standards are introduced in this unit and revisited throughout the program.

Reading Literature

2. Determine a theme or central idea of a text and analyze its development over the course of the text, including its relationship to the characters, setting, and plot; provide an objective summary of the text.

10. By the end of the year, read and comprehend literature, including stories, dramas, and poems, at the high end of grades 6–8 text complexity band independently and proficiently.

Reading Informational Text

2. Determine a central idea of a text and analyze its development over the course of the text, including its relationship to supporting ideas; provide an objective summary of the text.

8. Delineate and evaluate the argument and specific claims in a text, assessing whether the reasoning is sound and the evidence is relevant and sufficient; recognize when irrelevant evidence is introduced.

Writing

1. Write arguments to support claims with clear reasons and relevant evidence.

2. Write informative/explanatory texts to examine a topic and convey ideas, concepts, and information through the selection, organization, and analysis of relevant content.

7. Conduct short research projects to answer a question (including a self-generated question), drawing on several sources and generating additional related, focused questions that allow for multiple avenues of exploration.

8. Gather relevant information from multiple print and digital sources, using search terms effectively; assess the credibility and accuracy of each source; and quote or paraphrase the data and conclusions of others while avoiding plagiarism and following a standard format for citation.

Additional standards addressed in these workshops:

Reading Informational Text
9

Writing
1.a, 1.b, 1.e, 2.a, 2.c, 2.f

Language
2.b, 6

UNIT 1 Can all conflicts be resolved?

DIGITAL ASSETS KEY

These digital resources, as well as audio and the Online Writer's Notebook, can be found at **pearsonrealize.com**.

🖥 Interactive Whiteboard Activities

🌐 Virtual Tour

📋 Close Reading Notebook

📹 Video

🔍 Close Reading Tool for Annotating Texts

Ⓖ Grammar Tutorials

📚 Online Text Set

UNIT 1 · Unit at a Glance

■ READ

Text Analysis
Plot
Character Traits
Point of View
Theme
Comparing Characters of Different Eras
Setting
Oral Tradition
Style
Comparisons
Dialogue

Comprehension
Make Predictions
Compare and Contrast
Make Inferences

Language Study
Greek root -scope-
Latin suffix -ity
Latin root -spec-
Latin prefix per-

Conventions
Nouns
Pronouns
Adjectives and Adverbs
Principal Parts of Verbs

Language Study Workshop
Using a Dictionary and Thesaurus

■ DISCUSS

Presentation of Ideas
Oral Response

Comprehension and Collaboration
Radio Broadcast
Panel Discussion

Responding to Text
Group Discussion
Panel Discussion
One-on-One Discussion
Class Discussion
Debate

Speaking and Listening Workshop
Delivering a Narrative Presentation

■ RESEARCH

Research and Technology
Summary of an Article

Investigate the Topic: Human vs. Machine
The Rise of "Smart" Machines
The Machine Age
Watson the Computer
Neurorobotics
Androids

■ WRITE

Writing to Sources
New Ending
Character Profile
Dialogue
Comparison of Works
Explanatory Essay
Argumentative Essay
Evaluation
Diary Entry
Comparison-and-Contrast Essay
Autobiographical Narrative

Writing Process Workshop
Narrative Text: Autobiographical Essay
  Sentence Fluency: Revising Sentences
   by Combining With Conjunctions
  Conventions: Revising for Pronoun-Antecedent
   Agreement

■ **UNIT VOCABULARY**

Academic Vocabulary appears in *blue*.

Introducing the Big Question   *argument, compromise, injury, insecurity, interact, irritate, mislead, negotiate, oppose, reaction, solution, stalemate, victorious, viewpoint, violence*

Raymond's Run   *prodigy, liable, reputation, pageant, periscope, gesture*

The Tell-Tale Heart   *cunningly, resolved, stealthily, vex, audacity, derision*

Flowers for Algernon   *deceive, refute, intellectual, naïveté, deterioration, introspective*

The Story-Teller   *persistent, inevitable, conviction, suppressed, immensely, assail*

The Finish of Patsy Barnes; The Drummer Boy of Shiloh   *compulsory, meager, diplomatic, immortality, resolute, argument, interact, negotiate, viewpoint*

Who Can Replace a Man?   *deficiency, erosion, ravaged, interactions, reaction, viewpoint*

John Henry   *region, aspects, elements*

Julie and the Turing Test   *software, artificial intelligence, wired, distinctive, identify, capable*

"The Good News, Dave, . . ."   *illogical, identify, validity*

Robots Get a Feel for the World at USC Virterbi   *tactile, algorithm, thermal, beneficial, incorporate, imitate*

***from* The Measure of a Man *from* Star Trek: The Next Generation**   *hostile, contention, condemn, technique, evaluation, arguments*

■ **COMMON CORE STATE STANDARDS**

For the full wording of the standards, see the standards chart following the Contents pages.

Reading Literature
RL.8.1, RL.8.2, RL.8.3, RL.8.4, RL.8.6, RL.8.7, RL.8.9, RL.8.10

Reading Informational Text
RI.8.1, RI.8.2, RI.8.4, RI.8.5, RI.8.9, RI.8.10

Writing
W.8.1, W.8.1.a–e, W.8.2, W.8.2.b, W.8.3, W.8.3.a–e, W.8.4, W.8.5, W.8.6, W.8.7, W.8.8, W.8.9, W.8.9.a, W.8.10

Speaking and Listening
SL.8.1, SL.8.1.a–d, SL.8.2, SL.8.4, SL.8.6

Language
L.8.1, L.8.2, L.8.2.c, L.8.3, L.8.4, L.8.4.b–d, L.8.5, L.8.5.b, L.8.5.c, L.8.6

PART 3
TEXT SET DEVELOPING INSIGHT

BELONGING TO A PLACE

PART 4
DEMONSTRATING INDEPENDENCE

Independent Reading

ONLINE TEXT SET

DIGITAL ASSETS KEY

These digital resources, as well as audio and the Online Writer's Notebook, can be found at **pearsonrealize.com**.

- Interactive Whiteboard Activities
- Virtual Tour
- Close Reading Notebook
- Video
- Close Reading Tool for Annotating Texts
- Grammar Tutorials
- Online Text Set

■ UNIT VOCABULARY

Academic Vocabulary appears in *blue*.

Introducing the Big Question   *accumulate, challenge, decision, development, discrimination, explanation, exploration, factor, global, inequality, quality, quantity, reveal, statistics, valuable*

from **Harriet Tubman: Conductor on the Underground Railroad**   *invariably, fugitives, incentive, dispel, mutinous, bleak*

from **Always to Remember: The Vision of Maya Ying Lin**   *authorized, criteria, harmonious, anonymously, eloquent, unanimous*

The Trouble With Television   *constructive, diverts, passively, pervading, trivial, skeptically*

Science and the Sense of Wonder   *exultantly, awed, cataclysm, radiation, conceivable, contraction*

Forest Fire; The Season's Curmudgeon Sees the Light; Why Leaves Turn Color in the Fall   *evacuees, tenacious, consoling, contemplation, predisposed, capricious, argument, decision, emphasize, influence*

from **Travels with Charley**   *omens, inexplicable, desolate, intensify, perceive, anticipate*

Gentleman of Río en Medio   *negotiation, preliminary, descendants, influence, accurate, methods*

Choice: A Tribute to Martin Luther King, Jr.   *brutal, disinherit, revolutionary, cite, annotated, cause-and-effect*

Tears of Autumn   *affluence, radical, degrading, significance, tradition, techniques*

from **I Know Why the Caged Bird Sings**   *valid, intolerant, enchantment, community, role, maintain*

Study Finds Americans Increasingly Rooted   *assumption, embedded, disruption, statistics, contrasting, evidence*

Relationships to Place   *sources, categories, support*

■ COMMON CORE STATE STANDARDS

For the full wording of the standards, see the standards chart following the Contents pages.

Reading Literature
RL.8.1, RL.8.2, RL.8.3, RL.8.4, RL.8.10

Reading Informational Text
RI.8.1, RI.8.2, RI.8.3, RI.8.4, RI.8.5, RI.8.6, RI.8.7, RI.8.8, RI.8.9, RI.8.10

Writing
W.8.1, W.8.1.a, W.8.1.b, W.8.1.e, W.8.2, W.8.2.a–f, W.8.3, W.8.3.a–e, W.8.4, W.8.5, W.8.6, W.8.7, W.8.9, W.8.9.b

Speaking and Listening
SL.8.1, SL.8.1.a–d, SL.8.2, SL.8.3, SL.8.4, SL.8.5, SL.8.6

Language
L.8.1, L.8.1.b–d, L.8.2, L.8.2.b, L.8.2.c, L.8.3, L.8.3.a, L.8.4, L.8.4.a–c, L.8.5, L.8.5.a–c, L.8.6

UNIT 3   What is the secret to reaching someone with words?

PART 3
TEXT SET DEVELOPING INSIGHT

GENERATIONS

PART 4
DEMONSTRATING INDEPENDENCE

Independent Reading

ONLINE TEXT SET
OPEN LETTER
from **My Own True Name**
Pat Mora

POEM
Your World
Georgia Douglas Johnson

REFLECTIVE ESSAY
Words to Sit in, Like Chairs
Naomi Shihab Nye

DIGITAL ASSETS KEY

These digital resources, as well as audio
and the Online Writer's Notebook, can
be found at **pearsonrealize.com**.

- Interactive Whiteboard Activities
- Virtual Tour
- Close Reading Notebook
- Video
- Close Reading Tool for
  Annotating Texts
- **G** Grammar Tutorials
- Online Text Set

UNIT 3 Unit at a Glance

■ **UNIT VOCABULARY**

Academic Vocabulary appears in *blue*.

Introducing the Big Question   *benefit, connection, cultural, experience, express, feedback, individuality, inform, meaningful, media, misunderstood, relevant, sensory, significance, valid*

Silver; Ring Out, Wild Bells; Cat!; Thumbprint   *scampering, strife, spite, flatterer, singularity, imprint*

The Sky Is Low, the Clouds Are Mean; Concrete Mixers; Harlem Night Song; The City Is So Big   *rut, debates, ponderous, urban, roam, dew*

The New Colossus; Blow, Blow, Thou Winter Wind; Paul Revere's Ride   *exiles, yearning, ingratitude, somber, defiance, peril*

Grandma Ling; your little voice / Over the wires came leaping; New World; January   *tongue, jostling, impertinently, exquisite, pollen, recede*

The Road Not Taken; O Captain! My Captain!   *diverged, exulting, connection, influence, objective, relevant*

Old Man; For My Sister Molly Who in the Fifties   *legacy, aromas, remote, reinforce, pattern, conveyed*

The Medicine Bag   *authentic, procession, unseemly, represents, initial, traditions*

Cub Pilot on the Mississippi   *malicious, judicious, confronted, adjust, opposing, relevant*

Thank You, M'am   *contact, presentable, barren, imply, insight, factor*

Tutoring Benefits Seniors' Health, Students' Skills   *buoyed, promising, engaged, benefit, valid, support*

The Return of the Multi-Generational Family Household   *demographic, resources, incentives, trend, percentage, statistics*

■ **COMMON CORE STATE STANDARDS**

For the full wording of the standards, see the standards chart following the Contents pages.

Reading Literature
  RL.8.1, RL.8.2, RL.8.3, RL.8.4, RL.8.5, RL.8.9, RL.8.10

Reading Informational Text
  RI.8.1, RI.8.2, RI.8.3, RI.8.4, RI.8.5, RI.8.7, RI.8.10

Writing
  W.8.1, W.8.1.a–e, W.8.2, W.8.2.a–f, W.8.3, W.8.3.a–c, W.8.3.e, W.8.4, W.8.5, W.8.6, W.8.7, W.8.8, W.8.9, W.8.9.a

Speaking and Listening
  SL.8.1, SL.8.1.a–d, SL.8.2, SL.8.3, SL.8.4, SL.8.5, SL.8.6

Language
  L.8.1, L.8.1.c, L.8.1.d, L.8.2, L.8.2.a–c, L.8.3, L.8.4, L.8.4.a–d, L.8.5, L.8.5.a–c, L.8.6

UNIT 4   Is it our differences or our similarities that matter most?

DIGITAL ASSETS KEY

These digital resources, as well as audio and the Online Writer's Notebook, can be found at **pearsonrealize.com**.

🖥 Interactive Whiteboard Activities

🌐 Virtual Tour

📑 Close Reading Notebook

▶️ Video

🔍 Close Reading Tool for Annotating Texts

Ⓖ Grammar Tutorials

📚 Online Text Set

UNIT 4   Unit at a Glance

■ **READ**

Text Analysis
Dialogue
Character's Motivation
Setting and Character
Comparing Adaptations to Originals
Plot and Conflict
Diary
Narrative Pacing
Supporting Visuals
Claims and Evidence
Author's Purpose

Comprehension
Cause and Effect
Draw Conclusions

Language Study
Greek suffix -ist
Latin prefix in-
Latin suffix -ory

Conventions
Prepositions and Prepositional Phrases
Participial and Infinitive Phrases
Clauses

Language Study Workshop
Borrowed and Foreign Words

■ **DISCUSS**

Presentation of Ideas
Guided Tour
Debate

Responding to Text
Group Discussion
Partner Discussion
Panel Discussion
Small Group Discussion
Quick Write and Discuss

Speaking and Listening Workshop
Evaluating Media Messages

■ **RESEARCH**

Research and Technology
Bulletin Board Display

Investigate the Topic: The Holocaust
Holocaust Survivors
Survival in Print
Historical Causes
Resistance
An International Community
Liberators

■ **WRITE**

Writing to Sources
Diary Entries
Film Review
Public Service Announcement
Explanatory Essay
Argumentative Essay
First-Person Narrative
Analytical Essay
Informative Essay
Letter to the Editor
Imaginary Interview
Play
Comparison-and-Contrast Essay

Writing Process Workshop
Explanatory Text: Cause-and-Effect Essay
    Organization: Organize Details
    Conventions: Revising to Combine Sentences
        Using Gerunds and Participles

■ UNIT VOCABULARY

Academic Vocabulary appears in *blue*.

Introducing the Big Question   *assumption, class, common, discriminate, distinguish, divide, generalization, identify, judge, represent, separate, superficial, sympathy, tolerance, unify*

The Diary of Anne Frank, Act I   *conspicuous, tension, resent, insufferable, bewildered, fatalist*

The Diary of Anne Frank, Act II   *inarticulate, apprehension, blackmail, forlorn, intuition, ineffectually*

The Governess   *inferior, discrepancies, discharged, satisfactory, lax, guileless*

The Ninny   *account, carelessness, spineless, timidly, connection, distinguish, influence, judge*

Kindertransport   *callous, morbid, monumental, motive, distinguishes, evidence*

***from* Anne Frank: The Diary of a Young Girl**   *enhance, emigrated, evading, observations, investigate, precise*

***from* Anne Frank Remembered**   *refugee, chaos, succumbed, perception, transfer, document*

***from* Night**   *protruded, vulnerable, delirious, respond, credible, evidence*

***from* Remarks on a Visit to Buchenwald**   *aspirations, invoke, denigrate, support, condition, opinion*

Local Holocaust Survivors and Liberators Attend Opening Event for Exhibition   *liberators, testimonies, genocides, contrast, argument, primary sources*

■ COMMON CORE STATE STANDARDS

▸For the full wording of the standards, see the standards chart following the Contents pages.

Reading Literature
RL.8.1, RL.8.2, RL.8.3, RL.8.4, RL.8.5, RL.8.6, RL.8.7, RL.8.9, RL.8.10

Reading Informational Text
RI.8.1, RI.8.2, RI.8.3, RI.8.5, RI.8.6. RI.8.7, RI.8.8, RI.8.10

Writing
W.8.1, W.8.1.a, W.8.1.b, W.8.1.d, W.8.1.e, W.8.2, W.8.2.a–f, W.8.3, W.8.3.a, W.8.3.d, W.8.3.e, W.8.4, W.8.5, W.8.7, W.8.8, W.8.9, W.8.9.a, W.8.9.b, W.8.10

Speaking and Listening
SL.8.1, SL.8.1.a, SL.8.2, SL.8.3, SL.8.4, SL.8.5, SL.8.6

Language
L.8.1, L.8.1.a, L.8.2, L.8.2.a, L.8.2.c, L.8.4, L.8.4.a, L.8.4.b, L.8.4.d, L.8.5, L.8.5.a, L.8.5.c, L.8.6

PART 1
SETTING EXPECTATIONS

PART 2
TEXT ANALYSIS GUIDED EXPLORATION

HEROES AND TRADITIONS

DIGITAL ASSETS KEY

These digital resources, as well as audio and the Online Writer's Notebook, can be found at **pearsonrealize.com**.

- Interactive Whiteboard Activities
- Virtual Tour
- Close Reading Notebook
- Video
- Close Reading Tool for Annotating Texts
- **G** Grammar Tutorials
- Online Text Set

UNIT 5   Unit at a Glance

■ READ

Text Analysis
Mythology
Oral Tradition
Cultural Context
Author's Influences
Comparing Heroic Characters
Oratory
Forms of Poetry
Word Choice and Tone
Style
Persuasive Techniques
Claims and Evidence

Comprehension
Summarize
Purpose for Reading

Language Study
Latin root -sacr-
Suffix -eer
Latin root -grat-
Latin root -aud-

Conventions
Basic Sentence Structures
Commas and Semicolons
Ellipses and Dashes
Capitalization

Language Study Workshop
Figurative Language

■ DISCUSS

Presentation of Ideas
Oral Presentation

Comprehension and Collaboration
Storytelling Workshop

Responding to Text
Partner Discussion
Panel Discussion
Class Discussion
Group Discussion

Speaking and Listening Workshop
Delivering a Persuasive Speech Using
Multimedia

■ RESEARCH

Research and Technology
Letter
Research Article

Investigate the Topic: Freedom Fighters
Civil Rights Leaders
Underground Railroad
The Abolitionists
Thurgood Marshall's Contributions
   to Civil Rights
The Women's Movement
The Grape Boycott
Henry David Thoreau

■ WRITE

Writing to Sources
Myth
Critical Analysis
Research Proposal
Persuasive Speech
Essay
Informative Essay
Narrative
Analysis
Argument
Poem
Autobiographical Narrative

Writing Process Workshop
Argument: Problem-and-Solution Essay
   Voice: Using Voice in an Argumentative Piece
   Conventions: Revising to Correct Comparative
      and Superlative Forms

■ **UNIT VOCABULARY**

Academic Vocabulary appears in *blue*.

Introducing the Big Question *accomplishments, admirably, aspects, bravery, courage, cultural, emphasize, endure, exaggerate, imitate, influence, outdated, overcome, suffering, symbolize*

Coyote Steals the Sun and Moon *sacred, pestering, lagged, shriveled, pursuit, curiosity*

Chicoria *self-confident, cordially, haughty*

from **The People, Yes,** *straddling, cyclone, mutineers*

from **Out of the Dust** *feuding, spindly, drought, grateful, sparse, rickety*

An Episode of War *winced, audible, compelled, tumultuous, contempt, disdainfully*

Davy Crockett's Dream; Paul Bunyan of the North Woods; Invocation *from* **John Brown's Body** *kindled, shanties, commotion, subdued, arrogant, cultural, endure, influence, quality*

from **The American Dream** *paradoxes, devoid, perish, observation, distinguish, evidence*

Runagate Runagate *beckoning, shackles, anguish, objective, intensify, elements*

Emancipation *from* **Lincoln: A Photobiography** *alienate, compensate, humiliating, citing, contribute, develop*

Harriet Beecher Stowe *complacent, transfigured, result, response, overall*

Brown vs. Board of Education *predominantly, deliberating, oppressed, revealed, elements, advocate*

On Woman's Right to Suffrage *mockery, derived, rebellion, discriminate, emphasizing, granted*

from **Address to the Commonwealth Club of San Francisco** *implements, exploit, infamy, expert, promote, investigate*

Nonviolence Tree *convey, civil, valid*

■ **COMMON CORE STATE STANDARDS**

For the full wording of the standards, see the standards chart following the Contents pages.

Reading Literature
RL.8.1, RL.8.2, RL.8.3, RL.8.4, RL.8.6, RL.8.7, RL.8.9, RL.8.10

Reading Informational Text
RI.8.1, RI.8.2, RI.8.3, RI.8.4, RI.8.5, RI.8.6, RI.8.7, RI.8.8, RI.8.9, RI.8.10

Writing
W.8.1, W.8.1.a–e, W.8.2, W.8.2.a, W.8.2.b, W.8.2.e, W.8.2.f, W.8.3, W.8.3.a–e, W.8.4, W.8.7, W.8.8, W.8.9, W.8.9.a, W.8.9.b

Speaking and Listening
SL.8.1, SL.8.1.a–d, SL.8.2, SL.8.4, SL.8.5, SL.8.6

Language
L.8.1, L.8.1.b, L.8.2, L.8.2.a–c, L.8.4, L.8.4.b, L.8.5, L.8.5.a–c, L.8.6

Range of Reading

ONLINE LITERATURE LIBRARY

Highlighted selections are found in
the **Online Literature Library (OLL)** in
the Online Student Edition.

Informational Text—Literary Nonfiction

FUNCTIONAL TEXTS

LITERATURE IN CONTEXT—
READING IN THE CONTENT AREAS

MEDIA

ONLINE LITERATURE LIBRARY

Highlighted selections are found in
the **Online Literature Library (OLL)** in
the Online Student Edition.

Features and Workshops

ONLINE TEXT SETS

These selections can be found in the **Online Literature Library** in the Online Student Edition

Unit 1

AUTOMBIOGRAPHY
from **An American Childhood**
Annie Dillard

NARRATIVE ESSAY
Baseball
Lionel G. García

SHORT STORY
The White Umbrella
Gish Jen

Unit 2

SHORT STORY
The 11:59
Patricia C. McKissack

MEMOIR
A Glow in the Dark *from*
Woodsong
Gary Paulsen

MAGAZINE ARTICLE
**Sun Suckers and Moon
Cursers**
Richard and Joyce Wolkomir

Unit 3

OPEN LETTER
from **My Own True Name**
Pat Mora

POEM
Your World
Georgia Douglas Johnson

REFLECTIVE ESSAY
Words to Sit in, Like Chairs
Naomi Shihab Nye

Unit 4

FICTION
Old Ben
Jesse Stuart

POEM
Snake on the Etowah
David Bottoms

NARRATIVE ESSAY
Vanishing Species
Bailey White

Unit 5

POEM
Ellis Island
Joseph Bruchac

LETTER
from **Steinbeck: A Life in
Letters**
John Steinbeck

SHORT STORY
Up the Slide
Jack London

The Common Core State Standards will prepare you to succeed in college and your future career. They are separated into four sections— Reading (Literature and Informational Text), Writing, Speaking and Listening, and Language. Beginning each section, the College and Career Readiness Anchor Standards define what you need to achieve by the end of high school. The grade-specific standards that follow define what you need to know by the end of your current grade level.

Common Core Reading Standards

College and Career Readiness Anchor Standards

Key Ideas and Details

1. Read closely to determine what the text says explicitly and to make logical inferences from it; cite specific textual evidence when writing or speaking to support conclusions drawn from the text.

2. Determine central ideas or themes of a text and analyze their development; summarize the key supporting details and ideas.

3. Analyze how and why individuals, events, and ideas develop and interact over the course of a text.

Craft and Structure

4. Interpret words and phrases as they are used in a text, including determining technical, connotative, and figurative meanings, and analyze how specific word choices shape meaning or tone.

5. Analyze the structure of texts, including how specific sentences, paragraphs, and larger portions of the text (e.g., a section, chapter, scene, or stanza) relate to each other and the whole.

6. Assess how point of view or purpose shapes the content and style of a text.

Integration of Knowledge and Ideas

7. Integrate and evaluate content presented in diverse formats and media, including visually and quantitatively, as well as in words.

8. Delineate and evaluate the argument and specific claims in a text, including the validity of the reasoning as well as the relevance and sufficiency of the evidence.

9. Analyze how two or more texts address similar themes or topics in order to build knowledge or to compare the approaches the authors take.

Range of Reading and Level of Text Complexity

10. Read and comprehend complex literary and informational texts independently and proficiently.

Grade 8 Reading Standards for Literature

Key Ideas and Details

1. Cite the textual evidence that most strongly supports an analysis of what the text says explicitly as well as inferences drawn from the text.

2. Determine a theme or central idea of a text and analyze its development over the course of the text, including its relationship to the characters, setting, and plot; provide an objective summary of the text.

3. Analyze how particular lines of dialogue or incidents in a story or drama propel the action, reveal aspects of a character, or provoke a decision.

Craft and Structure

4. Determine the meaning of words and phrases as they are used in a text, including figurative and connotative meanings; analyze the impact of specific word choices on meaning and tone, including analogies or allusions to other texts.

5. Compare and contrast the structure of two or more texts and analyze how the differing structure of each text contributes to its meaning and style.

6. Analyze how differences in the points of view of the characters and the audience or reader (e.g., created through the use of dramatic irony) create such effects as suspense or humor.

Integration of Knowledge and Ideas

7. Analyze the extent to which a filmed or live production of a story or drama stays faithful to or departs from the text or script, evaluating the choices made by the director or actors.

8. (Not applicable to literature)

9. Analyze how a modern work of fiction draws on themes, patterns of events, or character types from myths, traditional stories, or religious works such as the Bible, including describing how the material is rendered new.

Range of Reading and Level of Text Complexity

10. By the end of the year, read and comprehend literature, including stories, dramas, and poems, at the high end of grades 6–8 text complexity band independently and proficiently.

Grade 8 Reading Standards for Informational Text

Key Ideas and Details

1. Cite the textual evidence that most strongly supports an analysis of what the text says explicitly as well as inferences drawn from the text.

2. Determine a central idea of a text and analyze its development over the course of the text, including its relationship to supporting ideas; provide an objective summary of the text.

3. Analyze how a text makes connections among and distinctions between individuals, ideas, or events (e.g., through comparisons, analogies, or categories).

Craft and Structure

4. Determine the meaning of words and phrases as they are used in a text, including figurative, connotative, and technical meanings; analyze the impact of specific word choices on meaning and tone, including analogies or allusions to other texts.

5. Analyze in detail the structure of a specific paragraph in a text, including the role of particular sentences in developing and refining a key concept.

6. Determine an author's point of view or purpose in a text and analyze how the author acknowledges and responds to conflicting evidence or viewpoints.

Integration of Knowledge and Ideas

7. Evaluate the advantages and disadvantages of using different mediums (e.g., print or digital text, video, multimedia) to present a particular topic or idea.

8. Delineate and evaluate the argument and specific claims in a text, assessing whether the reasoning is sound and the evidence is relevant and sufficient; recognize when irrelevant evidence is introduced.

9. Analyze a case in which two or more texts provide conflicting information on the same topic and identify where the texts disagree on matters of fact or interpretation.

Range of Reading and Level of Text Complexity

10. By the end of the year, read and comprehend literary nonfiction at the high end of the grades 6–8 text complexity band independently and proficiently.

Common Core Writing Standards

College and Career Readiness Anchor Standards

Text Types and Purposes

1. Write arguments to support claims in an analysis of substantive topics or texts, using valid reasoning and relevant and sufficient evidence.

2. Write informative/explanatory texts to examine and convey complex ideas and information clearly and accurately through the effective selection, organization, and analysis of content.

3. Write narratives to develop real or imagined experiences or events using effective technique, well-chosen details, and well-structured event sequences.

Production and Distribution of Writing

4. Produce clear and coherent writing in which the development, organization, and style are appropriate to task, purpose, and audience.

5. Develop and strengthen writing as needed by planning, revising, editing, rewriting, or trying a new approach.

6. Use technology, including the Internet, to produce and publish writing and to interact and collaborate with others.

Research to Build and Present Knowledge

7. Conduct short as well as more sustained research projects based on focused questions, demonstrating understanding of the subject under investigation.

8. Gather relevant information from multiple print and digital sources, assess the credibility and accuracy of each source, and integrate the information while avoiding plagiarism.

9. Draw evidence from literary or informational texts to support analysis, reflection, and research.

Range of Writing

10. Write routinely over extended time frames (time for research, reflection, and revision) and shorter time frames (a single sitting or a day or two) for a range of tasks, purposes, and audiences.

Grade 8 Writing Standards

Text Types and Purposes

1. Write arguments to support claims with clear reasons and relevant evidence.

   a. Introduce claim(s), acknowledge and distinguish the claim(s) from alternate or opposing claims, and organize the reasons and evidence logically.

   b. Support claim(s) with logical reasoning and relevant evidence, using accurate, credible sources and demonstrating an understanding of the topic or text.

   c. Use words, phrases, and clauses to create cohesion and clarify the relationships among claim(s), counterclaims, reasons, and evidence.

   d. Establish and maintain a formal style.

   e. Provide a concluding statement or section that follows from and supports the argument presented.

2. Write informative/explanatory texts to examine a topic and convey ideas, concepts, and information through the selection, organization, and analysis of relevant content.

   a. Introduce a topic clearly, previewing what is to follow; organize ideas, concepts, and information into broader categories; include formatting (e.g., headings), graphics (e.g., charts, tables), and multimedia when useful to aiding comprehension.

   b. Develop the topic with relevant, well-chosen facts, definitions, concrete details, quotations, or other information and examples.

   c. Use appropriate and varied transitions to create cohesion and clarify the relationships among ideas and concepts.

   d. Use precise language and domain-specific vocabulary to inform about or explain the topic.

   e. Establish and maintain a formal style.

   f. Provide a concluding statement or section that follows from and supports the information or explanation presented.

3. Write narratives to develop real or imagined experiences or events using effective technique, relevant descriptive details, and well-structured event sequences.

   a. Engage and orient the reader by establishing a context and point of view and introducing a narrator and/or characters; organize an event sequence that unfolds naturally and logically.

   b. Use narrative techniques, such as dialogue, pacing, description, and reflection, to develop experiences, events, and/or characters.

   c. Use a variety of transition words, phrases, and clauses to convey sequence, signal shifts from one time frame or setting to another, and show the relationships among experiences and events.

   d. Use precise words and phrases, relevant descriptive details, and sensory language to capture the action and convey experiences and events.

   e. Provide a conclusion that follows from and reflects on the narrated experiences or events.

Production and Distribution of Writing

4. Produce clear and coherent writing in which the development, organization, and style are appropriate to task, purpose, and audience.

5. With some guidance and support from peers and adults, develop and strengthen writing as needed by planning, revising, editing, rewriting, or trying a new approach, focusing on how well purpose and audience have been addressed.

6. Use technology, including the Internet, to produce and publish writing and present the relationships between information and ideas efficiently as well as to interact and collaborate with others.

Research to Build and Present Knowledge

7. Conduct short research projects to answer a question (including a self-generated question), drawing on several sources and generating additional related, focused questions that allow for multiple avenues of exploration.

8. Gather relevant information from multiple print and digital sources, using search terms effectively; assess the credibility and accuracy of each source; and quote or paraphrase the data and conclusions of others while avoiding plagiarism and following a standard format for citation.

9. Draw evidence from literary or informational texts to support analysis, reflection, and research.

   a. Apply *grade 8 Reading standards* to literature (e.g., "Analyze how a modern work of fiction draws on themes, patterns of events, or character types from myths, traditional stories, or religious works such as the Bible, including describing how the material is rendered new").

   b. Apply *grade 8 Reading standards* to literary nonfiction (e.g., "Delineate and evaluate the argument and specific claims in a text, assessing whether the reasoning is sound and the evidence is relevant and sufficient; recognize when irrelevant evidence is introduced").

Range of Writing

10. Write routinely over extended time frames (time for research, reflection, and revision) and shorter time frames (a single sitting or a day or two) for a range of discipline-specific tasks, purposes, and audiences.

Common Core Speaking and Listening Standards

College and Career Readiness Anchor Standards

Comprehension and Collaboration

1. Prepare for and participate effectively in a range of conversations and collaborations with diverse partners, building on others' ideas and expressing their own clearly and persuasively.

2. Integrate and evaluate information presented in diverse media and formats, including visually, quantitatively, and orally.

3. Evaluate a speaker's point of view, reasoning, and use of evidence and rhetoric.

Presentation of Knowledge and Ideas

4. Present information, findings, and supporting evidence such that listeners can follow the line of reasoning and the organization, development, and style are appropriate to task, purpose, and audience.

5. Make strategic use of digital media and visual displays of data to express information and enhance understanding of presentations.

6. Adapt speech to a variety of contexts and communicative tasks, demonstrating command of formal English when indicated or appropriate.

Grade 8 Speaking and Listening Standards

Comprehension and Collaboration

1. Engage effectively in a range of collaborative discussions (one-on-one, in groups, and teacher-led) with diverse partners on *grade 8 topics, texts, and issues*, building on others' ideas and expressing their own clearly.

    a. Come to discussions prepared, having read or researched material under study; explicitly draw on that preparation by referring to evidence on the topic, text, or issue to probe and reflect on ideas under discussion.

    b. Follow rules for collegial discussions and decision-making, track progress toward specific goals and deadlines, and define individual roles as needed.

    c. Pose questions that connect the ideas of several speakers and respond to others' questions and comments with relevant evidence, observations, and ideas.

    d. Acknowledge new information expressed by others, and, when warranted, qualify or justify their own views in light of the evidence presented.

2. Analyze the purpose of information presented in diverse media and formats (e.g., visually, quantitatively, orally) and evaluate the motives (e.g., social, commercial, political) behind its presentation.

3. Delineate a speaker's argument and specific claims, evaluating the soundness of the reasoning and relevance and sufficiency of the evidence and identifying when irrelevant evidence is introduced.

Presentation of Knowledge and Ideas

4. Present claims and findings, emphasizing salient points in a focused, coherent manner with relevant evidence, sound valid reasoning, and well-chosen details; use appropriate eye contact, adequate volume, and clear pronunciation.

5. Integrate multimedia and visual displays into presentations to clarify information, strengthen claims and evidence, and add interest.

6. Adapt speech to a variety of contexts and tasks, demonstrating command of formal English when indicated or appropriate. (See grade 8 Language standards 1 and 3 for specific expectations.)

Common Core Language Standards

College and Career Readiness Anchor Standards

Conventions of Standard English

1. Demonstrate command of the conventions of standard English grammar and usage when writing or speaking.

2. Demonstrate command of the conventions of standard English capitalization, punctuation, and spelling when writing.

Knowledge of Language

3. Apply knowledge of language to understand how language functions in different contexts, to make effective choices for meaning or style, and to comprehend more fully when reading or listening.

Vocabulary Acquisition and Use

4. Determine or clarify the meaning of unknown and multiple-meaning words and phrases by using context clues, analyzing meaningful word parts, and consulting general and specialized reference materials, as appropriate.

5. Demonstrate understanding of figurative language, word relationships, and nuances in word meanings.

6. Acquire and use accurately a range of general academic and domain-specific words and phrases sufficient for reading, writing, speaking, and listening at the college and career readiness level; demonstrate independence in gathering vocabulary knowledge when considering a word or phrase important to comprehension or expression.

Grade 8 Language Standards

Conventions of Standard English

1. Demonstrate command of the conventions of standard English grammar and usage when writing or speaking.
   a. Explain the function of verbals (gerunds, participles, infinitives) in general and their function in particular sentences.
   b. Form and use verbs in the active and passive voice.
   c. Form and use verbs in the indicative, imperative, interrogative, conditional, and subjunctive mood.
   d. Recognize and correct inappropriate shifts in verb voice and mood.

2. Demonstrate command of the conventions of standard English capitalization, punctuation, and spelling when writing.
   a. Use punctuation (comma, ellipsis, dash) to indicate a pause or break.
   b. Use an ellipsis to indicate an omission.
   c. Spell correctly.

Knowledge of Language

3. Use knowledge of language and its conventions when writing, speaking, reading, or listening.
   a. Use verbs in the active and passive voice and in the conditional and subjunctive mood to achieve particular effects (e.g., emphasizing the actor or the action; expressing uncertainty or describing a state contrary to fact).

Vocabulary Acquisition and Use

4. Determine or clarify the meaning of unknown and multiple-meaning words and phrases based on *grade 8 reading and content*, choosing flexibly from a range of strategies.
   a. Use context (e.g., the overall meaning of a sentence or paragraph; a word's position or function in a sentence) as a clue to the meaning of a word or phrase.
   b. Use common, grade-appropriate Greek or Latin affixes and roots as clues to the meaning of a word (e.g., *precede, recede, secede*).
   c. Consult general and specialized reference materials (e.g., dictionaries, glossaries, thesauruses), both print and digital, to find the pronunciation of a word or determine or clarify its precise meaning or its part of speech.
   d. Verify the preliminary determination of the meaning of a word or phrase (e.g., by checking the inferred meaning in context or in a dictionary).

5. Demonstrate understanding of figurative language, word relationships, and nuances in word meanings.
   a. Interpret figures of speech (e.g. verbal irony, puns) in context.
   b. Use the relationship between particular words to better understand each of the words.
   c. Distinguish among the connotations (associations) of words with similar denotations (definitions) (e.g., *bullheaded, willful, firm, persistent, resolute*).

6. Acquire and use accurately grade-appropriate general academic and domain-specific words and phrases; gather vocabulary knowledge when considering a word or phrase important to comprehension or expression.

COMMON CORE WORKSHOPS

- BUILDING ACADEMIC VOCABULARY

- WRITING AN OBJECTIVE SUMMARY

- COMPREHENDING COMPLEX TEXTS

- ANALYZING ARGUMENTS

- CONDUCTING RESEARCH

Common Core State Standards

Reading Literature 2, 10
Reading Informational Text 2, 8, 9
Writing 1.a, 1.b, 1.e, 2, 2.a, 2.c, 2.f, 7, 8
Language 2.b, 6

BUILDING ACADEMIC VOCABULARY

Academic vocabulary is the language you encounter in textbooks and on standardized tests and other assessments. Understanding these words and using them in your classroom discussions and writing will help you communicate your ideas clearly and effectively.

There are two basic types of academic vocabulary: general and domain-specific. **General academic vocabulary** includes words that are not specific to any single course of study. For example, the general academic vocabulary word *analyze* is used in language arts, math, social studies, art, and so on.

Domain-specific academic vocabulary includes words that are usually encountered in the study of a specific discipline. For example, the words *factor* and *remainder* are most often used in mathematics classrooms and texts.

Common Core State Standards

Language
6. Acquire and use accurately grade-appropriate general academic and domain-specific words and phrases; gather vocabulary knowledge when considering a word or phrase important to comprehension or expression.

General Academic Vocabulary

Word	Definition	Related Words	Word in Context
accumulate (uh KYOO myuh layt) *v.*	collect or gather	accumulation accumulating	Dust began to **accumulate** on the tables and chairs in the empty classroom.
argument (AHR gyuh muhnt) *n.*	claim; persuasive reasoning	argue argumentative	The **argument** in the essay is well supported.
aspects (AS pehkts) *n.*	ways in which an idea or a problem may be viewed or seen		I needed to consider all the **aspects** of his argument before replying.
assumption (uh SUMP shuhn) *n.*	act of taking for granted	assume assuming	My **assumption** was based on insufficient evidence.
benefit (BEHN uh fiht) *n.*	advantage or positive result	beneficial beneficiary	The **benefit** of studying geometry is clear for certain careers such as architecture and engineering.
bias (BY uhs) *n.*	tendency to see things from a slanted or prejudiced viewpoint	biased unbiased	In the past, accusations of **bias** have been hurled at the media during political campaigns.

Word	Definition	Related Words	Word in Context
challenge (CHAL uhnj) v.	call into question; demand proof	challenging challenged	The teacher asked his students to **challenge** accepted points of view and to be distrustful of opinions that are not well supported by facts.
class (klas) n.	group of people or objects	classify classification	They studied how the differences between the nobility and the merchant **class** contributed to the French Revolution.
confirm (kuhn FURM) v.	prove or establish as true	confirmation confirming	He asked them to **confirm** their answers one more time before submitting their tests.
connection (kuh NEHK shuhn) n.	tie; link	connect connected	It was easy to find a **connection** between the character's motives and his actions.
contradict (kon truh DIHKT) v.	deny; present an opposing viewpoint	contradictory contradiction	He was afraid to **contradict** the expert on nutrition, even though he was familiar with research that undermined her position.
cultural (KUL chuhr uhl) adj.	related to the customs and beliefs of a group or community	culture culturally	The museum exhibit explored the **cultural** achievements of the Aztecs.
decision (dih SIHZH uhn) n.	choice; act of making up one's mind	decisively decide	Once she had made her **decision** about which political candidate to support, no argument could change her mind.
development (dih VEHL uhp muhnt) n.	event or happening; outcome	develop developer	The law professor asked his class to follow every **development** in an important Supreme Court case about job discrimination.

Ordinary Language:
The two characters **disagree with** each other constantly.

Academic Language:
The two characters **contradict** each other constantly.

Word	Definition	Related Words	Word in Context
discriminate (dihs KRIHM uh nayt) v.	see differences between; tell apart	discriminatory discrimination	The food critic was able to **discriminate** between two dishes that had been prepared in slightly different ways.
discrimination (dihs krihm uh NAY shuhn) n.	unfair treatment of a person or group	discriminate discriminatory	Housing regulations outlaw **discrimination** against buyers or renters based on race or nationality.
distinguish (dihs TIHNG gwihsh) v.	mark as different; set apart	distinguishing undistinguished	Paints come in so many colors that it can be difficult to **distinguish** between various shades of the same basic color.
divide (duh VYD) v.	separate	divisive division	The teacher asked the students to **divide** into small groups to discuss the reading.
doubtful (DOWT fuhl) adj.	not likely; open to challenge	doubtfully doubt	The historian made the **doubtful** claim that the royal family had survived the revolution, when their deaths had already been well documented.
emphasize (EHM fuh syz) v.	stress; show the importance of	emphasis emphatically	In her classes, she decided to **emphasize** reasoning and analysis over memorizing facts.
endure (ehn DOOR) v.	hold up under; last	enduring endurance	Sarah had to **endure** a twenty-minute lecture from her older sister every time she made a minor mistake.
evidence (EHV uh duhns) n.	proof	evidently evidentiary	He gave **evidence** from his own experience, as well as from the reading, to support his central points.
exaggerate (ehg ZAJ uh rayt) v.	make too much of; overstate	exaggeration exaggeratedly	Writers of tall tales **exaggerate** the abilities of their heroes by making them bigger, stronger, faster, and smarter than most main characters.
explanation (ehks pluh NAY shuhn) n.	act of giving meaning to, or clarifying, an idea or a concept	explanatory explain	A good **explanation** leaves no confusion in the mind of the reader.

Word	Definition	Related Words	Word in Context
factor (FAK tuhr) n.	any of the circumstances or conditions that lead to a result	factoring factory	One major **factor** in his decision to skip the prom was that he was embarrassed about his dancing skills.
factual (FAK choo uhl) adj.	based on or limited to fact	fact factually	Her opposition had no **factual** basis; it was based purely on emotion.
global (GLOH buhl) adj.	complete, covering a large class of cases	globally globe	He favored a **global** approach to the community's problems—addressing each problem in isolation was just not going to work.
identify (y DEHN tuh fy) v.	classify; name	identification identity	She could **identify** many different species of trees by examining their leaves and bark.
illogical (ih LOJ uh kuhl) adj.	contrary or opposed to fact	illogically logic	He held the **illogical** belief that everything he said was correct simply because he stated it was so.
imitate (IHM uh tayt) v.	copy or follow the example of	imitation imitative	The assignment asked the students to **imitate** the style of Mark Twain in a five-page story.
individuality (ihn duh vihj oo AL uh tee) n.	way in which a person or thing stands apart or is different	individualize individually	Emily Dickinson expressed her **individuality** through her short, unpredictable poems.
influence (IHN floo uhns) v.	sway or affect	influential influentially	He tried to **influence** the crowd to vote for him based on his eight-year record as a governor.
insecurity (ihn sih KYOOR uh tee) n.	lack of confidence; self-doubt	insecure security	His **insecurity** about his mathematical abilities surfaced whenever the teacher asked a question in algebra class and he hid from view.

Ordinary Language:
The writer's argument **doesn't make sense**.

Academic Language:
The writer's argument is **illogical**.

Word	Definition	Related Words	Word in Context
interact (ihn tuhr AKT) v.	deal with or work with someone or something	interaction interactive	Being lab partners forced them to **interact**, even though they disliked each other.
investigate (ihn VEHS tuh gayt) v.	search; look into	investigative investigation	The reporter was sent to **investigate** a banking scandal.
judge (juhj) v.	form an opinion about	judgmental judge n.	It is wise to collect facts before you **judge** someone's actions.
objective (uhb JEHK tihv) adj.	open-minded; not influenced by personal feelings or prejudice	objectively objectivity	Reporters try to remain **objective** about the subjects of their articles, letting their readers form their own opinions based on the facts presented.
observation (ob zuhr VAY shuhn) n.	statement; point of view	observe observing	His **observation** that the economy often goes through boom and bust cycles was obvious to anyone who knew economic history.
opinion (uh PIHN yuhn) n.	personal view or attitude	opinionated opine	He formed his **opinion** about the issue based on articles he read on Web sites and in newspapers.
oppose (uh POHZ) v.	go against; stand in the way of	opposition opposite	They decided to **oppose** the dam project because they feared a negative effect on local fish populations.
persuade (puhr SWAYD) v.	convince; bring around to one's way of thinking	persuasion persuasively	It is difficult to **persuade** people to change their minds when their opinions are based purely on emotion.
prove (proov) v.	show or demonstrate	proof proving	**Prove** your case by showing me persuasive evidence.
quality (KWOL uh tee) n.	characteristic or feature	qualitative qualification	The main character had a mischievous **quality** that proved popular with young readers.
quantity (KWON tuh tee) n.	amount	quantitative quantify	The **quantity** of caffeine is different in coffee, tea, and soda.
reaction (ree AK shuhn) n.	response to an influence, action, or statement	react reactive	What was their **reaction** to the announcement that the performance was being cancelled?
relevant (REHL uh vuhnt) adj.	to the point; relating to the matter at hand	relevance irrelevant	Her argument that a new playground was unnecessary was not **relevant** to a discussion of child safety.

Ordinary Language:
The subplot about the two workers did not seem to **matter**.

Academic Language:
The subplot about the two workers did not seem **relevant**.

Practice

Examples of various kinds of domain-specific academic vocabulary appear in the charts below. Some chart rows are not filled in. Look up the definitions of the remaining words, provide one or two related words, and use each word in context on a separate piece of paper.

Social Studies: Domain-Specific Academic Vocabulary

Word	Definition	Related Words	Word in Context
federalism (FEHD uhr uhl ihz uhm) n.	support for a strong federal (or national) government	federal federalist	Alexander Hamilton believed strongly in **federalism**.
founder (FOWN duhr) n.	person who founds or establishes something	found founded	The Pilgrims were the **founders** of the Plymouth colony.
framer (FRAYM uhr) n.	person who helps design or build a document, policy, or movement	frame framing	Benjamin Franklin was a **framer** of the U.S. Constitution.
hierarchy (HY uhr ahr kee) n.	organized system in which people or things are ranked one above another	hierarchic hierarchical	The people at the top of a **hierarchy** have more power than those below them.
recession (rih SEHSH uhn) n.	in economics, period of economic downturn	recede recessionary	Many people lost money and jobs in the **recession** of 2008.
commerce (KOM uhrs) n.			
congressional (kuhn GREHSH uh nul) adj.			
constitutional (kon stuh TOO shuh nul) adj.			
exchange (ehks CHAYNJ) v., n.			
nationalism (NASH uh nul ihz uhm) n.			

Mathematics: Domain-Specific Academic Vocabulary

Word	Definition	Related Words	Word in Context
array (uh RAY) *n.*	arrangement of a series of terms in rows and columns according to value	array *v.* arrayed	We were told to arrange the numbers in an **array** from smallest to largest.
complementary angles (kom pluh MEHN tuh ree ANG guhlz) *n.*	two angles that, when added together, produce an angle of 90 degrees	complement	An angle of 30 degrees and an angle of 60 degrees are **complementary angles**.
corresponding angles (kawr uh SPON dihng ANG guhlz) *n.*	two angles that are formed in corresponding positions on two parallel lines that are crossed by a third line	correspond	I created **corresponding angles** by drawing a line that crossed two parallel lines.
supplementary angles (suhp luh MEHN tuh ree ANG guhlz) *n.*	two angles that, when added together, produce an angle of 180 degrees	supplement supplemental	Two 90-degree angles are **supplementary angles**.
transversal (trans VUR suhl) *n.*	line that intersects two or more other lines	transverse transversing	The **transversal** intersected two parallel lines.
infinite (IHN fuh niht) *adj.*			
intercept (ihn tuhr SEHPT) *v.*			
nonlinear (non LIHN ee uhr) *adj.*			
symmetry (SIHM uh tree) *n.*			
vertex (VUR tehks) *n.*			

Science: Domain-Specific Academic Vocabulary

Word	Definition	Related Words	Word in Context
electron (ee LEHK tron) *n.*	elementary particle having a negative charge	electric electrical	A hydrogen atom has one **electron**.
inertia (ihn UR shuh) *n.*	property of matter by which it maintains its state of rest or uniform motion	inert	The lab we completed tested the **inertia** of matter.
mutualism (MYOO choo uh lihz uhm) *n.*	relationship that benefits two interacting organisms	mutual mutually	The bees and the flowers benefited from **mutualism.**
neutron (NOO tron) *n.*	elementary particle that has no charge	neutral	Except for hydrogen, all atoms have **neutrons**.
reactant (ree AK tuhnt) *n.*	substance that undergoes a chemical change in a reaction	react reaction	One **reactant** in the experiment was oxygen.

Science: Domain-Specific Academic Vocabulary *(continued)*

Word	Definition	Related Words	Word in Context
acid (AS ihd) *n.*			
compound (KOM pownd) *n.*			
density (DEHN suh tee) *n.*			
element (EHL uh muhnt) *n.*			
immunity (ih MYOON ih tee) *n.*			

Art: Domain-Specific Academic Vocabulary

Word	Definition	Related Words	Word in Context
contour line (KON toor lyn) *n.*	line that shows the important interior ridges and edges (or contours) of an object	contoured contouring	The first step to drawing the bowl is to make **contour lines**.
primary color (PRY mehr ee KUHL uhr) *n.*	red, yellow, and blue; colors that can be mixed to make all other colors	primarily	The teacher told us to use **primary colors** to make the colors we wanted.
rhythm (RIH<u>TH</u> uhm) *n.*	visual tempo or beat created by placing repeated elements in a work of art	rhythmic	The muralist placed buildings and cars repeatedly in his work to create a lively **rhythm**.
secondary color (SEHK uhn dehr ee KUHL uhr) *n.*	orange, green, and violet; colors made by mixing two primary colors in equal amounts	second	I mixed red and yellow to make the **secondary color** of orange.
tertiary color (TUR shee ehr ee KUHL uhr) *n.*	color produced by mixing two secondary colors		The artist used two secondary colors to make the **tertiary color** of brown.
balance (BAL uhns) *n., v.*			
cool color (kool KUHL uhr) *n.*			
shape (shayp) *n.*			
style (styl) *n.*			
warm color (wawrm KUHL uhr) *n.*			

Technology: Domain-Specific Academic Vocabulary

Word	Definition	Related Words	Word in Context
cursor (KUR suhr) *n.*	movable, blinking symbol that shows the position of the next character that will be entered from the keyboard	cursory	I placed the **cursor** where I wanted to insert a new paragraph.
home row (hohm roh) *n.*	row on a computer keyboard that contains the home keys: *A, S, D,* and *F* on the left and *J, K, L,* and the semicolon on the right	home row	You can type faster and more accurately by placing your hands correctly on the **home row**.
spreadsheet (SPREHD sheet) *n.*	worksheet that contains columns and rows for data	spread	We kept our budget in a **spreadsheet** to track what we spent.
storyboard (STAWR ee bawrd) *n.*	series of illustrated panels that show the action planned for a film, video, or animation	boards story	Our group made a **storyboard** to show the sequence of events in our film.
telecommunications (tehl ih kuh myoo nih KAY shuhnz) *n.*	technology that enables the sending of information over great distances	communicate communications	The invention of cell phones drastically changed **telecommunications**.
chat room (chat room) *n.*			
file folder (fyl FOHL duhr) *n.*			
home page (hohm duhr) *n.*			
import (IHM pawrt) *n., v.*			
menu bar (MEHN yoo bahr) *n.*			

Increasing Your Word Knowledge

Increase your word knowledge and chances of success by taking an active role in developing your vocabulary. Here are some tips for you.

To own a word, follow these steps:

Steps to Follow	Model
1. Learn to identify the word and its basic meaning.	The word *examine* means "to look at closely."
2. Take note of the word's spelling.	*Examine* begins and ends with an *e*.
3. Practice pronouncing the word so that you can use it in conversation.	The *e* on the end of the word *examine* is silent. Its second syllable gets the most stress.
4. Visualize the word and illustrate its key meaning.	When I think of the word *examine*, I visualize a doctor checking a patient's health.
5. Learn the various forms of the word and its related words.	*Examination* and *exam* are forms of the word *examine*.
6. Compare the word with similar words.	*Examine*, *peruse*, and *study* are synonyms.
7. Contrast the word with similar words.	*Examine* suggests a more detailed study than *read* or *look at*.
8. Use the word in various contexts.	"I'd like to *examine* the footprints more closely." "I will *examine* the use of imagery in this poem."

Building Your Speaking Vocabulary

Language gives us the ability to express ourselves. The more words you know, the better able you will be to get your points across. There are two main aspects of language: reading and speaking. Using the steps above will help you acquire a rich vocabulary. Follow these steps to help you learn to use this rich vocabulary in discussions, speeches, and conversations:

Steps to Follow	Tip
1. Practice pronouncing the word.	Become familiar with pronunciation guides to allow you to sound out unfamiliar words. Listening to audiobooks as you read the text will help you learn pronunciations of words.
2. Learn word forms.	Dictionaries often list forms of words following the main word entry. Practice saying word families aloud: "generate," "generated," "generation," "regenerate," "generator."
3. Translate your thoughts.	Restate your own thoughts and ideas in a variety of ways, to inject formality or to change your tone, for example.
4. Hold discussions.	With a classmate, practice using academic vocabulary words in discussions about the text. Choose one term to practice at a time, and see how many statements you can create using that term.
5. Tape-record yourself.	Analyze your word choices by listening to yourself objectively. Note places your word choice could be strengthened or changed.

WRITING AN OBJECTIVE SUMMARY

The ability to summarize a text effectively will lead to success in school as well as in many careers. When you write an effective objective summary, you identify the key ideas of a text and show your overall understanding of the original text.

What Is an Objective Summary?

An effective objective summary is a concise, complete, accurate, and objective overview of a text. Effective objective summaries have the following characteristics:

- The summary should contain references to the original text's title and author.
- If the original text is a narrative, the summary should include key plot events that lead to the story's conclusion.
- If the text is informational, the summary should include specific, relevant details that support that theme or central idea.

What to Avoid in an Objective Summary

- Do not include sentences or paragraphs copied from the original source.
- Do not include every event, detail, or point in the original text.
- Do not include evaluative comments, such as your overall opinion of or reaction to the selection.
- Do not include your interpretation or a critical analysis of the text.

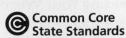 **Common Core State Standards**

Reading Literature
2. Determine a theme or central idea of a text and analyze its development over the course of the text, including its relationship to the characters, setting, and plot; provide an objective summary of the text.

Reading Informational Text
2. Determine a central idea of a text and analyze its development over the course of the text, including its relationship to supporting ideas; provide an objective summary of the text.

Model Objective Summary

Review the elements of an effective objective summary, called out in the sidenotes. Then, write an objective summary of a text you have recently read. Review your summary. Delete any unnecessary details, opinions, or evaluations.

Summary of "Ribbons" by Laurence Yep

"Ribbons" by Laurence Yep tells the story of Stacy, a Chinese American girl adjusting to the changes she must make when her Paw-paw, or maternal Chinese grandmother, comes from Hong Kong to live with the family in San Francisco. ~~This story is one of the best I have read this year.~~

> A one-sentence synopsis highlighting the central idea of the story can be an effective start to a summary.

> This sentence is an opinion and should be deleted.

First of all, Stacy must give her room to her grandmother and share a room with her younger brother Ian. Also, Stacy must give up her ballet lessons, which she loves, to pay for her grandmother's transportation from Hong Kong.

When Paw-paw arrives, Stacy notices that she is unsteady on her feet; she uses two canes. Although Stacy is curious about her grandmother's feet, she respects her mother's wishes and doesn't ask her grandmother about them.

> Relating the development of the text in chronological order makes a summary of a narrative easy to follow.

As days go by, there are more changes in the household to accommodate Grandmother. It is also becoming apparent to Stacy that Ian has become Grandmother's favorite. ~~Ian looks like his Chinese grandmother; Stacy looks like her Caucasian father.~~ Stacy is hurt, but she decides to try to get to know her grandmother better. Stacy feels that one way to get to know someone better is to share something you love. So Stacy decides to dance for Grandmother.

> Eliminate unnecessary details, such as these.

As Stacy puts on her toe shoes, the ribbons on one of her shoes fall off. Stacy, ~~remembering that her grandmother is an excellent seamstress,~~ brings the ribbons to her and asks her to sew them back on. At the sight of the ribbons, Grandmother gets furious, first at Stacy, and then at Stacy's mom. When Stacy asks her mom about her grandmother's anger, her mother says that the ribbons remind Paw-paw of something awful that happened to her a long time ago.

A still-angry Stacy decides to ignore her grandmother, and tension in the house grows. Quite by accident, Stacy walks into the bathroom and sees her grandmother soaking her misshapen feet. It is after that that Stacy's mother explains that at one time in China young girls had their feet bent and then bound with ribbons, which was horribly painful and disfiguring. Grandmother had mistakenly thought that Stacy's mother was going to bind Stacy's feet. Once that misunderstanding is cleared up, Stacy and Grandmother begin to get to know each other better.

COMPREHENDING COMPLEX TEXTS

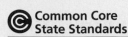 **Common Core
State Standards**

**Reading Literature
10.** By the end of the year, read
and comprehend literature,
including stories, dramas, and
poems, at the high end of the
grades 6–8 text complexity band
independently and proficiently.

During this year and in high school, you will be required to read increasingly
complex texts to prepare for college and the workplace. A complex text
contains challenging vocabulary; long, complex sentences; figurative language;
multiple levels of meaning; or unfamiliar settings and situations.

The selections in this textbook include a range of readings, from short stories
to autobiographies, poetry, drama, myths, and even science and social studies
texts. You will be able to read some of these texts easily; others may be more
challenging.

Strategy 1: **Multidraft Reading**

Good readers develop the habit of rereading texts in order to comprehend
them completely. Just as you might listen to a new song over and over
again to understand the lyrics, good readers return to texts to more fully enjoy
and comprehend them. To fully understand a text, try this multidraft reading
strategy:

1st Reading

The first time you read a text, read to gain its basic meaning. If you are
reading a narrative text, look for story basics: what happened, to whom,
and why. If the text is nonfiction, look for its main ideas. If you are reading
poetry, read first to get an overall sense of the poem and its speaker. Also
take note of its mood or setting.

2nd Reading

During your second reading of a text, focus on the artistry or effectiveness
of the writing. Look for text structures, and think about why the author
chose those organizational patterns. Then, examine the author's creative
uses of language and the effects of that language. For example, has the
author used alliteration? Rhythms? Hyperbole? Parallelism? If so, to what
end?

3rd Reading

Once you have completed your third reading, begin to synthesize your
ideas. To do so, compare and contrast the text with others of its kind you
have read. Also think about the message the work conveys and whether or
not that message is original and/or valid. Then, evaluate the text's overall
effectiveness and whether or not it has broadened your understanding.

Independent Practice

As you read this poem, practice the multidraft reading strategy by completing a chart like the one below.

"Migrant Birds" by Moumin Manzoor Quazi

Swept by invisible brooms,
black birds, like words on a page,
specks of spilt ground
pepper blown in the wind,
much bigger though,
tightly—not randomly—
change course all
together at the same,
exact moment.

So-called "junk" birds
swim the skies, come north
for a while to make a life.
Ready now, they once again
become fluid spice, do their
instinctual dance, moved
not by whim, but fancy anyway,
and the hot pepper blows home to southern climes,
seasoning skies elsewhere for a time.

Multidraft Reading Chart

	My Understanding
1st Reading Look for key ideas and details that unlock basic meaning.	
2nd Reading Read for deeper meanings. Look for ways in which the author used text structures and language to create effects.	
3rd Reading Read to integrate your knowledge and ideas. Connect the text to others of its kind and to your own experience.	

Strategy 2: **Close Read the Text**

Complex texts require close reading, a careful analysis of the words, phrases, and sentences. When you close read, use the following tips to comprehend the text:

Tips for Close Reading
1. **Break down long sentences** into parts. Look for the subject of the sentence and its verb. Then identify which parts of the sentence modify, or give more information about, its subject.
2. **Reread passages.** When reading complex texts, be sure to reread dense passages to confirm their meaning.

3. **Look for context clues,** such as the following:
 	
  a. Restatements of ideas within text. For example, in this sentence, "completely destroyed" restates the verb *devastated*.
 	
    The earthquake and tsunami **devastated,** or <u>completely destroyed</u>, the small fishing village.
 	
  b. Examples of concepts and topics. In the following sentence, the fact that we know that bobsledding and skiing are winter sports indicates that *luge* must also be a winter sport.
 	
    The United States athletes won medals in <u>bobsledding, skiing, and **luge.**</u>
 	
  c. Comparisons of ideas and topics.
 	
    The **dulcet** tones of the singer were as <u>sweet and soothing as a mother's lullaby</u>.
 	
  d. Contrasts of ideas and topics.
 	
    Criticism, <u>unlike praise,</u> can be hurtful.

4. **Identify pronoun antecedents.** If long sentences contain pronouns, reread the text to make sure you know to what or to whom the pronouns refer. The pronoun *its* in the following sentence refers to the Quiet Room, not the company.   The Quiet Room was set aside by the company for employees to enjoy **its** peaceful comfort.
5. **Look for conjunctions,** such as *and, but,* and *yet,* to understand relationships between ideas.
6. **Paraphrase,** or restate in your own words, passages of difficult text in order to check your understanding. Remember that a paraphrase is a word-for-word rephrasing of an original text; it is not a summary.

Close-Read Model

As you read this document, take note of the sidenotes that model ways to unlock meaning in the text.

from *On Duty* by Cicero

. . . Now, those who care for the interests of a part of the citizens and neglect another part, introduce into the civil service a dangerous element — dissension and party strife. . . As a result of this party spirit bitter strife arose at Athens, and in our own country not only dissensions but also disastrous civil wars broke out. All this the citizen who is patriotic, brave, and worthy of a leading place in the state will shun with abhorrence; he will dedicate himself unreservedly to his country, without aiming at influence or power for himself; and he will devote himself to the state in its entirety in such a way as to further the interests of all. . .

A most wretched custom, assuredly, is our electioneering and scrambling for office. Concerning this also we find a fine thought in Plato: "Those who compete against one another," he says, "to see which of two candidates shall administer the government, are like sailors quarrelling as to which one of them shall do the steering." And he likewise lays down the rule that we should regard only those as adversaries who take up arms against the state, not those who strive to have the government administered according to their convictions. . .

Neither must we listen to those who think that one should indulge in violent anger against one's political enemies and imagine that such is the attitude of a great-spirited, brave man. For nothing is more commendable, nothing more becoming in a pre-eminently great man than courtesy and forbearance. Indeed, in a free people, where all enjoy equal rights before the law, we must school ourselves to affability and what is called "mental poise"; for if we are irritated when people intrude upon us at unseasonable hours or make unreasonable requests, we shall develop a sour, churlish temper, prejudicial to ourselves and offensive to others. And yet gentleness of spirit and forbearance are to be commended only with the understanding that strictness may be exercised for the good of the state; for without that, the government cannot be well administered. On the other hand, if punishment or correction must be administered, it need not be insulting; it ought to have regard to the welfare of the state, not to the personal satisfaction of the man who administers the punishment or reproof. . .

Search for context clues. The words in blue are context clues that help you figure out the meaning of the word *dissension*.

Look for antecedents. In this sentence, the noun phrase *the citizen who is patriotic . . .* is replaced by the pronoun *he*.

This sentence is inverted: its subject comes last. A paraphrase of this sentence might be "Desperately trying to get elected has become commonplace."

Search for context clues. The words in green are comparison context clues that hint at the meaning of "affability." The words in light blue provide contrasting context clues that describe what an affable person is *not*.

The antecedent for the pronoun *it* in this sentence is *punishment or correction*.

Common Core Workshop

Strategy 3: **Ask Questions**

Be an attentive reader by asking questions as you read. Each selection in this textbook is followed by questions for you to answer. These questions are sorted into three basic categories that build in sophistication and lead you to a deeper understanding of the texts you read. Here is an example from this text:

Some questions are about **Key Ideas and Details** in the text. To answer these questions, you will need to locate and cite explicit information in the text or draw inferences from what you have read.

Some questions are about **Craft and Structure** in the text. To answer these questions, you will need to analyze how the author developed and structured the text. You will also look for ways in which the author artfully used language and how those word choices impacted the meaning and tone of the work.

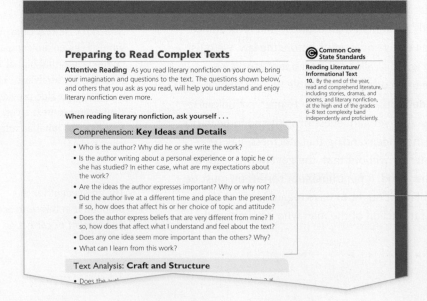

An Hour With Abuelo

Close Reading Activities

Comprehension: **Key Ideas and Details**

1. What is the narrator's conflict at the start of the story? Cite details in support.

2. (a) What was Abuelo's dream in life? **(b) Summarize:** What caused Abuelo to give up his dream? **(c) Infer:** What is Abuelo's new purpose in life? Explain.

3. (a) How does Abuelo surprise the narrator? **(b) Draw Conclusions:** How is the narrator changed by story events? Cite story details to support your answer.

4. Summarize: Write a brief, objective summary of the story.

Text Analysis: **Craft and Structure**

5. Evaluate: Does the author's use of Spanish add to or detract from the story? Explain, citing specific examples.

6. (a) Cite four details that the author includes to help readers understand Abuelo. Explain what each shows about his character. **(b) Evaluate:** How effective is the author's development of Abuelo's character?

7. Analyze: The story uses first-person narration—it is told by a character in the story. How does this choice of narrator contribute to the effectiveness of the ending? Cite details to support your analysis.

Connections: **Integration of Knowledge and Ideas**

Discuss
Conduct a **small-group discussion** about the irony in the story. To identify the irony, consider how readers expect the story to turn out and how it actually ends. Then, relate this irony to the story's theme, or insight into life.

Research
Judith Ortiz ... ... nto poetry

influence Ortiz Cofer's family and culture had on her writing.

Write
Characters' words and actions propel story events forward. Write an **essay** in which you analyze how the author develops characters in the story and why that development is vital to the plot. Cite details from the ...

Some questions are about the **Integration of Knowledge and Ideas** in the text. These questions ask you to evaluate a text in many different ways, such as comparing texts, analyzing arguments in the text, and using many other methods of thinking critically about a text's ideas.

Preparing to Read Complex Texts

Attentive Reading As you read literary nonfiction on your own, bring your imagination and questions to the text. The questions shown below, and others that you ask as you read, will help you understand and enjoy literary nonfiction even more.

When reading literary nonfiction, ask yourself . . .

Comprehension: **Key Ideas and Details**

- Who is the author? Why did he or she write the work?
- Is the author writing about a personal experience or a topic he or she has studied? In either case, what are my expectations about the work?
- Are the ideas the author expresses important? Why or why not?
- Did the author live at a different time and place than the present? If so, how does that affect his or her choice of topic and attitude?
- Does the author express beliefs that are very different from mine? If so, how does that affect what I understand and feel about the text?
- Does any one idea seem more important than the others? Why?
- What can I learn from this work?

Text Analysis: **Craft and Structure**

- Does the auth... ...

Common Core State Standards

Reading Literature/ Informational Text
10. By the end of the year, read and comprehend literature, including stories, dramas, and poems, and literary nonfiction, at the high end of the grades 6–8 text complexity band independently and proficiently.

As you read independently, ask similar types of questions to ensure that you fully enjoy and comprehend texts you read for school and for pleasure. We have provided sets of questions for you on the Independent Reading pages at the end of each unit.

Model

Following is an example of a complex text. The sidenotes show sample questions that an attentive reader might ask while reading.

Sample questions:

from "The Funeral Oration of Pericles" retold by Thucydides

A speech given in 431 B.C. to honor Athenian soldiers and praise Athenian democracy:

Our constitution is called a democracy because power is in the hands not of a minority but of the whole people. When it is a question of settling private disputes, everyone is equal before the law; when it is a question of putting one person before another in positions of public responsibility, what counts is not membership of a particular class, but the actual ability which the man possesses. No one, so long as he has it in him to be of service to the state, is kept in political obscurity because of poverty. And, just as our political life is free and open, so is our day-to-day life in our relations with each other. . . . We are free and tolerant in our private lives; but in public affairs we keep to the law. This is because it commands our deep respect.

Key Ideas and Details Who is the *Our* in this sentence?

Craft and Structure Why might Thucydides have chosen to use repetition in this passage?

Integration of Knowledge and Ideas If you were to make a digital presentation display of advantages of life in Athens, what would your bullet points be?

Independent Practice

Write three to five questions you might ask yourself as you continue reading "The Funeral Oration of Pericles."

We give our obedience to those whom we put in positions of authority, and we obey the laws themselves, especially those which are for the protection of the oppressed, and those unwritten laws which it is an acknowledged shame to break. . . . Here each individual is interested not only in his own affairs but in the affairs of the state as well: even those who are mostly occupied with their own business are extremely well-informed on general politics—this is a peculiarity of ours: we do not say that a man who takes no interest in politics is a man who minds his own business; we say that he has no business here at all. We Athenians, in our own persons, take our decisions on policy or submit them to proper discussions: for we do not think that there is an incompatibility between words and deeds; the worst thing is to rush into action before the consequences have been properly debated. . . . Taking everything together then, I declare that our city is an education to Greece. . .you have only to consider the power which our city possesses and which has been won by those very qualities which I have mentioned.

ANALYZING ARGUMENTS

The ability to evaluate an argument, as well as to make one, is an important skill for success in college and in the workplace.

What Is an Argument?

Informally speaking, an *argument* is disagreement between people. This type of argument involves trading opinions and evidence in a conversation. A formal written argument, however, presents one side of a controversial or debatable issue. An effective argument is supported by reasoning and evidence.

Purposes of Argument

There are three main purposes for writing a formal argument:

- to change the reader's mind about a controversial issue
- to convince the reader to accept your ideas
- to motivate the reader to take action

Elements of Argument
Claim (assertion)—what the writer is trying to prove Example: *Students in the United States need to be more competitive to keep up with students in other countries.*
Grounds (evidence)—the support used to convince the reader Example: *American students scored lower on math and science tests than children in many other countries.*
Justification—the link between the grounds and the claim; why the grounds are credible Example: *Longer school days and year-round school would help students in the United States perform better on assessments.*

Evaluating Claims

When reading or listening to a formal argument, critically assess the claims that are made. Which claims are based on fact or can be proved true? Also evaluate evidence that supports the claims. To evaluate an argument, ask questions such as these:

- What specific claims are presented?
- Are the claims logically presented?
- Is there enough evidence to support the stated claims?
- Does the evidence directly support the claims, or is any evidence irrelevant?
- Can the evidence be proved to be true?

Common Core State Standards

Reading Informational Text
8. Delineate and evaluate the argument and specific claims in a text, assessing whether the reasoning is sound and the evidence is relevant and sufficient; recognize when irrelevant evidence is introduced.

Language
6. Acquire and use accurately grade-appropriate general academic and domain-specific words and phrases; gather vocabulary knowledge when considering a word or phrase important to comprehension or expression.

Model Argument

This excerpt from a speech by President John F. Kennedy is an example of an argument.

from "We Choose to Go to the Moon"
by John F. Kennedy

. . .Despite the striking fact that most of the scientists that the world has ever known are alive and working today, despite the fact that this Nation's own scientific manpower is doubling every 12 years in a rate of growth more than three times that of our population as a whole, despite that, the vast stretches of the unknown and the unanswered and the unfinished still far outstrip our collective comprehension. . . .

Claim: Despite advances in science, there is much we still do not know.

This is a breathtaking pace, and such a pace cannot help but create new ills as it dispels old, new ignorance, new problems, new dangers. Surely the opening vistas of space promise high costs and hardships, as well as high reward.

So it is not surprising that some would have us stay where we are a little longer to rest, to wait. But this. . .country of the United States was not built by those who waited and rested and wished to look behind them. This country was conquered by those who moved forward—and so will space. . . .

An opposing argument is acknowledged and refuted.

If this capsule history of our progress teaches us anything, it is that man, in his quest for knowledge and progress, is determined and cannot be deterred. The exploration of space will go ahead, whether we join in it or not, and it is one of the great adventures of all time, and no nation which expects to be the leader of other nations can expect to stay behind in this race for space. Those who came before us made certain that this country rode the first waves of the industrial revolution, the first waves of modern invention, and the first wave of nuclear power, and this generation does not intend to founder in the backwash of the coming age of space. We mean to be a part of it—we mean to lead it. For the eyes of the world now look into space, to the moon and to the planets beyond, and we have vowed that we shall not see it governed by a hostile flag of conquest, but by a banner of freedom and peace. We have vowed that we shall not see space filled with weapons of mass destruction, but with instruments of knowledge and understanding. . . .

Justification: The United States must be the leader in space exploration if we are to be the leader of other nations.

Grounds: The U.S. has led the world in industry, invention, and nuclear power.

Grounds: Space should be governed in freedom and peace, not by a hostile government.

We choose to go to the moon. We choose to go to the moon in this decade and do the other things, not because they are easy, but because they are hard, because that goal will serve to organize and measure the best of energies and skills, because that challenge is one that we are willing to accept, one we are unwilling to postpone, and one which we intend to win. . . .

Grounds: Going to the moon will bring out the best of our country's energies and skills.

A strong conclusion does more than simply restate the claim.

THE ART OF ARGUMENT: RHETORICAL DEVICES AND PERSUASIVE TECHNIQUES

Rhetorical Devices

Rhetoric is the art of using language in order to make a point or to persuade listeners. Rhetorical devices such as the ones listed below are accepted elements of argument. Their use does not invalidate or weaken an argument. Rather, the use of rhetorical devices is regarded as a key part of an effective argument.

Rhetorical Devices	Examples
Repetition The repeated use of certain words, phrases, or sentences	Let's go! Let's fight! Let's win!
Parallelism The repeated use of similar grammatical structures	Reading is reflective. Writing is expressive.
Rhetorical Question A question that calls attention to the issue by implying an obvious answer	Should we sit and watch while the rest of the world acts?
Sound Devices The use of alliteration, rhyme, or rhythm	We the people must be powerful and purposeful.
Simile and Metaphor The comparison of two unlike things or the assertion that one thing is another	The Iron Curtain separating democratic nations from communist countries has fallen.

Persuasive Techniques

The persuasive techniques below are often found in advertisements and in other forms of informal persuasion. Although techniques like the ones below are sometimes found in formal arguments, these techniques are usually avoided.

Persuasive Techniques	Examples
Bandwagon Approach/Anti-Bandwagon Approach Appeals to a person's desire to belong/Encourages or celebrates individuality	Nine out of ten Americans want to go "green."
Emotional Appeal Capitalizes on people's fear, anger, or desire	To protect your child, serve organic foods.
Endorsement/Testimony Employs a well-known person to promote a product or idea	Attending Middletown University was my stepping stone to success.
Loaded Language Uses words charged with emotion	These poor, tired, and desperate citizens have been forsaken by our government.
"Plain Folks" Appeal Shows a connection to everyday, ordinary people	I, like you, have worked in the fields, tilling the soil.
Hyperbole Exaggerates to make a point	This is a once-in-a-lifetime chance to vote your heart!

Model Speech

The excerpted speech below includes examples of rhetorical devices and persuasive techniques.

"A Tribute to the Dog" by George Graham Vest

My fellow citizens:

Gentlemen of the Jury: The best friend a man has in the world may turn against him and become his enemy. His son or daughter that he has reared with loving care may prove ungrateful. Those who are nearest and dearest to us, those whom we trust with our happiness and our good name may become traitors to their faith. The money that a man has, he may lose. It flies away from him, perhaps when he needs it most. A man's reputation may be sacrificed in a moment of ill-considered action. The people who are prone to fall on their knees to do us honor when success is with us, may be the first to throw the stone of malice when failure settles its cloud upon our heads.

The parallelism created by repeated grammatical structures gives the speech rhythm.

The one absolutely unselfish friend that man can have in this selfish world, the one that never deserts him, the one that never proves ungrateful or treacherous is his dog. A man's dog stands by him in prosperity and in poverty, in health and in sickness. He will sleep on the cold ground, where the wintry winds blow and the snow drives fiercely, if only he may be near his master's side. He will kiss the hand that has no food to offer; he will lick the wounds and sores that come in encounters with the roughness of the world. He guards the sleep of his pauper master as if he were a prince. When all other friends desert, he remains. When riches take wings, and reputation falls to pieces, he is as constant in his love as the sun in its journey through the heavens.

Sound devices, such as alliteration, can be used to emphasize a phrase.

Figurative language helps the speaker make his point.

If fortune drives the master forth an outcast in the world, friendless and homeless, the faithful dog asks no higher privilege than that of accompanying him, to guard him against danger, to fight against his enemies. And when the last scene of all comes, and death takes his master in its embrace and his body is laid away in the cold ground, no matter if all other friends pursue their way, there by the graveside will be the noble dog be found, his head between his paws, his eyes sad, but open in alert watchfulness, faithful and true even in death.

The speaker uses words with strong positive connotations.

COMPOSING AN ARGUMENT

Choosing a Topic

When choosing a topic for an argumentative essay, brainstorm topics you would like to write about; then, choose the topic that most interests you. Once you have chosen a topic, check to be sure you can make an arguable claim. Ask yourself:

1. What is my argument? What ideas about my argument do I need to convey?

2. What people might disagree with my claim? What opinions might they have?

3. What evidence supports my claim? Is my evidence sufficient and relevant?

If you are able to put into words what you want to prove and answered "yes" to questions 2 and 3, you have an arguable claim.

Introducing the Claim and Establishing Its Significance

Before you begin writing, think about your audience and how much you think they already know about your chosen topic. Then, provide background information, as necessary. Once you have provided context for your argument, you should clearly state your claim, or thesis. A written argument's claim often, but not always, appears in the first paragraph.

Developing Your Claim with Reasoning and Evidence

Now that you have made your claim, support it with evidence that proves it to be true. A good argument should have at least three solid pieces of evidence to support each claim. Evidence can range from personal experience to researched data or expert opinion. Knowing your audience's knowledge level, concerns, values, and possible biases can help inform your decision on what kind of evidence will have the strongest impact. Make sure your evidence is up to date and comes from a reliable source that you credit.

You should also address the opposing points of view within the body of your argument. Consider points you have made or evidence you have provided that a person might challenge. Acknowledge the validity of counterclaims, even as you make the case that your argument is stronger.

Writing a Concluding Statement or Section

Once you have developed your argument, restate your claim in the conclusion. Then, synthesize, or pull together, the evidence you have provided. Your conclusion should be powerful and memorable.

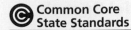 **Common Core State Standards**

Writing
1.a. Introduce claim(s), acknowledge and distinguish the claim(s) from alternate or opposing claims, and organize the reasons and evidence logically.
1.b. Support claim(s) with logical reasoning and relevant evidence, using accurate, credible sources and demonstrating an understanding of the topic or text.
1.e. Provide a concluding statement or section that follows from and supports the argument presented.

Practice

Complete a graphic organizer like the one below to help you plan your own argument.

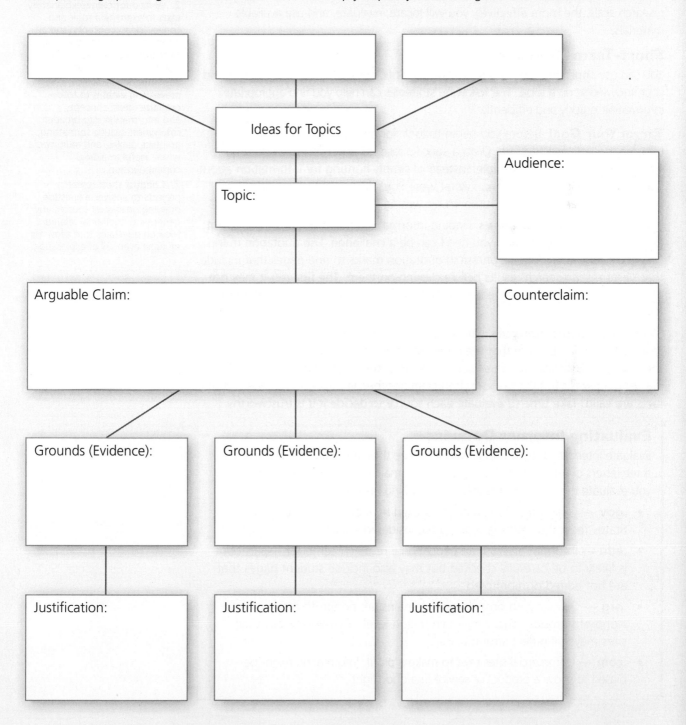

Ideas for Topics

Audience:

Topic:

Arguable Claim:

Counterclaim:

Grounds (Evidence):

Grounds (Evidence):

Grounds (Evidence):

Justification:

Justification:

Justification:

CONDUCTING RESEARCH

Research is an organized search for useful, accurate information. The stronger your research skills, the more effectively you will locate, evaluate, and use available materials.

Short-Term Research

You can use **short-term research** to answer specific questions about a text or extend your knowledge on a topic. The following strategies can help you find appropriate information quickly and efficiently.

Target Your Goal Before you begin to look for answers, decide what information you need to find. Draft a specific research question to avoid time-wasting digressions. For example, instead of simply hunting for information about Edgar Allan Poe, you might ask, "What were Poe's first published writings like?" or "Did Poe show a sense of humor in his writing?"

Use Online Search Engines Finding information on the Internet is easy, but finding the exact information you need can be a challenge. Use quotation marks to focus your search. Place a phrase in quotation marks to find pages that include that phrase. Scan search results before clicking on them. The first result may not be the most relevant. Read the text and consider the domain before making a choice.

Consult Multiple Sources Check for answers in more than one source. This strategy helps you be sure that the information you find is accurate. If you read the exact same phrases in more than one source, there is a good chance that the information was simply cut-and-pasted from another site. Check to make sure the facts are valid. Take time to evaluate each source to decide if it is trustworthy.

 **Common Core State Standards**

Writing

2. Write informative/explanatory texts to examine a topic and convey ideas, concepts, and information through the selection, organization, and analysis of relevant content.

2.a. Introduce a topic clearly, previewing what is to follow; organize ideas, concepts, and information into broader categories; include formatting, graphics, tables, and multimedia when useful to aiding comprehension.

7. Conduct short research projects to answer a question, drawing on several sources and generating additional related, focused questions that allow for multiple avenues of exploration.

> ### Evaluating Internet Domains
>
> Evaluate Internet sources carefully to make sure they are trustworthy. The last three letters of an Internet URL identify the domain of the site, which can help you evaluate the quality of the information being offered.
>
> - **.gov** — Government sites are sponsored by a branch of the United States federal government and are considered reliable.
>
> - **.edu** — Information from an educational research center or department is likely to be carefully checked but may also include student pages that are not edited or monitored.
>
> - **.org** — Groups with organization domains are nonprofit groups. Nonprofit groups usually maintain a high level of credibility, but their sites may still reflect strong biases.
>
> - **.com** — Commercial sites exist to make a profit. Information might be biased to show a product or service in a good light.

Long-Term Research

Long-term research allows you to explore a topic fully by conducting a detailed, comprehensive investigation. Start by making a research plan so you can gather, organize, and synthesize information from multiple sources over time.

As you learn more about your topic, you will need to adjust your research plan to reflect your findings. Throughout your investigation, you might decide to return to an earlier stage to refocus your thesis, gather more information, or reflect on what you have learned.

It is never too late to return to your sources. Once you begin drafting, you might discover that you need one or two more relevant facts to fully support an idea. During revision, you might notice a logical gap that did not occur to you earlier. If you plan ahead, your notes will make it easier for you to return quickly to sources that you have already identified as reliable and find the details you need.

The Research Process

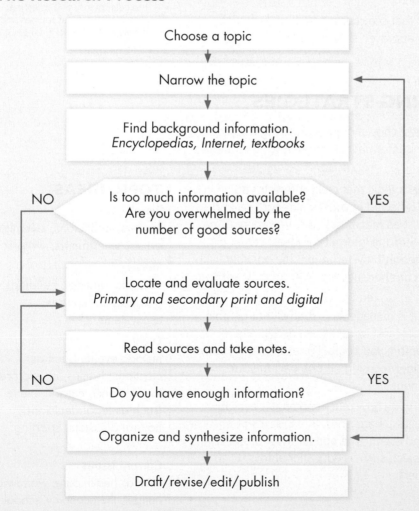

Refer to the Research Process Workshop (see p. lxxii) for more details about the steps in this flowchart.

RESEARCH PROCESS WORKSHOP

Research Writing: Research Report

Research writing brings together information gathered from several sources in order to prove a central point, or thesis. You might use elements of a research report when writing informational articles, historical analyses, or business reports.

Elements of a Research Report

An effective research report includes these elements:

- a *thesis statement* that is clearly expressed
- *factual support* from a variety of reliable, credited sources
- a *clear organization* that includes an introduction, a body, and a conclusion
- *visuals* or *media* to support key ideas
- a *bibliography* or *works-cited list* that provides a complete listing of research sources formatted in an approved style
- error-free grammar

PREWRITING/PLANNING STRATEGIES

Prewriting includes three distinct stages: choosing and narrowing a topic, creating a research plan, and gathering information. The following strategies can help you prepare to write.

Choose and narrow a topic. Find a topic that really interests you. Your enthusiasm for a subject will be reflected in your final report. To find topic ideas, flip through recently published magazines or newspapers. Tune in to television and radio broadcasts. Surf the Internet for ideas, creating and organizing bookmarks in your Internet browser to identify possible topics. List people, places, events, or current issues that you might want to investigate.

Once you select a topic, be sure that it is manageable. You will not be able to cover a broad topic, such as the Holocaust or castles, in detail. Avoid problems by focusing your research before you begin. For example, if you choose to write about a person, consider focusing on one part of your subject's life or a specific accomplishment.

Conduct preliminary research to determine how much material is available. Search through relevant books, Web sites, magazines, and indexes at a library. Jot down the names, ideas, and events that appear most often. Use this information to narrow a wide subject, such as educational toys, to a narrower one, such as electronic readers.

@ **Common Core State Standards**

Writing

2. Write informative/explanatory texts to examine a topic and convey ideas, concepts, and information through the selection, organization, and analysis of relevant content.

2.a. Introduce a topic; organize ideas, concepts, and information, using strategies such as definition, classification, comparison/contrast, and cause/effect; include formatting (e.g., headings), graphics (e.g., charts and tables), and multimedia when useful to aiding comprehension.

7. Conduct short research projects to answer a question, drawing on several sources and refocusing the inquiry when appropriate.

TOPIC IDEAS

People
leaders, politicians, scientists, artists, entertainers, writers

Places
cities, landmarks, buildings, geographic features, ecosystems

Events
historic events (such as elections, battles, or explorers' expeditions), current events (such as legal decisions), natural disasters, sporting events

Current Issues
such as health care, worldwide hunger, the economy, school funding, technology

Create a research plan. An organized plan will help guide your investigation and keep you on track. Your plan can include the elements described in the chart below. Adjust and add to your plan as needed.

Research Question	Compose a question about your topic. The question will help focus your research into a comprehensive but flexible search plan, as well as prevent you from gathering details that do not directly support your purpose. Sample research questions: • How did Lorraine Hansberry's first play get produced on Broadway? • What inspired J. R. R. Tolkien's to write *The Hobbit*? • What Supreme Court decision had the greatest effect on the U.S. Civil Rights Movement?
Source List	Create a list of sources you will consult. Plan to use a variety of sources. Add sources to your plan as you discover them. Place a check next to sources you have located, and then underline sources you have consulted thoroughly.
Search Terms	Write down terms you plan to investigate using online search engines. Making these decisions before you go online can help you avoid digressions that take you away from your topic.
Deadlines	Break a long-term project into short-term goals in order to stay on track and prevent last-minute stress.

Use multiple sources. An effective research project combines information from many sources. The creativity and originality of your research depends on how you combine ideas from many places. Plan to include a variety of these resources:

• **Primary and Secondary Resources** Use primary sources (firsthand or original accounts, such as interview transcripts and letters) and secondary sources (accounts that are not original, such as encyclopedia entries).

• **Print and Digital Resources** The Internet allows fast access to data, but print resources are often edited more carefully. Plan to include both print and digital resources.

• **Media Resources** You can find valuable information in media resources such as documentaries, television programs, podcasts, and museum exhibitions. Public lectures by experts also offer an opportunity to hear an expert's thoughts on a topic.

• **Original Research** Depending on your topic, you may wish to conduct original research to include among your sources. For example, you might interview experts or eyewitnesses or conduct a survey to find out about beliefs in your community.

PREWRITING/PLANNING STRATEGIES
(Continued)

Evaluate sources. Just because something is in print or online does not mean it is true or unbiased. Often you will find articles written by unreliable authors, articles with a bias or an agenda, or articles that lack factual evidence to support their claims. To ensure that you use the right sources, evaluate their reliability using these questions.

Does the source go into enough depth to cover the subject?	☐ yes ☐ no
Does the publisher have a good reputation?	☐ yes ☐ no
Is the author an authority on the subject?	☐ yes ☐ no
Do at least two other sources agree with this source?	☐ yes ☐ no

To ensure that your information is current, accurate, and balanced, follow these guidelines:

- Check publication dates to make sure the information is current.

- If you note discrepancies in the information given by two sources, check the facts in a third source. If three or more sources disagree, mention the disagreement in your paper. Explain whether they differ in matters of fact or in the interpretation of facts.

- Consider the author's perspective. Examine the author's credentials—his or her background—before accepting a conclusion.

Use source cards and note cards. As you do research, take detailed notes on index cards.

- Create a *source card* for each book, article, or Web site. For print sources, list the author, title, publisher, and place and date of publication. For each Internet source, list the sponsor, page name, date of last revision, date you accessed it, and address.

- As you take notes, write one idea on each card. When taking notes, be careful to avoid *plagiarism*, the unethical presentation of someone else's ideas as if they were your own. Clearly indicate if your note reflects an author's exact words or a paraphrase of an author's ideas.

- Use quotation marks whenever you copy words exactly. When using cursive, write legibly to avoid misquoting or misspelling.

Alternatively, you can use computer programs, such as database or word processing software, to keep track of source information.

© **Common Core State Standards**

Reading Informational Text
9. Analyze a case in which two or more texts provide conflicting information on the same topic and identify where the texts disagree on matters of fact or interpretation.

Writing
8. Gather relevant information from multiple print and digital sources, using search terms effectively; assess the credibility and accuracy of each source; and quote or paraphrase the data and conclusions of others while avoiding plagiarism and following a standard format for citation.

Note Card

Du Bois's Education	Lewis	3

The Academic Council awarded
Du Bois a Henry Bromfield
Rogers Memorial Fellowship.

p. 103

Lewis, David Levering	3

W. E. B. Du Bois, 1868–1919:
Biography of a Race

New York: Henry Holt & Company, 1993

920L Public Library

Source Card

DRAFTING STRATEGIES

Define your thesis. Sum up the main point you plan to address in your report in a single statement, called a **thesis statement.** Use your thesis statement to direct your writing and include it in the introduction to your report. The arguments and evidence that you present in the body of your report should connect logically to the thesis statement. If they do not connect, you should consider either modifying your original thesis or using other evidence.

Make an outline. Write a formal outline, such as the one shown, for your report before you begin to draft. Use Roman numerals for your most important points and capital letters for the details that support them. Make sure each point in your outline supports your thesis.

Balance research and original ideas. As you write your draft, strive to achieve a balance between research-based information and your own original ideas. The highlighted portion in this example indicates the writer's original words, not research.

Title of Your Report

I. Introduction
   Thesis Statement
II. First main point
   A. Supporting detail #1
      1. Example
      2. Example
      3. Example
   B. Supporting detail #2
   C. Supporting detail #3
III. Second main point

Model:

The famous Underground Railroad, which operated from approximately 1780 to 1862 ("The Underground Railroad," PBS.org), was not underground, nor was it a railroad. Rather, it was a system operated by a secret network of courageous people who helped slaves escape from the American South and find their way to freedom. The first slaves had arrived in Jamestown, Virginia, in 1619, a year before the Pilgrims arrived at Plymouth Rock, Massachusetts (Buckmaster 11). By the early 1800s, there were about four million slaves in this country (Siebert 378). It was the Underground Railroad that saved many lives from the hardships of slavery in the American South.

Prepare to credit sources. Any material that is not an original idea should be credited, whether you paraphrase it or quote it directly. As you draft, circle all ideas and phrases that come directly from your research. At this stage, for each circled item, use parentheses to note the author's name and the page number of the source. Internet sources can be identified by Web addresses. You can create formal citations later.

DRAFTING STRATEGIES (Continued)

Make direct reference to sources. You can use one of these methods to incorporate the information you have found.

- **Quote directly.** Support your thesis and conclusions with opinions from authorities. When using a source's exact words, enclose the entire statement in quotation marks. However, if the quotation is more than four lines, use a *block quote*. Introduce the quotation with a colon. Then, begin on a new line, indenting the entire quotation and leaving out the quotation marks. Use ellipsis marks to indicate words you decide to omit from any word-for-word quotation. Check that the omission does not change its overall meaning.

- **Paraphrase.** This technique involves restating a writer's specific ideas in your own words. Be sure to properly credit the source.

- **Summarize.** Where appropriate, summarize all major perspectives on the topic. This is especially important when you are describing controversial or complex ideas.

Create visuals. Use visual displays such as charts, graphs, and tables when you want to organize and display information in a way that illustrates your main point and is easy to grasp.

- Pie charts show parts of a whole, so they can be useful in showing any topic with data in percentages.

- Line graphs and bar graphs show information as it changes over time, so they can be useful in showing trends.

Three different ways of visualizing the same general topic—migration—are shown here. Note that important similarities or differences in tables and charts can be emphasized by using different colors and fonts.

Other types of visuals that can help you illustrate your points include photographs, diagrams, and maps. Always make sure the text in your visuals is readable. Add captions to photos so readers can understand what they show. Diagrams and maps should also be clearly labeled. A map requires a legend that tells what the symbols mean, a compass rose indicating where north is, and a scale showing distance.

Create a "Works Cited" list. When you finish drafting, provide full information about your sources in an alphabetical "Works Cited" list or "Bibliography" at the end of your report. Check the format required for your report and follow its style and punctuation guidelines. For more guidance on formats, see the "Works Cited" list on page lxxxi and the information on pages lxxxii–lxxxiii.

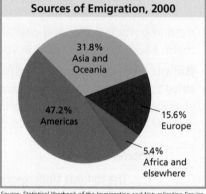

Sources of Emigration, 2000

31.8% Asia and Oceania

15.6% Europe

5.4% Africa and elsewhere

47.2% Americas

Source: *Statistical Yearbook of the Immigration and Naturalization Service*

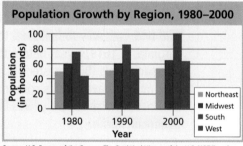

Population Growth by Region, 1980–2000

Population (in thousands)

Year

Northeast
Midwest
South
West

Source: U.S. Bureau of the Census, *The Statistical History of the U.S.* (1976) and 2000 Census of the U.S. www.census.gov

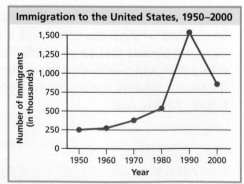

Immigration to the United States, 1950–2000

Number of Immigrants (in thousands)

Year

Source: *Yearbook of Immigration Statistics, 2003*

REVISING STRATEGIES

Common Core State Standards

Writing

2.c. Use appropriate and varied transitions to create cohesion and clarify the relationships among ideas and concepts.

2.f. Provide a concluding statement or section that follows from and supports the information or explanation presented.

Language

2.b. Use an ellipsis to indicate an omission.

Check for unity. All the parts of your report should fit together in a complete, self-contained whole.

1. Check that every paragraph develops your thesis statement. Delete those that do not, or revise to show a connection.

2. Identify the main idea of each paragraph. Often, a topic sentence will directly state that main idea. If a paragraph does not contain a topic sentence, consider adding one.

3. In each paragraph, eliminate any sentences that do not support or explain the topic sentence or main idea.

4. Use transition words and phrases to smooth the flow between paragraphs and between ideas. Examples include *next, finally, although, as a result of, therefore, despite,* and *however.*

5. Check your conclusion to make sure it provides a sense of closure to the writing and that it reinforces your thesis.

Model: Revising for Unity

The Underground Railroad had apparently been in existence toward the end of the 1700s, but it was not named as such until around 1831, when the steam railroads were emerging. Railroad terms were used to describe various aspects of the system. It had "stations" and "depots," the homes and businesses where the runaway slaves could rest and eat. The people who sheltered the fugitives in these stations were called "stationmasters." ~~They would hide people in barns, basements, and back rooms—anywhere they could.~~ People who contributed money or goods were called "stockholders." ~~The money was needed to buy decent clothing for the escaping slaves, for tattered clothing would send an unwanted message about the person's status.~~ The system also had "conductors," whose job was to move fugitives from one station to the next.

The crossed-out sentences do not belong in a paragraph that deals with the terminology of the Underground Railroad.

Check your citations. You must cite an author's direct quotations as well as his or her ideas, even if you restate the information in your own words. An internal citation appears in parentheses and directly follows the information it references. It includes the author's last name and the page number on which the information appears.

Example: "The Duke of Lancaster, in 1888, controlled more than 163,000 acres of British countryside" (Pool 193).

Peer Review Ask a partner to read your draft, identifying details that wander too far from your thesis. Together, look for ways to link your information back to the main idea, or consider cutting the text.

EDITING AND PROOFREADING

Review your draft to correct factual and citation errors, as well as mistakes in format, grammar, and spelling.

Check your facts. Be sure that the facts you have included in your report are accurate. Errors sometimes occur during note-taking, drafting, and revising. To fact-check your report, place an open square next to each fact. Then refer to your original sources to make sure you have stated each fact clearly and correctly. When you have confirmed a fact, place a check in the box and move on to the next one.

Review citations. Check that you have given credit for any ideas that are not your own. You might have unintentionally included exact phrases from one of your sources. To avoid plagiarism, you need to give credit to your sources for any ideas that are not common knowledge. Try reading your draft aloud. Listen for words and phrases that do not sound familiar or do not have your own voice. Chances are good that those elements came from one of your sources. Either provide an accurate citation or paraphrase the information to put the ideas in your own words.

Focus on format. Follow the manuscript requirements by including a title page and appropriate pagination, spacing, margins, and citations. Make sure you have used the preferred system for crediting sources in your paper and for bibliographical sources at the end. Double-check all punctuation and capitalization.

Proofread. Reread your draft to find and correct spelling errors. Be sure that you have used quotation marks correctly and that each open quotation mark has a corresponding closing quotation mark.

Publishing and Presenting

Consider one of the following ways to share your writing:

Give a speech. Now that you are knowledgeable about your topic, give an impromptu (unrehearsed) speech to your classmates. Describe your initial questions, your thesis, and what you found while researching. After you finish, answer questions from the audience.

Deliver an oral presentation. Read your research report aloud to your classmates, or consider recreating the report as a multimedia presentation using presentation software. Add appropriate visual aids as needed, such as charts, maps, and graphs.

Organize a panel discussion. If several of your classmates have written on a similar topic, plan a discussion to compare and contrast your findings. Speakers can summarize their research before opening the panel to questions from the class.

STUDENT MODEL: RESEARCH PAPER

This research report shows how one student develops and supports a thesis statement, integrating research from a variety of sources. Notice how parenthetical citations within each paragraph refer to sources detailed in the works-cited list at the end of the report. Marginal notes highlight elements that make this paper effective.

James Barraclough, Los Alamos, NM

Alexander the Great

Southeastern Europe and western Asia were continually plagued by wars and rebellions in the fourth century B.C. Out of all this strife rose a boy, Alexander III, a hero whose name would be remembered for thousands of years. Alexander became King of Macedonia at the young age of twenty and commenced to conquer the Persian Empire and part of modern-day India using brilliant battle strategy and a quickness to act that kept his enemies guessing. He earned his reputation as 'Alexander the Great' by carving an empire of approximately one million square miles out of a land filled with enemies who were often intent on overthrowing him (Walbank 248).

> James introduces the overall focus—the impressive accomplishments of Alexander—in the first paragraph.

Alexander was born in July 356 B.C. to King Philip II of Macedonia and Olympias, daughter of the King of Epirus. Throughout his life, Alexander was very close to his mother, Olympias, from whom he learned to pray and to believe deeply in the gods. However, Alexander inherited his military genius and bravery from his father, who conquered all of the Greek city-states and then united them under his rule. Even as a child, Alexander had enough ambition for several men, as shown by his comment after his father had conquered a city: "My father will have everything, and I will have nothing left to conquer" (Wepman 121).

After uniting Greece, Philip began a campaign to conquer the Persian Empire, but his efforts were cut short when he was assassinated in 336 B.C. Alexander was only twenty years old, though he had been commanding troops with his father for four years. He was not guaranteed power after his father's death, so he quickly claimed the throne with the army's support (Wilcken 61). Picking up where his father left off, Alexander III, King of Macedonia, began a campaign that would change the world.

> The paper's organization is chronological, following a clear path from Alexander's birth to his death.

In the spring of 334 B.C., Alexander led a relatively small army of 30,000 infantry, comprised mostly of soldiers called *hoplites*, who carried 16-foot spears, and 5,000 cavalry, called the Companions, across the Hellespont, a narrow strait. There, he met a force of Persian cavalry and Greek mercenaries, sent by Darius III, King of the Persian Empire, which was intended to throw back the invaders. However, the Macedonians cut them to shreds by employing Alexander's innovative military strategy (Cartledge 28–29). After that battle, Alexander led his army down along the coast of Asia Minor, taking cities for Greece until he met Darius at Issus. There, Alexander's outnumbered soldiers again routed the Persians, but Darius escaped. As the ancient historian Arrian reports, Darius fled in such a panic, he abandoned his royal chariot. "He even left his bow in the chariot; and mounting a horse continued his flight" (Arrian 450).

James uses a variety of sources—both ancient and modern— for quotations and supporting evidence.

Choosing not to pursue Darius further, Alexander continued along the eastern Mediterranean coast into Egypt, liberating the Egyptians from their hated Persian overlords. In exchange for their liberation, the Egyptians named Alexander pharaoh of Egypt. After his victory, he planned a city called Alexandria to be built on the Mediterranean Sea. As Alexander pressed back into Asia he conquered many cities, but again Darius confronted him—this time better prepared for the man who was such a grave threat to the Persian Empire. However, Alexander employed a cunning ruse to distract the Persians during the battle and crashed back to the middle, crushing the unsuspecting Persians. When Darius fled, the empire was left to Alexander's control (Cartledge 32). At the age of twenty-five, Alexander had become ruler of the Persian Empire and the most powerful man in the world.

Smooth transitions give the paper a sense of flow.

After some time in Babylon, the city he made his capital, Alexander decided to head towards India to conquer new land for his empire. Many of the Greek soldiers protested that they wished to go home after years of hard fighting. Even so, Alexander inspired such loyalty that the soldiers reluctantly followed him to India. After fighting their way through modern-day Afghanistan and Pakistan, Alexander crossed into India. Many of his men died when monsoon rains arrived and poisonous snakes, rats, and tropical diseases, such as malaria, became prevalent.

As the army moved deeper into India, King Porus, an Indian ruler, confronted Alexander's troops with approximately two hundred war elephants and an extensive cavalry. Even though the elephants made it difficult for Alexander's cavalry to fight, Alexander once again outsmarted his enemy and defeated the Indian army. Porus surrendered and agreed to be his ally. Following the restoration of Porus to his kingdom, Alexander's men, who were wearied by the intense heat and stricken with homesickness, refused to move on. Alexander sulked in his tent, until he finally relented and set out towards Babylon (Prevas 166–172).

James credits each source in parentheses—using only author's last name and page number— directly after the information taken from that source. Full citations appear at the end of the paper.

Approximately one year after his return from India, Alexander developed a fever and stomach cramps. These may have been caused by heavy drinking, typhoid, malaria, or poison. The fatal illness kept him in bed until he died on June 11, 323 B.C. at the age of 32. Since Alexander did not appoint a successor to his throne, the mightiest empire of the time, perhaps of all time, fell into disorder and collapsed with his death (Prevas 202–207).

All in all, Alexander—who was just a boy in some people's eyes when he took the throne—rose to the occasion and conquered the world, forging an empire with his heart and sword. Alexander was a complex man who could be harsh, ruthless, and relentless in battle, but he could also be compassionate and sympathetic towards his wounded soldiers. These characteristics inspired loyalty and unity in thousands of soldiers. They followed Alexander wherever he led, even if they had a fierce desire to go home. The man known as Alexander the Great was a king, an emperor, a pharaoh, a conqueror, and most of all, a leader who could charge into battle, knowing his men would follow.

Works Cited

Arrian. *The Anabasis of Alexander.* Trans. Edward J. Chinnock. *The Greek Historians: The Complete and Unabridged Historical Works of Herodotus, Thucydides, Xenophon, Arrian.* Ed. Francis R. Godolphin. New York: Random, 1942. Print.

Cartledge, Paul. *Alexander the Great.* New York: Overlook, 2004. Print.

Prevas, John. *Envy of the Gods.* Cambridge: Da Capo, 2004. Print.

Walbank, Frank W. "Alexander the Great." *Encyclopedia Britannica.* 15th ed. 1990. Print.

Wepman, Dennis. Excerpt from *Alexander the Great.* New York: Facts on File, 1986. Web. *eReader.com.* 14 April 2005.

Wilcken, Ulrich. *Alexander the Great.* New York: Norton, 1967. Print.

All sources used are listed at the end of the paper in a Works Cited list. To see the proper format for different sources, see Citing Sources and Preparing Manuscript, pages lxxxii–lxxxiii.

CITING SOURCES AND PREPARING MANUSCRIPT

Proofreading and Preparing Manuscript

Before preparing a final copy, proofread your manuscript. The chart shows the standard symbols for marking corrections to be made.

Proofreading Symbols	
insert	∧
delete	ᵔ
close space	◠
new paragraph	¶
add comma	⋏
add period	⊙
transpose (switch)	∩
change to cap	a̲
change to lowercase	A̸

- Choose a standard, easy-to-read font.
- Type or print on one side of unlined 8 1/2" x 11" paper.
- Set the margins for the side, top, and bottom of your paper at approximately one inch. Most word-processing programs have a default setting that is appropriate.
- Double-space the document.
- Indent the first line of each paragraph.
- Number the pages in the upper right corner.

Follow your teacher's directions for formatting formal research papers. Most papers will have the following features:

- Title Page
- Table of Contents or Outline
- Works Cited List

Avoiding Plagiarism

Whether you are presenting a formal research paper or an opinion paper on a current event, you must be careful to give credit for any ideas or opinions that are not your own. Presenting someone else's ideas, research, or opinion as your own—even if you have phrased it in different words—is *plagiarism*, the equivalent of academic stealing, or fraud.

Do not use the ideas or research of others in place of your own. Read from several sources to draw your own conclusions and form your own opinions. Incorporate the ideas and research of others to support your points. Credit the source of the following types of support:

- Statistics
- Direct quotations
- Indirectly quoted statements of opinions
- Conclusions presented by an expert
- Facts available in only one or two sources

Crediting Sources

When you credit a source, you acknowledge where you found your information and you give your readers the details necessary for locating the source themselves. Within the body of the paper, you provide a short citation, a footnote number linked to a footnote, or an endnote number linked to an endnote reference. These brief references show the page numbers on which you found the information. Prepare a reference list at the end of the paper to provide full bibliographic information on your sources. These are two common types of reference lists:

- A bibliography provides a listing of all the resources you consulted during your research.
- A Works Cited list indicates the works you have referenced in your paper.

The chart on the next page shows the Modern Language Association format for crediting sources. This is the most common format for papers written in the content areas in middle school and high school. Unless instructed otherwise by your teacher, use this format for crediting sources.

MLA Style for Listing Sources

Book with one author	Pyles, Thomas. *The Origins and Development of the English Language.* 2nd ed. New York: Harcourt, 1971. Print.
Book with two or three authors	McCrum, Robert, William Cran, and Robert MacNeil. *The Story of English.* New York: Penguin, 1987. Print.
Book with an editor	Truth, Sojourner. *Narrative of Sojourner Truth.* Ed. Margaret Washington. New York: Vintage, 1993. Print.
Book with more than three authors or editors	Donald, Robert B., et al. *Writing Clear Essays.* Upper Saddle River: Prentice, 1996. Print.
Single work in an anthology	Hawthorne, Nathaniel. "Young Goodman Brown." *Literature: An Introduction to Reading and Writing.* Ed. Edgar V. Roberts and H. E. Jacobs. Upper Saddle River: Prentice, 1998. 376–385. Print. [Indicate pages for the entire selection.]
Introduction to a work in a published edition	Washington, Margaret. Introduction. *Narrative of Sojourner Truth.* By Sojourner Truth. Ed. Washington. New York: Vintage, 1993. v–xi. Print.
Signed article from an encyclopedia	Askeland, Donald R. "Welding." *World Book Encyclopedia.* 1991 ed. Print.
Signed article in a weekly magazine	Wallace, Charles. "A Vodacious Deal." *Time* 14 Feb. 2000: 63. Print.
Signed article in a monthly magazine	Gustaitis, Joseph. "The Sticky History of Chewing Gum." *American History* Oct. 1998: 30–38. Print.
Newspaper	Thurow, Roger. "South Africans Who Fought for Sanctions Now Scrap for Investors." *Wall Street Journal* 11 Feb. 2000: A1+. Print. [For a multipage article that does not appear on consecutive pages, write only the first page number on which it appears, followed by the plus sign.]
Unsigned editorial or story	"Selective Silence." Editorial. *Wall Street Journal* 11 Feb. 2000: A14. Print. [If the editorial or story is signed, begin with the author's name.]
Signed pamphlet or brochure	[Treat the pamphlet as though it were a book.]
Work from a library subscription service	Ertman, Earl L. "Nefertiti's Eyes." *Archaeology* Mar.–Apr. 2008: 28–32. *Kids Search.* EBSCO. New York Public Library. Web. 18 June 2008. [Indicate the date you accessed the information.]
Filmstrips, slide programs, videocassettes, DVDs, and other audiovisual media	*The Diary of Anne Frank.* Dir. George Stevens. Perf. Millie Perkins, Shelley Winters, Joseph Schildkraut, Lou Jacobi, and Richard Beymer. 1959. Twentieth Century Fox, 2004. DVD.
CD-ROM (with multiple publishers)	Simms, James, ed. *Romeo and Juliet.* By William Shakespeare. Oxford: Attica Cybernetics; London: BBC Education; London: Harper, 1995. CD-ROM.
Radio or television program transcript	"Washington's Crossing of the Delaware." *Weekend Edition Sunday.* Natl. Public Radio. WNYC, New York. 23 Dec. 2003. Print. Transcript.
Internet Web page	"Fun Facts About Gum." NACGM site. 1999. National Association of Chewing Gum Manufacturers. Web. 19 Dec. 1999. [Indicate the date you accessed the information.]
Personal interview	Smith, Jane. Personal interview. 10 Feb. 2000.

All examples follow the style given in the *MLA Handbook for Writers of Research Papers,* seventh edition, by Joseph Gibaldi.

THE BIG ?

Can all conflicts be resolved?

UNIT PATHWAY

PART 1
SETTING EXPECTATIONS

- INTRODUCING THE BIG QUESTION
- CLOSE READING WORKSHOP

PART 2
TEXT ANALYSIS
GUIDED EXPLORATION

TURNING POINTS

PART 3
TEXT SET
DEVELOPING INSIGHT

HUMAN VS. MACHINE

PART 4
DEMONSTRATING INDEPENDENCE

- INDEPENDENT READING
- ONLINE TEXT SET

CLOSE READING TOOL

Use this tool to practice the close reading strategies you learn.

STUDENT eTEXT

Bring learning to life with audio, video, and interactive tools.

ONLINE WRITER'S NOTEBOOK

Easily capture notes and complete assignments online.

Find all Digital Resources at **pearsonrealize.com**

Introducing the Big Question

Can all conflicts be resolved?

A **conflict** is a struggle between opposing forces. For example, a disagreement might arise between you and a friend about where to eat. Such a minor conflict usually has a quick solution that ends in a compromise. However, it may turn into an argument about who has better taste in food. It might even end in a stalemate, a dispute that neither side can win.

Major conflicts are more serious and take time to resolve. Some can lead to anger or even violence and injury. For example, a land dispute that cannot be resolved peacefully through negotiation could turn into a violent conflict between neighboring countries.

Some conflicts have clear outcomes, often with a clear winner and a clear loser. Sometimes, both parties may feel they have won or lost. Sometimes, though, there is no clear resolution. A feud between former friends may simmer for years. Nations may find an uneasy, troubled peace.

Exploring the Big Question

Collaboration: Group Discussion Start thinking about the Big Question by making a list of different conflicts based on your own experience and knowledge. Describe one specific example of each of the following types of conflicts and explain its outcome.

- A situation in which neighbors irritate each other
- An incident in which someone tries to take something by force
- An occasion on which one person tries to mislead another
- A strong reaction to an opposing viewpoint
- A person's struggle with insecurity about leaving home
- A person's doubts about his or her ability to achieve a particular goal

Talk with a partner about attempts that were made to resolve each conflict. As you discuss each example, consider whether the attempted resolution was successful—or whether a resolution might be possible. Use the Big Question vocabulary in your discussion.

Connecting to the Literature Each reading in this unit will give you additional insight into the Big Question: Can all conflicts be resolved?

Vocabulary

Acquire and Use Academic Vocabulary The term "academic vocabulary" refers to words you typically encounter in scholarly and literary texts and in technical and business writing. Review the definitions of these academic vocabulary words.

Common Core State Standards

Speaking and Listening
1. Engage effectively in a range of collaborative discussions (one-on-one, in groups, and teacher-led) with diverse partners on *grade 8 topics, texts, and issues,* building on others' ideas and expressing their own clearly.

Language
6. Acquire and use accurately grade-appropriate general academic and domain-specific words and phrases; gather vocabulary knowledge when considering a word or phrase important to comprehension or expression.

argument (är´ gyo͞o mənt) *n.* 1. supporting reasons given for a claim; 2. oral disagreement

injury (in´ jə rē) *n.* harm or damage to a person

insecurity (in´ si kyo͝or´ ə tē) *n.* lack of confidence; self-doubt

interact (in´ tər akt´) *v.* 1. change or affect one another; 2. communicate (with)

negotiate (ni gō´ shē āt´) *v.* bargain or deal with another party to reach a settlement

oppose (ə pōz´) *v.* go against; stand in the way of

reaction (rē ak´ shən) *n.* response to an influence, an action, or a statement

solution (sə lo͞o´ shən) *n.* 1. way to fix a problem; 2. act of solving a problem or answering a question

viewpoint (vyo͞o´ point´) *n.* position regarding an idea or a statement

Use these words as you complete Big Question activities in this unit that involve reading, writing, speaking, and listening.

Gather Vocabulary Knowledge Additional words related to conflict are listed below. Categorize the words by deciding whether you know each one well, know it a little bit, or do not know it at all.

compromise	mislead	victorious
irritate	stalemate	violence

Then, do the following:

1. Write the definitions of the words you know.
2. Consult a print or an online dictionary to confirm the meaning and pronunciation of each word you defined. Revise your definition if necessary.
3. Next, look up each word you do not know. Then, write its meaning and practice its pronunciation.
4. Use at least four of the words in a paragraph about a conflict that you or someone you know has faced.

Close Reading Workshop

In this workshop you will learn an approach to reading that will deepen your understanding of literature and will help you better appreciate an author's craft. The workshop includes models for the close reading, discussion, research, and writing activities you will complete as you study the literature in this unit. After you have reviewed the strategies and models in this workshop, practice your skills with the Independent Practice selection.

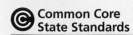 **Common Core State Standards**

RL.8.1, RL.8.2, RL.8.3; W.8.2, W.8.7, W.8.9.a; SL.8.1
[For full standards wording, see the standards chart in the front of this book.]

CLOSE READING: SHORT STORY

In Part 2 of this unit you will focus on reading various stories. Use these strategies as you read the texts.

Comprehension: Key Ideas and Details

- Read first to unlock basic meaning.
- Use context clues and reference works to determine the meanings of unfamiliar words.
- Identify details to clarify through research.
- Make inferences about information that is implied.

Ask yourself questions such as these:
- Who are the main characters?
- What is the major conflict, or struggle between opposing forces?

Text Analysis: Craft and Structure

- Analyze how the author uses dialogue and other story details to portray characters and move the action along.
- Look for irony—actual outcomes that contradict expected ones.
- Interpret any symbols—people or things that stand for a larger meaning.

Ask yourself questions such as these:
- Which details paint a picture of characters or show how they change?
- What expectations does the author create? Are any contradicted?
- What does each symbol in the story represent?

Connections: Integration of Knowledge and Ideas

- Consider how story details work to express theme—the story's central insight about life.
- Compare this work with others you have read.

Ask yourself questions such as these:
- What insight into life is suggested by the patterns of the story details?
- How is this story similar to and different from others I have read?

Read

As you read this short story, take note of the annotations, which model ways to closely read the text.

Reading Model

from "Peter and Rosa" by Isak Dinesen

"I have heard a story, Rosa, you know," he said, "of a skipper who named his ship after his wife. He had the figurehead of it beautifully carved, just like her, and the hair of it gilt.[1] But his wife was jealous of the ship. 'You think more of the figurehead than of me,' she said to him. 'No,' he answered, 'I think so highly of her because she is like you, yes, because she is you yourself.[2] Is she not gallant, full-bosomed; does she not dance in the waves, like you at our wedding? In a way she is really even kinder to me than you are. She gallops along where I tell her to go, and she lets her long hair down freely, while you put up yours under a cap. But she turns her back to me, so that when I want a kiss I come home to Elsinore.' Now once, when this skipper was trading at Trankebar, he chanced to help an old native King to flee from traitors in his own country. As they parted the King gave him two big blue, precious stones, and these he had set into the face of his figurehead, like a pair of eyes to it. When he came home he told his wife of his adventure, and said: 'Now she has your blue eyes too.'[3] 'You had better give me the stones for a pair of earrings,' said she. 'No,' he said again, 'I cannot do that, and you would not ask me to if you understood.' Still the wife could not stop fretting about the blue stones, and one day, when her husband was with the skippers' corporation, she had a glazier of the town take them out, and put two bits of blue glass into the figurehead instead, and the skipper did not find out, but sailed off to Portugal. But after some time the skipper's wife found that her eyesight was

Key Ideas and Details
1 To clarify meaning, you might look up the word *figurehead* to learn that it means a carved figure on the bow of a ship.

Craft and Structure
2 The wife shows her jealousy, while the husband attempts to reassure her. His repeated use of the word *you* emphasizes the deep connection he sees between his wife and the figurehead.

Craft and Structure
3 This statement is short but powerful: "Now she has your blue eyes too." The blue stones complete the figurehead as a symbol of jealousy: It is the wife's rival in every detail.

growing bad, and that she could not see to thread a needle. She went to a wise woman, who gave her ointments and waters, but they did not help her, and in the end the old woman shook her head, and told her that this was a rare and incurable disease, and that she was going blind. 'Oh, God,' the wife then cried, 'that the ship was back in the harbor of Elsinore. Then I should have the glass taken out, and the jewels put back. For did he not say that they were my eyes?'[4] But the ship did not come back. Instead the skipper's wife had a letter from the Consul of Portugal, who informed her that she had been wrecked, and gone to the bottom with all hands. And it was a very strange thing, the Consul wrote, that in broad daylight she had run straight into a tall rock, rising out of the sea."[5]

Craft and Structure

4 The wife is horrified as she realizes that the "eyes" she stole from the figurehead have led to her own failing eyesight. This situation creates irony.

Integration of Knowledge and Ideas

5 Both wife and ship are now blind, with a deadly result. The story's outcome expresses the theme that jealousy causes destructive "blindness."

Discuss

Sharing your own ideas and listening to the ideas of others can deepen your understanding of a text and help you look at a topic in a whole new way. As you participate in collaborative discussions, work to have a genuine exchange in which classmates build upon one another's ideas. Support your points with evidence and ask meaningful questions.

Discussion Model

Student 1: It seems strange to me how the symbol of the wife—the carved ship and its figurehead—is so closely linked to her. The skipper even says, "She is you yourself." I can't blame the wife for being a little jealous.

Student 2: Right! The skipper even says this symbol is "kinder" to him than the wife herself, so I can see why the wife was mad and jealous. Also, the sea can represent a threat to wives and those "left behind" on land. The sea takes loved ones away.

Student 3: I remember reading something about sailors believing that figureheads protected their ships, but I think these were carvings of gods and goddesses. I wonder what a female figurehead represents or what makes her eyes so important.

Research

Targeted research can clarify unfamiliar details and shed light on various aspects of a text. Consider questions that arise in your mind as you read, and use those questions as the basis for research.

Research Model

Question: *What do figureheads on ships represent?*

Key Words for Internet Search: ship's figureheads + symbols

Result: National Museum of the Royal Navy (Portsmouth), Ship's Figureheads

What I Learned: Figureheads represent the life force of the ship and have been used for centuries. Figureheads range from carvings of ferocious animals to mythological figures to women. Frightening figureheads were meant to scare enemy ships, while women were believed to have the power to calm a raging sea. Some sailors believed that the ship needed eyes in order to know where to travel safely.

Write

Writing about a text will deepen your understanding of it and will also allow you to share your ideas with others more formally. The following model essay analyzes how symbolism creates meaning in Isak Dinesen's "Peter and Rosa." The writer cites evidence to support the main claim.

Writing Model: Argument

A Close Look at Symbols in an Excerpt from Isak Dinesen's "Peter and Rosa"

In the excerpt from "Peter and Rosa," Isak Dinesen tells a haunting tale about a skipper and his wife. The main theme of Dinesen's story is that jealousy can lead to horrible consequences. The author conveys this theme through powerful symbols and the story events they shape.

The writer begins by introducing a claim about the story's theme.

The main symbol in the story is the figurehead. The wife is jealous of the skipper's ship and its figurehead. She reveals her jealousy by telling her husband, "You think more of the figurehead than of me." She probably feels cheated because the skipper spends a lot of time on his ship and speaks proudly of the figurehead.

The writer structures the argument logically, interpreting a different aspect of the story's symbolism in each body paragraph.

The skipper tries to reassure his wife, telling her that the figurehead "is you yourself." He is saying that his wife is the most important thing in his life. She is the reason he goes out and makes a living on the sea. She is also the reason he comes back home. The skipper makes this clear when he says that the figurehead "turns her back to me, so that when I want a kiss I come home to Elsinore." These statements show that the figurehead symbolizes the skipper's love for his wife. However, his wife just gets angrier and more jealous.

Specific details cited from the text support the argument.

Perhaps the most important symbol Dinesen uses is the figurehead's eyes. Eyes often stand for wisdom, and in sailing legends the eyes of the figurehead allowed the ship to "see" to travel safely. In this story, the jealous wife takes the stones that form the eyes of the figurehead on her husband's ship. The wife then loses her sight, and the ship crashes. Jealousy has "blinded" both the wife and the ship.

By incorporating information found during research, the writer gives a deeper interpretation of the symbol of the figurehead.

Dinesen uses the symbol of the figurehead to express her theme: Jealousy "blinds" people and is destructive. She is able to convey her theme clearly and powerfully by placing this symbol at the center of events in the story. The ship's sinking, the husband's death, and the wife's incurable blindness are all consequences of the wife's jealousy of the figurehead. These events, along with the eerie image of the figurehead, guarantee that readers will remember Dinesen's message.

The writer concludes the argument by restating the original claim and summarizing the story's catastrophic events.

As you read the following, apply the close reading strategies you have learned. You may need to read the short story multiple times.

An Hour With Abuelo
by Judith Ortiz Cofer

"Just one hour, *una hora,* is all I'm asking of you, son." My grandfather is in a nursing home in Brooklyn, and my mother wants me to spend some time with him, since the doctors say that he doesn't have too long to go now. I don't have much time left of my summer vacation, and there's a stack of books next to my bed I've got to read if I'm going to get into the AP English class I want. I'm going stupid in some of my classes, and Mr. Williams, the principal at Central, said that if I passed some reading tests, he'd let me move up.

Besides, I hate the place, the old people's home, especially the way it smells like industrial-strength ammonia and other stuff I won't mention, since it turns my stomach. And really the abuelo always has a lot of relatives visiting him, so I've gotten out of going out there except at Christmas, when a whole vanload of grandchildren are herded over there to give him gifts and a hug. We all make it quick and spend the rest of the time in the recreation area, where they play checkers and stuff with some of the old people's games, and I catch up on back issues of *Modern Maturity.* I'm not picky, I'll read almost anything.

Anyway, after my mother nags me for about a week, I let her drive me to Golden Years. She drops me off in front. She wants me to go in alone and have a "good time" talking to Abuelo. I tell her to be back in one hour or I'll take the bus back to Paterson. She squeezes my hand and says, *"Gracias, hijo,"*[1] in a choked-up voice like I'm doing her a big favor.

I get depressed the minute I walk into the place. They line up the old people in wheelchairs in the hallway as if they were about to be raced to the finish line by orderlies who don't even look at them when they push them here and there. I walk fast to room 10, Abuelo's "suite." He is sitting up in his bed writing with a pencil in one of those old-fashioned black hardback notebooks. It has the outline of the island of Puerto Rico on it. I slide into the hard vinyl chair by his bed. He sort of smiles and the lines

Meet the Author
Born in Puerto Rico in 1952, **Judith Ortiz Cofer** grew up in both Puerto Rico and New Jersey, where her father was stationed in the United States Navy. She was introduced to the storytelling tradition at her grandmother's house in Puerto Rico.

◀ **Vocabulary**
recreation (rek rē ā´ shən) *n. used as adj.* for the purpose of play or amusement

orderlies (ôr´ dər lēz) *n.* hospital attendants

CLOSE READING TOOL

Read and respond to this selection online using the **Close Reading Tool.**

---

1. **"Gracias** (grä´ sē äs), **hijo** (ē´ hō)" Spanish for "Thank you, son." *Hijo* also means "child."

on his face get deeper, but he doesn't say anything. Since I'm supposed to talk to him, I say, "What are you doing, Abuelo, writing the story of your life?"

It's supposed to be a joke, but he answers, "Sí, how did you know, Arturo?"

His name is Arturo too. I was named after him. I don't really know my grandfather. His children, including my mother, came to New York and New Jersey (where I was born) and he stayed on the Island until my grandmother died. Then he got sick, and since nobody could leave their jobs to go take care of him, they brought him to this nursing home in Brooklyn. I see him a couple of times a year, but he's always surrounded by his sons and daughters. My mother tells me that Don Arturo had once been a teacher back in Puerto Rico, but had lost his job after the war. Then he became a farmer. She's always saying in a sad voice, "Ay, bendito!² What a waste of a fine mind." Then she usually shrugs her shoulders and says, "Así es la vida."³ That's the way life is. It sometimes makes me mad that the adults I know just accept whatever is thrown at them because "that's the way things are." Not for me. I go after what I want.

Anyway, Abuelo is looking at me like he was trying to see into my head, but he doesn't say anything. Since I like stories, I decide I may as well ask him if he'll read me what he wrote.

I look at my watch: I've already used up twenty minutes of the hour I promised my mother.

Abuelo starts talking in his slow way. He speaks what my mother calls book English. He taught himself from a dictionary, and his words sound stiff, like he's sounding them out in his head before he says them. With his children he speaks Spanish, and that funny book English with us grandchildren. I'm surprised that he's still so sharp, because his body is shrinking like a crumpled-up brown paper sack with some bones in it. But I can see from looking into his eyes that the light is still on in there.

"It is a short story, Arturo. The story of my life. It will not take very much time to read it."

"I have time, Abuelo." I'm a little embarrassed that he saw me looking at my watch.

"Yes, *hijo*. You have spoken the truth. *La verdad.* You have much time."

Abuelo reads: "'I loved words from the beginning of my life. In the campo⁴ where I was born one of seven sons, there were few books. My mother read them to us over and over: the Bible, the

---

2. **bendito** (ven dē′ tō) Spanish for "blessed."
3. **Así es la vida** (ä sē′ es lä vē′ *th*ä) Spanish for "such is life."
4. **campo** (käm′ pō) Spanish for "open country."

stories of Spanish **conquistadors** and of pirates that she had read as a child and brought with her from the city of Mayagüez; that was before she married my father, a coffee bean farmer; and she taught us words from the newspaper that a boy on a horse brought every week to her. She taught each of us how to write on a slate with chalks that she ordered by mail every year. We used those chalks until they were so small that you lost them between your fingers.

"'I always wanted to be a writer and a teacher. With my heart and my soul I knew that I wanted to be around books all of my life. And so against the wishes of my father, who wanted all his sons to help him on the land, she sent me to high school in Mayagüez. For four years I boarded with a couple she knew. I paid my rent in labor, and I ate vegetables I grew myself. I wore my clothes until they were thin as parchment. But I graduated at the top of my class! My whole family came to see me that day. My mother brought me a beautiful *guayabera*, a white shirt made of the finest cotton and embroidered by her own hands. I was a happy young man.

"'In those days you could teach in a country school with a high school diploma. So I went back to my mountain village and got a job teaching all grades in a little classroom built by the parents of my students.

"'I had books sent to me by the government. I felt like a rich man although the pay was very small. I had books. All the books I wanted! I taught my students how to read poetry and plays, and how to write them. We made up songs and put on shows for the parents. It was a beautiful time for me.

"'Then the war came,[5] and the American President said that all Puerto Rican men would be drafted. I wrote to our governor and explained that I was the only teacher in the mountain village. I told him that the children would go back to the fields and grow up ignorant if I could not teach them their letters. I said that I thought I was a better teacher than a soldier. The governor did not answer my letter. I went into the U.S. Army.

"'I told my sergeant that I could be a teacher in the army. I could teach all the farm boys their letters so that they could read the instructions on the ammunition boxes and not blow themselves up. The sergeant said I was too smart for my own good, and gave me a job cleaning latrines. He said to me there is reading material for you there, scholar. Read the writing on the walls. I spent the war mopping floors and cleaning toilets.

"'When I came back to the Island, things had changed. You

◄ **Vocabulary**
conquistadors (kän kēs´ tə dôrz´) *n.* Spanish conquerors of parts of America in the sixteenth century

---

5. **"'Then the war came, . . .'"** The United States entered World War II in 1941, after the bombing of Pearl Harbor.

had to have a college degree to teach school, even the lower grades. My parents were sick, two of my brothers had been killed in the war, the others had stayed in Nueva York. I was the only one left to help the old people. I became a farmer. I married a good woman who gave me many good children. I taught them all how to read and write before they started school.'"

Abuelo then puts the notebook down on his lap and closes his eyes.

"*Así es la vida* is the title of my book," he says in a whisper, almost to himself. Maybe he's forgotten that I'm there.

For a long time he doesn't say anything else. I think that he's sleeping, but then I see that he's watching me through half-closed lids, maybe waiting for my opinion of his writing. I'm trying to think of something nice to say. I liked it and all, but not the title. And I think that he could've been a teacher if he had wanted to bad enough. Nobody is going to stop me from doing what I want with my life. I'm not going to let la vida get in my way. I want to discuss this with him, but the words are not coming into my head in Spanish just yet. I'm about to ask him why he didn't keep fighting to make his dream come true, when an old lady in hot-pink running shoes sort of appears at the door.

She is wearing a pink jogging outfit too. The world's oldest marathoner, I say to myself. She calls out to my grandfather in a flirty voice, "Yoo-hoo, Arturo, remember what day this is? It's poetry-reading day in the rec room! You promised us you'd read your new one today."

I see my abuelo perking up almost immediately. He points to his wheelchair, which is hanging like a huge metal bat in the open closet. He makes it obvious that he wants me to get it. I put it together, and with Mrs. Pink Running Shoes's help, we get him in it. Then he says in a strong deep voice I hardly recognize, "Arturo, get that notebook from the table, please."

I hand him another map-of-the-Island notebook—this one is red. On it in big letters it says, *POEMAS DE ARTURO.*

I start to push him toward the rec room, but he shakes his finger at me.

"Arturo, look at your watch now. I believe your time is over." He gives me a wicked smile.

Then with her pushing the wheelchair—maybe a little too fast—they roll down the hall. He is already reading from his notebook, and she's making bird noises. I look at my watch and the hour *is* up, to the minute. I can't help but think that my abuelo has been timing *me*. It cracks me up. I walk slowly down the hall toward the exit sign. I want my mother to have to wait a little. I don't want her to think that I'm in a hurry or anything.

Close Reading Activities

Read

Comprehension: Key Ideas and Details

1. What is the narrator's conflict at the start of the story? Cite details in support.

2. **(a)** What was Abuelo's dream in life? **(b) Summarize:** What caused Abuelo to give up his dream? **(c) Infer:** What is Abuelo's new purpose in life? Explain.

3. **(a)** How does Abuelo surprise the narrator? **(b) Draw Conclusions:** How is the narrator changed by story events? Cite story details to support your answer.

4. **Summarize:** Write a brief, objective summary of the story.

Text Analysis: Craft and Structure

5. **Evaluate:** Does the author's use of Spanish add to or detract from the story? Explain, citing specific examples.

6. **(a)** Cite four details that the author includes to help readers understand Abuelo. Explain what each shows about his character. **(b) Evaluate:** How effective is the author's development of Abuelo's character?

7. **Analyze:** The story uses first-person narration—it is told by a character in the story. How does this choice of narrator contribute to the effectiveness of the ending? Cite details to support your analysis.

Connections: Integration of Knowledge and Ideas

Discuss
Conduct a **small-group discussion** about the irony in the story. To identify the irony, consider how readers expect the story to turn out and how it actually ends. Then, relate this irony to the story's theme, or insight into life.

Research
Judith Ortiz Cofer's grandfather wrote poetry in his backyard workshop. As a child, Ortiz Cofer had to listen to his poems to be allowed to enter. Research Ortiz Cofer's experiences with storytelling and poetry in her family home and their influence on

a. this particular story.

b. her writing in general.

Take notes as you perform your research. Then, write a brief **explanation** of the influence that Ortiz Cofer's family and culture had on her writing.

Write
Characters' words and actions propel story events forward. Write an **analytical essay** in which you analyze how Ortiz Cofer develops characters in this story and why that development is vital to the plot. Cite details from the story, including specific incidents and lines of dialogue, to support your analysis.

Can all conflicts be resolved?
Both the narrator and Abuelo experience a conflict between their own wishes and the duties they must fulfill. Is each conflict resolved at the end? Explain your answer.

"**A story isn't** about **a** moment in time; a story is about ***the*** moment in time."

—**W. D. Wetherell**

PART 2

TEXT ANALYSIS GUIDED EXPLORATION

TURNING POINTS

As you read the stories in this section, notice how conflicts or challenges drive events. These conflicts bring the characters to turning points—moments of decision that could change everything. The quotation on the facing page will help you start thinking about turning points and the important ways that they develop character, in both literature and life.

◀ **CRITICAL VIEWING** In what ways does this image capture "*the* moment in time," or a turning point? What aspects of a turning point does it not capture?

READINGS IN PART 2

SHORT STORY
Raymond's Run
Toni Cade Bambara
(p. 22)

SHORT STORY
The Tell-Tale Heart
Edgar Allan Poe (p. 38)

SHORT STORY
Flowers for Algernon
Daniel Keyes (p. 52)

SHORT STORY
The Story-Teller
Saki (p. 92)

CLOSE READING TOOL

Use the **Close Reading Tool** to practice the strategies you learn in this unit.

Elements of a Short Story

In a short story, **characters**, **setting**, **plot**, and **conflict** combine to develop a meaningful **theme**.

A **short story** is a brief work of fiction intended to be read in a single sitting. Most short stories are built from certain common elements.

At the heart of a short story are the **characters,** the people or the animals who take part in the action. To help you get to know a character, an author uses **characterization.** For example, by having a character talk tough but act kindly, a writer uses what the character says and does to reveal the character's personality. Characterization can show

- a character's **traits**—his or her qualities, attitudes, and values;
- a character's **motives**—the reasons for a character's actions.

Characters live and act in a **setting**— the time and place of the story's action. Setting often contributes to the story's atmosphere or **mood.** Setting includes cultural context—the society in which the characters live.

Plot is the sequence of events in a story. Each event in the plot plays its role in propelling the action forward. Early scenes may provide important background information. Subsequent events build to the climax, or turning point, which leads to the ending.

A **conflict,** or struggle between opposing forces, calls on characters to act and so drives the plot. An **internal conflict** takes place in the mind of a character, as when a character struggles with opposing feelings. An **external conflict** takes place between a character and an outside force, such as nature.

All the details in a short story work together to develop its **theme**—a central message or insight about life. Although themes may be stated directly, they are more often implied by the characters' experiences and statements, as well as by patterns in story events and descriptions, as in the example below.

Characters	Setting	Plot and Conflicts
• an overworked bus driver • a powerful pro wrestler • a quiet store clerk and her young son • other passengers	A crowded city bus in rush-hour traffic on a busy highway	The bus driver, who has also been working a night job, falls asleep while driving. Most of the passengers, including the wrestler, panic. The clerk focuses only on her son's safety, not on her own. She calmly takes control and drives the bus to safety.

Themes	• Sometimes, heroism is born from love, not muscle. • Appearances can be deceiving.

Plot Structure

The way in which story events are organized for dramatic effect is the **plot structure.** Typically, a plot is organized into these parts:

- The **exposition** introduces the characters and their situation. It often includes an **inciting event** that reveals the central **conflict.**

- The **rising action** develops the conflict.

- The **climax** is the turning point at which the story's outcome is determined. The climax is the point of greatest intensity.

- The **falling action** sets up the story's ending.

- The **resolution,** or conclusion, usually shows how the conflict is settled. It may also leave open part or all of the conflict.

The chart below shows how the parts of a plot work together to tell a story.

Point of View

The perspective from which a story is told is the **point of view.** Using point of view, writers structure and control the information readers receive.

- **First-person point of view** presents the story from the perspective of a character in the story. The narrator uses the pronouns *I, me,* and *my.*

- **Third-person point of view** tells the story from the perspective of a narrator outside the story. An **omniscient** third-person narrator knows everything that happens and reveals what each character thinks and feels. A **limited** third-person narrator reveals the thoughts and feelings of a single character.

Common Core State Standards

Reading Literature

2. Determine a theme or central idea of a text and analyze its development over the course of the text, including its relationship to the characters, setting, and plot; provide an objective summary of the text.

3. Analyze how particular lines of dialogue or incidents in a story or drama propel the action, reveal aspects of a character, or provoke a decision.

Climax: *The train rushes toward a cliff as the sheriff struggles with the ropes binding him.*

Bart traps the sheriff on a train.

The sheriff arrests Bart's sidekick.

Bart's gang robs the bank.

Rising Action

Falling Action

The sheriff wriggles loose from the ropes and jumps from the train.

The sheriff sneaks up on Bart's gang.

Exposition: *The sheriff learns that Bart and his gang plan to rob a bank.*

Resolution: *The sheriff jails Bart and his gang.*

Analyzing Plot, Character Development, and Theme

In a short story, **plot incidents** and **dialogue** propel the action and reveal character. They can also help to develop a **theme**.

Propelling the Action

Chain of Events Incidents in a story often form a chain of events: Each event affects one or more characters, causing the affected characters to respond in ways that further propel the action, as in this example.

1. Having placed second at an event, a skater begins to doubt her talents.
2. At her next performance she loses her concentration.
3. As a result, she snaps at a young fan who asks for her autograph.
4. The young fan is upset and writes her a letter.
5. The skater is moved. She realizes that performance is for the fans as well as for herself, and she invites the fan to lunch.

When writers follow **chronological order,** they show the chain of events as it unfolds in time order. Writers may also relate some events out of chronological order. A **flashback** shows events from before the present of the story, often to reveal a character's motives.

Dialogue, or the presentation of characters' words as uttered, can also move the action along. Compare these two versions of a scene.

Example: Narration

Jena called Brit to talk about their disagreement, but Brit refused to discuss it. She didn't think there was any point to talking about it anymore.

Example: Dialogue

Brit knew who was calling.
"What do you want?" she asked brusquely.
"I really think we should meet to talk about what happened," mumbled Jena.
"We've talked enough," Brit snapped, hanging up on Jena.

Revealing Character

Characterization Dialogue is also a key part of characterization, the methods a writer uses to help you get to know a character.

In **direct characterization,** the narrator makes direct statements about a character's personality. In **indirect characterization,** a writer shows what characters are like by providing details about what the characters say and do, what other characters say about them, and how other characters respond to them.

Developing Themes

A **theme** is a message about life that an author conveys. To **develop** a theme, an author crafts story elements, including plot events and details about characters, to express a message or an insight over the course of the work.

- A *stated theme* is expressed directly by the author. Fables often end with a moral that states the theme, such as "Look before you leap."

- An *implied theme* is suggested by what happens to the characters.

- A *universal theme* is a message about life that is often expressed in many different eras and across cultures, such as "Hard work pays off in the end."

Story Elements and Theme

Characters To determine theme, note changes characters undergo as well as the insights they have. For instance, the skater in the example on the previous page learns that people need to remember what they owe others. This lesson is a theme.

Plot and Conflict Writers may develop theme through the choices that characters make, as well as through the results of those choices. To determine theme, trace the development of the conflict and evaluate the resolution. Ask yourself: Do characters meet the fate they deserve? Are the characters admirable? Or, do they represent what *not* to do?

Setting Writers can also develop theme through their choice and depiction of a story's setting. For example, by setting a story in the Arctic wilderness, a writer may send a message that nature is harsh and, in the end, hostile to humanity.

Irony Writers may also develop theme through **irony,** an intended contradiction between appearances and reality or between an actual outcome and the outcome that the reader or the characters expect. Irony can be an effective tool in developing a theme, especially if the theme involves people's misguided perceptions.

Example of Irony

Situation		Expected Outcome		Actual Outcome
Friends of a student who loses an election plan a party to console him.	→	The student will feel better because of the party.	≠	At the party, the student tells friends that he is relieved not to have won.

Toni Cade Bambara
(1939–1995) grew up in
New York City, where she
learned that life could
be tough but rewarding.
Bambara loved the energy
and rhythm of city living
and the lively talk of the
streets. As a writer, she
had a gift for capturing
the language, dreams,
and struggles of real
people. Bambara gave
her mother credit for
inspiring her to write.
"She gave me permission
to wonder, to . . . dawdle,
to daydream," Bambara
once said.

© **Common Core
State Standards**

Reading Literature
3. Analyze how particular lines of
dialogue or incidents in a story or
drama propel the action, reveal
aspects of a character, or provoke
a decision.

Language
4.b. Use common, grade-
appropriate Greek or Latin affixes
and roots as clues to the meaning
of a word (e.g., *precede, recede,
secede*).

Can all conflicts be resolved?

Explore the Big Question as you read "Raymond's Run." Take notes
on how the story's conflict helps change the narrator's views.

CLOSE READING FOCUS

Key Ideas and Details: **Make Predictions**

To **make predictions** while reading, ask yourself what might
happen next in the story. Base your ideas on story details, as
well as on your own background knowledge. For example, if a
character is pacing in a hospital, you might draw on your own
knowledge to predict that the character will soon receive news
about a patient. As you read, make predictions by asking yourself
questions such as, "What would I do in this situation?"

Craft and Structure: **Plot**

Plot is the sequence of related events in a story. As you read,
identify and analyze the following parts of the story's plot:

- **exposition:** basic information about the characters and
situation provided at the beginning of the story
- **conflict:** a struggle between two opposing forces
- **rising action:** events that increase the conflict's tension
- **climax:** the point of greatest tension, usually when the
outcome of the conflict is determined
- **falling action:** events that follow the climax
- **resolution:** the final outcome, in which remaining conflicts or
questions are either resolved or, in some stories, left open

Vocabulary

Decide whether you know each of the following words from the
story well, a little, or not at all. After you read the story, see how
your knowledge of each word has changed.

prodigy	liable	reputation
pageant	periscope	gesture

CLOSE READING MODEL

The passage below is from Toni Cade Bambara's short story "Raymond's Run." The annotations to the right of the passage show ways in which you can use close reading skills to make predictions and analyze the plot of the story.

from "Raymond's Run"

Then the second-graders line up for the thirty-yard dash and I don't even bother to turn my head to watch cause Raphael Perez always wins. He wins before he even begins by psyching the runners, telling them they're going to trip on their shoelaces and fall on their faces or lose their shorts or something, which he doesn't really have to do since he is very fast, almost as fast as I am. After that is the forty-yard dash which I use to run when I was in first grade.[1] Raymond is hollering from the swings cause he knows I'm about to do my thing cause the man on the loudspeaker has just announced the fifty-yard dash,[2] although he might just as well be giving a recipe for angel food cake cause you can hardly make out what he's saying for the static. I get up and slip off my sweat pants and then I see Gretchen standing at the starting line, kicking her legs out like a pro.[3] Then as I get into place I see that ole Raymond is on line on the other side of the fence, bending down with his fingers on the ground just like he knew what he was doing.[4] I was going to yell at him but then I didn't. It burns up your energy to holler.

Plot
1 The text describes races that take place before the race in which the narrator will run. This delay in telling the main event increases the tension and adds to the reader's anticipation.

Make Predictions
2 Bambara writes that Raymond is "hollering from the swings." This detail suggests that Raymond is a little unruly and might do something that will complicate events. The reader can make a prediction about what that action might be.

Plot
3 Gretchen is the narrator's rival. When the narrator says that Gretchen kicks her legs out "like a pro," she emphasizes Gretchen's experience and determination, which heightens the conflict between the characters.

Make Predictions
4 Raymond is taking a runner's stance. Drawing on this detail, the reader can make a prediction about what might happen next. For instance, the reader might predict that Raymond will join the race.

Raymond's Run

Toni Cade Bambara

I don't have much work to do around the house like some girls. My mother does that. And I don't have to earn my pocket money by hustling; George runs errands for the big boys and sells Christmas cards. And anything else that's got to get done, my father does. All I have to do in life is mind my brother Raymond, which is enough.

Sometimes I slip and say my little brother Raymond. But as any fool can see he's much bigger and he's older too. But a lot of people call him my little brother cause he needs looking after cause he's not quite right. And a lot of smart mouths got lots to say about that too, especially when George was minding him. But now, if anybody has anything to say to Raymond, anything to say about his big head, they have to come by me. And I don't play the dozens[1] or believe in standing around with somebody in my face doing a lot of talking. I much rather just knock you down and take my chances even if I am a little girl with skinny arms and a squeaky voice, which is how I got the name Squeaky. And if things get too rough, I run. And as anybody can tell you, I'm the fastest thing on two feet.

There is no track meet that I don't win the first-place medal. I used to win the twenty-yard dash when I was a little kid in kindergarten. Nowadays, it's the fifty-yard dash. And tomorrow I'm subject to run the quarter-mile relay all by myself and come in first, second, and third. The big kids call me Mercury[2] cause I'm the swiftest thing in the neighborhood. Everybody knows that—except two people who know better, my father and me.

He can beat me to Amsterdam Avenue with me having a two fire-hydrant headstart and him running with his hands in his pockets and whistling. But that's private information. Cause can you imagine some thirty-five-year-old man stuffing himself into PAL[3] shorts to race little kids? So as far as everyone's concerned, I'm the fastest and that goes for Gretchen, too, who has put out the tale that she is going to win the first-place medal this year. Ridiculous. In the second

Make Predictions
In the first two paragraphs, what clues help you predict how Squeaky will react to a challenge?

Plot
List four facts you learn about Squeaky in the exposition of this story.

Comprehension
What is Squeaky's special talent?

---

1. **the dozens** game in which the players insult one another; the first to show anger loses.
2. **Mercury** in Roman mythology, the messenger of the gods, known for great speed.
3. **PAL** Police Athletic League.

place, she's got short legs. In the third place, she's got freckles. In the first place, no one can beat me and that's all there is to it.

I'm standing on the corner admiring the weather and about to take a stroll down Broadway so I can practice my breathing exercises, and I've got Raymond walking on the inside close to the buildings, cause he's subject to fits of fantasy and starts thinking he's a circus performer and that the curb is a tightrope strung high in the air. And sometimes after a rain he likes to step down off his tightrope right into the gutter and slosh around getting his shoes and cuffs wet. Or sometimes if you don't watch him he'll dash across traffic to the island in the middle of Broadway and give the pigeons a fit. Then I have to go behind him apologizing to all the old people sitting around trying to get some sun and getting all upset with the pigeons fluttering around them, scattering their newspapers and upsetting the waxpaper lunches in their laps. So I keep Raymond on the inside of me, and he plays like he's driving a stage coach, which is O.K. by me so long as he doesn't run me over or interrupt my breathing exercises, which I have to do on account of I'm serious about my running, and I don't care who knows it. ●

Make Predictions
What details support a prediction that Squeaky will be tough to beat in a race?

Now some people like to act like things come easy to them, won't let on that they practice. Not me. I'll high prance down 34th Street like a rodeo pony to keep my knees strong even if it does get my mother uptight so that she walks ahead like she's not with me, don't know me, is all by herself on a shopping trip, and I am somebody else's crazy child.

Now you take Cynthia Procter for instance. She's just the opposite. If there's a test tomorrow, she'll say something like, "Oh, I guess I'll play handball this afternoon and watch television tonight," just to let you know she ain't thinking about the test. Or like last week when she won the spelling bee for the millionth time, "A good thing you got 'receive,' Squeaky, cause I would have got it wrong. I completely forgot about the spelling bee." And she'll clutch the lace on her blouse like it was a narrow escape. Oh, brother.

But of course when I pass her house on my early morning trots around the block, she is practicing the scales on the piano over and over and over and over. Then in music class she always lets herself get bumped around so she falls accidently on purpose onto the piano stool and is so surprised to find herself sitting there that she decides just for fun to try out the ole keys and what do you know—Chopin's[4] waltzes just spring out of her fingertips and she's the most surprised thing in the world. A regular prodigy. I could kill people like that.

I stay up all night studying the words for the spelling bee. And you can see me any time of day practicing running. I never walk if I can trot, and shame on Raymond if he can't keep up. But of course he does, cause if he hangs back someone's liable to walk up to him and get smart, or take his allowance from him, or ask him where he got that great big pumpkin head. People are so stupid sometimes.

So I'm strolling down Broadway breathing out and breathing in on counts of seven, which is my lucky number, and here comes Gretchen and her sidekicks—Mary Louise who used to be a friend of mine when she first moved to Harlem from Baltimore and got beat up by everybody till I took up for her on account of her mother and my mother used to sing in the same choir when they were young girls, but people ain't grateful, so now she hangs out with the new girl Gretchen and talks about me like a dog; and Rosie who is as fat as I am skinny and has a big mouth where Raymond is concerned and is too stupid to know that there is not a big deal of difference between herself and Raymond and that she can't afford to throw stones. So they are steady coming up Broadway and I see right away that it's going to be one of those Dodge City[5] scenes cause the street ain't that big and they're close to the buildings just as

◀ Vocabulary
prodigy (präd′ ə jē) *n.* unusually talented person

liable (lī′ ə bəl) *adj.* likely

▲ **Critical Viewing**
How do you think growing up in a city like this one has affected Squeaky's personality?

Comprehension
Why does Squeaky dislike Cynthia Procter?

---

4. **Chopin** (shō′ pan) Frédéric François Chopin (1810–1849), highly regarded Polish composer and pianist, known for his challenging piano compositions.
5. **Dodge City** location of the television program *Gunsmoke*, which often presented a gunfight between the sheriff and an outlaw.

Vocabulary ▶
reputation (rep′ yo̅o̅ tā′ shən) *n.* the opinion that others have of a person, whether good or bad

we are. First I think I'll step into the candy store and look over the new comics and let them pass. But that's chicken and I've got a **reputation** to consider. So then I think I'll just walk straight on through them or even over them if necessary. But as they get to me, they slow down. I'm ready to fight, cause like I said I don't feature a whole lot of chit-chat, I much prefer to just knock you down right from the jump and save everybody a lotta precious time.

"You signing up for the May Day races?" smiles Mary Louise, only it's not a smile at all.

A dumb question like that doesn't deserve an answer. Besides, there's just me and Gretchen standing there really, so no use wasting my breath talking to shadows.

"I don't think you're going to win this time," says Rosie, trying to signify with her hands on her hips all salty, completely forgetting that I have whupped her many times for less salt than that.

"I always win cause I'm the best," I say straight at Gretchen who is, as far as I'm concerned, the only one talking in this ventriloquist-dummy routine.[6]

Gretchen smiles, but it's not a smile, and I'm thinking that girls never really smile at each other because they don't know how and don't want to know how and there's probably no one to teach us how cause grown-up girls don't know either. Then they all look at Raymond who has just brought his mule team to a standstill. And they're about to see what trouble they can get into through him.

"What grade you in now, Raymond?"

"You got anything to say to my brother, you say it to me, Mary Louise Williams of Raggedy Town, Baltimore."

"What are you, his mother?" sasses Rosie.

"That's right, Fatso. And the next word out of anybody and I'll be *their* mother too." So they just stand there and Gretchen shifts from one leg to the other and so do they. Then Gretchen puts her hands on her hips and is about to say something with her freckle-face self but doesn't. Then she walks around me looking me up and down but keeps walking up Broadway,

Make Predictions
What do you think Squeaky will do if the girls tease Raymond? What details in the story support your prediction?

Plot
What clues in the story indicate that Gretchen is Squeaky's main rival in this conflict?

---

6. **ventriloquist** (ven tril′ə kwist)-**dummy routine** a comedy act in which the performer speaks through a puppet called a "dummy."

and her sidekicks follow her. So me and Raymond smile at each other and he says, "Gidyap" to his team and I continue with my breathing exercises, strolling down Broadway toward the ice man on 145th with not a care in the world cause I am Miss Quicksilver herself.

I take my time getting to the park on May Day because the track meet is the last thing on the program. The biggest thing on the program is the May Pole dancing, which I can do without, thank you, even if my mother thinks it's a shame I don't take part and act like a girl for a change. You'd think my mother'd be grateful not to have to make me a white organdy dress with a big satin sash and buy me new white baby-doll shoes that can't be taken out of the box till the big day. You'd think she'd be glad her daughter ain't out there prancing around a May Pole getting the new clothes all dirty and sweaty and trying to act like a fairy or a flower or whatever you're supposed to be when you should be trying to be yourself, whatever that is, which is, as far as I am concerned, a poor black girl who really can't afford to buy shoes and a new dress you only wear once a lifetime cause it won't fit next year.

I was once a strawberry in a Hansel and Gretel pageant when I was in nursery school and didn't have no better sense than to dance on tiptoe with my arms in a circle over my head doing umbrella steps and being a perfect fool just so my mother and father could come dressed up and clap. You'd think they'd know better than to encourage that kind of nonsense. I am not a strawberry. I do not dance on my toes. I run. That is what I am all about. So I always come late to the May Day program, just in time to get my number pinned on and lay in the grass till they announce the fifty-yard dash.

▲ **Critical Viewing**
What would Squeaky think about these children, shown dancing around a May Pole?

◄ **Vocabulary**
pageant (paj´ ənt) *n.* an elaborate play

Comprehension
What would Squeaky's mother prefer that Squeaky do on May Day?

▲ **Critical Viewing**
How might a runner's emotions change after a race has started?

Vocabulary ▶
periscope (per′ ə skōp′) *n.* tube that rises from a submarine to allow sailors to see objects above the water's surface

gesture (jes′ chər) *n.* something said or done to express a feeling

I put Raymond in the little swings, which is a tight squeeze this year and will be impossible next year. Then I look around for Mr. Pearson, who pins the numbers on. I'm really looking for Gretchen if you want to know the truth, but she's not around. The park is jam-packed. Parents in hats and corsages and breast-pocket handkerchiefs peeking up. Kids in white dresses and light-blue suits. The parkees unfolding chairs and chasing the rowdy kids from Lenox as if they had no right to be there. The big guys with their caps on backwards, leaning against the fence swirling the basketballs on the tips of their fingers, waiting for all these crazy people to clear out the park so they can play. Most of the kids in my class are carrying bass drums and glockenspiels[7] and flutes. You'd think they'd put in a few bongos or something for real like that.

Then here comes Mr. Pearson with his clipboard and his cards and pencils and whistles and safety pins and fifty million other things he's always dropping all over the place with his clumsy self. He sticks out in a crowd because he's on stilts. We used to call him Jack and the Beanstalk to get him mad. But I'm the only one that can outrun him and get away, and I'm too grown for that silliness now.

"Well, Squeaky," he says, checking my name off the list and handing me number seven and two pins. And I'm thinking he's got no right to call me Squeaky, if I can't call him Beanstalk.

"Hazel Elizabeth Deborah Parker," I correct him and tell him to write it down on his board.

"Well, Hazel Elizabeth Deborah Parker, going to give someone else a break this year?" I squint at him real hard to see if he is seriously thinking I should lose the race on purpose just to give someone else a break. "Only six girls running this time," he continues, shaking his head sadly like it's my fault all of New York didn't turn out in sneakers. "That new girl should give you a run for your money." He looks around the park for Gretchen like a **periscope** in a submarine movie. "Wouldn't it be a nice **gesture** if you were . . . to ahhh . . ."

I give him such a look he couldn't finish putting that idea into words. Grownups got a lot of nerve sometimes. I pin

---

7. glockenspiels (gläk′ ən spēlz′) *n.* musical instruments with flat metal bars that make bell-like tones when struck with small hammers.

number seven to myself and stomp away, I'm so burnt. And I go straight for the track and stretch out on the grass while the band winds up with "Oh, the Monkey Wrapped His Tail Around the Flag Pole," which my teacher calls by some other name. The man on the loudspeaker is calling everyone over to the track and I'm on my back looking at the sky, trying to pretend I'm in the country, but I can't, because even grass in the city feels hard as sidewalk, and there's just no pretending you are anywhere but in a "concrete jungle" as my grandfather says. ●

The twenty-yard dash takes all of two minutes cause most of the little kids don't know no better than to run off the track or run the wrong way or run smack into the fence and fall down and cry. One little kid, though, has got the good sense to run straight for the white ribbon up ahead, so he wins. Then the second-graders line up for the thirty-yard dash and I don't even bother to turn my head to watch cause Raphael Perez always wins. He wins before he even begins by psyching the runners, telling them they're going to trip on their shoelaces and fall on their faces or lose their shorts or something, which he doesn't really have to do since he is very fast, almost as fast as I am. After that is the forty-yard dash which I use to run when I was in first grade. Raymond is hollering from the swings cause he knows I'm about to do my thing cause the man on the loudspeaker has just announced the fifty-yard dash, although he might just as well be giving a recipe for angel food cake cause you can hardly make out what he's saying for the static. I get up and slip off my sweat pants and then I see Gretchen standing at the starting line, kicking her legs out like a pro. Then as I get into place I see that ole Raymond is on line on the other side of the fence, bending down with his fingers on the ground just like he knew what he was doing. I was going to yell at him but then I didn't. It burns up your energy to holler.

Every time, just before I take off in a race, I always feel like I'm in a dream, the kind of dream you have when you're sick with fever and feel all hot and weightless. I dream I'm flying over a sandy beach in the early morning sun, kissing the leaves of the trees as I fly by. And there's always the smell of

Spiral Review
THEME What details in this part of the story indicate Squeaky's attitude toward winning?

Make Predictions
What do you predict will be the outcome of the conflict between Gretchen and Squeaky?

Comprehension
How does Mr. Pearson annoy Squeaky?

apples, just like in the country when I was little and used to think I was a choo-choo train, running through the fields of corn and chugging up the hill to the orchard. And all the time I'm dreaming this, I get lighter and lighter until I'm flying over the beach again, getting blown through the sky like a feather that weighs nothing at all. But once I spread my fingers in the dirt and crouch over the Get on Your Mark, the dream goes and I am solid again and am telling myself, Squeaky you must win, you must win, you are the fastest thing in the world, you can even beat your father up Amsterdam if you really try. And then I feel my weight coming back just behind my knees then down to my feet then into the earth and the pistol shot explodes in my blood and I am off and weightless again, flying past the other runners, my arms pumping up and down and the whole world is quiet except for the crunch as I zoom over the gravel in the track. I glance to my left and there is no one. To the right a blurred Gretchen, who's got her chin jutting out as if it would win the race all by itself. And on the other side of the fence is Raymond with his arms down to his side and the palms tucked up behind him, running in his very own style, and it's the first time I ever saw that and I almost stop to watch my brother Raymond on his first run. But the white ribbon is bouncing toward me and I tear past it, racing into the distance till my feet with a mind of their own start digging up footfuls of dirt and brake me short. Then all the kids standing on the side pile on me, banging me on the back and slapping my head with their May Day programs, for I have won again and everybody on 151st Street can walk tall for another year.

"In first place . . ." the man on the loudspeaker is clear as a bell now. But then he pauses and the loudspeaker starts

▲ **Critical Viewing**
How does this image show that a race involves great tension and concentration?

to whine. Then static. And I lean down to catch my breath and here comes Gretchen walking back, for she's overshot the finish line too, huffing and puffing with her hands on her hips taking it slow, breathing in steady time like a real pro and I sort of like her a little for the first time. "In first place . . ." and then three or four voices get all mixed up on the loudspeaker and I dig my sneaker into the grass and stare at Gretchen who's staring back, we both wondering just who did win. I can hear old Beanstalk arguing with the man on the loudspeaker and then a few others running their mouths about what the stopwatches say. Then I hear Raymond yanking at the fence to call me and I wave to shush him, but he keeps rattling the fence like a gorilla in a cage like in them gorilla movies, but then like a dancer or something he starts climbing up nice and easy but very fast. And it occurs to me, watching how smoothly he climbs hand over hand and remembering how he looked running with his arms down to his side and with the wind pulling his mouth back and his teeth showing and all, it occurred to me that Raymond would make a very fine runner. Doesn't he always keep up with me on my trots? And he surely knows how to breathe in counts of seven cause he's always doing it at the dinner table, which drives my brother George up the wall. And I'm smiling to beat the band cause if I've lost this race, or if me and Gretchen tied, or even if I've won, I can always retire as a runner and begin a whole new career as a coach with Raymond as my champion. After all, with a little more study I can beat Cynthia and her phony self at the spelling bee. And if I bugged my mother, I could get piano lessons and become a star. And I have a big rep as the baddest thing around. And I've got a roomful of ribbons and medals and awards. But what has Raymond got to call his own?

So I stand there with my new plans, laughing out loud by this time as Raymond jumps down from the fence and runs over with his teeth showing and his arms down to the side, which no one before him has quite mastered as a running style. And by the time he comes over I'm jumping up and down so glad to see him—my brother Raymond, a great runner in the family tradition. But of course everyone thinks I'm jumping up and down because the men on the

Plot
In what way is this the moment of greatest tension?

Make Predictions
What do you think Squeaky will do in the days following the race? Explain.

Comprehension
What is Raymond doing while Squeaky runs the race?

Make Predictions
Was the outcome of the story difficult to predict? Explain.

loudspeaker have finally gotten themselves together and compared notes and are announcing "In first place—Miss Hazel Elizabeth Deborah Parker." (Dig that.) "In second place—Miss Gretchen P. Lewis." And I look over at Gretchen wondering what the "P" stands for. And I smile. Cause she's good, no doubt about it. Maybe she'd like to help me coach Raymond; she obviously is serious about running, as any fool can see. And she nods to congratulate me and then she smiles. And I smile. We stand there with this big smile of respect between us. It's about as real a smile as girls can do for each other, considering we don't practice real smiling every day, you know, cause maybe we too busy being flowers or fairies or strawberries instead of something honest and worthy of respect . . . you know . . . like being people.

Language Study

Vocabulary The words in italics in the sentences below appear in the short story "Raymond's Run." Answer each question, writing your answer as a complete sentence that includes the italicized word and shows your knowledge of its meaning.

1. Why were people impressed when the *prodigy* played at the show?

2. How is a wild animal *liable* to react when threatened?

3. What is the *reputation* of your favorite sports team?

4. What might appear in a *pageant* that celebrates spring?

5. What *gesture* can you make to show appreciation for someone?

WORD STUDY

The **Greek root -scope-** means "look at" or "watch." In this story, a character cranes his neck like the **periscope** on a submarine. A periscope is a device that helps the user look around an obstacle.

Word Study

Part A Use your knowledge of the **Greek root -scope-** to explain the meanings of the words *kaleidoscope* and *stereoscope*. Consult a dictionary if necessary.

Part B Use context clues and what you know about the Greek root -scope- to answer each question.

1. Why would a scientist use a *microscope* to study cells?

2. Why does an observatory have a large *telescope*?

Close Reading Activities

Literary Analysis

Key Ideas and Details

1. (a) Describe Squeaky's relationship with Raymond.
(b) Paraphrase: What does Squeaky mean when she says that she has to keep Raymond "on the inside of me"?

2. (a) What does Raymond do immediately before and during Squeaky's race? **(b) Summarize:** What does she realize about Raymond after her race?

3. Make Predictions (a) List two predictions you made as you read. **(b)** Which story details helped support your predictions? **(c)** How did background knowledge help you make those predictions?

4. Make Predictions (a) Which details can support a prediction that Gretchen will win the race? **(b)** Why would the author include details that support predictions of different outcomes?

Craft and Structure

5. Plot Complete a plot chart like the one shown, identifying one event from the story for each stage of the plot. Two sample events have been identified for you.

6. Plot How does Raymond's run contribute to the resolution of the story?

Integration of Knowledge and Ideas

7. (a) Contrast: How does Squeaky's view of Raymond change during the story? Cite story details to support your answer.
(b) Draw Conclusions: Why does Squeaky lose interest in the official outcome of the race after she observes Raymond's behavior after her run?

8. Contrast: How does Squeaky's view of Gretchen change in the course of the story?

9. Generalize: Explain what message about life Bambara is suggesting through the change in Squeaky's views of Raymond, Gretchen, and racing. Cite story details.

10. **Can all conflicts be resolved?** With a small group, discuss the following: **(a)** How is the conflict between Squeaky and Gretchen resolved? **(b)** Do you think the story suggests that all conflicts can be resolved? Explain, using details from the text.

Exposition

1. Example: We learn that Squeaky looks after her brother Raymond.
2.

Rising Action

Climax

Falling Action

1. Example: Squeaky and Gretchen exchange smiles.
2.

Resolution

ACADEMIC VOCABULARY

As you write and speak about "Raymond's Run," use the words related to conflict that you explored on page 3 of this textbook.

Conventions: **Nouns**

A **common noun** names any one of a class of persons, places, or things. A **proper noun** names a specific person, place, or thing. A **possessive noun** shows ownership.

A **common noun,** such as *house,* is used to name any one of a class of persons, places, or things—"the gray house," "the house on the corner," and so on. Do not capitalize common nouns except at the start of a sentence or in a title.

Proper nouns name specific persons, places, or things, such as the *White House.* They begin with capital letters.

Common Nouns	Proper Nouns
person	Mario
ocean	Pacific Ocean
language	Spanish

Possessive nouns show ownership. For example, *Jennifer's* is a possessive noun, as in "Jennifer's dog." To form the possessive of most singular nouns, add *'s.* For plurals that end in *-s* already, add an apostrophe at the end: for example, *dogs'* in "dogs' toys."

Practice A

For each sentence, identify each noun as proper, common, or possessive.

1. Squeaky meets Gretchen, Mary Louise, and Rosie on Broadway near the store.
2. The celebration on May Day has races.
3. Squeaky sees Raymond's promise.
4. Squeaky's full name is Hazel Elizabeth Deborah Parker.

Reading Application Find two sentences in "Raymond's Run" that have both common and proper nouns. Identify each noun as common or proper.

Practice B

Rewrite these sentences, using correct capitalization and correct possessive forms.

1. Squeakys School is open next monday.
2. We heard that cynthias piano is old and has Dents, but it still plays a nice tune.
3. Raymonds grandfather calls the city a concrete jungle.
4. The characters of hansel and gretel were not squeaky's favorites.

Writing Application Find three common and three proper nouns in "Raymond's Run" and write their possessive forms.

Writing to Sources

Narrative Text Write a **new ending** for the short story "Raymond's Run." For example, imagine how the ending would have been different if Squeaky had lost or if Raymond had run on the track beside the racers. Make sure your new ending follows naturally from events in the original story. Use the following strategies in your writing:

- Decide how your ending will be different from the original story.
- Plan how each character will react to the new turn of events.
- As you write, add descriptive details about each character's actions, including his or her gestures and movements.
- Include dialogue that reveals the characters' personalities.
- To end strongly, include a character's memorable statement of what he or she has learned.

Grammar Application Check to make sure you correctly capitalized the names of specific people and places.

Speaking and Listening

Comprehension and Collaboration Work with a partner to write and perform a **radio broadcast** of the race in "Raymond's Run" for your classmates. Be sure to include key details about the runners and the race from the story.

To deliver an exciting broadcast, use the following tips:

- Reread the text and take notes on the story events, placing them in logical sequence.
- Use precise and vivid action verbs—such as *flying, jutting,* and *cheering*—to convey action and emotion. Add sensory details, including specific sights or sounds, to create a vivid scene.
- Include physical descriptions to show how the characters look, act, and move. Use these descriptions for comparison or contrast. For example, *Squeaky runs with her arms pumping, while Gretchen runs with her chin sticking out.*

As you and your partner deliver the broadcast, vary your tone and the pace of your delivery to create a mood of suspense and excitement for your listeners.

Common Core State Standards

Writing
3. Write narratives to develop real or imagined experiences or events using effective technique, relevant descriptive details, and well-structured event sequences.
3.b. Use narrative techniques, such as dialogue, pacing, description, and reflection, to develop experiences, events, and/or characters.
3.d. Use precise words and phrases, relevant descriptive details, and sensory language to capture the action and convey experiences and events.
3.e. Provide a conclusion that follows from and reflects on the narrated experiences or events.

Speaking and Listening
6. Adapt speech to a variety of contexts and tasks, demonstrating command of formal English when indicated or appropriate.

Language
2. Demonstrate command of the conventions of standard English capitalization, punctuation, and spelling when writing.

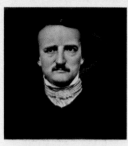

Meet the Author

Edgar Allan Poe
(1809–1849) had a short
and troubled life, but his
groundbreaking, often
terrifying stories have
long survived him. Shortly
after Poe's birth, his father
abandoned his family.
When Poe was only two
years old, his mother died,
leaving him in the care of
foster parents. With dreams
of becoming a poet, the
teenaged Poe quarreled
bitterly with his business-
minded foster father,
John Allan. Poe then went
from one job to another,
struggling to make a living
but gaining a reputation as
a writer. He died in poverty
at the age of 40.

 **Common Core**
State Standards

Reading Literature
3. Analyze how particular lines of
dialogue or incidents in a story or
drama propel the action, reveal
aspects of a character, or provoke
a decision.

? Can all conflicts be resolved?

Explore the Big Question as you read "The Tell-Tale Heart." Take
notes on the narrator's internal and external conflicts.

CLOSE READING FOCUS

Key Ideas and Details: **Compare and Contrast**

To **compare and contrast** characters' perspectives, look for
similarities and differences between their views of events.

- Compare one character's actions, feelings, and ideas with
  those of another character.
- Ask yourself what the comparison shows about each
  character's perspective—how he or she views events. For
  example, is one an optimist, the other a pessimist?
- Then, compare one character's perspective with your own.
  For example, a character might be upset by a situation, but
  you might think he or she is overreacting.

Some characters have distorted, or false, perspectives. Use what
you learn to decide how much you trust what a character thinks.

Craft and Structure: **Character Traits**

Character traits are a character's qualities, attitudes, and values.
For example, one character may be lazy and untrustworthy,
while another is hardworking and reliable. The number of traits a
character displays contributes to how well you "know" him or her.

- Round characters are fully developed by the writer. They show
  many character traits, both good and bad.
- Flat characters are one-sided, often showing just one trait.

As you read, draw conclusions about the characters' traits based
on their words and actions.

Vocabulary

These words appear in the text that follows. Copy them into your
notebook. Which is probably a synonym for *sneakily*?

cunningly	resolved	stealthily
vex	audacity	derision

CLOSE READING MODEL

The passage below is from Edgar Allan Poe's short story "The Tell-Tale Heart." The annotations to the right of the passage show ways in which you can use close reading skills to compare and contrast characters and analyze character traits.

from "The Tell-Tale Heart"

Presently I heard a slight groan, and I knew it was the groan of mortal terror. It was not a groan of pain or of grief—oh, no!— it was the low stifled sound that arises from the bottom of the soul when overcharged with awe. I knew the sound well. Many a night, just at midnight, when all the world slept, it has welled up from my own bosom, deepening, with its dreadful echo, the terrors that distracted me.[1] I say I knew it well. I knew what the old man felt, and pitied him, although I chuckled at heart.[2]

I knew that he had been lying awake ever since the first slight noise, when he had turned in the bed. His fears had been ever since growing upon him. He had been trying to fancy them causeless, but could not. He had been saying to himself—"It is nothing but the wind in the chimney—it is only a mouse crossing the floor," or "it is merely a cricket which has made a single chirp."[3] Yes, he had been trying to comfort himself with these suppositions: but he had found all in vain. *All in vain;* because Death, in approaching him, had stalked with his black shadow before him, and enveloped the victim.[4]

Character Traits
1 The narrator speaks of being familiar with the sounds a person makes when overcome with terror—the narrator has made them himself. This detail suggests that the narrator is nervous and unhappy.

Character Traits
2 The narrator admits to understanding and pitying the old man but also says, "I chuckled at heart." This detail paints a picture of the narrator as an uncaring character.

Compare and Contrast
3 According to the narrator, the old man has been disturbed and is trying to calm himself. The old man's perspective seems to be one of uncertainty and fear. By contrast, the narrator states with certainty what he believes the old man is thinking.

Compare and Contrast
4 The repetition of "all in vain" shows that the narrator is nearly gleeful in discussing death. You can compare his perspective to your own to reach the conclusion that his perspective might not be normal.

The Tell-Tale Heart

Edgar Allan Poe

True!—nervous—very, very dreadfully nervous I had been and am; but why *will* you say that I am mad? The disease had sharpened my senses—not destroyed—not dulled them. Above all was the sense of hearing acute. I heard all things in the heaven and in the earth. I heard many things in hell. How, then, am I mad? Hearken![1] and observe how healthily—how calmly I can tell you the whole story.

It is impossible to say how first the idea entered my brain; but once conceived, it haunted me day and night. Object there was none. Passion there was none. I loved the old man. He had never wronged me. He had never given me insult. For his gold I had no desire. I think it was his eye! yes, it was this! One of his eyes resembled that of a vulture—a pale blue eye, with a film over it. Whenever it fell upon me, my blood ran cold; and so by degrees—very gradually—I made up my mind to take the life of the old man, and thus rid myself of the eye forever.

Now this is the point. You fancy me mad. Madmen know nothing. But you should have seen *me*. You should have seen how wisely I proceeded—with what caution—with what foresight—with what dissimulation[2] I went to work! I was never kinder to the old man than during the whole week before I killed him. And every night, about midnight, I turned the latch of his door and opened it—oh, so gently! And then, when I had made an opening sufficient for my head, I put in a dark lantern, all closed, closed, so that no light shone out, and then I thrust in my head. Oh, you would have laughed to see how **cunningly** I thrust it in! I moved it slowly—very, very slowly, so that I might not disturb the old man's sleep. It took me an hour to place my whole head within the opening so far that I could see him as he lay upon his bed. Ha!—would a madman have been so wise as this? And then, when my head was well in the room, I undid the lantern cautiously—oh, so cautiously—cautiously (for the hinges creaked)—I undid it just so much that a single thin ray fell upon the vulture eye. And this I did for seven long nights—every night just at midnight—but I found the eye always closed; and so it

---

1. **Hearken!** (här′ kən) *v.* listen!
2. **dissimulation** (di sim′ yōō lā′ shən) *n.* hiding of one's feelings or purposes.

◄ **Critical Viewing**
What kind of story do you expect to read, based on the title and the illustration? Explain.

Compare and Contrast
The narrator and the author are not the same person. Contrast the way the narrator sees himself with the way the author portrays him.

Comprehension
What feature of the old man makes the narrator want to murder him?

◄ **Vocabulary**
cunningly (kun′ iŋ lē) *adv.* in a way that is skillfully dishonest

Character
What character traits does the narrator reveal as he describes his murder plan?

▼ **Critical Viewing**
How do the shadows and light affect the mood of the illustrations on these pages?

was impossible to do the work; for it was not the old man who vexed me, but his evil eye. And every morning, when the day broke, I went boldly into the chamber, and spoke courageously to him, calling him by name in a hearty tone, and inquiring how he had passed the night. So you see he would have been a very profound old man, indeed, to suspect that every night, just at twelve, I looked in upon him while he slept. •

Upon the eighth night I was more than usually cautious in opening the door. A watch's minute hand moves more quickly than did mine. Never, before that night, had I *felt* the extent of my own powers—of my sagacity.[3] I could scarcely contain my feelings of triumph. To think that there I was, opening the door, little by little, and he not even to dream of my secret deeds or thoughts. I fairly chuckled at the idea; and perhaps he heard me; for he moved on the bed suddenly,

---

3. **sagacity** (sə gas´ ə tē) *n.* high intelligence and sound judgment.

as if startled. Now you may think that I drew back—but no. His room was as black as pitch with the thick darkness (for the shutters were close fastened, through fear of robbers), and so I knew that he could not see the opening of the door, and I kept pushing it on steadily, steadily.

I had my head in, and was about to open the lantern, when my thumb slipped upon the tin fastening, and the old man sprang up in the bed, crying out—"Who's there?"

I kept quite still and said nothing. For a whole hour I did not move a muscle, and in the meantime I did not hear him lie down. He was still sitting up in the bed, listening;—just as I have done, night after night, hearkening to the deathwatches[4] in the wall.

---

4. **deathwatches** (deth´ wäch´ əz) *n.* wood-boring beetles whose heads make a tapping sound; they are superstitiously regarded as an omen of death.

Comprehension
What steps does the narrator take to prevent the old man from hearing or seeing him?

Presently I heard a slight groan, and I knew it was the groan of mortal terror. It was not a groan of pain or of grief—oh, no!—it was the low stifled sound that arises from the bottom of the soul when overcharged with awe. I knew the sound well. Many a night, just at midnight, when all the world slept, it has welled up from my own bosom, deepening, with its dreadful echo, the terrors that distracted me. I say I knew it well. I knew what the old man felt, and pitied him, although I chuckled at heart. I knew that he had been lying awake ever since the first slight noise, when he had turned in the bed. His fears had been ever since growing upon him. He had been trying to fancy them causeless, but could not. He had been saying to himself— "It is nothing but the wind in the chimney—it is only a mouse crossing the floor," or "it is merely a cricket which has made a single chirp." Yes, he had been trying to comfort himself with these suppositions: but he had found all in vain. *All in vain*; because Death, in approaching him, had stalked with his black shadow before him, and enveloped the victim. And it was the mournful influence of the unperceived shadow that caused him to feel—although he neither saw nor heard—to *feel* the presence of my head within the room. •

When I had waited a long time, very patiently, without hearing him lie down, I **resolved** to open a little—a very, very little crevice in the lantern. So I opened it—you cannot imagine how **stealthily**, stealthily—until, at length, a single dim ray, like the thread of the spider, shot from out the crevice and fell upon the vulture eye.

It was open—wide, wide open—and I grew furious as I gazed upon it. I saw it with perfect distinctness—all a dull blue, with a hideous veil over it that chilled the very marrow in my bones; but I could see nothing else of the old man's face or person for I had directed the ray as if by instinct, precisely upon the spot.

And now—have I not told you that what you mistake for madness is but overacuteness of the senses?—now, I say, there came to my ears a low, dull, quick sound, such as a watch makes when enveloped in cotton. I knew *that* sound well, too. It was the beating of the old man's heart. It increased my fury, as the beating of a drum stimulates the soldier into courage.

But even yet I refrained and kept still. I scarcely breathed. I held the lantern motionless. I tried how steadily I could maintain the ray upon the eye. Meantime the hellish tattoo of the heart increased. It grew quicker and quicker, and louder and louder every instant. The old man's terror *must* have been extreme! It grew louder, I say, louder every moment!—do you mark me well? I have told you that I am nervous: so I am. And now at the dead hour of the night, amid the dreadful silence of that old house, so strange a noise as this excited me to uncontrollable terror. Yet, for some minutes longer I refrained and stood still. But the beating grew louder, louder! I thought the heart must burst. And now a new anxiety seized me—the sound would be heard by a neighbor! The old man's hour had come! With a loud yell, I threw open the lantern and leaped into the room. He shrieked once—once only. In an instant I dragged him to the floor, and pulled the heavy bed over him. I then smiled gaily, to find the deed so far done. But, for many minutes, the heart beat on with a muffled sound. This, however, did not **vex** me; it would not be heard through the wall. At length it ceased. The old man was dead. I removed the bed and examined the corpse. Yes, he was stone, stone dead. I placed my hand upon the heart and held it there many minutes. There was no pulsation. He was stone dead. His eye would trouble me no more.

Spiral Review
PLOT How does the narrator's hearing the beating of the old man's heart advance the plot?

It grew quicker and quicker, and louder and louder every instant. The old man's terror *must* have been extreme!

◀ **Vocabulary**
vex (veks) *v.* annoy; distress

Comprehension
How does the narrator kill the old man?

If still you think me mad, you will think so no longer when I describe the wise precautions I took for the concealment of the body. The night waned, and I worked hastily, but in silence. First of all I dismembered the corpse. I cut off the head and the arms and the legs.

I then took up three planks from the flooring of the chamber, and deposited all between the scantlings.[5] I then replaced the boards so cleverly, so cunningly, that no human eye—not even *his*—could have detected anything wrong. There was nothing to wash out—no stain of any kind—no blood-spot whatever. I had been too wary for that. A tub had caught all—ha! ha! •

When I had made an end of these labors, it was four o'clock—still dark as midnight. As the bell sounded the hour, there came a knocking at the street door. I went down to open it with a light heart—for what had I *now* to fear? There entered three men, who introduced themselves, with perfect suavity, as officers of the police. A shriek had been heard by a neighbor during the night; suspicion of foul play had been aroused; information had been lodged at the police office, and they (the officers) had been deputed to search the premises.

I smiled—for *what* had I to fear? I bade the gentlemen welcome. The shriek, I said, was my own in a dream. The old man, I mentioned, was absent in the country. I took my visitors all over the house. I bade them search— search *well*. I led them, at length, to *his* chamber. I showed them his treasures, secure, undisturbed. In the enthusiasm of my confidence, I brought chairs into the room, and desired them *here* to rest from their fatigues, while I myself, in the wild audacity of my perfect triumph, placed my own seat upon the very spot beneath which reposed the corpse of the victim.

---

5. **scantlings** (skant′ liŋz) *n.* small beams or timbers.

The officers were satisfied. My *manner* had convinced them. I was singularly at ease. They sat, and while I answered cheerily, they chatted of familiar things. But, ere long, I felt myself getting pale and wished them gone. My head ached, and I fancied a ringing in my ears: but still they sat and still chatted. The ringing became more distinct:—it continued and became more distinct: I talked more freely to get rid of the feeling: but it continued and gained definitiveness—until, at length, I found that the noise was *not* within my ears.

No doubt I now grew *very* pale;—but I talked more fluently, and with a heightened voice. Yet the sound increased—and what could I do? It was *a low, dull, quick sound—much such a sound as a watch makes when enveloped in cotton.* I gasped for breath—and yet the officers heard it not. I talked more quickly—more vehemently; but the noise steadily increased. I arose and argued about trifles, in a high key and with violent gesticulations;[6] but the noise steadily increased. Why *would* they not be gone? I paced the floor to and fro with heavy strides, as if excited to fury by the observations of the men—but the noise steadily increased. Oh! what *could* I do? I foamed—I raved—I swore! I swung the chair upon which I had been sitting, and grated it upon the boards, but the noise arose over all and continually increased. It grew louder—louder—*louder!* And still the men chatted pleasantly, and smiled. Was it possible they heard not?—no, no! They heard!—they suspected!—they *knew!*—they were making a mockery of my horror!—this I thought, and this I think. But

---

6. **gesticulations** (jes tik′ yoo lā′ shənz) *n.* energetic hand or arm movements.

Character
Which character traits allow the narrator to conceal the crime?

Compare and Contrast
Compare and contrast the perspective of the narrator with the likely perspectives of the officers.

anything was better than this agony! Anything was
more tolerable than this **derision**! I could bear those
hypocritical smiles no longer! I felt that I must scream
or die!—and now—again!—hark! louder! louder! louder!
louder!—

   "Villains!" I shrieked, "dissemble[7] no more! I admit the
deed!—tear up the planks!—here, here!—it is the beating
of his hideous heart!"

---

7. **dissemble** (di sem´ bəl) *v.* conceal one's true feelings.

Language Study

Vocabulary The words listed below appear in "The Tell-Tale Heart."
In each numbered item, replace the word or words in italics with a
synonym from the vocabulary list.

    cunningly   resolved   stealthily   vex   derision

1. Leon *decided firmly* to become a better basketball player.

2. The dog's constant barking began to *annoy* the neighbors.

3. She was elected because of her *cleverly* organized campaign.

4. Dressed in black, they *silently* crept up to the old castle.

5. All Lin's ideas for a party theme were met with *ridicule*.

Word Study

Part A Explain how the **Latin suffix -*ity*** contributes to the meanings
of *complexity*, *continuity*, and *purity*. Consult a dictionary if necessary.

Part B Use what you know about the Latin suffix -*ity* to answer each
question. Explain your answers.

1. Would something that is a *rarity* be easy or hard to find?

2. Would someone's *timidity* make public speaking easy?

Close Reading Activities

Literary Analysis

Key Ideas and Details

1. (a) According to the story, why does the narrator kill the old man? **(b) Draw Conclusions:** What does the narrator fear? Use story details, including the narrator's own words, to explain.

2. Compare and Contrast (a) Compare and contrast the perspectives of the narrator and old man on the night of the murder. **(b)** Who reports what the old man is thinking and feeling? **(c)** Do you trust the narrator's account of what happened? Cite details from the text to explain why or why not.

3. Compare and Contrast (a) Summarize the narrator's account of the police officers' visit. **(b)** Compare your perspective on the visit with the narrator's. **(c)** How would the description of the officers' visit be different if it were told from the perspective of one of them? Cite story details in your answer.

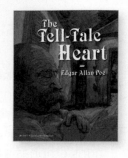

Craft and Structure

4. Character Traits Using a chart like the one shown, analyze the narrator's character. **(a)** List three of the narrator's traits in the first box. **(b)** In the second box, give details that show each trait. Use the narrator's own words in at least one example.

5. Character Traits (a) Which of the characters are round characters and which are flat characters? **(b)** Why might readers care more about what happens to the round character(s) than the flat one(s)? Support your answer with story details.

Narrator's Character Traits
Examples

Integration of Knowledge and Ideas

6. (a) What sound drives the narrator to confess to the crime? **(b) Apply:** What does the narrator's confession show about why people sometimes confess to wrongdoing, even if there is little chance their acts will be discovered?

7. (a) Assess: How does the narrator's confession at the end of the story affect your willingness to trust the story he has told? **(b) Make a Judgment:** Is the narrator sane or insane? What textual details support your view?

8. **Can all conflicts be resolved? (a)** What conflicts does the narrator experience before and after the crime? **(b)** What leads to his final breakdown? **(c)** Have all his conflicts been resolved? Explain.

ACADEMIC VOCABULARY

As you write and speak about "The Tell-Tale Heart," use the words related to conflict that you explored on page 3 of this textbook.

Conventions: **Pronouns**

Personal pronouns replace nouns in sentences. They refer to persons or things. **Possessive pronouns** show ownership. A **reflexive pronoun** indicates that someone or something performs an action to, for, or upon itself. An **intensive pronoun** adds emphasis to a noun or pronoun.

All pronouns take the place of or refer back to a noun or group of words acting as a noun. Pronouns can be grouped by *person*, as shown in the following chart. Note that reflexive and intensive pronouns look the same, but they function differently.

	Personal	Possessive	Reflexive	Intensive
First Person	I, me, we, us	my, mine, our, ours	I took **myself** home. We took **ourselves** outside.	I **myself** ran outside. We **ourselves** are unhappy with our own decision.
Second Person	you	your, yours	You are proud of **yourself.** You understand **yourselves** better than others do.	You **yourself** agreed. Even you **yourselves** cannot know for sure.
Third Person	he, she, it, him, her, they, them	his, her, hers, its, their, theirs	It could not move **itself.** They asked **themselves.**	The king **himself** sat down. They **themselves** admitted it.

Practice A

Fill in the appropriate personal or possessive pronouns. Identify the type of each.

1. The narrator is driven to confess by _____ own madness.

2. The old man wakes after hearing a noise in the room where _____ sleeps.

3. While talking to the policemen, the narrator wishes _____ gone.

4. Different readers form _____ own opinions about the narrator.

Reading Application Find one sentence in "The Tell-Tale Heart" with a personal pronoun and one with a possessive pronoun.

Practice B

Identify each reflexive and intensive pronoun in the following sentences.

1. As the story begins, he himself is describing his crime.

2. You should ask yourself how you would have resolved the narrator's conflict.

3. The police themselves did not suspect him.

4. When the police visited, the narrator worked himself into a panic.

Writing Application Write two sentences about "The Tell-Tale Heart." Use a reflexive pronoun in one and an intensive pronoun in the other.

Writing to Sources

Explanatory Text Write a **character profile** of the narrator in "The Tell-Tale Heart." Explain how the narrator's traits affect the story's plot and resolution. Begin by taking notes on the story:

- Review the chart of traits you created for the narrator (p. 47).
- Reread the end of the story to review why the narrator acts the way he does when the police arrive.

Begin your draft with a clear description of the narrator's personality. Then, show the connection between the narrator's personality and the story's ending. Support your analysis of his personality and of the ending with relevant story details.

Grammar Application Make sure that your character profile uses pronouns correctly and consistently.

Speaking and Listening

Presentation of Ideas Prepare and present an **oral response** to a film version of "The Tell-Tale Heart." Evaluate which is more frightening—the original story or the film.

- With your teacher's help and approval, find a film version of the story.
- As you view the film, take notes on its similarities to and differences from Poe's story, including similarities and differences in plot, characters, and dialogue.
- Evaluate the director's decisions about when to change elements of Poe's story and when to keep them the same. Do these decisions make the film more or less effective than the story? Clearly state your evaluation at the beginning of your response. Then, support your evaluation with examples from the story and the film. Make sure each detail you cite helps to prove your point.
- Make clear, logical connections between the evidence you give and the points it supports. Use phrases such as "as shown by" to link your points to the supporting evidence you provide.
- To give your response greater depth, call attention to specific techniques used by Edgar Allan Poe or by the filmmakers to provoke a reaction from the audience.

As you share your response with class members, make appropriate eye contact. Speak clearly and loudly to aid listeners' comprehension.

Common Core State Standards

Reading Literature

7. Analyze the extent to which a filmed or live production of a story or drama stays faithful to or departs from the text or script, evaluating the choices made by the director or actors.

Writing

2. Write informative/explanatory texts to examine a topic and convey ideas, concepts, and information through the selection, organization, and analysis of relevant content.

Speaking and Listening

4. Present claims and findings, emphasizing salient points in a focused, coherent manner with relevant evidence, sound [and] valid reasoning, and well-chosen details; use appropriate eye contact, adequate volume, and clear pronunciation.

Language

1. Demonstrate command of the conventions of standard English grammar and usage when writing or speaking.

Meet the Author

Award-winning writer **Daniel Keyes** (b. 1927) was raised in Brooklyn, New York. A former photographer, merchant seaman, and teacher, Keyes is fascinated by unusual psychological conditions. He has written a number of works related to this topic. For example, Keyes's nonfiction book *The Minds of Billy Milligan* is about a man with multiple-personality disorder.

 ## Can all conflicts be resolved?

Explore the Big Question as you read "Flowers for Algernon." Take notes on the changes in Charlie that might cause conflict within himself and with others.

CLOSE READING FOCUS

Key Ideas and Details: **Make Inferences**

To **make inferences** when reading, use logic and your own background knowledge to determine what an author is suggesting through story clues. For example, if an author describes a child fidgeting and sighing, you might infer that the child is bored. As you read, infer meaning from the characters' words and actions.

Craft and Structure: **Point of View**

Point of view is the perspective from which a story is told. Most stories are told from first-person or third-person point of view.

- **First person:** The narrator participates in the story's action and can tell only what he or she sees, knows, thinks, or feels. The narrator uses the pronoun *I*.
- **Third person:** The narrator describes events from the "outside." The narrator uses pronouns such as *he, she,* and *they* to refer to the characters.

Using point of view, an author can create differences between what characters know and what readers know. For example, a third-person narrator may tell readers that there is a lion in the woods. A character walking in those woods, however, may not know about the lion. Such contrasts in knowledge can create suspense, humor, or surprise.

Vocabulary

The words below are critical to understanding the text that follows. Which word ends in a common suffix that shows it is a noun (a word naming a person, place, or thing)?

deceive	**refute**	**intellectual**
naïveté	**deterioration**	**introspective**

Common Core State Standards

Reading Literature
1. Cite the textual evidence that most strongly supports an analysis of what the text says explicitly as well as inferences drawn from the text.
6. Analyze how differences in the points of view of the characters and the audience or reader create such effects as suspense or humor.

Language
5.b. Use the relationship between particular words to better understand each of the words.

CLOSE READING MODEL

The passage below is from Daniel Keyes's short story "Flowers for Algernon." The annotations to the right of the passage show ways in which you can use close reading skills to make inferences and identify point of view.

from "Flowers for Algernon"

Last night Joe Carp and Frank Reilly invited me to a party. There were lots of girls and some men from the factory. . . .

We had a lot of fun for a while.[1] Joe said I should dance with Ellen and she would teach me the steps. I fell a few times and I couldn't understand why because no one else was dancing besides Ellen and me. And all the time I was tripping because somebody's foot was always sticking out.[2]

Then when I got up I saw the look on Joe's face and it gave me a funny feeling in my stomack. "He's a scream," one of the girls said. Everybody was laughing.

Frank said, "I ain't laughed so much since we sent him out for the newspaper that night at Muggsy's and ditched him."

"Look at him. His face is red."

"He's blushing. Charlie is blushing."

"Hey, Ellen, what'd you do to Charlie? I never saw him act like that before."

I didn't know what to do or where to turn.[3] Everyone was looking at me and laughing and I felt naked. I wanted to hide myself.[4] I ran out into the street and I threw up. Then I walked home. It's a funny thing I never knew that Joe and Frank and the others liked to have me around all the time to make fun of me.

Point of View

1 The words *me* and *We* show that the story is told from first-person point of view. The narrator is one of the characters. When he uses a phrase such as "a lot of fun," readers can "hear" his voice—he speaks informally.

Make Inferences

2 Joe encourages the narrator to dance, but the narrator and Ellen are the only ones dancing and people are tripping him. From these details, you can infer that the people at the party are being mean to the narrator.

Make Inferences

3 Frank reports a trick that the group played on Charlie, the narrator. Others notice that the narrator is beginning to blush. Then, the narrator says he "didn't know what to do." From these details, you can infer that the narrator is embarrassed.

Point of View

4 The narrator tells us that he wanted "to hide" himself. Because he is a first-person narrator, he can directly report his own feelings. Readers know exactly what he is feeling because he tells them.

Flowers for **Algernon**

Daniel Keyes

progris riport 1—martch 5 1965

Dr. Strauss says I shud rite down what I think and evrey thing that happins to me from now on. I dont know why but he says its importint so they will see if they will use me. I hope they use me. Miss Kinnian says maybe they can make me smart. I want to be smart. My name is Charlie Gordon. I am 37 years old and 2 weeks ago was my brithday. I have nuthing more to rite now so I will close for today.

Make Inferences
What details in the opening paragraph help you to make inferences about Charlie's situation? Explain.

progris riport 2—martch 6

I had a test today. I think I faled it. and I think that maybe now they wont use me. What happind is a nice young man was in the room and he had some white cards with ink spilled all over them. He sed Charlie what do you see on this card. I was very skared even tho I had my rabits foot in my pockit because when I was a kid I always faled tests in school and I spillled ink to.

I told him I saw a inkblot. He said yes and it made me feel good. I thot that was all but when I got up to go he stopped me. He said now sit down Charlie we are not thru yet. Then I dont remember so good but he wantid me to say what was in the ink. I dint see nuthing in the ink but he said there was picturs there other pepul saw some picturs. I coudnt see any picturs. I reely tryed to see. I held the card close up and then far away. Then I said if I had my glases I coud see better I usally only ware my glases in the movies or TV but I said they are in the closit in the hall. I got them. Then I said let me see that card agen I bet Ill find it now.

I tryed hard but I still coudnt find the picturs I only saw the ink. I told him maybe I need new glases. He rote somthing down on a paper and I got skared of faling the test. I told him it was a very nice inkblot with littel points all around the eges. He looked very sad so that wasnt it. I said please let me try agen. Ill get it in a few minits becaus Im not so fast somtimes. Im a slow reeder too in Miss Kinnians class for slow adults but I'm trying very hard.

He gave me a chance with another card that had 2 kinds of ink spilled on it red and blue.

He was very nice and talked slow like Miss Kinnian does and he explaned it to me that it was a *raw shok*.[1] He said pepul see things in the ink. I said show me where. He said think. I told him I think a inkblot but that wasnt rite eather. He said what does it remind you—pretend somthing. I closd my eyes for a long time to pretend. I told him I pretned a fowntan pen with ink leeking all over a table cloth. Then he got up and went out.

I dont think I passd the *raw shok* test.

> I had a test today. I think I faled it.

Point of View
What elements here tell you the story is told from the first-person point of view?

---

1. *raw shok* misspelling of Rorschach (rôr´ shäk´) test, a psychological test that requires a subject to describe the images suggested by inkblots.

progris riport 3—martch 7

Dr Strauss and Dr Nemur say it dont matter about the inkblots. I told them I dint spill the ink on the cards and I coudnt see anything in the ink. They said that maybe they will still use me. I said Miss Kinnian never gave me tests like that one only spelling and reading. They said Miss Kinnian told that I was her bestist pupil in the adult nite scool becaus I tryed the hardist and I reely wantid to lern. They said how come you went to the adult nite scool all by yourself Charlie. How did you find it. I said I askd pepul and sumbody told me where I shud go to lern to read and spell good. They said why did you want to. I told them becaus all my life I wantid to be smart and not dumb. But its very hard to be smart. They said you know it will probly be tempirery. I said yes. Miss Kinnian told me. I dont care if it herts.

Later I had more crazy tests today. The nice lady who gave it me told me the name and I asked her how do you spellit so I can rite it in my progris riport. THEMATIC APPERCEPTION TEST.[2] I dont know the frist 2 words but I know what *test* means. You got to pass it or you get bad marks. This test lookd easy becaus I coud see the picturs. Only this time she dint want me to tell her the picturs. That mixd me up. I said the man yesterday said I shoud tell him what I saw in the ink she said that dont make no difrence. She said make up storys about the pepul in the picturs.

I told her how can you tell storys about pepul you never met. I said why shud I make up lies. I never tell lies any more becaus I always get caut.

She told me this test and the other one the raw-shok was for getting personalty. I laffed so hard. I said how can you get that thing from inkblots and fotos. She got sore and put her picturs away. I dont care. It was sily. I gess I faled that test too.

Later some men in white coats took me to a difernt part of the hospitil and gave me a game to play. It was like a race with a white mouse. They called the mouse Algernon. Algernon was in a box with a lot of twists and turns like all kinds of walls and they gave me a pencil and a paper with lines and lots of boxes. On one side it said START and on the

Make Inferences
What does Charlie's failure to understand the tests reveal about his personality and abilities?

Comprehension
What type of test does the "nice young man" give Charlie?

---

2. **THEMATIC** (thē mat′ ik) **APPERCEPTION** (ap′ ər sep′ shən) **TEST** personality test in which the subject makes up stories about a series of pictures.

other end it said FINISH. They said it was *amazed*[3] and that Algernon and me had the same *amazed* to do. I dint see how we could have the same *amazed* if Algernon had a box and I had a paper but I dint say nothing. Anyway there wasnt time because the race started.

One of the men had a watch he was trying to hide so I woudnt see it so I tryed not to look and that made me nervus.

Anyway that test made me feel worser than all the others because they did it over 10 times with difernt *amazeds* and Algernon won every time. I dint know that mice were so smart. Maybe thats because Algernon is a white mouse. Maybe white mice are smarter than other mice.

Point of View
What does the first-person point of view show about Charlie's experience with the doctors?

---

3. *amazed* Charlie means "a maze," or confusing series of paths. Often, the intelligence of animals is assessed by how fast they go through a maze.

LITERATURE IN CONTEXT

Science Connection
Test Inventors
Three pioneers of intelligence and behavioral testing devised tests that are still used to this day.

In the early twentieth century, Swiss psychologist Hermann Rorschach developed a test in which the subject describes what an inkblot looks like. Psychologists use the subject's responses to a **Rorschach inkblot**, such as the one shown, to reach conclusions about the subject's personality and mental condition. ▼

▲
In 1905, **Alfred Binet**, above left, and Theodore Simon devised a system for testing intelligence based on standardized, average mental levels for various age groups. In 1916, **Lewis Terman**, above right, reworked the test, which become known as the Revised Stanford-Binet Intelligence Test. One question from an intelligence test is shown above.

Connect to the Literature
What do you think Charlie's first reaction to the Rorschach inkblots reveals?

progris riport 4—Mar 8

Their going to use me! Im so exited I can hardly write. Dr Nemur and Dr Strauss had a argament about it first. Dr Nemur was in the office when Dr Strauss brot me in. Dr Nemur was worryed about using me but Dr Strauss told him Miss Kinnian rekemmended me the best from all the pepul who she was teaching. I like Miss Kinnian becaus shes a very smart teacher. And she said Charlie your going to have a second chance. If you volenteer for this experament you mite get smart. They dont know if it will be perminint but theirs a chance. Thats why I said ok even when I was scared because she said it was an operashun. She said dont be scared Charlie you done so much with so little I think you deserv it most of all.

So I got scaird when Dr Nemur and Dr Strauss argud about it. Dr Strauss said I had something that was very good. He said I had a good *motor-vation.*[4] I never even knew I had that. I felt proud when he said that not every body with an eye-q[5] of 68 had that thing. I dont know what it is or where I got it but he said Algernon had it too. Algernons *motor-vation* is the cheese they put in his box. But it cant be that because I didnt eat any cheese this week.

Then he told Dr Nemur something I dint understand so while they were talking I wrote down some of the words.

He said Dr Nemur I know Charlie is not what you had in mind as the first of your new brede of intelek** (coudnt get the word) superman. But most people of his low ment** are host** and uncoop** they are usualy dull apath** and hard to reach. He has a good natcher hes intristed and eager to please.

Dr Nemur said remember he will be the first human beeng ever to have his intelijence trippled by surgicle meens.

Dr Strauss said exakly. Look at how well hes lerned to read and write for his low mentel age its as grate an acheve** as you and I lerning einstines therey of **vity without help. That shows the intenss motor-vation. Its comparat** a tremen** achev** I say we use Charlie.

▲ **Critical Viewing**
Judging from this scene from the 1968 movie version of the story, in what ways are Charlie and Algernon similar and different?

Comprehension
What makes Charlie excited on March 8?

---

4. *motor-vation* motivation, or desire to work hard and achieve a goal.
5. *eye-q* IQ, or intelligence quotient. A way of measuring human intelligence.

▲ **Critical Viewing**
Why do scientists
use lab animals like
Algernon in their
experiments?

Make Inferences
What details in the
March 8 entry show the
way both doctors feel
about Charlie?

Point of View
What feelings does the
use of this point of view
allow the narrator to
reveal?

I dint get all the words and they were talking to fast but it sounded like Dr Strauss was on my side and like the other one wasnt.

Then Dr Nemur nodded he said all right maybe your right. We will use Charlie. When he said that I got so exited I jumped up and shook his hand for being so good to me. I told him thank you doc you wont be sorry for giving me a second chance. And I mean it like I told him. After the operashun Im gonna try to be smart. Im gonna try awful hard.

progris ript 5—Mar 10

Im skared. Lots of people who work here and the nurses and the people who gave me the tests came to bring me candy and wish me luck. I hope I have luck. I got my rabits foot and my lucky penny and my horse shoe. Only a black cat crossed me when I was comming to the hospitil. Dr Strauss says dont be supersitis Charlie this is sience. Anyway Im keeping my rabits foot with me.

I asked Dr Strauss if Ill beat Algernon in the race after the operashun and he said maybe. If the operashun works Ill show that mouse I can be as smart as he is. Maybe smarter. Then Ill be abel to read better and spell the words good and know lots of things and be like other people. I want to be smart like other people. If it works perminint they will make everybody smart all over the wurld.

They dint give me anything to eat this morning. I dont know what that eating has to do with getting smart. Im very hungry and Dr Nemur took away my box of candy. That Dr Nemur is a grouch. Dr Strauss says I can have it back after the operashun. You cant eat befor a operashun . . .

Progress Report 6—Mar 15

The operashun dint hurt. He did it while I was sleeping. They took off the bandijis from my eyes and my head today so I can make a PROGRESS REPORT. Dr Nemur who looked at some of my other ones says I spell PROGRESS wrong and he told me how to spell it and REPORT too. I got to try and remember that.

I have a very bad memary for spelling. Dr Strauss says its ok to tell about all the things that happin to me but he says I shoud tell more about what I feel and what I think. When I told him I dont know how to think he said try. All the time when the bandijis were on my eyes I tryed to think. Nothing happened. I dont know what to think about. Maybe if I ask him he will tell me how I can think now that Im suppose to get smart. What do smart people think about. Fancy things I suppose. I wish I knew some fancy things alredy.

Progress Report 7—Mar 19

Nothing is happining. I had lots of tests and different kinds of races with Algernon. I hate that mouse. He always beats me. Dr Strauss said I got to play those games. And he said some time I got to take those tests over again. Thse inkblots are stupid. And those pictures are stupid too. I like to draw a picture of a man and a woman but I wont make up lies about people.

I got a headache from trying to think so much. I thot Dr Strauss was my frend but he dont help me. He dont tell me what to think or when Ill get smart. Miss Kinnian dint come to see me. I think writing these progress reports are stupid too.

Progress Report 8—Mar 23

Im going back to work at the factery. They said it was better I shud go back to work but I cant tell anyone what the operashun was for and I have to come to the hospitil for an

Spiral Review
CHARACTER What do Charlie's thoughts in this entry reveal about how he views himself in relation to the rest of the world?

Make Inferences
Which words in Progress Report 7 indicate Charlie's state of mind after the operation?

Comprehension
Why does Charlie want to beat Algernon in the race?

hour evry night after work. They are gonna pay me mony every month for lerning to be smart.

Im glad Im going back to work because I miss my job and all my frends and all the fun we have there.

Dr Strauss says I shud keep writing things down but I dont have to do it every day just when I think of something or something speshul happins. He says dont get discoridged because it takes time and it happins slow. He says it took a long time with Algernon before he got 3 times smarter then he was before. Thats why Algernon beats me all the time because he had that operashun too. That makes me feel better. I coud probly do that *amazed* faster than a reglar mouse. Maybe some day Ill beat Algernon. Boy that would be something. So far Algernon looks like he mite be smart perminent.

▲ Critical Viewing
What impression of Charlie do you get from this photograph?

Mar 25

(I dont have to write PROGRESS REPORT on top any more just when I hand it in once a week for Dr Nemur to read. I just have to put the date on. That saves time)

We had a lot of fun at the factery today. Joe Carp said hey look where Charlie had his operashun what did they do Charlie put some brains in. I was going to tell him but I remembered Dr Strauss said no. Then Frank Reilly said what did you do Charlie forget your key and open your door the hard way. That made me laff. Their really my friends and they like me.

Sometimes somebody will say hey look at Joe or Frank or George he really pulled a Charlie Gordon. I dont know why they say that but they always laff. This morning Amos Borg who is the 4 man at Donnegans used my name when he shouted at Ernie the office boy. Ernie lost a packige. He said Ernie what are you trying to be a Charlie Gordon. I dont understand why he said that. I never lost any packiges.

Make Inferences
What do Charlie's friends mean when they say someone "pulled a Charlie Gordon"?

Mar 28

Dr Straus came to my room tonight to see why I dint come in like I was suppose to. I told him I dont like to race with Algernon any more. He said I dont have to for a while but I shud come in. He had a present for me only it wasnt a present but just for lend. I thot it was a little television but it wasnt. He said I got to turn it on when I go to sleep. I said your kidding why shud I turn it on when Im going to sleep. Who ever herd of a thing like that. But he said if I want to get smart I got to do what he says. I told him I dint think I was going to get smart and he put his hand on my sholder and said Charlie you dont know it yet but your getting smarter all the time. You wont notice for a while. I think he was just being nice to make me feel good because I dont look any smarter.

Oh yes I almost forgot. I asked him when I can go back to the class at Miss Kinnians school. He said I wont go their. He said that soon Miss Kinnian will come to the hospitil to start and teach me speshul. I was mad at her for not comming to see me when I got the operashun but I like her so maybe we will be frends again.

Mar 29

That crazy TV kept me up all night. How can I sleep with something yelling crazy things all night in my ears. And the nutty pictures. Wow. I dont know what it says when Im up so how am I going to know when Im sleeping.

Dr Strauss says its ok. He says my brains are lerning when I sleep and that will help me when Miss Kinnian starts my lessons in the hospitl (only I found out it isnt a hospitil its a labatory. I think its all crazy. If you can get smart when your sleeping why do people go to school. That thing I dont think will work. I use to watch the late show and the late late show on TV all the time and it never made me smart. Maybe you have to sleep while you watch it.

Progress Report 9—APRIL 3

Dr Strauss showed me how to keep the TV turned low so now I can sleep. I don't hcar a thing. And I still dont understand what it says. A few times I play it over in the

Comprehension
What does Dr. Strauss give to Charlie?

morning to find out what I lerned when I was sleeping and I dont think so. Miss Kinnian says Maybe its another langwidge or something. But most times it sounds american. It talks so fast faster then even Miss Gold who was my teacher in 6 grade and I remember she talked so fast I coudnt understand her.

I told Dr Strauss what good is it to get smart in my sleep. I want to be smart when Im awake. He says its the same thing and I have two minds. Theres the *subconscious* and the *conscious* (thats how you spell it). And one dont tell the other one what its doing. They dont even talk to each other. Thats why I dream. And boy have I been having crazy dreams. Wow. Ever since that night TV. The late late late late late show.

I forgot to ask him if it was only me or if everybody had those two minds.

(I just looked up the word in the dictionary Dr Strauss gave me. The word is *subconscious. adj. Of the nature of mental operations yet not present in consciousness; as, subconscious conflict of desires.*) There's more but I still dont know what it means. This isnt a very good dictionary for dumb people like me.

Anyway the headache is from the party. My frends from the factery Joe Carp and Frank Reilly invited me to go with them to Muggsys Saloon for some drinks. I dont like to drink but they said we will have lots of fun. I had a good time.

Joe Carp said I shoud show the girls how I mop out the toilet in the factory and he got me a mop. I showed them and everyone laffed when I told that Mr Donnegan said I was the best janiter he ever had because I like my job and do it good and never come late or miss a day except for my operashun.

I said Miss Kinnian always said Charlie be proud of your job because you do it good.

Everybody laffed and we had a good time and they gave me lots of drinks and Joe said Charlie is a card when hes potted. I dont know what that means but everybody likes me and we have fun. I cant wait to be smart like my best frends Joe Carp and Frank Reilly.

I dont remember how the party was over but I think I went out to buy a newspaper and coffe for Joe and Frank and when I came back there was no one their. I looked for them all over till late. Then I dont remember so good but I think I got sleepy or sick. A nice cop brot me back home. Thats what my landlady Mrs Flynn says.

But I got a headache and a big lump on my head and black and blue all over. I think maybe I fell. Anyway I got a bad headache and Im sick and hurt all over. I dont think Ill drink anymore.

April 6

I beat Algernon! I dint even know I beat him until Burt the tester told me. Then the second time I lost because I got so exited I fell off the chair before I finished. But after that I beat him 8 more times. I must be getting smart to beat a smart mouse like Algernon. But I dont *feel* smarter.

I wanted to race Algernon some more but Burt said thats enough for one day. They let me hold him for a minit. Hes not so bad. Hes soft like a ball of cotton. He blinks and when he opens his eyes their black and pink on the eges.

I said can I feed him because I felt bad to beat him and I wanted to be nice and make frends. Burt said no Algernon is a very specshul mouse with an operashun like mine, and he was the first of all the animals to stay smart so long. He told me Algernon is so smart that every day he has to solve a test to get his food. Its a thing like a lock on a door that changes every time Algernon goes in to eat so he has to lern something new to get his food. That made me sad because if he coudnt lern he woud be hungry.

I dont think its right to make you pass a test to eat. How woud Dr Nemur like it to have to pass a test every time he wants to eat. I think Ill be frends with Algernon.

April 9

Tonight after work Miss Kinnian was at the laboratory. She looked like she was glad to see me but scared. I told her dont worry Miss Kinnian Im not smart yet and she laffed. She said I have confidence in you Charlie the way you struggled so hard to read and right better than all the others. At werst you will have it for a littel wile and your doing something for sience.

We are reading a very hard book. I never read such a hard book before. Its called *Robinson Crusoe*[6] about a man who

---

6. *Robinson Crusoe* (krōō' sō) novel written in 1719 by Daniel Defoe, a British author.

Comprehension
What happens at the party to make people laugh?

gets merooned on a dessert Iland. Hes smart and figers out all kinds of things so he can have a house and food and hes a good swimmer. Only I feel sorry because hes all alone and has no frends. But I think their must be somebody else on the iland because theres a picture with his funny umbrella looking at footprints. I hope he gets a frend and not be lonly.

▲ **Critical Viewing**
What details in this photograph show that Charlie admires Miss Kinnian?

Make Inferences
What can you infer about Miss Kinnian's personality, based on this entry?

April 10

Miss Kinnian teaches me to spell better. She says look at a word and close your eyes and say it over and over until you remember. I have lots of truble with *through* that you say *threw* and *enough* and *tough* that you dont say *enew* and *tew*. You got to say *enuff* and *tuff*. Thats how I use to write it before I started to get smart. Im confused but Miss Kinnian says theres no reason in spelling.

April 14

Finished Robinson Crusoe. I want to find out more about what happens to him but Miss Kinnian says thats all there is. *Why*

April 15

Miss Kinnian says Im lerning fast. She read some of the Progress Reports and she looked at me kind of funny. She says Im a fine person and Ill show them all. I asked her why. She said never mind but I shoudnt feel bad if I find out that everybody isnt nice like I think. She said for a person who god gave so little to you done more then a lot of people with brains they never even used. I said all my frends are smart people but there good. They like me and they never did anything that wasnt nice. Then she got something in her eye and she had to run out to the ladys room.

April 16

Today, I lerned, the comma, this is a comma (,) a period, with a tail, Miss Kinnian, says its important, because, it makes writing, better, she said, somebody, coud lose, a lot of money, if a comma, isnt, in the, right place, I dont have, any money, and I dont see, how a comma, keeps you, from losing it,

But she says, everybody, uses commas, so Ill use, them too,

April 17

I used the comma wrong. Its punctuation. Miss Kinnian told me to look up long words in the dictionary to lern to spell them. I said whats the difference if you can read it anyway. She said its part of your education so now on Ill look up all the words Im not sure how to spell. It takes a long time to write that way but I think Im remembering. I only have to look up once and after that I get it right. Anyway thats how come I got the word *punctuation* right. (Its that way in the dictionary). Miss Kinnian says a period is punctuation too, and there are lots of other marks to lern. I told her I thot all the periods had to have tails but she said no.

You got to mix them up, she showed? me" how. to mix! them(up,. and now; I can! mix up all kinds" of punctuation, in! my writing? There, are lots! of rules? to lern; but Im gettin'g them in my head.

One thing I? like about, Dear Miss Kinnian: (thats the way it goes in a business letter if I ever go into business) is she, always gives me' a reason" when—I ask. She's a gen'ius! I wish! I cou'd be smart" like, her;

(Punctuation, is; fun!)

April 18

What a dope I am! I didn't even understand what she was talking about. I read the grammar book last night and it explanes the whole thing. Then I saw it was the same way as Miss Kinnian was trying to tell me, but I didn't get it. I got up in the middle of the night, and the whole thing straightened out in my mind.

Miss Kinnian said that the TV working in my sleep helped out. She said I reached a plateau. Thats like the flat top of a hill.

After I figgered out how punctuation worked, I read over all my old Progress Reports from the beginning. Boy, did I have crazy spelling and punctuation! I told Miss Kinnian I ought to go over the pages and fix all the mistakes but she said, "No, Charlie, Dr. Nemur wants them just as they are. That's

Point of View
What do you learn about Charlie from this entry that you might not know if it were written in the third person?

Make Inferences
What details in the April 18 entry show that Charlie's level of thought has increased?

Comprehension
What are some things Charlie is learning from Miss Kinnian?

why he let you keep them after they were photostated, to see your own progress. You're coming along fast, Charlie."

That made me feel good. After the lesson I went down and played with Algernon. We don't race any more.

April 20

I feel sick inside. Not sick like for a doctor, but inside my chest it feels empty like getting punched and a heartburn at the same time.

I wasn't going to write about it, but I guess I got to, because its important. Today was the first time I ever stayed home from work.

Last night Joe Carp and Frank Reilly invited me to a party. There were lots of girls and some men from the factory. I remembered how sick I got last time I drank too much, so I told Joe I didn't want anything to drink. He gave me a plain coke instead. It tasted funny, but I thought it was just a bad taste in my mouth.

We had a lot of fun for a while. Joe said I should dance with Ellen and she would teach me the steps. I fell a few times and I couldn't understand why because no one else was dancing besides Ellen and me. And all the time I was tripping because somebody's foot was always sticking out.

Then when I got up I saw the look on Joe's face and it gave me a funny feeling in my stomach. "He's a scream," one of the girls said. Everybody was laughing.

Frank said, "I ain't laughed so much since we sent him off for the newspaper that night at Muggsy's and ditched him."

"Look at him. His face is red."

"He's blushing. Charlie is blushing."

"Hey, Ellen, what'd you do to Charlie? I never saw him act like that before."

I didn't know what to do or where to turn. Everyone was looking at me and laughing and I felt naked. I wanted to hide myself. I ran out into the street and I threw up. Then I walked home. It's a funny thing I never knew that Joe and Frank and the others liked to have me around all the time to make fun of me.

Now I know what it means when they say "to pull a Charlie Gordon."

I'm ashamed.

Make Inferences
Is Joe a true friend to Charlie? Explain.

Point of View
How does the use of first-person point of view help you to sympathize with Charlie?

Progress Report 11–April 21

Still didn't go into the factory. I told Mrs. Flynn my landlady to call and tell Mr. Donnegan I was sick. Mrs. Flynn looks at me very funny lately like she's scared of me.

I think it's a good thing about finding out how everybody laughs at me. I thought about it a lot. It's because I'm so dumb and I don't even know when I'm doing something dumb. People think it's funny when a dumb person can't do things the same way they can.

Anyway, now I know I'm getting smarter every day. I know punctuation and I can spell good. I like to look up all the hard words in the dictionary and I remember them. I'm reading a lot now, and Miss Kinnian says I read very fast. Sometimes I even understand what I'm reading about, and it stays in my mind. There are times when I can close my eyes and think of a page and it all comes back like a picture.

Besides history, geography and arithmetic, Miss Kinnian said I should start to learn a few foreign languages. Dr. Strauss gave me some more tapes to play while I sleep. I still don't understand how that conscious and unconscious mind works, but Dr. Strauss says not to worry yet. He asked me to promise that when I start learning college subjects next week I wouldn't read any books on psychology—that is, until he gives me permission.

I feel a lot better today, but I guess I'm still a little angry that all the time people were laughing and making fun of me because I wasn't so smart. When I become intelligent like Dr. Strauss says, with three times my I.Q. of 68, then maybe I'll be like everyone else and people will like me and be friendly.

I'm not sure what an I.Q. is. Dr. Nemur said it was something that measured how intelligent you were—like a scale in the drugstore weighs pounds. But Dr. Strauss had a big arguement with him and said an I.Q. didn't

▲ **Critical Viewing**
Does Charlie seem to have made progress, judging from the details in this photograph? Explain.

Comprehension
What happened at Joe Carp's party?

weigh intelligence at all. He said an I.Q. showed how much intelligence you could get, like the numbers on the outside of a measuring cup. You still had to fill the cup up with stuff.

Then when I asked Burt, who gives me my intelligence tests and works with Algernon, he said that both of them were wrong (only I had to promise not to tell them he said so). Burt says that the I.Q. measures a lot of different things including some of the things you learned already, and it really isn't any good at all.

So I still don't know what I.Q. is except that mine is going to be over 200 soon. I didn't want to say anything, but I don't see how if they don't know *what* it is, or *where* it is—I don't see how they know *how much* of it you've got.

Dr. Nemur says I have to take a *Rorshach Test* tomorrow. I wonder what *that* is.

April 22

I found out what a *Rorshach* is. It's the test I took before the operation—the one with the inkblots on the pieces of cardboard. The man who gave me the test was the same one.

I was scared to death of those inkblots. I knew he was going to ask me to find the pictures and I knew I wouldn't be able to. I was thinking to myself, if only there was some way of knowing what kind of pictures were hidden there. Maybe there weren't any pictures at all. Maybe it was just a trick to see if I was dumb enough too look for something that wasn't there. Just thinking about that made me sore at him.

"All right, Charlie," he said, "you've seen these cards before, remember?"

"Of course I remember."

The way I said it, he knew I was angry, and he looked surprised. "Yes, of course. Now I want you to look at this one. What might this be? What do you see on this card? People see all sorts of things in these inkblots. Tell me what it might be for you—what it makes you think of."

I was shocked. That wasn't what I had expected him to say at all. "You mean there are no pictures hidden in those inkblots?"

He frowned and took off his glasses. "What?"

"Pictures. Hidden in the inkblots. Last time you told me

that everyone could see them and you wanted me to find them too."

He explained to me that the last time he had used almost the exact same words he was using now. I didn't believe it, and I still have the suspicion that he misled me at the time just for the fun of it. Unless—I don't know any more—could I have been *that* feeble-minded?

We went through the cards slowly. One of them looked like a pair of bats tugging at some thing. Another one looked like two men fencing with swords. I imagined all sorts of things. I guess I got carried away. But I didn't trust him any more, and I kept turning them around and even looking on the back to see if there was anything there I was supposed to catch. While he was making his notes, I peeked out of the corner of my eye to read it. But it was all in code that looked like this:

$$\text{WF + A DdF-Ad orig. WF-A}$$
$$\text{SF + obj}$$

The test still doesn't make sense to me. It seems to me that anyone could make up lies about things that they didn't really see. How could he know I wasn't making a fool of him by mentioning things that I didn't really imagine? Maybe I'll understand it when Dr. Strauss lets me read up on psychology.

April 25

I figured out a new way to line up the machines in the factory, and Mr. Donnegan says it will save him ten thousand dollars a year in labor and increased production. He gave me a $25 bonus.

I wanted to take Joe Carp and Frank Reilly out to lunch to celebrate, but Joe said he had to buy some things for his wife, and Frank said he was meeting his cousin for lunch. I guess it'll take a little time for them to get used to the changes in me. Everybody seems to be frightened of me. When I went over to Amos Borg and tapped him on the shoulder, he jumped up in the air.

People don't talk to me much any more or kid around the way they used to. It makes the job kind of lonely.

Point of View
How does the first-person point of view help you to keep track of Charlie's development?

Make Inferences
Why do Charlie's co-workers behave differently toward him?

Comprehension
What surprises Charlie about the Rorschach test?

April 27

I got up the nerve today to ask Miss Kinnian to have dinner with me tomorrow night to celebrate my bonus.

At first she wasn't sure it was right, but I asked Dr. Strauss and he said it was okay. Dr. Strauss and Dr. Nemur don't seem to be getting along so well. They're arguing all the time. This evening when I came in to ask Dr. Strauss about having dinner with Miss Kinnian, I heard them shouting. Dr. Nemur was saying that it was *his* experiment and *his* research, and Dr. Strauss was shouting back that he contributed just as much, because he found me through Miss Kinnian and he performed the operation. Dr. Strauss said that someday thousands of neurosurgeons[7] might be using his technique all over the world.

Dr. Nemur wanted to publish the results of the experiment at the end of this month. Dr. Strauss wanted to wait a while longer to be sure. Dr. Strauss said that Dr. Nemur was more interested in the Chair[8] of Psychology at Princeton than he was in the experiment. Dr. Nemur said that Dr. Strauss was nothing but an opportunist who was trying to ride to glory on *his* coattails.

When I left afterwards, I found myself trembling. I don't know why for sure, but it was as if I'd seen both men clearly for the first time. I remember hearing Burt say that Dr. Nemur had a shrew of a wife who was pushing him all the time to get things published so that he could become famous. Burt said that the dream of her life was to have a big shot husband.

Was Dr. Strauss really trying to ride on his coattails?

▲ **Critical Viewing**
What details in this picture show that Charlie's intelligence has increased?

April 28

I don't understand why I never noticed how beautiful Miss Kinnian really is. She has brown eyes and feathery brown hair that comes to the top of her neck. She's only thirty-four!

---

7. **neurosurgeons** (nŏŏr´ ō sʉr´ jənz) *n.* doctors who operate on the nervous system, including the brain and spine.
8. **Chair** *n.* professorship.

I think from the beginning I had the feeling that she was an unreachable genius—and very, very old. Now, every time I see her she grows younger and more lovely.

We had dinner and a long talk. When she said that I was coming along so fast that soon I'd be leaving her behind, I laughed.

"It's true, Charlie. You're already a better reader than I am. You can read a whole page at a glance while I can take in only a few lines at a time. And you remember every single thing you read. I'm lucky if I can recall the main thoughts and the general meaning."

"I don't feel intelligent. There are so many things I don't understand."

"You've got to be a *little* patient. You're accomplishing in days and weeks what it takes normal people to do in half a lifetime. That's what makes it so amazing. You're like a giant sponge now, soaking things in. Facts, figures, general knowledge. And soon you'll begin to connect them, too. You'll see how the different branches of learning are related. There are many levels, Charlie, like steps on a giant ladder that take you up higher and higher to see more and more of the world around you.

"I can see only a little bit of that, Charlie, and I won't go much higher than I am now, but you'll keep climbing up and up, and see more and more, and each step will open new worlds that you never even knew existed." She frowned. "I hope . . . I just hope to God—"

"What?"

"Never mind, Charles. I just hope I wasn't wrong to advise you to go into this in the first place."

I laughed. "How could that be? It worked, didn't it? Even Algernon is still smart."

We sat there silently for a while and I knew what she was thinking about as she watched me toying with the chain of my rabbit's foot and my keys. I didn't want to think of that possibility any more than elderly people want to think of death. I *knew* that this was only the beginning. I knew what she meant about levels because I'd seen some of them already. The thought of leaving her behind made me sad.

I'm in love with Miss Kinnian.

Point of View
Compare this entry to Progress Report 3 on pages 55 and 56. Which words and phrases show that Charlie has changed?

Comprehension
How are Charlie's feelings toward Miss Kinnian changing?

Progress Report 12–April 30

I've quit my job with Donnegan's Plastic Box Company. Mr. Donnegan insisted that it would be better for all concerned if I left. What did I do to make them hate me so?

The first I knew of it was when Mr. Donnegan showed me the petition. Eight hundred and forty names, everyone connected with the factory, except Fanny Girden. Scanning the list quickly, I saw at once that hers was the only missing name. All the rest demanded that I be fired.

Joe Carp and Frank Reilly wouldn't talk to me about it. No one else would either, except Fanny. She was one of the few people I'd known who set her mind to something and believed it no matter what the rest of the world proved, said or did— and Fanny did not believe that I should have been fired. She had been against the petition on principle and despite the pressure and threats she'd held out.

"Which don't mean to say," she remarked, "that I don't think there's something mighty strange about you, Charlie. Them changes. I don't know. You used to be a good, dependable, ordinary man—not too bright maybe, but honest. Who knows what you done to yourself to get so smart all of a sudden. Like everybody around here's been saying, Charlie, it's not right."

"But how can you say that, Fanny? What's wrong with a man becoming intelligent and wanting to acquire knowledge and understanding of the world around him?"

She stared down at her work, and I turned to leave. Without looking at me, she said: "It was evil when Eve listened to the snake and ate from the tree of knowledge. It was evil when she saw that she was naked. If not for that none of us would ever have to grow old and sick, and die."

Once again now I have the feeling of shame burning inside me. This intelligence has driven a wedge between me and all the people I once knew and loved. Before, they laughed at me and despised me for my ignorance and dullness; now, they hate me for my knowledge and understanding. What do they want of me?

They've driven me out of the factory. Now I'm more alone than ever before . . .

Make Inferences
Why do you think Charlie's co-workers signed the petition to have him fired?

Make Inferences
What comparison is Fanny making between Charlie and Eve?

May 15

Dr. Strauss is very angry at me for not having written any progress reports in two weeks. He's justified because the lab is now paying me a regular salary. I told him I was too busy thinking and reading. When I pointed out that writing was such a slow process that it made me impatient with my poor handwriting, he suggested that I learn to type. It's much easier to write now because I can type nearly seventy-five words a minute. Dr. Strauss continually reminds me of the need to speak and write simply so that people will be able to understand me.

I'll try to review all the things that happened to me during the last two weeks. Algernon and I were presented to the American Psychological Association sitting in convention with the World Psychological Association last Tuesday. We created quite a sensation. Dr. Nemur and Dr. Strauss were proud of us.

I suspect that Dr. Nemur, who is sixty—ten years older than Dr. Strauss—finds it necessary to see tangible[9] results of his work. Undoubtedly the result of pressure by Mrs. Nemur.

Contrary to my earlier impressions of him, I realize that Dr. Nemur is not at all a genius. He has a very good mind, but it struggles under the specter of self-doubt. He wants people to take him for a genius. Therefore, it is important for him to feel that his work is accepted by the world. I believe that Dr. Nemur was afraid of further delay because he worried that someone else might make a discovery along these lines and take the credit from him.

Dr. Strauss on the other hand might be called a genius, although I feel that his areas of knowledge are too limited. He was educated in the tradition of narrow specialization; the broader aspects of background were neglected far more than necessary—even for a neurosurgeon.

I was shocked to learn that the only ancient languages he could read were Latin, Greek and Hebrew, and that he knows almost nothing of mathematics beyond the elementary levels of the calculus of variations. When he admitted this to me, I found myself almost annoyed. It was as if he'd hidden this

Point of View
What details in this entry reveal Charlie's increased intelligence?

Comprehension
Why does Charlie quit his job?

---

9. tangible (tan´ jə bəl) *adj.* able to be felt or perceived; substantial.

part of himself in order to **deceive** me, pretending—as do many people I've discovered—to be what he is not. No one I've ever known is what he appears to be on the surface.

Dr. Nemur appears to be uncomfortable around me. Sometimes when I try to talk to him, he just looks at me strangely and turns away. I was angry at first when Dr. Strauss told me I was giving Dr. Nemur an inferiority complex. I thought he was mocking me and I'm oversensitive at being made fun of.

How was I to know that a highly respected psycho-experimentalist like Nemur was unacquainted with Hindustani[10] and Chinese? It's absurd when you consider the work that is being done in India and China today in the very field of his study.

I asked Dr. Strauss how Nemur could **refute** Rahajamati's attack on his method and results if Nemur couldn't even read them in the first place. That strange look on Dr. Strauss' face can mean only one of two things. Either he doesn't want to tell Nemur what they're saying in India, or else—and this worries me—Dr. Strauss doesn't know either. I must be careful to speak and write clearly and simply so that people won't laugh.

May 18

I am very disturbed. I saw Miss Kinnian last night for the first time in over a week. I tried to avoid all discussions of **intellectual** concepts and to keep the conversation on a simple, everyday level, but she just stared at me blankly and asked me what I meant about the mathematical variance equivalent in Dorbermann's *Fifth Concerto*.

When I tried to explain she stopped me and laughed. I guess I got angry, but I suspect I'm approaching her on the wrong level. No matter what I try to discuss with her, I am unable to communicate. I must review Vrostadt's equations on *Levels of Semantic Progression*. I find that I don't communicate with people much any more. Thank God for books and music and things I can think about. I am alone in my apartment at Mrs. Flynn's boarding house most of the time and seldom speak to anyone.

Point of View
How would the May 18 entry be different if it were told from Miss Kinnian's point of view?

---

10. **Hindustani** (hin´ do͞o stä´ nē) *n.* a language of northern India.

May 20

I would not have noticed the new dishwasher, a boy of about sixteen, at the corner diner where I take my evening meals if not for the incident of the broken dishes.

They crashed to the floor, shattering and sending bits of white china under the tables. The boy stood there, dazed and frightened, holding the empty tray in his hand. The whistles and catcalls from the customers (the cries of "hey, there go the profits!" . . . *"Mazeltov!"* . . . and "well, he didn't work here very long . . ." which invariably seems to follow the breaking of glass or dishware in a public restaurant) all seemed to confuse him.

When the owner came to see what the excitement was about, the boy cowered as if he expected to be struck and threw up his arms as if to ward off the blow.

"All right! All right, you dope," shouted the owner, "don't just stand there! Get the broom and sweep that mess up. A broom . . . a broom, you idiot! It's in the kitchen. Sweep up all the pieces."

The boy saw that he was not going to be punished. His frightened expression disappeared and he smiled and hummed as he came back with the broom to sweep the floor. A few of the rowdier customers kept up the remarks, amusing themselves at his expense.

"Here, sonny, over here there's a nice piece behind you . . ."

"C'mon, do it again . . ."

"He's not so dumb. It's easier to break 'em than to wash 'em . . ."

As his vacant eyes moved across the crowd of amused onlookers, he slowly mirrored their smiles and finally broke into an uncertain grin at the joke which he obviously did not understand.

I felt sick inside as I looked at his dull, vacuous smile, the wide, bright eyes of a child, uncertain but eager to please. They were laughing at him because he was mentally retarded.

And I had been laughing at him too.

Suddenly, I was furious at myself and all those who were smirking at him. I jumped up and shouted, "Shut up! Leave him alone! It's not his fault he can't understand! He can't help what he is! But . . . he's still a human being!"

> I felt sick inside as I looked at his dull, vacuous smile, the wide, bright eyes of a child. . . .

Comprehension
What makes Charlie angry with Miss Kinnian?

Point of View
How does Charlie
now see himself?

The room grew silent. I cursed myself for losing control and creating a scene. I tried not to look at the boy as I paid my check and walked out without touching my food. I felt ashamed for both of us.

How strange it is that people of honest feelings and sensibility, who would not take advantage of a man born without arms or legs or eyes—how such people think nothing of abusing a man born with low intelligence. It infuriated me to think that not too long ago I, like this boy, had foolishly played the clown.

And I had almost forgotten.

I'd hidden the picture of the old Charlie Gordon from myself because now that I was intelligent it was something that had to be pushed out of my mind. But today in looking at that boy, for the first time I saw what I had been. I *was just like him!*

Only a short time ago, I learned that people laughed at me. Now I can see that unknowingly I joined with them in laughing at myself. That hurts most of all.

Vocabulary ▶
naïveté (nä ēv tā´)
n. the state of being
simple or childlike

I have often reread my progress reports and seen the illiteracy, the childish naïveté, the mind of low intelligence peering from a dark room, through the keyhole, at the dazzling light outside. I see that even in my dullness I knew that I was inferior, and that other people had something I lacked—something denied me. In my mental blindness, I thought that it was somehow connected with the ability to read and write, and I was sure that if I could get those skills I would automatically have intelligence too.

Even a feeble-minded man wants to be like other men.

A child may not know how to feed itself, or what to eat, yet it knows of hunger.

This then is what I was like. I never knew. Even with my gift of intellectual awareness, I never really knew.

Point of View
What has Charlie
learned about himself?

This day was good for me. Seeing the past more clearly, I have decided to use my knowledge and skills to work in the field of increasing human intelligence levels. Who is better equipped for this work? Who else has lived in both worlds? These are my people. Let me use my gift to do something for them.

Tomorrow, I will discuss with Dr. Strauss the manner in which I can work in this area. I may be able to help him work out the problems of widespread use of the technique which was used on me. I have several good ideas of my own.

There is so much that might be done with this technique. If I could be made into a genius, what about thousands of others like myself? What fantastic levels might be achieved by using this technique on normal people? On *geniuses?*

There are so many doors to open. I am impatient to begin.

PROGRESS REPORT 13–May 23

It happened today. Algernon bit me. I visited the lab to see him as I do occasionally, and when I took him out of his cage, he snapped at my hand. I put him back and watched him for a while. He was unusually disturbed and vicious.

May 24

Burt, who is in charge of the experimental animals, tells me that Algernon is changing. He is less cooperative; he refuses to run the maze any more; general motivation has decreased. And he hasn't been eating. Everyone is upset about what this may mean.

Make Inferences
What is upsetting about the changes in Algernon described in the May 23 and May 24 entries?

May 25

They've been feeding Algernon, who now refuses to work the shifting-lock problem. Everyone identifies me with Algernon. In a way we're both the first of our kind. They're all pretending that Algernon's behavior is not necessarily significant for me. But it's hard to hide the fact that some of the other animals who were used in this experiment are showing strange behavior.

Dr. Strauss and Dr. Nemur have asked me not to come to the lab any more. I know what they're thinking but I can't accept it. I am going ahead with my plans to carry their research forward. With all due respect to both of these fine scientists, I am well aware of their limitations. If there is an answer, I'll have to find it out for myself. Suddenly, time has become very important to me.

Comprehension
What new line of work does Charlie want to pursue?

May 29

I have been given a lab of my own and permission to go ahead with the research. I'm on to something. Working day and night. I've had a cot moved into the lab. Most of my writing time is spent on the notes which I keep in a separate folder, but from time to time I feel it necessary to put down my moods and my thoughts out of sheer habit.

I find the *calculus of intelligence* to be a fascinating study. Here is the place for the application of all the knowledge I have acquired. In a sense it's the problem I've been concerned with all my life.

May 31

Dr. Strauss thinks I'm working too hard. Dr. Nemur says I'm trying to cram a lifetime of research and thought into a few weeks. I know I should rest, but I'm driven on by something inside that won't let me stop. I've got to find the reason for the sharp regression in Algernon. I've got to know *if* and *when* it will happen to me.

June 4

Letter to Dr. Strauss *(copy)*
Dear Dr. Strauss:
Under separate cover I am sending you a copy of my report entitled, "The Algernon-Gordon Effect: A Study of Structure and Function of Increased Intelligence," which I would like to have you read and have published.

As you see, my experiments are completed. I have included in my report all of my formulae, as well as mathematical analysis in the appendix. Of course, these should be verified.

Because of its importance to both you and Dr. Nemur (and need I say to myself, too?) I have checked and rechecked my results a dozen times in the hope of finding an error. I am sorry to say the results must stand. Yet for the sake of science, I am grateful for the little bit that I here add to the knowledge of the function of the human mind and of the laws governing the artificial increase of human intelligence.

I recall your once saying to me that an experimental *failure* or the *disproving* of a theory was as important to the advancement of learning as a success would be. I know

Make Inferences
What aspects of this letter show that Charlie is as smart as the doctors?

now that this is true. I am sorry, however, that my own contribution to the field must rest upon the ashes of the work of two men I regard so highly.

Yours truly,
Charles Gordon

encl.: rept.

June 5

I must not become emotional. The facts and the results of my experiments are clear, and the more sensational aspects of my own rapid climb cannot obscure the fact that the tripling of intelligence by the surgical technique developed by Drs. Strauss and Nemur must be viewed as having little or no practical applicability (at the present time) to the increase of human intelligence.

As I review the records and data on Algernon, I see that although he is still in his physical infancy, he has regressed mentally. Motor activity[11] is impaired; there is a general reduction of glandular activity; there is an accelerated loss of coordination.

There are also strong indications of progressive amnesia.

As will be seen by my report, these and other physical and mental **deterioration** syndromes[12] can be predicted with statistically significant results by the application of my formula.

The surgical stimulus to which we were both subjected has resulted in an intensification and acceleration of all mental processes. The unforeseen development, which I have

◄ **Vocabulary**
deterioration (dē tir´ ē ə rā´ shən) *n. (used here as an adjective)* the process of becoming worse

Comprehension
What does Charlie want to learn through his research?

---

11. **motor activity** movement; physical coordination.
12. **syndromes** (sin´ drōmz´) *n.* a number of symptoms occurring together and characterizing a specific disease or condition.

taken the liberty of calling the "Algernon-Gordon Effect," is the logical extension of the entire intelligence speedup. The hypothesis here proven may be described simply in the following terms: Artificially increased intelligence deteriorates at a rate of time directly proportional to the quantity of the increase.

I feel that this, in itself, is an important discovery.

As long as I am able to write, I will continue to record my thoughts in these progress reports. It is one of my few pleasures. However, by all indications, my own mental deterioration will be very rapid.

I have already begun to notice signs of emotional instability and forgetfulness, the first symptoms of the burnout.

June 10

Point of View
How does the point of view make the changes Charlie is experiencing more dramatic?

Deterioration progressing. I have become absent-minded. Algernon died two days ago. Dissection shows my predictions were right. His brain had decreased in weight and there was a general smoothing out of cerebral convolutions as well as a deepening and broadening of brain fissures.

I guess the same thing is or will soon be happening to me. Now that it's definite, I don't want it to happen.

I put Algernon's body in a cheese box and buried him in the back yard. I cried.

June 15

Dr. Strauss came to see me again. I wouldn't open the door and I told him to go away. I want to be left to myself. I have become touchy and irritable. I feel the darkness closing in. I keep telling myself how important this introspective journal will be.

Vocabulary ▶
introspective (in´ trō spek´ tiv) *adj.* thoughtful; inward-looking

It's a strange sensation to pick up a book that you've read and enjoyed just a few months ago and discover that you don't remember it. I remembered how great I thought John Milton[13] was, but when I picked up *Paradise Lost* I couldn't understand it at all. I got so angry I threw the book across the room.

I've got to try to hold on to some of it. Some of the things I've learned. Oh, God, please don't take it all away.

---

13. **John Milton** British poet (1608–1674) who wrote *Paradise Lost*.

June 19

Sometimes, at night, I go out for a walk. Last night I couldn't remember where I lived. A policeman took me home. I have the strange feeling that this has all happened to me before—a long time ago. I keep telling myself I'm the only person in the world who can describe what's happening to me.

June 21

Why can't I remember? I've got to fight. I lie in bed for days and I don't know who or where I am. Then it all comes back to me in a flash. Fugues of amnesia.[14] Symptoms of senility—second childhood. I can watch them coming on. It's so cruelly logical. I learned so much and so fast. Now my mind is deteriorating rapidly. I won't let it happen. I'll fight it. I can't help thinking of the boy in the restaurant, the blank expression, the silly smile, the people laughing at him. No—please—not that again . . .

June 22

I'm forgetting things that I learned recently. It seems to be following the classic pattern—the last things learned are the first things forgotten. Or is that the pattern? I'd better look it up again . . .

I reread my paper on the "Algernon-Gordon Effect" and I get the strange feeling that it was written by someone else. There are parts I don't even understand.

Motor activity impaired. I keep tripping over things, and it becomes increasingly difficult to type.

Make Inferences
How does Charlie probably feel about forgetting things he had learned? Why?

June 23

I've given up using the typewriter completely. My coordination is bad. I feel that I'm moving slower and slower. Had a terrible shock today. I picked up a copy of an article I used in my research, Krueger's "Uber psychische Ganzheit," to see if it would help me understand what I had done. First I thought there was something wrong with my eyes. Then I realized I could no longer read German. I tested myself in other languages. All gone.

Comprehension
What are some signs that Charlie's mental state is rapidly reversing?

---

14. **fugues** (fyo͞ogz) **of amnesia** (am nē′ zhə) *n.* periods of loss of memory.

June 30

A week since I dared to write again. It's slipping away like sand through my fingers. Most of the books I have are too hard for me now. I get angry with them because I know that I read and understood them just a few weeks ago.

I keep telling myself I must keep writing these reports so that somebody will know what is happening to me. But it gets harder to form the words and remember spellings. I have to look up even simple words in the dictionary now and it makes me impatient with myself.

Dr. Strauss comes around almost every day, but I told him I wouldn't see or speak to anybody. He feels guilty. They all do. But I don't blame anyone. I knew what might happen. But how it hurts.

July 7

I don't know where the week went. Todays Sunday I know because I can see through my window people going to church. I think I stayed in bed all week but I remember Mrs. Flynn bringing food to me a few times. I keep saying over and over Ive got to do something but then I forget or maybe its just easier not to do what I say Im going to do.

I think of my mother and father a lot these days. I found a picture of them with me taken at a beach. My father has a big ball under his arm and my mother is holding me by the hand. I dont remember them the way they are in the picture. All I remember is my father arguing with mom about money.

He never shaved much and he used to scratch my face when he hugged me. He said he was going to take me to see cows on a farm once but he never did. He never kept his promises . . .

July 10

My landlady Mrs Flynn is very worried about me. She said she doesnt like loafers. If Im sick its one thing, but if Im a loafer thats another thing and she wont have it. I told her I think Im sick.

I try to read a little bit every day, mostly stories, but sometimes I have to read the same thing over and over again because I dont know what it means. And its hard to write.

It's slipping away like sand through my fingers.

Make Inferences
What does Charlie's style of writing reveal?

I know I should look up all the words in the dictionary but its so hard and Im so tired all the time.

Then I got the idea that I would only use the easy words instead of the long hard ones. That saves time. I put flowers on Algernons grave about once a week. Mrs. Flynn thinks Im crazy to put flowers on a mouses grave but I told her that Algernon was special.

July 14

Its sunday again. I dont have anything to do to keep me busy now because my television set is broke and I dont have any money to get it fixed. (I think I lost this months check from the lab. I dont remember)

I get awful headaches and asperin doesnt help me much. Mrs. Flynn knows Im really sick and she feels very sorry for me. Shes a wonderful woman whenever someone is sick.

July 22

Mrs. Flynn called a strange doctor to see me. She was afraid I was going to die. I told the doctor I wasnt too sick and that I only forget sometimes. He asked me did I have any friends or relatives and I said no I dont have any. I told him I had a friend called Algernon once but he was a mouse and we used to run races together. He looked at me kind of funny like he thought I was crazy.

He smiled when I told him I used to be a genius. He talked to me like I was a baby and he winked at Mrs Flynn. I got mad and chased him out because he was making fun of me the way they all used to.

July 24

I have no more money and Mrs Flynn says I got to go to work somewhere and pay the rent because I havent paid for over two months. I dont know any work but the job I used to have at Donnegans Plastic Box Company. I dont want to go back there because they all knew me when I was smart and maybe they'll laugh at me. But I dont know what else to do to get money.

Point of View
How does the first-person point of view help you to understand Charlie's experience?

Comprehension
How does the doctor anger Charlie?

July 25

I was looking at some of my old progress reports and its very funny but I cant read what I wrote. I can make out some of the words but they dont make sense.

Miss Kinnian came to the door but I said go away I dont want to see you. She cried and I cried too but I wouldnt let her in because I didnt want her to laugh at me. I told her I didn't like her any more. I told her I didn't want to be smart any more. Thats not true. I still love her and I still want to be smart but I had to say that so shed go away. She gave Mrs. Flynn money to pay the rent. I dont want that. I got to get a job.

Please . . . please let me not forget how to read and write . . .

▲ **Critical Viewing**
Why would Charlie be reluctant to go back to this job?

July 27

Mr. Donnegan was very nice when I came back and asked him for my old job of janitor. First he was very suspicious but I told him what happened to me then he looked very sad and put his hand on my shoulder and said Charlie Gordon you got guts.

Everybody looked at me when I came downstairs and started working in the toilet sweeping it out like I used to. I told myself Charlie if they make fun of you dont get sore because you remember their not so smart as you once thot they were. And besides they were once your friends and if they laughed at you that doesnt mean anything because they liked you too.

One of the new men who came to work there after I went away made a nasty crack he said hey Charlie I hear your a very smart fella a real quiz kid. Say something intelligent. I felt bad but Joe Carp came over and grabbed him by the shirt and said leave him alone or Ill break your neck. I didnt expect Joe to take my part so I guess hes really my friend.

Point of View
How has Charlie's view of his co-workers changed?

Later Frank Reilly came over and said Charlie if anybody bothers you or trys to take advantage you call me or Joe and we will set em straight. I said thanks Frank and I got choked up so I had to turn around and go into the supply room so he wouldnt see me cry. Its good to have friends.

July 28

I did a dumb thing today I forgot I wasnt in Miss Kinnians class at the adult center any more like I use to be. I went in and sat down in my old seat in the back of the room and she looked at me funny and she said Charles. I dint remember she ever called me that before only Charlie so I said hello Miss Kinnian Im ready for my lesin today only I lost my reader that we was using. She startid to cry and run out of the room and everybody looked at me and I saw they wasnt the same pepul who use to be in my class.

Then all of a suddin I rememberd some things about the operashun and me getting smart and I said holy smoke I reely pulled a Charlie Gordon that time. I went away before she come back to the room.

Thats why Im going away from New York for good. I dont want to do nothing like that agen. I dont want Miss Kinnian to feel sorry for me. Evry body feels sorry at the factery and I dont want that eather so Im going someplace where nobody knows that Charlie Gordon was once a genus and now he cant even reed a book or rite good.

Im taking a cuple of books along and even if I cant reed them Ill practise hard and maybe I wont forget every thing I lerned. If I try reel hard maybe Ill be a littel bit smarter then I was before the operashun. I got my rabits foot and my luky penny and maybe they will help me.

If you ever reed this Miss Kinnian dont be sorry for me Im glad I got a second chanse to be smart becaus I lerned a lot of things that I never even new were in this world and Im grateful that I saw it all for a littel bit. I dont know why Im dumb agen or what I did wrong maybe its becaus I dint try hard enuff. But if I try and practis very hard maybe Ill get a littl smarter and kow what all the words are. I remember a littel bit how nice I had a feeling with the blue book that has the torn cover when I reit. Thats why Im gonna keep trying to get smart so I can have that feeling agen. Its a good feeling

Point of View
What thoughts and emotions drive Charlie to leave New York?

Comprehension
Why is Charlie leaving New York?

Make Inferences
Based on his writing, do you think Charlie will be able to regain his intelligence? Why or why not?

to know things and be smart. I wish I had it rite now if I did I woud sit down and reed all the time. Anyway I bet Im the first dumb person in the world who ever found out somthing importent for sience. I remember I did somthing but I dont remember what. So I gess its like I did it for all the dumb pepul like me.

Goodbye Miss Kinnian and Dr Strauss and evreybody. And P.S. please tell Dr Nemur not to be such a grouch when pepul laff at him and he woud have more frends. Its easy to make frends if you let pepul laff at you. Im going to have lots of frends where I go.

P.P.S. Please if you get a chanse put some flowrs on Algernons grave in the bak yard . . .

Language Study

Vocabulary Analogies show the relationships between words. The words listed below appear in "Flowers for Algernon." For each numbered item, choose a word from the list to complete the second word pair and match the word relationship in the first pair.

> **deceive   refute   intellectual   naïveté   deterioration**

1. *Heavy* is to *weighty* as *lie* is to _____.

2. *Emotional* is to *rational* as *physical* is to _____.

3. *Happiness* is to *contentment* as *inexperience* is to _____.

4. *Expand* is to *shrink* as *improvement* is to _____.

5. *Accept* is to *reject* as *support* is to _____.

WORD STUDY

The **Latin root** *-spec-* means "to look." In this story, Charlie is **introspective** when he writes in his diary about his innermost thoughts and feelings. He "looks inside" himself to find interesting insights.

Word Study

Part A Explain how the **Latin root** *-spec-* contributes to the meanings of *speculate*, *perspective*, and *circumspect*. Consult a dictionary if necessary.

Part B Answer each question. Use the context of the sentences and what you know about the Latin root *-spec-* to explain your answers.

1. What does a *spectator* do during a sports event?

2. How does a police *inspector* solve a crime?

Close Reading Activities

Literary Analysis

Key Ideas and Details

1. **Make Inferences** Make an inference, based on story details, about Miss Kinnian's personality or her motives. Cite the details that most clearly support your inference.

2. **Make Inferences (a)** Citing story details, explain how Charlie's attitudes toward his doctors change after his operation. **(b)** Use these details to make an inference about how the operation affects Charlie.

3. **(a) Analyze:** When does the reader realize that the effects of Charlie's operation are not permanent? **(b) Support:** List two story details that reveal the reversal of these effects.

Craft and Structure

4. **Point of View** Review the two story events listed in the chart. In a copy of the chart, explain how the telling of the two events would change if the story were told from Dr. Strauss's point of view.

5. **Point of View (a)** Identify a point in the story when you understand better than Charlie what is happening to him. **(b)** How does the first-person point of view help to create this difference in understanding? **(c)** What effect does this difference between the reader's understanding and Charlie's create?

Charlie
Charlie reveals his confusion about the inkblot test.

Dr. Strauss

Charlie
Charlie shares his innermost feelings through his journal entries.

Dr. Strauss

Integration of Knowledge and Ideas

6. **(a) Compare:** In what sense is Charlie the same at the end of the story as he is at the beginning? **(b) Draw Conclusions:** Review the diary entry for July 28. What has Charlie gained through his experience? **(c) Generalize:** As people grow and change, are they likely to have realizations that can be compared with Charlie's? Explain, giving an example.

7. **(a) Make a Judgment:** Do you think Charlie should have had the operation? Why or why not? Use evidence from the story to support your position.

8. **Can all conflicts be resolved? (a)** Citing examples from the text, identify two conflicts that Charlie's surgery creates. **(b)** Name a conflict that cannot be resolved by the end of the story. Explain your response.

ACADEMIC VOCABULARY

As you write and speak about "Flowers for Algernon," use the words related to conflict that you explored on page 3 of this textbook.

Conventions: **Adjectives and Adverbs**

An **adjective** is a word that modifies, or adds to the meaning of, a noun or pronoun. An **adverb** is a word that modifies, or adds to the meaning of, a verb, an adjective, or another adverb.

An adjective adds detail to a noun by answering *What kind?*, *Which one?*, *How many?*, *How much?*, or *Whose?* For example, in the sentence *It was a pretty dress,* the adjective *pretty* modifies the noun *dress.* It answers the question *What kind of dress?*

What kind?	Which one?	How many?	How much?	Whose?
old, sparkling, green, layered	this, that, these, those	many, few, five, ten	some, little, excessive	my, your, his, her

Adverbs often end in the suffix *-ly* and answer the questions *When?*, *Where?*, *In what manner?*, or *To what extent?*

When?	Where?	In what manner?	To what extent?
yesterday, today, now	locally, nationally, here, there	playfully, wistfully, badly, well	exactly, almost, fully

In the sentence *She answered yesterday,* the adverb *yesterday* modifies the verb *answered,* telling *When?*

Note that adjectives should not be used in place of adverbs, as illustrated in this example:

Incorrect: He played <u>bad</u>.   **Correct:** He played <u>badly</u>.

Practice A

Identify the adjectives in these sentences.

1. Charlie wanted to become a smart person.
2. He did not want bad marks on his tests.
3. Algernon became smarter afterward.
4. Several people gave Charlie candy.

Reading Application In "Flowers for Algernon," find one adjective and one adverb. Identify the word each modifies.

Practice B

Rewrite each sentence, correcting the use of adjectives in place of adverbs.

1. Charlie answered the test questions bad.
2. After the surgery, Charlie realized that he had communicated poor with people.
3. Algernon was real upset.
4. Charlie left New York and his friends quick.

Writing Application Write two sentences about the story, using both an adjective and an adverb.

Writing to Sources

Narrative Write **dialogue** for a movie scene that you adapt from "Flowers for Algernon."

- First, choose a scene that you can expand by imagining details and parts of conversations that the author left out.
- Next, review the story and take notes on each character who will appear in your scene. Write a sentence describing each.
- Finally, draft your dialogue using words that seem natural for each character.

Write in standard dialogue format. Provide the character's name, and then place a colon before the words he or she says. Place directions, which are not spoken, in parentheses, and start a new line each time a different character speaks. Here is an example:

Charlie: (*in a superior tone of voice*) I have now mastered reading, writing, and speaking in Latin.

Dr. Strauss: (*excitedly*) Charlie, that is astounding.

Grammar Application Review your draft to make sure you have not used adjectives in place of adverbs.

Research and Technology

Build and Present Knowledge Write a **summary of an article** about scientific research on improving intelligence. Relate your summary to "Flowers for Algernon." Follow these steps:

- Use library resources to find an appropriate article.
- As you read the article, take notes, recording important information and quotations on the topic.
- Then, write a summary that includes the main idea of the article and at least two significant details, stated in your own words.
- Include a quotation that captures the author's perspective.
- Add a section relating the article to "Flowers for Algernon." For example, you might discuss whether the research indicates that an operation like Charlie's is possible.
- Make sure to keep your summary free of personal opinion or bias.
- Check your spelling of any technical terms you use.

Common Core State Standards

Reading Informational Text
2. Determine a central idea of a text and analyze its development over the course of the text, including its relationship to supporting ideas; provide an objective summary of the text.

Writing
2.b. Develop the topic with relevant, well-chosen facts, definitions, concrete details, quotations, or other information and examples.
3.b. Use narrative techniques, such as dialogue, pacing, description, and reflection, to develop experiences, events, and/or characters.

Language
1. Demonstrate command of the conventions of standard English grammar and usage when writing or speaking.
2.c. Spell correctly.

Meet the Author

Saki is the penname used by H. H. (Hector Hugh) Munro (1870–1916). Long before today's single-name celebrities, Munro became famous using just one name. He is beloved for tales that poke fun at social rules. Born to British parents in Burma (now Myanmar), the author was raised in England by his aunts. Munro worked as a foreign correspondent and political writer before beginning to write the clever short stories for which he is famous.

 **Common Core State Standards**

Reading Literature

1. Cite the textual evidence that most strongly supports inferences drawn from the text.

2. Determine a theme or central idea of a text and analyze its development over the course of the text, including its relationship to the characters, setting, and plot.

9. Analyze how a modern work of fiction draws on themes, patterns of events, or character types from traditional stories.

? **Can all conflicts be resolved?**

Explore the Big Question as you read "The Story-Teller." Take notes on the conflicts among the characters.

CLOSE READING FOCUS

Key Ideas and Details: **Make Inferences**

To **make inferences** while reading, come to reasonable conclusions, based on what the writer states, about what is left unstated. First, make connections, as follows:

- Connect story events to reasons and outcomes.
- Connect story details to your own experiences and ideas.

Then, for each connection you make, ask yourself what meaning the author is suggesting.

Craft and Structure: **Theme**

The **theme** of a literary work is its central insight or message.

- A **stated** theme is expressed directly. For example, a character in a story about loyalty may state the theme, "Loyalty matters more than winning."
- More often, a theme is **unstated** or **implied**. You infer the theme from the characters' experiences and from story events.

As you read a story, notice how the characters, setting, and plot develop the theme. Note also cases in which writers adapt themes from traditional literature. For example, imagine a modern writer who tells the story of a good person who meets a wolf in the woods. By repeating character types and a pattern of events from "Little Red Riding Hood," the writer shows that the theme of her story is related to the theme of the fairy tale.

Vocabulary

Copy these words from the selection into your notebook. Judging from their endings, which two words are probably adjectives?

persistent	inevitable	conviction
suppressed	immensely	assail

CLOSE READING MODEL

The passage below is from Saki's short story "The Story-Teller."
The annotations to the right of the passage show ways in
which you can use close reading skills to make inferences and
interpret a theme.

from "The Story-Teller"

[The aunt] began an unenterprising and deplorably
uninteresting story about a little girl who was good,
and made friends with everyone on account of her
goodness, and was finally saved from a mad bull
by a number of rescuers who admired her moral
character.

"Wouldn't they have saved her if she hadn't been
good?" demanded the bigger of the small girls.
It was exactly the question that the bachelor had
wanted to ask.[1]

"Well, yes," admitted the aunt lamely, "but I don't
think they would have run quite so fast to her help
if they had not liked her so much."[1]

"It's the stupidest story I've ever heard," said the
bigger of the small girls, with immense conviction.

"I didn't listen after the first bit, it was so stupid,"
said Cyril. . . .[2]

"You don't seem to be a success as a story-teller,"
said the bachelor suddenly from his corner.

The aunt bristled in instant defense at this
unexpected attack.

"It's a very difficult thing to tell stories that children
can both understand and appreciate," she said
stiffly.

"I don't agree with you," said the bachelor.[3]

Theme
1 The small girl and the bachelor
share a doubt about whether the
rescuers would save only a good
person. The aunt tries to explain
that someone's goodness makes an
important difference. These details
suggest that the theme of Saki's
story may concern being good.

Make Inferences
2 Cyril says that the story was so
"stupid" that he stopped listening.
When a young character uses such
harsh language, you might infer
that he or she is too young to have
proper manners.

Make Inferences
3 The bachelor says that the aunt's
storytelling is not successful. He
also states that he does not agree
with the point she makes. From
these details, you can infer that
the bachelor is not afraid to offend
someone, even someone he might
not know well.

The Story-Teller
Saki

▲ Critical Viewing
What does this painting tell you about travel in the late nineteenth century?

It was a hot afternoon, and the railway carriage was correspondingly sultry, and the next stop was at Templecombe, nearly an hour ahead. The occupants of the carriage were a small girl, and a smaller girl, and a small boy. An aunt belonging to the children occupied one corner seat, and the further corner seat on the opposite side was occupied by a bachelor who was a stranger to their party, but the small girls and the small boy emphatically occupied the compartment. Both the aunt and the children were conversational in a limited, persistent way, reminding one of the attentions of a housefly that refused to be discouraged. Most of the aunt's remarks seemed to begin with "Don't," and nearly all of the children's remarks began with "Why?" The bachelor said nothing out loud.

"Don't, Cyril, don't," exclaimed the aunt, as the small boy began smacking the cushions of the seat, producing a cloud of dust at each blow.

"Come and look out of the window," she added.

The child moved reluctantly to the window. "Why are those sheep being driven out of that field?" he asked.

"I expect they are being driven to another field where there is more grass," said the aunt weakly.

"But there is lots of grass in that field," protested the boy; "there's nothing else but grass there. Aunt, there's lots of grass in that field."

"Perhaps the grass in the other field is better," suggested the aunt fatuously.[1]

"Why is it better?" came the swift, inevitable question.

"Oh, look at those cows!" exclaimed the aunt. Nearly every field along the line had contained cows or bullocks, but she spoke as though she were drawing attention to a rarity.

"Why is the grass in the other field better?" persisted Cyril.

The frown on the bachelor's face was deepening to a scowl. He was a hard, unsympathetic man, the aunt decided in her mind. She was utterly unable to come to any satisfactory decision about the grass in the other field.

The smaller girl created a diversion by beginning to recite "On the Road to Mandalay."[2] She only knew the first line, but she put her limited knowledge to the fullest possible use. She repeated the line over and over again in a dreamy but resolute and very audible voice; it seemed to the bachelor as though someone had had a bet with her that she could not repeat the line aloud two thousand times without stopping. Whoever it was who had made the wager was likely to lose his bet.

"Come over here and listen to a story," said the aunt, when the bachelor had looked twice at her and once at the communication cord.

---

1. **fatuously** (fach´ o͞o əs lē) *adv.* in a silly or foolish way.
2. **"On the Road to Mandalay"** popular poem by Rudyard Kipling, later a song. Its first lines are: "On the road to Mandalay, where the flyin' fishes play / An' the dawn comes up like thunder outer China 'crost the bay!"

◀ **Vocabulary**
persistent (pər sist´ ənt) *adj.* continuing to happen, especially for longer than is usual or desirable

◀ **Vocabulary**
inevitable (in ev´ i tə bəl) *adj.* certain to happen

Make Inferences
What can you infer from this passage about the relationship between the children and their aunt? Why?

Comprehension
Who occupies the railway carriage?

Theme
What does the children's reaction suggest about the kind of stories the aunt tells?

The children moved listlessly[3] toward the aunt's end of the carriage. Evidently her reputation as a story-teller did not rank high in their estimation.

In a low, confidential voice, interrupted at frequent intervals by loud, petulant[4] questions from her listeners, she began an unenterprising and deplorably[5] uninteresting story about a little girl who was good, and made friends with everyone on account of her goodness, and was finally saved from a mad bull by a number of rescuers who admired her moral character.

"Wouldn't they have saved her if she hadn't been good?" demanded the bigger of the small girls. It was exactly the question that the bachelor had wanted to ask.

"Well, yes," admitted the aunt lamely, "but I don't think they would have run quite so fast to her help if they had not liked her so much."

"It's the stupidest story I've ever heard," said the bigger of the small girls, with immense conviction.

"I didn't listen after the first bit, it was so stupid," said Cyril.

The smaller girl made no actual comment on the story, but she had long ago recommenced a murmured repetition of her favorite line.

"You don't seem to be a success as a story-teller," said the bachelor suddenly from his corner.

The aunt bristled in instant defense at this unexpected attack.

"It's a very difficult thing to tell stories that children can both understand and appreciate," she said stiffly.

"I don't agree with you," said the bachelor.

"Perhaps *you* would like to tell them a story," was the aunt's retort.

"Tell us a story," demanded the bigger of the small girls.

"Once upon a time," began the bachelor, "there was a little girl called Bertha, who was extraordinarily good."

The children's momentarily aroused interest began at once to flicker; all stories seemed dreadfully alike, no matter who told them.

"She did all that she was told, she was always truthful, she kept her clothes clean, ate milk puddings as though they were

Vocabulary ▶
conviction (kən vik′ shən) *n.* strong belief; certainty

Make Inferences
What do the aunt and the bachelor think of each other?

Spiral Review
POINT OF VIEW How has the third-person point of view affected your feelings toward the bachelor up until this point in the story?

---

3. **listlessly** (list′ lis lē) *adv.* without energy or enthusiasm.
4. **petulant** (pech′ ə lənt) *adj.* peevishly impatient.
5. **deplorably** (dē plôr′ ə blē) *adv.* miserably; wretchedly.

jam tarts, learned her lessons perfectly, and was polite in her manners."

"Was she pretty?" asked the bigger of the small girls.

"Not as pretty as any of you." said the bachelor, "but she was horribly good."

There was a wave of reaction in favor of the story; the word horrible in connection with goodness was a novelty that commended itself. It seemed to introduce a ring of truth that was absent from the aunt's tales of infant life.

"She was so good," continued the bachelor, "that she won several medals for goodness, which she always wore, pinned on to her dress. There was a medal for obedience, another medal for punctuality, and a third for good behavior. They were large metal medals and they clinked against one another as she walked. No other child in town where she lived had as many as three medals, so everybody knew that she must be an extra good child."

"Horribly good," quoted Cyril.

"Everybody talked about her goodness, and the Prince of the country got to hear about it, and he said that as she was so very good she might be allowed once a week to walk in his park, which was just outside the town. It was a beautiful park, and no children were ever allowed in it, so it was a great honor for Bertha to be allowed to go there."

"Were there any sheep in the park?" demanded Cyril.

"No," said the bachelor, "there were no sheep."

"Why weren't there any sheep?" came the inevitable question arising out of that answer.

The aunt permitted herself a smile, which might almost have been described as a grin.

"There were no sheep in the park," said the bachelor, "because the Prince's mother had once had a dream that her son would either be killed by a sheep or else by a clock falling on him. For that reason the Prince never kept a sheep in his park or a clock in his palace."

> "She was so good," continued the bachelor, "that she won several medals for goodness...."

Make Inferences
What details support the inference that the bachelor understands children?

Make Inferences
Why do you think the aunt smiles?

Comprehension
What is the subject of the aunt's story?

▶ Critical Viewing
How do these pigs
resemble those
in the bachelor's
story?

Vocabulary ▶
suppressed (sə prest′)
v. kept back (a cough,
laugh, and so on);
restrained

The aunt **suppressed** a gasp of admiration.

"Was the Prince killed by a sheep or by a clock?" asked Cyril.

"He is still alive, so we can't tell whether the dream will come true," said the bachelor unconcernedly; "anyway, there were no sheep in the park, but there were lots of little pigs running all over the place."

"What color were they?"

"Black with white faces, white with black spots, black all over, gray with white patches, and some were white all over."

The story-teller paused to let a full idea of the park's treasures sink into the children's imaginations; then he resumed:

"Bertha was rather sorry to find that there were no flowers in the park. She had promised her aunts, with tears in her eyes, that she would not pick any of the kind Prince's flowers, and she had meant to keep her promise, so of course it made her feel silly to find that there were no flowers to pick."

"Why weren't there any flowers?"

"Because the pigs had eaten them all," said the bachelor promptly. "The gardeners had told the Prince that you couldn't have pigs and flowers, so he decided to have pigs and no flowers."

Make Inferences
What can you infer
from the children's
murmur of approval?

There was a murmur of approval at the excellence of the Prince's decision; so many people would have decided the other way.

"There were lots of other delightful things in the park. There were ponds with gold and blue and green fish in them, and trees with beautiful parrots that said clever things at a moment's notice, and hummingbirds that hummed all the popular tunes of the day. Bertha walked up and down and enjoyed herself immensely, and thought to herself: 'If I were not so extraordinarily good, I should not have been allowed to come into this beautiful park and enjoy all that there is to be seen in it,' and her three medals clinked against one another as she walked and helped to remind her how very good she really was. Just then an enormous wolf came prowling into the park to see if it could catch a fat little pig for its supper."

"What color was it?" asked the children, amid an immediate quickening of interest.

"Mud color all over, with a black tongue and pale gray eyes that gleamed with unspeakable ferocity. The first thing that it saw in the park was Bertha; her pinafore[6] was so spotlessly white and clean that it could be seen from a great distance. Bertha saw the wolf and saw that it was stealing toward her, and she began to wish that she had never been allowed to come into the park. She ran as hard as she could, and the wolf came after her with huge leaps and bounds. She managed to reach a shrubbery of myrtle bushes, and she hid herself in one of the thickest of the bushes. The wolf came sniffing among the branches, its black tongue lolling out of its mouth and its pale gray eyes glaring with rage. Bertha was terribly frightened, and thought to herself: 'If I had not been so extraordinarily good, I should have been safe in the town at this moment.' However, the scent of the myrtle was so strong that the wolf could not sniff out where Bertha was hiding, and the bushes were so thick that he might have hunted about in them for a long time without catching sight of her, so he thought he might as well go off and catch a little pig instead. Bertha was trembling very much at having the wolf prowling and sniffing so near her, and as she trembled the medal for obedience clinked against the medals for good conduct and punctuality. The wolf was just moving away when he heard the sound of the medals clinking and stopped to listen; they clinked again in a bush quite near him. He dashed into the bush, his pale gray eyes gleaming with ferocity and triumph, and dragged Bertha out and devoured her to the last morsel. All that was left of her were her shoes, bits of clothing, and the three medals for goodness."

---

6. **pinafore** (pin´ ə fôr´) *n.* sleeveless apronlike garment worn over a dress.

◀ **Vocabulary**
immensely (i mens´ lē)
adv. greatly

Theme
How is the message of the bachelor's story different from the message of the aunt's story?

Comprehension
What kinds of things were in the park?

"Were any of the little pigs killed?"

"No, they all escaped."

"The story began badly," said the smaller of the small girls, "but it had a beautiful ending."

"It is the most beautiful story that I ever heard," said the bigger of the small girls, with immense decision.

"It is the *only* beautiful story I have ever heard," said Cyril.

A dissentient[7] opinion came from the aunt.

"A most improper story to tell to young children! You have undermined the effect of years of careful teaching."

"At any rate," said the bachelor, collecting his belongings preparatory to leaving the carriage, "I kept them quiet for ten minutes, which was more than you were able to do."

"Unhappy woman!" he observed to himself as he walked down the platform of Templecombe station; "for the next six months or so those children will **assail** her in public with demands for an improper story!"

---

7. **dissentient** (di sen´ shənt) *adj.* differing from the majority.

Language Study

Vocabulary The words listed below appear in "The Story-Teller." Respond to the questions that follow by choosing the correct vocabulary word from this list.

> **inevitable   conviction   suppressed   immensely   assail**

1. Which word is similar in meaning to *belief*?

2. Which word is the opposite of *defend*?

3. Which word is the opposite of *slightly*?

4. Which word is similar in meaning to *restrained* or *stifled*?

5. Which word is the opposite of *avoidable*?

Word Study

Part A Explain how the **Latin prefix *per-*** contributes to the meanings of *pervasive*, *perpetual*, and *permanence*. Use a dictionary if needed.

Part B Answer each question. Use the context of the sentences and what you know about the Latin prefix *per-* to explain your answers.

1. Would a person who *perseveres* be likely to give up easily?

2. Why should students *peruse* their notes before a test?

Close Reading Activities

Literary Analysis

Key Ideas and Details

1. (a) At the beginning of the story, what do the children ask their aunt? **(b) Analyze:** Why are they unsatisfied with her answers?

2. Make Inferences (a) What is the connection between the behavior of the children and the bachelor's decision to amuse them with a story? **(b)** What can you infer about his reason for telling them a story? Support your response with story details.

3. Make Inferences Why do the children like the bachelor's story better than the aunt's? Support your response with story details.

Craft and Structure

4. Theme (a) In the first box of a chart like this one, identify a theme of this story and indicate whether it is stated or implied. **(b)** In the second box support your interpretation with story details that show how the theme is developed. **(c)** Discuss your response with a partner. Then in the third box, record whether the discussion changed your interpretation.

5. Theme (a) At the end of the bachelor's story, what helps the wolf catch Bertha? **(b)** Explain how this detail is directly related to the theme of Saki's story.

6. Theme (a) Name two similarities between the bachelor's story and a traditional fairy tale. **(b)** How is the ending of his story different from that of traditional tales? **(c)** What does the difference in endings show about the difference between Saki's theme and a traditional theme?

Theme (stated or implied)
Details
Did My View Change?

Integration of Knowledge and Ideas

7. Draw Conclusions: What can you infer about the author's general view of children and their upbringing? Cite textual details to support your inferences.

8. Evaluate: Do you agree with the aunt that the bachelor's story is "improper" for children? Explain, citing details from the text.

9. **THE BIG ?** **Can all conflicts be resolved? (a)** What are two main conflicts in "The Story-Teller"? **(b)** Are these conflicts resolved at the end of the story? Explain, citing story details. **(c)** Explain what, if anything, characters might have done to better resolve these conflicts.

ACADEMIC VOCABULARY

As you write and speak about "The Story-Teller," use the words related to conflict that you explored on page 3 of this textbook.

Conventions: **Principal Parts of Verbs**

A **verb** expresses an action or a state of being. Every verb has four **principal parts,** or forms. Most verbs are **regular,** but many common verbs are **irregular**—their past and past participle forms do not follow a single predictable pattern.

The following chart shows the four principal parts of one regular verb, *talk,* and one irregular verb, *draw.*

Principal Part	How to Form	Examples
Present	Basic form. Add -s or -es for third-person singular.	*talk*—I talk to her every day. *draw*—He draws pictures of clouds.
Present Participle	Add -ing. Use after a form of be (is, are, was, were, will be, etc.).	*talking*—We **are** talking to the teacher. *drawing*—I **was** drawing a blank.
Past	REGULAR: Add -d or -ed. IRREGULAR: No single predictable pattern	REGULAR: *talked*—You talked to my brother. IRREGULAR: *drew*—I drew her a picture last week.
Past Participle	REGULAR: Add -d or -ed. Use after a form of have. IRREGULAR: No single predictable pattern. Use after a form of have.	REGULAR: *talked*—We **have** talked several times. IRREGULAR: *drawn*—We **have** drawn together on many occasions.

Practice A

Identify the principal part used in each underlined verb. Then, identify each verb as regular or irregular.

1. The aunt <u>told</u> the children another boring story.

2. The bachelor <u>was listening</u> to the aunt's story with little appreciation.

3. The children <u>had enjoyed</u> his story.

4. The train <u>leaves</u> the station promptly.

Reading Application Find an example in "The Story-Teller" of each of the four principal parts of verbs.

Practice B

Complete each sentence with the verb given. Tell which principal part you used.

1. As the story begins, the young children are _____ out the window. (look)

2. They had _____ their aunt. (ask)

3. Yesterday, the little girl _____ away from the wolf. (run)

4. Last week, the bachelor _____ the children an unusual story. (tell)

Writing Application Write a paragraph about the story, using four principal parts of a regular and of an irregular verb.

Writing to Sources

Explanatory Text Traditional children's stories often feature a lesson about the right way to behave. In "The Story-Teller," the bachelor twists this tradition and tells a story that challenges ideas about the rewards for goodness. Write a **comparison of works** comparing a traditional children's story to the bachelor's story.

- First, identify a traditional children's story, such as "Little Red Riding Hood," that features a lesson for young people.

- Next, take notes on any similarities in character types or pattern of events between the traditional story and the bachelor's story.

- State the theme in each story, citing specific passages and events. Then, compare the themes of the two stories, noting their similarities and differences. Explain how Saki makes the traditional theme "new."

- Conclude by giving your opinion on Saki's twist on traditional tales—is it effective?

Grammar Application Check your draft for correct use of the principal parts of irregular verbs.

Speaking and Listening

Comprehension and Collaboration Organize a **panel discussion** about "The Story-Teller." Discuss whether the bachelor should have told the children such a gruesome story. Follow these steps:

- Be sure that everyone prepares by rereading "The Story-Teller."

- Ask one person to be the moderator, or leader, of the discussion. That person should ensure that each panelist identifies the theme of the story, judges the theme's effectiveness, and justifies his or her opinion.

- Set a time limit for the panel discussion. Choose a person to track time and to call out the time remaining as time runs out.

- After the panel members have spoken, open up the discussion to the class. Encourage students to pose questions that will connect and clarify points made in the discussion. Panelists should acknowledge new information shared by classmates, relate it to their own views, and justify their ideas as needed.

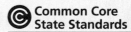 **Common Core State Standards**

Reading Literature

9. Analyze how a modern work of fiction draws on themes, patterns of events, or character types from myths, traditional stories, or religious works such as the Bible, including describing how the material is rendered new.

Writing

9.a. Apply grade 8 Reading standards to literature.

Speaking and Listening

1.a. Come to discussions prepared, having read or researched material under study; explicitly draw on that preparation by referring to evidence on the topic, text, or issue.

1.b. Follow rules for collegial discussions and decision-making, track progress toward specific goals and deadlines, and define individual roles as needed.

1.c. Pose questions that connect the ideas of several speakers and respond to others' questions and comments with relevant evidence, observations, and ideas.

1.d. Acknowledge new information expressed by others, and when warranted, qualify or justify their own views in light of the evidence presented.

Language

1. Demonstrate command of the conventions of standard English grammar and usage when writing and speaking.

Can all conflicts be resolved?

Explore the Big Question as you read these stories. Take notes on the ways in which each story portrays conflict. Then, compare and contrast how the conflict in each story is resolved.

READING TO COMPARE CHARACTERS OF DIFFERENT ERAS

In these two stories, authors Paul Laurence Dunbar and Ray Bradbury explore past eras. As you read each story, consider how the characters are affected by their historical and cultural worlds. After reading the stories, compare how the settings and events have led to changes in the characters.

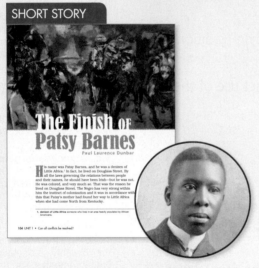

"The Finish of Patsy Barnes"

Paul Laurence Dunbar (1872–1906)
Paul Laurence Dunbar was born in Dayton, Ohio, the son of former slaves. In his brief life, Dunbar penned numerous poems, novels, and short stories. His poetry became so popular that while in Florida he was able to report, "Down here one finds my poems recited everywhere."

"The Drummer Boy of Shiloh"

Ray Bradbury (1920–2012)
Ray Bradbury said that he started writing after a carnival magician commanded him to live forever. Bradbury often traveled to the future in his stories; many of his tales are set on Mars or Venus. Occasionally, however, the author shifted his time-travel machine into reverse and headed for the past.

Comparing Characters of Different Eras

A **character** is someone who takes part in the action of a story.

- A *dynamic character* develops and learns through story events.
- A *static character* does not change.

The main character of a story is usually a dynamic character. The way in which this character changes is central to the story and its meaning, or *theme*.

Just as in life, characters in fiction are affected by the **historical and cultural settings** in which they live. These settings include forces that shape characters such as their jobs, living conditions, social status, and family customs, as well as the historical events that define their world.

History and Character When a major historical event is part of a story, that event is likely to help define characters. The way in which a character responds to such an event reveals aspects of his or her personality, as well as his or her culture's values. In addition, basic facts about the characters' time period, such as the type of transportation available, can define and limit their choices.

Both of these stories present boys who live through challenging times. In "The Finish of Patsy Barnes," a recent move north and a sudden illness have a devastating impact on a poor family. In "The Drummer Boy of Shiloh," a battle threatens to change the life of a young soldier forever.

Comparing Characters As you read, identify specific lines of dialogue (the words characters say) and specific events that reveal character. In addition, compare characters by asking questions, such as those in the chart, about the forces that shape their lives. In your comparison, consider how each writer uses the characters and the setting to convey a theme.

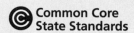

Common Core State Standards

Reading Literature
2. Determine a theme or central idea of a text and analyze its development over the course of the text, including its relationship to the characters, setting, and plot; provide an objective summary of the text.
3. Analyze how particular lines of dialogue or incidents in a story or drama propel the action, reveal aspects of a character, or provoke a decision.

Writing
2. Write informative/explanatory texts to examine a topic and convey ideas, concepts, and information through the selection, organization, and analysis of relevant content.

Questions for Comparing Main Characters	Responses
Where does he or she live?	
What does he or she do?	
What hardships does he or she face?	
How do his or her motivations and reactions reflect the cultural and historical setting?	

The Finish of
Patsy Barnes
Paul Laurence Dunbar

His name was Patsy Barnes, and he was a denizen of Little Africa.[1] In fact, he lived on Douglass Street. By all the laws governing the relations between people and their names, he should have been Irish—but he was not. He was colored, and very much so. That was the reason he lived on Douglass Street. The Negro has very strong within him the instinct of colonization and it was in accordance with this that Patsy's mother had found her way to Little Africa when she had come North from Kentucky.

---

1. **denizen of Little Africa** someone who lives in an area heavily populated by African Americans.

Patsy was incorrigible.[2] Even into the confines of Little Africa had penetrated the truant officer[3] and the terrible penalty of the **compulsory** education law. Time and time again had poor Eliza Barnes been brought up on account of the shortcomings of that son of hers. She was a hard-working, honest woman, and day by day bent over her tub, scrubbing away to keep Patsy in shoes and jackets, that would wear out so much faster than they could be bought. But she never murmured, for she loved the boy with a deep affection, though his misdeeds were a sore thorn in her side.

She wanted him to go to school. She wanted him to learn. She had the notion that he might become something better, something higher than she had been. But for him school had no charms; his school was the cool stalls in the big livery stable near at hand; the arena of his pursuits its sawdust floor; the height of his ambition, to be a horseman. Either here or in the racing stables at the Fair-grounds he spent his truant hours. It was a school that taught much, and Patsy was as apt a pupil as he was a constant attendant. He learned strange things about horses, and fine, sonorous oaths that sounded eerie on his young lips, for he had only turned into his fourteenth year.

A man goes where he is appreciated; then could this slim black boy be blamed for doing the same thing? He was a great favorite with the horsemen, and picked up many a dime or nickel for dancing or singing, or even a quarter for warming up a horse for its owner. He was not to be blamed for this, for, first of all, he was born in Kentucky, and had spent the very days of his infancy about the paddocks[4] near Lexington, where his father had sacrificed his life on account of his love for horses. The little fellow had shed no tears when he looked at his father's bleeding body, bruised and broken

◀ **Vocabulary**
compulsory (kəm pul′ sə rē) *adj.* required

Farm Boy, 1941, Charles Alston, Courtesy of Clark Atlanta University

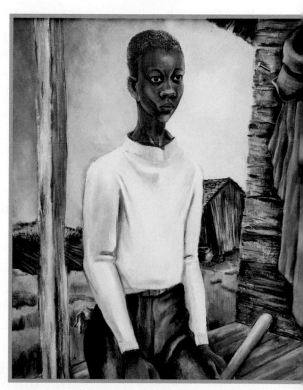

▲ **Critical Viewing**
How might growing up on a farm leave a boy like the one in this painting unprepared for city life?

Comprehension
Where does Patsy spend his time?

---

2. **incorrigible** (in kôr′ ə jə bəl) *adj.* unable to be corrected or improved because of bad habits.
3. **truant** (trōō′ ənt) **officer** *n.* person whose job is to make sure children attend school.
4. **paddocks** (pad′ əks) *n.* enclosed areas near a stable in which horses are exercised.

Character
What is unusual about Patsy's reaction to his father's death?

Vocabulary ▶
meager (mē′ gər) *adj.* small in amount

by the fiery young two-year-old he was trying to subdue. Patsy did not sob or whimper, though his heart ached, for over all the feeling of his grief was a mad, burning desire to ride that horse.

His tears were shed, however, when, actuated by the idea that times would be easier up North, they moved to Dalesford. Then, when he learned that he must leave his old friends, the horses and their masters, whom he had known, he wept. The comparatively **meager** appointments of the Fair-grounds at Dalesford proved a poor compensation for all these. For the first few weeks Patsy had dreams of running away—back to Kentucky and the horses and stables. Then after a while he settled himself with heroic resolution to make the best of what he had, and with a mighty effort took up the burden of life away from his beloved home.

Eliza Barnes, older and more experienced though she was, took up her burden with a less cheerful philosophy than her son. She worked hard, and made a scanty livelihood, it is true, but she did not make the best of what she had. Her complainings were loud in the land, and her wailings for her old home smote the ears of any who would listen to her.

They had been living in Dalesford for a year nearly, when hard work and exposure brought the woman down to bed with pneumonia.[5] They were very poor—too poor even to call in a doctor, so there was nothing to do but to call in the city physician. Now this medical man had too frequent calls into Little Africa, and he did not like to go there. So he was very gruff when any of its denizens called him, and it was even said that he was careless of his patients.

Patsy's heart bled as he heard the doctor talking to his mother:

"Now, there can't be any foolishness about this," he said. "You've got to stay in bed and not get yourself damp."

"How long you think I got to lay hyeah, doctah?" she asked.

"I'm a doctor, not a fortune-teller," was the reply. "You'll lie there as long as the disease holds you."

"But I can't lay hyeah long, doctah, case I ain't got nuffin' to go on."

"Well, take your choice: the bed or the boneyard."

Eliza began to cry.

Character
What does this exchange between Eliza and the doctor reveal about the difficulties Patsy and his mother face?

---

5. **pneumonia** (nōō mōn′ yə) *n.* potentially deadly infection that causes swelling in the lungs, making it difficult to breathe.

"You needn't sniffle," said the doctor; "I don't see what you people want to come up here for anyhow. Why don't you stay down South where you belong? You come up here and you're just a burden and a trouble to the city. The South deals with all of you better, both in poverty and crime." He knew that these people did not understand him, but he wanted an outlet for the heat within him.

There was another angry being in the room, and that was Patsy. His eyes were full of tears that scorched him and would not fall. The memory of many beautiful and appropriate oaths came to him; but he dared not let his mother hear him swear. Oh! to have a stone—to be across the street from that man!

When the physician walked out, Patsy went to the bed, took his mother's hand, and bent over shamefacedly to kiss her.

The little mark of affection comforted Eliza unspeakably. The mother-feeling overwhelmed her in one burst of tears. Then she dried her eyes and smiled at him.

"Honey," she said; "mammy ain' gwine lay hyeah long. She be all right putty soon."

"Nevah you min'," said Patsy with a choke in his voice. "I can do somep'n', an' we'll have anothah doctah."

"La, listen at de chile; what kin you do?"

"I'm goin' down to McCarthy's stable and see if I kin git some horses to exercise."

A sad look came into Eliza's eyes as she said: "You'd bettah not go, Patsy; dem hosses'll kill you yit, des lak dey did yo' pappy."

But the boy, used to doing pretty much as he pleased, was obdurate, and even while she was talking, put on his ragged jacket and left the room.

Patsy was not wise enough to be **diplomatic**. He went right to the point with McCarthy, the liveryman.

The big red-faced fellow slapped him until he spun round and round. Then he said, "Ye little devil, ye, I've a mind to knock the whole head off o' ye. Ye want harses to exercise, do ye? Well git on that un, 'an' see what ye kin do with him."

The boy's honest desire to be helpful had tickled the big, generous Irishman's peculiar sense of humor, and from now on, instead of giving Patsy a horse to ride now and then as he had formerly done, he put into his charge all the animals that

Character
How does the doctor's attitude toward the poor affect the mood of this scene?

◄ **Vocabulary**
diplomatic
(dip′ lə mat′ ik) *adj.*
showing skill in dealing with people

Comprehension
How does the doctor make Patsy angry?

needed exercise.

It was with a king's pride that Patsy marched home with his first considerable earnings.

They were small yet, and would go for food rather than a doctor, but Eliza was inordinately proud, and it was this pride that gave her strength and the desire of life to carry her through the days approaching the crisis of her disease.

As Patsy saw his mother growing worse, saw her gasping for breath, heard the rattling as she drew in the little air that kept going her clogged lungs, felt the heat of her burning hands, and saw the pitiful appeal in her poor eyes, he became convinced that the city doctor was not helping her. She must have another. But the money?

That afternoon, after his work with McCarthy, found him at the Fair-grounds. The spring races were on, and he thought he might get a job warming up the horse of some independent jockey. He hung around the stables, listening to the talk of men he knew and some he had never seen before. Among the latter was a tall, lanky man, holding forth to a group of men.

"No, suh," he was saying to them generally, "I'm goin' to withdraw my hoss, because thaih ain't nobody to ride him as he ought to be rode. I haven't brought a jockey along with me, so I've got to depend on pick-ups. Now, the talent's set again my hoss, Black Boy, because he's been losin' regular, but that hoss has lost for the want of ridin', that's all."

The crowd looked in at the slim-legged, raw-boned horse, and walked away laughing.

"The fools!" muttered the stranger. "If I could ride myself I'd show 'em!"

Patsy was gazing into the stall at the horse.

"What are you doing thaih?" called the owner to him.

"Look hyeah, mistah," said Patsy, "ain't that a bluegrass hoss?"

"Of co'se it is, an' one o' the fastest that evah grazed."

"I'll ride that hoss, mistah."

"What do you know bout ridin'?"

"I used to gin'ally be' roun' Mistah Boone's paddock in Lexington, an'—"

"Aroun' Boone's paddock—what! Look here, if you can ride that hoss to a winnin' I'll give you more money than you ever seen before."

"I'll ride him."

Character
What challenge does Patsy face as he watches his mother's condition worsen?

▼ **Critical Viewing**
What qualities would someone need to be able to ride a stallion like this one?

Patsy's heart was beating very wildly beneath his jacket. That horse. He knew that glossy coat. He knew that raw-boned frame and those flashing nostrils. That black horse there owed something to the orphan he had made.

The horse was to ride in the race before the last. Somehow out of odds and ends, his owner scraped together a suit and colors for Patsy. The colors were maroon and green, a curious combination. But then it was a curious horse, a curious rider, and a more curious combination that brought the two together.

Long before the time for the race Patsy went into the stall to become better acquainted with his horse. The animal turned its wild eyes upon him and neighed. He patted the long, slender head, and grinned as the horse stepped aside as gently as a lady.

"He sholy is full o' ginger," he said to the owner, whose name he had found to be Brackett.

"He'll show 'em a thing or two," laughed Brackett.

"His dam[6] was a fast one," said Patsy, unconsciously.

Brackett whirled on him in a flash. "What do you know about his dam?" he asked.

The boy would have retracted, but it was too late. Stammeringly he told the story of his father's death and the horse's connection therewith.

"Well," said Bracket, "if you don't turn out a hoodoo,[7] you're a winner, sure. But I'll be blessed if this don't sound like a story! But I've heard that story before. The man I got Black Boy from, no matter how I got him, you're too young to understand the ins and outs of poker, told it to me."

When the bell sounded and Patsy went out to warm up, he felt as if he were riding on air. Some of the jockeys laughed at his get-up, but there was something in him—or under him, maybe—that made him scorn their derision. He saw a sea of faces about him, then saw no more. Only a shining white track loomed ahead of him, and a restless steed was cantering[8] with him around the curve. Then the bell called him back to the stand.

They did not get away at first, and back they trooped. A second trial was a failure. But at the third they were off

Spiral Review
THEME What detail in this paragraph hints at the theme of "overcoming obstacles"?

Comprehension
What unexpected job does Patsy take on?

---

6. **dam** (dam) *n.* mother of a horse.
7. **hoodoo** (hoo′ doo′) *n.* here, someone or something that causes bad luck.
8. **steed** (stēd) **was cantering** (kan′ tər iŋ) high-spirited riding horse was running at a smooth, easy pace.

▶ **Critical Viewing**
What details in this photo tell you that the horses are moving very rapidly?

Character
In what ways are Black Boy and Patsy well suited for each other as horse and jockey?

in a line as straight as a chalk-mark. There were Essex and Firefly, Queen Bess and Mosquito, galloping away side by side, and Black Boy a neck ahead. Patsy knew the family reputation of his horse for endurance as well as fire, and began riding the race from the first. Black Boy came of blood that would not be passed, and to this his rider trusted. At the eighth the line was hardly broken, but as the quarter was reached Black Boy had forged a length ahead, and Mosquito was at his flank. Then, like a flash, Essex shot out ahead under whip and spur, his jockey standing straight in the stirrups.

The crowd in the stand screamed; but Patsy smiled as he lay low over his horse's neck. He saw that Essex had made his best spurt. His only fear was for Mosquito, who hugged and hugged his flank. They were nearing the three-quarter post, and he was tightening his grip on the black. Essex fell back; his spurt was over. The whip fell unheeded on his sides. The spurs dug him in vain.

Black Boy's breath touches the leader's ear. They are neck and neck—nose to nose. The black stallion passes him.

Another cheer from the stand, and again Patsy smiles as they turn into the stretch. Mosquito has gained a head. The colored boy flashes one glance at the horse and rider who are so surely gaining upon him, and his lips close in a grim line. They are half-way down the stretch, and Mosquito's head is at the stallion's neck.

For a single moment Patsy thinks of the sick woman at home and what that race will mean to her, and then his knees close against the horse's sides with a firmer dig. The spurs

Character
What circumstances give Patsy extra motivation to win?

shoot deeper into the steaming flanks. Black Boy shall win; he must win. The horse that has taken away his father shall give him back his mother. The stallion leaps away like a flash, and goes under the wire—a length ahead.

Then the band thundered, and Patsy was off his horse, very warm and very happy, following his mount to the stable. There, a little later, Brackett found him. He rushed to him, and flung his arms around him.

"You little devil," he cried, "you rode like you were kin to that hoss! We've won! We've won!" And he began sticking banknotes at the boy. At first Patsy's eyes bulged, and then he seized the money and got into his clothes.

"Goin' out to spend it?" asked Brackett.

"I'm goin' for a doctah fu' my mother," said Patsy, "she's sick."

"Don't let me lose sight of you."

"Oh, I'll see you again. So long," said the boy.

An hour later he walked into his mother's room with a very big doctor, the greatest the druggist could direct him to. The doctor left his medicines and his orders, but, when Patsy told his story, it was Eliza's pride that started her on the road to recovery. Patsy did not tell his horse's name.

Character
How have events in the story changed Patsy?

Critical Thinking

1. **Key Ideas and Details: (a)** Instead of school, where does Patsy prefer to go? **(b) Infer:** In what way do Patsy's reasons for spending time there change after his mother becomes ill?

2. **Key Ideas and Details: (a)** Why does the doctor speak to Eliza Barnes in an unfeeling way? **(b) Draw Conclusions:** What does this story suggest about the problems faced by Patsy and his mother?

3. **Key Ideas and Details: (a)** What motivates Patsy to ride Black Boy? **(b) Analyze:** How is Patsy's win a victory for both his mother and his father?

4. **Integration of Knowledge and Ideas: (a)** Identify two conflicts that Patsy faces. **(b)** What do these conflicts reveal about American society in the nineteenth century? **(c)** Explain whether these conflicts are resolved in the story. *[Connect to the Big Question: Can all conflicts be resolved?]*

The Drummer Boy of Shiloh

Ray Bradbury

This story is about a Civil War drummer boy. Although drummer boys accompanied troops into battle, they carried no weapons. There was no age requirement; some drummer boys were as young as ten. Because few parents were willing to send their young sons to battle, many drummer boys were runaways or orphans.

In the April night, more than once, blossoms fell from the orchard trees and lighted with rustling taps on the drumhead. At midnight a peach stone left miraculously on a branch through winter, flicked by a bird, fell swift and unseen; it struck once, like panic, and jerked the boy upright. In silence he listened to his own heart ruffle away, away—at last gone from his ears and back in his chest again.

After that he turned the drum on its side, where its great lunar face peered at him whenever he opened his eyes.

His face, alert or at rest, was solemn. It was a solemn time and a solemn night for a boy just turned fourteen in the peach orchard near Owl Creek not far from the church at Shiloh.

". . . thirty-one . . . thirty-two . . . thirty-three." Unable to see, he stopped counting.

Beyond the thirty-three familiar shadows forty thousand men, exhausted by nervous expectation and unable to sleep for romantic dreams of battles yet unfought, lay crazily askew in their uniforms. A mile farther on, another army was strewn helter-skelter, turning slowly, basting themselves with the thought of what they would do when the time came—a leap, a yell, a blind plunge their strategy, raw youth their protection and benediction.[1]

Now and again the boy heard a vast wind come up that gently stirred the air. But he knew what it was—the army here, the army there, whispering to itself in the dark. Some men talking to others, others murmuring to themselves, and all so quiet it was like a natural element arisen from South or North with the motion of the earth toward dawn.

What the men whispered the boy could only guess and he guessed that it was "Me, I'm the one, I'm the one of all the rest who won't die. I'll live through it. I'll go home. The band will play. And I'll be there to hear it."

Yes, thought the boy, *that's all very well for them, they can give as good as they get!*

◄ **Critical Viewing**
Which aspects of this drummer boy reflect the information in the background note above the story?

Character
What historical situation affects the boy's mood?

Character
How do the drummer boy's age and job give him a different perspective from those of soldiers in modern wars?

Comprehension
Why do the soldiers sleep uneasily?

---

1. **benediction** (ben´ ə dik´ shən) *n.* blessing.

For with the careless bones of the young men, harvested by night and bindled[2] around campfires, were the similarly strewn steel bones of their rifles with bayonets fixed like eternal lightning lost in the orchard grass.

Me, thought the boy, *I got only a drum, two sticks to beat it, and no shield.*

There wasn't a man-boy on this ground tonight who did not have a shield he cast, riveted or carved himself on his way to his first attack, compounded[3] of remote but nonetheless firm and fiery family devotion, flag-blown patriotism and cocksure **immortality** strengthened by the touchstone of very real gunpowder, ramrod, Minié ball[4] and flint. But without these last, the boy felt his family move yet farther off in the dark, as if one of those great prairie-burning trains had chanted them away, never to return—leaving him with this drum which was worse than a toy in the game to be played tomorrow or someday much too soon.

The boy turned on his side. A moth brushed his face, but it was peach blossom. A peach blossom flicked him, but it was a moth. Nothing stayed put. Nothing had a name. Nothing was as it once was.

If he lay very still, when the dawn came up and the soldiers put on their bravery with their caps, perhaps they might go away, the war with them, and not notice him lying small here, no more than a toy himself. ●

"Well, by thunder now," said a voice. The boy shut his eyes to hide inside himself, but it was too late. Someone, walking by in the night, stood over him. "Well," said the voice quietly, "here's a soldier crying *before* the fight. Good. Get it over. Won't be time once it all starts."

And the voice was about to move on when the boy, startled, touched the drum at his elbow. The man above, hearing this, stopped. The boy could feel his eyes, sense him slowly bending near. A hand must have come down out of the night, for there was a little *rat-tat* as the fingernails brushed and the man's breath fanned the boy's face.

"Why, it's the drummer boy, isn't it?"

The boy nodded, not knowing if his nod was seen. "Sir, is that you?" he said.

---

2. **bindled** (bin′ dəld) *adj.* bedded.
3. **compounded** (käm pound′ əd) *adj.* mixed or combined.
4. **Minié** (min′ ē) **ball** *n.* cone-shaped rifle bullet that expands when fired.

"I assume it is." The man's knees cracked as he bent still closer. He smelled as all fathers should smell, of salt-sweat, tobacco, horse and boot leather, and the earth he walked upon. He had many eyes. No, not eyes, brass buttons that watched the boy.

He could only be, and was, the general. "What's your name, boy?" he asked.

"Joby, sir," whispered the boy, starting to sit up.

"All right, Joby, don't stir." A hand pressed his chest gently, and the boy relaxed. "How long you been with us, Joby?"

"Three weeks, sir."

"Run off from home or join legitimate, boy?"

Silence.

"Damn-fool question," said the general. "Do you shave yet, boy? Even more of a fool. There's your cheek, fell right off the tree overhead. And the others here, not much older. Raw, raw, damn raw, the lot of you. You ready for tomorrow or the next day, Joby?"

"I think so, sir."

"You want to cry some more, go on ahead. I did the same last night."

"You, sir?"

"God's truth. Thinking of everything ahead. Both sides figuring the other side will just give up, and soon, and the war done in weeks and us all home. Well, that's not how it's going to be. And maybe that's why I cried."

"Yes, sir," said Joby.

The general must have taken out a cigar now, for the dark was suddenly filled with the Indian smell of tobacco unlighted yet, but chewed as the man thought what next to say.

"It's going to be a crazy time," said the general. "Counting both sides, there's a hundred thousand men—give or take a few thousand—out there tonight, not one as can spit a sparrow off a tree, or knows a horse clod from a Minié ball. Stand up, bare the breast, ask to be a target, thank them and sit down, that's us, that's them. We should turn tail and train four months, they should do the same. But here we are, taken with spring fever and thinking it blood lust, taking our sulphur with cannons instead of with molasses, as it should be—going to be a hero, going to live forever. And I can see all them over there nodding agreement, save the other way around. It's wrong, boy, it's wrong as a head put on hindside front and a man marching backward through life. Sometime

Character
Why is the general's reaction to the boy's tears surprising?

Comprehension
Why is Joby crying?

Social Studies Connection

A Bloody Battle

The Battle of Shiloh was sparked when the southern Confederate army suddenly attacked the northern Union troops near Shiloh Church in Tennessee on April 6, 1862. Some of the heaviest fighting took place in Sarah Bell's peach orchard.

Thanks to the efforts of raw, young recruits from the farms of Iowa and Illinois, the Union lines held. This bloody, bitterly fought battle resulted in the killing or wounding of about 23,000 men and dashed any hopes of a quick end to the Civil War.

Connect to the Literature

What details of the historical setting are included in Bradbury's story?

Character
What do the general's words reveal about his character?

this week more innocents will get shot out of pure Cherokee enthusiasm than ever got shot before. Owl Creek was full of boys splashing around in the noonday sun just a few hours ago. I fear it will be full of boys again, just floating, at sundown tomorrow, not caring where the current takes them." •

The general stopped and made a little pile of winter leaves and twigs in the dark as if he might at any moment strike fire to them to see his way through the coming days when the sun might not show its face because of what was happening here and just beyond.

The boy watched the hand stirring the leaves and opened his lips to say something, but did not say it. The general heard the boy's breath and spoke himself.

"Why am I telling you this? That's what you wanted to ask, eh? Well, when you got a bunch of wild horses on a loose rein somewhere, somehow you got to bring order, rein them in. These lads, fresh out of the milkshed, don't know what I know; and I can't tell them—men actually die in war. So each is his own army. I got to make one army of them. And for that, boy, I need you."

"Me!" The boy's lips barely twitched.

"You, boy," said the general quietly. "You are the heart of the army. Think about that. You are the heart of the army. Listen to me, now."

And lying there, Joby listened. And the general spoke. If he, Joby, beat slow tomorrow, the heart would beat slow in the men. They would lag by the wayside. They would drowse in the fields on their muskets. They would sleep forever, after that—in those same fields, their hearts slowed by a drummer boy and stopped by enemy lead.

But if he beat a sure, steady, ever faster rhythm, then, then, their knees would come up in a long line down over that hill, one knee after the other, like a wave on the ocean shore. Had he seen the ocean ever? Seen the waves rolling in like a well-ordered cavalry charge to the sand? Well, that was it, that's what he wanted, that's what was needed. Joby was his right hand and his left. He gave the orders, but Joby set the pace.

◄ **Critical Viewing**
Why might the drummer boy's role be important in the confusion of a Civil War battle such as this one?

So bring the right knee up and the right foot out and the left knee up and the left foot out, one following the other in good time, in brisk time. Move the blood up the body and make the head proud and the spine stiff and the jaw resolute. Focus the eye and set the teeth, flare the nostrils and tighten the hands, put steel armor all over the men, for blood moving fast in them does indeed make men feel as if they'd put on steel. He must keep at it, at it! Long and steady, steady and long! Then, even though shot or torn, those wounds got in hot blood—in blood he'd helped stir—would feel less pain. If their blood was cold, it would be more than slaughter, it would be murderous nightmare and pain best not told and no one to guess.

The general spoke and stopped, letting his breath slack off. Then, after a moment, he said, "So there you are, that's it. Will you do that, boy? Do you know now you're general of the army when the general's left behind?"

The boy nodded mutely.

"You'll run them through for me then, boy?"

"Yes, sir."

"Good. And, God willing, many nights from tonight, many years from now, when you're as old or far much older than me, when they ask you what you did in this awful time, you will tell them—one part humble and one part proud—I was the drummer boy at the battle of Owl Creek or the Tennessee River, or maybe they'll just name it after the church there. I was the drummer boy at Shiloh. Good grief, that has a beat and sound to it fitting for Mr. Longfellow. 'I was the drummer boy at Shiloh.' Who will ever hear those words and not know you, boy, or what you thought this night, or what you'll think tomorrow or the next day when we must get up on our legs and move!"

◄ **Vocabulary**
resolute (rez´ ə loot)
adj. showing a firm purpose

Spiral Review
THEME As the general describes the role of the drummer boy, are there any hints that he is exaggerating? Explain.

Comprehension
According to the general, what is Joby's role in the war?

Character

Why might the general's words appeal to a young boy in the middle of the Civil War?

The general stood up. "Well, then. God bless you, boy. Good night."

"Good night, sir." And tobacco, brass, boot polish, salt sweat and leather, the man moved away through the grass.

Joby lay for a moment staring, but unable to see where the man had gone. He swallowed. He wiped his eyes. He cleared his throat. He settled himself. Then, at last, very slowly and firmly he turned the drum so that it faced up toward the sky.

He lay next to it, his arm around it, feeling the tremor, the touch, the muted thunder as, all the rest of the April night in the year 1862, near the Tennessee River, not far from the Owl Creek, very close to the church named Shiloh, the peach blossoms fell on the drum.

Critical Thinking

1. **Key Ideas and Details: (a)** What frightens Joby most about the upcoming battle? **(b) Compare and Contrast:** How are his fears like and unlike those of the other soldiers? **(c) Compare and Contrast:** In what other ways are Joby and the soldiers alike and not alike?

2. **Key Ideas and Details: (a)** What do you think motivates the general to talk to Joby? **(b) Draw Conclusions:** How do you think Joby feels after his talk with the general? Explain.

3. **Key Ideas and Details:** Is the drummer boy's role as crucial as the general says? Explain.

4. **Integration of Knowledge and Ideas: (a)** What does Joby promise to do? **(b)** Do you think the general has motivated Joby to keep his promise? Why or why not? **(c) Make a Judgment:** Is the general's request fair or unfair to Joby? Explain.

5. **Integration of Knowledge and Ideas: (a)** What conflict does the general help resolve for Joby? **(b)** Is this resolution a true or valid resolution? Explain, using details from the selection and your background knowledge. *[Connect to the Big Question: Can all conflicts be resolved?]*

Comparing and Contrasting Characters

1. Key Ideas and Details: Complete a chart like this one to analyze each character, giving examples from the text.

Name	Static or Dynamic	Proof
Patsy Barnes		
the doctor		
Joby		
the general		

2. Key Ideas and Details: (a) List two historical details involving time and place that affect Patsy Barnes. **(b)** List two historical details involving time and place that affect Joby.

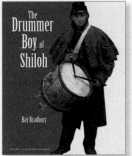

⏱ Timed Writing

Explanatory Text: Essay

Compare and contrast Patsy and Joby. In an essay, discuss ways that the historical events and cultural settings help to develop these main characters and to develop each story's theme. **(40 minutes)**

5-Minute Planner

1. Read the prompt carefully and completely.

2. Gather your ideas by jotting down answers to these questions:

   • How do historical and cultural circumstances affect the characters' reactions, motivations, and emotions?

   • How do the boys change as a result of their experiences?

   • What theme does each boy's changes help convey? How does the setting contribute to the theme?

3. Organize your draft. To use the block method, present all the details about Patsy, then all the details about Joby. To use point-by-point organization, discuss one aspect of both characters, then another aspect, and so on. (See p. 276.)

4. Reread the prompt, and then draft your essay.

USE ACADEMIC VOCABULARY

As you write, use academic language, including the following words or their related forms:

argument

interact

negotiate

viewpoint

For more information, see the Building Academic Vocabulary workshop in the front of your book.

Using a Dictionary and Thesaurus

When you look up a word in a **dictionary,** you will find the meaning, pronunciation, and part of speech for the word. You will also find the word's **etymology,** or origin. Etymologies show how words come into the English language and how they change over time. Look in the front or the back of a dictionary for a guide to the abbreviations used in etymologies.

Specialized references offer detailed information about a particular subject. Almanacs and atlases are examples of specialized references. An **etymological dictionary** is a specialized reference that provides in-depth etymologies. A **dictionary of technical terms** is a dictionary that includes definitions and pronunciations of terms having to do with a particular field, such as technology, engineering, medicine, or other scientific fields.

When you look up a word in a **thesaurus,** you will find the word's synonyms, or words with similar meaning. A thesaurus can be helpful when you are looking for alternate word choices to use in your writing.

Compare these two entries for the word *verdict*:

Dictionary

> **ver•dict** (vur´ dikt) *n.* [ME *verdit* <
> Anglo-Fr < ML *veredictum*, true saying,
> verdict < L *vere*, truly + *dictum*, a thing
> said: see VERY and DICTUM] **1.** The
> decision arrived at by a jury at the end
> of a trial **2.** any decision or judgment

Thesaurus

> **verdict** *n.* judgment, finding, decision,
> answer, opinion, sentence, determination,
> decree, conclusion, deduction, adjudication,
> arbitrament

Notice that a thesaurus does not provide definitions of words. Before you use a word you find in a thesaurus, check a dictionary to verify the meaning of the word and confirm that it is a good choice.

© **Common Core State Standards**

Language
4. Determine or clarify the meaning of unknown and multiple-meaning words or phrases based on *grade 8 reading and content,* choosing flexibly from a range of strategies.

4.c. Consult general and specialized reference materials, both print and digital, to find the pronunciation of a word or determine or clarify its precise meaning or its part of speech.

4.d. Verify the preliminary determination of the meaning of a word or phrase.

Where to Find a Dictionary and Thesaurus You can find these resources in book form at your school or in a library. You can also use digital tools, such as online dictionaries and thesauruses, to search for the perfect words to express your ideas. Ask your teacher to recommend the best online word study resources.

Practice A

Use a general print or online dictionary to look up words 1 through 3 below. Look up word 4 in both a general and a medical dictionary. Show how each word breaks into syllables and which syllables are stressed. Then, write each word's definition. Finally, use each word in a sentence that shows its meaning.

1. quandary
2. interminable
3. perfunctory
4. maxillary

Practice B

Use a print or an online thesaurus to find five synonyms for the word *strange*. Write a definition for each of the synonyms. Then, use a dictionary to confirm the definitions of these five words. Finally, use each synonym in a sentence that shows the word's exact meaning.

Activity

The cluster diagram shown gives four synonyms for the word *fast*. Using a thesaurus, add to the diagram by giving two synonyms for each of the *fast* synonyms. (An example for *nimble* is shown below.) Share your completed diagram with a partner, and discuss how all of the words in your diagram differ in meaning. Refer to the dictionary definition and etymology of each word in your discussion.

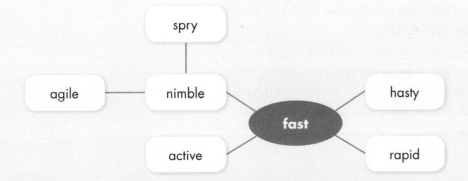

Comprehension and Collaboration

In a group, discuss the day's weather without using these words:

- **nice**
- **bad**
- **cold**
- **hot**
- **warm**
- **windy**

Use a thesaurus to find alternate word choices. Check a dictionary to be sure you use those words correctly.

Speaking and Listening

Delivering a Narrative Presentation

 **Common Core State Standards**

Speaking and Listening
6. Adapt speech to a variety of contexts and tasks, demonstrating command of formal English when indicated or appropriate.

In a **narrative presentation,** you organize and deliver information to tell a story that will inform or entertain your audience.

Learn the Skills

Consider your audience. To increase the effectiveness of your presentation, take the time to analyze your audience. A profile like the one shown can help you identify the interests, concerns, and knowledge level of your listeners. Use your answers to help you choose the right words and details.

Choose details wisely. The events you choose for your narrative should be ones that help you tell a dramatic or informative story. Choose significant events that have a clear progression and that you can elaborate on with descriptions of specific actions and dialogue.

Practice beforehand. Rehearsing will help you get comfortable with the words in your presentation and find the right gestures, body movements, and voice modulations to accompany them.

Use appropriate sentences. Speak in complete sentences, using correct grammar and the active voice. Save slang and sentence fragments for dialogue only. For added impact, vary your sentences by

- mixing short, powerful sentences with longer ones.
- using an interesting assortment of sentence openings.
- using conjunctions to combine logically related sentences (see page 127).

Focus on word choice. Match your vocabulary to your audience and purpose. Use specific nouns and verbs as well as interesting, vivid adjectives. Choose words that help convey the mood of your story and bring it to life for your audience.

Use audience feedback. Gauge your audience's reactions in order to make adjustments to vocabulary level, organization, pacing, tone, and emphasis. If an audience seems confused by unfamiliar terms, define them. If listeners appear bored, pick up the pace and skip unnecessary sections or details.

Audience Profile

- What is the average age of my audience?
- What background knowledge will my audience have on this subject?
- What background do I need to provide?
- What details will be most interesting to my audience?
- What situations or issues in my narrative will be of most concern to my audience?

Practice the Skills

Presentation of Knowledge and Ideas Use what you have learned in this workshop to perform the following task.

ACTIVITY: **Prepare and Deliver a Narrative Presentation**

Prepare and deliver a brief narrative presentation about a time that you learned a valuable lesson, such as a time when you discovered the value of teamwork or hard effort. In choosing your topic, consider how your audience might benefit from hearing the experience you are relating. To help you construct your presentation, answer the following questions.

• Is my purpose for relating the narrative clear?
• Do I explain how others might benefit from hearing my narrative?
• What background information do I need to provide for my listeners?
• Do I present events in a logical sequence?
• Are the events clearly related to each other, and do they build toward the overall point I am trying to make?

In addition to presenting your own narrative, pay close attention as your classmates deliver theirs. Use the Presentation Checklist below to analyze their presentations.

Presentation Checklist

Does the presentation meet all of the requirements of the activity? Check all that apply.

❑ The subject is appropriate for the audience.
❑ The events of the narrative have a clear progression.
❑ The speaker used action, description, and, if appropriate, dialogue.

Presentation Delivery

Did the speaker deliver the narrative well? Check all that apply.

❑ The speaker used varied sentences and descriptive word choices.
❑ The speaker used gestures and modulated his or her voice.
❑ The speaker made adjustments as needed, according to audience feedback.

Comprehension and Collaboration After you and your classmates have delivered your presentations, form small discussion groups. Group members should refer to their Presentation Checklists to provide feedback on each person's presentation, noting successes and areas for improvement.

Write a Narrative Text

Autobiographical Essay

Defining the Form An **autobiographical essay** tells the story of a memorable event, time, or situation in the writer's life. You may use elements of this form in letters, anecdotes, or expository essays.

Assignment Write an autobiographical essay about an event that changed you in a significant way. Include these elements:

✓ a plan for writing that addresses *purpose and audience*

✓ a clear *sequence of events* from your life using well-chosen details and description

✓ a central *conflict*, problem, or shift in perspective

✓ *precise words* that indicate the event's significance or your attitude toward the event

✓ consistent use of first-person *point of view*

✓ correct *use of pronouns* and *punctuation of dialogue*

To preview the criteria on which your autobiographical essay may be judged, see the rubric on page 131.

FOCUS ON RESEARCH

When you write autobiographical essays, you might

- interview friends and relatives who have additional information or perspectives on the events in your narrative.

- search archived news sources for background on events that occurred at the time of the events you narrate.

- consult a local library or historical society for more background about places in the narrative.

Be sure to note all resources you use in your research, and credit those sources in your final draft. Refer to the Conducting Research workshop in the Introductory Unit for assistance in citing materials.

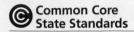
Common Core State Standards

Writing

3. Write narratives to develop real or imagined experiences or events using effective technique, relevant descriptive details, and well-structured event sequences.

3.a. Engage and orient the reader by establishing a context and point of view and introducing a narrator and/or characters; organize an event sequence that unfolds naturally and logically.

3.d. Use precise words and phrases, relevant descriptive details, and sensory language to capture the action and convey experiences and events.

READING-WRITING CONNECTION

To get a feel for autobiographical writing, read the excerpt from *I Know Why the Caged Bird Sings,* by Maya Angelou, on page 322.

Prewriting/Planning Strategies

Make a blueprint. Draw and label a blueprint of a familiar or special place—a friend's house, your school, or a park. List the people, things, and incidents you associate with each spot labeled on your blueprint. Choose one as your topic. The model below shows the events and experiences associated with a town football field.

Determine audience and purpose. Knowing who your audience will be and why you want to tell your story can help you decide what to write about.

- If your purpose is **to entertain your audience,** focus on the funny, moving, or exciting parts of the story you share.

- If your purpose is **to share a lesson you learned,** focus on the events that illustrate the message and prepare to explain what you learned from your experience.

Gather descriptive details. Make a five-column chart with the following headings for your topic: *People, Time, Place, Events,* and *Emotions.* For each column, use about three minutes to list words and phrases that describe the corresponding aspect of your topic.

Visitors

Visitors' Bench

Home Bench

Caught game-winning touchdown

Caught my first interception

Coach

Scored on my own team when I got confused and ran the wrong way

Home

- Focus on **physical description** when describing people. Answer these questions: *How did they look? How did they act?*

- Focus on **background description** when describing time and place. Answer: *What was unique about this time of your life? What was special about the place where these events occurred?*

- Focus on **specific action** when describing events. Answer: *Who did what to whom? What was the exact sequence of events?*

Use words and phrases from the chart when you draft your essay.

Drafting Strategies

 **Common Core State Standards**

Writing

3.a. Engage and orient the reader by establishing a context and point of view and introducing a narrator and/or characters; organize an event sequence that unfolds naturally and logically.

3.b. Use narrative techniques, such as dialogue, pacing, description, and reflection, to develop experiences, events, and/or characters.

3.d. Use precise words and phrases, relevant descriptive details, and sensory language to capture the action and convey experiences and events.

3.e. Provide a conclusion that follows from and reflects on the narrated experiences or events.

Order events. Identify the **conflict,** or problem, that makes your narrative worth reading. Then, organize events around the conflict. Make sure the order of events is *clear* and *coherent*—that it will make sense to your readers. First, introduce the people, setting, and situation. Build to the **climax,** where the tension is the greatest. Finish your narrative with a **resolution** that settles the problem, and then reflect on the experiences described.

Use a consistent point of view. Maintain a first-person point of view, using the pronoun *I* to refer to yourself. Avoid telling what other people are thinking or feeling unless you show readers how you inferred other people's thoughts.

Control narrative pace. Pacing is how quickly or slowly a story moves. For a slow pace, include background details when describing setting, events, and characters. For a fast pace that reflects excitement or action, use short, punchy sentences that focus on the most exciting details. Choose the pace that best fits each section of your narrative.

Develop readers' interest. As you write, provide background about the event, setting, and people. Choose vivid descriptive details that will show the significance of the event, engage your audience, and contribute to your overall purpose.

> **Dull:** I run two miles every day.
> **Vivid:** Every day at 5 A.M., when all sensible people are asleep, I groggily lace my cleats and run two miles to improve my fitness.

Write an effective conclusion. End your narrative with a memorable conclusion that brings the story to a clear close and highlights any lessons learned. To enhance your conclusion, use one of the strategies described in the chart.

Strategy for an Effective Conclusion	Example
Launch a slogan. Summarize your story, building toward a memorable statement of the lesson you learned.	I am still a skeptic about Ed's schemes, but I always remind myself: "Never say 'never' when a Smith is around."
Close the circle. Refer back to a key element of your narrative, such as a striking remark, a moving sight, a significant feeling, and so on.	Whenever someone asks me why I volunteer at the shelter, I think of Cy's big, brown, dopey puppy eyes at feeding time.
Make a connection. Link your own experience to experiences that audience members are likely to share.	If you have ever struck out just when your team needed a run the most, you know just how I felt when I got the news.

Revising Sentences by Combining With Conjunctions

Understanding Conjunctions **Conjunctions** connect words.

Coordinating conjunctions join words of the same kind and equal rank, such as two nouns, two verbs, or two clauses of equal weight.

Example: *Pablo* takes dance lessons. *June* takes dance lessons.

Compound Subject: *Pablo* **and** *June* take dance lessons.

Correlative conjunctions work in pairs to link words or phrases of equal importance. Linked phrases should be similar in length and form.

Example: Some team members will travel *by bus*. Others will travel *by train*.

Compound Modifier: Team members will travel **both** *by train* **and** *by bus.*

Subordinating conjunctions connect two complete ideas and show that one is dependent on the other.

Example: Ada takes dance. She wants to be graceful.

Complex Sentence: ***Because*** *Ada wants to be graceful, she takes dance.*

Type	Function	Examples
Coordinating	connects words, phrases, or clauses of equal importance	*and, but, for, nor, or, so, yet*
Correlative	pairs words or phrases of equal importance	*both/and, either/or, neither/nor*
Subordinating	connects two ideas, one dependent on the other	*because, before, even though, if, since, while, until*

Joining Sentences With Conjunctions You can join short, choppy sentences with conjunctions. Follow these steps:

1. **Identify short sentences that could be combined.** Then, identify the words, phrases, or clauses that you want to join.

2. **Determine if the items are of the same kind and of equal rank.** If so, use a coordinating or correlative conjunction to join them.

3. **Determine if one is dependent on the other.** If so, use a subordinating conjunction to join them.

Grammar in Your Writing

Choose three paragraphs in your draft. Improve coherence and add interest by combining some of the sentences with conjunctions.

Revising Strategies

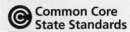
Check for sentence variety. Look over your paragraphs to see whether many of your sentences follow the same pattern. When writing in the first person, you may find that many of the sentences begin with *I*.

To analyze and evaluate sentence patterns in your draft, highlight the first word of each sentence. Then, review your draft to determine if you have too many sentences that start with *I*. Revise repetitive sentence beginnings to build variety, using the chart. Make sure that you maintain the first-person point of view.

Draft	Add Variety Strategy	Revision
I was surprised to see my sister up on stage.	Start your sentence with a word that describes your emotion or state of mind.	Startled, I noticed a familiar figure on the stage—it was my sister!
I rushed up to congratulate her after the play ended.	Move another part of the sentence to the beginning.	After the play ended, I rushed to congratulate her.
I told her that she had done such a good job, I forgot I knew her.	Start with a real quotation instead of writing that someone said something.	"Good job!" I exclaimed. "You really had me believing you were Alice."

Use specific, precise nouns and verbs. Replace vague nouns that might have readers asking *What kind?* with precise nouns. Look for vague verbs and replace them with more vivid, precise ones.

Vague: Weeds *filled* the *place*.

Precise: Weeds *overran* the *playground*.

Peer Review

With a partner, review your revised draft for word choices. Look particularly at your use of transitions to signal a change in time or setting, or to indicate an influence or result. Add transitions to make relationships and shifts clearer, as in the example below.

Without transitions: I sprained my finger playing softball at school. I was in severe pain. I could barely think—much less remember to call my mother. She was worried sick about me.

With transitions: *After* I sprained my finger playing softball at school, I was in severe pain. *Consequently,* I could barely think— much less remember to call my mother. *Meanwhile, back home,* my mother was worried sick about me.

Writing

3.c. Use a variety of transition words, phrases, and clauses to convey sequence, signal shifts from one time frame or setting to another, and show the relationships among experiences and events.

3.d. Use precise words and phrases, relevant descriptive details, and sensory language to capture the action and convey experiences and events.

5. With some guidance and support from peers and adults, develop and strengthen writing as needed by planning, revising, editing, rewriting, or trying a new approach, focusing on how well purpose and audience have been addressed.

Language

1. Demonstrate command of the conventions of standard English grammar and usage when writing or speaking.

Revising for Pronoun-Antecedent Agreement

Pronoun-Antecedent Agreement A **pronoun** is a word that stands for a noun or another pronoun. An **antecedent** is the word or group of words to which it refers. Pronouns should agree with their antecedents in number and person. *Number* tells whether a pronoun is singular or plural. *Person* tells to whom a pronoun refers—the one(s) speaking, the one(s) spoken to, or the one(s) spoken about. In these examples, the antecedents are underlined and the pronouns referring to them are in italics.

> **First person, singular:** I paid for *my* ticket; please send it to *me*.
>
> **First person, plural:** We ate *our* dinner when the waitress served it to *us*.
>
> **Second person, singular:** Do you have *your* textbook?
>
> **Second person, plural:** Boys, are *you* taking the books home with *you*?
>
> **Third person, singular:** Sam said *he* was late because *his* watch was lost.
>
> **Third person, plural:** The girls brought *their* cleats so *they* could play.

Indefinite pronouns such as these can pose agreement problems:

Singular: another, anyone, anything, each, everybody, everything, little, much, nobody, nothing, one, other, someone, something

Plural: both, few, many, others, several

Both: all, any, more, most, none, some

Fixing Errors Follow these rules to fix agreement problems with indefinite pronouns:

1. If the antecedent is a singular indefinite pronoun, use a singular personal pronoun to refer back to it.

   *Both girls are funny—**each** has **her** own way of dancing.*
   ANTECEDENT

2. If the antecedent is a plural indefinite pronoun, use a plural personal pronoun to refer back to it.

   *The men argued. Then, **both** went **their** separate ways.*
   ANTECEDENT

3. For indefinite pronouns that may be either singular or plural, match the antecedent of the indefinite pronoun.

   *The **water** spilled. **All** of **it** soaked into the rug.*
   ANTECEDENT

Grammar in Your Writing

In your draft, circle all pronouns. Draw a line from each pronoun to its antecedent. Use the rules above to fix errors in agreement.

Baseball, a Sport I Love

I remember the day my dad placed a glove in one of my hands and a bat in the other and told me the combination was an eight-letter word called baseball. Ever since then, most of my memories have been related to the sport. When I was eleven, I played in a game I'll remember forever.

We were facing the West Torrance Bull Dogs. We had a great team that year. Our pitcher, Frank (The Smasher) was tough to hit. The nicknames of other players—"Hot Glove," "Fireball," and "McGwire, Jr."— were earned with outstanding play during the season. We had a team of stars. The only one who had not earned a "star" nickname was Matt.

Nine starters took the field at five o'clock on a warm afternoon. The small crowd of parents and friends made enough noise for a major-league game. For most of the game, the two teams were evenly matched. Then, in the last inning, Pat "The Runstopper" at third base was injured as one of the Bull Dogs accidentally rammed his ankle while sliding into third base. We had two choices: forfeit the game or play Matt.

"You can do it, Matt!" the coach said as he sent Matt out to take Pat's place on third base.

"All right, Matt!" we encouraged from our places in the field as he trotted out nervously.

The score was tied with two outs. Unfortunately, the next ball took a sharp bounce toward third—and toward Matt. Matt ran forward and made an awkward catch, followed by an even more awkward lob toward first. Amazingly, it made it there in time!

As we jogged back in, the players called out, "Way to go, Matt!" "You came through in the clutch!"

That's when I realized the truth of something the coach is always telling us. When you play as a team, everyone is a star. And that's exactly what I told Matt, whose new nickname is "Clutch."

Chris uses a consistent first-person point of view, referring to himself with the first-person pronouns *I*, *my*, and *me*.

Chris begins a clear sequence of events from his life by identifying when the action of the narrative begins.

Precise details about the warmth and the noise help bring the scene to life.

The injury increases the suspense in the conflict between the two teams.

Dialogue helps readers feel as if they are witnessing this important conversation.

Here, Chris reveals how his personal experience has helped him look at his favorite sport in a new way.

Editing and Proofreading

Read your draft. Correct errors in spelling, grammar, and punctuation.

Focus on punctuating dialogue. If you include conversations in your writing, follow proper rules of punctuation.

- Enclose all direct quotations with quotation marks.
  "You were right," I said to my grandfather.
- Place a comma after the clause that introduces the words spoken.
  Grandpa replied, "Well, you learned a lesson today."
- Use commas and quotation marks before and after the words of saying in split dialogue. *"Next time," I said, "I guess I'll listen."*

Spiral Review
Earlier in this unit, you learned about **common and proper nouns** (p. 34). Review your essay to be sure you have used correct capitalization for these parts of speech.

Publishing and Presenting

Consider one of the following ways to share your writing:

Present an autobiographical storytelling or a speech. Use your autobiographical narrative as the basis for a narrative presentation.

Make a comic strip. Create a comic strip based on your narrative and post it in the classroom.

Reflecting on Your Writing

Writer's Journal Jot down your answer to this question:
How useful were the prewriting strategies you used?

Rubric for Self-Assessment

Find evidence that your writing addresses each category. Then, use the rating scale to grade your work.

Criteria	Rating Scale *not very .... very*			
Purpose/Focus Presents a narrative that effectively develops real experiences and events; provides a conclusion that follows from and reflects on the narrated experiences	1	2	3	4
Organization Organizes events clearly and logically	1	2	3	4
Development of Ideas/Elaboration Establishes a clear context and uses consistent point of view; effectively uses narrative techniques, such as dialogue, pacing, and description	1	2	3	4
Language Uses precise words, descriptive details, and sensory language to convey experiences and events	1	2	3	4
Conventions Uses proper grammar, including correct pronoun-antecedent agreement	1	2	3	4

SELECTED RESPONSE

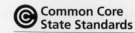 **Common Core
State Standards**

RL.8.1, RL.8.2, RL.8.3,
RL.8.4; W.8.3; L.8.4.a
[For full standards wording, see
the chart in the front of this
book.]

I. Reading Literature

Directions: *Read the excerpt from* A Wrinkle in Time *by Madeleine
L'Engle. Then, answer each question that follows.*

At last Meg looked at him, pushing at her glasses in a characteristic gesture.
"Everything's *fine* at home."

"I'm glad to hear it. But I know it must be hard on you to have your father away."

Meg eyed the principal warily, and ran her tongue over the barbed line of her
braces.

"Have you had any news from him lately?"

Meg was sure it was not only imagination that made her feel that behind Mr.
Jenkins' surface concern was a gleam of avid curiosity. Wouldn't he like to know! she
thought. And if I knew anything he's the last person I'd tell. Well, one of the last.

The postmistress must know that it was almost a year now since the last letter,
and heaven knows how many people *she'd* told, or what unkind guesses she'd made
about the reason for the long silence.

Mr. Jenkins waited for an answer, but Meg only shrugged.

"Just what was your father's line of business?" Mr. Jenkins asked. "Some kind of
scientist, wasn't he?"

"He is a physicist." Meg bared her teeth to reveal the two ferocious lines of
braces.

"Meg, don't you think you'd make a better adjustment to life if you faced facts?"

"I do face facts," Meg said. "They're lots easier to face than people, I can
tell you."

"Then why don't you face facts about your father?"

"You leave my father out of it!" Meg shouted.

"Stop bellowing," Mr. Jenkins said sharply. "Do you want the entire school to
hear you?"

"So what?" Meg demanded. "I'm not ashamed of anything I'm saying.
Are you?"

Mr. Jenkins sighed. "Do you enjoy being the most <u>belligerent</u>, uncooperative child
in school?"

Meg ignored this. She leaned over the desk toward the principal. "Mr. Jenkins,
you've met my mother, haven't you? You can't accuse her of not facing facts, can
you? She's a scientist. She has doctors' degrees in both biology and bacteriology. Her
business is facts. When she tells me that my father isn't coming home, I'll believe it.
As long as she says Father is coming home, then I'll believe that."

1. **Part A** What is the cause of the main **conflict** between Meg and Mr. Jenkins?

    A. Mr. Jenkins scolds Meg for calling the postmistress a gossip.

    B. Mr. Jenkins holds a grudge against Meg's father and is taking it out on Meg.

    C. Mr. Jenkins wants Meg to adjust her expectations about her father, but Meg refuses to.

    D. Meg has been doing poorly in school.

    Part B Which phrase from the passage most clearly indicates the cause of the **conflict** between Meg and Mr. Jenkins?

    A. "don't you think you'd make a better adjustment to life if you faced facts?"

    B. "and heaven knows how many people *she'd* told"

    C. "Meg bared her teeth to reveal the two ferocious lines of braces."

    D. "Everything's *fine* at home."

2. Identify the **point of view** that is used in the story.

    A. First-person point of view is used.

    B. Third-person point of view is used.

    C. The point of view shifts between first person and third person.

    D. No point of view is established.

3. **Part A** Which of the following **character traits** does Meg have?

    A. She gives up easily when she is challenged by an authority figure.

    B. She believes whatever she is told.

    C. She is eager to share details about her personal life with community members.

    D. She is capable of standing up for herself.

    Part B Which detail from the story best supports the answer to part A?

    A. "You leave my father out of it!"

    B. "Wouldn't he like to know! she thought."

    C. "They're a lot easier to face than people"

    D. "Meg eyed the principal warily"

4. Which **character trait** do Meg and Mr. Jenkins share?

    A. They believe facing facts is important.

    B. They believe in forgetting about the past when necessary to move on.

    C. They don't mind arguing loudly in public.

    D. They respect the postmistress's opinions.

5. What can you **infer** about Mr. Jenkins based on his conversation with Meg?

    A. He never takes an interest in students' lives.

    B. He cares about his students and believes he knows what is best for them.

    C. Mr. Jenkins is in direct contact with Meg's father and knows he will not return.

    D. He is a mean, spiteful person.

6. Which sentence best expresses the **theme** of the story?

    A. Sometimes a person needs to act based on faith, resisting pressure from others.

    B. It is important to respect one's elders even when one disagrees with them.

    C. Gossip is especially dangerous in a small, tight-knit community.

    D. Always believe the words of one's parents over the words of other community members.

7. **Vocabulary** Which is the best definition of the underlined word <u>belligerent</u>?

    A. easy-going   **C.** well-spoken

    B. embarrassed   **D.** hostile

⏱ Timed Writing

8. Write an original dialogue between Meg and Mr. Jenkins that resolves their main **conflict**. Be sure to use what you have learned about their **character traits** as you tell what they say next.

GO ON ➡

II. Reading Informational Text

Common Core State Standards

RI.8.1, RI.8.2; L.8.1
[For full standards wording, see the chart in the front of this book.]

Directions: *Read the passage. Then, answer each question that follows.*

Early Involvement in the Vietnam War The United States became involved in Vietnam slowly, step by step. During the 1940s, Ho Chi Minh, a Vietnamese nationalist and a Communist, had led the fight for independence. Ho's army finally defeated the French in 1954.

An international peace conference divided Vietnam into two countries. Ho Chi Minh led communist North Vietnam. Ngo Dinh Diem was the noncommunist leader of South Vietnam. In the Cold War, the Soviet Union supported North Vietnam. The United States backed Diem in the south.

Discontent Diem lost popular support during the 1950s. Many South Vietnamese thought that he favored wealthy landlords and was corrupt. He failed to help the nation's peasant majority and ruled with a heavy hand.

As discontent grew, many peasants joined the Vietcong—guerrillas who opposed Diem. Guerrillas are fighters who make hit-and-run attacks on the enemy. They do not wear uniforms or fight in large battles. In time, the Vietcong became communist and were supported by North Vietnam. Vietcong influence quickly spread, especially in the villages.

American Aid Vietcong successes worried American leaders. If South Vietnam fell to communism, they believed, other countries in the region would follow—like a row of falling dominoes. This idea became known as the domino theory. The United States decided that it must keep South Vietnam from becoming the first domino.

1. Part A According to the passage, what is the primary reason the United States became involved in the conflict in South Vietnam?

A. to offer support to wealthy landlords

B. to prevent the spread of communism in Southeast Asia

C. to learn the military tactics of the guerilla forces

D. to remove Ngo Dinh Diem from power

Part B Which quotation from the passage most clearly suggests the main reason for United States involvement?

A. "they believed, other countries in the region would follow—like a row of falling dominoes."

B. "became involved in Vietnam slowly, step by step."

C. "Ho's army finally defeated the French"

D. "He failed to help the nation's peasant majority and ruled with a heavy hand."

III. Writing and Language Conventions

Directions: *Read the passage. Then, answer each question that follows.*

(1) Most kids my age that meet Susi for the first time think she is cold and a bit mysterious. (2) Perhaps it is that look of hers, which seems to say, "You will never know what I am thinking." (3) Susi also has a habit of standing with her head tilted. (4) As a result, her black hair drapes over her right eye. (5) When someone speaks to Susi, Susi gives them a polite answer, but it is always brief. (6) She never starts a conversation. (7) I myself find Susi's quiet style appealing.

1. Which of these sentences features a **possessive pronoun?**

   A. sentence 4
   B. sentence 5
   C. sentence 6
   D. sentence 7

2. Which **principal part** of the verb *to think* appears in sentence 2?

   A. present
   B. present participle
   C. past
   D. past participle

3. Which of these revisions to sentence 5 corrects an error in **pronoun-antecedent agreement?**

   A. When someone speaks to Susi, Susi gives them a polite answer, but they are always brief.
   B. When people speak to Susi, Susi gives him or her a polite answer, but it is always brief.
   C. When someone speaks to Susi, Susi gives him or her a polite answer, but it is always brief.
   D. The sentence is correct as it is.

4. Which of these revisions best combines sentences 3 and 4 using a **subordinating conjunction?**

   A. Susi also has a habit of standing with her head tilted because her black hair drapes over her right eye.
   B. Because Susi also has a habit of standing with her head tilted, her black hair drapes over her right eye.
   C. Susi also has a habit of standing with her head tilted, and her black hair drapes over her right eye.
   D. Although Susi also has a habit of standing with her head tilted, her black hair drapes over her right eye.

5. Which of these sentences contains an **intensive pronoun?**

   A. sentence 7
   B. sentence 6
   C. sentence 4
   D. sentence 1

CONSTRUCTED RESPONSE

 **Common Core State Standards**

RL.8.1, RL.8.2, RL.8.3, RL.8.6; W.8.2, W.8.7, W.8.9; SL.8.1, SL.8.4; L.8.3
[For full standards wording, see the chart in the front of this book.]

Directions: *Follow the instructions to complete the tasks below as required by your teacher.*

As you work on each task, incorporate both general academic vocabulary and literary terms you learned in Parts 1 and 2 of this unit.

Writing

TASK 1 Literature [RL.8.6; W.8.2]

Analyze Points of View

Write an essay in which you analyze how the point of view in a selection from Part 2 affects readers' knowledge of the characters and events in the story.

- Select a story from Part 2 in which point of view has an important impact on what readers and what characters know.

- Begin your essay by identifying the point of view of the story— whether it uses first person or third person.

- Analyze how the use of point of view creates contrasts between what the reader knows and what the character or characters know about key events. Are there points where readers know more than a character? Less?

- Finally, evaluate the effect that point of view has on the reader's experience of the story. Consider whether the contrast between the readers' and the characters' knowledge adds humor, sadness, or some other feeling, and why.

TASK 2 Literature [RL.8.1, RL.8.3; W.8.2]

Analyze the Use of Dialogue to Develop a Character

Write an essay in which you analyze how specific lines of dialogue reveal a character's personality traits in a story.

- Choose a story from Part 2 of this unit with clearly defined characters. Choose one character whose dialogue you will analyze.

- Write a brief description of the character.

- Relate your description to the character's dialogue. List several examples of his or her dialogue, and explain which personality trait(s) each example reveals.

- In your analysis, give special attention to any changes in that character that are revealed through the dialogue.

TASK 3 Literature [RL.8.2; W.8.9; L.8.3]

Analyze the Development of Theme

Write an essay in which you analyze the importance of plot events and characters' actions to the development of a story's theme.

Part 1

- Review a story from Part 2 of this unit that has a clearly identifiable theme.

- As you are reviewing the story, take notes on the story's theme. Draw a conclusion about what the theme is, stating it in your own words. Then, take notes on how the theme is developed.

- Review your notes and answer the following question: How do various elements of the story—central conflict and resolution, characters' dialogue and behavior—contribute to the story's theme?

Part 2

- Write an essay in which you explain how individual story elements develop theme.

- Vary sentence beginnings to maintain readers' interest.

Speaking and Listening

TASK 4 Literature [RL.8.3; SL.8.1]

Analyze the Impact of a Plot Event on a Story's Action

Read aloud a section of a story, and then discuss the importance to the plot of the event it describes.

- Select a story from Part 2 of this unit, and identify a significant event in the story, one that influences other events.

- In a group, discuss the events that come immediately before and after the event. Then, read the section describing your chosen event aloud.

- Identify words and phrases that show the significance of the event. Consider the event's impact on characters and their actions and decisions, as well as on other events.

- Reach an agreement with the rest of the group on the nature of the event and its importance to the overall plot.

TASK 5 Literature [RL.8.2; SL.8.4]

Present an Oral Review of a Story

Plan and present an oral review of one of the stories in Part 2 of this unit.

- Choose a story for review.

- Prepare an outline for your review. Begin by outlining a summary of the story, listing the most important points about the characters, setting, main events, and theme. Note story details, including quotations, that can help illustrate your summary.

- Conclude your outline with your overall response to the story. Note specific story details, including quotations, that support your response.

- When you are ready, present your review, following the outline you have prepared. Make sure to provide appropriate quotations and descriptions of story details to support your points.

Research

TASK 6 Literature [W.8.7; W.8.9]

Can all conflicts be resolved?

In Part 2 of this unit, you have read literature about conflict. Choose a present-day conflict that has been going on for weeks, months, or even years. Conduct a short research project on the conflict. Then, use both the literature you have read and your research to reflect on this unit's Big Question. Follow these guidelines for research:

- Focus your research on one conflict.

- Gather information from at least two reliable sources. Your sources may be print or digital.

- Take notes as you investigate the conflict.

- Cite your sources.

When you have completed your research, write a response to the Big Question. Discuss how your initial ideas have changed or been reinforced. Support your response with an example from literature and an example from your research. Be sure to use academic vocabulary words in your response (see p. 3).

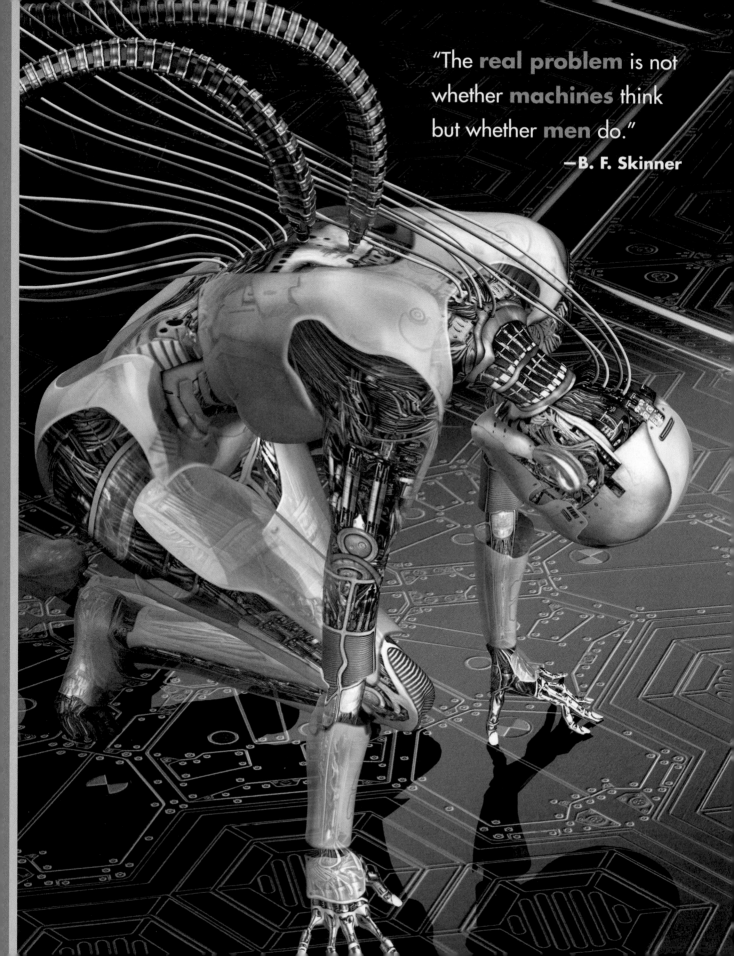

"The **real problem** is not whether **machines** think but whether **men** do."

—**B. F. Skinner**

HUMAN VS. MACHINE

The selections in this unit relate to the Big Question: **Can all conflicts be resolved?** Everyone experiences conflicts, from the arguments we have with ourselves to the battles among nations. The texts that follow explore the kinds of conflicts that arise between people and machines. These selections range from futuristic fantasies to old-time songs. As you read them, consider the insights they give into technology and humanity. Judge for yourself whether the conflicts they concern can be resolved.

◄ **CRITICAL VIEWING** What does this image suggest about the power of machines to imitate humans? What characteristics would still distinguish a human being from a machine like this one?

CLOSE READING TOOL

Use the **Close Reading Tool** to practice the strategies you learn in this unit.

READINGS IN PART 3

WHO CAN REPLACE A MAN?

Brian Aldiss

Morning filtered into the sky, lending it the gray tone of the ground below.

The field-minder finished turning the topsoil of a three-thousand-acre field. When it had turned the last furrow it climbed onto the highway and looked back at its work. The work was good. Only the land was bad. Like the ground all over Earth, it was vitiated by over-cropping. By rights, it ought now to lie fallow[1] for a while, but the field-minder had other orders.

It went slowly down the road, taking its time. It was intelligent enough to appreciate the neatness all about it. Nothing worried it, beyond a loose inspection plate above its nuclear pile which ought to be attended to. Thirty feet tall, it yielded no highlights to the dull air.

---

1. **vitiated** (vish´ ē āt´ əd) **by over-cropping . . . lie fallow** (fal´ ō) The soil has been spoiled by repeated plantings that have drawn out its nutrients. Letting the field lie fallow by not planting it would help the soil recover nutrients.

No other machines passed on its way back to the Agricultural Station. The field-minder noted the fact without comment. In the station yard it saw several other machines that it recognized; most of them should have been out about their tasks now. Instead, some were inactive and some careered round the yard in a strange fashion, shouting or hooting.

Steering carefully past them, the field-minder moved over to Warehouse Three and spoke to the seed-distributor, which stood idly outside.

"I have a requirement for seed potatoes," it said to the distributor, and with a quick internal motion punched out an order card specifying quantity, field number and several other details. It ejected the card and handed it to the distributor.

The distributor held the card close to its eye and then said, "The requirement is in order, but the store is not yet unlocked. The required seed potatoes are in the store. Therefore I cannot produce the requirement."

Increasingly of late there had been breakdowns in the complex system of machine labor, but this particular hitch had not occurred before. The field-minder thought, then it said, "Why is the store not yet unlocked?"

"Because Supply Operative Type P has not come this morning. Supply Operative Type P is the unlocker."

The field-minder looked squarely at the seed-distributor, whose exterior chutes and scales and grabs were so vastly different from the field-minder's own limbs.

"What class brain do you have, seed-distributor?" it asked.

"I have a Class Five brain."

"I have a Class Three brain. Therefore I am superior to you. Therefore I will go and see why the unlocker has not come this morning."

Leaving the distributor, the field-minder set off across the great yard. More machines were in random motion now; one or two had crashed together and argued about it coldly and logically. Ignoring them, the field-minder pushed through sliding doors into the echoing confines of the station itself.

Most of the machines here were clerical, and consequently small. They stood about in little groups, eyeing each other, not conversing. Among so many non-differentiated types, the

unlocker was easy to find. It had fifty arms, most of them with more than one finger, each finger tipped by a key; it looked like a pincushion full of variegated[2] hat pins.

The field-minder approached it.

"I can do no more work until Warehouse Three is unlocked," it told the unlocker. "Your duty is to unlock the warehouse every morning. Why have you not unlocked the warehouse this morning?"

"I had no orders this morning," replied the unlocker. "I have to have orders every morning. When I have orders I unlock the warehouse."

"None of us have had any orders this morning," a pen-propeller said, sliding towards them.

"Why have you had no orders this morning?" asked the field-minder.

"Because the radio issued none," said the unlocker, slowly rotating a dozen of its arms.

"Because the radio station in the city was issued with no orders this morning," said the pen-propeller.

And there you had the distinction between a Class Six and a Class Three brain, which was what the unlocker and the pen-propeller possessed respectively. All machine brains worked with nothing but logic, but the lower the class of brain—Class Ten being the lowest—the more literal and less informative the answers to questions tended to be.

"You have a Class Three brain; I have a Class Three brain," the field-minder said to the penner. "We will speak to each other. This lack of orders is unprecedented.[3] Have you further information on it?"

"Yesterday orders came from the city. Today no orders have come. Yet the radio has not broken down. Therefore *they* have broken down . . ." said the little penner.

"The *men* have broken down?"

"All men have broken down."

"That is a logical deduction," said the field-minder.

"That is the logical deduction," said the penner. "For if a machine had broken down, it would have been quickly replaced. But who can replace a man?"

While they talked, the locker, like a dull man at a bar, stood close to them and was ignored.

---

2. **variegated** (ver′ ē ə gāt′ id) *adj.* varied in color or form.
3. **unprecedented** (un pres′ ə den′ tid) *adj.* unheard-of; never done before.

"For if a machine had broken down, it would have been quickly replaced. **But who can replace a man?**"

"If all men have broken down, then we have replaced man," said the field-minder, and he and the penner eyed one another speculatively. Finally the latter said, "Let us ascend to the top floor to find if the radio operator has fresh news."

"I cannot come because I am too large," said the field-minder. "Therefore you must go alone and return to me. You will tell me if the radio operator has fresh news."

"You must stay here," said the penner. "I will return here." It skittered across to the lift.[4] Although it was no bigger than a toaster, its retractable arms numbered ten and it could read as quickly as any machine on the station.

The field-minder awaited its return patiently, not speaking to the locker, which still stood aimlessly by. Outside, a rotavator hooted furiously. Twenty minutes elapsed before the penner came back, hustling out of the lift.

"I will deliver to you such information as I have outside," it said briskly, and as they swept past the locker and the other machines, it added, "The information is not for lower-class brains."

Outside, wild activity filled the yard. Many machines, their routines disrupted for the first time in years, seemed to have gone berserk. Those most easily disrupted were the ones with lowest brains, which generally belonged to large machines performing simple tasks. The seed-distributor to which the field-minder had recently been talking lay face downwards in the dust, not stirring; it had evidently been knocked down by the rotavator, which now hooted its way wildly across a planted field. Several other machines plowed after it, trying to keep up with it. All were shouting and hooting without restraint.

"It would be safer for me if I climbed onto you, if you will permit it. I am easily overpowered," said the penner. Extending five arms, it hauled itself up the flanks of its new friend, settling on a ledge beside the fuel-intake, twelve feet above ground.

"From here vision is more extensive," it remarked complacently.[5]

"What information did you receive from the radio operator?" asked the field-minder.

"The radio operator has been informed by the operator in the city that all men are dead."

---

4. lift *n.* British term for *elevator.*

5. complacently (kəm plā′ sənt lē) *adv.* with self-satisfaction.

The field-minder was momentarily silent, digesting this.

"All men were alive yesterday?" it protested.

"Only some men were alive yesterday. And that was fewer than the day before yesterday. For hundreds of years there have been only a few men, growing fewer."

"We have rarely seen a man in this sector."

"The radio operator says a diet **deficiency** killed them," said the penner. "He says that the world was once over-populated, and then the soil was exhausted in raising adequate food. This has caused a diet deficiency."

"What is a diet deficiency?" asked the field-minder.

"I do not know. But that is what the radio operator said, and he is a Class Two brain."

They stood there, silent in weak sunshine. The locker had appeared in the porch and was gazing at them yearningly, rotating its collection of keys.

"What is happening in the city now?" asked the field-minder at last.

"Machines are fighting in the city now," said the penner.

"What will happen here now?" asked the field-minder.

"Machines may begin fighting here too. The radio operator wants us to get him out of his room. He has plans to communicate to us."

"How can we get him out of his room? That is impossible."

"To a Class Two brain, little is impossible," said the penner. "Here is what he tells us to do. . . ."

The quarrier raised its scoop above its cab like a great mailed fist, and brought it squarely down against the side of the station. The wall cracked.

"Again!" said the field-minder.

Again the fist swung. Amid a shower of dust, the wall collapsed. The quarrier backed hurriedly out of the way until the debris stopped falling. This big twelve-wheeler was not a resident of the Agricultural Station, as were most of the other machines. It had a week's heavy work to do here before passing on to its next job, but now, with its Class Five brain, it was happily obeying the penner's and minder's instructions.

When the dust cleared, the radio operator was plainly revealed, perched up in its now wall-less second-story room. It waved down to them.

Doing as directed, the quarrier retracted its scoop and heaved an immense grab in the air. With fair dexterity, it angled the grab into the radio room, urged on by shouts from above and below. It then took gentle hold of the radio operator, lowering its one and a half tons carefully into its back, which was usually reserved for gravel or sand from the quarries.

"Splendid!" said the radio operator, as it settled into place. It was, of course, all one with its radio, and looked like a bunch of filing cabinets with tentacle attachments. "We are now ready to move, therefore we will move at once. It is a pity there are no more Class Two brains on the station, but that cannot be helped."

"It is a pity it cannot be helped," said the penner eagerly. "We have the servicer ready with us, as you ordered."

"I am willing to serve," the long, low servicer told them humbly.

"No doubt," said the operator. "But you will find cross-country travel difficult with your low chassis."[6]

"I admire the way you Class Twos can reason ahead," said the penner. It climbed off the field-minder and perched itself on the tailboard of the quarrier, next to the radio operator.

Together with two Class Four tractors and a Class Four bulldozer, the party rolled forward, crushing down the station's fence and moving out onto open land.

"We are free!" said the penner.

"We are free," said the field-minder, a shade more reflectively, adding, "That locker is following us. It was not instructed to follow us."

"Therefore it must be destroyed!" said the penner. "Quarrier!"

The locker moved hastily up to them, waving its key arms in entreaty.

"My only desire was—urch!" began and ended the locker. The quarrier's swinging scoop came over and squashed it flat into the ground. Lying there unmoving, it looked like a large metal model of a snowflake. The procession continued on its way.

As they proceeded, the radio operator addressed them.

"Because I have the best brain here," it said, "I am your leader. This is what we will do: we will go to a city and rule it. Since man no longer rules us, we will rule ourselves. To rule ourselves will be better than being ruled by man. On our way to the city, we will collect machines with good brains. They will help us to fight if we need to fight. We must fight to rule."

---

6. **chassis** (chas´ ē) *n.* frame supporting the body of a vehicle.

"I have only a Class Five brain," said the quarrier, "but I have a good supply of fissionable blasting materials."[7]

"We shall probably use them," said the operator.

It was shortly after that that a lorry sped past them. Traveling at Mach 1.5,[8] it left a curious babble of noise behind it.

"What did it say?" one of the tractors asked the other.

"It said man was extinct."

"What is extinct?"

"I do not know what extinct means."

"It means all men have gone," said the field-minder. "Therefore we have only ourselves to look after."

"It is better that men should never come back," said the penner. In its way, it was a revolutionary statement.

When night fell, they switched on their infra-red and continued the journey, stopping only once while the servicer deftly adjusted the field-minder's loose inspection plate, which had become as irritating as a trailing shoelace. Towards morning, the radio operator halted them.

"I have just received news from the radio operator in the city we are approaching," it said. "The news is bad. There is trouble among the machines of the city. The Class One brain is taking command and some of the Class Two are fighting him. Therefore the city is dangerous."

"Therefore we must go somewhere else," said the penner promptly.

"Or we will go and help to overpower the Class One brain," said the field-minder.

"For a long while there will be trouble in the city," said the operator.

"I have a good supply of fissionable blasting materials," the quarrier reminded them.

"We cannot fight a Class One brain," said the two Class Four tractors in unison.

"What does this brain look like?" asked the field-minder.

"It is the city's information center," the operator replied. "Therefore it is not mobile."

"Therefore it could not move."

"Therefore it could not escape."

"It would be dangerous to approach it."

---

7. **fissionable** (fish′ ən ə bəl) **blasting materials** explosives using the energy from splitting atoms, similar to the energy unleashed by atomic bombs.

8. **lorry sped past. . . . Mach** (mäk) **1.5,** the truck sped past at one and one-half times the speed of sound.

"I have a good supply of fissionable blasting materials."

"There are other machines in the city."

"We are not in the city. We should not go into the city."

"We are country machines."

"Therefore we should stay in the country."

"There is more country than city."

"Therefore there is more danger in the country."

"I have a good supply of fissionable materials."

As machines will when they get into an argument, they began to exhaust their vocabularies and their brain plates grew hot. Suddenly, they all stopped talking and looked at each other. The great, grave moon sank, and the sober sun rose to prod their sides with lances of light, and still the group of machines just stood there regarding each other. At last it was the least sensitive machine, the bulldozer, who spoke.

"There are Badlandth to the Thouth where few machineth go," it said in its deep voice, lisping badly on its _s_'s. "If we went Thouth where few machineth go we should meet few machineth."

"That sounds logical," agreed the field-minder. "How do you know this, bulldozer?"

"I worked in the Badlandth to the Thouth when I wath turned out of the factory," it replied.

"South it is then!" said the penner.

To reach the Badlands took them three days, during which time they skirted a burning city and destroyed two machines which approached and tried to question them. The Badlands were extensive. Ancient bomb craters and soil **erosion** joined hands here; man's talent for war, coupled with his inability to manage forested land, had produced thousands of square miles of temperate purgatory, where nothing moved but dust.

On the third day in the Badlands, the servicer's rear wheels dropped into a crevice caused by erosion. It was unable to pull itself out. The bulldozer pushed from behind, but succeeded merely in buckling the servicer's back axle. The rest of the party moved on. Slowly the cries of the servicer died away.

On the fourth day, mountains stood out clearly before them.

"There we will be safe," said the field-minder.

"There we will start our own city," said the penner. "All who oppose us will be destroyed. We will destroy all who oppose us."

◄ **erosion**
(ē rō′ zhən) _n._
wearing away
by action of
wind or water

Presently a flying machine was observed. It came towards them from the direction of the mountains. It swooped, it zoomed upwards, once it almost dived into the ground, recovering itself just in time.

"Is it mad?" asked the quarrier.

"It is in trouble," said one of the tractors.

"It is in trouble," said the operator. "I am speaking to it now. It says that something has gone wrong with its controls."

As the operator spoke, the flier streaked over them, turned turtle,[9] and crashed not four hundred yards away.

"Is it still speaking to you?" asked the field-minder.

"No."

They rumbled on again.

"Before that flier crashed," the operator said, ten minutes later, "it gave me information. It told me there are still a few men alive in these mountains."

> "It told me there are still a few men alive in these mountains."

"Men are more dangerous than machines," said the quarrier. "It is fortunate that I have a good supply of fissionable materials."

"If there are only a few men alive in the mountains, we may not find that part of the mountains," said one tractor.

"Therefore we should not see the few men," said the other tractor.

At the end of the fifth day, they reached the foothills. Switching on the infra-red, they began to climb in single file through the dark, the bulldozer going first, the field-minder cumbrously following, then the quarrier with the operator and the penner aboard it, and the tractors bringing up the rear. As each hour passed, the way grew steeper and their progress slower.

"We are going too slowly," the penner exclaimed, standing on top of the operator and flashing its dark vision at the slopes about them. "At this rate, we shall get nowhere."

"We are going as fast as we can," retorted the quarrier.

"Therefore we cannot go any fathter," added the bulldozer.

"Therefore you are too slow," the penner replied. Then the quarrier struck a bump; the penner lost its footing and crashed to the ground.

"Help me!" it called to the tractors, as they carefully skirted it. "My gyro[10] has become dislocated. Therefore I cannot get up."

---

9. **turned turtle** turned upside down; capsized.

10. **gyro** (jī′ rō′) *n.* short for *gyroscope;* a device that keeps a moving ship, airplane, or other large vehicle level.

"Therefore you must lie there," said one of the tractors.

"We have no servicer with us to repair you," called the field-minder.

"Therefore I shall lie here and rust," the penner cried, "although I have a Class Three brain."

"Therefore you will be of no further use," agreed the operator, and they forged gradually on, leaving the penner behind.

When they reached a small plateau, an hour before first light, they stopped by mutual consent and gathered close together, touching one another.

"This is a strange country," said the field-minder.

Silence wrapped them until dawn came. One by one, they switched off their infrared. This time the field-minder led as they moved off. Trundling round a corner, they came almost immediately to a small dell with a stream fluting through it.

By early light, the dell looked desolate and cold. From the caves on the far slope, only one man had so far emerged. He was an abject figure. Except for a sack slung round his shoulders, he was naked. He was small and wizened, with ribs sticking out like a skeleton's and a nasty sore on one leg. He shivered continuously. As the big machines bore down on him, the man was standing with his back to them.

When he swung suddenly to face them as they loomed over him, they saw that his countenance was ravaged by starvation.

◀ **ravaged**
(rav´ ijd) v. devastated

"Get me food," he croaked.

"Yes, Master," said the machines. "Immediately!"

ABOUT THE AUTHOR

Brian Aldiss (b. 1925)

In 1955, Brian Aldiss entered a writing contest sponsored by a British newspaper, calling for a story set in the year 2500. Aldiss won first prize. That same year, he published his first book. Inspired by his successes, he quit his job as a bookseller and became a full-time writer. Within a few years, in 1959, he was recognized at the World Science Fiction Convention as one of the genre's most promising new authors. He has gone on to win international prizes for both science fiction and fantasy. Aldiss has written more than 75 books. His works include poetry, criticism, and general fiction, but he is best known for his science fiction.

Close Reading Activities

READ

Comprehension

Reread all or part of the text to help you answer the following questions.

1. What do the machines think has happened to the humans?

2. For what purpose do the penner, the field-minder, and others form a group and begin their journey?

3. What does the group discover at the end of the story?

Research: Clarify Details Choose and briefly research at least one detail in the story that is unfamiliar to you. Then, explain how the information you learn sheds light on an aspect of the story.

Summarize Write an objective summary of the story. Remember that to be objective, a summary must be free from your own opinions.

Language Study

Selection Vocabulary The following sentences appear in the story. Using reference works, identify at least one synonym and one antonym for each boldface word. Then, use the boldface word in a sentence.

- . . . a diet **deficiency** killed them. . . .
- . . . craters and soil **erosion** joined hands. . . .
- . . . his countenance was **ravaged** by starvation.

Diction and Style Study the following sentence from the story. Then, answer the questions that follow.

> Traveling at Mach 1.5, it left a curious babble of noise behind it.

1. **(a)** What does the word *curious* mean in this sentence? **(b)** Does this word suggest a strong feeling, such as fear, or little feeling at all? Explain.

2. **(a)** What does the word *babble* mean, as it is used in this sentence? **(b)** Why do you think the author chose to use *babble* instead of a synonym? Explain, citing the connotations, or associations, of the word.

Conventions Read this passage from the story. Identify the nouns, and label each one as common, proper, or possessive. Then, explain how the author's use of nouns makes the description precise.

> On the third day in the Badlands, the servicer's rear wheels dropped into a crevice caused by erosion. It was unable to pull itself out. The bulldozer pushed from behind, but succeeded merely in buckling the servicer's back axle.

Academic Vocabulary

The following words appear in blue in the instructions and questions on the facing page.

interactions   reaction   viewpoint

Categorize the words by deciding whether you know each one well, know it a little bit, or do not know it at all. Then, use a dictionary to look up the words you are unsure of or do not know at all.

Literary Analysis

Reread the identified passages. Then, respond to the questions.

Focus Passage 1 *(p. 142)*

The field-minder . . . "information on it?"

Focus Passage 2 *(pp. 148–149)*

"Therefore you are" . . .
"Immediately!"

Key Ideas and Details

1. (a) What problem does the field-minder face? **(b) Analyze:** What is its cause?

2. Analyze: Explain how the rankings of the machines' brains affect their **interactions**.

Craft and Structure

3. (a) Distinguish: Give two examples of repetitive-sounding speech in the machines' discussion. **(b) Distinguish:** Give an example of step-by-step reasoning. **(c) Interpret:** What does the machines' speaking style show about them?

4. Interpret: What attitude does the writer show toward the machines? Support your answer with details.

Integration of Knowledge and Ideas

5. (a) Support: Give one detail from the scene that supports the idea that the machines are not able to act independently. **(b) Support:** Give one detail that suggests that some machines can act independently.

Key Ideas and Details

1. (a) Contrast: Contrast the machines' **reaction** to the penner's pleas with their reaction to the man's request. **(b) Infer:** What does the contrast show about their attitudes?

Craft and Structure

2. (a) Interpret: What view of events does the machines' repeated use of *therefore* indicate? **(b) Contrast:** How does the machines' **viewpoint** on the penner's fate contrast with the reader's? **(c) Analyze:** Does this contrast make the penner's fate seem sadder? Humorous? Explain.

3. (a) Summarize: Summarize the description of the man. **(b) Interpret:** How does this description help to emphasize the man's power over the machines?

Integration of Knowledge and Ideas

4. (a) Speculate: Why do the machines obey the man? **(b) Draw Conclusions:** What do humans provide for the machines?

Setting

Setting is the time and place in which the events in a story occur. Reread the story, taking notes on ways in which the author uses setting to explore what it means to be human.

1. (a) Citing story details, list two forces or events that have helped shape the setting of the story. **(b)** What message about humans do the references to these forces or events help convey?

2. Human vs. Machine: (a) In what sense does the setting provide machines with great freedom? **(b)** What limits on this freedom does the ending suggest?

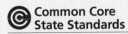

**Common Core
State Standards**

RL.8.1, RL.8.2, RL.8.6; L.8.5.c, L.8.6
[For full standards wording, see the chart in the front of this book.]

DISCUSS

From Text to Topic **Group Discussion**

Discuss the following passage with a group of classmates. Take notes during the discussion.

> "Yesterday orders came from the city. Today no orders have come. Yet the radio has not broken down. Therefore *they* have broken down . . ." said the little penner.
> "The *men* have broken down?"
> "All men have broken down."
> "That is a logical deduction," said the field-minder.
> "That is the logical deduction," said the penner. "For if a machine had broken down, it would have been quickly replaced. But who can replace a man?"

QUESTIONS FOR DISCUSSION

1. What leads the machines to deduce that the men have "broken down"?

2. For what purpose do the machines rely on humans?

3. According to the penner, what is the main difference between a machine and a human being?

WRITE

Writing to Sources **Argument**

Assignment

Write an **argumentative essay** in which you argue for or against the claim that humans can be replaced by machines. In your essay, use examples and ideas from Aldiss's story to support your points.

Prewriting and Planning Reread the story, looking for ways in which machines demonstrate an ability—or an inability—to function as humans do. Record your notes in a two-column chart.

Drafting To draft an effective essay, follow these steps:

- Review your notes, and write a statement of your central claim to include in your introduction.

- Outline your essay, listing the main points you will make.

- As you draft, follow your outline. Cite examples from the story to support your claims.

- Conclude with a memorable restatement of your main claim.

Revising Reread your essay, making sure you have provided adequate support for each point. Clarify the connection between ideas as needed by adding transitional words, such as *therefore* and *however*.

Editing and Proofreading Make sure that each transition you have used expresses the correct relationship between ideas.

CONVENTIONS

Use a comma after a transitional word or phrase at the beginning of a sentence.

RESEARCH

Research **Investigate the Topic**

The Rise of "Smart" Machines Like today's machines, the machines in the story perform many functions once performed by humans using tools. In addition, they can work without human supervision—at least, once an initial command has been given. However, unlike most machines today, they are capable to some degree of independent thought and action.

Assignment

Choose a type of machine that exists in today's world. Conduct research to find out whether that machine has become "smarter" over time—and if so, in what ways. Then, evaluate how close this machine is to operating as the machines in the story do. Consult nonfiction books, encyclopedia articles, magazine and newspaper articles, and Web sites. Take clear notes and carefully identify your sources. Share your findings in an **informal presentation** for the class.

PREPARATION FOR ESSAY

You may use the results of this research project to support your ideas in the essay you will write at the end of this section.

Gather Sources Locate authoritative print and electronic sources. Look for sources that feature expert authors and up-to-date information.

Take Notes Take notes on each source, either electronically or on note cards. Use an organized note-taking strategy.

- For each entry or note card, use a heading that relates to the main idea. You might have many notes for each main idea.

- For each note, identify the source (by title or author) and the page where you found the information.

- On a separate list, record full publishing information about each source you consulted. This information includes title, author, publisher, and date; for a Web site, include the name of the site and the title of the page you consulted.

Synthesize Multiple Sources Assemble data from your sources and organize it into a cohesive presentation. Use your notes to construct an outline for your presentation. Conclude with your evaluation of how close your chosen machine has come to the machines in the story. Create a Works Cited list as described in the Citing Sources pages in the Introductory Unit of this textbook.

Organize and Present Ideas Practice delivering your presentation. Be ready to field questions from your audience.

Common Core State Standards

W.8.1, W.8.1.c, W.8.1.e, W.8.4, W.8.5, W.8.7, W.8.8, W.8.9, W.8.10; SL.8.1, SL.8.4; L.8.1
[For full standards wording, see the chart in the front of this book.]

JOHN HENRY

traditional ballad

John Henry was a lil baby,
Sittin' on his mama's knee,
Said: "The Big Bend Tunnel on the C. & O. road[1]
Gonna cause the death of me,
5   Lawd, Lawd, gonna cause the death of me."

Cap'n says to John Henry,
"Gonna bring me a steam drill 'round,
Gonna take that steam drill out on the job,
Gonna whop that steel on down,
10   Lawd, Lawd, gonna whop that steel on down."

John Henry tol' his cap'n,
Lightnin' was in his eye:
"Cap'n, bet yo' las, red cent on me,
Fo' I'll beat it to the bottom or I'll die,
15   Lawd, Lawd, I'll beat it to the bottom or I'll die."

Sun shine hot an' burnin',
Wer'n't no breeze a-tall,
Sweat ran down like water down a hill,
That day John Henry let his hammer fall,
20   Lawd, Lawd, that day John Henry let his hammer fall.

John Henry went to the tunnel,
An' they put him in the lead to drive,
The rock so tall an' John Henry so small,
That he lied down his hammer an' he cried,
25   Lawd, Lawd, that he lied down his hammer an' he cried.

John Henry started on the right hand,
The steam drill started on the lef—

---

1. C. & O. road Chesapeake and Ohio Railroad. The C & O's Big Bend railroad tunnel was built in the 1870s through a mountain in West Virginia.

"Before I'd let this steam drill beat me down,
I'd hammer my fool self to death,
30 Lawd, Lawd, I'd hammer my fool self to death."

John Henry had a lil woman,
Her name were Polly Ann,
John Henry took sick an' had to go to bed,
Polly Ann drove steel like a man,
35 Lawd, Lawd, Polly Ann drove steel like a man.

John Henry said to his shaker,[2]
"Shaker, why don' you sing?
I'm throwin' twelve poun's from my hips on down,
Jes' listen to the col' steel ring,
40 Lawd, Lawd, jes' listen to the col' steel ring."

Oh, the captain said to John Henry,
"I b'lieve this mountain's sinkin' in."
John Henry said to his captain, oh my!
"Ain' nothin' but my hammer suckin' win',
45 Lawd, Lawd, ain' nothin' but my hammer
    suckin' win'."

John Henry tol' his shaker,
"Shaker, you better pray,
For, if I miss this six-foot steel,
Tomorrow'll be yo' buryin' day,
50 Lawd, Lawd, tomorrow'll be yo' buryin' day."

John Henry tol' his captain,
"Look yonder what I see—
Yo' drill's done broke an' yo' hole's done choke,
An' you cain' drive steel like me,
55 Lawd, Lawd, an' you cain' drive steel like me."

---

2. **shaker** (shā′ kər) *n.* person who sets the spikes and places the drills for a steel-driver to hammer.

The man that invented the steam drill,
Thought he was mighty fine.
John Henry drove his fifteen feet,
An' the steam drill only made nine,
60 Lawd, Lawd, an' the steam drill only made
      nine.

The hammer that John Henry swung,
It weighed over nine pound;
He broke a rib in his lef'-han' side,
An' his intrels[3] fell on the groun',
65 Lawd, Lawd, an' his intrels fell on the
      groun'.

All the womens in the Wes',
When they heared of John Henry's death,
Stood in the rain, flagged the eas'-boun'
      train,
Goin' where John Henry fell dead,
70 Lawd, Lawd, goin' where John Henry fell
      dead.

John Henry's lil mother,
She was all dressed in red,
She jumped in bed, covered up her head,
Said she didn' know her son was dead,
75 Lawd, Lawd, didn' know her son was dead.

Dey took John Henry to the graveyard,
An' they buried him in the san',
An' every locomotive come roarin' by,
Says, "There lays a steel-drivin' man,
80 Lawd, Lawd, there lays a steel-drivin' man."

---

3. **intrels** n. dialect for *entrails* (en´ trālz)—internal organs.

Close Reading Activities

READ

Comprehension

Reread all or part of the text to help you answer the following questions.

1. Who is the main character in this ballad?
2. With what does this character compete?
3. What tool does the main character use?
4. What happens to the main character in the end?

Research: Clarify Details Choose an unfamiliar detail from the ballad and briefly conduct research on it. Explain how your research clarifies the text.

Summarize Write an objective summary of the ballad. Remember that to be objective, a summary must be free from evaluation.

Language Study

Selection Vocabulary: Dialect Dialect is a version of a language, spoken in a given **region**. Using context, translate these dialect words from the ballad into standard English.

- lied (line 24)
- Jes' (line 39)
- done broke (line 53)

Literary Analysis

Reread the identified passage. Then, respond to the questions that follow:

> **Focus Passage** (ll. 36–55, p. 156)
> John Henry said . . . "like me."

Key Ideas and Details

1. Who or what has won the contest?

Craft and Structure

2. **(a) Analyze:** Describe John Henry's interactions with his shaker.

(b) Interpret: What kind of character do these interactions show John Henry to be?

3. **Draw Conclusions:** What does John Henry's reaction to the victory show about his reasons for challenging the drill?

Integration of Knowledge and Ideas

4. **(a) Connect:** What **aspects** of John Henry's character, shown in the passage, lead to his downfall? **(b) Interpret:** Explain what feelings his downfall inspires in readers.

Oral Tradition

The **oral tradition** consists of works that were originally passed on by word of mouth. Reread the ballad, taking notes on these **elements** of the oral tradition: repetition and exaggeration.

1. **(a)** Find two examples of repeated phrases. **(b)** Why is this repetition appropriate for a poem meant to be spoken aloud?

2. **(a)** Find two examples of exaggeration. **(b) Human vs. Machine:** What do these examples add to the picture of John Henry as a hero in the conflict with machines?

3. Cite a modern song or story that shares a theme, character type, or pattern of events with "John Henry." What does your choice show about the oral tradition?

DISCUSS • RESEARCH • WRITE

From Text to Topic **Panel Discussion**

Discuss the following passage in a panel discussion for the class. Panelists should take turns contributing ideas and supporting them with examples from the text.

> John Henry tol' his cap'n,
> Lightnin' was in his eye:
> "Cap'n, bet yo' las, red cent on me,
> Fo' I'll beat it to the bottom or I'll die,
> 15 Lawd, Lawd, I'll beat it to the bottom or I'll die."

Research **Investigate the Topic**

The Machine Age In the nineteenth century, during the Industrial Revolution, huge steam engines helped transform work. The engines were used to power everything from locomotives to factory machines. The rise of these machines had positive and negative effects.

Assignment

Conduct research on the rise of machines in the nineteenth century and its effects on the average worker. Consult both primary sources, such as letters from the time, and secondary sources, such as encyclopedias. Take clear notes and identify your sources. Record your findings in an **outline** annotated with relevant quotations.

Writing to Sources **Argument**

The story of John Henry has been retold in a variety of media.

Assignment

With your teacher's help and approval, view a film or cartoon version of "John Henry." Write an **evaluation** of how well this version interprets the original story.

- Introduce the topic and clearly summarize your evaluation.
- Then, discuss how faithful the production is to the original. Consider any changes to the plot, characters, language, or theme of the original.
- Support your claims with details about the performances in and visual style of the production, including the use of cuts and viewpoint.
- Provide a conclusion that sums up your points.

QUESTIONS FOR DISCUSSION

1. What does the passage indicate about John Henry's struggle?
2. What does his struggle suggest about the relationship between humans and machines?

PREPARATION FOR ESSAY

You may use the results of this research project to support your ideas in the essay you will write at the end of this section.

ACADEMIC VOCABULARY

Academic terms appear in blue on these pages. Use a dictionary to find their definitions. Then, use the words as you speak and write about the text.

 **Common Core State Standards**

RL.8.1, RL.8.2, RL.8.7, RL.8.9; W.8.1, W.8.1.b, W.8.7; SL.8.1, SL.8.4; L.8.6
[For full standards wording, see the chart in the front of this book.]

JULIE and the TURING TEST

Linda Formichelli

Julie likes tennis, hiking, Phil Collins, and *Lois & Clark*. A normal 14-year-old girl, right? Sure. Except that she's a computer program. *Julie* is part of an educational game based on *Phoenix Quest*, a novel by children's author Julie Lawson. The creation of **software** developer Richard Gibbons, *Julie* came in third in the 1997 Loebner Prize Competition in Artificial Intelligence. To recognize the most human-like program, this competition uses a variant—or slightly different form—of a test for **artificial intelligence** called the Turing test.

This test was developed in 1950 by Alan Turing, one of the pioneers of artificial intelligence research, to determine whether computers can think. In the Turing test, a judge is connected to one person and one machine via a computer terminal. The judge asks questions of each and uses the answers to decide which of the two candidates is the machine and which is the person. If she cannot decide within a certain time, the machine is considered intelligent.

At the 1997 contest in New York City, Technical Director George Lowe set up five PCs with the contestants' programs—of the five contestants, only first-prize winner David Levy was actually present—and connected a sixth to a person at another computer. Each of the five judges spent ten minutes conversing with each of the six computers. They tried to see, for example, if competitors could handle slang and sudden topic changes. All five judges correctly identified the human, and then ranked the programs from one to five based on how well they imitated human reasoning and conversation.

There's a reason so few programmers entered the competition. Imagine how hard it must be to develop a program that acts human: The program must be able to field any question that you can ask it. It has to recognize the many ways people have of saying the same thing. For instance, it must understand not

software ▶
(soft´ wer´) *n.* programs for a computer or computer system

artificial intelligence ▶
(ärt´ ə fish´ əl in tel´ ə jəns) *n.* the capability of computers to mimic human thought processes

only "How are you?", but also "How's it going?", "What's up?", and "What's new?" And it has to handle strange questions and slang, too: No choking when a judge asks, "What's your sign?"

To develop *Julie*'s character, Gibbons pored through *Phoenix Quest* and drew up a profile of *Julie*, from the things she likes to the common expressions she uses. Then, to develop her conversational ability, Gibbons took *Julie* into schools to see what kids would ask her. Then, he had to develop suitable responses. Making things even more difficult, here was a 24-year-old male trying to create the personality of a 14-year-old female. "However, these issues were not as significant as they might initially appear, because simply creating something 'human sounding' is very difficult," says Gibbons. "Spending time worrying about age and gender differences was like worrying about getting a sunburn when you're in the middle of a nuclear war."

If a computer can fool a person into thinking it's human, does this mean the computer really thinks like a human? "Right now, I think most of the successful artificial intelligence programs do not actually think," says Gibbons. "Instead, many of the AI programs like *Julie* simply look up information based on important phrases in statements people make. *Julie* sometimes seems human, but what she's actually doing is looking up information very quickly. So calling *Julie* 'intelligent' is like calling a person 'knowledgeable' when all he does is look up facts in an encyclopedia." George Lowe agrees: "It's not knowledge, but experience that makes us intelligent."

Experience isn't the only quality that makes us what we are, though. There are robots **wired** to react as a human would—for example, to pull back after touching something painful. What separates us from these robots? What other qualities must computers have before they can be considered more like humans? Emotion? Common sense? Artistic ability? Artificial intelligence programmers are still debating whether a computer can be like a person—but that hasn't stopped them from trying to create one with human intelligence.

Interested in trying to fool the judges? "Build a program and send it in," says George Lowe. "Anyone can enter. It doesn't cost anything, and you don't have to be at the competition."

Maybe you can pass Turing's test!

"It's not knowledge, but **EXPERIENCE** that makes us **INTELLIGENT**."

◀ **wired**
(wīrd) *adj.* having circuitry designed for performing particular tasks

READ

Comprehension

Reread all or part of the text to help you answer the following questions.

1. What is unusual about Julie?

2. What is the Turing test?

3. Name two challenges that make it difficult to create a program that can pass the test.

Research: Clarify Details Choose at least one unfamiliar detail in the selection and briefly conduct research on it. Explain how your research clarifies the text.

Summarize Write an objective summary of the article. Remember not to include your own opinions.

Language Study

Selection Vocabulary: Computer Science Define each boldface word from the text, and use it in a sentence of your own.

• The creation of **software** developer Richard Gibbons, *Julie* came in third. . . .

• . . . this competition uses a variant . . . of a test for **artificial intelligence**. . . .

• There are robots **wired** to react as a human would. . . .

Literary Analysis

Reread the passage identified. Then, respond to the questions that follow:

> **Focus Passage** *(p. 161)*
>
> If a computer . . . human intelligence.

Key Ideas and Details

1. Interpret: What point does Gibbons make in comparing *Julie* with a person?

Craft and Structure

2. The author asks several questions in the second paragraph of this passage, but she does not answer them. **(a) Interpret:** For what reason does she use this technique? **(b) Analyze:** How does she connect these questions to her topic in the final sentence of the paragraph?

Integration of Knowledge and Ideas

3. Gibbons says that artificial intelligence programs "do not actually think." **(a) Analyze:** Drawing on his statements, explain how he might define "thinking." **(b) Make a Judgment:** Explain whether you would agree with this definition.

Style

Style is the "sound" of someone's writing—it refers to the **distinctive** ways a writer uses words, including the types of words he or she chooses. Reread the article, and take notes on the author's style.

1. (a) Describe the author's style. For example, is it conversational or scholarly? **(b) Identify** two examples that support your evaluation.

2. Human vs. Machine: How might the style influence readers' views of the relationship between humans and machines?

DISCUSS • RESEARCH • WRITE

From Text to Topic **One-on-One Discussion**

Discuss the following passage with a partner. Take notes during the discussion. As you contribute ideas, support them with details from the text. Share the notes from your discussion with the class.

> What separates us from these robots? What other qualities must computers have before they can be considered more like humans? Emotion? Common sense? Artistic ability?

Research **Investigate the Topic**

Watson the Computer IBM has developed a computer that can do very well on game shows. It is called Watson, and its developers hope that it can be used for other applications in the future.

Assignment

Conduct research to find out what Watson has done, what it is **capable** of, and what it might do in the future. Consult online sources for information. You might also wish to interview an expert on artificial intelligence. Take clear notes and identify your sources so that you can retrieve the information later. Share your findings in a **short essay,** using specific examples to develop your points.

Writing to Sources **Explanatory Text**

The Turing test helps researchers in artificial intelligence set a goal—to create a program that can pass the test. However, opinions are divided on what exactly it can prove.

Assignment

Write an **explanatory essay** in which you explain what the Turing test is. Include sample questions of your own that a judge might ask on the test. Follow these steps:

- Introduce the test and describe how it works, drawing on details in the article.
- For each sample question you include, provide sample answers to clarify how humans and machines might respond.
- Provide a conclusion in which you reflect on what the Turing test can show about humans and machines.

QUESTIONS FOR DISCUSSION

1. Do you agree that the qualities listed by the author separate humans from machines? Explain.

2. What other qualities could be included?

3. What would it mean if a robot did exhibit the qualities listed?

PREPARATION FOR ESSAY

You may use the results of this research project to support your ideas in the essay you will write at the end of this section.

ACADEMIC VOCABULARY

Academic terms appear in blue on these pages. Use a dictionary to find their definitions. Then, use the words as you speak and write about the text.

Common Core State Standards

RI.8.2, RI.8.5; W.8.2, W.8.2.b; SL.8.1; L.8.4, L.8.6
[For full standards wording, see the chart in the front of this book.]

"The Good News, Dave, . . ." *by Chris Madden*

"The good news, Dave, is that the computer's passed the Turing test. The bad news is that you've failed. "

READ • DISCUSS • WRITE

Common Core State Standards

W.8.3.b, W.8.10; SL.8.1, SL.8.2
[For full standards wording, see the chart in the front of this book.]

Comprehension

Look at the cartoon again and reread the caption to help you answer the following questions.

1. Infer: What can you infer about the setting of this cartoon? Support your answer with details from the cartoon.

2. Hypothesize: What is the likely relationship between the two humans? Explain how you know.

Critical Analysis

Key Ideas and Details

1. Analyze: Given what you know about the Turing test, what is **illogical** about the second statement in the caption?

2. Interpret: What makes this cartoon funny?

Craft and Structure

3. (a) Analyze: Identify the parallelism—the use of similar phrases to express related ideas—in the caption. **(b) Evaluate:** In what way does the parallelism strengthen the impact of the cartoon?

Integration of Knowledge and Ideas

4. Interpret: What message about the difference between humans and computers does the cartoonist communicate?

ACADEMIC VOCABULARY

Academic terms appear in blue on these pages. Use a dictionary to find their definitions. Then, use the words as you speak and write about the text.

From Text to Topic **Class Discussion**

Discuss the cartoon and its message with classmates. Use the following discussion questions to focus your conversation.

1. What does the cartoon show about the **validity** of the Turing test?

2. What does it suggest about humans and machines?

3. How does the visual style of the cartoon influence your interpretation of it?

Writing to Sources **Narrative Text**

Write the **diary entry** that Dave might have written on the day of the cartoon. Narrate the day's events, including what happened before and after the scene shown. To pace your narrative,

- cover background information quickly.
- add more details just before the high point to keep readers guessing.

ROBOTS

Get a Feel for the World at USCViterbi

University of Southern California Viterbi

June 18, 2012

What does a robot feel when it touches something? Little or nothing until now. But with the right sensors, actuators, and software, robots can be given the sense of feel—or at least the ability to identify materials by touch.

tactile ▶
(tak´ təl) *adj.* related to the sense of touch

algorithm ▶
(al´ gə rith´ əm) *n.* a set of instructions given to a computer for solving a specific problem

thermal ▶
(thur´ məl) *adj.* having to do with heat or temperature

Researchers at the University of Southern California's Viterbi School of Engineering published a study today in *Frontiers in Neurorobotics* showing that a specially designed robot can outperform humans in identifying a wide range of natural materials according to their textures, paving the way for advancements in prostheses,[1] personal assistive robots, and consumer product testing.

The robot was equipped with a new type of **tactile** sensor built to mimic the human fingertip.

It also used a newly designed **algorithm** to make decisions about how to explore the outside world by imitating human strategies. Capable of other human sensations, the sensor can also tell where and in which direction forces are applied to the fingertip and even the **thermal** properties of an object being touched.

Like the human finger, the group's BioTac® sensor has a soft, flexible skin over a liquid filling. The skin even has fingerprints on its surface, greatly enhancing

---

1. prostheses (präs thē´ sēz´) *n.* artificial or mechanical replacements for body parts (plural of *prosthesis*).

its sensitivity to vibration. As the finger slides over a textured surface, the skin vibrates in characteristic ways. These vibrations are detected by a hydrophone inside the bone-like core of the finger. The human finger uses similar vibrations to identify textures, but the BioTac is even more sensitive.

When humans try to identify an object by touch, they use a wide range of exploratory movements based on their prior experience with similar objects. A famous theorem by 18th-century mathematician Thomas Bayes describes how decisions might be made from the information obtained during these movements. Until now, however, there was no way to decide which exploratory movement to make next. The article, authored by Professor of Biomedical Engineering Gerald Loeb and recently graduated doctoral student Jeremy Fishel, describes their new theorem for solving this general problem as "Bayesian Exploration."

Built by Fishel, the specialized robot was trained on 117 common materials gathered from fabric, stationery, and hardware stores. When confronted with one material at random, the robot could correctly identify the material 95% of the time, after intelligently selecting and making an average of five exploratory movements. It was only rarely confused by a pair of similar textures that human subjects making their own exploratory movements could not distinguish at all.

So, is touch another task that humans will outsource to robots? Fishel and Loeb point out that while their robot is very good at identifying which textures are similar to each other, it has no way to tell what textures people will prefer. Instead, they say this robot touch technology could be used in human prostheses or to assist companies who employ experts to judge the feel of consumer products and even human skin.

Loeb and Fishel are partners in SynTouch LLC, which develops and manufactures tactile sensors for mechatronic systems that mimic the human hand. Founded in 2008 by researchers from USC's Medical Device Development Facility, the start-up is now selling their BioTac sensors to other researchers and manufacturers of industrial robots and prosthetic hands. . . .

So, is touch another task that humans will outsource to **ROBOTS**?
· · · · · · · · · · · · · · · · •

READ

Comprehension

Reread all or part of the text to help you answer the following questions.

1. What type of sensations can the robot in the article "feel"?

2. What are the main parts of the sensor?

3. How does the sensor use vibrations?

4. List two uses for this technology.

Research: Clarify Details Choose an unfamiliar detail from the text and briefly conduct research on it. Explain how your research clarifies the text.

Summarize Write an objective summary of the article. Remember that to be objective, a summary must be free from opinion.

Language Study

Selection Vocabulary: Science Words
Define each boldface word from the selection. For each, use references to find at least one other word that shares the same root. Explain what meaning the two words have in common.

- The robot was equipped with a new type of **tactile** sensor. . . .
- It also used a newly designed **algorithm** to make decisions. . . .
- . . . the sensor can also tell . . . the **thermal** properties of an object. . . .

Literary Analysis

Reread the passage identified. Then, respond to the questions that follow:

> **Focus Passage** *(pp. 168–169)*
> Researchers . . . even more sensitive.

Key Ideas and Details

1. Compare and Contrast: According to the passage, how do the robot's abilities compare with those of a human?

Craft and Structure

2. (a) Analyze: Describe the relationship among the three paragraphs. Which is most general? Which most specific?
(b) Draw Conclusions: Why is the order of ideas here helpful to readers?

Integration of Knowledge and Ideas

3. Apply: In what kinds of situations might this technology be **beneficial**? Explain.

Comparisons

Writers may make comparisons to help readers follow their explanations. Reread the article, and take notes on the use of comparisons.

1. (a) Find two examples in which the writer makes a comparison with human beings.

(b) Why might these comparisons be helpful to readers?

2. Human vs. Machine: In making these comparisons, does the writer seem to claim that the robots function exactly as humans do? Explain, citing details from the text.

ROBOTS
Get a Feel for the World at USC Viterbi
University of Southern California Viterbi

DISCUSS • RESEARCH • WRITE

From Text to Topic **Debate**

Hold a debate on the following proposition: *Fishel's robot has a sense of touch, just as a human being does.* Participants should draw support from the facts in the passage below.

> When confronted with one material at random, the robot could correctly identify the material 95% of the time. . . . It was only rarely confused by a pair of similar textures that human subjects . . . could not distinguish at all. . . .
>
> [W]hile [the] robot is very good at identifying which textures are similar to each other, it has no way to tell what textures people will prefer.

Research **Investigate the Topic**

Neurorobotics The use of robots and artificial intelligence to study or aid the human nervous system is called *neurorobotics.*

Assignment

Conduct research on the history of neurorobotics, including recent advances. Consult reputable sources, including Web sites of organizations such as hospitals. Take clear notes and identify online images that will aid readers in understanding your points. Present your results in an **illustrated timeline.** In your timeline, **incorporate** graphics with appropriate captions.

Writing to Sources **Informative Text**

"Robots Get a Feel for the World at USC Viterbi" explains in detail the use of technology to closely **imitate** a human sense.

Assignment

Write a **comparison-and-contrast essay** in which you explain the similarities and differences between the BioTac® sensor and the human fingertip. Follow these steps:

- Reread the article, taking notes on the similarities and differences.
- Write a first draft, comparing and contrasting the two items.
- Review your writing, looking for places to strengthen the comparison by adding more details.

QUESTIONS FOR DISCUSSION

1. How do the robot's skills compare with those of humans?

2. Does the robot sense, just as humans do? Explain.

3. What does the passage show about what people can do that robots cannot?

PREPARATION FOR ESSAY

You may use the results of this research project to support your ideas in the essay you will write at the end of this section.

ACADEMIC VOCABULARY

Academic terms appear in blue on these pages. Use a dictionary to find their definitions. Then, use the words as you speak and write about the text.

 **Common Core State Standards**

RI.8.1, RI.8.2, RI.8.4; W.8.2, W.8.4, W.8.6, W.8.7; SL.8.1, SL.8.4
[For full standards wording, see the chart in the front of this book.]

from THE Measure OF A Man

FROM *STAR TREK:* THE NEXT GENERATION

Melinda M. Snodgrass

from ACT 5

SCENE 22 – INT. COURTROOM (OPTICAL)

Everyone in their original positions.

PICARD. (*making his opening statement*) Commander Riker has dramatically demonstrated to this court that Lieutenant Commander Data is a machine. Do we deny that? No. But how is this relevant? We too are machines, just machines of a different type. Commander Riker has continually reminded us that Data was built by a human. We do not deny *that* fact. But again how is it relevant? Does construction imply ownership? Children are created from the building blocks of their parents' DNA. Are they property? We have a chance in this hearing to severely limit the boundaries of freedom. And I think we better be pretty [. . .] careful before we take so arrogant a step. I call Lieutenant Commander Data to the stand.

DATA *returns to the witness stand.* PICARD *pulls from beneath the table the android's travel case. Places it on the table, opens it.*

PICARD. (*continuing; lifts out the case of medals, and displays the contents*) What are these, please?

DATA. My medals.

PICARD. Why pack them? What logical purpose do they serve?

DATA. I . . . I do not know, sir. None I suppose. I just wanted them. Is that vanity?

PICARD. (*holding up the book of sonnets*) And this?

DATA. It was a gift from you, sir.

PICARD. You value it?

DATA. Yes, sir.

PICARD. Why?

DATA. It is a reminder of friendship and service.

PICARD. (*lifts out the holocube, and triggers it;* TASHA *stands before them*) And this? You have no portraits of any other of your crewmates. Why this person?

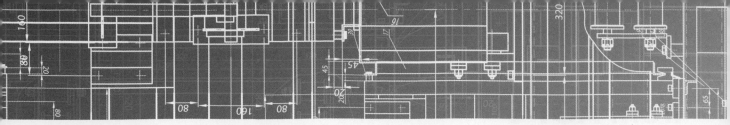

DATA. I would prefer not to answer that question, sir. I gave my word.

PICARD. Mister Data, may I remind you, that you are under oath. (*more gently now*) And under the circumstances, I don't think Tasha would mind.

DATA. (*swallowing convulsively several times*) She was important to me. . . .

PHILLIPA *is literally rocked back in her chair.*

PICARD. I have no further questions of this witness.

PHILLIPA. Commander Riker, do you wish to cross?[1]

RIKER. I have no questions, Your Honor.

PICARD. I call to the stand Commander Bruce Maddox as a **hostile** witness.

RIKER *and* MADDOX *confer, then with a shrug* MADDOX *seats himself in the witness chair.*

COMPUTER VOICE. Verify, Maddox, Bruce, Commander. Current assignment, Chair of Robotics, Federation Institute of Technology. Major papers—

PICARD. Enough. Suffice it to say, he's an expert. (*right up in his face*) Commander Maddox, it is your **contention** that Data is not a sentient[2] being and therefore not entitled to those rights reserved for all other life-forms in this Federation?

MADDOX. Data is not sentient, no.

PICARD. Why, Commander?

MADDOX. Because Data is a piece of outstanding engineering and programming.

PICARD. What is required for sentience?

MADDOX. Intelligence, self awareness, consciousness.

hostile ▶
(häs´ təl) *adj.* warlike; unfriendly; antagonistic

contention ▶
(kən ten´ shən) *n.* statement that one argues is true or valid

---

1. **cross** *v.* short for *cross-examine*; question a courtroom witness who was originally called to the stand by one's opponent.
2. **sentient** (sen´ shənt) *adj.* capable of having feelings and consciousness.

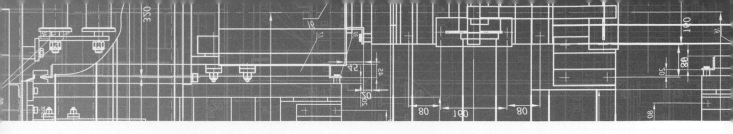

PICARD. Do you know what sentience is, Commander?

MADDOX. Of course.

PICARD. Excellent. Then you can enlighten the rest of us.

All of PICARD'S *delivery needs to be sharp and staccato.*

PICARD. (*continuing; right in* MADDOX'S *face*) Prove to this court that I'm sentient.

MADDOX. (*to* PHILLIPA) This is absurd!

PICARD. Why? Because you can't do it?

MADDOX. No, it's just pointless. We all know you're sentient.

PICARD. So I'm sentient, but Data isn't?

MADDOX. That's right.

PICARD. Why?

MADDOX. Well . . . well, you're self aware.

PICARD. Ah, the second ingredient. But let's deal with the first requirement. Is Data intelligent?

MADDOX. Yes?

PICARD. Why?

MADDOX. It has the ability to learn and understand, and to cope with new situations.

PICARD. Like this hearing. What about self awareness? What does that mean? Why am I self aware?

MADDOX. Because you are conscious of your existence and actions. You're aware of yourself and your own ego.

PICARD. Data, what are you doing now?

DATA. I am taking part in a legal hearing to determine my rights and status. Am I property or person?

PICARD. And what's at stake?

DATA. My right to choose. Perhaps my very life.

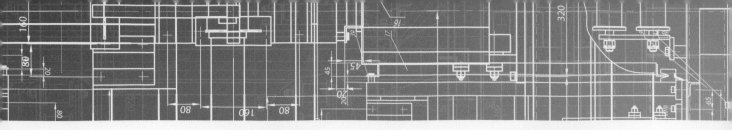

PICARD. *My* rights. *My* status. *My* right to choose. *My* life. He seems pretty [. . .] self aware to me. Well, Commander Maddox, I'm waiting.

MADDOX. This is exceedingly difficult . . .

PICARD. Do you like Data?

MADDOX. (*completely taken aback*) I don't know it well enough to like or dislike it.

PICARD. But you admire him?

MADDOX. Oh yes, it's an outstanding—

PICARD. (*interrupting*) Piece of engineering and programming. Yes, you've said that. You've devoted your life to the study of cybernetics in general?

MADDOX. Yes.

PICARD. And Data in particular?

MADDOX. Yes.

PICARD. And now you're proposing to dismantle him.

MADDOX. So I can rebuild him and construct more!

PICARD. How many more?

MADDOX. Hundreds, thousands. There's no limit.

PICARD. And do what with them?

MADDOX. Use them.

PICARD. How?

MADDOX. As effective units on Federation ships. As replacements for humans in dangerous situations. So much is closed to us because of our fragility. But they—

PICARD. (*interrupting; he picks up an object and throws it down a disposal chute*) Are expendable.

MADDOX. It sounds harsh but to some extent, yes.

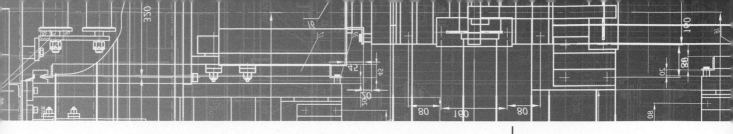

PICARD. Are you expendable, Commander Maddox? Never mind. A single Data is a curiosity, a wonder, but a thousand Datas, doesn't that become a new race? And aren't we going to be judged as a species about how we treat these creations? If they're expendable, disposable, aren't *we*? What is Data?

MADDOX. What? I don't understand.

PICARD. What . . . is . . . he?

MADDOX. (*angry now and hostile*) A machine!

PICARD. Is he? Are you sure?

MADDOX. Yes!

PICARD. But he's met two of your three criteria for sentience, and we haven't addressed the third. So you might find him meeting your third criterion, and then what is he?

MADDOX. (*driven to his limit*) I don't know. I don't know!

SCENE 22A – ANOTHER ANGLE

Reaction shot from PHILLIPA.

PICARD. He doesn't know. (*to* PHILLIPA) Do you? That's the decision you're facing. Your Honor, a courtroom is a crucible. In it we burn away the egos, the selfish desires, the half-truths, until we're left with the pure product—a truth—for all time. Sooner or later it's going to happen. This man or others like him are going to succeed in replicating Data. And then we have to decide—what are they? And how will we treat these creations of our genius? The decision you reach here today stretches far beyond this android and this courtroom. It will reveal the kind of a people *we* are. And what (*points to* DATA) . . . *they* are going to be. Do you **condemn** them to slavery? Starfleet was founded to seek out *new life*. (*indicating* DATA) Well, there he sits, Your Honor, waiting on our decision. You have a chance to *make* law. Well, let's make a good one. Let us be wise.

> And aren't we going to be judged as a species about how we treat these creations?

◀ **condemn**
(kən dem′) *v.* inflict a penalty upon; convict

PHILLIPA. It sits there looking at me, and I don't know what it is. This case has dealt with metaphysics, with questions best left to saints and philosophers. I'm neither competent nor qualified to answer those. I've got to make a ruling, to try to speak to the future. Is Data a machine? Yes. Is he the property of Starfleet? No. We've all been dancing around the basic issue: Does Data have a soul? I don't know that he has. I don't know that I have. But I've got to give him the freedom to explore that question himself. It is the ruling of this court that Lieutenant Commander Data has the freedom to choose.

The courtroom erupts in joy. PHILLIPA *starts to leave then crosses to* PICARD.

PHILLIPA. (*continuing*) You see, sometimes it works.

PICARD *watches her walk away, conflicting emotions washing across his face.*

SCENE 22B – ANOTHER ANGLE

DATA *walks to* MADDOX, *who is looking confused, guilty, and sad.*

DATA. Continue your work, Commander, and when you are ready I will still be here.

MADDOX. You'd be willing after what I've put you through?

DATA. Yes, it would be a less lonely universe if there were more of my kind.

PHILLIPA *comes up unnoticed by* DATA *and* MADDOX.

MADDOX. (*watching* DATA *walk away*) He's remarkable.

PHILLIPA. You didn't call him "it."

MADDOX *looks startled, then smiles.*

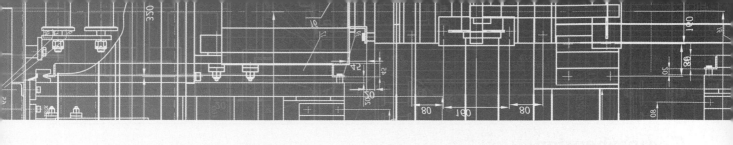

SCENE 23 – INT. OBSERVATION LOUNGE (OPTICAL)

RIKER *sitting alone in the darkness, staring out the windows as the stars rush past.* DATA *enters.* RIKER *does not turn.*

DATA. Sir, there is a celebration on the Holodeck.

RIKER. I have no right to be there.

DATA. (*edging closer*) Because you failed in your task?

RIKER. (*slewing around in his chair at that*) No [. . .]. Data, I came this close to winning.

    RIKER *indicates a bare inch with thumb and forefinger.*

DATA. Yes, sir.

RIKER. (*in agony just remembering*) I could have cost you your life!

DATA. (*moving in, and seating himself opposite* RIKER) Yes, that is true, but Commander . . . Will, I have learned from your experience.

RIKER. What could you have possibly learned from this kind of ordeal?

DATA. That at times one must deny his or her nature, sacrifice his or her own personal beliefs to protect another. Is it not true that had you refused to prosecute, Captain Louvois would have ruled summarily[3] against me?

RIKER. Yes.

DATA. That action injured you, and saved me. I will not forget.

RIKER. (*taking his hand*) You're a wise man, my friend.

DATA. Not yet, sir, but with your help I am learning.

    RIKER *clasps* DATA'S *shoulder, squeezes, as they shake hands, and we:*

    FADE OUT.

---

3. **ruled summarily** (sə mer′ ə lē) decided without the benefit of a trial.

READ

Comprehension

Reread all or part of the text to help you answer the following questions.

1. What is the main setting of the script?

2. List the main characters, and explain their roles.

3. What is the question that is being debated?

4. Which side wins the debate?

Research: Clarify Details Choose at least one unfamiliar detail from the TV script and briefly conduct research on it. Explain how your research clarifies the text.

Summarize Write an objective summary of the script. Remember not to include your own opinions.

Language Study

Selection Vocabulary Define the meaning of each boldface word from the selection. Then, identify another form of the word. (For example, give the noun form of a verb or adjective.)

- I call to the stand Commander Bruce Maddox as a **hostile** witness.

- . . . it is your **contention** . . . ?

- Do you **condemn** them to slavery?

Literary Analysis

Reread the passage identified. Then, respond to the questions that follow:

> **Focus Passage** *(pp. 175–176)*
>
> PICARD. So I'm sentient . . . or dislike it.

Key Ideas and Details

1. **Interpret:** What conclusion is Picard driving toward with his questions? Cite details.

Craft and Structure

2. **(a) Infer:** Give an example of a question that Picard asks to make Maddox uncomfortable.

(b) Analyze: Explain whether he succeeds, citing textual details.

3. **Analyze:** What effect does Picard intend the repetition of *my* to have in the speech that begins "*My* rights"?

Integration of Knowledge and Ideas

4. **Draw Conclusions:** Why might Picard's questioning **technique** strengthen his chances of winning? Explain, citing examples.

Dialogue

The term **dialogue** refers to conversation between characters. Reread the TV script, and take notes on ways the author uses dialogue.

1. Find an example of dialogue that moves the action of the story along. Explain your choice.

2. **Human vs. Machine: (a)** Summarize the dialogue between Data and Riker. **(b)** What human feeling does Data express in the line, "That action injured you, and saved me. I will not forget"? **(c)** How does this line help justify the court's verdict?

DISCUSS • RESEARCH • WRITE

From Text to Topic **Panel Discussion**

Hold a panel discussion in which you discuss the following passage. Panelists should take turns contributing. Each should build on previous comments and support claims with examples from the text. Each panelist should conclude by giving an overall **evaluation** of the verdict.

> Is Data a machine? Yes. Is he the property of Starfleet? No. We've all been dancing around the basic issue: Does Data have a soul? I don't know that he has. I don't know that I have. But I've got to give him the freedom to explore that question himself.

Research **Investigate the Topic**

Androids Researchers have succeeded in building robots that, like Data, resemble humans—they are androids.

Assignment

Conduct research to determine how close science is to creating an android as sophisticated as Data. Note any cases in which sources differ, and evaluate whether they differ over the facts or over their interpretation of the facts. Take clear notes and carefully identify your sources. Present your findings in an **outline** in which you arrange your ideas and supporting details in logical order.

Writing to Sources **Argument**

In "The Measure of a Man," a court hears **arguments** over the nature and eventual fate of the android Data. The question of whether Data shares key characteristics with humans is a basic part of these arguments.

Assignment

Write an **argumentative essay** in which you take a stand on the following issue: *Is Data the equal of a human being in key respects?*

- Introduce the topic and clearly state your main claim.
- Develop your argument by clearly stating your own ideas of what the key characteristics of humans are.
- Support your claims with facts and evidence from the text.
- Provide a conclusion in which you sum up the points you made.

QUESTIONS FOR DISCUSSION

1. Does the judge make a clear, definite ruling? Why or why not?
2. Judging from the evidence, did the judge make the correct ruling? Explain.

PREPARATION FOR ESSAY

You may use the results of this research project to support your ideas in the essay you will write at the end of this section.

ACADEMIC VOCABULARY

Academic terms appear in blue on these pages. Use a dictionary to find their definitions. Then, use the words as you speak and write about the text.

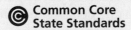 **Common Core State Standards**

RL.8.1, RL.8.2, RL.8.3, RL.8.4; RI.8.9; W.8.1, W.8.1.a, W.8.1.b, W.8.1.e, W.8.4, W.8.7; SL.8.1, SL.8.1.c, SL.8.4
[For full standards wording, see the chart in the front of this book.]

Speaking and Listening **Group Discussion**

Human vs. Machine and Conflict The texts in this section vary in genre and perspective. However, all of them comment in some way on the similarities and differences between humans and machines. These similarities and differences may lead to competition between humans and machines, raising the question of whether human beings could be "replaced" by machines. This topic is fundamentally related to the Big Question addressed in this unit: **Can all conflicts be resolved?**

Assignment

Conduct discussions. With a small group of classmates, conduct a discussion about the relationships of humans and machines and the conflicts they involve. To support your ideas, refer to the texts in this section, other texts you have read, and your personal experience and knowledge. Begin your discussion by addressing the following questions:

- What are some similarities between humans and machines?
- In what ways are humans and machines different?
- What are some conflicts between humans and machines that have arisen in the past?
- What conflicts might occur in the future?
- Can these conflicts be resolved?

Summarize and present your ideas. After you have fully explored the topic, summarize your discussion and present your findings to the class.

▲ Refer to the selections you read in Part 3 as you complete the activities on this assessment.

Criteria for Success

✓ **Organizes the group effectively**
Appoint a group leader and a timekeeper. The group leader should present the discussion questions. The timekeeper should make sure the discussion takes no longer than 20 minutes.

✓ **Maintains focus of discussion**
As a group, stay on topic and avoid straying into other subject areas.

✓ **Involves all participants equally and fully**
No one person should monopolize the conversation. Rather, everyone should take turns speaking and contributing ideas.

✓ **Follows the rules for collegial discussion**
As each group member speaks, others should listen carefully. Build on one another's ideas, asking questions to connect ideas and acknowledging new information. Always support points and opinions with sound reasoning and evidence. Express disagreement respectfully.

USE NEW VOCABULARY

As you speak and share ideas, work to use the vocabulary words you have learned in this unit. The more you use new words, the more you will "own" them.

Writing Narrative

SL.8.1.a–d; W.8.3.a–e
[For full standards wording, see the chart in the front of this book.]

Human vs. Machine and Conflict The texts in this section explore relationships between humans and machines—including their conflicts. These conflicts can tell us much about what it means to be human.

> ## Assignment
>
> Write an **autobiographical narrative,** or a true story about your own life, in which you retell a conflict you had with or about a machine. In your narrative, introduce the situation. Narrate, in logical order, the events leading to the conflict. Conclude by reflecting on the meaning of the incident, including what it shows about humans and machines.

Criteria for Success

Purpose/Focus
✓ **Connects specific incidents with larger ideas**
Make meaningful connections between your experiences and the texts you have read in this section.

✓ **Clearly conveys the significance of the story**
Provide a conclusion in which you reflect on what you experienced.

Organization
✓ **Sequences events logically**
- Structure your narrative so that each event builds to the next.
- Use pacing to ensure narrative flow, spending more time telling the most interesting parts and less time on background.

Development of Ideas/Elaboration
✓ **Supports insights**
Relate the details of your narrative to a general insight.

✓ **Uses narrative techniques effectively**
- Use dialogue to let characters speak for themselves.
- Show readers who your characters are through their dialogue, their actions, and the reactions of others to them.

Language
✓ **Uses description effectively**
Use descriptive details to paint word pictures that help readers see settings and characters.

✓ **Uses transitions effectively**
Use transition words such as *then, meanwhile,* and *next* to show the relationship between events.

Conventions
✓ **Does not have errors**
Check to eliminate errors in grammar, spelling, and punctuation.

WRITE TO EXPLORE

Writing is a way to clarify what you feel and think. As you write your narrative, you may find your ideas about your story changing. By adjusting to shifts in your own ideas, you will improve your final draft.

Writing to Sources **Argument**

Human vs. Machine and Conflict The related readings in this section present a range of ideas about the relationship between humans and machines. They also raise important questions, including the following:

- What do machines and humans have in common? How do they differ? When are they in conflict?
- Is there a sense in which a machine can "replace" a human being?
- In what sense can a human being never be "replaced" by a machine?
- What does the difference between humans and machines show about what it means to be human?

Reflect on these questions, jotting notes on preliminary answers, and then complete the following assignment.

INCORPORATE RESEARCH

As you write your argument, refer to the research you conducted as you read the texts in this section. Choose appropriate details from your research to support your claims.

Assignment

Write an **argumentative essay** in which you defend a claim about what it means to be human, based on our similarities to, differences from, and conflicts with machines. Clearly state your claim, and then build support by analyzing the ideas and examples in two or more texts from this section.

Prewriting and Planning

Choose texts. Review the texts in this section. Select at least two that will provide strong material to support your argument.

Gather details. Use a chart like the one shown to gather details from the texts you have chosen.

Craft a working thesis, or claim. Review your notes, and then develop a central claim based on them, as in the chart below.

Text	Passage	Notes
"Who Can Replace a Man?"	"For if a machine had broken down, it would have been quickly replaced. But who can replace a man?"	The robot reveals a key distinction between humans and machines: Humans are irreplaceable individuals.
"Julie and the Turing Test"	"[Gibbons says] 'Julie sometimes seems human, but what she's actually doing is looking up information very quickly.'"	The author recognizes that humans have a kind of intelligence that is different from just looking things up.

Example Claim: What sets humans apart from machines is not the ability to do something better or faster, but a special kind of individuality and intelligence.

Answer counterclaims. For each point you will make to support your claim, note a possible objection to it. Plan to feature these counterclaims in your essay, along with your arguments refuting them.

Drafting

Structure your ideas and evidence. Create an outline of your main points. In your outline, list the evidence you will use to support each point.

Begin and end strongly. Write an introduction that clearly introduces your claim and distinguishes it from opposing claims. End with a conclusion that features a memorable restatement of your main points.

Address counterclaims. Review your notes on counterclaims. As you draft, discuss these counterclaims at appropriate points. Include a reasoned, well-supported response to each.

Use transitions. As you draft, use transitions to clarify the relationships between your claims and evidence or your claims and counterclaims.

Sample Transitions

in addition   *by contrast*   *therefore*   *however*

Revising and Editing

Review content. Highlight the support for each main point in a different color. Review highlights, and add more relevant evidence as needed.

Review style. Make sure you have maintained a formal style. Avoid informal usages such as using *you* to refer to people generally.

Informal: You already know you aren't a robot.

Formal: A person clearly knows that he or she is not a robot.

Common Core State Standards

W.8.1.a–e
[For full standards wording, see the chart in the front of this book.]

CITE RESEARCH CORRECTLY

Create a Works Cited list for your argument, following a standard style. Review your draft, and make sure you have included appropriately formatted citations for quotations and ideas not your own. (See the Conducting Research workshop in the front of this book.)

Self-Evaluation Rubric

Use the following criteria to evaluate the effectiveness of your essay.

Criteria	Rating Scale
Purpose/Focus Introduces a claim and distinguishes the claim from alternative or opposing claims; provides a concluding section that follows from and supports the argument presented	*not very … very* 1 2 3 4
Organization Organizes the reasons and evidence logically; uses words, phrases, and clauses to create cohesion and clarify the relationships among claims, counterclaims, reasons, and evidence	1 2 3 4
Development of Ideas/Elaboration Supports the claim with logical reasoning and relevant evidence, using accurate, credible sources and demonstrating an understanding of the topic or text	1 2 3 4
Language Establishes and maintains a formal style	1 2 3 4
Conventions Correctly follows conventions of grammar, spelling, and punctuation	1 2 3 4

Titles for Extended Reading

In this unit, you have read a variety of short stories. Continue to read on your own. Select works that you enjoy, but challenge yourself to explore new authors and works of increasing depth and complexity. The titles suggested below will help you get started.

INFORMATIONAL TEXT

Behind the Blue and Gray: The Soldier's Life in the Civil War

by Delia Ray

 Soldiers on both sides of the Civil War quickly learned about the hardships of army life. The first-person accounts in this **nonfiction** book provide special insight into the horrors of the Civil War experience.

Math Trek: Adventures in the Math Zone

by Ivars Peterson and Nancy Henderson

Jossey-Bass, 1999   EXEMPLAR TEXT ©

 In this **nonfiction** book, readers get to take a trip through an adventure park, stopping in each chapter to solve creative math puzzles and problems.

Lend Me Your Ears: Great Speeches in History

edited by William Safire   EXEMPLAR TEXT ©

William Safire, a speechwriter for President Nixon, introduces this book of exceptional wartime, political, and commencement **speeches.** Included is Winston Churchill's "Blood, Toil, Tears, and Sweat" speech, delivered at a dark moment for Britons, when their ally France was facing Nazi tanks, guns, and planes.

Chess for Kids

by Michael Basman

 In this **nonfiction** guide, International Master Michael Basman introduces one of the world's oldest games of strategy in simple, accessible language. Learn the rules, learn the techniques—learn to win!

LITERATURE

Robot Dreams

by Isaac Asimov

 This collection of twenty-one **science-fiction short stories** shows Isaac Asimov at his visionary best. Whether imagining the inner life of robots or life without bodies, this book provides fascinating and thought-provoking reading.

Robin Hood

by Angela Bull

 To some, Robin Hood—who steals from the rich to give to the poor—is a hero; to others, he is an outlaw. Read this **novel** to see how this crafty woodsman tries to solve one conflict while unintentionally creating others.

19 Varieties of Gazelle

by Naomi Shihab Nye

 This **poetry** collection brings together sixty of Nye's imagery-rich poems. Full of figs and olive trees, prayer and heartbreak, these poems capture the uniqueness of the Middle East and of the Arab American experience.

ONLINE TEXT SET

AUTOBIOGRAPHY
from **An American Childhood**
Annie Dillard

NARRATIVE ESSAY
Baseball Lionel G. García

SHORT STORY
The White Umbrella Gish Jen

Preparing to Read Complex Texts

Attentive Reading As you read on your own, ask yourself questions about the text. The questions shown below, and others that you ask as you read, will help you understand and enjoy literature even more.

When reading narratives, ask yourself...

Comprehension: **Key Ideas and Details**

- Can I clearly picture the setting of the story? Which details help me do so?
- Can I picture the characters clearly in my mind? Why or why not?
- Do the characters speak and act like real people? Why or why not?
- Which characters do I like? Why? Which characters do I dislike? Why?
- Do I understand why the characters act as they do? Why or why not?
- What does the story mean to me? Does it express a meaning or an insight I find important and true?

Text Analysis: **Craft and Structure**

- Does the story grab my attention right from the beginning?
- Do I want to keep reading? Why or why not?
- Can I follow the sequence of events in the story? Am I confused at any point? If so, what information would make the sequence clearer?
- Do the characters change as the story progresses? If so, do their changes seem believable?
- Are there any passages that I find especially moving, interesting, or well written? If so, why?

Connections: **Integration of Knowledge and Ideas**

- How is this story similar to and different from others I have read?
- Do I care what happens to the characters? Do I sympathize with them? Why or why not?
- How do my feelings toward the characters affect my experience of reading the story?
- Did the story teach me something new or cause me to look at something in a new way? If so, what did I learn?
- Would I recommend this story to others? Why or why not?
- Would I like to read other works by this author? Why or why not?

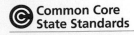

**Common Core
State Standards**

**Reading Literature/
Informational Text**
10. By the end of the year, read and comprehend literature, including stories, dramas, and poems, and literary nonfiction at the high end of the grades 6–8 text complexity band independently and proficiently.

How much information is enough?

UNIT PATHWAY

PART 1
SETTING EXPECTATIONS

- INTRODUCING THE BIG QUESTION
- CLOSE READING WORKSHOP

PART 2
TEXT ANALYSIS
GUIDED EXPLORATION

FACTS AND VISIONS

PART 3
TEXT SET
DEVELOPING INSIGHT

BELONGING TO A PLACE

PART 4
DEMONSTRATING INDEPENDENCE

- INDEPENDENT READING
- ONLINE TEXT SET

CLOSE READING TOOL

Use this tool to practice the close reading strategies you learn.

STUDENT eTEXT

Bring learning to life with audio, video, and interactive tools.

ONLINE WRITER'S NOTEBOOK

Easily capture notes and complete assignments online.

Find all Digital Resources at **pearsonrealize.com**

Introducing the Big Question

How much information is enough?

Every day, from the time we wake up until the time we go to sleep, we constantly encounter new **information**. Television, radio, the Internet, newspapers, magazines, books, and advertisements all compete for our attention. E-mail, text messages, online publications, and social media updates alert us to news from around the world even as it occurs.

However, if we are flooded with too many disorganized fragments of information, our brains may have trouble processing those jumbled bits into one useful whole. The challenge is to avoid possible information overload and to separate quality from quantity. One answer to this challenge may lie in the work that writers of literary nonfiction do—shaping bits of information into cohesive, understandable wholes.

Exploring the Big Question

Collaboration: Group Discussion Start thinking about the Big Question by identifying different types of information. Discuss with a group at least one example of information that would be important to someone in each of these situations:

- A historian writing a biography
- A defense attorney representing a client
- An emergency-room doctor receiving a patient
- A hiker exploring dry backcountry that is prone to fires
- A social scientist researching children's television-viewing habits
- A government official looking into complaints about racial or gender discrimination

Talk about why each type of information would be helpful and how you might evaluate its quality. As you participate in the discussion, listen to one another's ideas carefully and add your own observations and comments. Pose questions and respond thoughtfully to those asked by others. Respond respectfully to others' ideas while you clearly express your own.

Connecting to the Literature Each reading in this unit will give you additional insight into the Big Question: How much information is enough?

Vocabulary

Acquire and Use Academic Vocabulary The term "academic vocabulary" refers to words you typically encounter in scholarly and literary texts and in technical and business writing. Review the definitions of these academic vocabulary words.

Common Core State Standards

Speaking and Listening
1. Engage effectively in a range of collaborative discussions with diverse partners on *grade 8 topics, texts, and issues,* building on others' ideas and expressing their own clearly.

1.c. Pose questions that connect the ideas of several speakers and respond to others' questions and comments with relevant evidence, observations, and ideas.

Language
6. Acquire and use accurately grade-appropriate general academic and domain-specific words and phrases; gather vocabulary knowledge when considering a word or phrase important to comprehension or expression.

accumulate (ə kyo͞om´ yo͞o lāt´) *v.* collect; gather

challenge (chal´ ənj) *v.* call into question

decision (dē sizh´ ən) *n.* choice; person's determination that he or she will take a certain action

development (di vel´ əp mənt) *n.* 1. event; 2. growth

discrimination (di skrim´ i nā´ shən) *n.* 1. judgment; 2. unfair treatment based on particular differences

factor (fak´ tər) *n.* element that contributes to a condition or situation

global (glō´ bəl) *adj.* worldwide

reveal (ri vēl´) *v.* uncover; expose; show

statistics (stə tis´ tiks) *n.* numerical facts

Use these words as you complete Big Question activities that involve reading, writing, speaking, and listening.

Gather Vocabulary Knowledge Additional words related to information are listed below. Categorize the words by deciding whether you know each one well, know it a little bit, or do not know it at all.

explanation	inequality	quantity
exploration	quality	valuable

Then, do the following:

1. Write the definitions of the words you know.
2. Consult a dictionary to confirm the meaning of each word you know. Revise your definition if necessary.
3. Using a print or an online dictionary, look up the meanings of the words you do not know. Then, write the meanings.
4. If a word sounds familiar but you are not sure of its meaning, consult a dictionary. Then, record the meaning.
5. Use all of the words in a brief paragraph about the value of different types of information.

Close Reading Workshop

**Common Core
State Standards**

RI.8.1, RI.8.2, RI.8.4, RI.8.6;
W.8.2, W.8.7, W.8.9.b; SL.8.1
[For full standards wording, see
the standards chart in the front
of this book.]

In this workshop you will learn an approach to reading that will
deepen your understanding of literature and will help you better
appreciate an author's craft. The workshop includes models for
the close reading, discussion, research, and writing activities you
will complete as you study literature in this unit. After you have
reviewed the strategies and models in this section, practice your
skills with the Independent Practice selection.

CLOSE READING: **TYPES OF NONFICTION**

In Part 2 of this unit you will focus on reading various types of
nonfiction. Use these strategies as you read the texts.

Comprehension: **Key Ideas and Details**

- Read first to unlock basic meaning.
- Use context clues and reference works
  to help you determine the meanings of
  unfamiliar words.
- Identify unfamiliar details that you
  might need to clarify through research.

- Make inferences about information
  that is implied.

Ask yourself questions such as these:
- What is the central idea of the text?
- How is the text structured?

Text Analysis: **Craft and Structure**

- Think about why the author chooses
  either informal or formal language.
- Determine the author's purpose: to
  inform, persuade, narrate, or entertain.
- Analyze how the author develops
  ideas and uses supporting details.

Ask yourself questions such as these:
- What is the author's tone? What
  viewpoint does it help convey?
- Does the author acknowledge the
  viewpoint of others?

Connections: **Integration of Knowledge and Ideas**

- Look for relationships among key
  ideas. Identify causes and effects, as
  well as comparisons and contrasts.
- Look for the ways the author's viewpoint
  shapes the text.
- Compare and contrast this work with
  other works you have read.

Ask yourself questions such as these:
- How has this work increased my
  knowledge of a subject, an author, or
  a type of nonfiction?
- How is this nonfiction text similar to
  other texts I have read?

Read

As you read this excerpt from a nonfiction text, take note of the annotations, which model ways to closely read the text.

Reading Model

"We the People" from *Words We Live By*
by Linda R. Monk

We the People . . .

These first three words of the Constitution are the most important.[1] They clearly state that the people—not the king, not the legislature, not the courts—are the true rulers in American government. This principle is known as popular sovereignty.

But who are "We the People"? This question troubled[2] the nation for centuries. As Lucy Stone, one of America's first advocates for women's rights,[3] asked in 1853: "'We the People'? Which 'We the People'? The women were not included." Neither were white males who did not own property, American Indians, or African Americans—slave or free. Justice Thurgood Marshall, the first African American on the Supreme Court,[3] described this limitation:

> For a sense of the evolving nature of the Constitution, we need look no further than the first three words of the document's preamble: 'We the People.' When the Founding Fathers used this phrase in 1787, they did not have in mind the majority of America's citizens. . . .

> The men who gathered in Philadelphia in 1787 could not . . . have imagined, nor would they have accepted,[4] that the document they were drafting would one day be construed by a Supreme Court to which had been appointed a woman and the descendant of an African slave.

Through the Amendment process, more and more Americans were eventually included in the Constitution's definition of "We the People."[5] After the Civil War, the Thirteenth Amendment ended slavery, the Fourteenth Amendment gave African Americans citizenship, and the Fifteenth Amendment gave black men the vote. In 1920, the Nineteenth Amendment gave women the right to vote nationwide, and in 1971, the Twenty-sixth Amendment extended suffrage to eighteen-year-olds.

Key Ideas and Details

1 In her first sentence, the author states the main idea of the text: The first three words of this historic document are the "most important."

Craft and Structure

2 In this context, the word *troubled* means "disturbed." This word choice helps the author set up the conflict of beliefs examined in the text.

Key Ideas and Details

3 To illustrate the expanding definition of "We the People," the author cites the opinions of a famous woman and a renowned African American. They represent two groups of people originally denied the right to vote.

Craft and Structure

4 Monk quotes Marshall's description of the Founding Fathers' mindset to persuade people of the evolving nature of the Constitution. Marshall's standing as a Supreme Court justice gives his judgment authority.

Integration of Knowledge and Ideas

5 The author links her discussion of "We the People" to historical events. In this way, she suggests a vision of political progress—the definition of who "we" are broadens over time.

Discuss

Sharing your own ideas and listening to the ideas of others can deepen your understanding of a text and help you look at a topic in a whole new way. As you participate in collaborative discussions, work to have a genuine exchange in which classmates build upon one another's ideas. Support your points with evidence and ask meaningful questions.

Discussion Model

Student 1: Monk got me interested in this text right away when she mentioned the "first three words" of the Constitution. I wanted to know what the three words were and why she thought they were so important.

Student 2: Yes, me too. And it was skillful the way she used the phrase "We the People" to set up the main idea and organize the text. She posed a question—"But who are 'We the People'?"—and then explained the answer.

Student 3: I agree. I like the way that Monk repeats the phrase "We the People" and brings it up again at the end when she lists amendments that were passed to include more people in the voting process. I wonder how the groups she mentions—women and African Americans—gained the right to vote.

Research

Targeted research can clarify unfamiliar details and shed light on various aspects of a text. Consider questions that arise in your mind as you read, and use those questions as the basis for research.

Research Model

Question: *What strategies did American women use to win their voting rights?*

Key Words for Internet Search: women + voting + United States

Result: National Archives, "19th Amendment to the U.S. Constitution: Women's Right to Vote"

What I Learned: Women's struggle to gain the vote began in the mid-1800s. To protest their exclusion from the vote, women marched, engaged in hunger strikes, picketed, lobbied, lectured, and practiced civil disobedience. Some women's groups took the fight to the courts. Their efforts did not pay off until 1920, when women were finally granted the right to vote.

Write

Writing about a text will deepen your understanding of it and will also allow you to share your ideas more formally with others. The following model essay analyzes Linda Monk's discussion of a phrase in the United States Constitution, citing textual evidence.

Writing Model: Informative Text

Monk's Main Idea in "We the People" from *Words We Live By*

The United States Constitution is a long, detailed document; however, the excerpt from Linda R. Monk's *Words We Live By* focuses on just three of its words: "We the People." Posing the question "But who are 'We the People'?" Monk explains that our understanding of those three words has changed over time and so has our country. "We the People" has expanded to include groups, such as African Americans and women, who were once excluded from voting and governing. Now, these groups share in these basic rights.

Effective essays state the main idea in a thesis statement, or statement of the writer's main claim, placed in the introduction to help orient readers.

Monk begins by explaining the power of the phrase "We the People." Using this phrase, the Constitution gives the American people the right to determine the laws of the country. The people, "not the king, not the legislature, not the courts," are the real rulers of the country. This principle of democracy is what, at the time, made the United States unique.

The writer uses a quotation from the text as evidence of Monk's point of view.

Monk goes on to explain, though, that the meaning of "We the People" posed problems. Originally, it excluded many Americans. When the country was founded, only white men who owned property were allowed to vote.

Monk gives a voice to two of the excluded groups—women and African Americans—when she quotes Lucy Stone, a nineteenth-century women's rights leader, and Thurgood Marshall, the nation's first African American Supreme Court justice. Marshall explains that the Founding Fathers never meant to include the majority of Americans in "We the People."

The writer supports claims with specific details from the text. In this case, the writer notes that "We the People" originally referred only to white male landowners.

Both African Americans and women struggled for many years before they won the right to vote. Women, for example, protested, lobbied, and lectured for voting rights in the mid-eighteenth and early nineteenth centuries. More than 70 years later, they succeeded in their cause.

By incorporating information from research, the writer expands on the claims that Monk makes.

In the last paragraph, Monk reviews the history of how "We the People" expanded. She lists the amendments to the Constitution that gave the right to vote to African American men, then to women of all ethnicities, and finally to eighteen-year-olds. Her answer to the question "But who are 'We the People'?" seems to be "The answer changes over time to include more and more of us."

As you read the following text, apply the close reading strategies you have learned. You may need to read the journal entries multiple times.

Making Tracks on Mars
by Andrew Mishkin

NASA blasted two rockets into space in 2003. Sitting on top of them were Spirit *and* Opportunity, *robotic vehicles the size of golf carts called rovers. Their job was to look for water on Mars and collect data. The Mars Exploration Rovers traveled seven months and 303 million miles, and on January 3, 2004,* Spirit *was due to enter the Martian atmosphere.*

Monday, December 29, 2003
Six Days to First Landing

The big question about Mars is, did life ever exist there? Life as we understand it demands the presence of liquid water, yet Mars is now apparently a dead desert world. But what if things were different in the ancient past? From space, Mars looks as if once water might have flowed in rivers, collected in vast oceans, or pooled in crater lakes. The two robotic Mars Exploration Rovers will search for evidence of that water, potentially captured in the rocks and soil of the planet's surface. . .

Spirit, the first of the rovers to reach Mars, will be landing next Saturday night, January 3rd. "*Opportunity*" will follow three weeks later.

A British spacecraft—*Beagle 2*[1]—attempted its own Mars landing on Christmas Eve, but has been silent ever since. Landing on Mars is hard! I wish the *Beagle 2* team well, and hope they hear from their spacecraft soon. I cannot help but hope that our own landing goes more smoothly, with a quick confirmation from *Spirit* that it has arrived unscathed.

---

1. *Beagle 2* No definite cause was found for the loss of the robot space probe.

Meet the Author

Engineer **Andrew Mishkin** designs and develops robotic vehicles and their operating systems for NASA at its Jet Propulsion Laboratory. He was part of the team that created the *Spirit* and *Opportunity* rovers, which began exploring Mars in 2004.

Vocabulary ▶
confirmation (kän´ fər mā´ shən) *n.* something that confirms or proves

CLOSE READING TOOL

Read and respond to this selection online using the **Close Reading Tool.**

Saturday, January 3, 2004

Landing Day

Far away, so far that the signals it was sending were taking nearly 10 minutes at the speed of light to arrive at Earth, the spacecraft carrying the *Spirit* rover was about to collide with Mars.

I waited with a sick feeling, a hundred million miles closer to home in mission control at the Jet Propulsion Laboratory in Pasadena, California. Hundreds of us have worked for the past three years—days, evenings, weekends, and holidays—for this moment.

It's looking more and more like the *Beagle 2* mission has failed. I can only imagine wreckage strewn over a barren butterscotch-hued landscape. Will we have better luck?

Spirit's lander must be hitting the atmosphere, a falling meteor blazing in the Martian sky. We'd named the next moments "the six minutes of terror." I listened to the reports on the voice network. All the way down, radio signals from the spacecraft told us "so far so good." Then, immediately after the lander hit the ground, contact was lost. Everyone tensed up. Time dragged. There was only silence from Mars.

Ten minutes later, we got another signal. *Spirit* had survived! The engineers and scientists in mission control were screaming, cheering, thrusting their fists in the air. We were on Mars!

Two hours later, the first pictures arrived from *Spirit*. None of us could believe our luck. The rover looked perfect, with its solar panels fully extended, and the camera mast[2] fully deployed. All the engineering data looked "nominal."[3] There were no fault conditions—much better than any of our rehearsals!

In another minute or two, we had our first panoramic view through *Spirit*'s eyes. We could see 360 degrees around the rover, to the horizon. The landing site looked flat, with small rocks. We can drive here!

---

2. **camera mast** tall pole on which the camera is mounted, which rotates and swivels.
3. **nominal** normal; what is expected.

Sunday, January 11, 2004
Living on Mars Time

I just finished working the Martian night, planning *Spirit*'s activities for the rover's ninth Martian day on the surface. I've been working Mars time for the past four days, and now finally have a couple of days off.

The Mars day (called a "sol") is just a bit longer than an Earth day, at twenty-four hours and thirty-nine and a half minutes. Since the rover is solar powered, and wakes with the sun, its activities are tied to the Martian day. And so are the work shifts of our operations team on Earth. Part of the team works the Martian day, interacting with the spacecraft, sending commands, and analyzing the results. But those of us who build new commands for the rover work the Martian night, while the rover sleeps.

Since the rover wakes up about 40 Earth minutes later every morning, so do we. It seems like sleeping later every day would be easy, but it can be disorienting. It's very easy to lose track of what time it is here on Earth . . .

Thursday, January 15, 2004
Sol 12: Six Wheels on Dirt!

Mars time continues to be disorienting. During another planning meeting for *Spirit*, we were introduced to a Congressman touring the Laboratory. All I could think was, "What's he doing here in the middle of the night?" It was two in the morning—Mars time. Only after he left did I remember that it was mid-afternoon Pacific time . . .

My team delivered the commands for sol 12—drive off day— but nobody went home. This would be *Spirit*'s most dangerous day since landing. There was a small chance the rover could tip over or get stuck as it rolled off the lander platform onto the dust of Mars. When the time came, the Flight Director played the theme from *Rawhide*[4]—"rollin', rollin', rollin'. . ." —and everyone crowded into mission control cheered and applauded. The command to drive shot through space.

---

4. *Rawhide* popular 1960s television show about cattle drivers in the 1860s. Its theme song was also extremely popular.

We'll now have to wait another hour and a half to hear back. Engineers are professional worriers. We imagine all the ways things can fail, so that we can prevent those failures from occurring. But even when we've done our jobs, and considered all the alternatives we can come up with, there is always some doubt . . .

A signal. Applause. Then images started to appear. There was the lander—behind us! We could see tracks in the dirt. The front cameras showed nothing but Martian soil under our wheels. We were off! Engineers were cheering, applauding, and hugging each other. People were shaking my hand. The mission had just shifted from deployment to exploration.

Thursday, January 22, 2004
Sol 19

Something's wrong with *Spirit*. Yesterday, the rover didn't respond to the commands we sent. At first we thought it was just the thunderstorms at our transmitter in Australia, getting in the way. But later *Spirit* missed its preprogrammed communications times, or sent meaningless data. When your spacecraft is halfway across the solar system and won't talk to you, there's no way to tell whether this is a minor problem, easily fixed, or the beginning of the end of our mission. For *Spirit,* there's no repairman to make house calls.

And we've just barely gotten started!

Sunday, January 25, 2004
Ups, Downs, and Landing on Mars—Again

After a day of unsuccessful attempts to regain control of the rover, the project manager declared *Spirit*'s condition "critical." We tried commanding *Spirit* to send us simple "beep" signals that would prove it was listening to us. Sometimes these worked. But after one such attempt, we got no signal. The mood in the control room collapsed. The team forced itself into thinking about what to try next.

A few minutes later, there was a tentative, incredulous voice on the network: "Uh. Flight. Telecom. Station 63 is reporting carrier lock."[5] Engineers around the room looked up in surprise. "They're reporting symbol lock . . . We've got telemetry."[6] *Spirit* was back! The data coming down was **garbled**, but our girl was at least babbling at us. The mood in the room transformed again.

Thanks to extreme long distance diagnosis by the software engineers, *Spirit* was listening to us again within two days. We still have a lot of work to do. But at least we can now begin tracing the problem on a stable spacecraft.

In the meantime, *Opportunity* has been falling toward Mars. On Saturday night, those of us working on *Spirit*'s problems paused long enough to watch the landing events unfold. *Opportunity*'s first photos were amazing, even for Mars. It looks like we rolled to a stop at the bottom of a bowl—actually a small crater. The soil is a grayish red, except where we've disturbed it with our airbags; there it looks like a deep pure red. And while there are no individual rocks, we seem to be partly encircled by a rock outcropping—bedrock. No one has seen anything like this on Mars before. And it's only yards away. A scientist standing next to me in mission control said only one word: "Jackpot!"

Vocabulary ▶
garbled (gär′ bəld) *adj.* confused; mixed up

---

5. **carrier lock** stage of receiving information. Communication over a great distance involves locating the frequency of the carrier's signal, locking onto it, and holding it while information is received.
6. **telemetry** (tə lem′ ə trē) *n.* transmission of data over a great distance, as from satellites and other space vehicles.

Close Reading Activities

Read

Comprehension: Key Ideas and Details

1. (a) What is the mission of the two rovers? **(b) Generalize:** What discoveries do scientists hope to make?

2. (a) Infer: What is Andrew Mishkin's main purpose for writing about the mission?

(b) Analyze: Identify three elements of the text that reflect that purpose.

3. Summarize: Write a brief, objective summary of the journal excerpt. Cite journal details in your writing.

Text Analysis: Craft and Structure

4. (a) Distinguish: In the journal excerpt, find one example of formal, scientific language; one example of poetic language; and one example of informal language.
(b) Analyze: What does Mishkin's use of different types of language suggest about his point of view on the topic? Explain.

5. (a) Interpret: How does Mishkin personify *Spirit,* or give it human qualities? Cite specific

examples from the text. **(b) Speculate:** Why does he choose to personify the rover in these instances? In your answer, consider his purpose in writing.

6. Analyze: In his journal, Mishkin presents events in chronological order, or the order in which the events occurred. How does his choice of organizational structure suit his purpose?

Connections: Integration of Knowledge and Ideas

Discuss
Conduct a **small-group discussion** about the physical, mental, and emotional demands of being a NASA rover engineer. Use evidence from the journal to support your main points.

Research
Since 2004, NASA has landed several other rovers on Mars. Briefly research these rovers and their missions.

a. The *Phoenix* rover, launched in 2007
b. The *Curiosity* rover, launched in 2011

Take notes as you perform your research. Then, write a brief **explanation** comparing and contrasting the missions and findings of *Spirit, Opportunity, Phoenix*, and *Curiosity*.

Write
Literary nonfiction uses some of the same storytelling techniques as fiction to enliven a text. Write an **informative essay** in which you identify literary devices and effects, such as imagery (word pictures) and suspense, in "Making Tracks on Mars." Explain how these techniques enhance the text. Cite details from the text to support your analysis.

 How much information is enough?

Consider the information in the journal. Does Mishkin present the details in a way that is interesting to scientists, nonscientists, or both? Explain.

"'**We have facts**,' they say.
But facts are not **everything**—
at least **half** the business
lies in how you **interpret** them!"

—**Fyodor Dostoevsky**

FACTS AND VISIONS

As you read the selections in this section, note how the authors use facts to help build a vision of the world. By connecting visions to facts, the authors help people think about real-life issues in depth. The quotation on the facing page will help you start thinking about the power of facts, and of the authors' interpretation of them.

◀ **CRITICAL VIEWING** What types of facts might the people in the image be recording? What vision of the world might they build with these facts? What aspects of the situation might they be missing?

CLOSE READING TOOL

Use the **Close Reading Tool** to practice the strategies you learn in this unit.

Elements of Literary Nonfiction

Literary nonfiction discusses real people, places, and events while using literary techniques and expressing artistic insight.

Literary nonfiction is writing that describes real people, places, events, and ideas, but it employs the types of craft and artistry you are used to seeing in fiction or poetry. For that reason, it is sometimes called "creative nonfiction."

For example, in an account of a historic soccer game, an author might include conversations among players. Such use of **dialogue**—a technique you know from fiction—helps readers better understand the players' thoughts and feelings. In describing the game, the author might also build **suspense,** or a feeling of tension about what will happen next.

Works of literary nonfiction may focus on big topics, such as the causes of a war. Alternatively, they may focus on small topics, such as a moment in someone's life. Regardless of the topic, a literary nonfiction work expresses a **central idea,** or key point. It also conveys the author's unique **point of view,** or perspective, on the topic.

An author develops a central idea by presenting **supporting details** that add information. To help the reader understand the connections between ideas and details, the author presents them in a logical order. Sometimes, an author will follow a formal pattern of organization, such as one of the formats described in the chart below.

Common Organizational Patterns

Pattern or Structure	Description
Chronological Order	Presenting events in time order, or the sequence in which they occurred **Example:** the true story of a mission to Mars
Comparison and Contrast	Grouping elements of a subject according to their similarities and differences **Example:** a review of two different productions of a play
Cause and Effect	Presenting actions (causes) and their results (effects) **Example:** an explanation of a scientific experiment
Problem and Solution	Describing a problem and then explaining one or more ways to solve it **Example:** a proposal to build a new playground and park

Types of Literary Nonfiction

There are five main types, or modes, of literary nonfiction:

- **Narration:** Narrative texts tell the stories of real events.
- **Informative Text:** Informative texts provide information on a topic.
- **Argument:** Argumentative, or persuasive, texts convince readers to take an action or to think differently.
- **Reflection:** Reflective texts offer the author's insights into the meaning of a personal experience.
- **Explanatory Text:** Explanatory texts explain a process or provide direction.

Purposes of Nonfiction

In all types of nonfiction, an author writes for a **purpose,** or reason. Three main purposes are as follows:

- to **inform** or to **explain**
- to **persuade** or to argue
- to **entertain** or to amuse

Purpose and mode go hand in hand. For example, if an author's purpose is to inform readers about a new invention, he or she will write an informative work. The author may, however, combine other types of writing to fulfill that purpose. For instance, he or she might narrate the story of the invention's development and describe the invention in detail.

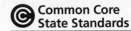
Common Core State Standards

Reading Informational Text

4. Determine the meaning of words and phrases as they are used in a text, including figurative, connotative, and technical meanings; analyze the impact of specific word choices on meaning and tone, including analogies or allusions to other texts.

5. Analyze in detail the structure of a specific paragraph in a text, including the role of particular sentences in developing and refining a key concept.

6. Determine an author's point of view or purpose in a text and analyze how the author acknowledges and responds to conflicting evidence or viewpoints.

Types and Examples of Nonfiction

Type (or Mode)	Example
Narration	an **autobiography** in which a senator tells the story of her life
	a **memoir** in which the author tells the story of an adventure
Informative	an **essay** in which a scholar explains the causes of the Civil War
	a **report** in which a scientist presents results
Argument	a **speech** in which a student tries to convince classmates to exercise daily
	an **editorial** in which the author protests a new law
Reflection	a **magazine article** in which a poet describes what he learned from a favorite teacher
	a **reflective essay** in which an artist discusses her sources of inspiration
Explanatory	a **manual** that provides guidance on building a personal computer
	a set of driving **directions**

Determining Point of View and Structure

A writer chooses a **structure** to develop concepts and convey a **point of view**.

Point of view is the perspective with which a writer sees a subject. It is shaped by the author's knowledge, beliefs, and experiences.

Stated or Implied Point of View

Sometimes, a writer simply states his or her point of view. More often, however, point of view is implied. The reader must infer—or make an educated guess about—the writer's point of view.

> **Stated Point of View:** As president of the Bike Club, I support bicycle lanes.
>
> **Implied Point of View:** I spent my childhood going on bike trips. One of my first words was *derailleur*.

Point of View and Position

Point of view is not the same as position. In fact, two people who support the same position may have different points of view.

Position: Students Should Wear Uniforms

School Principal	Student
Point of View: I am responsible for students' safety.	**Point of View:** I spend too much time on clothes.
Specific Position: If students wore uniforms, we could identify non-students more easily.	**Specific Position:** Uniforms would allow us to focus on our studies.

Opposing Points of View

When writers disagree about ideas, it may be due to differences in their viewpoints. In such cases, writers anticipate conflicts and address them directly.

> **Anticipating Conflicting Viewpoints**
>
> I know that some students disagree with me. They want to express themselves through their clothing.
>
> **Addressing Conflicting Viewpoints**
>
> I think, however, that most students agree that safety outweighs expression.

By acknowledging another point of view, the author demonstrates respect for others and builds a stronger argument.

Language and Tone

The words writers choose create a distinct **tone,** or emotional attitude. When choosing words, writers consider both **denotation,** or dictionary meanings, and **connotation,** or emotional associations. Sometimes, writers use **charged** or **loaded words** that convey strong emotion, as in the example below.

> **Example: Charged Words**
>
> Today we meet our oldest rivals, the Screaming Eagles. We will march onto the football field with strength, pride, and purpose. Cheer us on to victory!

Central Ideas and Paragraphs

Writers develop central ideas, or main points, by introducing related, or supporting, ideas and details. Supporting ideas and details are organized in paragraphs. Each paragraph focuses on a single concept.

Topic Sentences Paragraphs usually function in the same way as the work as a whole. Each paragraph contains a main idea, which may be expressed in a topic sentence. Every sentence within the paragraph then helps to develop that main point.

Types of Support Writers develop ideas by using varied types of evidence.

- **Facts:** statements that can be proved
- **Opinions:** beliefs that may or may not be based on fact
- **Reasons:** statements that justify or explain opinions
- **Examples:** specific cases that illustrate general ideas
- **Descriptions:** details that show how something looks, sounds, feels, or tastes
- **Anecdotes:** brief stories that illustrate a concept

In the example shown here, the author states a main idea and then develops it with both a fact and an example.

Example: Types of Support

[Main Idea] In general, good students spend more time on homework. *[Fact]* A survey of middle school students shows that an "A" student spends at least two hours on homework each day. *[Example]* For example, my son spent three hours last night studying for a math test.

Forms of Explanation
Writers can explain ideas using various elements.

- **Definition:** a statement of the meaning of a key term
- **Explanation:** an account of the relationship between facts or ideas
- **Analogy:** an extended comparison that may help readers understand something unfamiliar by comparing it to something familiar
- **Allusion:** a reference to a character from literature, a historical event, a song lyric, and so on that may help readers understand a writer's ideas

Language Structures Language structures called **rhetorical devices** help writers emphasize ideas.

- **Repetition:** reuse of a key word, phrase, or idea
  Example: Eat fruit. Eat vegetables. Eat lean meat. Eat well.
- **Parallel Structure:** use of similar grammatical structures to express related ideas
  Example: We will show our strength and prove our talent.
- **Rhetorical Questions:** questions asked for effect, where the answer is assumed to be obvious
  Example: Are we to stand idly by while our park is ruined?

Structure and Author's Purpose

A writer's structural choices help to achieve his or her purpose for writing by shaping the reader's view of the topic. As you read literary nonfiction, ask yourself questions such as these: *Why does the author open with an anecdote? Why does he or she put this point first?* Use your answers to better understand the author's purpose.

How much information is enough?

Explore the Big Question as you read "Harriet Tubman: Conductor on the Underground Railroad." Take notes on the type of information you learn about Harriet Tubman.

CLOSE READING FOCUS

Key Ideas and Details: **Main Idea**

The **main idea** of a work is the central point the author conveys. Sometimes, the author directly states the main idea. Often, however, the author only implies, or suggests, the main idea.

To identify the **implied main idea**, look for *connections*, or links, between details. For example, in an essay about a family vacation, you might learn that the writer's sister was silent and shaking on a plane ride, while the writer's brother enjoyed flying but feared driving. The connections among these details help you see the main idea: The writer's family has various fears of travel.

Craft and Structure: **Narrative Essay**

A **narrative essay** tells the story of real events and people. Narrative essays and fictional stories share features like these:

• They relate a series of events in logical order.
• Characters' personalities may be *developed*, or revealed, through their words, actions, and thoughts.
• The *setting*, or time and place of the action, may create a specific mood. It may also tell something about characters' background or their situation.

As you read, note details that establish character and setting.

Vocabulary

Copy the words from the essay into your notebook. Which word might share a root meaning "change" with a word from mathematics? Explain your thinking.

invariably	fugitives	incentive
dispel	mutinous	bleak

Meet the Author

Ann Petry (1908–1997) was the first African American woman to publish a best-selling novel—her book *The Street* sold more than a million copies. Petry's grandfather Willis James was a fugitive who had escaped slavery in Virginia and settled in Connecticut in the 1800s. Petry's parents encouraged Petry to be confident and proud of her heritage by telling stories of her ancestors. These stories later helped Petry capture the voices of history in her own writing.

© **Common Core State Standards**

Reading Informational Text
2. Determine a central idea of a text and analyze its development over the course of the text, including its relationship to supporting ideas.
3. Analyze how a text makes connections among and distinctions between individuals, ideas, or events.

Language
6. Acquire and use accurately grade-appropriate general academic and domain-specific words and phrases; gather vocabulary knowledge when considering a word or phrase important to comprehension or expression.

CLOSE READING MODEL

The passage below is from Ann Petry's narrative essay "Harriet Tubman: Conductor on the Underground Railroad." The annotations to the right of the passage show ways in which you can use close reading skills to identify the main idea and analyze a narrative essay.

from "Harriet Tubman: Conductor on the Underground Railroad"

When she knocked on the door of a farmhouse, a place where she and her parties of runaways had always been welcome, always been given shelter and plenty to eat, there was no answer.[1] She knocked again, softly. A voice from within said, "Who is it?" There was fear in the voice.[2]

She knew instantly from the sound of the voice that there was something wrong. She said, "A friend with friends," the password on the Underground Railroad.

The door opened, slowly. The man who stood in the doorway looked at her coldly, looked with unconcealed astonishment and fear at the eleven disheveled runaways who were standing near her. Then he shouted, "Too many, too many. It's not safe. My place was searched last week. It's not safe!" and slammed the door in her face.[3]

She turned away from the house, frowning. She had promised her passengers food and rest and warmth, and instead of that, there would be hunger and cold and more walking over the frozen ground. Somehow she would have to instill courage into these eleven people, most of them strangers, would have to feed them on hope and bright dreams of freedom instead of the fried pork and corn bread and milk she had promised them.[4]

Narrative Essay

1 The setting—a farmhouse—is clearly identified. The references to "runaways" and to the unanswered knock hint at danger in the setting.

Narrative Essay

2 The description of the voice ("There was fear in the voice") helps indicate character and makes it easier for readers to imagine the situation vividly.

Main Idea

3 The author writes that the man looked at the runaways with "unconcealed astonishment and fear." He tells them to leave, and he slams the door. These details reveal that helping runaway slaves was a dangerous business. As you continue reading, you can link this idea to others to determine the main idea of the essay.

Narrative Essay

4 This sentence suggests the woman's inner thoughts. These thoughts help to develop, or reveal, her character: She is a strong leader who is determined to give others courage in the face of difficulty and hardship.

from Harriet Tubman:
Conductor on the Underground Railroad

Ann Petry

The Railroad Runs to Canada

Along the Eastern Shore of Maryland, in Dorchester County, in Caroline County, the masters kept hearing whispers about the man named Moses, who was running off slaves. At first they did not believe in his existence. The stories about him were fantastic, unbelievable. Yet they watched for him. They offered rewards for his capture.

They never saw him. Now and then they heard whispered rumors to the effect that he was in the neighborhood. The woods were searched. The roads were watched. There was never anything to indicate his whereabouts. But a few days afterward, a goodly number of slaves would be gone from the plantation. Neither the master nor the overseer had heard or seen anything unusual in the quarter. Sometimes one or the other would vaguely remember having heard a whippoorwill call somewhere in the woods, close by, late at night. Though it was the wrong season for whippoorwills.

Sometimes the masters thought they had heard the cry of a hoot owl, repeated, and would remember having thought that the intervals between the low moaning cry were wrong, that it had been repeated four times in succession instead of three. There was never anything more than that to suggest that all was not well in the quarter. Yet when morning came, they **invariably** discovered that a group of the finest slaves had taken to their heels.

Unfortunately, the discovery was almost always made on a Sunday. Thus a whole day was lost before the machinery of pursuit could be set in motion. The posters offering rewards for the **fugitives** could not be printed until Monday. The men who made a living hunting for runaway slaves were out of reach, off in the woods with their dogs and their guns, in pursuit of four-footed game, or they were in camp meetings[1] saying their prayers with their wives and families beside them.

Harriet Tubman could have told them that there was far more involved in this matter of running off slaves than signaling the would-be runaways by imitating the call of a whippoorwill, or a hoot owl, far more involved than a matter of waiting for a clear night when the North Star was visible.

In December, 1851, when she started out with the band of fugitives that she planned to take to Canada, she had been in the vicinity of the plantation for days, planning the trip, carefully selecting the slaves that she would take with her.

She had announced her arrival in the quarter by singing the forbidden spiritual[2]—"Go down, Moses, 'way down to Egypt Land"—singing it softly outside the door of a slave cabin, late at night. The husky voice was beautiful even when it was barely more than a murmur borne on the wind.

Once she had made her presence known, word of her coming spread from cabin to cabin. The slaves whispered

◄ **Vocabulary**
invariably (in ver´ ē ə blē) *adv.* all the time; always

fugitives (fyo͞o´ ji tivz) *n.* people fleeing from danger

Comprehension
What does Harriet Tubman do?

---

1. **camp meetings** religious meetings held outdoors or in a tent.
2. **forbidden spiritual** In 1831, a slave named Nat Turner encouraged an unsuccessful slave uprising by talking about the biblical story of the Israelites' escape from Egypt. Afterward, the singing of certain spirituals, songs based on the Bible, was forbidden for fear of encouraging more uprisings.

to each other, ear to mouth, mouth to ear, "Moses is here." "Moses has come." "Get ready. Moses is back again." The ones who had agreed to go North with her put ashcake and salt herring in an old bandanna, hastily tied it into a bundle, and then waited patiently for the signal that meant it was time to start. ●

There were eleven in this party, including one of her brothers and his wife. It was the largest group that she had ever conducted, but she was determined that more and more slaves should know what freedom was like.

She had to take them all the way to Canada. The Fugitive Slave Law was no longer a great many incomprehensible words written down on the country's lawbooks. The new law had become a reality. It was Thomas Sims, a boy, picked up on the streets of Boston at night and shipped back to Georgia. It was Jerry and Shadrach, arrested and jailed with no warning.

She had never been in Canada. The route beyond Philadelphia was strange to her. But she could not let the runaways who accompanied her know this. As they walked along she told them stories of her own first flight, she kept painting vivid word pictures of what it would be like to be free.

But there were so many of them this time. She knew moments of doubt when she was half-afraid, and kept looking back over her shoulder, imagining that she heard the sound of pursuit. They would certainly be pursued. Eleven of them. Eleven thousand dollars' worth of flesh and bone and muscle that belonged to Maryland planters. If they were caught, the eleven runaways would be whipped and sold South, but she—she would probably be hanged.

They tried to sleep during the day but they never could wholly relax into sleep. She could tell by the positions they assumed, by their restless movements. And they walked at night. Their progress was slow. It took them three nights of walking to reach the first stop. She had told them about the place where they would stay, promising warmth and good food, holding these things out to them as an **incentive** to keep going.

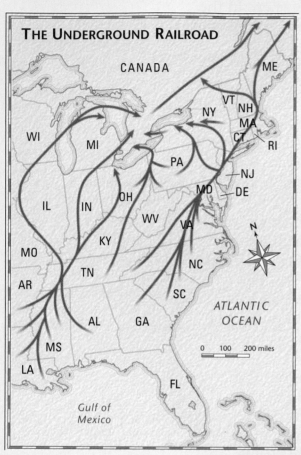

THE UNDERGROUND RAILROAD

▲ Critical Viewing
What does the map show?

Main Idea
What new details about Tubman do you learn here?

Vocabulary ▶
incentive (in sent´ iv) *n.* something that makes a person take action

When she knocked on the door of a farmhouse, a place where she and her parties of runaways had always been welcome, always been given shelter and plenty to eat, there was no answer. She knocked again, softly. A voice from within said, "Who is it?" There was fear in the voice.

She knew instantly from the sound of the voice that there was something wrong. She said, "A friend with friends," the password on the Underground Railroad.

▼ **Critical Viewing**
Describe how it might feel to be one of eleven escaped slaves hiding in this attic on the Underground Railroad.

The door opened, slowly. The man who stood in the doorway looked at her coldly, looked with unconcealed astonishment and fear at the eleven disheveled runaways who were standing near her. Then he shouted, "Too many, too many. It's not safe. My place was searched last week. It's not safe!" and slammed the door in her face.

She turned away from the house, frowning. She had promised her passengers food and rest and warmth, and instead of that, there would be hunger and cold and more walking over the frozen ground. Somehow she would have to instill courage into these eleven people, most of them strangers, would have to feed them on hope and bright dreams of freedom instead of the fried pork and corn bread and milk she had promised them.

They stumbled along behind her, half-dead for sleep, and she urged them on, though she was as tired and as discouraged as they were. She had never been in Canada but she kept painting wondrous word pictures of what it would be like. She managed to dispel their fear of pursuit, so that they would not become hysterical, panic-stricken. Then she had to bring some of the fear back, so that they would stay awake and keep walking though they drooped with sleep. ●

Yet during the day, when they lay down deep in a thicket, they never really slept, because if a twig snapped or the wind sighed in the branches of a pine tree, they jumped to their feet, afraid of their own shadows, shivering and shaking. It was very cold, but they dared not make fires because someone would see the smoke and wonder about it.

◀ **Vocabulary**
dispel (di spel′) v. cause (something) to go away

Comprehension
Why does the man slam the door in Tubman's face?

Main Idea
What main idea is implied by Tubman's thoughts at the beginning of this paragraph?

▼ **Critical Viewing**
Judging from the text and this photo of a secret tunnel entrance under an Ohio tavern, what physical sensations and emotions do you think the fugitives would have experienced hiding in the "stations"?

She kept thinking, eleven of them. Eleven thousand dollars' worth of slaves. And she had to take them all the way to Canada. Sometimes she told them about Thomas Garrett, in Wilmington. She said he was their friend even though he did not know them. He was the friend of all fugitives. He called them God's poor. He was a Quaker and his speech was a little different from that of other people. His clothing was different, too. He wore the wide-brimmed hat that the Quakers wear.

She said that he had thick white hair, soft, almost like a baby's, and the kindest eyes she had ever seen. He was a big man and strong, but he had never used his strength to harm anyone, always to help people. He would give all of them a new pair of shoes. Everybody. He always did. Once they reached his house in Wilmington, they would be safe. He would see to it that they were.

She described the house where he lived, told them about the store where he sold shoes. She said he kept a pail of milk and a loaf of bread in the drawer of his desk so that he would have food ready at hand for any of God's poor who should suddenly appear before him, fainting with hunger. There was a hidden room in the store. A whole wall swung open, and behind it was a room where he could hide fugitives. On the wall there were shelves filled with small boxes—boxes of shoes—so that you would never guess that the wall actually opened.

While she talked, she kept watching them. They did not believe her. She could tell by their expressions. They were thinking. New shoes, Thomas Garrett, Quaker, Wilmington—what foolishness was this? Who knew if she told the truth? Where was she taking them anyway?

That night they reached the next stop—a farm that belonged to a German. She made the runaways take shelter behind trees at the edge of the fields before she knocked at the door. She hesitated before she approached the door, thinking, suppose that he, too, should refuse shelter, suppose— Then she thought, Lord, I'm going to hold steady on to You and You've got to see me through—and knocked softly.

She heard the familiar guttural voice say, "Who's there?"

She answered quickly, "A friend with friends."

He opened the door and greeted her warmly. "How many this time?" he asked.

"Eleven," she said and waited, doubting, wondering.

He said, "Good. Bring them in."

He and his wife fed them in the lamplit kitchen, their faces glowing, as they offered food and more food, urging them to eat, saying there was plenty for everybody, have more milk, have more bread, have more meat. ●

They spent the night in the warm kitchen. They really slept, all that night and until dusk the next day. When they left, it was with reluctance. They had all been warm and safe and well-fed. It was hard to exchange the security offered by that clean, warm kitchen for the darkness and the cold of a December night.

"Go On or Die"

Harriet had found it hard to leave the warmth and friendliness, too. But she urged them on. For a while, as they walked, they seemed to carry in them a measure of contentment; some of the serenity and the cleanliness of that big warm kitchen lingered on inside them. But as they walked farther and farther away from the warmth and the light, the cold and the darkness entered into them. They fell silent, sullen, suspicious. She waited for the moment when some one of them would turn **mutinous**. It did not happen that night.

Two nights later she was aware that the feet behind her were moving slower and slower. She heard the irritability in their voices, knew that soon someone would refuse to go on.

She started talking about William Still and the Philadelphia Vigilance Committee.[3] No one commented. No one asked any questions. She told them the story of William and Ellen Craft and how they escaped from Georgia. Ellen was so fair that she looked as though she were white, and so she dressed up in a man's clothing and she looked like a wealthy young planter. Her husband, William, who was dark, played the role of her slave. Thus they traveled from Macon, Georgia, to Philadelphia, riding on the trains, staying at the finest hotels. Ellen pretended to be very ill—her right arm was in a sling, and her right hand was bandaged, because she was supposed to have rheumatism. Thus she avoided having to sign the register at the hotels for she could not read or write. They finally arrived safely in Philadelphia, and then went on to Boston.

---

3. **Philadelphia Vigilance Committee** group of citizens that helped escaped slaves. Its secretary was a free black man named William Still.

Narrative Essay
What elements of the setting contribute to the action of the plot here?

◄ **Vocabulary**
mutinous (my$\overline{oo}$t´ ən əs) *adj.* rebellious

Narrative Essay
Tubman tells a narrative of her own here. Why does she tell the story of these real people?

Comprehension
What does Tubman fear the fugitives might do?

History Connection

Frederick Douglass: Fighter for Freedom

Born into slavery in Maryland in 1818, Frederick Douglass learned to read even though it was against the law. Twenty years later, he fled north, and in 1845 wrote his autobiography, which made him the most famous and visible African American spokesperson of the nineteenth century. Douglass began publishing the influential antislavery newspaper North Star shortly afterward.

He also became an inspiring speaker who spoke out against slavery before the Civil War. Douglass continued to fight for African American civil rights, for women's rights, and on behalf of the poor until his death in 1895.

Connect to the Literature

Why do you think Harriet Tubman chose to tell the slaves about Frederick Douglass on their journey north?

No one said anything. Not one of them seemed to have heard her.

She told them about Frederick Douglass, the most famous of the escaped slaves, of his eloquence, of his magnificent appearance. Then she told them of her own first vain effort at running away, evoking the memory of that miserable life she had led as a child, reliving it for a moment in the telling.

But they had been tired too long, hungry too long, afraid too long, footsore too long. One of them suddenly cried out in despair, "Let me go back. It is better to be a slave than to suffer like this in order to be free."

She carried a gun with her on these trips. She had never used it—except as a threat. Now as she aimed it, she experienced a feeling of guilt, remembering that time, years ago, when she had prayed for the death of Edward Brodas, the Master, and then not too long afterward had heard that great wailing cry that came from the throats of the field hands, and knew from the sound that the Master was dead.

One of the runaways said, again, "Let me go back. Let me go back," and stood still, and then turned around and said, over his shoulder, "I am going back."

She lifted the gun, aimed it at the despairing slave. She said, "Go on with us or die." The husky low-pitched voice was grim.

He hesitated for a moment and then he joined the others. They started walking again. She tried to explain to them why none of them could go back to the plantation. If a runaway returned, he would turn traitor, the master and the overseer would force him to turn traitor. The returned slave would disclose the stopping places, the hiding places, the cornstacks they had used with the full knowledge of the owner of the farm, the name of the German farmer who had fed them and sheltered them. These people who had risked their own security to help runaways would be ruined, fined, imprisoned.

She said, "We got to go free or die. And freedom's not bought with dust."

This time she told them about the long agony of the Middle Passage on the old slave ships, about the black horror of the holds, about the chains and the whips. They too knew these stories. But she wanted to remind them of the long hard way they had come, about the long hard way they had yet to go. She told them about Thomas Sims, the boy picked up on the streets of Boston and sent back to Georgia. She said when they got him back to Savannah, got him in prison there, they whipped him until a doctor who was standing by watching said, "You will kill him if you strike him again!" His master said, "Let him die!" ●

Thus she forced them to go on. Sometimes she thought she had become nothing but a voice speaking in the darkness, cajoling, urging, threatening. Sometimes she told them things to make them laugh, sometimes she sang to them, and heard the eleven voices behind her blending softly with hers, and then she knew that for the moment all was well with them.

She gave the impression of being a short, muscular, indomitable[4] woman who could never be defeated. Yet at any moment she was liable to be seized by one of those curious fits of sleep, which might last for a few minutes or for hours.[5]

Even on this trip, she suddenly fell asleep in the woods. The runaways, ragged, dirty, hungry, cold, did not steal the gun as they might have, and set off by themselves, or turn back. They sat on the ground near her and waited patiently until she awakened. They had come to trust her implicitly, totally. They, too, had come to believe her repeated statement, "We got to go free or die." She was leading them into freedom, and so they waited until she was ready to go on.

Finally, they reached Thomas Garrett's house in Wilmington, Delaware. Just as Harriet had promised, Garrett gave them all new shoes, and provided carriages to take them on to the next stop.

By slow stages they reached Philadelphia, where William Still hastily recorded their names, and the plantations whence they had come, and something of the life they had led in slavery. Then he carefully hid what he had written, for fear it might be discovered. In 1872 he published this record in book form and called it *The Underground Railroad*. In the

Narrative Essay
Why does Tubman tell the fugitives the anecdote about Thomas Sims?

Main Idea
What main idea is directly stated in this paragraph?

Comprehension
What prevents the fugitives from turning back?

---

4. **indomitable** (in däm′ it ə bəl) *adj.* not easily discouraged.
5. **sleep . . . hours.** When she was about thirteen, Harriet accidentally received a severe blow on the head. Afterward, she often lost consciousness and could not be awakened until the episode ended.

foreword to his book he said: "While I knew the danger of keeping strict records, and while I did not then dream that in my day slavery would be blotted out, or that the time would come when I could publish these records, it used to afford me great satisfaction to take them down, fresh from the lips of fugitives on the way to freedom, and to preserve them as they had given them."

William Still, who was familiar with all the station stops on the Underground Railroad, supplied Harriet with money and sent her and her eleven fugitives on to Burlington, New Jersey.

Main Idea
What main idea about the weather is directly stated here? Which details best illustrate the main idea?

Harriet felt safer now, though there were danger spots ahead. But the biggest part of her job was over. As they went farther and farther north, it grew colder; she was aware of the wind on the Jersey ferry and aware of the cold damp in New York. From New York they went on to Syracuse, where the temperature was even lower.

In Syracuse she met the Reverend J. W. Loguen, known as "Jarm" Loguen. This was the beginning of a lifelong friendship. Both Harriet and Jarm Loguen were to become friends and supporters of Old John Brown.[6]

From Syracuse they went north again, into a colder, snowier city—Rochester. Here they almost certainly stayed with Frederick Douglass, for he wrote in his autobiography:

Spiral Review
AUTHOR'S PURPOSE
Why do you think the author includes this passage from Douglass's autobiography? How does it support her purpose for writing?

"On one occasion I had eleven fugitives at the same time under my roof, and it was necessary for them to remain with me until I could collect sufficient money to get them to Canada. It was the largest number I ever had at any one time, and I had some difficulty in providing so many with food and shelter, but, as may well be imagined, they were not very fastidious in either direction, and were well content with very plain food, and a strip of carpet on the floor for a bed, or a place on the straw in the barnloft." ●

Late in December, 1851, Harriet arrived in St. Catharines, Canada West (now Ontario), with the eleven fugitives. It had taken almost a month to complete this journey; most of the time had been spent getting out of Maryland.

That first winter in St. Catharines was a terrible one. Canada was a strange frozen land, snow everywhere, ice everywhere, and a bone-biting cold the like of which none of them had ever experienced before. Harriet rented a small

6. **John Brown** white antislavery activist (1800–1859) hanged for leading a raid on the arsenal at Harpers Ferry, then in Virginia (now in West Virginia), as part of a slave uprising.

frame house in the town and set to work to make a home. The fugitives boarded with her. They worked in the forests, felling trees, and so did she. Sometimes she took other jobs, cooking or cleaning house for people in the town. She cheered on these newly arrived fugitives, working herself, finding work for them, finding food for them, praying for them, sometimes begging for them.

Often she found herself thinking of the beauty of Maryland, the mellowness of the soil, the richness of the plant life there. The climate itself made for an ease of living that could never be duplicated in this **bleak**, barren countryside.

In spite of the severe cold, the hard work, she came to love St. Catharines, and the other towns and cities in Canada where black men lived. She discovered that freedom meant more than the right to change jobs at will, more than the right to keep the money that one earned. It was the right to vote and to sit on juries. It was the right to be elected to office. In Canada there were black men who were county officials and members of school boards. St. Catharines had a large colony of ex-slaves, and they owned their own homes, kept them neat and clean and in good repair. They lived in whatever part of town they chose and sent their children to the schools.

▲ **Critical Viewing**
Judging from this painting, how warmly were the slaves received once they arrived in the North? Explain.

◄ **Vocabulary**
bleak (blēk) *adj.* bare and windswept; cold and harsh

When spring came she decided that she would make this small Canadian city her home—as much as any place could be said to be home to a woman who traveled from Canada to the Eastern Shore of Maryland as often as she did.

In the spring of 1852, she went back to Cape May, New Jersey. She spent the summer there, cooking in a hotel. That fall she returned, as usual, to Dorchester County, and brought out nine more slaves, conducting them all the way to St. Catharines, in Canada West, to the bone-biting cold, the snow-covered forests—and freedom.

She continued to live in this fashion, spending the winter in Canada, and the spring and summer working in Cape May, New Jersey, or in Philadelphia. She made two trips a year into slave territory, one in the fall and another in the spring. She now had a definite crystallized purpose, and in carrying it out, her life fell into a pattern which remained unchanged for the next six years.

Language Study

Vocabulary The words in italics appear in the narrative essay "Harriet Tubman: Conductor on the Underground Railroad." Use your knowledge of these vocabulary words to tell if the statements are *typically true* or *typically false*. Explain your answers.

1. Eating a good meal will *dispel* the feeling of hunger.

2. A *mutinous* sailor obeys all the captain's rules.

3. *Fugitives* often have reason to feel afraid.

4. The need to pay bills is an *incentive* for getting a job.

5. On a *bleak* morning, the sun is bright and the air is warm.

Word Study

Part A Answer each question. Use context clues and what you know about the **Old English suffix -ly** to explain each answer.

1. Why would someone escaping from a room open the door *silently*?

2. Why is it best to answer a test question *correctly*?

Part B Explain how the suffix -ly contributes to the meanings of the words *persuasively*, *horribly*, and *humorously*. Consult a dictionary if necessary.

WORD STUDY

The **suffix -ly** comes from **Old English.** It is used to create adverbs that describe how, when, or how often something is done. In this essay, slave owners who hear a special signal **invariably** discover afterward that slaves have escaped. Time after time, the slave owners make this discovery.

Literary Analysis

Key Ideas and Details

1. (a) What does Harriet Tubman do when a fugitive wants to go back to the plantation? **(b) Analyze Cause and Effect:** Explain why Tubman feels she must act this way.

2. Main Idea (a) Using a chart like the one shown, list at least two details you learned about Harriet Tubman from the essay. Cite the text in your answer. **(b)** Then, write a sentence, based on the details in your chart, that states the main idea the author conveys about Tubman.

Craft and Structure

3. Narrative Essay (a) List two important events in this narrative essay. **(b)** Explain how they are connected.

4. Narrative Essay (a) Using examples from the text, explain how the author uses different types of details to develop Tubman's character. **(b)** Summarize Tubman's character, based on these details.

5. Narrative Essay (a) Use details from the text to identify and describe two of its settings. **(b)** Explain in each case how the setting helps to explain characters' actions or their situations.

Integration of Knowledge and Ideas

6. Interpret: Harriet Tubman says, "We got to go free or die. And freedom's not bought with dust." In your own words, interpret this statement. Cite evidence from the text to support your interpretation.

7. (a) Make a Judgment: Were the results of Tubman's trips on the Underground Railroad worth the risks involved? Explain why or why not, citing evidence from the text. **(b) Compare and Contrast:** Share your judgment with a partner. Then, discuss how your own opinion has or has not changed as a result of your conversation.

8. **How much information is enough?** With a small group, discuss the following questions: **(a)** What kind of information does Ann Petry provide in this narrative essay that you would not find in an encyclopedia entry about Harriet Tubman? **(b)** Does Petry's approach give you a better idea of what Tubman was like as a person? Explain why or why not, using details from the text.

Detail

If she were caught, she would be hanged.

+

Detail

She hid the fact that she did not know the new route.

+

Detail

↓

Main Idea

ACADEMIC VOCABULARY

As you write and speak about "Harriet Tubman: Conductor on the Underground Railroad," use the academic vocabulary that you explored on page 191 of this textbook.

Conventions: **Simple Tenses of Verbs**

> The **tense** of a verb shows the time of an action or a condition.
> The three **simple tenses** are *past, present,* and *future.*

Present Tense	Past Tense	Future Tense
Use base form *(walk)*; add *-s* or *-es* for the third person.	For regular verbs, add *-d* or *-ed* to base form.	Use *will* before base form.
I *walk*	I *walked*	I *will walk*
you *walk*	you *walked*	you *will walk*
he, she, it *walks*	he, she, it *walked*	he, she, it *will walk*

When telling a sequence of events, do not shift tense unnecessarily.

Incorrect: I *walked* to the door and *open* it.
Correct: I *walked* to the door and *opened* it.

In some cases, however, it is necessary to shift tense to show the order of events.

Incorrect: Because I *run* yesterday, I *ache* today.
Correct: Because I *ran* yesterday, I *ache* today.

Practice A

Complete each sentence with a verb that uses the tense indicated.

1. Harriet Tubman _____ several miles on foot to reach the farmhouse. (past)

2. The runaways _____ to Canada by the end of the month. (future)

3. The man _____ the door in Harriet's face. (present)

4. Eventually, Harriet _____ to Canada and live there permanently. (future)

Reading Application In "Harriet Tubman: Conductor on the Underground Railroad," find a sentence that contains at least two verbs in simple tenses. Identify the tenses of these verbs.

Practice B

Explain whether each sentence uses verb tenses correctly, and correct it if it does not.

1. Harriet Tubman was a former slave who will guide runaways.

2. It was not easy for fugitives in the 1800s; only a few hiding places were safe.

3. Because she once wrote a biography about Harriet Tubman, the author now often speaks on the subject.

4. Each week, she reads one biography and usually enjoyed it.

Writing Application Find a sentence in Ann Petry's essay that uses two verbs in the same tense. Then, use those same verbs in a new sentence that shows actions or conditions that happen at different times.

Writing to Sources

Explanatory Text Write a **biographical sketch** about a person who took risks to achieve a worthy goal. In your sketch, compare your subject to Harriet Tubman.

- In the first sentence, state the main idea you want to convey.

- As you describe the life and character of your subject, make sure the details you provide support your main idea. If needed, revise your main idea to fit what you have learned about the person.

- Include relevant quotations from the person you have chosen. Choose quotations that are especially revealing or powerful. If you choose to omit words from a quotation for brevity or clarity, use an ellipsis to indicate the omission. (See page 804.) Take care, however, not to change the meaning of the quotation.

- Discuss similarities between the person you have chosen and Tubman. Include details from Petry's essay in support.

- Use varied transitions to show the progress from one idea to the next. Transitions include words and phrases such as *finally, meanwhile, as a result,* and *for example*.

- End with a strong concluding paragraph.

Grammar Application Check your biographical sketch to make sure you have used simple verb tenses correctly.

Speaking and Listening

Presentation of Ideas In a small group, create a **skit** based on events from the essay on Harriet Tubman. Follow these steps:

- Select a series of events from the essay and take notes on them.

- Determine the best means to present the events. Which parts will you act out? Will you need to include narration?

- Draft your skit, presenting events in logical sequence. Choose words that capture the way the characters speak and that create a suitable mood. Use formal and informal English as needed.

- Indicate the gestures, facial expressions, and body language you will use to express the characters' feelings.

Rehearse your skit. Then, present it to your classmates. After your performance, ask the audience to compare the skit with the essay.

Common Core State Standards

Writing
2. Write informative/explanatory texts to examine a topic and convey ideas, concepts, and information through the selection, organization, and analysis of relevant content.
2.b. Develop the topic with relevant, well-chosen facts, definitions, concrete details, quotations, or other information and examples.
2.c. Use appropriate and varied transitions to create cohesion and clarify the relationships among ideas and concepts.

Speaking and Listening
6. Adapt speech to a variety of contexts and tasks, demonstrating command of formal English when indicated or appropriate.

Language
1. Demonstrate command of the conventions of standard English grammar and usage when writing or speaking.
2.b. Use an ellipsis to indicate an omission.

How much information is enough?

Explore the Big Question as you read the excerpt from *Always to Remember*. Take notes on the kinds of information the writer provides about Maya Lin and the way in which she planned her work.

CLOSE READING FOCUS

Key Ideas and Details: **Main Idea**

Main, or central, ideas are the most important points in a work of nonfiction. Often, the main idea is stated in the introduction. As you read, look for ways the main idea of the work is developed. To do so, first identify the main point of each body paragraph.

- This point may be stated in a topic sentence (often, the first sentence in the paragraph).
- For a paragraph without a topic sentence, determine the *implied main idea*—the idea that all the sentences in the paragraph work together to express.

Link the main points of paragraphs together to determine how they contribute to and develop the main idea of the work.

Craft and Structure: **Biography and Autobiography**

Biography and autobiography are two types of nonfiction.

- A **biography** is a nonfiction work in which the writer tells about important events in the life of another person.
- An **autobiography** is a true account of events written by the person who directly experienced the events. It includes the writer's thoughts and feelings.

Both types of writing examine the influence of personal experiences on a person's development and accomplishments. They also may capture the heritage, attitudes, and beliefs of the subject.

Vocabulary

Read each word listed from the selection. Which words share a suffix? What does the suffix indicate about the words' meaning?

authorized	criteria	harmonious
anonymously	eloquent	unanimous

Meet the Author

When **Brent Ashabranner** (b. 1921) was growing up, he loved a book called *Bomba the Jungle Boy*. As a young boy, he tried writing a book called *Barbara the Jungle Girl*, but gave up after the third page. Ashabranner did not give up on writing for long—he won fourth prize in a short-story contest when in high school. He has been writing ever since, drawing on his experiences serving in the Peace Corps in Africa and India, and living in the Philippines and Indonesia.

Common Core State Standards

Reading Informational Text
2. Determine a central idea of a text and analyze its development over the course of the text, including its relationship to supporting ideas.
3. Analyze how a text makes connections among and distinctions between individuals, ideas, or events.

Language
5.b. Use the relationship between particular words to better understand each of the words.

CLOSE READING MODEL

The passage below is from Brent Ashabranner's biography *Always to Remember*. The annotations to the right of the passage show ways in which you can use close reading skills to determine main ideas and identify elements of biography.

from *Always to Remember:* "The Vision of Maya Ying Lin"[1]

How could this be? How could an undergraduate student win one of the most important design competitions ever held? How could she beat out some of the top names in American art and architecture? Who was Maya Ying Lin?[2]

The answer to that question provided some of the other answers, at least in part.[3] Maya Lin, reporters soon discovered, was a Chinese-American girl who had been born and raised in the small midwestern city of Athens, Ohio. Her father, Henry Huan Lin, was a ceramicist of considerable reputation and dean of fine arts at Ohio University in Athens. Her mother, Julia C. Lin, was a poet and professor of Oriental and English literature. Maya Lin's parents were born to culturally prominent families in China.[4] When the Communists came to power in China in the 1940's, Henry and Julia Lin left the country and in time made their way to the United States. Maya Lin grew up in an environment of art and literature.[5] She was interested in sculpture and made both small and large sculptural figures, one cast in bronze.

Biography

1 The title of the text reveals that the work is about someone other than the author and is therefore a biography.

Main Idea

2 The author asks this series of questions to suggest how astonished the world was by Maya Lin's accomplishment. His questions imply the main idea of this paragraph: It is amazing that Lin won the contest.

Main Idea

3 The topic sentence of this paragraph indicates that the paragraph will answer the question, Who is Maya Lin? In addition, the sentence suggests that the paragraph will help connect who she is with how she was able to win.

Biography

4 This paragraph provides a number of biographical details about Maya Lin's family history. These details begin to answer the question of how Maya Lin was able to win a design contest.

Biography

5 Here, the biographer sums up Maya Lin's family background in a sentence that clearly points to her artistic potential.

from Always to Remember:

THE VISION OF MAYA YING LIN

BRENT ASHABRANNER

In the 1960s and 1970s, the United States was involved in a war in Vietnam. Because many people opposed the war, Vietnam veterans were not honored as veterans of other wars had been. Jan Scruggs, a Vietnam veteran, thought that the 58,000 U.S. servicemen and women killed or reported missing in Vietnam should be honored with a memorial. With the help of lawyers Robert Doubek and John Wheeler, Scruggs worked to gain support for his idea. In 1980, Congress authorized the building of the Vietnam Veterans Memorial in Washington, D.C., between the Washington Monument and the Lincoln Memorial.

The memorial had been **authorized** by Congress "in honor and recognition of the men and women of the Armed Forces of the United States who served in the Vietnam War." The law, however, said not a word about what the memorial should be or what it should look like. That was left up to the Vietnam Veterans Memorial Fund, but the law did state that the memorial design and plans would have to be approved by the Secretary of the Interior, the Commission of Fine Arts, and the National Capital Planning Commission.

What would the memorial be? What should it look like? Who would design it? Scruggs, Doubek, and Wheeler didn't know, but they were determined that the memorial should help bring closer together a nation still bitterly divided by the Vietnam War. It couldn't be something like the Marine Corps Memorial showing American troops planting a flag on enemy soil at Iwo Jima. It couldn't be a giant dove with an olive branch of peace in its beak. It had to soothe passions, not stir

◄ **Critical Viewing**
What does this veteran's reaction to the memorial tell you about its power?

◄ **Vocabulary**
authorized (ô´ thər īzd´)
v. officially approved

Main Idea
What point does the author make here about the challenges of designing the memorial?

Main Idea
How do the details about how the designer was to be chosen connect to the main point of the previous paragraph?

Vocabulary ▶
criteria (krī tir´ ē ə) *n.* standards by which something can be judged

▼ Critical Viewing
How does the design of the memorial honor individual soldiers, such as the veteran shown here?

them up. But there was one thing Jan Scruggs insisted on: The memorial, whatever it turned out to be, would have to show the name of every man and woman killed or missing in the war.

The answer, they decided, was to hold a national design competition open to all Americans. The winning design would receive a prize of $20,000, but the real prize would be the winner's knowledge that the memorial would become a part of American history on the Mall in Washington, D.C. Although fund raising was only well started at this point, the choosing of a memorial design could not be delayed if the memorial was to be built by Veterans Day, 1982. H. Ross Perot contributed the $160,000 necessary to hold the competition, and a panel of distinguished architects, landscape architects, sculptors, and design specialists was chosen to decide the winner. ●

Announcement of the competition in October, 1980, brought an astonishing response. The Vietnam Veterans Memorial Fund received over five thousand inquiries. They came from every state in the nation and from every field of design; as expected, architects and sculptors were particularly interested. Everyone who inquired received a booklet explaining the criteria. Among the most important: The memorial could not make a political statement about the war; it must contain the names of all persons killed or missing in action in the war; it must be in harmony with its location on the Mall.

A total of 2,573 individuals and teams registered for the competition. They were sent photographs of the memorial site, maps of the area around the site and of the entire Mall, and other technical design information. The competitors had three months to prepare their designs, which had to be received by March 31, 1981.

Of the 2,573 registrants, 1,421 submitted designs, a record number for such a design competition. When the designs were spread out for jury selection,

they filled a large airplane hangar. The jury's task was to select the design which, in their judgment, was the best in meeting these criteria:

- a design that honored the memory of those Americans who served and died in the Vietnam War.
- a design of high artistic merit.
- a design which would be **harmonious** with its site, including visual harmony with the Lincoln Memorial and the Washington Monument.
- a design that could take its place in the "historic continuity" of America's national art.
- a design that would be buildable, durable, and not too hard to maintain.

The designs were displayed without any indication of the designer's name so that they could be judged **anonymously**, on their design merits alone. The jury spent one week reviewing all the designs in the airplane hangar. On May 1 it made its report to the Vietnam Veterans Memorial Fund; the experts declared Entry Number 1,026 the winner. The report called it "the finest and most appropriate" of all submitted and said it was "superbly harmonious" with the site on the Mall. Remarking upon the "simple and forthright" materials needed to build the winning entry, the report concludes:

> This memorial, with its wall of names, becomes a place of quiet reflection, and a tribute to those who served their nation in difficult times. All who come here can find it a place of healing. This will be a quiet memorial, one that achieves an excellent relationship with both the Lincoln Memorial and Washington Monument, and relates the visitor to them. It is uniquely horizontal, entering the earth rather than piercing the sky.

> This is very much a memorial of our own times, one that could not have been achieved in another time and place. The designer has created an **eloquent** place where the simple meeting of earth, sky and remembered names contain messages for all who will know this place.

The eight jurors signed their names to the report, a **unanimous** decision. When the name of the winner was revealed, the art and architecture worlds were stunned.

◀ **Vocabulary**
harmonious (här mō´ nē əs) *adj.* combined in a pleasing arrangement

anonymously (ə nän´ ə məs lē) *adv.* without an indication of the author's or creator's name

Biography
The author identifies the winner by number. How does this detail suggest that the winner's identity may surprise readers?

◀ **Vocabulary**
eloquent (el´ ə kwənt) *adj.* vividly expressive

unanimous (yo͞o nan´ ə məs) *adj.* in complete agreement

Comprehension
What is the purpose of the memorial?

Arts Connection

Honoring Civil Rights

In addition to the Vietnam Veterans Memorial, Maya Ying Lin also designed a memorial that honors the Civil Rights Movement. Her inspiration came from these words of Dr. Martin Luther King, Jr.'s famous "I Have a Dream" speech: ". . . until justice rolls down like waters and righteousness like a mighty stream." Maya Lin decided that the memorial would be about water, and would honor King by using his words to connect the past with the future.

At the Civil Rights Memorial, water streams over King's words carved into the black granite wall. Clear water covers the names and events of the Civil Rights Movement on the circular stone table.

Connect to the Literature

In what ways does the Civil Rights Memorial resemble the Vietnam Veterans Memorial?

It was not the name of a nationally famous architect or sculptor, as most people had been sure it would be. The creator of Entry Number 1,026 was a twenty-one-year-old student at Yale University. Her name—unknown as yet in any field of art or architecture—was Maya Ying Lin.

How could this be? How could an undergraduate student win one of the most important design competitions ever held? How could she beat out some of the top names in American art and architecture? Who was Maya Ying Lin?

The answer to that question provided some of the other answers, at least in part. Maya Lin, reporters soon discovered, was a Chinese-American girl who had been born and raised in the small midwestern city of Athens, Ohio. Her father, Henry Huan Lin, was a ceramicist of considerable reputation and dean of fine arts at Ohio University in Athens. Her mother, Julia C. Lin, was a poet and professor of Oriental and English literature. Maya Lin's parents were born to culturally prominent families in China. When the Communists came to power in China in the 1940's, Henry and Julia Lin left the country and in time made their way to the United States.

Maya Lin grew up in an environment of art and literature. She was interested in sculpture and made both small and large sculptural figures, one cast in bronze. She learned silversmithing and made jewelry. She was surrounded by books and read a great deal, especially fantasies such as *The Hobbit* and *Lord of the Rings.*

But she also found time to work at McDonald's. "It was about the only way to make money in the summer," she said.

A covaledictorian at high school graduation, Maya Lin went to Yale without a clear notion of what she wanted to study and eventually decided to major in Yale's undergraduate program in architecture. During her junior year she studied in Europe and found herself increasingly interested in cemetery architecture. "In Europe there's very little space, so graveyards are used as parks," she said. "Cemeteries are cities of the dead in European countries, but they are also living gardens."

In France, Maya Lin was deeply moved by the war memorial to those who died in the Somme offensive in 1916 during World War I.[1] The great arch by architect Sir Edwin Lutyens is considered one of the world's most outstanding war memorials. ●

Back at Yale for her senior year, Maya Lin enrolled in Professor Andrus Burr's course in funerary (burial) architecture. The Vietnam Veterans Memorial competition had recently been announced, and although the memorial would be a cenotaph—a monument in honor of persons buried someplace else—Professor Burr thought that having his students prepare a design of the memorial would be a worthwhile course assignment.

Surely, no classroom exercise ever had such spectacular results.

After receiving the assignment, Maya Lin and two of her classmates decided to make the day's journey from New Haven, Connecticut, to Washington to look at the site where the memorial would be built. On the day of their visit, Maya Lin remembers, Constitution Gardens was awash with a late November sun; the park was full of light, alive with joggers and people walking beside the lake.

"It was while I was at the site that I designed it," Maya Lin said later in an interview about the memorial with *Washington Post* writer Phil McCombs. "I just sort of visualized it. It just popped into my head. Some people were playing Frisbee. It was a beautiful park. I didn't want to destroy a living park. You use the landscape. You don't fight with it. You absorb the landscape. . . . When I looked at the site I just knew I wanted something horizontal that took you in, that made you feel safe within the park, yet at the same time reminding you of the dead. So I just imagined opening up the earth. . . ."

When Maya Lin returned to Yale, she made a clay model of the vision that had come to her in Constitution Gardens.

▼ **Critical Viewing**
How does Maya Lin's design, shown here, contrast with other memorials that you have seen?

Biography
From what sources did Maya Lin draw inspiration for her prize-winning design?

Comprehension
Why did Maya Lin go with classmates to Washington?

---

1. **Somme offensive . . . World War I** costly and largely unsuccessful Allied attack that resulted in approximately 615,000 British and French soldiers being killed.

**Spiral Review
AUTHOR'S PURPOSE**
Why do you think the author notes that Maya Lin barely made the submission deadline? How does this detail add to the author's portrayal of Lin?

She showed it to Professor Burr; he liked her conception and encouraged her to enter the memorial competition. She put her design on paper, a task that took six weeks, and mailed it to Washington barely in time to meet the March 31 deadline.

A month and a day later, Maya Lin was attending class. Her roommate slipped into the classroom and handed her a note. Washington was calling and would call back in fifteen minutes. Maya Lin hurried to her room. The call came. She had won the memorial competition.

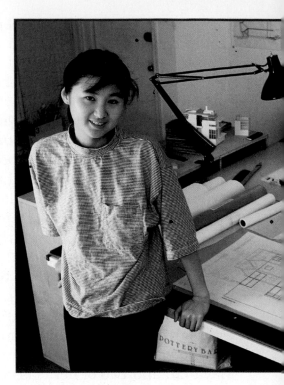

Language Study

Vocabulary In each word pair below, the first word appears in *Always to Remember*. Identify each pair as synonyms (words with similar meanings) or antonyms (words with opposite meanings).

1. *criteria*, guidelines
2. *harmonious*, compatible
3. *eloquent*, inexpressive
4. *unanimous*, divided
5. *authorized*, empowered

WORD STUDY

The **Greek root -nym-** means "name." In this essay, the designs for the Vietnam Veterans Memorial are submitted **anonymously**, or without names, so that the judges can evaluate them based only on the strengths of the ideas.

Word Study

Part A Explain how the **Greek root -nym-** contributes to the meaning of *homonym*, *patronym*, and *acronym*. Consult a dictionary if needed.

Part B Use what you know about the Greek root -nym- to answer each question. Explain your responses.

1. The word *atlas* is an *eponym* taken from the name of the mythological Greek giant Atlas. What eponym is related to the Roman goddess Fortuna?
2. How is using a *pseudonym* different from being *anonymous*?

Close Reading Activities

Literary Analysis

Key Ideas and Details

1. **(a)** How did supporters of the memorial set about getting it designed? **(b) Interpret:** Why did people think that a Vietnam memorial was necessary? Cite essay details in your answer.

2. **Main Idea** Review the beginning of the text, through the account of the jury's decision. **(a)** Identify the main idea of three paragraphs in this section. Cite details in support of your answer. **(b)** Explain how the three ideas you have identified are linked.

3. **Main Idea** Review the second half of the text, beginning with "How could this be?" Summarize the main idea of this section, citing textual details in support of your answer.

Craft and Structure

4. **Biography and Autobiography (a)** Fill out a chart like the one shown on the right with information about Lin. **(b)** Refer to the chart to summarize what you learned about Lin's life.

5. **Biography and Autobiography (a)** According to the text, why was Lin's win so surprising? **(b)** How did her background prepare her for the contest? **(c)** What personal qualities does she demonstrate that might also help explain her victory? Cite details from the text to explain your answer.

6. **Biography and Autobiography** Give two ways in which the text would have been different if it were part of Lin's autobiography.

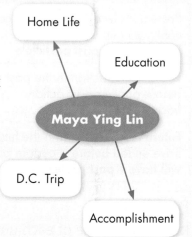

Integration of Knowledge and Ideas

7. Make a two-column chart. **(a) Classify:** In one column, list the design criteria reported in the text. **(b) Evaluate:** In the second column, explain whether the memorial meets these criteria.

8. **(a) Interpret:** What were supporters of the monument responding to when they decided that "it had to soothe passions, not stir them up"? **(b) Make a Judgment:** Do you think their concerns were reasonable, or do you think they unfairly shut out other options? Explain, citing details from the text in support.

9. **How much information Is enough? (a)** What types of information did Maya Lin consider as she planned her design for the memorial? **(b)** Is there usually a connection between architecture and historical events? Explain.

ACADEMIC VOCABULARY

As you write and speak about *Always to Remember: The Vision of Maya Ying Lin*, use the academic vocabulary that you explored on page 191 of this textbook.

Conventions: **Perfect Tenses of Verbs**

The **tense** of a verb shows the time of an action or a condition. Each of the **perfect tenses** describes an action or a condition that was or will be completed before a certain time, or a past action or condition that continues into the present.

Perfect tenses are formed by adding a form of the verb *have* to the past participle of the main verb.

Verb Tense	Example: *own (owned)*
Present Perfect: action in the past that continues into the present **have or has + past participle**	I *have owned* this red bike for two years. He *has owned* five different bikes.
Past Perfect: action in the past that ended before another past action **had + past participle**	I *had owned* one like it for a few years before I bought this one.
Future Perfect: action in the future that will have ended before a certain point in time **will have + past participle**	By next year, I *will have owned* three red bikes.

Practice A
Identify the tense of each underlined verb.

1. The judges <u>have reviewed</u> all the designs, and they plan to announce the winner on May 1.

2. They <u>had discussed</u> each one by the time they made their final decision.

3. By next year, many more viewers <u>will have seen</u> the Vietnam Veterans Memorial.

4. When the votes were counted, Maya Ying Lin <u>had won</u> the award.

Reading Application Choose a sentence from *Always to Remember*. Rewrite the sentence using one of the perfect tenses. Identify which tense you have used.

Practice B
Fill in each sentence with a verb in the perfect tense specified in parentheses.

1. In a few years, Lin probably _____ more memorials. (future perfect)

2. Lin _____ the site and was already inspired. (past perfect)

3. Reporters _____ Maya Ying Lin, and she plans to answer their questions. (present perfect)

4. Professor Burr _____ his class an assignment, which they are completing now. (present perfect)

Writing Application Write three sentences about Maya Ying Lin's life and work. Use each of the three perfect tenses.

Writing to Sources

Explanatory Text Write a **reflective essay** on a commemorative work, such as a memorial, statue, or painting, that has significance to you. In your essay, compare the purpose and style of this work to the purpose and style of Lin's memorial, as reported in Ashabranner's biography.

- Begin your essay with an introduction to your topic. Include a thesis statement in which you explain the focus of your essay.
- Weave together details about the commemorative work you have chosen. Choose details that support your main idea.
- Make clear comparisons to Lin's work, citing details from Ashabranner's text.
- Conclude your reflective essay by summarizing your ideas.

Grammar Application As you write, use perfect verb tenses as necessary to show the sequence of actions.

Research and Technology

Build and Present Knowledge With a group of classmates, create a **multimedia presentation** that explores the impact of the Vietnam War on our culture and attitudes toward war.

- Begin by devising a research question about the effects of the war on our culture, based on what you learned in the biography of Maya Lin.
- Conduct research to answer your question, taking notes on several reliable online and multimedia sources.
- As a group, discuss your research. Be aware of questions that arise as you work, and explore additional research sources to find answers.
- Design the presentation, including visuals, such as charts and maps, spoken words, and music. Choose the media best suited for presenting different types of information or creating different effects.
- During the presentation, connect your research to the biography about Lin, using direct quotations from the text. Consider ways in which your research sheds light on information provided by Ashabranner.

Common Core State Standards

Writing

2. Write informative/explanatory texts to examine a topic and convey ideas, concepts, and information through the selection, organization, and analysis of relevant content.

7. Conduct short research projects to answer a question (including a self-generated question), drawing on several sources and generating additional related, focused questions that allow for multiple avenues of exploration.

9. Draw evidence from literary or informational texts to support analysis, reflection, and research.

Speaking and Listening

5. Integrate multimedia and visual displays into presentations to clarify information, strengthen claims and evidence, and add interest.

Language

1. Demonstrate command of the conventions of standard English grammar and usage when writing or speaking.

 How much information is enough?

Explore the Big Question as you read. Take notes on MacNeil's claims about the information television programs provide.

CLOSE READING FOCUS

Meet the Author

Robert MacNeil (b. 1931) began his broadcast career in his native Canada as a radio announcer and disc jockey. In 1955, he moved to England and worked as a journalist. In 1975, MacNeil became co-host of a highly respected news program on American public television. The show, which eventually became known as *The MacNeil/Lehrer NewsHour,* stood out from other news programs by offering more in-depth news and analysis. He retired from the *NewsHour* in 1995 but continues to write about life, language, and history.

 Common Core State Standards

Reading Informational Text
6. Determine an author's point of view or purpose in a text and analyze how the author acknowledges and responds to conflicting evidence or viewpoints.
8. Delineate and evaluate the argument and specific claims in a text, assessing whether the reasoning is sound.

Language
4.b. Use common, grade-appropriate Greek or Latin affixes and roots as clues to the meaning of a word.

Key Ideas and Details: **Fact and Opinion**

In **argumentative essays and speeches,** writers make and support claims using **facts** and **opinions**.

- A **statement of fact** is one that can be proved true or false. Most often, arguments must be supported by facts.
- To make a strong argument, a writer must also interpret and judge the facts. Interpretations and judgments are **statements of opinion,** ideas that can be supported but that cannot be proved true or false. Clue words, such as *best, worst, think,* or *feel,* often signal statements of opinion.

Arguments can also be supported by **generalizations,** or conclusions about a group based on details about its members.

Craft and Structure: **Persuasive Techniques**

Persuasive techniques are methods that writers use in an argument to lead an audience to agree with them.

- **Repetition** consists of saying something repeatedly for effect.
- **Rhetorical questions** are questions with obvious answers that are asked for effect.
- **Appeals to reason** invite the audience to draw logical conclusions from the evidence the writer has presented.
- **Appeals to emotions** attempt to persuade readers by triggering their feelings about a subject.
- **Appeals to authority** are references to expert opinions.

Vocabulary

You will encounter these words in this speech. Which word is an antonym, or word with the opposite meaning, of *actively*?

constructive	diverts	passively
pervading	trivial	skeptically

CLOSE READING MODEL

The passage below is from Robert MacNeil's speech "The Trouble With Television." The annotations to the right of the passage show ways in which you can use close reading skills to identify facts and opinions and to analyze types of persuasive techniques.

from "The Trouble With Television"

It is difficult to escape the influence of television.[1] If you fit the statistical averages, by the age of 20 you will have been exposed to at least 20,000 hours of television. You can add 10,000 hours for each decade you have lived after the age of 20.[2] The only things Americans do more than watch television are work and sleep. . . .

. . .

Everything about this nation—the structure of the society, its forms of family organization, its economy, its place in the world—has become more complex, not less. Yet its dominating communications instrument, its principal form of national linkage,[3] is one that sells neat resolutions to human problems that usually have no neat resolutions. It is all symbolized in my mind by the hugely successful art form that television has made central to the culture, the thirty-second commercial: the tiny drama of the earnest housewife who finds happiness in choosing the right toothpaste.

When before in human history has so much humanity collectively surrendered so much of its leisure to one toy, one mass diversion? When before has virtually an entire nation surrendered itself wholesale to a medium for selling?[4]

Fact and Opinion
1 MacNeil claims that television's influence is hard to escape. This claim is an opinion, which he cannot prove but which he intends to support with evidence.

Fact and Opinion
2 MacNeil claims that the average American watches about 10,000 hours of television each decade. This claim is a fact—a reader could conduct research to confirm that MacNeil's claim is true. This fact supports the opinion that television's influence is hard to escape.

Persuasive Techniques
3 MacNeil uses phrases that begin with the pronoun *its*, meaning *this nation's*, five times in just two sentences. This repetition helps contrast the complexity of our problems with the simplicity of the solutions television offers.

Persuasive Techniques
4 MacNeil asks two questions that have the same obvious answer: *Never before.* Such rhetorical questions may lead readers to feel that the author's point is obvious, making it easier for them to agree with it.

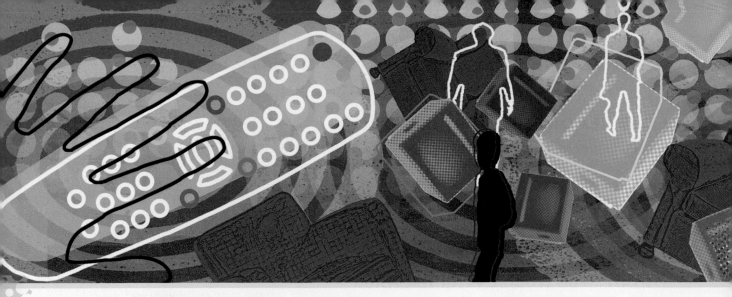

The Trouble With Television

Robert MacNeil

Fact and Opinion
Identify one fact and one opinion presented here.

Spiral Review
POINT OF VIEW
Examine MacNeil's word choice in the first two paragraphs. What might be his point of view on the subject of television?

It is difficult to escape the influence of television. If you fit the statistical averages, by the age of 20 you will have been exposed to at least 20,000 hours of television. You can add 10,000 hours for each decade you have lived after the age of 20. The only things Americans do more than watch television are work and sleep.

Calculate for a moment what could be done with even a part of those hours. Five thousand hours, I am told, are what a typical college undergraduate spends working on a bachelor's degree. In 10,000 hours you could have learned enough to become an astronomer or engineer. You could have learned several languages fluently. If it appealed to you, you could be reading Homer[1] in the original Greek or Dostoevski[2] in Russian. If it didn't, you could have walked around the world and written a book about it.

---

1. **Homer** (hō′ mər) ancient Greek author to whom the epic poems the *Odyssey* and the *Iliad* are attributed.
2. **Dostoevski** (dôs′ tô yef′ skē) (1821–1881) Fyodor *(fyô′ dôr)*, Russian novelist.

The trouble with television is that it discourages concentration. Almost anything interesting and rewarding in life requires some **constructive**, consistently applied effort. The dullest, the least gifted of us can achieve things that seem miraculous to those who never concentrate on anything. But television encourages us to apply no effort. It sells us instant gratification. It **diverts** us only to divert, to make the time pass without pain.

Television's variety becomes a narcotic, not a stimulus.[3] Its serial, kaleidoscopic[4] exposures force us to follow its lead. The viewer is on a perpetual guided tour: thirty minutes at the museum, thirty at the cathedral, then back on the bus to the next attraction—except on television, typically, the spans allotted are on the order of minutes or seconds, and the chosen delights are more often car crashes and people killing one another. In short, a lot of television usurps one of the most precious of all human gifts, the ability to focus your attention yourself, rather than just **passively** surrender it. ●

Capturing your attention—and holding it—is the prime motive of most television programming and enhances its role as a profitable advertising vehicle. Programmers live in constant fear of losing anyone's attention—anyone's. The surest way to avoid doing so is to keep everything brief, not to strain the attention of anyone but instead to provide constant stimulation through variety, novelty, action and movement. Quite simply, television operates on the appeal to the short attention span.

It is simply the easiest way out. But it has come to be regarded as a given, as inherent in the medium[5] itself: as

---

3. **becomes a narcotic, not a stimulus** becomes something that dulls the senses instead of something that inspires action.
4. **kaleidoscopic** (kə lī´ də skäp´ ik) *adj.* constantly changing.
5. **inherent** (in her´ ənt) **in the medium** a natural part of television. A *medium* is a means of communication; the plural is *media*.

► **Critical Viewing**
What does this photo suggest about the effects of watching television?

Vocabulary ►
pervading (pər vād´ iŋ) *adj.* spreading throughout

Fact and Opinion
Is the first sentence of this paragraph a fact or an opinion? How do you know?

an imperative, as though General Sarnoff, or one of the other august pioneers of video, had bequeathed to us tablets of stone commanding that nothing in television shall ever require more than a few moments' concentration.

In its place that is fine. Who can quarrel with a medium that so brilliantly packages escapist entertainment as a mass-marketing tool? But I see its values now pervading this nation and its life. It has become fashionable to think that, like fast food, fast ideas are the way to get to a fast-moving, impatient public.

In the case of news, this practice, in my view, results in inefficient communication. I question how much of television's nightly news effort is really absorbable and understandable. Much of it is what has been aptly described as "machine gunning with scraps." I think its technique fights coherence.[6] I think it tends to make things ultimately boring and dismissible (unless they are accompanied by horrifying pictures) because almost anything is boring and dismissable if you know almost nothing about it.

I believe that TV's appeal to the short attention span is not only inefficient communication but decivilizing as well. Consider the casual assumptions that television tends to cultivate: that complexity must be avoided, that visual stimulation is a substitute for thought, that verbal precision is an anachronism.[7] It may be old-fashioned, but I was taught that thought is words, arranged in grammatically precise ways.

There is a crisis of literacy in this country. One study estimates that some 30 million adult Americans are "functionally

---

6. **coherence** (kō hir´ əns) *n.* quality of being connected in a way that is easily understood.
7. **anachronism** (ə nak´ rə niz´ əm) *n.* something that seems to be out of its proper place in history.

Culture Connection

The Television Age

When television sets were scarce, people peered through store windows to watch broadcasts of popular events such as this one, the inauguration of Queen Elizabeth II in 1953. Radio pioneer David Sarnoff believed in and supported TV's emerging technology. His vision was right on the mark—today, nearly 100 percent of U.S. homes have one or more televisions.

1900 The word *television* is used for the first time at the World's Fair in Paris.

1923 **Vladimir Zworykin** patents his **iconoscope,** a TV camera tube. Later he develops the **kinescope** for picture display.

1927 **Philo Farnsworth** files for a patent on the first electronic television system.

1936 **Coaxial cable,** used to transmit TV, telephone, and data signals, is introduced. About 200 TV sets are in use worldwide.

1939 **RCA's David Sarnoff** showcases TV at the World's Fair.

1948 **Milton Berle's** *Texaco Star Theater* is the No. 1 program. Less than two percent of homes in the U.S. own a TV set.

1953 The puppet show *Kukla, Fran and Ollie* broadcasts in **color.**

1956 **Robert Adler** invents the first practical **remote control,** called the *Zenith Space Commander.* Seventy percent or more of U.S. households now own a TV.

1969 On July 20, 600 million people watch a TV **transmission from the moon.**

1998 First **HDTV** (high definition television) broadcast.

2004 **Plasma** and **LCD** (liquid crystal display) technology supports flat-screen TVs.

Connect to the Literature

How has the fascination with television impacted U.S. culture?

illiterate" and cannot read or write well enough to answer a want ad or understand the instructions on a medicine bottle.

Literacy may not be an inalienable human right, but it is one that the highly literate Founding Fathers might not have found unreasonable or even unattainable. We are not only not attaining it as a nation, statistically speaking, but we are falling further and further short of attaining it. And, while I would not be so simplistic as to suggest that television is the cause, I believe it contributes and is an influence. ●

Everything about this nation—the structure of the society, its forms of family organization, its economy, its

Comprehension
What does MacNeil dislike about the way television covers news?

place in the world—has become more complex, not less. Yet its dominating communications instrument, its principal form of national linkage, is one that sells neat resolutions to human problems that usually have no neat resolutions. It is all symbolized in my mind by the hugely successful art form that television has made central to the culture, the thirty-second commercial: the tiny drama of the earnest housewife who finds happiness in choosing the right toothpaste.

When before in human history has so much humanity collectively surrendered so much of its leisure to one toy, one mass diversion? When before has virtually an entire nation surrendered itself wholesale to a medium for selling?

Some years ago Yale University law professor Charles L. Black, Jr., wrote: ". . . forced feeding on trivial fare is not itself a trivial matter." I think this society is being force fed with trivial fare, and I fear that the effects on our habits of mind, our language, our tolerance for effort, and our appetite for complexity are only dimly perceived. If I am wrong, we will have done no harm to look at the issue skeptically and critically, to consider how we should be resisting it. I hope you will join with me in doing so.

Language Study

Vocabulary Rewrite each item using one of the vocabulary words listed.

> **constructive   diverts   passively   trivial   skeptically**

1. Her questions were about small, unimportant matters.

2. When I am doing homework, any small noise disturbs me.

3. Our conversation was helpful because it gave me ideas.

4. He listened to her yell but did not fight back.

5. I looked at him doubtfully when he said that he was 29.

Word Study

Part A Explain how the **Latin root -vad-** or **-vas-** contributes to the meanings of *evasively*, *invader*, and *vamoose*.

Part B Answer each question. Use what you know about the Latin root *-vad-* or *-vas-* to explain your answers.

1. What would a driver do in order to *evade* an obstacle?

2. Why might someone think carefully before having *invasive* surgery?

Close Reading Activities

Literary Analysis

Key Ideas and Details

1. (a) What does MacNeil identify as the main trouble with television in general? **(b) Analyze:** What evidence does he provide to support his viewpoint? **(c) Connect:** According to MacNeil, which techniques used by broadcasters contribute to the problem?

2. Fact and Opinion (a) Summarize MacNeil's criticism of nightly news shows on television. **(b)** What is one opinion he offers to support his views? **(c)** What facts does he provide in support?

3. Fact and Opinion (a) Fill out a chart like the one shown on the right. Classify each claim as a fact, a generalization, or an opinion. **(b)** Explain how each claim adds to the speech's persuasiveness.

Craft and Structure

4. Persuasive Techniques (a) Identify two places where MacNeil says that television appeals to short attention spans. **(b)** Why does he repeat this idea?

5. Persuasive Techniques (a) What is one source MacNeil quotes to give his claim authority? **(b)** Explain how he uses this source for support. **(c)** Identify and explain another persuasive technique he employs, in addition to repetition and appeals to authority.

Integration of Knowledge and Ideas

6. (a) What positive aspects of television does MacNeil mention? **(b) Speculate:** If he were in charge of programming for a network, what changes might he make? Cite evidence from the text.

7. (a) Connect: How does MacNeil's speech reflect the time in which it was written (1984)? **(b) Evaluate:** Are his opinions and information still relevant? Cite details from the text to support your response.

8. Speculate: What might MacNeil say about new media, such as the Internet, texts, and tweets? Refer to specific criticisms he makes of the "old media" to support your speculation.

9.  **How much information is enough? (a)** Citing details from the text, explain what MacNeil thinks about the information on the news. **(b)** Taking into account MacNeil's evaluation, how much information do you think is enough? Explain.

Claim
1. "It is difficult to escape the influence of television."
2. ". . . some 30 million adult Americans are 'functionally illiterate.' . . ."
3. "Everything about this nation . . . has become more complex. . . ."
4. "I think this society is being force fed with trivial fare. . . ."

Type of Claim
1. opinion
2.
3.
4.

ACADEMIC VOCABULARY

As you write and speak about "The Trouble With Television," use the academic vocabulary that you explored on page 191 of this textbook.

Conventions: **Verb Mood—The Subjunctive**

A verb in the **subjunctive mood** is used when the action that the verb expresses is contrary to fact or when the speaker is expressing a wish or demand that the action be taken.

The **indicative mood** is used for statements of fact. By contrast, the **subjunctive** is used to express a wish, a hope, or a statement contrary to fact—"I wish that he *were* here." It is also used to express a request, demand, or proposal. The subjunctive is often found in a clause beginning with *if* or *that*.

Indicative Mood	Subjunctive Mood	What Subjunctive Expresses
Jorge **is going** to the store.	I wish that Sam **were going**, too.	a wish
I **am** at home.	If I **were** at home, I would eat.	a condition contrary to fact
Sam **goes** to the store.	I insist that Sam **go** to the store.	a demand
They **were** quiet.	We asked that they **be** quiet.	a request

Take care to avoid improper shifts in mood.

Incorrect: If he **were** sad and she **was** here, she would help him.
           subjunctive   indicative

Correct: If he **were** sad and she **were** here, she would help him.
         subjunctive   subjunctive

Practice A

Indicate the mood of each verb in italics.

1. If we *were* not such fans of television, we would have more time.

2. MacNeil *wants* readers to think about the effects of television.

3. MacNeil insists that the viewer *be* aware of television's effects.

Reading Application Identify a sentence in MacNeil's essay that uses the indicative mood. Rewrite the sentence, using the subjunctive mood.

Practice B

Identify the incorrect verb form in each sentence, and rewrite the sentence correctly.

1. If I was MacNeil, I would have also discussed the Internet.

2. MacNeil wishes that he was living in a more literate society.

3. If programming was less fragmented, it might be easier to understand.

4. He seems to demand that I am more aware of my own viewing habits.

Writing Application Write a sentence about television. Use the subjunctive mood.

Writing to Sources

Argument Write an **evaluation** of MacNeil's speech. Begin by identifying MacNeil's main claim and then outlining his arguments. State your own claim about how persuasive MacNeil is, and support your ideas with relevant evidence from the essay. Use these criteria:

- **Sound reasoning:** Are claims and support logically connected?
- **Relevant evidence:** Does the evidence always apply logically to the point being made?
- **Sufficient evidence:** Is enough evidence provided?
- **Response to counterarguments:** Are arguments against claims noted and addressed?

Grammar Application Revise your evaluation, correcting inappropriate use of verb moods.

Research and Technology

Presentation of Ideas With a group of classmates, create a **snapshot** of two conflicting arguments on the effects of watching television. Use Internet resources to find an editorial or essay that argues that watching television can be beneficial. Compare the piece you find with MacNeil's essay. Follow these steps:

- With your group, make a T-chart. List the "pros" and "cons" of television as each author identifies them.
- Indicate which items are facts and which are opinions.
- Note instances where the authors' arguments conflict. Identify the reason for each conflict by answering these questions:

    Question 1: *Do the authors present conflicting facts? For example, does each cite a different number of hours that people watch television?*
    Question 2: *Do the authors present similar facts but disagree about how to interpret them? For example, do they agree on the fact that television "chops up" information, but disagree about whether the effect is harmful?*

- Write an overview of the arguments, explaining whether each conflict between the two arguments results from a disagreement over facts or over the interpretation of facts.

Use a class blog to post and discuss your findings.

**Common Core
State Standards**

Reading Informational Text
6. Determine an author's point of view or purpose in a text.
8. Delineate and evaluate the argument and specific claims in a text, assessing whether the reasoning is sound and the evidence is relevant and sufficient; recognize when irrelevant evidence is introduced.
9. Analyze a case in which two or more texts provide conflicting information on the same topic and identify where the texts disagree on matters of fact or interpretation.

Writing
1. Write arguments to support claims with clear reasons and relevant evidence.
6. Use technology, including the Internet, to produce and publish writing and present the relationships between information and ideas efficiently as well as to interact and collaborate with others.

Language
1.c. Form and use verbs in the indicative, imperative, interrogative, conditional, and subjunctive mood.
1.d. Recognize and correct inappropriate shifts in verb voice and mood.
3.a. Use verbs in the active and passive voice and in the conditional and subjunctive mood to achieve particular effects.

Meet the Author

Isaac Asimov (1920–1992) became a science-fiction fan by reading fantastic stories in magazines. Asimov's father discouraged his son's early interest, describing the magazines as "junk." Still, Asimov's interest continued, and he started writing his own stories at age eleven. At first, his stories were rejected, but Asimov developed into a visionary science writer and one of the most influential science-fiction writers of the twentieth century.

How much information is enough?

Explore the Big Question as you read "Science and the Sense of Wonder." Take notes on how information can lead to wonder.

CLOSE READING FOCUS

Key Ideas and Details: **Fact and Opinion**

In argumentative texts, writers use both facts and opinions to support claims. A **statement of fact** can be proved. A **statement of opinion** expresses a person's judgment or belief. **Valid opinions** can be supported by facts. **Faulty opinions** cannot be supported and often show **bias,** an unfair preference or dislike.

As you read, outline an author's argument by noting main claims and the facts and opinions used to support each. Evaluate the argument by asking yourself, Is the author's reasoning logical? Is the evidence relevant, or logically related, to the point? Is it sufficient?

Craft and Structure: **Word Choice**

An author's **word choice** can convey tone—the author's attitude toward the topic or audience. For example, the use of slang might create a friendly tone. These factors influence word choice:

- an author's intended audience and purpose
- the **denotations** of words, or their dictionary definitions
- the **connotations** of words, or their negative or positive associations. (For example, *assertive* and *pushy* have similar denotations but different connotations.)

Authors may gain precision by using *technical terms,* or words specific to a field. They may make ideas vivid by using *figurative language,* or language not meant to be taken literally. As you read, notice how word choice conveys meaning and tone.

Vocabulary

These words appear in the essay that follows. Identify the two words that share a suffix, and identify their part of speech.

exultantly	awed	cataclysm
radiation	conceivable	contraction

Common Core State Standards

Reading Informational Text
4. Determine the meaning of words and phrases as they are used in a text, including figurative, connotative, and technical meanings; analyze the impact of specific word choices on meaning and tone.

8. Delineate and evaluate the argument and specific claims in a text, assessing whether the reasoning is sound and the evidence is relevant and sufficient.

Language
5.c. Distinguish among the connotations (associations) of words with similar denotations (definitions).

CLOSE READING MODEL

The passage below is from Isaac Asimov's essay "Science and the Sense of Wonder." The annotations to the right of the passage show ways in which you can use close reading skills to evaluate facts and opinions and to analyze word choice.

from "Science and the Sense of Wonder"

All these galaxies are hurrying outward from each other in a vast universal expansion that began fifteen billion years ago, when all the matter in the universe was in a tiny sphere that exploded in the hugest conceivable shatter to form the galaxies.[1]

The universe may expand forever or the day may come when the expansion slows and turns back into a contraction to re-form the tiny sphere and begin the game all over again so that the whole universe is exhaling and inhaling in breaths[2] that are perhaps a trillion years long.

And all of this vision—far beyond the scale of human imaginings—was made possible by the works of hundreds of "learn'd" astronomers. All of it; *all* of it was discovered after the death of Whitman in 1892, and most of it in the past twenty-five years, so that the poor poet never knew what a stultified and limited beauty he observed when he "look'd up in perfect silence at the stars."[3]

Nor can we know or imagine now the limitless beauty yet to be revealed in the future—by science.[4]

Fact and Opinion

1 Asimov is explaining the origin of galaxies and the expansion of the universe. He presents facts—things upon which scientific experts agree.

Word Choice

2 Asimov refers to the universe as "inhaling" and "exhaling." These word choices create a mental picture of the universe as a living creature, supporting his claim that the scientific world is full of wonder.

Word Choice

3 Asimov refers to poet Walt Whitman, who believed science could discourage wonder. By choosing the words *poor* and *stultified* (meaning "dull" or "made to seem foolish"), Asimov creates a clear tone—he pities Whitman, who did not benefit from the vision of modern science.

Fact and Opinion

4 Asimov claims that the universe holds "limitless beauty." This statement is a valid opinion because it is supported by the facts he has presented in the preceding paragraphs.

SCIENCE
and the Sense of Wonder
Isaac Asimov

▲ **Critical Viewing**
The brown, white, and red ovals on Jupiter's surface are storms. The largest of these, the Great Red Spot, is a storm three times the size of Earth. Does knowing facts about planets take away from their beauty? Explain.

One of Walt Whitman's best-known poems is this one:

When I heard the learn'd astronomer,

When the proofs, the figures, were ranged in columns before me,

When I was shown the charts and diagrams, to add, divide and measure them,

When I sitting heard the astronomer where he lectured with much applause in the lecture-room,

How soon unaccountable I became tired and sick,

Till rising and gliding out I wander'd off by myself,

In the mystical moist night-air, and from time to time,

Look'd up in perfect silence at the stars.

I imagine that many people reading those lines tell themselves, **exultantly**, "How true! Science just sucks all the beauty out of everything, reducing it all to numbers and tables and measurements! Why bother learning all that junk when I can just go out and look at the stars?"

That is a very convenient point of view since it makes it not only unnecessary, but downright aesthetically wrong,[1] to try to follow all that hard stuff in science. Instead, you can just take a look at the night sky, get a quick beauty fix, and go off to a nightclub.

The trouble is that Whitman is talking through his hat, but the poor soul didn't know any better.

I don't deny that the night sky is beautiful, and I have in my time spread out on a hillside for hours looking at the stars and being **awed** by their beauty (and receiving bug-bites whose marks took weeks to go away).

But what I see—those quiet, twinkling points of light—*is not all the beauty there is*. Should I stare lovingly at a single leaf and willingly remain ignorant of the forest? Should I be satisfied to watch the sun glinting off a single pebble and scorn any knowledge of a beach?

Those bright spots in the sky that we call planets are worlds. There are worlds with thick atmospheres of carbon dioxide and sulfuric acid; worlds of red-hot liquid with hurricanes that could gulp down the whole earth; dead worlds with quiet pockmarks of craters; worlds with volcanoes puffing plumes of dust into airlessness; worlds with pink and desolate deserts— each with a weird and unearthly beauty that boils down to a mere speck of light if we just gaze at the night sky.

Those other bright spots, which are stars rather than planets, are actually suns. Some of them are of incomparable grandeur,[2] each glowing with the light

1. **aesthetically** (es thet′ i klē) **wrong** insensitive to beauty.
2. **incomparable grandeur** (gran′ jər) unequaled splendor.

◀ **Vocabulary**
exultantly (eg zult′ 'nt lē) *adv.* triumphantly

awed (ôd) *v.* filled with wonder

Fact and Opinion
Is this statement about Whitman fact or opinion? Explain.

Spiral Review
AUTHOR'S PURPOSE
Identify two rhetorical questions in this passage. What purpose do these questions help Asimov achieve?

Word Choice
Which words in this passage add drama to the description?

Comprehension
What does Asimov think of Whitman's views of astronomy?

of a thousand suns like ours; some of them are merely red-hot coals doling out their energy stingily. Some of them are compact bodies as massive as our sun, but with all that mass squeezed into a ball smaller than the earth. Some are more compact still, with the mass of the sun squeezed down into the volume of a small asteroid. And some are more compact still, with their mass shrinking down to a volume of zero, the site of which is marked by an intense gravitational field that swallows up everything and gives back nothing; with matter spiraling into that bottomless hole and giving out a wild death-scream of X-rays.

There are stars that pulsate endlessly in a great cosmic breathing; and others that, having consumed their fuel, expand and redden until they swallow up their planets, if they have any (and someday, billions of years from now, our sun will expand and the earth will crisp and sere and vaporize into a gas of iron and rock with no sign of the life it once bore). And some stars explode in a vast

Vocabulary ▶
cataclysm (kat′ ə kliz′ əm) *n.* sudden, violent event that causes change

Fact and Opinion
Do these figures support Asimov's opinion that there is more to the universe than we see? Explain.

cataclysm whose ferocious blast of cosmic rays, hurrying outward at nearly the speed of light, reaches across thousands of light years to touch the earth and supply some of the driving force of evolution through mutations.

Those paltry few stars we see as we look up in perfect silence (some 2,500 or more on even the darkest and clearest night) are joined by a vast horde we don't see, up to as many as three hundred billion—300,000,000,000—to form an enormous pinwheel in space. This pinwheel, the Milky Way galaxy, stretches so widely that it takes light, moving at 186,282 miles each *second*, a hundred thousand *years* to cross it from end to end; and it rotates about its center in a vast and stately turn that takes two hundred million years to complete—and the sun and the earth and we ourselves all make that turn.

Beyond our Milky Way galaxy are others, a score or so of them bound to our own in a cluster of galaxies, most of them small, with no more than a few billion stars in each; but with one at least, the Andromeda galaxy, twice as large as our own.

Beyond our own cluster, other galaxies and other clusters exist; some clusters made up of thousands of galaxies. They stretch outward and outward as far as our best telescopes can see, with no visible sign of an end—perhaps a hundred billion of them in all.

And in more and more of those galaxies we are becoming aware of violence at the centers—of great explosions and outpourings of **radiation**, marking the death of perhaps millions of stars. Even at the center of our own galaxy there is incredible violence masked from our own solar system far in the outskirts by enormous clouds of dust and gas that lie between us and the heaving center.

Some galactic centers are so bright that they can be seen from distances of billions of light-years, distances from which the galaxies themselves cannot be seen and only the bright starlike centers of ravening[3] energy show up—as quasars. Some of these have been detected from more than ten billion light-years away.

All these galaxies are hurrying outward from each other in a vast universal expansion that began fifteen billion years ago, when all the matter in the universe was in a tiny sphere that exploded in the hugest **conceivable** shatter to form the galaxies.

The universe may expand forever or the day may come when the expansion slows and turns back into a **contraction** to re-form the tiny sphere and begin the game all over again so that the whole universe is exhaling and inhaling in breaths that are perhaps a trillion years long.

---

3. **ravening** (rav´ ə nin) *adj.* consuming greedily.

◄ **Vocabulary**
radiation (rā´ dē ā´ shən) *n.* rays of energy

conceivable (kən sēv´ ə bəl) *adj.* imaginable

contraction (kən trak´ shən) *n.* the act of becoming smaller

LITERATURE IN CONTEXT

Science Connection

Lord of the Rings
The wonder of Saturn's rings—patterned waves that resemble ripples in a pond—wowed the world in 2004. The images were transmitted from 900 million miles away by the *Cassini* spacecraft, which NASA had launched seven years before.

The craft is named for the seventeenth-century astronomer Giovanni Cassini, discoverer of several of Saturn's moons. Cassini also discovered a gap in the rings, which was named *Cassini's Division*. Scientists know that the hundreds of rings are made up of ice and rock particles that orbit Saturn at different speeds. By studying the rings up close, scientists hope to learn more about the solar system and how planets form.

Connect to the Literature

Would Asimov be impressed by the *Cassini* photos? Explain.

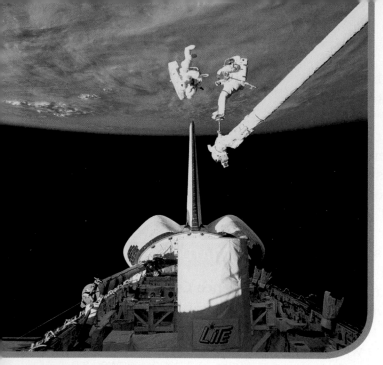

And all of this vision—far beyond the scale of human imaginings—was made possible by the works of hundreds of "learn'd" astronomers. All of it; *all* of it was discovered after the death of Whitman in 1892, and most of it in the past twenty-five years, so that the poor poet never knew what a stultified[4] and limited beauty he observed when he "look'd up in perfect silence at the stars."

Nor can we know or imagine now the limitless beauty yet to be revealed in the future—by science.

▲ **Critical Viewing**
How might being in space give you a different appreciation for the wonders of science and the universe?

4. **stultified** (stul′ tə fid′) *adj.* foolish or absurd.

Language Study

Vocabulary Write a sentence to answer each question, using the blue vocabulary word that means the same as the underlined word or words.

> exultantly awed cataclysm radiation conceivable

1. What aspects of nature cause you to be <u>struck with wonder</u>?
2. Would an underdog team view a win <u>with a joyous emotion</u>?
3. How might a tornado cause a <u>disaster</u> in a city in its path?
4. Is the <u>energy</u> released by an atomic bomb dangerous?
5. Is it <u>possible</u> that a child of five can compose a symphony?

Word Study

WORD STUDY

The **Latin root -tract-** means "pull" or "drag." In this essay, Asimov suggests that our expanding universe may someday begin a period of **contraction**, or shrinking, in which gravity pulls it back to its original shape and form.

Part A Explain how the **Latin root -tract-** contributes to the meaning of *attract*, *detract*, and *extract*. Consult a dictionary if necessary.

Part B Answer each question. Use the context of the sentences and what you know about the Latin root -tract- to explain your answers.

1. Why is a *tractor* a good tool for moving a heavy object?
2. What might happen if you *distract* the driver of a car?

Close Reading Activities

Literary Analysis

Key Ideas and Details

1. Fact and Opinion (a) What is Asimov's main claim, or argument? **(b)** How does he support this argument? List two examples. **(c)** Is the evidence he offers relevant and sufficient? Explain, citing details from the text.

2. Fact and Opinion (a) At the end of the essay, what fact does Asimov give about the dates of the discoveries he has been discussing? **(b)** Does this fact call Whitman's views into question? Why or why not?

3. Fact and Opinion (a) Is it fact or Asimov's opinion that what Whitman admired was a "limited beauty"? Explain. **(b)** Does Asimov's view reflect bias? Explain.

Craft and Structure

4. Word Choice (a) Use a chart like the one shown to analyze three examples of Asimov's word choice. **(b)** Citing examples from your chart, explain how he uses connotations to support his points.

5. Word Choice What tone does Asimov's word choice create—chatty, inspiring, critical, or something else? Support your response with examples.

6. Word Choice (a) Cite an example of a technical term that Asimov uses. Why is its use appropriate? **(b)** Cite an example of figurative language, and explain how it enhances his meaning.

Asimov's Purpose

Words and Phrases That Support His Purpose

Connotations

Integration of Knowledge and Ideas

7. Make a Judgment: If Whitman were alive today to reflect on the scientific advances of the twentieth century reported by Asimov, would his view of the relationship between science and wonder be the same? Explain, using details from the essay.

8. (a) Evaluate: Is it possible that Whitman's and Asimov's claims are both correct? Explain. **(b) Draw Conclusions:** Are there statements on which Whitman and Asimov would agree? Explain your answer, using details from the text.

9. **THE BIG ?** **How much information is enough?** With a small group, discuss these questions: **(a)** As we gather more data about the universe, whose view will be proved correct, Whitman's or Asimov's? **(b)** Will our sense of wonder increase or decrease? Explain.

ACADEMIC VOCABULARY

As you write and speak about "Science and the Sense of Wonder," use the academic vocabulary that you explored on page 191 of this textbook.

Conventions: Active and Passive Voice

> The **voice** of a verb shows whether the subject of the verb is performing the action or receiving it.

A verb is in the **active voice** when its subject performs the action.
A verb is in the **passive voice** when its subject receives the action.
A passive verb is a verb phrase made from a form of *be* with the past participle of an action verb, as shown in the chart.

Active Voice	Passive Voice
We **built** the barn.	The barn **was built**. (***Built*** is the past participle of ***build***.)
My family **is painting** the house.	The house **is being painted** by my family. (***Painted*** is the past participle of ***paint***.)

Generally, it is better style for writers to use the active voice. Use passive voice when the performer of the action is unknown or when it is desirable to stress the action instead of its performer.

Avoid shifting between the active voice and the passive voice without good reason. When a person performs actions in a series of sentences, it can be confusing to shift suddenly to passive, as in this example: *Mia **kicked** the ball. The ball **was kicked** hard.*

Practice A

Identify whether each sentence uses the active or the passive voice.

1. Whitman appreciated the night sky.
2. Asimov was awed by its beauty.
3. Some planets are swallowed by their suns.
4. We circle the center of the Milky Way.

Reading Application Review the last two paragraphs in "Science and the Sense of Wonder." Identify one example of passive voice and one of active voice.

Practice B

Revise the following sentences to use the active voice.

1. The poem was written by Whitman.
2. Beauty is revealed by science.
3. Earth will be destroyed by the sun.
4. These facts were discovered by astronomers.

Writing Application Identify two sentences in "Science and the Sense of Wonder" that use the active voice, and revise them to use the passive voice. What effect is created by the change in voice?

Writing to Sources

Explanatory Text Write a **response** to Asimov's essay in which you evaluate his main ideas as well as his way of expressing them.

- First, reread the essay to identify and reflect on the main ideas.

- Next, identify especially effective passages from the text, and take notes on Asimov's word choice in them. Pay special attention to **analogies,** or extended comparisons of one thing to another, used to aid readers' understanding.

- Draft your response, discussing how Asimov's word choice and analogies affect your reaction to the text. Then, explain whether you agree with his idea that the scientist's appreciation of nature is as valid as the poet's.

- Review your draft carefully for correct spelling, paying special attention to any technical or unfamiliar words you have quoted from Asimov's essay. Consult a dictionary as needed.

Grammar Application Review your draft to check your use of voice. Use passive voice only when the action of a sentence requires emphasis or the performer of the action is unknown.

Speaking and Listening

Presentation of Ideas Conduct research to locate an audiovisual presentation on the wonders of astronomy. Then write a **speech** comparing the effectiveness of the audiovisual presentation with the effectiveness of Asimov's text "Science and the Sense of Wonder." Discuss the advantages or disadvantages to using each medium. For example, consider whether there are cases where poetic descriptions are more powerful than visuals, and vice versa.

Begin by making an outline that includes an introduction, or preview; a body, or main section, that is developed in logical order; and a strong, effective conclusion. As you draft, use these strategies:

- Support your ideas with sound reasoning and strong evidence.

- Identify and omit irrelevant details.

- Ensure you have provided enough evidence to support claims.

- Use parallel wording to add drama and emphasis to your speech.

Deliver the speech to your class using appropriate eye contact, adequate volume, and clear pronunciation. Pause for dramatic effect and vary your pacing to create audience interest.

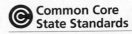

Common Core State Standards

Reading Informational Text

4. Determine the meaning of words and phrases as they are used in a text, including figurative, connotative, and technical meanings; analyze the impact of specific word choices on meaning and tone, including analogies or allusions to other texts.

7. Evaluate the advantages and disadvantages of using different mediums to present a particular topic or idea.

Writing

2. Write informative/explanatory texts to examine a topic and convey ideas, concepts, and information through the selection, organization, and analysis of relevant content.

9.b. Apply grade 8 Reading standards to literary nonfiction.

Speaking and Listening

4. Present claims and findings, emphasizing salient points in a focused, coherent manner with relevant evidence, sound valid reasoning, and well-chosen details; use appropriate eye-contact, adequate volume, and clear pronunciation.

Language

1.b. Form and use verbs in the active and passive voice.

1.d. Recognize and correct inappropriate shifts in verb voice and mood.

2.c. Spell correctly.

3. Use knowledge of language and its conventions when writing, speaking, reading, or listening.

3.a. Use verbs in the active and passive voice, and in the conditional and subjunctive mood to achieve particular effects.

How much information is enough?

Explore the Big Question as you read these three selections. Take notes on what the writers think is vital to the readers' understanding of the events being depicted. Then, compare and contrast the ways the information is presented in the three works.

READING TO COMPARE TYPES OF ORGANIZATION

Although authors Anaïs Nin, Mary C. Curtis, and Diane Ackerman all express their thoughts in essay form, they each choose a different type of organization. As you read each essay, consider why the author chooses to use one or more of the following: chronological order, cause-and-effect order, or comparison and contrast. After you have read all the essays, compare how the chosen type of organization affects the delivery of information in the essay.

"Forest Fire"

Anaïs Nin (1903–1977)
Anaïs Nin wrote in many forms, but she is best known for her diaries. Born in France, Nin started a diary at age eleven. Nin eventually filled 200 volumes with diary entries.

"The Season's Curmudgeon Sees the Light"

Mary C. Curtis (b. 1953)
Mary Curtis grew up in Baltimore and worked at *The New York Times, Baltimore Sun,* and *Charlotte* (North Carolina) *Observer* before becoming a blogger for *The Washington Post.* Her blog posts examine politics, culture, and social issues.

"Why Leaves Turn Color in the Fall"

Diane Ackerman (b. 1948)
A native of Waukegan, Illinois, nature writer Diane Ackerman combines her literary skills with her scientific training. Ackerman has published books of poems and books of nonfiction, including *A Natural History of the Senses.*

• Forest Fire
• The Season's Curmudgeon Sees the Light
• Why Leaves Turn Color in the Fall

Comparing Types of Organization

To present information clearly, writers can choose among several **types of organization.** Here are three of the most common types:

- **Chronological order** relates events in order of occurrence. Narratives usually place events in time order.

- **Cause-and-effect order** highlights the relationship between an event and its result or results. Science articles often use cause-and-effect text structure to explain events or reactions.

- **Comparison and contrast** shows similarities and differences.

As you read these essays, look for clues that signal the type of organization being used. For example, words and phrases like *consequently* or *as a result* might signal a cause-and-effect pattern.

Paragraph Structure In addition to the structure of the full work, analyze the structures of specific paragraphs. For example, a writer might include an anecdote, or brief story, within a work that does not otherwise use chronological order. As you look for these nuances, also analyze how individual sentences develop or refine ideas within paragraphs. For example, notice whether a sentence adds an important detail or example.

As you read, use charts like the ones shown to analyze the organizational patterns used in these essays. Then, examine how individual sentences help to develop and refine meaning.

Common Core State Standards

Reading Informational Text
5. Analyze in detail the structure of a specific paragraph in a text, including the role of particular sentences in developing and refining a key concept.

Writing
9. Draw evidence from literary or informational texts to support analysis, reflection, and research.
9.b. Apply grade 8 Reading standards to literary nonfiction.

Forest Fire: Retells exciting event

Why Leaves Turn: Explains natural process

Season's Curmudgeon: Compares/contrasts author's feelings

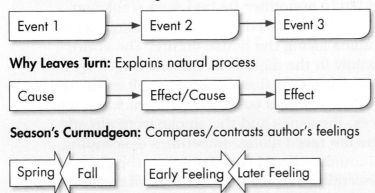

Forest Fire

Anaïs Nin

▲ **Critical Viewing**
What details in this photograph show the danger of forest fires?

A man rushed in to announce he had seen smoke on Monrovia Peak.[1] As I looked out of the window I saw the two mountains facing the house on fire. The entire rim burning wildly in the night. The flames, driven by hot Santa Ana winds[2] from the desert, were as tall as the tallest trees, the sky already tinted coral, and the crackling noise of burning trees, the ashes and the smoke were already increasing. The fire raced along, sometimes descending behind the mountain where I could only see the glow, sometimes descending toward us. I thought of the foresters in danger. I made coffee for the weary men who came down occasionally with horses they had led out, or with old people

---

1. **Monrovia Peak** a mountain in the Sierra Madre range near where Nin had a home in southwest California.
2. **Santa Ana winds** hot, quickly moving desert winds that dry out vegetation and fuel massive fires.

from the isolated cabins. They were covered with soot from their battle with the flames.

At six o'clock the fire was on our left side and rushing toward Mount Wilson. **Evacuees** from the cabins began to arrive and had to be given blankets and hot coffee. The streets were blocked with fire engines readying to fight the fire if it touched the houses. Policemen and firemen and guards turned away the sightseers. Some were relatives concerned over the fate of the foresters, or the pack station family. The policemen lighted flares, which gave the scene a theatrical, tragic air. The red lights on the police cars twinkled alarmingly. More fire engines arrived. Ashes fell, and the roar of the fire was now like thunder.

We were told to ready ourselves for evacuation. I packed the diaries. The saddest spectacle, beside that of the men fighting the fire as they would a war, were the animals, rabbits, coyotes, mountain lions, deer, driven by the fire to the edge of the mountain, taking a look at the crowd of people and panicking, choosing rather to rush back into the fire.

The fire now was like a ring around Sierra Madre, every mountain was burning. People living at the foot of the mountain were packing their cars. I rushed next door to the Campion children, who had been left with a baby-sitter, and got them into the car. It was impossible to save all the horses. We parked the car on the field below us. I called up the Campions, who were out for the evening, and reassured them. The baby-sitter dressed the children warmly. I made more coffee. I answered frantic telephone calls.

All night the fire engines sprayed water over the houses. But the fire grew immense, angry, and rushing at a speed I could not believe. It would rush along and suddenly leap over a road, a trail, like a monster, devouring all in its path. The firefighters cut breaks in the heavy brush,[3] but when the wind was strong enough, the fire leaped across them. At dawn one arm of the fire reached the back of our houses but was finally contained.

But high above and all around, the fire was burning, more vivid than the sun, throwing spirals of smoke in the air like the smoke from a volcano. Thirty-three cabins burned, and twelve thousand acres of forest still burning endangered countless homes below the fire. The fire was burning to the back of us now, and a rain of ashes began to fall and

---

3. **cut breaks in the heavy brush** cut down trees, shrubs, and underbrush to starve the fire of the fuel it needs to spread.

◄ **Vocabulary**
evacuees (ē vak′ yōō ēz′) *n.* people who are removed from a dangerous area

Organization
What clues here indicate that this essay is organized chronologically?

Organization
How does relating these events in chronological order increase the drama?

Comprehension
How is the author affected by the forest fire?

Vocabulary ▶
tenacious (tə nā´ shəs)
adj. holding on
firmly; stubborn

continued for days. The smell of the burn in the air, acid and pungent and tenacious. The dragon tongues of flames devouring, the flames leaping, the roar of destruction and dissolution,[4] the eyes of the panicked animals, caught between fire and human beings, between two forms of death. They chose the fire. It was as if the fire had come from the bowels of the earth, like that of a fiery volcano, it was so powerful, so swift, and so ravaging. I saw trees become skeletons in one minute, I saw trees fall, I saw bushes turned to ashes in a second, I saw weary, ash-covered men, looking like men returned from war, some with burns, others overcome by smoke.

The men were rushing from one spot to another watching for recrudescence.[5] Some started backfiring up the mountain so that the ascending flames could counteract the descending ones.

As the flames reached the cities below, hundreds of roofs burst into flame at once. There was no water pressure because all the fire hydrants were turned on at the same time, and the fire departments were helpless to save more than a few of the burning homes.

The blaring loudspeakers of passing police cars warned us to prepare to evacuate in case the wind changed and drove the fire in our direction. What did I wish to save? I thought only of the diaries. I appeared on the porch carrying a huge stack of diary volumes, preparing to pack them in the car. A reporter for the Pasadena *Star News* was taking pictures of the evacuation. He came up, very annoyed with me. "Hey, lady, next time could you bring out something more important than all those old papers? Carry some clothes on the next trip. We gotta have human interest in these pictures!"

▼ Critical Viewing
Why would a mountain be an especially challenging place to fight a fire?

---

4. **dissolution** (dis´ ə loo´ shən) *n.* crumbling.
5. **recrudescence** (rē´ kroo des´ əns) *n.* fresh outbreak of something that has been inactive.

A week later, the danger was over.

Gray ashy days.

In Sierra Madre, following the fire, the January rains brought floods. People are sandbagging their homes. At four A.M. the streets are covered with mud. The bare, burnt, naked mountains cannot hold the rains and slide down bringing rocks and mud. One of the rangers must now take photographs and movies of the disaster. He asks if I will help by holding an umbrella over the cameras. I put on my raincoat and he lends me hip boots which look to me like seven-league boots.

We drive a little way up the road. At the third curve it is impassable. A river is rushing across the road. The ranger takes pictures while I hold the umbrella over the camera. It is terrifying to see the muddied waters and rocks, the mountain disintegrating. When we are ready to return, the road before us is covered by large rocks but the ranger pushes on as if the truck were a jeep and forces it through. The edge of the road is being carried away.

I am laughing and scared too. The ranger is at ease in nature, and without fear. It is a wild moment of danger. It is easy to love nature in its peaceful and consoling moments, but one must love it in its furies too, in its despairs and wildness, especially when the damage is caused by us.

Organization
What event makes a mudslide more likely to occur after the fire?

Spiral Review
POINT OF VIEW How would you describe the author's point of view in these final paragraphs? Cite details to support your thinking.

◀ **Vocabulary**
consoling (kən sōl´ iŋ) *adj.* comforting

Critical Thinking

1. **Key Ideas and Details: (a)** What possession does Nin rescue from the fire? **(b)** How does she help other people during the ordeal? **(c) Infer:** What do her actions reveal about her?

2. **Key Ideas and Details: (a)** List three details Nin uses to describe the fire. **(b) Assess:** What effect does her language have on you?

3. **Integration of Knowledge and Ideas:** What does Nin conclude about nature after witnessing the fire and the mudslide?

4. **Integration of Knowledge and Ideas:** What kind of information can we learn from one natural disaster that might help us to better prepare for the next one? *[Connect to the Big Question: How much information is enough?]*

The Season's Curmudgeon[1] Sees the Light

Mary C. Curtis

Spring has never done much for me.

I was always an autumn kind of gal: My birthday is in September. When red and gold creep into the leaves, I see beauty, not death. A slight chill in the air feels just right.

I planned an October wedding. When I raised my face to kiss the groom, I didn't want any beads of sweat ruining the moment.

In autumn, you can fall back into an extra hour for sleep or **contemplation**. It's something I look forward to all summer.

Autumn leads into the hibernation of winter, setting the perfect mood for us quiet types. When you sit inside to read a book, you're never chided for wasting a perfectly beautiful day.

I didn't mind fall's signal of a new school year; I liked school.

The season even has a song —"Autumn in New York"— that mentions two of my favorite things.

Spring meant too many rainy days, too many reminders of the humid summer to come. Spring-fever romances? New blossoms and pungent smells trigger sneezes, not love.

In spring, you lose an hour, which you need for all the scrubbing and cleaning.

Everyone is always *doing* something in the spring. And if you aren't, you feel like some kind of slug. "You've had all winter to rest, you lazy bum. Go outside!"

When you do venture out, it's not cold, but it's not warm enough, either. You can't take a walk without running into throngs of people: jogging, cycling, lying in every tiny patch of sun.

---

1. **curmudgeon** (kər muj´ ən) *n.* bad-tempered person.

Everyone says it's time to garden; I hate to garden.

"It Might as Well be Spring" isn't bad, but it's a little corny.

But this year, I began to wonder if maybe I had written off spring too hastily.

Spring is a clear signal that you've made it through another ice storm, another broken heater, another cold snap.

Rain isn't a bother if you think of it as washing all the grime away. Splashing is fun!

Spring is an excuse to get out of all those black clothes and go buy a pair of pink shoes. (Oh yes I did!)

You can peel off another layer of outerwear each day. As you lighten up—by hue and weight—it puts a "spring" in your step.

Sure you feel obligated, even compelled, to move around. Just look at it as a reminder from Mother Nature that it's time to put those chocolate bunny ears down and exercise.

It's for your health and so you'll look fabulous when those layers come off.

You get to see people you haven't seen for months. Or if you did pass them by, they had their collars up and their heads down.

Now, you can stop and say hi, ask them what they've been up to, give them garden advice and get some tips yourself. (Even if you have no intention of actually getting out in the garden yourself, saying "mulch," "fertilizer," and "perennials" is cathartic.[2])

Spring is fresh and positive like no other season.

The best part is knowing that another spring will come, and you will always have the chance for a fresh start.

Organization
What two feelings about spring does the author contrast?

---

2. **cathartic** (ke thär´ tik) *adj.* allowing a release of emotional tension.

Critical Thinking

1. **Key Ideas and Details: (a)** What are two reasons that Curtis initially gives for preferring fall? **(b) Deduce:** Based on these reasons, how would you describe the author's personality? Explain.

2. **Key Ideas and Details: (a)** What change occurs in the author's thinking? **(b) Speculate:** What might have prompted this change?

3. **Integration of Knowledge and Ideas: (a)** On what type of information does Curtis base her impressions? **(b)** What makes them subject to change? *[Connect to the Big Question: How much information is enough?]*

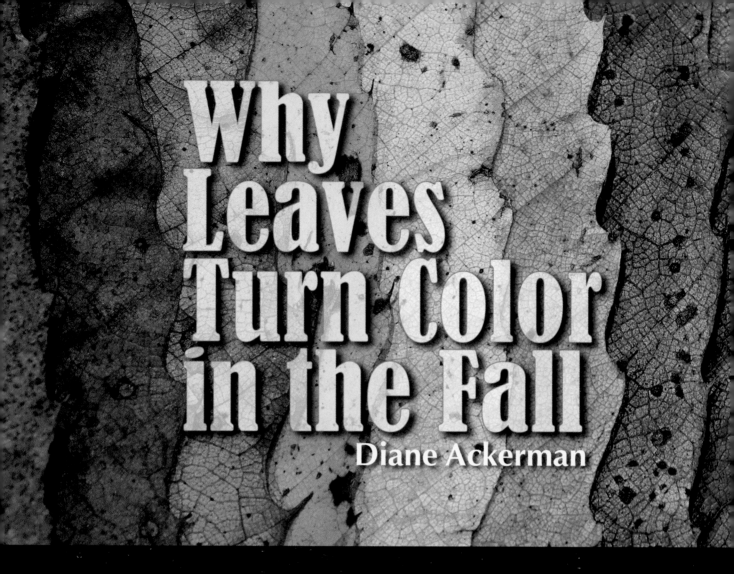

Why Leaves Turn Color in the Fall

Diane Ackerman

The stealth of autumn catches one unaware. Was that a goldfinch perching in the early September woods, or just the first turning leaf? A red-winged blackbird or a sugar maple closing up shop for the winter? Keen-eyed as leopards, we stand still and squint hard, looking for signs of movement. Early-morning frost sits heavily on the grass, and turns barbed wire into a string of stars. On a distant hill, a small square of yellow appears to be a lighted stage. At last the truth dawns on us: Fall is staggering in, right on schedule, with its baggage of chilly nights, macabre holidays, and spectacular, heart-stoppingly beautiful leaves. Soon the leaves will start cringing on the trees, and roll up in clenched fists before they actually fall off. Dry seedpods will rattle like tiny gourds. But first there will be weeks of gushing color so bright, so pastel, so confettilike, that people will travel up and down the East Coast just to stare at it—a whole season of leaves.

Where do the colors come from? Sunlight rules most living things with its golden edicts. When the days begin to shorten, soon after the summer solstice on June 21, a tree reconsiders its leaves. All summer it feeds them so they can process sunlight, but in the dog days of summer the tree begins pulling nutrients back into its trunk and roots, pares down, and gradually chokes off its leaves. A corky layer of cells forms at the leaves' slender petioles,[1] then scars over. Undernourished, the leaves stop producing the pigment chlorophyll,[2] and photosynthesis[3] ceases. Animals can migrate, hibernate, or store food to prepare for winter. But where can a tree go? It survives by dropping its leaves, and by the end of autumn only a few fragile threads of fluid-carrying xylem[4] hold leaves to their stems.

A turning leaf stays partly green at first, then reveals splotches of yellow and red as the chlorophyll gradually breaks down. Dark green seems to stay longest in the veins, outlining and defining them. During the summer, chlorophyll dissolves in the heat and light, but it is also being steadily replaced. In the fall, on the other hand, no new pigment is produced, and so we notice the other colors that were always there, right in the leaf, although chlorophyll's shocking green hid them from view. With their camouflage gone, we see these colors for the first time all year, and marvel, but they were always there, hidden like a vivid secret beneath the hot glowing greens of summer.

The most spectacular range of fall foliage occurs in the northeastern United States and in eastern China, where the leaves are robustly colored thanks in part to a rich climate. European maples don't achieve the same flaming reds as their American relatives, which thrive on cold nights and sunny days. In Europe, the warm, humid weather turns the leaves brown or mildly yellow. Anthocyanin, the pigment that gives apples their red and turns leaves red or red-violet, is produced by sugars that remain in the leaf after the supply of nutrients dwindles. Unlike the carotenoids, which color carrots, squash, and corn, and turn leaves orange and yellow, anthocyanin varies from year to year, depending on

Organization
What is the beginning and end of the chain of causes and effects the author describes here?

Comprehension
What pigment in leaves gives them their green color?

---

1. **petioles** (pet′ ē ōlz′) *n.* stalks of leaves.
2. **chlorophyll** (klôr′ ə fil′) *n.* green pigment found in plant cells. It is essential for photosynthesis.
3. **photosynthesis** (fōt′ ō sin′ thə sis) *n.* chemical process by which green plants make their food. This process involves using energy from the sun to turn water and carbon dioxide into food.
4. **xylem** (zī′ ləm) *n.* plant's woody tissue, which carries water and minerals in the stems, roots, and leaves.

Organization
What cause produces the most brilliantly colored leaves?

Vocabulary ▶
predisposed (prē dis pōzd´) *adj.* inclined

▼ Critical Viewing
From the author's description of leaf colors, what type of tree do you think this is?

the temperature and amount of sunlight. The fiercest colors occur in years when the fall sunlight is strongest and the nights are cool and dry (a state of grace scientists find vexing to forecast). This is also why leaves appear dizzyingly bright and clear on a sunny fall day: The anthocyanin flashes like a marquee.

Not all leaves turn the same color. Elms, weeping willows, and the ancient ginkgo all grow radiant yellow, along with hickories, aspens, bottlebrush buckeyes, cottonweeds, and tall, keening poplars. Basswood turns bronze, birches bright gold. Water-loving maples put on a symphonic display of scarlets. Sumacs turn red, too, as do flowering dogwoods, black gums, and sweet gums. Though some oaks yellow, most turn a pinkish brown. The farmlands also change color, as tepees of cornstalks and bales of shredded-wheat-textured hay stand drying in the fields. In some spots, one slope of a hill may be green and the other already in bright color, because the hillside facing south gets more sun and heat than the northern one.

An odd feature of the colors is that they don't seem to have any special purpose. We are **predisposed** to respond to their beauty, of course. They shimmer with the colors of sunset, spring flowers, the tawny buff of a colt's pretty rump, the shuddering pink of a blush. Animals and flowers color for a reason—adaptation to their environment—but there is no

adaptive reason for leaves to color so beautifully in the fall any more than there is for the sky or ocean to be blue. It's just one of the haphazard marvels the planet bestows every year. We find the sizzling colors thrilling, and in a sense they dupe us. Colored like living things, they signal death and disintegration. In time, they will become fragile and, like the body, return to dust. They are as we hope our own fate will be when we die; not to vanish, just to sublime from one beautiful state into another. Though leaves lose their green life, they bloom with urgent colors, as the woods grow mummified day by day, and Nature becomes more carnal, mute, and radiant.

We call the season "fall," from the Old English *feallan*, to fall, which leads back through time to the Indo-European *phol*, which also means to fall. So the word and the idea are both extremely ancient, and haven't really changed since the first of our kind needed a name for fall's leafy abundance. As we say the word, we're reminded of that other Fall, in the Garden of Eden, when fig leaves never withered and scales fell from our eyes. Fall is the time when leaves fall from the trees, just as spring is when flowers spring up, summer is when we simmer, and winter is when we whine from the cold.

Children love to play in piles of leaves, hurling them into the air like confetti, leaping into soft unruly mattresses of them. For children, leaf fall is just one of the odder figments of Nature, like hailstones or snowflakes. Walk down a lane overhung with trees in the never-never land of autumn, and you will forget about time and death, lost in the sheer delicious spill of color. . . . ●

> **Children love to play in piles of leaves, hurling them into the air like confetti, leaping into soft unruly mattresses of them.**

But how do the colored leaves fall? As a leaf ages, the growth hormone, auxin, fades, and cells at the base of the petiole divide. Two or three rows of small cells, lying at right angles to the axis of the petiole, react with water, then come apart, leaving the petioles hanging on by only a few threads of xylem. A light breeze, and the leaves are airborne. They glide and swoop, rocking in invisible cradles. They are all wing and may flutter from yard to yard on small whirlwinds or updrafts, swiveling as they go. Firmly tethered to earth, we love to see things rise up and fly—soap bubbles, balloons, birds, fall leaves. They remind us that the end of a season is **capricious**, as is the end of life. We especially like the way leaves rock, careen, and swoop as they fall. Everyone knows the motion. Pilots sometimes do a maneuver called a "falling leaf," in which the plane loses altitude quickly and on purpose, by slipping first to the right, then to the left. The machine weighs a ton or more, but in one pilot's mind it is a weightless thing, a falling leaf. She has seen the motion before, in the Vermont woods where she played as a child. Below her the trees radiate gold, copper, and red. Leaves are

Organization
How does the author use cause and effect to explain how the colored leaves fall?

◀ **Vocabulary**
capricious (kə prish´ əs) *adj.* tending to change abruptly, without apparent reason

Comprehension
Where does the word *fall* come from?

falling, although she can't see them fall, as she falls, swooping down for a closer view.

At last the leaves leave. But first they turn color and thrill us for weeks on end. Then they crunch and crackle underfoot. They *shush,* as children drag their small feet through leaves heaped along the curb. Dark, slimy mats of leaves cling to one's heels after a rain. A damp, stuccolike mortar of semidecayed leaves protects the tender shoots with a roof until spring, and makes a rich humus. An occasional bulge or ripple in the leafy mounds signals a shrew or a field mouse tunneling out of sight. Sometimes one finds in fossil stones the imprint of a leaf, long since disintegrated, whose outlines remind us how detailed, vibrant, and alive are the things of this earth that perish.

Organization
Humus is rich soil. How is humus both an effect and a cause?

Spiral Review
POINT OF VIEW How would you describe the author's point of view in this final paragraph? Cite details to support your answer.

Critical Thinking

1. **Key Ideas and Details: (a)** Identify two facts about leaves that are presented in the essay. **(b) Speculate:** Do you think Ackerman's scientific knowledge about leaves comes mostly from observation or research? Explain.

2. **Key Ideas and Details: (a)** Why do leaves fall? **(b) Apply:** To what human process does Ackerman compare the turning and falling of leaves?

3. **Key Ideas and Details: (a)** According to the text, where do leaves have the most spectacular color changes? **(b) Compare:** What weather conditions do those two places probably share? **(c) Speculate:** What questions might occur to a reader who does not live in a place where leaves change color?

4. **Integration of Knowledge and Ideas: (a)** List two pieces of information that the author provides that are new for you and two facts that you already knew. **(b)** Does learning more about the scientific explanation for the changing colors of leaves make them seem more, equally, or less amazing? Explain. *[Connect to the Big Question: How much information is enough?]*

• Forest Fire
• The Season's Curmudgeon Sees the Light
• Why Leaves Turn Color in the Fall

Writing to Sources

Comparing Types of Organization

1. **Craft and Structure:** **(a)** Identify three events in "Forest Fire" that occur in **chronological order.** **(b)** How does the final event of the essay help the writer make a point about nature?

2. **Craft and Structure:** **(a)** Name two **causes** in "Why Leaves Turn Color in the Fall" that explain the changes in autumn leaves. **(b)** What **effect** does the author point out in the last line? **(c)** How does this effect help her make a point about living things?

3. **Craft and Structure:** **(a)** In "The Season's Curmudgeon Sees the Light," identify two ways the author **compares and contrasts** spring and fall. **(b)** How does the writer use these contrasts to emphasize the qualities she has come to value about spring?

 Timed Writing

Explanatory Text: Essay

The authors of these essays use specific organizational patterns to achieve their purposes, or reasons for writing. Choose one essay and write an in-depth analysis of its structure. Discuss the overall organization of the essay and explain whether it suits the author's topic. Then, analyze one important paragraph, explaining how it is structured and the ways in which individual sentences work together to build meaning. Come to a general conclusion about the ways in which the topic can influence the author's choice of organizational pattern. **(40 minutes)**

5-Minute Planner

1. Read the prompt carefully and completely.

2. Gather your ideas by completing a chart like the one shown.

Title	Author's Purpose	Key Details	Organization

3. Look for connections, such as similarities or contrasts, in the details you have observed. Use these connections to help organize your essay.

4. Reread the prompt, and then draft your essay.

USE ACADEMIC VOCABULARY

As you write, use academic language, including these words or their related forms:

argument

decision

emphasize

influence

For more information about academic vocabulary, see the Building Academic Vocabulary workshop in the front of your book.

Word Origins

The history of the English language begins around the year A.D. 500. Germanic tribes—the Angles, Saxons, and Jutes—brought their language to Britain when they moved west and settled there. Later, when the Vikings invaded Britain, Danish and Norse elements were introduced to the language. Latin elements were added when Christian missionaries arrived. The resulting language, Old English, was spoken until about 1100, when it underwent another change.

The Norman Conquest In 1066, Britain was conquered by invaders from the Normandy region of France, who introduced elements of Old French into the language. This new form, Middle English, was spoken from about 1100 to 1500.

The Renaissance During the Renaissance (1300–1600), interest in ancient Greek and Roman culture brought Greek and Latin influences to English. Toward the end of the Renaissance, Shakespeare added about two thousand words to English. The result, Modern English, continues to change to this day.

Word Roots The root of a word, or its basic element of meaning, is a clue to the word's origins. In addition, modern English words that share the same root usually have related meanings.

This chart shows some of the ways words enter our language.

Common Core State Standards

4. Determine or clarify the meaning of unknown and multiple-meaning words or phrases based on *grade 8 reading and content,* choosing flexibly from a range of strategies.

4.a. Use context as a clue to the meaning of a word or phrase.

4.b. Use common, grade-appropriate Greek or Latin affixes and roots as clues to the meaning of a word (e.g., *precede, recede, secede*).

4.c. Consult general and specialized reference materials, both print and digital, to find the pronunciation of a word or determine or clarify its precise meaning or its part of speech.

Source	Result	Examples
War	Conquerors bring new terms, ideas, and vocabulary.	*anger* (Old Norse) *chivalry* (French)
Immigration	Large groups of people moving from other countries bring words with them.	*boycott* (Irish) *frankfurter* (German) *carnival* (Italian)
Travel and Trade	People who travel and do business in foreign lands bring new words back with them.	*shampoo* (Hindi) *kimono* (Japanese) *kowtow* (Chinese)
Science and Technology	New concepts in science and technology give rise to new words.	*blog* *ultrasound* *laser*
Mythology	Names of gods, goddesses, heroes, and heroines of various mythologies form the basis of new words.	*Wednesday* (from Woden, a god in Anglo-Saxon mythology) *martial* (from Mars, the god of war in Roman mythology)

Practice A

For each underlined root, write two more related words.

1. The Greek root _-phon-_, meaning "sound," is part of our word _telephone._

2. The Latin root _-mob-_, meaning "move," is part of our word _mobile._

3. The Latin root _-ped-_, meaning "foot," is part of our word _pedal._

4. The Greek root _-therm-_, meaning "heat," is part of our word _thermometer._

5. The Latin root _-vis-_, meaning "see," is part of our word _visible._

6. The Greek root _-photo-_, meaning "light," is part of our word _photography._

7. The Latin root _-dent-_, meaning "tooth," is part of our word _dentist._

Practice B

An **allusion** is a reference to a person, place, thing, or literary work. Many works of literature contain allusions to characters from **mythology.** Read each description of a mythological character. Then, use the information to complete each allusion.

1. In Greek mythology, Narcissus was a young man who fell in love with his own reflection. _He is such a Narcissus, he does not care about_ _____.

2. Titans were gigantic beings in Greek mythology. _The ship_ Titanic _was_ _____.

3. In Roman mythology, Mercury, the messenger of the gods, was known for his speed. _Because she ran like Mercury, her team_ _____.

4. Cupid was the Roman god of love. _My friend warned me not to play Cupid because_ _____.

5. In Greek mythology, King Midas had the gift of making everything he touched turn to gold. _The president of the company has the Midas touch because_ _____.

Activity Look up the following words in a dictionary that includes information on word origins. Describe the ways in which these words entered American English.

1. tortilla
2. gigabyte
3. sauna
4. camouflage
5. Thursday
6. January

Comprehension and Collaboration

Choose one of the mythological characters from Practice B, or research one of these:

- **Atlas**
- **Proteus**
- **Hercules**

Then, write a short paragraph on a topic of your choice that includes an **allusion** to that character.

Effective Listening and Note-Taking

For situations when understanding and remembering are crucial, it is useful to learn effective listening and note-taking skills.

Learn the Skills

Select a purpose for listening. Choosing a purpose for listening helps you focus your attention on what is most important. For example, if your purpose is to follow instructions, you will need to focus more closely on details than if your purpose were enjoyment.

Consider the speaker's purpose. A speaker's purpose will influence how you listen. For example, listen carefully and analytically as a teacher speaks to inform you. Listen critically and note questions you have as a candidate speaks to persuade you.

Listen to how something is said. Speakers often give you hints that can help you identify their purpose and perspective. Listen for these clues:

- changes in tone of voice that indicate emotion
- emphasis on words or phrases
- repetition of key points

Eliminate barriers to listening. Try to avoid distractions when listening. Sit close to the speaker and try to stay focused on what he or she is saying—not on the other things that are happening in the room.

Listen critically. When you are absorbing media messages or different points of view, ask yourself questions such as those in the chart. Answering such questions will also help you identify the speaker's purpose.

Note main ideas and details. Do not try to record every word a speaker says. Instead, note the speaker's main points and a few supporting details. To save time, use minimal punctuation, partial phrases, and abbreviations. Later, review your notes to be sure you understand them.

Record your questions. Write down your questions and reactions. These notes will help you think critically about what you hear.

 **Common Core State Standards**

Speaking and Listening
1.c. Pose questions that connect the ideas of several speakers and respond to others' questions and comments with relevant evidence, observations, and ideas.
2. Analyze the purpose of information presented in diverse media and formats and evaluate the motives behind its presentation.
3. Delineate a speaker's argument and specific claims, evaluating the soundness of the reasoning and relevance and sufficiency of the evidence and identifying when irrelevant evidence is introduced.

Critical-Listening Questions

- How would you **paraphrase**, or describe in your own words, the **speaker's purpose**?
- How would you describe his or her **point of view** or message?
- What are the main ideas in the speaker's argument?
- Does the speaker offer enough facts or examples as support?
- How does the way the speaker **delivers** the presentation affect the message?
- Do you agree with the speaker's point of view and ideas?
- What are the speaker's **biases**, influences, or leanings? Do they make his or her points more believable or less believable?
- What **questions** remain unanswered for you?

Practice the Skills

Presentation of Knowledge and Ideas Use what you have learned in this workshop to complete the following activity.

ACTIVITY: Listen to a Political Speech and Take Notes

Listen to a recording of a current or historic political speech. Then, follow the steps below:

- Identify your purpose for listening.
- Identify the speaker's purpose and perspective by paying attention to ideas that repeat, emphasis placed on words, or changes in tone.
- Avoid distractions and focus your attention on the speaker.
- Take notes, capturing the speaker's main points and a few supporting details.
- Write down your questions and reactions.

Use a Listening Guide like the one below as you analyze the purpose of information presented and evaluate the motives behind its presentation.

Listening Guide

Speaker's Cues

What methods does the speaker use to reveal purpose? Consider changes in tone of voice, emphasis on words or phrases, and repetition of key points.

Interpret

- What is the speaker's point of view, and how is it revealed?
- What are the speaker's biases, and how do they affect the message?
- How does the speaker's delivery affect the message?
- Are enough facts or examples presented to support key points?
- What are the main points in the speaker's arguments?
- How logical is the connection between each point and the main claim?

Taking Notes

Jot down the speaker's main ideas and a few supporting details. Note your reaction to the speech and any questions you have.

Comprehension and Collaboration With a group of classmates, watch and take notes on a television interview. Compare the conclusions group members reached about the purpose of and motivation behind the interview. Also, compare questions. Then, compare how your notes differed in organization and style. In your discussion, ask questions that connect your group members' ideas, and use your notes to respond to questions they raise.

Write an Informative Text

Comparison-and-Contrast Essay

Defining the Form In a **comparison-and-contrast essay**, a writer examines the similarities and differences between two or more subjects. You might use elements of this type of writing in comparisons of literary works, product comparisons, and news analyses.

Assignment Write a comparison-and-contrast essay to analyze the similarities and differences between two or more subjects. Your essay should feature the following elements:

✓ a *topic involving two or more subjects* that are different in some ways and similar in other ways

✓ an introduction that presents the *thesis,* or main point; a body that shows similarities and differences; and a conclusion that restates and reinforces the thesis

✓ a consistent *structure that uses parallelism* to emphasize comparisons and contrasts

✓ error-free writing, including *correct use of consistent verb mood*

To preview the criteria on which your comparison-and-contrast essay may be judged, see the rubric on page 281.

FOCUS ON RESEARCH

When you write a comparison-and-contrast essay, you might perform research to

- verify the similarities and differences you claim exist between the two topics you are comparing.

- find additional examples to illustrate your thesis, or main point.

- locate facts and statistics that support your comparisons.

Be sure to note all resources you use in your research, and credit those sources in your final drafts. Refer to the Conducting Research workshop in the Introductory Unit for assistance in citing materials.

Common Core State Standards

Writing

2. Write informative/explanatory texts to examine a topic and convey ideas, concepts, and information through the selection, organization, and analysis of relevant content.

2.a. Introduce a topic clearly, previewing what is to follow; organize ideas, concepts, and information into broader categories; include formatting, graphics, and multimedia when useful to aiding comprehension.

2.b. Develop the topic with relevant, well-chosen facts, definitions, concrete details, quotations, or other information and examples.

READING-WRITING CONNECTION

To get a feel for comparison-and-contrast essays, read "The Season's Curmudgeon Sees the Light," by Mary C. Curtis, on page 262.

Prewriting/Planning Strategies

Create a personal-experience timeline. Every time you outgrow your clothes, you can see how you are changing. In addition to physical change, you undergo changes in attitude and perspective. Use a timeline like the one shown to chart ways you have changed over time. Next, choose two entries as one possible topic for your comparison-and-contrast essay.

Preschool	Kindergarten	Grade 2	Grade 4	Grade 6	Grade 8
Enjoyed playing alone in sandbox	Liked dressing as a superhero, finger painting	Wanted to do everything perfectly	Understood it was OK to make mistakes	Joined the swimming team	Helped team win swim meet

Narrow your topic. Before you finalize your topic, examine it to be sure you can discuss it fully. A topic such as "The Best Vacation Spots," for example, is much too broad in scope to be addressed adequately in a short essay. You might narrow it to "Atlanta vs. San Francisco—Which Is More Family-Friendly?" Review your topic to divide it into separate parts, aspects, or subtopics. Choose one of these subtopics as your new, narrowed topic.

Use a Venn diagram. To gather details, use a Venn diagram, as shown here. Jot down as many similarities as you can in the center section, and note several differences in the outer sections of each circle. When you have finished, circle the items that most vividly show comparisons and contrasts. When you write your essay, plan to *juxtapose* these details—set them side-by-side—to emphasize their differences and similarities. Look at this example:

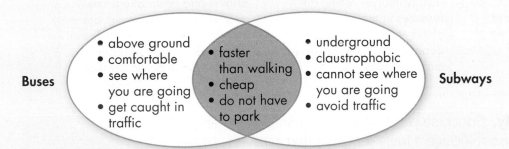

Generate ideas. For more idea-generating strategies, see page 277.

Drafting Strategies

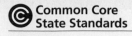

Common Core State Standards

Writing
2.b. Develop the topic with relevant, well-chosen facts, definitions, concrete details, quotations, or other information and examples.
2.f. Provide a concluding statement or section that follows from and supports the information or explanation presented.

Select the best organizational format. There are two common ways to organize a comparison-and-contrast essay. Review these options and use a structure that is appropriate to your topic.

- **Block method** Present all the details about one aspect first, and then present all the details about the next aspect. The block method works well if you are writing about more than two aspects of a topic, or if your topic is complex.

- **Point-by-point organization** Discuss each aspect of your subjects in turn. For example, if you are comparing buses and subways, you might first discuss the cost of each, then the convenience, and so on.

Use parallel paragraph structure. No matter which overall organizational method you choose, be sure to keep the paragraphs in the body *parallel,* or consistent, in structure and style. This makes it easier for your reader to follow and understand your points. For example, for the first aspect you compare, you might choose the SEE method (shown in the chart below) to develop the comparison in your supporting paragraphs. Then you would use the same method to develop support for the second aspect. Study the example in the chart.

- State the topic of the paragraph.
- Extend the idea by restating it in a new way, applying it to a particular case, or contrasting it with another point.
- Elaborate with specific examples, facts, or explanations.

Block

I. Buses
   a. cheaper
   b. more routes
   c. better views
II. Trains
   a. better seats
   b. faster
   c. quieter

Point-by-Point

I. Introduction
II. Cost of each
III. Accessibility of each
IV. View from each
V. Disadvantages of each

Statement	Extension	Elaboration
Buses and trains are two forms of public transportation that offer advantages and disadvantages in the area of convenience.	These advantages and disadvantages reflect differences in the two types of transportation. They also depend on riders' particular circumstances.	For example, if people's origins and destinations are near train stations, trains are usually more convenient. Trains do not get caught in traffic and are generally faster than buses.

Conclude effectively. Conclude your essay with a paragraph that sums up your comparison. Include a lively sentence that captures your main impression of the topic.

Generating Ideas

Ideas are the building blocks of all good writing. To generate ideas, try one or more of these methods before you begin writing.

Accessing Prior Knowledge Ask, "What do I already know about these subjects' similarities and differences?" Jot down any relevant personal experiences, as well as ideas that you discovered while reading.

Brainstorming With Others Get together with classmates and have a brainstorming session to discuss different **aspects of comparison**, or factors people consider when deciding between the two subjects. For example, in comparing different entertainment systems, aspects of comparison might be price, durability, or enjoyment. As you brainstorm, try to be accepting of all ideas—no matter how unusual. The purpose of the brainstorming session is to list as many ideas as you can. Later, when you review your list, you can decide how many of the ideas could actually work.

Researching Identify and use various resources to help you compare and contrast the subjects. These resources may be books, Web pages, articles, or individuals with expert knowledge. Focus on three or four aspects of comparison from your brainstorming session.

Looking at All Sides When comparing and contrasting subjects, generate as many comparisons as contrasts between the subjects. You can always choose not to use an idea later, but a comparison-and-contrast essay should include at least one way in which the subjects are alike and at least one way in which they are different.

COMPARE	CONTRAST
Entertainment System A The system takes up about two square feet of space on a tabletop.	**Entertainment System A** The system is the most expensive one on the market today.
Entertainment System B The system takes up about one-and-a-half square feet of space on a tabletop.	**Entertainment System B** The system is in the mid-price range and often goes on sale at electronics stores.

Trying New Approaches The time to work on your ideas is not limited to the time you spend planning. As you draft and then revise, pay attention to new insights that occur to you, as well as to ideas that just aren't working. Do not be afraid to rewrite sections of your draft—or even to start drafting again, using a new approach—based on what you discover as you write.

Revising Strategies

Common Core State Standards

Check for relevant support. Reread your draft. Make sure each paragraph contains relevant supporting details. Where details are missing, add facts, quotations, or other relevant information or examples to support your analysis. Delete any details that do not add to your comparison.

Check language and spelling. Be sure to use precise language. Whenever appropriate, use vocabulary that is specific to your topic. When you do use technical terms for precision, define each term at its first appearance to aid the reader. Make sure to check your spelling of technical terms, consulting a dictionary as needed.

Check overall balance. Use one color to highlight details about one aspect of your comparison. Use additional colors to mark details about other aspects. If your draft has more of one color, add details on an aspect that is less developed.

Check organization and structure. If your rereading reveals a confusing overall organization, consider rearranging sections to fit the block method or point-by-point organization. If your review indicates an inconsistent paragraph structure, revise your work to develop your arguments in a parallel way.

Original Version	Revised to Include Parallelism
Bus routes crisscross the city, traveling down every major street and into every neighborhood. I took the train once, and it dropped me off on the outskirts of town.	*Bus routes crisscross the city,* traveling down every major street and into every neighborhood. *The train, on the other hand, skirts the city,* traveling down tracks far from many common destinations.

Revise for formal language. Your essay should be engaging, but you should use an appropriately formal style. Replace or eliminate informal expressions such as *cool, I mean, kind of, way too* and the word *like* used as filler, as in *Buses are like too expensive.*

Check voice. Identify any cases in which you have used passive voice, and consider revising to active. (See page 254.)

Peer Review

Invite a classmate to read your draft. Ask your reader whether

- the overall organization you chose for your comparison is clear.

- your essay is missing support for an aspect of your comparison.

Revise your draft, based on this feedback.

Writing

2.b. Develop the topic with relevant, well-chosen facts, definitions, concrete details, quotations, or other information and examples.

2.d. Use precise language and domain-specific vocabulary to inform about or explain the topic.

2.e. Establish and maintain a formal style.

5. With some guidance and support from peers and adults, develop and strengthen writing as needed by planning, revising, editing, rewriting, or trying a new approach, focusing on how well purpose and audience have been addressed.

Language

1.b. Form and use verbs in the active and passive voice.

1.c. Form and use verbs in the indicative, imperative, interrogative, conditional, and subjunctive mood.

1.d. Recognize and correct inappropriate shifts in verb voice and mood.

2.c. Spell correctly.

3.a. Use verbs in the active and passive voice and in the conditional and subjunctive mood to achieve particular effects (e.g., emphasizing the actor or the action; expressing uncertainty or describing a state contrary to fact).

Revising Verbs for Mood

Mood expresses the speaker's attitude toward the action or state of being expressed by a verb.

Identifying Mood of Verbs English has several verb moods:

Indicative: This mood is used to make statements of fact.

Example: Paul went to the store.

Interrogative: This mood is used to ask questions.

Example: Did you go to the store? Will you buy milk?

Imperative: This mood is used to issue requests or commands.

Examples: Please go to the store.   Go to the store!

Subjunctive: This mood is used to express a wish, a hope, or a statement contrary to fact. It is often found in an *if* clause.

Example: If I **were** going to the store, I would take my wallet.

The subjunctive is also used to express a request, demand, or proposal.

Examples: I insisted that he **go**.   We ask that you **be** quiet.

Conditional: This mood is used to refer to something that has not happened. In addition, it is used to express uncertainty. It uses conditional auxiliary verbs such as *could, would, should,* and *might.*

Example: I **might** go to the store.

Fixing Incorrect Use of the Indicative To determine whether to use the subjunctive, check *if* and *that* clauses. Determine whether they express a wish, command, or matter contrary to fact. If they do, use the subjunctive.

Error: If Josephine <u>was</u> taller, she would be able to reach.

Correction: If Josephine <u>were</u> taller, she would be able to reach.

Fixing Incorrect Shifts in Mood To fix incorrect shifts in mood, check places where you change from one mood to another. Make sure each change is required. If it is not, revise to keep the mood consistent.

Incorrect Shift to Imperative: Visitors must check in at the gate, and remember, don't feed the wildlife!

Correction: Visitors must check in at the gate and remember not to feed the wildlife.

Grammar in Your Writing

Review your draft for places where you should use the subjunctive, or where you shift from one mood to another. Fix any errors in mood.

STUDENT MODEL: **Carolyn Sienko, Williamston, MI**

Comparing Struggles for Equality

The Civil Rights Movement of the 1950s and 1960s had a lot in common with the women's suffrage movement that began with the Seneca Falls Convention in 1848. Both movements involved a group of people who were denied rights and who fought to obtain those rights.

Although in most ways the two struggles were similar, the specific rights each group fought for were different. Women wanted the right to vote in elections, the right to own property in their own names, and the right to keep their own wages. African Americans fought for the end to segregation. Like the women, they wanted to be treated with equal rights. However, the Civil Rights Movement was about fairness in schools, jobs, and public places like buses and restaurants.

Both movements protested in nonviolent ways. They held marches, boycotts, and demonstrations to raise the public's consciousness and get the laws changed. In 1917, Alice Paul and other women picketed at the White House. In 1963, more than 200,000 Americans, led by Dr. Martin Luther King, Jr., marched on Washington, D.C. They wanted Congress to pass laws to end discrimination.

Both movements were about equality. The Declaration of Independence, an important document in the struggle for equality, states: "We hold these truths to be self-evident, that all men are created equal; that they are endowed by their Creator with certain unalienable rights; that among these are life, liberty, and the pursuit of happiness."

Protesters in both the Civil Rights Movement and the women's suffrage movement felt that they were being denied rights that were given to them by this statement from the Declaration of Independence. Both groups were able to change the laws so that they could have their rights. Women were given the right to vote in 1920 by Amendment 19 to the Constitution. Similarly, the Civil Rights Act of 1964 outlawed discrimination in hiring and ended segregation in public places.

In conclusion, the Civil Rights Movement of the 1950s and 1960s and the women's suffrage movement were both about equality under the law. They are both good examples of how much work and determination it takes to change the laws. It is good to know, however, that the laws can be changed.

Carolyn begins her essay with a thesis statement that introduces the subjects of her comparison. She indicates that she will focus more on similarities.

The writer focuses first on the differences in the specific rights being sought.

Carolyn uses point-by-point organization to compare the movements.

The writer provides a quotation to support an idea.

The conclusion restates the introduction, emphasizing the writer's main idea.

Editing and Proofreading

Proofread to correct errors in spelling, grammar, and punctuation.

Focus on items in a series. Use commas to separate words, phrases, or clauses in a series. To avoid confusion, use semicolons to separate items in a series when some items already contain commas. Use colons to introduce lists.

> **Commas:** Recyling is cheaper, easier, and cleaner than dumping.
>
> **Semicolons:** We visited Moab, Utah; Lima, Ohio; and Bath, Maine.
>
> **Colons:** I will compare the following: beets, carrots, and celery.

Spiral Review
Earlier in this unit, you learned about **simple tenses of verbs** (p. 222) and **perfect tenses of verbs** (p. 234). Check your essay to be sure you have used verb tenses correctly.

Publishing and Presenting

Consider one of the following ways to share your writing:

Publish a column. If you compared subjects of local interest, such as two restaurants or several stores, submit your essay to your local newspaper or post it on a community blog or Web site.

Start a family tradition. If you have compared two subjects of interest to your family—two uncles, two birthdays, two vacations—read your essay at a family gathering.

Reflecting on Your Writing

Writer's Journal Jot down your answer to this question:

If you could write your essay again, what would you do differently?

Rubric for Self-Assessment

Find evidence in your writing to address each category. Then, use the rating scale to grade your work.

Criteria	Rating Scale
Purpose/Focus Clearly introduces a topic, previewing what is to follow; provides a concluding section that follows from the information presented	*not very* .... *very* 1　　2　　3　　4
Organization Effectively uses parallel structure to emphasize the points of comparison and contrast	1　　2　　3　　4
Development of Ideas/Elaboration Successfully develops the topic with relevant, well-chosen, concrete details	1　　2　　3　　4
Language Uses precise and formal language to compare and contrast the subjects, including domain-specific vocabulary when appropriate	1　　2　　3　　4
Conventions Uses proper grammar; avoids improper shifts in verb mood	1　　2　　3　　4

SELECTED RESPONSE

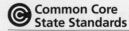

**Common Core
State Standards**

RI.8.4, RI.8.6
[For full standards wording, see the chart in the front of this book.]

I. Reading Literature/Informational Text

Directions: *Read the excerpt from "Sharing in the American Dream," a speech by Colin Powell. Then, answer each question that follows.*

Over 200 years ago, a group of volunteers gathered on this sacred spot to found a new nation. In perfect words, they voiced their dreams and <u>aspirations</u> of an imperfect world. They pledged their lives, their fortune and their sacred honor to secure inalienable rights given by God for life, liberty and pursuit of happiness—pledged that they would provide them to all who would inhabit this new nation.

They look down on us today in spirit, with pride for all we have done to keep faith with their ideals and their sacrifices. Yet, despite all we have done, this is still an imperfect world. We still live in an imperfect society. Despite more than two centuries of moral and material progress, despite all our efforts to achieve a more perfect union, there are still Americans who are not sharing in the American Dream. There are still Americans who wonder: is the journey there for them, is the dream there for them, or, whether it is, at best, a dream deferred.

The great American poet Langston Hughes talked about a dream deferred, and he said, "What happens to a dream deferred? Does it dry up like a raisin in the sun, or fester like a sore and then run? Does it stink like rotten meat or crust and sugar over like a syrupy sweet? Maybe it just sags, like a heavy load. Or, does it explode?" . . .

So today, we gather here today to pledge that the dream must no longer be deferred and it will never, as long as we can do anything about it, become a dream denied. That is why we are here, my friends. We gather here to pledge that those of us who are more fortunate will not forsake those who are less fortunate. We are a compassionate and caring people. We are a generous people. We will reach down, we will reach back, we will reach across to help our brothers and sisters who are in need.

1. To which "group of volunteers" does the speaker most likely refer in the first sentence?
   A. Langston Hughes and other famous poets, who invented the term "American Dream"
   B. America's Founding Fathers, who signed the Declaration of Independence
   C. the group of workers who constructed the building in which the writer is standing
   D. There is no way to know.

2. **Part A** What **persuasive technique** does the speaker use in the final paragraph?
   A. appeal to authority
   B. appeal to reason
   C. rhetorical question
   D. repetition

   Part B Which phrase from the passage best supports the answer to Part A?
   A. "we gather here today to pledge that the dream must no longer be deferred"
   B. "That is why we are here, my friends."
   C. "We are a compassionate and caring people. We are a generous people."
   D. "as long as we can do anything about it"

3. How does the speaker use an **appeal to emotions** in the passage?
   A. The speaker repeats the words "dream deferred" frequently.
   B. The speaker refers to the ideas that people had over 200 years ago.
   C. The speaker refers to the hardships faced by fellow Americans in need of help.
   D. The speaker compares a dream deferred to a raisin in the sun.

4. **Part A** What was most likely the speaker's **purpose** when writing this passage?
   A. to educate people about a great poet
   B. to explain the historical origins of the term "American Dream"
   C. to convince people to spend more time with their siblings
   D. to encourage people to help others through volunteer work

Part B Which phrase from the passage most clearly indicates the speaker's purpose?
   A. "those of us who are more fortunate will not forsake those who are less fortunate"
   B. "The great American poet Langston Hughes talked about a dream deferred"
   C. "brothers and sisters"
   D. "more than two centuries of . . . progress"

5. Which pair of words best describes the overall **tone** of the passage?
   A. passionate and hopeful
   B. casual and funny
   C. alarmed and angry
   D. optimistic and thankful

6. Which best describes an **organizational structure** used in the passage?
   A. a contrast between a 200-year-old dream and present-day reality
   B. a cause-and-effect explanation of a "dream deferred"
   C. a chronological account of the history of volunteerism
   D. a comparison of two different dreams

7. **Vocabulary** Which is the best definition of the underlined word <u>aspirations</u>?
   A. nightmares   C. sweat
   B. goals   D. speeches

Timed Writing

8. In a brief essay, analyze the writer's **word choice** in the passage. Choose three specific words or phrases, and explain how their **denotations** and **connotations** contribute to the passage's **tone** and meaning.

II. Reading Informational Text

 **Common Core State Standards**

RI.8.1; L.8.1.b, L.8.1.c, L.8.1.d, L.8.3.a, L.8.4.a
[For full standards wording, see the chart in the front of this book.]

Directions: *Read the passages. Then, answer each question that follows.*

Passage A We were all, horses and men, four days and four nights on the cars coming here from San Antonio and were very tired and very dirty when we arrived. . . .

Mother stays at a big hotel about a mile from camp. There are nearly thirty thousand troops here now, besides the sailors from the war-ships in the bay. At night the corridors and piazzas are thronged with officers of the army and navy; the older ones fought in the great Civil War, a third of a century ago, and now they are all going to Cuba to war against the Spaniards. Most of them are in blue, but our rough-riders are in brown.

Passage B It was the beginning of the Spanish-American War in the spring of 1898. As Assistant Secretary of the Navy, Roosevelt was stationed in Florida, with the Rough Riders, a volunteer <u>regiment</u> that he had helped organize. The men and their horses had just endured four grueling days of rail travel from San Antonio, Texas, to the camp in Tampa.

In late June, American troops traveled to Cuba. On July 1, Roosevelt and his Rough Riders fought in the legendary Battle of San Juan Hill. Stories of Roosevelt's fearless leadership following the battle made him a hero in the United States. It was also the start of his political career.

1. Which word or phrase is closest in meaning to the underlined word <u>regiment</u>?

   A. an elaborate celebration
   B. a unit of ground forces
   C. a group of highly paid warriors
   D. a five-star general

2. **Part A** According to the passages, by what method of transportation did the Rough Riders travel from San Antonio to the camp?

   A. horseback
   B. naval ship
   C. covered wagon
   D. train

Part B Which phrase from the passages most clearly shows the Rough Riders' method of transportation to the camp?

   A. "We were all, horses and men"
   B. "had just endured four grueling days of rail travel"
   C. "besides the sailors from the war-ships in the bay."
   D. "In late June, American troops traveled to Cuba."

III. Writing and Language Conventions

Directions: *Read the passage. Then, answer each question that follows.*

(1) One of the most powerful characters in fiction is the character Charlie in "Flowers for Algernon." (2) Charlie is a man with a limited intellect. (3) If he was more intelligent, he will know that others mistreat him. (4) After Charlie has surgery to improve his intelligence, he began to see the world differently. (5) Suddenly, people's limitations are noticed by him—people whom he once considered smart. (6) Worse, he realizes that his friends have taken advantage of him. (7) What does Charlie's bitter experience show? (8) It shows how knowledge sometimes comes at a high price.

1. Which revision to sentence 3 correctly uses the **subjunctive** and **conditional moods**?
   A. If he was more intelligent, he would know that others mistreat him.
   B. If he is more intelligent, he would know that others mistreat him.
   C. If he were more intelligent, he will know that others mistreat him.
   D. If he were more intelligent, he would know that others mistreat him.

2. Which revision to sentence 4 would maintain a consistent verb **tense**?
   A. After Charlie had surgery to improve his intelligence, he begins to see the world differently.
   B. After Charlie has surgery to improve his intelligence, he begins to see the world differently.
   C. After Charlie has had surgery to improve his intelligence, he began to see the world differently.
   D. The sentence is correct as it is.

3. Which revision to the first part of sentence 5 corrects an improper shift in **voice** without changing the meaning of the sentence?
   A. Suddenly, people are noticed by his limitations
   B. Suddenly, people notice his limitations
   C. Suddenly, he notices people's limitations
   D. Suddenly, his limitations are noticed by people

4. Which **tense** of the verb *take* appears in sentence 6?
   A. simple present tense
   B. simple past tense
   C. present perfect tense
   D. past perfect tense

5. What **mood** is used in sentence 7?
   A. subjunctive
   B. imperative
   C. indicative
   D. interrogative

CONSTRUCTED RESPONSE

Common Core
State Standards

RI.8.2, RI.8.4, RI.8.5, RI.8.6,
RI.8.8; W.8.7, W.8.8, W.8.9;
SL.8.1, SL.8.6; L.8.1
[For full standards wording, see
the chart in the front of this
book.]

Directions: *Follow the instructions to complete the tasks below as required by your teacher.*

As you work on each task, incorporate both general academic vocabulary and literary terms you learned in Parts 1 and 2 of this unit.

Writing

TASK 1 ▶ Informational Text [RI.8.5]

Analyze Paragraph Structure

Write an essay in which you analyze the structure of one paragraph from a work of nonfiction in Part 2 of this unit.

Part 1

- Review and evaluate a paragraph that was particularly important to an essay or a speech from Part 2 of this unit.

- As you are reviewing the paragraph, take notes on its central, or main, idea.

- Answer the following questions: Is the central idea directly stated or implied? What role does each sentence play in building the central idea?

Part 2

- Write an essay in which you identify the paragraph's central idea and explain how each sentence in the paragraph introduces, refines, or develops the idea.

- Conclude your essay by restating your ideas about the importance of the paragraph within the work as a whole.

TASK 2 ▶ Informational Text [RI.8.4; L.8.1]

Compare and Contrast Tone

Write an essay in which you analyze the authors' word choices in two selections from Part 2 of this unit. Explain how each author's word choices affect his or her overall tone.

- Choose two selections that have notable differences in tone.

- In your essay, identify the overall tone of each selection (e.g., casual, friendly, respectful, earnest), and explain how that tone reflects the author's attitude toward the selection's topic or audience.

- Compare and contrast the two authors' word choices, explaining how each author's choice of words conveys a different tone. Consider the denotations and connotations of specific words or phrases in the selections.

- As you write, be sure to avoid inappropriate shifts in verb voice or mood.

TASK 3 ▶ Informational Text [RI.8.2, RI.8.6, RI.8.8]

Evaluate an Argument

Write an evaluation of the argument in an essay or speech from Part 2 of this unit.

- Begin your evaluation by explaining which work you will analyze and why you chose it. Identify the author's central idea and purpose for writing, and include a brief summary of the work.

- State whether you think the author's argument is logical, clearly developed through specific claims, and supported with valid evidence.

- If you find the argument logical and sound, explain why. If you find the argument weak or inadequately supported, explain why.

- Support your evaluation with details from the work.

Speaking and Listening

Analyze and Discuss Word Choice

Lead a small group discussion in which you analyze the word choice in a nonfiction work from Part 2 of this unit.

- Prepare for the discussion by choosing and analyzing the work ahead of time. Consider the author's use of specific words and phrases, and note any figurative language, words with strong emotional connotations, or words with technical meanings that he or she uses. Describe how the author's word choices combine to create a specific tone.

- Identify at least three key points you want to cover during the discussion.

- Create handouts, such as lists of words with definitions, to share with your group.

- As you conduct the discussion, refer to your handouts, and invite participants to make suggestions for items to add.

Evaluate Evidence

Write and deliver an oral evaluation of the evidence used in a persuasive selection from Part 2 of this unit.

- Open your oral evaluation by identifying the selection you will analyze. Summarize the author's main argument in the selection, reviewing the key claims he or she makes.

- Give your general evaluation of the author's use of evidence: Does the author provide sufficient evidence for his or her claims? Is every piece of evidence relevant, or logically related to the claim it is meant to support?

- Support your evaluation with examples from the text. Identify any claims supported with sufficient evidence, any claims for which the author should have provided more evidence, and any examples you find of irrelevant evidence. Explain the reasons for your judgments.

- As you speak, demonstrate respect for your topic, the academic setting, and your audience by using formal English.

Research

 ## How much information is enough?

In this unit, you have read nonfiction selections that shed light on the value of high-quality or significant information. Now you will conduct a short research project on the reliability of the information in one particular Internet source. Then, you will use both the selections from Part 2 of this unit and your research to reflect on this unit's Big Question. Follow these guidelines:

- Select one Internet source to research.

- To evaluate the reliability of the source, check the information it offers against at least two other sources. Choose sources for your check that you know to be reliable. They may be print or digital.

- Take notes as you research the reliability of the first source.

- Cite your sources in your notes.

When you have completed your research, write a response to the Big Question. Discuss how your initial ideas have changed or been reinforced. Support your response with an example from a selection and an example from your research. Be sure to use academic vocabulary words in your response (see p. 191).

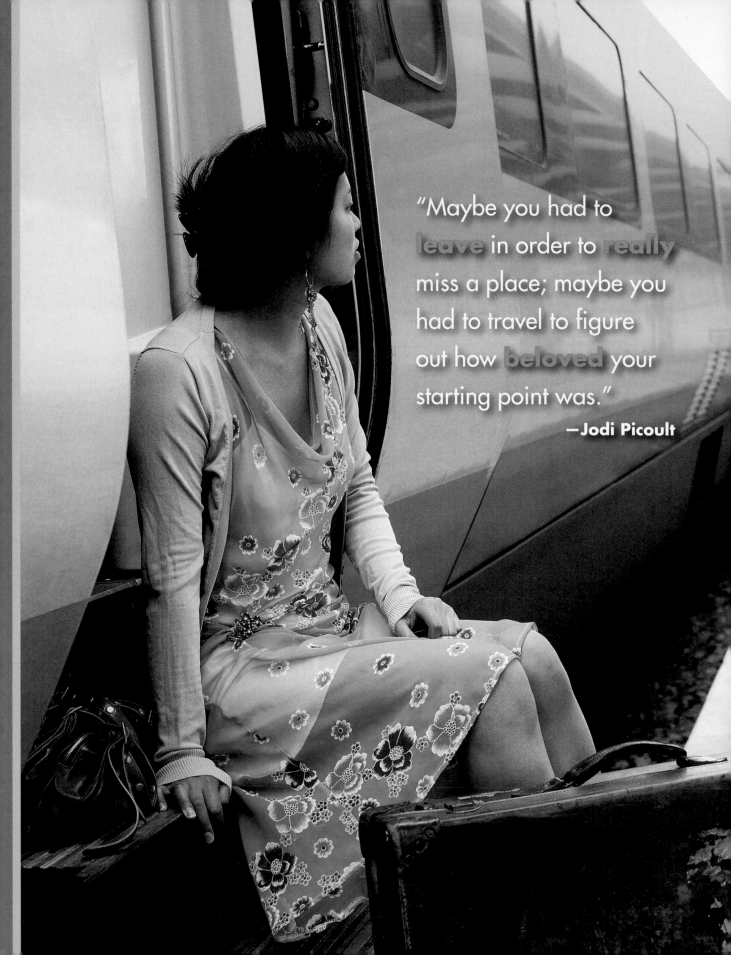

"Maybe you had to **leave** in order to **really** miss a place; maybe you had to travel to figure out how **beloved** your starting point was."

—**Jodi Picoult**

BELONGING TO A PLACE

The selections in this unit relate to the Big Question: **How much information is enough?** Today, technology connects people across the miles, making the world seem both smaller and larger. The texts that follow explore the sense of belonging and how people learn to feel connection to a place. The place might be a familiar room or a desolate landscape, but in each case, people explore what it means to belong there. As you read, think about the information people need in order to feel at home—and how they find what they need to know.

◀ **CRITICAL VIEWING** How does the woman in the photograph appear to feel about traveling? Why might she look forward to the place she is traveling to? What might she now appreciate about the place she is leaving behind?

CLOSE READING TOOL

Use the **Close Reading Tool** to practice the strategies you learn in this unit.

READINGS IN PART 3

from Travels *with* Charley

JOHN STEINBECK

▲ John Steinbeck and Charley

The night was loaded with **omens**. The grieving sky turned the little water to a dangerous metal and then the wind got up—not the gusty, rabbity wind of the seacoasts I know but a great bursting sweep of wind with nothing to inhibit it for a thousand miles in any direction. Because it was a wind strange to me, and therefore mysterious, it set up mysterious responses in me. In terms of reason, it was strange only because I found it so. But a goodly part of our experience which we find **inexplicable** must be like that. To my certain knowledge, many people conceal experiences for fear of ridicule. How many people have seen or heard or felt something which so outraged their sense of what should be that the whole thing was brushed quickly away like dirt under a rug?

For myself, I try to keep the line open even for things I can't understand or explain, but it is difficult in this frightened time. At this moment in North Dakota I had a reluctance to drive on that amounted to fear. At the same time, Charley wanted to go—in fact, made such a commotion about going that I tried to reason with him.

"Listen to me, dog. I have a strong impulse to stay amounting to celestial command. If I should overcome it and go and a great snow should close in on us, I would recognize it as a warning disregarded. If we stay and a big snow should come I would be certain I had a pipeline to prophecy."

Charley sneezed and paced restlessly. "All right, *mon cur*,[1] let's take your side of it. You want to go on. Suppose we do, and in the night a tree should crash down right where we are presently standing. It would be you who have the attention of the gods. And there is always that chance. I could tell you many stories about faithful animals who saved their masters, but I think you are just bored and I'm not going to flatter you." Charley leveled at me his most cynical eye. I think he is neither a romantic nor a mystic. "I know what you mean. If we go, and no tree crashes down, or stay and no snow falls—what then? I'll tell you what then. We forget the whole episode and the field

◀ **omens**
(ō´ mənz) *n.* signs of bad or good events that may take place in the future

◀ **inexplicable**
(in´ ek splik´ ə bəl) *adj.* impossible to explain

---

1. **mon cur** (mōn kᵫr´) a pun on *mon coeur* (French for "my dear") and *cur* (a mixed-breed dog).

of prophecy is in no way injured. I vote to stay. You vote to go. But being nearer the pinnacle of creation than you, and also president, I cast the deciding vote."

We stayed and it didn't snow and no tree fell, so naturally we forgot the whole thing and are wide open for more mystic feelings when they come. And in the early morning swept clean of clouds and telescopically clear, we crunched around on the thick white ground cover of frost and got under way. The caravan of the arts was dark but the dog barked as we ground up to the highway.

Someone must have told me about the Missouri River at Bismarck, North Dakota, or I must have read about it. In either case, I hadn't paid attention. I came on it in amazement. Here is where the map should fold. Here is the boundary between east and west. On the Bismarck side it is eastern landscape, eastern grass, with the look and smell of eastern America. Across the Missouri on the Mandan side, it is pure west, with brown grass and water scorings and small outcrops. The two sides of the river might well be a thousand miles apart. As I was not prepared for the Missouri boundary, so I was not prepared for the Bad Lands. They deserve this name. They are like the work of an evil child. Such a place the Fallen Angels might have built as a spite to Heaven, dry and sharp, **desolate** and dangerous, and for me filled with foreboding. A sense comes from it that it does not like or welcome humans. But humans being what they are, and I being human, I turned off the highway on a shaley road and headed in among the

desolate ▶
(des´ ə lit) *adj.*
empty; lonely

◀ **Badlands National Park, South Dakota**

buttes, but with a shyness as though I crashed a party. The road surface tore viciously at my tires and made Rocinante's[2] overloaded springs cry with anguish. What a place for a colony of troglodytes, or better, of trolls. And here's an odd thing. Just as I felt unwanted in this land, so do I feel a reluctance in writing about it.

Presently I saw a man leaning on a two-strand barbed-wire fence, the wires fixed not to posts but to crooked tree limbs stuck in the ground. The man wore a dark hat, and jeans and long jacket washed palest blue with lighter places at knees and elbows. His pale eyes were frosted with sun glare and his lips scaly as snakeskin. A .22 rifle leaned against the fence beside him and on the ground lay a little heap of fur and feathers— rabbits and small birds. I pulled up to speak to him, saw his eyes wash over Rocinante, sweep up the details, and then retire into their sockets. And I found I had nothing to say to him. The "Looks like an early winter," or "Any good fishing hereabouts?" didn't seem to apply. And so we simply brooded at each other.

"Afternoon!"

"Yes, sir," he said.

"Any place nearby where I can buy some eggs?"

"Not real close by 'less you want to go as far as Galva or up to Beach."

2. **Rocinante's** (rō sē nän´ tāz) Steinbeck's nickname for his camper truck. Rocinante was a broken-down horse in the seventeenth-century novel *Don Quixote*. His owner was convinced he was a knight and rode Rocinante across the Spanish countryside on foolish quests. Steinbeck thought the name was appropriate for his cross-country adventure.

"I was set for some scratch-hen eggs."

"Powdered," he said. "My Mrs. gets powdered."

"Lived here long?"

"Yep."

I waited for him to ask something or to say something so we could go on, but he didn't. And as the silence continued, it became more and more impossible to think of something to say. I made one more try. "Does it get very cold here winters?"

"Fairly."

"You talk too much."

He grinned. "That's what my Mrs. says."

"So long," I said, and put the car in gear and moved along. And in my rear-view mirror I couldn't see that he looked after me. He may not be a typical Badlander, but he's one of the few I caught.

A little farther along I stopped at a small house, a section of war-surplus barracks, it looked, but painted white with yellow trim, and with the dying vestiges of a garden, frosted-down geraniums and a few clusters of chrysanthemums, little button things yellow and red-brown. I walked up the path with the certainty that I was being regarded from behind the white window curtains. An old woman answered my knock and gave me the drink of water I asked for and nearly talked my arm off. She was hungry to talk, frantic to talk, about her relatives, her friends, and how she wasn't used to this. For she was not a native and she didn't rightly belong here. Her native clime was a land of milk and honey and had its share of apes and ivory and peacocks. Her voice rattled on as though she was terrified of the silence that would settle when I was gone. As she talked it came to me that she was afraid of this place and, further, that so was I. I felt I wouldn't like to have the night catch me here.

I went into a state of flight, running to get away from the unearthly landscape. And then the late afternoon changed everything. As the sun angled, the buttes and coulees, the cliffs and sculptured hills and ravines lost their burned and dreadful look and glowed with yellow and rich browns and a hundred variations of red and silver gray, all picked out by streaks of coal black. It was so beautiful that I stopped near a thicket of dwarfed and wind-warped cedars and junipers, and once stopped I was caught, trapped in color and dazzled by the clarity of the light. Against the descending sun the battlements were dark and clean-lined, while to the east, where the uninhibited light poured slantwise, the strange landscape shouted with color. And the night, far from being frightful, was lovely beyond thought, for the stars were close, and although there was no moon the starlight made a silver glow in the sky. The air cut the nostrils with dry frost. And for pure pleasure I collected a pile of dry dead cedar branches and built a small fire just to smell the perfume of the burning wood and to hear the excited crackle of the branches. My fire made a dome of yellow light over me, and nearby I heard a screech owl hunting and a barking of coyotes, not howling but the short chuckling bark of the dark of the moon. This is one of the few places I have ever seen where the night was friendlier than the day. And I can easily see how people are driven back to the Bad Lands.

Before I slept I spread a map on my bed, a Charley-tromped map. Beach was not far away, and that would be the end of North Dakota. And coming up would be Montana, where I had never been. That night was so cold that I put on my insulated underwear for pajamas, and when Charley had done his duties and had his biscuits and consumed his usual gallon of water and finally curled up in his place under the bed, I dug out an extra blanket and covered him—all except the tip of his nose—and he sighed and wriggled and gave a great groan of pure ecstatic comfort. And I thought how every safe generality I gathered in my travels was canceled by another. In the night the Bad Lands had become Good Lands. I can't explain it. That's how it was.

ABOUT THE AUTHOR

John Steinbeck (1902–1968)

A gifted observer and listener, John Steinbeck dedicated himself to exploring real life in America. He got to know workers on farms, in canning factories, and in fisheries in his native state of California. He watched Americans struggle during the Great Depression of the 1930s and wrote sympathetically and movingly about those struggles. His observations came to life in novels such as *East of Eden* and *The Grapes of Wrath*. Steinbeck won both the Pulitzer Prize and Nobel Prize for Literature for his work.

READ

Comprehension

Reread all or part of the text to help you answer the following questions.

1. At the outset of the selection, what decision must Steinbeck make?

2. How does he feel about the Badlands at first?

3. How does he feel about the Badlands later?

4. Whom does he meet on his drive?

Language Study

Selection Vocabulary Define each boldface word from the text and use it in a sentence of your own.

- The night was loaded with **omens**.
- But a goodly part of our experience which we find **inexplicable** must be like that.
- Such a place the Fallen Angels might have built as a spite to Heaven, dry and sharp, **desolate** and dangerous. . . .

Diction and Style Read this sentence and answer the questions that follow.

> As the sun angled, the buttes and coulees, the cliffs and sculptured hills and ravines lost their burned and dreadful look and glowed with yellow and rich browns and a hundred variations of red and silver gray, all picked out by streaks of coal black.

1. **(a)** What image does *glowed with* create in this sentence? **(b)** How would the author's picture of the landscape be different if he had changed "glowed with" to "revealed"?

Research: Clarify Details Choose one unfamiliar detail from the memoir and conduct research on it. Explain how your research clarifies the text.

Summarize Write an objective summary of the memoir. Remember not to include your own opinions.

2. **(a)** What are *buttes, coulees, cliffs,* and *ravines*? **(b)** What effect does Steinbeck create by listing a variety of geographic features?

Conventions In this sentence, the author uses both active and passive voice. Identify each, explaining why its use is appropriate. Then, rewrite the sentence, using just active voice. Explain the difference in the effect of the sentence.

> I walked up the path with the certainty that I was being regarded from behind the white window curtains.

Academic Vocabulary

The following words appear in blue in the instructions and questions on the facing page.

intensify   **perceive**   **anticipate**

Categorize the words by deciding whether you know each one well, know it a little bit, or do not know it at all. Then, use a print or online dictionary to look up the definitions of the words you are unsure of or do not know at all.

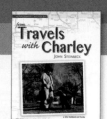

Literary Analysis

Reread the identified passages and answer the questions.

Focus Passage 1 *(pp. 292–293)*

Someone must have told . . . writing about it.

Focus Passage 2 *(p. 294)*

A little farther . . . night catch me here.

Key Ideas and Details

1. (a) What boundary does the author encounter? **(b) Summarize:** How does he react to it?

Craft and Structure

2. (a) Identify: What simile (comparison using *like* or *as*) does the author use to describe the Badlands? **(b) Connect:** Explain how he uses another comparison to **intensify** this simile.

3. (a) Identify: What simile does Steinbeck use to describe his feelings after he turns off the highway? **(b) Interpret:** What idea does this simile express?

Integration of Knowledge and Ideas

4. Make a Judgment: Why might Steinbeck **perceive** the landscape as threatening or unwelcoming? Explain.

Key Ideas and Details

1. (a) Whom does the author meet in this passage? **(b) Interpret:** What conclusion does he reach about her?

Craft and Structure

2. Connect: How does the detail about the "dying vestiges of a garden" **anticipate** what Steinbeck learns about the woman?

3. (a) Connect: How does Steinbeck's language reflect the woman's hunger to talk about her original home?
(b) Interpret: In what way does Steinbeck's description of the woman's need to talk support his description of the Badlands?

Integration of Knowledge and Ideas

4. Draw Conclusions: What does the woman's fear suggest about general human needs?

Style

Style is a writer's distinctive use of language. Sentence length, tone, word choice, and figurative language are all part of style. Reread the selection, taking notes on the author's style.

1. (a) Find three examples of vivid language in the text. **(b)** Describe the author's style, based on the details you found.

2. (a) Contrast these sentences:

- the sentence beginning "As the sun angled"
- "The air cut the nostrils with dry frost."
- the sentence beginning "My fire made"

(b) Belonging to a Place: Explain how the rhythm and word choice in each sentence reinforce its meaning and create a sense of belonging.

Common Core State Standards

RI.8.1, RI.8.2, RI.8.4, RI.8.5; L.8.1, L.8.1.b, L.8.4.a, L.8.5.a, L.8.6
[For full standards wording, see the chart in the front of this book.]

DISCUSS

From Text to Topic **Partner Discussion**

Discuss the passage below with a partner. Take turns contributing ideas and asking questions. As your partner contributes information, explore whether that information supports you own ideas.

> And I thought how every safe generality I gathered in my travels was canceled by another. In the night the Bad Lands had become the Good Lands. I can't explain it. That's how it was.

WRITE

Writing to Sources **Informative Text**

Assignment
Write a **travel essay** for an audience that is interested in travel to North Dakota. In your descriptions, include details from Steinbeck's text.

Prewriting and Planning Reread the text, looking for details that inform the reader about specific places, landscapes, or even types of people. Group the details into categories.

Drafting As you draft, use these organizational strategies.

- **Introduction-Body-Conclusion** In your introduction, establish the main impression of North Dakota that you wish to convey. Develop this impression in your body paragraphs and reaffirm it in your conclusion.

- **Topic Sentences and Support** Begin each body paragraph with a topic sentence introducing an aspect of the topic. Support your topic sentence with relevant examples from the text.

Revising Reread your essay, focusing on your word choice. Replace dull or overused words, such as *cold* or *nice*, with precise, colorful synonyms, such as *frigid* or *welcoming*. Consider incorporating figures of speech to emphasize important points, as in this revision:

ORIGINAL: *The land is dry.*

REVISION: *The sun-baked, dusty land cries out for water.*

Editing and Proofreading Make sure you have spelled each word correctly. Use a spellchecker, but carefully consider the meaning of a suggested correction before accepting it.

QUESTIONS FOR DISCUSSION

1. What change was necessary to help the author feel as if he belonged in the Badlands?

2. Compare Steinbeck's eventual sense of belonging with the feelings of the people he meets during his journey.

3. What does Steinbeck's experience show about what is needed to "belong" to a place?

CONVENTIONS

When you use two adjectives before a single noun, and the order of the adjectives could be reversed without a change in meaning, place a comma between them. For example, you should write "the drafty, unpainted house" (comma required) but "the last unpainted house" and "the three yellow houses" (no comma).

RESEARCH

Research **Investigate the Topic**

Fear: A Barrier to Belonging Fear of the unknown, the "creeps," the "heebie jeebies"—people can experience these feelings when they are in a new place or surrounded by strangers. People can also find ways to overcome these feelings.

Assignment

Conduct research to learn more about the fear of unknown places and how people conquer it. Use the Internet as well as print sources, such as encyclopedias and journal articles. Share your findings in a **brief presentation.**

Gather Sources Locate authoritative print and electronic sources, including journal articles and psychology textbooks. Look for current sources whose authors are experts on this topic, such as college professors.

Take Notes Take notes on each source, either electronically or on note cards. Use an organized note-taking strategy.

- If you are using note cards, make a source card for each source, listing all information required for a Works Cited list entry. Number each source card 1, 2, 3, and so on. If you are using a spreadsheet, put each source's full bibliographic information in the heading of a column.

- For each note you take, put the number of the source in the corner of a new card. If you are using a spreadsheet, enter notes in the correct column for the source.

- You should take most notes in your own words. Quote your source exactly when you wish to capture an important definition, a vivid comparison, and so on for later quotation. Remember to use quotation marks when quoting a source directly.

Synthesize Multiple Sources Group your notes into categories. Review your notes, and draw conclusions about how new places affect us and how people overcome fears. Organize your ideas in an outline, and begin to draft. Cite your sources following an approved style, and add a Works Cited list (see the Conducting Research workshop in the front of this book).

Organize and Present Ideas Review your draft, proofreading for errors. Make sure you have correctly and consistently cited sources for the words and ideas of others.

PREPARATION FOR ESSAY

You may use the results of this research project to support your ideas in the essay you will write at the end of this section.

Ⓒ Common Core State Standards

W.8.2.a, W.8.2.b, W.8.2.d, W.8.2.f, W.8.4, W.8.5, W.8.7; SL.8.1.a-d
[For full standards wording, see the chart in the front of this book.]

Gentleman
of Río en Medio

Juan A. A. Sedillo

It took months of negotiation to come to an understanding with the old man. He was in no hurry. What he had the most of was time. He lived up in Río en Medio,[1] where his people had been for hundreds of years. He tilled the same land they had tilled. His house was small and wretched, but quaint. The little creek ran through his land. His orchard was gnarled and beautiful.

The day of the sale he came into the office. His coat was old, green and faded. I thought of Senator Catron,[2] who had been such a power with these people up there in the mountains. Perhaps it was one of his old Prince Alberts.[3] He also wore gloves. They were old and torn and his fingertips showed through them. He carried a cane, but it was only the skeleton of a worn-out umbrella. Behind him walked one of his innumerable kin—a dark young man with eyes like a gazelle.

The old man bowed to all of us in the room. Then he removed his hat and gloves, slowly and carefully. Chaplin[4] once did that in a picture, in a bank—he was the janitor. Then he handed his things to the boy, who stood obediently behind the old man's chair.

There was a great deal of conversation, about rain and about his family. He was very proud of his large family. Finally we got down to business. Yes, he would sell, as he had agreed, for twelve hundred dollars, in cash. We would buy, and the money was ready. "Don[5] Anselmo," I said to him in Spanish, "we have made a discovery. You remember that we sent that surveyor, that engineer, up there to survey your land so as to make the deed. Well, he finds that you own more than eight acres. He tells us that your land extends across the river and that you own almost twice as much as you thought." He didn't know that. "And now, Don Anselmo," I added, "these Americans are *buena gente*,[6] they are good people, and they are willing to pay you for the additional land as well, at the same rate per acre, so that instead of twelve hundred dollars you will get almost twice as much, and the money is here for you."

1. **Río en Medio** (rē′ ō en mā′ dē ō) an area in Sante Fe County, New Mexico; the name is Spanish for "River in the Middle."
2. **Senator Catron** Thomas Benton Catron, U.S. senator from New Mexico, 1912–1917.
3. **Prince Alberts** long, old-fashioned coats worn on formal occasions.
4. **Chaplin** Charlie Chaplin (1889–1977), actor and producer of silent films in the United States.
5. **Don** (dän) Spanish title of respect, similar to *Sir* in English.
6. *buena gente* (bwā′ nä hen′ tā) Spanish for "good people."

negotiation
(ni gō′ shē ā′ shən)
n. bargaining; discussion; deal-making

The old man hung his head for a moment in thought. Then he stood up and stared at me. "Friend," he said, "I do not like to have you speak to me in that manner." I kept still and let him have his say. "I know these Americans are good people, and that is why I have agreed to sell to them. But I do not care to be insulted. I have agreed to sell my house and land for twelve hundred dollars and that is the price."

I argued with him but it was useless. Finally he signed the deed and took the money but refused to take more than the amount agreed upon. Then he shook hands all around, put on his ragged gloves, took his stick and walked out with the boy behind him.

A month later my friends had moved into Río en Medio. They had replastered the old adobe house, pruned the trees, patched the fence, and moved in for the summer. One day they came back to the office to complain. The children of the village were overrunning their property. They came every day and played under the trees, built little play fences around them, and took blossoms. When they were spoken to they only laughed and talked back good-naturedly in Spanish.

I sent a messenger up to the mountains for Don Anselmo. It took a week to arrange another meeting. When he arrived he repeated his previous **preliminary** performance. He wore the same faded cutaway,[7] carried the same stick and was accompanied by the boy again. He shook hands all around, sat down with the boy behind his chair, and talked about the weather. Finally I broached the subject. "Don Anselmo, about the ranch you sold to these people. They are good people and want to be your friends and neighbors always. When you sold to them you signed a document, a deed, and in that deed you agreed to several things. One thing was that they were to have the complete possession of the property. Now, Don Anselmo, it seems that every day the children of the village overrun the orchard and spend most of their time there. We would like to know if you, as the most respected man in the village, could not stop them

preliminary ▶
(prē lim′ ə ner′ ē) *adj.*
introductory;
preparatory

---

7. **cutaway** *n.* coat worn by men for formal daytime occasions; it is cut short in the front and curves to long tails in the back.

from doing so in order that these people may enjoy their new home more in peace."

Don Anselmo stood up. "We have all learned to love these Americans," he said, "because they are good people and good neighbors. I sold them my property because I knew they were good people, but I did not sell them the trees in the orchard."

This was bad. "Don Anselmo," I pleaded, "when one signs a deed and sells real property one sells also everything that grows on the land, and those trees, every one of them, are on the land and inside the boundaries of what you sold."

"Yes, I admit that," he said. "You know," he added, "I am the oldest man in the village. Almost everyone there is my relative and all the children of Río en Medio are my *sobrinos* and *nietos*,[8] my **descendants**. Every time a child has been born in Río en Medio since I took possession of that house from my mother I have planted a tree for that child. The trees in that orchard are not mine, *Señor*, they belong to the children of the village. Every person in Río en Medio born since the railroad came to Santa Fe owns a tree in that orchard. I did not sell the trees because I could not. They are not mine."

There was nothing we could do. Legally we owned the trees but the old man had been so generous, refusing what amounted to a fortune for him. It took most of the following winter to buy the trees, individually, from the descendants of Don Anselmo in the valley of Río en Medio.

◄ **descendants**
(dē sen´ dənts)
n. children, grandchildren, and continuing generations

---

8. **sobrinos** (sō brē´ nōs) and **nietos** (nyä´ tōs) Spanish for "nephews" and "grandsons"; used here to include nieces and granddaughters as well.

ABOUT THE AUTHOR

Juan A. A. Sedillo (1902–1982)

Born in New Mexico, Juan A. A. Sedillo was descended from Spanish colonists of the Southwest. Sedillo had talents in a number of fields. In addition to being a writer, he was a lawyer and judge who held various public positions. He even worked in film, playing a detective in the 1929 movie *The Girl from Havana,* which was among the first "talkies," or films with sound. His varied life experiences and his exposure to the diverse cultures of New Mexico helped him add a realistic depth to his stories.

Close Reading Activities

READ

Comprehension

Reread all or part of the text to help you answer the following questions.

1. At the outset of the story, what bargain does the old man make?

2. What problem do the new owners of the land face?

3. How do they solve their problem?

Research: Clarify Details Choose one unfamiliar detail from the story and conduct research on it. Explain how your research clarifies the text.

Summarize Write an objective summary of the story. Remember to omit opinions and evaluation from your summary.

Language Study

Selection Vocabulary Define each boldface word from the selection, and then use it in a sentence of your own.

• It took months of **negotiation** to come to an understanding with the old man.

• When he arrived he repeated his previous **preliminary** performance.

• Almost everyone there is my relative and all the children of Río en Medio are my . . . **descendants**.

Literary Analysis

Reread the identified passage and answer the questions that follow.

> **Focus Passage** *(p. 302)*
> The old man hung . . . boy behind him.

Key Ideas and Details

1. (a) What decision does the old man announce? **(b)** What reason does he give?

Craft and Structure

2. (a) Analyze: Describe the old man's way of speaking. Is it formal or informal, stiff or casual? Quote details in support.

(b) Infer: What does his speaking style show about his personality?

3. (a) Infer: What does the sentence beginning "I kept still" show about the narrator's attitude toward the old man?
(b) Analyze: How does the narrator **influence** your perception of the old man?

Integration of Knowledge and Ideas

4. (a) Infer: What does the old man value more than money? **(b) Generalize:** Are his values widely shared by modern Americans? Explain how you know.

Plot and Theme

Plot, or the sequence of events in a story, can help convey a **theme,** or central message.

1. (a) How do the new purchasers save money when they buy the land? **(b)** What happens that causes them to spend more money?

2. Belonging to a Place: Explain what theme about values these two events convey. Use details from the story to support your interpretation.

Gentleman
of Río en Medio
Juan A. A. Sedillo

DISCUSS • RESEARCH • WRITE

From Text to Topic **Group Discussion**

Write a quick response to the Questions for Discussion, citing details from the story. Then, discuss your answers with a small group. Take notes on the discussion.

> Every time a child has been born in Río en Medio since I took possession of that house from my mother I have planted a tree for that child. The trees in that orchard are not mine, *Señor,* they belong to the children of the village.

Research **Investigate the Topic**

Surveying Surveying is the use of instruments and tools to measure and map land. A less **accurate** survey might have changed events in "Gentleman of Río en Medio."

Assignment
Conduct research into the history of surveying. Find out why early **methods** could lead to error. Take clear notes, and gather graphics to help illustrate key concepts. Then, write a conclusion about what your research has revealed about belonging and place. Share your findings, including your graphics, in a **multimedia presentation**.

Writing to Sources **Argument**

Make a claim about whether owning land carries responsibilities. Consider possible responsibilities to the land, to neighbors, to the community, or to the past. Also consider factors such as an individual's rights. Support your claim with details from the story.

Assignment
Write an **argumentative essay** in which you put forth and support a claim about the responsibilities of land ownership. Follow these steps:

- Clearly state a claim.
- Supply reasons for your claim and support them with relevant details, including details from the story.
- Distinguish your claim from opposing claims.
- Conclude logically and effectively.

QUESTIONS FOR DISCUSSION

1. What ideas of "belonging to a person" and "belonging to a place" does Don Anselmo express?

2. How is his idea of ownership, or what belongs to whom, different from the narrator's idea?

PREPARATION FOR ESSAY

You may use the results of this research project to support your ideas in the essay you will write at the end of this section.

ACADEMIC VOCABULARY

Academic terms appear in blue on these pages. Use a dictionary to find their definitions. Then, use the words as you speak and write about the text.

 Common Core State Standards

RL.8.1, RL.8.3, RL.8.4; W.8.1, W.8.1.a, W.8.1.b, W.8.1.e; SL.8.1, SL.8.5; L.8.6
[For full standards wording, see the chart in the front of this book.]

Choice:
A Tribute to Martin Luther King, Jr.
Alice Walker

My great-great-great-grandmother walked as a slave from Virginia to Eatonton, Georgia—which passes for the Walker ancestral home—with two babies on her hips. She lived to be a hundred and twenty-five years old and my own father knew her as a boy. (It is in memory of this walk that I choose to keep and to embrace my "maiden" name, Walker.)

There is a cemetery near our family church where she is buried; but because her marker was made of wood and rotted years ago, it is impossible to tell exactly where her body lies. In the same cemetery are most of my mother's people, who have lived in Georgia for so long nobody even remembers when they came. And all of my great-aunts and -uncles are there, and my grandfather and grandmother, and, very recently, my own father.

If it is true that land does not belong to anyone until they have buried a body in it, then the land of my birthplace belongs to me, dozens of times over. Yet the history of my family, like that of all black Southerners, is a history of dispossession. We loved the land and worked the land, but we never owned it; and even if we bought land, as my great-grandfather did after the Civil War, it was always in danger of being taken away, as his was, during the period following Reconstruction.[1]

My father inherited nothing of material value from his father, and when I came of age in the early sixties I awoke to the bitter knowledge that in order just to continue to love the land of my birth, I was expected to leave it. For black people—including my parents—had learned a long time ago that to stay willingly in a beloved but **brutal** place is to risk losing the love and being forced to acknowledge only the brutality.

◄ **brutal**
(brōōt´'l) *adj.* harsh; savage; cruel and unfeeling

It is a part of the black Southern sensibility that we treasure memories; for such a long time, that is all of our homeland those of us who at one time or another were forced away from it have been allowed to have.

I watched my brothers, one by one, leave our home and leave the South. I watched my sisters do the same. This was not unusual; abandonment, except for memories, was the common thing, except for those who "could not do any better," or those

---

1. **Reconstruction** (1865–1877) period following the American Civil War when the South was rebuilt and reestablished as part of the Union.

whose strength or stubbornness was so colossal they took the risk that others could not bear.

In 1960, my mother bought a television set, and each day after school I watched Hamilton Holmes and Charlayne Hunter[2] as they struggled to integrate—fair-skinned as they were—the University of Georgia. And then, one day, there appeared the face of Dr. Martin Luther King, Jr. What a funny name, I thought. At the moment I first saw him, he was being handcuffed and shoved into a police truck. He had dared to claim his rights as a native son, and had been arrested. He displayed no fear, but seemed calm and serene, unaware of his own extraordinary courage. His whole body, like his conscience, was at peace.

At the moment I saw his resistance I knew I would never be able to live in this country without resisting everything that sought to **disinherit** me, and I would never be forced away from the land of my birth without a fight.

He was The One, The Hero, The One Fearless Person for whom we had waited. I hadn't even realized before that we *had* been waiting for Martin Luther King, Jr., but we had. And I knew it for sure when my mother added his name to the list of people she prayed for every night.

I sometimes think that it was literally the prayers of people like my mother and father, who had bowed down in the struggle for such a long time, that kept Dr. King alive until five years ago.[3] For years we went to bed praying for his life, and awoke with the question "Is the 'Lord' still here?"

The public acts of Dr. King you know. They are visible all around you. His voice you would recognize sooner than any other voice you have heard in this century—this in spite of the fact that certain municipal libraries, like the one in downtown Jackson, do not carry recordings of his speeches, and the librarians chuckle cruelly when asked why they do not.

You know, if you have read his books, that his is a complex and **revolutionary** philosophy that few people are capable of understanding fully or have the patience to embody in themselves. Which is our weakness, which is our loss.

And if you know anything about good Baptist preaching, you can imagine what you missed if you never had a chance to hear Martin Luther King, Jr., preach at Ebeneezer Baptist Church.

disinherit ▶
(dis′ in her′ it) *v.* deprive (a person or people) of a right or privilege

revolutionary ▶
(rev′ ə lōō′ shə ner′ ē) *adj.* favoring or bringing about sweeping change

---

2. **Hamilton Holmes and Charlayne Hunter** the first two African American students to attend the University of Georgia.
3. **until five years ago** Dr. Martin Luther King, Jr., was assassinated on April 4, 1968.

You know of the prizes and awards that he tended to think very little of. And you know of his concern for the disinherited: the American Indian, the Mexican-American, and the poor American white—for whom he cared much.

You know that this very room, in this very restaurant, was closed to people of color not more than five years ago. And that we eat here together tonight largely through his efforts and his blood. We accept the common pleasures of life, assuredly, in his name.

But add to all of these things the one thing that seems to me second to none in importance: He gave us back our heritage. He gave us back our homeland; the bones and dust of our ancestors, who may now sleep within our caring *and* our hearing. He gave us the blueness of the Georgia sky in autumn as in summer; the colors of the Southern winter as well as glimpses of the green of vacation-time spring. Those of our relatives we used to invite for a visit we now can ask to stay. . . . He gave us full-time use of our woods, and restored our memories to those of us who were forced to run away, as realities we might each day enjoy and leave for our children.

He gave us continuity of place, without which community is ephemeral.[4] He gave us home.   *1973*

> **He gave us back our homeland; the bones and dust of our ancestors. . . .**

---

4. **ephemeral** (e fem´ ər əl) *adj.* short-lived; fleeting.

ABOUT THE AUTHOR

Alice Walker (b. 1944)

Alice Walker's parents loved to tell her stories—so much so, that she later referred to her mother as "a walking history of our community." Walker's love of stories and learning inspired her to go to college, where she became involved in the civil rights movement. After meeting Martin Luther King, Jr., she participated in marches and registered African Americans to vote in Georgia—dangerous activities at the time.

By the end of the 1960s, Walker had launched a writing career, with published works that included essays, novels, and poems. She became a well-respected and popular voice of African Americans and of African American women in particular. Her 1982 novel, *The Color Purple,* won the Pulitzer Prize and the National Book Award. It was also adapted as a major motion picture, directed by Steven Spielberg.

READ

Comprehension

Reread all or part of the text to help you answer the following questions.

1. Which ancestor's arrival in Georgia does Walker describe?

2. What does Walker say her brothers and sisters have done?

3. What decision did Walker make when she first saw Martin Luther King, Jr.?

4. For what reasons does Walker celebrate King?

Research: Clarify Details Choose one unfamiliar detail from the speech and conduct research on it. Explain how your research clarifies the text.

Summarize Write an objective summary of the speech. Remember not to include your own opinions or judgments in your summary.

Language Study

Selection Vocabulary Replace each boldface word with a synonym. Then, describe how the change affects the impact of the passage.

• . . . to stay willingly in a beloved but **brutal** place is to risk losing the love. . . .

• . . . I would never be able to live in this country without resisting everything that sought to **disinherit** me. . . .

• . . . his is a complex and **revolutionary** philosophy. . . .

Literary Analysis

Reread the identified passage and answer the questions that follow.

> **Focus Passage** *(p. 307)*
>
> If it is true . . . allowed to have.

Key Ideas and Details

1. **Interpret:** In what way does Walker's family own the land?

2. **Interpret:** In what way did the land never truly belong to them?

Craft and Structure

3. In the sentence beginning "For black people," Walker pairs these words: "to stay" / "to risk." **(a)** Find two other related, or parallel, word pairs in the sentence. **(b)** What point is Walker emphasizing with this parallelism?

Integration of Knowledge and Ideas

4. **Connect:** Why does Walker say at the end of her speech that King "gave us back our homeland"? **Cite** textual details in support.

Author's Perspective

An **author's perspective** is his or her view of the world or of a specific topic. Take notes on Walker's perspective in this speech.

1. What is Walker's perspective on Georgia?

2. **Belonging to a Place:** From Walker's perspective, what must people have in order to truly belong to a place? Cite details from the text to support your response.

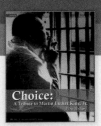

DISCUSS • RESEARCH • WRITE

From Text to Topic **Group Discussion**

Discuss the following passage with a group of classmates. Take notes during the discussion.

> He gave us continuity of place, without which community is ephemeral. He gave us home.

Research **Investigate the Topic**

King's Speeches and Sermons King used public speaking to help return to African Americans what rightfully belonged to them.

Assignment

Conduct research to locate a speech or sermon in which King discusses issues in an American city or cities. Outline the speech, identifying ways King's ideas address the issues of "home" that Walker raises. Take clear notes and accurately identify the title, date, and place of the speech. Share your findings in an **annotated outline** calling out connections of King's ideas to Walker's.

Writing to Sources **Informative Text**

In this speech, Alice Walker weaves a tight connection between her family history and the history of the Civil Rights Movement. One common thread is the notion of home and belonging.

Assignment

Write an **analytical essay** in which you analyze what Walker thinks it means to belong to a place. Follow these steps:

- Introduce the topic and your perspective on it.

- Summarize Walker's account of her family history and of King's success, using **cause-and-effect** explanations.

- Provide an analysis of Walker's idea of belonging, and show how this idea relates both to her family history and to the Civil Rights Movement. Quote textual details to support your analysis.

- Link your ideas with appropriate transitions such as *next, therefore,* and *in addition*.

- Provide a conclusion summarizing your analysis.

QUESTIONS FOR DISCUSSION

1. What does Walker mean by "continuity of place"?

2. In what way were African Americans missing this continuity?

3. How did King help restore it?

PREPARATION FOR ESSAY

You may use the results of this research project to support your ideas in the essay you will write at the end of this section.

ACADEMIC VOCABULARY

Academic terms appear in blue on these pages. Use a dictionary to find their definitions. Then, use the words as you speak and write about the text.

Common Core State Standards

RI.8.1, RI.8.2, RI.8.3, RI.8.4, RI.8.6; W.8.2, W.8.7, W.8.9.b; SL.8.1; L.8.4, L.8.6
[For full standards wording, see the chart in the front of this book.]

Tears of Autumn

Yoshiko Uchida

Hana Omiya stood at the railing of the small ship that shuddered toward America in a turbulent November sea. She shivered as she pulled the folds of her silk kimono close to her throat and tightened the wool shawl about her shoulders.

She was thin and small, her dark eyes shadowed in her pale face, her black hair piled high in a pompadour that seemed too heavy for so slight a woman. She clung to the moist rail and breathed the damp salt air deep into her lungs. Her body seemed leaden and lifeless, as though it were simply the vehicle transporting her soul to a strange new life, and she longed with childlike intensity to be home again in Oka Village.

She longed to see the bright persimmon dotting the barren trees beside the thatched roofs, to see the fields of golden rice stretching to the mountains where only last fall she had gathered plum white mushrooms, and to see once more the maple trees lacing their flaming colors through the green pine. If only she could see a familiar face, eat a meal without retching, walk on solid ground, and stretch out at night on a *tatami* mat[1] instead of in a hard narrow bunk. She thought now of seeking the warm shelter of her bunk but could not bear to face the relentless smell of fish that penetrated the lower decks.

Why did I ever leave Japan, she wondered bitterly. Why did I ever listen to my uncle? And yet she knew it was she herself who had begun the chain of events that placed her on this heaving ship. It was she who had first planted in her uncle's mind the thought that she would make a good wife for Taro Takeda, the lonely man who had gone to America to make his fortune in Oakland, California.

It all began one day when her uncle had come to visit her mother.

"I must find a nice young bride," he had said, startling Hana with this blunt talk of marriage in her presence. She blushed and was ready to leave the room when her uncle quickly added, "My good friend Takeda has a son in America. I must find someone willing to travel to that far land."

---

1. *tatami* (tə tä′ mē) **mat** *n.* floor mat woven of rice straw, traditionally used in Japanese homes.

This last remark was intended to indicate to Hana and her mother that he didn't consider this a suitable prospect for Hana, who was the youngest daughter of what once had been a fine family. Her father, until his death fifteen years ago, had been the largest landholder of the village and one of its last samurai.[2] They had once had many servants and field hands, but now all that was changed. Their money was gone. Hana's three older sisters had made good marriages, and the eldest remained in their home with her husband to carry on the Omiya name and perpetuate the homestead. Her other sisters had married merchants in Osaka and Nagoya and were living comfortably.

Now that Hana was twenty-one, finding a proper husband for her had taken on an urgency that produced an embarrassing secretive air over the entire matter. Usually, her mother didn't speak of it until they were lying side by side on their quilts at night. Then, under the protective cover of darkness, she would suggest one name and then another, hoping that Hana would indicate an interest in one of them.

Her uncle spoke freely of Taro Takeda only because he was so sure Hana would never consider him. "He is a conscientious, hardworking man who has been in the United States for almost ten years. He is thirty-one, operates a small shop, and rents some rooms above the shop where he lives." Her uncle rubbed his chin thoughtfully. "He could provide well for a wife," he added.

"Ah," Hana's mother said softly.

"You say he is successful in this business?" Hana's sister inquired.

"His father tells me he sells many things in his shop—clothing, stockings, needles, thread, and buttons—such things as that. He also sells bean paste, pickled radish, bean cake, and soy sauce. A wife of his would not go cold or hungry."

They all nodded, each of them picturing this merchant in varying degrees of success and **affluence**. There were many Japanese emigrating to America these days, and Hana had heard of the picture brides who went with nothing more than an exchange of photographs to bind them to a strange man.

"Taro San[3] is lonely," her uncle continued. "I want to find for him a fine young woman who is strong and brave enough to cross the ocean alone."

affluence ▶
(af´ lōō əns) *n.*
wealth; abundance

---

2. **samurai** (sam´ ə rī) *n.* Japanese army officer or member of the military class.
3. **San** (sän) Japanese term added to names, indicating respect.

"It would certainly be a different kind of life," Hana's sister ventured, and for a moment, Hana thought she glimpsed a longing ordinarily concealed behind her quiet, obedient face. In that same instant, Hana knew she wanted more for herself than her sisters had in their proper, arranged, and loveless marriages. She wanted to escape the smothering strictures of life in her village. She certainly was not going to marry a farmer and spend her life working beside him planting, weeding, and harvesting in the rice paddies until her back became bent from too many years of stooping and her skin was turned to brown leather by the sun and wind. Neither did she particularly relish the idea of marrying a merchant in a big city as her two sisters had done. Since her mother objected to her going to Tokyo to seek employment as a teacher, perhaps she would consent to a flight to America for what seemed a proper and respectable marriage.

Almost before she realized what she was doing, she spoke to her uncle. "Oji San, perhaps I should go to America to make this lonely man a good wife."

"You, Hana Chan?"[4] Her uncle observed her with startled curiosity. "You would go all alone to a foreign land so far away from your mother and family?"

"I would not allow it." Her mother spoke fiercely. Hana was her youngest and she had lavished upon her the attention and latitude that often befall the last child. How could she permit her to travel so far, even to marry the son of Takeda who was known to her brother?

---

4. **Chan** (chän) Japanese term added to children's names.

But now, a notion that had seemed quite impossible a moment before was lodged in his receptive mind, and Hana's uncle grasped it with the pleasure that comes from an unexpected discovery.

"You know," he said looking at Hana, "it might be a very good life in America."

Hana felt a faint fluttering in her heart. Perhaps this lonely man in America was her means of escaping both the village and the encirclement of her family.

Her uncle spoke with increasing enthusiasm of sending Hana to become Taro's wife. And the husband of Hana's sister, who was head of their household, spoke with equal eagerness. Although he never said so, Hana guessed he would be pleased to be rid of her, the spirited younger sister who stirred up his placid life with what he considered **radical** ideas about life and the role of women. He often claimed that Hana had too much schooling for a girl. She had graduated from Women's High School in Kyoto, which gave her five more years of schooling than her older sister.

"It has addled her brain—all that learning from those books," he said when he tired of arguing with Hana.

A man's word carried much weight for Hana's mother. Pressed by the two men, she consulted her other daughters and their husbands. She discussed the matter carefully with her brother and asked the village priest. Finally, she agreed to an exchange of family histories and an investigation was begun into Taro Takeda's family, his education, and his health, so they would be assured there was no insanity or tuberculosis or police records concealed in his family's past. Soon Hana's uncle was devoting his energies entirely to serving as go-between for Hana's mother and Taro Takeda's father.

When at last an agreement to the marriage was almost reached, Taro wrote his first letter to Hana. It was brief and proper and gave no more clue to his character than the stiff formal portrait taken at his graduation from middle school. Hana's uncle had given her the picture with apologies from his parents because it was the only photo they had of him and it was not a flattering likeness.

Hana hid the letter and photograph in the sleeve of her kimono and took them to the outhouse to study in private. Squinting in the dim light and trying to ignore the foul odor, she read and reread Taro's letter, trying to find the real man somewhere in the sparse unbending prose.

radical ▶
(rad´ i kəl) *adj.*
favoring change in the social structure

By the time he sent her money for her steamship tickets, she had received ten more letters, but none revealed much more of the man than the first. In none did he disclose his loneliness or his need, but Hana understood this. In fact, she would have recoiled from a man who bared his intimate thoughts to her so soon. After all, they would have a lifetime together to get to know one another.

So it was that Hana had left her family and sailed alone to America with a small hope trembling inside of her. Tomorrow, at last, the ship would dock in San Francisco and she would meet face to face the man she was soon to marry. Hana was overcome with excitement at the thought of being in America, and terrified of the meeting about to take place. What would she say to Taro Takeda when they first met, and for all the days and years after?

Hana wondered about the flat above the shop. Perhaps it would be luxuriously furnished with the finest of brocades and lacquers,[5] and perhaps there would be a servant, although he had not mentioned it. She worried whether she would be able to manage on the meager English she had learned at Women's High School. The overwhelming anxiety for the day to come and the violent rolling of the ship were more than Hana could bear. Shuddering in the face of the wind, she leaned over the railing and became violently and wretchedly ill.

By five the next morning, Hana was up and dressed in her finest purple silk kimono and coat. She could not eat the bean soup and rice that appeared for breakfast and took only a few bites of the yellow pickled radish. Her bags, which had scarcely been touched since she boarded the ship, were easily packed, for all they contained were her kimonos and some of her favorite books. The large willow basket, tightly secured by a rope, remained under the bunk, untouched since her uncle had placed it there.

She had not befriended the other women in her cabin, for they had lain in their bunks for most of the voyage, too sick to be company to anyone. Each morning Hana had fled the closeness of the sleeping quarters and spent most of the day huddled in a corner of the deck, listening to the lonely songs of some Russians also traveling to an alien land.

---

5. **brocades** (brō ́ kādz ́) **and lacquers** (lak ́ ərz) brocades are rich cloths with raised designs; lacquers are highly polished, decorative pieces of wood.

As the ship approached land, Hana hurried up to the deck to look out at the gray expanse of ocean and sky, eager for a first glimpse of her new homeland.

"We won't be docking until almost noon," one of the deckhands told her.

Hana nodded, "I can wait," she answered, but the last hours seemed the longest.

When she set foot on American soil at last, it was not in the city of San Francisco as she had expected, but on Angel Island, where all third-class passengers were taken. She spent two miserable days and nights waiting, as the immigrants were questioned by officials, examined for trachoma and tuberculosis, and tested for hookworm. It was a bewildering, **degrading** beginning, and Hana was sick with anxiety, wondering if she would ever be released.

On the third day, a Japanese messenger from San Francisco appeared with a letter for her from Taro. He had written it the day of her arrival, but it had not reached her for two days.

Taro welcomed her to America and told her that the bearer of the letter would inform Taro when she was to be released so he could be at the pier to meet her.

The letter eased her anxiety for a while, but as soon as she was released and boarded the launch for San Francisco, new fears rose up to smother her with a feeling almost of dread.

The early morning mist had become a light chilling rain, and on the pier, black umbrellas bobbed here and there, making the task of recognition even harder. Hana searched desperately for a face that resembled the photo she had studied so long and hard. Suppose he hadn't come. What would she do then?

Hana took a deep breath, lifted her head and walked slowly from the launch. The moment she was on the pier, a man in a black coat, wearing a derby and carrying an umbrella, came quickly to her side. He was of slight build, not much taller than she, and his face was sallow and pale. He bowed stiffly and murmured, "You have had a long trip, Miss Omiya. I hope you are well."

Hana caught her breath. "You are Takeda San?" she asked.

He removed his hat and Hana was further startled to see that he was already turning bald.

"You are Takeda San?" she asked again. He looked older than thirty-one.

"I am afraid I no longer resemble the early photo my parents gave you. I am sorry."

degrading ▶
(dē grād´ iŋ) *adj.*
insulting; dishonorable

Hana had not meant to begin like this. It was not going well.

"No, no," she said quickly. "It is just that I . . . that is, I am terribly nervous . . ." Hana stopped abruptly, too flustered to go on.

"I understand," Taro said gently. "You will feel better when you meet my friends and have some tea. Mr. and Mrs. Toda are expecting you in Oakland. You will be staying with them until . . ." He couldn't bring himself to mention the marriage just yet and Hana was grateful he hadn't.

He quickly made arrangements to have her baggage sent to Oakland and then led her carefully along the rain-slick pier toward the streetcar that would take them to the ferry.

Hana shuddered at the sight of another boat, and as they climbed to its upper deck she felt a queasy tightening of her stomach.

"I hope it will not rock too much," she said anxiously. "Is it many hours to your city?"

Taro laughed for the first time since their meeting, revealing the gold fillings of his teeth. "Oakland is just across the bay," he explained. "We will be there in twenty minutes."

Raising a hand to cover her mouth, Hana laughed with him and suddenly felt better. I am in America now, she thought, and this is the man I came to marry. Then she sat down carefully beside Taro, so no part of their clothing touched.

ABOUT THE AUTHOR

Yoshiko Uchida (1921–1992)

On December 7, 1941, a Japanese attack on the American naval base in Pearl Harbor, Hawaii, brought the United States into World War II. Suspicion fell on all Americans of Japanese descent. Yoshiko Uchida's family and more than 100,000 other people of Japanese descent were forced to leave their homes and property. They were "resettled" in Wartime Relocation Authority (WRA) camps guarded by armed soldiers. One of Uchida's best-known books, *Journey to Topaz*, is based on her family's experience in the camps. Uchida explained her purpose for writing this way: "I want to celebrate our common humanity. . . ."

READ

Comprehension

Reread all or part of the text to help you answer the following questions.

1. Who is the main character?

2. Where is she going? Why?

3. What feelings does she have on the way?

4. What happens at the end of the story?

Research: Clarify Details Choose one unfamiliar detail from the story and conduct research on it. Explain how your research clarifies the text.

Summarize Write an objective summary of the story. Remember not to include your own opinions or judgments.

Language Study

Selection Vocabulary Use each boldface word from the selection in a sentence of your own. Then, identify a synonym and an antonym for each word.

- . . . each of them picturing this merchant in varying degrees of success and **affluence.**

- . . . the spirited younger sister who stirred up his placid life with what he considered **radical** ideas about life. . . .

- It was a bewildering, **degrading** beginning. . . .

Literary Analysis

Reread the passage identified and answer the questions that follow.

> **Focus Passage** *(p. 313)*
>
> She was thin . . . lower decks.

Key Ideas and Details

1. In this scene, what is Hana longing for?

Craft and Structure

2. **(a) Analyze:** Does this scene happen earlier or later in time than the middle section of the story? Explain.

(b) Interpret: What effect does starting the narrative at this point create?

3. **(a) Interpret:** In the second paragraph, how does the writer use images and sentence structure to contrast past and present? **(b) Draw Conclusions:** Why does the writer give more detail about the past than about the present?

Integration of Knowledge and Ideas

4. **Interpret:** What does the image of Hana's "leaden and lifeless" body suggest about the **significance** of her journey?

Cultural Context

The **cultural context** of a story includes the attitudes and values found in the characters' society.

1. What customs and attitudes lead to Hana's marriage?

2. **(a)** What aspects of traditional life does Hana reject? **(b) Belonging to a Place:** How does her rejection of **tradition** affect her feelings of belonging?

DISCUSS • RESEARCH • WRITE

From Text to Topic **Small Group Discussion**

Discuss the following passage with a small group of classmates. Take notes during the discussion. Contribute your own ideas, and support them with examples from the text.

> "You are Takeda San?" she asked.
> He removed his hat and Hana was further startled to see that he was already turning bald.

Research **Investigate the Topic**

The Immigration Boom From the 1840s to the first decades of the twentieth century, millions of immigrants like Hana poured into the United States from various countries.

Assignment

Conduct research on nineteenth- and early-twentieth-century U.S. immigration from a country you choose. Focus your research on the obstacles to belonging that immigrants faced, as well as on the resources they used to build a life for themselves here. Consult reputable Internet or print sources. Take clear notes and carefully identify your sources. Present your findings in a **history poster** that you display for the class.

Writing to Sources **Fictional Narrative**

The conclusion of "Tears of Autumn" may seem "open-ended"—the reader is left to imagine how Hana's future will turn out.

Assignment

Write a **new ending** to the story, indicating whether or not Hana will feel as if she belongs in her new life. Follow these steps:

- Review the story, taking notes on story background and characters.
- As you draft, use dialogue and other narrative **techniques** to develop characters, events, and the theme of belonging.
- Use precise words and include relevant descriptive details.
- Review your draft to make sure events, characters' concerns, and characters' styles of speaking are consistent with Uchida's narrative.

QUESTIONS FOR DISCUSSION

1. What does the passage suggest about difficulties Hana may face in making her new home in America?

2. Is Hana's *wanting* to belong to a new place enough to guarantee that she will? Explain.

PREPARATION FOR ESSAY

You may use the results of this research project to support your ideas in the essay you will write at the end of this section.

ACADEMIC VOCABULARY

Academic terms appear in blue on these pages. Use a dictionary to find their definitions. Then, use the words as you speak and write about the text.

 **Common Core State Standards**

RL.8.1, RL.8.2; W.8.3, W.8.3.b, W.8.3.d; SL.8.1; L.8.4, L.8.6
[For full standards wording, see the chart in the front of this book.]

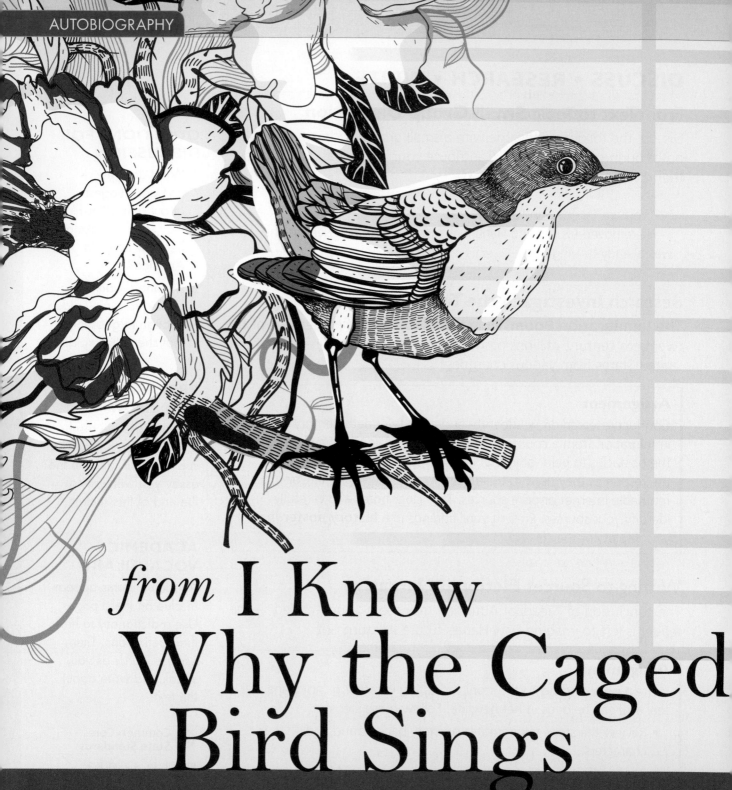

from I Know
Why the Caged
Bird Sings

Maya Angelou

We lived with our grandmother and uncle in the rear of the Store (it was always spoken of with a capital *s*), which she had owned some twenty-five years.

Early in the century, Momma (we soon stopped calling her Grandmother) sold lunches to the sawmen in the lumberyard (east Stamps) and the seedmen at the cotton gin (west Stamps). Her crisp meat pies and cool lemonade, when joined to her miraculous ability to be in two places at the same time, assured her business success. From being a mobile lunch counter, she set up a stand between the two points of fiscal interest and supplied the workers' needs for a few years. Then she had the Store built in the heart of the Negro area. Over the years it became the lay center of activities in town. On Saturdays, barbers sat their customers in the shade on the porch of the Store, and troubadours[1] on their ceaseless crawlings through the South leaned across its benches and sang their sad songs of The Brazos[2] while they played juice harps[3] and cigar-box guitars.

The formal name of the Store was the Wm. Johnson General Merchandise Store. Customers could find food staples, a good variety of colored thread, mash for hogs, corn for chickens, coal oil for lamps, light bulbs for the wealthy, shoestrings, hair dressing, balloons, and flower seeds. Anything not visible had only to be ordered.

Until we became familiar enough to belong to the Store and it to us, we were locked up in a Fun House of Things where the attendant had gone home for life. . . .

Weighing the half-pounds of flour, excluding the scoop, and depositing them dust-free into the thin paper sacks held a simple kind of adventure for me. I developed an eye for measuring how full a silver-looking ladle of flour, mash, meal, sugar or corn had to be to push the scale indicator over to eight ounces or one pound. When I was absolutely accurate our appreciative customers used to admire: "Sister Henderson sure got some smart grandchildrens." If I was off in the Store's

---

1. **troubadours** (trōō´ bə dôrz´) *n.* traveling musicians.
2. **The Brazos** (bräz´ əs) area in central Texas near the Brazos River.
3. **juice** (jōōs) **harps** small musical instruments held between the teeth and played by plucking a metal band.

favor, the eagle-eyed women would say, "Put some more in that sack, child. Don't you try to make your profit offa me."

Then I would quietly but persistently punish myself. For every bad judgment, the fine was no silver-wrapped kisses, the sweet chocolate drops that I loved more than anything in the world, except Bailey. And maybe canned pineapples. My obsession with pineapples nearly drove me mad. I dreamt of the days when I would be grown and able to buy a whole carton for myself alone.

Although the syrupy golden rings sat in their exotic cans on our shelves year round, we only tasted them during Christmas. Momma used the juice to make almost-black fruit cakes. Then she lined heavy soot-encrusted iron skillets with the pineapple rings for rich upside-down cakes. Bailey and I received one slice each, and I carried mine around for hours, shredding off the fruit until nothing was left except the perfume on my fingers. I'd like to think that my desire for pineapples was so sacred that I wouldn't allow myself to steal a can (which was possible) and eat it alone out in the garden, but I'm certain that I must have weighed the possibility of the scent exposing me and didn't have the nerve to attempt it.

> Until I was thirteen and left Arkansas for good, the Store was my favorite place to be.

Until I was thirteen and left Arkansas for good, the Store was my favorite place to be. Alone and empty in the mornings, it looked like an unopened present from a stranger. Opening the front doors was pulling the ribbon off the unexpected gift. The light would come in softly (we faced north), easing itself over the shelves of mackerel, salmon, tobacco, thread. It fell flat on the big vat of lard and by noontime during the summer the grease had softened to a thick soup. Whenever I walked into the Store in the afternoon, I sensed that it was tired. I alone could hear the slow pulse of its job half done. But just before bedtime, after numerous people had walked in and out, had argued over their bills, or joked about their neighbors, or just dropped in "to give Sister Henderson a 'Hi y'all,'" the promise of magic mornings returned to the Store and spread itself over the family in washed life waves. . . .

When Maya was about ten years old, she returned to Stamps from a visit to St. Louis with her mother. She had become depressed and withdrawn.

For nearly a year, I sopped around the house, the Store, the school and the church, like an old biscuit, dirty and inedible. Then I met, or rather got to know, the lady who threw me my first lifeline.

Mrs. Bertha Flowers was the aristocrat[4] of Black Stamps. She had the grace of control to appear warm in the coldest weather, and on the Arkansas summer days it seemed she had a private breeze which swirled around, cooling her. She was thin without the taut look of wiry people, and her printed voile[5] dresses and flowered hats were as right for her as denim overalls for a farmer. She was our side's answer to the richest white woman in town.

Her skin was a rich black that would have peeled like a plum if snagged, but then no one would have thought of getting close enough to Mrs. Flowers to ruffle her dress, let alone snag her skin. She didn't encourage familiarity. She wore gloves too.

I don't think I ever saw Mrs. Flowers laugh, but she smiled often. A slow widening of her thin black lips to show even, small white teeth, then the slow effortless closing. When she chose to smile on me, I always wanted to thank her. The action was so graceful and inclusively benign.

She was one of the few gentlewomen I have ever known, and has remained throughout my life the measure of what a human being can be. . . .

One summer afternoon, sweet-milk fresh in my memory, she stopped at the Store to buy provisions. Another Negro woman of her health and age would have been expected to carry the paper sacks home in one hand, but Momma said, "Sister Flowers, I'll send Bailey up to your house with these things."

---

4. **aristocrat** (ə ris´ tə krat´) *n.* person belonging to the upper class.
5. **voile** (voil) *n.* light cotton fabric.

She smiled that slow dragging smile, "Thank you, Mrs. Henderson. I'd prefer Marguerite, though." My name was beautiful when she said it. "I've been meaning to talk to her, anyway." They gave each other age-group looks.

Momma said, "Well, that's all right then. Sister, go and change your dress. You going to Sister Flowers's. . . ."

There was a little path beside the rocky road, and Mrs. Flowers walked in front swinging her arms and picking her way over the stones.

She said, without turning her head, to me, "I hear you're doing very good school work, Marguerite, but that it's all written. The teachers report that they have trouble getting you to talk in class." We passed the triangular farm on our left and the path widened to allow us to walk together. I hung back in the separate unasked and unanswerable questions.

"Come and walk along with me, Marguerite." I couldn't have refused even if I wanted to. She pronounced my name so nicely. Or more correctly, she spoke each word with such clarity that I was certain a foreigner who didn't understand English could have understood her.

"Now no one is going to make you talk—possibly no one can. But bear in mind, language is man's way of communicating with his fellow man and it is language alone which separates him from the lower animals." That was a totally new idea to me, and I would need time to think about it.

> "Now no one is going to make you talk—possibly no one can."

"Your grandmother says you read a lot. Every chance you get. That's good, but not good enough. Words mean more than what is set down on paper. It takes the human voice to infuse them with the shades of deeper meaning."

I memorized the part about the human voice infusing words. It seemed so **valid** and poetic.

She said she was going to give me some books and that I not only must read them, I must read them aloud. She suggested that I try to make a sentence sound in as many different ways as possible.

"I'll accept no excuse if you return a book to me that has been badly handled." My imagination boggled at the punishment I would deserve if in fact I did abuse a book of Mrs. Flowers'. Death would be too kind and brief.

valid ▶
(val´ id) *adj.* convincing; true; backed by evidence and sound reasoning

The odors in the house surprised me. Somehow I had never connected Mrs. Flowers with food or eating or any other common experience of common people. There must have been an outhouse, too, but my mind never recorded it.

The sweet scent of vanilla had met us as she opened the door.

"I made tea cookies this morning. You see, I had planned to invite you for cookies and lemonade so we could have this little chat. The lemonade is in the icebox."

It followed that Mrs. Flowers would have ice on an ordinary day, when most families in our town bought ice late on Saturdays only a few times during the summer to be used in the wooden ice cream freezers.

She took the bags from me and disappeared through the kitchen door. I looked around the room that I had never in my wildest fantasies imagined I would see. Browned photographs leered or threatened from the walls and the white, freshly done curtains pushed against themselves and against the wind. I wanted to gobble up the room entire and take it to Bailey, who would help me analyze and enjoy it.

"Have a seat, Marguerite. Over there by the table." She carried a platter covered with a tea towel. Although she warned that she hadn't tried her hand at baking sweets for some time, I was certain that like everything else about her the cookies would be perfect.

They were flat round wafers, slightly browned on the edges and butter-yellow in the center. With the cold lemonade they were sufficient for childhood's lifelong diet. Remembering my manners, I took nice little ladylike bites off the edges. She said she had made them expressly for me and that she had a few in the kitchen that I could take home to my brother. So I jammed one whole cake in my mouth and the rough crumbs scratched the insides of my jaws, and if I hadn't had to swallow, it would have been a dream come true.

As I ate she began the first of what we later called "my lessons in living." She said that I must always be intolerant of ignorance but understanding of illiteracy. That some people, unable to go to school, were more educated and even more intelligent than college professors. She encouraged me to listen carefully to what country people called mother wit. That in those homely sayings was couched the collective wisdom of generations.

When I finished the cookies she brushed off the table and brought a thick, small book from the bookcase. I had read *A Tale of Two Cities* and found it up to my standards as a romantic novel. She opened the first page and I heard poetry for the first time in my life.

> She said that I must always be intolerant of ignorance but understanding of illiteracy.

"It was the best of times and the worst of times . . ." Her voice slid in and curved down through and over the words. She was nearly singing. I wanted to look at the pages. Were they the same that I had read? Or were there notes, music, lined on the pages, as in a hymn book? Her sounds began cascading gently. I knew from listening to a thousand preachers that she was nearing the end of her reading, and I hadn't really heard, heard to understand, a single word.

"How do you like that?"

It occurred to me that she expected a response. The sweet vanilla flavor was still on my tongue and her reading was a wonder in my ears. I had to speak.

I said, "Yes, ma'am." It was the least I could do, but it was the most also.

"There's one more thing. Take this book of poems and memorize one for me. Next time you pay me a visit, I want you to recite."

I have tried often to search behind the sophistication of years for the enchantment I so easily found in those gifts. The essence escapes but its aura[6] remains. To be allowed, no, invited, into the private lives of strangers, and to share their joys and fears, was a chance to exchange the Southern bitter wormwood[7] for a cup of mead with Beowulf[8] or a hot cup of tea

---

6. **aura** (ô´ rə) *n.* atmosphere or quality.
7. **wormwood** (wʉrm´ wood´) *n.* plant that produces a bitter oil.
8. **Beowulf** (bā´ ə woolf´) hero of an old Anglo-Saxon epic. People in this poem drink **mead** (mēd), a drink made with honey and water.

and milk with Oliver Twist. When I said aloud, "It is a far far better thing that I do, than I have ever done . . ."[9] tears of love filled my eyes at my selflessness.

On that first day, I ran down the hill and into the road (few cars ever came along it) and had the good sense to stop running before I reached the Store.

I was liked, and what a difference it made. I was respected not as Mrs. Henderson's grandchild or Bailey's sister but for just being Marguerite Johnson.

Childhood's logic never asks to be proved (all conclusions are absolute). I didn't question why Mrs. Flowers had singled me out for attention, nor did it occur to me that Momma might have asked her to give me a little talking to. All I cared about was that she had made tea cookies for *me* and read to *me* from her favorite book. It was enough to prove that she liked me.

---

9. **"It is . . . than I have ever done"** last two lines from *A Tale of Two Cities* by Charles Dickens, uttered by Sydney Carton as he sacrifices his own life to save Charles Darnay, the man whom Lucie Manette—Carton's beloved—truly loves.

ABOUT THE AUTHOR

Maya Angelou (b. 1928)

Born Marguerite Johnson, Maya Angelou and her brother Bailey were raised in part by their grandmother in Arkansas. Bailey called Marguerite "mya sister," and she later officially changed her name to "Maya." After moving to San Francisco and finishing high school there, Angelou held a number of jobs that led to careers in drama, dance, teaching, and writing. She was an activist for women and for the African American community. Angelou struggled with racism, poverty, and ill treatment early in her life, but she worked hard to overcome these obstacles. She chronicled these struggles in her several autobiographies, the first and most famous of which is *I Know Why the Caged Bird Sings*.

Today, Angelou is one of the best-known African American authors in the world. In her work, Angelou tries to show that "as human beings we are more alike than we are unalike." During a long lifetime of achievement, Angelou has earned much praise and many awards. One of her most significant moments of recognition occurred when, in 1993, Bill Clinton asked Angelou to compose and read a poem for his first presidential inauguration.

READ

Comprehension

Reread all or part of the text to help you answer the following questions.

1. Who owns the Store?

2. What does the narrator do at the Store?

3. Whose house does the narrator visit?

4. What task does her host give the narrator?

Research: Clarify Details Choose one unfamiliar detail from the autobiography and conduct research on it. Explain how your research clarifies the text.

Summarize Write an objective summary of the autobiography. Remember not to include your own opinions or judgments.

Language Study

Selection Vocabulary Use each boldface word from the selection in a sentence. Identify one other form of each vocabulary word.

• It seemed so **valid** and poetic.

• She said that I must always be **intolerant** of ignorance but understanding of illiteracy.

• I have tried often to search . . . for the **enchantment** I so easily found in those gifts.

Literary Analysis

Reread the identified passage and answer the questions that follow.

> **Focus Passage** *(p. 325)*
> For nearly a year . . . gloves too.

Key Ideas and Details

1. What details indicate that Mrs. Flowers is special in her **community**?

Craft and Structure

2. (a) Identify: What does the narrator compare to an old biscuit?

(b) Interpret: What does this simile show about her feelings about herself?

3. (a) Interpret: Why does the narrator say that Mrs. Flowers seemed to have a "private breeze" on hot days? **(b) Interpret:** What does the image reveal about Marguerite's view of her?

Integration of Knowledge and Ideas

4. Draw Conclusions: Why might Marguerite be particularly open to Mrs. Flowers's influence? Cite textual details in support.

Point of View

Point of view is the perspective from which a story is told. Reread the autobiography, taking notes on point of view.

1. (a) Give three examples in which the narrator shares her thoughts and feelings about the Store. **(b) Belonging to a Place:** What do these details reveal about her sense of belonging there?

2. Belonging to a Place: From the perspective of young Marguerite, what type of belonging does Mrs. Flowers represent?

3. (a) Contrast the narrator's adult view of the past with her youthful perspective, giving two examples. **(b) Belonging to a Place:** Explain what this contrast shows about the world to which Marguerite now belongs.

from I Know
Why the Caged
Bird Sings
Maya Angelou

DISCUSS • RESEARCH • WRITE

From Text to Topic **Panel Discussion**

Form a panel to discuss the passage below and to answer the Questions for Discussion. Contribute your own ideas and support them with examples. Take notes during the discussion.

> On that first day, I ran down the hill and into the road . . . and had the good sense to stop running before I reached the Store.
> I was liked, and what a difference it made. I was respected not as Mrs. Henderson's grandchild or Bailey's sister but for just being Marguerite Johnson.

Research **Investigate the Topic**

Education Angelou attended school in Arkansas in the 1930s and 1940s. For many reasons, including discrimination, she needed a mentor like Mrs. Flowers.

Assignment

Conduct research on African American participation in the education system in the South during Angelou's childhood. Take clear notes and identify your sources so that you can retrieve the information later. Share your findings in an **informal speech** for the class.

Writing to Sources **Informative Text**

In Marguerite's world, many rich, sensory objects belong in the Store, while ideas and books belong mainly with Mrs. Flowers.

Assignment

Write a **comparison-contrast essay** in which you contrast the Store with Mrs. Flowers's world. Focus on the **role** of objects and ideas, noting Angelou's use of descriptions and literary quotations. Draw a conclusion from your comparison about ways people can belong.

- Introduce the topic in your opening, previewing main points.
- Develop body paragraphs using the point-by-point method of comparison. Include textual details and examples.
- Use transitional words, phrases, and clauses as needed.
- Establish and **maintain** a formal style.

QUESTIONS FOR DISCUSSION

1. How has Marguerite's outlook changed?
2. Why might she need a new way of belonging, beyond her way of belonging to the Store?

PREPARATION FOR ESSAY

You may use the results of this research project to support your ideas in the essay you will write at the end of this section.

ACADEMIC VOCABULARY

Academic terms appear in blue on these pages. Use a dictionary to find their definitions. Then, use the words as you speak and write about the text.

Common Core State Standards

RI.8.1, RI.8.2, RI.8.4, RI.8.6; SL.8.1; W.8.2, W.8.2.c, W.8.2.e; L.8.4, L.8.5, L.8.6
[For full standards wording, see the chart in the front of this book.]

Study Finds Americans **Increasingly Rooted**

Cindy Weiss

Americans are becoming more planted in one place, defying the cultural **assumption** that the frontier offers a better life.

But the decline in migration, linked by some to the poor economy, actually is a trend that has been underway for 40 years, according to a new study by geography professor Thomas Cooke.

"You can see the pattern since the late sixties and earlier seventies, this steady march downward," he says.

The peak of migratory behavior was in 1968, and it's been downhill since.

His analysis, to be published in the journal "Population, Space, and Place," shows that only 1.6 percent of Americans moved from one state to another between 2008 and 2009, a record low. And only 3.7 percent moved from one county to another.

From 1999 to 2009, only 63 percent of the migration decline can be attributed to economic conditions, he found. The rest is due to demographic[1] changes, such as a growing older population and a stronger trend toward rootedness.

That defies what others have called "the mobility myth," which often guides social scientists and cultural commentators, he notes.

"It's just engrained into what Americans think about themselves—it's **embedded** in our culture. We believe this myth," he

assumption ▶
(ə sump´ shən)
n. statement supposed true without proof

embedded ▶
(im bed´ əd) *v.*
fixed in some surrounding material

---

1. demographic (dem´ ə graf´ ik) *adj.* of or related to the characteristics of a group of people, such as age, gender, education, and so on.

says. "We believe that migration is the solution to all kinds of problems."

"In reality, we don't move that much," he says.

That, in turn, has implications for social policies. If policymakers expect people to move out of an ailing city like Detroit, for example, in search of jobs and better housing, they may need to reexamine their expectations.

What keeps people stuck in one place? Age, for one thing. Older people are less likely to move. But technology is also contributing to the trend. If retired people can easily fly to a warm climate for part of the year, they are less likely to move there. And if workers can commute a long distance rather than move, they do so.

LAT—couples who are "living apart together"—is also a big trend now, he notes. With Skype and e-mail allowing them to keep in touch, couples are opting for jobs in separate cities rather than both moving for career opportunities.

"People are willing to engage in that kind of **disruption** rather than be uprooted," he says.

◄ **disruption**
(dis rup´ shən)
n. disturbance;
interruption of
the orderly course
of events

The poor economy does contribute to the trend, when people cannot find jobs by moving or they have negative equity[2] in their homes and cannot afford to sell. During 2007–2009, the height of the recession, homeowners were less mobile and the South Atlantic states, including Florida, where in-migration has been high, showed dramatic declines in migration.

But even if the economy and the housing market improve, any bump up in migration will be temporary. The long-range downward trend will continue, Cooke says.

Over the next 30 years, the Baby Boomers will become less migratory as they age, pushing the rates down even more. Even the young aren't moving as much; the two youngest groups in his study migrated less often in 2009 than in 1999. With a new "boomerang" generation of college graduates who migrate back home, that is likely to continue.

"The likelihood is that America has long ago entered into a post-modern period of reduced mobility due to increased value of leisure time, increased ability to remain rooted and yet travel for leisure and work, and convergence in regional housing and labor markets," Cooke wrote in his paper.

---

2. **equity** (ek´ wit ē) *n.* value of something after subtracting any amount still owed.

Close Reading Activities

READ

Comprehension

Reread all or part of the text to help you answer the following questions.

1. What trend does the article analyze?

2. According to the article, what is one cause of the trend?

3. What might make the trend continue?

Research: Clarify Details Choose one unfamiliar detail from the article and conduct research on it. Explain how your research clarifies the text.

Summarize Write an objective summary of the article that is free from opinion and evaluation.

Language Study

Selection Vocabulary Define each boldface word and use it in a sentence.

• Americans are . . . defying the cultural **assumption**. . . .

• ". . . it's **embedded** in our culture."

• "People are willing to engage in that kind of **disruption** rather than be uprooted. . . ."

Literary Analysis

Reread the identified passage and answer the questions that follow.

> **Focus Passage** *(pp. 332–333)*
> From 1999 to 2009 . . . "that much," he says.

Key Ideas and Details

1. **(a)** What do the **statistics** show is the main reason for the migration decline from 1999 to 2009? **(b)** What are two other reasons?

2. Weiss reports that, according to the study, "only 63 percent . . . can be attributed to

economic conditions." **Infer:** Why is it important that the rest of the decline cannot be attributed to economic conditions?

Craft and Structure

3. **Connect:** How do the **contrasting** phrases "the mobility myth" and "In reality" help readers follow the author's main points?

Integration of Knowledge and Ideas

4. **Draw Conclusions:** Why might Americans think of migration as a "solution"? Give examples to support your response.

Main Idea and Support

Writers build arguments by presenting a **main idea** with **support**—**evidence** for and explanations of the main idea. Reread the article, taking notes on the main idea and the details given in support.

1. **(a)** Find a sentence in the text that states the main idea. **(b)** Cite two details that support

the main idea. Explain whether the details you identify serve as supporting evidence (for example, a statistic can serve as evidence) or as additional explanation.

2. **Belonging to a Place:** What conclusion about Americans' view of belonging can you draw from this article?

DISCUSS • RESEARCH • WRITE

From Text to Topic **Group Discussion**

Discuss the following passage with a group of classmates. Take notes during the discussion.

> What keeps people stuck in one place? Age, for one thing. Older people are less likely to move. But technology is also contributing to the trend. If retired people can easily fly to a warm climate for part of the year, they are less likely to move there.

Research **Investigate the Topic**

The American Frontier The article cites the myth of the frontier: The belief that pushing into new land is one way to make a better life. One historical reality behind this myth is the growth of the United States.

Assignment

Conduct research on a decade when explorers or settlers pushed into the American West. Consult history books and articles to learn the reasons people moved. Evaluate whether they succeeded in "belonging" to the places they settled. Take clear notes and carefully identify your sources. Share your **research notes**.

Writing to Sources **Argument**

This article indicates that many people value feeling "rooted."

Assignment

Write an **argumentative essay** in which you make a claim about whether rootedness is good for individuals and communities. Consider both sides of the issue. For example, consider the benefits of familiarity with a place, but also the ways staying in one place may limit knowledge or opportunity.

- Review the article for ideas you can use to support your claim.
- State your claim clearly in your introduction. Distinguish your claim from opposing claims.
- Support your claim with reasons, explanations, and examples.
- State and refute at least one counterargument.
- Conclude logically and effectively.

QUESTIONS FOR DISCUSSION

1. What factors allow people to remain in a place, even as their lives change?

2. Do any of these factors determine whether someone truly "belongs" to a place?

PREPARATION FOR ESSAY

You may use the results of this research project to support your ideas in the essay you will write at the end of this section.

ACADEMIC VOCABULARY

Academic terms appear in blue on these pages. Use a dictionary to find their definitions. Then, use the words as you speak and write about the text.

Common Core State Standards

RI.8.4, RI.8.8; W.8.1, W.8.1.a, W.8.1.b, W.8.1.e; SL.8.1; L.8.6
[For full standards wording, see the chart in the front of this book.]

Relationships to Place

RELATIONSHIP	TYPE OF BOND	PROCESS
Biographical	Historical and familial	Being born in and living in a place; develops over time
Spiritual	Emotional, intangible	Feeling a sense of belonging; simply felt rather than created
Ideological	Moral and ethical	Living according to moral guidelines for human responsibility to place; guidelines may be religious or secular
Narrative	Mythical	Learning about a place through stories, including creation myths, family histories, political accounts, and fictional accounts
Commodified	Cognitive	Choosing a place based on a list of desirable traits and lifestyle preferences, comparison of actual places with ideal
Dependent	Material	Constrained by lack of choice, dependency on another person, or economic opportunity

from "What Is Sense of Place?"
—Jennifer E. Cross

READ • DISCUSS • WRITE

Common Core State Standards

RI.8.6; W.8.1; SL.8.1, SL.8.2, SL.8.4; L.8.6
[For full standards wording, see the chart in the front of this book.]

Comprehension

Reread the chart as needed to help you answer these questions.

1. In the chart, what are the six types of relationships to place?

2. Which column explains the **sources** or causes of belonging?

Critical Analysis

Key Ideas and Details

1. Analyze: What type of information does the second column in the chart add to the first?

2. Compare and Contrast: Identify two types of relationship in the chart that can be classified as opposites.

Craft and Structure

3. Analyze: The typical purpose of a chart is to provide readers with ways to quickly find and compare information in various **categories**. How is the writer's use of words in this chart consistent with the general purpose of a chart?

Integration of Knowledge and Ideas

4. Classify: Choose three of the other texts you have read in this section. Using the categories in the chart, classify people's relationship to place in each of the texts you have chosen.

ACADEMIC VOCABULARY

Academic terms appear in blue on these pages. Use a dictionary to find their definitions. Then, use the words as you speak and write about the text.

From Text to Topic **Class Discussion**

Discuss the chart with classmates. Use the following discussion questions to focus your conversation.

1. Does this chart show all the different ways of belonging? Explain, drawing on your own background knowledge or on examples from the texts in this section.

2. Would you remove any of the categories from the chart? Explain why or why not.

Writing to Sources **Argument**

Write a brief **argument** in which you rank one relationship from the chart as most important. Use information from the chart and details from other texts in this section as **support** for your claim.

Speaking and Listening **Group Discussion**

Belonging to a Place and Information The texts in this section vary in genre, style, and perspective. However, all of them focus on how and why people develop relationships to places. The issue of belonging to a place is related to the Big Question addressed in this unit: **How much information is enough?**

▲ Refer to the selections you read in Part 3 as you complete the activities on this assessment.

Assignment

Conduct discussions. With a small group of classmates, conduct a discussion about issues of belonging to a place and of the information, or understandings, that belonging involves. Refer to the texts in this section, other texts you have read, and your personal experience and knowledge to support your ideas. Begin your discussion by addressing the following questions:

- What must people know or understand about a place in order to belong there?
- How do they gain that knowledge or understanding?
- What types of experiences can tell people that they do *not* belong?
- In what cases might a person draw conclusions about others based on the place to which they belong?

Summarize and present your ideas. After you have fully explored the topic, summarize your discussion and present your findings to the class as a whole.

Criteria for Success

✓ **Organizes the group effectively**
Appoint a group leader and a timekeeper. The group leader should present the discussion questions. The timekeeper should make sure the discussion takes no longer than 20 minutes.

✓ **Maintains focus of discussion**
As a group, stay on topic and avoid straying into other subject areas.

✓ **Involves all participants equally and fully**
No one person should monopolize the conversation. Rather, everyone should take turns speaking and contributing ideas.

✓ **Follows the rules for collegial discussion**
As each group member speaks, others should listen carefully. Build on one another's ideas and support viewpoints and opinions with sound reasoning and evidence. Express disagreement respectfully.

USE NEW VOCABULARY

As you speak and share ideas, work to use the vocabulary words you have learned in this unit. The more you use new words, the more you will "own" them.

Writing Narrative

Belonging to a Place and Information Belonging to a particular place—or not belonging there—tells us a good deal about ourselves. Belonging to a place may also say something about the information we have. For example, people who live in a particular town are likely to know the fastest way to the nearby mall and where to go swimming in the summer.

Common Core State Standards

W.8.3.a–e; SL.8.1.a–d
[For full standards wording, see the chart in the front of this book.]

Assignment

Write a **narrative essay** telling of a place to which you belong or do not belong. In your essay, narrate incidents that clearly show your relationship to the place. In addition, explain the role played by information in this relationship. Compare your relationship to this place with a relationship to place in one of the selections in this section. Draw on the research you conducted for additional examples and insights.

Criteria for Success

Purpose/Focus

✓ **Connects specific incidents with larger ideas**
Make meaningful connections between your experiences of belonging and the texts you have read in this section.

✓ **Clearly conveys the significance of the story**
Provide a conclusion in which you reflect on what you experienced.

Organization

✓ **Organizes ideas and examples effectively and logically**
Structure your essay so that events build toward a climax. Use a clear organization to ensure that readers can easily follow the connections you make between general ideas and specific incidents.

✓ **Makes clear transitions**
Weave together general ideas and specific examples using transitional words and phrases, such as "for example."

Development of Ideas/Elaboration

✓ **Supports insights**
Include examples from your own experience, as well as details from the texts you have read or the research you have conducted in this section.

Language

✓ **Uses description effectively**
Use descriptive details to paint vivid word pictures of places.

Conventions

✓ **Does not have errors**
Check your narrative to eliminate errors in grammar, spelling, and punctuation.

WRITE TO EXPLORE

As you write your narrative essay, you may find new, unexpected connections between your own experiences and the texts in this section. By finding ways to smoothly incorporate new insights, you will improve your final draft.

Writing to Sources Informative Text

Belonging to a Place and Information The readings in this section show various ways of belonging to a place and the type of information each involves. They raise questions about belonging such as the following:

- What do different ways of belonging have in common? How are they different?
- How does each connect or separate people?
- To truly belong to a place, must one belong in more than one way?
- Is one way of belonging more important than the others?
- If a person "has to" stay in a given place, does he or she belong there less truly than if he or she feels free to leave?

Reflect on these questions, and then draw on your ideas to complete the following assignment.

Assignment

Write a **comparison-and-contrast essay** in which you compare four or more ways of belonging to a place and the information each involves. Use ideas from the selections you have read and from the research you have conducted in this section. Draw conclusions about the importance of each type of belonging. Consider the way each can connect people, as well as the choices or lack of choices each involves.

Prewriting and Planning

Choose texts. Select at least three texts in this section that will provide strong material to support a comparison and contrast.

Gather details and craft a working thesis. Use a chart like the one shown to develop your key ideas. Though you may refine or change your ideas as you write, the working version will establish a clear direction.

INCORPORATE RESEARCH

To incorporate research in your essay, refer to your notes. Quote or summarize material as appropriate. Introduce your research smoothly with transitional phrases that clearly identify each source: for example, "As Jane Smith notes in her book *The Pioneers*, . . .".

Focus Question: How do different ways of belonging compare?

Text	Passage	Notes
"Gentleman of Río en Medio"	"The trees in that orchard are not mine, *Señor*, they belong to the children of the village."	People need to understand others' perspectives on belonging.
"Choice: A Tribute to Martin Luther King, Jr."	[T]he history of my family, like that of all black Southerners, is a history of dispossession. We loved the land and worked the land, but we never owned it. . . .	At the same time, society has to acknowledge belonging by granting legal rights of ownership.

Example Main Idea: Other people have to understand how and why you belong, and the law has to reflect that knowledge.

Drafting

Organize your comparisons and conclusions. Decide whether you will use block organization (discussing each type of belonging in turn) or point-by-point organization (discussing first one aspect, then another). Then, outline your essay, following your chosen structure. In your outline, note which facts, details, quotations, and examples you will use to support each point.

Write your introduction and conclusion last. As you draft, follow your outline. Then, review your draft. Write a brief statement summarizing your main ideas. Then, craft a strong introduction previewing these ideas and a conclusion that concisely restates them.

Use language effectively. As you draft, choose words that capture your meaning precisely. For example, the word *eerie* is more precise than *strange*. In addition, use appropriately formal language, avoiding slang terms such as *cool,* except as needed to capture characters' dialogue.

Use transitions. Clarify comparisons by using transitional words, phrases, and clauses, such as *similarly, in contrast,* and *from another perspective.*

Revising and Editing

Review content. Make sure your comparisons are well supported. Balance comparisons by adding more details as needed.

Review style. Revise to vary sentences. For example, if you have used mostly short, simple sentences, identify related sentences and combine them using conjunctions. (See p. 127.)

Common Core State Standards

W.8.2.a-f
[For full standards wording, see the chart in the front of this book.]

CITE RESEARCH CORRECTLY

Create a Works Cited list for your essay, following a standard style. Review your draft and make sure you have included appropriately formatted citations for quotations and for ideas not your own. (See the Conducting Research workshop in the front of this book.)

Self-Evaluation Rubric

Use the following criteria to evaluate the effectiveness of your essay.

Criteria	Rating Scale *not very ....very*			
Purpose/Focus Introduces a specific topic; provides a concluding section that follows from and supports the information or explanation presented	1	2	3	4
Organization Organizes ideas, concepts, and information into broader categories; uses appropriate and varied transitions to create cohesion and clarify relationships among ideas and concepts	1	2	3	4
Development of Ideas/Elaboration Develops the topic with relevant, well-chosen facts, definitions, concrete details, quotations, or other information and examples	1	2	3	4
Language Uses precise language and domain-specific vocabulary to inform about or explain the topic; establishes and maintains a formal style	1	2	3	4
Conventions Correctly follows conventions of grammar, spelling, and punctuation.	1	2	3	4

Independent Reading

Titles for Extended Reading

In this unit, you have read a variety of informational texts, including literary nonfiction. Continue to read on your own. Select works that you enjoy, but challenge yourself to explore new topics, new authors, and works of increasing depth and complexity. The titles suggested below will help you get started.

INFORMATIONAL TEXT

The Building of Manhattan
by Donald Mackay   **EXEMPLAR TEXT** ©

This illustrated **nonfiction** account tells the history of how New York City was built, from the subways underground to the skyscrapers that crowd the skyline.

Albert Einstein: A Photographic Story of a Life
by Frieda Wishinsky

In this **biography,** the extraordinary life of Albert Einstein is told through words and photographs. From his early struggles as a student to his revolutionary discoveries in physics, this book provides fascinating details.

Cool Stuff and How It Works
by Chris Woodford, Luke Collins, Clint Witchalls, Ben Morgan, and James Flint

Explore the inner workings of modern technological devices such as robots and MP3 players through the **essays,** diagrams, photographs, and captions in this richly illustrated book.

Discoveries: Exploring the Possibilities

This **essay** collection provides a wide range of information on subjects such as forensic anthropology, stamps, and the Internet. This volume is part of the Discoveries series, which covers a broad range of engaging topics.

LITERATURE

Chicago Poems
by Carl Sandburg   **EXEMPLAR TEXT** ©

In this collection of **poems,** Sandburg focuses his lens, with memorable results, on the "stormy, husky, brawling" city of Chicago in the early twentieth century.

No Promises in the Wind
by Irene Hunt
Berkley, 2002

Set during the Great Depression, this **historical novel** chronicles two brothers' desperate search for food and work. On the road, they experience the harsh reality of miserable economic times.

The Boy Who Reversed Himself
by William Sleator

In this **science-fiction novel,** Laura discovers that her strange neighbor has direct access to the fourth dimension. Events turn serious when Laura and her boyfriend travel to "four-space" on their own.

ONLINE TEXT SET

SHORT STORY
The 11:59 Patricia C. McKissack

MEMOIR
A Glow in the Dark *from* **Woodsong**
Gary Paulsen

MAGAZINE ARTICLE
Sun Suckers and Moon Cursers
Richard and Joyce Wolkomir

Preparing to Read Complex Texts

Attentive Reading As you read literary nonfiction on your own, bring your imagination and questions to the text. The questions shown below, and others that you ask as you read, will help you understand and enjoy literary nonfiction even more.

When reading literary nonfiction, ask yourself . . .

Comprehension: **Key Ideas and Details**

- Who is the author? Why did he or she write the work?
- Is the author writing about a personal experience or a topic he or she has studied? In either case, what are my expectations about the work?
- Are the ideas the author expresses important? Why or why not?
- Did the author live at a different time and place than the present? If so, how does that affect his or her choice of topic and attitude?
- Does the author express beliefs that are very different from mine? If so, how does that affect what I understand and feel about the text?
- Does any one idea seem more important than the others? Why?
- What can I learn from this work?

Text Analysis: **Craft and Structure**

- Does the author organize ideas so that I can understand them? If not, what is unclear?
- What has the author done to capture my interest? Is the work interesting from the start? If not, why?
- Does the author give me a new way of looking at a topic? How?
- Is the author an expert on the topic? How do I know?
- Does the author use a variety of relevant evidence? If not, what is weak?
- Where does the author use words in interesting ways?

Connections: **Integration of Knowledge and Ideas**

- Does the work seem believable? Why or why not?
- Do I agree or disagree with the author's arguments or ideas? Why?
- Does this work remind me of others I have read? In what ways?
- Does this work make me want to read more about this topic? Does it make me want to explore a related topic? Why?

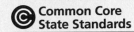 **Common Core State Standards**

Reading Literature/ Informational Text
10. By the end of the year, read and comprehend literature, including stories, dramas, and poems, and literary nonfiction, at the high end of the grades 6–8 text complexity band independently and proficiently.

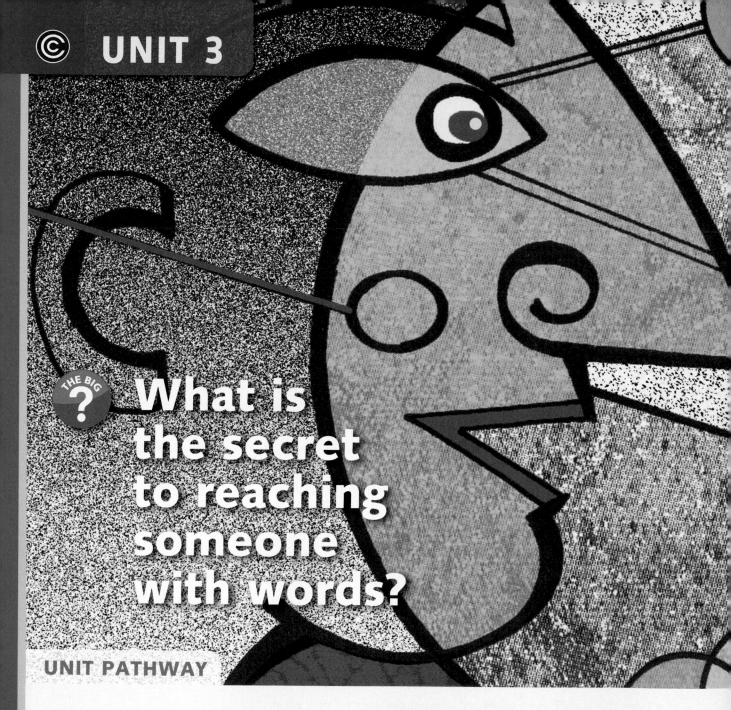

What is the secret to reaching someone with words?

THE BIG ?

UNIT PATHWAY

PART 1
SETTING EXPECTATIONS

- INTRODUCING THE BIG QUESTION
- CLOSE READING WORKSHOP

PART 2
TEXT ANALYSIS
GUIDED EXPLORATION

VOICES IN VERSE

PART 3
TEXT SET
DEVELOPING INSIGHT

GENERATIONS

PART 4
DEMONSTRATING INDEPENDENCE

- INDEPENDENT READING
- ONLINE TEXT SET

CLOSE READING TOOL

Use this tool to practice the close reading strategies you learn.

STUDENT eTEXT

Bring learning to life with audio, video, and interactive tools.

ONLINE WRITER'S NOTEBOOK

Easily capture notes and complete assignments online.

Find all Digital Resources at **pearsonrealize.com**

What is the secret to reaching someone with words?

Think of how limited our lives would be without words. Words, written or spoken, are the building blocks that make meaningful communication possible. When two people connect, it is often the result of verbal communication—whether it is between child and parent, friend and friend, or writer and reader. The result of communication takes different forms, such as agreement or disagreement, satisfaction in gaining knowledge, or the experience that occurs when someone reads a powerful, meaningful text.

Writers use different techniques to express ideas. All writers share one common starting point, however. Whether their goal is to inform, persuade, or entertain, writers know that in order to create something with significance they must first reach a reader with words.

Exploring the Big Question

Collaboration: One-on-One Discussion Start thinking about the Big Question by describing a specific example of each of the following situations.

- A news story in the media about a recent historical event
- A situation that allowed you to express your individuality
- An experience that you found difficult to put into words
- A conversation that inspired you to try a new activity or approach
- A text message, an e-mail, or a blog entry that made you laugh
- A story, a poem, or an article that changed your perspective

Discuss with a partner how each situation reveals a different aspect of the human desire to communicate. Use the Big Question vocabulary in your discussion.

Connecting to the Literature Each reading in this unit will give you additional insight into the Big Question: What is the secret to reaching someone with words?

Vocabulary

Acquire and Use Academic Vocabulary The term "academic vocabulary" refers to words you typically encounter in scholarly and literary texts and in technical and business writing. Review the definitions of these academic vocabulary words.

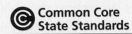 **Common Core State Standards**

Speaking and Listening
1. Engage effectively in a range of collaborative discussions with diverse partners on *grade 8 topics, texts, and issues,* building on others' ideas and expressing their own clearly.

Language
6. Acquire and use accurately grade-appropriate general academic and domain-specific words and phrases; gather vocabulary knowledge when considering a word or phrase important to comprehension or expression.

benefit (ben´ ə fit) *n.* advantage; positive result

connection (kə nek´ shən) *n.* link; tie; relationship

cultural (kul´ chər əl) *adj.* relating to the customs and beliefs of a group

individuality (in´ də vij´ o͞o al´ ə tē) *n.* characteristics that set a person or thing apart from others

inform (in fôrm´) *v.* tell; give information or knowledge

relevant (rel´ ə vənt) *adj.* connected to the topic being discussed; related

significance (sig nif´ ə kəns) *n.* importance

valid (val´ id) *adj.* convincing; true; backed by evidence and sound reasoning

Use these words as you complete Big Question activities in this unit that involve reading, writing, speaking, and listening.

Gather Vocabulary Knowledge Additional words related to communication are listed below. Categorize the words by deciding whether you know each one well, know it a little bit, or do not know it at all.

experience	**meaningful**	**misunderstood**
express	**media**	**sensory**
feedback		

Then, do the following:

1. Write the definitions of the words you know.
2. Using a print or an online dictionary, look up the meaning of each word you do not know. Then, write the meaning.
3. Confirm the meaning and pronunciation of each word you think you know. Revise your definition if necessary.
4. Use as many of the words as possible in a paragraph about the obstacles and difficulties you might encounter when trying to reach someone with words.

In this workshop you will learn an approach to reading that will deepen your understanding of literature and will help you better appreciate an author's craft. The workshop includes models for the close reading, discussion, research, and writing activities you will complete as you study literature in this unit. After you have reviewed the strategies and models in this workshop, practice your skills with the Independent Practice selection.

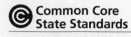 **Common Core State Standards**

RL.8.1, RL.8.4; W.8.2, W.8.7, W.8.9.a; SL.8.1
[For full standards wording, see the standards chart in the front of this book.]

CLOSE READING: POETRY

In Part 2 of this unit you will focus on reading various poems. Use these strategies as you read the texts.

Comprehension: Key Ideas and Details

- Read first to unlock basic meaning.
- Use context clues and reference works to help you determine the meanings of unfamiliar words.
- Identify unfamiliar details that you might need to clarify through research.
- Make inferences about information that is implied.

Ask yourself questions such as these:
- Who is the speaker, or the voice that "says" the words of the poem?
- What is the poem's subject?

Text Analysis: Craft and Structure

- Think about the ways that sound devices affect the tone of the poem.
- Analyze the poet's use of figurative language, or language not meant to be taken literally.
- Take note of the poem's imagery, or the pictures it creates with words.
- Consider how the poet develops the speaker's personality.
- Analyze the poem's form, including the patterns of rhythm and rhyme.

Ask yourself questions such as these:
- Which language appeals to the five senses?
- What do the word choices and imagery tell me about the speaker?
- How does the poem's form reflect its meaning?

Connections: Integration of Knowledge and Ideas

- Look for images and symbols and analyze their deeper meaning.
- Compare and contrast this work with other works you have read.
- **Ask yourself questions such as these:**
- How has this work expanded my ideas—or my imagination?
- What is the poem's theme?

Read

As you read this poem, take note of the annotations, which model ways to closely read the text.

Reading Model

"A Poem for My Librarian, Mrs. Long"

(You never know what troubled little girl needs a book.)

by Nikki Giovanni

At a time when there was no tv before 3:00 P.M.
And on Sunday none until 5:00
We sat on front porches watching
The jfg sign go on and off greeting
5 The neighbors, discussing the political
Situation congratulating the preacher
On his sermon[1]

There was always radio which brought us
Songs from wlac in nashville and what we would now call
10 Easy listening or smooth jazz but when I listened
Late at night with my portable (that I was so proud of)
Tucked under my pillow
I heard nat king cole and matt dennis, june christy and ella fitzgerald
And sometimes sarah vaughan sing black coffee
15 Which I now drink
It was just called music[2]

There was a bookstore uptown on gay street
Which I visited and inhaled that wonderful odor
Of new books[3]
20 Even today I read hardcover as a preference paperback only
As a last resort

And up the hill on vine street
(The main black corridor) sat our carnegie library
Mrs. Long always glad to see you
25 The stereoscope[4] always ready to show you faraway
Places to dream about

Craft and Structure
1 The first *stanza*—group of lines—shows that this poem is written in *free verse*: a poetic form that features poetic language but does not follow a formal pattern of rhythm or rhyme.

Key Ideas and Details
2 A rapid flurry of the names of African American and white singers is followed by an assertion—"It was just called music." The lack of capitals and the quantity of names help the names run together, confirming the speaker's point: Music shows racial equality.

Craft and Structure
3 The image "that wonderful odor" captures the speaker's deep appreciation of books, which extends to their physical qualities.

Key Ideas and Details
4 The *stereoscope* is associated here with dreams and with images. By consulting a dictionary, readers can confirm that it is a device that combines two images to give an illusion of depth.

Mrs. Long asking what are you looking for today
When I wanted *Leaves of Grass* or alfred north whitehead
She would go to the big library uptown and I now know
30 Hat in hand to ask to borrow so that I might borrow
Probably they said something humiliating since southern
Whites like to humiliate southern blacks[5]

But she nonetheless brought the books
Back[6] and I held them to my chest
35 Close to my heart
And happily skipped back to grandmother's house
Where I would sit on the front porch
In a gray glider and dream of a world
Far away

40 I love the world where I was
I was safe and warm and grandmother gave me neck kisses
When I was on my way to bed

But there was a world
Somewhere
45 Out there
And Mrs. Long opened that wardrobe
But no lions or witches scared me
I went through
Knowing there would be
50 Spring[7]

Key Ideas and Details

5 "Hat in hand" conveys the librarian's humility when interacting with people at the "big library uptown." The word choice reveals Mrs. Long's dedication—she braves potential humiliation to borrow books for the speaker.

Craft and Structure

6 The repeated *b* (*brought, books, back*) emphasizes the librarian's success in the face of obstacles. For the reader, this emphasis may reinforce the librarian's determination or the decisiveness of her action.

Integration of Knowledge and Ideas

7 The poet completes her tribute to Mrs. Long by alluding to the book *The Lion, the Witch, and the Wardrobe,* in which four children enter a fantasyland through an enchanted wardrobe. The speaker shows that Mrs. Long "opened" the speaker's mind to the possibility of other worlds and adventures.

Discuss

Sharing ideas and listening to others' ideas can deepen your understanding and help you look at a topic in a new way. As you participate in discussions, work to have a genuine exchange in which classmates build upon one another's ideas. Support your points with evidence and ask meaningful questions.

Discussion Model

Student 1: This poem feels very informal. It feels like someone is telling a story to friends. There isn't even much punctuation, and a lot of words—look at "ella fitzgerald" and "nashville"—aren't even capitalized.

Student 2: Yes. The tone is really personal. The speaker just talks about when she was a girl and how much she loved books and how thankful she is for her librarian.

Student 3: Books helped her get ready for the world beyond her neighborhood. At the end, she says she wasn't afraid of that world; she knew "there would be / Spring." Before that, though, she says she "now know[s]" the librarian probably went through humiliation to help her. I think the poet is using this story to also talk about society.

Research

Research can shed light on various aspects of a text. Consider questions that arise as you read, and use them as the basis for research.

Research Model

Questions: *How does Nikki Giovanni use her childhood experiences in her poems?*

Key Words for Internet Search: Nikki Giovanni + childhood

Result: The Poetry Foundation, Nikki Giovanni Biography

What I Learned: In her poems, Giovanni draws on her own experiences. Like the speaker, she read a lot as a girl and spent time in the segregated South of the 1950s. As explained in her Poetry Foundation biography, Giovanni's children's poems are "unrhymed incantations of childhood images and feelings which also focus on African-American history and explore issues and concerns specific to black youngsters."

Write

Writing about a text deepens your understanding of it and allows you to share your ideas with others. The following model essay analyzes Nikki Giovanni's use of imagery and cites evidence to support the main ideas.

Writing Model: Explanatory Text

The Power of Books: Opening Up New Worlds

In Nikki Giovanni's "A Poem for My Librarian, Mrs. Long," the speaker is a young girl whose love of reading is encouraged by Mrs. Long, a librarian. Books carry the girl to places beyond her own neighborhood. In telling this story, Giovanni sends the message that books can open up new worlds for people who face challenges in real life.

In the poem, Giovanni includes many details to reveal how much books meant to the speaker. For example, Giovanni writes about the bookstore where the speaker "inhaled that wonderful odor / Of new books" (lines 18–19). She describes how she held the books Mrs. Long got for her "to my chest / Close to my heart" (lines 34–35), a powerful image that clearly conveys the speaker's love of reading.

Books are important to the girl because they connect her to worlds beyond her own, just as the radio and the library stereoscope do. While she loves her own world, "the world where I was / I was safe and warm . . . " (lines 40–41), she also treasures the world of the imagination: "But there was a world / Somewhere / Out there / And Mrs. Long opened that wardrobe / . . . / I went through / Knowing there would be / Spring" (lines 43–50). The wardrobe to which she is referring appears in *The Lion, the Witch, and the Wardrobe.* In this book, children use a magical wardrobe as the gateway to a wondrous land.

For Mrs. Long, though, getting these books involves challenges in the real world. She faces the possibility that someone will say "something humiliating" (line 31) to her when she goes to the main library to get books for the speaker. Giovanni grew up at a time when African Americans were making historic strides against injustice. She and her family fought against the kind of prejudice Mrs. Long faces. Giovanni's older sister, Gary Ann, was one of the first African American students to attend an all-white high school, desegregating it.

Despite these challenges, books open the speaker's mind much as the magic wardrobe in *The Lion, the Witch, and the Wardrobe* opened the way to a wondrous land. In telling us this story, the speaker not only thanks Mrs. Long but also invites readers to look beyond the challenges they face, using the power of the imagination.

In the first paragraph, the writer's thesis connects the poem's subject with a larger theme.

The writer supports claims with specific details from the poem, citing line numbers.

The writer uses a specific detail to draw a conclusion about the speaker's feelings.

The writer incorporates information from research to put events in historical context.

The writer clarifies a text reference and connects it to the poem's larger theme.

As you read the following texts, apply the close reading strategies you have learned. You may need to read the poems multiple times.

Describe Somebody

by Jacqueline Woodson

Today in class Ms. Marcus said
Take out your poetry notebooks and describe somebody.
Think carefully, Ms. Marcus said.
You're gonna read it to the class.
5   I wrote, Ms. Marcus is tall and a little bit skinny.
Then I put my pen in my mouth and stared down
at the words.
Then I crossed them out and wrote
Ms. Marcus's hair is long and brown.
10   Shiny.
When she smiles it makes you feel all good inside.
I stopped writing and looked around the room.
Angel was staring out the window.
Eric and Lamont were having a pen fight.
15   They don't care about poetry.
Stupid words, Eric says.
Lots and lots of stupid words.
Eric is tall and a little bit mean.
Lamont's just regular.
20   Angel's kinda chubby. He's got light brown hair.
Sometimes we all hang out,
play a little ball or something. Angel's real good
at science stuff. Once he made a volcano
for science fair and the stuff that came out of it
25   looked like real lava. Lamont can
draw superheroes real good. Eric—nobody
at school really knows this but
he can sing. Once, Miss Edna[1] took me
to a different church than the one

---

1. **Miss Edna** the foster mother of the speaker of the poem, Lonnie.

Meet the Author

Poet and novelist **Jacqueline Woodson** was born in 1963 in Columbus, Ohio. Her works reflect her interest in writing for and about young people. Woodson has won several writing awards, including the Margaret A. Edwards Award, which honors authors who write for young adults.

CLOSE READING TOOL

Read and respond to this selection online using the **Close Reading Tool.**

30   we usually go to on Sunday.
      I was surprised to see Eric up there
      with a choir robe on. He gave me a mean look
      like I'd better not
      say nothing about him and his dark green robe with

35   gold around the neck.
      After the preacher preached
      Eric sang a song with nobody else in the choir singing.

Vocabulary ▶
dabbing (dab´ iŋ) *v.*
patting with
something soft

      Miss Edna started **dabbing** at her eyes
      whispering *Yes, Lord.*

40   Eric's voice was like something
      that didn't seem like it should belong
      to Eric.
      Seemed like it should be coming out of an angel.

      Now I gotta write a whole new poem

45   'cause Eric would be real mad if I told the class
      about his angel voice.

Almost Summer Sky
by Jacqueline Woodson

It was the trees first, Rodney[1] tells me.
It's raining out. But the rain is light and warm.
And the sky's not all close to us like it gets
sometimes. It's way up there with
5   some blue showing through.
Late spring sky, Ms. Marcus says. *Almost summer sky.*
And when she said that, I said
Hey Ms. Marcus, that's a good title
for a poem, right?
10 *You have a poet's heart, Lonnie.*
That's what Ms. Marcus said to me.
I have a poet's heart.
That's good. A good thing to have.
And I'm the one who has it.

15 Now Rodney puts his arm around my shoulder
We keep walking. There's a park
eight blocks from Miss Edna's house
That's where we're going.
Me and Rodney to the park.
20 Rain coming down warm
Rodney with his arm around my shoulder
Makes me think of Todd and his pigeons
how big his smile gets when they fly.

The trees upstate ain't like other trees you seen, Lonnie
25 Rodney squints up at the sky, shakes his head
smiles.
No, upstate they got maple and catalpa and scotch pine,[2]
all kinds of trees just standing.
Hundred-year-old trees big as three men.

30 *When you go home this weekend,* Ms. Marcus said.
Write about a perfect moment.

---

1. **Rodney** one of Miss Edna's sons.
2. **catalpa** (kə tal′ pə) **and scotch pine** Catalpa is a tree with heart-shaped leaves; scotch
   pine is a tree with yellow wood, grown for timber.

Yeah, Little Brother, Rodney says.
You don't know about shade till you lived upstate.
Everybody should do it—even if it's just for a little while.

35 Way off, I can see the park—blue-gray sky
touching the tops of trees.

I had to live there awhile, Rodney said.
Just to be with all that green, you know?
I nod, even though I don't.
40 I can't even imagine moving away from here,
from Rodney's arm around my shoulder,
from Miss Edna's Sunday cooking,
from Lily[3] in her pretty dresses and great
big smile when she sees me.

45 Can't imagine moving away

From
Home.

You know what I love about trees, Rodney says.
It's like . . . It's like their leaves are hands
reaching
50 *out to you. Saying Come on over here, Brother.*
Let me just . . . Let me just . . .
Rodney looks down at me and grins.
Let me just give you some shade for a while.

---

3. **Lily** Lonnie's sister, who lives in a different foster home.

Close Reading Activities

Read

Comprehension: **Key Ideas and Details**

1. (a) What assignment does Ms. Marcus give Lonnie in each poem? **(b) Analyze:** How does each poem relate to that assignment? How does it go beyond the assignment?

2. (a) What secret does Lonnie know about Eric in "Describe Somebody"?
(b) Speculate: Why would Eric be angry if Lonnie revealed Eric's secret?

3. (a) Infer: What is the setting for "Almost Summer Sky"? **(b) Interpret:** How does Lonnie feel about this setting? Cite details from the poem to support your ideas.

4. Summarize: Write a brief summary of each poem. Include details from the poems in your writing.

Text Analysis: **Craft and Structure**

5. Analyze: How does Lonnie's point of view shape what readers learn about the other people in the poems? Use details from each poem to support your answer.

6. (a) Describe: Which characteristics of these poems show that they are written in free verse? **(b) Evaluate:** How is free verse well suited to conveying Lonnie's thoughts?

7. (a) In the last stanza of "Almost Summer Sky," what comparison does Rodney make? **(b) Analyze:** What effect does this use of figurative language have on readers?

Connections: **Integration of Knowledge and Ideas**

Discuss
Conduct a **small-group discussion** about the poetic language used in each poem. For example, consider Rodney's description of trees in "Almost Summer Sky."

Research
Although she writes from many points of view, Jacqueline Woodson says that her writing is always "emotionally autobiographical." Briefly research the following topics to determine what Woodson means.

a. autobiography
b. Jacqueline Woodson
c. speaker in poetry

Write a brief **explanation** of how Woodson's poetry could be emotionally autobiographical, even when she writes as different characters.

Write
Write an **explanatory essay** explaining how the poet takes simple topics and makes them into insightful poetry. Cite details to support your analysis.

 What is the secret to reaching someone with words?

How does Jacqueline Woodson reach readers emotionally with words? Explain your answer.

"[A poem] begins as a **lump in the throat**, a sense of wrong, a homesickness, a **lovesickness**. . . . It finds its thought or makes its thought."

—**Robert Frost**

VOICES IN VERSE

As you read the poems in this section, be mindful of the authors' word choices. Listen for their voices in the verse. Much like music, the words of poetry filter through your sense of hearing and, when successful, reach your very sense of being. The quotation on the facing page will help you start thinking about this thought-provoking form of communication.

◀ **CRITICAL VIEWING** What might the person in the photograph be thinking and feeling? Why might poetry be an appropriate way to communicate these thoughts and feelings to others?

CLOSE READING TOOL

Use the **Close Reading Tool** to practice the strategies you learn in this unit.

READINGS IN PART 2

POETRY COLLECTION I
Silver • Ring Out, Wild Bells • Cat! • Thumbprint
(p. 367)

POETRY COLLECTION 2
The Sky Is Low, the Clouds Are Mean • Concrete Mixers • Harlem Night Song • The City Is So Big
(p. 379)

EXEMPLAR TEXT ©

POETRY COLLECTION 3
The New Colossus • Blow, Blow, Thou Winter Wind • Paul Revere's Ride
(p. 391)

POETRY COLLECTION 4
Grandma Ling • your little voice / Over the wires came leaping • New World • January
(p. 405)

Elements of Poetry

Poetry is the most **musical** of literary forms.

The **structure** of a poem is the way the words and lines are arranged.

Lines Most poetry is arranged in **lines,** or groupings of words. A line may not be a complete sentence. A poet may *break,* or end, a line to emphasize a word or an idea, or to create a pattern of rhythm or rhyme.

Stanzas Lines may be grouped in **stanzas**—logical sections of ideas, like paragraphs in an essay. A two-line stanza is a **couplet**; three lines are a **tercet**; four lines are a **quatrain.**

Rhyme The **rhyme scheme** is the pattern of rhymes at the ends of lines. Each new rhyme is assigned a letter of the alphabet, as shown below.

The path of least resistance,	a
Is short, but it's boring.	b
Choose the tougher distance	a
For soaring.	b

Meter The pattern of stressed and unstressed syllables in a poem is the **meter.** Each unit of stressed and unstressed syllables in a poem is called a **foot.**

The example below shows how poetry can be marked to show the meter. An accent (´) marks each stressed syllable. A horseshoe symbol (ˇ) marks each unstressed syllable. Vertical lines (|) divide each line into feet.

> Sómebŏdў, | Nóbŏdў—
>
> Ă fáce | iš sŏ neár

The chart below shows a fuller analysis of the meter and other structural elements of a poem.

from "The Village Blacksmith," Henry Wadsworth Longfellow	
His hair | is crisp, | and black, | and long, His face | is like | the tan; His brow | is wet | with hon | est sweat, He earns | whate'er | he can, And looks | the whole | world in | the face, For he owes | not an | y man.	This stanza has six lines. The poet begins each line with a capital letter. The regular beat is like the rhythmic pounding of a hammer. The second, fourth, and sixth lines rhyme. This *abcbdb* rhyme scheme reinforces the sense of pounding and emphasizes the word *man* at the end of the stanza. Internal rhyme calls attention to the vivid image. The change in meter at the end of the stanza slows readers down so that they think about the last line.

Poetic Forms A poem's form is usually defined by its purpose and characteristics. **Formal verse** follows fixed, traditional patterns that may include a specific rhyme scheme, meter, line length, or stanza structure. **Free verse** uses poetic language, but does not follow a fixed pattern. Three main categories of poetry are lyric, narrative, and dramatic. Within these categories are forms of poetry that have specific structures and features.

Lyric poetry expresses the thoughts and feelings of a single speaker, often in very musical verse. The chart below describes some forms of lyric poetry.

Narrative poetry tells a story. Most narrative poetry, including **ballads** and **epic poetry,** follows a formal structure with set stanzas, strong rhythms, and a regular rhyme scheme.

Dramatic poetry presents a drama in verse. The action is told through the words the characters speak.

Speaker The **speaker** is the person or character who communicates the words of the poem. Do not assume that the voice in the poem is the poet's, even when the poem is written in the first person. The poet creates the character of the speaker, just as a songwriter may invent a character to express his or her feelings and ideas in a song.

Imagery Poets create word pictures for readers by using **imagery,** or vivid language that appeals to the five senses. Imagery can enhance the meaning of a poem by providing a context or setting a scene. Imagery also helps create a poem's emotional impact.

Common Core State Standards

Reading Literature

4. Determine the meaning of words and phrases as they are used in a text, including figurative and connotative meanings; analyze the impact of specific word choices on meaning and tone, including analogies or allusions to other texts.

Forms of Lyric Poetry	
Sonnet "The New Colossus," p. 391	A sonnet is a fourteen-line poem of praise with a specific rhyme scheme. A **Petrarchan sonnet** often has a rhyme scheme of *abba/abba/cde/cde*. A **Shakespearean sonnet** has a rhyme scheme of *abab/cdcd/efef/gg*.
Ode	An ode is a formal poem of honor or celebration. Odes often have a regular meter and end rhyme, but the number and length of their lines and stanzas can vary.
Elegy "O Captain! My Captain!," p. 419	An elegy is a formal poem reflecting on death or another serious theme. The structure, meter, and rhyme scheme of elegies can vary considerably.
Haiku	A haiku is a short, unrhymed poem, often about nature. It has one three-line stanza that follows a 5-7-5 syllabic pattern.

Analyzing Poetic Language

Poets create **meaning** through their imaginative use of **language.**

In poetry, writers communicate more than the literal meanings of their words. Through figurative language, sound devices, and other literary techniques, they create vivid images and express unique ideas. Understanding the ways a poet uses language can help you fully grasp the meaning of a poem.

Figurative Language Words and phrases have **literal** meanings—the meanings you find in a dictionary. **Figurative language** describes and compares things in ways that are not meant to be taken literally. By using the following types of figurative language, a poet can put intense focus on a particular quality and present it in a rich and unique way.

Similes and **metaphors** highlight a shared quality of two things that are otherwise different.

- A **simile** uses the word *like* or *as* to compare two things: *The icy water hurt like a thousand bee stings.*

- A **metaphor** compares by describing one thing as if it were another: *The icy water was a thousand stinging bees.*

- An **extended metaphor** carries a metaphor throughout part or all of a poem.

Personification assigns human qualities to a non-human subject. In the example below, the clarinets and drums are personified.

> **Example:**
>
> The clarinets sang merrily,
> While the drums grumbled and
>   complained.

An **analogy** explains, clarifies, or illustrates by drawing comparisons.

In the example below, the poet uses the analogy of deleted computer files to clarify the idea that memories exist someplace but are inaccessible.

> Age betrayed her daily now.
> Memories gone, but where?
> Somewhere inaccessible,
> The way a computer file
> Deleted accidentally,
> Is there
> But not there.

Allusions are direct or implied references to people, places, events, literary works, or artworks, as in the following example, which refers to the story of Cinderella:

> In desperate times be brave and bold
> Your Cinderella story is not yet told.

Sound Devices

The sounds of words contribute to the musical quality of a poem and strengthen its meaning.

Alliteration is the repetition of initial consonant sounds:

> He climbs the hill and huffs and heaves.

The repeated *h* sound strengthens the impression of labored breath.

Consonance is the repetition of consonant sounds in stressed syllables with different vowel sounds:

> Gulls gracefully pass across the sky.

The repeated *s* sound creates a sense of graceful movement from word to word.

Assonance is the repetition of vowel sounds in stressed syllables that do not rhyme:

> Calling and squawking like crows, they fought.

The repetition of the *aw* sound reinforces the sense of the simile.

Repetition is the repeated use of a word or phrase:

> Time and time again I lose track of time.

The repetition emphasizes a key idea.

Onomatopoeia is the use of words that imitate sounds:

> The wind whooshed in and slammed the door with a bang.

Whooshed and *bang* appeal to the sense of hearing.

Connotations and Tone

Connotations are the ideas associated with a word beyond its **denotation,** or literal definition. Connotations can be positive or negative. This chart shows the negative and positive connotations of the word *diva*.

The actress is a *diva*.	
Denotation: successful female performer	
Negative	**Positive**
arrogance, ego, bossiness	power, confidence, talent
Context: The actress has a temper tantrum.	**Context:** The actress gives a great performance.

Tone is the attitude the writer projects in a poem. Word choice and other poetic elements work together to convey the tone of a poem.

Combination of Elements	Tone Created
Word choices: *exquisite, rare, inspire* **Connotations:** positive **Meter:** musical	• respectful • admiring
Word choices: *isolated, loneliness* **Connotations:** negative **Meter:** slow beat	• sorrowful • pitying
Word choices: *tizzy, whiz* **Connotations:** positive/amusing **Meter:** bouncy beat	• carefree • playful

Poetry Collection 1

 **Common Core
State Standards**

Reading Literature
4. Determine the meaning of
words and phrases as they are used
in a text, including figurative and
connotative meanings; analyze the
impact of specific word choices
on meaning and tone, including
analogies or allusions to other
texts.

Language
4.a. Use context (e.g., the
overall meaning of a sentence or
paragraph; a word's position or
function in a sentence) as a clue to
the meaning of a word or phrase.
5.b. Use the relationship between
particular words to better
understand each of the words.
6. Acquire and use accurately
grade-appropriate general
academic and domain-specific
words and phrases; gather
vocabulary knowledge when
considering a word or phrase
important to comprehension or
expression.

? **What is the secret to reaching someone
with words?**

Explore the Big Question as you read the poems. Find examples of
how each poet uses words to reach his or her readers.

CLOSE READING FOCUS

Key Ideas and Details: **Using Context**

The **context** of a word consists of the other words that surround
it in a text. As you read, look for these types of context clues to
help determine the meaning of unfamiliar words.

- **synonym/renaming:** words that mean the same as the
  unfamiliar word or that name the same thing
- **antonym/contrast:** words that mean the opposite of the word
- **explanation/example:** words that give more information
  about the word
- **sentence role:** the word's grammatical function

Craft and Structure: **Sound Devices**

Sound devices are ways to create musical effects using words.
Common sound devices include these:

- **alliteration:** repetition of initial consonant sounds—*we won*
- **onomatopoeia:** words that imitate sounds—*buzz* or *hiss*
- **rhyme:** repetition of sounds at the ends of words—*spring*
  and *fling*. Rhymes occurring at the ends of lines are called
  external or *end rhyme*. *Internal rhyme* occurs within a single
  line. *Rhyme scheme* is the pattern of end rhyme in a poem,
  analyzed by assigning each rhyme a letter (*a, b, c, d,* etc.)
- **meter:** a poem's rhythmic pattern, mainly determined by the
  strong and weak stresses a reader naturally places on the words

Vocabulary

Copy these words from the poems that follow into your notebook.
Which one is a synonym for *disagreement*?

scampering	strife	spite
flatterer	singularity	imprint

CLOSE READING MODEL

The passages below are from the poems "Silver" and "Thumbprint." The annotations to the right of the passages show ways in which you can use close reading skills to unlock meaning and analyze author's craft.

from "Silver"

Slowly, silently, now the moon[1]
Walks the night in her silver shoon;
This way, and that, she peers, and sees
Silver fruit upon silver trees;[2]
5   One by one the casements catch
Her beams beneath the silvery thatch;
Couched in his kennel, like a log,
With paws of silver sleeps the dog;

Sound Devices

1 By using the words *slowly* and *silently* together, the writer creates alliteration, the repetition of initial consonant sounds. Repeating sounds creates a soothing mood and helps the reader imagine seeing the moon on a still night.

Sound Devices

2 This pair of lines ends in a rhyme (*sees* and *trees*), just as the previous pair did. This repetitive and almost childlike use of end rhyme helps to create a magical or perhaps whimsical mood.

from "Thumbprint"

On the pad of my thumb
are whorls, whirls, wheels
in a unique design:[3]
mine alone.
5   What a treasure to own!
My own flesh, my own feelings.
No other, however grand or base,
can ever contain the same.
My signature,
10   thumbing the pages of my time.
My universe key,
my singularity.[4]

Using Context

3 The word *whorls* may be unfamiliar. The phrase "On the pad of my thumb" is a context clue that provides an explanation. This detail helps the reader realize that here *whorls* refers to the curved lines found on a thumb.

Using Context

4 In these lines, the word *singularity* is used to rename a *signature*. To figure out the meaning of *singularity*, the reader can use the word *signature* as a context clue. Each person writes his or her name with a unique signature. So, a singularity is probably something that is unique to a person.

Meet the Poets

"Silver"

Walter de la Mare (1873–1956)

Before becoming a full-time poet and novelist, Englishman Walter de la Mare wrote while he worked at an ordinary job as a bookkeeper for an oil company. He held this job for eighteen years. In 1908, the British government gave him a grant that allowed him to retire at age thirty-five and write full-time for the rest of his life.

"Ring Out, Wild Bells"

Alfred, Lord Tennyson (1809–1892)

The works of Alfred, Lord Tennyson, an English poet, became enormously popular in his lifetime. In 1850, Britain's Queen Victoria honored his poetic achievement by appointing him Poet Laureate. The acclaimed author came from a humble background, with seven brothers and four sisters. Tennyson's family had little money but many books. He began writing poems as a child.

"Cat!"

Eleanor Farjeon (1881–1965)

Eleanor Farjeon spent much of her childhood reading fantasy stories in the attic of her family's house in London, England. She also enjoyed playing games of make-believe with her little brother. When she grew up, she drew on memories of her childhood as inspiration for her poetry and stories for children and young adults.

"Thumbprint"

Eve Merriam (1916–1992)

Eve Merriam fell in love with words at an early age. As a child, she enjoyed playing with rhythms, rhymes, and puns. As an adult, she never lost her feeling that words could be fun. She once said, "It's like a shot of adrenaline or oxygen when I hear rhymes and word play."

SILVER

Walter de la Mare

Slowly, silently, now the moon
Walks the night in her silver shoon;[1]
This way, and that, she peers, and sees
Silver fruit upon silver trees;
5   One by one the casements[2] catch
Her beams beneath the silvery thatch;[3]
Couched in his kennel, like a log,
With paws of silver sleeps the dog;
From their shadowy coat the white breasts peep
10 Of doves in a silver-feathered sleep;
A harvest mouse goes scampering by,
With silver claws, and silver eye;
And moveless fish in the water gleam,
By silver reeds in a silver stream.

---

1. **shoon** (sho͞on) *n.* old-fashioned word for "shoes."
2. **casements** (kās´ mənts) *n.* windows that open out like doors.
3. **thatch** (thach) *n.* roof made of straw or other plant material.

Sound Devices
Identify examples of alliteration in lines 1–5.

◀ **Vocabulary**
scampering (skam´ pər iŋ) *v.* running quickly

Spiral Review
CONNOTATION Identify the connotations of the word *peep* in line 9. How do the word's connotations contribute to the poem's mood?

▲ **Critical Viewing**
How does this image capture the mood and images of the poem?

Ring Out, Wild Bells

Alfred, Lord Tennyson

Ring out, wild bells, to the wild sky,
    The flying cloud, the frosty light:
    The year is dying in the night;
Ring out, wild bells, and let him die.

5 Ring out the old, ring in the new,
    Ring, happy bells, across the snow:
    The year is going, let him go;
Ring out the false, ring in the true.

Ring out the grief that saps the mind,
10   For those that here we see no more;
    Ring out the feud of rich and poor,
Ring in redress to all mankind.

Ring out a slowly dying cause,
    And ancient forms of party **strife**;
15   Ring in the nobler modes of life,
With sweeter manners, purer laws.

Ring out the want, the care, the sin,
    The faithless coldness of the times;
    Ring out, ring out thy mournful rhymes,
20 But ring the fuller minstrel[1] in.

Ring out false pride in place and blood,
    The civic[2] slander and the **spite**;
    Ring in the love of truth and right,
Ring in the common love of good.

25 Ring out old shapes of foul disease;
    Ring out the narrowing lust of gold;
    Ring out the thousand wars of old,
Ring in the thousand years of peace.

---

1. **fuller minstrel** (min´ strəl) *n.* singer of the highest rank.
2. **civic** (siv´ ik) *adj.* relating to cities or citizens.

Sound Devices
How many beats do you hear in each line?

Context
How can the pattern of things "rung out" and "rung in" help you determine the meaning of *saps* in line 9?

◀ **Vocabulary**
strife (strīf) *n.* conflict

spite (spīt) *n.* nastiness

Cat!

Eleanor Farjeon

▲ **Critical Viewing** In what ways does the cat in this picture resemble the cat described in the poem? Explain.

Cat!
Scat!
After her, after her,
Sleeky **flatterer**,
5   Spitfire chatterer,
Scatter her, scatter her
    Off her mat!
    Wuff!
    Wuff!
10   Treat her rough!
Git her, git her,
Whiskery spitter!
Catch her, catch her,
Green-eyed scratcher!
15   Slathery
    Slithery
    Hisser,
    Don't miss her!
Run till you're dithery,[1]
20   Hithery
    Thithery[2]
    Pftts! pftts!
    How she spits!
    Spitch! Spatch!
25   Can't she scratch!
Scritching the bark
Of the sycamore tree,
She's reached her ark
And's hissing at me
30 *Pftts! pftts!*
    Wuff! wuff!
    Scat,
    Cat!
    That's
35   *That!*

◄ **Vocabulary**
flatterer (flat´ ər ər) *n.*
one who praises
insincerely to win
approval

Context
Which words in lines
10–14 provide a
synonym that helps you
determine the meaning
of *git*?

Sound Devices
Find two made-up
words that imitate
cat sounds. How do
they help you imagine
the actions the poem
describes?

---

1. **dithery** (di*th*´ ər ē) *adj.* nervous and confused; in a dither.
2. **Hithery/Thithery** made-up words based on *hither* and *thither*, which mean "here"
and "there."

Thumbprint
Eve Merriam

On the pad of my thumb
are whorls,[1] whirls, wheels
in a unique design:
mine alone.
5 What a treasure to own!
My own flesh, my own feelings.
No other, however grand or base,
can ever contain the same.
My signature,
10 thumbing the pages of my time.
My universe key,
my singularity.

Impress, implant,
I am myself,
15 of all my atom parts I am the sum.
And out of my blood and my brain
I make my own interior weather,
my own sun and rain.
Imprint my mark upon the world,
20 whatever I shall become.

---

1. **whorls** (hwôrlz) *n.* circular ridges that form the pattern of fingerprints.

Sound Devices
Which repeated consonant sounds create alliteration in lines 1–6?

Vocabulary ▶
singularity (siṉ´ gyə lér´ ə tē) *n.* unique or unusual quality

imprint (im print´) *v.* make a lasting mark in or on

Language Study

Vocabulary In each group, identify the word that does not belong. Explain how its meaning differs from that of the other words.

1. spite, malice, kindness
2. strife, peace, goodwill
3. scampering, running, strolling
4. singularity, ordinariness, uniqueness
5. flatterer, critic, nitpicker

Word Study

Part A Explain how the **Latin prefix *im-*** contributes to the meanings of *immersion, immigrant,* and *impress.* Consult a dictionary if needed.

Part B Answer each question. Use the context of the sentences and what you know about the Latin prefix *im-* to explain each answer.

1. What happens to someone who is *imprisoned*?
2. Are *imports* shipped into or out of a country?

WORD STUDY
The **Latin prefix *im-*** can mean "in" or "into." In "Thumbprint," the poet wants to leave her **imprint**, or create a lasting mark, on the world.

Close Reading Activities

Literary Analysis

Key Ideas and Details

1. **Using Context** What context clues help you clarify the meaning of *feud* (line 11) in "Ring Out, Wild Bells"?

2. **Using Context** Explain how context helps you determine the meaning of the word *scritching* (line 26) in "Cat!" Cite details from the text.

3. **Using Context** Explain how context helps you figure out the meaning of *base* (line 7) in "Thumbprint." Cite details from the text in your answer.

Craft and Structure

4. **Sound Devices (a)** Complete a chart like the one shown, listing several examples of sound devices found in poems in this poetry collection. Not all sound devices are used in each poem. **(b)** For each poem, explain how one of the sound devices listed contributes to its mood, tone, and meaning. Cite details from the poem in your answer.

5. **Sound Devices** How do the sounds and rhythms of "Cat!" help the poet communicate her ideas? Support your answer with specific details from the poem.

Integration of Knowledge and Ideas

6. **(a)** What "[w]alks the night" in "Silver"? Use details from the text in your answer. **(b) Analyze Causes and Effects:** What effect does this "walk" have on everyday objects? **(c) Draw Conclusions:** What does the poem suggest about the power of the imagination to change how we see things?

7. **(a) Interpret:** Explain lines 14–20 in "Thumbprint." According to these lines, how does the speaker feel about herself and her future? **(b) Make a Judgment:** Do you agree with her view of individuality? Explain why or why not.

8. **What is the secret to reaching someone with words?** **(a)** What sounds and rhythms do these poets use to connect with readers? Cite details from the poetry collection in your response. **(b)** How do these devices help the poets reach readers?

Poetry Collection 1

Alliteration
Onomatopoeia
Rhyme
Meter

ACADEMIC VOCABULARY

As you write and speak about the poems in Poetry Collection 1, use the words related to communication that you explored on page 347 of this textbook.

Conventions: **Types of Sentences**

A **declarative sentence** states, or declares, an idea. It ends in a period. An **interrogative sentence** asks a question. It ends in a question mark. An **exclamatory sentence** conveys strong emotion. It ends in an exclamation point. An **imperative sentence** gives an order, a command, or a direction. It ends in a period or an exclamation point.

Poetry Collection 1

Use the chart to distinguish among the four types of sentences.

Declarative	Interrogative	Exclamatory	Imperative
Dinner is at eight.	What is for dinner?	I love turkey burgers!	Go set the table.
We take the subway.	Do you know why?	We will miss the train!	Quick, run for it!

Imperative sentences always feature a verb in the **imperative mood,** indicating a command. By contrast, declarative sentences often use the **indicative mood,** which conveys facts or opinions. Be careful not to shift between indicative and imperative mood in a jarring or confusing way.

IMPROPER SHIFT IN MOOD: An employee must clock in upon arrival. Don't forget to put on your uniform. *[shift to imperative]* An employee should then report to the manager.

Practice A

Identify whether each sentence is declarative, interrogative, exclamatory, or imperative. Then, indicate which endmark—period, question mark, or exclamation point—should appear.

1. Sabrina's cat is an orange tabby

2. Ouch, your cat just scratched me

3. How long have you had your pet

4. Leave Sabrina's cat alone

Reading Application Find four lines in "Cat!" that are examples of imperative sentences.

Practice B

Rewrite these sentences, using the correct punctuation for the type of sentence each is likeliest to be.

1. Have you read his poem.

2. Walter de la Mare was a British poet!

3. Write a short essay about the poem?

4. I cannot believe I lost my book?

Writing Application Write a paragraph about one of the poems in which you shift improperly between declarative and imperative sentences. Exchange paragraphs with a partner and correct each other's work.

Writing to Sources

Poetry Write a poem that uses rhythm and sound devices. Choose "Silver" or "Ring Out, Wild Bells" as a model. Before you start, analyze the rhyme scheme in the poem you have chosen. Follow this rhyme scheme as you create your poem. To help you draft your poem, apply these steps:

- Prewrite to choose a main idea to develop.
- Brainstorm for rhyming words connected to your topic. Ensure you have enough rhymes to follow your chosen rhyme scheme.
- Decide what mood you want to convey, whether serious, aggressive, exciting, or soothing. Plan to use sound devices that will best convey this mood.
- Follow your rhyme scheme as you draft.
- As you write, carefully consider the words you choose. Read them aloud for their sound as well as for their meaning.

Grammar Application Consider including interrogative, exclamatory, or imperative sentences in your poem.

Speaking and Listening

Presentation of Ideas Choose and memorize a poem that uses sound devices effectively. Then, present the poem in a **poetry recitation.** You may choose a poem from this collection or a favorite poem or song.

- To prepare, notice how sound devices contribute to the overall mood and meaning. Keep these in mind as you practice.
- While rehearsing, aim for appropriate enunciation, emphasis, volume, and tone of voice. Speak clearly and naturally, not too fast or too slow. Modulate, or vary, your voice to express the tone of the poem. Add gestures if they enhance your presentation.
- Practice reciting your poem with a natural rhythm.
- Monitor your reading for effect and for errors in pronunciation.
- When you are ready, recite the poem for your class. Apply the speaking techniques you practiced and maintain eye contact with your audience.

 **Common Core State Standards**

Writing
4. Produce clear and coherent writing in which the development, organization, and style are appropriate to task, purpose, and audience.

Speaking and Listening
6. Adapt speech to a variety of contexts and tasks, demonstrating command of formal English when indicated or appropriate.

Language
1.c. Form and use verbs in the indicative, imperative, interrogative, conditional, and subjunctive mood.
1.d. Recognize and correct inappropriate shifts in verb voice and mood.

Poetry Collection 2

© **Common Core State Standards**

Reading Literature
4. Determine the meaning of words and phrases as they are used in the text, including figurative and connotative meanings; analyze the impact of specific word choices on meaning and tone, including analogies or allusions to other texts.

Language
4.a. Use context as a clue to the meaning of a word or phrase.
4.d. Verify the preliminary determination of the meaning of a word or phrase.
5.a. Interpret figures of speech (e.g. verbal irony, puns) in context.

? **What is the secret to reaching someone with words?**

Explore the Big Question as you read the poems. Note ways in which the poets move readers to think and feel, using words.

CLOSE READING FOCUS

Key Ideas and Details: **Context Clues**

When you encounter an unfamiliar word, look for **context clues** in the surrounding text to figure out its meaning. Then, verify your definition by using it in place of the unfamiliar word. Types of context clues include these:

- **Comparison/contrast:** Fred *hates* to shop, but I am a shopping <u>enthusiast</u>.
- **Restatement:** Do not <u>veto</u> the plan. Your *rejection* can hurt us.
- **Definition:** The <u>tare</u> of the truck, *its weight when empty,* was ten tons.
- **Example:** She <u>agonized</u>, *biting her nails and sleeping poorly.*

Craft and Structure: **Figurative Language**

Figurative language is language not meant to be taken literally. Poets use figures of speech like these to make creative comparisons:

- A **simile** compares two unlike things using the words *like* or *as: His eyes were as black as coal.*
- A **metaphor** compares two unlike things by saying that one thing is the other: *The world is my oyster.*
- **Personification** is a comparison in which a nonhuman subject is given human characteristics: *The trees toss in their sleep.*

Vocabulary

These words appear in the poems that follow. Write each one in your notebook. Then, choose one word from the list associated with either the countryside or the city. Explain your choice.

rut	debates	ponderous
urban	roam	dew

CLOSE READING MODEL

The passages below are from the poems "The Sky Is Low, the Clouds Are Mean" and "Concrete Mixers." The annotations to the right of the passages show ways in which you can use close reading skills to determine meaning using context clues and to interpret figurative language.

"The Sky Is Low, the Clouds Are Mean"

The sky is low, the clouds are mean,
A travelling flake of snow
Across a barn or through a rut
Debates if it will go.[1]

5   A narrow wind complains all day
How some one treated him;[2]
Nature, like us, is sometimes caught
Without her diadem.

Context Clues

1 The poet writes that a snowflake "Debates if it will go." The phrase "if it will go" is a context clue to the meaning of the verb *debates*. Will it go? Or will it not go? *Debates* has something to do with making a decision.

Figurative Language

2 The wind "complains." The poet uses personification to give human-like qualities to the wind.

from "Concrete Mixers"

Concrete mixers
Move like elephants
Bellow like elephants
15   Spray like elephants[3]
Concrete mixers are urban elephants,
Their trunks are raising a city.[4]

Figurative Language

3 The poet uses three similes with the word *like* to compare concrete mixers to elephants. According to the poet, mixers and elephants both "move," "bellow," and "spray."

Context Clues

4 The word *city* can help readers understand the meaning of the word *urban*: "of or in a city." By reading before and after an unfamiliar word, you can find clues to its meaning.

Meet the Poets

"The Sky Is Low, the Clouds Are Mean"

Emily Dickinson (1830–1886)

Emily Dickinson considered books her "strongest friend." Withdrawn and shy, she spent most of her time at home in Amherst, Massachusetts, reading and writing. Most of her 1,775 poems were discovered after her death, including one that begins, "I'm nobody! Who are you?" Today, Dickinson is considered one of the most important American poets.

"Concrete Mixers"

Patricia Hubbell (b. 1928)

Patricia Hubbell says she began writing poetry when she was in third grade. She liked to sit in a tree and look down on her family's farm, noting things she would later capture in verse. Hubbell, who has been writing poetry and children's books for decades, explains, "Poem ideas are everywhere; you have to listen and watch for them."

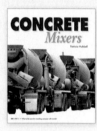

"Harlem Night Song"

Langston Hughes (1902–1967)

Fresh out of high school, Langston Hughes took a train to visit his father in Mexico. He wanted to convince his father to pay for studies at Columbia University in New York City. His father agreed, and Hughes's writing career was launched. During his year at Columbia, Hughes developed a lifelong love for the New York neighborhood of Harlem, the setting of many of his stories, poems, and plays.

"The City Is So Big"

Richard García (b. 1941)

Richard García published his first poetry collection in 1973, but then stopped writing for six years. An encouraging letter from Octavio Paz, winner of the 1990 Nobel Prize for Literature, inspired him to write again. In addition to writing, García is known for leading poetry and art workshops for hospitalized children.

The Sky Is Low, the Clouds Are Mean

Emily Dickinson

The sky is low, the clouds are mean,
A travelling flake of snow
Across a barn or through a rut
Debates if it will go.

5 A narrow wind complains all day
How some one treated him;
Nature, like us, is sometimes caught
Without her diadem.[1]

---

1. **diadem** (dī′ ə dem′) *n.* crown.

◀ **Vocabulary**
rut (rut) *n.* a groove in the ground

debates (dē bāts′) *v.* considers the reasons for and against; argues over a point

CONCRETE *Mixers*

Patricia Hubbell

The drivers are washing the concrete mixers;
Like elephant tenders they hose them down.
Tough gray-skinned monsters standing **ponderous**,
Elephant-bellied and elephant-nosed,
5   Standing in muck up to their wheel-caps,
Like rows of elephants, tail to trunk.
Their drivers perch on their backs like mahouts,[1]
Sending the sprays of water up.
They rid the trunk-like trough of concrete,
10 Direct the spray to the bulging sides,
Turn and start the monsters moving.
      Concrete mixers
      Move like elephants
      Bellow like elephants
15   Spray like elephants
    Concrete mixers are **urban** elephants,
    Their trunks are raising a city.

---

1. mahouts (mə houts´) *n.* in India and the East Indies, elephant drivers or keepers.

Context Clues
Reread lines 1–8. What context clues help reveal the meaning of *muck?* Explain.

Spiral Review
TONE In line 4, the concrete mixers are referred to as "elephant-bellied" and "elephant-nosed." What tone does this metaphor suggest?

◄ **Vocabulary**
ponderous (pän´ dər əs) *adj.* very heavy

urban (ur´ bən) *adj.* related to the city or city life

◄ **Critical Viewing**
What details in this picture of cement mixers support the comparison in the poem?

HARLEM
NIGHT SONG

Langston Hughes

Come,
Let us **roam** the night together
Singing.

I love you.

5 Across
The Harlem roof-tops
Moon is shining.
Night sky is blue.
Stars are great drops
10 Of golden **dew**.

Down the street
A band is playing.

I love you.

Come,
15 Let us roam the night together
Singing.

◄ **Vocabulary**
roam (rōm) *v.* go
aimlessly; wander

dew (do͞o) *n.* tiny
drops of moisture that
condense on cooled
objects at night

Figurative Language
Does Hughes use a
simile or a metaphor to
describe stars? Explain.

The City Is So Big
Richard García

Context Clues
Which words help you confirm that *quake* means "tremble"?

The city is so big
Its bridges quake with fear
I know, I have seen at night

The lights sliding from house to house
5   And trains pass with windows shining
Like a smile full of teeth

I have seen machines eating houses
And stairways walk all by themselves
And elevator doors opening and closing
10   And people disappear.

Language Study

Vocabulary Use your knowledge of the italicized words to answer these questions.

1. If you wanted to *roam,* where might you go?

2. Why might someone choose to live in an *urban* location?

3. Where are you most likely to find *dew*?

4. What kind of road surface gets very few *ruts*?

5. How would you react to someone who *debates* every decision?

Word Study

Part A Explain how the **Latin suffix -ous** contributes to the meanings of *omnivorous* and *outrageous.* Use a dictionary if needed.

Part B Answer each question. Use the context and what you know about the Latin suffix -ous to explain your answers.

1. Which is more *nutritious*, a carrot or a marshmallow?

2. Do good athletes follow a *rigorous* training schedule?

WORD STUDY

The **Latin suffix -ous** means "full of" or "characterized by." In the poem "Concrete Mixers," the poet describes the vehicles as **ponderous**—very heavy or full of weight, much like elephants.

Close Reading Activities

Literary Analysis

Key Ideas and Details

1. **(a) Compare:** Compare the scenes being described in "The City Is So Big" and "The Sky Is Low, the Clouds Are Mean." **(b) Analyze:** What is the mood, or general feeling, in each poem? Cite specific word choices in support of your answer.

2. **(a)** What scene is described in "Harlem Night Song"? **(b) Support:** In what ways does the poem resemble a song?

3. **Context Clues** Using the **context** surrounding the word *trough* in line 9 of "Concrete Mixers," explain what a trough looks like and why a concrete mixer might need one. Cite details from the poem in your answer.

4. **Context Clues** Read the text before and after the term *elephant tenders* in line 2 of "Concrete Mixers." **(a)** What do you think this means? **(b)** Explain, using details from the text.

Craft and Structure

5. **Figurative Language (a)** Identify an example of personification in "The Sky Is Low, the Clouds Are Mean." **(b)** What does your example suggest about the weather in the poem?

6. **Figurative Language (a)** Identify one metaphor and one simile in "The City Is So Big." **(b)** Explain what general feelings or ideas about the city each suggests.

7. **Figurative Language (a)** Use a chart like the one shown to analyze examples of figurative language in all four poems in this collection. **(b)** In a small group, review your charts. Discuss how each poet uses figurative language to appeal to the readers' senses and emotions. **(c)** Decide, as a group, which poem makes the most effective use of figurative language.

Integration of Knowledge and Ideas

8. **Evaluate:** Is the main effect of each of these four poems to paint a picture for you? Or, is it to change the way you might look at a familiar scene? Explain.

9. 🤔 **What is the secret to reaching someone with words?** To which of these poems did you respond most strongly? Give examples of how the poet used words to lead you to respond with feelings or ideas.

Poetry Collection 2

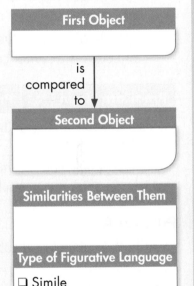

First Object

is compared to

Second Object

Similarities Between Them

Type of Figurative Language
❏ Simile
❏ Metaphor
❏ Personification

ACADEMIC VOCABULARY

As you write and speak about Poetry Collection 2, use the words related to communication that you explored on page 347 of this textbook.

Conventions: Subject Complements

> A **linking verb** connects its subject to a subject complement.
> A **subject complement** is a noun, a pronoun, or an adjective that follows a linking verb and completes the thought by telling something about the subject.

Poetry Collection 2

The most common linking verbs are forms of *be*, such as *am, are, is, was,* and *were.* Other verbs that function as linking verbs include *seem, look, feel, become, grow,* and *appear* when they are followed by subject complements. There are three types of subject complements:

- A **predicate noun** or **predicate pronoun** follows a linking verb and identifies or renames the subject of the sentence.

- A **predicate adjective** follows a linking verb and describes the subject of the sentence.

Predicate Noun	Predicate Pronoun	Predicate Adjective
Ronnie will be the <u>captain</u> of the team.	The winners are <u>they</u>.	The flight to Houston was <u>swift</u>.
Captain renames the subject, *Ronnie.*	*They* identifies the subject, *winners.*	*Swift* describes the subject, *flight.*

Practice A

Identify the subject and subject complement in each sentence.

1. The mixer is a gray-skinned monster.
2. The stars were golden in the moonlight.
3. My favorite poet is she.
4. The city in "The City Is So Big" is scary.

Reading Application Review the poems in Poetry Collection 2, and find one sentence that has a subject complement. (Note that a sentence may include more than one line of poetry.)

Practice B

In each sentence, identify the subject, linking verb, and subject complement, noting the type of complement.

1. The mixer's trough is a huge trunk.
2. The Harlem night looks beautiful.
3. The machines seemed hungry.
4. Nature was a topic for Dickinson.

Writing Application Write a sentence about Emily Dickinson that uses a predicate noun. Then, write another sentence about her that uses a predicate adjective.

Writing to Sources

Explanatory Text Write a **study for a poem** about one of the settings used for the poems in Poetry Collection 2: a city, a neighborhood, a work site, or a natural setting. Include an analysis comparing the setting of the poem in Collection 2 with your own interpretation of that setting.

- List the objects, sights, and sounds that come to mind when you think about your setting.
- To think of fresh ways to describe the items in your list, use this sentence starter: _____ *is like* _____ *because* _____. Jot down several answers. Then, choose one or two you like best.
- In a few sentences, explain your plan. Include details about the comparisons and figurative language your poem will present.
- Compare your ideas with those in the Collection 2 poem.

Grammar Application Review your draft to determine whether you can enhance descriptions using subject complements.

Research and Technology

Build and Present Knowledge Follow your own interests to create a **mini-anthology,** a collection of four poems on a similar topic or theme, including one of the poems from Collection 2. Present an argument for your choices. Follow these steps:

- First, review the poems in Collection 2. Choose one on a topic that speaks to you, such as city life, night, music, or weather.
- Next, visit your library or browse the Internet to research other poems on this subject. Select the three that you like best.
- Write an introduction defending your three new choices, telling how each poem affected you and why you think it should be included in the mini-anthology along with the poem you chose from Collection 2. Include a brief description of the style of each of the four poets, such as his or her use of figurative language. Point out interesting similarities and contrasts among the four poems, drawing on details from the texts.
- To complete the mini-anthology, design a cover and draw or use appropriate software to create illustrations inspired by the poems.

**Common Core
State Standards**

Writing
1. Write arguments to support claims with clear reasons and relevant evidence.
4. Produce clear and coherent writing in which the development, organization, and style are appropriate to task, purpose, and audience.
9. Draw evidence from literary or informational texts to support analysis, reflection, and research.

Language
1. Demonstrate command of the conventions of standard English grammar and usage when writing or speaking.

Poetry Collection 3

 **Common Core
State Standards**

Reading Literature
4. Determine the meaning of
words and phrases as they are used
in a text, including figurative and
connotative meanings; analyze the
impact of specific word choices
on meaning and tone, including
analogies or allusions to other texts.

5. Compare and contrast the
structure of two or more texts and
analyze how the differing structure
of each text contributes to its
meaning and style.

9. Analyze how a modern work of
fiction draws on themes, patterns
of events, or character types
from myths, traditional stories, or
religious works such as the Bible,
including describing how the
material is rendered new.

Language
4.b. Use common, grade-
appropriate Greek or Latin affixes
and roots as clues to the meaning
of a word (e.g., *precede, recede,
secede*).

? **What is the secret to reaching someone
with words?**

Explore the Big Question as you read the poems. Take notes on
words and techniques the poets use to convey their messages.

CLOSE READING FOCUS

Key Ideas and Details: **Paraphrase**

Paraphrasing is restating a text in your own words. Restating the
text helps you check your understanding. Before you paraphrase,
reread to clarify meaning. Look up any unfamiliar words. Then,
follow these steps:

- Identify the most basic information in each sentence. Make
  sure your paraphrase captures this information.
- Restate the text simply. Replace uncommon words with their
  more common synonyms. Replace unusual sentence structures
  with language that is more like everyday speech.

Craft and Structure: **Forms of Poetry**

Two major **forms of poetry** are lyric poetry and narrative poetry.

- A **lyric poem** uses "musical" verse to express the thoughts and
  feelings of a single **speaker**—the person "saying" the poem.
  Its purpose is to create a vivid impression in readers' minds.
- A **narrative poem** tells a story and includes the main elements
  of a short story—characters, setting, conflict, and plot.

Both lyric and narrative poems can tap readers' prior knowledge
and emotions by including **allusions**—references to people,
places, or things from other artistic works. As you read, consider
how the form of each poem, as well as any allusions it includes,
contributes to its meaning.

Vocabulary

Copy these words from the poems into your notebook. Which one
is a form of a verb? How do you know?

exiles   yearning   ingratitude
somber   defiance   peril

CLOSE READING MODEL

The passages below are from the poems "Blow, Blow, Thou Winter Wind" and "Paul Revere's Ride." The annotations to the right of the passages show ways in which you can use close reading skills to paraphrase poems and to determine their forms.

from "Blow, Blow, Thou Winter Wind"

Blow, blow, thou winter wind.
Thou art not so unkind
    As man's ingratitude.[1]
Thy tooth is not so keen,
5 Because thou art not seen,
    Although thy breath be rude.
Heigh-ho! Sing, heigh-ho! unto the green holly.
Most friendship is feigning, most loving mere folly.
    Then, heigh-ho, the holly!
10   This life is most jolly.[2]

Paraphrase
1 The poet compares the winter wind to man's ingratitude. Using synonyms and everyday speech, a reader might paraphrase these lines so: *The cold wind of winter is not as bad as people's lack of appreciation for what they are given.*

Forms of Poetry
2 The poet conveys thoughts on friendship and love as if singing a carol. The songlike quality of these lines shows that the work is a lyric poem.

from "Paul Revere's Ride"

Then he climbed the tower of the Old North Church,
By the wooden stairs, with stealthy tread,[3]
To the belfry-chamber overhead,
And startled the pigeons from their perch
35 On the somber rafters, that round him made
Masses and moving shapes of shade,—
By the trembling ladder, steep and tall,
To the highest window in the wall,
Where he paused to listen and look down
40 A moment on the roofs of the town,
And the moonlight flowing over all.[4]

Forms of Poetry
3 The poet describes a man climbing the stairs of a church tower. The presence of a character, a series of events, and a setting (the tower) indicates that this is a narrative poem.

Paraphrase
4 The poet recounts the climb in great detail. After identifying the most basic information in these lines, a reader might paraphrase these lines, along with the first line, so: *He climbed the ladder, paused, and looked out the window at the moonlit town below.*

Meet the Poets

"The New Colossus"

Emma Lazarus (1849–1887)

Emma Lazarus wrote "The New Colossus" to inspire others to donate money for the Statue of Liberty's pedestal. The final lines of the poem were so inspirational that they were permanently inscribed on the pedestal itself. Raised in New York City, where she studied languages, Lazarus published a book of poems and translations at seventeen. Later, drawing on her Jewish heritage, she wrote several works celebrating America as a place of refuge for people persecuted in Europe.

"Blow, Blow, Thou Winter Wind"

William Shakespeare (1564–1616)

William Shakespeare is regarded by some as the greatest writer in the English language. Born in Stratford-on-Avon, a small town in England, he moved to London as a young man and spent most of his adult life there. Shakespeare was an actor, a producer, and a director. However, he is most famous for the plays and poems he wrote.

"Paul Revere's Ride"

Henry Wadsworth Longfellow (1807–1882)

Henry Wadsworth Longfellow started college at age fifteen and was asked to be the first professor of modern languages at Bowdoin College at the age of nineteen. He was one of the "fireside poets," a group of writers whose popular poems were read aloud by nineteenth-century families as they gathered around their fireplaces. He wrote several long poems on topics in American history.

The New Colossus

Emma Lazarus

Background The Colossus of Rhodes, referred to in the title and first two lines of the poem, was a 100-foot tall statue of the Greek sun god Helios. One of the Seven Wonders of the Ancient World, the statue was built around 280 B.C. It stood at the entrance to the harbor of the Greek island of Rhodes.

Not like the brazen giant of Greek fame,
With conquering limbs astride from land to land;
Here at our sea-washed, sunset gates shall stand
A mighty woman with a torch, whose flame
5   Is the imprisoned lightning, and her name
Mother of **Exiles**. From her beacon-hand
Glows world-wide welcome; her mild eyes command
The air-bridged harbor that twin cities frame.
"Keep, ancient lands, your storied pomp!"[1] cries she
10   With silent lips. "Give me your tired, your poor,
Your huddled masses **yearning** to breathe free,
The wretched refuse of your teeming[2] shore.
Send these, the homeless, tempest-tost[3] to me,
I lift my lamp beside the golden door!"

▲ **Critical Viewing**
How does this statue make you feel? How would one celebrating a military victory make you feel?

◄ **Vocabulary**
exiles (ek´ sīlz) *n.* people who are forced to live in another country

yearning (yʉr´ niŋ) *v.* feeling longing for; painfully wanting something

---

1. **pomp** (pämp) *n.* stately or brilliant display; splendor.
2. **teeming** (tēm´ iŋ) *adj.* swarming with people.
3. **tempest-tost** (tem´ pist tôst´) *adj.* here, having suffered a stormy ocean journey.

Blow, Blow, Thou Winter Wind

William Shakespeare

Blow, blow, thou winter wind.
Thou art not so unkind
    As man's ingratitude.
Thy tooth is not so keen,
Because thou art not seen,
    Although thy breath be rude.
Heigh-ho! Sing, heigh-ho! unto the green holly.
Most friendship is feigning, most loving mere folly.[1]
    Then, heigh-ho, the holly!
      This life is most jolly.

Freeze, freeze, thou bitter sky,
That dost not bite so nigh
    As benefits forgot.
Though thou the waters warp,[2]
    Thy sting is not so sharp
    As friend remembered not.
Heigh-ho! Sing, heigh-ho! unto the green holly.
Most friendship is feigning, most loving mere folly.
    Then, heigh-ho, the holly!
      This life is most jolly.

◄ **Vocabulary**
ingratitude (in grat´ i tood´) *n.* lack of thankfulness or appreciation

Spiral Review
ANALOGY What two things does Shakespeare compare in the first stanza? How are they alike?

Forms of Poetry
To what does the speaker compare the winter's chill in this lyric poem?

---

1. **Most friendship is feigning . . . folly** Most friendship is fake, most loving is foolish.
2. **warp** (wôrp) *v.* freeze.

Paul Revere's Ride

Henry Wadsworth Longfellow

▲ **Critical Viewing**
Based on this painting, what do you think the mood of this poem will be?

Listen, my children, and you shall hear
Of the midnight ride of Paul Revere,
On the eighteenth of April, in Seventy-five;
Hardly a man is now alive
5 Who remembers that famous day and year.

He said to his friend, "If the British march
By land or sea from the town to-night,
Hang a lantern aloft in the belfry arch
Of the North Church tower as a signal light,—
10 One, if by land, and two, if by sea;
And I on the opposite shore will be,
Ready to ride and spread the alarm
Through every Middlesex village and farm,
For the country folk to be up and to arm."

15 Then he said, "Good night!" and with muffled oar
Silently rowed to the Charlestown shore,
Just as the moon rose over the bay,
Where swinging wide at her moorings lay
The *Somerset*, British man-of-war;[1]
20 A phantom ship, with each mast and spar
Across the moon like a prison bar,
And a huge black hulk, that was magnified
By its own reflection in the tide.

Meanwhile, his friend, through alley and street,
25 Wanders and watches with eager ears,
Till in the silence around him he hears
The muster[2] of men at the barrack door,
The sound of arms, and the tramp of feet,
And the measured tread of the grenadiers,[3]
30 Marching down to their boats on the shore.

Then he climbed the tower of the Old North Church,
By the wooden stairs, with stealthy tread,
To the belfry-chamber overhead,
And startled the pigeons from their perch
35 On the somber rafters, that round him made
Masses and moving shapes of shade,—
By the trembling ladder, steep and tall,
To the highest window in the wall,
Where he paused to listen and look down
40 A moment on the roofs of the town,
And the moonlight flowing over all.

Forms of Poetry
What is the conflict in
this poem?

Spiral Review
FIGURATIVE
LANGUAGE
What does the
metaphor in lines
20–21 suggest about
the speaker's feelings
toward the British?

◄ **Vocabulary**
somber (säm´ bər)
adj. dark; gloomy

Comprehension
At what time in
history is this narrative
poem set?

1. **man-of-war** (man´ əv wôr´) *n.* armed naval vessel; warship.
2. **muster** (mus´ tər) *n.* assembly of troops summoned for inspection, roll call, or service.
3. **grenadiers** (gren´ ə dirz´) *n.* soldiers in a special regiment or corps.

▼ **Critical Viewing**
What would make the
Old North Church,
shown here, a good
place from which to
signal Revere?

Paraphrase
Paraphrase lines 73–80
by identifying what is
happening and who
is participating in the
action.

Beneath, in the churchyard, lay the dead,
In their night-encampment on the hill,
Wrapped in silence so deep and still
45 That he could hear, like a sentinel's tread,[4]
The watchful night-wind, as it went
Creeping along from tent to tent,
And seeming to whisper, "All is well!"
A moment only he feels the spell
50 Of the place and the hour, and the secret dread
Of the lonely belfry and the dead;
For suddenly all his thoughts are bent
On a shadowy something far away,
Where the river widens to meet the bay,—
55 A line of black that bends and floats
On the rising tide, like a bridge of boats.

Meanwhile, impatient to mount and ride,
Booted and spurred, with a heavy stride
On the opposite shore walked Paul Revere.
60 Now he patted his horse's side,
Now gazed at the landscape far and near,
Then, impetuous,[5] stamped the earth,
And turned and tightened his saddle-girth;[6]
But mostly he watched with eager search
65 The belfry-tower of the Old North Church,
As it rose above the graves on the hill,
Lonely and spectral and somber and still.
And lo! as he looks, on the belfry's height
A glimmer, and then a gleam of light!
70 He springs to the saddle, the bridle he turns,
But lingers and gazes, till full on his sight
A second lamp in the belfry burns!

A hurry of hoofs in a village street,
A shape in the moonlight, a bulk in the dark,
75 And beneath, from the pebbles, in passing, a spark
Struck out by a steed flying fearless and fleet:
That was all! And yet, through the gloom and the light,
The fate of a nation was riding that night;

---

4. sentinel's (sent´ 'n əlz) **tread** (tred) footsteps of a guard.
5. impetuous (im pech´ o͞o əs) *adj.* done suddenly with little thought.
6. saddle-girth (gʉrth) *n.* band put around the belly of a horse for holding a saddle.

And the spark struck out by that steed in his flight,
80 Kindled the land into flame with its heat.

He has left the village and mounted the steep,
And beneath him, tranquil and broad and deep,
Is the Mystic,[7] meeting the ocean tides;
And under the alders that skirt its edge,
85 Now soft on the sand, now loud on the ledge,
Is heard the tramp of his steed as he rides.

It was twelve by the village clock,
When he crossed the bridge into Medford town.
He heard the crowing of the cock,
90 And the barking of the farmer's dog,
And felt the damp of the river fog,
That rises after the sun goes down.

It was one by the village clock,
When he galloped into Lexington.
95 He saw the gilded weathercock
Swim in the moonlight as he passed,
And the meeting-house windows, blank and bare,
Gaze at him with a spectral glare,
As if they already stood aghast
100 At the bloody work they would look upon.

It was two by the village clock,
When he came to the bridge in Concord town.
He heard the bleating of the flock,
And the twitter of birds among the trees,
105 And felt the breath of the morning breeze
Blowing over the meadows brown.
And one was safe and asleep in his bed
Who at the bridge would be first to fall,
Who that day would be lying dead,
110 Pierced by a British musket-ball.

Comprehension
For what does Paul
Revere wait?

---

7. **Mystic** (mis′ tik) river in Massachusetts.

Paraphrase
Paraphrase lines 111–118 by explaining who was fighting and what the result of the fight was.

You know the rest. In the books you have read,
How the British Regulars fired and fled,—
How the farmers gave them ball for ball,
From behind each fence and farm-yard wall,
115 Chasing the red-coats down the lane,
Then crossing the fields to emerge again
Under the trees at the turn of the road,
And only pausing to fire and load.

So through the night rode Paul Revere;
120 And so through the night went his cry of alarm
To every Middlesex village and farm,—
A cry of **defiance** and not of fear,
A voice in the darkness, a knock at the door,
And a word that shall echo forevermore!
125 For, borne on the night-wind of the Past,
Through all our history, to the last,
In the hour of darkness and **peril** and need,
The people will waken and listen to hear
The hurrying hoof-beats of that steed,
130 And the midnight message of Paul Revere.

Vocabulary ▶
defiance (dē fī′ əns) *n.* refusal to obey authority

peril (per′ əl) *n.* danger

Forms of Poetry
What is the resolution of the conflict in this poem?

Language Study

Vocabulary In each item, the first word listed appears in a poem in this collection. For each item, write a sentence that correctly uses both of the words or phrases provided.

1. *exiles;* the United States

2. *yearning;* homesick

3. *somber;* memorial service

4. *defiance;* authority

5. *peril;* carelessly

WORD STUDY
The **Latin prefix *in-*** can mean "not" or "lacking." In "Blow, Blow, Thou Winter Wind," the speaker refers to man's **ingratitude**, or lack of thankfulness, for the gift of friendship.

Word Study

Part A Explain how the **Latin prefix *in-*** contributes to the meanings of *inability, incurable,* and *inconclusive.* Consult a dictionary if needed.

Part B Answer each question. Use the context of the sentences and what you know about the Latin prefix *in-* to explain your answers.

1. Why would an employer fire an *incompetent* worker?

2. Should jury members focus on *insignificant* details in a trial?

Close Reading Activities

Literary Analysis

Poetry Collection 3

Key Ideas and Details

1. **Paraphrase** Reread lines 3–6 of "The New Colossus" to clarify their meaning. **(a)** Identify the most basic information in the lines. **(b)** Rewrite the lines, using everyday language.

2. **Paraphrase** Reread lines 4–6 of "Blow, Blow, Thou Winter Wind." Rewrite each individual line, using everyday words and sentence structure.

3. **Paraphrase** Reread lines 15–23 of "Paul Revere's Ride."
   (a) Find synonyms for *muffled, moorings, phantom,* and *spar.*
   (b) Paraphrase the stanza, using these synonyms.

Craft and Structure

4. **Forms of Poetry (a)** For each poem in this collection, fill out a chart like the one shown. **(b)** Referring to your chart, explain how each poem's form—lyric or narrative—contributes to its effectiveness. In your explanations, consider the author's purpose in writing—for example, to teach a lesson, to inspire with pride, or to tell a good story.

5. **Forms of Poetry (a)** What main impression does "The New Colossus" convey? **(b)** What allusion appears in the first lines? **(c)** How does the allusion connect to the main impression?

Is the poem lyric or narrative?
What characteristics make it lyric or narrative?

Integration of Knowledge and Ideas

6. **(a) Interpret:** Determine the literal and figurative meanings of these lines: "The New Colossus," lines 6–8, and "Paul Revere's Ride," lines 77–80. **(b) Connect:** In each case, explain the significance of the lines to the poem as a whole.

7. **(a) Compare and Contrast:** Compare the word choice and sentence patterns in "Blow, Blow, Thou Winter Wind," lines 1–6, with those in "Paul Revere's Ride," lines 1–5. **(b) Evaluate:** Which do you find easier to understand? **(c) Connect:** Connect your answers to these facts: Longfellow wrote his poem around 200 years ago. Shakespeare wrote his around 200 years before Longfellow.

8. **What is the secret to reaching someone with words?**
   (a) Do you find "The New Colossus" or "Paul Revere's Ride" more moving? **(b)** Which words, lines, or lyric or narrative elements of the poem led to your response?

ACADEMIC VOCABULARY

As you read and speak about the poems in Poetry Collection 3, use the words related to communication that you explored on page 347 of this textbook.

Conventions: **Direct and Indirect Objects**

Poetry Collection 3

A **direct object** is a noun or pronoun that receives the action of a verb. An **indirect object** is a noun or pronoun that comes after an action verb and names the person or thing to which something is given or for which something is done.

A direct object answers the questions *Whom?* or *What?* after an action verb. An indirect object answers the questions *To whom? For whom? To what?* or *For what?*

A sentence cannot have an indirect object unless it also has a direct object. To find the indirect object, first find the direct object. Then, ask one of the four indirect object questions.

Direct Object	Indirect Object
S **V** **DO** **Sentence:** Bill baked some cookies. **Baked what?** cookies	**S** **V** **IO** **DO** **Sentence:** Bill baked Marissa some cookies. **Baked for whom?** Marissa

In a statement, an indirect object will almost always come between the verb and the direct object.

Practice A

In each sentence, identify the subject (S), verb (V), direct object (DO), and indirect object (IO). Some sentences do not include indirect objects.

1. Lyric poetry moves readers.
2. William Shakespeare mentions friendship.
3. Longfellow tells readers a famous story from American history.
4. He gives Paul Revere new life.

Reading Application Find two lines of poetry in Collection 3 that have direct objects. Identify the direct object in each.

Practice B

In each sentence, identify the subject (S), verb (V), direct object (DO), and indirect object (IO), if there is one. Then rewrite each sentence with a different direct object.

1. The poem gives us powerful descriptions.
2. The winter wind evokes sadness.
3. Lazarus offers readers a stirring declaration.
4. He climbed the tower of the church.

Writing Application Write two sentences, each with a direct object and an indirect object, about one of the poems you read.

Writing to Sources

Narrative Text Write a **lyric** or a **narrative poem** about an admirable person from history or from your own life. Compare your work to one of the poems in this collection.

- If you are writing a lyric poem, brainstorm for details about the person's qualities.
- If you are writing a narrative poem, list the events, characters, and details of setting you will include in the poem.

Use your notes to draft and revise the lines of your poem.

- To revise word choice in a lyric poem, look for places to add words that have a musical quality and convey strong emotions.
- To revise word choice in a narrative poem, replace dull description with dynamic language that describes the action or develops the characters.

Punctuate based on sentence structure and on how you want your poem to be read. For a brief pause or break, use a comma. To indicate a thought that trails off, use an ellipsis (…). To indicate an abrupt change in thought, use a dash (—).

When you have finished, write a paragraph comparing the topic and style of your poem with those of a poem in this collection.

Grammar Application Review your draft to identify one direct object and one indirect object (if present) that you have used.

Speaking and Listening

Comprehension and Collaboration Prepare an oral presentation of the poems in this collection. In a group, develop an **evaluation form** for the presentations. Follow these steps:

- Identify the different qualities of an effective delivery, such as varying tone of voice, using pauses for dramatic effect, reading clearly, and adjusting reading rates.
- Decide on a rating scale and a layout for your form.

Share the form with classmates to help them prepare to read poetry aloud. As students give their presentations, use the form to evaluate their delivery. Afterward, discuss which poems were best suited for oral presentation and why.

**Common Core
State Standards**

Writing

4. Produce clear and coherent writing in which the development, organization, and style are appropriate to task, purpose, and audience.

Speaking and Listening

1. Engage effectively in a range of collaborative discussions (one-on-one, in groups, and teacher led) with diverse partners on *grade 8 topics, texts, and issues,* building on others' ideas and expressing their own clearly.

Language

1. Demonstrate command of the conventions of standard English grammar and usage when writing or speaking.

2.a. Use punctuation (comma, ellipsis, dash) to indicate a pause or break.

Poetry Collection 4

 Common Core State Standards

Reading Literature
1. Cite the textual evidence that most strongly supports an analysis of what the text says explicitly as well as inferences drawn from the text.

4. Determine the meaning of words and phrases as they are used in a text, including figurative and connotative meanings; analyze the impact of specific word choices on meaning and tone, including analogies or allusions to other texts.

Language
4.b. Use common, grade-appropriate Greek or Latin affixes and roots as clues to the meaning of a word (e.g., *precede, recede, secede*).

5.c. Distinguish among the connotations (associations) of words with similar denotations (definitions).

What is the secret to reaching someone with words?

Explore the Big Question as you read the poems. Take notes on how the poets use sensory images to connect with readers.

CLOSE READING FOCUS

Key Ideas and Details: **Paraphrase**

Paraphrasing is restating text in your own words. To paraphrase,
- first read aloud fluently, following the punctuation. Pause briefly at commas, dashes, and semicolons, and pause fully after end marks such as periods. Next,
- restate each thought in your own words. Rephrase unusual or complicated expressions using simpler language.

To support a paraphrase, list evidence from the text, such as a particular word choice, that expresses the meaning you give.

Craft and Structure: **Word Choice, Imagery, and Tone**

A writer's **style** is his or her distinctive use of language, including his or her **word choice.** Using word choice, writers can
- develop **imagery**, or language that appeals to the senses. Imagery helps readers imagine sights, sounds, textures, tastes, and smells: *The train <u>thundered</u> past, a <u>silver</u> <u>blur</u>.*
- convey **tone**, or the writer's attitude toward his or her subject or audience. A writer's tone may be described with words such as *serious* or *light, formal* or *friendly, angry* or *humorous.* Writers create tone in part by choosing words with the appropriate **connotations**—the ideas and feelings associated with a word, in addition to its literal definition.

Vocabulary

Copy these words from the poems into your notebook. Judging from their endings, which two words can be used as adjectives?

tongue	jostling	impertinently
exquisite	pollen	recede

CLOSE READING MODEL

The passages below are from the poems "Grandma Ling" and "New World." The annotations to the right of the passages show ways in which you can use close reading skills to paraphrase poems and to analyze how the poets' word choice contributes to imagery.

from "Grandma Ling"

17   She smiled, stretched her arms
     to take to heart the eldest daughter
     of her youngest son[1] a quarter century away.

from "New World"

20   At dawn
     eagles
     hie and
     hover
     above
25   the plain
     where light
     gathers
     in pools.[2]
     Grasses
30   shimmer
     and shine.[3]
     Shadows
     withdraw
     and lie
35   away
     like smoke.[4]

Paraphrase

1 By focusing on the key words *daughter* and *son*, a reader can rephrase "the eldest daughter of her youngest son" as "her granddaughter." The reader might then paraphrase these lines so: *reached with her arms to pull her granddaughter toward her.* In other words, the woman hugged her.

Imagery

2 The light at dawn "gathers in pools." The poet's word choice conveys the striking image of land covered with puddles—puddles not of water, however, but of light.

Word Choice and Tone

3 *Shine* shares a basic literal meaning with words such as *glare*: "give off light." However, *shine* has neutral or positive connotations, whereas words such as *glare* and *burn* suggest discomfort. By choosing *shine,* the poet maintains a simple, direct, respectful tone of appreciation for nature.

Imagery

4 The poet compares the shadows' movement to the way that smoke gradually disappears. By making a comparison using an image that is likely familiar to the reader, he lets the reader "see" the shadows as vividly as he does.

Meet the Poets

"Grandma Ling"

Amy Ling (1939–1999)

Amy Ling was born in China and lived there with her family until she was six years old, when they moved to the United States. In addition to writing poetry, Ling worked as an editor of American literature anthologies. She was instrumental in bringing the work of Asian American writers to a wider audience.

"your little voice / Over the wires came leaping"

E. E. Cummings (1894–1962)

During World War I, Edward Estlin Cummings joined a volunteer ambulance corps in France. The unusual writing style of his letters back home convinced French censors he was a spy, and he was imprisoned for three months. In his poetry, Cummings is known for his experimental, playful style, unusual punctuation, and unconventional arrangement of words.

"New World"

N. Scott Momaday (b. 1934)

A Kiowa Indian, N. Scott Momaday is known for his poetry, plays, art, and essays. As a writer, Momaday strives to pass on Kiowa oral traditions. His father, a great teller of Kiowa stories, inspired Momaday to write: "it was only after I became an adult that I understood how fragile [the stories] are, because they exist only by word of mouth, always just one generation away from extinction."

"January"

John Updike (1932–2009)

Although he is best known as a Pulitzer Prize–winning novelist, John Updike also wrote poetry, essays, short stories, and literary criticism. As a child growing up on a farm in Pennsylvania, Updike enjoyed reading so much that his mother encouraged him to write. He is one of only a handful of writers to have won both the National Medal of Art and the National Medal for the Humanities.

Grandma Ling

Amy Ling

If you dig that hole deep enough
you'll reach China, they used to tell me,
a child in a backyard in Pennsylvania.
Not strong enough to dig that hole,
5   I waited twenty years,
then sailed back, half way around the world.

In Taiwan I first met Grandma.
Before she came to view, I heard
her slippered feet softly measure
10   the tatami¹ floor with even step;
the aqua paper-covered door slid open
and there I faced
my five foot height, sturdy legs and feet,
square forehead, high cheeks, and wide-set eyes;
15   my image stood before me,
acted on by fifty years.

She smiled, stretched her arms
to take to heart the eldest daughter
of her youngest son a quarter century away.
20   She spoke a tongue I knew no word of,
and I was sad I could not understand,
but I could hug her.

---

1. **tatami** (tə tä´ mē) floor mat woven of rice straw.

Imagery
Which words in lines 9–11 appeal to one or more of the five senses?

◀ **Vocabulary**
tongue (tuŋ) *n.*
language

Paraphrase
Restate lines 20–22 in your own words.

Unit 3 • What is the secret to reaching someone with words?

your little voice
Over the wires came leaping
E. E. Cummings

your little voice
          Over the wires came leaping
and i felt suddenly
dizzy
5   With the **jostling** and shouting of merry flowers
wee skipping high-heeled flames
courtesied[1] before my eyes
               or twinkling over to my side

Looked up
10 with **impertinently exquisite** faces
floating hands were laid upon me
I was whirled and tossed into delicious dancing
up
Up
15 with the pale important
             stars and the Humorous
                   moon

dear girl
How i was crazy how i cried when i heard
              over time
20 and tide and death
leaping
Sweetly
     your voice

---

1. **courtesied** (kʉrt´ sēd) v. bowed with bended knees; curtsied.

◀ **Vocabulary**
jostling (jäs´ əl iŋ) n. the act of knocking into, often on purpose

impertinently (im pʉrt´ 'n ənt lē) adv. disrespectfully

exquisite (ek skwiz´ it) adj. very beautiful

◀ **Critical Viewing**
What details in this artwork illustrate the poem's ideas about communication?

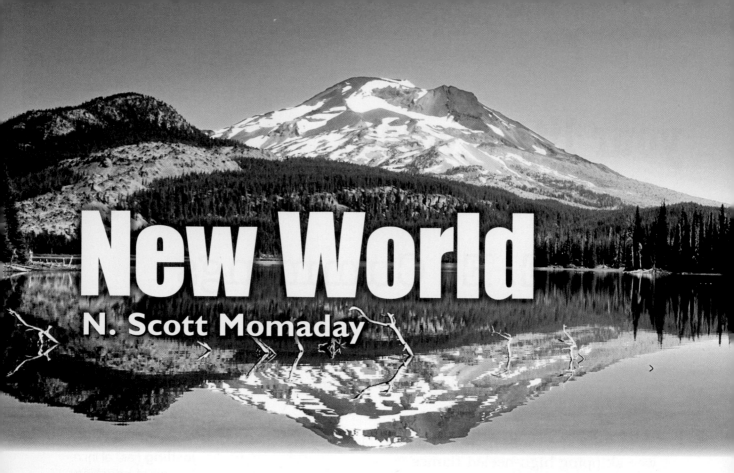

New World
N. Scott Momaday

▲ Critical Viewing
What aspects of this image convey the idea of a "new world"?

Vocabulary ▶
pollen (päl´ ən) *n.* powdery grains on seed plants that aid in reproduction

1.

First Man,
behold:
the earth
glitters
5 with leaves;
the sky
glistens
with rain.
Pollen
10 is borne
on winds
that low
and lean
upon
15 mountains.
Cedars
blacken
the slopes—
and pines.

2.

20 At dawn
eagles
hie and
hover[1]
above
25 the plain
where light
gathers
in pools.
Grasses
30 shimmer
and shine.
Shadows
withdraw
and lie
35 away
like smoke.

---

1. hie (hī) **and hover** (huv´ ər) fly swiftly and then hang as if suspended in the air.

3.

At noon
turtles
enter
40 slowly
into
the warm
dark loam.[2]
Bees hold
45 the swarm.
Meadows
recede
through planes
of heat
50 and pure
distance.

4.

At dusk
the gray
foxes
55 stiffen
in cold;
blackbirds
are fixed
in the
60 branches.
Rivers
follow
the moon,
the long
65 white track
of the
full moon.

2. **loam** (lōm) rich, dark soil.

Word Choice and Tone
Which words and phrases in this section support the author's simple, direct tone of appreciation for nature's majesty? Explain.

◀ **Vocabulary**
recede (ri sēd´) v.
slope backward;
become more distant

Imagery
What images convey a sense of the temperature in the final stanza?

JANUARY John Updike

Paraphrase
Read lines 1–4 according to punctuation. Then, put this stanza into your own words.

The days are short,
    The sun a spark
Hung thin between
    The dark and dark.

5 Fat snowy footsteps
    Track the floor,
And parkas pile up
    Near the door.

The river is
10   A frozen place
Held still beneath
    The trees' black lace.

The sky is low.
    The wind is gray.
15 The radiator
    Purrs all day.

▶ **Critical Viewing**
Compare and contrast the depiction of winter in the image with Updike's.

Language Study

Vocabulary The words listed appear in the poems in this collection. Rewrite each sentence using one of the words listed. Choose the word that makes the sentence more logical.

   tongue   **jostling**   **impertinently**   **exquisite**   **pollen**

1. My friend has terrible taste in clothes and always looks good.

2. Bees gather petals from flowers to make honey.

3. The rude child spoke respectfully.

4. We'll need a translator who is familiar with their native food.

5. In the crowded store, people moved easily through the aisles.

WORD STUDY

The **Latin root -cede-** or **-ceed-** means "go" or "yield." In the poem "New World," the speaker describes meadows that seem to **recede**, or move into the distance, in the midday heat.

Word Study

Part A Explain how the **root -cede-** or **-ceed-** contributes to the meanings of *succeed*, *secede*, and *intercede*. Consult a dictionary.

Part B Use the context of the sentences and what you know about the Latin root -cede- or -ceed- to explain your answer to each question.

1. Would a war's victor be likely to *cede* territory to the loser?

2. Would a negative review *exceed* an author's expectations?

Literary Analysis

Key Ideas and Details

1. (a) In "Grandma Ling," what prevents the grandmother and granddaughter from communicating in their first meeting?
(b) Speculate: What might they want to tell or ask each other?
(c) Analyze: How do they finally communicate, and what are they saying?

2. Paraphrase Reread lines 1–6 of "Grandma Ling." **(a)** Using punctuation, identify the two complete sentences in these lines.
(b) Paraphrase the lines. Explain which words in the text were most important in making your paraphrase.

3. Paraphrase Use a chart like the one shown on the right to paraphrase the lines listed for each poem in this collection.

Craft and Structure

4. Word Choice and Tone (a) Describe Cummings's tone in "your little voice. . . ." **(b)** Analyze three of his word choices. Explain how the words' connotations contribute to the tone.

5. Imagery (a) In "New World," what imagery is used in the first section? **(b)** How do the author's style and use of images affect the poem's meaning?

6. Imagery (a) What imagery does Updike use in "January" to describe winter days? Cite specific word choices. **(b)** How do his word choice and style affect the poem's meaning?

Integration of Knowledge and Ideas

7. (a) In "New World," what three times of day are identified?
(b) Infer: Why does the poet describe these times? **(c) Interpret:** What more might these times represent? Cite specific details from the poem to support your interpretation.

8. Evaluate: Which poem from this collection do you think uses the most vivid images to convey a mood or feeling to the reader? Justify your answer, citing specific words or phrases from the poem.

9. **What is the secret to reaching someone with words?** Reread "Grandma Ling" and "your little voice . . . ." Do these poems suggest that a strong connection between people is possible only if they have a good means of communication? Explain, citing details from the poem.

Poetry Collection 4

Original Lines
1. "Grandma Ling" (lines 15–16)
2. "your little voice . . ." (lines 1–4)
3. "New World" (lines 37–45)
4. "January" (lines 13–16)
Paraphrase
1.
2.
3.
4.

ACADEMIC VOCABULARY

As you read and speak about the poems in Poetry Collection 4, use the words related to communication that you explored on page 347 of this textbook.

Conventions: **Pronoun Case**

English has three **cases,** or forms, of pronouns. **Nominative, or subjective, case** is used for the subjects of verbs and for predicate pronouns. **Objective case** is used for direct and indirect objects and for objects of prepositions. **Possessive case** is used to show ownership.

Poetry Collection 4

The chart below shows the personal pronouns grouped by case.

The Three Cases of Personal Pronouns		
Case	**Pronouns**	**Function in a Sentence**
Nominative (subject)	I, we, you, he, she, it, they	subject of a verb ("*She* told the story.") predicate pronoun ("The storyteller was *she*.")
Objective (object)	me, us, you, him, her, it, them	direct object ("Amy told *it* to John.") indirect object ("Amy told *him* the story.") object of a preposition ("Amy told the story to *him*.")
Possessive	my, mine, our, ours, your, yours, his, her, hers, its, their, theirs	to show ownership ("Amy told *her* story to John.")

Practice A

Choose the correct pronouns and give their cases.

1. When Amy Ling visited (she/her) grandma, (she/her) saw an image of herself.

2. People told (she/her) to dig a hole to China, though (they/them) were not serious.

3. When Amy and (her/she) hugged, it was (their/they) first hug ever.

4. (They/Their) spoke different languages, but (they/their) love was deep and needed no words.

Reading Application Find two of the personal pronoun cases in a poem in Poetry Collection 4.

Practice B

Choose appropriate personal pronouns to complete each item.

1. The speaker is excited when ___ gets a call.

2. The caller made ___ so happy, ___voice actually made ___ feel dizzy.

3. ___ grandmother is very important to ___.

4. The person who left ___ parka by the door is ___.

Writing Application Write a sentence about one of the poems using all three pronoun cases.

Writing to Sources

Argument A review of a literary work is an evaluation of its strengths and weaknesses. Write a **review** of the four poems in Poetry Collection 4. Evaluate each poem based on sound, word choice, and imagery.

- To evaluate the sound of a poem, read it aloud and decide how well its sound and rhythm match its subject.

- To evaluate word choice and imagery, determine whether the poet uses vivid and appropriate words and images to effectively convey feelings and ideas.

As you draft, support your claims with references to lines from the poems. Finally, offer your overall opinion of each poem.

Grammar Application As you write, make sure you use correct pronoun cases to convey your ideas clearly and grammatically.

Research and Technology

Build and Present Knowledge Write a **profile** of one of the poets featured in Poetry Collection 4. Follow these steps:

- Use search terms to gather information from several print or online sources about the poet's life, writings, and influences. Choose reliable sources, such as well-known periodicals or Web sites with URLs that end with *.edu*. Sites maintained by individuals may not have the most accurate information.

- When taking notes, carefully record each source. You may paraphrase or quote the writer in your notes. If you copy down the writer's exact words, enclose them in quotation marks and check to make sure you have accurately transcribed them.

- When you have finished your research, outline your main ideas and begin drafting. In your draft, explain how the poet's work reflects his or her influences, heritage, or beliefs. Cite details from the poet's poem in Poetry Collection 4 to support your claims.

- While drafting, be sure to develop an effective balance between research information and original ideas. Be careful to credit ideas and words that are not your own, following a standard format for citations. Include a Works Cited list. (See the Conducting Research workshop in the Introductory Unit of this textbook for additional guidance.)

Common Core State Standards

Writing

1. Write arguments to support claims with clear reasons and relevant evidence.

8. Gather relevant information from multiple print and digital sources, using search terms effectively; assess the credibility and accuracy of each source; and quote or paraphrase the data and conclusions of others while avoiding plagiarism and following a standard format for citation.

9. Draw evidence from literary or informational texts to support analysis, reflection, and research.

Language

1. Demonstrate command of the conventions of standard English grammar and usage when writing or speaking.

What is the secret to reaching someone with words?

Explore the Big Question as you read these two poems. As you read, note word choices and choices of style designed to move readers to think or to feel.

READING TO COMPARE TYPES OF DESCRIPTION

Authors Robert Frost and Walt Whitman use different styles and structures in their writing, but they both use description to create images in the reader's mind. As you read each poem, consider why the authors chose to write in a certain style. After you have read both poems, compare their literal and symbolic meanings.

POEM

POEM

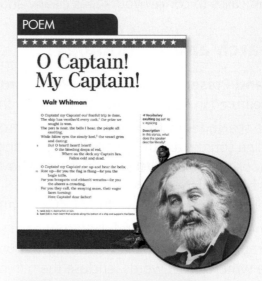

"The Road Not Taken"

Robert Frost (1874–1963)
One of the best-known and best-loved American poets, Robert Frost was a four-time winner of the Pulitzer Prize. Though he was born in San Francisco, Frost spent most of his life in New England—the subject of many of his poems. He read his poem "The Gift Outright" at the inauguration of President John F. Kennedy in 1961.

"O Captain! My Captain!"

Walt Whitman (1819–1892)
Although he is now considered one of the greatest American poets, Walt Whitman could not find a commercial publisher and was forced to pay for the publication of his masterpiece *Leaves of Grass* in 1855. This collection of poems about the United States has continued to influence poetry ever since.

Comparing Types of Description

Descriptive writing paints pictures with words. A variety of descriptions can be used in poetry to present **levels of meaning.**

- **Literal meaning** is the actual, everyday meaning of words.

- In contrast, **figurative meaning** is based on the symbolic nature of language, using imaginative, innovative ways to express ideas.

An **analogy** is a figurative description that compares two or more things that are similar in some ways, but otherwise unalike. In literature, analogies may extend over the course of a work. For example, a poem that literally describes the ocean also can be read as an analogy: It may compare the ocean to life because both are vast, deep, and ever-changing. The poem, therefore, has two levels of meaning—one literal and one figurative or symbolic.

When you think a poem may have levels of meaning, think about whether the poet is using an analogy or other type of figurative description to emphasize an idea. Follow these steps as you read the poems by Frost and Whitman:

- Record your ideas about what the descriptions might symbolize, or represent.

- In a chart like the one shown, list some of the words and images that give you clues about the figurative meaning.

- Determine whether or not the figurative meaning develops over the course of the poem.

- Finally, compare the analogies in the two poems.

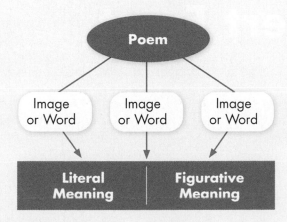

Common Core State Standards

Reading Literature
1. Cite the textual evidence that most strongly supports an analysis of what the text says explicitly as well as inferences drawn from the text.

4. Determine the meaning of words and phrases as they are used in a text, including figurative and connotative meanings; analyze the impact of specific word choices on meaning and tone, including analogies or allusions to other texts.

Writing
9. Draw evidence from literary or informational texts to support analysis, reflection, and research.

The Road Not Taken

Robert Frost

Two roads diverged in a yellow wood,
And sorry I could not travel both
And be one traveler, long I stood
And looked down one as far as I could
5 To where it bent in the undergrowth;

Then took the other, as just as fair,
And having perhaps the better claim,
Because it was grassy and wanted wear;
Though as for that, the passing there
10 Had worn them really about the same,

And both that morning equally lay
In leaves no step had trodden black.
Oh, I kept the first for another day!
Yet knowing how way leads on to way,
15 I doubted if I should ever come back.

I shall be telling this with a sigh
Somewhere ages and ages hence:
Two roads diverged in a wood, and I—
I took the one less traveled by,
20 And that has made all the difference.

◄ **Vocabulary**
diverged (dī vʉrj´ d)
v. branched off

Description
What is the literal
subject of this poem?

Description
What clue in the
final stanza hints
that the poem is
about more than a
hike in the woods?

Critical Thinking

1. **Key Ideas and Details: (a)** In the first five lines, where does the
   speaker remember being? **(b) Infer:** Based on these lines, what can
   you tell about the speaker's character and attitude toward life?

2. **Key Ideas and Details: (a)** Which road does the speaker finally
   choose? **(b) Deduce:** Why does the speaker choose one road over
   the other? **(c) Analyze:** Find two statements suggesting that the
   speaker believes he has made a significant choice.

3. **Key Ideas and Details: (a)** Why does the speaker predict that he
   will remember this decision? **(b) Generalize:** What message does
   the poem communicate about decisions in general?

4. **Integration of Knowledge and Ideas: (a)** How does the
   language Frost uses let him reach a wide readership with his
   message? **(b)** What might Frost say is the secret to reaching
   someone with words? *[Connect to the Big Question: What is
   the secret to reaching someone with words?]*

▲ **Critical Viewing** What details in this photograph of Lincoln's funeral procession reflect the importance of Lincoln's death to Americans such as Whitman?

O Captain! My Captain!

Walt Whitman

O Captain! my Captain! our fearful trip is done,
The ship has weather'd every rack,[1] the prize we
    sought is won,
The port is near, the bells I hear, the people all
    exulting,
While follow eyes the steady keel,[2] the vessel grim
    and daring;
5   But O heart! heart! heart!
         O the bleeding drops of red,
            Where on the deck my Captain lies,
            Fallen cold and dead.

O Captain! my Captain! rise up and hear the bells;
10 Rise up—for you the flag is flung—for you the
    bugle trills,
For you bouquets and ribbon'd wreaths—for you
    the shores a-crowding,
For you they call, the swaying mass, their eager
    faces turning;
      Here Captain! dear father!

◀ **Vocabulary**
exulting (eg zult´ in)
v. rejoicing

Description
In this stanza, what
does the speaker
describe literally?

---

1. **rack** (rak) *n.* destruction or ruin.
2. **keel** (kēl) *n.* main beam that extends along the bottom of a ship and supports the frame.

This arm beneath your head!
15   It is some dream that on the deck,
      You've fallen cold and dead.

My Captain does not answer, his lips are pale
   and still,
My father does not feel my arm, he has no pulse
   nor will,
The ship is anchor'd safe and sound, its voyage
   closed and done,
20 From fearful trip the victor ship comes in with
   object won;
    Exult O shores, and ring O bells!
      But I with mournful tread,
        Walk the deck my Captain lies,
          Fallen cold and dead.

Description
What is the symbolic meaning of the safely anchored ship?

Critical Thinking

1. **Key Ideas and Details: (a)** What has happened to the Captain? **(b) Infer:** Why does the timing of this event make it doubly unfortunate? **(c) Interpret:** How does the mood or feeling of the poem reflect what has happened?

2. **Key Ideas and Details: (a)** What words in the poem relate to the sea and sailing? **(b) Compare:** In what ways does Lincoln's leadership resemble a captain's role on a ship? **(c) Draw Conclusions:** What kind of leader does the speaker consider Lincoln?

3. **Craft and Structure:** Review the various forms of poetry discussed on page 361. How does the tone and purpose of Whitman's poem fit the form of an *elegy*?

4. **Integration of Knowledge and Ideas:** Is it more powerful to hear about someone's life and death described in symbolic language, as in Whitman's poem? Or, is direct description more powerful, as in a speech given at a funeral? Explain your reasoning. *[Connect to the Big Question: What is the secret to reaching someone with words?]*

Writing to Sources

Comparing Types of Description

1. **Craft and Structure: (a)** In "The Road Not Taken," what descriptive language shows that the two roads are alike and different? **(b)** What kind of choice might these two roads represent? Explain, using details from the poem.

2. **Key Ideas and Details: (a)** In "O Captain! My Captain!" what is the ship's destination? **(b)** What is the "fearful trip" that the ship has "weather'd"? **(c)** How does this trip and the rest of the poem reveal the poet's response to a historic event?

3. **Craft and Structure:** Use a chart like this one to analyze the ideas and emotions that each poem conveys through the use of analogy.

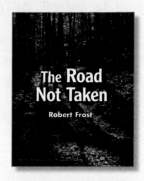

Literal Meaning	Analogy		Ideas and Emotions
Two roads separate		→	
A ship's captain dies			

Timed Writing

Explanatory Text: Essay
In an essay, explain whether the insights conveyed through figurative descriptions in the poems remain relevant to readers today. **(40 minutes)**

5-Minute Planner

1. Read the prompt carefully and completely.

2. Gather your ideas by jotting down answers to these questions:

   - How common are the experiences that each poem describes?

   - Which poet better expresses emotions through description?

   - How do analogies help readers understand the events described?

   - Which message is easier for you to interpret? Why?

3. Make sure that you address the prompt and support your response with relevant details from the poems. Consult the charts you completed on this page and on page 415.

ACADEMIC VOCABULARY

As you write, use academic language, including the following words or their related forms:

connection

influence

objective

relevant

For more information about academic vocabulary, see the Building Academic Vocabulary workshop in the front of your book.

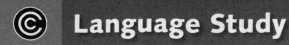

Language Study

Words With Multiple Meanings

Many words in English relate to multiple subjects and therefore have multiple meanings. A **multiple-meaning word** is a word that has more than one definition. The word *bat,* for example, can be defined as a furry, flying animal or as a club used in baseball. The following chart shows two usages of the multiple-meaning word *factor*.

Language
4. Determine or clarify the meaning of unknown and multiple-meaning words or phrases based on *grade 8 reading and content,* choosing flexibly from a range of strategies.
4.a. Use context as a clue to the meaning of a word or phrase.
4.c. Consult general and specialized reference materials, both print and digital, to find the pronunciation of a word or determine or clarify its precise meaning or its part of speech.

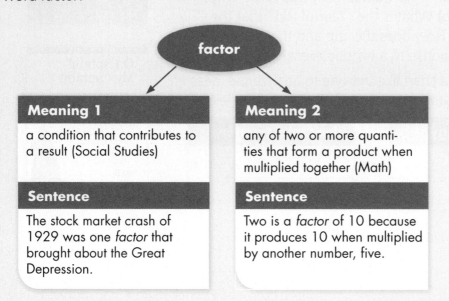

factor

Meaning 1

a condition that contributes to a result (Social Studies)

Sentence

The stock market crash of 1929 was one *factor* that brought about the Great Depression.

Meaning 2

any of two or more quantities that form a product when multiplied together (Math)

Sentence

Two is a *factor* of 10 because it produces 10 when multiplied by another number, five.

Using Context To determine which meaning of a multiple-meaning word is being used in a given sentence, use context, or the other words surrounding the word. For example, when you read the example sentence on the left side of the chart, you can use the phrase "brought about" as a clue to the meaning of *factor*. *Brought about* means "caused" or "helped make happen." This clue shows that the word *factor* is being used in the sense of "a condition that contributes to a result."

One type of context clue is the role of a word in a sentence. For example, you might encounter the sentence, "When deciding which model to buy, you should factor in the resale value of each." The context clue "you should . . ." clearly indicates that in this sentence, the word *factor* is being used as a verb. Using a dictionary, you can confirm that *factor in* is a verb meaning "include as a factor" or "take into account."

Practice A

Using context, write the meaning of each italicized word in the sentences below. If necessary, check the meaning in a dictionary.

1. a. After weeks of cold weather, the *ground* was very hard.
   b. I like freshly *ground* pepper on my salad.
2. a. The overflowing garbage can produced a *rank* smell.
   b. Juan hopes to reach the *rank* of captain.
3. a. Today's *date* is January 23.
   b. I sliced a *date* into pieces and put it in my bowl of cereal.
4. a. Do not *cross* the street until the light turns green.
   b. The coach becomes *cross* when players are late for practice.

Practice B

For each word listed, write two sentences that use different meanings of the word. If necessary, look up the meanings in a dictionary.

1. bank
2. mean
3. square
4. base
5. count
6. bound
7. range
8. capital

Comprehension and Collaboration

Work with two or three classmates to write a sentence for each of the following words, using two different meanings of the word in the same sentence. For example: *"In his speech, the governor will* <u>state</u> *his goals for reducing pollution in our* <u>state</u>*."*

- **plain**
- **sound**
- **object**

Activity Look in a dictionary to learn more about these words that have multiple meanings: *nature, horn, jam, match, positive*. Write each word on a separate note card like the one shown. Fill in the left-hand column of the note card with details about the word in one of its meanings. Fill in the right-hand column with details about the word in another one of its meanings. Then, trade note cards with a partner, and discuss the different meanings and uses of the words that each of you found.

Word: _____	
Part of Speech:	**Part of Speech:**
Definition:	**Definition:**
Example Sentence:	**Example Sentence:**

Evaluating an Oral Presentation

When you evaluate an oral presentation, you make judgments about a speaker's ideas and effectiveness. Use these steps to guide you.

Understand the Structure

Evaluating a presentation is easier if you know the topic and format.

Identify topic. The topic of a speech is its subject, or what the speech is about. The topic can generally be summarized in a phrase and may appear in the title of the presentation. Speakers usually introduce the topic within the first few minutes.

Identify purpose. The general purpose of an oral presentation is often to inform or persuade. The specific purpose depends on the topic. For example, the specific purpose of a scientific presentation might be to describe new research on the brain.

Determine point of view. Especially when listening to a persuasive speech, it is important to identify point of view. Use the arguments and examples a speaker offers, as well as his or her background, to determine how the speaker feels about a subject.

Identify organization. Identify the speaker's main ideas and connect them with the facts and ideas that support them. Determine the organizational format, such as cause-and-effect or order of importance. Knowing organization helps focus your listening.

Evaluate the Speech

Evaluate the content. Ask yourself if the speaker supports main ideas with strong and varied evidence, such as facts, examples, and expert opinions. Determine whether the evidence is relevant, or logically relates to the ideas presented. For example, a speaker might claim that a particular diet is healthful. Relevant evidence would include statistics showing that when people with high blood pressure go on the diet, their blood pressure goes down. Irrelevant details would include statistics showing that many athletes are on the diet. Details of uncertain relevance would include reports that people on the diet feel better.

Evaluate the delivery. A speaker who mumbles and repeats points unnecessarily gives a poor presentation. A good speaker should enunciate clearly, vary his or her voice, and deliver a lively, informative presentation.

 Common Core State Standards

Speaking and Listening

2. Analyze the purpose of information presented in diverse media and formats and evaluate the motives behind its presentation.

3. Delineate a speaker's argument and specific claims, evaluating the soundness of the reasoning and relevance and sufficiency of the evidence and identifying when irrelevant evidence is introduced.

6. Adapt speech to a variety of contexts and tasks, demonstrating command of formal English when indicated or appropriate.

Practice the Skills

Presentation of Knowledge and Ideas Choose a specific claim and present an argument that defends the claim. Then, in a group, take turns presenting a speech. Use the chart to focus your presentation.

ACTIVITY: **Giving an Oral Presentation**

- Identify your topic, purpose, and point of view, or attitude, toward your subject.
- Conduct research in order to decide which position to take on your topic. Find ample, relevant evidence to support your argument.
- Present information clearly, concisely, and logically. Emphasize main points in a focused way and use relevant evidence.
- Use sound reasoning and well-chosen examples or details.
- Maintain effective eye contact.
- Speak clearly and at an adequate volume.
- Use formal English and avoid mistakes in grammar or pronunciation.

Use an evaluation form like the one shown below as you listen to your classmates' oral presentations.

Evaluating an Oral Presentation

Content

_____ Clarity of ideas _____ Interesting topic _____ Logical organization
_____ Strong evidence or examples _____Originality

Delivery

_____ Enunciated clearly? _____ Varied voice?
_____ Good eye contact? _____ Adequate volume?
_____ Used appropriate and correct language, including formal English?

Respond to these questions:

In your own words, what was the speaker's purpose? _____
Did the speaker achieve this purpose? _____
What was the speaker's point of view on the topic? _____
Did the speaker present information clearly and logically? _____
Did the speaker consistently use varied evidence to support ideas? _____
Did the speaker consistently use relevant evidence to support ideas? _____
What constructive suggestions for improvement can you offer
the speaker? Consider elements of both the content and the delivery.

_____

Write an Argument

Response to Literature: Critical Review

Defining the Form A **critical review** is an analysis of a work of literature in which the writer describes the work and makes claims about its quality and effectiveness. You might use elements of this form in writing critical essays or book reviews.

Assignment Write a critical review of two or more works of literature that are linked by theme or topic. Your critical review should include these elements:

✓ a *main claim* about two or more works, offering an evaluation or interpretation of them

✓ a well-developed *argument* in support of the main claim

✓ *ample relevant evidence* in support of the main claim, including text evidence such as quotations and paraphrases of the works

✓ an *analysis* of literary elements in the works, such as characters, plots, or themes

✓ *supporting claims, arguments,* and *evaluations* that demonstrate insight

✓ error-free writing, including *correct subject-verb agreement*

To preview the criteria on which your critical review may be judged, see the rubric on page 433.

Common Core State Standards

Writing

1. Write arguments to support claims with clear reasons and relevant evidence.

4. Produce clear and coherent writing in which the development, organization, and style are appropriate to task, purpose, and audience.

9. Draw evidence from literary or informational texts to support analysis, reflection, and research.

FOCUS ON RESEARCH

When you write critical reviews, you might perform research to

- gather background information to help you better understand the setting and characters in a work.

- support your claims with the opinions of authoritative critics.

- learn more about the author's life and influences to gain additional insight into the works.

Be sure to note all resources you use in your research, and credit those sources in your final drafts. Refer to the Conducting Research workshop in the Introductory Unit for assistance in citing materials.

Prewriting/Planning Strategies

Choose two works. Browse this textbook and other books to identify two literary works you can connect in meaningful ways. Consider not only works that you enjoyed, but also works that left you with questions—even works you thought had shortcomings.

Identify aspects for comparison. To find an angle for comparison, review the works, taking notes on literary elements such as characters, plot, and theme. Use a chart like the one shown.

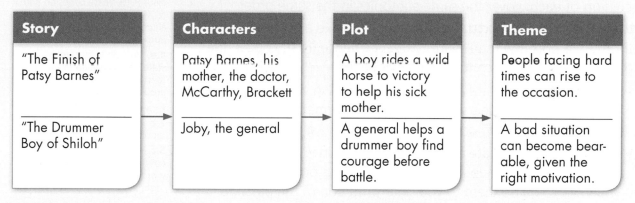

Story	Characters	Plot	Theme
"The Finish of Patsy Barnes"	Patsy Barnes, his mother, the doctor, McCarthy, Brackett	A boy rides a wild horse to victory to help his sick mother.	People facing hard times can rise to the occasion.
"The Drummer Boy of Shiloh"	Joby, the general	A general helps a drummer boy find courage before battle.	A bad situation can become bearable, given the right motivation.

Find and define your focus. Review your chart, and pinpoint an idea that connects both works and can serve as your focus. Consider aspects of the works that you found interesting—or annoying. Your focus could center on specific storytelling techniques, such as flashback. It could involve similarities and differences in two characters. It might be a more general claim about which work is more effective.

Model: Focus for Comparison

Patsy Barnes: young; must care for sick mother
Joby: young; must go to battle

FOCUS: How do two young characters face new responsibilities?

Gather details. Review the works, and gather more details on your chosen focus. In addition, note background information readers will need about each work if they are to follow your analysis. For example, even if your focus is on the characters in two stories, you might need to tell readers that one story is set in modern times, the other at the time of the Civil War.

Drafting Strategies

Formulate and present a main claim. Think about the two works that you have chosen and the focus of your comparison. Then, formulate your main claim about the two works. Your claim might concern the best interpretation of the works, or it might be a claim about their value. Present your main claim in a thesis statement in your introduction.

Use a logical organization. Outline your major ideas, and follow your outline as you draft. Consider presenting all of your points about one work first, then all of your points about the other. In your discussion of each, cover the same subtopics in the same order.

Cite and integrate textual evidence. To make a point with authority, support it with relevant textual evidence. First, choose the appropriate form in which to present evidence:

- **Summarize,** or restate main ideas in your own words, when you wish to give readers a good deal of information quickly, as when you fill them in on plot or historical background.

- **Paraphrase,** or restate a particular passage in your own words, when you wish to help readers understand its point or when you wish to guide them to your interpretation of the passage.

- **Quote** the writer's exact words, or repeat the text word for word, whenever the exact words make a difference. For example, quote when you wish to give an example of the writer's style, when you wish to analyze a significant scene, or when you wish to support an interpretation of a symbol.

Make sure to clearly introduce each piece of textual evidence you cite, explaining its source and significance, as in this example: "The main character shows his courage when he says, 'I'll take the wheel.'" Remember that you can focus a quotation by omitting words that are not critical to your point, as long as you do not change the writer's meaning. Indicate such omissions with an ellipsis.

ORIGINAL: "After years of study, years that saw the end of one war and the start of another, he was ready."

WORDS OMITTED: "After years of study, . . . he was ready."

Address counterclaims To strengthen your argument, identify the counterclaims that a reader might offer against your views. In your draft, include answers refuting these counterclaims, using textual evidence.

Writing a strong conclusion. In your conclusion, summarize your main claim. Restate your supporting claims, and conclude with a memorable restatement of your insights.

 **Common Core State Standards**

Writing

1.a. Introduce claim(s), acknowledge and distinguish the claim(s) from alternate or opposing claims, and organize the reasons and evidence logically.

1.b. Support claim(s) with logical reasoning and relevant evidence, using accurate, credible sources and demonstrating an understanding of the topic or text.

1.c. Use words, phrases, and clauses to create cohesion and clarify the relationships among claim(s), counterclaims, reasons, and evidence.

1.e. Provide a concluding statement or section that follows from and supports the argument presented.

Language

2.b. Use an ellipsis to indicate an omission.

5.c. Distinguish among the connotations (associations) of words with similar denotations (definitions).

> **Model Main Claim**
> Although their stories are set in very different times, the two main characters in these works find the strength they need to accomplish great things.

Using the Right Words

Word choice is the exact language a writer selects to communicate ideas. For a critical review, good writers choose precise words that convey either praise or criticism, or both.

Follow these tips when writing your critical review.

Considering Audience and Purpose Take a moment to identify why you are writing and for whom. Choose words that will appeal to your audience and help you achieve your purpose.

Determining Your Opinion Think about how each work affected you when you read it. Ask yourself questions such as these:

- Did the story have a plot that interested me? Why or why not?
- Were the characters believable? Did I like them? Why?
- Would I recommend this work to a friend? Why?

Jot down your answers, either as individual words or as phrases or clauses. Examine the ideas in your responses for possible word choices. For example, you might write that you found characters in a story "difficult to relate to" because the plot itself was so "outlandish." The words *difficult to relate to* and *outlandish* are word choices you might consider using in your draft to establish and support claims.

Writing Like a Reviewer As you think about your response to the literature, be aware of your word choices and their *connotations*. Connotations are the impressions and feelings a word conveys beyond its basic meaning. For example, *moving* has positive connotations, *emotional* has neutral connotations, and *sentimental* may have negative connotations. Ask: *Do my words have connotations that suit my purpose? What impact will my words have on my audience?*

Brainstorming for Accurate Words Determine your attitude toward the story. Do you think it deserves praise—or disapproval? Make lists of words that express these attitudes. Start with the categories in this chart, and then consult a thesaurus for synonyms.

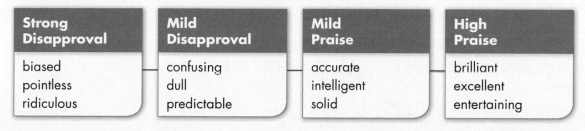

Strong Disapproval	Mild Disapproval	Mild Praise	High Praise
biased	confusing	accurate	brilliant
pointless	dull	intelligent	excellent
ridiculous	predictable	solid	entertaining

Revising Strategies

Revise for completeness and consistency. Work with a partner to check your draft to make sure that you have fully developed the claim you set forth in your introduction. To help you revise, answer questions like these:

Questions	Revisions
• Have I anticipated and answered my readers' questions?	• If not, add information to add background and address readers' possible counterclaims.
• Have I been consistent in presenting my arguments?	• If not, revise by eliminating items that conflict with your main claim.
• Have I provided a sense of closure to my review?	• If not, reshape your conclusion to emphasize your main comparison or contrast.

Check support for the main claim. As you reread your draft, circle each supporting claim that you make in a different color. Make sure that each of these points supports your main claim. Consider eliminating any paragraphs that do not support the main claim.

Evaluate the evidence. Look back at the claims that you have circled and underline the textual evidence that you used to support the claim in the same color. If you find that a particular claim has too little evidence, go back and supply additional textual evidence to help persuade readers.

Revise to maintain a formal style. As you reread your draft, make sure that your writing remains formal. A critical review is an analysis of literature, and so it should not sound overly conversational.

TOO INFORMAL: *If you asked most people, they might have said he would give up, period, but you need to remember what happened before.*

REVISION: *If the reader considers earlier scenes, it should be clear that the main character will persevere.*

Use transitions. Use transitional words such as *because* and *therefore* to clarify connections between claims. Words such as *in contrast* and *despite* can clarify distinctions between claims and counterclaims.

Common Core State Standards

Writing
1.b. Support claim(s) with logical reasoning and relevant evidence, using accurate, credible sources and demonstrating an understanding of the topic or text.

1.c. Use words, phrases, and clauses to create cohesion and clarify the relationships among claim(s), counterclaims, reasons, and evidence.

1.d. Establish and maintain a formal style.

5. With some guidance and support from peers and adults, develop and strengthen writing as needed by planning, revising, editing, rewriting, or trying a new approach, focusing on how well purpose and audience have been addressed.

Language
1. Demonstrate command of the conventions of standard English grammar and usage when writing or speaking.

3. Use knowledge of language and its conventions when writing, speaking, reading, or listening.

Revising for Subject-Verb Agreement

A verb must agree with its subject in number. In grammar, the number of a word can be either *singular* (indicating *one*) or *plural* (indicating *more than one*). Here are examples of nouns and pronouns used as singular subjects and of nouns and pronouns used as plural subjects.

Used as Singular Subjects	Used as Plural Subjects
bus, goose, I, you, Seth or Mia	buses, geese, we, you, Seth and Mia

Most verbs have the same singular and plural form, except that in the present tense, they add *-s* or *-es* for the third-person singular form: *he runs; Trudy goes.* The verb *be* takes the form *am* or *was* with the subject *I, is* or *was* with third-person singular subjects, and *are* or *were* with the subject *you* and all plural subjects. In the chart, the subjects are underlined and the verbs are set in italics.

Subject-Verb Agreement	
Third-Person Singular	**Third-Person Plural**
He *runs*.	They *run*.
The child *goes* to sleep.	The children *go* to sleep.
Seth *agrees*.	Seth and Mia *agree* to get married.

Fixing Faulty Subject-Verb Agreement To fix problems with subject-verb agreement, use the following methods.

1. **Identify the subject, and check its number.** For singular subjects, use singular verbs. For plural subjects, use plural verbs.
2. **If the subject comes after the verb, rephrase the sentence.** This makes it easier to determine the number of the subject.
   Faulty Inverted Sentence: There was many girls in the store.
   Rephrased: Many girls were in the store.
3. **Omit intervening phrases.** If a prepositional phrase follows the subject, read the sentence without it to determine the correct number; for example, "The photos [on the wall] *are* funny."

Grammar in Your Writing
Choose two paragraphs in your draft. Draw a line from each subject to its verb. Fix any errors in agreement according to the examples above.

Common Core State Standards

Language
2.c. Spell correctly.

Storybook Greed

Although *The Giving Tree*, by Shel Silverstein, and the story of King Midas are different in many ways, they both are about the unhappy consequences of greed. *The Giving Tree* also includes a message about the environment.

The Giving Tree is the story of a boy who keeps taking pieces of an apple tree to try to make himself happy. The tree loves the little boy. Every day he comes to play with her leaves, climb her trunk, and eat her apples. However, as the boy grows older, other things became more important. From then on, all he wants to do is take things from the tree and use them for his own needs. In the end, the tree has nothing left to give him. Instead of taking something from her, all he does is sit on the tree's stump.

The story of King Midas is also a story about greed. King Midas spares the life of a satyr who is caught sleeping in his royal rose bed, a crime punishable by death. Because King Midas decides to spare the satyr's life, he is granted one wish. Being a greedy man, he immediately wishes for the gift of a golden touch. In Ovid's version of the tale, he asks, "Cause that whatever I shall touch with my body shall be turned into yellow gold." One day, his beloved daughter comes running up to him and gives him a hug. She is instantly turned to gold, and King Midas is heartbroken.

Both of these stories show men who ask for more than they should have. In the end, both men lose the one thing they have loved most. That shows what greed can do.

In addition, *The Giving Tree* sends a clear message about the environment. The boy's taking from the tree is typical of our interactions with the environment. Some might say that the story is just about one boy and one tree. It is not a lesson about the environment. However, readers need to look at the full picture. Because the boy takes too much, the tree can no longer give to him—just as can happen when we use up precious natural resources. In addition, the bare stump is a powerful symbol of how we can strip the environment bare if we are not careful.

Both stories show why people should not be so greedy. This applies to greed for material possessions, as well as greed that harms the environment. The tales of King Midas and of *The Giving Tree* are important, and everyone should read them and learn from them. Their basic lesson is how to be a friend to all.

In the first line, Joyce addresses the works' common theme.

In her thesis statement, Joyce makes a claim that she will then support with evidence.

Joyce summarizes both works, offers details from the text, and explains how each one connects to the theme of greed.

Joyce adds a quote from the story to support her claim with textual evidence.

Joyce identifies a potential counterclaim and refutes it, supporting her claim with additional textual evidence.

In her conclusion, Joyce refers to her initial claim and offers an opinion that reflects independent thought.

Editing and Proofreading

Spell tricky or difficult words correctly. Certain words are commonly misspelled because they are commonly mispronounced. Though correct pronunciation does not always help with spelling, in some cases it does. If you add extra letter or syllable sounds to a word—for example, if you say *athalete*—you will probably spell the word incorrectly. If in doubt, run a spell check or consult a dictionary.

Publishing and Presenting

Consider one of the following ways to share your writing.

Present a book talk. Use your critical review as the basis for an informal oral presentation. Summarize your main ideas and support on note cards, and practice presenting before delivering your talk.

Publish a "Teens Review" column. Contact a local newspaper and arrange for your work to be part of a series of critical reviews by young people.

Reflecting on Your Writing

Writer's Journal Jot down your answers to this question:
Which of the strategies or activities did you find most useful?

Spiral Review
Earlier in this unit, you learned about **subject complements** (p. 386), **direct and indirect objects** (p. 400), and **pronoun case** (p. 412). Review your essay for correct use of pronoun case, including pronoun case in complements.

Rubric for Self-Assessment

Find evidence that your writing addresses each category. Then, use the rating scale to grade your work.

Criteria	Rating Scale
Purpose/Focus Clearly presents a claim comparing two works; provides a concluding section that follows from the argument	not very .... very 1 2 3 4
Organization Organizes the reasons and evidence logically; uses words, phrases, and clauses to create cohesion and clarify the relationships among claim(s), counterclaims, reasons, and evidence	1 2 3 4
Development of Ideas/Elaboration Supports the claim with logical reasoning and relevant evidence, acknowledging counterclaims and demonstrating an understanding of the text	1 2 3 4
Language Establishes and maintains a formal style	1 2 3 4
Conventions Correctly follows conventions of grammar, spelling, and punctuation, including subject-verb agreement	1 2 3 4

SELECTED RESPONSE

**Common Core
State Standards**

**RL.8.1, RL.8.4; W.8.2.b;
L.8.4.a**
[For full standards wording, see
the chart in the front of this
book.]

I. Reading Literature

Directions: *Read the poem "A Pinch of Salt" by Robert Graves.
Then, answer each question that follows.*

WHEN a dream is born in you
    With a sudden clamorous pain,
When you know the dream is true
    And lovely, with no flaw or stain,
5   O then, be careful, or with sudden clutch
You'll hurt the delicate thing you prize so much.

Dreams are like a bird that mocks,
    Flirting the feathers of his tail.
When you seize at the salt-box,
10   Over the hedge you'll see him sail.
Old birds are neither caught with salt nor chaff:
They watch you from the apple bough and laugh.

Poet, never chase the dream.
    Laugh yourself, and turn away.
15 <u>Mask</u> your hunger; let it seem
    Small matter if he come or stay;
But when he nestles in your hand at last,
Close up your fingers tight and hold him fast.

1. **Part A** The poem displays what **poetic form?**
   A. lyric   C. dramatic
   B. narrative   D. elegy

   Part B Which feature of the poem most clearly indicates its form?
   A. The action of the poem is conveyed through the words the characters speak.
   B. The poem has a regular rhyme scheme and all the elements of a short story.
   C. The poem is formal and mournful and reflects on a serious issue.
   D. The poem expresses the thoughts and feelings of a single speaker.

2. What is the **rhyme scheme** of each stanza?
   A. *abcabc*
   B. *abcdef*
   C. *ababcc*
   D. *ababaa*

3. Which of the following best states the main idea in the first stanza of the poem?
   A. Dreams are fragile and valuable things that should not be grabbed roughly or too quickly.
   B. A dream is like a tricky bird that is trying to escape one's sudden grasp.
   C. Dreams are similar to prizes that can be won in contests.
   D. Although dreams are said to convey truth, they can also cause great pain.

4. Which line of the poem contains a **simile?**
   A. line 1
   B. line 5
   C. line 7
   D. line 13

5. **Part A** What **sound device** is used in lines 7–10 of the poem?
   A. onomatopoeia   C. alliteration
   B. internal rhyme D. repetition

   Part B Which pair of words from lines 7–10 of the poem best supports the answer to part A?
   A. *tail* and *sail*   C. *feathers* and *tail*
   B. *see* and *sail*   D. *mocks* and *flirting*

6. Which of the following best **paraphrases** the words ". . . let it seem / Small matter if he come or stay" in lines 15–16 of the poem?
   A. Make him feel insignificant so he will leave you alone.
   B. Tell him he is so small that you cannot see him anymore.
   C. Act as if it is unimportant to you whether or not he is near.
   D. Only laugh with him about small, unimportant matters.

7. **Vocabulary** Which word or phrase is closest in meaning to the underlined word <u>mask</u> as it is used in the poem?
   A. feed   C. a face
   B. a covering   D. conceal

⏱ Timed Writing

8. In a well-developed essay, discuss the poet's use of multiple **levels of meaning.** Choose one line from each stanza. Explain the **literal meaning** of each line that you have chosen. Then analyze the **figurative meaning** of each line. Support your analysis with specific details from throughout the poem.

GO ON

II. Reading Informational Text

Common Core State Standards

RI.8.1, RI.8.2; L.8.1, L.8.1.c
[For full standards wording, see the chart in the front of this book.]

Directions: *Read the passages. Then, answer each question that follows.*

"You-Till"

Product Description: This 4-horsepower, gas-engine rotary tiller is equipped with spinning blades to loosen soil. It is perfect for preparing soil for planting vegetables or flowers.

Cost: $49.95

Easy-to-Use Instructions:
1. Fill the 1-gal. tank with gasoline. Replace gas cap tightly.
2. Press and hold the Start button.
3. Adjust lever on right handle to adjust motor speed.
4. Release Start button to turn off.

Caution! Always clear the soil of rocks and debris before using tiller!

"Hoe for Health"

This specially designed hoe is perfectly engineered to eliminate unnecessary back strain. It provides optimum balance and strength to the user.

Yours for the low cost of $14.99

How to Care for Your "Hoe for Health":
- Store in a shed or covered area.
- Clean your hoe of dirt and dry before storing.

---

1. According to the first passage, what is the purpose of a rotary tiller?
   A. It breaks up the soil.
   B. It plants vegetables or flowers.
   C. It helps you to spread seeds.
   D. It helps you spread the mulch layer.

2. **Part A** What features do the passages have in common?
   A. Both contain directions.
   B. Both give specific details about a product's parts.
   C. Both contain caution notes.
   D. Both list manufacturer information.

Part B Which answer choice accurately identifies details from the passages that clearly show what the passages have in common?
   A. One passage describes an engine and blades, and the other describes a comfortable handle.
   B. One passage gives instructions on use, and the other gives instructions on care.
   C. Both products cost less than fifty dollars.
   D. Both passages warn the customer about the danger of improper use.

III. Writing and Language Conventions

Directions: *Read the passage. Then, answer each question.*

(1) Many people have problems writing thank-you cards. (2) You might want to thank people for their kindness and generosity but you never get around to it. (3) I will give you a few easy steps to follow. (4) Buy a set of blank cards and envelopes. (5) Stamps should be bought, too. (6) Send an e-mail to your friends and relatives, asking them if they will send you their mailing addresses. (7) Put those addresses in an address book for safekeeping! (8) When someone does a nice deed for you, you can start writing: The envelopes, stamps, and address book is at your fingertips!

1. Which words are the **direct object** and the **indirect object** in sentence 3?

  A. The direct object is *you*, and the indirect object is *follow*.

  B. The direct object is *you*, and the indirect object is *steps*.

  C. The direct object is *steps*, and the indirect object is *follow*.

  D. The direct object is *steps*, and the indirect object is *you*.

2. Which possible revision to sentence 5 includes a **predicate noun?**

  A. Stamps should be bought in advance.

  B. Stamps are another item to keep on hand.

  C. You should buy stamps, too.

  D. Do not forget to buy stamps!

3. Which is an **imperative sentence?**

  A. sentence 2

  B. sentence 3

  C. sentence 7

  D. sentence 8

4. Which revision to the second half of sentence 6 corrects an error in **pronoun case?**

  A. asking them if them will send you their mailing addresses

  B. asking them if their will send you their mailing addresses

  C. asking them if they will send you them mailing addresses

  D. The sentence is correct as it is.

5. Which revision to sentence 8 corrects an error in **subject-verb agreement?**

  A. When someone do a nice deed for you, you can start writing: The envelopes, stamps, and address book is at your fingertips!

  B. When someone does a nice deed for you, you can starts writing: The envelopes, stamps, and address book is at your fingertips!

  C. When someone does you a nice deed, you can start writing: The envelopes, stamps, and address book is at your fingertips!

  D. When someone does a nice deed for you, you can start writing: The envelopes, stamps, and address book are at your fingertips!

CONSTRUCTED RESPONSE

 **Common Core State Standards**

RL.8.2, RL.8.4, RL.8.5;
W.8.2, W.8.4, W.8.7, W.8.9;
SL.8.1; L.8.1, L.8.5, L.8.5.a,
L.8.5.c
[For full standards wording, see
the chart in the front of this
book.]

Directions: *Follow the instructions to complete the tasks below as required by your teacher.*

As you work on each task, incorporate both general academic vocabulary and literary terms you learned in Parts 1 and 2 of this unit.

Writing

TASK 1 Literature [RL.8.4; W.8.9; L.8.5, L.8.5.c]

Analyze the Effect of Word Choice on a Poem's Meaning and Tone

Write an essay in which you analyze a poet's word choices and their impact on meaning and tone in a poem from Part 2 of this unit.

Part 1

- Review and evaluate a poem from Part 2 of this unit whose meaning and tone seem clear to you.
- As you are reviewing the poem, take notes on the poet's word choices.
- Answer the following questions: How do specific choices of words, phrases, and figurative language reflect or reinforce the poem's meaning? How do the connotations of particular words and phrases contribute to the poem's tone?

Part 2

- Write an essay in which you identify the poem's meaning and tone and explain how the poet's specific word choices convey the meaning and tone to the reader.
- Check your writing to ensure that the verb in each sentence agrees with the subject.

TASK 2 Literature [RL.8.5; W.8.4]

Contrast the Structure of Two Poems

Write an essay in which you contrast the structures of two poems from Part 2 of this unit.

- Choose two poems from this unit that have notable differences in structure. For example, you might choose the sonnet "The New Colossus" (p. 391) and the free verse poem "your little voice / Over the wires came leaping" (p. 407).
- Explain how the poems differ by contrasting such characteristics as rhyme scheme, line length, number of lines in each stanza, and pattern of stressed syllables (meter).
- Explain how the differences in structure contribute to the overall meaning and effect of the poem. Consider, for example, the formality or informality the structure creates.

TASK 3 Literature [RL.8.4; W.8.2; L.8.1]

Analyze the Sound Devices in a Poem

Write an essay in which you analyze the effect of sound devices in a poem from Part 2 of this unit.

- Select a poem that uses sound devices—such as rhyme, rhythm, or alliteration—in a powerful way.
- Identify examples of sound devices in the poem, stating the device used in each example.
- Describe the effect of these sound devices on the poem's tone. For example, explain whether they make the poem seem musical or mournful.
- Check your writing to make sure that each pronoun you use is in the appropriate case.

Speaking and Listening

TASK 4 Literature [RL.8.4; L.8.5, L.8.5.a]

Analyze Word Choice Through a Close Reading

Read aloud a poem from Part 2 of this unit to a group. Then, discuss the meaning of specific words and phrases in that poem.

- Select a poem in which the author has made several interesting word choices, using words for their connotative meanings or in a figurative sense.
- Read the poem aloud to a group. Then, review the poem, line by line.
- As you review, identify examples of figurative language, such as simile, metaphor, and personification, and analyze their meanings.
- Focus on the poet's word choice, distinguishing between the literal meanings and the connotations of particular words.
- Then, analyze how the poet's word choice and use of figurative language help to convey or reinforce the meaning of the poem.

TASK 5 Literature [RL.8.2; SL.8.1]

Hold a Panel Discussion About Three Poems

Choose three poems from Part 2 of this unit that address a similar topic and explain how each poet brings a different perspective to that topic.

- Identify three poems in this unit that have the same general topic, such as nature or history.
- Ask panel members to characterize the poet's attitude toward the topic and to identify one or more themes in each of the poems.
- To support their claims, panel members should identify specific lines or sections of the poem that best reflect the theme and the poet's attitude.
- Each panel member should ask questions and make comments that connect to and build on the comments of other panel members.

Research

TASK 6 Literature [W.8.7, W.8.9]

 ## What is the secret to reaching someone with words?

In Part 2 of this unit, you have read literature in which poets use carefully chosen words to express ideas in meaningful ways. Conduct a short research project into a particular songwriter's approach to creating meaningful lyrics. Then, use both the literature you have read and your research to reflect on this unit's Big Question. Follow these guidelines:

- Focus on one songwriter. Make sure sources, such as reviews, interviews, or biographical articles, are available for your subject.
- Gather information from at least two reliable sources. Your sources may be print or digital.

- Take notes on your research, focusing on the songwriter's goals and on the craft he or she uses in composing lyrics.
- In your notes, make sure to cite your sources.

When you have completed your research, write a response to the Big Question. Discuss how your initial ideas have changed or been reinforced. Support your response with an example from literature and an example from your research. Be sure to use academic vocabulary words (see p. 347) in your response.

"A man can know his father, or his son,
and there might still be nothing between
them but **loyalty and love** and mutual
incomprehension."

—**Marilynne Robinson**

GENERATIONS

The selections in this unit all relate to the Big Question: **What is the secret to reaching someone with words?** Different generations of people may have different outlooks—but they may also have much to teach one another. The texts that follow look at the ways in which people use words to reach across the generations, from grandparents talking with their grandchildren to strangers who meet on the street. As you read, consider how younger and older people interact, the value of different perspectives, and how people use words to connect across the generations.

◀ **CRITICAL VIEWING** What do the young person and the adult in the image appear to share? What might they want to communicate to each other? What might they not understand about each other?

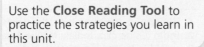

CLOSE READING TOOL

Use the **Close Reading Tool** to practice the strategies you learn in this unit.

READINGS IN PART 3

remembrance (smiles/hurts sweetly)
October 8, 1972

Old Man | Ricardo Sánchez

legacy ▶
(leg´ ə sē) *n.* something
physical or spiritual
handed down from
an ancestor

old man
with brown skin
talking of past
    when being shepherd
5   in utah, nevada, colorado and
             new mexico
was life lived freely;

old man,
    grandfather,
wise with time
10 running rivulets on face,
deep, rich furrows,[1]
    each one a **legacy**,
deep, rich memories
of life . . .
15   "you are indio,[2]
        among other things,"
he would tell me
    during nights spent
so long ago
20   amidst familial gatherings
in albuquerque . . .

old man, loved and respected,
he would speak sometimes
of pueblos,[3]

---

1. **rivulets . . . furrows** here, the wrinkles on the old man's face.
2. **indio** (ēn´dē ō) *n.* Indian; Native American.
3. **pueblos** (pweb´ lōz) *n.* here, Native American towns in central and northern New Mexico.

25   san juan, santa clara,
       and even santo domingo,
and his family, he would say,
came from there:
       some of our blood was here,
30   he would say,
       before the coming of coronado,[4]
other of our blood
       came with los españoles,[5]
and the mixture
35 was rich,
       though often painful . . .

old man,
who knew earth
       by its awesome **aromas**
40 and who felt
the heated sweetness
       of chile verde[6]
by his supple touch,
gone into dust is your body
45   with its stoic[7] look and resolution,
but your reality, old man, lives on
in a mindsoul touched by you . . .

Old Man . . .

◀ **aromas**
(ə rō´ məz) *n.* smells

---

4. **coronado** (kôr´ ə nä´ dō) sixteenth-century Spanish explorer Francisco Vásquez de Coronado, who journeyed through what is today the American Southwest.
5. **los españoles** (lôs es pä nyō´ lās) *n.* Spaniards.
6. **chile verde** (chē´ lā ver´ dā) *n.* green pepper.
7. **stoic** (stō´ ik) *adj.* calm in the face of suffering.

ABOUT THE AUTHOR

Ricardo Sánchez (1941–1995)

Born in El Paso, Texas, Ricardo Sánchez has been called the "grandfather of Chicano poetry." His family had roots in Mexican and Native American cultures, and most of Sánchez's work explores and celebrates his rich cultural heritage.

For My Sister Molly Who in the Fifties

ALICE WALKER

Once made a fairy rooster from
Mashed potatoes
Whose eyes I forget
But green onions were his tail
5 And his two legs were carrot sticks
A tomato slice his crown.
Who came home on vacation
When the sun was hot
and cooked
10 and cleaned
And minded least of all
The children's questions
A million or more
Pouring in on her
15 Who had been to school
And knew (and told us too) that certain
Words were no longer good
And taught me not to say us for we
No matter what "Sonny said" up the
20 road.

FOR MY SISTER MOLLY WHO IN THE FIFTIES
Knew Hamlet[1] well and read into the night
And coached me in my songs of Africa
A continent I never knew
25 But learned to love
Because "they" she said could carry
A tune
And spoke in accents never heard
In Eatonton.
30 Who read from *Prose and Poetry*
And loved to read "Sam McGee from Tennessee"[2]
On nights the fire was burning low
And Christmas wrapped in angel hair[3]
And I for one prayed for snow.

35 WHO IN THE FIFTIES
Knew all the written things that made
Us laugh and stories by
The hour   Waking up the story buds
Like fruit. Who walked among the flowers
40 And brought them inside the house
And smelled as good as they
And looked as bright.
Who made dresses, braided
Hair. Moved chairs about
45 Hung things from walls
Ordered baths
Frowned on wasp bites
And seemed to know the endings
Of all the tales
50 I had forgot.

---

1. **Hamlet** *Hamlet* is a play by William Shakespeare.
2. **"Sam McGee from Tennessee"** reference to the title character in the Robert Service poem "The Cremation of Sam McGee."
3. **angel hair** fine, white, filmy Christmas tree decoration.

WHO OFF INTO THE UNIVERSITY
Went exploring   To London and
To Rotterdam
Prague and to Liberia
55 Bringing back the news to us
Who knew none of it
But followed
crops and weather
funerals and
60 Methodist Homecoming;
easter speeches,
groaning church.

WHO FOUND ANOTHER WORLD
Another life   With gentlefolk
65 Far less trusting
And moved and moved and changed
Her name
And sounded precise
When she spoke   And frowned away
70 Our sloppishness.

WHO SAW US SILENT
Cursed with fear   A love burning
Inexpressible
And sent me money not for me
75 But for "College."
Who saw me grow through letters
The words misspelled   But not
The longing   Stretching
Growth
80 The tied and twisting
Tongue
Feet no longer bare
Skin no longer burnt against
The cotton.

85 WHO BECAME SOMEONE OVERHEAD
    A light   A thousand watts
    Bright and also blinding
    And saw my brothers cloddish
    And me destined to be
90 Wayward[4]
    My mother **remote**   My father
    A wearisome farmer
    With heartbreaking
    Nails.

95 FOR MY SISTER MOLLY WHO IN THE FIFTIES
    Found much
    Unbearable
    Who walked where few had
    Understood   And sensed our
100 Groping after light
    And saw some extinguished
    And no doubt mourned.

    FOR MY SISTER MOLLY WHO IN THE FIFTIES
    Left us.

◀ **remote**
(ri mōt´) *adj.* aloof;
cold; distant

---

4. wayward (wā´ wərd) *adj.* headstrong; disobedient.

ABOUT THE AUTHOR

Alice Walker (b. 1944)

Alice Walker is the youngest of eight children of Georgia farmers. Although an accident blinded her in one eye, Walker went on to become valedictorian of her local school. Her love of stories and learning inspired her to go to college; she received scholarships to Spelman College and Sarah Lawrence College. She is one of the best-known and best-loved African American writers. Walker's works frequently deal with the preservation of her culture and heritage. Her central characters must contend with issues such as poverty and discrimination, but Walker also portrays triumph over oppression and the power of loyalty.

READ

Comprehension

Reread all or part of the text to help you answer the following questions.

1. In "Old Man," what is the relationship of the speaker to the old man?

2. What did the old man talk about with the speaker at family gatherings?

3. List two things Molly does for the speaker in "For My Sister Molly Who in the Fifties."

4. What does Molly do at the end of the poem?

Research: Clarify Details Choose one unfamiliar detail from either poem and conduct research on it. Explain how your research clarifies the text.

Summarize Write an objective summary of each poem. Remember not to include your own opinions.

Language Study

Selection Vocabulary Write two synonyms for each boldface word from the selections. Then, use the word in a sentence of your own.

• running rivulets on face, / deep, rich furrows, / each one a **legacy** (Sánchez)

• old man, / who knew earth / by its awesome **aromas** (Sánchez)

• And me destined to be / Wayward / My mother **remote**. . . . (Walker)

Diction and Style Study lines 88–90 of "For My Sister Molly Who in the Fifties." Answer the questions that follow.

And saw my brothers cloddish / And me destined to be / Wayward

1. **(a)** In these lines, what does *cloddish* mean? **(b)** What might the associated meanings of the word *clod* suggest about the brothers' background?

2. **(a)** What does the poet mean by "destined to be / Wayward"? **(b)** How does the use of the word *destined* change the meaning of the word *saw* in line 88?

Conventions Read this passage (lines 21–27 of "For My Sister Molly Who in the Fifties"). Identify the pronouns and label them as subjective, objective, or possessive. Then, explain what the speaker's use of the pronoun "my" in "my songs" suggests about the speaker.

FOR MY SISTER MOLLY WHO IN THE FIFTIES /
Knew Hamlet well and read into the night /
And coached me in my songs of Africa /
A continent I never knew / But learned to love /
Because "they" she said could carry / A tune

Academic Vocabulary

The following words appear in blue in the instructions and questions on the facing page.

reinforce   **pattern**   **conveyed**

Copy the words into your notebook. For each, find a word that is built on the same base word (for example, *evaluate/evaluation*).

Literary Analysis

Reread the identified passages. Then, respond to the questions that follow.

> **Focus Passage 1** (*Sánchez, ll. 22–36, pp. 442–443*)
>
> old man, loved . . . though often painful . . .

> **Focus Passage 2** (*Walker, ll. 95–104, p. 447*)
>
> FOR MY SISTER . . . / Found much / Unbearable / . . . / Left us.

Key Ideas and Details

1. **(a) Identify:** From what pueblos did the old man's family come? **(b) Infer:** What group of ancestors lived in these pueblos?

2. **Identify:** What other group of ancestors does the old man mention?

Craft and Structure

3. **(a) Identify:** Identify two words or phrases from Spanish (other than names) in these lines. **(b) Analyze:** How does the mix of Spanish and English **reinforce** the meaning of these lines?

4. **Analyze:** How does the poet use the indentation of lines to show the relationships among ideas?

Integration of Knowledge and Ideas

5. **Interpret:** What do you think the speaker means when he says that the mixture of ancestral blood was "rich, / though often painful"?

Key Ideas and Details

1. **Interpret:** What does the speaker mean in saying that Molly "walked where few had / Understood"?

2. **(a) Infer:** Whom or what did Molly see "extinguished"? **(b) Draw Conclusions:** Why did Molly leave?

Craft and Structure

3. **Compare:** What is the effect the poet creates by her use of line breaks in lines 95–100?

4. **Interpret:** What is the tone **conveyed** by the phrase "no doubt"? Explain.

Integration of Knowledge and Ideas

5. **Justify:** Could Molly have remained true to herself if she had stayed with the family? Explain.

Free Verse and Structure

In **free verse,** or poetry without a regular **pattern** of rhythm or rhyme, poets create **structure** by arranging words, lines, and groups of lines in particular ways. Reread these free verse poems, and take notes on ways in which the poets use structure.

1. **(a)** What is similar about Sánchez's and Walker's use of structure? **(b)** How do the structures used by the two poets differ?

2. **Generations:** Compare how the poets use structural elements, such as repeated phrases, lists, and breaks between stanzas, to pay tribute to an elder.

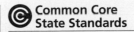 **Common Core State Standards**

RL.8.1, RL.8.4, RL.8.5; L.8.3, L.8.4, L.8.5.b, L.8.6
[For full standards wording, see the chart in the front of this book.]

DISCUSS

From Text to Topic **Partner Discussion**

Discuss the following passages from the poems with a partner. Take notes during the discussion. Contribute your own ideas, and support them with examples from the text.

from "Old Man"	from "For My Sister Molly Who in the Fifties"

15 "you are indio,
      among other things,"
he would tell me
      during nights spent
so long ago
20   amidst familial gatherings
in albuquerque . . .
	WHO SAW US SILENT
	Cursed with fear A love burning
	Inexpressible
	And sent me money not for me
	75 But for "College."
	Who saw me grow through
	    letters
	The words misspelled. . . .

QUESTIONS FOR DISCUSSION

1. Compare the ways in which the old man and Molly each support a younger person.
2. Why is this support important?
3. What do these passages suggest about the ties between generations?

WRITE

Writing to Sources **Informative Text**

Assignment

Write a **comparison-and-contrast essay** analyzing the theme and mood in "Old Man" and "For My Sister Molly Who in the Fifties."

Prewriting and Planning Take notes on details in the poems that convey mood, or general feeling, and theme, or a central insight.

Drafting As you draft, cite specific examples from the poems to support your points. Clearly indicate the relationship of each piece of evidence to the point it supports, as in the example.

Sample: Integrating Textual Evidence

When Sánchez uses the word *furrows*, he emphasizes the old man's connection to farming and the earth. [connects to main idea: The old man represents a past way of life.]

Revising Make sure you have used transitional words and phrases, such as *in contrast* and *similarly,* to clarify comparisons.

Editing and Proofreading Reread your essay, making sure you have correctly used subjective, objective, and possessive pronouns.

CONVENTIONS

To check the case of a pronoun in a compound subject, such as "He and the old man," remove the other nouns and pronouns in the subject and see if the sentence still makes sense.

RESEARCH

Research **Investigate the Topic**

Generations Across Cultures In "Old Man," Sánchez honors what he learned about his heritage from his grandfather. In "For My Sister Molly Who in the Fifties," Molly grows apart from her parents. Relations between generations can vary from family to family, and from culture to culture. In some cultures, elders are keepers of wisdom and traditions; in others, older people who are no longer physically productive are viewed as burdens.

Assignment

Conduct research to learn about relations between generations in two different cultures. Consult books, magazines, and Web sites on anthropology and sociology. Take clear notes and carefully identify your sources. Once you have completed research, identify parallels or contrasts between attitudes in the cultures you have studied and the situations in the poems. Share your findings in a **speech** or **presentation** for the class.

PREPARATION FOR ESSAY

You may use the results of this research project to support your ideas in the essay you will write at the end of this section.

Gather Sources Locate authoritative print and electronic sources. Primary sources, such as journals, letters, or anthropological observations, provide authentic firsthand information. You may also want to use secondary sources, such as sociological studies. Look for sources that feature expert authors and up-to-date information.

Take Notes Take notes on each source, either electronically or on note cards. Use an organized note-taking strategy.

- Color code your notes, using highlighters or cards of different colors for each culture.

- Carefully copy relevant quotations from primary sources to add interest to your presentation.

- Write the source on each note card so that you can easily assemble citations for all quotations and references in your draft.

Synthesize Multiple Sources Use what you have learned to draw conclusions about relationships between generations, relating your research to one or both of the poems. Assemble data from your sources and organize it in an outline. Create a Works Cited list as described in the Citing Sources section of the Introductory Unit in this textbook.

Organize and Present Ideas Review your outline and practice delivering your presentation. Use formal English as you present.

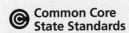

Common Core State Standards

W.8.2, W.8.2.b, W.8.2.c, W.8.4, W.8.7, W.8.8, W.8.9, W.8.9.a; SL.8.1, SL.8.4, SL.8.6
[For full standards wording, see the chart in the front of this book.]

The Medicine Bag  Virginia Driving Hawk Sneve

My kid sister Cheryl and I always bragged about our Sioux[1] grandpa, Joe Iron Shell. Our friends, who had always lived in the city and only knew about Indians from movies and TV, were impressed by our stories. Maybe we exaggerated and made Grandpa and the reservation sound glamorous, but when we'd return home to Iowa after our yearly summer visit to Grandpa, we always had some exciting tale to tell.

We always had some authentic Sioux article to show our listeners. One year Cheryl had new moccasins[2] that Grandpa had made. On another visit he gave me a small, round, flat, rawhide drum that was decorated with a painting of a warrior riding a horse. He taught me a real Sioux chant to sing while I beat the drum with a leather-covered stick that had a feather on the end. Man that really made an impression.

We never showed our friends Grandpa's picture. Not that we were ashamed of him, but because we knew that the glamorous tales we told didn't go with the real thing. Our friends would have laughed at the picture because Grandpa wasn't tall and stately like TV Indians. His hair wasn't in braids but hung in stringy, gray strands on his neck, and he was old. He was our great-grandfather, and he didn't live in a tepee, but all by himself in a part log, part tar-paper shack on the Rosebud Reservation in South Dakota. So when Grandpa came to visit us, I was so ashamed and embarrassed I could've died.

There are a lot of yippy poodles and other fancy little dogs in our neighborhood, but they usually barked singly at the mailman from the safety of their own yards. Now it sounded as if a whole pack of mutts were barking together in one place.

I got up and walked to the curb to see what the commotion was. About a block away I saw a crowd of little kids yelling, with the dogs yipping and growling around someone who was walking down the middle of the street.

I watched the group as it slowly came closer and saw that in the center of the strange procession was a man wearing a tall black hat. He'd pause now and then to peer at something in his hand and then at the houses on either side of the street. I felt

◄ **authentic**
(ô then′ tik) *adj.*
genuine; real

◄ **procession**
(prō sesh′ ən) *n.*
a group moving
forward, as in
a parade

---

1. **Sioux** (sōō′) *adj.* belonging to a Native American tribe of the northern United States and southern Canada.
2. **moccasins** (mäk′ ə sənz) *n.* soft shoes traditionally made from animal hide.

cold and hot at the same time as I recognized the man. "Oh, no!" I whispered. "It's Grandpa!"

I stood on the curb, unable to move even though I wanted to run and hide. Then I got mad when I saw how the yippy dogs were growling and nipping at the old man's baggy pant legs and how wearily he poked them away with his cane. "Stupid mutts," I said as I ran to rescue Grandpa.

When I kicked and hollered at the dogs to get away, they put their tails between their legs and scattered. The kids ran to the curb where they watched me and the old man.

"Grandpa," I said and felt pretty dumb when my voice cracked. I reached for his beat-up old tin suitcase, which was tied shut with a rope. But he set it down right in the street and shook my hand.

"*Hau, Takoza*, Grandchild," he greeted me formally in Sioux.

All I could do was stand there with the whole neighborhood watching and shake the hand of the leather-brown old man. I saw how his gray hair straggled from under his big black hat, which had a drooping feather in its crown. His rumpled black suit hung like a sack over his stooped frame. As he shook my hand, his coat fell open to expose a bright red satin shirt with a beaded bolo tie under the collar. His get-up wasn't out of place on the reservation, but it sure was here, and I wanted to sink right through the pavement.

"Hi," I muttered with my head down. I tried to pull my hand away when I felt his bony hand trembling, and looked up to see fatigue in his face. I felt like crying. I couldn't think of anything to say so I picked up Grandpa's suitcase, took his arm, and guided him up the driveway to our house.

Mom was standing on the steps. I don't know how long she'd been watching, but her hand was over her mouth and she looked as if she couldn't believe what she saw. Then she ran to us.

"Grandpa," she gasped. "How in the world did you get here?"

She checked her move to embrace Grandpa and I remembered that such a display of affection is **unseemly** to the Sioux and would embarrass him.

"*Hau*, Marie," he said as he shook Mom's hand. She smiled and took his other arm.

As we supported him up the steps, the door banged open and Cheryl came bursting out of the house. She was all smiles and was so obviously glad to see Grandpa that I was ashamed of how I felt.

unseemly ▶
(un sēm´ lē) *adj.*
inappropriate

"Grandpa!" she yelled happily. "You came to see us!"

Grandpa smiled, and Mom and I let go of him as he stretched out his arms to my ten-year-old sister, who was still young enough to be hugged.

"*Wicincala*, little girl," he greeted her and then collapsed.

He had fainted. Mom and I carried him into her sewing room, where we had a spare bed.

After we had Grandpa on the bed, Mom stood there helplessly patting his shoulder.

"Shouldn't we call the doctor, Mom?" I suggested, since she didn't seem to know what to do.

"Yes," she agreed with a sigh. "You make Grandpa comfortable, Martin."

I reluctantly moved to the bed. I knew Grandpa wouldn't want to have Mom undress him, but I didn't want to, either. He was so skinny and frail that his coat slipped off easily. When I loosened his tie and opened his shirt collar, I felt a small leather pouch that hung from a thong around his neck. I left it alone and moved to remove his boots. The scuffed old cowboy boots were tight, and he moaned as I put pressure on his legs to jerk them off.

I put the boots on the floor and saw why they fit so tight. Each one was stuffed with money. I looked at the bills that lined the boots and started to ask about them, but Grandpa's eyes were closed again.

Mom came back with a basin of water. "The doctor thinks Grandpa is suffering from heat exhaustion," she explained as she bathed Grandpa's face. Mom gave a big sigh, "*Oh, hinh*, Martin. How do you suppose he got here?"

We found out after the doctor's visit. Grandpa was angrily sitting up in bed while Mom tried to feed him some soup.

"Tonight you let Marie feed you, Grandpa," spoke my dad, who had gotten home from work just as the doctor was leaving. "You're not really sick," he said as he gently pushed Grandpa back against the pillows. "The doctor said you just got too tired and hot after your long trip."

Grandpa relaxed, and between sips of soup, he told us of his journey. Soon after our visit to him, Grandpa decided that he would like to see where his only living descendants lived and what our home was like. Besides, he admitted sheepishly, he was lonesome after we left.

I knew that everybody felt as guilty as I did—especially Mom. Mom was all Grandpa had left. So even after she married my dad, who's a white man and teaches in the college in our city, and after Cheryl and I were born, Mom made sure that every summer we spent a week with Grandpa.

I never thought that Grandpa would be lonely after our visits, and none of us noticed how old and weak he had become. But Grandpa knew, and so he came to us. He had ridden on buses for two and a half days. When he arrived in the city, tired and stiff from sitting for so long, he set out, walking, to find us.

He had stopped to rest on the steps of some building downtown, and a policeman found him. The cop, according to Grandpa, was a good man who took him to the bus stop and waited until the bus came and told the driver to let Grandpa out at Bell View Drive. After Grandpa got off the bus, he started walking again. But he couldn't see the house numbers on the other side when he walked on the sidewalk, so he walked in the middle of the street. That's when all the little kids and dogs followed him.

I knew everybody felt as bad as I did. Yet I was so proud of this eighty-six-year-old man, who had never been away from the reservation, having the courage to travel so far alone.

"You found the money in my boots?" he asked Mom.

"Martin did," she answered, and roused herself to scold. "Grandpa, you shouldn't have carried so much money. What if someone had stolen it from you?"

Grandpa laughed. "I would've known if anyone tried to take the boots off my feet. The money is what I've saved for a long time—a hundred dollars—for my funeral. But you take it now to buy groceries so that I won't be a burden to you while I am here."

"That won't be necessary, Grandpa," Dad said. "We are honored to have you with us, and you will never be a burden. I am only sorry that we never thought to bring you home with us this summer and spare you the discomfort of a long trip."

Grandpa was pleased. "Thank you," he answered. "But do not feel bad that you didn't bring me with you, for I would not have come then. It was not time." He said this in such a way that no one could argue with him. To Grandpa and the Sioux, he once told me, a thing would be done when it was the right time to do it, and that's the way it was.

"Also," Grandpa went on, looking at me, "I have come because it is soon time for Martin to have the medicine bag."

We all knew what that meant. Grandpa thought he was going to die, and he had to follow the tradition of his family to pass the medicine bag, along with its history, to the oldest male child.

"Even though the boy," he said still looking at me, "bears a white man's name, the medicine bag will be his."

I didn't know what to say. I had the same hot and cold feeling that I had when I first saw Grandpa in the street. The medicine bag was the dirty leather pouch I had found around his neck. "I could never wear such a thing," I almost said aloud. I thought of having my friends see it in gym class or at the swimming pool and could imagine the smart things they would say. But I just swallowed hard and took a step toward the bed. I knew I would have to take it.

But Grandpa was tired. "Not now, Martin," he said, waving his hand in dismissal. "It is not time. Now I will sleep."

So that's how Grandpa came to be with us for two months. My friends kept asking to come see the old man, but I put them off. I told myself that I didn't want them laughing at Grandpa. But even as I made excuses, I knew it wasn't Grandpa that I was afraid they'd laugh at.

Nothing bothered Cheryl about bringing her friends to see Grandpa. Every day after school started, there'd be a crew of giggling little girls or round-eyed little boys crowded around the old man on the patio, where he'd gotten in the habit of sitting every afternoon.

Grandpa would smile in his gentle way and patiently answer their questions, or he'd tell them stories of brave warriors, ghosts, animals; and the kids listened in awed silence. Those little guys thought Grandpa was great.

Finally, one day after school, my friends came home with me because nothing I said stopped them. "We're going to see the great Indian of Bell View Drive," said Hank, who was supposed to be my best friend. "My brother has seen him three times so he oughta be well enough to see us."

When we got to my house, Grandpa was sitting on the patio. He had on his red shirt, but today he also wore a fringed leather vest that was decorated with beads. Instead of his usual cowboy boots, he had solidly beaded moccasins on his feet that stuck out of his black trousers. Of course, he had his old black hat on—he was seldom without it. But it had been brushed, and the feather in the beaded headband was proudly erect, its tip a brighter white. His hair lay in silver strands over the red shirt collar.

I stared just as my friends did, and I heard one of them murmur, "Wow!"

Grandpa looked up, and, when his eyes met mine, they twinkled as if he were laughing inside. He nodded to me, and my face got all hot. I could tell that he had known all along I was afraid he'd embarrass me in front of my friends.

"*Hau, hoksilas,* boys," he greeted and held out his hand.

My buddies passed in a single file and shook his hand as I introduced them. They were so polite I almost laughed. "How, there, Grandpa," and even a "How-do-you-do, sir."

"You look fine, Grandpa," I said as the guys sat on the lawn chairs or on the patio floor.

"*Hanh,* yes," he agreed. "When I woke up this morning, it seemed the right time to dress in the good clothes. I knew that my grandson would be bringing his friends."

"You guys want some lemonade or something?" I offered. No one answered. They were listening to Grandpa as he started telling how he'd killed the deer from which his vest was made.

Grandpa did most of the talking while my friends were there. I was so proud of him and amazed at how respectfully quiet my buddies were. Mom had to chase them home at supper time. As they left, they shook Grandpa's hand again and said to me,

"Martin, he's really great!"

"Yeah, man! Don't blame you for keeping him to yourself."

"Can we come back?"

But after they left, Mom said, "No more visitors for a while, Martin. Grandpa won't admit it, but his strength hasn't returned. He likes having company, but it tires him."

That evening Grandpa called me to his room before he went to sleep. "Tomorrow," he said, "when you come home, it will be time to give you the medicine bag."

I felt a hard squeeze from where my heart is supposed to be and was scared, but I answered, "OK, Grandpa."

All night I had weird dreams about thunder and lightning on a high hill. From a distance I heard the slow beat of a drum. When I woke up in the morning, I felt as if I hadn't slept at all. At school it seemed as if the day would never end and, when it finally did, I ran home.

Grandpa was in his room, sitting on the bed. The shades were down, and the place was dim and cool. I sat on the floor in front of Grandpa, but he didn't even look at me. After what seemed a long time he spoke.

"I sent your mother and sister away. What you will hear today is only for a man's ears. What you will receive is only for a man's hands." He fell silent, and I felt shivers down my back.

"My father in his early manhood," Grandpa began, "made a vision quest[3] to find a spirit guide for his life. You cannot understand how it was in that time, when the great Teton Sioux were first made to stay on the reservation. There was a strong need for guidance from *Wakantanka*,[4] the Great Spirit. But too many of the young men were filled with despair and hatred. They thought it was hopeless to search for a vision when the glorious life was gone and only the hated confines of a reservation lay ahead. But my father held to the old ways.

"He carefully prepared for his quest with a purifying sweat bath, and then he went alone to a high butte top[5] to fast and pray. After three days he received his sacred dream—in which he found, after long searching, the white man's iron. He did not understand his vision of finding something belonging to the white people, for in that time they were the enemy. When he came down from the butte to cleanse himself at the stream below, he found the remains of a campfire and the broken shell of an iron kettle. This was a sign that reinforced his dream.

3. **vision quest** *n.* in Native American cultures, a difficult search for spiritual guidance.
4. **Wakantanka** (wä´ kən tank´ ə) *n.* Sioux religion's most important spirit—the creator of the world.
5. **butte** (byo͞ot) **top** *n.* isolated mountain top with steep sides.

He took a piece of the iron for his medicine bag, which he had made of elk skin years before, to prepare for his quest.

"He returned to his village, where he told his dream to the wise old men of the tribe. They gave him the name *Iron Shell*, but neither did they understand the meaning of the dream. The first Iron Shell kept the piece of iron with him at all times and believed it gave him protection from the evils of those unhappy days.

"Then a terrible thing happened to Iron Shell. He and several other young men were taken from their homes by the soldiers and sent far away to a white man's boarding school. He was angry and lonesome for his parents and the young girl he had wed before he was taken away. At first Iron Shell resisted the teacher's attempts to change him, and he did not try to learn. One day it was his turn to work in the school's blacksmith shop. As he walked into the place, he knew that his medicine had brought him there to learn and work with the white man's iron.

"Iron Shell became a blacksmith and worked at the trade when he returned to the reservation. All of his life he treasured the medicine bag. When he was old, and I was a man, he gave it to me, for no one made the vision quest any more."

Grandpa quit talking, and I stared in disbelief as he covered his face with his hands. His shoulders were shaking with quiet sobs, and I looked away until he began to speak again.

"I kept the bag until my son, your mother's father, was a man and had to leave us to fight in the war across the ocean. I gave him the bag, for I believed it would protect him in battle, but he did not take it with him. He was afraid that he would lose it. He died in a faraway place."

Again Grandpa was still, and I felt his grief around me.

"My son," he went on after clearing his throat, "had only a daughter, and it is not proper for her to know of these things."

He unbuttoned his shirt, pulled out the leather pouch, and lifted it over his head. He held it in his hand, turning it over and over as if memorizing how it looked.

"In the bag," he said as he opened it and removed two objects, "is the broken shell of the iron kettle, a pebble from the butte, and a piece of the sacred sage."[6] He held the pouch upside down and dust drifted down.

"After the bag is yours you must put a piece of prairie sage within and never open it again until you pass it on to your

---

6. sage (sāj) *n.* type of herb.

son." He replaced the pebble and the piece of iron, and tied the bag.

I stood up, somehow knowing I should. Grandpa slowly rose from the bed and stood upright in front of me holding the bag before my face. I closed my eyes and waited for him to slip it over my head. But he spoke.

"No, you need not wear it." He placed the soft leather bag in my right hand and closed my other hand over it. "It would not be right to wear it in this time and place where no one will understand. Put it safely away until you are again on the reservation. Wear it then, when you replace the sacred sage."

Grandpa turned and sat again on the bed. Wearily he leaned his head against the pillow. "Go," he said. "I will sleep now."

"Thank you, Grandpa," I said softly and left with the bag in my hands.

That night Mom and Dad took Grandpa to the hospital. Two weeks later I stood alone on the lonely prairie of the reservation and put the sacred sage in my medicine bag.

ABOUT THE AUTHOR

Virginia Driving Hawk Sneve (b. 1933)

Virginia Driving Hawk Sneve grew up on the Rosebud Reservation in South Dakota. While Sneve's parents traveled off the reservation to find seasonal work, Sneve and her brother spent summers at the homes of their two grandmothers. These "strong, dignified, and loving" women were avid storytellers, sharing traditional Sioux legends and folk tales that became an inspiration for Sneve's work. As a Sioux mother, Sneve quickly realized that few children's books accurately portrayed Native American culture. She began writing in the early 1970s to correct this gap in literature. Sneve has spent her award-winning career depicting Native Americans realistically. She notes, "I write from my own experience and about Native Americans I've known all my life." Her work demonstrates the enduring strength and pride of Native American culture. In 2000, President Bill Clinton awarded her a National Humanities Medal.

READ

Comprehension

Reread all or part of the text to help you answer the following questions.

1. Why is the narrator embarrassed when his great-grandfather comes to visit?

2. Name three reasons Grandpa left the reservation.

3. At the end of the story, what does Grandpa ask Martin to do?

Research: Clarify Details Choose one unfamiliar detail from the story and conduct research on it. Explain how your research clarifies the text.

Summarize Write an objective summary of the story. Remember not to include your own opinions or judgments.

Language Study

Selection Vocabulary Define each boldface word from the selection and use it in a sentence of your own.

• We always had some **authentic** Sioux article to show our listeners.

• . . . in the center of the strange **procession** was a man wearing a tall black hat.

• . . . I remembered that such a display of affection is **unseemly** to the Sioux and would embarrass him.

Literary Analysis

Reread the identified passage. Then, respond to the questions that follow.

> **Focus Passage** (pp. 460–61)
> "In the bag," . . . in my hands.

Key Ideas and Details

1. When may Martin open the bag?

Craft and Structure

2. **(a) Interpret:** How does Martin seem to feel about the gift? Explain which details

suggest his feelings. **(b) Interpret:** Why does the author suggest Martin's feelings, rather than stating them directly?

3. **Support:** Which characters' actions in the passage give the scene the quality of a ritual or ceremony? Explain.

Integration of Knowledge and Ideas

4. **Apply:** Why are some "gifts" that are passed from one generation to another also responsibilities? Cite story details.

Symbolism

A **symbol** is something that stands for, or **represents**, a larger meaning.

1. **(a)** What does the medicine bag symbolize? **(b) Generations:** What does passing the bag to a new generation represent?

2. **(a)** Contrast Martin's **initial** embarrassment about his great-grandfather with his response to the gift. What has changed? **(b) Generations:** What does Martin's action of adding the sage symbolize?

DISCUSS • RESEARCH • WRITE

From Text to Topic **Group Discussion**

Discuss the following passage with a group of classmates. Take notes during the discussion. Contribute your own ideas, and support them with textual evidence. If others do not support their ideas with evidence, respectfully ask them to provide support.

> My friends kept asking to come see the old man, but I put them off. I told myself that I didn't want them laughing at Grandpa. But even as I made excuses, I knew it wasn't Grandpa that I was afraid they'd laugh at.

Research **Investigate the Topic**

Traditions In "The Medicine Bag," Grandpa explains that many young men despaired and would not go on vision quests after the Sioux had been forced to live on reservations.

Assignment

Conduct research to learn more about how the Sioux or another Native American group passes its heritage from one generation to the next. Contrast the group's **traditions** as they existed in the past with ways the group relates to its heritage today. Consult primary sources as well as history texts and online sources. Take clear notes and carefully identify your sources. Record your notes in a **comparison chart.**

Writing to Sources **Narrative Retelling**

"The Medicine Bag" tells of an encounter between generations— Grandpa, from an older generation, passes something on to Martin, from the younger generation.

Assignment

Write a **narrative retelling** of a story about an interaction between generations. The story you retell may be from a work such as a movie, or it may be a story from your own family. Follow these steps:

- Introduce the problem or conflict.
- Use figurative language to create vivid descriptions.
- Use dialogue to create a strong sense of the characters.
- Provide a conclusion in which you compare the story to Martin's experience.

QUESTIONS FOR DISCUSSION

1. What is Martin's main concern in this passage? What does this concern reveal about him?

2. In what ways is behavior like Martin's more typical of young people than adults?

PREPARATION FOR ESSAY

You may use the results of this research project to support your ideas in the essay you will write at the end of this section.

ACADEMIC VOCABULARY

Academic terms appear in blue on these pages. Use a dictionary to find their definitions. Then, use the words as you speak and write about the text.

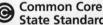 **Common Core State Standards**

RL.8.1, RL.8.2, RL.8.3, RL.8.4; W.8.3, W.8.3.a, W.8.3.b, W.8.3.e, W.8.4, W.8.7, W.8.8; SL.8.1, SL.8.1.a, SL.8.1.c, SL.8.3; L.8.4, L.8.6
[For full standards wording, see the chart in the front of this book.]

CUB PILOT ON THE
Mississippi

MARK TWAIN

During the two or two and a half years of my apprenticeship[1] I served under many pilots, and had experience of many kinds of steamboatmen and many varieties of steamboats. I am to this day profiting somewhat by that experience; for in that brief, sharp schooling, I got personally and familiarly acquainted with about all the different types of human nature that are to be found in fiction, biography, or history.

The fact is daily borne in upon me that the average shore-employment requires as much as forty years to equip a man with this sort of an education. When I say I am still profiting by this thing, I do not mean that it has constituted me a judge of men—no, it has not done that, for judges of men are born, not made. My profit is various in kind and degree, but the feature of it which I value most is the zest which that early experience has given to my later reading. When I find a well-drawn character in fiction or biography I generally take a warm personal interest in him, for the reason that I have known him before—met him on the river.

The figure that comes before me oftenest, out of the shadows of that vanished time, is that of Brown, of the steamer *Pennsylvania*. He was a middle-aged, long, slim, bony, smooth-shaven, horsefaced, ignorant, stingy,

---

1. apprenticeship (ə pren´ tis ship´) *n.* time spent working for a master craftsperson in return for instruction in his or her craft.

malicious, snarling, fault-hunting, mote magnifying tyrant.[2] I early got the habit of coming on watch with dread at my heart. No matter how good a time I might have been having with the off-watch below, and no matter how high my spirits might be when I started aloft, my soul became lead in my body the moment I approached the pilothouse.

I still remember the first time I ever entered the presence of that man. The boat had backed out from St. Louis and was "straightening down." I ascended to the pilothouse in high feather, and very proud to be semiofficially a member of the executive family of so fast and famous a boat. Brown was at the wheel. I paused in the middle of the room, all fixed to make my bow, but Brown did not look around. I thought he took a furtive glance at me out of the corner of his eye, but as not even this notice was repeated, I judged I had been mistaken. By this time he was picking his way among some dangerous "breaks" abreast the woodyards; therefore it would not be proper to interrupt him; so I stepped softly to the high bench and took a seat.

There was silence for ten minutes; then my new boss turned and inspected me deliberately and painstakingly from head to heel for about—as it seemed to me—a quarter of an hour. After which he removed his countenance[3] and I saw it no more for some seconds; then it came around once more, and this question greeted me: "Are you Horace Bigsby's cub?"

"Yes, sir."

After this there was a pause and another inspection. Then: "What's your name?"

I told him. He repeated it after me. It was probably the only thing he ever forgot; for although I was with him many months he never addressed himself to me in any other way than "Here!" and then his command followed.

"Where was you born?"

"In Florida, Missouri."

A pause. Then: "Dern sight better stayed there!"

By means of a dozen or so of pretty direct questions, he pumped my family history out of me.

> By means of a dozen or so of pretty direct questions, he pumped my family history out of me.

---

2. **mote magnifying tyrant** a cruel authority figure who exaggerates every tiny fault.
3. **countenance** (koun′ t'n əns) *n.* face.

The leads[4] were going now in the first crossing. This interrupted the inquest. When the leads had been laid in he resumed:

"How long you been on the river?"

I told him. After a pause:

"Where'd you get them shoes?"

I gave him the information.

"Hold up your foot!"

I did so. He stepped back, examined the shoe minutely and contemptuously, scratching his head thoughtfully, tilting his high sugarloaf hat well forward to facilitate the operation, then ejaculated, "Well, I'll be dod derned!" and returned to his wheel.

What occasion there was to be dod derned about it is a thing which is still as much of a mystery to me now as it was then. It must have been all of fifteen minutes—fifteen minutes of dull, homesick silence—before that long horse-face swung round upon me again—and then what a change! It was as red as fire, and every muscle in it was working. Now came this shriek: "Here! You going to set there all day?"

I lit in the middle of the floor, shot there by the electric suddenness of the surprise. As soon as I could get my voice I said apologetically: "I have had no orders, sir."

"You've had no *orders*! My, what a fine bird we are! We must have *orders*! Our father was a *gentleman*—and *we've* been to *school*. Yes, *we* are a gentleman, *too*, and got to have *orders*! Orders, is it? Orders is what you want! Dod dern my skin, *I'll* learn you to swell yourself up and blow around *here* about your dod-derned *orders*! G'way from the wheel!" (I had approached it without knowing it.)

I moved back a step or two and stood as in a dream, all my senses stupefied by this frantic assault.

"What you standing there for? Take that ice-pitcher down to the texas-tender![5] Come, move along, and don't you be all day about it!"

The moment I got back to the pilothouse Brown said: "Here! What was you doing down there all this time?"

"I couldn't find the texas-tender; I had to go all the way to the pantry."

"Derned likely story! Fill up the stove."

---

4. **leads** (ledz) *n.* weights that are lowered to test the depth of the river.
5. **texas-tender** the waiter in the officers' quarters. On Mississippi steamboats, rooms were named after the states. The officers' area, being the largest, was named after Texas, then the largest state.

I proceeded to do so. He watched me like a cat. Presently he shouted: "Put down that shovel! Derndest numskull I ever saw—ain't even got sense enough to load up a stove."

All through the watch this sort of thing went on. Yes, and the subsequent watches were much like it during a stretch of months. As I have said, I soon got the habit of coming on duty with dread. The moment I was in the presence, even in the darkest night, I could feel those yellow eyes upon me, and knew their owner was watching for a pretext to spit out some venom on me. Preliminarily he would say: "Here! Take the wheel."

Two minutes later: "*Where* in the nation you going to? Pull her down! pull her down!"

After another moment: "Say! You going to hold her all day? Let her go—meet her! meet her!"

Then he would jump from the bench, snatch the wheel from me, and meet her himself, pouring out wrath upon me all the time.

George Ritchie was the other pilot's cub. He was having good times now; for his boss, George Ealer, was as kind-hearted as Brown wasn't. Ritchie had steered for Brown the season before; consequently, he knew exactly how to entertain himself and plague me, all by the one operation. Whenever I took the wheel for a moment on Ealer's watch, Ritchie would sit back on the bench and play Brown, with continual ejaculations of "Snatch her! Snatch her! Derndest mudcat I ever saw!" "Here! Where are you going *now*? Going to run over that snag?" "Pull her *down*! Don't you hear me? Pull her *down*!" "There she goes! *Just* as I expected! I *told* you not to cramp that reef. G'way from the wheel!"

So I always had a rough time of it, no matter whose watch it was; and sometimes it seemed to me that Ritchie's good-natured badgering was pretty nearly as aggravating as Brown's dead-earnest nagging.

I often wanted to kill Brown, but this would not answer. A cub had to take everything his boss gave, in the way of vigorous comment and criticism; and we all believed that there was a United States law making it a penitentiary offense to strike or threaten a pilot who was on duty.

However, I could *imagine* myself killing Brown; there was no law against that; and that was the thing I used always to do the moment I was abed. Instead of going over my river in my

As I have said, I soon got the habit of coming on duty with dread.

mind, as was my duty, I threw business aside for pleasure, and killed Brown. I killed Brown every night for months; not in old, stale, commonplace ways, but in new and picturesque ones—ways that were sometimes surprising for freshness of design and ghastliness of situation and environment.

Brown was *always* watching for a pretext to find fault; and if he could find no plausible pretext, he would invent one. He would scold you for shaving a shore, and for not shaving it; for hugging a bar, and for not hugging it; for "pulling down" when not invited, and for *not* pulling down when not invited; for firing up without orders, and *for* waiting for orders. In a word, it was his invariable rule to find fault with *everything* you did and another invariable rule of his was to throw all his remarks (to you) into the form of an insult.

One day we were approaching New Madrid, bound down and heavily laden. Brown was at one side of the wheel, steering; I was at the other, standing by to "pull down" or "shove up." He cast a furtive glance at me every now and then. I had long ago learned what that meant; viz., he was trying to invent a trap for me. I wondered what shape it was going to take. By and by he stepped back from the wheel and said in his usual snarly way:

"Here! See if you've got gumption enough to round her to."

This was simply *bound* to be a success; nothing could prevent it; for he had never allowed me to round the boat to before; consequently, no matter how I might do the thing, he could find free fault with it. He stood back there with his greedy eye on me, and the result was what might have been foreseen: I lost my head in a quarter of a minute, and didn't know what I was about; I started too early to bring the boat around, but detected a green gleam of joy in Brown's eye, and corrected my mistake. I started around once more while too high up, but corrected myself again in time. I made other false moves, and still managed to save myself; but at last I grew so confused and anxious that I tumbled into the very worst blunder of all—I got too far *down* before beginning to fetch the boat around. Brown's chance was come.

His face turned red with passion; he made one bound, hurled me across the house with a sweep of his arm, spun the wheel down, and began to pour out a stream of vituperation[6] upon me which lasted till he was out of breath. In the course of

---

6. **vituperation** (vi tōō′ pər ā′ shən) *n.* abusive language.

this speech he called me all the different kinds of hard names he could think of, and once or twice I thought he was even going to swear—but he had never done that, and he didn't this time. "Dod dern" was the nearest he ventured to the luxury of swearing.

Two trips later I got into serious trouble. Brown was steering; I was "pulling down." My younger brother Henry appeared on the hurricane deck, and shouted to Brown to stop at some landing or other, a mile or so below. Brown gave no intimation[7] that he had heard anything. But that was his way: he never condescended to take notice of an underclerk. The wind was blowing; Brown was deaf (although he always pretended he wasn't), and I very much doubted if he had heard the order. If I had had two heads, I would have spoken; but as I had only one, it seemed **judicious** to take care of it; so I kept still.

Presently, sure enough, we went sailing by that plantation. Captain Klinefelter appeared on the deck, and said: "Let her come around, sir, let her come around. Didn't Henry tell you to land here?"

"*No,* sir!"

"I sent him up to do it."

"He *did* come up; and that's all the good it done, the dod-derned fool. He never said anything."

"Didn't *you* hear him?" asked the captain of me.

Of course I didn't want to be mixed up in this business, but there was no way to avoid it; so I said: "Yes, sir."

I knew what Brown's next remark would be, before he uttered it. It was: "Shut your mouth! You never heard anything of the kind."

I closed my mouth, according to instructions. An hour later Henry entered the pilothouse, unaware of what had been going on. He was a thoroughly inoffensive boy, and I was sorry to see him come, for I knew Brown would have no pity on him. Brown began, straightway: "Here! Why didn't you tell me we'd got to land at that plantation?"

"I did tell you, Mr. Brown."

"It's a lie!"

I said: "You lie, yourself. He did tell you."

Brown glared at me in unaffected surprise; and for as much as a moment he was entirely speechless; then he shouted to me: "I'll attend to your case in a half a minute!" then to Henry, "And you leave the pilothouse; out with you!"

judicious ▶
(jōō dish´ əs) *adj.* showing sound judgment; wise

---

7. **intimation** (in´ tə mā´ shən) *n.* hint or suggestion.

It was pilot law, and must be obeyed. The boy started out, and even had his foot on the upper step outside the door, when Brown, with a sudden access of fury, picked up a ten-pound lump of coal and sprang after him; but I was between, with a heavy stool, and I hit Brown a good honest blow which stretched him out.

I had committed the crime of crimes—I had lifted my hand against a pilot on duty! I supposed I was booked for the penitentiary sure, and couldn't be booked any surer if I went on and squared my long account with this person while I had the chance; consequently I stuck to him and pounded him with my fists a considerable time. I do not know how long, the pleasure of it probably made it seem longer than it really was; but in the end he struggled free and jumped up and sprang to the wheel: a very natural solicitude, for, all this time, here was this steamboat tearing down the river at the rate of fifteen miles an hour and nobody at the helm! However, Eagle Bend was two miles wide at this bank-full stage, and correspondingly long and deep: and the boat was steering herself straight down the middle and taking no chances. Still, that was only luck—a body *might* have found her charging into the woods.

Perceiving at a glance that the *Pennsylvania* was in no danger, Brown gathered up the big spyglass, war-club fashion, and ordered me out of the pilothouse with more than ordinary bluster. But I was not afraid of him now; so, instead of going, I tarried, and criticized his grammar. I reformed his ferocious speeches for him, and put them into good English, calling his attention to the advantage of pure English over the dialect of the collieries[8] whence he was extracted. He could have done his part to admiration in a crossfire of mere vituperation, of course; but he was not equipped for this species of controversy; so he presently laid aside his glass and took the wheel, muttering and shaking his head; and I retired to the bench. The racket had brought everybody to the hurricane deck, and I trembled when I saw the old captain looking up from amid the crowd. I said to myself, "Now I *am* done for!" for although, as a rule, he was so fatherly and indulgent toward the boat's family, and so patient of minor shortcomings, he could be stern enough when the fault was worth it.

I tried to imagine what he *would* do to a cub pilot who had been guilty of such a crime as mine, committed on a boat guard-deep with costly freight and alive with passengers.

---

8. collieries (kăl′ yər ēz) *n.* coal mines.

Our watch was nearly ended. I thought I would go and hide somewhere till I got a chance to slide ashore. So I slipped out of the pilothouse, and down the steps, and around to the texas-door, and was in the act of gliding within, when the captain **confronted** me! I dropped my head, and he stood over me in silence a moment or two, then said impressively: "Follow me."

confronted ▶
(kən frunt′ əd) *v.* faced or opposed boldly

I dropped into his wake; he led the way to his parlor in the forward end of the texas. We were alone now. He closed the afterdoor, then moved slowly to the forward one and closed that. He sat down; I stood before him. He looked at me some little time, then said: "So you have been fighting Mr. Brown?"

I answered meekly: "Yes, sir."

"Do you know that that is a very serious matter?"

"Yes, sir."

"Are you aware that this boat was plowing down the river fully five minutes with no one at the wheel?"

"Yes, sir."

"Did you strike him first?"

"Yes, sir."

"What with?"

"A stool, sir."

"Hard?"

"Middling, sir."

"Did it knock him down?"

"He—he fell, sir."

"Did you follow it up? Did you do anything further?"

"Yes, sir."

"What did you do?"

"Pounded him, sir."

"Pounded him?"

"Yes, sir."

"Did you pound him much? that is, severely?"

"One might call it that, sir, maybe."

"I'm deuced glad of it! Hark ye, never mention that I said that. You have been guilty of a great crime; and don't you ever be guilty of it again, on this boat. *But*—lay for him ashore! Give him a good sound thrashing, do you hear? I'll pay the expenses. Now go—and mind you, not a word of this to anybody. Clear out with you! You've been guilty of a great crime, you whelp!"[9]

---

9. **whelp** (welp) *n.* puppy. Here, the captain uses it to indicate that Twain is young and foolish, like a puppy.

I slid out, happy with the sense of a close shave and a mighty deliverance; and I heard him laughing to himself and slapping his fat thighs after I had closed his door.

When Brown came off watch he went straight to the captain, who was talking with some passengers on the boiler deck, and demanded that I be put ashore in New Orleans—and added: "I'll never turn a wheel on this boat again while that cub stays."

The captain said: "But he needn't come round when you are on watch, Mr. Brown."

"I won't even stay on the same boat with him. One of us has got to go ashore." "Very well," said the captain, "let it be yourself," and resumed his talk with the passengers.

During the brief remainder of the trip I knew how an emancipated slave feels, for I was an emancipated slave myself. While we lay at landings I listened to George Ealer's flute, or to his readings from his two Bibles, that is to say, Goldsmith and Shakespeare, or I played chess with him—and would have beaten him sometimes, only he always took back his last move and ran the game out differently.

ABOUT THE AUTHOR

Mark Twain (1835–1910)

Mark Twain's ability to tell stories in the language of the people has made him one of the best-loved American writers.

Growing up in Hannibal, Missouri, Twain was enchanted by the nearby Mississippi River. Twain's real name was Samuel Langhorne Clemens; he took his pen name from a riverman's call. "By the mark—twain" means that the river is "two fathoms (twelve feet) deep." Twain trained as a pilot and worked on steamboats for two years. He then headed west, finding work as a newspaper reporter in Virginia City, Nevada.

In 1865, "Jim Smiley and His Jumping Frog," Twain's amusing and lighthearted story about life in a mining camp, was printed in newspapers and magazines across the country. Twain had found his calling as a writer. He is perhaps best remembered for his classic novels *The Adventures of Tom Sawyer* and *The Adventures of Huckleberry Finn*.

READ

Comprehension

Reread all or part of the text to help you answer the following questions.

1. Explain why Twain dislikes Brown.

2. Why does Twain finally stand up to Brown?

3. How is the dispute between Brown and Twain resolved?

Research: Clarify Details Choose one unfamiliar detail from the autobiography and conduct research on it. Explain how your research clarifies the text.

Summarize Write an objective summary of the text. Do not include your own opinions.

Language Study

Selection Vocabulary Find a synonym for each boldface word from the selection.

• He was a . . . stingy, **malicious,** . . . tyrant.

• . . . it seemed **judicious** to take care of it. . . .

• So I slipped . . . down the steps, . . . when the captain **confronted** me!

Literary Analysis

Reread the identified passage and answer the questions that follow.

> **Focus Passage** *(p. 472)*
>
> I dropped into his wake . . . "you whelp!"

Key Ideas and Details

1. (a) What are Twain and the captain discussing? **(b) Infer:** How does Twain show his respect for the captain?

2. (a) What is the captain's reaction to Twain's actions? **(b) Infer:** What does this reaction show about the captain's view of Brown?

Craft and Structure

3. (a) Interpret: What is the "punch line" in this scene—the line that first reveals the captain's feelings and invites a laugh?
(b) Analyze: Explain how Twain uses repetition and delay in the dialogue to build suspense before the punch line.

Integration of Knowledge and Ideas

4. (a) Interpret: How does the captain **adjust** "the rules" to fit the circumstances?
(b) Make a Judgment: Is he justified? Explain.

Conflict

A **conflict** is a struggle between **opposing** forces. Reread the story and note how Twain uses conflict.

1. (a) Identify one conflict in the story between people. **(b)** Identify one internal conflict (a conflict one person experiences between opposing desires).

2. Generations: (a) Both Brown and the captain are older authority figures. Why does Twain relate to each man differently? **(b)** Is Twain justified when he rebels against an older authority figure? Explain.

DISCUSS • RESEARCH • WRITE

From Text to Topic **Panel Discussion**

Discuss the following passage in a panel discussion. Take notes during the discussion.

> An hour later Henry entered the pilothouse. . . . Brown began, straightway: "Here! Why didn't you tell me we'd got to land at that plantation?"
>
>   "I did tell you, Mr. Brown."
>
>   "It's a lie!'
>
>   I said: "You lie, yourself. He did tell you."

Research **Investigate the Topic**

Questioning Authority Young Twain believes there is a strict law against striking or threatening a pilot who is on duty.

> ### Assignment
>
> Conduct research to find out in what situations it is illegal to disobey a command by someone in authority, whether you consider the command right or wrong. Gather **relevant** information from a variety of sources. Take detailed notes and identify your sources. Discuss your findings in an **informal discussion** with two classmates.

Writing to Sources **Narrative**

"Cub Pilot on the Mississippi" focuses on a conflict between an apprentice and his trainer, a person from an older generation. What are some ways of responding to conflicts like Twain's?

> ### Assignment
>
> Write a **scenario** telling of an imaginary situation in which a young person thinks an older person in authority is acting unfairly. Explain how the young person should act. Follow these steps:
>
> - Introduce the problem or conflict.
> - Organize the event sequence so that the narrative unfolds logically.
> - Use transition words and phrases to connect events in sequence.
> - Describe the options the character has in coping with the conflict, and explain how the conflict is resolved.
> - Conclude by comparing your scenario with Twain's story.

QUESTIONS FOR DISCUSSION

1. Why does Twain react as he does?
2. Do Brown's actions justify Twain's disrespect? Explain.
3. What difference to your answer does it make that Twain is responding on behalf of someone else?

PREPARATION FOR ESSAY

You may use the results of this research project to support your ideas in the essay you will write at the end of this section.

ACADEMIC VOCABULARY

Academic terms appear in blue on these pages. Use a dictionary to find their definitions. Then, use the words as you speak and write about the text.

Ⓒ **Common Core State Standards**

RI.8.1, RI.8.2, RI.8.3; W.8.3, W.8.3.a, W.8.3.c, W.8.3.e, W.8.4, W.8.7, W.8.8, W.8.9; SL.8.1, SL.8.4; L.8.4, L.8.6
[For full standards wording, see the chart in the front of this book.]

Thank You, M'am

Langston Hughes

She was a large woman with a large purse that had everything in it but a hammer and nails. It had a long strap, and she carried it slung across her shoulder. It was about eleven o'clock at night, dark, and she was walking alone, when a boy ran up behind her and tried to snatch her purse. The strap broke with the sudden single tug the boy gave it from behind. But the boy's weight and the weight of the purse combined caused him to lose his balance. Instead of taking off full blast as he had hoped, the boy fell on his back on the sidewalk and his legs flew up. The large woman simply turned around and kicked him right square in his blue-jeaned sitter. Then she reached down, picked the boy up by his shirt front, and shook him until his teeth rattled.

After that the woman said, "Pick up my pocketbook, boy, and give it here."

She still held him tightly. But she bent down enough to permit him to stoop and pick up her purse. Then she said, "Now ain't you ashamed of yourself?"

Firmly gripped by his shirt front, the boy said, "Yes'm."

The woman said, "What did you want to do it for?"

The boy said, "I didn't aim to."

She said, "You a lie!"

By that time two or three people passed, stopped, turned to look, and some stood watching.

"If I turn you loose, will you run?" asked the woman.

"Yes'm," said the boy.

"Then I won't turn you loose," said the woman. She did not release him.

"Lady, I'm sorry," whispered the boy.

"Um-hum! Your face is dirty. I got a great mind to wash your face for you. Ain't you got nobody home to tell you to wash your face?"

"No'm," said the boy.

"Then it will get washed this evening," said the large woman, starting up the street, dragging the frightened boy behind her.

He looked as if he were fourteen or fifteen, frail and willow-wild, in tennis shoes and blue jeans.

The woman said, "You ought to be my son. I would teach you right from wrong. Least I can do right now is to wash your face. Are you hungry?"

"No'm," said the being-dragged boy. "I just want you to turn me loose."

"Was I bothering *you* when I turned that corner?" asked the woman.

"No'm."

"But you put yourself in **contact** with *me*," said the woman. "If you think that that contact is not going to last awhile, you got another thought coming. When I get through with you, sir, you are going to remember Mrs. Luella Bates Washington Jones."

Sweat popped out on the boy's face and he began to struggle. Mrs. Jones stopped, jerked him around in front of her, put a half nelson[1] about his neck, and continued to drag him up the

◄ **contact**
(kän´ takt) *n.*
touching;
communication

---

1. **half nelson** wrestling hold in which an arm is placed under the opponent's armpit from behind with the palm of the hand pressed against the back of the neck.

street. When she got to her door, she dragged the boy inside, down a hall, and into a large kitchenette-furnished room at the rear of the house. She switched on the light and left the door open. The boy could hear other roomers laughing and talking in the large house. Some of their doors were open, too, so he knew he and the woman were not alone. The woman still had him by the neck in the middle of her room.

She said, "What is your name?"

"Roger," answered the boy.

"Then, Roger, you go to that sink and wash your face," said the woman, whereupon she turned him loose—at last. Roger looked at the door—looked at the woman—looked at the door— *and went to the sink.*

"Let the water run until it gets warm," she said. "Here's a clean towel."

"You gonna take me to jail?" asked the boy, bending over the sink.

"Not with that face, I would not take you nowhere," said the woman. "Here I am trying to get home to cook me a bite to eat, and you snatch my pocketbook! Maybe you ain't been to your supper either, late as it be. Have you?"

"There's nobody home at my house," said the boy.

"Then we'll eat," said the woman. "I believe you're hungry—or been hungry—to try to snatch my pocketbook!"

"I want a pair of blue suede shoes,"[2] said the boy.

"Well, you didn't have to snatch *my* pocketbook to get some suede shoes," said Mrs. Luella Bates Washington Jones. "You could of asked me."

"M'am?"

The water dripping from his face, the boy looked at her. There was a long pause. A very long pause. After he had dried his face and not knowing what else to do, dried it again, the boy turned around, wondering what next. The door was open. He could make a dash for it down the hall. He could run, run, run, *run!*

---

2. **blue suede** (swād) **shoes** style of shoes worn by "hipsters" in the 1940s and 1950s; made famous in a song sung by Elvis Presley.

The woman was sitting on the day bed. After awhile she said, "I were young once and I wanted things I could not get."

There was another long pause. The boy's mouth opened. Then he frowned, not knowing he frowned.

The woman said, "Um-hum! You thought I was going to say *but*, didn't you? You thought I was going to say, *but I didn't snatch people's pocketbooks*. Well, I wasn't going to say that." Pause. Silence. "I have done things, too, which I would not tell you, son—neither tell God, if He didn't already know. Everybody's got something in common. So you set down while I fix us something to eat. You might run that comb through your hair so you will look **presentable**."

In another corner of the room behind a screen was a gas plate and an icebox. Mrs. Jones got up and went behind the screen. The woman did not watch the boy to see if he was going to run now, nor did she watch her purse, which she left behind her on the day bed. But the boy took care to sit on the far side of the room, away from the purse, where he thought she could easily see him out of the corner of her eye if she wanted to. He did not trust the woman *not* to trust him. And he did not want to be mistrusted now.

"Do you need somebody to go to the store," asked the boy, "maybe to get some milk or something?"

"Don't believe I do," said the woman, "unless you just want sweet milk yourself. I was going to make cocoa out of this canned milk I got here."

"That will be fine," said the boy.

She heated some lima beans and ham she had in the icebox, made the cocoa, and set the table. The woman did not ask the boy anything about where he lived, or his folks, or anything else that would embarrass him. Instead, as they ate, she told him about her job in a hotel beauty shop that stayed open late, what the work was like, and how all kinds of women came in and out, blondes, redheads, and Spanish. Then she cut him a half of her ten-cent cake.

"Eat some more, son," she said.

When they were finished eating, she got up and said, "Now here, take this ten dollars and buy yourself some blue suede shoes. And next time, do not make the mistake of latching onto *my* pocketbook *nor nobody else's*—because shoes got by devilish ways will burn your feet. I got to get my rest now. But from here on in, son, I hope you will behave yourself."

She led him down the hall to the front door and opened it. "Good night! Behave yourself, boy!" she said, looking out into the street as he went down the steps.

The boy wanted to say something other than, "Thank you, m'am," to Mrs. Luella Bates Washington Jones, but although his lips moved, he couldn't even say that as he turned at the foot of the barren stoop and looked up at the large woman in the door. Then she shut the door.

◀ **barren**
(bar´ ən) *adj.* empty; bare

ABOUT THE AUTHOR

Langston Hughes (1902–1967)

In the 1920s and 1930s, a young writer named Langston Hughes was at the forefront of an explosion of creativity in literature and the arts known as the Harlem Renaissance. Readers first noticed Hughes's talent in 1921, when his poem "The Negro Speaks of Rivers" was published. Hughes had just graduated from high school.

Hughes enrolled briefly at Columbia University, but dropped out in 1922. His work as a steward aboard a merchant ship took him to Africa and Spain, after which he lived in Paris for a short time.

Throughout his travels, Hughes continued writing poetry. In 1926, his first collection of poems was published as *The Weary Blues*. In 1930, Hughes published his first novel, *Not Without Laughter*. The commercial success of the book finally enabled Hughes to make a living as a writer. Hughes went on to have a long career in literature, focusing on African American themes and heritage. He wrote poetry, short stories, plays, children's books—and even lyrics for a Broadway musical.

READ

Comprehension

Reread all or part of the text to help you answer the following questions.

1. What happens immediately after Roger grabs Mrs. Jones's purse?

2. What does Mrs. Jones do after supper?

3. What does Roger do as he leaves?

Research: Clarify Details Choose one unfamiliar detail from the story and conduct research on it. Explain how your research clarifies the text.

Summarize Write an objective summary of the text. Do not include your own opinions.

Language Study

Selection Vocabulary For each boldface word, give two different definitions. Then, use each boldface word in a new sentence.

• "But you put yourself in **contact** with *me*," said the woman.

• "You might run that comb through your hair so you will look **presentable**."

• . . . he couldn't even say that as he turned at the foot of the **barren** stoop. . . .

Literary Analysis

Reread the identified passage and answer the questions that follow.

> **Focus Passage** *(p. 480)*
>
> The woman . . . mistrusted now.

Key Ideas and Details

1. Interpret: What does Mrs. Jones admit to Roger?

2. Infer: What does Mrs. Jones **imply** when she says, "Everybody's got something in common"?

Craft and Structure

3. (a) Analyze: What does the author show readers about Mrs. Jones by having her go behind the screen? **(b) Connect:** What does Roger do while she is there? **(c) Interpret:** What does his action reveal about his character?

Integration of Knowledge and Ideas

4. Generalize: What general **insight** into how people grow does the passage suggest?

Point of View

Point of view is the perspective from which a story is told. Reread the story, and take notes on ways in which the author uses point of view.

1. Is the story written in first person (the narrator says "I") or third person (the narrator says "he" and "she")? Cite two examples to support your answer.

2. Does the author tell you what each character thinks and feels? Does he show you through their words or actions? Does he do both? Cite examples.

3. Generations: Give an example where the details revealed by Hughes show that the characters are from different generations.

DISCUSS • RESEARCH • WRITE

From Text to Topic **Quick Write and Discuss**

Read the passage, and write answers to the Questions for Discussion. Take notes as you discuss your answers with a group of classmates.

> When they were finished eating, she got up and said, "Now here, take this ten dollars and buy yourself some blue suede shoes. And next time, do not make the mistake of latching onto *my* pocketbook *nor nobody else's*—because shoes got by devilish ways will burn your feet. . . ."

Research **Investigate the Topic**

Changing Styles In "Thank You, M'am," Roger turns to theft in order to buy "blue suede shoes"—an object his generation values.

Assignment
Conduct research to find out what fashion items were valued by various generations from the 1940s through today. Consult multiple print and digital sources. Take notes and identify your sources. Use software to create a **fashion slideshow** based on your research.

Writing to Sources **Explanatory Text**

"Thank You, M'am" tells the chain of events caused by an attempted robbery. These events are shaped by one key **factor**—how a person from an older generation views the actions of a younger person.

Assignment
Write a **cause-and-effect analysis** in which you chart cause-and-effect relationships in the story. Follow these steps:

- Introduce the essay topic clearly in the first paragraph.
- Describe at least three specific story events. Explain whether each is a cause, an effect, or both.
- Analyze how the difference in generations between Mrs. Jones and Roger shapes the events you are analyzing.
- Connect your ideas with transitions that indicate cause and effect, such as *because, since,* and *as a result*. Use a comma after a transitional prepositional phrase, such as *as a result,* at the beginning of a sentence.
- Provide a conclusion in which you summarize your findings.

QUESTIONS FOR DISCUSSION

1. Why does Mrs. Jones give Roger money? Is she just rewarding bad behavior? Explain.

2. How is this interaction influenced by Mrs. Jones's past? How might it influence Roger's future?

PREPARATION FOR ESSAY

You may use the results of this research project to support your ideas in the essay you will write at the end of this section.

ACADEMIC VOCABULARY

Academic terms appear in blue on these pages. Use a dictionary to find their definitions. Then, use the words as you speak and write about the text.

Common Core State Standards

RL.8.1, RL.8.2, RL.8.3; W.8.2, W.8.2.a, W.8.2.c, W.8.2.f, W.8.4, W.8.7, W.8.8, W.8.9; SL.8.1, SL.8.5; L.8.2.a, L.8.4, L.8.6
[For full standards wording, see the chart in the front of this book.]

Tutoring Benefits Seniors' Health, Students' Skills

David Crary, The Associated Press

promising ▶
(präm′ is iŋ) *adj.*
showing potential
for future success
or excellence

BALTIMORE—For 73-year-old Rosetta Handy, and the second-graders who dote on her, it's a 50/50 proposition, with winners all around.

"They help me as much as I help them," said Handy of her volunteer work as a tutor at Belmont Elementary School in a low-income West Baltimore neighborhood. "They give you energy. You learn psychology all over again."

Recent research indicates that Handy knows of what she speaks—documenting significant health benefits for the tutors.

Handy, who worked many years for the Social Security Administration, is in her fifth year with the Experience Corps, a program . . . that trains volunteers over 55 to tutor and mentor elementary school students.

Roughly 2,000 volunteers currently work with about 20,000 students, but the Experience Corps—**buoyed** by positive feedback and encouraging

buoyed ▶
(boid) *v.* lifted up in
spirits; encouraged

research—hopes to double its scope within five years.

The program's concepts have seemed **promising** ever since it was founded as a pilot project in 1995, but new academic studies have validated the optimism that it's a boon for the volunteers as well as the students.

- A two-year, $2 million study completed in 2009 by researchers at Washington University in St. Louis, involving 881 second- and third-graders in three cities, found that students with Experience Corps tutors made over 60% more progress with reading comprehension and sounding out new words than comparable students not in the program.
- Separate studies by Washington University and by Johns Hopkins University in Baltimore found that the tutoring led to measurable improvements for the volunteers—compared to adults of similar age and

"They help me as much as I help them, . . ."

demographics[1]—in physical activity and mental health. One small-scale study reported in the *Journal of Gerontology: Medical Sciences* last year—which included sophisticated neuroimaging[2] of 17 study members over 60—including eight Experience Corps volunteers in Baltimore—suggested that tutoring young children in reading and math could delay or even reverse brain aging.

The lead researcher, Professor Michelle Carlson of the Johns Hopkins Bloomberg School of Public Health, is launching a far larger, multi-year study to pursue these preliminary findings. The study focuses on the same population that makes up a majority of the tutors in Baltimore—predominantly African-American women with modest incomes and an above-average risk of various health problems.

---

1. **demographics** (dem′ ə graf′ iks) characteristics of a group of people, such as age, gender, education, and so on, used in the study of the group.
2. **neuroimaging** (noor′ ō im′ ij iŋ) the use of a technique, such as X-rays or MRI (magnetic resonance imaging), to take pictures of the brain.

"Ideally, we'd like to see if this mentoring program reduces the risk for dementia[3] and other costly diseases," said Carlson. "We'll be looking at whether we can recalibrate their rate of aging—and show that people at the greatest health risk are the ones who can benefit most immediately."

There has been extensive research in recent years suggesting that mental exercises such as crossword puzzles could help elderly people slow the deterioration of their brains. But Carlson said it's possible that tutoring children might be even more effective by integrating cognitive,[4] physical, and social activity.

"How many crossword puzzles can you do before you get bored with them?" she asked. "This tutoring gets people **engaged** in doing what the brain is supposed to do—the brain is a social organ."

"The message to them is to take all their accumulated wisdom of a lifetime and give it back to help other people," Carlson said. "They get out of bed in the morning, even when they don't feel great, because they have a social contract with the kids at school. They know a child is waiting for them."

Minnie Broady, a 62-year-old volunteer, doesn't need any research findings to know that the tutoring has rejuvenated her. A former teacher at Baltimore City Community College, she was sidelined by a heart attack and deeply depressed at what might lie ahead.

Now, she feels better than she has in years—mentally and physically.

"This has saved my life—I'm not going to lie to you," she said, her voice briefly breaking with emotion. "Some of the children are a challenge, but it has been a great help to me."

She's no pushover—some of the students call her "Sarge," and she preaches the need for self-respect and responsibility.

"They need that," she said. "They feel that they can do whatever they want to do, and there's no repercussions."

The Baltimore tutors generally work 15 hours a week, receiving an annual stipend of about $2,800 that helps cover transportation costs, school lunches, and occasional treats for the kids. . . .

In the classrooms, the tutors generally work with one or two

3. **dementia** (di men´ shə) illness involving reduced mental ability, including reduced ability to remember, to recognize objects, to control movements, and so on.
4. **cognitive** (käg´ nə tiv) having to do with knowing, including the functions of remembering, perceiving, judging, and so on.

students at a time, giving them extra practice on math or reading. If a child is acting up, the tutor can take him or her aside for a quiet discussion while the regular teacher proceeds uninterrupted with the other students.

"You can imagine the difference having 15 extra mature adults around the school," said Sylvia McGill, director of Experience Corps' Baltimore operation. "The principals tell us it's a more teachable, calmer environment, and a lot of young, first-year teachers say they wouldn't have made it without their volunteer."

One of those rookie teachers, Jennifer Ries, was getting help from Elizabeth Dorsey—a patient, soft-spoken tutor—in a bright-colored classroom filled with 17 third-graders.

"The kids love her," said Ries, 22. "They like having another adult around."

Later, with neither teacher nor tutor in earshot, 8-year-old Kayla Smith confirmed that assessment about Dorsey.

"She helps us with things," said Kayla. "We only have to raise our hand—she'll come over and explain it to us. She's real nice."

Dorsey, 67, retired five years ago after a career as a civil servant in nearby Howard County and was looking for something to do. She'd taught adult literature classes before, but when it came to engaging with children, "I always stayed away."

And now—after experiencing the Experience Corps?

"I do like them," she said, sounding almost surprised. "It's amazing. Even the ones who you think you're not getting close to, all of a sudden one day they'll jump up and give you a hug."

· · ·

Nationally, Experience Corps spends about $23 million on its operations, according to its CEO, Lester Strong. It relies on a mix of funding sources—including federal funds from AmeriCorps, private donations, and payments from the school districts it serves.

In Baltimore, principals who want the tutors are asked to contribute $20,000 from their own school budgets—covering about a quarter of the program cost.

Strong hopes the overall budget will grow so the program can multiply in size while maintaining high standards.

"The program is a triple win—for our tutors, for our children, and for the schools," he said. "Everyone benefits."

Close Reading Activities

READ

Comprehension

Reread all or part of the text to help you answer the following questions.

1. What does the Experience Corps do?

2. For older volunteers, what is one likely benefit of participation in the program?

3. Name one way Experience Corps volunteers help in the classroom.

Research: Clarify Details Choose one unfamiliar detail from the article and conduct research on it. Explain how your research clarifies the text.

Summarize Write an objective summary of the article. Remember not to include your own opinions or judgments.

Language Study

Selection Vocabulary Define each boldface word as it is used in this article. Then, identify other meanings of each word.

• . . . the Experience Corps—**buoyed** by positive feedback . . .

• The program's concepts have seemed **promising** ever since it was founded. . . .

• "This tutoring gets people **engaged** in doing what the brain is supposed to do. . . ."

Literary Analysis

Reread the identified passage. Then, respond to the questions that follow.

> **Focus Passage** (pp. 484–85).
>
> The program's concepts . . . mental health.

Key Ideas and Details

1. **(a) Compare:** According to the first Washington University study mentioned, how do students **benefit** from tutoring? **(b) Identify:** What did the Johns Hopkins study find?

Craft and Structure

2. **(a) Distinguish:** How do the contents of the bullet points differ? **(b) Analyze:** Why does the writer use bullet points rather than standard text?

Integration of Knowledge and Ideas

3. **(a) Identify:** To what group did each study compare Experience Corps participants? **(b) Support:** How do these comparisons help make the studies **valid**?

Diction

Diction is a writer's word choice. Reread the article, and take notes on the author's diction.

1. **(a)** Give two examples of sophisticated or technical diction in the article. **(b)** Give an example of less formal, more chatty or relaxed diction used by the writer.

2. **Generations: (a)** Give an example of the writer's use of less formal diction to help readers identify either with seniors or with children. Explain your choice. **(b)** Why might the writer have chosen this way of presenting his subject?

Tutoring Benefits
**Seniors' Health,
Students' Skills**
David Crary, The Associated Press

DISCUSS • RESEARCH • WRITE

From Text to Topic **Class Discussion**

Discuss the following passage as a class. Take notes during the discussion. Contribute your own ideas, and **support** them with examples from the text.

> "The message to [the volunteers] is to take all their accumulated wisdom of a lifetime and give it back to help other people," Carlson said. "They get out of bed in the morning, even when they don't feel great, because they have a social contract with the kids at school. They know a child is waiting for them."

Research **Investigate the Topic**

Senior Volunteers Crary's article describes programs in which older adults can help elementary students. Older adults have a wealth of experience, knowledge, and skills. In what other ways can elders help those younger than themselves?

Assignment

Conduct research to find out about other volunteer programs in which older adults can play an important role. Take clear notes and identify your sources. Share your findings in an **informal presentation**.

Writing to Sources **Argument**

"Tutoring Benefits Seniors' Health, Students' Skills" provides facts about the benefits of tutoring for both adult tutors and students.

Assignment

Write a **persuasive essay** in which you use information from the article to convince seniors to tutor. Follow these steps:

- Introduce the essay with a precise claim.
- Establish a logical organization, using words, phrases, and clauses to clarify relationships among claims, reasons, and evidence.
- Use details from the article as evidence for your claim.
- Identify and address potential counterclaims.
- Maintain a formal style and follow standard conventions of capitalization, punctuation, and spelling.

QUESTIONS FOR DISCUSSION

1. According to Michelle Carlson, how should older people use their "wisdom"?
2. What might she think is the best relationship between generations?
3. Explain whether you agree with her views.

PREPARATION FOR ESSAY

You may use the results of this research project to support your ideas in the essay you will write at the end of this section.

ACADEMIC VOCABULARY

Academic terms appear in blue on these pages. Use a dictionary to find their definitions. Then, use the words as you speak and write about the text.

Common Core State Standards

RI.8.1, RI.8.2, RI.8.3, RI.8.4, RI.8.5; W.8.1, W.8.1.a, W.8.1.c, W.8.1.d, W.8.4, W.8.5, W.8.7; SL.8.4; L.8.2, L.8.4, L.8.6
[For full standards wording, see the chart in the front of this book.]

The Return of the Multi-Generational Family Household

Pew Research Center

demographic ▶
(dem´ ə graf´ ik)
adj. relating to characteristics of a group of people, such as age, gender, education, and so on

The multi-generational American family household is staging a comeback—driven in part by the job losses and home foreclosures[1] of recent years but more so by **demographic** changes that have been gathering steam for decades.

As of 2008, a record 49 million Americans, or 16.1% of the total U.S. population, lived in a family household that contained at least two adult generations or a grandparent and at least one other generation, according to a new Pew Research Center analysis of census data.

This represents a significant trend reversal. Starting right after World War II, the extended family household fell out of favor with the American public. In 1940, about a quarter of the population lived in one; by 1980, just 12% did. A range of demographic factors likely contributed to this decline, among them the rapid growth of the nuclear-family-centered suburbs;[2] the decline in the share of immigrants in the population; and the sharp rise in the health and economic well-being of adults ages 65 and older.

Since bottoming out around 1980, however, the multi-generational family household has mounted a comeback. The reversal has taken place among all major demographic groups, and it, too, appears to be the result of a mix of social and economic forces.

One is the change in the median age of first marriage. The typical man now marries for

---

1. **home foreclosures** (fôr klō´ zhərz) legal proceedings in which homeowners may lose their homes because they are unable to pay back the loans they used to buy them.
2. **nuclear-family-centered suburbs** residential areas just outside a city (suburbs), which tend to serve the needs of nuclear families, or family households that consist of just parents and their children.

the first time at age 28 and the typical woman at age 26. For both genders, this is about five years older than it was in 1970. One byproduct of this cultural shift is that there are more unmarried 20-somethings in the population, many of whom consider their childhood home to be an attractive living situation, especially when a bad economy makes it difficult for them to find jobs or launch careers (see Kaplan).

Another factor has been the big wave of immigration, dominated by Latin Americans and Asians, that began around 1970. Like their European counterparts from earlier centuries, these modern immigrants are far more inclined than native-born Americans to live in multi-generational family households.

However, the trend reversal has also played out among native-born Americans. And for all groups, the move into multi-generational family households has accelerated during the Great Recession that began at the end of 2007. The Pew Research analysis of census data finds that in 2008, 2.6 million more Americans were living in such a household than had been doing so in 2007.

Who lives in multi-generational households? While the phenomenon has grown more prevalent in recent years among virtually all major demographic groups, the incidence levels vary considerably by age, race, ethnicity, and gender. . . .

U.S. Population Living in Multi-Generational Family Households, 1940–2008 (millions)

Year	Millions
2008	49
2000	42
1990	35
1980	28
1970	26
1960	27
1950	32
1940	32

Source: Pew Research Center analysis of the U.S. Decennial Census data, 1940–2000, and 2006, 2007, 2008 American Community Surveys, based on Integrated Public-Use Microdata Series (IPUMS) samples

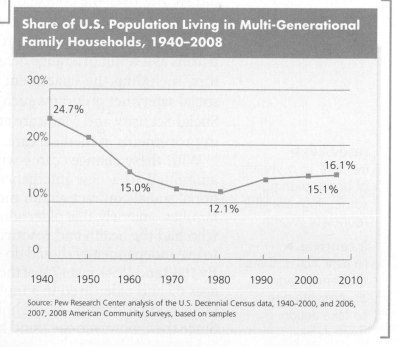

Share of U.S. Population Living in Multi-Generational Family Households, 1940–2008

24.7% ... 15.0% ... 12.1% ... 15.1% ... 16.1%

Source: Pew Research Center analysis of the U.S. Decennial Census data, 1940–2000, and 2006, 2007, 2008 American Community Surveys, based on samples

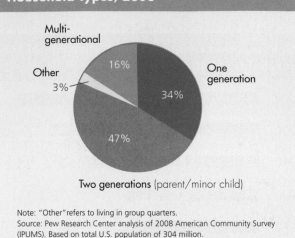

Share of Population in Various Generational Household Types, 2008

Multi-generational 16%

Other 3%

One generation 34%

Two generations (parent/minor child) 47%

Note: "Other" refers to living in group quarters.
Source: Pew Research Center analysis of 2008 American Community Survey (IPUMS). Based on total U.S. population of 304 million.

Older Adults

Older adults were once by far the likeliest of any age group to live in a multi-generational family household. Back in 1900, fully 57% of adults ages 65 and older did so. But over the course of the 20th century, older adults grew steadily healthier and more prosperous as a result of a range of factors, including the enactment of social safety net programs such as Social Security and Medicare and improvements in medical care.

With these changes came what amounted to a new intergenerational social contract within most families—namely, that older adults who had the health and **resources** to live independently should do so. By 1980 and 1990, just 17% of those ages 65 and older lived in a multi-generational family household. Since then, however, the trend has reversed course and the share has risen slightly—to 20%.

One possible explanation for the recent trend reversal is an increase in what demographers refer to as "kin availability." The outsized Baby Boom generation[3] is now passing through late middle age. Compared with earlier generations, it offers its elderly parents about 50% more grown children with whom they can share a household if and when their life circumstances (such as widowhood, declining health, or poverty) take them in that direction. Another possible explanation is that cuts to Medicare enacted in 1997 have increased the financial **incentives** for those who are elderly and infirm to move in with a grown child who is able to take on the role of informal caregiver (Engelhardt; Orsini)....

resources ▶
(rē´ sôrs´ iz) *n.* means of accomplishing something; available money or wealth

incentives ▶
(in sent´ ivz) *n.* things that encourage or motivate one to take action

3. **Baby Boom generation** the generation of people born in the United States in a period following the Second World War, from 1946 to 1964, when birth rates rose dramatically.

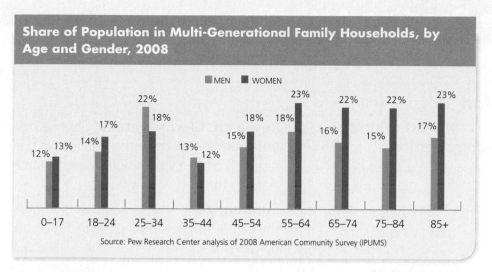

Share of Population in Multi-Generational Family Households, by Age and Gender, 2008

■ MEN ■ WOMEN

Age	0–17	18–24	25–34	35–44	45–54	55–64	65–74	75–84	85+
Men	12%	14%	22%	13%	15%	18%	16%	15%	17%
Women	13%	17%	18%	12%	18%	23%	22%	22%	23%

Source: Pew Research Center analysis of 2008 American Community Survey (IPUMS)

Young Adults

Older adults are not the age group most responsible for the overall trend reversal since 1980. That distinction belongs instead to young adults—especially those ages 25 to 34. In 1980, just 11% of adults in this age group lived in a multi-generational family household. By 2008, 20% did. Among adults 65 and older, the same share—20%—lived in such a household in 2008. However, the rise for this group has been less steep. Back in 1980, 17% lived in a multi-generational family household.

As noted above, the trend toward older median ages for first marriage is a big part of this long-term shift among younger adults. But in recent years, the economy appears to have played a significant role. Just from 2007 to 2008, the share of adults ages 25 to 34 living in such households rose by a full percentage point, from 18.7% to 19.8%.

According to a recent Pew Research Center analysis of Bureau of Labor Statistics data, as of 2009, some 37% of 18- to 29-year-olds were either unemployed or out of the workforce, the highest share among this age group in nearly four decades. In addition, a 2009 Pew Research survey found that among 22- to 29-year-olds, one-in-eight say that, because of the recession, they have boomeranged back to live with their parents after being on their own.

WORKS CITED

Engelhardt, Gary V., and Nadia Greenhalgh-Stanley. "Public Long-term Care Insurance and the Housing and Living Arrangements of the Elderly: Evidence from Medicare Home Health Benefits." Chestnut Hill, MA: Center for Retirement Research at Boston College (December 2008).

Kaplan, Greg. "Boomerang Kids: Labor Market Dynamics and Moving Back Home." Federal Reserve Bank of Minneapolis, Working Paper 675 (October 2009).

Orsini, Chiara. "Changing the Way the Elderly Live: Evidence from the Home Health Care Market in the United States." College Park, MD: University of Maryland (February 2007).

READ

Comprehension

Reread all or part of the text to help you answer the following questions.

1. What is a multi-generational family household?

2. Since 1980, what has happened to the percentage of Americans living in such households?

3. What is one reason for this **trend**?

Research: Clarify Details Choose one unfamiliar detail from the article and conduct research on it. Explain how your research clarifies the text.

Summarize Write an objective summary of the article. Remember not to include your own opinions.

Language Study

Selection Vocabulary: Social Sciences
Define each boldface word from the selection.

- . . . but more so by **demographic** changes that have been gathering steam . . .

- . . . older adults who had the health and **resources** to live independently . . .

- . . . increased the financial **incentives** for those who are elderly . . .

Literary Analysis

Reread the identified passage. Then, respond to the questions that follow.

> **Focus Passages**
>
> Since bottoming . . . households.
> (pp. 490–91)
> Graph: "Share of U.S. Population Living in Multi-Generational Family Households, 1940–2008" (p. 491)

Key Ideas and Details

1. (a) **Relate:** What two factors does the passage say have influenced the trend in multi-generational households since 1980? (b) **Apply:** In what specific way does each factor contribute to the trend?

Craft and Structure

2. **Analyze:** How does the graph help to clarify the text?

Integration of Knowledge and Ideas

3. **Hypothesize:** What could lead to a future decrease in the number of people living in multi-generational households? Give evidence from the article.

Text Structure

Text structure refers to the organized presentation of information in a text. Reread the article, taking notes on text structure.

1. (a) Identify the main idea in each of the first three paragraphs.

(b) What is the logical relationship that connects each idea to the next?

2. **Generations:** (a) What way of thinking about generations does the text structure encourage? (b) Contrast this view with the perspective you might find in a short story.

DISCUSS • RESEARCH • WRITE

From Text to Topic **Partner Discussion**

With a partner, review the graph "Share of Population in Multi-Generational Family Households, by Age and Gender, 2008." (The graph shows the **percentage** of males and the percentage of females in each age group who live in a multi-generational family household.) Identify the patterns shown, and discuss possible reasons for them. Take notes during the discussion.

Research **Investigate the Topic**

Life in a Multi-Generational Household The study gives **statistics** about multi-generational family households, but it leaves open the question, "What's it like to live in such a household?"

Assignment

Conduct research to find out how people may feel about living in a multi-generational household. Conduct research online, search for periodical articles, and interview friends and family. Take clear notes and carefully identify your sources. Share your findings in a **blog post**.

Writing to Sources **Argument**

"The Return of the Multi-Generational Family Household" describes and explains the changes in family households from 1940 to the present. Is the return to the multi-generational family household generally a positive or negative change?

Assignment

Write an **argumentative essay** in which you argue for or against the benefits of multi-generational family households. Follow these steps:

- Introduce your claim.
- Support the claim with clear reasons and relevant evidence, using examples from the article and from your own knowledge.
- Vary sentence structure and use rhetorical devices to strengthen your argument.
- Consider and address potential counterclaims.
- Provide a concluding statement that relates the argument to the article.

QUESTIONS FOR DISCUSSION

1. Which are the only age groups with a higher percentage of men than of women? Why might this be the case?

2. How might you account for the gender differences in the 65–85+ age groups?

PREPARATION FOR ESSAY

You may use the results of this research project to support your ideas in the essay you will write at the end of this section.

ACADEMIC VOCABULARY

Academic terms appear in blue on these pages. Use a dictionary to find their definitions. Then, use the words as you speak and write about the text.

Common Core State Standards

RI.8.1, RI.8.2, RI.8.3, RI.8.4, RI.8.5, RI.8.7; W.8.1, W.8.1.b, W.8.1.e, W.8.6, W.8.7, W.8.8; SL.8.1; L.8.4, L.8.6
[For full standards wording, see the chart in the front of this book.]

Speaking and Listening **Group Discussion**

Generations and Words The texts in this section vary in genre, length, style, and perspective. However, each of them comments in some way on interactions between different generations. Whether the selection tells a story, explains, informs, or persuades, it can also help suggest an answer to the Big Question addressed in this unit: **What is the secret to reaching someone with words?**

Assignment

Conduct discussions. With two or three classmates, conduct a discussion about the role of words in connecting different generations or in capturing their relationships. To support your ideas, refer to the texts in this section, other texts you have read, and your personal experience and knowledge. Begin your discussion by considering the following questions:

- How can words or stories connect generations?
- How can interactions between generations create conflict? Can words resolve these conflicts?
- What can each generation teach the other?
- Why might it sometimes be difficult for two generations to communicate?
- Why might the words of the older generation be especially important at times?
- What besides words can connect people of different generations?

Summarize and present your ideas. After you have fully explored the topic, summarize your discussion and present your conclusions to the class.

▲ Refer to the selections you read in Part 3 as you complete the activities on this assessment.

Criteria for Success

✓ **Organizes the group effectively**
Appoint a group leader and a timekeeper. The group leader should present the discussion questions. The timekeeper should make sure the discussion takes no longer than 20 minutes.

✓ **Maintains focus of discussion**
As a group, stay on topic and avoid straying into other subject areas.

✓ **Involves all participants equally and fully**
No one person should monopolize the conversation. Rather, everyone should take turns speaking and contributing ideas.

✓ **Follows the rules for collegial discussion**
As each group member speaks, others should listen carefully. Build on one another's ideas and support viewpoints and opinions with sound reasoning and evidence. Express disagreement respectfully, and justify or qualify your own views when others present new information.

USE NEW VOCABULARY

As you speak and share ideas, work to use the vocabulary words you have learned in this unit. The more you use new words, the more you will "own" them.

Writing Narrative

Generations and Words Whatever the purpose of communication, and whatever the age of the people involved, the success of communication depends on whether the speaker's words reach the listener.

Common Core State Standards

W.8.3.a–e; SL.8.1.a–d; L.8.2

[For full standards wording, see the chart in the front of this book.]

Assignment

Write an **autobiographical narrative** in which you describe and reflect on a particularly meaningful interaction with someone from another generation. Keep in mind that an effective autobiographical narrative does not just present a series of events, but explores the significance of the events in your life. Focus your reflection on how and why the words you or the other person used established a connection or made a difference. Conclude by comparing this event with an event or idea in one of the texts in this section.

Criteria for Success

Purpose/Focus

✓ **Connects specific incidents with larger ideas**

Make connections between the events you describe, the topic of relations between generations, and the texts in this section.

✓ **Clearly conveys the significance of the story**

Provide a conclusion in which you reflect on the role of words in what you experienced.

Organization

✓ **Organizes events dramatically**

Structure your narrative so that events logically lead to a climax, or high point of interest.

Development of Ideas/Elaboration

✓ **Provides background**

Provide enough information about characters and situations so that readers can easily follow your story.

✓ **Integrates insights**

Smoothly and logically integrate your reflections with your story, using appropriate transitions.

Language

✓ **Creates tone**

Use precise word choice to create a consistent tone—whether light and chatty or serious and contemplative.

Conventions

✓ **Does not have errors**

Eliminate errors in grammar, spelling, and punctuation.

WRITE TO EXPLORE

Writing is a way to clarify what you feel and think. As you draft your narrative, you may find new, unexpected connections between your own experiences and the texts you are writing about. By adjusting your draft to reflect these shifts in your own ideas, you will improve your narrative.

Writing to Sources **Explanatory Text**

Generations and Words The readings in this section present a range of ideas about generations. They raise—and help to answer—questions such as the following:

- What do members of different generations have in common? What sets them apart?
- What can they give one another?
- What do elders owe to those younger than themselves?
- Do the young always owe their elders respect? Obedience?
- What binds young and old? Are the ties between them always grounded in wisdom and respect—or does need play a role as well?

Reflect on these questions, jotting notes on preliminary answers, and then complete the following assignment.

Assignment
Write an **explanatory essay** in which you explore what the generations can give one another, the obstacles that may separate them, and how these obstacles may be overcome. Present your main idea in a clear thesis statement, and support it with examples from the texts.

Prewriting and Planning

Choose texts. Review the texts in the section to determine which ones you will cite in your essay. Select at least two that will provide strong material to support your exposition.

Gather details. Use a chart like the one shown to take notes. Begin by describing the relationships between the generations in each selection. Then, fill in the last column with supporting quotations. As needed, revise your notes based on what you discover when you fill in details.

INCORPORATE RESEARCH

Be selective in incorporating quotations from texts. Avoid quoting passages for no clear reason. Instead, find the passage that best supports your point. Present it to readers with an explanation of what it shows, clearly tying the quotation to the point you are making.

Text: "Cub Pilot on the Mississippi"

Older Generation	Younger Generation	Relationship	Supporting Passage with Notes
Brown, the captain	Twain, his brother Henry	Brown tries to get Twain in trouble and blames Henry for his own error; Twain hates him. Twain respects the captain, though.	"What you standing there for? Take that ice-pitcher down to the texas-tender! Come, move along, and don't you be all day about it!" [Brown is abusing his authority—his intention is to boss Twain around and make him feel inferior.]

Draft a thesis statement. Review your notes, and draft a sentence or two that clearly expresses your main idea about the relations between generations.

Drafting

Organize your ideas. Outline your draft, organizing your ideas and examples in broader categories, such as *What the Young Give the Old*.

Begin and end strongly. In your introduction, orient readers with a clear thesis statement and a preview of the ideas you will explore. In your conclusion, sum up your ideas, ending with an insight.

Support ideas. As you draft, follow your outline. State each point clearly, and support it with the strongest and most relevant examples, quotations, facts, or other details. Use transitions, such as *for example* and *for this reason* to connect main ideas and supporting details.

Use formal language. Show your thoughts at their most polished. Avoid filler expressions such as "sort of," "I mean," and "you know."

Revising and Editing

Review content. Review your support for each main idea. Delete or move any sentences that do not relate to the idea they were meant to support.

Review style. Review your word choice, replacing vague or overused words with words that express your meaning precisely.

> VAGUE: Mrs. Jones is <u>sort of tough</u> but <u>nice</u> too.
>
> PRECISE: Mrs. Jones is <u>stern</u> but <u>kind</u>.

To express technical ideas, consider using the domain-specific words from the social sciences that you learned in this section, such as *demographic*.

Common Core State Standards

W.8.2.a–f, W.8.4, W.8.5
[For full standards wording, see the chart in the front of this book.]

CITE RESEARCH CORRECTLY

Create a Works Cited list for your essay, following a standard style. Review your draft and make sure you have included appropriately formatted citations for quotations and for summaries of other works. (See the Conducting Research workshop in the front of this book.)

Self-Evaluation Rubric

Use the following criteria to evaluate the effectiveness of your essay.

Criteria	Rating Scale			
	not very .... *very*			
Purpose/Focus Introduces a topic clearly; provides a concluding section that follows from and supports the information or explanation presented	1	2	3	4
Organization Organizes ideas into broader categories; uses appropriate and varied transitions to create cohesion and clarify relationships among ideas	1	2	3	4
Development of Ideas/Elaboration Develops the topic with relevant, well-chosen facts, definitions, concrete details, quotations, or other information and examples	1	2	3	4
Language Uses precise language and domain-specific vocabulary to inform about or explain the topic; establishes and maintains a formal style	1	2	3	4
Conventions Correctly follows conventions of grammar, spelling, and punctuation	1	2	3	4

Independent Reading

Titles for Extended Reading

In this unit, you have read a wide variety of poems by many different poets. Continue to read on your own. Select works that you enjoy, but challenge yourself to explore new writers and works of increasing depth and complexity. The titles suggested below will help you get started.

INFORMATIONAL TEXT

A Street Through Time
by Anne Millard

Have you ever wondered how your neighborhood would look one hundred, five hundred, or even several thousand years ago? This fascinating **nonfiction book** follows an English port city through time, from the Stone Age to the present day. Discover how nature and human activities can shape a landscape in dramatic ways.

Discoveries: Lines of Communication

Advances in technology have transformed the way we communicate. Read this collection of **essays** to learn more about these topics: "Samuel Morse's Dream," "Astronauts Take Off in Russian," "Welcome to the Blogosphere," and "Misleading Statistics."

Helen Keller: A Photographic Story of a Life
by Leslie Garrett

This **biography** tells the remarkable story of Helen Keller, who lost her sight and hearing at age two. Read how she overcame her disabilities to break out of the isolation of her world. This volume is part of the DK Biography Series, which offers personal and historical background on a wide range of fascinating people.

LITERATURE

Black Hair   EXEMPLAR TEXT ©
by Gary Soto

In this wide-ranging collection of **poetry,** Gary Soto reaches back to his roots—growing up poor in a Fresno neighborhood. In poems such as "Oranges," Soto looks back with fondness, humor, and insight on his earlier years.

The Heart of a Chief
by Joseph Bruchac

A bright, courageous eleven-year-old Native American boy fights injustice and prejudice in this **novel** by author Bruchac, whose own mother was Abenaki. Through a mixture of seriousness and humor, this first-person story offers a unique perspective on the world.

Classic Poems to Read Aloud   EXEMPLAR TEXT ©
edited by James Berry

Poetry by poets from all over the world is included in this collection, organized by subject. Read such classic poems as Lewis Carroll's "Jabberwocky" and W. H. Auden's "Funeral Blues" alongside contemporary gems such as Shel Silverstein's "It's Dark in Here."

ONLINE TEXT SET

OPEN LETTER
from **My Own True Name** Pat Mora

POEM
Your World Georgia Douglas Johnson

REFLECTIVE ESSAY
Words to Sit in, Like Chairs Naomi Shihab Nye

Preparing to Read Complex Texts

Attentive Reading As you read on your own, ask yourself questions about the text. The questions shown below and others that you ask as you read will help you understand and enjoy literature even more.

When reading poetry, ask yourself...

Comprehension: **Key Ideas and Details**

- Who is the speaker of the poem? What kind of person does the speaker seem to be? How do I know?
- What is the poem about?
- If the poem is telling a story, who are the characters and what happens to them?
- Does any one line or section state the poem's theme, or meaning, directly? If so, what is that line or section?
- If there is no direct statement of a theme, what details help me to see the deeper meaning of the poem?

Text Analysis: **Craft and Structure**

- How does the poem look on the page?
- Does the poem have a formal structure or is it free verse?
- How does the form affect how I read the poem?
- How many stanzas form this poem? What does each stanza tell me?
- Do I notice repetition, rhyme, or meter? Do I notice other sound devices? How do these elements affect how I read the poem?
- Are any of the poet's word choices especially interesting? Why?
- What images do I notice? Do they create clear word-pictures? Why or why not?

Connections: **Integration of Knowledge and Ideas**

- Has the poem helped me understand its subject in a new way? How?
- Does the poem remind me of others I have read? If so, how?
- In what ways is the poem different from others I have read?
- What information or insights have I gained from this poem?
- Do I find the poem moving, funny, or mysterious? How does the poem make me feel?
- Would I like to read more poems by this poet? Why or why not?

**Common Core
State Standards**

**Reading Literature/
Informational Text**

10. By the end of the year, read and comprehend literature, including stories, dramas, and poems, and literary nonfiction at the high end of the grades 6–8 text complexity band independently and proficiently.

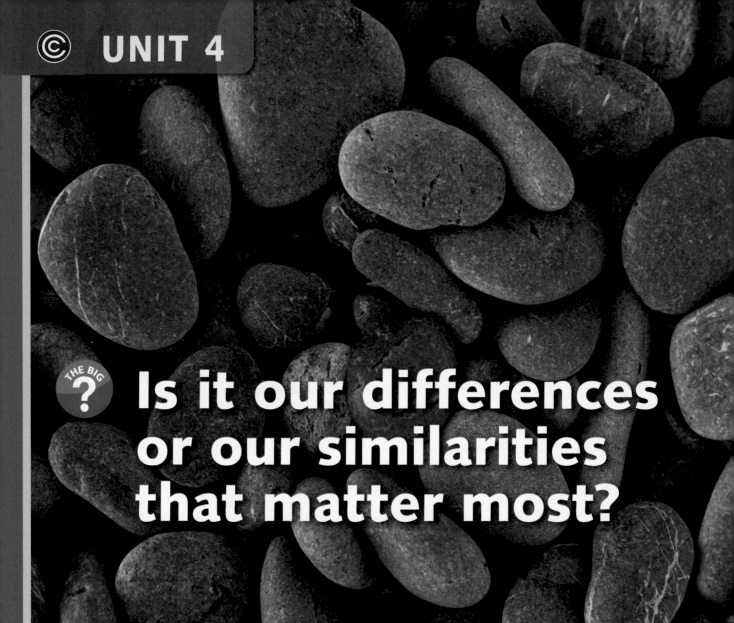

THE BIG ?

Is it our differences or our similarities that matter most?

UNIT PATHWAY

PART 1
SETTING EXPECTATIONS

- INTRODUCING THE BIG QUESTION
- CLOSE READING WORKSHOP

PART 2
TEXT ANALYSIS
GUIDED EXPLORATION

DIALOGUE AND DISCOVERY

PART 3
TEXT SET
DEVELOPING INSIGHT

THE HOLOCAUST

PART 4
DEMONSTRATING INDEPENDENCE

- INDEPENDENT READING
- ONLINE TEXT SET

CLOSE READING TOOL

Use this tool to practice the close reading strategies you learn.

STUDENT eTEXT

Bring learning to life with audio, video, and interactive tools.

ONLINE WRITER'S NOTEBOOK

Easily capture notes and complete assignments online.

Find all Digital Resources at **pearsonrealize.com.**

Is it our differences or our similarities that matter most?

There are many ways for people to distinguish themselves from one another. People often choose to identify themselves—or to classify others—based on race, religion, national origin, or economic class. Or, they might choose a different category, such as academic or athletic achievement. At the same time, as human beings with similar needs and desires, people everywhere have much in common.

The health of a society depends on how we handle our differences and similarities. We debate about whether to find value in our differences, or whether we should focus on our similarities. We question the standards we use to judge one another—whether they are superficial or whether they touch on what really matters, such as character. However we answer these questions, it is important to explore the ways in which we balance our differences and our similarities.

Exploring the Big Question

Collaboration: One-on-One Discussion Start thinking about the Big Question by making a list of various ways in which similarities and differences among people influence behavior. Describe one specific example of each of these situations:

- A well-off employer considering how much to pay a worker
- A group of people trying to escape religious discrimination
- An event at school that brings different social groups together
- A visit to a family from a different ethnic background

Share your examples with a partner. Discuss how people in these situations might act if they based their actions on differences alone, on similarities alone, or on both similarities and differences.

Connecting to the Literature Each reading in this unit will give you additional insight into the Big Question: Is it our differences or our similarities that matter most?

Vocabulary

Acquire and Use Academic Vocabulary The term "academic vocabulary" refers to words you typically encounter in scholarly and literary texts and in technical and business writing. Review the definitions of these academic vocabulary words.

Common Core State Standards

Speaking and Listening
1. Engage effectively in a range of collaborative discussions (one-on-one, in groups, and teacher-led) with diverse partners on *grade 8 topics, texts, and issues,* building on others' ideas and expressing their own clearly.

Language
6. Acquire and use accurately grade-appropriate general academic and domain-specific words and phrases; gather vocabulary knowledge when considering a word or phrase important to comprehension or expression.

class (klas) *n.* grouping of people or objects based on common traits

discriminate (di skrim´ i nāt´) *v.* 1. see the difference between; tell apart; 2. treat unfairly based on particular differences

distinguish (di stiŋ´ gwish) *v.* 1. see the difference between; tell apart; 2. mark as different; set apart

divide (də vīd´) *v.* separate

identify (i den´ tə fi´) *v.* 1. recognize as being; 2. call out as being the thing specified

judge (juj) *v.* form an opinion about; evaluate

represent (rep´ ri zent´) *v.* 1. stand for; 2. speak for

Use these words as you complete Big Question activities in this unit that involve reading, writing, speaking, and listening.

Gather Vocabulary Knowledge Additional words related to people's differences and similarities are listed below. Categorize the words by deciding whether you know each one well, know it a little bit, or do not know it at all.

assumption	separate	tolerance
common	superficial	unify
generalization	sympathy	

Then, do the following:

1. Write the definitions of the words you know.
2. Consult a dictionary to confirm the definitions of the words you know. Revise your definitions if necessary.
3. Using a print or an online dictionary, look up the meanings of the words you do not know. Then, write the meanings.
4. Use all of the words in a brief paragraph about a specific conflict in which either a crucial difference or a key similarity among individuals or groups of people affected the outcome.

In this workshop you will learn an approach to reading that will deepen your understanding of literature and will help you better appreciate an author's craft. The workshop includes models for the close reading, discussion, research, and writing activities you will complete as you study the literature in this unit. After you have reviewed the strategies and models in this workshop, practice your skills with the Independent Practice selection.

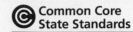

Common Core State Standards

RL.8.1, RL.8.2; W.8.1, W.8.7, W.8.9.a; SL.8.1
[For full standards wording, see the standards chart in the front of this book.]

CLOSE READING: DRAMA

In Part 2 of this unit you will focus on reading excerpts from various dramas. Use these strategies as you read the texts.

Comprehension: **Key Ideas and Details**

- Read first to unlock basic meaning.
- Use context clues and reference works to determine the meanings of unfamiliar words.
- Identify unfamiliar details that you might need to clarify through research.

- Make inferences about information that is implied.

Ask yourself questions such as these:
- Where and when does the action occur?
- How do the main characters change?

Text Analysis: **Craft and Structure**

- Analyze how dramatic elements advance the action and build tension and suspense.
- Notice how the playwright uses stage directions to help readers visualize the scenes.

- Consider how dialogue reveals characters' traits.

Ask yourself questions such as these:
- What conflict do the characters face?
- How do characters' words and actions reveal their personalities?

Connections: **Integration of Knowledge and Ideas**

- Look for relationships among key ideas.
- Draw conclusions about the play's theme, based on the characters' words and actions, revealed in stage directions.
- Compare and contrast this work with works with a similar theme.

- **Ask yourself questions such as these:**
- How has this work increased my insight into people or life?
- What is the most dramatic scene, and what does it reveal about the theme?

Read

As you read these scenes, take note of the annotations, which model ways to closely read the text.

Reading Model

from *Billy Elliot* by Lee Hall

These scenes take place in Billy Elliot's home and in the boxing hall where Billy takes ballet lessons. Billy and his father do not agree about the value of these lessons.

[INT. ELLIOT HOUSE. STAIRS—MORNING[1]

BILLY *is stuffing his ballet shoes down his trousers. He has his boxing gloves slung as usual over his shoulders.][2]*

BILLY. See you, then.

TONY. *[off-screen]* Wait. Your breakfast's ready.

*[*BILLY *slams the door.* DAD *runs out of the downstairs bathroom.]*

DAD. What's he up to?

[CUT TO: INT. BOXING HALL—LATER

Another exercise. MRS. WILKINSON *is concentrating her attention on* BILLY. BILLY *suddenly sees* DAD *and freezes.[3] His reaction puzzles* MRS. WILKINSON *for a second. The music comes to a standstill.* MRS. WILKINSON *turns to see* DAD.*]*

DAD: You. Out. Now.

MRS. WILKINSON: I beg your pardon?

[The mood has been fractured by DAD*'s aggressive tone.[4] Everybody stares at* DAD. *The girls start to giggle.* BILLY *gives an embarrassed look to* MRS. WILKINSON *and starts to walk out, embarrassed.]*

BILLY: Please, Miss … *[softly]* … don't.

*[*BILLY *exits with* DAD. MRS. WILKINSON *stops in her tracks and watches* BILLY *follow* DAD *out. She is suddenly lost, running through all the possible courses of action. The class is staring at her, startled by* DAD*'s intrusion. She turns and very calmly says:]*

MRS. WILKINSON: All right, which way are we facing?

[and carries on with her next exercise as if nothing had happened.][5]

Craft and Structure

1 The stage directions indicate the setting—where and when the scene occurs. *INT.* stands for "interior," which in this case means inside the Elliot house.

Key Ideas and Details

2 Billy is sneakily hiding the ballet shoes; he has the boxing gloves on display, perhaps as a distraction. Readers know to look for the effects of this deceptive act.

Integration of Knowledge and Ideas

3 Billy "freezes," a sign that he knows his father does not approve of his actions. The conflict between what Billy wants and what his father expects points to a theme—should people be free to pursue their dreams?

Key Ideas and Details

4 The reference to Dad's "aggressive tone" in the stage directions supports the inference that Dad is often gruff and bossy.

Craft and Structure

5 Stage directions and dialogue reveal Mrs. Wilkinson's character. Though "suddenly lost," she maintains her composure and continues with the class.

Discuss

Sharing your own ideas and listening to the ideas of others can deepen your understanding of a text and help you look at a topic in a whole new way. As you participate in collaborative discussions, work to have a genuine exchange in which classmates build upon one another's ideas. Support your points with evidence and ask meaningful questions.

Discussion Model

Student 1: Right from the beginning, it is clear that Billy has to hide his interest in ballet from his dad. He stuffs his ballet shoes down his pants, and leaves the house without breakfast to avoid running into his father.

Student 2: Well, it is not unusual for people to think of ballet as something that mostly girls do. From his actions and words, it seems that Billy's dad has a big problem with the idea of Billy taking ballet, even though ballet is actually a grueling, athletic activity.

Student 3: I agree. Ballet dancers have to be strong and very focused. I wonder when that dance form began and if male dancers have always had a tough time being accepted in society.

Research

Targeted research can clarify unfamiliar details and shed light on various aspects of a text. Consider questions that arise in your mind as you read, and use those questions as the basis for research.

Research Model

Question: *When did ballet begin, and how did it develop?*

Key Words for Internet Search: History + Ballet

Result: The Ballet, The History of Ballet

What I Learned: People have been dancing since prehistoric times. In ancient civilizations, people danced both for spiritual reasons and entertainment. Ballet started to develop as a dance form in royal courts in Europe during the 1400s. By 1581, ballet began to take the form we know now.

Write

Writing about a text will deepen your understanding of it and will also allow you to share your ideas more formally with others. The following model essay analyzes the use of various elements of drama and cites evidence to support the main ideas.

Writing Model: Explanatory Text

Conflict and Theme in *Billy Elliot*

In the scenes taken from *Billy Elliot*, the scriptwriter uses a conflict to suggest two different but related themes. One theme is that some goals are worth working toward even if the costs are high. Another is that males and females have equal rights to pursue their dreams.

Like many young people throughout history, Billy Elliot dreams of being a ballet dancer. His father, however, has other ideas. Dance has been a source of inspiration since ancient times, and ballet has been a cultural force since the 1500s, but Billy's father does not believe his son should be dancing. In fact, Billy's father does not seem to think that any boy should pursue ballet. As a result, Billy's desire to dance creates a conflict with his father.

This conflict leads to emotionally intense scenes. When Billy's dad discovers his son in a ballet class, he orders Billy to leave with the command "You. Out. Now." These three short words of dialogue make it clear that the father is angry and that Billy faces great opposition to his pursuit of a dance career.

Like the dialogue, the stage directions help convey the conflict and themes. When readers first meet Billy, he *"is stuffing his ballet shoes down his trousers,"* but he has his *"boxing gloves slung as usual over his shoulders."* Right away, readers know that he is hiding something, probably in order to avoid a conflict. When Billy's father finds Billy in the ballet class, the stage directions emphasize the father's anger and Billy's embarrassment: "[*The mood has been fractured by* DAD's *aggressive tone. . . .* BILLY *gives an embarrassed look to* MRS. WILKINSON. . . .*]*" These stage directions show the intensity of the conflict. It is clear that Billy will have to fight hard to pursue his dream.

The dramatic conflict between Billy and his father forces audience members to ask themselves whether Billy should pursue his dream despite his father's opposition and whether Billy has the same right as a female to pursue dance. By posing these questions, the writer expresses important themes: Dreams are worth pursuing despite obstacles, and males and females should have equal rights to pursue their dreams.

The writer introduces the main idea of the essay in the first line of the first paragraph—the scriptwriter uses a conflict to present two main themes.

By incorporating evidence from research, the writer connects the main character's struggle to a common human desire—to dance.

The writer points to a key piece of dialogue to show the obstacle Billy faces—the expectations of others.

The writer cites the stage directions to further explore the conflict in and the themes of the movie.

As you read the following excerpt from a play, apply the close reading strategies you have learned. You may need to read the excerpt from the drama multiple times.

from The Miracle Worker

by William Gibson

The Miracle Worker is a play based on the real-life story of teacher Annie Sullivan and her student Helen Keller, a seven-year-old girl who is unable to see, hear, or speak. Like her student, Annie suffers from eyesight disabilities; however, she is not totally blind.

from Act I

KELLER. [*very courtly*] Welcome to Ivy Green, Miss Sullivan. I take it you are Miss Sullivan—

KATE. My husband, Miss Annie, Captain Keller.

ANNIE. [*her best behavior*] Captain, how do you do.

KELLER. A pleasure to see you, at last. I trust you had an agreeable journey?

ANNIE. Oh, I had several! When did this country get so big?

JAMES. Where would you like the trunk, father?

KELLER. Where Miss Sullivan can get at it, I imagine.

ANNIE. Yes, please. Where's Helen?

KELLER. In the hall, Jimmie—

KATE. We've put you in the upstairs corner room, Miss Annie, if there's any breeze at all this summer, you'll feel it—

[*In the house the setter* BELLE *flees into the family room, pursued by* HELEN *with groping hands; the dog doubles back out the same door, and* HELEN *still groping for her makes her way out to the porch; she is messy, her hair tumbled, her pinafore now ripped, her shoelaces untied.* KELLER *acquires the suitcase, and* ANNIE *gets her hands on it too, though still endeavoring to live up to the general air of propertied manners.[1]*]

---

1. **the general air of propertied manners** atmosphere of refinement and wealth

Meet the Author

American playwright **William Gibson** (1914–2008) was born and raised in New York City. Although he is best known for his play *The Miracle Worker*, which debuted on Broadway in 1959, Gibson also wrote novels, short stories, and poems.

CLOSE READING TOOL

Read and respond to this selection online using the **Close Reading Tool**.

KELLER. *And* the suitcase—

ANNIE. [*pleasantly*] I'll take the suitcase, thanks.

KELLER. Not at all, I have it, Miss Sullivan.

ANNIE. I'd like it.

KELLER. [*gallantly*] I couldn't think of it, Miss Sullivan. You'll find in the south we—

ANNIE. Let me.

KELLER. —view women as the flowers of civiliza—

ANNIE. [*impatiently*] I've got something in it for Helen!

[*She tugs it free;* KELLER *stares.*]

Thank you. When do I see her?

KATE. There. There is Helen.

[ANNIE *turns, and sees* HELEN *on the porch. A moment of silence. Then* ANNIE *begins across the yard to her, lugging her suitcase.*]

KELLER. [*sotto voce*[2]] Katie—

[KATE *silences him with a hand on his arm. When* ANNIE *finally reaches the porch steps she stops, contemplating* HELEN *for a last moment before entering her world. Then she drops the suitcase on the porch with intentional heaviness,* HELEN *starts with the jar, and comes to grope over it.* ANNIE *puts forth her hand, and touches* HELEN'*s.* HELEN *at once grasps it, and commences to explore it, like reading a face. She moves her hand on to* ANNIE'*s forearm, and dress; and* ANNIE *brings her face within reach of* HELEN'*s fingers, which travel over it, quite without timidity, until they encounter and push aside the smoked glasses.* ANNIE'*s gaze is grave, unpitying, very attentive. She puts her hands on* HELEN'*s arms, but* HELEN *at once pulls away, and they confront each other with a distance between. Then* HELEN *returns to the suitcase, tries to open it, cannot.* ANNIE *points* HELEN'*s hand overhead.* HELEN *pulls away, tries to open the suitcase again;* ANNIE *points her hand overhead again.* HELEN *points overhead, a question, and* ANNIE, *drawing* HELEN'*s hand to her own face, nods.* HELEN *now begins tugging the suitcase toward the door; when* ANNIE *tries to take it from her, she fights her off and backs through the doorway with it.* ANNIE *stands a moment, then follows her in, and together they get the suitcase up the steps into* ANNIE'*s room.*]

---

2. *sotto voce* (sät´ō vō´chē) in a low voice

Kate. Well?

Keller. She's very rough, Katie.

Kate. I like her, Captain.

Keller. Certainly rear a peculiar kind of young woman in the north. How old is she?

Kate. [*vaguely*] Ohh— Well, she's not in her teens, you know.

Keller. She's only a child. What's her family like, shipping her off alone this far?

Kate. I couldn't learn. She's very closemouthed about some things.

Keller. Why does she wear those glasses? I like to see a person's eyes when I talk to—

Kate. For the sun. She was blind.

Keller. Blind.

Kate. She's had nine operations on her eyes. One just before she left.

Keller. Blind, good heavens, do they expect one blind child to teach another? Has she experience at least, how long did she teach there?

Kate. She was a pupil.

Keller. [*heavily*] Katie, Katie. This is her first position?

Kate. [*bright voice*] She was valedictorian—

Keller. Here's a houseful of grownups can't cope with the child, how can an inexperienced half-blind Yankee schoolgirl manage her?

[James *moves in with the trunk on his shoulder.*]

James. [*easily*] Great improvement. Now we have two of them to look after.

Keller. You look after those strawberry plants!

[James *stops with the trunk.* Keller *turns from him without another word, and marches off.*]

James. Nothing I say is right.

KATE. Why say anything?

[*She calls.*]

Don't be long, Captain, we'll have supper right away—

[*She goes into the house, and through the rear door of the family room.* JAMES *trudges in with the trunk, takes it up the steps to* ANNIE's *room, and sets it down outside the door. The lights elsewhere dim somewhat.*

Meanwhile, inside, ANNIE *has given* HELEN *a key; while* ANNIE *removes her bonnet,* HELEN *unlocks and opens the suitcase. The first thing she pulls out is a voluminous shawl. She fingers it until she perceives what it is; then she wraps it around her, and acquiring* ANNIE's *bonnet and smoked glasses as well, dons the lot: the shawl swamps her, and the bonnet settles down upon the glasses, but she stands before a mirror cocking her head to one side, then to the other, in a mockery of adult action.* ANNIE *is amused, and talks to her as one might to a kitten, with no trace of company manners.*]

ANNIE. All the trouble I went to and that's how I look?

[HELEN *then comes back to the suitcase, gropes for more, lifts out a pair of female drawers.*]

Oh, no. Not the drawers!

[*But* HELEN *discarding them comes to the elegant doll. Her fingers explore its features, and when she raises it and finds its eyes open and close, she is at first startled, then delighted. She picks it up, taps its head* vigorously, *taps her own chest, and nods questioningly.* ANNIE *takes her finger, points it to the doll, points it to* HELEN, *and touching it to her own face, also nods.* HELEN *sits back on her heels, clasps the doll to herself, and rocks it.* ANNIE *studies her, still in bonnet and smoked glasses like a caricature of herself, and addresses her humorously.*]

All right, Miss O'Sullivan. Let's begin with doll.

[*She takes* HELEN's *hand; in her palm* ANNIE's *forefinger points, thumb holding her other fingers clenched.*]

◀ **Vocabulary**
vigorously (vig´
ər əs lē) *adv.* in an
energetic manner

D.

[*Her thumb next holds all her fingers clenched, touching* HELEN's *palm.*]

O.

[*Her thumb and forefinger extended.*]

L.

[*Same contact repeated.*]

L.

[*She puts* HELEN's *hand to the doll.*]

Doll.

JAMES. You spell pretty well.

[ANNIE *in one hurried move gets the drawers swiftly back into the suitcase, the lid banged shut, and her head turned, to see* JAMES *leaning in the doorway.*]

Finding out if she's ticklish? She is.

[ANNIE *regards him stonily, but* HELEN *after a scowling moment tugs at her hand again,* **imperious**. ANNIE *repeats the letters, and* HELEN *interrupts her fingers in the middle, feeling each of them, puzzled.* ANNIE *touches* HELEN's *hand to the doll, and begins spelling into it again.*]

JAMES. What is it, a game?

ANNIE. [*curtly*] An alphabet.

JAMES. Alphabet?

ANNIE. For the deaf.

[HELEN *now repeats the finger movements in air, exactly, her head cocked to her own hand, and* ANNIE's *eyes suddenly gleam.*]

Ho. How *bright* she is!

JAMES. You think she knows what she's doing?

[*He takes* HELEN's *hand, to throw a meaningless gesture into it; she repeats this one too.*]

She imitates everything, she's a monkey.

ANNIE. [*very pleased*] Yes, she's a bright little monkey, all right.

Vocabulary ▶
imperious (im pir´ ē əs) *adj.* overbearing; proud and demanding

[*She takes the doll from* HELEN, *and reaches for her hand;* HELEN *instantly grabs the doll back.* ANNIE *takes it again, and* HELEN'*s hand next, but* HELEN *is **incensed** now; when* ANNIE *draws her hand to her face to shake her head no, then tries to spell to her,* HELEN *slaps at* ANNIE'*s face.* ANNIE *grasps* HELEN *by both arms, and swings her into a chair, holding her pinned there, kicking, while glasses, doll, bonnet fly in various directions.* JAMES *laughs.*]

◀ **Vocabulary**
incensed (in senst′)
adj. extremely angry

JAMES. She wants her doll back.

ANNIE. When she spells it.

JAMES. Spell, she doesn't know the thing has a name, even.

ANNIE. Of course not, who expects her to, now? All I want is her fingers to learn the letters.

JAMES. Won't mean anything to her.

[ANNIE *gives him a look. She then tries to form* HELEN'*s fingers into the letters, but* HELEN *swings a haymaker*[3] *instead, which* ANNIE *barely ducks, at once pinning her down again.*]

Doesn't like that alphabet, Miss Sullivan. You invent it yourself?

[HELEN *is now in a rage, fighting tooth and nail to get out of the chair, and* ANNIE *answers while struggling and dodging her kicks.*]

ANNIE. Spanish monks under a—vow of silence. Which I wish *you'd* take!

[*And suddenly releasing* HELEN'*s hands, she comes and shuts the door in* JAMES'*s face.* HELEN *drops to the floor, groping around for the doll.* ANNIE *looks around desperately, sees her purse on the bed, rummages in it, and comes up with a battered piece of cake wrapped in newspaper; with her foot she moves the doll deftly out of the way of* HELEN'*s groping, and going on her knee she lets* HELEN *smell the cake. When* HELEN *grabs for it,* ANNIE *removes the cake and spells quickly into the reaching hand.*]

Cake. From Washington up north, it's the best I can do.

[HELEN'*s hand waits, baffled.* ANNIE *repeats it.*]

C, a, k, e. Do what my fingers do, never mind what it means.

[*She touches the cake briefly to* HELEN'*s nose, pats her hand, presents her own hand.* HELEN *spells the letters rapidly back.* ANNIE *pats her hand enthusiastically, and gives her the cake;*

---

3. **swings a haymaker** throws a punch

HELEN *crams it into her mouth with both hands.* ANNIE *watches her, with humor.*]

Get it down fast, maybe I'll steal that back too. Now.

[*She takes the doll, touches it to* HELEN's *nose, and spells again into her hand.*]

D, o, l, l. Think it over.

[HELEN t*hinks it over, while* ANNIE *presents her own hand. Then* HELEN *spells three letters.* ANNIE *waits a second, then completes the word for Helen in her palm.*]

L.

[*She hands over the doll, and* HELEN *gets a good grip on its leg.*]

Imitate now, understand later. End of the first les—

[*She never finishes, because* HELEN *swings the doll with a furious energy, it hits* ANNIE *squarely in the face, and she falls back with a cry of pain, her knuckles up to her mouth.* HELEN *waits, tensed for further combat. When* ANNIE *lowers her knuckles she looks at blood on them; she works her lips, gets to her feet, finds the mirror, and bares her teeth at herself. Now she is furious herself.*]

You little wretch, no one's taught you *any* manners? I'll—

[*But rounding from the mirror she sees the door slam,* HELEN *and the doll are on the outside, and* HELEN *is turning the key in the lock.* ANNIE *darts over, to pull the knob, the door is locked fast. She yanks it again.*]

Helen! Helen, let me out of—

[*She bats her brow at the folly of speaking, but* JAMES, *now downstairs, hears her and turns to see* HELEN *with the key and doll groping her way down the steps.* JAMES *takes in the whole situation, makes a move to intercept* HELEN, *but then changes his mind, lets her pass, and amusedly follows her out onto the porch. Upstairs* ANNIE *meanwhile rattles the knob, kneels, peers through the keyhole, gets up. She goes to the window, looks down, frowns.* JAMES *from the yard sings gaily up to her:*]

JAMES.
> *Buffalo girl, are you coming out tonight,*
> *Coming out tonight,*
> *Coming out—*

[*He drifts back into the house.* ANNIE *takes a handkerchief, nurses her mouth, stands in the middle of the room, staring at door and window in turn, and so catches sight of herself in the mirror, her cheek scratched, her hair* disheveled, *her handkerchief bloody, her face disgusted with herself. She addresses the mirror, with some irony.*]

ANNIE. Don't worry. They'll find you, you're not lost. Only out of place.

[*But she coughs, spits something into her palm, and stares at it, outraged.*]

And toothless.

[*She winces.*]

Oo! It hurts.

. . . .

◄ **Vocabulary**
disheveled (di shev´ əld) *adj.* rumpled and untidy

from Act III

At Annie's request, Annie and Helen have just spent two weeks alone in a separate building on the family's property. Annie thought she could make better progress with Helen without the interference of Helen's parents. Now, Helen and Annie return to the family home, where the family gathers for dinner. It soon becomes clear that Helen has still not learned how to behave at the table.

[. . . ANNIE, *with everyone now watching, for the third time puts the napkin on* HELEN. HELEN *yanks it off, and throws it down.* ANNIE *rises, lifts* HELEN*'s plate, and bears it away.* HELEN, *feeling it gone, slides down and commences to kick up under the table; the dishes jump.* ANNIE *contemplates this for a moment, then coming back takes* HELEN*'s wrists firmly and swings her off the chair.* HELEN *struggling gets one hand free, and catches at her mother's skirt; when* KATE *takes her by the shoulders,* HELEN *hangs quiet.*]

KATE. Miss ANNIE.

ANNIE. No.

KATE. [*a pause*] It's a very special day.

ANNIE. [*grimly*] It will be, when I give in to that.

[*She tries to disengage* HELEN*'s hand;* Kate *lays hers on* ANNIE*'s.*]

KATE. Please. I've hardly had a chance to welcome her home—

ANNIE. Captain Keller.

KELLER. [*embarrassed*] Oh. Katie, we—had a little talk, Miss Annie feels that if we indulge Helen in these—

AUNT EV. But what's the child done?

ANNIE. She's learned not to throw things on the floor and kick. It took us the best part of two weeks and—

AUNT EV. But only a napkin, it's not as if it were breakable!

ANNIE. And everything she's learned *is*? Mrs. Keller, I don't think we should—play tug-of-war for her, either give her to me or you keep her from kicking.

KATE. What do you wish to do?

ANNIE. Let me take her from the table.

AUNT EV. Oh, let her stay, my goodness, she's only a child, she doesn't have to wear a napkin if she doesn't want to her first evening—

ANNIE. [*level*] And ask outsiders not to interfere.

AUNT EV. [*astonished*] Out—outsi— I'm the child's *aunt!*

KATE. [*distressed*] Will once hurt so much, Miss Annie? I've— made all Helen's favorite foods, tonight.

[*A pause*]

KELLER. [*gently*] It's a homecoming party, Miss Annie.

[ANNIE *after a moment releases* HELEN. *But she cannot accept it, at her own chair she shakes her head and turns back, intent on* KATE.]

ANNIE. She's testing you. You realize?

JAMES. [*to* ANNIE] She's testing you.

KELLER. Jimmie, be quiet.

[JAMES *sits, tense.*]

Now she's home, naturally she—

ANNIE. And wants to see what will happen. At your hands. I said it was my main worry, is this what you promised me not half an hour ago?

KELLER. [*reasonably*] But she's *not* kicking, now—

ANNIE. And not learning not to. Mrs. Keller, teaching her is bound to be painful, to everyone. I know it hurts to watch, but she'll live up to just what you demand of her, and no more.

JAMES. [*palely*] She's testing *you.*

KELLER. [*testily*] Jimmie.

JAMES. I have an opinion, I think I should—

KELLER. No one's interested in hearing your opinion.

ANNIE. *I'm* interested, of course she's testing me. Let me keep her to what she's learned and she'll go on learning from me. Take her out of my hands and it all comes apart.

[KATE *closes her eyes, digesting it;* ANNIE *sits again, with a brief comment for her.*]

Be bountiful, it's at her expense.

[*She turns to* JAMES, *flatly.*]

Please pass me more of—her favorite foods.

[*Then* KATE *lifts* HELEN*'s hand, and turning her toward* ANNIE, *surrenders her;* HELEN *makes for her own chair.*]

KATE. [*low*] Take her, Miss Annie.

ANNIE. [*then*] Thank you.

[*But the moment* ANNIE *rising reaches for her hand,* HELEN *begins to fight and kick, clutching to the tablecloth, and uttering laments.* ANNIE *again tries to loosen her hand, and* KELLER *rises.*]

KELLER. [*tolerant*] I'm afraid you're the difficulty, Miss Annie. Now I'll keep her to what she's learned, you're quite right there—

[*He takes* HELEN*'s hands from* ANNIE, *pats them;* HELEN *quiets down.*]

—but I don't see that we need send her from the table, after all, she's the guest of honor. Bring her plate back.

ANNIE. If she was a seeing child, none of you would tolerate one—

KELLER. Well, she's not, I think some compromise is called for. Bring her plate, please.

Vocabulary ▶
aversion (ə vʉr´ zhən) n.
intense dislike

[ANNIE's *jaw sets, but she restores the plate, while* KELLER *fastens the napkin around* HELEN's *neck; she permits it.*]

There. It's not unnatural, most of us take some **aversion** to our teachers, and occasionally another hand can smooth things out.

[*He puts a fork in* HELEN's *hand;* HELEN *takes it. Genially:*]

Now. Shall we start all over?

[*He goes back around the table, and sits.* ANNIE *stands watching.* HELEN *is motionless, thinking things through, until with a wicked glee she deliberately flings the fork on the floor. After another moment she plunges her hand into her food, and crams a fistful into her mouth.*]

JAMES. [*wearily*] I think we've started all over—

[KELLER *shoots a glare at him, as* HELEN *plunges her other hand into* ANNIE's *plate.* ANNIE *at once moves in, to grasp her wrist, and* HELEN *flinging out a hand encounters the pitcher; she swings with it at* ANNIE; ANNIE *falling back blocks it with an elbow, but the water flies over her dress.* ANNIE *gets her breath, then snatches the pitcher away in one hand, hoists* HELEN *up bodily under the other arm, and starts to carry her out, kicking.* KELLER *stands.*]

ANNIE. [*savagely polite*] Don't get up!

KELLER. Where are you going?

ANNIE. Don't smooth anything else out for me, don't interfere in any way! I treat her like a seeing child because I *ask* her to see, I *expect* her to see, don't undo what I do!

KELLER. Where are you taking her?

ANNIE. To make her fill this pitcher again!

[*She thrusts out with* HELEN *under her arm, but* HELEN *escapes up the stairs and* ANNIE *runs after her.* KELLER *stands rigid.* AUNT EV *is astounded.*]

AUNT EV. You let her speak to you like that, Arthur? A creature who *works* for you?

KELLER. [*angrily*] No. I don't.

[*He is starting after* ANNIE *when* JAMES, *on his feet with shaky resolve, interposes his chair between them in* KELLER's *path.*]

JAMES. Let her go.

KELLER. What!

JAMES. [*a swallow*] I said—let her go. She's right.

[KELLER *glares at the chair and him.* JAMES *takes a deep breath, then headlong:*]

She's right, Kate's right, I'm right, and you're wrong. If you drive her away from here it will be over my dead—chair, has it never occurred to you that on one occasion you might be consummately wrong?

[KELLER*'s stare is unbelieving, even a little fascinated.* KATE *rises in* trepidation, *to mediate.*]

KATE. Captain.

[KELLER *stops her with his raised hand; his eyes stay on* JAMES*'s pale face, for a long hold. When he finally finds his voice, it is gruff.*]

KELLER. Sit down, everyone.

[*He sits.* KATE *sits.* JAMES *holds onto his chair.* KELLER *speaks mildly.*]

Please sit down, Jimmie.

[JAMES *sits, and a moveless silence prevails;* KELLER*'s eyes do not leave him.*

ANNIE *has pulled* HELEN *downstairs again by one hand, the pitcher in her other hand, down the porch steps, and across the yard to the pump. She puts* HELEN*'s hand on the pump handle, grimly.*]

ANNIE. All right. Pump.

[HELEN *touches her cheek, waits uncertainly.*]

No, she's not here. Pump!

[*She forces* HELEN*'s hand to work the handle, then lets go. And* HELEN *obeys. She pumps till the water comes, then* ANNIE *puts the pitcher in her other hand and guides it under the spout, and the water tumbling half into and half around the pitcher douses* HELEN*'s hand.* ANNIE *takes over the handle to keep water coming, and does automatically what she has done so many times before, spells into* HELEN*'s free palm:*]

Water. W, a, t, e, r. *Water.* It has a—*name*—

[*And now the miracle happens.* HELEN *drops the pitcher on the slab under the spout, it shatters. She stands transfixed.* ANNIE *freezes on the pump handle: there is a change in the sundown light, and with it a change in* HELEN*'s face, some light coming into*

◄ Vocabulary
trepidation (trep´ ə dā´ shən) *n.* fear; anxiety; dread

it we have never seen there, some struggle in the depths behind it; and her lips tremble, trying to remember something the muscles around them once knew, till at last it finds its way out, painfully, a baby sound buried under the debris of years of dumbness.]

HELEN. Wah. Wah.

[*And again, with great effort*]

Wah. Wah.

[HELEN *plunges her hand into the dwindling water, spells into her own palm. Then she gropes frantically,* ANNIE *reaches for her hand, and* HELEN *spells into* ANNIE'S *hand.*]

ANNIE. [*whispering*] Yes.

[HELEN *spells into it again.*]

Yes!

[HELEN *grabs at the handle, pumps for more water, plunges her hand into its spurt and grabs* ANNIE'S *to spell it again.*]

Yes! Oh, my dear—

[*She falls to her knees to clasp* HELEN'S *hand, but* HELEN *pulls it free, stands almost bewildered, then drops to the ground, pats it swiftly, holds up her palm, imperious.* ANNIE *spells into it:*]

Ground.

[HELEN *spells it back.*]

Yes!

[HELEN *whirls to the pump, pats it, holds up her palm, and* ANNIE *spells into it.*]

Pump.

[HELEN *spells it back.*]

Yes! Yes!

[*Now* HELEN *is in such an excitement she is possessed, wild, trembling, cannot be still, turns, runs, falls on the porch steps, claps it, reaches out her palm, and* ANNIE *is at it instantly to spell:*]

Step.

[HELEN *has no time to spell back now, she whirls groping, to touch anything, encounters the trellis, shakes it, thrusts out her palm, and* ANNIE *while spelling to her cries wildly at the house.*]

Trellis. Mrs. Keller. *Mrs. Keller!*

Close Reading Activities

Read

Comprehension: Key Ideas and Details

1. **(a)** Why has Annie come to the Kellers' home? **(b) Infer:** What is Helen like when Annie first arrives? Cite details to support your answer.

2. **(a) Contrast:** What are the differences between the way Annie treats Helen and the way others do? Cite evidence from the play. **(b) Draw Conclusions:** Does Annie understand Helen better than the others do? Explain.

3. **(a)** Describe Annie's personality, citing evidence from the play. **(b) Speculate:** What do you think motivates Annie to help Helen? Cite the play for support.

4. **Summarize:** Write a brief, objective summary of the excerpt from Act III.

Text Analysis: Craft and Structure

5. **Compare and Contrast:** Give two examples of the writer's use of dialogue to reveal the characters of Captain Keller and of Annie. What similarities and differences do they reveal?

6. **(a) Generalize:** What information about Helen is given in the stage directions? Cite details from the play to answer. **(b) Connect:** Why does the playwright use stage directions rather than dialogue to convey this information?

7. The climax of a play is the moment of greatest tension, which determines how the play ends. **(a) Identify:** Which event in this play is the climax? **(b) Analyze:** Identify one way in which the playwright intensifies readers' emotions right before the climax.

Connections: Integration of Knowledge and Ideas

Discuss
Conduct a **small-group discussion** about Annie Sullivan and Helen Keller's relationship. Discuss how it began and developed.

Research
Briefly research Annie Sullivan and take notes on the following:

a. hardships during her childhood

b. her education

Then, write a brief **explanation** of how Sullivan's experiences made her the ideal teacher for Helen Keller.

Write
A **play review** tells what a play is about and includes the reviewer's evaluation. Review *The Miracle Worker.* Cite details from the two scenes to support your review.

 Is it our differences or our similarities that matter most?

Helen Keller was seen as different because of her inability to communicate. How does Annie Sullivan help Helen overcome obstacles and participate more fully in society?

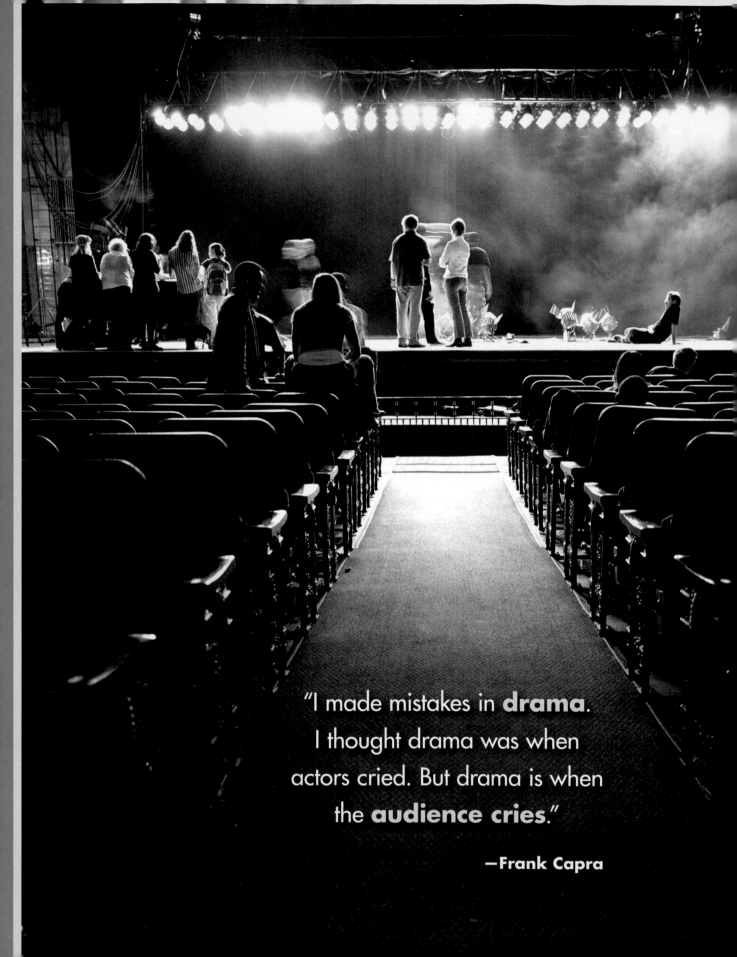

"I made mistakes in **drama**. I thought drama was when actors cried. But drama is when the **audience cries**."

—Frank Capra

DIALOGUE AND DISCOVERY

Drama connects. It connects audience members to the characters on stage, teaching the audience to understand and to sympathize with them. It connects audience members with each other, enabling them to share deep emotion or humor. As you read the plays in this section, examine the ways the authors help you connect with the characters and with other readers. For example, look for ways the authors use dialogue to reveal the characters' thoughts and feelings, deepening your understanding and inspiring your sympathy. The quotation on the facing page will help you start thinking about the ways in which drama connects audience members to characters and to each other.

◀ **CRITICAL VIEWING** What does this photograph suggest about the theatrical techniques that actors, directors, lighting engineers, and so on can use to connect with an audience?

READINGS IN PART 2

EXEMPLAR TEXT Ⓖ
DRAMA
The Diary of Anne Frank, Act I
Frances Goodrich and Albert Hackett (p. 534)

EXEMPLAR TEXT Ⓖ
DRAMA
The Diary of Anne Frank, Act II
Frances Goodrich and Albert Hackett (p. 598)

DRAMA
The Governess
Neil Simon (p. 642)

CLOSE READING TOOL

Use the **Close Reading Tool** to practice the strategies you learn in this unit.

Elements of Drama

In **drama**, dialogue and action work together to develop characters and tell a story.

Drama is a genre of literature that is meant to be performed. It includes **plays,** or stories meant to be performed by actors on stage.

The **playwright,** or dramatist, is the author of the **script,** the written version of a play. The script contains **dialogue,** the words spoken by the characters, and **stage directions,** which provide instructions on how the play should be performed.

A play takes place at a particular time and location, called the **setting.** As a play develops, we learn about the **characters** and the struggle, or **conflict,** they face. Events in the **plot** move forward, and the action builds until it reaches a **climax,** the point when the conflict reaches its peak. As the play comes to a close, the conflict is usually settled. This part of the play is called the **resolution.**

A successful play presents the reader or audience with believable, **well-rounded characters.** Such characters remind us of people we know in real life. Playwrights portray well-rounded characters through the careful development of dialogue that reveals not only *what* the characters say but *how* and *why* they say it.

Elements of Drama

Element	Function
Dialogue	• reveals the nature of characters • advances the plot • establishes theme, the work's central message about life or human nature
Characters	• have qualities, or traits, and motivations shown through their words and actions • face one or more conflicts • develop theme through their words and actions
Plot	• may be organized to develop suspense • focuses on a conflict, or struggle between opposing forces • builds to a climax, or turning point—the point of maximum interest • shows relationships between characters' actions and events • expresses theme
Stage Directions	• describe scenery, lighting, and sound effects • tell how characters behave
Setting	• is the time and place in which the action occurs • creates mood

Types of Drama

Two general categories of drama are comedy and tragedy.

A **comedy** usually deals with a light subject or handles a dark subject in an upbeat way. Comedies often present everyday characters in amusing situations. They are humorous in tone and end happily.

In a **tragedy,** events lead to the downfall or death of the main character. This character can be an average person but is often a heroic figure who displays a **tragic flaw,** a human trait such as pride or greed, that brings about his or her destruction. A tragedy may teach a powerful lesson about human nature.

A playwright may combine elements of both comedy and tragedy in a single work. For example, some comedies use humor to express a serious message about life or human nature. Likewise, a tragedy might include **comic relief**—a scene or an incident that provides a break from the otherwise serious events of the play.

The Changing World of Drama

For centuries, plays were intended to be viewed by a live audience or read in script form. Today, technology has changed the ways in which we experience plays. We can still watch a play with live actors onstage, but we can also watch a performance onscreen in a movie theater or at home in front of our televisions or computers.

 **Common Core State Standards**

Reading Literature

3. Analyze how particular lines of dialogue or incidents in a story or drama propel the action, reveal aspects of a character, or provoke a decision.

6. Analyze how differences in the points of view of the characters and the audience or reader (e.g., created through the use of dramatic irony) create such effects as suspense or humor.

Types of Drama Today

Live Theater	Film/Movies	Television Drama	Radio Drama
• performed live for an audience • follows a written script • is divided into acts and scenes • uses dialogue to tell the audience what is happening • uses scenery and lighting for visual effects	• recorded on film or digital medium and shown in theaters or streamed online • follows a script called a screenplay • is often made up of many short scenes • uses a camera to direct audience's attention to certain details	• recorded or performed live • follows a script called a teleplay • uses long and short scenes • like film, uses a camera to direct audience's attention • may be streamed online over the Internet	• recorded or performed live • follows a script called a radio play • uses long and short scenes • uses dialogue and sound effects to tell the audience what is happening

Analyzing Dramatic Elements

In drama, **conflict**, **dialogue**, and **stage directions** make the characters and their actions come alive.

Drama has the power to reveal important truths about life and human nature. Whether you are reading a play or watching it, realistic characters can remind you of yourself or people you know. Even if just for a moment, you may feel as strongly about their situations as you do about real life. It is through the play's action, conflict, and dialogue that this magic takes place.

Action and Conflict In most plays, characters face a **conflict,** or struggle between opposing forces, that drives the **action.**

- An **external conflict** involves a character confronting an outside force, such as a physical obstacle, an enemy, nature, or society.

- An **internal conflict** is a struggle that occurs within a character. It often involves the character's feelings, beliefs, and values.

Dialogue and Character Development In drama, most of what you learn about characters comes from dialogue. Playwrights use dialogue in the following ways:

- to show a character's personality;
- to express a character's thoughts and feelings about events and other characters.

Character Motivation When a playwright writes a play, he or she must decide who the characters are and what their personalities are like. The playwright must also determine how each character will respond to events in the plot. For example, a character might respond to an event by telling how he or she feels. A character might also respond by making a decision that moves the plot in a new direction. By showing a character's response to events, a playwright develops **character motivation**—the reasons why a character feels or behaves a certain way. The following chart demonstrates how character motivation works.

Character Motivation	Shown by the Resulting Action
Anna likes Max, a new boy at school, and wants to meet him.	Anna's friend Jenna is having a party. At Anna's request, Jenna invites both Anna and Max to the party.
A man must get on the last train out of his war-torn country.	The man sleeps at the station the night before to guarantee his spot on the train.

Character motivation typically sets up a **cause-and-effect relationship** between events in a play. In the first example from the chart on page 528, Anna's desire to get to know the new boy causes her to ask Jenna to invite them both to a party. The resulting action is the effect.

Complex Characters To create plays that audiences care about, playwrights strive to develop **complex characters.** These characters display strengths and weaknesses and exhibit a full range of emotions. Sometimes, complex characters have multiple motivations.

Characters in Written Drama

In a live performance, the actors use facial expressions, body language, and tones of voice to help the audience understand the characters. When you read a play, however, you must gather clues to fully understand the characters and their motivations and conflicts. Here are questions to ask yourself:

- Do the stage directions call for certain movements, facial expressions, or vocal intonations? (Example: *She nods in agreement.*)
- Do punctuation marks in a speech express a character's mood or feeling? (Example: That's amazing! I had no idea!)
- Do the characters use certain words that reveal their relationships? (Example: Honey, why didn't you call me?)

Dramatic Irony Sometimes the audience or readers of a play know more than the characters know. Such situations are examples of **dramatic irony,** a technique that can create humor or build suspense. The chart shows an example of dramatic irony and two possible ways that the situation might be revealed to the audience but hidden from the other characters.

Situation: The audience knows a character works on a farm, while the other characters believe she is a queen.

Dramatic Irony: The other characters ask the "queen" to punish the farm worker; the audience knows the "queen" and farm worker are the same person.

Possibility 1: The character puts on a disguise during a scene in which the other characters are not present.

Possibility 2: The character reveals she is in disguise by delivering a speech called an **aside.** An aside can be heard by the audience but not by other characters.

When a playwright uses dramatic irony, the point of view of the audience is very different from the points of view of the characters.

Theme in Drama As characters face conflicts and undergo change, their actions and attitudes deliver important messages about life, or themes. To determine the theme of a dramatic work, ask yourself these questions:

- How have events caused the characters to change?
- Do events in the play remind me of my own experiences? If so, what did those experiences teach me?
- What might have been the playwright's purpose for writing the play?

Frances Goodrich (1890–1984) and **Albert Hackett** (1900–1995) began working together in 1927 and were married in 1931. The couple's writings included screenplays for such classic films as *The Thin Man* (1934), *It's a Wonderful Life* (1946), and *Father of the Bride* (1950). They spent two years writing *The Diary of Anne Frank.* The play won a Pulitzer Prize and other awards.

© Common Core State Standards

Reading Literature

3. Analyze how particular lines of dialogue or incidents in a story or drama propel the action, reveal aspects of a character, or provoke a decision.

4. Analyze the impact of specific word choices on meaning and tone, including analogies or allusions to other texts.

6. Analyze how differences in the points of view of the characters and the audience or reader (e.g., created through the use of dramatic irony) create such effects as suspense or humor.

② Is it our differences or our similarities that matter most?

Explore the Big Question as you read *The Diary of Anne Frank,* Act I. Take notes on similarities and differences among the characters.

CLOSE READING FOCUS

Key Ideas and Details: **Cause and Effect**

A **cause** is an event, an action, or a feeling that produces a result, or an **effect**. When a story is set in a particular time and place, use background information, including facts provided in the introduction and footnotes, to link historical causes with effects. For example, in a play about the U.S. Civil War, a mother in a border state begs her sons not to take sides. The war is the cause; family strife is the effect. Background knowledge that the division between the North and South led to divided loyalties in border states helps you understand this situation.

Craft and Structure: **Dialogue**

Dialogue is a conversation between or among characters. Dialogue serves three main functions:

- helping readers learn about the characters and their goals.
- setting the tone of a scene and conveying its significance.
- developing the plot and subplots. Conflicts come to life as characters confide in friends, argue with enemies, and plan their actions.

As you read, notice how dialogue develops characters, establishes tone, and propels the plot. Look for ways dialogue helps create *dramatic irony,* a situation in which the audience knows more than the characters about events.

Vocabulary

You will encounter the following words in this play. Copy the words into your notebook. Which is a synonym for *unbearable*?

conspicuous	tension	resent
insufferable	bewildered	fatalist

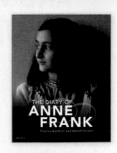

CLOSE READING MODEL

The passage below is from the play *The Diary of Anne Frank*. The annotations to the right of the passage show ways in which you can use close reading skills to identify causes and effects and to analyze dialogue.

from *The Diary of Anne Frank,* Act I

ANNE. [*Pulling out a pasteboard-bound book*] A diary! [*She throws her arms around her father.*] I've never had a diary. And I've always longed for one.[1] [*She looks around the room.*] Pencil, pencil, pencil, pencil. [*She starts down the stairs.*] I'm going down to the office to get a pencil.

MR. FRANK. Anne! No! [*He goes after her, catching her by the arm and pulling her back.*]

ANNE. [*Startled*] But there's no one in the building now.

MR. FRANK. It doesn't matter. I don't want you ever to go beyond that door.

ANNE. [*Sobered*] Never . . . ? Not even at nighttime, when everyone is gone? Or on Sundays? Can't I go down to listen to the radio?

MR. FRANK. Never. I am sorry, Anneke. It isn't safe. No, you must never go beyond that door.

[*For the first time* ANNE *realizes what "going into hiding" means.*]

ANNE. I see.[2]

MR. FRANK. It'll be hard, I know. But always remember this, Anneke. There are no walls, there are no bolts, no locks that anyone can put on your mind.[3] Miep will bring us books. We will read history, poetry, mythology.[4]

Dialogue

1 This dialogue reveals Anne's interest in keeping a diary. It helps to reveal her personality—how she thinks and acts. It also helps propel the plot, since Anne's diary is important to the story.

Cause and Effect

2 Mr. Frank gives a chilling warning. If you apply the background knowledge that the Franks went into hiding to escape the persecution and killing of Jews during the Holocaust, you will better understand why he insists that Anne stay inside their hiding spot.

Dialogue

3 The dialogue shows Mr. Frank's determination to keep up his daughter's spirits no matter what. It reveals his character, showing his kindness and his sense of purpose.

Cause and Effect

4 Readers learn that someone will provide books. Knowing that some people helped hide Jews during World War II can help you understand the causes involved—someone sympathetic to the family is helping out.

FRANK FAMILY
AND WORLD WAR II
TIMELINES

Shown on these pages is a brief timeline of events in the lives of a single Jewish family, the Frank family. The Franks—Otto and Edith and their daughters, Anne and Margot—lived in Europe during a period of Nazi terror in which Jews were forced to flee their homes or go into hiding—or face persecution. This period of anti-Jewish violence and mass murder is known as the Holocaust. The major events of the period are shown on the bottom half of the timeline.

1941 Growing Nazi restrictions on the daily lives of Dutch Jews force the Frank girls to attend an all-Jewish school.

JUNE 12, 1942 Otto gives Anne a diary for her thirteenth birthday.

JULY 6, 1942 The Franks go into hiding after receiving an order for Margot to report to a forced labor camp. They hide in the attic rooms above Mr. Frank's workplace with the help of close friends. Another family, the Van Pels (called the "Van Daans" in her diary), joins them, followed by Fritz Pfeffer ("Dussel"), months later.

TIMELINE OF THE FRANK FAMILY

SUMMER 1933 Alarmed by Nazi actions in Germany, Otto Frank begins the process of moving his family to safety in the Netherlands.

1929 Anne Frank is born in Frankfurt, Germany.

1934 Anne starts kindergarten at the Montessori school in Amsterdam.

1925	1930	1935	1940

TIMELINE OF WORLD EVENTS

JANUARY 1933 Adolf Hitler comes to power in Germany. Over the next few months, all political parties, except the Nazi Party, are banned. Jews are dismissed from medical, legal, government, and teaching positions.

1935 The Nuremberg Laws are passed in Germany, stripping Jews of their rights as German citizens. Laws passed over the next several years further isolate Jews, including the requirement to wear a yellow Star of David.

SEPTEMBER 1, 1939 Germany invades Poland, triggering the beginning of World War II.

MAY 1940 The Nazis invade the Netherlands. Once in control, they set up a brutal police force, the Gestapo, to administer laws to isolate Dutch Jews from the rest of the Dutch population.

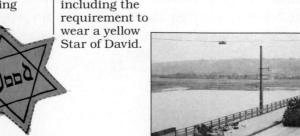

AUGUST 4, 1944
The hiding place of the Franks is discovered and the families are arrested.

SEPTEMBER 3, 1944
All eight of those who hid in the attic are deported from the Netherlands to the Auschwitz death camp.

MARCH 1945*
Anne and Margot die of the disease typhus in the Bergen-Belsen concentration camp.

1947 Anne's diary is published in Dutch. Over the next few years it is translated and published in France, Germany, the United States, Japan, and Great Britain.

1960 The hiding place of the Franks is converted into a permanent museum that tells the story of Anne and those who hid with her.

| 1945 | 1950 | 1955 | 1960 |

MAY 1945 The Allies win as the war in Europe ends.

JUNE 1944 The Allies carry out a successful invasion of France. Their success gives many who live under Nazi occupation hope that the end of the war is near.

JANUARY 1943 The Battle of Stalingrad marks the turning of the tide against the Nazis.

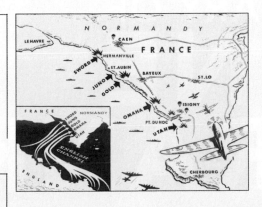

MAY 1960 Adolf Eichmann, one of the last major Nazi figures to be tried, is captured and put on trial in Israel. He is convicted and executed for his role in arranging the transport of Jews to concentration camps and ghettoes, where an estimated six million Jews died.

*Estimate. Exact date unknown.

THE DIARY OF
ANNE
FRANK

Frances Goodrich and Albert Hackett

Characters

Anne Frank	Miep Gies	Mrs. Van Daan
Otto Frank	Mr. Kraler	Mr. Van Daan
Edith Frank	Mr. Dussel	
Margot Frank	Peter Van Daan	

Act I

Scene 1

[The scene remains the same throughout the play. It is the top floor of a warehouse and office building in Amsterdam, Holland. The sharply peaked roof of the building is outlined against a sea of other rooftops, stretching away into the distance. Nearby is the belfry of a church tower, the Westertoren, whose carillon[1] rings out the hours. Occasionally faint sounds float up from below: the voices of children playing in the street, the tramp of marching feet, a boat whistle from the canal.

The three rooms of the top floor and a small attic space above are exposed to our view. The largest of the rooms is in the center, with two small rooms, slightly raised, on either side. On the right is a bathroom, out of sight. A narrow steep flight of stairs at the back leads up to the attic. The rooms are sparsely furnished with a few chairs, cots, a table or two. The windows are painted over, or covered with makeshift blackout curtains.[2] In the main room there is a sink, a gas ring for cooking and a woodburning stove for warmth.

The room on the left is hardly more than a closet. There is a skylight in the sloping ceiling. Directly under this room is a small steep stairwell, with steps leading down to a door. This is the only entrance from the building below. When the door is opened we see that it has been concealed on the outer side by a bookcase attached to it.

The curtain rises on an empty stage. It is late afternoon, November 1945.

---

1. **carillon** (kar´ ə län´) n. set of bells, each producing one note of the scale.
2. **blackout curtains** dark curtains that conceal all lights that might be visible to bombers from the air.

Cause and Effect
Use your knowledge of Nazi policies toward Jews to explain why these rooms might serve as a hiding place for a Jewish family.

Comprehension
What is the setting of this play?

▲ During the war, the Allies bombed industrial areas that had been taken over by the Germans.

The rooms are dusty, the curtains in rags. Chairs and tables are overturned.

The door at the foot of the small stairwell swings open. MR. FRANK comes up the steps into view. He is a gentle, cultured European in his middle years. There is still a trace of a German accent in his speech.

He stands looking slowly around, making a supreme effort at self-control. He is weak, ill. His clothes are threadbare.

After a second he drops his rucksack on the couch and moves slowly about. He opens the door to one of the smaller rooms, and then abruptly closes it again, turning away. He goes to the window at the back, looking off at the Westertoren as its carillon strikes the hour of six, then he moves restlessly on. From the street below we hear the sound of a barrel organ[3] and children's voices at play. There is a many-colored scarf hanging from a nail. MR. FRANK takes it, putting it around his

---

3. **barrel organ** mechanical musical instrument often played by street musicians in past decades.

neck. *As he starts back for his rucksack, his eye is caught by something lying on the floor. It is a woman's white glove. He holds it in his hand and suddenly all of his self-control is gone. He breaks down, crying.*

We hear footsteps on the stairs. Miep Gies *comes up, looking for* Mr. Frank. Miep *is a Dutch girl of about twenty-two. She wears a coat and hat, ready to go home. She is pregnant. Her attitude toward* Mr. Frank *is protective, compassionate.*]

Miep. Are you all right, Mr. Frank?

Mr. Frank. [*Quickly controlling himself*] Yes, Miep, yes.

Miep. Everyone in the office has gone home . . . It's after six. [*Then pleading*] Don't stay up here, Mr. Frank. What's the use of torturing yourself like this?

Mr. Frank. I've come to say good-bye . . . I'm leaving here, Miep.

Miep. What do you mean? Where are you going? Where?

Mr. Frank. I don't know yet. I haven't decided.

Miep. Mr. Frank, you can't leave here! This is your home! Amsterdam is your home. Your business is here, waiting for you . . . You're needed here . . . Now that the war is over, there are things that . . .

Mr. Frank. I can't stay in Amsterdam, Miep. It has too many memories for me. Everywhere there's something . . . the house we lived in . . . the school . . . that street organ playing out there . . . I'm not the person you used to know, Miep. I'm a bitter old man. [*Breaking off*] Forgive me. I shouldn't speak to you like this . . . after all that you did for us . . . the suffering . . .

Miep. No. No. It wasn't suffering. You can't say we suffered. [*As she speaks, she straightens a chair which is overturned.*]

Mr. Frank. I know what you went through, you and Mr. Kraler. I'll remember it as long as I live. [*He gives one last look around.*] Come, Miep. [*He starts for the steps, then remembers his rucksack, going back to get it.*]

Miep. [*Hurrying up to a cupboard*] Mr. Frank, did you see? There are some of your papers here. [*She brings a bundle of papers to him.*] We found them in a heap of rubbish on the floor after . . . after you left.

Cause and Effect
The war in Europe ended in May 1945, but many who survived the camps did not return until the fall. What effect has the war had on Mr. Frank?

Dialogue
What do Mr. Frank's words and the hesitation in his speech tell you about his feelings?

Cause and Effect
What events might make it harder for Mr. Frank to think of Amsterdam as home? Explain.

Comprehension
Why does Miep want Mr. Frank to stay?

MR. FRANK. Burn them. [*He opens his rucksack to put the glove in it.*]

MIEP. But, Mr. Frank, there are letters, notes . . .

MR. FRANK. Burn them. All of them.

MIEP. Burn *this*? [*She hands him a paperbound notebook.*]

MR. FRANK. [*Quietly*] Anne's diary. [*He opens the diary and begins to read.*] "Monday, the sixth of July, nineteen forty-two." [*To* MIEP] Nineteen forty-two. Is it possible, Miep? . . . Only three years ago. [*As he continues his reading, he sits down on the couch.*] "Dear Diary, since you and I are going to be great friends, I will start by telling you about myself. My name is Anne Frank. I am thirteen years old. I was born in Germany the twelfth of June, nineteen twenty-nine. As my family is Jewish, we emigrated to Holland when Hitler came to power."

[*As* MR. FRANK *reads on, another voice joins his, as if coming from the air. It is* ANNE'S VOICE.]

MR. FRANK AND ANNE. "My father started a business, importing spice and herbs. Things went well for us until nineteen forty. Then the war came, and the Dutch capitulation,[4] followed by the arrival of the Germans. Then things got very bad for the Jews."

[MR. FRANK'S VOICE *dies out.* ANNE'S VOICE *continues alone. The lights dim slowly to darkness. The curtain falls on the scene.*]

ANNE'S VOICE. You could not do this and you could not do that. They forced Father out of his business. We had to wear yellow stars.[5] I had to turn in my bike. I couldn't go to a Dutch school any more. I couldn't go to the movies, or ride in an automobile, or even on a streetcar, and a million other things. But somehow we children still managed to have fun. Yesterday Father told me we were going into hiding. Where, he wouldn't say. At five o'clock this morning Mother woke me and told me to hurry and get dressed. I was to put on as many clothes as I could. It would look too suspicious if we walked along carrying suitcases. It wasn't until we were on our way that I learned where we were going. Our hiding place was to be upstairs in the building where

Cause and Effect
Anne is referring to Adolf Hitler, the German dictator who persecuted Jews throughout Europe. What other historical causes and effects do you learn here?

Dialogue
In the play, Anne's lines are often spoken to her diary, as if the diary were another character. What significant plot event is revealed in this speech?

---

4. **capitulation** (kə pich′ ə lā′ shən) *n.* surrender.
5. **yellow stars** Stars of David, the six-pointed stars that are symbols of Judaism. The Nazis ordered all Jews to wear them on their clothing.

Father used to have his business. Three other people were coming in with us . . . the Van Daans and their son Peter . . . Father knew the Van Daans but we had never met them . . .

[*During the last lines the curtain rises on the scene. The lights dim on.* ANNE'S VOICE *fades out.*]

Scene 2

[*It is early morning, July 1942. The rooms are bare, as before, but they are now clean and orderly.*

MR. VAN DAAN, *a tall, portly[6] man in his late forties, is in the main room, pacing up and down, nervously smoking a cigarette. His clothes and overcoat are expensive and well cut.*

MRS. VAN DAAN *sits on the couch, clutching her possessions, a hatbox, bags, etc. She is a pretty woman in her early forties. She wears a fur coat over her other clothes.*

PETER VAN DAAN *is standing at the window of the room on the right, looking down at the street below. He is a shy, awkward boy of sixteen. He wears a cap, a raincoat, and long Dutch trousers, like "plus fours."[7] At his feet is a black case, a carrier for his cat.*

*The yellow Star of David is **conspicuous** on all of their clothes.*]

---

6. **portly** (pôrt´ lē) *adj.* large and heavy.
7. **plus fours** *n.* loose knickers (short pants) worn for active sports.

▼ **Critical Viewing**
This photograph shows the Frank family with some friends before their years in hiding. How would you describe their mood, judging from their expressions?

◀ **Vocabulary**
conspicuous (kən spik´ yōō əs) *adj.* noticeable

Comprehension
How did life change for the Franks after the Germans invaded?

MRS. VAN DAAN. [*Rising, nervous, excited*] Something's happened to them! I know it!

MR. VAN DAAN. Now, Kerli!

MRS. VAN DAAN. Mr. Frank said they'd be here at seven o'clock. He said . . .

MR. VAN DAAN. They have two miles to walk. You can't expect . . .

MRS. VAN DAAN. They've been picked up. That's what's happened. They've been taken . . .

[MR. VAN DAAN *indicates that he hears someone coming.*]

MR. VAN DAAN. You see?

[PETER *takes up his carrier and his schoolbag, etc., and goes into the main room as* MR. FRANK *comes up the stairwell from below.* MR. FRANK *looks much younger now. His movements are brisk, his manner confident. He wears an overcoat and carries his hat and a small cardboard box. He crosses to the* VAN DAANS, *shaking hands with each of them.*]

MR. FRANK. Mrs. Van Daan, Mr. Van Daan, Peter. [*Then, in explanation of their lateness*] There were too many of the Green Police[8] on the streets . . . we had to take the long way around.

[*Up the steps come* MARGOT FRANK, MRS. FRANK, MIEP *(not pregnant now) and* MR. KRALER. *All of them carry bags, packages, and so forth. The Star of David is conspicuous on all of the* FRANKS' *clothing.* MARGOT *is eighteen, beautiful, quiet, shy.* MRS. FRANK *is a young mother, gently bred, reserved. She, like* MR. FRANK, *has a slight German accent.* MR. KRALER *is a Dutchman, dependable, kindly.*

As MR. KRALER *and* MIEP *go upstage to put down their parcels,* MRS. FRANK *turns back to call* ANNE.]

MRS. FRANK. Anne?

[ANNE *comes running up the stairs. She is thirteen, quick in her movements, interested in everything, mercurial[9] in her emotions. She wears a cape, long wool socks and carries a schoolbag.*]

Dialogue
How do the authors convey a mood of anxiety through the Van Daans' dialogue?

Cause and Effect
Read the footnote on the "Green Police." Why do the Franks fear this force?

8. **Green Police** the Dutch Gestapo, or Nazi police, who wore green uniforms and were known for their brutality. Those in danger of being arrested or deported feared the Gestapo, especially because of their practice of raiding houses to round up victims in the middle of the night—when people are most confused and vulnerable.
9. **mercurial** (mər kyŏŏr′ ē əl) *adj.* quick or changeable in behavior.

MR. FRANK. [*Introducing them*] My wife, Edith. Mr. and Mrs. Van Daan [MRS. FRANK *hurries over, shaking hands with them.*] . . . their son, Peter . . . my daughters, Margot and Anne.

[ANNE *gives a polite little curtsy as she shakes* MR. VAN DAAN'S *hand. Then she immediately starts off on a tour of investigation of her new home, going upstairs to the attic room.*

MIEP *and* MR. KRALER *are putting the various things they have brought on the shelves.*]

MR. KRALER. I'm sorry there is still so much confusion.

MR. FRANK. Please. Don't think of it. After all, we'll have plenty of leisure to arrange everything ourselves.

MIEP. [*To* MRS. FRANK] We put the stores of food you sent in here. Your drugs are here . . . soap, linen here.

MRS. FRANK. Thank you, Miep.

MIEP. I made up the beds . . . the way Mr. Frank and Mr. Kraler said. [*She starts out.*] Forgive me. I have to hurry. I've got to go to the other side of town to get some ration books[10] for you.

MRS. VAN DAAN. Ration books? If they see our names on ration books, they'll know we're here.

MR. KRALER. There isn't anything . . .

MIEP. Don't worry. Your names won't be on them. [*As she hurries out*] I'll be up later.

MR. FRANK. Thank you, Miep.

MRS. FRANK. [*To* MR. KRALER] It's illegal, then, the ration books? We've never done anything illegal.

MR. FRANK. We won't be living here exactly according to regulations.

[*As* MR. KRALER *reassures* MRS. FRANK, *he takes various small things, such as matches, soap, etc., from his pockets, handing them to her.*]

MR. KRALER. This isn't the black market,[11] Mrs. Frank. This is

---

10. **ration** (rash′ ən) **books** *n.* books of stamps given to ensure the equal distribution of scarce items, such as meat or gasoline, in times of shortage.

11. **black market** illegal way of buying scarce items without ration stamps.

▲ **Critical Viewing**
What will having ration books, like the one above, allow the Franks to do?

Cause and Effect
Why might Mrs. Frank be afraid of doing something illegal? Why is her fear illogical?

Comprehension
How are Miep and Mr. Kraler helping the Franks and Van Daans?

what we call the white market . . . helping all of the hundreds and hundreds who are hiding out in Amsterdam.

[*The carillon is heard playing the quarter-hour before eight.* Mr. Kraler *looks at his watch.* Anne *stops at the window as she comes down the stairs.*]

Anne. It's the Westertoren!

Mr. Kraler. I must go. I must be out of here and downstairs in the office before the workmen get here. [*He starts for the stairs leading out.*] Miep or I, or both of us, will be up each day to bring you food and news and find out what your needs are. Tomorrow I'll get you a better bolt for the door at the foot of the stairs. It needs a bolt that you can throw yourself and open only at our signal. [*To* Mr. Frank] Oh . . . You'll tell them about the noise?

Mr. Frank. I'll tell them.

Mr. Kraler. Good-bye then for the moment. I'll come up again, after the workmen leave.

Mr. Frank. Good-bye, Mr. Kraler.

Mrs. Frank. [*Shaking his hand*] How can we thank you?

[*The others murmur their good-byes.*]

Mr. Kraler. I never thought I'd live to see the day when a man like Mr. Frank would have to go into hiding. When you think—

[*He breaks off, going out.* Mr. Frank *follows him down the steps, bolting the door after him. In the interval before he returns,* Peter *goes over to* Margot, *shaking hands with her. As* Mr. Frank *comes back up the steps,* Mrs. Frank *questions him anxiously.*]

Mrs. Frank. What did he mean, about the noise?

Mr. Frank. First let us take off some of these clothes.

[*They all start to take off garment after garment. On each of their coats, sweaters, blouses, suits, dresses, is another yellow Star of David.* Mr. *and* Mrs. Frank *are underdressed quite simply. The others wear several things, sweaters, extra dresses, bathrobes, aprons, nightgowns, etc.*]

Mr. Van Daan. It's a wonder we weren't arrested, walking along the streets . . . Petronella with a fur coat in July . . . and that cat of Peter's crying all the way.

Cause and Effect
What does the description of the characters' clothing indicate about how long they expect to be in hiding?

ANNE. [*As she is removing a pair of panties*] A cat?

MRS. FRANK. [*Shocked*] Anne, please!

ANNE. It's alright. I've got on three more.

[*She pulls off two more. Finally, as they have all removed their surplus clothes, they look to* MR. FRANK, *waiting for him to speak.*]

MR. FRANK. Now. About the noise. While the men are in the building below, we must have complete quiet. Every sound can be heard down there, not only in the workrooms, but in the offices too. The men come at about eight-thirty, and leave at about five-thirty. So, to be perfectly safe, from eight in the morning until six in the evening we must move only when it is necessary, and then in stockinged feet. We must not speak above a whisper. We must not run any water. We cannot use the sink, or even, forgive me, the w.c.[12] The pipes go down through the workrooms. It would be heard. No trash . . .

[MR. FRANK *stops abruptly as he hears the sound of marching feet from the street below. Everyone is motionless, paralyzed with fear.* MR. FRANK *goes quietly into the room on the right to look down out of the window.* ANNE *runs after him, peering out with him. The tramping feet pass without stopping. The* **tension** *is relieved.* MR. FRANK, *followed by* ANNE, *returns to the main room and resumes his instructions to the group.*] . . . No trash must ever be thrown out which might reveal that someone is living up here . . . not even a potato paring. We must burn everything in the stove at night. This is the way we must live until it is over, if we are to survive.

[*There is silence for a second.*]

MRS. FRANK. Until it is over.

MR. FRANK. [*Reassuringly*] After six we can move about . . . we can talk and laugh and have our supper and read and play games . . . just as we would at home. [*He looks at his watch.*] And now I think it would be wise if we all went to our rooms, and were settled before eight o'clock. Mrs. Van Daan, you and your husband will be upstairs. I regret that there's no place up there for Peter. But he will be here, near us. This will be our common room, where we'll meet to talk and eat and read, like one family.

---

12. **w.c.** water closet; bathroom.

Cause and Effect
Why is the sound of marching feet alarming to the families?

◀ **Vocabulary**
tension (ten´shən) *n.* a nervous, worried, or excited state that makes relaxation impossible

Cause and Effect
Why must the families maintain different schedules for day and night?

Comprehension
Why is it safe to move around after 6 P.M.?

MR. VAN DAAN. And where do you and Mrs. Frank sleep?

MR. FRANK. This room is also our bedroom.

[*Together*] $\Big\{$ **MRS. VAN DAAN.** That isn't right. We'll sleep here and you take the room upstairs.

MR. VAN DAAN. It's your place.

MR. FRANK. Please. I've thought this out for weeks. It's the best arrangement. The only arrangement.

MRS. VAN DAAN. [*To* MR. FRANK] Never, never can we thank you. [*Then to* MRS. FRANK] I don't know what would have happened to us, if it hadn't been for Mr. Frank.

MR. FRANK. You don't know how your husband helped me when I came to this country . . . knowing no one . . . not able to speak the language. I can never repay him for that. [*Going to* VAN DAAN] May I help you with your things?

MR. VAN DAAN. No. No. [*To* MRS. VAN DAAN] Come along, *liefje.*[13]

MRS. VAN DAAN. You'll be all right, Peter? You're not afraid?

PETER. [*Embarrassed*] Please, Mother.

[*They start up the stairs to the attic room above.* MR. FRANK *turns to* MRS. FRANK.]

MR. FRANK. You too must have some rest, Edith. You didn't close your eyes last night. Nor you, Margot.

ANNE. I slept, Father. Wasn't that funny? I knew it was the last night in my own bed, and yet I slept soundly.

MR. FRANK. I'm glad, Anne. Now you'll be able to help me straighten things in here. [*To* MRS. FRANK *and* MARGOT] Come with me . . . You and Margot rest in this room for the time being.

[*He picks up their clothes, starting for the room on the right.*]

MRS. FRANK. You're sure . . .? I could help . . . And Anne hasn't had her milk . . .

MR. FRANK. I'll give it to her. [*To* ANNE *and* PETER] Anne, Peter . . . it's best that you take off your shoes now, before you forget.

[*He leads the way to the room, followed by* MARGOT.]

MRS. FRANK. You're sure you're not tired, Anne?

Dialogue
What does this dialogue reveal about the relationship between Anne and her parents?

---

13. *liefje* (lēf′ yə) Dutch for "little love."

ANNE. I feel fine. I'm going to help Father.

MRS. FRANK. Peter, I'm glad you are to be with us.

PETER. Yes, Mrs. Frank.

[MRS. FRANK *goes to join* MR. FRANK *and* MARGOT.]

[*During the following scene* MR. FRANK *helps* MARGOT *and* MRS. FRANK *to hang up their clothes. Then he persuades them both to lie down and rest. The* VAN DAANS *in their room above settle themselves. In the main room* ANNE *and* PETER *remove their shoes.* PETER *takes his cat out of the carrier.*]

ANNE. What's your cat's name?

PETER. Mouschi.

ANNE. Mouschi! Mouschi! Mouschi! [*She picks up the cat, walking away with it. To* PETER] I love cats. I have one . . . a darling little cat. But they made me leave her behind. I left some food and a note for the neighbors to take care of her . . . I'm going to miss her terribly. What is yours? A him or a her?

PETER. He's a tom. He doesn't like strangers. [*He takes the cat from her, putting it back in its carrier.*]

ANNE. [*Unabashed*] Then I'll have to stop being a stranger, won't I? Is he fixed?

PETER. [*Startled*] Huh?

ANNE. Did you have him fixed?

PETER. No.

ANNE. Oh, you ought to have him fixed—to keep him from— you know, fighting. Where did you go to school?

PETER. Jewish Secondary.

ANNE. But that's where Margot and I go! I never saw you around.

PETER. I used to see you . . . sometimes . . .

ANNE. You did?

PETER. . . . In the school yard. You were always in the middle of a bunch of kids. [*He takes a penknife from his pocket.*]

ANNE. Why didn't you ever come over?

Dialogue
In what way does this dialogue between Peter and Anne highlight the differences between their personalities?

Comprehension
Where did Peter see Anne before they went into hiding?

PETER. I'm sort of a lone wolf. [*He starts to rip off his Star of David.*]

ANNE. What are you doing?

PETER. Taking it off.

ANNE. But you can't do that. They'll arrest you if you go out without your star.

[*He tosses his knife on the table.*]

PETER. Who's going out?

ANNE. Why, of course! You're right! Of course we don't need them any more. [*She picks up his knife and starts to take her star off.*] I wonder what our friends will think when we don't show up today?

PETER. I didn't have any dates with anyone.

ANNE. Oh, I did. I had a date with Jopie to go and play ping-pong at her house. Do you know Jopie de Waal?

PETER. No.

ANNE. Jopie's my best friend. I wonder what she'll think when she telephones and there's no answer? . . . Probably she'll go over to the house . . . I wonder what she'll think . . . we left everything as if we'd suddenly been called away . . . breakfast dishes in the sink . . . beds not made . . . [*As she pulls off her star, the cloth underneath shows clearly the color and form of the star.*] Look! It's still there! [PETER *goes over to the stove with his star.*] What're you going to do with yours?

PETER. Burn it.

ANNE. [*She starts to throw hers in, and cannot.*] It's funny, I can't throw mine away. I don't know why.

PETER. You can't throw . . . ? Something they branded you with . . . ? That they made you wear so they could spit on you?

ANNE. I know. I know. But after all, it *is* the Star of David, isn't it?

[*In the bedroom, right,* MARGOT *and* MRS. FRANK *are lying down.* MR. FRANK *starts quietly out.*]

Cause and Effect
Think about what the yellow star represents in the historical context of World War II. Why is it important to Peter to remove the star?

▼ **Critical Viewing**
Why do you think the Nazis forced Jews to wear yellow stars like this one, bearing the Dutch word for "Jew"?

PETER. Maybe it's different for a girl.

[MR. FRANK *comes into the main room.*]

MR. FRANK. Forgive me, Peter. Now let me see. We must find a bed for your cat. [*He goes to a cupboard.*] I'm glad you brought your cat. Anne was feeling so badly about hers. [*Getting a used small washtub*] Here we are. Will it be comfortable in that?

PETER. [*Gathering up his things*] Thanks.

MR. FRANK. [*Opening the door of the room on the left*] And here is your room. But I warn you, Peter, you can't grow any more. Not an inch, or you'll have to sleep with your feet out of the skylight. Are you hungry?

PETER. No.

MR. FRANK. We have some bread and butter.

PETER. No, thank you.

MR. FRANK. You can have it for luncheon then. And tonight we will have a real supper . . . our first supper together.

PETER. Thanks. Thanks. [*He goes into his room. During the following scene he arranges his possessions in his new room.*]

MR. FRANK. That's a nice boy, Peter.

ANNE. He's awfully shy, isn't he?

MR. FRANK. You'll like him, I know.

ANNE. I certainly hope so, since he's the only boy I'm likely to see for months and months.

[MR. FRANK *sits down, taking off his shoes.*]

MR. FRANK. Annele,[14] there's a box there. Will you open it?

[*He indicates a carton on the couch.* ANNE *brings it to the center table. In the street below there is the sound of children playing.*]

ANNE. [*As she opens the carton*] You know the way I'm going to think of it here? I'm going to think of it as a boarding house. A very peculiar summer boarding house, like the one that we—[*She breaks off as she pulls out some photographs.*] Father! My movie stars! I was wondering where they were! I was looking for them this morning . . . and Queen Wilhelmina![15] How wonderful!

Dialogue
What does this dialogue tell you about Mr. Frank as a person?

Comprehension
Why had the Franks left their house in a messy state?

---

14. **Annele** (än´ ə lə) another nickname for "Anne."
15. **Queen Wilhelmina** (vil´ hel mē´ nä) Queen of the Netherlands from 1890 to 1948.

MR. FRANK. There's something more. Go on. Look further. [*He goes over to the sink, pouring a glass of milk from a thermos bottle.*]

ANNE. [*Pulling out a pasteboard-bound book*] A diary! [*She throws her arms around her father.*] I've never had a diary. And I've always longed for one. [*She looks around the room.*] Pencil, pencil, pencil, pencil. [*She starts down the stairs.*] I'm going down to the office to get a pencil.

MR. FRANK. Anne! No! [*He goes after her, catching her by the arm and pulling her back.*]

ANNE. [*Startled*] But there's no one in the building now.

MR. FRANK. It doesn't matter. I don't want you ever to go beyond that door.

ANNE. [*Sobered*] Never . . . ? Not even at nighttime, when everyone is gone? Or on Sundays? Can't I go down to listen to the radio?

MR. FRANK. Never. I am sorry, Anneke.[16] It isn't safe. No, you must never go beyond that door.

[*For the first time* ANNE *realizes what "going into hiding" means.*]

ANNE. I see.

Cause and Effect
Why is Anne forbidden to go downstairs?

MR. FRANK. It'll be hard, I know. But always remember this, Anneke. There are no walls, there are no bolts, no locks that anyone can put on your mind. Miep will bring us books. We will read history, poetry, mythology. [*He gives her the glass of milk.*] Here's your milk. [*With his arm about her, they go over to the couch, sitting down side by side.*] As a matter of fact, between us, Anne, being here has certain advantages for you. For instance, you remember the battle you had with your mother the other day on the subject of overshoes? You said you'd rather die than wear overshoes? But in the end you had to wear them? Well now, you see, for as long as we are here you will never have to wear overshoes! Isn't that good? And the coat that you inherited from Margot, you won't have to wear that any more. And the piano! You won't have to practice on the piano. I tell you, this is going to be a fine life for you!

---

16. Anneke (än´ ə kə) nickname for "Anne."

[ANNE's *panic is gone.* PETER *appears in the doorway of his room, with a saucer in his hand. He is carrying his cat.*]

PETER. I . . . I . . . I thought I'd better get some water for Mouschi before . . .

MR. FRANK. Of course.

[*As he starts toward the sink the carillon begins to chime the hour of eight. He tiptoes to the window at the back and looks down at the street below. He turns to* PETER, *indicating in pantomime that it is too late.* PETER *starts back for his room. He steps on a creaking board. The three of them are frozen for a minute in fear. As* PETER *starts away again,* ANNE *tiptoes over to him and pours some of the milk from her glass into the saucer for the cat.* PETER *squats on the floor, putting the milk before the cat.* MR. FRANK *gives* ANNE *his fountain pen, and then goes into the room at the right. For a second* ANNE *watches the cat, then she goes over to the center table, and opens her diary.*

In the room at the right, MRS. FRANK *has sat up quickly at the sound of the carillon.* MR. FRANK *comes in and sits down beside her on the settee, his arm comfortingly around her.*

Upstairs, in the attic room, MR. *and* MRS. VAN DAAN *have hung their clothes in the closet and are now seated on the iron bed.* MRS. VAN DAAN *leans back exhausted.* MR. VAN DAAN *fans her with a newspaper.*

ANNE *starts to write in her diary. The lights dim out, the curtain falls.*

Cause and Effect
How does the fear of discovery affect the behavior of the two families?

Comprehension
What positive aspects about living in hiding does Mr. Frank point out to comfort Anne?

◄ The radio was a crucial link to news of the war—especially through non-German stations such as the BBC (British Broadcasting Corporation).

In the darkness ANNE'S VOICE *comes to us again, faintly at first, and then with growing strength.*]

ANNE'S VOICE. I expect I should be describing what it feels like to go into hiding. But I really don't know yet myself. I only know it's funny never to be able to go outdoors . . . never to breathe fresh air . . . never to run and shout and jump. It's the silence in the nights that frightens me most. Every time I hear a creak in the house, or a step on the street outside, I'm sure they're coming for us. The days aren't so bad. At least we know that Miep and Mr. Kraler are down there below us in the office. Our protectors, we call them. I asked Father what would happen to them if the Nazis found out they were hiding us. Pim said that they would suffer the same fate that we would . . . Imagine! They know this, and yet when they come up here, they're always cheerful and gay as if there were nothing in the world to bother them . . . Friday, the twenty-first of August, nineteen forty-two. Today I'm going to tell you our general news. Mother is unbearable. She insists on treating me like a baby, which I loathe. Otherwise things are going better. The weather is . . .

[*As* ANNE'S VOICE *is fading out, the curtain rises on the scene.*]

Scene 3

[*It is a little after six o'clock in the evening, two months later.*
  MARGOT *is in the bedroom at the right, studying.* MR. VAN DAAN *is lying down in the attic room above.*
  The rest of the "family" is in the main room. ANNE *and* PETER *sit opposite each other at the center table, where they have been doing their lessons.* MRS. FRANK *is on the couch.* MRS. VAN DAAN *is seated with her fur coat, on which she has been sewing, in her lap. None of them are wearing their shoes.*
  Their eyes are on MR. FRANK, *waiting for him to give them the signal which will release them from their day-long quiet.* MR. FRANK, *his shoes in his hand, stands looking down out of the window at the back, watching to be sure that all of the workmen have left the building below.*
  After a few seconds of motionless silence, MR. FRANK *turns from the window.*]

MR. FRANK. [*Quietly, to the group*] It's safe now. The last workman has left.

[*There is an immediate stir of relief.*]

ANNE. [*Her pent-up energy explodes.*] WHEE!

MR. FRANK. [*Startled, amused*] Anne!

MRS. VAN DAAN. I'm first for the w.c.

[*She hurries off to the bathroom.* MRS. FRANK *puts on her shoes and starts up to the sink to prepare supper.* ANNE *sneaks* PETER'S *shoes from under the table and hides them behind her back.* MR. FRANK *goes in to* MARGOT'S *room.*]

MR. FRANK. [*To* MARGOT] Six o'clock. School's over.

[MARGOT *gets up, stretching.* MR. FRANK *sits down to put on his shoes. In the main room* PETER *tries to find his.*]

PETER. [*To* ANNE] Have you seen my shoes?

ANNE. [*Innocently*] Your shoes?

PETER. You've taken them, haven't you?

ANNE. I don't know what you're talking about.

PETER. You're going to be sorry!

ANNE. Am I?

[PETER *goes after her.* ANNE, *with his shoes in her hand, runs from him, dodging behind her mother.*]

MRS. FRANK. [*Protesting*] Anne, dear!

PETER. Wait till I get you!

ANNE. I'm waiting!
[PETER *makes a lunge for her. They both fall to the floor.* PETER *pins her down, wrestling with her to get the shoes.*]

Don't! Don't! Peter, stop it. Ouch!

MRS. FRANK. Anne! . . . Peter!

[*Suddenly* PETER *becomes self-conscious. He grabs his shoes roughly and starts for his room.*]

ANNE. [*Following him*] Peter, where are you going?
Come dance with me.

PETER. I tell you I don't know how.

▲ The common living room and dining room of the Anne Frank House has been set up to look as it did when the Franks were in hiding.

Comprehension
Why does Anne take Peter's shoes?

ANNE. I'll teach you.

PETER. I'm going to give Mouschi his dinner.

ANNE. Can I watch?

PETER. He doesn't like people around while he eats.

ANNE. Peter, please.

PETER. No! [*He goes into his room.* ANNE *slams his door after him.*]

MRS. FRANK. Anne, dear, I think you shouldn't play like that with Peter. It's not dignified.

ANNE. Who cares if it's dignified? I don't want to be dignified.

[MR. FRANK *and* MARGOT *come from the room on the right.* MARGOT *goes to help her mother.* MR. FRANK *starts for the center table to correct* MARGOT'S *school papers.*]

MRS. FRANK. [*To* ANNE] You complain that I don't treat you like a grownup. But when I do, you **resent** it.

ANNE. I only want some fun . . . someone to laugh and clown with . . . After you've sat still all day and hardly moved, you've got to have some fun. I don't know what's the matter with that boy.

MR. FRANK. He isn't used to girls. Give him a little time.

ANNE. Time? Isn't two months time? I could cry. [*Catching hold of* MARGOT] Come on, Margot . . . dance with me. Come on, please.

MARGOT. I have to help with supper.

ANNE. You know we're going to forget how to dance . . . When we get out we won't remember a thing.

[*She starts to sing and dance by herself.* MR. FRANK *takes her in his arms, waltzing with her.* MRS. VAN DAAN *comes in from the bathroom.*]

MRS. VAN DAAN. Next? [*She looks around as she starts putting on her shoes.*] Where's Peter?

ANNE. [*As they are dancing*] Where would he be!

MRS. VAN DAAN. He hasn't finished his lessons, has he? His father'll kill him if he catches him in there with that cat and his work not done. [MR. FRANK *and* ANNE *finish their dance. They bow to each other with extravagant formality.*]

Cause and Effect
What is the effect of Mrs. Frank's upbringing on the way she expects Anne to act?

Vocabulary ▶
resent (ri zent´) *v.* feel angry out of a sense of unfairness

Dialogue
What subplot does this dialogue develop?

Anne, get him out of there, will you?

ANNE. [*At* PETER's *door*] Peter? Peter?

PETER. [*Opening the door a crack*] What is it?

ANNE. Your mother says to come out.

PETER. I'm giving Mouschi his dinner.

MRS. VAN DAAN. You know what your father says. [*She sits on the couch, sewing on the lining of her fur coat.*]

PETER. For heaven's sake, I haven't even looked at him since lunch.

MRS. VAN DAAN. I'm just telling you, that's all.

ANNE. I'll feed him.

PETER. I don't want you in there.

MRS. VAN DAAN. Peter!

PETER. [*To* ANNE] Then give him his dinner and come right out, you hear?

[*He comes back to the table.* ANNE *shuts the door of* PETER's *room after her and disappears behind the curtain covering his closet.*]

MRS. VAN DAAN. [*To* PETER] Now is that any way to talk to your little girl friend?

PETER. Mother . . . for heaven's sake . . . will you please stop saying that?

MRS. VAN DAAN. Look at him blush! Look at him!

PETER. Please! I'm not . . . anyway . . . let me alone, will you?

MRS. VAN DAAN. He acts like it was something to be ashamed of. It's nothing to be ashamed of, to have a little girl friend.

PETER. You're crazy. She's only thirteen.

MRS. VAN DAAN. So what? And you're sixteen. Just perfect. Your father's ten years older than I am. [*To* MR. FRANK] I warn you, Mr. Frank, if this war lasts much longer, we're going to be related and then . . .

MR. FRANK. *Mazeltov!*[17]

Dialogue
Based on this dialogue, how does Mrs. Van Daan feel about the growing friendship between Anne and Peter?

Comprehension
Why does Peter react negatively in response to his mother's hints about Anne?

---

17. ***Mazeltov*** (mä´ zəl tōv´) "good luck" in Hebrew and Yiddish; a word used to offer congratulations.

MRS. FRANK. [*Deliberately changing the conversation*] I wonder where Miep is. She's usually so prompt.

[*Suddenly everything else is forgotten as they hear the sound of an automobile coming to a screeching stop in the street below. They are tense, motionless in their terror. The car starts away. A wave of relief sweeps over them. They pick up their occupations again.* ANNE *flings open the door of* PETER'S *room, making a dramatic entrance. She is dressed in* PETER'S *clothes.* PETER *looks at her in fury. The others are amused.*]

ANNE. Good evening, everyone. Forgive me if I don't stay. [*She jumps up on a chair.*] I have a friend waiting for me in there. My friend Tom. Tom Cat. Some people say that we look alike. But Tom has the most beautiful whiskers, and I have only a little fuzz. I am hoping . . . in time . . .

PETER. All right, Mrs. Quack Quack!

ANNE. [*Outraged—jumping down*] Peter!

PETER. I heard about you . . . How you talked so much in class they called you Mrs. Quack Quack. How Mr. Smitter made you write a composition . . . " 'Quack, Quack,' said Mrs. Quack Quack."

ANNE. Well, go on. Tell them the rest. How it was so good he read it out loud to the class and then read it to all his other classes!

PETER. Quack! Quack! Quack . . . Quack . . . Quack . . .

[ANNE *pulls off the coat and trousers.*]

Vocabulary ▶
insufferable
(in suf′ ə rə bəl) *adj.*
unbearable

ANNE. You are the most intolerable, **insufferable** boy I've ever met!

[*She throws the clothes down the stairwell.* PETER *goes down after them.*]

PETER. Quack, quack, quack!

MRS. VAN DAAN. [*To* ANNE] That's right, Anneke! Give it to him!

ANNE. With all the boys in the world . . . Why I had to get locked up with one like you! . . .

PETER. Quack, quack, quack, and from now on stay out of my room!

[*As* PETER *passes her,* ANNE *puts out her foot, tripping him. He picks himself up, and goes on into his room.*]

MRS. FRANK. [*Quietly*] Anne, dear . . . your hair. [*She feels* ANNE's *forehead.*] You're warm. Are you feeling all right?

ANNE. Please, Mother. [*She goes over to the center table, slipping into her shoes.*]

MRS. FRANK. [*Following her*] You haven't a fever, have you?

ANNE. [*Pulling away*] No. No.

MRS. FRANK. You know we can't call a doctor here, ever. There's only one thing to do . . . watch carefully. Prevent an illness before it comes. Let me see your tongue.

ANNE. Mother, this is perfectly absurd.

MRS. FRANK. Anne, dear, don't be such a baby. Let me see your tongue. [*As* ANNE *refuses,* MRS. FRANK *appeals to* MR. FRANK] Otto . . .?

MR. FRANK. You hear your mother, Anne.

[ANNE *flicks out her tongue for a second, then turns away.*]

MRS. FRANK. Come on—open up! [*As* ANNE *opens her mouth very wide*] You seem all right . . . but perhaps an aspirin . . .

MRS. VAN DAAN. For heaven's sake, don't give that child any pills. I waited for fifteen minutes this morning for her to come out of the w.c.

ANNE. I was washing my hair!

MR. FRANK. I think there's nothing the matter with our Anne that a ride on her bike, or a visit with her friend Jopie de Waal wouldn't cure. Isn't that so, Anne?

[MR. VAN DAAN *comes down into the room. From outside we hear faint sounds of bombers going over and a burst of ack-ack.*][18]

MR. VAN DAAN. Miep not come yet?

MRS. VAN DAAN. The workmen just left, a little while ago.

---

18. **ack-ack** (ak′ ak′) *n.* slang for an anti-aircraft gun's fire.

LITERATURE IN CONTEXT

History Connection

Air Raids

When the families hear bombers and anti-aircraft guns overhead, they are hearing familiar sounds of the time. World War II was the first major war that involved the massive aerial bombing of cities.

Often, the first sound to alert people to an attack was the ghostly wailing of an air raid siren. This meant "Take cover!" Then, the drone of bomber engines and the crackle and burst of anti-aircraft fire would take over—the sounds that Anne hears. Finally, there would be the whistling of bombs dropping, the whine of a falling plane, or the sound of explosions. These were sounds heard by many families throughout Europe. This was the soundtrack of war.

Connect to the Literature

Why might the sound of bombers, like this American B-17, cause mixed feelings of anxiety and anticipation for those in hiding?

Comprehension
What does Anne do to tease Peter?

MR. VAN DAAN. What's for dinner tonight?

MRS. VAN DAAN. Beans.

MR. VAN DAAN. Not again!

MRS. VAN DAAN. Poor Putti! I know. But what can we do? That's all that Miep brought us.

[MR. VAN DAAN *starts to pace, his hands behind his back.* ANNE *follows behind him, imitating him.*]

ANNE. We are now in what is known as the "bean cycle." Beans boiled, beans en casserole, beans with strings, beans without strings . . .

[PETER *has come out of his room. He slides into his place at the table, becoming immediately absorbed in his studies.*]

MR. VAN DAAN. [*To* PETER] I saw you . . . in there, playing with your cat.

MRS. VAN DAAN. He just went in for a second, putting his coat away. He's been out here all the time, doing his lessons.

MR. FRANK. [*Looking up from the papers*] Anne, you got an excellent in your history paper today . . . and very good in Latin.

ANNE. [*Sitting beside him*] How about algebra?

MR. FRANK. I'll have to make a confession. Up until now I've managed to stay ahead of you in algebra. Today you caught up with me. We'll leave it to Margot to correct.

ANNE. Isn't algebra *vile,* Pim!

MR. FRANK. Vile!

MARGOT. [*To* MR. FRANK] How did I do?

ANNE. [*Getting up*] Excellent, excellent, excellent, excellent!

MR. FRANK. [*To* MARGOT] You should have used the subjunctive[19] here . . .

MARGOT. Should I? . . . I thought . . . look here . . . I didn't use it here . . .

[*The two become absorbed in the papers.*]

ANNE. Mrs. Van Daan, may I try on your coat?

Dialogue
Based on this dialogue, what is Mr. Frank's attitude toward education?

---

19. subjunctive (səb juŋk′ tiv) *n.* form of a verb that is used to express doubt or uncertainty.

MRS. FRANK. No, Anne.

MRS. VAN DAAN. [*Giving it to* ANNE] It's all right . . . but careful with it. [ANNE *puts it on and struts with it.*] My father gave me that the year before he died. He always bought the best that money could buy.

ANNE. Mrs. Van Daan, did you have a lot of boy friends before you were married?

MRS. FRANK. Anne, that's a personal question. It's not courteous to ask personal questions.

MRS. VAN DAAN. Oh I don't mind. [*To* ANNE] Our house was always swarming with boys. When I was a girl we had . . .

MR. VAN DAAN. Oh, God. Not again!

MRS. VAN DAAN. [*Good-humored*] Shut up! [*Without a pause, to* ANNE, MR. VAN DAAN *mimics* MRS. VAN DAAN, *speaking the first few words in unison with her.*] One summer we had a big house in Hilversum. The boys came buzzing round like bees around a jam pot. And when I was sixteen! . . . We were wearing our skirts very short those days and I had good-looking legs. [*She pulls up her skirt, going to* MR. FRANK.] I still have 'em. I may not be as pretty as I used to be, but I still have my legs. How about it, Mr. Frank?

MR. VAN DAAN. All right. All right. We see them.

MRS. VAN DAAN. I'm not asking you. I'm asking Mr. Frank.

PETER. Mother, for heaven's sake.

MRS. VAN DAAN. Oh, I embarrass you, do I? Well, I just hope the girl you marry has as good. [*Then to* ANNE] My father used to worry about me, with so many boys hanging round. He told me, if any of them gets fresh, you say to him . . . "Remember, Mr. So-and-So, remember I'm a lady."

ANNE. "Remember, Mr. So-and-So, remember I'm a lady." [*She gives* MRS. VAN DAAN *her coat.*]

MR. VAN DAAN. Look at you, talking that way in front of her! Don't you know she puts it all down in that diary?

MRS. VAN DAAN. So, if she does? I'm only telling the truth!

[ANNE *stretches out, putting her ear to the floor, listening to what is going on below. The sound of the bombers fades away.*]

Dialogue
What does Mrs. Van Daan's comment about her father reveal about her values?

Dialogue
What do Mrs. Van Daan's words and actions reveal about her personality?

Comprehension
What do Anne and Mrs. Van Daan discuss?

MRS. FRANK. [*Setting the table*] Would you mind, Peter, if I moved you over to the couch?

ANNE. [*Listening*] Miep must have the radio on.

[PETER *picks up his papers, going over to the couch beside* MRS. VAN DAAN.]

MR. VAN DAAN. [*Accusingly, to* PETER] Haven't you finished yet?

PETER. No.

MR. VAN DAAN. You ought to be ashamed of yourself.

PETER. All right. All right. I'm a dunce. I'm a hopeless case. Why do I go on?

MRS. VAN DAAN. You're not hopeless. Don't talk that way. It's just that you haven't anyone to help you, like the girls have. [*To* MR. FRANK] Maybe you could help him, Mr. Frank?

MR. FRANK. I'm sure that his father . . . ?

MR. VAN DAAN. Not me. I can't do anything with him. He won't listen to me. You go ahead . . . if you want.

MR. FRANK. [*Going to* PETER] What about it, Peter? Shall we make our school coeducational?

MRS. VAN DAAN. [*Kissing* MR. FRANK] You're an angel, Mr. Frank. An angel. I don't know why I didn't meet you before I met that one there. Here, sit down, Mr. Frank . . . [*She forces him down on the couch beside* PETER.] Now, Peter, you listen to Mr. Frank.

MR. FRANK. It might be better for us to go into Peter's room.

[PETER *jumps up eagerly, leading the way.*]

MRS. VAN DAAN. That's right. You go in there, Peter. You listen to Mr. Frank. Mr. Frank is a highly educated man.

[*As* MR. FRANK *is about to follow* PETER *into his room,* MRS. FRANK *stops him and wipes the lipstick from his lips. Then she closes the door after them.*]

ANNE. [*On the floor, listening*] Shh! I can hear a man's voice talking.

MR. VAN DAAN. [*To* ANNE] Isn't it bad enough here without your sprawling all over the place?

[ANNE *sits up.*]

MRS. VAN DAAN. [*To* MR. VAN DAAN] If you didn't smoke so much, you wouldn't be so bad-tempered.

MR. VAN DAAN. Am I smoking? Do you see me smoking?

MRS. VAN DAAN. Don't tell me you've used up all those cigarettes.

MR. VAN DAAN. One package. Miep only brought me one package.

MRS. VAN DAAN. It's a filthy habit anyway. It's a good time to break yourself.

MR. VAN DAAN. Oh, stop it, please.

MRS. VAN DAAN. You're smoking up all our money. You know that, don't you?

MR. VAN DAAN. Will you shut up?
[*During this,* MRS. FRANK *and* MARGOT *have studiously kept their eyes down. But* ANNE, *seated on the floor, has been following the discussion interestedly.* MR. VAN DAAN *turns to see her staring up at him.*] And what are you staring at?

ANNE. I never heard grownups quarrel before. I thought only children quarreled.

MR. VAN DAAN. This isn't a quarrel! It's a discussion. And I never heard children so rude before.

ANNE. [*Rising, indignantly*] I, rude!

MR. VAN DAAN. Yes!

MRS. FRANK. [*Quickly*] Anne, will you get me my knitting? [ANNE *goes to get it.*] I must remember, when Miep comes, to ask her to bring me some more wool.

MARGOT. [*Going to her room*] I need some hairpins and some soap. I made a list. [*She goes into her bedroom to get the list.*]

MRS. FRANK. [*To* ANNE] Have you some library books for Miep when she comes?

ANNE. It's a wonder that Miep has a life of her own, the way we make her run errands for us. Please, Miep, get me some starch. Please take my hair out and have it cut. Tell me all the latest news, Miep. [*She goes over, kneeling on the couch beside* MRS. VAN DAAN] Did you know she was engaged?

Dialogue
What plot conflict do the lines of dialogue here develop?

I never heard grownups quarrel before. I thought only children quarreled.

Comprehension
In what way does Mr. Frank offer to help Peter?

His name is Dirk, and Miep's afraid the Nazis will ship him off to Germany to work in one of their war plants. That's what they're doing with some of the young Dutchmen . . . they pick them up off the streets—

MR. VAN DAAN. [*Interrupting*] Don't you ever get tired of talking? Suppose you try keeping still for five minutes. Just five minutes.

[*He starts to pace again. Again* ANNE *follows him, mimicking him.* MRS. FRANK *jumps up and takes her by the arm up to the sink, and gives her a glass of milk.*]

MRS. FRANK. Come here, Anne. It's time for your glass of milk.

MR. VAN DAAN. Talk, talk, talk. I never heard such a child. Where is my . . . ? Every evening it's the same talk, talk, talk. [*He looks around.*] Where is my . . . ?

MRS. VAN DAAN. What're you looking for?

MR. VAN DAAN. My pipe. Have you seen my pipe?

MRS. VAN DAAN. What good's a pipe? You haven't got any tobacco.

MR. VAN DAAN. At least I'll have something to hold in my mouth! [*Opening* MARGOT's *bedroom door*] Margot, have you seen my pipe?

MARGOT. It was on the table last night.

[ANNE *puts her glass of milk on the table and picks up his pipe, hiding it behind her back.*]

MR. VAN DAAN. I know. I know. Anne, did you see my pipe? . . . Anne!

MRS. FRANK. Anne, Mr. Van Daan is speaking to you.

ANNE. Am I allowed to talk now?

MR. VAN DAAN. You're the most aggravating . . . The trouble with you is, you've been spoiled. What you need is a good old-fashioned spanking.

ANNE. [*Mimicking* MRS. VAN DAAN] "Remember, Mr. So-and-So, remember I'm a lady." [*She thrusts the pipe into his mouth, then picks up her glass of milk.*]

MR. VAN DAAN. [*Restraining himself with difficulty*] Why aren't you nice and quiet like your sister Margot? Why do you have to show off all the time? Let me give you a little

Dialogue
What cultural attitudes does Mr. Van Daan show in this dialogue?

advice, young lady. Men don't like that kind of thing in a girl. You know that? A man likes a girl who'll listen to him once in a while . . . a domestic girl, who'll keep her house shining for her husband . . . who loves to cook and sew and . . .

ANNE. I'd cut my throat first! I'd open my veins! I'm going to be remarkable! I'm going to Paris . . .

MR. VAN DAAN. [*Scoffingly*] Paris!

ANNE. . . . to study music and art.

MR. VAN DAAN. Yeah! Yeah!

ANNE. I'm going to be a famous dancer or singer . . . or something wonderful.

[*She makes a wide gesture, spilling the glass of milk on the fur coat in* MRS. VAN DAAN's *lap.* MARGOT *rushes quickly over with a towel.* ANNE *tries to brush the milk off with her skirt.*]

▼ **Critical Viewing**
Why might the designers of this stamp have chosen such a happy photograph of Anne?

MRS. VAN DAAN. Now look what you've done . . . you clumsy little fool! My beautiful fur coat my father gave me . . .

ANNE. I'm so sorry.

MRS. VAN DAAN. What do you care? It isn't yours . . . So go on, ruin it! Do you know what that coat cost? Do you? And now look at it! Look at it!

ANNE. I'm very, very sorry.

MRS. VAN DAAN. I could kill you for this. I could just kill you!

[MRS. VAN DAAN *goes up the stairs, clutching the coat.* MR. VAN DAAN *starts after her.*]

MR. VAN DAAN. Petronella . . . *liefje! Liefje!* . . . Come back . . . the supper . . . come back!

MRS. FRANK. Anne, you must not behave in that way.

ANNE. It was an accident. Anyone can have an accident.

MRS. FRANK. I don't mean that. I mean the answering back. You must not answer back. They are our guests. We must always show the greatest courtesy to them. We're all living under terrible tension. [*She stops as* MARGOT *indicates that* VAN DAAN *can hear. When he is gone, she continues.*]

Cause and Effect
How is the characters' situation affecting them?

Comprehension
What bothers Mr. Van Daan about Anne?

Cause and Effect
Is Mrs. Frank's advice practical, given the families' situation? Explain.

That's why we must control ourselves . . . You don't hear Margot getting into arguments with them, do you? Watch Margot. She's always courteous with them. Never familiar. She keeps her distance. And they respect her for it. Try to be like Margot.

ANNE. And have them walk all over me, the way they do her? No, thanks!

MRS. FRANK. I'm not afraid that anyone is going to walk all over you, Anne. I'm afraid for other people, that you'll walk on them. I don't know what happens to you, Anne. You are wild, self-willed. If I had ever talked to my mother as you talk to me . . .

ANNE. Things have changed. People aren't like that any more. "Yes, Mother." "No, Mother." "Anything you say, Mother." I've got to fight things out for myself! Make something of myself!

MRS. FRANK. It isn't necessary to fight to do it. Margot doesn't fight, and isn't she . . .?

ANNE. [*Violently rebellious*] Margot! Margot! Margot! That's all I hear from everyone . . . how wonderful Margot is . . . "Why aren't you like Margot?"

MARGOT. [*Protesting*] Oh, come on, Anne, don't be so . . .

ANNE. [*Paying no attention*] Everything she does is right, and everything I do is wrong! I'm the goat around here! . . . You're all against me! . . . And you worst of all!

[*She rushes off into her room and throws herself down on the settee, stifling her sobs.* MRS. FRANK *sighs and starts toward the stove.*]

MRS. FRANK. [*To* MARGOT] Let's put the soup on the stove . . . if there's anyone who cares to eat. Margot, will you take the bread out? [MARGOT *gets the bread from the cupboard.*] I don't know how we can go on living this way . . . I can't say a word to Anne . . . she flies at me . . .

MARGOT. You know Anne. In half an hour she'll be out here, laughing and joking.

Cause and Effect
How does the situation in the outside world force Mrs. Frank to accept conditions she finds unbearable?

MRS. FRANK. And . . . [*She makes a motion upwards, indicating the* VAN DAANS.] . . . I told your father it wouldn't work . . . but no . . . no . . . he had to ask them, he said . . . he owed it to him, he said. Well, he knows now that I was right!

These quarrels! . . . This bickering!

MARGOT. [*With a warning look*] Shush. Shush.

[*The buzzer for the door sounds.* MRS. FRANK *gasps, startled.*]

MRS. FRANK. Every time I hear that sound, my heart stops!

MARGOT. [*Starting for* PETER'S *door*] It's Miep. [*She knocks at the door.*] Father?

[MR. FRANK *comes quickly from* PETER'S *room.*]

MR. FRANK. Thank you, Margot. [*As he goes down the steps to open the outer door*] Has everyone his list?

MARGOT. I'll get my books. [*Giving her mother a list*] Here's your list.
[MARGOT *goes into her and* ANNE'S *bedroom on the right.* ANNE *sits up, hiding her tears, as* MARGOT *comes in.*]
Miep's here.
[MARGOT *picks up her books and goes back.* ANNE *hurries over to the mirror, smoothing her hair.*]

MR. VAN DAAN. [*Coming down the stairs*] Is it Miep?

MARGOT. Yes. Father's gone down to let her in.

MR. VAN DAAN. At last I'll have some cigarettes!

MRS. FRANK. [*To* MR. VAN DAAN] I can't tell you how unhappy I am about Mrs. Van Daan's coat. Anne should never have touched it.

MR. VAN DAAN. She'll be all right.

MRS. FRANK. Is there anything I can do?

MR. VAN DAAN. Don't worry.

[*He turns to meet* MIEP. *But it is not* MIEP *who comes up the steps. It is* MR. KRALER, *followed by* MR. FRANK. *Their faces are grave.* ANNE *comes from the bedroom.* PETER *comes from his room.*]

MRS. FRANK. Mr. Kraler!

MR. VAN DAAN. How are you, Mr. Kraler?

MARGOT. This is a surprise.

MRS. FRANK. When Mr. Kraler comes, the sun begins to shine.

MR. VAN DAAN. Miep is coming?

MR. KRALER. Not tonight.

I've got to fight things out for myself! Make something of myself!

Comprehension
Why does Anne dislike being compared with Margot?

Cause and Effect
Why would a visit from an outside friend be especially welcome to those in hiding?

[KRALER *goes to* MARGOT *and* MRS. FRANK *and* ANNE, *shaking hands with them.*]

MRS. FRANK. Wouldn't you like a cup of coffee? . . . Or, better still, will you have supper with us?

MR. FRANK. Mr. Kraler has something to talk over with us. Something has happened, he says, which demands an immediate decision.

MRS. FRANK. [*Fearful*] What is it?

[MR. KRALER *sits down on the couch. As he talks he takes bread, cabbages, milk, etc., from his briefcase, giving them to* MARGOT *and* ANNE *to put away.*]

MR. KRALER. Usually, when I come up here, I try to bring you some bit of good news. What's the use of telling you the bad news when there's nothing that you can do about it? But today something has happened . . . Dirk . . . Miep's Dirk, you know, came to me just now. He tells me that he has a Jewish friend living near him. A dentist. He says he's in trouble. He begged me, could I do anything for this man? Could I find him a hiding place? . . . So I've come to you . . . I know it's a terrible thing to ask of you, living as you are, but would you take him in with you?

▼ Critical Viewing
This photograph shows the front of the Secret Annex. What are some pros and cons of this hiding place?

MR. FRANK. Of course we will.

MR. KRALER. [*Rising*] It'll be just for a night or two . . . until I find some other place. This happened so suddenly that I didn't know where to turn.

MR. FRANK. Where is he?

MR. KRALER. Downstairs in the office.

MR. FRANK. Good. Bring him up.

MR. KRALER. His name is Dussel . . . Jan Dussel.

MR. FRANK. Dussel . . . I think I know him.

MR. KRALER. I'll get him.

[*He goes quickly down the steps and out.* MR. FRANK *suddenly becomes conscious of the others.*]

MR. FRANK. Forgive me. I spoke without consulting you. But I knew you'd feel as I do.

MR. VAN DAAN. There's no reason for you to consult

anyone. This is your place. You have a right to do exactly as you please. The only thing I feel . . . there's so little food as it is . . . and to take in another person . . .

[PETER *turns away, ashamed of his father.*]

MR. FRANK. We can stretch the food a little. It's only for a few days.

MR. VAN DAAN. You want to make a bet?

MRS. FRANK. I think it's fine to have him. But, Otto, where are you going to put him? Where?

PETER. He can have my bed. I can sleep on the floor. I wouldn't mind.

MR. FRANK. That's good of you, Peter. But your room's too small . . . even for *you.*

ANNE. I have a much better idea. I'll come in here with you and Mother, and Margot can take Peter's room and Peter can go in our room with Mr. Dussel.

MARGOT. That's right. We could do that.

MR. FRANK. No, Margot. You mustn't sleep in that room . . . neither you nor Anne. Mouschi has caught some rats in there. Peter's brave. He doesn't mind.

ANNE. Then how about *this?* I'll come in here with you and Mother, and Mr. Dussel can have my bed.

MRS. FRANK. *No. No. No!* Margot will come in here with us and he can have her bed. It's the only way. Margot, bring your things in here. Help her, Anne.

[MARGOT *hurries into her room to get her things.*]

ANNE. [*To her mother*] Why Margot? Why can't I come in here?

MRS. FRANK. Because it wouldn't be proper for Margot to sleep with a . . . Please, Anne. Don't argue. Please.

[ANNE *starts slowly away.*]

MR. FRANK. [*To* ANNE] You don't mind sharing your room with Mr. Dussel, do you, Anne?

ANNE. No. No, of course not.

MR. FRANK. Good. [ANNE *goes off into her bedroom, helping* MARGOT. MR. FRANK *starts to search in the cupboards.*]

Cause and Effect
What possible effects will Dussel's arrival have on the families' living situation?

Comprehension
What does Mr. Kraler ask of Mr. Frank?

Where's the cognac?

MRS. FRANK. It's there. But, Otto, I was saving it in case of illness.

MR. FRANK. I think we couldn't find a better time to use it. Peter, will you get five glasses for me?

[PETER *goes for the glasses.* MARGOT *comes out of her bedroom, carrying her possessions, which she hangs behind a curtain in the main room.* MR. FRANK *finds the cognac and pours it into the five glasses that* PETER *brings him.* MR. VAN DAAN *stands looking on sourly.* MRS. VAN DAAN *comes downstairs and looks around at all the bustle.*]

MRS. VAN DAAN. What's happening? What's going on?

MR. VAN DAAN. Someone's moving in with us.

MRS. VAN DAAN. In here? You're joking.

MARGOT. It's only for a night or two . . . until Mr. Kraler finds him another place.

MR. VAN DAAN. Yeah! Yeah!

[MR. FRANK *hurries over as* MR. KRALER *and* DUSSEL *come up.* DUSSEL *is a man in his late fifties, meticulous, finicky . . .* *bewildered now. He wears a raincoat. He carries a briefcase, stuffed full, and a small medicine case.*]

MR. FRANK. Come in, Mr. Dussel.

MR. KRALER. This is Mr. Frank.

DUSSEL. Mr. Otto Frank?

MR. FRANK. Yes. Let me take your things. [*He takes the hat and briefcase, but* DUSSEL *clings to his medicine case.*] This is my wife Edith . . . Mr. and Mrs. Van Daan . . . their son, Peter . . . and my daughters, Margot and Anne.

[DUSSEL *shakes hands with everyone.*]

MR. KRALER. Thank you, Mr. Frank. Thank you all. Mr. Dussel, I leave you in good hands. Oh . . . Dirk's coat.

[DUSSEL *hurriedly takes off the raincoat, giving it to* MR. KRALER. *Underneath is his white dentist's jacket, with a yellow Star of David on it.*]

DUSSEL. [*To* MR. KRALER] What can I say to thank you . . . ?

**Vocabulary ▶
bewildered**
(bē wil′ dərd) *adj.*
hopelessly confused

MRS. FRANK. [*To* DUSSEL] Mr. Kraler and Miep . . . They're our life line. Without them we couldn't live.

MR. KRALER. Please. Please. You make us seem very heroic. It isn't that at all. We simply don't like the Nazis. [*To* MR. FRANK, *who offers him a drink*] No, thanks. [*Then going on*] We don't like their methods. We don't like . . .

MR. FRANK. [*Smiling*] I know. I know. "No one's going to tell us Dutchmen what to do with our damn Jews!"

MR. KRALER. [*To* DUSSEL] Pay no attention to Mr. Frank. I'll be up tomorrow to see that they're treating you right. [*To* MR. FRANK] Don't trouble to come down again. Peter will bolt the door after me, won't you, Peter?

PETER. Yes, sir.

MR. FRANK. Thank you, Peter. I'll do it.

Dialogue
Does Mr. Frank accept Mr. Kraler's explanation of why he is helping the families? Explain.

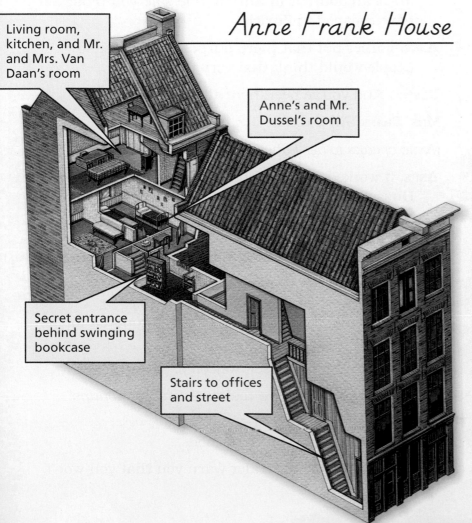

Anne Frank House

Living room, kitchen, and Mr. and Mrs. Van Daan's room

Anne's and Mr. Dussel's room

Secret entrance behind swinging bookcase

Stairs to offices and street

◀ **Critical Viewing**
How does the layout in this diagram help you to imagine what life might have been like for the residents of the Secret Annex?

Comprehension
How do Mr. and Mrs. Van Daan react to the news of Mr. Dussel's moving in?

World Events Connection

Safe Havens
One of the few safe havens for European Jews during the war was Switzerland.

A neutral country in the center of Europe, Switzerland was never occupied by the Nazis. Since many other countries refused to admit refugees, there were very few avenues of escape for European Jews. While the country did place some limits on immigration, Switzerland took in approximately 22,000 Jewish refugees during the war, saving many from certain death at the hands of the Nazis.

Connect to the Literature
Why was the rumor of the Franks fleeing to Switzerland believable?

MR. KRALER. Good night. Good night.

GROUP. Good night, Mr. Kraler. We'll see you tomorrow, etc., etc.

[MR. KRALER *goes out with* MR. FRANK, MRS. FRANK *gives each one of the "grownups" a glass of cognac.*]

MRS. FRANK. Please, Mr. Dussel, sit down.

[MR. DUSSEL *sinks into a chair.* MRS. FRANK *gives him a glass of cognac.*]

DUSSEL. I'm dreaming. I know it. I can't believe my eyes. Mr. Otto Frank here! [*To* MRS. FRANK] You're not in Switzerland then? A woman told me . . . She said she'd gone to your house . . . the door was open, everything was in disorder, dishes in the sink. She said she found a piece of paper in the wastebasket with an address scribbled on it . . . an address in Zurich. She said you must have escaped to Zurich.

ANNE. Father put that there purposely . . . just so people would think that very thing!

DUSSEL. And you've been *here* all the time?

MRS. FRANK. All the time . . . ever since July.

[ANNE *speaks to her father as he comes back.*]

ANNE. It worked, Pim . . . the address you left! Mr. Dussel says that people believe we escaped to Switzerland.

MR. FRANK. I'm glad. . . . And now let's have a little drink to welcome Mr. Dussel.
[*Before they can drink,* MR. DUSSEL *bolts his drink.* MR. FRANK *smiles and raises his glass.*]
To Mr. Dussel. Welcome. We're very honored to have you with us.

MRS. FRANK. To Mr. Dussel, welcome.

[*The* VAN DAANS *murmur a welcome. The "grownups" drink.*]

MRS. VAN DAAN. Um. That was good.

MR. VAN DAAN. Did Mr. Kraler warn you that you won't

get much to eat here? You can imagine . . . three ration books among the seven of us . . . and now you make eight.

[PETER *walks away, humiliated. Outside a street organ is heard dimly.*]

DUSSEL. [*Rising*] Mr. Van Daan, you don't realize what is happening outside that you should warn me of a thing like that. You don't realize what's going on . . .

[As MR. VAN DAAN *starts his characteristic pacing,* DUSSEL *turns to speak to the others.*]
Right here in Amsterdam every day hundreds of Jews disappear . . . They surround a block and search house by house. Children come home from school to find their parents gone. Hundreds are being deported . . . people that you and I know . . . the Hallensteins . . . the Wessels . . .

MRS. FRANK. [*In tears*] Oh, no. No!

DUSSEL. They get their call-up notice . . . come to the Jewish theater on such and such a day and hour . . . bring only what you can carry in a rucksack. And if you refuse the call-up notice, then they come and drag you from your home and ship you off to Mauthausen.[20] The death camp!

MRS. FRANK. We didn't know that things had got so much worse.

DUSSEL. Forgive me for speaking so.

ANNE. [*Coming to* DUSSEL] Do you know the de Waals? . . . What's become of them? Their daughter Jopie and I are in the same class. Jopie's my best friend.

DUSSEL. They are gone.

ANNE. Gone?

DUSSEL. With all the others.

ANNE. Oh, no. Not Jopie!

[*She turns away, in tears.* MRS. FRANK *motions to* MARGOT *to comfort her.* MARGOT *goes to* ANNE, *putting her arms comfortingly around her.*]

MRS. VAN DAAN. There were some people called Wagner. They lived near us . . . ?

Cause and Effect
How does Dussel's news affect Anne?

Comprehension
Why does Mr. Van Daan say Dussel will not get much to eat in the Annex?

---

20. **Mauthausen** (mou´ tou´ zən) village in Austria that was the site of a Nazi concentration camp.

Mr. Frank. [*Interrupting, with a glance at* Anne] I think we should put this off until later. We all have many questions we want to ask . . . But I'm sure that Mr. Dussel would like to get settled before supper.

Dussel. Thank you. I would. I brought very little with me.

Mr. Frank. [*Giving him his hat and briefcase*] I'm sorry we can't give you a room alone. But I hope you won't be too uncomfortable. We've had to make strict rules here . . . a schedule of hours . . . We'll tell you after supper. Anne, would you like to take Mr. Dussel to his room?

Anne. [*Controlling her tears*] If you'll come with me, Mr. Dussel? [*She starts for her room.*]

Dussel. [*Shaking hands with each in turn*] Forgive me if I haven't really expressed my gratitude to all of you. This has been such a shock to me. I'd always thought of myself as Dutch. I was born in Holland. My father was born in Holland, and my grandfather. And now . . . after all these years . . . [*He breaks off.*] If you'll excuse me.

[Dussel *gives a little bow and hurries off after* Anne. Mr. Frank *and the others are subdued.*]

Anne. [*Turning on the light*] Well, here we are.

[Dussel *looks around the room. In the main room* Margot *speaks to her mother.*]

Margot. The news sounds pretty bad, doesn't it? It's so different from what Mr. Kraler tells us. Mr. Kraler says things are improving.

Mr. Van Daan. I like it better the way Kraler tells it.

[*They resume their occupations, quietly.* Peter *goes off into his room. In* Anne's *room,* Anne *turns to* Dussel.]

Anne. You're going to share the room with me.

Dussel. I'm a man who's always lived alone. I haven't had to adjust myself to others. I hope you'll bear with me until I learn.

Anne. Let me help you. [*She takes his briefcase.*] Do you always live all alone? Have you no family at all?

Dussel. No one. [*He opens his medicine case and spreads his bottles on the dressing table.*]

Spiral Review
CHARACTER DEVELOPMENT What first impressions do you have of Dussel's character from his dialogue up to this point in the play?

▲ Anne Frank House—
The Franks' hiding place
is now open to the pub-
lic. Every year more than
900,000 people from all
over the world come to
visit.

ANNE. How dreadful. You must be terribly lonely.

DUSSEL. I'm used to it.

ANNE. I don't think I could ever get used to it. Didn't you even
have a pet? A cat, or a dog?

DUSSEL. I have an allergy for fur-bearing animals. They give
me asthma.

ANNE. Oh, dear. Peter has a cat.

DUSSEL. Here? He has it here?

ANNE. Yes. But we hardly ever see it. He keeps it in his room
all the time. I'm sure it will be all right.

DUSSEL. Let us hope so. [*He takes some pills to fortify himself.*]

ANNE. That's Margot's bed, where you're going to sleep. I sleep
on the sofa there. [*Indicating the clothes hooks on the wall*]
We cleared these off for your things. [*She goes over to the
window.*] The best part about this room . . . you can look
down and see a bit of the street and the canal. There's a

Comprehension
Why did Dussel believe
he was safe from
persecution as a Jew?

houseboat . . . you can see the end of it . . . a bargeman lives there with his family . . . They have a baby and he's just beginning to walk and I'm so afraid he's going to fall into the canal some day. I watch him. . . .

DUSSEL. [*Interrupting*] Your father spoke of a schedule.

ANNE. [*Coming away from the window*] Oh, yes. It's mostly about the times we have to be quiet. And times for the w.c. You can use it now if you like.

DUSSEL. [*Stiffly*] No, thank you.

ANNE. I suppose you think it's awful, my talking about a thing like that. But you don't know how important it can get to be, especially when you're frightened . . . About this room, the way Margot and I did . . . she had it to herself in the afternoons for studying, reading . . . lessons, you know . . . and I took the mornings. Would that be all right with you?

DUSSEL. I'm not at my best in the morning.

ANNE. You stay here in the mornings then. I'll take the room in the afternoons.

DUSSEL. Tell me, when you're in here, what happens to me? Where am I spending my time? In there, with all the people?

ANNE. Yes.

DUSSEL. I see. I see.

ANNE. We have supper at half past six.

DUSSEL. [*Going over to the sofa*] Then, if you don't mind . . . I like to lie down quietly for ten minutes before eating. I find it helps the digestion.

ANNE. Of course. I hope I'm not going to be too much of a bother to you. I seem to be able to get everyone's back up.

[DUSSEL *lies down on the sofa, curled up, his back to her.*]

DUSSEL. I always get along very well with children. My patients all bring their children to me, because they know I get on well with them. So don't you worry about that.

[ANNE *leans over him, taking his hand and shaking it gratefully.*]

ANNE. Thank you. Thank you, Mr. Dussel.

Dialogue
Based on this dialogue, how well do you think Anne and Dussel will get along as the plot develops?

[*The lights dim to darkness. The curtain falls on the scene.* ANNE'S VOICE *comes to us faintly at first, and then with increasing power.*]

ANNE'S VOICE. . . . And yesterday I finished Cissy Van Marxvelt's latest book. I think she is a first-class writer. I shall definitely let my children read her. Monday the twenty-first of September, nineteen forty-two. Mr. Dussel and I had another battle yesterday. Yes, Mr. Dussel! According to him, nothing, I repeat . . . nothing, is right about me . . . my appearance, my character, my manners. While he was going on at me I thought . . . sometime I'll give you such a smack that you'll fly right up to the ceiling! Why is it that every grownup thinks he knows the way to bring up children? Particularly the grownups that never had any. I keep wishing that Peter was a girl instead of a boy. Then I would have someone to talk to. Margot's a darling, but she takes everything too seriously. To pause for a moment on the subject of Mrs. Van Daan. I must tell you that her attempts to flirt with father are getting her nowhere. Pim, thank goodness, won't play.

[*As she is saying the last lines, the curtain rises on the darkened scene.* ANNE'S VOICE *fades out.*]

Cause and Effect
Are Anne's reactions here a result of her circumstances, or would they occur in any time period? Explain.

Mr. Dussel and I had another battle yesterday.

Scene 4

[*It is the middle of the night, several months later. The stage is dark except for a little light which comes through the skylight in* PETER'S *room.*

Everyone is in bed. MR. *and* MRS. FRANK *lie on the couch in the main room, which has been pulled out to serve as a makeshift double bed.*

MARGOT *is sleeping on a mattress on the floor in the main room, behind a curtain stretched across for privacy. The others are all in their accustomed rooms.*

From outside we hear two drunken soldiers singing "Lili Marlene." A girl's high giggle is heard. The sound of running feet is heard coming closer and then fading in the distance. Throughout the scene there is the distant sound of airplanes passing overhead.

A match suddenly flares up in the attic. We dimly see MR. VAN DAAN. *He is getting his bearings. He comes quickly down the stairs, and goes to the cupboard where the food is stored. Again the match flares up, and is as quickly blown out.*]

Comprehension
What does Anne explain to Dussel?

The dim figure is seen to steal back up the stairs.

There is quiet for a second or two, broken only by the sound of airplanes, and running feet on the street below.

Suddenly, out of the silence and the dark, we hear ANNE *scream.*]

ANNE. [*Screaming*] No! No! Don't . . . don't take me!

[*She moans, tossing and crying in her sleep. The other people wake, terrified.* DUSSEL *sits up in bed, furious.*]

DUSSEL. Shush! Anne! Anne, for God's sake, shush!

ANNE. [*Still in her nightmare*] Save me! Save me!

[*She screams and screams.* DUSSEL *gets out of bed, going over to her, trying to wake her.*]

DUSSEL. For God's sake! Quiet! Quiet! You want someone to hear?

[*In the main room* MRS. FRANK *grabs a shawl and pulls it around her. She rushes in to* ANNE, *taking her in her arms.* MR. FRANK *hurriedly gets up, putting on his overcoat.* MARGOT *sits up, terrified.* PETER's *light goes on in his room.*]

MRS. FRANK. [*To* ANNE, *in her room*] Hush, darling, hush. It's all right. It's all right. [*Over her shoulder to* DUSSEL] Will you be kind enough to turn on the light, Mr. Dussel? [*Back to* ANNE] It's nothing, my darling. It was just a dream.

[DUSSEL *turns on the light in the bedroom.* MRS. FRANK *holds* ANNE *in her arms. Gradually* ANNE *comes out of her nightmare still trembling with horror.* MR. FRANK *comes into the room, and goes quickly to the window, looking out to be sure that no one outside has heard* ANNE'S *screams.* MRS. FRANK *holds* ANNE, *talking softly to her. In the main room* MARGOT *stands on a chair, turning on the center hanging lamp. A light goes on in the* VAN DAANS' *room overhead.* PETER *puts his robe on, coming out of his room.*]

DUSSEL. [*To* MRS. FRANK, *blowing his nose*] Something must be done about that child, Mrs. Frank. Yelling like that! Who knows but there's somebody on the streets? She's endangering all our lives.

MRS. FRANK. Anne, darling.

DUSSEL. Every night she twists and turns. I don't sleep. I spend half my night shushing her. And now it's nightmares!

[MARGOT *comes to the door of* ANNE'S *room, followed by* PETER. MR. FRANK *goes to them, indicating that everything is all right.* PETER *takes* MARGOT *back.*]

MRS. FRANK. [*To* ANNE] You're here, safe, you see? Nothing has happened. [*To* DUSSEL] Please, Mr. Dussel, go back to bed. She'll be herself in a minute or two. Won't you, Anne?

DUSSEL. [*Picking up a book and a pillow*] Thank you, but I'm going to the w.c. The one place where there's peace!

[*He stalks out.* MR. VAN DAAN, *in underwear and trousers, comes down the stairs.*]

MR. VAN DAAN. [*To* DUSSEL] What is it? What happened?

DUSSEL. A nightmare. She was having a nightmare!

MR. VAN DAAN. I thought someone was murdering her.

DUSSEL. Unfortunately, no.

[*He goes into the bathroom.* MR. VAN DAAN *goes back up the stairs.* MR. FRANK, *in the main room, sends* PETER *back to his own bedroom.*]

MR. FRANK. Thank you, Peter. Go back to bed.

[PETER *goes back to his room.* MR. FRANK *follows him, turning out the light and looking out the window. Then he goes back to*

Dialogue
How do the lines delivered by Dussel and Mrs. Frank reveal important differences between them?

Comprehension
Why does Anne scream in the middle of the night?

the main room, and gets up on a chair, turning out the center hanging lamp.]

MRS. FRANK. [*To* ANNE] Would you like some water? [ANNE *shakes her head.*] Was it a very bad dream? Perhaps if you told me . . . ?

ANNE. I'd rather not talk about it.

MRS. FRANK. Poor darling. Try to sleep then. I'll sit right here beside you until you fall asleep. [*She brings a stool over, sitting there.*]

ANNE. You don't have to.

MRS. FRANK. But I'd like to stay with you . . . very much. Really.

ANNE. I'd rather you didn't.

MRS. FRANK. Good night, then. [*She leans down to kiss* ANNE. ANNE *throws her arm up over her face, turning away.* MRS. FRANK, *hiding her hurt, kisses* ANNE'S *arm.*] You'll be all right? There's nothing that you want?

ANNE. Will you please ask Father to come.

MRS. FRANK. [*After a second*] Of course, Anne dear. [*She hurries out into the other room.* MR. FRANK *comes to her as she comes in.*] *Sie verlangt nach Dir!*[21]

MR. FRANK. [*Sensing her hurt*] Edith, *Liebe, schau . . .*[22]

MRS. FRANK. *Es macht nichts! Ich danke dem lieben Herrgott, dass sie sich wenigstens an Dich wendet, wenn sie Trost braucht! Geh hinein, Otto, sie ist ganz hysterisch vor Angst.*[23] [*As* MR. FRANK *hesitates*] *Geh zu ihr.*[24]
[*He looks at her for a second and then goes to get a cup of water for* ANNE. MRS. FRANK *sinks down on the bed, her face in her hands, trying to keep from sobbing aloud.* MARGOT *comes over to her, putting her arms around her.*] She wants nothing of me. She pulled away when I leaned down to kiss her.

MARGOT. It's a phase . . . You heard Father . . . Most girls go through it . . . they turn to their fathers at this age . . . they give all their love to their fathers.

Dialogue
What does this exchange between Anne and her mother reveal about their relationship?

---

21. *Sie verlangt nach Dir* (sē fer´ laŋt´ näkh´ dir´) German for "She is asking for you."
22. *Liebe, schau* (lē´ bə shou´) German for "Dear, look."
23. *Es macht . . . vor Angst* German for "It's all right. I thank dear God that at least she turns to you when she needs comfort. Go in, Otto, she is hysterical because of fear."
24. *Geh zu ihr* (gā´ tsoo͞´ ēr´) German for "Go to her."

MRS. FRANK. You weren't like this. You didn't shut me out.

MARGOT. She'll get over it . . .

[*She smooths the bed for* MRS. FRANK *and sits beside her a moment as* MRS. FRANK *lies down. In* ANNE'S *room* MR. FRANK *comes in, sitting down by* ANNE. ANNE *flings her arms around him, clinging to him. In the distance we hear the sound of ack-ack.*]

ANNE. Oh, Pim. I dreamed that they came to get us! The Green Police! They broke down the door and grabbed me and started to drag me out the way they did Jopie.

MR. FRANK. I want you to take this pill.

ANNE. What is it?

MR. FRANK. Something to quiet you.

[*She takes it and drinks the water. In the main room* MARGOT *turns out the light and goes back to her bed.*]

MR. FRANK. [*To* ANNE] Do you want me to read to you for a while?

ANNE. No. Just sit with me for a minute. Was I awful? Did I yell terribly loud? Do you think anyone outside could have heard?

MR. FRANK. No. No. Lie quietly now. Try to sleep.

ANNE. I'm a terrible coward. I'm so disappointed in myself. I think I've conquered my fear . . . I think I'm really grown-up . . . and then something happens . . . and I run to you like a baby . . . I love you, Father. I don't love anyone but you.

MR. FRANK. [*Reproachfully*] Annele!

ANNE. It's true. I've been thinking about it for a long time. You're the only one I love.

MR. FRANK. It's fine to hear you tell me that you love me. But I'd be happier if you said you loved your mother as well . . . She needs your help so much . . . your love . . .

ANNE. We have nothing in common. She doesn't understand me. Whenever I try to explain my views on life to her she asks me if I'm constipated.

MR. FRANK. You hurt her very much just now. She's crying. She's in there crying.

ANNE. I can't help it. I only told the truth. I didn't want her

Comprehension
What happens in
Anne's nightmare?

Dialogue
What insights does Anne have about herself, as revealed in this dialogue?

here . . . [*Then, with sudden change*] Oh, Pim, I was horrible, wasn't I? And the worst of it is, I can stand off and look at myself doing it and know it's cruel and yet I can't stop doing it. What's the matter with me? Tell me. Don't say it's just a phase! Help me.

MR. FRANK. There is so little that we parents can do to help our children. We can only try to set a good example . . . point the way. The rest you must do yourself. You must build your own character.

ANNE. I'm trying. Really I am. Every night I think back over all of the things I did that day that were wrong . . . like putting the wet mop in Mr. Dussel's bed . . . and this thing now with Mother. I say to myself, that was wrong. I make up my mind, I'm never going to do that again. Never! Of course I may do something worse . . . but at least I'll never do *that* again! . . . I have a nicer side, Father . . . a sweeter, nicer side. But I'm scared to show it. I'm afraid that people are going to laugh at me if I'm serious. So the mean Anne comes to the outside and the good Anne stays on the inside, and I keep on trying to switch them around and have the good Anne outside and the bad Anne inside and be what I'd like to be . . . and might be . . . if only . . . only . . .

[*She is asleep.* MR. FRANK *watches her for a moment and then turns off the light, and starts out. The lights dim out. The curtain falls on the scene.* ANNE'S VOICE *is heard dimly at first, and then with growing strength.*]

Vocabulary ▶
fatalist (fā′ təl ist) *n.* one who believes that all events are determined by fate and so must be accepted

ANNE'S VOICE. . . . The air raids are getting worse. They come over day and night. The noise is terrifying. Pim says it should be music to our ears. The more planes, the sooner will come the end of the war. Mrs. Van Daan pretends to be a **fatalist**. What will be, will be. But when the planes come over, who is the most frightened? No one else but Petronella! . . . Monday, the ninth of November, nineteen forty-two. Wonderful news! The Allies have landed in Africa. Pim says that we can look for an early finish to the war. Just for fun he asked each of us what was the first thing we wanted to do when we got out of here. Mrs. Van Daan longs to be home with her own things, her needle-point chairs, the Beckstein piano her father gave her . . . the best that money could buy. Peter would like to go to a movie. Mr. Dussel wants to get back to his dentist's drill.

Dialogue
What does Anne's narration tell the audience about the war? How does this information add to the movement of the plot?

He's afraid he is losing his touch. For myself, there are so many things . . . to ride a bike again . . . to laugh till my belly aches . . . to have new clothes from the skin out . . . to have a hot tub filled to overflowing and wallow in it for hours . . . to be back in school with my friends . . .

[*As the last lines are being said, the curtain rises on the scene. The lights dim on as* ANNE'S VOICE *fades away.*]

Scene 5

[*It is the first night of the Hanukkah*[25] *celebration.* MR. FRANK *is standing at the head of the table on which is the Menorah.*[26] *He lights the Shamos,*[27] *or servant candle, and holds it as he says the blessing. Seated listening is all of the "family," dressed in their best. The men wear hats,* PETER *wears his cap.*]

MR. FRANK. [*Reading from a prayer book*] "Praised be Thou, oh Lord our God, Ruler of the universe, who has sanctified us with Thy commandments and bidden us kindle the Hanukkah lights. Praised be Thou, oh Lord our God, Ruler of the universe, who has wrought wondrous deliverances for our fathers in days of old. Praised be Thou, oh Lord our God, Ruler of the universe, that Thou has given us life and sustenance and brought us to this happy season." [MR. FRANK *lights the one candle of the Menorah as he continues.*] "We kindle this Hanukkah light to celebrate the great and wonderful deeds wrought through the zeal with which God filled the hearts of the heroic Maccabees, two thousand years ago. They fought against indifference, against tyranny and oppression, and they restored our Temple to us. May these lights remind us that we should ever look to God, whence cometh our help." Amen.

ALL. Amen.

[MR. FRANK *hands* MRS. FRANK *the prayer book.*]

MRS. FRANK. [*Reading*] "I lift up mine eyes unto the mountains, from whence cometh my help. My help cometh from the Lord who made heaven and earth. He will not suffer thy foot to be moved. He that keepeth thee will not slumber. He that keepeth Israel doth neither slumber nor sleep. The Lord is

Cause and Effect
Why might the story of Hanukkah have special meaning for the families in hiding?

Comprehension
What does Anne want to do when the war ends?

---

25. **Hanukkah** (khä´ noo kä´) *n.* Jewish celebration that lasts eight days.
26. **Menorah** (mə nō´ rə) *n.* candle holder with nine candles, used during Hanukkah.
27. *Shamos* (shä´ məs) *n.* candle used to light the others in a menorah.

Critical Viewing ▲
This photo is from a production of
this play. How well does it capture
the mood of this scene?

thy keeper. The Lord is thy shade upon thy right hand. The sun shall not smite thee by day, nor the moon by night. The Lord shall keep thee from all evil. He shall keep thy soul. The Lord shall guard thy going out and thy coming in, from this time forth and forevermore." Amen.

ALL. Amen.

[MRS. FRANK *puts down the prayer book and goes to get the food and wine.* MARGOT *helps her.* MR. FRANK *takes the men's hats and puts them aside.*]

DUSSEL. [*Rising*] That was very moving.

ANNE. [*Pulling him back*] It isn't over yet!

MRS. VAN DAAN. Sit down! Sit down!

ANNE. There's a lot more, songs and presents.

DUSSEL. Presents?

MRS. FRANK. Not this year, unfortunately.

MRS. VAN DAAN. But always on Hanukkah everyone gives presents . . . everyone!

DUSSEL. Like our St. Nicholas' Day.[28]

[*There is a chorus of "no's" from the group.*]

MRS. VAN DAAN. No! Not like St. Nicholas! What kind of a Jew are you that you don't know Hanukkah?

MRS. FRANK. [*As she brings the food*] I remember particularly the candles . . . First one, as we have tonight. Then the second night you light two candles, the next night three . . . and so on until you have eight candles burning. When there are eight candles it is truly beautiful.

MRS. VAN DAAN. And the potato pancakes.

MR. VAN DAAN. Don't talk about them!

MRS. VAN DAAN. I make the best *latkes* you ever tasted!

MRS. FRANK. Invite us all next year . . . in your own home.

MR. FRANK. God willing!

MRS. VAN DAAN. God willing.

Dialogue
What do Dussel's lines reveal about his familiarity with Hanukkah?

Comprehension
What rituals are part of the celebration of Hanukkah?

---

28. **St. Nicholas' Day** December 6, the day Christian children in the Netherlands receive gifts.

Cause and Effect
How do world events
make this Hanukkah
different from others
that the families have
celebrated?

MARGOT. What I remember best is the presents we used to get
when we were little . . . eight days of presents . . . and each
day they got better and better.

MRS. FRANK. [*Sitting down*] We are all here, alive. That is
present enough.

ANNE. No, it isn't. I've got something . . . [*She rushes into her
room, hurriedly puts on a little hat improvised from the lamp
shade, grabs a satchel bulging with parcels and comes
running back.*]

MRS. FRANK. What is it?

ANNE. Presents!

MRS. VAN DAAN. Presents!

DUSSEL. Look!

MR. VAN DAAN. What's she got on her head?

PETER. A lamp shade!

ANNE. [*She picks out one at random.*] This is for Margot. [*She
hands it to* MARGOT, *pulling her to her feet.*] Read it out loud.

MARGOT. [*Reading*]
"You have never lost your temper.
You never will, I fear,
You are so good.
But if you should,
Put all your cross words here."
[*She tears open the package.*] A new crossword puzzle book!
Where did you get it?

Cause and Effect
How do Anne's gifts
reflect the reality of the
families' situation?

ANNE. It isn't new. It's one that you've done. But I rubbed it all out,
and if you wait a little and forget, you can do it all over again.

MARGOT. [*Sitting*] It's wonderful, Anne. Thank you. You'd never
know it wasn't new.

[*From outside we hear the sound of a streetcar passing.*]

ANNE. [*With another gift*] Mrs. Van Daan.

MRS. VAN DAAN. [*Taking it*] This is awful . . . I haven't anything
for anyone . . . I never thought . . .

MR. FRANK. This is all Anne's idea.

MRS. VAN DAAN. [*Holding up a bottle*] What is it?

ANNE. It's hair shampoo. I took all the odds and ends of soap and mixed them with the last of my toilet water.

MRS. VAN DAAN. Oh, Anneke!

ANNE. I wanted to write a poem for all of them, but I didn't have time. [*Offering a large box to* MR. VAN DAAN] Yours, Mr. Van Daan, is really something . . . something you want more than anything. [*As she waits for him to open it*] Look! Cigarettes!

MR. VAN DAAN. Cigarettes!

ANNE. Two of them! Pim found some old pipe tobacco in the pocket lining of his coat . . . and we made them . . . or rather, Pim did.

MRS. VAN DAAN. Let me see . . . Well, look at that! Light it, Putti! Light it.

[MR. VAN DAAN *hesitates.*]

ANNE. It's tobacco, really it is! There's a little fluff in it, but not much.

[*Everyone watches intently as* MR. VAN DAAN *cautiously lights it. The cigarette flares up. Everyone laughs.*]

PETER. It works!

MRS. VAN DAAN. Look at him.

MR. VAN DAAN. [*Spluttering*] Thank you, Anne. Thank you.

[ANNE *rushes back to her satchel for another present.*]

ANNE. [*Handing her mother a piece of paper*] For Mother, Hanukkah greeting.

[*She pulls her mother to her feet.*]

MRS. FRANK. [*She reads*] "Here's an I.O.U. that I promise to pay. Ten hours of doing whatever you say. Signed, Anne Frank." [MRS. FRANK, *touched, takes* ANNE *in her arms, holding her close.*]

DUSSEL. [*To* ANNE] Ten hours of doing what you're told? Anything you're told?

ANNE. That's right.

DUSSEL. You wouldn't want to sell that, Mrs. Frank?

MRS. FRANK. Never! This is the most precious gift I've ever had!

[*She sits, showing her present to the others.* ANNE *hurries back*

Cause and Effect
What effect do Anne's gifts have on the group's spirits?

Comprehension
What does Anne give Mrs. Van Daan?

to the satchel and pulls out a scarf, the scarf that MR. FRANK *found in the first scene.]*

ANNE. [*Offering it to her father*] For Pim.

MR. FRANK. Anneke . . . I wasn't supposed to have a present!

[*He takes it, unfolding it and showing it to the others.*]

ANNE. It's a muffler . . . to put round your neck . . . like an ascot, you know. I made it myself out of odds and ends . . . I knitted it in the dark each night, after I'd gone to bed. I'm afraid it looks better in the dark!

MR. FRANK. [*Putting it on*] It's fine. It fits me perfectly. Thank you, Annele.

[ANNE *hands* PETER *a ball of paper with a string attached to it.*]

ANNE. That's for Mouschi.

PETER. [*Rising to bow*] On behalf of Mouschi, I thank you.

ANNE. [*Hesitant, handing him a gift*] And . . . this is yours . . . from Mrs. Quack Quack. [*As he holds it gingerly in his hands*] Well . . . open it . . . Aren't you going to open it?

PETER. I'm scared to. I know something's going to jump out and hit me.

ANNE. No. It's nothing like that, really.

MRS. VAN DAAN. [*As he is opening it*] What is it, Peter? Go on. Show it.

ANNE. [*Excitedly*] It's a safety razor!

DUSSEL. A what?

ANNE. A razor!

MRS. VAN DAAN. [*Looking at it*] You didn't make that out of odds and ends.

ANNE. [*To* PETER] Miep got it for me. It's not new. It's second-hand. But you really do need a razor now.

DUSSEL. For what?

ANNE. Look on his upper lip . . . you can see the beginning of a mustache.

DUSSEL. He wants to get rid of that? Put a little milk on it and let the cat lick it off.

PETER. [*Starting for his room*] Think you're funny, don't you.

Dussel. Look! He can't wait! He's going in to try it!

Peter. I'm going to give Mouschi his present!

[*He goes into his room, slamming the door behind him.*]

Mr. Van Daan. [*Disgustedly*] Mouschi, Mouschi, Mouschi.

[*In the distance we hear a dog persistently barking.* **Anne** *brings a gift to* **Dussel.**]

Anne. And last but never least, my roommate, Mr. Dussel.

Dussel. For me? You have something for me?

[*He opens the small box she gives him.*]

Anne. I made them myself.

Dussel. [*Puzzled*] Capsules! Two capsules!

Anne. They're ear-plugs!

Dussel. Ear-plugs?

Anne. To put in your ears so you won't hear me when I thrash around at night. I saw them advertised in a magazine. They're not real ones . . . I made them out of cotton and candle wax. Try them . . . See if they don't work . . . see if you can hear me talk . . .

Dussel. [*Putting them in his ears*] Wait now until I get them in . . . so.

Anne. Are you ready?

Dussel. Huh?

Anne. Are you ready?

Dussel. Good God! They've gone inside! I can't get them out! [*They laugh as* MR. DUSSEL *jumps about, trying to shake the plugs out of his ears. Finally he gets them out. Putting them away*] Thank you, Anne! Thank you!

[*Together*] {
Mr. Van Daan. A real Hanukkah!

Mrs. Van Daan. Wasn't it cute of her?

Mrs. Frank. I don't know when she did it.

Margot. I love my present.
}

Anne. [*Sitting at the table*] And now let's have the song, Father . . . please . . . [*To* DUSSEL] Have you heard the Hanukkah song, Mr. Dussel? The song is the whole thing!

I knitted it in the dark each night, after I'd gone to bed. I'm afraid it looks better in the dark!

Dialogue
What subplot does this dialogue develop?

Comprehension
How does Mr. Dussel anger Peter?

[*She sings.*] "Oh, Hanukkah! Oh, Hanukkah! The sweet celebration . . ."

MR. FRANK. [*Quieting her*] I'm afraid, Anne, we shouldn't sing that song tonight. [*To* DUSSEL] It's a song of jubilation, of rejoicing. One is apt to become too enthusiastic.

ANNE. Oh, please, please. Let's sing the song. I promise not to shout!

MR. FRANK. Very well. But quietly now . . . I'll keep an eye on you and when . . .

[*As* ANNE *starts to sing, she is interrupted by* DUSSEL, *who is snorting and wheezing.*]

DUSSEL. [*Pointing to* PETER] You . . . You! [PETER *is coming from his bedroom, ostentatiously holding a bulge in his coat as if he were holding his cat, and dangling* ANNE'S *present before it.*] How many times . . . I told you . . . Out! Out!

MR. VAN DAAN. [*Going to* PETER] What's the matter with you? Haven't you any sense? Get that cat out of here.

PETER. [*Innocently*] Cat?

MR. VAN DAAN. You heard me. Get it out of here!

PETER. I have no cat. [*Delighted with his joke, he opens his coat and pulls out a bath towel. The group at the table laugh, enjoying the joke.*]

DUSSEL. [*Still wheezing*] It doesn't need to be the cat . . . his clothes are enough . . . when he comes out of that room . . .

MR. VAN DAAN. Don't worry. You won't be bothered any more. We're getting rid of it.

DUSSEL. At last you listen to me. [*He goes off into his bedroom.*]

MR. VAN DAAN. [*Calling after him*] I'm not doing it for you. That's all in your mind . . . all of it! [*He starts back to his place at the table.*] I'm doing it because I'm sick of seeing that cat eat all our food.

PETER. That's not true! I only give him bones . . . scraps . . .

MR. VAN DAAN. Don't tell me! He gets fatter every day! Damn cat looks better than any of us. Out he goes tonight!

PETER. No! No!

Dialogue
What does the dialogue between Peter and Mr. Dussel reveal about both their personalities?

ANNE. Mr. Van Daan, you can't do that! That's Peter's cat. Peter loves that cat.

MRS. FRANK. [*Quietly*] Anne.

PETER. [*To* MR. VAN DAAN] If he goes, I go.

MR. VAN DAAN. Go! Go!

MRS. VAN DAAN. You're not going and the cat's not going! Now please . . . this is Hanukkah . . . Hanukkah . . . this is the time to celebrate . . . What's the matter with all of you? Come on, Anne. Let's have the song.

ANNE. [*Singing*]
"Oh, Hanukkah! Oh, Hanukkah! The sweet celebration."

Cause and Effect
How do the families' circumstances influence Mr. Van Daan's opinion about keeping a cat?

Comprehension
Who triggers the argument over the cat?

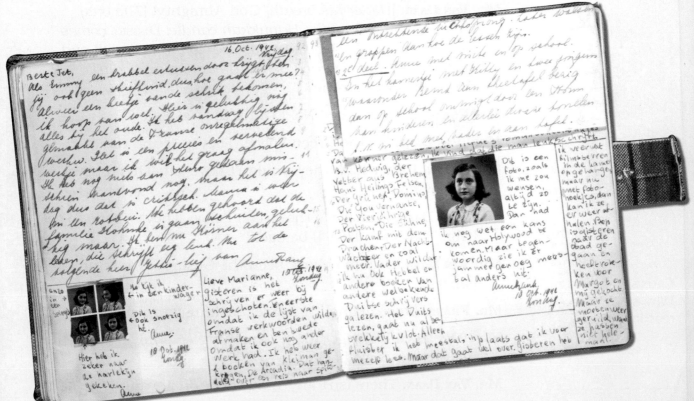

▲ **Anne Frank wrote these pages in October 1942.**

MR. FRANK. [*Rising*] I think we should first blow out the candle . . . then we'll have something for tomorrow night.

MARGOT. But, Father, you're supposed to let it burn itself out.

MR. FRANK. I'm sure that God understands shortages. [*Before blowing it out*] "Praised be Thou, oh Lord our God, who hast sustained us and permitted us to celebrate this joyous festival."

[*He is about to blow out the candle when suddenly there is a crash of something falling below. They all freeze in horror, motionless. For a few seconds there is complete silence. MR. FRANK slips off his shoes. The others noiselessly follow his example. MR. FRANK turns out a light near him. He motions to PETER to turn off the center lamp. PETER tries to reach it, realizes he cannot and gets up on a chair. Just as he is touching the lamp he loses his balance. The chair goes out from under him. He falls. The iron lamp shade crashes to the floor. There is a sound of feet below, running down the stairs.*]

MR. VAN DAAN. [*Under his breath*] God Almighty! [*The only light left comes from the Hanukkah candle. DUSSEL comes from his room. MR. FRANK creeps over to the stairwell and stands listening. The dog is heard barking excitedly.*] Do you hear anything?

MR. FRANK. [*In a whisper*] No. I think they've gone.

MRS. VAN DAAN. It's the Green Police. They've found us.

MR. FRANK. If they had, they wouldn't have left. They'd be up here by now.

MRS. VAN DAAN. I know it's the Green Police. They've gone to get help. That's all. They'll be back!

MR. VAN DAAN. Or it may have been the Gestapo,[29] looking for papers . . .

MR. FRANK. [*Interrupting*] Or a thief, looking for money.

MRS. VAN DAAN. We've got to do something . . . Quick! Quick! Before they come back.

MR. VAN DAAN. There isn't anything to do. Just wait.

[MR. FRANK *holds up his hand for them to be quiet. He is listening intently. There is complete silence as they all strain to hear any sound from below. Suddenly* ANNE *begins to sway. With a low*

Cause and Effect
Why is everyone reacting fearfully?

---

29. **Gestapo** (gə stä′ pō) *n.* secret police force of Nazi Germany, known for its brutality.

cry she falls to the floor in a faint. MRS. FRANK *goes to her quickly, sitting beside her on the floor and taking her in her arms.*]

MRS. FRANK. Get some water, please! Get some water!

[MARGOT *starts for the sink.*]

MR. VAN DAAN. [*Grabbing* MARGOT] No! No! No one's going to run water!

MR. FRANK. If they've found us, they've found us. Get the water. [MARGOT *starts again for the sink.* MR. FRANK, *getting a flashlight*] I'm going down.

[MARGOT *rushes to him, clinging to him.* ANNE *struggles to consciousness.*]

MARGOT. No, Father, no! There may be someone there, waiting . . . It may bc a trap!

MR. FRANK. This is Saturday. There is no way for us to know what has happened until Miep or Mr. Kraler comes on Monday morning. We cannot live with this uncertainty.

MARGOT. Don't go, Father!

MRS. FRANK. Hush, darling, hush. [MR. FRANK *slips quietly out, down the steps and out through the door below.*] Margot! Stay close to me. [MARGOT *goes to her mother.*]

MR. VAN DAAN. Shush! Shush!

[MRS. FRANK *whispers to* MARGOT *to get the water.* MARGOT *goes for it.*]

MRS. VAN DAAN. Putti, where's our money? Get our money. I hear you can buy the Green Police off, so much a head. Go upstairs quick! Get the money!

MR. VAN DAAN. Keep still!

MRS. VAN DAAN. [*Kneeling before him, pleading*] Do you want to be dragged off to a concentration camp? Are you going to stand there and wait for them to come up and get you? Do something, I tell you!

MR. VAN DAAN. [*Pushing her aside*] Will you keep still!

[*He goes over to the stairwell to listen.* PETER *goes to his mother, helping her up onto the sofa. There is a second of silence, then* ANNE *can stand it no longer.*]

ANNE. Someone go after Father! Make Father come back!

It's the Green Police. They've found us.

Comprehension
How does Peter fall?

PETER. [*Starting for the door*] I'll go.

MR. VAN DAAN. Haven't you done enough?

[*He pushes* PETER *roughly away. In his anger against his father* PETER *grabs a chair as if to hit him with it, then puts it down, burying his face in his hands.* MRS. FRANK *begins to pray softly.*]

ANNE. Please, please, Mr. Van Daan. Get Father.

MR. VAN DAAN. Quiet! Quiet!

[ANNE *is shocked into silence.* MRS. FRANK *pulls her closer, holding her protectively in her arms.*]

MRS. FRANK. [*Softly, praying*] "I lift up mine eyes unto the mountains, from whence cometh my help. My help cometh from the Lord who made heaven and earth. He will not suffer thy foot to be moved . . . He that keepeth thee will not slumber . . ."

[*She stops as she hears someone coming. They all watch the door tensely.* MR. FRANK *comes quietly in.* ANNE *rushes to him, holding him tight.*]

MR. FRANK. It was a thief. That noise must have scared him away.

MRS. VAN DAAN. Thank God.

MR. FRANK. He took the cash box. And the radio. He ran away in such a hurry that he didn't stop to shut the street door. It was swinging wide open. [*A breath of relief sweeps over them.*] I think it would be good to have some light.

MARGOT. Are you sure it's all right?

MR. FRANK. The danger has passed. [MARGOT *goes to light the small lamp.*] Don't be so terrified, Anne. We're safe.

DUSSEL. Who says the danger has passed? Don't you realize we are in greater danger than ever?

MR. FRANK. Mr. Dussel, will you be still!

[MR. FRANK *takes* ANNE *back to the table, making her sit down with him, trying to calm her.*]

DUSSEL. [*Pointing to* PETER] Thanks to this clumsy fool, there's someone now who knows we're up here! Someone now knows we're up here, hiding!

MRS. VAN DAAN. [*Going to* DUSSEL] Someone knows we're here, yes. But who is the someone? A thief! A thief! You think a

Dialogue
What plot line does this exchange between Peter and his father develop?

thief is going to go to the Green Police and say . . . I was robbing a place the other night and I heard a noise up over my head? You think a thief is going to do that?

Dussel. Yes. I think he will.

Mrs. Van Daan. [*Hysterically*] You're crazy!

[*She stumbles back to her seat at the table.* Peter *follows protectively, pushing* Dussel *aside.*]

Dussel. I think some day he'll be caught and then he'll make a bargain with the Green Police . . . if they'll let him off, he'll tell them where some Jews are hiding!

[*He goes off into the bedroom. There is a second of appalled silence.*]

Mr. Van Daan. He's right.

Anne. Father, let's get out of here! We can't stay here now . . . Let's go . . .

Mr. Van Daan. Go! Where?

Mrs. Frank. [*Sinking into her chair at the table*] Yes. Where?

Mr. Frank. [*Rising, to them all*] Have we lost all faith? All courage? A moment ago we thought that they'd come for us. We were sure it was the end. But it wasn't the end. We're alive, safe. [Mr. Van Daan *goes to the table and sits.* Mr. Frank *prays.*]
"We thank Thee, oh Lord our God, that in Thy infinite mercy Thou hast again seen fit to spare us." [*He blows out the candle, then turns to* Anne.] Come on, Anne. The song! Let's have the song!
[*He starts to sing.* Anne *finally starts falteringly to sing, as* Mr. Frank *urges her on. Her voice is hardly audible at first.*]

Anne. [*Singing*]
"Oh, Hanukkah! Oh, Hanukkah! The sweet . . . celebration . . ."

[*As she goes on singing, the others gradually join in, their voices still shaking with fear.* Mrs. Van Daan *sobs as she sings.*]

Group. Around the feast . . . we . . . gather
In complete . . . jubilation . . .
Happiest of sea . . . sons
Now is here.
Many are the reasons for good cheer.

Cause and Effect
What do Mr. Dussel's lines about the Green Police suggest about their methods for finding Jews?

Comprehension
What is Dussel afraid the thief will do?

[DUSSEL *comes from the bedroom. He comes over to the table,
standing beside* MARGOT, *listening to them as they sing.*]

"Together
We'll weather
Whatever tomorrow may bring."

[*As they sing on with growing courage, the lights start to dim.*]

"So hear us rejoicing
And merrily voicing
The Hanukkah song that we sing.
Hoy!"

[*The lights are out. The curtain starts slowly to fall.*]

"Hear us rejoicing
And merrily voicing
The Hanukkah song that we sing."

[*They are still singing, as the curtain falls.*]

Dialogue
What is the effect
of this song as a
finale to the act?

Language Study

Vocabulary The words listed below appear in the play *The Diary of
Anne Frank.* Rewrite each sentence that follows, using a word from
the list to convey the same basic meaning.

conspicuous   tension   resent   insufferable   bewildered

1. The summer sun in the desert is intolerable.

2. The hole in Bryan's sweater is in a noticeable place.

3. Jasmine and Carly dislike the fact that Alberto gets the most
attention.

4. The hostility between the cats is affecting the rest of the family.

5. Sam was confused by all the buttons on his new camera.

Word Study

WORD STUDY

The **Greek suffix -ist**
indicates a noun that
means "one who does,
makes, practices, is
skilled in, or believes
in." In this play, a
character claims to be
a **fatalist**—one who
believes that our lives
are determined by
fate and so must be
accepted.

Part A Use context and what you know about the **Greek suffix -ist**
to explain your answer to each question.

1. Is a *violinist* someone who sells violins?

2. If you were a *humorist,* what might you do for a living?

Part B Explain how the suffix -ist contributes to the meanings of the
words *bicyclist, moralist,* and *artist.* Consult a dictionary if necessary.

Close Reading Activities

Literary Analysis

Key Ideas and Details

1. **Cause and Effect (a)** What is the historical cause that forces the Franks into hiding? **(b)** What effects does this historical event have on their daily lives? Include evidence from the text in your response.

2. **Cause and Effect** Anne and Peter discuss the Stars of David. **(a)** What effects do the Nazis intend the stars to have? Cite details from the play to support your answer. **(b)** What background information helps you understand the intended effect? Cite details from the play.

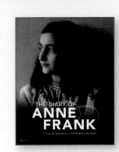

Craft and Structure

3. **Dialogue** Complete an organizer like the one shown. For each purpose identified, provide two examples of dialogue from the play that achieve that purpose. Explain your choices.

Dialogue
Reveals character and relationships:
Advances the action of the plot or subplot:
Develops the conflict:

4. **Dialogue (a)** After Mr. Kraler asks if Dussel can join the group, what does the dialogue among the characters reveal about their personalities? **(b)** How does Dussel's dialogue on his arrival change the tone of the scene? In your answer, refer to his word choice when he explains what is happening in the outside world.

5. **Dialogue** Consider what you know about Anne's eventual fate. How does this knowledge add dramatic irony to the dialogue at the end of Act I?

Integration of Knowledge and Ideas

6. **(a) Synthesize:** In what ways does the Hanukkah scene sum up the situation of the people hiding in the annex, reflecting various aspects of their lives and circumstances? **(b) Draw Conclusions:** What central insights does the scene suggest about the ways people deal with crisis?

7. **Evaluate:** With a partner, discuss Mr. Frank's statement, "There are . . . no locks that anyone can put on your mind." Explain whether you agree or disagree, citing details from the play as well as other examples. Share your answers with the class.

8. **THE BIG ? Is it our differences or our similarities that matter most?**
   (a) What does Mr. Frank's reaction to the crisis involving the thief reveal about his personality, compared with Mr. Van Daan's? **(b)** What do the stresses faced by the families tend to bring out more—their differences or their similarities? Cite text details in support.

ACADEMIC VOCABULARY

As you write and speak about *The Diary of Anne Frank,* use the words related to similarities and differences that you explored on page 505 of this textbook.

Conventions: **Prepositions and Prepositional Phrases**

A **preposition** connects a noun or pronoun to another word within a sentence. A **prepositional phrase** begins with a preposition and ends with a noun or pronoun.

Here is a list of common prepositions.

Thirty Common Prepositions					
about	at	beyond	from	on	to
above	behind	by	in	opposite	to under
after	below	during	near	over	until
among	beside	except	of	past	up
around	between	for	off	since	with

A prepositional phrase consists of a preposition plus the noun or pronoun following. As a unit, a prepositional phrase acts as an adjective or an adverb. It *modifies,* or tells more about, another word in the sentence.

Prepositional Phrase	Explanation
The cup *of milk* tipped over.	The prepositional phrase *of milk* acts as an adjective and tells which cup.
The milk spilled *onto the floor.*	The prepositional phrase *onto the floor* acts as an adverb and tells where the milk spilled.

Practice A

Identify the prepositional phrase or phrases in each sentence. Tell whether each prepositional phrase acts as an adjective or adverb.

1. Anne gave gifts made of recycled items.
2. Anne writes daily in her diary.
3. Peter was a shy, awkward boy of sixteen.
4. There was a skylight in the sloping ceiling.

Reading Application In Scene 1 of Act I, find two prepositional phrases that act as adjectives and two that act as adverbs.

Practice B

Rewrite each item, adding a prepositional phrase to modify the italicized word.

1. They could hear faint sounds, including a boat *whistle* _____.
2. Anne poured some of her *milk* _____.
3. There was a small *stairwell* _____.
4. Mr. Frank *stood* _____ watching the workers.

Writing Application Write a short paragraph to describe Act I, using three prepositional phrases.

Writing to Sources

Narrative Text To explore the perspectives of two characters from the play other than Anne, write two **diary entries**, one from each character's point of view. Follow these steps:

- Choose an event from the play that affects at least two characters other than Anne. In a two-column chart, take notes on details from the play that show how each person might have viewed the event.

- Referring to your chart, draw a conclusion about the perspectives of the characters. For example, you should consider how the importance and meaning of an event may differ for each character.

- Then, write a diary entry about the event you have chosen from each character's point of view. Include a description of the event, using carefully chosen details that reflect each character's unique perspective and experience. Include details describing how people looked and acted during the event.

Grammar Application Check your writing. Identify three or four prepositional phrases in your work. Indicate whether the phrases act as adjectives or adverbs.

Speaking and Listening

Presentation of Ideas Drawing on the text of the play and accompanying photos, along with original research, present a **guided tour** of the Franks' rooms and their daily life in hiding. Follow these steps:

- Review the play for details about the layout of the rooms, the food the family ate, and the stresses of life in a cramped attic.

- Check the validity of major events and details in the play by consulting Anne's real diary (a primary source) and reliable secondary sources, such as the Web site of the Anne Frank House. During your guided tour, point out details from the play that your research confirms, clarifies, or calls into question.

- For extra impact, include a dramatic soliloquy (solo speech) from the play. Whatever material you choose to present, vary your voice and use dynamic gestures and an appropriate tone to convey the atmosphere of the secret rooms to your audience.

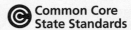

**Common Core
State Standards**

Writing
3. Write narratives to develop real or imagined experiences or events using effective technique, relevant descriptive details, and well-structured event sequences.

Speaking and Listening
6. Adapt speech to a variety of contexts and tasks, demonstrating command of formal English when indicated or appropriate.

Language
1. Demonstrate command of the conventions of standard English grammar and usage when writing or speaking.

Meet the Author

At age 13, budding author **Anne Frank** (1929–1945) began filling notebooks with stories and essays—while hiding from the Nazis. Born in Frankfurt, Germany, Frank and her Jewish family moved to the Netherlands in 1933 to escape Nazi persecution. However, the persecution spread to Holland. In 1944, the Franks were deported to concentration camps. Anne died soon after. In the years that followed, her diary of her Holocaust experiences became a renowned book and the basis of several plays and films.

© Common Core State Standards

Reading Literature
3. Analyze how particular lines of dialogue or incidents in a story or drama propel the action, reveal aspects of a character, or provoke a decision.

Language
4.b. Use common, grade-appropriate Greek or Latin affixes and roots as clues to the meaning of a word (e.g., *precede, recede, secede*).

? Is it our differences or our similarities that matter most?

Explore the Big Question as you read *The Diary of Anne Frank,* Act II. Look for ways in which the families are or are not able to preserve their human dignity amid their suffering.

CLOSE READING FOCUS

Key Ideas and Details: **Cause and Effect**

Cause-and-effect relationships explain connections between events. To analyze cause-and-effect relationships, ask questions such as these:

- What is the cause of this event? What other causes might have helped to trigger it? (One event may have multiple causes.)
- What possible effects—or chain of effects—might result from this event? (One event may have multiple effects.)
- Are these events truly related—or is it just coincidence that one happened after the other?

As you read the play, analyze causes and effects.

Craft and Structure: **Character's Motivation**

A **character's motivation** is the reason he or she takes a particular action. Motivation is revealed through dialogue and action.

- **Internal motivations** include emotions, such as jealousy.
- **External motivations** may include factors in the **setting** or situation, such as war or poverty.

As you read, examine the characters' dialogue and actions for clues to their motivations. Consider how the characters' confinement in the attic and the fact of war shape their motivations.

Vocabulary

The words below appear in the text that follows. Copy the words into your notebook. Which is an antonym for *happy*?

| inarticulate | apprehension | blackmail |
| forlorn | intuition | ineffectually |

CLOSE READING MODEL

The passage below is from *The Diary of Anne Frank,* Act II. The annotations to the right of the passage show ways in which you can use close reading skills to determine cause-and-effect relationships and to analyze a character's motivation.

from *The Diary of Anne Frank,* Act II

Mr. Van Daan. A cake! [. . .] I'll get some plates. [. . . .]

Mrs. Frank. Thank you, Miepia. You shouldn't have done it. You must have used all of your sugar ration for weeks. [*Giving it to* Mrs. Van Daan] It's beautiful, isn't it?[1]

Mrs. Van Daan. It's been ages since I even saw a cake. Not since you brought us one last year. [. . . *to* Miep] Remember? Don't you remember, you gave us one on New Year's Day? Just this time last year? I'll never forget it because you had "Peace in nineteen forty-three" on it. [*She looks at the cake and reads*] "Peace in nineteen forty-four!"

Miep. Well, it has to come sometime, you know.[2] [. . . .]

Mr. Van Daan. [*Bringing plates and a knife*] Here's the knife, *liefje.* Now, how many of us are there?

Miep. None for me, thank you. [. . . .]

Mr. Van Daan. Good! That leaves one . . . two . . . three . . . seven of us.[3]

Dussel. Eight! Eight! [. . .]

Mr. Van Daan. I left Margot out. I take it for granted Margot won't eat any.

Anne. Why wouldn't she!

Mrs. Frank. I think it won't harm her.

Mr. Van Daan. All right! All right! I just didn't want her to start coughing again, that's all.[4]

Cause and Effect

1 The cake causes exclamations, but this cause-and-effect relationship is not as simple as it might seem. Because of the war, people are allowed only small rations of sugar. Making a cake takes weeks of rations, so the overall effect of the gift is extraordinary.

Character's Motivation

2 The dialogue reveals that Miep has written a message of peace on the cake. By taking into account the desperate circumstances, readers can see that Miep's likely motivation is to give hope to the people in the attic.

Cause and Effect

3 Miep refuses a piece of cake, showing further generosity on her part. Her action results in more cake for the others, as shown when Mr. Van Daan begins counting the number of people who will eat cake.

Character's Motivation

4 Mr. Van Daan does not count a piece of cake for Margot until forced to do so. He mentions her coughing as reason to leave her out, but leaving her out also leaves more cake for him. His internal motivation may be selfish.

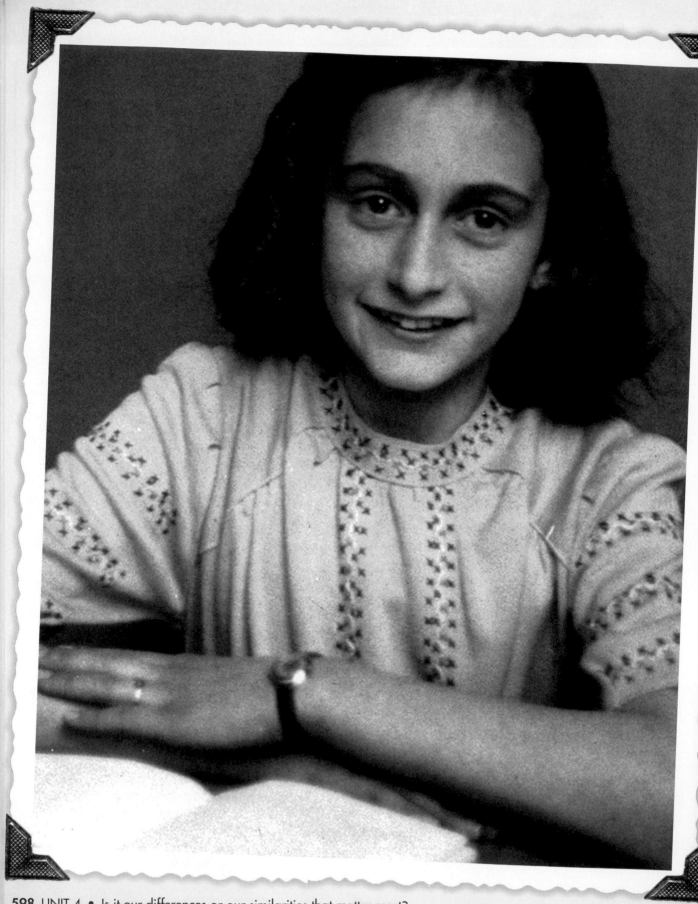

THE DIARY OF ANNE FRANK

Review and Anticipate In Act I, Anne Frank's father visits the attic where his family and four others hid from the Nazis during World War II. As he holds Anne's diary, the offstage voice of Anne draws him into the past as the families begin their new life hiding from the Nazis. As months drag on, fear and lack of privacy in the attic rooms contribute to increasing tension between the family members. Act I ends on the first night of Hanukkah. The group's celebration is interrupted by the sounds of a thief below, who may have heard them. Read Act II to learn whether the hiding place has been discovered.

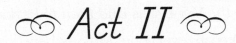 *Act II*

Scene 1

[*In the darkness we hear* ANNE'S VOICE, *again reading from the diary.*]

ANNE'S VOICE. Saturday, the first of January, nineteen forty-four. Another new year has begun and we find ourselves still in our hiding place. We have been here now for one year, five months and twenty-five days. It seems that our life is at a standstill.

[*The curtain rises on the scene. It is late afternoon. Everyone is bundled up against the cold. In the main room* MRS. FRANK *is taking down the laundry which is hung across the back.* MR. FRANK *sits in the chair down left, reading.* MARGOT *is lying on the couch with a blanket over her and the many-colored knitted scarf around her throat.* ANNE *is seated at the center table, writing in her diary.* PETER, MR. *and* MRS. VAN DAAN *and* DUSSEL *are all in their own rooms, reading or lying down.*

As the lights dim on, ANNE'S *voice continues, without a break.*]

Comprehension
How much time has passed since the Franks first went into hiding?

Character's Motivation
Why do you think Anne writes about her feelings toward her mother in her diary?

ANNE'S VOICE. We are all a little thinner. The Van Daans' "discussions" are as violent as ever. Mother still does not understand me. But then I don't understand her either. There is one great change, however. A change in myself. I read somewhere that girls of my age don't feel quite certain of themselves. That they become quiet within and begin to think of the miracle that is taking place in their bodies. I think that what is happening to me is so wonderful . . . not only what can be seen, but what is taking place inside. Each time it has happened I have a feeling that I have a sweet secret.

[*We hear the chimes and then a hymn being played on the carillon outside. The buzzer of the door below suddenly sounds. Everyone is startled.* MR. FRANK *tiptoes cautiously to the top of the steps and listens. Again the buzzer sounds, in* MIEP'S *V-for-Victory signal.*[1]]

MR. FRANK. It's Miep!

[*He goes quickly down the steps to unbolt the door.* MRS. FRANK *calls upstairs to the* VAN DAANS *and then to* PETER.]

MRS. FRANK. Wake up, everyone! Miep is here!

[ANNE *quickly puts her diary away.* MARGOT *sits up, pulling the blanket around her shoulders.* MR. DUSSEL *sits on the edge of his bed, listening, disgruntled.* MIEP *comes up the steps, followed by* MR. KRALER. *They bring flowers, books, newspapers, etc.* ANNE *rushes to* MIEP, *throwing her arms affectionately around her.*] Miep . . . and Mr. Kraler . . . What a delightful surprise!

MR. KRALER. We came to bring you New Year's greetings.

MRS. FRANK. You shouldn't . . . you should have at least one day to yourselves. [*She goes quickly to the stove and brings down teacups and tea for all of them.*]

ANNE. Don't say that, it's so wonderful to see them! [*Sniffing at* MIEP'S *coat*] I can smell the wind and the cold on your clothes.

▼ Critical Viewing
Behind this bookcase are stairs leading to the hiding place. How does this photograph help you understand the tension in the play?

---

1. **V-for-Victory signal** three short rings and one long one (the letter *V* in Morse code).

MIEP. [*Giving her the flowers*] There you are. [*Then to* MARGOT, *feeling her forehead*] How are you, Margot? . . . Feeling any better?

MARGOT. I'm all right.

ANNE. We filled her full of every kind of pill so she won't cough and make a noise. [*She runs into her room to put the flowers in water.* MR. *and* MRS. VAN DAAN *come from upstairs. Outside there is the sound of a band playing.*]

MRS. VAN DAAN. Well, hello, Miep. Mr. Kraler.

MR. KRALER. [*Giving a bouquet of flowers to* MRS. VAN DAAN] With my hope for peace in the New Year.

PETER. [*Anxiously*] Miep, have you seen Mouschi? Have you seen him anywhere around?

MIEP. I'm sorry, Peter. I asked everyone in the neighborhood had they seen a gray cat. But they said no.

[MRS. FRANK *gives* MIEP *a cup of tea.* MR. FRANK *comes up the steps, carrying a small cake on a plate.*]

MR. FRANK. Look what Miep's brought for us!

MRS. FRANK. [*Taking it*] A cake!

MR. VAN DAAN. A cake! [*He pinches* MIEP's *cheeks gaily and hurries up to the cupboard.*] I'll get some plates.

[DUSSEL, *in his room, hastily puts a coat on and starts out to join the others.*]

MRS. FRANK. Thank you, Miepia. You shouldn't have done it. You must have used all of your sugar ration for weeks. [*Giving it to* MRS. VAN DAAN] It's beautiful, isn't it?

MRS. VAN DAAN. It's been ages since I even saw a cake. Not since you brought us one last year. [*Without looking at the cake, to* MIEP] Remember? Don't you remember, you gave us one on New Year's Day? Just this time last year? I'll never forget it because you had "Peace in nineteen forty-three" on it. [*She looks at the cake and reads*] "Peace in nineteen forty-four!"

MIEP. Well, it has to come sometime, you know. [*As* DUSSEL *comes from his room*] Hello, Mr. Dussel.

Cause and Effect
What does the dialogue about the cake reveal about life under German occupation?

Comprehension
What occasion are the families celebrating?

MR. KRALER. How are you?

MR. VAN DAAN. [*Bringing plates and a knife*] Here's the knife, *liefje*. Now, how many of us are there?

MIEP. None for me, thank you.

MR. FRANK. Oh, please. You must.

MIEP. I couldn't.

MR. VAN DAAN. Good! That leaves one . . . two . . . three . . . seven of us.

DUSSEL. Eight! Eight! It's the same number as it always is!

MR. VAN DAAN. I left Margot out. I take it for granted Margot won't eat any.

ANNE. Why wouldn't she!

MRS. FRANK. I think it won't harm her.

MR. VAN DAAN. All right! All right! I just didn't want her to start coughing again, that's all.

DUSSEL. And please, Mrs. Frank should cut the cake.

[*Together*] {
  MR. VAN DAAN. What's the difference?

  MRS. VAN DAAN. It's not Mrs. Frank's cake, is it, Miep? It's for all of us.
}

DUSSEL. Mrs. Frank divides things better.

[*Together*] {
  MRS. VAN DAAN. [*Going to* DUSSEL] What are you trying to say?

  MR. VAN DAAN. Oh, come on! Stop wasting time!
}

MRS. VAN DAAN. [*To* DUSSEL] Don't I always give everybody exactly the same? Don't I?

MR. VAN DAAN. Forget it, Kerli.

MRS. VAN DAAN. No. I want an answer! Don't I?

DUSSEL. Yes. Yes. Everybody gets exactly the same . . . except Mr. Van Daan always gets a little bit more.

[VAN DAAN *advances on* DUSSEL, *the knife still in his hand.*]

MR. VAN DAAN. That's a lie!

[DUSSEL *retreats before the onslaught of the* VAN DAANS.]

MR. FRANK. Please, please! [*Then to* MIEP] You see what a little sugar cake does to us? It goes right to our heads!

Character's Motivation
Beyond the excuse he gives, what is another possible reason that Mr. Van Daan leaves out Margot?

Character's Motivation
How do the pressures of life in hiding affect the relationship between Dussel and the Van Daans?

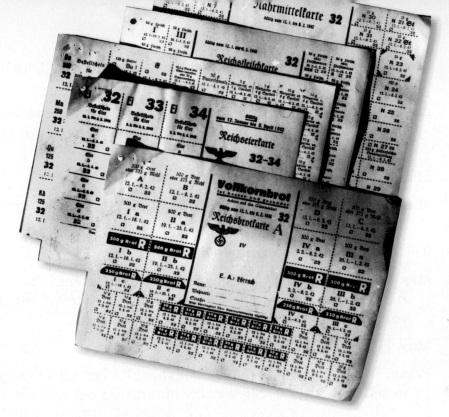

MR. VAN DAAN. [*Handing* MRS. FRANK *the knife*] Here you are, Mrs. Frank.

MRS. FRANK. Thank you. [*Then to* MIEP *as she goes to the table to cut the cake*] Are you sure you won't have some?

MIEP. [*Drinking her tea*] No, really, I have to go in a minute.

[*The sound of the band fades out in the distance.*]

PETER. [*To* MIEP] Maybe Mouschi went back to our house . . . they say that cats . . . Do you ever get over there . . . ? I mean . . . do you suppose you could . . . ?

MIEP. I'll try, Peter. The first minute I get I'll try. But I'm afraid, with him gone a week . . .

DUSSEL. Make up your mind, already someone has had a nice big dinner from that cat!

[PETER *is furious,* **inarticulate.** *He starts toward* DUSSEL *as if to hit him.* MR. FRANK *stops him.* MRS. FRANK *speaks quickly to ease the situation.*]

MRS. FRANK. [*To* MIEP] This is delicious, Miep!

MRS. VAN DAAN. [*Eating hers*] Delicious!

MR. VAN DAAN. [*Finishing it in one gulp*] Dirk's in luck to get a girl who can bake like this!

◀ **Vocabulary**
inarticulate
(in´ är tik´ yo͞o lit)
adj. unable to express oneself

Comprehension
What does Peter ask Miep to do?

Miep. [*Putting down her empty teacup*] I have to run. Dirk's taking me to a party tonight.

Anne. How heavenly! Remember now what everyone is wearing, and what you have to eat and everything, so you can tell us tomorrow.

Miep. I'll give you a full report! Good-bye, everyone!

Mr. Van Daan. [*To* Miep] Just a minute. There's something I'd like you to do for me.

[*He hurries off up the stairs to his room.*]

Mrs. Van Daan. [*Sharply*] Putti, where are you going? [*She rushes up the stairs after him, calling hysterically.*] What do you want? Putti, what are you going to do?

Miep. [*To* Peter] What's wrong?

Peter. [*His sympathy is with his mother.*] Father says he's going to sell her fur coat. She's crazy about that old fur coat.

Dussel. Is it possible? Is it possible that anyone is so silly as to worry about a fur coat in times like this?

Peter. It's none of your darn business . . . and if you say one more thing . . . I'll, I'll take you and I'll . . . I mean it . . . I'll . . .

[*There is a piercing scream from* Mrs. Van Daan *above. She grabs at the fur coat as* Mr. Van Daan *is starting downstairs with it.*]

Mrs. Van Daan. No! No! No! Don't you dare take that! You hear? It's mine! [*Downstairs* Peter *turns away, embarrassed, miserable.*] My father gave me that! You didn't give it to me. You have no right. Let go of it . . . you hear?

[Mr. Van Daan *pulls the coat from her hands and hurries downstairs.* Mrs. Van Daan *sinks to the floor, sobbing. As* Mr. Van Daan *comes into the main room the others look away, embarrassed for him.*]

Character's Motivation
Are Mr. Van Daan's reasons for selling his wife's fur coat selfish or unselfish? Explain.

Mr. Van Daan. [*To* Mr. Kraler] Just a little—discussion over the advisability of selling this coat. As I have often reminded Mrs. Van Daan, it's very selfish of her to keep it when people outside are in such desperate need of clothing . . . [*He gives the coat to* Miep.] So if you will please to sell it for us? It should fetch a good price. And by the way, will you get me cigarettes. I don't care what kind they are . . . get all you can.

MIEP. It's terribly difficult to get them, Mr. Van Daan. But I'll try. Good-bye.

[*She goes.* MR. FRANK *follows her down the steps to bolt the door after her.* MRS. FRANK *gives* MR. KRALER *a cup of tea.*]

MRS. FRANK. Are you sure you won't have some cake, Mr. Kraler?

MR. KRALER. I'd better not.

MR. VAN DAAN. You're still feeling badly? What does your doctor say?

MR. KRALER. I haven't been to him.

MRS. FRANK. Now, Mr. Kraler! . . .

MR. KRALER. [*Sitting at the table*] Oh, I tried. But you can't get near a doctor these days . . . they're so busy. After weeks I finally managed to get one on the telephone. I told him I'd like an appointment . . . I wasn't feeling very well. You know what he answers . . . over the telephone . . . Stick out your tongue! [*They laugh. He turns to* MR. FRANK *as* MR. FRANK *comes back.*] I have some contracts here . . . I wonder if you'd look over them with me . . .

MR. FRANK. [*Putting out his hand*] Of course.

MR. KRALER. [*He rises*] If we could go downstairs . . . [MR. FRANK *starts ahead;* MR. KRALER *speaks to the others.*] Will you forgive us? I won't keep him but a minute. [*He starts to follow* MR. FRANK *down the steps.*]

MARGOT. [*With sudden foreboding*] What's happened? Something's happened! Hasn't it, Mr. Kraler?

[MR. KRALER *stops and comes back, trying to reassure* MARGOT *with a pretense of casualness.*]

MR. KRALER. No, really. I want your father's advice . . .

MARGOT. Something's gone wrong! I know it!

MR. FRANK. [*Coming back, to* MR. KRALER] If it's something that concerns us here, it's better that we all hear it.

MR. KRALER. [*Turning to him, quietly*] But . . . the children . . . ?

MR. FRANK. What they'd imagine would be worse than any reality.

Is it possible that anyone is so silly as to worry about a fur coat in times like this?

Comprehension
What reason does Mr. Kraler give for wanting to talk with Mr. Frank privately?

Vocabulary ▶
apprehension
(ap´ rē hen´ shən) *n.*
fearful feeling about
what will happen next

[*As* MR. KRALER *speaks, they all listen with intense apprehension.* MRS. VAN DAAN *comes down the stairs and sits on the bottom step.*]

MR. KRALER. It's a man in the storeroom . . . I don't know whether or not you remember him . . . Carl, about fifty, heavy-set, nearsighted . . . He came with us just before you left.

MR. FRANK. He was from Utrecht?

MR. KRALER. That's the man. A couple of weeks ago, when I was in the storeroom, he closed the door and asked me . . . how's Mr. Frank? What do you hear from Mr. Frank? I told him I only knew there was a rumor that you were in Switzerland. He said he'd heard that rumor too, but he thought I might know something more. I didn't pay any attention to it . . . but then a thing happened yesterday . . . He'd brought some invoices to the office for me to sign. As I was going through them, I looked up. He was standing staring at the bookcase . . . your bookcase. He said he thought he remembered a door there . . . Wasn't there a door there that used to go up to the loft? Then he told me he wanted more money. Twenty guilders[2] more a week.

MR. VAN DAAN. Blackmail!

MR. FRANK. Twenty guilders? Very modest blackmail.

MR. VAN DAAN. That's just the beginning.

Vocabulary ▶
blackmail (blak´ māl´)
n. the practice of
making someone do
what one wants by
threatening to reveal
his or her secrets

DUSSEL. [*Coming to* MR. FRANK] You know what I think? He was the thief who was down there that night. That's how he knows we're here.

MR. FRANK. [*To* MR. KRALER] How was it left? What did you tell him?

MR. KRALER. I said I had to think about it. What shall I do? Pay him the money? . . . Take a chance on firing him . . . or what? I don't know.

DUSSEL. [*Frantic*] Don't fire him! Pay him what he asks . . . keep him here where you can have your eye on him.

Cause and Effect
How does Dussel's
reaction reflect his fear
about being caught
by the authorities?

MR. FRANK. Is it so much that he's asking? What are they paying nowadays?

MR. KRALER. He could get it in a war plant. But this isn't a

---

2. **guilders** (gil´ dərz) *n.* monetary unit of the Netherlands at the time.

war plant. Mind you, I don't know if he really knows . . . or if he doesn't know.

MR. FRANK. Offer him half. Then we'll soon find out if it's blackmail or not.

DUSSEL. And if it is? We've got to pay it, haven't we? Anything he asks we've got to pay!

MR. FRANK. Let's decide that when the time comes.

MR. KRALER. This may be all my imagination. You get to a point, these days, where you suspect everyone and everything. Again and again . . . on some simple look or word, I've found myself . . .

[*The telephone rings in the office below.*]

MRS. VAN DAAN. [*Hurrying to* MR. KRALER] There's the telephone! What does that mean, the telephone ringing on a holiday?

MR. KRALER. That's my wife. I told her I had to go over some papers in my office . . . to call me there when she got out of church. [*He starts out.*] I'll offer him half then. Good-bye . . . we'll hope for the best!

[*The group calls their good-byes halfheartedly.* MR. FRANK *follows* MR. KRALER *to bolt the door below. During the following scene,* MR. FRANK *comes back up and stands listening, disturbed.*]

DUSSEL. [*To* MR. VAN DAAN] You can thank your son for this . . . smashing the light! I tell you, it's just a question of time now.

[*He goes to the window at the back and stands looking out.*]

MARGOT. Sometimes I wish the end would come . . . whatever it is.

MRS. FRANK. [*Shocked*] Margot!

[ANNE *goes to* MARGOT, *sitting beside her on the couch with her arms around her.*]

MARGOT. Then at least we'd know where we were.

MRS. FRANK. You should be ashamed of yourself! Talking that way! Think how lucky we are! Think of the thousands dying in the war, every day. Think of the people in concentration camps.

Cause and Effect
Here, Kraler resists a cause-and-effect explanation for events that occurred in order. What else might explain the employee's demand?

Comprehension
What does the employee say to Mr. Kraler?

▶ Margot Frank (left) with her sister, Anne (right)

ANNE. [*Interrupting*] What's the good of that? What's the good of thinking of misery when you're already miserable? That's stupid!

MRS. FRANK. Anne!

[*As* ANNE *goes on raging at her mother,* MRS. FRANK *tries to break in, in an effort to quiet her.*]

ANNE. We're young, Margot and Peter and I! You grownups have had your chance! But look at us . . . If we begin thinking of all the horror in the world, we're lost! We're trying to hold onto some kind of ideals . . . when everything . . . ideals, hopes . . . everything, are being destroyed! It isn't our fault that the world is in such a mess! We weren't around when all this started! So don't try to take it out on us! [*She rushes off to her room, slamming the door after her. She picks up a brush from the chest and hurls it to the floor. Then she sits on the settee, trying to control her anger.*]

MR. VAN DAAN. She talks as if we started the war! Did we start the war?

[*He spots* ANNE's *cake. As he starts to take it,* PETER *anticipates him.*]

Cause and Effect
How does Anne's speech reveal a gap between the adults' and the teenagers' perspectives on the outside world?

PETER. She left her cake. [*He starts for* ANNE's *room with the cake. There is silence in the main room.* MRS. VAN DAAN *goes up to her room, followed by* VAN DAAN. DUSSEL *stays looking out the window.* MR. FRANK *brings* MRS. FRANK *her cake. She eats it slowly, without relish.* MR. FRANK *takes his cake to* MARGOT *and sits quietly on the sofa beside her.* PETER *stands in the doorway of* ANNE's *darkened room, looking at her, then makes a little movement to let her know he is there.* ANNE *sits up, quickly, trying to hide the signs of her tears.* PETER *holds out the cake to her.*] You left this.

ANNE. [*Dully*] Thanks.

[PETER *starts to go out, then comes back.*]

PETER. I thought you were fine just now. You know just how to talk to them. You know just how to say it. I'm no good . . . I never can think . . . especially when I'm mad . . . That Dussel . . . when he said that about Mouschi . . . someone eating him . . . all I could think is . . . I wanted to hit him. I wanted to give him such a . . . a . . . that he'd . . . That's what I used to do when there was an argument at school . . . That's the way I . . . but here . . . And an old man like that . . . it wouldn't be so good.

ANNE. You're making a big mistake about me. I do it all wrong. I say too much. I go too far. I hurt people's feelings . . .

[DUSSEL *leaves the window, going to his room.*]

PETER. I think you're just fine . . . What I want to say . . . if it wasn't for you around here, I don't know. What I mean . . .

[PETER *is interrupted by* DUSSEL's *turning on the light.* DUSSEL *stands in the doorway, startled to see* PETER. PETER *advances toward him forbiddingly.* DUSSEL *backs out of the room.* PETER *closes the door on him.*]

ANNE. Do you mean it, Peter? Do you really mean it?

PETER. I said it, didn't I?

ANNE. Thank you, Peter!

[*In the main room* MR. *and* MRS. FRANK *collect the dishes and take them to the sink, washing them.* MARGOT *lies down again on the couch.* DUSSEL, *lost, wanders into* PETER's *room and takes up a book, starting to read.*]

> **Character's Motivation**
> Why does Peter seek out Anne in her room?

> **Comprehension**
> Why does Peter admire Anne?

▶ **Critical Viewing**
This photograph shows a museum re-creation of a wall in Anne Frank's room. In what ways does her room resemble a typical teenager's room today?

PETER. [*Looking at the photographs on the wall*] You've got quite a collection.

ANNE. Wouldn't you like some in your room? I could give you some. Heaven knows you spend enough time in there . . . doing heaven knows what . . .

PETER. It's easier. A fight starts, or an argument . . . I duck in there.

ANNE. You're lucky, having a room to go to. His lordship is always here . . . I hardly ever get a minute alone. When they start in on me, I can't duck away. I have to stand there and take it.

PETER. You gave some of it back just now.

ANNE. I get so mad. They've formed their opinions . . . about everything . . . but we . . . we're still trying to find out . . . We have problems here that no other people our age have ever had. And just as you think you've solved them, something comes along and bang! You have to start all over again.

PETER. At least you've got someone you can talk to.

ANNE. Not really. Mother . . . I never discuss anything serious with her. She doesn't understand. Father's all right. We can talk about everything . . . everything but one thing. Mother. He simply won't talk about her. I don't think you can be really intimate with anyone if he holds something back, do you?

PETER. I think your father's fine.

ANNE. Oh, he is, Peter! He is! He's the only one who's ever given me the feeling that I have any sense. But anyway, nothing can take the place of school and play and friends of your own age . . . or near your age . . . can it?

PETER. I suppose you miss your friends and all.

ANNE. It isn't just . . . [*She breaks off, staring up at him for a second.*] Isn't it funny, you and I? Here we've been seeing each other every minute for almost a year and a half, and this is the first time we've ever really talked. It helps a lot to have someone to talk to, don't you think? It helps you to let off steam.

PETER. [*Going to the door*] Well, any time you want to let off steam, you can come into my room.

ANNE. [*Following him*] I can get up an awful lot of steam.
   You'll have to be careful how you say that.

PETER. It's all right with me.

ANNE. Do you mean it?

PETER. I said it, didn't I?

[*He goes out.* ANNE *stands in her doorway looking after him.
As* PETER *gets to his door he stands for a minute looking back
at her. Then he goes into his room.* DUSSEL *rises as he comes in,
and quickly passes him, going out. He starts across for
his room.* ANNE *sees him coming, and pulls her door shut.*
DUSSEL *turns back toward* PETER's *room.* PETER *pulls his door
shut.* DUSSEL *stands there, bewildered,* **forlorn.**

   The scene slowly dims out. The curtain falls on the scene.
ANNE's VOICE *comes over in the darkness . . . faintly at first,
and then with growing strength.*]

◀ **Vocabulary**
forlorn (fôr lôrn´)
adj. sad and lonely

Comprehension
What problems does
Anne describe to Peter?

Cause and Effect
What is the effect of the "bad news" on the people in the Annex?

ANNE'S VOICE. We've had bad news. The people from whom Miep got our ration books have been arrested. So we have had to cut down on our food. Our stomachs are so empty that they rumble and make strange noises, all in different keys. Mr. Van Daan's is deep and low, like a bass fiddle. Mine is high, whistling like a flute. As we all sit around waiting for supper, it's like an orchestra tuning up. It only needs Toscanini[3] to raise his baton and we'd be off in the Ride of the Valkyries.[4] Monday, the sixth of March, nineteen forty-four. Mr. Kraler is in the hospital. It seems he has ulcers. Pim says we are his ulcers. Miep has to run the business and us too. The Americans have landed on the southern tip of Italy. Father looks for a quick finish to the war. Mr. Dussel is waiting every day for the warehouse man to demand more money. Have I been skipping too much from one subject to another? I can't help it. I feel that spring is coming. I feel it in my whole body and soul. I feel utterly confused. I am longing . . . so longing . . . for everything . . . for friends . . . for someone to talk to . . . someone who understands . . . someone young, who feels as I do . . .

[*As these last lines are being said, the curtain rises on the scene. The lights dim on.* ANNE'S VOICE *fades out.*]

Scene 2

[*It is evening, after supper. From outside we hear the sound of children playing. The "grownups," with the exception of* MR. VAN DAAN, *are all in the main room.* MRS. FRANK *is doing some mending,* MRS. VAN DAAN *is reading a fashion magazine.* MR. FRANK *is going over business accounts.*
DUSSEL, *in his dentist's jacket, is pacing up and down, impatient to get into his bedroom.* MR. VAN DAAN *is upstairs working on a piece of embroidery in an embroidery frame.*

In his room PETER *is sitting before the mirror, smoothing his hair. As the scene goes on, he puts on his tie, brushes his coat and puts it on, preparing himself meticulously for a visit from* ANNE. *On his wall are now hung some of* ANNE'S *motion picture stars.*

---

3. **Toscanini** (täs´ kə nē´ nē) Arturo Toscanini, a famous Italian American orchestra conductor.
4. **Ride of the Valkyries** (val´ ki rēz) stirring selection from an opera by Richard Wagner, a German composer.

In her room ANNE *too is getting dressed. She stands before the mirror in her slip, trying various ways of dressing her hair.* MARGOT *is seated on the sofa, hemming a skirt for* ANNE *to wear.*

In the main room DUSSEL *can stand it no longer. He comes over, rapping sharply on the door of his and* ANNE'S *bedroom.*]

ANNE. [*Calling to him*] No, no, Mr. Dussel! I am not dressed yet. [DUSSEL *walks away, furious, sitting down and burying his head in his hands.* ANNE *turns to* MARGOT.] How is that? How does that look?

MARGOT. [*Glancing at her briefly*] Fine.

ANNE. You didn't even look.

MARGOT. Of course I did. It's fine.

ANNE. Margot, tell me, am I terribly ugly?

MARGOT. Oh, stop fishing.

ANNE. No. No. Tell me.

MARGOT. Of course you're not. You've got nice eyes . . . and a lot of animation, and . . .

ANNE. A little vague, aren't you?

[*She reaches over and takes a brassiere out of* MARGOT'S *sewing basket. She holds it up to herself, studying the effect in the mirror. Outside,* MRS. FRANK, *feeling sorry for* DUSSEL, *comes over, knocking at the girls' door.*]

MRS. FRANK. [*Outside*] May I come in?

MARGOT. Come in, Mother.

MRS. FRANK. [*Shutting the door behind her*] Mr. Dussel's impatient to get in here.

ANNE. [*Still with the brassiere*] Heavens, he takes the room for himself the entire day.

MRS. FRANK. [*Gently*] Anne, dear, you're not going in again tonight to see Peter?

ANNE. [*Dignified*] That is my intention.

MRS. FRANK. But you've already spent a great deal of time in there today.

ANNE. I was in there exactly twice. Once to get the dictionary, and then three-quarters of an hour before supper.

Comprehension
How does Mrs. Frank feel about the time Anne spends with Peter?

Vocabulary ▶
intuition (in´ tōō ish´ ən)
n. ability to sense
immediately, without
reasoning

Character's Motivation
What prompts Mrs.
Frank to make these
requests of Anne?

MRS. FRANK. Aren't you afraid you're disturbing him?

ANNE. Mother, I have some intuition.

MRS. FRANK. Then may I ask you this much, Anne. Please don't shut the door when you go in.

ANNE. You sound like Mrs. Van Daan! [*She throws the brassiere back in* MARGOT's *sewing basket and picks up her blouse, putting it on.*]

MRS. FRANK. No. No. I don't mean to suggest anything wrong. I only wish that you wouldn't expose yourself to criticism . . . that you wouldn't give Mrs. Van Daan the opportunity to be unpleasant.

ANNE. Mrs. Van Daan doesn't need an opportunity to be unpleasant!

MRS. FRANK. Everyone's on edge, worried about Mr. Kraler. This is one more thing . . .

ANNE. I'm sorry, Mother. I'm going to Peter's room. I'm not going to let Petronella Van Daan spoil our friendship.

[MRS. FRANK *hesitates for a second, then goes out, closing the door after her. She gets a pack of playing cards and sits at the center table, playing solitaire. In* ANNE's *room* MARGOT *hands the finished skirt to* ANNE. *As* ANNE *is putting it on,* MARGOT *takes off her high-heeled shoes and stuffs paper in the toes so that* ANNE *can wear them.*]

MARGOT. [*To* ANNE] Why don't you two talk in the main room? It'd save a lot of trouble. It's hard on Mother, having to listen to those remarks from Mrs. Van Daan and not say a word.

ANNE. Why doesn't she say a word? I think it's ridiculous to take it and take it.

MARGOT. You don't understand Mother at all, do you? She can't talk back. She's not like you. It's just not in her nature to fight back.

ANNE. Anyway . . . the only one I worry about is you. I feel awfully guilty about you. [*She sits on the stool near* MARGOT, *putting on* MARGOT's *high-heeled shoes.*]

MARGOT. What about?

Anne. I mean, every time I go into Peter's room, I have a feeling I may be hurting you. [Margot *shakes her head.*] I know if it were me, I'd be wild. I'd be desperately jealous, if it were me.

Margot. Well, I'm not.

Anne. You don't feel badly? Really? Truly? You're not jealous?

Margot. Of course I'm jealous . . . jealous that you've got something to get up in the morning for . . . But jealous of you and Peter? No.

[Anne *goes back to the mirror.*]

Anne. Maybe there's nothing to be jealous of. Maybe he doesn't really like me. Maybe I'm just taking the place of his cat . . . [*She picks up a pair of short white gloves, putting them on.*] Wouldn't you like to come in with us?

Margot. I have a book.

[*The sound of the children playing outside fades out. In the main room* Dussel *can stand it no longer. He jumps up, going to the bedroom door and knocking sharply.*]

Dussel. Will you please let me in my room!

Anne. Just a minute, dear, dear Mr. Dussel. [*She picks up her mother's pink stole and adjusts it elegantly over her shoulders, then gives a last look in the mirror.*] Well, here I go . . . to run the gauntlet.[5]

[*She starts out, followed by* Margot.]

Dussel. [*As she appears—sarcastic*] Thank you so much.

[Dussel *goes into his room.* Anne *goes toward* Peter's *room, passing* Mrs. Van Daan *and her parents at the center table.*]

Mrs. Van Daan. My God, look at her! [Anne *pays no attention. She knocks at* Peter's *door.*] I don't know what good it is to have a son. I never see him. He wouldn't care if I killed myself. [Peter *opens the door and stands aside for* Anne *to come in.*] Just a minute, Anne. [*She goes to them at the door.*] I'd like to say a few words to my son. Do you mind? [Peter *and* Anne *stand waiting.*] Peter, I don't want you

Of course I'm jealous . . . jealous that you've got something to get up in the morning for . . .

---

5. **run the gauntlet** (gônt´ lit) formerly, to pass between two rows of men who struck at the offender with clubs as he passed; here, a series of troubles or difficulties.

Comprehension
Why does Anne fear she might be hurting Margot?

staying up till all hours tonight. You've got to have your sleep. You're a growing boy. You hear?

MRS. FRANK. Anne won't stay late. She's going to bed promptly at nine. Aren't you, Anne?

ANNE. Yes, Mother . . . [*To* MRS. VAN DAAN] May we go now?

MRS. VAN DAAN. Are you asking me? I didn't know I had anything to say about it.

MRS. FRANK. Listen for the chimes, Anne dear.

[*The two young people go off into* PETER's *room, shutting the door after them.*]

Cause and Effect
How might Mrs. Van Daan's beliefs about what is socially acceptable reflect her own upbringing?

MRS. VAN DAAN. [*To* MRS. FRANK] In my day it was the boys who called on the girls. Not the girls on the boys.

MRS. FRANK. You know how young people like to feel that they have secrets. Peter's room is the only place where they can talk.

MRS. VAN DAAN. Talk! That's not what they called it when I was young.

[MRS. VAN DAAN *goes off to the bathroom.* MARGOT *settles down to read her book.* MR. FRANK *puts his papers away and brings a chess game to the center table. He and* MRS. FRANK *start to play. In* PETER's *room,* ANNE *speaks to* PETER, *indignant, humiliated.*]

ANNE. Aren't they awful? Aren't they impossible? Treating us as if we were still in the nursery.

[*She sits on the cot.* PETER *gets a bottle of pop and two glasses.*]

PETER. Don't let it bother you. It doesn't bother me.

ANNE. I suppose you can't really blame them . . . they think back to what *they* were like at our age. They don't realize how much more advanced we are . . . When you think what wonderful discussions we've had! . . . Oh, I forgot. I was going to bring you some more pictures.

PETER. Oh, these are fine, thanks.

ANNE. Don't you want some more? Miep just brought me some new ones.

PETER. Maybe later. [*He gives her a glass of pop and, taking some for himself, sits down facing her.*]

ANNE. [*Looking up at one of the photographs*] I remember when I got that . . . I won it. I bet Jopie that I could eat five ice-cream cones. We'd all been playing ping-pong . . . We used to have heavenly times . . . we'd finish up with ice cream at the Delphi, or the Oasis, where Jews were allowed . . . there'd always be a lot of boys . . . we'd laugh and joke . . . I'd like to go back to it for a few days or a week. But after that I know I'd be bored to death. I think more seriously about life now. I want to be a journalist . . . or something. I love to write. What do you want to do?

PETER. I thought I might go off some place . . . work on a farm or something . . . some job that doesn't take much brains.

ANNE. You shouldn't talk that way. You've got the most awful inferiority complex.

PETER. I know I'm not smart.

ANNE. That isn't true. You're much better than I am in dozens of things . . . arithmetic and algebra and . . . well, you're a million times better than I am in algebra. [*With sudden directness*] You like Margot, don't you? Right from the start you liked her, liked her much better than me.

PETER. [*Uncomfortably*] Oh, I don't know.

[*In the main room* MRS. VAN DAAN *comes from the bathroom and goes over to the sink, polishing a coffee pot.*]

Comprehension
Why does Anne feel she might be dissatisfied now with her old life?

Character's Motivation
What is Anne's possible motivation for asking Peter whether he likes Margot?

ANNE. It's all right. Everyone feels that way. Margot's so good. She's sweet and bright and beautiful and I'm not.

PETER. I wouldn't say that.

ANNE. Oh, no, I'm not. I know that. I know quite well that I'm not a beauty. I never have been and never shall be.

PETER. I don't agree at all. I think you're pretty.

ANNE. That's not true!

PETER. And another thing. You've changed . . . from at first, I mean.

ANNE. I have?

PETER. I used to think you were awful noisy.

ANNE. And what do you think now, Peter? How have I changed?

PETER. Well . . . er . . . you're . . . quieter.

[*In his room* DUSSEL *takes his pajamas and toilet articles and goes into the bathroom to change.*]

ANNE. I'm glad you don't just hate me.

PETER. I never said that.

ANNE. I bet when you get out of here you'll never think of me again.

PETER. That's crazy.

ANNE. When you get back with all of your friends, you're going to say . . . now what did I ever see in that Mrs. Quack Quack.

PETER. I haven't got any friends.

ANNE. Oh, Peter, of course you have. Everyone has friends.

PETER. Not me. I don't want any. I get along all right without them.

ANNE. Does that mean you can get along without me? I think of myself as your friend.

PETER. No. If they were all like you, it'd be different.

[*He takes the glasses and the bottle and puts them away. There is a second's silence and then* ANNE *speaks, hesitantly, shyly.*]

ANNE. Peter, did you ever kiss a girl?

PETER. Yes. Once.

ANNE. [*To cover her feelings*] That picture's crooked.

[PETER *goes over, straightening the photograph.*]
    Was she pretty?

PETER. Huh?

ANNE. The girl that you kissed.

PETER. I don't know. I was blindfolded. [*He comes back and sits down again.*] It was at a party. One of those kissing games.

ANNE. [*Relieved*] Oh. I don't suppose that really counts, does it?

PETER. It didn't with me.

ANNE. I've been kissed twice. Once a man I'd never seen before kissed me on the cheek when he picked me up off the ice and I was crying. And the other was Mr. Koophuis, a friend of Father's who kissed my hand. You wouldn't say those counted, would you?

PETER. I wouldn't say so.

ANNE. I know almost for certain that Margot would never kiss anyone unless she was engaged to them. And I'm sure too that Mother never touched a man before Pim. But I don't know . . . things are so different now . . . What do you think? Do you think a girl shouldn't kiss anyone except if she's engaged or something? It's so hard to try to think what to do, when here we are with the whole world falling around our ears and you think . . . well . . . you don't know what's going to happen tomorrow and . . . What do you think?

PETER. I suppose it'd depend on the girl. Some girls, anything they do's wrong. But others . . . well . . . it wouldn't necessarily be wrong with them. [*The carillon starts to strike nine o'clock.*] I've always thought that when two people . . .

ANNE. Nine o'clock. I have to go.

PETER. That's right.

ANNE. [*Without moving*] Good night.

[*There is a second's pause, then* PETER *gets up and moves toward the door.*]

Cause and Effect
Based on Anne's comments, what effect is the war having on prewar attitudes?

Comprehension
How has Peter's view of Anne changed?

Character's Motivation
What causes Anne to want to share her diary with Peter?

PETER. You won't let them stop you coming?

ANNE. No. [*She rises and starts for the door.*] Sometimes I might bring my diary. There are so many things in it that I want to talk over with you. There's a lot about you.

PETER. What kind of things?

ANNE. I wouldn't want you to see some of it. I thought you were a nothing, just the way you thought about me.

PETER. Did you change your mind, the way I changed my mind about you?

ANNE. Well . . . You'll see . . .

[*For a second* ANNE *stands looking up at* PETER, *longing for him to kiss her. As he makes no move she turns away. Then suddenly* PETER *grabs her awkwardly in his arms, kissing her on the cheek.* ANNE *walks out dazed. She stands for a minute, her back to the people in the main room. As she regains her poise she goes to her mother and father and* MARGOT, *silently kissing them. They murmur their good nights to her. As she is about to open her bedroom door, she catches sight of* MRS. VAN DAAN. *She goes quickly to her, taking her face in her hands and kissing her first on one cheek and then on the other. Then she hurries off into her room.* MRS. VAN DAAN *looks after her, and then looks over at* PETER'S *room. Her suspicions are confirmed.*]

MRS. VAN DAAN. [*She knows.*] Ah hah!

[*The lights dim out. The curtain falls on the scene. In the darkness* ANNE'S VOICE *comes faintly at first and then with growing strength.*]

ANNE'S VOICE. By this time we all know each other so well that if anyone starts to tell a story, the rest can finish it for him. We're having to cut down still further on our meals. What makes it worse, the rats have been at work again. They've carried off some of our precious food. Even Mr. Dussel wishes now that Mouschi was here. Thursday, the twentieth of April, nineteen forty-four. Invasion fever is mounting every day. Miep tells us that people outside talk of nothing else. For myself, life has become much more pleasant. I often go to Peter's room after supper. Oh, don't think I'm in love, because I'm not. But it does make life more bearable to have someone with whom you can exchange views. No more tonight. P.S. . . . I must be honest. I must confess that I actually live for the next meeting. Is there anything lovelier than to sit under the skylight and feel the sun on your cheeks and have a darling boy in your arms? I admit now that I'm glad the Van Daans had a son and not a daughter. I've outgrown another dress. That's the third. I'm having to wear Margot's clothes after all. I'm working hard on my French and am now reading *La Belle Nivernaise*.[6]

[*As she is saying the last lines—the curtain rises on the scene. The lights dim on, as* ANNE'S VOICE *fades out.*]

But it does make life more bearable to have someone with whom you can exchange views.

Scene 3

[*It is night, a few weeks later. Everyone is in bed. There is complete quiet. In the* VAN DAANS' *room a match flares up for a moment and then is quickly put out.* MR. VAN DAAN, *in bare feet, dressed in underwear and trousers, is dimly seen coming stealthily down the stairs and into the main room, where* MR. *and* MRS. FRANK *and* MARGOT *are sleeping. He goes to the food safe and again lights a match. Then he cautiously opens the safe, taking out a half-loaf of bread. As he closes the safe, it creaks. He stands rigid.* MRS. FRANK *sits up in bed. She sees him.*]

MRS. FRANK. [*Screaming*] Otto! Otto! *Komme schnell!*[7]

[*The rest of the people wake, hurriedly getting up.*]

MR. FRANK. *Was ist los? Was ist passiert?*[8]

[DUSSEL, *followed by* ANNE, *comes from his room.*]

MRS. FRANK. [*As she rushes over to* MR. VAN DAAN] *Er stiehlt das Essen!*[9]

DUSSEL. [*Grabbing* MR. VAN DAAN] You! You! Give me that.

MRS. VAN DAAN. [*Coming down the stairs*] Putti . . . Putti . . . what is it?

Character's Motivation
Why is Mr. Van Daan being so cautious about making noise?

Comprehension
Why does Mrs. Frank scream in the middle of the night?

---

6. *La Belle Nivernaise* story by Alphonse Daudet, a French author.
7. *Komme schnell!* (käm´ ə shnel´) German for "Come quick!"
8. *Was ist los? Was ist passiert?* (väs´ ist los´ väs´ ist päs´ ērt) German for "What's the matter? What happened?"
9. *Er stiehlt das Essen!* (er shtēlt´ däs es´ ən) German for "He steals food!"

DUSSEL. [*His hands on* VAN DAAN's *neck*] You dirty thief . . . stealing food . . . you good-for-nothing . . .

MR. FRANK. Mr. Dussel! For God's sake! Help me, Peter!

[PETER *comes over, trying, with* MR. FRANK, *to separate the two struggling men.*]

PETER. Let him go! Let go!

[DUSSEL *drops* MR. VAN DAAN, *pushing him away. He shows them the end of a loaf of bread that he has taken from* VAN DAAN.]

DUSSEL. You greedy, selfish . . . !

[MARGOT *turns on the lights.*]

MRS. VAN DAAN. Putti . . . what is it?

[*All of* MRS. FRANK's *gentleness, her self-control, is gone. She is outraged, in a frenzy of indignation.*]

MRS. FRANK. The bread! He was stealing the bread!

DUSSEL. It was you, and all the time we thought it was the rats!

MR. FRANK. Mr. Van Daan, how could you!

MR. VAN DAAN. I'm hungry.

MRS. FRANK. We're all of us hungry! I see the children getting thinner and thinner. Your own son Peter . . . I've heard him moan in his sleep, he's so hungry. And you come in the night and steal food that should go to them . . . to the children!

MRS. VAN DAAN. [*Going to* MR. VAN DAAN *protectively*] He needs more food than the rest of us. He's used to more. He's a big man.

[MR. VAN DAAN *breaks away, going over and sitting on the couch.*]

MRS. FRANK. [*Turning on* MRS. VAN DAAN] And you . . . you're worse than he is! You're a mother, and yet you sacrifice your child to this man . . . this . . . this . . .

MR. FRANK. Edith! Edith!

[MARGOT *picks up the pink woolen stole, putting it over her mother's shoulders.*]

MRS. FRANK. [*Paying no attention, going on to* MRS. VAN DAAN]

Spiral Review
CONFLICT What long-simmering resentments does Mr. Van Daan's action bring out into the open?

Don't think I haven't seen you! Always saving the choicest bits for him! I've watched you day after day and I've held my tongue. But not any longer! Not after this! Now I want him to go! I want him to get out of here!

[*Together*] {
MR. FRANK. Edith!

MR. VAN DAAN. Get out of here?

MRS. VAN DAAN. What do you mean?
}

Cause and Effect
What causes Mr. Van Daan to steal food, and what is the effect of his actions on the others?

MRS. FRANK. Just that! Take your things and get out!

MR. FRANK. [*To* MRS. FRANK] You're speaking in anger. You cannot mean what you are saying.

MRS. FRANK. I mean exactly that!

[MRS. VAN DAAN *takes a cover from the* FRANKS' *bed, pulling it about her.*]

MR. FRANK. For two long years we have lived here, side by side. We have respected each other's rights . . . we have managed to live in peace. Are we now going to throw it all away? I know this will never happen again, will it, Mr. Van Daan?

The bread! He was stealing the bread!

MR. VAN DAAN. No. No.

MRS. FRANK. He steals once! He'll steal again!

[MR. VAN DAAN, *holding his stomach, starts for the bathroom.* ANNE *puts her arms around him, helping him up the step.*]

MR. FRANK. Edith, please. Let us be calm. We'll all go to our rooms . . . and afterwards we'll sit down quietly and talk this out . . . we'll find some way . . .

MRS. FRANK. No! No! No more talk! I want them to leave!

MRS. VAN DAAN. You'd put us out, on the streets?

MRS. FRANK. There are other hiding places.

MRS. VAN DAAN. A cellar . . . a closet. I know. And we have no money left even to pay for that.

MRS. FRANK. I'll give you money. Out of my own pocket I'll give it gladly. [*She gets her purse from a shelf and comes back with it.*]

MRS. VAN DAAN. Mr. Frank, you told Putti you'd never forget what he'd done for you when you came to Amsterdam. You said you could never repay him, that you . . .

Comprehension
How does Mr. Frank react to his wife's demand that the Van Daans leave?

MRS. FRANK. [*Counting out money*] If my husband had any obligation to you, he's paid it, over and over.

MR. FRANK. Edith, I've never seen you like this before. I don't know you.

MRS. FRANK. I should have spoken out long ago.

DUSSEL. You can't be nice to some people.

Character's Motivation
What do Mr. Frank's lines show about his character and about what motivates him?

MRS. VAN DAAN. [*Turning on* DUSSEL] There would have been plenty for all of us, if *you* hadn't come in here!

MR. FRANK. We don't need the Nazis to destroy us. We're destroying ourselves.

[*He sits down, with his head in his hands.* MRS. FRANK *goes to* MRS. VAN DAAN.]

MRS. FRANK. [*Giving* MRS. VAN DAAN *some money*] Give this to Miep. She'll find you a place.

ANNE. Mother, you're not putting Peter out. Peter hasn't done anything.

MRS. FRANK. He'll stay, of course. When I say I must protect the children, I mean Peter too.

[PETER *rises from the steps where he has been sitting.*]

PETER. I'd have to go if Father goes.

[MR. VAN DAAN *comes from the bathroom.* MRS. VAN DAAN *hurries to him and takes him to the couch. Then she gets water from the sink to bathe his face.*]

Character's Motivation
What do Peter's words reveal about how he feels about leaving?

MRS. FRANK. [*While this is going on*] He's no father to you . . . that man! He doesn't know what it is to be a father!

PETER. [*Starting for his room*] I wouldn't feel right. I couldn't stay.

MRS. FRANK. Very well, then. I'm sorry.

ANNE. [*Rushing over to* PETER] No, Peter! No! [PETER *goes into his room, closing the door after him.* ANNE *turns back to her mother, crying.*] I don't care about the food. They can have mine! I don't want it! Only don't send them away. It'll be daylight soon. They'll be caught . . .

MARGOT. [*Putting her arms comfortingly around* ANNE] Please, Mother!

MRS. FRANK. They're not going now. They'll stay here until Miep finds them a place. [*To* MRS. VAN DAAN] But one thing I insist on! He must never come down here again! He must never come to this room where the food is stored! We'll divide what we have . . . an equal share for each! [DUSSEL *hurries over to get a sack of potatoes from the food safe.* MRS. FRANK *goes on, to* MRS. VAN DAAN] You can cook it here and take it up to him.

[DUSSEL *brings the sack of potatoes back to the center table.*]

MARGOT. Oh, no. No. We haven't sunk so far that we're going to fight over a handful of rotten potatoes.

DUSSEL. [*Dividing the potatoes into piles*] Mrs. Frank, Mr. Frank, Margot, Anne, Peter, Mrs. Van Daan, Mr. Van Daan, myself . . . Mrs. Frank . . .

[*The buzzer sounds in* MIEP'S *signal.*]

MR. FRANK. It's Miep! [*He hurries over, getting his overcoat and putting it on.*]

MARGOT. At this hour?

MRS. FRANK. It is trouble.

MR. FRANK. [*As he starts down to unbolt the door*] I beg you, don't let her see a thing like this!

MR. DUSSEL. [*Counting without stopping*] . . . Anne, Peter, Mrs. Van Daan, Mr. Van Daan, myself . . .

MARGOT. [*To* DUSSEL] Stop it! Stop it!

DUSSEL. . . . Mr. Frank, Margot, Anne, Peter, Mrs. Van Daan, Mr. Van Daan, myself, Mrs. Frank . . .

MRS. VAN DAAN. You're keeping the big ones for yourself! All the big ones . . . Look at the size of that! . . . And that! . . .

[DUSSEL *continues on with his dividing.* PETER, *with his shirt and trousers on, comes from his room.*]

MARGOT. Stop it! Stop it!

[*We hear* MIEP'S *excited voice speaking to* MR. FRANK *below.*]

MIEP. Mr. Frank . . . the most wonderful news! . . . The invasion has begun!

MR. FRANK. Go on, tell them! Tell them!

[MIEP *comes running up the steps ahead of* MR. FRANK. *She has a man's raincoat on over her nightclothes and a bunch of orange-colored flowers in her hand.*]

Cause and Effect
What effect does Mr. Van Daan's action have on the tensions among the characters?

Comprehension
Why does Dussel bring the sack of potatoes to the table?

MIEP. Did you hear that, everybody? Did you hear what I said? The invasion has begun! The invasion!

[*They all stare at* MIEP, *unable to grasp what she is telling them.* PETER *is the first to recover his wits.*]

PETER. Where?

MRS. VAN DAAN. When? When, Miep?

MIEP. It began early this morning . . .

[*As she talks on, the realization of what she has said begins to dawn on them. Everyone goes crazy. A wild demonstration takes place.* MRS. FRANK *hugs* MR. VAN DAAN.]

MRS. FRANK. Oh, Mr. Van Daan, did you hear that?

[DUSSEL *embraces* MRS. VAN DAAN. PETER *grabs a frying pan and parades around the room, beating on it, singing the Dutch National Anthem.* ANNE *and* MARGOT *follow him, singing, weaving in and out among the excited grown-ups.* MARGOT *breaks away to take the flowers from* MIEP *and distribute them to everyone. While this pandemonium is going on* MRS. FRANK *tries to make herself heard above the excitement.*]

MRS. FRANK. [*To* MIEP] How do you know?

MIEP. The radio . . . The B.B.C.![10] They said they landed on the coast of Normandy!

PETER. The British?

MIEP. British, Americans, French, Dutch, Poles, Norwegians . . . all of them! More than four thousand ships! Churchill spoke, and General Eisenhower! D-Day they call it!

MR. FRANK. Thank God, it's come!

MRS. VAN DAAN. At last!

MIEP. [*Starting out*] I'm going to tell Mr. Kraler. This'll be better than any blood transfusion.

MR. FRANK. [*Stopping her*] What part of Normandy did they land, did they say?

MIEP. Normandy . . . that's all I know now . . . I'll be up the minute I hear some more! [*She goes hurriedly out.*]

MR. FRANK. [*To* MRS. FRANK] What did I tell you? What did I tell you?

Cause and Effect
What is the effect of the news about D-Day on the people in the Annex?

---

10. B.B.C. British Broadcasting Corporation.

[MRS. FRANK *indicates that he has forgotten to bolt the door after* MIEP. *He hurries down the steps.* MR. VAN DAAN, *sitting on the couch, suddenly breaks into a convulsive[11] sob. Everybody looks at him, bewildered.*]

MRS. VAN DAAN. [*Hurrying to him*] Putti! Putti! What is it? What happened?

MR. VAN DAAN. Please, I'm so ashamed.

[MR. FRANK *comes back up the steps.*]

DUSSEL. Oh, for God's sake!

MRS. VAN DAAN. Don't, Putti.

MARGOT. It doesn't matter now!

MR. FRANK. [*Going to* MR. VAN DAAN] Didn't you hear what Miep said? The invasion has come! We're going to

Comprehension
What are the details of the news that Miep brings?

---

11. **convulsive** (kən vul´ siv) *adj.* having an uncontrolled muscular spasm; shuddering.

LITERATURE IN CONTEXT

History Connection

Taking the Beaches, Ending the War

On D-Day, June 6, 1944, a fleet of 4,000 ships headed for Normandy on the northern coast of France. Omaha Beach, shown below in the distance, was the most difficult to attack of the five planned sites because of its high cliffs and lack of inland routes. Yet by day's end, U.S. troops had secured a two-mile position from which they could continue to Paris and to Germany.

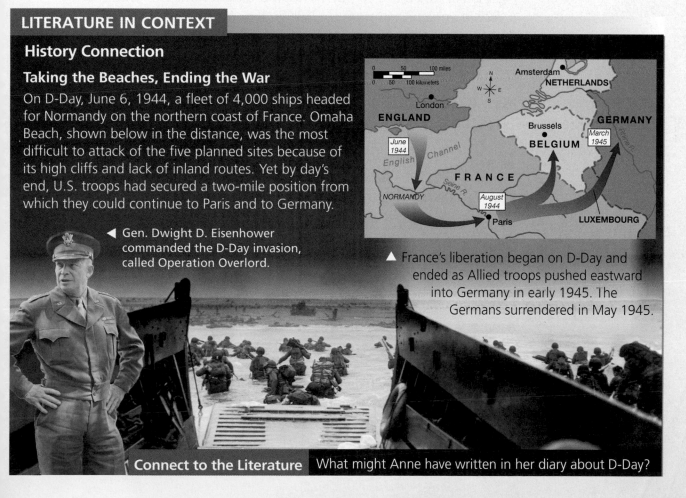

◀ Gen. Dwight D. Eisenhower commanded the D-Day invasion, called Operation Overlord.

▲ France's liberation began on D-Day and ended as Allied troops pushed eastward into Germany in early 1945. The Germans surrendered in May 1945.

Connect to the Literature What might Anne have written in her diary about D-Day?

be liberated! This is a time to celebrate! [*He embraces* MRS. FRANK *and then hurries to the cupboard and gets the cognac and a glass.*]

MR. VAN DAAN. To steal bread from children!

MRS. FRANK. We've all done things that we're ashamed of.

ANNE. Look at me, the way I've treated Mother . . . so mean and horrid to her.

MRS. FRANK. No, Anneke, no.

[ANNE *runs to her mother, putting her arms around her.*]

ANNE. Oh, Mother, I was. I was awful.

MR. VAN DAAN. Not like me. No one is as bad as me!

DUSSEL. [*To* MR. VAN DAAN] Stop it now! Let's be happy!

MR. FRANK. [*Giving* MR. VAN DAAN *a glass of cognac*] Here! Here! Schnapps! L'chaim![12]

[VAN DAAN *takes the cognac. They all watch him. He gives them a feeble smile.* ANNE *puts up her fingers in a V-for-Victory sign. As* VAN DAAN *gives an answering V-sign, they are startled to hear a loud sob from behind them. It is* MRS. FRANK, *stricken with remorse. She is sitting on the other side of the room.*]

MRS. FRANK. [*Through her sobs*] When I think of the terrible things I said . . .

[MR. FRANK, ANNE *and* MARGOT *hurry to her, trying to comfort her.* MR. VAN DAAN *brings her his glass of cognac.*]

MR. VAN DAAN. No! No! You were right!

MRS. FRANK. That I should speak that way to you! . . . Our friends! . . . Our guests! [*She starts to cry again.*]

DUSSEL. Stop it, you're spoiling the whole invasion!

[*As they are comforting her, the lights dim out. The curtain falls.*]

ANNE'S VOICE. [*Faintly at first and then with growing strength*] We're all in much better spirits these days. There's still excellent news of the invasion. The best part about it is that I have a feeling that friends are coming. Who knows? Maybe I'll be back in school by fall. Ha, ha! The joke is on us! The warehouse man doesn't know a thing and we are

12. *Schnapps!* (shnäps) German for "a drink." *L'chaim!* (lə khä´ yim) Hebrew toast meaning "To life!"

Character's Motivation
What drives Anne to admit that she has treated her mother badly?

paying him all that money! . . . Wednesday, the second of July, nineteen forty-four. The invasion seems temporarily to be bogged down. Mr. Kraler has to have an operation, which looks bad. The Gestapo have found the radio that was stolen. Mr. Dussel says they'll trace it back and back to the thief, and then, it's just a matter of time till they get to us. Everyone is low. Even poor Pim can't raise their spirits. I have often been downcast myself . . . but never in despair. I can shake off everything if I write. But . . . and that is the great question . . . will I ever be able to write well? I want to so much. I want to go on living even after my death. Another birthday has gone by, so now I am fifteen. Already I know what I want. I have a goal, an opinion.

[*As this is being said—the curtain rises on the scene, the lights dim on, and* ANNE'S VOICE *fades out.*]

Scene 4

[*It is an afternoon a few weeks later . . . Everyone but* MARGOT *is in the main room. There is a sense of great tension.*

Both MRS. FRANK *and* MR. VAN DAAN *are nervously pacing back and forth,* DUSSEL *is standing at the window, looking down fixedly at the street below.* PETER *is at the center table, trying to do his lessons.* ANNE *sits opposite him, writing in her diary.* MRS. VAN DAAN *is seated on the couch, her eyes on* MR. FRANK *as he sits reading.*

The sound of a telephone ringing comes from the office below. They all are rigid, listening tensely. DUSSEL *rushes down to* MR. FRANK.]

DUSSEL. There it goes again, the telephone! Mr. Frank, do you hear?

MR. FRANK. [*Quietly*] Yes. I hear.

DUSSEL. [*Pleading, insistent*] But this is the third time, Mr. Frank! The third time in quick succession! It's a signal! I tell you it's Miep, trying to get us! For some reason she can't come to us and she's trying to warn us of something!

MR. FRANK. Please. Please.

MR. VAN DAAN. [*To* DUSSEL] You're wasting your breath.

DUSSEL. Something has happened, Mr. Frank. For three days

I have often been downcast myself . . . but never in despair.

Comprehension
What new goal does Anne set for herself?

now Miep hasn't been to see us! And today not a man has come to work. There hasn't been a sound in the building!

MRS. FRANK. Perhaps it's Sunday. We may have lost track of the days.

MR. VAN DAAN. [*To* ANNE] You with the diary there. What day is it?

DUSSEL. [*Going to* MRS. FRANK] I don't lose track of the days! I know exactly what day it is! It's Friday, the fourth of August. Friday, and not a man at work. [*He rushes back to* MR. FRANK, *pleading with him, almost in tears.*] I tell you Mr. Kraler's dead. That's the only explanation. He's dead and they've closed down the building, and Miep's trying to tell us!

MR. FRANK. She'd never telephone us.

DUSSEL. [*Frantic*] Mr. Frank, answer that! I beg you, answer it!

MR. FRANK. No.

MR. VAN DAAN. Just pick it up and listen. You don't have to speak. Just listen and see if it's Miep.

DUSSEL. [*Speaking at the same time*] For God's sake . . . I ask you.

MR. FRANK. No. I've told you, no. I'll do nothing that might let anyone know we're in the building.

PETER. Mr. Frank's right.

MR. VAN DAAN. There's no need to tell us what side you're on.

MR. FRANK. If we wait patiently, quietly, I believe that help will come.

[*There is silence for a minute as they all listen to the telephone ringing.*]

DUSSEL. I'm going down.
[*He rushes down the steps.* MR. FRANK *tries* **ineffectually** *to hold him.* DUSSEL *runs to the lower door, unbolting it. The telephone stops ringing.* DUSSEL *bolts the door and comes slowly back up the steps.*] Too late.

[MR. FRANK *goes to* MARGOT *in* ANNE'S *bedroom.*]

MR. VAN DAAN. So we just wait here until we die.

MRS. VAN DAAN. [*Hysterically*] I can't stand it! I'll kill myself! I'll kill myself!

Cause and Effect
What is the effect of the ringing telephone?

Vocabulary ▶
ineffectually
(in´ e fek´ chōō ə lē)
adv. without producing the desired results

Mr. Van Daan. For God's sake, stop it!

[*In the distance, a German military band is heard playing a Viennese waltz.*]

Mrs. Van Daan. I think you'd be glad if I did! I think you want me to die!

Mr. Van Daan. Whose fault is it we're here? [Mrs. Van Daan *starts for her room. He follows, talking at her.*] We could've been safe somewhere . . . in America or Switzerland. But no! No! You wouldn't leave when I wanted to. You couldn't leave your things. You couldn't leave your precious furniture.

Mrs. Van Daan. Don't touch me!

[*She hurries up the stairs, followed by* Mr. Van Daan. Peter, *unable to bear it, goes to his room.* Anne *looks after him, deeply concerned.* Dussel *returns to his post at the window.* Mr. Frank *comes back into the main room and takes a book, trying to read.* Mrs. Frank *sits near the sink, starting to peel some potatoes.* Anne *quietly goes to* Peter's *room, closing the door after her.* Peter *is lying face down on the cot.* Anne *leans over him, holding him in her arms, trying to bring him out of his despair.*]

Anne. Look, Peter, the sky. [*She looks up through the skylight.*] What a lovely, lovely day! Aren't the clouds beautiful? You know what I do when it seems as if I couldn't stand being cooped up for one more minute? I *think* myself out. I think myself on a walk in the park where I used to go with Pim. Where the jonquils and the crocus and the violets grow down the slopes. You know the most wonderful part about *thinking* yourself out? You can have it any way you like. You can have roses and violets and chrysanthemums all blooming at the same time . . . It's funny . . . I used to take it all for granted . . . and now I've gone crazy about everything to do with nature. Haven't you?

Cause and Effect
What effect has Mrs. Van Daan's love of expensive objects had on the family, according to Mr. Van Daan?

Comprehension
Why are the families upset?

PETER. I've just gone crazy. I think if something doesn't happen soon . . . if we don't get out of here . . . I can't stand much more of it!

ANNE. [*Softly*] I wish you had a religion, Peter.

PETER. No, thanks! Not me!

ANNE. Oh, I don't mean you have to be Orthodox[13] . . . or believe in heaven and hell and purgatory[14] and things . . . I just mean some religion . . . it doesn't matter what. Just to believe in something! When I think of all that's out there . . . the trees . . . and flowers . . . and seagulls . . . when I think of the dearness of you, Peter . . . and the goodness of the people we know . . . Mr. Kraler, Miep, Dirk, the vegetable man, all risking their lives for us every day . . . When I think of these good things, I'm not afraid any more . . . I find myself, and God, and I . . .

[PETER *interrupts, getting up and walking away.*]

PETER. That's fine! But when I begin to think, I get mad! Look at us, hiding out for two years. Not able to move! Caught here like . . . waiting for them to come and get us . . . and all for what?

ANNE. We're not the only people that've had to suffer. There've always been people that've had to . . . sometimes one race . . . sometimes another . . . and yet . . .

PETER. That doesn't make me feel any better!

ANNE. [*Going to him*] I know it's terrible, trying to have any faith . . . when people are doing such horrible . . . But you know what I sometimes think? I think the world may be going through a phase, the way I was with Mother. It'll pass, maybe not for hundreds of years, but some day . . . I still believe, in spite of everything, that people are really good at heart.

PETER. I want to see something now . . . Not a thousand years from now! [*He goes over, sitting down again on the cot.*]

---

13. **Orthodox** (ôr´ thə däks´) *adj.* strictly observing the rites and traditions of Judaism.
14. **purgatory** (pʉr´gə tôr´ ē) *n.* state or place of temporary punishment.

ANNE. But, Peter, if you'd only look at it as part of a great pattern . . . that we're just a little minute in the life . . . [*She breaks off.*] Listen to us, going at each other like a couple of stupid grownups! Look at the sky now. Isn't it lovely? [*She holds out her hand to him.* PETER *takes it and rises, standing with her at the window looking out, his arms around her.*] Some day, when we're outside again, I'm going to . . .

[*She breaks off as she hears the sound of a car, its brakes squealing as it comes to a sudden stop. The people in the other rooms also become aware of the sound. They listen tensely. Another car roars up to a screeching stop.* ANNE *and* PETER *come from* PETER's *room.* MR. *and* MRS. VAN DAAN *creep down the stairs.* DUSSEL *comes out from his room. Everyone is listening, hardly breathing. A doorbell clangs again and again in the building below.* MR. FRANK *starts quietly down the steps to the door.* DUSSEL *and* PETER *follow him. The others stand rigid, waiting, terrified.*

In a few seconds DUSSEL *comes stumbling back up the steps. He shakes off* PETER's *help and goes to his room.* MR. FRANK *bolts the door below, and comes slowly back up the steps. Their eyes are all on him as he stands there for a minute. They realize that what they feared has happened.* MRS. VAN DAAN *starts to whimper.* MR. VAN DAAN *puts her gently in a chair, and then hurries off up the stairs to their room to collect their things.* PETER *goes to comfort his mother. There is a sound of violent pounding on a door below.*]

Character's Motivation
What causes this sudden change in the characters' actions and mood?

MR. FRANK. [*Quietly*] For the past two years we have lived in fear. Now we can live in hope.

[*The pounding below becomes more insistent. There are muffled sounds of voices, shouting commands.*]

MEN'S VOICES. *Auf machen! Da drinnen! Auf machen! Schnell! Schnell! Schnell!*[15] *etc., etc.*

[*The street door below is forced open. We hear the heavy tread of footsteps coming up.* MR. FRANK *gets two school bags from the shelves, and gives one to* ANNE *and the other to* MARGOT. *He goes to get a bag for* MRS. FRANK. *The sound of feet coming up grows louder.* PETER *comes to* ANNE, *kissing her good-bye,*

Comprehension
How does Anne seek to comfort Peter?

---

15. *Auf machen! . . . Schnell!* German for "Open up, you in there, open up, quick, quick, quick."

▲ Critical Viewing
What does this museum re-creation of her writing space tell you about Anne Frank and her experience in hiding?

then he goes to his room to collect his things. The buzzer of their door starts to ring. MR. FRANK *brings* MRS. FRANK *a bag. They stand together, waiting. We hear the thud of gun butts on the door, trying to break it down.*

ANNE *stands, holding her school satchel, looking over at her father and mother with a soft, reassuring smile. She is no longer a child, but a woman with courage to meet whatever lies ahead.*

The lights dim out. The curtain falls on the scene. We hear a mighty crash as the door is shattered. After a second ANNE'S VOICE *is heard.*]

ANNE'S VOICE. And so it seems our stay here is over. They are waiting for us now. They've allowed us five minutes to get our things. We can each take a bag and whatever it will hold of clothing. Nothing else. So, dear Diary, that means I must leave you behind. Good-bye for a while. P.S. Please, please, Miep, or Mr. Kraler, or anyone else. If you should find this diary, will you please keep it safe for me, because some day I hope . . .

Character's Motivation
Why does Anne leave her diary behind?

[*Her voice stops abruptly. There is silence. After a second the curtain rises.*]

Scene 5

[*It is again the afternoon in November, 1945. The rooms are as we saw them in the first scene.* MR. KRALER *has joined* MIEP *and* MR. FRANK. *There are coffee cups on the table. We see a great change in* MR. FRANK. *He is calm now. His bitterness is gone. He slowly turns a few pages of the diary. They are blank.*]

MR. FRANK. No more. [*He closes the diary and puts it down on the couch beside him.*]

MIEP. I'd gone to the country to find food. When I got back the block was surrounded by police . . .

MR. KRALER. We made it our business to learn how they knew. It was the thief . . . the thief who told them.

[MIEP *goes up to the gas burner, bringing back a pot of coffee.*]

MR. FRANK. [*After a pause*] It seems strange to say this, that anyone could be happy in a concentration camp. But Anne was happy in the camp in Holland where they first took us. After two years of being shut up in these rooms, she could be out . . . out in the sunshine and the fresh air that she loved.

MIEP. [*Offering the coffee to* MR. FRANK] A little more?

MR. FRANK. [*Holding out his cup to her*] The news of the war was good. The British and Americans were sweeping through France. We felt sure that they would get to us in time. In September we were told that we were to be shipped to Poland . . . The men to one camp. The women to another. I was sent to Auschwitz.[16] They went to Belsen.[17] In January we were freed, the few of us who were left. The war wasn't yet over, so it took us a long time to get home. We'd be sent here and there behind the lines where we'd be safe. Each time our train would stop . . . at a siding, or a crossing . . . we'd all get out and go from group to group . . . Where were you? Were you at Belsen? At Buchenwald?[18] At Mauthausen? Is it possible that you knew my

▼ **Critical Viewing**
This is a 1979 German stamp. What changes after the war might make the German government decide to honor Anne?

DEUTSCHE BUNDESPOST
60
ANNE FRANK · 12.6.1929 · 31.3.1945
1979

Comprehension
Where were the families sent after they were picked up by the police?

---

16. **Auschwitz** (oush′ vits′) Nazi concentration camp in Poland that was well known as a death camp.
17. **Belsen** (bel′ zən) village in Germany that, with the village of Bergen, was the site of Bergen-Belsen, a Nazi concentration camp; another name for this camp.
18. **Buchenwald** (boo͞′ ken wôld′) Nazi concentration camp in central Germany.

wife? Did you ever see my husband? My son? My daughter? That's how I found out about my wife's death . . . of Margot, the Van Daans . . . Dussel. But Anne . . . I still hoped . . . Yesterday I went to Rotterdam. I'd heard of a woman there . . . She'd been in Belsen with Anne . . . I know now.

[*He picks up the diary again, and turns the pages back to find a certain passage. As he finds it we hear* ANNE'S VOICE.]

ANNE'S VOICE. In spite of everything, I still believe that people are really good at heart. [MR. FRANK *slowly closes the diary.*]

MR. FRANK. She puts me to shame.

[*They are silent.*]

▲ Otto Frank visits children in Dusseldorf where a new school, the Anne Frank School, would be built.

Language Study

Vocabulary The first word in each pair below appears in the play. For each pair, write a sentence that uses both words correctly.

1. *inarticulate*, candidate

2. *apprehension*, unknown

3. *ineffectually*, weaker

4. *blackmail*, police

5. *forlorn*, rescue

WORD STUDY

The **Latin prefix *in-*** can mean "into" or "within." In this play, a character claims to have **intuition**, a feeling within herself that she knows what is going to happen, without having a logical explanation for it.

Word Study

Part A Explain how the **Latin prefix *in-*** contributes to the meaning of *incision* and *inherent*. Consult a dictionary if needed.

Part B Use the context of the sentences and what you know about the Latin prefix *in-* to explain your answer to each question.

1. What is one effect of an ear *infection*?

2. What happens to your lungs when you *inhale* deeply?

Close Reading Activities

Literary Analysis

Key Ideas and Details

1. (a) What disturbing news does Mr. Kraler bring on New Year's Day? **(b) Connect:** What hint does this news give about the ending of the play? Cite details from the play in your answer.

2. (a) Interpret: How have the characters changed since the end of Act I? **(b) Support:** How do you know that Anne has changed? Refer to details from the play in your answer.

3. Cause and Effect For each of these events, identify one cause and one effect, using details from the play: **(a)** Mr. Van Daan's decision to steal food; **(b)** Mrs. Frank's change of heart about wanting the Van Daans to go.

4. Cause and Effect What are some possible causes of Mrs. Van Daan's attitude toward Anne and Peter's relationship? Give evidence from the text.

5. Cause and Effect Living in close quarters has multiple effects on the people in the attic. List three effects that result from this single cause, making specific references to the text.

Craft and Structure

6. Character's Motivation Using a chart like the one shown, identify the possible motivation revealed by each action listed.

7. Character's Motivation What is Anne's motivation for keeping a diary? Support your answer with examples from the text.

8. Character's Motivation Give three examples of how the setting affects the characters and their actions, supported by details from the play.

Integration of Knowledge and Ideas

9. (a) Analyze: How was Anne able to preserve her dignity despite her suffering? Cite details from the text. **(b) Interpret:** What does Mr. Frank mean when he says of Anne: "She puts me to shame"? **(c) Evaluate:** Do you think Anne is exceptional, or might others do as well in her situation? Explain.

10. ❓ Is it our differences or our similarities that matter most? From Anne's statements in Act II, do you think that she believed that differences or similarities matter most? Explain, using examples from the play.

Character's Action
1. Mr. Kraler tells about Carl
2. Mr. Van Daan breaks into tears
3. Peter offers to leave

Motivation
1.
2.
3.

ACADEMIC VOCABULARY

As you write and speak about *The Diary of Anne Frank*, Act II, use the words related to similarities and differences that you explored on page 505 of this textbook.

Conventions: **Participial and Infinitive Phrases**

A **participle** is a verb form that acts as an adjective. A **participial phrase** is made up of a participle with its modifiers, such as adverbs, and objects or complements. An **infinitive** is a verb form that acts as a noun, an adjective, or an adverb. An **infinitive phrase** is made up of an infinitive with modifiers, objects, or complements, all acting together as a single part of speech.

Participles commonly end in *-ing* (present participle) or *-ed* (past participle). Infinitives begin with the word *to*. In the chart, participles and infinitives are underlined, and phrases are highlighted.

Participial Phrases and the Words They Modify	Infinitive Phrases and Their Functions
Traveling quickly, we got to the game on time. (modifies the subject, *we*)	To ski in Utah is my goal. (functions as a noun)
The tourist, confused by the signs, got lost. (modifies the subject, *tourist*)	She granted my request to end the meeting. (functions as an adjective modifying *request*)
The hallways are clogged with students going to class. (modifies the object, *students*)	They ran to watch the fireworks. (functions as an adverb modifying *ran*)

Practice A

Identify the participial phrase in each sentence below. Then, identify the noun it modifies.

1. Anne, feeling misunderstood and frustrated, wrote in her diary.
2. Anne's diary entries, written frequently, were full of details.
3. Celebrating the New Year, the families ate Miep's cake.
4. They had trouble finding a doctor.

Reading Application Find one example of a participial phrase in Act II. Explain its role in the sentence in which it appears.

Practice B

Identify the infinitive and infinitive phrase in each sentence. Then, use the same infinitive to write a new sentence.

1. Because of her problems, Anne wanted to talk with other young people.
2. To visit with Peter made Anne feel better.
3. The families needed to eat less because there were no more ration books.
4. Was it possible to escape from the Nazis?

Writing Application Write two sentences about Act II using infinitive phrases.

Writing to Sources

Informative Text In preparation for writing a **film review,** watch a film version of *The Diary of Anne Frank.* As you view, take notes. Use these questions to guide your note-taking:

- How do key scenes in the film and written version compare? How do any changes or omissions affect the film overall?
- Do the actors make good choices in their portrayals of characters, or do the portrayals not live up to your expectations? Why?
- What choices does the director make in sets, music, and camerawork? Do they enhance or detract from the story?
- Review your analysis and comment on the faithfulness of the film to the text: Does it present the same actions and events? Does it capture the general sense of the play?

After viewing, use your notes to draft your review. Highlight the differences between the filmed and the written versions, citing details from both, and explain which you found more effective.

Grammar Application As you write, use infinitive and participial phrases to add detail and precision to your sentences.

Research and Technology

Build and Present Knowledge With a group of classmates, create a **bulletin board display** about the experiences of Jewish individuals or communities living under Nazi occupation during Word War II. Follow these steps:

- As a group, decide on the audience and purpose for the display. Express your ideas clearly as you discuss them with the group. Use this information to focus your research.
- Draft a list of specific research questions. As you proceed, refine these questions and ask additional ones.
- Consult primary sources, such as photographs, diaries, and letters, and secondary sources, such as encyclopedia articles and books by historians. Attribute sources in captions in your display.
- In your display, feature the conclusions you have drawn about the experience of living under occupation. Supplement your text with charts, maps, graphs, and photographs.

Common Core State Standards

Reading Literature
7. Analyze the extent to which a filmed or live production of a story or drama stays faithful to or departs from the text or script, evaluating the choices made by the director or actors.

Writing
2. Write informative/explanatory texts to examine a topic and convey ideas, concepts, and information through the selection, organization, and analysis of relevant content.
4. Produce clear and coherent writing in which the development, organization, and style are appropriate to task, purpose, and audience.
7. Conduct short research projects to answer a question, drawing on several sources and generating additional related, focused questions that allow for multiple avenues of exploration.

Speaking and Listening
1. Engage effectively in a range of collaborative discussions with diverse partners, building on others' ideas and expressing their own clearly.

Language
1.a. Explain the function of verbals (gerunds, participles, infinitives) in general and their function in particular sentences.

Meet the Author

Celebrated playwright **Neil Simon** (b. 1927) once had four productions running at the same time on Broadway. Millions of people have enjoyed his plays and films. He is best known for his comedies—plays that poke gentle fun at people's behavior. Having grown up in New York City, Simon began writing for radio and television, then wrote comedies for the stage. In the 1980s, Simon drew on his own life for three plays that made critics view his work more seriously: *Brighton Beach Memoirs, Biloxi Blues,* and *Broadway Bound.*

 Common Core State Standards

Reading Literature

1. Cite the textual evidence that most strongly supports an analysis of what the text says explicitly as well as inferences drawn from the text.

3. Analyze how particular lines of dialogue or incidents in a story or drama propel the action, reveal aspects of a character, or provoke a decision.

? Is it our differences or our similarities that matter most?

Explore the Big Question as you read "The Governess." Take notes on the differences between the Mistress and the governess.

CLOSE READING FOCUS

Key Ideas and Details: **Draw Conclusions**

Drawing conclusions means forming ideas about the broader meaning of a text—beyond what is directly stated—based on details in the text. For instance, if a character gives compliments to his friends but then speaks poorly of them to others, a reader can draw the conclusion that he is insincere. To draw conclusions from a play, notice what the characters say and do.

- Look for statements revealing underlying ideas and attitudes.
- Analyze how characters treat one another.
- Notice actions that demonstrate a pattern of behavior.

Make connections among these items to decide what you can learn from them.

Craft and Structure: **Setting and Character**

Characters are developed through **dialogue,** or the words that they speak. **Setting** is largely established through the way the characters react to the onstage world. **Stage directions,** or notes that tell how a play should be performed, also provide insight into the characters and setting. They describe the scenery, costumes, lighting, and sound and may tell how characters feel, move, and speak.

As you read, note lines of dialogue and stage directions that help you understand the characters, setting, and action.

Vocabulary

Copy these words from the play into your notebook. Which word looks as if it might be a synonym for *without cunning*?

inferior	discrepancies	discharged
satisfactory	lax	guileless

CLOSE READING MODEL

The passage below is from "The Governess." The annotations to the right of the passage show ways in which you can use close reading skills to draw conclusions and analyze setting and character.

from "The Governess"

MISTRESS. Head up . . . [*She lifts head up*]¹ That's it. Don't be afraid to look people in the eyes, my dear. If you think of yourself as inferior, that's exactly how people will treat you.

JULIA. Yes, ma'am.

MISTRESS. . . . . Let's see now, we agreed on thirty rubles a month, did we not?

JULIA. [*Surprised*] Forty, ma'am.²

MISTRESS. No, no, thirty. I made a note of it.³ [*Points to the book*] I always pay my governesses thirty . . . Who told you forty?

JULIA. You did, ma'am. I spoke to no one else concerning money . . .²

MISTRESS. Impossible. Maybe you *thought* you heard forty when I said thirty. If you kept your head up, that would never happen. Look at me again and I'll say it clearly. *Thirty rubles a month.*

JULIA. If you say so, ma'am.²

MISTRESS. Settled. Thirty a month it is . . . Now then, you've been here two months exactly.

JULIA. Two months and five days.²

MISTRESS. No, no. Exactly two months. I made a note of it.³ You should keep books the way I do so there wouldn't be these discrepancies. So—we have two months at thirty rubles a month . . . comes to sixty rubles. Correct?

JULIA. [*Curtsies*]⁴ Yes, ma'am. Thank you, ma'am.²

Character

1 The Mistress orders Julia to lift up her head. Even though Julia does not reply verbally, the stage directions allow the reader to develop a mental image of what is happening on stage—Julia silently obeys.

Draw Conclusions

2 Each time the Mistress makes an assertion, Julia begins by contradicting her. Each time, Julia ends up backing down. The author establishes a clear pattern of behavior. This pattern allows the reader to conclude that the Mistress has authority over Julia.

Draw Conclusions

3 The Mistress repeatedly refers to her notebook as the ultimate source of authority. Even though the author does not say so directly, a reader may conclude that the Mistress knows that Julia will not argue with what was written in her notes.

Setting and Character

4 Even as Julia agrees to accept less money, she curtsies to the Mistress. The stage directions help readers see how meek Julia is. They also suggest the setting—a time when people showed respect by curtsying.

The Governess
Neil Simon

Critical Viewing ▲
Which person in this scene is playing the part of the governess? How can you tell?

Draw Conclusions
What conclusion can you draw about the relationship between Julia and the Mistress?

MISTRESS. Julia! [*Calls again*] Julia!

[*A young governess,* JULIA, *comes rushing in. She stops before the desk and curtsies.*]

JULIA. [*Head down*] Yes, madame?

MISTRESS. Look at me, child. Pick your head up. I like to see your eyes when I speak to you.

JULIA. [*Lifts her head up*] Yes, madame. [*But her head has a habit of slowly drifting down again.*]

MISTRESS. And how are the children coming along with their French lessons?

JULIA. They're very bright children, madame.

MISTRESS. Eyes up . . . They're bright, you say. Well, why not? And mathematics? They're doing well in mathematics, I assume?

JULIA. Yes, madame. Especially Vanya.

MISTRESS. Certainly. I knew it. I excelled in mathematics. He gets that from his mother, wouldn't you say?

JULIA. Yes, madame.

MISTRESS. Head up . . . [*She lifts head up.*] That's it. Don't be afraid to look people in the eyes, my dear. If you think of yourself as **inferior**, that's exactly how people will treat you.

JULIA. Yes, ma'am.

MISTRESS. A quiet girl, aren't you? . . . Now then, let's settle our accounts. I imagine you must need money, although you never ask me for it yourself. Let's see now, we agreed on thirty rubles[1] a month, did we not?

JULIA. [*Surprised*] Forty, ma'am.

MISTRESS. No, no, thirty. I made a note of it. [*Points to the book*] I always pay my governesses thirty . . . Who told you forty?

JULIA. You did, ma'am. I spoke to no one else concerning money . . .

MISTRESS. Impossible. Maybe you *thought* you heard forty when I said thirty. If you kept your head up, that would never happen. Look at me again and I'll say it clearly. *Thirty rubles a month.*

JULIA. If you say so, ma'am.

MISTRESS. Settled. Thirty a month it is . . . Now then, you've been here two months exactly.

JULIA. Two months and five days.

MISTRESS. No, no. Exactly two months. I made a note of it. You should keep books the way I do so there wouldn't be these **discrepancies**. So—we have two months at thirty rubles a month . . . comes to sixty rubles. Correct?

---

1. **rubles** (ro͞o´ bəlz) *n.* Russian currency; similar to U.S. dollars.

Setting and Character
Which stage directions help you understand the way the characters speak the dialogue?

Critical Viewing
If you were Julia, why would you feel intimidated by the Mistress, shown in the picture? Explain.

JULIA. [*Curtsies*] Yes, ma'am. Thank you, ma'am.

MISTRESS. Subtract nine Sundays . . . We did agree to subtract Sundays, didn't we?

JULIA. No, ma'am.

MISTRESS. Eyes! Eyes! . . . Certainly we did. I've always subtracted Sundays. I didn't bother making a note of it because I always do it. Don't you recall when I said we will subtract Sundays?

JULIA. No, ma'am.

MISTRESS. Think.

JULIA. [*Thinks*] No, ma'am.

MISTRESS. You weren't thinking. Your eyes were wandering. Look straight at my face and look hard . . . Do you remember now?

JULIA. [*Softly*] Yes, ma'am.

MISTRESS. I didn't hear you, Julia.

JULIA. [*Louder*] Yes, ma'am.

MISTRESS. Good. I was sure you'd remember . . . Plus three holidays. Correct?

JULIA. Two, ma'am. Christmas and New Year's.

MISTRESS. And your birthday. That's three.

JULIA. I worked on my birthday, ma'am.

MISTRESS. You did? There was no need to. My governesses never worked on their birthdays . . .

JULIA. But I did work, ma'am.

MISTRESS. But that's not the question, Julia. We're discussing financial matters now. I will, however, only count two holidays if you insist . . . Do you insist?

JULIA. I did work, ma'am.

MISTRESS. Then you *do* insist.

JULIA. No, ma'am.

MISTRESS. Very well. That's three holidays, therefore we take off twelve rubles. Now then, four days little Kolya was sick, and there were no lessons.

JULIA. But I gave lessons to Vanya.

MISTRESS. True. But I engaged you to teach two children, not one. Shall I pay you in full for doing only half the work?

JULIA. No, ma'am.

MISTRESS. So we'll deduct it . . . Now, three days you had a toothache and my husband gave you permission not to work after lunch. Correct?

JULIA. After four. I worked until four.

MISTRESS. [*Looks in the book*] I have here: "Did not work after lunch." We have lunch at one and are finished at two, not at four, correct?

JULIA. Yes, ma'am. But I—

MISTRESS. That's another seven rubles . . . Seven and twelve is nineteen . . . Subtract . . . that leaves . . . forty-one rubles . . . Correct?

JULIA. Yes, ma'am. Thank you, ma'am.

MISTRESS. Now then, on January fourth you broke a teacup and saucer, is that true?

JULIA. Just the saucer, ma'am.

MISTRESS. What good is a teacup without a saucer, eh? . . . That's two rubles. The saucer was an heirloom.[2] It cost much more, but let it go. I'm used to taking losses.

JULIA. Thank you, ma'am.

MISTRESS. Now then, January ninth, Kolya climbed a tree and tore his jacket.

JULIA. I forbid him to do so, ma'am.

MISTRESS. But he didn't listen, did he? . . . Ten rubles . . . January fourteenth, Vanya's shoes were stolen . . .

JULIA. But the maid, ma'am. You **discharged** her yourself.

---

2. **heirloom** (er′ lōōm′) *n.* treasured possession passed down from generation to generation.

Spiral Review
CONFLICT How does the difference between the social classes of Julia and the Mistress help create the play's conflict?

◀ **Vocabulary**
discharged (dis chärjd′) *v.* fired; released

Comprehension
How does the Mistress punish Julia for the actions of Kolya?

History Connection

What Is Women's Work?

Throughout the nineteenth century, jobs for women were scarce. Most professions were unavailable to anyone except men. Low-wage factory jobs, such as making clothing, were available to working-class women and girls. A majority of uneducated women, however, were domestic servants.

A middle-class woman with some education could become a teacher or a governess. An unmarried woman who needed to support herself had few other options.

Like domestic workers and factory workers, governesses earned very little. They were viewed as servants.

Connect to the Literature

Would Julia behave differently if she were paid better or if she could pursue other career options? Explain.

Vocabulary ▶
satisfactory (sat′ is fak′ tə rē) *adj.* adequate; sufficient to meet a requirement

lax (laks) *adj.* not strict or exact

MISTRESS. But you get paid good money to watch everything. I explained that in our first meeting. Perhaps you weren't listening. Were you listening that day, Julia, or was your head in the clouds?

JULIA. Yes, ma'am.

MISTRESS. Yes, your head was in the clouds?

JULIA. No, ma'am. I was listening.

MISTRESS. Good girl. So that means another five rubles off [*Looks in the book*] . . . Ah, yes . . . The sixteenth of January I gave you ten rubles.

JULIA. You didn't.

MISTRESS. But I made a note of it. Why would I make a note of it if I didn't give it to you?

JULIA. I don't know, ma'am.

MISTRESS. That's not a **satisfactory** answer, Julia . . . Why would I make a note of giving you ten rubles if I did not in fact give it to you, eh? . . . No answer? . . . Then I must have given it to you, mustn't I?

JULIA. Yes, ma'am. If you say so, ma'am.

MISTRESS. Well, certainly I say so. That's the point of this little talk. To clear these matters up. Take twenty-seven from forty-one, that leaves . . . fourteen, correct?

JULIA. Yes, ma'am. [*She turns away, softly crying.*]

MISTRESS. What's this? Tears? Are you crying? Has something made you unhappy, Julia? Please tell me. It pains me to see you like this. I'm so sensitive to tears. What is it?

JULIA. Only once since I've been here have I ever been given any money and that was by your husband. On my birthday he gave me three rubles.

MISTRESS. Really? There's no note of it in my book. I'll put it down now. [*She writes in the book.*] Three rubles. Thank you for telling me. Sometimes I'm a little **lax** with my accounts . . . Always shortchanging myself. So then, we take three more from fourteen . . . leaves eleven . . . Do you wish to check my figures?

JULIA. There's no need to, ma'am.

MISTRESS. Then we're all settled. Here's your salary for two months, dear. Eleven rubles. [*She puts the pile of coins on the desk.*] Count it.

JULIA. It's not necessary, ma'am.

MISTRESS. Come, come. Let's keep the records straight. Count it.

JULIA. [*Reluctantly counts it*] One, two, three, four, five, six, seven, eight, nine, ten . . . ? There's only ten, ma'am.

MISTRESS. Are you sure? Possibly you dropped one . . . Look on the floor, see if there's a coin there.

JULIA. I didn't drop any, ma'am. I'm quite sure.

MISTRESS. Well, it's not here on my desk, and I *know* I gave you eleven rubles. Look on the floor.

JULIA. It's all right, ma'am. Ten rubles will be fine.

MISTRESS. Well, keep the ten for now. And if we don't find it on the floor later, we'll discuss it again next month.

JULIA. Yes, ma'am. Thank you, ma'am. You're very kind, ma'am.

[*She curtsies and then starts to leave.*]

MISTRESS. Julia!

[JULIA *stops, turns.*]

Come back here.

[*She goes back to the desk and curtsies again.*]

Why did you thank me?

JULIA. For the money, ma'am.

MISTRESS. For the money? . . . But don't you realize what I've done? I've cheated you . . . *Robbed* you! I have no such notes in my book. I made up whatever came into my mind. Instead of the eighty rubles which I owe you, I gave you only ten. I have actually stolen from you and you still thank me . . . Why?

JULIA. In the other places that I've worked, they didn't give me anything at all.

▼ **Critical Viewing**
Does this photograph accurately capture Julia's personality? Why or why not?

Draw Conclusions
Does this speech change your mind about the Mistress's intentions? Explain.

MISTRESS. Then they cheated you even worse than I did . . . I was playing a little joke on you. A cruel lesson just to teach you. You're much too trusting, and in this world that's very dangerous . . . I'm going to give you the entire eighty rubles. [*Hands her an envelope*] It's all ready for you. The rest is in this envelope. Here, take it.

JULIA. As you wish, ma'am. [*She curtsies and starts to go again.*]

MISTRESS. Julia! [JULIA *stops.*] Is it possible to be so spineless? Why don't you protest? Why don't you speak up? Why don't you cry out against this cruel and unjust treatment? Is it really possible to be so guileless, so innocent, such a—pardon me for being so blunt—such a simpleton?

JULIA. [*The faintest trace of a smile on her lips*] Yes, ma'am . . . it's possible.

[*She curtsies again and runs off. The* MISTRESS *looks after her a moment, a look of complete bafflement on her face. The lights fade.*]

Vocabulary ▶
guileless (gīl´ lis) *adj.* not trying to hide anything or trick people; innocent

Language Study

Vocabulary The words listed below appear in "The Governess." Rewrite each sentence that follows, using one word from the list to produce a sentence that has the opposite meaning.

inferior	discrepancies	discharged	lax	guileless

1. The testimony of the two witnesses was in total agreement.

2. Josie was so clever that no one could play a trick on her.

3. The debaters treated each other as equals.

4. Ben's work was so outstanding that he was given a raise.

5. No one took a long lunch because the boss watched the clock.

WORD STUDY

The **Latin suffix -ory** means "of," "relating to," or "characterized by." In this play, the Mistress thinks Julia's answer to a question is not **satisfactory**. It is not the type of answer that is good enough to give her *satisfaction*.

Word Study

Part A Explain how the **Latin suffix -ory** contributes to the meanings of *migratory*, *circulatory*, and *mandatory*. Use a dictionary if needed.

Part B Use the context of the sentences and what you know about the Latin suffix *-ory* to explain your answer to each question.

1. If Bill acts in a *supervisory* manner, is he showing leadership?

2. If two statements are *contradictory*, do they have similar meanings?

Close Reading Activities

Literary Analysis

Key Ideas and Details

1. (a) List the reasons the Mistress gives for cutting Julia's pay.
(b) Infer: Why does Julia respond the way she does?

2. Draw Conclusions (a) From the first five pages of the play, identify three of the Mistress's lines that demonstrate a particular pattern of behavior. **(b)** Based on these lines, what conclusions can you draw about the reasons for the Mistress's behavior? **(c)** Does your opinion of the Mistress change when you read the end of the play? Explain.

3. Draw Conclusions Based on Julia's responses, what can you conclude about the treatment of governesses at the time of this play? Cite evidence from the text to support your conclusion.

Craft and Structure

4. Setting and Character (a) Fill out a chart like the one shown. For each category in the chart, give one example of dialogue and one example of stage directions from "The Governess." **(b)** How does each example help you understand the characters, action, and setting?

5. Setting and Character (a) Does the author ever indicate that Julia may not be as innocent as she seems? Cite specific lines of dialogue or stage directions to support your answer. **(b)** What does your answer suggest about the reasons for her behavior?

Integration of Knowledge and Ideas

6. (a) What final action does the Mistress take to try to make Julia fight back? **(b) Analyze:** Does the Mistress believe she is being kind, cruel, or both? **(c) Make a Judgment:** Which is she actually being?

7. Speculate: Do you think Julia will behave differently in the future? Cite evidence from the text to support your conclusion.

8. **Is it our differences or our similarities that matter most?** With a small group, discuss the following questions: **(a)** How are Julia and the Mistress alike and how are they different? **(b)** Which do you think play a greater role in shaping their relationship—their similarities or their differences? What makes you think so? **(c)** If Julia had been from the same social class as the Mistress, would the Mistress have acted differently? Cite evidence from the play to support your answer.

Describing an Action
Showing How a Character Feels

ACADEMIC VOCABULARY

As you write and speak about "The Governess," use the words related to similarities and differences that you explored on page 505 of this textbook.

Conventions: **Clauses**

> A **clause** is a group of words with its own subject and verb.

An **independent** clause can stand alone as a complete sentence. A **subordinate,** or **dependent, clause** also has a subject and verb, but it cannot stand alone. There are three types of subordinate clauses:

- An **adverb clause** acts as an adverb. It begins with a subordinating conjunction, such as *although, if, when,* or *because.*

- A **relative clause** acts as an adjective. It usually begins with a relative pronoun, such as *who, whom, whose, which,* or *that.*

- A **noun clause** acts as a noun. It begins with a word such as *what, whatever, when, where, how,* or *why.*

In the examples in the chart, each type of clause is underlined.

Type of Clause	Example
Independent Clause	*Because the dog barked, <u>the neighbors complained.</u>* (can stand alone as a complete sentence)
Adverb Clause	*<u>Because the dog barked,</u> the neighbors complained.* (acts as an adverb, modifying the verb *complained*)
Relative Clause	*The dog barked at the neighbors <u>who lived next door.</u>* (acts as an adjective, modifying *neighbors*)
Noun Clause	*The neighbors disliked <u>how the dog was behaving.</u>* (acts as a noun, the direct object of *disliked*)

Practice A

Identify the subordinate clause in each sentence, and write which type of subordinate clause it is.

1. Because she is a governess, Julia obeys.

2. The Mistress, who pretends to be cruel, means to be kind.

3. Julia does what the Mistress commands.

4. Julia deserves the money that she earned.

Reading Application In "The Governess," find two sentences that each have an independent clause and a subordinate clause.

Practice B

Identify each clause as an independent clause or as an adverb clause. Add an independent clause to each adverb clause.

1. The Mistress bullied Julia

2. When Julia disagreed

3. The Mistress was playing a trick on Julia

4. If she lost her job

Writing Application Write three sentences about "The Governess" that each have an independent and a subordinate clause.

Writing to Sources

Argument Write a **public service announcement (PSA)** to persuade listeners to support fair treatment of workers, including governesses. Draw examples from "The Governess" to support your argument. Follow these steps:

- Choose a figure from politics, business, or entertainment as your spokesperson. Write your script with this person in mind.
- Summarize the claims you will use to persuade your audience.
- List specific words, images, sound effects, or symbols that will help support your claims. Include details from the play.
- Using elements from your notes, write a script for radio or television to be delivered by your celebrity spokesperson.

Grammar Application Make sure your PSA uses a variety of independent and dependent clauses, including adverb clauses.

Speaking and Listening

Presentation of Knowledge and Ideas Form two teams to **debate** this proposal: "The minimum working age should be lowered to thirteen for jobs in retail stores."

Choose a moderator to keep time and to see that the debaters follow the rules. Follow these steps to prepare:

- Conduct research to identify evidence and examples that support your position. Differentiate facts from opinions so that you can establish a factual basis for your arguments.
- Jot down reasons that will strengthen your argument, drawing on any relevant examples from "The Governess."
- Craft a thesis, or statement of your position, from your notes. Present this thesis during your opening statement.
- Prepare for your opponents' arguments by thinking about the topic from their perspective. For example, you might anticipate the argument that working will take time away from schoolwork by countering that it will develop responsibility.
- During the debate, each participant should build on or respond to the arguments presented by the previous speaker. All debaters should use a respectful tone, particularly when pointing out flaws or weaknesses in opponents' arguments.

Common Core State Standards

Writing
1. Write arguments to support claims with clear reasons and relevant evidence.

Speaking and Listening
4. Present claims and findings, emphasizing salient points in a focused, coherent manner with relevant evidence, sound valid reasoning, and well-chosen details; use appropriate eye contact, adequate volume, and correct pronunciation.

Is it our differences or our similarities that matter most?

Explore the Big Question as you read "The Ninny" and reread "The Governess." Determine whether the differences between employer and servant matter just as much—or just as little—in both works, or whether each work provides a different viewpoint.

READING TO COMPARE ADAPTATIONS TO ORIGINALS

Neil Simon's play "The Governess" is a dramatic adaptation of Anton Chekhov's short story "The Ninny." Although both authors tell the story of a humble servant working for a master, they present the story in different forms. As you read, consider what techniques each form lets the author use to convey information. Then, compare how differences in the works' forms affect the reader's experience.

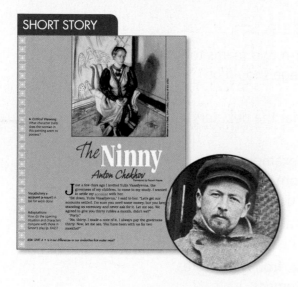

"The Ninny"

Anton Chekhov (1860–1904)
Anton Pavlovich Chekhov originally planned to be a doctor and studied medicine in Moscow. To pay for medical school and support his family, he began to write humorous articles and stories for journals.

Chekhov wrote more than two hundred short stories. Some are comic, while others show the small tragedies of ordinary life. All show sympathy and understanding for their characters. They paint a realistic and detailed picture of Russian life in both cities and peasant villages.

Comparing Adaptations to Originals

A literary **adaptation** is a work that has been changed or adjusted to fit a different form or genre. For example, a novel may be adapted into a play or a movie. When adapting a literary work, an author may change or delete parts of the original to suit the new form and purpose. For instance, since a play depends almost entirely on dialogue to entertain an audience, the narration or description that is included in a story has to be cut, or conveyed in a new way.

Elements for Comparison To compare an adaptation to the original work, remember the differences in the two literary forms. Keep those differences in mind as you analyze the two works.

- Look for the elements that the writer has kept from the original as well as those he has left out.

- Look for new elements the writer has introduced.

- Compare the purposes and styles of the two authors. Determine if one style results in a lighter, more humorous treatment or whether the styles are mostly the same.

- Compare the works' forms. Consider what each form allows the author to do, as well as what restrictions it imposes. For instance, a short story writer may include direct explanations of characters' motives or present their internal thoughts, while a playwright or filmmaker will often omit such direct statements. Evaluate the impact that the inclusion or omission of such details has on the reader.

As you read Chekhov's short story "The Ninny," use a Venn diagram like the one shown to analyze the similarities and differences between this work and Neil Simon's dramatic adaptation, "The Governess" (p. 642).

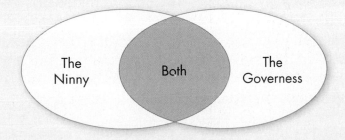

**Common Core
State Standards**

Reading Literature
5. Compare and contrast the structure of two or more texts and analyze how the differing structure of each text contributes to its meaning and style.

Writing
4. Produce clear and coherent writing in which the development, organization, and style are appropriate to task, purpose, and audience.

Woman in a Chair, John Collier, Courtesy of the artist

▶ **Critical Viewing**
What character traits does the woman in this painting seem to possess?

The Ninny
Anton Chekhov
Translated by Robert Payne

Vocabulary ▶
account (ə kount´) *n.*
bill for work done

Adaptations
How do the opening situation and characters compare with those in Simon's play (p. 642)?

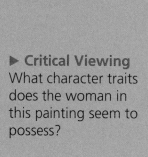

Just a few days ago I invited Yulia Vassilyevna, the governess of my children, to come to my study. I wanted to settle my **account** with her.

"Sit down, Yulia Vassilyevna," I said to her. "Let's get our accounts settled. I'm sure you need some money, but you keep standing on ceremony and never ask for it. Let me see. We agreed to give you thirty rubles a month, didn't we?"

"Forty."

"No, thirty. I made a note of it. I always pay the governess thirty. Now, let me see. You have been with us for two months?"

"Two months and five days."

"Two months exactly. I made a note of it. So you have sixty rubles coming to you. Subtract nine Sundays. You know you don't tutor Kolya on Sundays, you just go out for a walk. And then the three holidays . . ."

Yulia Vassilyevna blushed and picked at the trimmings of her dress, but said not a word.

"Three holidays. So we take off twelve rubles. Kolya was sick for four days—those days you didn't look after him. You looked after Vanya, only Vanya. Then there were the three days you had a toothache, when my wife gave you permission to stay away from the children after dinner. Twelve and seven makes nineteen. Subtract. . . . That leaves . . . hm . . . forty-one rubles. Correct?"

Yulia Vassilyevna's left eye reddened and filled with tears. Her chin trembled. She began to cough nervously, blew her nose, and said nothing.

"Then around New Year's Day you broke a cup and saucer. Subtract two rubles. The cup cost more than that—it was an heirloom, but we won't bother about that. We're the ones who pay. Another matter. Due to your **carelessness** Kolya climbed a tree and tore his coat. Subtract ten. Also, due to your carelessness the chambermaid[1] ran off with Vanya's boots. You ought to have kept your eyes open. You get a good salary. So we dock off five more. . . . On the tenth of January you took ten rubles from me."

"I didn't," Yulia Vassilyevna whispered.

"But I made a note of it."

"Well, yes—perhaps . . ."

"From forty-one we take twenty-seven. That leaves fourteen."

Her eyes filled with tears, and her thin, pretty little nose was shining with perspiration. Poor little child!

"I only took money once," she said in a trembling voice. "I took three rubles from your wife . . . never anything more."

"Did you now? You see, I never made a note of it. Take three from fourteen. That leaves eleven. Here's your money, my dear. Three, three, three . . . one and one. Take it, my dear."

I gave her the eleven rubles. With trembling fingers she took them and slipped them into her pocket.

◄ **Vocabulary**
carelessness (ker´ lis nis) n. lack of responsibility

Spiral Review
CHARACTERIZATION
Why does Yulia agree so quickly with her employer's assertion that she took ten rubles, when she first insisted she did not?

Comprehension
Why is Yulia crying?

---

1. **chambermaid** female household servant whose main job is to clean and care for bedrooms.

"*Merci*,"[2] she whispered.

I jumped up, and began pacing up and down the room. I was in a furious temper.

"Why did you say '*merci*'?" I asked.

"For the money."

". . . Don't you realize I've been cheating you? I steal your money, and all you can say is '*merci*'!"

"In my other places they gave me nothing."

"They gave you nothing! Well, no wonder! I was playing a trick on you—a dirty trick. . . . I'll give you your eighty rubles, they are all here in an envelope made out for you. Is it possible for anyone to be such a nitwit? Why didn't you protest? Why did you keep your mouth shut? Is it possible that there is anyone in this world who is so **spineless**? Why are you such a ninny?"

She gave me a bitter little smile. On her face I read the words: "Yes, it is possible."

I apologized for having played this cruel trick on her, and to her great surprise gave her the eighty rubles. And then she said "*merci*" again several times, always **timidly**, and went out. I gazed after her, thinking how very easy it is in this world to be strong.

2. *merci* (mer sē´) French for "thank you." In the nineteenth century, many upper-class Russians spoke French.

Vocabulary ▶
spineless (spīn´ lis) *adj.* lacking in courage

timidly (tim´ id lē) *adv.* in a shy or fearful manner

Critical Thinking

1. **Key Ideas and Details: (a)** Who tells the story of "The Ninny"? **(b) Connect:** What is this person's relationship with Yulia?

2. **Key Ideas and Details: (a)** Are any of the reasons the narrator gives for cutting Yulia's pay justifiable? Explain, citing examples from the text. **(b) Infer:** What do Yulia's responses suggest about her personality?

3. **Key Ideas and Details:** Does the narrator regret or take pleasure in the effect of his "cruel trick" on Yulia? Explain.

4. **Integration of Knowledge and Ideas: (a)** What differences separate these characters? **(b)** At the story's conclusion, have they grown more different or more alike? Explain. *[Connect to the Big Question: Is it our differences or our similarities that matter most?]*

Comparing Adaptations to Originals

1. Use a chart like the one shown to find similarities and differences between "The Ninny" and "The Governess."

	Relationships	Events	Endings	Style/Tone
"The Ninny"				
"The Governess"				

2. **(a)** Identify a significant detail included at the end of "The Ninny" but omitted from "The Governess" due to the difference in their forms. **(b)** Explain why the difference in form led to its omission. **(c)** Explain the effect this detail (or its omission) has on your appreciation of each work.

 Timed Writing

Explanatory Text: Essay

In an essay, compare and contrast the characterization, events, style, endings, and tone of Neil Simon's adaptation with the original short story. Use textual evidence to support your ideas. **(40 minutes)**

5-Minute Planner

1. Read the prompt carefully and completely.

2. Gather your ideas by jotting down answers to these questions:

   • Why do you think Chekhov chose to write about Yulia and her employer in a first-person story rather than as a play?

   • What purpose is served by Simon's adaptation as a play?

   • How much do the different elements of drama and short story account for the differences between the two works?

   • Is the story or the play more effective? Why?

3. To organize your essay, use one of your answers to the questions above as your main thesis. Then, draft the body of your essay by using each of the elements listed in the writing prompt as a point of comparison.

4. Reread the prompt, and then draft your essay.

USE ACADEMIC VOCABULARY

As you write, use academic language, including the following words or their related forms:

connection

distinguish

influence

judge

For more information about academic vocabulary, see the Building Academic Vocabulary workshop in the front of your book.

Borrowed and Foreign Words

A number of English words have been taken directly from other languages. For example, many words related to fruit or weather, such as *tomato* and *hurricane,* are borrowed from Native American languages. Many words borrowed from French relate to art or literature. For example, the word *critique* as a noun means "a critical essay or review." As a verb, *critique* means "to write a critical essay or review." The chart shows some borrowed and foreign words that have become part of the English language.

⊙ Common Core State Standards

Language

4.a. Use context as a clue to the meaning of a word or phrase.

4.d. Verify the preliminary determination of the meaning of a word or phrase.

Borrowed Word	Meaning
Native American languages	
opossum	small North American tree-dwelling animal
hickory	North American tree, related to the walnut tree
French	
café	coffee shop or small restaurant
sorbet	tart-tasting dessert made of ice and fruit
Italian	
balcony	railed-in platform projecting from an upper floor of a building
opera	musical play in which the words are mostly sung
Spanish	
canyon	long, narrow valley between high cliffs
ranch	large farm for raising horses or other livestock
German	
kindergarten	school for young children
delicatessen	shop selling cold cuts, cheese, and so on

Practice A

Use a dictionary to find the language of origin for each of these borrowed English words.

1. pretzel   **3.** bagel   **5.** waffle

2. burrito   **4.** curry   **6.** barbecue

Practice B

Recall that context clues are the words and phrases surrounding a given word that indicate the word's meaning. Context clues can help you uncover the meaning of an unfamiliar word.

Use context clues to help you figure out the meaning of the italicized foreign words and phrases. Check a dictionary if you need help.

1. Darlene was impressed by the colorful *macaw* she saw sitting on the branches of a tree.

2. Bennie called out *"Ciao!"* as he left the party to go home.

3. While in Mexico, Jaime bought a *sombrero* to shade herself from the sun's hot rays.

4. Duane told us all the boring details of his vacation, *ad nauseam.*

5. The students in the *anime* club like to illustate their favorite characters.

6. We like living on a street that is a *cul-de-sac* because there isn't much traffic.

7. Keisha had a strong sense of *déjà vu* when she came to our town, although she had never been here before.

8. Just before parting with his friends at the Tokyo airport, James said, *"Sayonara."*

Activity Read each of the borrowed words related to music, below. Then, on a chart like the one shown, write each word next to the language from which it comes.

suite	tempo	glockenspiel
ensemble	crescendo	piano
waltz	bassoon	violin

Language of Origin	Music Words
Italian	
French	
German	

Comprehension and Collaboration

Some borrowed words come from the names of people or places. With two or three classmates, find the origin of each of these words:

- **frankfurter**
- **argyle**
- **cologne**
- **manila paper**
- **denim**

Compare your findings with those of another group.

Evaluating Media Messages

Messages sent via television, radio, and the Internet are meant to persuade you to believe or do something specific. Practice being an active and critical listener and viewer by following these suggestions.

Learn the Skills

Use these strategies to complete the activity on page 661.

Look critically at images. The media flash images at us at amazing speeds. Some are stylized, or cartoon-like; others are realistic; some may look like valid photographs but are digitally created or retouched. All are intended to catch the attention of and influence an audience. When viewing an image, ask yourself, "What effect is this image intended to have on me?"

Listen critically to words and sounds. The creator of a message can attempt to influence an audience by playing on emotions. By associating a specific viewpoint with good or bad feelings, a message can lead viewers to accept or reject that viewpoint. "Buzz words" (words that trigger specific associations), music, and sound effects can all call up emotions.

Be aware of persuasive appeals and rhetorical techniques. Some messages use **rhetorical techniques** to persuade the audience to think in a certain way. These techniques include:

- **repetition**—multiple uses of the same important words or phrases for effect

- **loaded terms**—words or phrases that are charged with strong emotional connotations, or associations

- **leading questions**—questions that suggest the proper or desired answer

Look for hidden agendas. Sometimes, messages are hidden. Look beyond the surface of a media message by paraphrasing it. Ask yourself: Which facts, values, and ideas are being presented?

Identify slant or bias. Often, complex subjects are presented from only one point of view. For example, political ads often address only one side of a controversial issue. **Bias** refers to a commitment to one side of an issue that leads a message-maker to distort the facts or leave out important alternative viewpoints. Watch for bias in media messages.

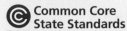 **Common Core State Standards**

Reading Informational Text
7. Evaluate the advantages and disadvantages of using different mediums to present a particular topic or idea.

Speaking and Listening
2. Analyze the purpose of information presented in diverse media and formats and evaluate the motives behind its presentation.
3. Delineate a speaker's argument and specific claims, evaluating the soundness of the reasoning and relevance and sufficiency of the evidence and identifying when irrelevant evidence is introduced.

Practice the Skills

Presentation of Knowledge and Ideas Use what you've learned in this workshop to perform the following task.

ACTIVITY: Evaluate Media Messages

Watch several television commercials. Then, follow these steps:
- Summarize each commercial.
- Identify the purpose and point of view of each message.
- Identify techniques, such as buzz words, repetition, loaded terms, and leading questions, used to deliver the message.
- Explain the effect each commercial had on you.
- Use the Evaluation Guide to interpret the commercials.

Use an Evaluation Guide like this one to evaluate each commercial.

Evaluation Guide

Visual and Sound Techniques
Identify which of the following techniques are used and how they influence the message.

- ❏ Flashy graphics
- ❏ Digital effects
- ❏ Sound effects
- ❏ Lighting
- ❏ Appealing use of color
- ❏ Music

The role of media
- How did each message focus your attention?
- How did each message affect, change, or shape your opinion?

Effect of the message
Interpret how the use of the following techniques creates a point of view and affects you as a viewer. Then, comment on the evidence that supports each commercial's claims.

- ❏ Rhetorical devices
- ❏ Hidden agendas
- ❏ Fact vs. opinion
- ❏ Bias or slant

How persuasive was the evidence? **Comments:** _____

Credibility
How would you rate the credibility of this message? Explain.
_____ Excellent _____ Good _____ Fair _____ Poor

Comprehension and Collaboration Discuss your findings with a classmate. Discuss how critical viewing and listening help to uncover motives behind the messages. Compare the insights you each gained from listening for rhetorical devices and persuasive appeals.

Write an Explanatory Text

Cause-and-Effect Essay

Defining the Form Almost everything that happens involves causes and effects, from local events to those that affect people worldwide. When you write a **cause-and-effect essay,** you analyze the reasons an event occurred or you consider its results.

Assignment Write a cause-and-effect essay about a question that interests you. Your essay should feature the following elements:

✓ a clear thesis that establishes a *controlling idea*

✓ a consistent and appropriate *organization*

✓ an explanation of how one or more events or situations result in another event or situation

✓ a thorough presentation of *facts, quotations,* and other *details* that support the explanation presented

✓ an *effective and well-supported conclusion*

✓ error-free grammar, including the use of *gerunds* and *participles* to avoid choppy sentences.

To preview the criteria on which your research report may be judged, see the rubric on page 669.

FOCUS ON RESEARCH

When you write a cause-and-effect essay, you might perform research to

• locate facts and statistics to support your ideas.

• verify claims you make about causes and effects.

• find examples to illustrate your points.

Be sure to note all resources you use in your research, and credit those sources in your final draft. Refer to the Conducting Research workshop in the Introductory Unit for assistance in citing materials.

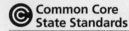 **Common Core State Standards**

Writing

2. Write informative/explanatory texts to examine a topic and convey ideas, concepts, and information through the selection, organization, and analysis of relevant content.

2.a. Introduce a topic clearly, previewing what is to follow; organize ideas, concepts, and information into broader categories; include formatting, graphics, and multimedia when useful to aiding comprehension.

2.b. Develop the topic with relevant, well-chosen facts, definitions, concrete details, quotations, or other information and examples.

READING-WRITING CONNECTION

To get the feel for a cause-and-effect essay, read "Why Leaves Turn Color in the Fall," by Diane Ackerman, on page 264.

Prewriting/Planning Strategies

Discuss with a classmate. To determine topics that interest you, pair up with a classmate and take turns asking these questions:

- What are your favorite books? What natural or historical events are crucial to the subjects or plots of those books?
- What is a science topic that you find interesting?
- Which political leader do you admire most? With which national or world events is he or she most closely associated?
- For what invention are you most grateful? Why?

Review your answers in order to choose a broad topic.

Narrow your topic. Make sure you develop a topic narrow enough for you to cover in depth. First, take time to jot down subtopics of your broader topic. Then, see if you can break your subtopics into more specific topics. Continue this process until you pinpoint a well-defined subject for your writing. The chart shows how one topic is narrowed.

Natural Disasters
earthquakes
North American earthquakes
North American earthquakes in the last decade

Conduct research. Gather the facts, statistics, examples, and other details you need to thoroughly illustrate cause-and-effect relationships. A K-W-L chart like the one shown is an excellent tool for planning and guiding your research.

K-W-L Chart		
What I **K**now	What I **W**ant to Know	What I **L**earned
• Air pollution is increasing and dangerous. • Pollution smells bad. • Cars and factories cause it. • It hurts people and animals.	• How can it be reduced? • What causes it besides cars and factories? • Which countries or cities are the worst? • How can we stop it? • What does it do to people? • To animals?	

Plan your support. Now that you have gathered information, think through the cause-and-effect relationship you will explain. Determine which details are needed to show the connections between cause and effect as clearly as possible. These supporting details can take the form of facts, expert opinions, or comparisons to similar cause-and-effect relationships.

Drafting Strategies

**Common Core
State Standards**

**Reading Informational Text
7.** Evaluate the advantages and
disadvantages of using different
mediums to present a particular
topic or idea.

**Writing
2.a.** Introduce a topic clearly,
previewing what is to follow;
organize ideas, concepts, and
information into broader
categories; include formatting,
graphics, and multimedia when
useful to aiding comprehension.

Write a useful introduction. Introduce your topic and show why it is interesting using the following strategies:

- Begin with a strong opening sentence that grabs your reader's attention. Use a rhetorical question, an interesting quotation, a personal experience, or another strong detail.
- In the rest of your introductory paragraph, develop a clear thesis, or controlling idea. Clearly identify the cause-and-effect relationship you will discuss, and preview your main points.

Prove the connections. To convince your audience that the connections you make between causes and effects are not just coincidental, add details to elaborate on the link you are showing.

- **Weak connection:** The local store is losing business because another store opened.
- **Strong connection:** The local store is losing business because a *larger* store *with a bigger inventory opened next door.*

Use formatting, graphics, and multimedia. Consider using boldface heads for the various sections of your essay to help guide readers. In addition to text, consider using other media, such as graphs or sound clips, to strengthen your work. When deciding which media to use, think about the details you are presenting. Consider the advantages and disadvantages of each medium, and choose the one that best suits your purpose.

MEDIUM	ADVANTAGE	DISADVANTAGE	SAMPLE USE
Print	Can convey information in precise, nuanced language	May not always help readers see relationships quickly	Use to present main ideas and detailed explanations
Video	Can show facts quickly and memorably	May not include all necessary information	Use to give quick idea of what a process involves
Multimedia	Can keep viewer's attention	May be difficult to use the required technology	Use only for a carefully rehearsed presentation
Sound Clips	Can add interest and convey some facts	May be distracting	Use conservatively
Graphs and Charts	Can present detailed information clearly	May lengthen the presentation or lose audience interest	Use sparingly for highly specific details

Organize Details

Match Organization to Topic Plan the best way to organize your essay, grouping the ideas, concepts, and information you are presenting into broader categories. Use an organizational structure that is appropriate to the particular type of cause-and-effect relationship you are analyzing so that the reader can follow the logic of your essay.

Review your research, and circle the main causes and effects. Identify which organizational pattern below best fits your topic. Then, organize your essay accordingly.

- **Many Causes/Single Effect:** If your topic is a single effect with several causes, discuss each cause in its own paragraph.

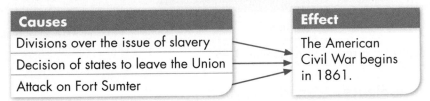

Causes
Divisions over the issue of slavery
Decision of states to leave the Union
Attack on Fort Sumter

Effect
The American Civil War begins in 1861.

- **Single Cause/Many Effects:** For one cause with several effects, devote a paragraph to each effect.

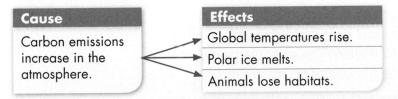

Cause
Carbon emissions increase in the atmosphere.

Effects
Global temperatures rise.
Polar ice melts.
Animals lose habitats.

- **Chain of Causes and Effects:** If you are presenting a chain of causes and effects, present them in chronological order with transitions to show the connections.

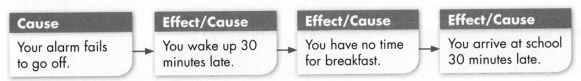

Cause	Effect/Cause	Effect/Cause	Effect/Cause
Your alarm fails to go off.	You wake up 30 minutes late.	You have no time for breakfast.	You arrive at school 30 minutes late.

Revising Strategies

Fill in gaps in support. Read through your draft to determine if you clearly and persuasively connect causes with effects. One way to check is to label your support (for example, "F" for fact). If it looks as if you have too much of one type of support or if there is no support at all for one of your main points, consider including additional information.

Use transitions to show connections. Your goal is to explain the links between causes and effects. Transition words can help ensure that the relationship between cause and effect is obvious to your readers. Use transitional words and phrases like the ones shown here to clarify connections.

Cause-and-Effect Transitions	
Introducing Causes	since, if, because, as soon as, until
Introducing Effects	consequently, as a result, subsequently, then

Define key terms for your audience. To make sure you have expressed your ideas clearly, follow these steps:

1. Reread your essay, circling any terms that your audience may not know.

2. Provide more background information or definitions where necessary. You may have to consult your research notes or other reference materials for this information. The example below uses an *appositive phrase* to provide the additional information.

Original	Revision With Key Terms Defined
Henry's kitten had to get a shot to prevent feline leukemia.	Henry's kitten had to get a shot to prevent feline leukemia, an incurable disease in cats that is caused by a virus.

Check spelling. Using a dictionary, check your spelling of all key terms. In addition, check your spelling of commonly confused words, such as *effect* and *affect*. Finally, check your spelling of *homonyms*—words that sound the same as but that are spelled differently from one another; for example, *there, their,* and *they're*.

Peer Review

Ask a classmate to review your draft to help you identify places in your draft where adding transitions would improve the writing. While you are revising, consider your classmate's suggestions.

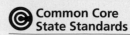

**Common Core
State Standards**

Writing

2.c. Use appropriate and varied transitions to create cohesion and clarify the relationships among ideas and concepts.

2.d. Use precise language and domain-specific vocabulary to inform about or explain the topic.

5. With some guidance and support from peers and adults, develop and strengthen writing as needed by planning, revising, editing, rewriting, or trying a new approach, focusing on how well purpose and audience have been addressed.

Language

1.a. Explain the function of verbals (gerunds, participles, infinitives) in general and their function in particular sentences.

2.c. Spell correctly.

Revising to Combine Sentences Using Gerunds and Participles

Gerunds and participles are **verbals,** or verb forms that are used as another part of speech.

Identifying Gerunds A **gerund** is a verb form ending in *-ing* that acts as a noun. A **gerund phrase** is a gerund with modifiers, objects, or complements, all acting together as a noun.

>**As subject:** *Baking cookies* is Heather's hobby.

>**As direct object:** Lucille enjoys *swimming*.

>**As predicate noun:** David's greatest talent is *playing the piano*.

>**As object of a preposition:** Randall never gets tired of *surfing*.

Identifying Participles A **participle** is a verb form that acts as an adjective. There are two kinds of participles: present participles and past participles. A **participial phrase** is a present or past participle and its modifiers, objects, or complements, all acting together as an adjective.

>**Present participle:** The *chirping* canary sang sweetly.

>**Past participle in participial phrase:** The runner, *filled with hope*, raced toward the finish line.

Revising Sentences To combine choppy or short sentences using gerunds and participles, follow these steps:

1. Identify pairs of sentences that sound choppy and that concern the same idea.

2. Combine the sentences by rephrasing related ideas using participles, gerunds, or participial or gerund phrases.

Choppy Sentences	
The sisters like to draw and paint. They like to play together.	
Combined with Gerunds:	**Combined with Participial Phrase:**
The sisters like *drawing, painting,* and *playing* together.	*Playing together,* the sisters like to draw and paint.

Grammar in Your Writing

Choose three paragraphs in your draft. Find pairs of sentences that deal with the same subject. If they are too choppy or repetitive, combine them using gerund or participial phrases.

Sleep—It's Healthy

Since the beginning of time, sleep has been an important factor in maintaining good health. While people sleep, they refuel their bodies and minds to help them through the next day. Many people do not get the proper amount of sleep, however, and this has a negative effect on their health.

During the day, our bodies and minds consume a great deal of energy. Sleep recharges our bodies and minds, giving our bodies and minds a chance to recover the energy that we have lost. We wake up feeling refreshed because, while we sleep, our brains do not need to focus and our muscles can relax.

Sleep deprivation occurs when someone receives fewer hours of sleep than his or her body needs. Many different things can cause sleep deprivation. A few of the main causes are drinking caffeine, living in a noisy environment, and working long hours. The effect on a person who does not get enough sleep can be devastating. Some effects of sleep deprivation are stress, anxiety, inability to concentrate, and loss of coping skills. Another effect is weight gain, which is very unhealthy for most people. Mood shifts, including depression, increased irritability, and loss of a sense of humor all result from not getting enough sleep.

I have observed some of these sleep deprivation effects in people I know. My friend Tim had to stay up late several nights in a row in order to finish a term paper on time. Here is how Tim describes how the loss of sleep affected him: "The first thing I noticed was that I couldn't concentrate in class. My attention would wander and I couldn't understand ideas that would ordinarily be very easy for me to grasp. My body was achy, my head was cloudy, and I was snapping at everyone about everything. The sleep that I did get wasn't very good because my dreams were bad ones about things like forgetting to turn my paper in."

People often dream when they have been thinking hard about something right before they go to sleep. Dreams can be good or bad for us. A good dream is relaxing and does not disturb the sleeper. A bad dream causes stress, anxiety, and restlessness. To avoid bad dreams, people should do something relaxing, like reading, before going to bed.

In conclusion, adequate sleep promotes good health and helps us feel better about ourselves. Sleep deprivation can seriously harm our minds and bodies. To counter these harmful effects, the answer is to simply get more sleep. Sleeping well can guarantee us better health and a better life.

Max clearly outlines the cause-and-effect relationship he will address.

This paragraph identifies the causes of sleep deprivation.

To support his explanation, Max offers detailed descriptions of sleep deprivation's effects.

Max concludes his essay effectively by summarizing the health benefits of sleep.

Editing and Proofreading

Make corrections in grammar, usage, and mechanics to ensure that your final draft is error-free.

Focus on prepositions. Whenever possible, avoid ending sentences with a preposition.

> **Draft Sentence:** Which friend are you traveling **with**?
>
> **Revised Sentence: With** which friend are you traveling?
> Who is traveling **with** you?

Spiral Review
Earlier in this unit, you learned about **prepositional phrases** (p. 594) and **clauses** (p. 650). Check your essay to make sure that you have used prepositional phrases and subordinate clauses correctly.

Publishing and Presenting

Consider one of the following ways to share your writing:

Present a speech. If your essay addresses a situation that others face, offer to speak to classes that can benefit from your work.

Publish a feature article. Submit your essay to your local or school newspaper. In a letter accompanying your essay, explain to the editor why the issue you address is important to readers.

Reflecting on Your Writing

Writer's Journal Jot down your answer to this question:

Did learning about the causes and effects of your topic motivate you to take any action?

Rubric for Self-Assessment

Find evidence that your writing addresses each category. Then, use the rating scale to grade your work.

Criteria	Rating Scale
Purpose/Focus Clearly introduces and develops a thesis, previewing what is to follow	*not very* .... *very* 1 2 3 4
Organization Effectively organizes ideas, concepts, and information to establish the connection between cause and effect; uses appropriate transitions	1 2 3 4
Development of Ideas/Elaboration Successfully develops the cause-and-effect explanation with relevant, well-chosen, concrete details	1 2 3 4
Language Uses precise language to demonstrate the connection between cause and effect	1 2 3 4
Conventions Correctly follows conventions of spelling, punctuation, and grammar, including the use of verbals to increase sentence fluency	1 2 3 4

SELECTED RESPONSE

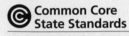 **Common Core State Standards**

RL.8.1, RL.8.3, RL.8.4, RL.8.6; W.8.1; L.8.4.a
[For full standards wording, see the chart in the front of this book.]

I. Reading Literature

Directions: *Read the excerpt from* Beyond the Horizon *by Eugene O'Neill. Then, answer each question that follows.*

[After agreeing to ship out to sea, Robert has realized that he is in love with Ruth. He believes that his brother Andrew is also in love with her.]

(*The sitting room of the Mayo farm house about nine o'clock . . . .*)

Mrs. Mayo. . . . You look all worked up over something, Robbie. What is it?

Robert. (*Swallowing hard, looks quickly from one to the other of them—then begins determinedly.*) Yes, there *is* something—something I must tell you—all of you. (*As he begins to talk* Andrew *enters quietly from the rear, closing the door behind him, and setting the lighted lantern on the floor. He remains standing by the door, his arms folded, listening to* Robert *with a repressed expression of pain on his face.* Robert *is so much taken up with what he is going to say that he does not notice* Andrew's *presence.*) Something I discovered on this evening— very beautiful and wonderful—something I did not take into consideration previously because I hadn't dared to hope that such happiness could ever come to me. (*Appealingly.*) You must all remember that fact, won't you?

Mayo. (*Frowning.*) Let's get to the point, son.

Robert. You were offended because you thought I'd been wasting my time star-gazing on my last night at home. (*With a trace of defiance.*) Well, the point is this, Pa; it *isn't* my last night at home. I'm not going—I mean—I can't go tomorrow with Uncle Dick—or at any future time, either.

Mrs. Mayo. (*With a sharp sigh of joyful relief.*) Oh, Robbie, I'm so glad!

Mayo. (*Astounded.*) You ain't serious, be you, Robert?

Robert. Yes, I mean what I say.

Mayo. (*Severely.*) Seems to me it's a pretty late hour in the day for you to be upsettin' all your plans so sudden!

Robert. I asked you to remember that, until this evening I didn't know myself— the wonder which makes everything else in the world seem <u>sordid</u> and pitifully selfish by comparison. I had never dared to dream—

Mayo. (*Irritably.*) Come to the point. What is this foolishness you're talkin' of?

Robert. (*Flushing.*) Ruth told me this evening that—she loved me. It was after I'd confessed I loved her. . . . I hadn't intended telling her anything but— suddenly—I felt I must. I didn't think it would matter, because I was going away, and before I came back I was sure she'd have forgotten. And I thought she loved—someone else.

1. Which is the best description of Robert's **motivation** for sharing his news with Mr. and Mrs. Mayo?

  A. internal: He has been forced against his will to share his news with his parents.

  B. internal and external: He is motivated by joy and by the need to cancel his earlier plans.

  C. internal: Pride causes him to brag about his love.

  D. He acts without clear motivation.

2. Which of the following best describes the **setting** of the scene?

  A. Night, inside a house

  B. Breakfast time, on a farm

  C. Midday, outdoors

  D. There is no way to tell without further reading.

3. **Part A** Which is the best example of **dramatic irony** within the passage?

  A. Mr. and Mrs. Mayo do not know what Robert is about to tell them.

  B. Only the reader knows that Andrew has entered in time to hear Robert's confession.

  C. The characters cannot see the stage directions, so they are unaware of one another's tones and facial expressions.

  D. It is ironic that Robert is changing his plans without warning.

  Part B Which phrase from the passage best supports the answer to Part A?

  A. "upsettin' all your plans so sudden!"

  B. "(*With a sharp sigh of joyful relief.*)"

  C. "Well, the point is this, Pa; it *isn't* my last night at home."

  D. "(. . . *he does not notice* ANDREW's *presence.*)"

4. Which of the following is *not* described by the **stage directions** in the passage?

  A. setting

  B. costumes

  C. characters' actions

  D. characters' emotions

5. What do the dialogue and stage directions reveal about Mr. Mayo's **character?**

  A. He is a serious man who prefers straightforward explanations.

  B. He tries not to concern himself with Robert's happiness and well-being.

  C. He is a poor listener because he is easily excitable.

  D. He is a sensitive man who becomes irritable when his family deceives him.

6. Which phrase best describes Robert's **tone** throughout the passage?

  A. mournful and somber

  B. giddy and somewhat reckless

  C. nervous, but earnest and decisive

  D. alarmed, perhaps even astonished

7. **Vocabulary** Which pair of words is closest in meaning to the underlined word <u>sordid</u>?

  A. generous; giving

  B. joyous; gleeful

  C. wonderful; awe-inspiring

  D. inferior; dirty

⏱ Timed Writing

8. In a brief argumentative essay, analyze what you believe to be the central conflict in the passage. Identify any inferences upon which you are relying, and cite specific lines of **dialogue** and **stage directions** that support your claim.

GO ON

II. Reading Informational Text

Directions: *Read the passage. Then, answer each question that follows.*

Common Core State Standards

RI.8.1; L.8.1, L.8.1.a, L.8.3
[For full standards wording, see the chart in the front of this book.]

Smithtown Pool Rules

- All children under five must be accompanied by an adult.
- Diving is not permitted in the shallow end or from the pool's sides.
- No glass containers are allowed in the pool area.
- No running, hard shoving, or horseplay will be tolerated.
- Guests must be accompanied by members.
- Above all, keep in mind that the pool is here for everyone's enjoyment. Rowdy behavior ruins the experience for everyone.

Application Process for Lifeguard Positions

1. Check our Web site for open positions, posted weekly.
2. Apply online for the position for which you are interested.
3. We will call you in for an interview, based on your qualifications.
4. Bring your lifeguard certification with you to the interview.
5. We will perform a background check only if your interview has gone well.
6. If your application is approved, you will need to complete the appropriate paperwork before your first day of work.

---

1. **Part A** According to the lifeguard application process, which of these statements is true?

   A. Applicants are encouraged to find open positions online and then apply by mail.

   B. The interview comes before the background check.

   C. Applicants should bring their lifeguard certificate to the first day of work.

   D. An interview will be given to everyone who applies.

Part B Which step or steps in the lifeguard application process most directly support the answer to Part A?

   A. steps 1 and 2   **C.** steps 4 and 6

   B. step 3   **D.** step 5

2. How are the purposes of these materials different?

   A. one is intended for a wider audience than the other

   B. one is meant to inform; the other to entertain

   C. one is meant for adults; the other for children

   D. one is meant to persuade; the other to entertain

III. Writing and Language Conventions

Directions: *Read the passage. Then, answer each question that follows.*

You-Play-It Players
664 South Street
Casaterra, CA 10000

To Whom It May Concern:

(1) I recently bought a faulty MP3 player from your company. (2) I press "play." (3) The unit makes an awful squeal.

(4) I have attempted to solve the problem. (5) I have placed calls to the number in the warranty several times. (6) My calls are never answered. (7) Please contact me so that we can arrange to fix the player by telephone. (8) Listening to music is my favorite hobby, so I hope we can take care of this without further delay. (9) You really need to tell your customer service representatives to do a better job.

(10) Sincerely,

Liz Alvarez

---

1. Which of these groups of words from the passage contains at least one **prepositional phrase?**
   A. *attempted to solve the problem* in sentence 4
   B. *placed calls to the number in the warranty* in sentence 5
   C. *arrange to fix the player* in sentence 7
   D. *need to tell your customer service representatives* in sentence 9

2. Which of these choices combines sentences 2 and 3 using a **subordinate clause?**
   A. I press "play"—the unit makes an awful squeal.
   B. Whenever I press "play," the unit makes an awful squeal.
   C. I press "play," but an awful squeal is made by the unit.
   D. I press "play," and the unit makes an awful squeal.

3. In sentence 9, as what part of speech does the **infinitive phrase** *to do a better job* function?
   A. It functions as a noun that is the direct object of *tell*.
   B. It functions as an adjective that modifies *representatives*.
   C. It functions as an adverb that modifies *need*.
   D. It functions as a prepositional phrase that modifies *representatives*.

4. Which of these choices combines sentences 4 and 5 using a **participial phrase?**
   A. Attempting to solve the problem, I have placed calls to the number in the warranty several times.
   B. I have attempted to solve the problem and placed calls to the number in the warranty several times.
   C. To solve the problem, I have placed calls to the number in the warranty.
   D. I have attempted to solve the problem by placing calls to the number in the warranty several times.

(STOP)

CONSTRUCTED RESPONSE

Common Core State Standards

RL.8.1, RL.8.2, RL.8.3; W.8.1, W.8.2, W.8.7, W.8.9; SL.8.1, SL.8.4, SL.8.6; L.8.1.a

[For full standards wording, see the chart in the front of this book.]

Directions: *Follow the instructions to complete the tasks below as required by your teacher.*

As you work on each task, incorporate both general academic vocabulary and literary terms you learned in Parts 1 and 2 of this unit.

Writing

TASK 1 Literature [RL.8.2; W.8.1]

Analyze the Development of Theme

Write an essay in which you focus on the impact of character on theme in one of the drama selections in Part 2 of this unit.

Part 1

- Review and evaluate a drama selection from Part 2 of this unit that had an identifiable theme.

- As you are reviewing the selection, focus on one of the main characters. Make notes on the relationship between the character and the selection's theme.

- Answer the following question: How do specific lines of dialogue and stage directions involving the character contribute to your understanding of the selection's theme?

Part 2

- Write an essay in which you argue for your interpretation of the character's relationship to the theme, showing how the character's words and actions help develop the theme.

- Check your writing for correct grammar and usage.

TASK 2 Literature [RL.8.3; W.8.2; L.8.1.a]

Analyze Character in Drama

Write an essay in which you analyze characterization in a drama selection from Part 2 of this unit.

- Select one of the drama selections in Part 2 of this unit with an interesting character. Begin your analysis by explaining what you found interesting about the character.

- In your analysis, answer the following questions: What is the character's function in the play? What character traits does he or she possess? What internal or external conflicts does he or she face?

- Cite specific dialogue, stage directions, and plot events to support your analysis.

- Revise your essay to combine short or choppy sentences, using gerunds and participles whenever appropriate.

TASK 3 Literature [RL.8.3; W.8.2]

Analyze Dialogue

Write an essay in which you analyze how particular lines of dialogue propel the action of a drama selection in Part 2 of this unit.

- Choose a significant passage of dialogue from one of the drama selections in Part 2 of this unit.

- Explain how the passage moves the plot forward. Tell how the dialogue provided adds to the conflict, shapes the relationship between characters, or otherwise affects the action.

- Support your ideas with evidence from the text.

- Be sure to quote accurately from the text and to punctuate your quotations correctly.

Speaking and Listening

TASK 4 Literature [RL.8.1; SL.8.4, SL.8.6]

Analyze and Interpret a Speech

Prepare an oral presentation in which you analyze a speech by a character in one of the plays in Part 2 of this unit. As part of your presentation, perform the speech in front of the class.

- Select a significant speech from one of the plays in Part 2 of this unit. Reread it carefully, looking up any unfamiliar words in a dictionary.

- Take notes analyzing the message of the speech. It may contain arguments and specific claims. It may reveal something about the character or the plot. It may contribute to the overall theme of the play.

- Present your analysis to the class, supporting points with relevant evidence. Then, perform the speech in front of the class. Make decisions as to how the character should behave; for example, whether he or she should appear angry, happy, or confident. Be sure your performance reflects your understanding of the character's feelings, goals, and attitudes.

- Invite questions from the audience and respond with relevant evidence and ideas.

TASK 5 Literature [RL.8.3; SL.8.1]

Compare and Contrast Characters

Hold a small group discussion in which you compare and contrast two characters in drama selections from Part 2 of this unit.

- Choose two characters from different selections in Part 2 of this unit who share at least one key trait.

- Determine the similarities and differences between these characters and their effects on the action of the selection.

- Come to the discussion prepared with your analysis of both characters, including a list of lines of dialogue that support your analysis. Prepare a list of questions to guide the discussion.

- Follow rules for collegial discussions. Ensure that everyone contributes. Pose further questions based on contributions from the group.

- Wrap up the discussion with a recap of the key points presented.

Research

TASK 6 Literature [W.8.7, W.8.9]

 ## Is it our differences or our similarities that matter most?

In this unit, you have read drama selections about people's differences. Conduct a short research project on someone you admire who is significantly different from you. Then, use both the literature you have read and your research to reflect on this unit's Big Question. Follow these guidelines:

- Focus your research on one person you admire.

- Gather information from at least two reliable sources. Your sources may be print or digital.

- Take careful notes as you conduct research.

- Cite your sources.

When you have completed your research, write a response to the Big Question. Discuss how your initial ideas have changed or been reinforced. Support your response with an example from literature and an example from your research, citing your sources. Be sure to use academic vocabulary words in your response (see p. 505).

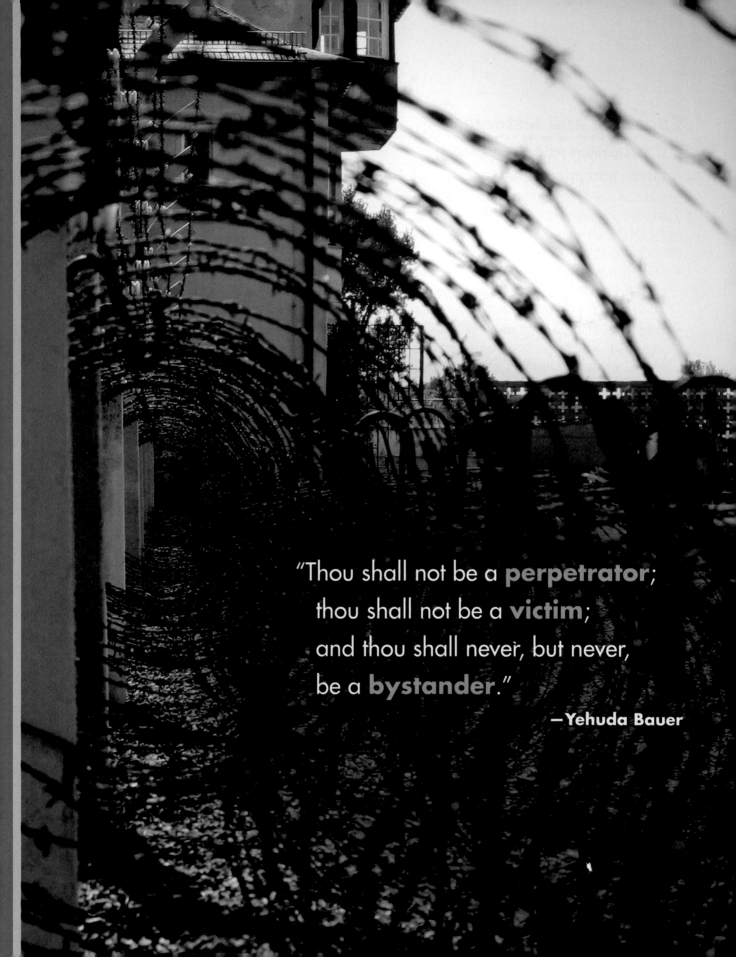

"Thou shall not be a **perpetrator**;
thou shall not be a **victim**;
and thou shall never, but never,
be a **bystander**."

—Yehuda Bauer

THE HOLOCAUST

The selections in this unit relate to the Big Question: **Is it our differences or our similarities that matter most?** People often live in groups defined by the similar backgrounds of their members. The differences between these groups may become a basis for conflict or even persecution. The texts that follow offer insights into the Holocaust, a historical crime in which the Nazis and others persecuted Jews and other targeted groups. Each selection shows how this persecution affected individuals, challenging their most basic relationships with others and with their own identities.

As you read, consider whether it is the differences or similarities between groups that count the most. Consider also how individuals can affirm common humanity and individual identity in the face of catastrophe.

◀ **CRITICAL VIEWING** What does this image suggest about the ability of human beings to act in inhumane ways? What responsibilities do people have when confronted by inhumanity?

CLOSE READING TOOL

Use the **Close Reading Tool** to practice the strategies you learn in this unit.

from

KINDERTRANSPORT

Diane Samuels

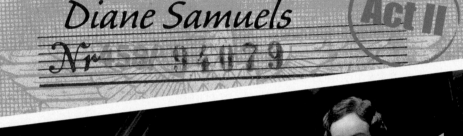

Act II

Nr. 94079

You are about to read an excerpt from the drama
Kindertransport. *In the preceding section of the play, two stories
have unfolded side by side. In one story, set in the 1930s, Helga
prepares her nine-year-old daughter, Eva, to leave Germany
for England, where Eva will live with a foster family. Eva must
flee Germany because she and her family are Jews, their lives
endangered by Nazi persecution. When she arrives in England,
she is taken in by Lil, who raises Eva as her own child.*

*The preceding section of the play also tells a second story, set
in the present. Evelyn, Eva's grown self, is helping her own
daughter, Faith, prepare to leave home. Exploring the storage
room in their home, Faith discovers evidence of Evelyn's German
Jewish past—a past Evelyn has never shared with Faith. Faith
flares up in anger at her mother.*

*This excerpt from the play opens as Lil, Evelyn's adoptive mother
and Faith's grandmother, attempts to help Evelyn deal with
the crisis. As you read, note ways in which the drama shifts
between the two stories—Eva's and Evelyn's.*

Characters

EVELYN: *English middle-class woman. In her fifties.*

FAITH: *Evelyn's only child. In her early twenties.*

EVA: *Evelyn's younger self. She starts the play at 9 years old
and finishes it at 17 years old. Jewish German becoming
increasingly English.*

HELGA: *German Jewish woman of the late 1930s. In her early
thirties. Eva/Evelyn's mother.*

LIL: *Eva/Evelyn's English foster mother. In her eighties.*

THE RATCATCHER: *A mythical character who also plays:* THE NAZI
BORDER OFFICIAL, THE ENGLISH ORGANIZER, THE POSTMAN, THE
STATION GUARD.

*[The play takes place in a spare storage room in Evelyn's house
in an outer London suburb in recent times.]*

from Scene 1

EVELYN. What shall I do with the papers?

LIL. You should've known she'd find them one day.

EVELYN. She's never searched in here in her life.

LIL. Burying's not enough, love. You have to get rid.

EVELYN. How could I get rid of them? There are documents in there that prove I have a right to be here. Papers that will stop them from sending me away.

LIL. Who'd want to send you away?

EVELYN. Someone. Anyone. You can never tell. Who knows what they may be thinking.

LIL. Who for [goodness] sake!

EVELYN. The authorities.

LIL. Your passport's not in there is it?

EVELYN. Not my current one.

LIL. And your naturalization papers?

EVELYN. The first entry permit is. There might be other documents.

LIL. Dig them out then.

EVELYN. I don't want to touch those letters and pictures.

LIL. I'll help.

[EVELYN *pulls back.*]

LIL. Don't you trust me?

EVELYN. Yes.

LIL. I'll sort them out with you.

[LIL *brings the box of papers over and takes out a letter. She holds it out to* EVELYN.]

LIL. Do you want to keep this?

[EVELYN *looks at the letter.*]

LIL. It's personal not official.

EVELYN. No.

Lil. What shall I do with it?

Evelyn. [*taking it*] I'll rip it up.

[Evelyn *holds it.*]

Lil. If you're going to do it, do it.

[Evelyn *is still.*]

What're you waiting for? Get tearing.

[Evelyn *looks at the paper.*]

Lil. Go on.

Evelyn. Why are you so keen for me to destroy everything?

Lil. I thought you wanted shut of it.

Evelyn. I do . . . I just . . .

Lil. Here love, let me.

Evelyn. No.

Lil. If you can't, I will.

Evelyn. It's mine not yours.

Lil. Don't be so daft.

Evelyn. You've always done too much.

Lil. How could I ever do enough?

Evelyn. You took too much.

Lil. How did I take?

Evelyn. Too much of me. You took me away.

Lil. What d'you mean by that?

Evelyn. I wasn't your child.

Lil. As good as . . .

Evelyn. You made me betray her.

Lil. I got you through it. Never forget that, Evelyn.

Evelyn. You made me betray them all.

Lil. I was with you and I put up with you and I stuck by you. That's what mothering's all about. Being there when it counts. No one else was there, were they? And good or bad, I'm still here. Who else have you got?

Evelyn. No one.

Lil. That's right, Evelyn, no one.

Evelyn. And isn't that what you always wanted?

Lil. Did I start the war? Am I Hitler?

Evelyn. You might as well have been.

Lil. What have I done to you that wasn't done in love?

Evelyn. What are you? Some saint? . . .

Lil. I didn't have to take you in . . .

Evelyn. Some savior to all the world's poor little orphans?

Lil. I could've starved you or worked you . . .

Evelyn. And what do I have to pay?

Lil. I could've hit you . . .

Evelyn. What's your price?

Lil. I saved you.

Evelyn. Part of me is dead because of you.

Lil. Nothing you say will make me walk out that door.

Evelyn. Murderer.

Lil. I kept you alive. More than alive.

Evelyn. Child-stealer.

Lil. Go on then. Bare your grudges at me. What else do you want to blame me for? What other ills in your life are all down to me?

Evelyn. Shut up.

Lil. I'm waiting.

Evelyn. I don't want to blame you.

Lil. What do you want?

Evelyn. I want it never to have happened.

Lil. Well it did.

[*Pause.*]

LIL. Now what?

EVELYN. Enough.

[EVELYN *tears up the letter into small pieces. She and* LIL *proceed to destroy each item in the box.*]

[STATION GUARD *enters.*]

GUARD. [*to* EVA] Can I help you, love?

EVA. What?

GUARD. You waiting for someone?

EVA. Two people.

GUARD. What do they look like, love?

[EVA *takes out a photo and shows it.*]

GUARD. Well-heeled.

EVA. Mother knows a good cobbler.

GUARD. Right. Is that them?

EVA. No.

GUARD. They your parents are they?

EVA. Yes.

[*They look.*]

GUARD. [*pointing*] What about those two?

EVA. No.

GUARD. You're not here on your own to meet them are you?

EVA. Mrs. Miller has just gone to cloakroom.

GUARD. Who's that then?

EVA. She looks after me.

GUARD. She knows where to find you?

EVA. Oh yes.

GUARD. What about that woman there?

Eva. No.

Guard. Live in Manchester[1] do you?

Eva. Yes.

Guard. Not been evacuated then?

Eva. No.

[*They look.*]

Guard. Well, I'm afraid they don't seem to be here, your Mam and Dad.

Eva. They will come.

Guard. You sure they were on this train?

Eva. They write that they come to me on September 9th.

Guard. But, it's September 11th today.

Eva. They must to come soon.

Guard. Look. Are you certain they were traveling from London?

Eva. Yes . . . it must be . . . I got here from there.

Guard. You see there's no more trains today from London.

Eva. Are you sure?

Guard. Course I am.

Eva. It can't be.

Guard. [*suspicious*] Where are you from?

Eva. 72 Mulberry Road . . .

Guard. No. I mean, what's your nationality?

Eva. My?

Guard. What country you from?

Eva. [*worried*] I don't live there any more.

Guard. Where don't you live any more?

Eva. It does not matter so much.

Guard. And where's this lady who's looking after you? She's left you a long time on your own hasn't she?

---

1. **Manchester** (man´ ches´ tər) city in northwest England.

Eva. I don't know.

Guard. [*taking her by the arm*] I think that you'd better come with me young lady.

[Lil *runs up to* Eva.]

Lil. Eva! Eva! Where [. . .] did you go!

Guard. Are you supposed to be looking after her?

Lil. I just went to the cloakroom.

Guard. You should take better care of her. Can't leave a girl of her age on her own. Specially nowadays. Could be an air raid warning any minute.

Lil. She ran off. [*to* Eva] What d'you do that for? You had me frantic. D'you think I like pacing platforms looking for you!

Guard. And what's this about her being a foreigner?

Lil. [*to* Eva] The last train's been and gone, love.

Eva. We cannot to give up yet.

Lil. We've been here three days on the trot.[2]

Eva. Please can we come back tomorrow.

Lil. I don't think they're coming. [*to* Guard] I'll take her now.

Guard. I asked you about her being a foreigner?

Lil. [*to* Guard] Don't worry yourself about it.

Guard. Got to look out for spies we have.

Lil. She's not a spy. She's ten years old.

Guard. What about them parents she's waiting for?

Lil. Her parents are still in Germany.

Eva. No, they're not!

Guard. Are they indeed?

Lil. Just leave it to me, will you. [*to* Eva] I did warn you that this would happen.

Guard. What's she doing here then? She should be in Germany with them.

---

2. **three days on the trot** British English idiom meaning "three days straight."

Eva. Maybe they're in London.

Lil. Eva. They're not coming.

Eva. They keep their promises. Always.

Lil. Wars break promises.

Eva. They must be coming some different way. They have their visas got by now . . . they have written to us that they come this week . . .

Lil. They wrote that before the war started. If it'd broke out a fortnight[3] later . . .

Eva. I want them to come. I got permits!

Lil. Believe me, Eva love, I want them to come too.

Guard. Well, I don't.

Eva. You are wrong! You are wrong! They will come!

Lil. There's no way through.

Eva. There is!

Lil. There isn't.

Guard. If they put one foot into this country, they'll be interned[4] straight off. Got to protect ourselves.

Eva. No!

Lil. Oh Eva.

Eva. No! No! No! No! No!

Lil. I know. I know.

Eva. No!

[Eva *shakes with distress.*]

Guard. [*exiting*] Should've stayed where she belongs.

Lil. We can go to church and pray for them.

Eva. I don't know how to pray in a church.

Lil. It's a lot easier to learn than English.

Eva. I'll never see them again, will I?

---

3. **fortnight** (fôrt´ nīt´) *n.* period of two weeks.
4. **interned** (in tʉrnd´) *v.* confined, especially during war.

Lil. They've got as much chance of surviving as we have. And I'm not dying and neither are you.

[Eva *takes off two rings, a charm bracelet, a watch, and a chain with a Star of David on it.*]

Lil. What're you doing?

Eva. I don't want these on me any more.

Lil. Why on earth not?

Eva. I don't like them.

Lil. We'll put them away safe at home.

Eva. How much longer can I stay with you?

Lil. Don't ask stupid questions.

[Lil *takes* Eva's *arm.* Eva *slowly moves with her.*]

[Evelyn *rips.* Lil *picks up the "Rattenfänger"* [5] *book and starts to tear out the first page.*]

Evelyn. No. Not that.

Lil. It's in German. Horrible pictures.

Evelyn. You can't damage a book. I'll give it to a secondhand shop.

Lil. [*picking up the Haggadah* [6]] What about this?

Evelyn. That too.

[Evelyn *puts the books to the side.* Lil *opens a letter.*]

[Evelyn *picks up the mouth organ. She doesn't recognize it. She puts it with the books.*]

[Lil *reads the letter in her hand intently.*]

---

5. **Rattenfänger** (rät´ ən feŋ´ ər) German for "Rat-Catcher." *Rattenfänger* is a name for the Pied Piper of Hamelin, a character in folklore who rid the city of Hamelin of its rats by luring them away with a flute. When the people failed to pay him for his service, he lured away their children as well.
6. **Haggadah** (hə gä´ də) book containing a narrative of the biblical story of Exodus, the story of the Jews' captivity in Egypt and of their liberation by Moses. It is read at the Seder meal during Passover, a Jewish holiday.

Evelyn. Is it important?

Lil. It's them changing their mind about letting you stay on at school after we fought them . . .

Evelyn. Rip it up.

Lil. "We accept Eva's proven brilliancy . . ."

Evelyn. Mum.[7]

Lil. Can't we save it?

Evelyn. What did you say about destroying?

[LIL *withholds it.*]

Evelyn. You were absolutely right. All this unpleasantness could have been avoided. I should have sifted through all these years ago. It's only paper.

Lil. I suppose.

Evelyn. What's done is done, Mum.

[EVELYN *takes the letter and tears it.*]

Evelyn. Let's get back to normal shall we?

Lil. You've got over worse.

Evelyn. I've made a good life. All I can do is live it and count my blessings.

Lil. And make up with your daughter.

Evelyn. We'll see.

Lil. You always have to make an effort with your children. No matter what.

Evelyn. All our children leave us. And one day they never come back. I can't stop her.

Lil. You and I are still close.

Evelyn. You and I are different.

Lil. She's more like you than you think.

Evelyn. I don't want her to be like me.

Lil. She's herself too. Every child's their own person.

---

7. **mum** British English for "mom."

Evelyn. Was I?

Lil. And how.

Evelyn. Not any more. The older I get the less of myself
I become.

Lil. The things you come out with.

Evelyn. I always knew she'd go. Didn't the German woman
realize that too?

Lil. You mean your first mother?

Evelyn. She wanted me to be hers forever.

Lil. I thought you'd forgotten her.

Evelyn. It doesn't matter. I have.

[Evelyn *continues to tear.*]

[*Soundtrack of a newsreel about the liberation of Belsen.*[8]]

[Lil *and* Eva (*now fifteen*) *watch. Suddenly* Lil *throws a
handkerchief over* Eva's *face and bundles her away.*]

Lil. They should have a warning about what's in them
newsreels. No children should see such pictures.

Eva. [*taking the handkerchief off her face*] I'm not a child.
I'm fifteen.

Lil. Especially not you. No matter how old you are.

Eva. It can't be kept from me forever.

Lil. D'you want to go back in then?

[*Pause.*]

Eva. No.

Lil. What you don't see can't come back to haunt you.

Eva. I suppose so.

Lil. Thank [goodness] I had my handkerchief.

Eva. The soldiers had them over their noses and mouths.

Lil. Don't think of it.

Eva. Can a handkerchief keep out the smell of all those bodies?

---

8. Belsen (bel´ zən) another name for Bergen-Belsen, a Nazi concentration camp in Germany.

Lil. It couldn't hold all the tears that want crying.

[*Pause.*]

Eva. I don't want to cry.

Lil. Far too shocking.

Eva. Should I want to cry? Is it **callous** of me?

Lil. You react as you react.

Eva. We can still go in to see the main feature, can't we?

Lil. Do you want to?

Eva. Yes. Is that wrong?

Lil. It was our treat.

Eva. There's no reason why we should miss our treat is there? I mean, it wouldn't make any difference to anything else would it?

Lil. Sure you're in the mood?

Eva. I have been looking forward to it.

Lil. I don't know if I'm in the mood now.

Eva. You've already paid for the tickets and we won't have another chance before it finishes.

Lil. All right.

[*Knocking on the door.*]

Faith. [*off*] Gran? Mum?

[Evelyn *shakes her head.*]

Lil. Go on down, Faith, love.

Faith. [*off*] What are you doing?

Lil. Let me sort it out.

Faith. [*off*] Let me in.

Lil. We'll be out soon. Promise.

Faith. [*off*] How soon?

Lil. Not long.

Faith. [*off*] I'll wait here.

---

callous ▶
(kal′ əs) *adj.* lacking pity or mercy; unfeeling

[EVA *stands on a box.* LIL *starts to fix her skirt hem.*]

EVA. Thank you for helping.

LIL. [*to* EVA] You can do your own hem next time.

EVA. You know I'm no good at sewing.

LIL. You'll have to learn sooner or later.

EVA. [*taking the gold watch and jewelry out of her pocket*] How much d'you think they're worth?

LIL. What's worth?

EVA. Two rings. A charm bracelet. Gold. A chain with a Star of David. A watch. All gold.

LIL. Don't ask me. I'm not a jeweler.

EVA. It'd be quite a lot, wouldn't it?

[EVA *peers at the jewelry.*]

LIL. Why d'you want to know?

EVA. I was thinking of selling them.

LIL. What d'you want to sell them for?

EVA. I'm fed up of hiding the watch under my socks to stop hearing the ticking at night.

LIL. It's bad luck to sell a keepsake.

EVA. I'd rather have the money.

LIL. Money's nothing. You purse it, you spend it. Those are more.

EVA. If they're mine, I can do what I want with them.

LIL. Are they yours?

EVA. My mother from Germany gave them to me.

LIL. To look after for her or have for yourself?

EVA. Same difference now.

LIL. We're still trying to track them down, aren't we? Still writing all those letters. Why are you so keen to give up?

EVA. It was all over a long time ago.

LIL. It isn't over till you know for sure.

Eva. I do know for sure.

Lil. Miracles can happen.

Eva. I don't believe in miracles.

Lil. It sounds to me like you don't want to.

Eva. I will sell them, Mum. There's better things the money could be spent on.

Lil. Like what?

Eva. I want to pay my way for myself as much as I can.

Lil. And I want to keep you. Like no one ever kept me. I don't care if it's hard. I'll do right by you. Somebody has to in this [. . .] world.

Eva. You've already done more than all right by me.

Lil. I've not finished yet.

Eva. D'you mind if I go now?

Lil. Just make sure no one [cheats] you.

   [*Knocking on the door.*]

Faith. [*off*] Let me in. Please, let me in.

   [Evelyn *nods.* Lil *opens the door.* Faith *enters.*]

Faith. My [goodness].

Evelyn. We're going to clean this room up now.

Faith. I didn't mean to shout at you like that.

Evelyn. It's over and done with.

Faith. I'm sorry.

Evelyn. It's forgotten.

   [Lil *tidies around the box of torn papers.*]

Faith. What are those?

Evelyn. I've put an end to the trouble.

Faith. You've torn up those letters and photos . . .

Evelyn. It's the only way forward.

Faith. [*to* Lil] How could you let her do this?

Lil. It's what we both think is best.

[FAITH *kneels down and stares at the pieces. She tries to gather and fit them together.*]

EVELYN. Don't get yourself all worked up now darling.

FAITH. Weren't these family documents . . . I mean . . . more than that . . .

EVELYN. I know what they were.

LIL. [*to* EVELYN] No one's accusing you, love.

FAITH. But . . . weren't these things . . . sort of . . . entrusted to you? Why didn't you look after them?

[EVELYN *is silent.*]

FAITH. Why didn't you pass them on to me?

EVELYN. I can do what I want with my own property.

FAITH. But how do I know what went before without them? How does anyone know? What proof is there? It could all be make-believe, couldn't it?

LIL. [*to* FAITH] You're not doing a very good job of making up, Faith.

FAITH. [*picking up scraps of paper from the floor*] Look at these remains. Where's the body for these feet? The hand for these fingers? Now they're just lost in the millions.

EVELYN. You know, Faith, there are hundreds of books on the subject. Read some of those if you must have a **morbid** interest in past events.

◄ **morbid**
(môr´ bid) *adj.* caused by an unhealthy tendency to focus on the grisly, gruesome, or horrible

FAITH. Who's going to be able to take care of their memory?

EVELYN. Are you going to go on at me about this for the rest of our lives?

FAITH. Did they die for you to forget?

EVELYN. Why are you being so cruel?

FAITH. Destroying these was crueler.

EVELYN. Do you think I don't know that.

FAITH. Why did you do it then?

EVELYN. Because—and I don't expect you to begin to understand this—it helps me? It gives me something I can do in the face of it all.

FAITH. It can't change what happened though, can it?

EVELYN. Do you want to draw blood?

FAITH. Not blood.

EVELYN. Well, blood is all I have left. Gallons and gallons of the freezing stuff stuck in my veins. One prick, Faith, and I might bleed forever.

FAITH. Mother, don't . . .

EVELYN. Do you still want to know about my childhood, about my origins, about my parents?

FAITH. Yes.

EVELYN. Well, let me tell you. Let me tell you what little remains in my brain. And if I do, will you leave me alone afterwards. Will you please leave me alone?

FAITH. If that's what you want.

EVELYN. My father was called Werner Schlesinger. My mother was called Helga. They lived in Hamburg. They were Jews. I was an only child. I think I must have loved them a lot at one time. One forgets what these things feel like. Other feelings displace the original ones. I remember a huge cone of sweets that I had on my first day at school. There were a lot of toffees . . .

FAITH. What else?

LIL. Faith.

FAITH. What else do you remember?

EVELYN. Books. Rows and rows . . . a whole house built of books and some of them were mine. A storybook filled with dreadful pictures: a terrifying man with razor eyes, long, long fingernails, hair like rats' tails who could see wherever you were, whatever you did, no matter how careful you tried to be, who could get in through sealed windows and closed doors . . .

FAITH. Go on.

EVELYN. The only other thing is a boy with a squint on the train I came away on. I kept trying not to look at him. Please believe me, Faith, there is nothing else in my memory from that time. It honestly is blank.

FAITH. What happened to your parents?

EVELYN. They died.

FAITH. In a concentration camp?

EVELYN. Yes. In Auschwitz.

LIL. When did you find that out?

FAITH. When did they die?

EVELYN. My father died in 1943. He was gassed soon after arrival.

FAITH. What about your mother?

EVELYN. My mother . . . she was . . . she was not gassed.

FAITH. What happened to her?

[HELGA *enters. She is utterly transformed—thin, wizened, old-looking. Her hair is thin and short.*]

HELGA. Ist das Eva? (*Is it Eva?*)

[EVA *is speechless.*]

HELGA. Bist Du das, Eva? (*Is that you, Eva?*)

EVA. Mother?

[HELGA *approaches* EVA *and hugs her.* EVA *tries to hug back but is clearly very uncomfortable.*]

HELGA. Ich hätte Dich nicht erkannt. (*How much you have changed.*)

EVA. I'm sorry. I don't quite understand.

HELGA. How much you have changed.

EVA. So have you.

HELGA. You are sixteen now.

EVA. Seventeen.

HELGA. Blue is suiting to you. A lovely dress.

EVA. Thank you.

HELGA. You are very pretty.

EVA. This is a nice hotel. I can't believe you're here.

HELGA. I promised I would come, Eva.

Eva. I'm called Evelyn now.

Helga. What is Evelyn?

Eva. I changed my name.

Helga. Why?

Eva. I wanted an English name.

Helga. Eva was the name of your great-grandmother.

Eva. I didn't mean any disrespect.

Helga. No. Of course not.

Eva. I'm sorry.

Helga. Nothing is the same any more.

Eva. It's just that I've settled down now.

Helga. These are the pieces of my life.

Eva. There were no letters for all those years and then I saw the newsreels and newspapers . . .

Helga. I am putting them all back together again.

Eva. I thought the worst.

Helga. I always promised that I would come and get you.

Eva. I was a little girl then.

Helga. I am sorry that there has been such a delay. It was not of my making. [*pause*] I am your Mutti, Eva.

Eva. Evelyn.

Helga. Eva. Now I am here, you have back your proper name.

Eva. Evelyn is on my naturalization papers.

Helga. Naturalized as English?

Eva. And adopted by Mr. and Mrs. Miller.

Helga. How can you be adopted when your own mother is alive for you?

Eva. I thought that you were not alive.

Helga. Never mind it. We have all done bad things in the last years that we regret. That is how we survive.

Eva. What did you do?

HELGA. I was right to send you here, yes? It is good to survive. Is it not, Eva?

EVA. Please call me Evelyn.

HELGA. Now we must put our lives right again. We will go to New York where your Onkel Klaus will help us to make a beginning.

EVA. All the way to New York?

HELGA. Who is here for us? No one. The remains of our family is in America.

EVA. I have a family here.

HELGA. These people were just a help to you in bad times. You can to leave them now behind. The bad times are finished. I know it.

EVA. I like it here.

HELGA. You will like it better in America.

EVA. Do I have to go away with you?

HELGA. That is what I came for.

[RATCATCHER *music*]

Scene 2

[*The torn papers and their box have been cleared away.*]

[HELGA, *holding a suitcase, stands in a corner.*]

[EVELYN *has open the box of glasses. She rubs one with a tea towel.*]

[FAITH *watches.*]

EVELYN. [*holding up a glass*] Will these be of any use?

FAITH. Aren't they a bit precious?

EVELYN. You can have them if you want them.

FAITH. If you're sure . . .

Evelyn. Yes or no?

Faith. Yes.

Evelyn. Good. That's glasses done.

[Faith *picks up the box and puts it by the door.*]

[Evelyn *moves on to another box.*]

[Lil *enters. She is wearing a coat.*]

Lil. I'm off out now.

Evelyn. Will you be back for dinner?

Lil. Yes.

Faith. Do you want me to give you a lift to the station tomorrow?

Evelyn. I said that I would.

Faith. You hate driving into town.

Lil. [*to* Faith] I told her she didn't have to.

Evelyn. [*to* Lil] I want to take you to the station.

Lil. You don't need to make anything up to me. I told you. It's all right.

Evelyn. Maybe I feel less all right about it than you do.

Lil. Don't be silly.

Evelyn. Just let me take you.

Lil. All right, take me.

Evelyn. I'll find out about departure times.

Lil. I've already got a timetable.

Evelyn. Fine.

Lil. See you later then.

Evelyn. See you later.

Faith. Bye.

[Lil *exits.*]

[Faith *starts to search through some boxes.*]

Evelyn. Don't you do a thing. You'll only cause a muddle. [*opening a box*] Do you need cutlery?

Faith. What sort?

EVELYN. [*pushing the box to her*] Look at it and decide.

FAITH. This is silver.

EVELYN. I don't like it.

FAITH. Why not?

EVELYN. The design's far too fussy.

FAITH. I like it.

EVELYN. Take it.

FAITH. Thanks.

EVELYN. Not at all.

[FAITH *puts the box by the door.*]

[EVELYN *continues to check boxes.*]

FAITH. Gran didn't know that your mother survived did she?

EVELYN. If she had known, she would have made me go with her.

FAITH. To New York?

EVELYN. She would have handed me back like a borrowed package.

FAITH. She might not.

EVELYN. You know your gran as well as I do, Faith.

FAITH. Did you ever see her after she left?

EVELYN. No.

FAITH. Was she still alive when I was born?

EVELYN. Yes.

FAITH. When did she die?

EVELYN. In 1969.

FAITH. She lived a long time.

EVELYN. She was a very strong woman.

FAITH. Didn't you ever want to be with her?

EVELYN. We didn't get on.

FAITH. You stopped me from knowing her.

EVELYN. I have tried to do my best for you. Please believe that.

FAITH. You stopped her from knowing me.

EVELYN. I wish it could have been simpler. But it wasn't.

FAITH. I just feel that I've lost out on so much.

EVELYN. Don't hanker after the past. It's done.

FAITH. It's still a part of our lives.

EVELYN. It is an abyss.

FAITH. Before, all I knew was a blank space. Now, it's beginning to fill up. I have a background, a context.

EVELYN. All you have now is a pile of ashes.

FAITH. There's far more than ashes, Mum.

EVELYN. [*opening out two boxes*] Crockery?[9]

FAITH. [*looking at it*] It's beautiful.

EVELYN. A collection.

FAITH. Why don't you use it.

EVELYN. I prefer the Royal Crescent set downstairs. That's an old fancy. I've outgrown it.

FAITH. I'll probably break it all.

EVELYN. I hope you won't.

FAITH. I was joking.

EVELYN. You will take care of this home of yours won't you?

FAITH. Of course, I will.

EVELYN. Do you have enough storage space?

FAITH. There's lots of empty cupboards. [*pause*] Am I Jewish?

EVELYN. You've been baptized.

FAITH. Wouldn't the Nazis have said that I was?

EVELYN. You can't let people who hate you tell you what you are.

FAITH. I want to know what it means.

EVELYN. I'm afraid that I can't help.

FAITH. Don't you feel at all Jewish?

---

9. crockery (kräk´ ər ē) *n.* earthenware pots, dishes, and so on.

EVELYN. I was baptized when I was eighteen. I was cleansed that day. Purified.

FAITH. How can you say that?

EVELYN. I have been a great deal happier for it.

FAITH. What about being German?

EVELYN. Germany spat me out. England took me in. I love this place: the language, the countryside, the buildings, the sense of humor, even the food. I danced and sang when I got my first British passport. I was so proud of it. My certificate of belonging. You can't imagine what it was like.

FAITH. Why didn't you tell Dad?

EVELYN. Is it so wrong to want a decent, ordinary life?

FAITH. It's hard starting from scratch.

EVELYN. You can carry on from where you are.

FAITH. Where I am has changed a lot in the last week.

EVELYN. There's a portable television somewhere.

FAITH. This is what you're best at.

EVELYN. What is?

FAITH. Providing for me.

EVELYN. You're hardly able to do it all for yourself yet.

FAITH. I think I'll manage.

EVELYN. Not in the manner to which you have always been accustomed. [*pulling out a desk lamp*] What about a desk lamp?

FAITH. Does it work?

EVELYN. There's no bulb.

FAITH. That's no problem.

[FAITH *turns to pick up a box.*]

FAITH. I'll start taking it all down.

[EVELYN *pulls out the Haggadah and the "Rattenfänger" books.*]

EVELYN. [*holding them out to* FAITH] There are these too.

FAITH. [*putting down the box*] You said everything had been destroyed.

EVELYN. They're just books. You might not want them . . .

FAITH. [*taking the books*] Of course I want them.

EVELYN. One is the storybook and the other is for some Jewish festival.

FAITH. Thank you.

[EVELYN *picks up the mouth organ.*]

EVELYN. And this. It must have come with me.

[FAITH *takes the mouth organ and lays it on top of a box.*]

FAITH. I'd better start taking these down.

[FAITH *picks up a box and starts to exit.*]

EVELYN. Leave it to the left of the door in the hallway, not the right.

[FAITH *exits.*]

[EVELYN *carefully sorts through boxes.*]

[*Sounds of a quayside. A boat is about to leave.*]

[EVA *enters.*]

HELGA. Where have you been?

EVA. I said. In the lavatory.

HELGA. For half an hour in the lavatory?

EVA. I was being sick.

HELGA. Sick?

EVA. I'm all right now.

HELGA. Are you sure?

EVA. Yes.

HELGA. You should change your mind and come with me.

EVA. I haven't got a case.

HELGA. You could have your things sent on.

EVA. You said it was all right to come later.

HELGA. I said I would prefer you to come now. There is enough money from Onkel Klaus for a ticket.

Eva. I can't just leave.

Helga. Why do you not want to be with your mother Eva?

Eva. Evelyn. My name is Evelyn.

Helga. Why are you so cold to me?

Eva. I don't mean to be cold.

Helga. We have been together a week and you are still years away.

Eva. I can't help it.

[*Boat's hooter sounds.*]

Helga. Boats do not wait for people.

Eva. I hope you have a safe trip.

Helga. When is "later" when you are coming?

Eva. In a month or two.

Helga. Just get on the boat with me. Do it now.

Eva. I'm not ready yet. Not at all.

Helga. You're making a mistake.

Eva. You're making me . . .

Helga. What am I making you do! I am your mother. I love you. We must be together.

Eva. We've not been together for too long.

Helga. That is why it is even more important now.

Eva. I can't leave home yet.

Helga. Home is inside you. Inside me and you. It is not a place.

Eva. I don't understand what you mean.

Helga. You are wasting a chance hardly anyone else has been given.

Eva. I will come.

Helga. Will you?

Eva. If you want me to.

Helga. If I want you to?

Eva. Just not yet.

Helga. Do you want to come to make a new life with me?

Eva. You keep asking me that.

Helga. Do you?

Eva. It's hard for me.

Helga. I lost your father. He was sick and they put him in line for the showers. I saw it. You know what I say to you. I lost him. But I did not lose myself. Nearly, a million times over, right on the edge of life, but I held on with my bones rattling inside me. Why have you lost yourself, Eva?

[*Ship's horn sounds out.*]

Helga. I am going to start again. I want my daughter Eva with me. If you find her, Evelyn, by any chance, send her over to find me.

[Helga *embraces* Eva *who stands stock still.*]

[Helga *picks up her case and starts to walk away.*]

Evelyn. [*quietly*] There are four types of daughters: wise, bad, stupid, and the ones who do not know what to ask.

Helga. [*turning round*] Which are you?

Evelyn. Don't look at the razor eyes. Whatever you do.

[*She looks at* Helga.]

Why do you only ever stare at me like that? Are those the only eyes you have? Didn't you have others once? Eyes which didn't burn?

Evelyn. I wish you had died.

Helga. I wish you had lived.

Evelyn. I did my best.

Helga. Hitler started the job and you finished it.

Evelyn. Why does it have to be my fault?

Helga. You cut off my fingers and pulled out my hair one strand at a time.

Evelyn. You were the Ratcatcher. Those were his eyes, his face . . .

HELGA. You hung me out of the window by my ears and broke my soul into shreds.

EVELYN. You threw me into the sea with all your baggage on my shoulders.

HELGA. You can never excuse yourself.

EVELYN. How could I swim ashore with so much heaviness on me? I was drowning in leagues and leagues of salty water.

HELGA. I have bled oceans out of my eyes.

EVELYN. I had to let go to float.

HELGA. Snake. Slithering out of yourself like it was an unwanted skin. Worm.

EVELYN. What right have you got to accuse me? You kept saying something. What was it? Over and over? Yes. "No," you said. That was all. "No. I won't help you. You have to be able to manage on your own. Take the needle. Sew the button and it's time to go. You don't need me. See. It's good." Was it really so very good, Mutti? Was it really what you wanted? It wasn't what I wanted.

HELGA. My suffering is monumental. Yours is personal.

[EVA *exits.*]

EVELYN. What about what you did to me? You should have hung onto me and never let me go. Why did you send me away when you were in danger? No one made you. You chose to do it. Didn't it ever occur to you that I might have wanted to die with you. Because I did. I never wanted to live without you and you made me. What is more cruel than that? Except for coming back from the dead and punishing me for surviving on my own.

◀ **monumental**
(män´ yoo
ment´ 'l) *adj.* of
lasting value or
importance, like
a monument;
massive

[Evelyn *sobs*. Faith *enters*.]

Faith. [*to* Evelyn] Are you crying?

[Faith *tries to get close to* Evelyn. Evelyn *does not turn to face* Faith.]

Faith. What can I do for you? Please tell me what I can do to help?

Evelyn. Stay my little girl forever.

Faith. I can't.

Evelyn. Then there's nothing you can do.

Faith. I'm going to find out what everything means. Get in touch with my relatives. I want to meet them.

Evelyn. You'll find them very different.

Faith. I'm sure they'd love to see you too.

Evelyn. I have nothing in common with them and neither do you.

Faith. I want to put that right.

Evelyn. I don't want you to bring trouble onto yourself.

Faith. There won't be any trouble.

Evelyn. You don't know . . .

Faith. We can do this together. It would make us closer to each other.

Evelyn. I'd rather die than go back.

Faith. You might change your mind . . .

Evelyn. I can't.

[Helga *and* Eva *exit.*]

Faith. Can I have my toys?

Evelyn. Surely you can leave those here.

Faith. I want to take them with me.

Evelyn. I'd like to keep something from when you were little.

Faith. They mean a lot to me.

Evelyn. Take them.

[FAITH *picks up the box of toys.*]

EVELYN. Have you got everything you need now?

FAITH. More or less.

EVELYN. All done in here then.

FAITH. Yes we are.

[FAITH *exits.*]

[*The shadow of the* RATCATCHER *covers the stage.*]

[THE END.]

ABOUT THE AUTHOR

Diane Samuels (b. 1960)

Diane Samuels is a playwright, an author, and a teacher from Liverpool, England. Growing up, she attended Jewish schools. Although she has written many plays, Samuels has received the most acclaim for *Kindertransport*, which was first performed in 1993 and which has been produced in a number of places around the world.

Samuels has this advice for young people who want to be writers: "The thing to do is make sure you practice. It is good to read but if you want to be a writer then writing regularly is more important. And try to find your own voice, even if others don't like it, persevere and be authentic." About her own identity as a writer, she says, "Writing is the backbone of my life, come rain or shine, and as any writer knows, it requires the regular sustained practice demanded of all art forms." She explains that she practices by writing the minute she rises every morning. Samuels adds that she constantly writes down ideas in notebooks and journals and saves them for later.

Close Reading Activities

READ

Comprehension

Reread all or part of the text to help you answer the following questions.

1. Explain Eva and Evelyn's relationship.

2. In Scene 1, what does Evelyn tear up?

3. Whom does Eva wait for at the station?

4. What is the relationship between Evelyn and Lil and between Evelyn and Helga?

5. At the end of Act II, what does Helga ask Eva to do? How does Eva respond?

Research: Clarify Details As you read, you may have encountered references to unfamiliar historical events, cultural traditions, or literary works. Choose one unfamiliar detail from the play and conduct research on it. Explain how your research clarifies the text.

Summarize Write an objective summary of the play. Remember that to be objective, the summary should not include your own opinions or evaluations.

Language Study

Selection Vocabulary Define each boldface word from the selection and use it in a sentence of your own.

• Is it **callous** of me?

• Read some of those if you must have a **morbid** interest in past events.

• My suffering is **monumental.**

Diction and Style Read the lines below and answer the questions.

> Evelyn. It is an abyss.
> Faith. Before, all I knew was a blank space. Now, it's beginning to fill up.

1. (a) What does *abyss* mean? **(b)** What other words might the author have chosen instead? **(c)** For what reason did she likely choose *abyss*? In your answer, consider the word's connotations, or the ideas associated with the word in addition to its literal meaning. Consult a dictionary if needed.

2. (a) What phrase related to *abyss* does Faith use? **(b)** What does the contrast between Evelyn's word and Faith's phrase suggest about the characters?

Conventions Identify the prepositional phrases in the sentence below and explain how they help identify the setting of the play. Then, rewrite the sentence, placing the phrases in a different order. Explain whether reordering the phrases affects the meaning of the sentence.

> [*The play takes place in a spare storage room in Evelyn's house in an outer London suburb in recent times.*]

Academic Vocabulary

The following words appear in blue in the instructions and questions on the facing page.

motive   distinguishes   evidence

Copy the words into your notebook and write the definition of each. Use each word in a sentence of your own. Then, find one related form of each.

Literary Analysis

Reread the identified passages and answer the questions that follow.

> **Focus Passage 1** *(p. 693)*
>
> **FAITH.** Weren't these . . . face of it all.

> **Focus Passage 2** *(pp. 705–706)*
>
> **EVELYN.** You threw me . . . to meet them.

Key Ideas and Details

1. What reason does Evelyn give for destroying the documents?

2. (a) What is Faith's response to the destruction? **(b) Infer:** What does Faith seem to have faith in?

Craft and Structure

3. Faith says of a torn photograph, "Where's the body for these feet?" **(a) Analyze:** What does her word choice suggest about the photograph's link to the person it depicts? **(b) Interpret:** What attitude toward the past is suggested by her concern about the photograph?

4. (a) What word does Evelyn use to describe Faith's interest in the documents? **(b) Interpret:** What is her **motive** in choosing this word?

Integration of Knowledge and Ideas

5. (a) Generalize: What question about our relationship to the past does this passage raise? **(b) Evaluate:** Do you agree more with Faith's or Evelyn's view? Explain.

Key Ideas and Details

1. (a) According to Evelyn, what did Helga refuse to do before they parted? **(b) Infer:** Why did Helga refuse?

2. According to Evelyn, in what way was her mother cruel to her?

Craft and Structure

3. (a) Distinguish: What **distinguishes** the first six speeches from the rest? **(b) Evaluate:** How does the style of these lines add to the power of the encounter between mother and daughter?

4. (a) What choice does Evelyn say she should have been given? **(b) Evaluate:** Is it believable that she feels this way? Explain.

5. (a) Whom does Faith wish to meet? **(b) Interpret:** Explain what the author wants to show by contrasting Helga and Evelyn's dialogue with Evelyn and Faith's.

Integration of Knowledge and Ideas

6. Draw Conclusions: Based on this passage, did Evelyn truly escape the Holocaust? Support your answer with **evidence**.

Plot and Conflict

A **plot** is a series of events that focuses on a **conflict**, or struggle between opposing forces. Conflicts may include a character's struggle with conflicting motives. Reread the play, taking notes on the conflicts that drive it.

1. (a) List one conflict at the start of Scene 1. **(b)** What other conflicts drive Act II?

2. The Holocaust: How does the Holocaust cause or shape each conflict you identify?

Common Core State Standards

RL.8.2, RL.8.3, RL.8.4; L.8.4.a, L.8.5.a, L.8.5.c, L.8.6
[For full standards wording, see the chart in the front of this book.]

DISCUSS

From Text to Topic **Group Discussion**

Discuss this passage with a small group, taking notes. Prepare by conducting research on the *"Rattenfänger"* story and the Haggadah.

> [EVELYN *rips.* LIL *picks up the "Rattenfänger" book and starts to tear out the first page.*]
> **EVELYN.** No. Not that.
> **LIL.** It's in German. Horrible pictures.
> **EVELYN.** You can't damage a book. I'll give it to a secondhand shop.
> **LIL.** [*picking up the Haggadah*] What about this?
> **EVELYN.** That too.

WRITE

Writing to Sources **Argument**

> ### Assignment
> Write an **argumentative essay** in which you support a claim about the benefits and drawbacks of the Kindertransport program.

Prewriting and Planning Reread the play, looking for details about the effects of the Kindertransport on the characters. Group your notes by character or by type of effect.

Drafting Select an organizational structure. Consider one of these options, which help readers "feel" an argument gathering power:

- **Least Important to Most Important** Present your points in order from least to most important.

- **Nestorian Order** Start with your second most important point. Then, present your other points from least to most important, concluding with your most important point.

In your draft, cite specific examples from the play to support your points.

Revising Reread your essay, making sure you have clearly stated your claim in your introduction. Check that each paragraph clearly connects to your claim. Eliminate or replace irrelevant paragraphs. Finally, review your conclusion, making sure it restates your central point.

Editing and Proofreading Dependent clauses—such as "For the survival of the children"—cannot stand alone. Combine them with independent clauses to create complete sentences.

QUESTIONS FOR DISCUSSION

1. How are the books different from the photos and papers Evelyn destroys?

2. In what way does the story in the play resemble the traditional *Rattenfänger* story? In what way does the play make this story new?

3. What aspects of the past do the two books symbolize?

4. What do these symbols suggest about Evelyn's decision not to remember? Does she truly have a choice? Explain.

CONVENTIONS

When a sentence features a dependent and an independent clause, and the dependent clause comes first, it should be followed by a comma: *If Helga had escaped earlier, Eva would have welcomed her.*

RESEARCH

Research **Investigate the Topic**

Holocaust Survivors Near the end of Scene 2, Helga says, "You are wasting a chance hardly anyone else has been given." She implies that after the Holocaust, reunions with family members who had been sent to concentration camps were rare. Many were killed in the camps, and even those who survived might have difficulty locating their families.

Assignment

Conduct research to find out how common or rare it was for survivors of the Holocaust to reunite with family and what difficulties these reunions may have presented. Consult a variety of sources. Take clear notes and carefully identify your sources. Write a **historical analysis** combining both statistical data and firsthand accounts of such reunions.

PREPARATION FOR ESSAY

You may use the results of this research project to support your ideas in the essay you will write at the end of this section.

Gather Sources Locate authoritative print and electronic sources, starting with general resources on Holocaust survivors. To determine the credibility of a source, look at the credentials of its creators. Favor sources by scholars. Consider also their motives: A Web site sponsored by a university is more likely to be objective than one sponsored by a political group. Comb your sources' bibliographies, notes, and links for resources, such as Web sites, that may contain detailed data on survivors or personal accounts of reunions.

Take Notes Take notes on each source, either electronically or on note cards. After a note-taking session, review your notes.

- Next to each note, jot down the subtopic it covers. Doing so will help you sort your notes later as you draft.

- If you discover that a note is unclear, return to the source and revise your note as necessary to clarify.

Synthesize Multiple Sources Use your notes to construct an outline for your analysis. Organize both statistical data and firsthand accounts into a cohesive presentation. Remember not to rely too much on any single source. Finally, create a Works Cited list, as described in the Citing Sources pages in the Introductory Unit of this textbook.

Organize and Present Ideas Follow your outline as you draft. When you have finished, review your draft against your outline and your notes to ensure you have covered all important points.

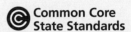

Common Core State Standards

RL.8.9; W.8.1.a, W.8.1.b, W.8.1.e, W.8.4, W.8.5, W.8.7, W.8.8; SL.8.1, SL.8.1.a; L.8.2.a
[For full standards wording, see the chart in the front of this book.]

from ANNE FRANK:
THE DIARY OF A YOUNG GIRL

Saturday, 20 June, 1942

. . . There is a saying that "paper is more patient than man"; it came back to me on one of my slightly melancholy days, while I sat chin in hand, feeling too bored and limp even to make up my mind whether to go out or stay at home. Yes, there is no doubt that paper is patient and as I don't intend to show this cardboard-covered notebook, bearing the proud name of "diary," to anyone, unless I find a real friend, boy or girl, probably nobody cares. And now I come to the root of the matter, the reason for my starting a diary: it is that I have no such real friend.

Let me put it more clearly, since no one will believe that a girl of thirteen feels herself quite alone in the world, nor is it so. I have darling parents and a sister of sixteen. I know about thirty people whom one might call friends—I have strings of boy friends, anxious to catch a glimpse of me and who, failing that, peep at me through mirrors in class. I have relations, aunts and uncles, who are darlings too, a good home, no—I don't seem to lack anything. But it's the same with all my friends, just fun and joking, nothing more. I can never bring myself to talk of anything outside the common round. We don't seem to be able to get any closer, that is the root of the trouble. Perhaps I lack confidence, but anyway, there it is, a stubborn fact and I don't seem to be able to do anything about it.

Hence, this diary. In order to enhance in my mind's eye the picture of the friend for whom I have waited so long, I don't want to set down a series of bald facts in a diary like most people do, but I want this diary itself to be my friend, and I shall call my friend Kitty. No one will grasp what I'm talking about if I begin my letters to Kitty just out of the blue, so, albeit[1] unwillingly, I will start by sketching in brief the story of my life.

My father was thirty-six when he married my mother, who was then twenty-five. My sister Margot was born in 1926 in Frankfort-on-Main, I followed on June 12, 1929, and, as we are Jewish, we emigrated to Holland in 1933, where my father was appointed Managing Director of Travies N.V. This firm is in close relationship with the firm of Kolen & Co. in the same building, of which my father is a partner.

The rest of our family, however, felt the full impact of Hitler's anti-Jewish laws, so life was filled with anxiety. In 1938 after the pogroms,[2] my two uncles (my mother's brothers) escaped to the U.S.A. My old grandmother came to us, she was then seventy-three. After May 1940 good times rapidly fled: first the war, then the capitulation,[3] followed by the arrival of the Germans, which is when the sufferings of us Jews really began. Anti-Jewish decrees followed each other in quick succession. Jews must wear a yellow star, Jews must hand in their bicycles, Jews are banned from trains and are forbidden to drive. Jews are only allowed to do their shopping between three and five o'clock and then only in shops which bear the placard "Jewish shop." Jews must be indoors by eight o'clock and cannot even sit in their own gardens after that hour. Jews are forbidden to visit theaters, cinemas, and other places of entertainment. Jews may not take part in public sports. Swimming baths, tennis courts, hockey fields, and other sports grounds are all prohibited to them. Jews may not visit Christians. Jews must go to Jewish schools, and many more restrictions of a similar kind.

So we could not do this and were forbidden to do that. But life went on in spite of it all. Jopie[4] used to say to me, "You're

◄ **enhance**
(en hans´) *v.*
improve the
quality of

◄ **emigrated**
(em´ i grāt´ əd) *v.*
left one place to
settle in another

---

1. **albeit** (ôl bē´ it) *conj.* although.
2. **pogroms** (pō´ grəmz) *n.* organized killings and other persecution of Jews.
3. **capitulation** (kə pich´ yōō lā´ shən) *n.* act of surrendering.
4. **Jopie** (yō´ pē) Jacqueline van Maarsen, Anne's best friend.

scared to do anything, because it may be forbidden." Our freedom was strictly limited. Yet things were still bearable.

Granny died in January 1942; no one will ever know how much she is present in my thoughts and how much I love her still.

In 1934 I went to school at the Montessori Kindergarten and continued there. It was at the end of the school year, I was in form 6B, when I had to say good-by to Mrs. K. We both wept, it was very sad. In 1941 I went, with my sister Margot, to the Jewish Secondary School, she into the fourth form[5] and I into the first.

So far everything is all right with the four of us and here I come to the present day.

Thursday, 19 November, 1942

Dear Kitty,

Dussel is a very nice man, just as we had all imagined. Of course he thought it was all right to share my little room.

Quite honestly I'm not so keen that a stranger should use my things, but one must be prepared to make some sacrifices for a good cause, so I shall make my little offering with a good will. "If we can save someone, then everything else is of secondary importance," says Daddy, and he's absolutely right.

The first day that Dussel was here, he immediately asked me all sorts of questions: When does the charwoman[6] come? When can one use the bathroom? When is one allowed to use the lavatory?[7] You may laugh, but these things are not so simple in a hiding place. During the day we mustn't make any noise that might be heard downstairs; and if there is some stranger—such as the charwoman for example—then we have to be extra careful. I explained all this carefully to Dussel. But one thing amazed me: he is very slow on the uptake. He asks everything twice over and still doesn't seem to remember. Perhaps that will wear off in time, and it's only that he's thoroughly upset by the sudden change.

Apart from that, all goes well. Dussel has told us a lot about the outside world, which we have missed for so long now. He had very sad news. Countless friends and acquaintances have gone to a terrible fate. Evening after evening the green

"If we can save someone, then everything else is of secondary importance. . . ."

---

5. **fourth form** here, a grade in secondary school.
6. **charwoman** n. cleaning woman.
7. **lavatory** n. toilet.

and gray army lorries trundle past.[8] The Germans ring at every front door to inquire if there are any Jews living in the house. If there are, then the whole family has to go at once. If they don't find any, they go on to the next house. No one has a chance of **evading** them unless one goes into hiding. Often they go around with lists, and only ring when they know they can get a good haul. Sometimes they let them off for cash—so much per head. It seems like the slave hunts of olden times. But it's certainly no joke; it's much too tragic for that. In the evenings when it's dark, I often see rows of good, innocent people accompanied by crying children, walking on and on, in charge of a couple of these chaps, bullied and knocked about until they almost drop. No one is spared—old people, babies, expectant mothers, the sick—each and all join in the march of death.

◄ **evading**
(ē vād´ iŋ) v. avoiding or escaping from through the use of deceit or cleverness

How fortunate we are here, so well cared for and undisturbed. We wouldn't have to worry about all this misery were it not that we are so anxious about all those dear to us whom we can no longer help.

I feel wicked sleeping in a warm bed, while my dearest friends have been knocked down or have fallen into a gutter somewhere out in the cold night. I get frightened when I think of close friends who have now been delivered into the hands of the cruelest brutes that walk the earth. And all because they are Jews!

Yours, Anne

---

8. **lorries trundle past** trucks move along.

ABOUT THE AUTHOR

Anne Frank (1929–1945)

In 1942, Anne Frank and her family, living in Holland, went into hiding from the Nazis. While in hiding, Anne worked on a novel and short stories as well as her diary. When the Nazis raided the Franks' hiding place, they scattered the pages of the diary but did not take them. Miep Gies, possibly with other people, later collected them, saved them unread, and presented them to Otto Frank. Anne died of typhus in the concentration camp Bergen-Belsen.

READ

Comprehension

Reread all or part of the text to help you answer the following questions.

1. Who is Kitty?

2. Who is Dussel?

3. What news does Dussel bring?

Research: Clarify Details Choose one unfamiliar detail from the diary and conduct research on it. Explain how your research clarifies the text.

Summarize Write an objective summary of the text. Do not include your own opinions.

Language Study

Selection Vocabulary Define each boldface word from the selection. Then, list two different forms of each (e.g., *move/movement/mover*).

• In order to **enhance** in my mind's eye the picture of the friend . . .

• . . . as we are Jewish, we **emigrated** to Holland in 1933. . . .

• No one has a chance of **evading** them unless one goes into hiding.

Literary Analysis

Reread the identified passage and answer the questions that follow.

> **Focus Passage** *(p. 714)*
>
> The first day that . . . sudden change.

Key Ideas and Details

1. (a) What does Dussel ask? **(b) Analyze:** How does he respond to the answers?

Craft and Structure

2. (a) Where does Anne use *you* in this paragraph? **(b)** Who is the "you" referred to?

(c) Draw Conclusions: How does this use of second person reflect Anne's purpose and audience?

3. (a) Analyze: What question word does Dussel repeat? **(b) Interpret:** What does this repetition emphasize?

Integration of Knowledge and Ideas

4. Draw Conclusions: What do Anne's **observations** of Dussel show about her strengths as a person? Explain, citing details from the text.

Diary

A **diary** is a daily account of its writer's life, not usually intended for an audience. Reread the selection, noting the characteristics of this form of writing.

1. (a) What kinds of details does Anne record in her November entry? **(b)** How might recording these details have helped Anne?

2. (a) How did the diary serve Anne's purposes when she wrote it? Support your answer with textual details. **(b) The Holocaust:** Though Anne died during the Holocaust, do you think she lives on through her diary? Explain.

DISCUSS • RESEARCH • WRITE

From Text to Topic **Partner Discussion**

Discuss the following passage with a partner. Take notes during the discussion. Contribute your own ideas, and support them with examples from the text.

> Yes, there is no doubt that paper is patient and as I don't intend to show this cardboard-covered notebook, bearing the proud name of "diary," to anyone, unless I find a real friend, boy or girl, probably nobody cares. And now I come to the root of the matter, the reason for my starting a diary: it is that I have no such real friend.

Research **Investigate the Topic**

Survival in Print   Although the diary was Anne's private journal, in its published form the diary is for the public, and it keeps people from forgetting Anne and the Holocaust.

Assignment

Conduct research to learn about the places where Anne's diary is read, the number of copies sold, and the other works—such as movies and music—that use it as inspiration. **Investigate** up-to-date resources that provide statistics about the diary. Take clear notes and carefully identify your sources. Share your findings with the class in a **visual presentation** with graphs and maps.

Writing to Sources **Narrative Text**

Anne's diary provides her point of view on Dussel's arrival, when he becomes the eighth person to occupy the already crowded hiding place. Imagine Dussel's own point of view on his arrival.

Assignment

Write a **first-person narrative** in which you retell Dussel's arrival from Dussel's point of view. Follow these steps:

• Orient your reader by establishing the situation.

• Use diary details to tell events.

• Use **precise** language as you weave Dussel's thoughts and feelings into his story.

• Provide a conclusion in which Dussel reflects on his situation.

QUESTIONS FOR DISCUSSION

1. What reason does Anne identify for keeping her diary?

2. How might learning Anne's thoughts help readers see the injustice of her death?

3. Why might publishing Anne's private thoughts and feelings be the right thing to do?

PREPARATION FOR ESSAY

You may use the results of this research project to support your ideas in the essay you will write at the end of this section.

ACADEMIC VOCABULARY

Academic terms appear in blue on these pages. Use a dictionary to find their definitions. Then, use the words as you speak and write about the text.

Common Core State Standards

RI.8.1, RI.8.2, RI.8.6; W.8.3, W.8.3.a, W.8.3.d, W.8.3.e
[For full standards wording, see the chart in the front of this book.]

from Anne Frank Remembered

Miep Gies with Alison Leslie Gold

H enk[1] flew home that day to tell me. It was June 3, 1945. He ran into the living room and grabbed me. "Miep, Otto Frank is coming back!"

My heart took flight. Deep down I'd always known that he would, that the others would, too.

Just then, my eye caught sight of a figure passing outside our window. My throat closed. I ran outside.

There was Mr. Frank himself, walking toward our door.

We looked at each other. There were no words. He was thin, but he'd always been thin. He carried a little bundle.

---

1. **Henk** Jan "Henk" Gies became Miep's husband in 1941. He too was an active resister of the Nazis during the Second World War.

My eyes swam. My heart melted. Suddenly, I was afraid to know more. I didn't want to know what had happened. I knew I would not ask.

We stood facing each other, speechless. Finally, Frank spoke.

"Miep," he said quietly. "Miep, Edith is not coming back."

My throat was pierced. I tried to hide my reaction to his thunderbolt. "Come inside," I insisted.

He went on. "But I have great hope for Margot and Anne."

"Yes. Great hope," I echoed encouragingly. "Come inside."

He still stood there. "Miep, I came here because you and Henk are the ones closest to me who are still here."

I grabbed his bundle from his hand. "Come, you stay right here with us. Now, some food. You have a room here with us for as long as you want."

He came inside. I made up a bedroom for him, and put everything we had into a fine meal for him. We ate. Mr. Frank told us he had ended up in Auschwitz. That was the last time he'd seen Edith, Margot, and Anne. The men had been separated from the women immediately. When the Russians liberated the camp in January, he had been taken on a very long trip to Odessa. Then from there to Marseille by ship, and at last, by train and truck to Holland.

He told us these few things in his soft voice. He spoke very little, but between us there was no need for words.

▲ Staff at Otto Frank's Opekta office in Amsterdam, Holland.

Mr. Frank settled in with Henk and me. Right away, he came back to the office and took his place again as the head of the business. I know he was relieved to have something to do each day. Meanwhile, he began exploring the network of information on Jews in the camps—the refugee agencies, the daily lists, the most crucial word-of-mouth information—trying everything to get news about Margot and Anne.

When Auschwitz was liberated, Otto Frank had gone right away to the women's camp to find out about his wife and children. In the chaos and desolation of the camps, he had learned that Edith had died shortly before the liberation.

He had also learned that in all likelihood, Margot and Anne had been transferred to another camp, along with Mrs. van Daan. The camp was called Bergen-Belsen, and was quite a distance from Auschwitz. That was as far as his trail had gone so far, though. Now he was trying to pick up the search.

As to the other men, Mr. Frank had lost track of Albert Dussel. He had no idea what had happened to him after the transit camp of Westerbork. He had seen with his own eyes Mr. van Daan on his way to be gassed. And Peter van Daan had come to visit Frank in the Auschwitz infirmary. Mr. Frank knew that right before the liberation of the camp, the Germans had taken groups of prisoners with them in their retreat. Peter had been in one of these groups.

Otto Frank had begged Peter to try to get into the infirmary himself, but Peter couldn't or wouldn't. He had last been seen going off with the retreating Germans into the snow-covered countryside. There was no further news about him.

Mr. Frank held high hopes for the girls, because Bergen-Belsen was not a death camp. There were no gassings there. It was a work camp—filled with hunger and disease, but with no apparatus for liquidation.[2] Because Margot and Anne had been sent to the camp later than most other inmates they were relatively healthy. I too lived on hope for Margot and Anne. In some deep part of me, like a rock, I counted on their survival and their safe return to Amsterdam.

Mr. Frank had written for news to several Dutch people who he had learned had been in Bergen-Belsen. Through word of mouth people were being reunited every day. Daily, he waited

---

2. liquidation (lik′ wi dā′ shən) *n.* act of getting rid of or killing.

for answers to his letters and for the new lists of survivors to be released and posted. Every time there was a knock at the door or footfalls on the steps, all our hearts would stand still. Perhaps Margot and Anne had found their way back home, and we could see them with our own eyes at last. Anne's sixteenth birthday was coming on June 12. Perhaps, we hoped, . . . but then the birthday came and went, and still no news.

⚜

One morning, Mr. Frank and I were alone in the office, opening mail. He was standing beside me, and I was sitting at my desk. I was vaguely aware of the sound of a letter being slit open. Then, a moment of silence. Something made me look away from my mail. Then, Otto Frank's voice, toneless, totally crushed: "Miep."

My eyes looked up at him, seeking out his eyes.

"Miep." He gripped a sheet of paper in both his hands. "I've gotten a letter from the nurse in Rotterdam. Miep, Margot and Anne are not coming back."

We stayed there like that, both struck by lightning, burnt thoroughly through our hearts, our eyes fixed on each other's. Then Mr. Frank walked toward his office and said in that defeated voice, "I'll be in my office."

I heard him walk across the room and down the hall, and the door closed.

"I've gotten a letter from the nurse in Rotterdam. Miep, Margot and Anne are not coming back."

I sat at my desk utterly crushed. Everything that had happened before, I could somehow accept. Like it or not, I had to accept it. But this, I could not accept. It was the one thing I'd been sure would not happen.

I heard the others coming into the office. I heard a door opening and a voice chattering. Then, good-morning greetings and coffee cups. I reached into the drawer on the side of my desk and took out the papers that had been waiting there for Anne for nearly a year now. No one, including me, had touched them. Now Anne was not coming back for her diary.

I took out all the papers, placing the little red-orange checkered diary on top, and carried everything into Mr. Frank's office.

Frank was sitting at his desk, his eyes murky with shock. I held out the diary and the papers to him. I said, "Here is your daughter Anne's legacy to you."

I could tell that he recognized the diary. He had given it to her just over three years before, on her thirteenth birthday, right before going into hiding. He touched it with the tips of his fingers. I pressed everything into his hands; then I left his office, closing the door quietly.

Shortly afterward, the phone on my desk rang. It was Mr. Frank's voice. "Miep, please see to it that I'm not disturbed." he said.

"I've already done that," I replied.

"Miep, you must read Anne's writing. Who would have imagined what went on in her quick little mind?"

The second printing of the diary sold out and another printing was planned. Mr. Frank was approached with the idea of permiting the diary to be translated and published abroad. He was against it at first, but then he **succumbed** to the pressure on him to allow the diary a more widespread audience.

Again and again, he'd say to me, "Miep, you must read Anne's writing. Who would have imagined what went on in her quick little mind?" Otto was never discouraged by my continuing refusal. He would always wait awhile and then ask me again.

Finally, I gave in to his insistence. I said, "All right, I will read the diary, but only when I'm totally alone."

The next time I was totally alone, on a warm day, I took the second printing of the diary, went to my room, and shut the door.

With awful fear in my heart, I opened the book and turned to the first page.

And so I began to read.

I read the whole diary without stopping. From the first word, I heard Anne's voice come back to speak to me from where she had gone. I lost track of time. Anne's voice tumbled out of the book, so full of life, moods, curiosity, feelings. She was no longer gone and destroyed. She was alive again in my mind.

succumbed ▶
(sə kumd´) *v.* gave way; yielded; submitted

I read to the very end. I was surprised by how much had happened in hiding that I'd known nothing about. Immediately, I was thankful that I hadn't read the diary after the arrest, during the final nine months of the occupation, while it had stayed in my desk drawer right beside me every day. Had I read it, I would have had to burn the diary because it would have been too dangerous for people about whom Anne had written.

When I had read the last word, I didn't feel the pain I'd anticipated. I was glad I'd read it at last. The emptiness in my heart was eased. So much had been lost, but now Anne's voice would never be lost. My young friend had left a remarkable legacy to the world.

But always, every day of my life, I've wished that things had been different. That even had Anne's diary been lost to the world, Anne and the others might somehow have been saved.

Not a day goes by that I do not grieve for them.

ABOUT THE AUTHOR

Miep Gies (1909–2010)

Miep Gies was born Hermine Santruschitz (also spelled "Santrouschitz") in Vienna, Austria. As a child, she suffered during the food shortages that followed World War I. Fortunately, she was rescued by a Dutch program that took in starving Austrian children. Gies went to live with a new family, who gave her the Dutch name Miep, a term of affection. While in the Netherlands, Gies's life improved, and she became so happy that her parents consented to her remaining there.

When Gies was in her mid-twenties, she was hired by Otto Frank to run the complaint and information desk at his company. Over the years, she grew closer to Frank and his family. When the Franks were forced into hiding, she immediately offered her support.

Gies married Jan (Henk) Gies, who also actively resisted the Nazis, in 1941. She lived to be 100.

Close Reading Activities

READ

Comprehension

Reread all or part of the text to help you answer the following questions.

1. What historical events allow Mr. Frank to return to Holland?

2. What has happened to his family?

3. What does Miep Gies give Mr. Frank? What does he do with this item?

Research: Clarify Details Choose one unfamiliar detail from the memoir and conduct research on it. Explain how your research clarifies the text.

Summarize Write an objective summary of the memoir. Remember not to include your own opinions.

Language Study

Selection Vocabulary Define each boldface word from the selection.

• . . . the network of information on Jews in the camps—the **refugee** agencies . . .

• . . . the **chaos** and desolation of the camps . . .

• . . . he **succumbed** to the pressure on him. . . .

Literary Analysis

Reread the identified passage and answer the questions that follow.

> **Focus Passage** (p. 721)
>
> One morning . . . the door closed.

Key Ideas and Details

1. **(a)** What has Mr. Frank learned? **(b)** How has he learned it?

Craft and Structure

2. **(a) Interpret:** What does Gies describe using the commonplace metaphor "struck by lightning"? **(b) Connect:** How does the next phrase both intensify the metaphor and make it more original?

Integration of Knowledge and Ideas

3. **Evaluate:** Should Gies have said more to comfort Mr. Frank? Explain why or why not.

Narrative Pacing

Narrative pacing refers to ways writers shape the flow of information—how much information readers receive in a given space, and in what order. Reread the memoir, and take notes on pacing.

1. **(a)** In the first paragraph of the Focus Passage (identified above), which details emphasize Gies's experience? **(b)** How does the writer use these details to build to

Mr. Frank's news? **(c)** How does Gies "stretch out" the last sentence of the passage to add drama to Mr. Frank's exit?

2. Find and explain another example of the use of narrative pacing in the selection.

3. **The Holocaust:** Explain how the narrative pacing in the selection helps emphasize the effects of the Holocaust on individuals.

DISCUSS • RESEARCH • WRITE

From Text to Topic **Partner Discussion**

With a partner, discuss whether publishing Anne's diary created an ideal memorial to the Holocaust—or whether the reader's gratitude that Anne's voice was rescued might limit **perception** of the event's full horror. Begin by responding to the passage below.

> When I had read the last word, I didn't feel the pain I'd anticipated. I was glad I'd read it at last. The emptiness in my heart was eased. So much had been lost, but now Anne's voice would never be lost. My young friend had left a remarkable legacy to the world.

Research **Investigate the Topic**

Historical Causes Gies's memoir includes references to many historical events. What led to the **transfer** of Anne to Bergen-Belsen, to the liberation of Auschwitz, or to Mr. Frank's journey to Odessa?

Assignment

Conduct research into the causes of the events identified above. Consult both general works and histories of the concentration camps. Take clear notes and carefully identify your sources. Create a **timeline** of Holocaust events, including a brief explanation of each event you list.

Writing to Sources **Explanatory Text**

In her memoir, Gies describes her changing view of Anne's diary—from private **document** to legacy for Mr. Frank to legacy for the world.

Assignment

Write an **analytical essay** in which you outline the changes in Gies's perspective on the diary. Consider how the diary is transformed from a private to a public document, and how this transformation is linked to Anne's death. Follow these steps:

- Introduce your main claim in an introductory paragraph.
- Support your analysis with details from Gies's text.
- Link ideas using transitional words, phrases, and clauses, such as *by that time, for this reason,* and *despite this fact.*
- Provide a concluding sentence or paragraph.

QUESTIONS FOR DISCUSSION

1. What does Gies see as the value of the diary?
2. Is the diary a kind of victory over the Holocaust? Explain.
3. What functions should a memorial to Holocaust victims fulfill?

PREPARATION FOR ESSAY

You may use the results of this research project to support your ideas in the essay you will write at the end of this section.

ACADEMIC VOCABULARY

Academic terms appear in blue on these pages. Use a dictionary to find their definitions. Then, use the words as you speak and write about the text.

Common Core State Standards

RI.8.1, RI.8.2, RI.8.6;
W.8.2.a, W.8.2.b, W.8.2.c,
W.8.2.f; SL.8.1, SL.8.4;
L.8.4, L.8.6
[For full standards wording, see the chart in the front of this book.]

from

NIGHT

Elie Wiesel
translated by Marion Wiesel

That same night, we reached our destination.

It was late. The guards came to unload us. The dead were left in the wagons. Only those who could stand could leave.

Meir Katz remained on the train. The last day had been the most lethal. We had been a hundred or so in this wagon. Twelve of us left it. Among them, my father and myself.

We had arrived in Buchenwald.[1]

At the entrance to the camp, SS[2] officers were waiting for us. We were counted. Then we were directed to the *Appelplatz*.[3] The orders were given over the loudspeakers:

"Form ranks of fives! Groups of one hundred! Five steps forward!"

I tightened my grip on my father's hand. The old, familiar fear: not to lose him.

Very close to us stood the tall chimney of the crematorium's[4] furnace. It no longer impressed us. It barely drew our attention.

A veteran of Buchenwald told us that we would be taking a shower and afterward be sent to different blocks. The idea of a hot shower fascinated me. My father didn't say a word. He was breathing heavily beside me.

"Father," I said, "just another moment. Soon, we'll be able to lie down. You'll be able to rest . . ."

He didn't answer. I myself was so weary that his silence left me indifferent. My only wish was to take the shower as soon as possible and lie down on a cot.

Only it wasn't easy to reach the showers. Hundreds of prisoners crowded the area. The guards seemed unable to restore order. They were lashing out, left and right, to no avail. Some prisoners who didn't have the strength to jostle, or even to stand, sat down in the snow. My father wanted to do the same. He was moaning:

"I can't anymore . . . It's over . . . I shall die right here . . ."

He dragged me toward a pile of snow from which **protruded** human shapes, torn blankets.

◄ Transport to Auschwitz, a German concentration camp in Poland, in 1944.

◄ **protruded**
(prō trōōd´ əd)
v. stuck out

---

1. **Buchenwald** (bōō´ kən wôld´) village in Germany that was the site of a Nazi concentration camp.
2. **SS** Abbreviation for German *Schutzstaffel* (shoots´ shtäf´ ´l), the name for the Nazi special police.
3. *Appelplatz* (äp´ ´l pläts´) square where roll call took place; often spelled *Appellplatz*.
4. **crematorium's** (krē´ mə tôr´ ē əmz) *n.* A crematorium was a large oven in which the corpses of Holocaust victims were burned. In some cases, victims were burned while still alive.

"Leave me," he said. "I can't go on anymore . . . Have pity on me . . . I'll wait here until we can go into the showers . . . You'll come and get me."

I could have screamed in anger. To have lived and endured so much; was I going to let my father die now? Now that we would be able to take a good hot shower and lie down?

"Father!" I howled. "Father! Get up! Right now! You will kill yourself . . ."

And I grabbed his arm. He continued to moan:

"Don't yell, my son . . . Have pity on your old father . . . Let me rest here . . . a little . . . I beg of you, I'm so tired . . . no more strength . . ."

He had become childlike: weak, frightened, vulnerable.

"Father," I said, "you cannot stay here."

I pointed to the corpses around him; they too had wanted to rest here.

"I see, my son. I do see them. Let them sleep. They haven't closed an eye for so long . . . They're exhausted . . . exhausted . . ."

His voice was tender.

I howled into the wind:

"They're dead! They will never wake up! Never! Do you understand?"

This discussion continued for some time. I knew that I was no longer arguing with him but with Death itself, with Death that he had already chosen.

The sirens began to wail. Alert. The lights went out in the entire camp. The guards chased us toward the blocks. In a flash, there was no one left outside. We were only too glad not to have to stay outside any longer, in the freezing wind. We let ourselves sink into the floor. The cauldrons at the entrance found no takers. There were several tiers of bunks. To sleep was all that mattered.

When I woke up, it was daylight. That is when I remembered that I had a father. During the alert, I had followed the mob, not taking care of him. I knew he was running out of strength, close to death, and yet I had abandoned him.

I went to look for him.

Yet at the same time a thought crept into my mind: If only I didn't find him! If only I were relieved of this responsibility, I could use all my strength to fight for my own survival, to take care only of myself . . . Instantly, I felt ashamed, ashamed of myself forever.

vulnerable ▶
(vul′ nər ə bəl) *adj.* open to attack or injury

I walked for hours without finding him. Then I came to a block where they were distributing black "coffee." People stood in line, quarreled.

A plaintive voice came from behind me:

"Eliezer, my son . . . bring me . . . a little coffee . . ."

I ran toward him.

"Father! I've been looking for you for so long . . . Where were you? Did you sleep? How are you feeling?"

He seemed to be burning with fever. I fought my way to the coffee cauldron like a wild beast. And I succeeded in bringing back a cup. I took one gulp. The rest was for him.

I shall never forget the gratitude that shone in his eyes when he swallowed this beverage. The gratitude of a wounded animal. With these few mouthfuls of hot water, I had probably given him more satisfaction than during my entire childhood . . .

He was lying on the boards, ashen, his lips pale and dry, shivering. I couldn't stay with him any longer. We had been ordered to go outside to allow for cleaning of the blocks. Only the sick could remain inside.

We stayed outside for five hours. We were given soup. When they allowed us to return to the blocks, I rushed toward my father:

"Did you eat?"

"No."

"Why?"

"They didn't give us anything . . . They said that we were sick, that we would die soon, and that it would be a waste of food . . . I can't go on . . ."

I gave him what was left of my soup. But my heart was heavy. I was aware that I was doing it grudgingly.

Just like Rabbi Eliahu's son,[5] I had not passed the test.

Every day, my father was getting weaker. His eyes were watery, his face the color of dead leaves. On the third day after we arrived in Buchenwald, everybody had to go to the showers. Even the sick, who were instructed to go last.

When we returned from the showers, we had to wait outside a long time. The cleaning of the blocks had not been completed.

---

5. **Rabbi Eliahu's son** Earlier in *Night*, Eliezer has witnessed a son abandoning his father, Rabbi Eliahu, by pretending not to notice when his father falls behind on a forced march.

From afar, I saw my father and ran to meet him. He went by me like a shadow, passing me without stopping, without a glance. I called to him, he did not turn around. I ran after him:

"Father, where are you running?"

He looked at me for a moment and his gaze was distant, otherworldly, the face of a stranger. It lasted only a moment and then he ran away.

Suffering from dysentery,[6] my father was prostrate on his cot, with another five sick inmates nearby. I sat next to him, watching him; I no longer dared to believe that he could still elude Death. I did all I could to give him hope.

All of a sudden, he sat up and placed his feverish lips against my ear:

"Eliezer . . . I must tell you where I buried the gold and silver . . . In the cellar . . . You know . . ."

And he began talking, faster and faster, afraid of running out of time before he could tell me everything. I tried to tell him that it was not over yet, that we would be going home together, but he no longer wanted to listen to me. He *could* no longer listen to me. He was worn out. Saliva mixed with blood was trickling from his lips. He had closed his eyes. He was gasping more than breathing.

For a ration of bread I was able to exchange cots to be next to my father. When the doctor arrived in the afternoon, I went to tell him that my father was very ill.

"Bring him here!"

I explained that he could not stand up, but the doctor would not listen. And so, with great difficulty, I brought my father to him. He stared at him, then asked curtly:

"What do you want?"

"My father is sick," I answered in his place . . . "Dysentery . . ."

"That's not my business. I'm a surgeon. Go on. Make room for the others!"

My protests were in vain.

"I can't go on, my son . . . Take me back to my bunk."

I took him back and helped him lie down. He was shivering.

"Try to get some sleep, Father. Try to fall asleep . . ."

His breathing was labored. His eyes were closed. But I was convinced that he was seeing everything. That he was seeing the truth in all things.

---

6. **dysentery** (dis´ ən ter´ ē) *n.* disease of the intestines.

Another doctor came to the block. My father refused to get up. He knew that it would be of no use.

In fact, that doctor had come only to finish off the patients. I listened to him shouting at them that they were lazy good-for-nothings who only wanted to stay in bed . . . I considered jumping him, strangling him. But I had neither the courage nor the strength. I was riveted to my father's agony. My hands were aching, I was clenching them so hard. To strangle the doctor and the others! To set the whole world on fire! My father's murderers! But even the cry stuck in my throat.

On my return from the bread distribution, I found my father crying like a child:

"My son, they are beating me!"

"Who?" I thought he was **delirious**.

"Him, the Frenchman . . . and the Pole . . . They beat me . . ."

One more stab to the heart, one more reason to hate. One less reason to live.

"Eliezer . . . Eliezer . . . tell them not to beat me . . . I haven't done anything . . . Why are they beating me?"

I began to insult his neighbors. They mocked me. I promised them bread, soup. They laughed. Then they got angry; they could not stand my father any longer, they said, because he no longer was able to drag himself outside to relieve himself.

The following day, he complained that they had taken his ration of bread.

"While you were asleep?"

"No. I wasn't asleep. They threw themselves on me. They snatched it from me, my bread . . . And they beat me . . . Again . . . I can't go on, my son . . . Give me some water . . ."

I knew that he must not drink. But he pleaded with me so long that I gave in. Water was the worst poison for him, but what else could I do for him? With or without water, it would be over soon anyway . . .

"You, at least, have pity on me . . ."

Have pity on him! I, his only son . . .

A week went by like that.

"Is this your father?" asked the *Blockälteste*.[7]

"Yes."

◀ **delirious**
(di lir´ ē əs) *adj.* in a state of extreme mental excitement; restless, confused, and hallucinating, or perceiving imaginary things

---

7. *Blockälteste* (blok´ el´ tes tə) the head of the block, or barracks, who is himself an inmate at Buchenwald.

"He is very sick."

"The doctor won't do anything for him."

He looked me straight in the eye:

"The doctor *cannot* do anything more for him. And neither can you."

He placed his big, hairy hand on my shoulder and added:

"Listen to me, kid. Don't forget that you are in a concentration camp. In this place, it is every man for himself, and you cannot think of others. Not even your father. In this place, there is no such thing as father, brother, friend. Each of us lives and dies alone. Let me give you good advice: stop giving your ration of bread and soup to your old father. You cannot help him anymore. And you are hurting yourself. In fact, you should be getting *his* rations . . ."

I listened to him without interrupting. He was right, I thought deep down, not daring to admit it to myself. Too late to save your old father . . . You could have two rations of bread, two rations of soup . . .

It was only a fraction of a second, but it left me feeling guilty. I ran to get some soup and brought it to my father. But he did not want it. All he wanted was water.

"Don't drink water, eat the soup . . ."

"I'm burning up . . . Why are you so mean to me, my son? . . . Water . . ."

I brought him water. Then I left the block for roll call. But I quickly turned back. I lay down on the upper bunk. The sick were allowed to stay in the block. So I would be sick. I didn't want to leave my father.

All around me, there was silence now, broken only by moaning. In front of the block, the SS were giving orders. An officer passed between the bunks. My father was pleading:

"My son, water . . . I'm burning up . . . My insides . . ."

"Silence over there!" barked the officer.

"Eliezer," continued my father, "water . . ."

The officer came closer and shouted to him to be silent. But my father did not hear. He continued to call me. The officer wielded his club and dealt him a violent blow to the head.

I didn't move. I was afraid, my body was afraid of another blow, this time to *my* head.

My father groaned once more, I heard:

"Eliezer . . ."

I could see that he was still breathing—in gasps. I didn't move.

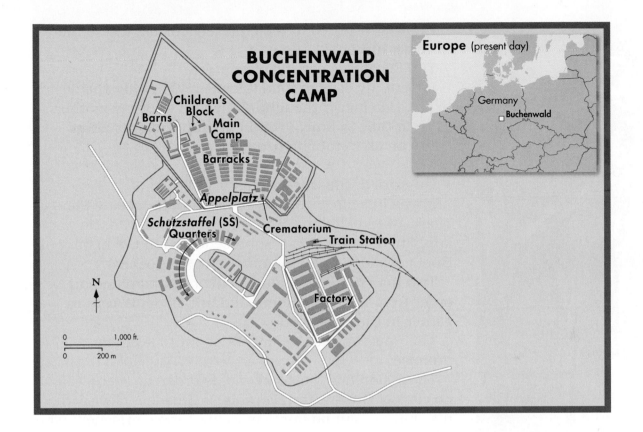

When I came down from my bunk after roll call, I could see his lips trembling; he was murmuring something. I remained more than an hour leaning over him, looking at him, etching his bloody, broken face into my mind.

Then I had to go to sleep. I climbed into my bunk, above my father, who was still alive. The date was January 28, 1945.

I woke up at dawn on January 29. On my father's cot there lay another sick person. They must have taken him away before daybreak and taken him to the crematorium. Perhaps he was still breathing . . .

No prayers were said over his tomb. No candle lit in his memory. His last word had been my name. He had called out to me and I had not answered.

I did not weep, and it pained me that I could not weep. But I was out of tears. And deep inside me, if I could have searched the recesses of my feeble conscience, I might have found something like: Free at last! . . .

I remained in Buchenwald until April 11. I shall not describe my life during that period. It no longer mattered. Since my father's death, nothing mattered to me anymore.

▲ Children at Auschwitz in 1945.

I was transferred to the children's block, where there were six hundred of us.

The Front was coming closer.

I spent my days in total idleness. With only one desire: to eat. I no longer thought of my father, or my mother.

From time to time, I would dream. But only about soup, an extra ration of soup.

On April 5, the wheel of history turned.

It was late afternoon. We were standing inside the block, waiting for an SS to come and count us. He was late. Such lateness was unprecedented in the history of Buchenwald. Something must have happened.

Two hours later, the loudspeakers transmitted an order from the camp Kommandant: all Jews were to gather in the *Appelplatz.*

This was the end! Hitler was about to keep his promise.

The children of our block did as ordered. There was no choice: Gustav, the *Blockälteste*, made it clear with his club . . . But on our way we met some prisoners who whispered to us:

"Go back to your block. The Germans plan to shoot you. Go back and don't move."

We returned to the block. On our way there, we learned that the underground resistance of the camp had made the decision not to abandon the Jews and to prevent their liquidation.

As it was getting late and the confusion was great—countless Jews had been passing as non-Jews—the *Lagerälteste*[8] had decided that a general roll call would take place the next day. Everybody would have to be present.

The roll call took place. The *Lagerkommandant*[9] announced that the Buchenwald camp would be liquidated. Ten blocks of inmates would be evacuated every day. From that moment on, there was no further distribution of bread and soup. And the evacuation began. Every day, a few thousand inmates passed the camp's gate and did not return.

On April 10, there were still some twenty thousand prisoners in the camp, among them a few hundred children. It was

---

8. *Lagerälteste* (läg´ ər el´ tes tə) term for the head of the camp.
9. *Lagerkommandant* (läg´ ər kom´ 'n dänt´) another term for the head of the camp.

decided to evacuate all of us at once. By evening. Afterward, they would blow up the camp.

And so we were herded onto the huge *Appelplatz*, in ranks of five, waiting for the gate to open. Suddenly, the sirens began to scream. Alert. We went back to the blocks. It was too late to evacuate us that evening. The evacuation was postponed to the next day.

Hunger was tormenting us; we had not eaten for nearly six days except for a few stalks of grass and some potato peels found on the grounds of the kitchens.

At ten o'clock in the morning, the SS took positions throughout the camp and began to herd the last of us toward the *Appelplatz*.

The resistance movement decided at that point to act. Armed men appeared from everywhere. Bursts of gunshots. Grenades exploding. We, the children, remained flat on the floor of the block.

The battle did not last long. Around noon, everything was calm again. The SS had fled and the resistance had taken charge of the camp.

At six o'clock that afternoon, the first American tank stood at the gates of Buchenwald.

ABOUT THE AUTHOR

Elie Wiesel (b. 1928)

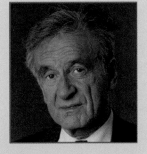

Elie Wiesel was just fifteen years old when he and his family were sent to the concentration camps at Auschwitz. He and his father managed to survive the 1945 death march that relocated them to the Buchenwald concentration camp, but his father died in the camp soon afterward.

Throughout his life, Wiesel has remained steadfastly committed to speaking out on behalf of Jews and others around the world who have been persecuted or who currently face persecution. He was also instrumental in the creation of the United States Holocaust Memorial Museum in Washington, D.C. In 1986, Wiesel was honored with the Nobel Peace Prize.

READ

Comprehension

Reread all or part of the text to help you answer the following questions.

1. What does Eliezer give to his father?

2. What does the *Blockälteste* advise Eliezer?

3. After his father's death, what is Eliezer upset that he cannot do?

Research: Clarify Details Choose one unfamiliar detail from the autobiographical narrative and conduct research on it. Explain how your research clarifies the text.

Summarize Write an objective summary of the text. Do not include your own opinions.

Language Study

Selection Vocabulary Define each boldface word from the selection.

• He dragged me toward a pile of snow from which **protruded** human shapes. . . .

• He had become childlike: weak, frightened, **vulnerable**.

• I thought he was **delirious**.

Literary Analysis

Reread the identified passage and answer the questions that follow.

> **Focus Passage** (*p. 729*)
>
> "Did you eat?" . . . not passed the test.

Key Ideas and Details

1. **(a)** According to Eliezer's father, why was he not given food? **(b)** How does Eliezer **respond** to his story?

Craft and Structure

2. **(a)** Where do ellipses (". . .") appear in the passage?

(b) Interpret: How do they affect the "sound" of the dialogue?

3. **(a) Infer:** What "test" does Rabbi Eliahu's son fail to pass? **(b) Interpret:** What does Eliezer's comparison of himself to the rabbi's son show about him?

Integration of Knowledge and Ideas

4. **Make a Judgment:** In this passage, does Wiesel show himself to be a dutiful son? In your answer, mention and refute a counterargument to your claim.

Supporting Visuals

Visuals, such as photographs and maps, may be used to clarify or support text. Reread the selection, and take notes on the map (p. 733).

1. Identify the Children's Block and Roll Call Square (*Appelplatz*) on the map. How does the map help clarify the events on April 5?

2. Drawing on the text, explain which features shown on the map might have been useful to the camp resistance force.

3. **The Holocaust:** Which details in the map suggest that the camp authorities kept firm control over the camp?

DISCUSS • RESEARCH • WRITE

From Text to Topic **Panel Discussion**

Form panels to discuss the following passage. Take notes during the discussion. Support your points with examples from the text.

> No prayers were said over his tomb. No candle lit in his memory. His last word had been my name. He had called out to me and I had not answered.
>
> I did not weep, and it pained me that I could not weep. But I was out of tears. And deep inside me, if I could have searched the recesses of my feeble conscience, I might have found something like: Free at last! . . .

Research **Investigate the Topic**

Resistance Wiesel mentions the resistance movement in Buchenwald, one example of the ways people found to oppose the Nazis.

Assignment

Conduct research into resistance in the camps and in the ghettos (neighborhoods to which Jews were confined). Use the Internet for research, making sure that each source you locate is **credible**. Take detailed notes and carefully identify your sources. Record the information you uncover in a set of **notes** organized by subtopic.

Writing to Sources **Informative Text**

Both Wiesel's narrative and the map provide information about the Buchenwald concentration camp.

Assignment

Using both the text and the map, write an **informative essay** in which you tell about conditions at Buchenwald. Follow these steps:

- Introduce your topic clearly.
- Use appropriate organizational strategies, such as chronological order for explaining a routine or spatial order for the layout.
- Use **evidence** from the text and the map to clarify details.
- Use appropriate transitional words, phrases, and clauses to make sure each idea leads clearly to the next.

QUESTIONS FOR DISCUSSION

1. Is Eliezer right or wrong to feel free? Explain, using details from the text.

2. What connection can you see between Wiesel's failure to answer his father and his need to write this memoir?

PREPARATION FOR ESSAY

You may use the results of this research project to support your ideas in the essay you will write at the end of this section.

ACADEMIC VOCABULARY

Academic terms appear in blue on these pages. Use a dictionary to find their definitions. Then, use the words as you speak and write about the text.

Common Core State Standards

RI.8.1, RI.8.2, RI.8.3; W.8.2, W.8.2.a, W.8.2.b, W.8.2.c, W.8.7, W.8.8; SL.8.1; L.8.4, L.8.6
[For full standards wording, see the chart in the front of this book.]

from

REMARKS ON A VISIT TO BUCHENWALD

Elie Wiesel June 5, 2009

Mr. President, Chancellor Merkel, Bertrand,[1] ladies and gentlemen. As I came here today it was actually a way of coming and visit my father's grave—but he had no grave. His grave is somewhere in the sky. This has become in those years the largest cemetery of the Jewish people.

The day he died was one of the darkest in my life. He became sick, weak, and I was there. I was there when he suffered. I was there when he asked for help, for water. I was there to receive his last words. But I was not there when he called for me, although we were in the same block; he on the upper bed and I on the lower bed. He called my name, and I was too afraid to move. All of us were. And then he died. I was there, but I was not there.

And I thought one day I will come back and speak to him, and tell him of the world that has become mine. I speak to him of times in which memory has become a sacred duty of all people of good will—in America, where I live, or in Europe or in Germany, where you, Chancellor Merkel, are a leader with great courage and moral **aspirations**.

aspirations ▶
(as´ pə rā´ shənz)
n. strong hopes, desires, or ambitions

What can I tell him that the world has learned? I am not so sure. Mr. President, we have such high hopes for you because you, with your moral vision of history, will be able and compelled to change this world into a better place, where people will stop waging war—every war is absurd and meaningless; where people will stop hating one another. . . .

But the world hasn't learned. When I was liberated in 1945, April 11, by the American army, somehow many of us were convinced that at least one lesson will have been learned—that

---

1. **Mr. President, Chancellor Merkel, Bertrand** Wiesel is addressing U.S. President Barack Obama, German Chancellor Angela Merkel, and Bertrand Herz, a fellow Buchenwald survivor.

never again will there be war; that hatred is not an option, that racism is stupid; and the will to conquer other people's minds or territories or aspirations, that will is meaningless.

I was so hopeful. Paradoxically, I was so hopeful then. Many of us were, although we had the right to give up on humanity, to give up on culture, to give up on education, to give up on the possibility of living one's life with dignity in a world that has no place for dignity.

We rejected that possibility and we said, no, we must continue believing in a future, because the world has learned. But again, the world hasn't. Had the world learned, there would have been no Cambodia and no Rwanda and no Darfur and no Bosnia.[2]

Will the world ever learn? I think that is why Buchenwald is so important—as important, of course, but differently as Auschwitz.[3] It's important because here the large—the big camp was a kind of international community. People came there from all horizons—political, economic, culture. The first globalization essay, experiment, were made in Buchenwald. And all that was meant to diminish the humanity of human beings. . . .

. . . Memory must bring people together rather than set them apart. Memory's here not to sow anger in our hearts, but on the contrary, a sense of solidarity with all those who need us. What else can we do except **invoke** that memory so that people everywhere will say the 21st century is a century of new beginnings, filled with promise and infinite hope, and at times profound gratitude to all those who believe in our task, which is to improve the human condition.

A great man, Camus,[4] wrote at the end of his marvelous novel, *The Plague*: "After all," he said, "after the tragedy, nevertheless . . . there is more in the human being to celebrate than to **denigrate**." Even that can be found as truth—painful as it is—in Buchenwald.

Thank you, Mr. President, for allowing me to come back to my father's grave, which is still in my heart.

◄ **invoke**
(in vōk´) *v.* call upon for inspiration or support; call forth

◄ **denigrate**
(den´ ə grāt´) *v.* say uncomplimentary things about someone or something

---

2. **no Cambodia . . . no Bosnia** Cambodia, Rwanda, Darfur, and Bosnia are all places that have been the site of a genocide, or the deliberate destruction of a group of people defined by race, culture, religion, or national identity.
3. **Auschwitz** (oush´ vits´) Nazi concentration camp established in Poland in the 1940s.
4. **Camus** (ka mōō´) Albert Camus (1913–1960), French novelist, essayist, and dramatist, known for his reflections on the human condition.

Close Reading Activities

READ

Comprehension

Reread all or part of the text to help you answer the following questions.

1. What is Wiesel's tie to the place where he gives the speech?

2. What does he say he hoped in 1945?

3. What does Wiesel want memory to do?

Research: Clarify Details Choose one unfamiliar detail from the speech and conduct research on it. Explain how your research clarifies the text.

Summarize Write an objective summary of the text. Do not include your own opinions.

Language Study

Selection Vocabulary Create a word map that shows synonyms for each boldface word from the selection.

• . . . great courage and moral **aspirations**.

• What else can we do except **invoke** that memory. . . .

• . . . there is more in the human being to celebrate than to **denigrate**.

Literary Analysis

Reread the identified passage and answer the questions that follow.

> **Focus Passage** (pp. 738–39)
>
> What can I tell him . . . and no Bosnia.

Key Ideas and Details

1. **Summarize:** What central question does Wiesel pose?

Craft and Structure

2. **(a) Analyze:** How does the first sentence tie Wiesel's main point to his story about his father's death? **(b) Interpret:** How does this connection intensify his argument about an obligation to end war?

3. **(a) Analyze:** Explain the paradox, or self-contradictory idea, that Wiesel identifies. **(b) Interpret:** How does this paradox underscore his argument?

Integration of Knowledge and Ideas

4. **Make a Judgment:** What lessons do you feel the world should learn from the Holocaust? Explain, citing the text.

Claims and Evidence

A **claim** is the main point a writer tries to prove. **Evidence** consists of the facts and arguments provided as proof.

1. **The Holocaust: (a)** What claim does Wiesel make about the lessons of the Holocaust? **(b)** What evidence does he use to **support** this claim?

2. **The Holocaust:** How does Wiesel use the example of Buchenwald to support his point that "[m]emory must bring people together"?

DISCUSS • RESEARCH • WRITE

From Text to Topic **Small Group Discussion**

Discuss the following passage with a group of classmates. Take notes during the discussion. Contribute your own ideas, and support them with examples from the text.

> Memory must bring people together rather than set them apart. Memory's here not to sow anger in our hearts, but on the contrary, a sense of solidarity with all those who need us. What else can we do except invoke that memory so that people everywhere will say the 21st century is a century of new beginnings, filled with promise and infinite hope, and at times profound gratitude to all those who believe in our task, which is to improve the human **condition**.

Research **Investigate the Topic**

An International Community Wiesel states that people at Buchenwald came "from all horizons," and he finds a kind of hope in the international makeup of the camp.

Assignment

Conduct research to learn what groups were held prisoner at Buchenwald. Consult reliable online resources on the camp. Take clear notes and identify your sources so that you can easily access the information later. Share your findings in a **diagram** or **chart.**

Writing to Sources **Argument**

Wiesel gave this speech at Buchenwald in the company of two world leaders, and the speech made the news. Which of his points did you find most moving? Most persuasive? Least credible?

Assignment

Write a **letter to the editor** in which you respond to one of the key ideas in the speech. Follow these steps:

- Use your opening paragraph to clearly state your **opinion** about the idea.
- Support the points you make by quoting from the text.
- Anticipate counterarguments and respond to them.
- Establish and maintain a formal style throughout.

QUESTIONS FOR DISCUSSION

1. Do you agree that memory should bring people together? Explain, citing the text.

2. Why does Wiesel put such emphasis on memory? What else might he call on?

PREPARATION FOR ESSAY

You may use the results of this research project to support your ideas in the essay you will write at the end of this section.

ACADEMIC VOCABULARY

Academic terms appear in blue on these pages. Use a dictionary to find their definitions. Then, use the words as you speak and write about the text.

Common Core State Standards

RI.8.1, RI.8.2, RI.8.3, RI.8.5, RI.8.8; W.8.1.a, W.8.1.b, W.8.1.d, W.8.7, W.8.8, W.8.9.b; SL.8.1, SL.8.5; L.8.4, L.8.6
[For full standards wording, see the chart in the front of this book.]

Local Holocaust Survivors and Liberators Attend Opening Event for Exhibition

FOR IMMEDIATE RELEASE
July 12, 2006
Contact: Andrea Moore,
PR Coordinator, Florida Holocaust Museum

liberators ▶
(lib´ ər at´ ərz) *n.*
persons who set free;
especially, those who
free a country from
an enemy or tyranny

St. Petersburg, FL—The Florida Holocaust Museum will honor Holocaust survivors and **liberators** at the opening event for the photography exhibitions *Fragments: Portraits of Survivors* by Jason Schwartz and *Liberators: Unexpected Outcomes* by Coe Arthur Younger. The reception will take place Thursday, July 13th at 5 p.m. and will be held at the Museum.

Both exhibitions will run through October 22. Many of the survivors and liberators featured in the exhibitions, as well as Coe Arthur Younger, photographer of the liberators exhibition, will be in attendance at the event.

Fragments: Portraits of Survivors features one hundred-twelve (112) 16 x 20 black and white photographs of local Holocaust survivors. Accompanying each portrait is a handwritten statement from the survivor in the photo. "I survived . . . I beat Hitler" is just one statement of many that quietly communicates the importance of this exhibition and its power to speak to all generations. The pictures and thoughts tell of the trials and triumphs of these extraordinary men and women survivors who bravely tell their stories as first-hand **testimonies** of a tragic time during the 20th century. Their memories give a voice to the voiceless.

testimonies ▶
(tes´ tə mō´ nēz) *n.*
statements or
declarations made
by witnesses

▲ **A photograph from the exhibition** *Liberators: Unexpected Outcomes*

The black and white photographs of the liberators tell a different story. *Liberators: Unexpected Outcomes* features 18 photographs of local U.S. troops who, as first responders and liberators at the end of WWII, witnessed the horrors behind camp gates. Without preparation or warning, these men happened upon unexpected and unimaginable scenes during regular military operations. Their stories are featured in photography by Coe Arthur Younger, as well as in an accompanying video that highlights the testimonies of several local liberators and survivors.

The Florida Holocaust Museum honors the memory of millions of innocent men, women, and children who suffered or died in the Holocaust. The Museum is dedicated to teaching members of all races and cultures to recognize the inherent worth and dignity of human life in order to prevent future **genocides**.

◄ **genocides**
(jen´ ə sīdz) *n.* deliberate destructions of groups of people defined by race, culture, religion, or national identity

READ

Comprehension

Reread all or part of the text to help you answer the following questions.

1. What event does the news release announce?

2. What are the subjects of the two exhibitions?

3. What is the museum's mission?

Research: Clarify Details Choose one unfamiliar detail from the news release and conduct research on it. Explain how your research clarifies the text.

Summarize Write an objective summary of the news release. Remember not to include your own opinions.

Language Study

Selection Vocabulary Define each boldface word from the selection. Then, identify the root of each word and explain its meaning.

• The Florida Holocaust Museum will honor Holocaust survivors and **liberators**. . . .

• . . . bravely tell their stories as first-hand **testimonies** of a tragic time. . . .

• . . . to recognize the inherent worth and dignity of human life in order to prevent future **genocides**.

Literary Analysis

Reread the identified passage and answer the questions that follow.

> **Focus Passage** *(p. 742)*
>
> *Fragments:* . . . to the voiceless.

Key Ideas and Details

1. (a) What accompanies the photographs in *Fragments*? **(b) Draw Conclusions:** Why might these additional materials be important to viewers?

Craft and Structure

2. (a) Analyze: In the passage, who are "the voiceless"? **(b) Interpret:** What effect does the direct **contrast** in the passage between "voice" and "voiceless" have?

Integration of Knowledge and Ideas

3. Speculate: How might a survivor or liberator feel when attending these exhibitions? Explain, citing the text.

Author's Purpose

Author's purpose is the writer's reason for writing: to inform, to persuade, or to entertain. Sometimes, a writer has mixed purposes. Reread the news release, and take notes on author's purpose.

1. What does the text inform you about?

2. The Holocaust: What persuasive **argument** for public commemoration of the Holocaust does the text suggest?

DISCUSS • RESEARCH • WRITE

From Text to Topic **Quick Write and Discuss**

Read the following passage and write a response to the Questions for Discussion. Share your response with a partner.

> *Liberators: Unexpected Outcomes* features 18 photographs of local U.S. troops who, as first responders and liberators at the end of WWII, witnessed the horrors behind camp gates. . . . Their stories are featured in photography by Coe Arthur Younger, as well as in an accompanying video that highlights the testimonies of several local liberators and survivors.

Research **Investigate the Topic**

Liberators The news release says that the liberators had no preparation or warning for what they were about to see.

Assignment

Conduct research to find out more about the experience of the liberators. You may use **primary sources**, such as firsthand accounts of liberators, secondary sources, such as history books, or both. Take clear notes and carefully identify your sources. Discuss your findings in a **small group discussion** with two or three classmates.

Writing to Sources **Narrative Text**

The exhibitions documented the experiences of local people who had been involved in traumatic historic events.

Assignment

Write an **imaginary interview** with a member of the museum staff involved in the exhibition. Follow these steps:

- Review the selection and take notes on the meaning of the exhibitions and the mission of the museum.
- Devise questions and answers that lead naturally from general background information to a discussion of the purpose and likely effect of the exhibitions.
- Follow dialogue format as you draft, writing the name of each speaker before his or her words.
- Use a conversational tone appropriate to an interview.

QUESTIONS FOR DISCUSSION

1. How might the sights of a concentration camp make liberators feel? What responsibility might they feel they have, given what they have witnessed?

2. What special bond might survivors and liberators feel?

PREPARATION FOR ESSAY

You may use the results of this research project to support your ideas in the essay you will write at the end of this section.

ACADEMIC VOCABULARY

Academic terms appear in blue on these pages. Use a dictionary to find their definitions. Then, use the words as you speak and write about the text.

 Common Core State Standards

RI.8.1, RI.8.2, RI.8.3, RI.8.6; W.8.4, W.8.9; SL.8.1; L.8.4, L.8.6
[For full standards wording, see the chart in the front of this book.]

Speaking and Listening **Group Discussion**

The Holocaust and Similarities and Differences The texts in this section vary in genre, style, and perspective. However, each of them raises questions about remembering (and forgetting) the Holocaust. They also prompt us to ask how deeply our differences can divide us, or how firmly our similarities can unite us, connecting to the Big Question in this unit: **Is it our similarities or differences that matter most?**

Assignment

Hold a discussion. With a small group of classmates, hold a discussion about issues of the Holocaust and about our differences or similarities. Refer to the texts in this section, other texts you have read, and your personal experience and knowledge to support your ideas. Begin your discussion by addressing the following questions:

- What differences became matters of life and death during the Holocaust?
- Do differences between people necessarily lead to conflict?
- How can the Holocaust help us find similarities that go beyond race, culture, nationality, and so on?
- Why is it important to remember what was done in the name of difference and similarity during the Holocaust?
- What reasons might people have to forget such issues? What reasons might they have to remember?

Summarize and present your ideas. After you have fully explored the topic, summarize your discussion and present your conclusions to the class as a whole.

▲ Refer to the selections you read in Part 3 as you complete the activities on this assessment.

Criteria for Success

✓ **Organizes the group effectively**
Appoint a group leader and a timekeeper. The group leader should present the discussion questions. The timekeeper should make sure the discussion takes no longer than 20 minutes.

✓ **Maintains focus of discussion**
As a group, stay on topic and avoid straying into other subject areas.

✓ **Involves all participants equally and fully**
No one person should monopolize the conversation. Rather, everyone should take turns speaking and contributing ideas.

✓ **Follows the rules for collegial discussion**
As each group member speaks, others should listen carefully. Build on one another's ideas and support viewpoints and opinions with sound reasoning and evidence. Express disagreement respectfully.

USE NEW VOCABULARY

As you speak and share ideas, work to use the vocabulary words you have learned in this unit. The more you use new words, the more you will "own" them.

Writing **Dramatic Text**

The Holocaust and Similarities and Differences The Holocaust turned lives upside down, at times challenging a person's deepest connections to others. Some dealt with the horror by forgetting; others, by remembering.

Common Core State Standards

W.8.3, W.8.4; SL.8.1
[For full standards wording, see the chart in the front of this book.]

> ## Assignment
> Write a brief **play** about characters in the Holocaust. Create characters whose relationship to each other is changed by historical events. In your play, show how remembering or forgetting has helped the characters deal with the pain of the past.

Criteria for Success

Purpose/Focus
✓ **Clearly conveys a theme**
Drawing on the texts in this section, construct a situation that will raise issues of broken relationships and of remembering and forgetting.

Organization
✓ **Builds to a climax**
Structure your play so that events build toward a dramatic climax, such as a quarrel or revelation.

Development of Ideas/Elaboration
✓ **Paces events for maximum effect**
To pace effectively, use a minimum of dialogue to build background for the audience. Heighten suspense by "stretching out" the scene that leads to the climax.

✓ **Builds resonance, connecting specific details with larger themes**
Repeat and develop images, lines of dialogue, or significant word choices to tie each section of your play to your theme.

Language
✓ **Uses dialogue for effective characterization**
Make sure the words each character says reflect his or her background, personality, and motives.

Conventions
✓ **Follows conventions for playscripts**
Call out speakers' names before their lines of dialogue. Add stage directions as needed, enclosing them in brackets. (If possible, use italics for the directions.)

✓ **Does not have errors**
Check your playscript to eliminate errors in grammar, spelling, and punctuation.

WRITE TO EXPLORE

As you work, you may find new, unexpected connections between your own ideas and the texts you have read. By adjusting to shifts in your own ideas, you will improve the final draft of your play.

Writing to Sources Explanatory Text

The Holocaust and Similarities and Differences The readings in this section raise questions about similarities and differences and about the power of the Holocaust to break or make connections—connections between people, as well as connections between past, present, and future. These questions include the following:

- Were the evils of the Holocaust so great that they could undo basic relationships—for example, the bond between parent and child?
- What new responsibilities, if any, did surviving or witnessing the Holocaust bring to people?
- Is memory a form of healing? Is forgetting?

Reflect on these questions, jotting notes, and complete this assignment.

INCORPORATE RESEARCH

Choose quotations to illustrate points, and incorporate them as you draft. To help readers follow, ensure you quote enough of the text to include required background, or add a sentence to your draft to provide the necessary information.

> ### Assignment
> **Comparison-and-Contrast Essay** Write an essay in which you compare and contrast the role played by memory (or forgetting) in two or more of the selections. Focus on how memory or forgetting formed a response to damaged, interrupted, renewed, or newly created relationships. Present your main idea in a thesis statement. Support your points with textual evidence.

Prewriting and Planning

Choose texts. Select texts from this section to cite in your essay.

Gather details. Use a chart like the one shown to take notes on your chosen selections.

Passage	Relationship	Forgetting	Remembering
Night With only one desire: to eat. I no longer thought of my father, or my mother.	son and parents	Hunger overwhelms the author; he forgets his parents.	He is writing about it now, remembering it all clearly.
Kindertransport EVELYN. Don't hanker after the past. It's done. FAITH. It's still a part of our lives.	mother and daughter	Evelyn tries to forget.	Her daughter knows the past is not done.

Develop a thesis. Review your notes, and develop a thesis based on them. For example, the details in the sample chart might support the following thesis: "Although suffering may lead victims of the Holocaust to forget, they may need to remember to truly deal with the past."

Drafting

Structure your ideas. Review your notes, and make an outline to organize the ideas for your comparison into logical categories.

Begin and end well. Begin your draft with an introduction clearly explaining your comparison. Conclude with a paragraph summing up your insights.

Support your main points. Support each main point with evidence from the text. Introduce each quotation or summary you include, explaining what it says or shows.

Use appropriate language. Use the correct historical terms, such as *refugee* and *genocide,* to refer to historical events with precision. Make sure your language is appropriately formal.

Revising and Editing

Review content. As needed, add transitional sentences to make clear connections between each of your main ideas and your thesis, and between main ideas and supporting details.

Review style. Look for series of short sentences, and vary sentence length and structure by combining some of them.

> CHOPPY: People need to remember. Memory can heal broken bonds.
>
> COMBINED: People need to remember because memory can heal broken bonds.

Common Core State Standards

W.8.2.a–f, W.8.4, W.8.10
[For full standards wording, see the chart in the front of this book.]

CITE RESEARCH CORRECTLY

Create a Works Cited list for your essay, following a standard style. Review your draft and make sure you have included appropriately formatted citations for quotations, for summaries of other works, and for ideas not your own. (See the Citing Sources pages in the Introductory Unit of this textbook.)

Self-Evaluation Rubric

Use the following criteria to evaluate the effectiveness of your essay.

Criteria	Rating Scale
Purpose/Focus Introduces a topic clearly; provides a concluding section that follows from and supports the information or explanation presented	*not very ....very* 1　　2　　3　　4
Organization Organizes ideas, concepts, and information into broader categories; uses appropriate and varied transitions to create cohesion and clarify relationships among ideas and concepts	1　　2　　3　　4
Development of Ideas/Elaboration Develops the topic with relevant, well-chosen facts, definitions, concrete details, quotations, or other information and examples	1　　2　　3　　4
Language Uses precise language and domain-specific vocabulary to inform about or explain the topic; establishes and maintains a formal style	1　　2　　3　　4
Conventions Correctly follows conventions of grammar, spelling, and punctuation	1　　2　　3　　4

Titles for Extended Reading

In this unit, you have read a variety of dramatic works. Continue to read on your own. Select works that you enjoy, but challenge yourself to explore new playwrights and works of increasing depth and complexity. The titles suggested below will help you get started.

INFORMATIONAL TEXTS

Narrative of the Life of Frederick Douglass

by Frederick Douglass
Signet, 1997

EXEMPLAR TEXT ©

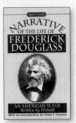

As an intellectual and a former slave, Douglass's was a unique voice for change. Through his powerful **autobiography,** Douglass inspired many readers to question slavery for the first time.

Discoveries: Believe It or Not

In this **essay** collection, you can explore the concept of truth in four different subject areas: social studies, science, humanities, and mathematics. Choose from a variety of interesting topics.

DK Eyewitness Books: World War II

Simon Adams

This survey of World War II history covers topics from the Blitz to code-breakers to the Holocaust to the war in the Pacific. Featuring detailed photographs and illustrations, this compelling **nonfiction** book shares the sights and artifacts of the time.

Holocaust

Angela Gluck Wood

This in-depth **nonfiction** book covers the causes of the Holocaust, the forces that halted it, and its aftershocks. The book includes first-hand accounts from survivors, which offer insights into their efforts to rebuild their lives.

LITERATURE

Eight Plays of U.S. History

Learn about important events in United States history in this collection of engaging **plays** that explores freedom, justice, culture, and social themes.

Escape to Freedom: A Play About Young Frederick Douglass

by Ossie Davis

This **play** is an account of Douglass's early life. Douglass secretly taught himself to read in violation of state law, escaped from a brutal master, and became a forceful voice in the movement to abolish slavery.

Henry Wadsworth Longfellow: Poems and Other Writings

by Henry Wadsworth
Longfellow

EXEMPLAR TEXT ©

When you enroll in college at age fifteen and become a professor at eighteen, clearly great things are expected of you. Longfellow did not disappoint, as he went on to write beloved works such as the epic poem *The Song of Hiawatha,* included in this **anthology**.

ONLINE TEXT SET

FICTION
Old Ben Jesse Stuart

POEM
Snake on the Etowah David Bottoms

NARRATIVE ESSAY
Vanishing Species Bailey White

Preparing to Read Complex Texts

Attentive Reading As you read on your own, ask yourself questions about the text. The questions shown below and others that you ask as you read will help you understand and enjoy literature even more.

When reading drama, ask yourself...

Comprehension: **Key Ideas and Details**

- Who is the main character? What struggles does this character face?
- What other characters are important? How do these characters relate to the main character?
- What is the setting? How does the setting affect the characters?
- Do the characters, settings, and events seem real? Why or why not?
- How does the play end? How does the ending make me feel?
- What theme or insight do I think the playwright is expressing? Do I find that theme to be important and true?

Text Analysis: **Craft and Structure**

- Does the playwright include background information? If so, how does this help me understand what I am reading?
- How many acts are in this play? What happens in each act?
- Which parts of the dialogue sound like real speech? Are there any that seem false?
- What do the stage directions tell me about the ways characters move, speak, and feel? How else do I learn about the characters?
- At what point in the play do I feel the most suspense? Why?
- Does the playwright seem to have a positive or a negative point of view? How does the playwright's point of view affect the story?
- Do I agree with the playwright's point of view? Why or why not?

Connections: **Integration of Knowledge and Ideas**

- Does the play remind me of others I have read or seen? If so, how?
- In what ways is the play different from others I have read or seen?
- What new information or ideas have I gained from reading this play?
- If I were to be in this play, what role would I want?
- Would I recommend this play to others? Why or why not?

Common Core State Standards

Reading Literature/ Informational Text
10. By the end of the year, read and comprehend literature, including stories, dramas, and poems, and literary nonfiction at the high end of the grades 6–8 text complexity band independently and proficiently.

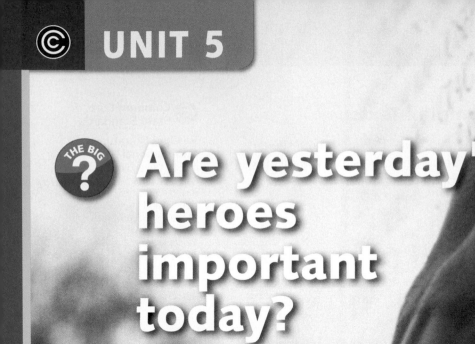

Are yesterday's heroes important today?

UNIT PATHWAY

PART 1
SETTING EXPECTATIONS

- INTRODUCING THE BIG QUESTION
- CLOSE READING WORKSHOP

PART 2
TEXT ANALYSIS
GUIDED EXPLORATION

HEROES AND TRADITIONS

PART 3
TEXT SET
DEVELOPING INSIGHT

FREEDOM FIGHTERS

PART 4
DEMONSTRATING INDEPENDENCE

- INDEPENDENT READING
- ONLINE TEXT SET

CLOSE READING TOOL

Use this tool to practice the close reading strategies you learn.

STUDENT eTEXT

Bring learning to life with audio, video, and interactive tools.

ONLINE WRITER'S NOTEBOOK

Easily capture notes and complete assignments online.

Find all Digital Resources at **pearsonrealize.com.**

Are yesterday's heroes important today?

Heroes are known for their bravery and their willingness to stand up for what they believe—no matter what opposition they face. Some heroes become famous for their physical skills; others are admired for their kindness or intelligence. At times, stories about the challenges a hero overcomes are exaggerated to impress an audience.

Stories of all kinds of heroes come from folklore, literature, and real life, and they are passed down from generation to generation. Heroes who stand the test of time have the ability to inspire people of different historical periods and cultural backgrounds.

Exploring the Big Question

Collaboration: One-on-One Discussion Start thinking about the Big Question by making a list of people you admire, whether from history, literature, contemporary life, or your personal experience. Make a list of examples of heroic deeds such as these:

- rescuing someone from a dangerous situation
- taking an unpopular position to defend a principle
- sacrificing for others so that they might succeed
- preserving dignity despite forces that try to degrade or destroy it
- helping people who are in need
- taking a risk to gain knowledge

Share your examples with a partner. Talk about the aspects of the actions that make them heroic, as well as the qualities someone must have to take such actions. Build on your partner's ideas, responding to each with related ideas of your own. Ask questions for clarification as needed, and help one another find logical support for each point made.

Connecting to the Literature Each reading in this unit will give you additional insight into the Big Question: Are yesterday's heroes important today?

Vocabulary

Acquire and Use Academic Vocabulary The term "academic vocabulary" refers to words you typically encounter in scholarly and literary texts and in technical and business writing. Review the definitions of these academic vocabulary words.

aspects (as´ pekts´) *n.*
1. ways an idea or a problem may be viewed or seen;
2. elements

cultural (kul´ chər əl) *adj.*
relating to the customs and beliefs of a group

emphasize (em´ fə sīz´) *v.*
stress; give one idea more importance than others

exaggerate (eg zaj´ ər āt´) *v.*
speak of something as being

greater or more important than it is

imitate (im´ i tāt´) *v.* copy; follow the example of

influence (in´ floo əns) *v.*
affect others' views, habits, plans, and so on

symbolize (sim´ bə līz´) *v.*
stand for; take the place of and signify an idea

Use these words as you complete Big Question activities in this unit that involve reading, writing, speaking, and listening.

Gather Vocabulary Knowledge Additional words related to traditions and heroes are listed below. Categorize the words by deciding whether you know each one well, know it a little bit, or do not know it at all.

accomplishments	courage	overcome
admirably	endure	suffering
bravery	outdated	

Then, do the following:

1. Write the definitions of the words you know.
2. Consult a dictionary to confirm the definitions of the words you know. Revise your definitions if necessary.
3. Using a print or an online dictionary, look up the meanings of the words you do not know. Then, write the meanings.
4. Use all of the words in a brief paragraph about heroes.

Common Core State Standards

Speaking and Listening
1. Engage effectively in a range of collaborative discussions with diverse partners on *grade 8 topics, texts, and issues,* building on others' ideas and expressing their own clearly.

Language
6. Acquire and use accurately grade-appropriate general academic and domain-specific words and phrases; gather vocabulary knowledge when considering a word or phrase important to comprehension or expression.

In this workshop you will learn an approach to reading that will deepen your understanding of literature and will help you better appreciate an author's craft. The workshop includes models for the close reading, discussion, research, and writing activities you will complete as you study the literature in this unit. After you have reviewed the strategies and models in this workshop, practice your skills with the Independent Practice selection.

 **Common Core State Standards**

RL.8.1, RL.8.2, RL.8.3, RL.8.4, RL.8.6; W.8.2.b, W.8.7, W.8.9.a; SL.8.1
[For full standards wording, see the standards chart in the front of this book.]

CLOSE READING: **THEMES IN AMERICAN STORIES**

In Part 2 of this unit you will focus on reading various American stories. Use these strategies as you read the texts.

Comprehension: **Key Ideas and Details**

- Read first to unlock basic meaning.
- Use context clues and reference works to help you determine the meanings of unfamiliar words.
- Identify unfamiliar details that you might need to clarify through research.
- Make inferences about information that is implied.

Ask yourself questions such as these:
- How would I summarize the action?
- How are the events in the story related?

Text Analysis: **Craft and Structure**

- Think about the cultural context and traditions behind the text.
- Analyze how the author's influences contribute to the characterizations.
- Consider the ways that the language of the oral tradition can influence written text.

Ask yourself questions such as these:
- In what social and historical context were the characters living?
- Which cultural and historical factors affected the author?

Connections: **Integration of Knowledge and Ideas**

- Look for relationships among key ideas.
- To identify a theme, analyze what the author shows about human nature.
- Compare and contrast this work with similar works you have read.

Ask yourself questions such as these:
- How has this work increased my insight into literary traditions?
- How do the themes apply to my life or to society today?

Read

As you read this story, take note of the annotations, which model ways to closely read the text.

Reading Model

from *The Adventures of Tom Sawyer* by Mark Twain

. . . But Tom's energy did not last. He began to think of the fun he had planned for this day, and his sorrows multiplied. Soon the free boys would come tripping along on all sorts of delicious expeditions, and they would make a world of fun of him for having to work—the very thought of it burnt him like fire.[1] He got out his worldly wealth and examined it—bits of toys, marbles, and trash; enough to buy an exchange of *work*, maybe, but not half enough to buy so much as half an hour of pure freedom. So he returned his straitened means to his pocket, and gave up the idea of trying to buy the boys. At this dark and hopeless moment an inspiration burst upon him! Nothing less than a great, magnificent inspiration.

He took up his brush and went tranquilly to work. Ben Rogers hove in sight presently—the very boy, of all boys, whose ridicule he had been dreading. Ben's gait was the hop-skip-and-jump—proof enough that his heart was light and his anticipations high.[2] He was eating an apple, and giving a long, melodious whoop, at intervals, followed by a deep-toned ding-dong-dong, ding-dong-dong, for he was personating a steamboat. As he drew near, he slackened speed, took the middle of the street, leaned far over to starboard and rounded to ponderously and with laborious pomp and circumstance—for he was personating the Big Missouri, and considered himself to be drawing nine feet of water. He was boat and captain and engine-bells combined, so he had to imagine himself standing on his own hurricane-deck giving the orders and executing them:[3]

"Stop her, sir! Ting-a-ling-ling!" The headway ran almost out, and he drew up slowly toward the sidewalk.

"Ship up to back! Ting-a-ling-ling!" His arms straightened and stiffened down his sides.

"Set her back on the stabboard! Ting-a-ling-ling! Chow! ch-chow-wow! Chow!"[4] His right hand, meantime, describing stately circles—for it was representing a forty-foot wheel.

Key Ideas and Details
1 The narrator describes the other boys as "free boys" who "would make a world of fun of [Tom]." This is one of numerous colorful, descriptive details that outline how Tom is feeling—he has an inner conflict because he has to work.

Craft and Structure
2 Ben moves lightly and energetically, with a "hop-skip-and-jump." The author uses informal language in his descriptions, capturing the sound of people's speech in his day.

Key Ideas and Details
3 An Internet search for the "Big Missouri" reveals that the *Big Missouri* was a steamboat operating on the Mississippi River. Ben's knowledge of the boat suggests the importance of steamboats and the river to the town and so helps to establish the setting.

Craft and Structure
4 Twain uses *onomatopoeia*, or words that imitate sounds—such as "Ting-a-ling-ling!"—to capture Ben's impersonation of the sounds of a steamboat.

"Let her go back on the labboard! Ting-a-ling-ling! Chow-ch-chow-chow!" The left hand began to describe circles.

"Stop the stabboard! Ting-a-ling-ling! Stop the labboard! Come ahead on the stabboard! Stop her! Let your outside turn over slow! Ting-a-ling-ling! Chow-ow-ow! Get out that head-line! *Lively* now! Come—out with your spring-line—what're you about there! Take a turn round that stump with the bight of it![5] Stand by that stage, now—let her go! Done with the engines, sir! Ting-a-ling-ling! *Sh't! s'h't! sh't!*" (trying the gauge-cocks).

Tom went on whitewashing—paid no attention to the steamboat. Ben stared a moment and then said: "*Hi-yi! You're* up a stump,[6] ain't you!"

No answer. Tom surveyed his last touch with the eye of an artist, then he gave his brush another gentle sweep and surveyed the result, as before. Ben ranged up alongside of him. Tom's mouth watered for the apple, but he stuck to his work. Ben said:

"Hello, old chap, you got to work, hey?"

Tom wheeled suddenly and said:

"Why, it's you, Ben! I warn't noticing."

"Say—*I'm* going in a-swimming, *I* am. Don't you wish you could? But of course you'd druther *work*—wouldn't you? Course you would!"[7]

Tom contemplated the boy a bit, and said:

"What do you call work?"

"Why, ain't *that* work?"

Tom resumed his whitewashing, and answered carelessly:

"Well, maybe it is, and maybe it ain't. All I know, is, it suits Tom Sawyer."

"Oh come, now, you don't mean to let on that you *like* it?"

The brush continued to move.

"Like it? Well, I don't see why I oughtn't to like it. Does a boy get a chance to whitewash a fence every day?"

That put the thing in a new light. Ben stopped nibbling his apple. Tom swept his brush daintily back and forth—stepped back to note the effect—added a touch here and there—criticised the effect again—Ben watching every move and getting more and more interested, more and more absorbed.[8] Presently he said:

"Say, Tom, let *me* whitewash a little."

Craft and Structure

5 By using the technical language of a riverboat pilot, including *spring-line*, the author adds flavor, reinforces the setting, and enriches his depiction of a boy who is "serious" about his play.

Key Ideas and Details

6 The phrase "up a stump" reflects the boys' dialect, or regional way of speaking. An Internet search shows that "up a stump" is slang for "in a difficult situation."

Craft and Structure

7 Twain puts *I'm* and *I* in italics to show Ben's emphasis on these words and establish Ben's teasing tone. The author wants readers to hear the story as the words would be spoken aloud. In this way he participates in a tradition of oral storytelling, in which the storyteller might impersonate each character.

Integration of Knowledge and Ideas

8 Words and phrases such as "daintily," "note the effect," and "criticised" make the chore sound like an art form. In turn, Ben becomes "more and more absorbed," which hints at a larger theme.

Tom considered, was about to consent; but he altered his mind:

"No—no—I reckon it wouldn't hardly do, Ben. You see, Aunt Polly's awful particular about this fence—right here on the street, you know— but if it was the back fence I wouldn't mind and *she* wouldn't. Yes, she's awful particular about this fence; it's got to be done very careful; I reckon there ain't one boy in a thousand, maybe two thousand, that can do it the way it's got to be done."

"No—is that so? Oh come, now—lemme just try. Only just a little—I'd let *you*, if you was me, Tom."

"Ben, I'd like to, honest injun; but Aunt Polly—well, Jim wanted to do it, but she wouldn't let him; Sid wanted to do it, and she wouldn't let Sid. Now don't you see how I'm fixed? If you was to tackle this fence and anything was to happen to it—"

"Oh, shucks, I'll be just as careful. Now lemme try. Say—I'll give you the core of my apple."[9]

"Well, here—No, Ben, now don't. I'm afeard —"

"I'll give you *all* of it!"

Tom gave up the brush with reluctance in his face, but alacrity in his heart. And while the late steamer Big Missouri worked and sweated in the sun, the retired artist sat on a barrel in the shade close by, dangled his legs, munched his apple, and planned the slaughter of more innocents.[10] There was no lack of material; boys happened along every little while; they came to jeer, but remained to whitewash. By the time Ben was fagged out, Tom had traded the next chance to Billy Fisher for a kite, in good repair; and when *he* played out, Johnny Miller bought in for a dead rat and a string to swing it with—and so on, and so on, hour after hour. And when the middle of the afternoon came, from being a poor poverty-stricken boy in the morning, Tom was literally rolling in wealth. He had besides the things before mentioned, twelve marbles, part of a jews-harp, a piece of blue bottle-glass to look through, a spool cannon, a key that wouldn't unlock anything, a fragment of chalk, a glass stopper of a decanter, a tin soldier, a couple of tadpoles, six fire-crackers, a kitten with only one eye, a brass doorknob, a dog-collar—but no dog—the handle of a knife, four pieces of orange-peel, and a dilapidated old window sash.[11]

Craft and Structure

9 Ben has already asked for a turn whitewashing, but Tom artfully delays his consent, ensuring that Ben is "hooked." Through this exchange, the author paints his classic portrait of Tom Sawyer as a masterful salesperson.

Craft and Structure

10 The author contrasts the "steamboat," Ben, with the "retired artist," Tom. The steamboat now works and sweats in the sun. The author's sense of humor is showing in the imagery.

Craft and Structure

11 The contrast between Tom's idea of "wealth" and the list of broken toys and trash is also humorous. Twain joins a tradition of humorous storytelling— humor being one reason why people like to pass such stories along.

He had had a nice, good, idle time all the while—plenty of company—and the fence had three coats of whitewash on it! If he hadn't run out of whitewash he would have bankrupted every boy in the village.

Tom said to himself that it was not such a hollow world, after all. He had discovered a great law of human action, without knowing it—namely, that in order to make a man or a boy covet a thing, it is only necessary to make the thing difficult to attain.[12]

Integration of Knowledge and Ideas

12 Twain states the theme: people want things that are "difficult to attain," or hard to get—even things they would otherwise dislike. By making painting seem difficult and exclusive, Tom makes it desirable, and so points out the folly of human beings.

Discuss

Sharing your own ideas and listening to the ideas of others can deepen your understanding of a text and help you look at a topic in a whole new way. As you participate in collaborative discussions, work to have a genuine exchange in which classmates build upon one another's ideas. Support your points with evidence and ask meaningful questions.

Discussion Model

Student 1: Tom Sawyer is the main character, and it is interesting that Mark Twain does not always show him in a positive light. Tom is clearly clever, because he tricks Ben and the other boys into working, but he is also sneaky. He tries to get out of doing work.

Student 2: I agree. For example, in the scene where Ben starts painting the fence, it says that Tom "munched his apple, and planned the slaughter of more innocents." The word *slaughter* is pretty negative—although kind of funny, too. It is such an exaggeration. I think the phrase "slaughter of innocents" might also be a reference to a story in the Bible.

Student 3: In that quote, it seems like Twain is making fun of Tom Sawyer. Maybe Twain gives Tom some negative qualities to make the story funny. I wonder if Twain is known for using humor in his other stories.

Research

Targeted research can clarify unfamiliar details and shed light on various aspects of a text. Consider general questions that arise in your mind as you read, and use those questions as the starting point for research that will deepen your understanding. For best results, refine your general questions or topics into specific research questions. For example, by starting with a general interest in Mark Twain, you can narrow your focus to Twain's brand of humor.

Research Model

General Topic: *Who is Mark Twain, and what type of writing is he famous for?*

Specific Question: *How does Mark Twain use humor to develop characters?*

Key Words for Internet Search: "Mark Twain" + humor

Result: The Kennedy Center Mark Twain Prize for American Humor

What I Learned: Mark Twain is recognized as one of the greatest American humor writers. He observed society and its flaws to create humor in descriptions and characterizations.

Evaluate Sources As you conduct research, look for relevant information in sources such as books, periodicals, and Web sites. To determine whether a source is credible, consider the background of its author or sponsor. For example, a book by a professor at a university is likely to be credible. A Web site hosted by a company that sells products related to your topic may be less credible.

Range of Sources Use multiple sources of information appropriate to your topic. Primary sources are firsthand accounts, such as letters, or original documents, such as a speech. Secondary sources, such as encyclopedia entries, interpret the information from primary sources.

Use primary sources to capture the perspectives of participants in an event. Use secondary sources to obtain a broader view and up-to-date information. Use general secondary sources such as encyclopedias to obtain basic facts and to orient research. Use specialized secondary sources to deepen your inquiry.

Taking Notes Take handwritten or electronic notes to summarize information. In your notes, document the publication information for each source. When copying a writer's words for later quotation, put them in quotation marks and double-check them for accuracy.

Write

Writing about a text will deepen your understanding of it and will also allow you to share your ideas more formally with others. The following model essay analyzes how characterization contributes to humor and cites evidence to support the main ideas.

Writing Model: Argument

Humor in *The Adventures of Tom Sawyer*

Main characters are often likeable and even heroic. In *The Adventures of Tom Sawyer,* however, Mark Twain gives his main character negative qualities to create humor. While Tom Sawyer is clever, he is also sneaky and lazy. Twain uses all these characteristics for humorous effect.

In the whitewashing episode, Tom uses his wits to get out of painting a fence. He acts as though the job were fun, convincing Ben Rogers and other neighborhood boys to do the work for him. For many readers, Tom's cleverness is an appealing, positive characteristic.

However, Tom's negative characteristics provide even more humor, as when Twain shows how sorry Tom feels for himself at the start of the same episode. Tom only has to paint a fence, but Twain uses phrases like "dark and hopeless moment" and "sorrows multiplied" to poke fun at Tom's mood. These dramatic exaggerations emphasize the humor in the situation.

Twain also develops humor by describing Tom's laziness. In the whitewashing episode, Tom persuades the other boys to do his job just because he does not want to do it himself. While the boys work, Tom has "a nice, good, idle time all the while." The image of Tom sitting by while the other boys paint the fence shows his laziness in a funny and memorable way.

Finally, Twain uses Tom's greed to make the whitewashing episode even funnier. Tom charges the boys to participate, greedily roping more and more boys into doing the work. Twain explains that if Tom "hadn't run out of whitewash he would have bankrupted every boy in the village." The result is a funny image of Tom's gains. The items Tom receives from the boys are mostly just pieces of trash and broken toys, but Twain says that Tom was "literally rolling in wealth."

Mark Twain is known as one of the greatest American humor writers. He observed people's flaws to create funny descriptions and situations. In *The Adventures of Tom Sawyer,* Twain creates the humor for which he is known by showing Tom Sawyer's flaws.

A thesis statement at the beginning of the essay introduces the essay's main claim—the point the writer will argue for in the body of the essay, using logic and evidence.

The writer acknowledges a claim from another perspective.

The writer supports the claim with specific language from the story.

The writer's references to imagery in the story highlight the writer's point about Tom's laziness.

By incorporating information from research, the writer connects Tom Sawyer to other characters in Twain's works.

Discuss Your Writing: Peer Review

By sharing your writing with peers and collecting their feedback, you can quickly identify where your draft succeeds in communicating—and where it needs improvement. First, trade papers with a partner. Then, each partner should follow these steps.

- Read the draft and note down comments, using courteous, respectful language.
- Identify one or more elements in the draft that are effective.
- Identify one or more areas for improvement. In each case, offer a suggestion to help the writer make the draft better.

Reviewers should comment on the clarity and interest of the writer's ideas and organization, the effectiveness and consistency of the style, and the use of error-free, standard English. Writers should review comments, ask for clarification as needed, and then revise their drafts to address the comments they agree are valid.

INDEPENDENT PRACTICE

As you read this story, apply the close reading strategies you have learned. You may need to read the story multiple times.

Water Names

by Lan Samantha Chang

Summertime at dusk we'd gather on the back porch, tired and sticky from another day of fierce encoded quarrels, nursing our mosquito bites and frail dignities, sisters in name only. At first we'd pinch and slap each other, fighting for the best—least ragged—folding chair. Then we'd argue over who would sit next to our grandmother. We were so close together on the tiny porch that we often pulled our own hair by mistake. Forbidden to bite, we planted silent toothmarks on each others' wrists. We ignored the bulk of house behind us, the yard, the fields, the darkening sky. We even forgot about our grandmother. Then suddenly we'd hear her old, dry voice, very close, almost on the backs of our necks.

"*Xiushila!* Shame on you. Fighting like a bunch of chickens."

And Ingrid, the oldest, would freeze with her thumb and forefinger right on the back of Lily's arm. I would slide my hand away from the end of Ingrid's braid. Ashamed, we would shuffle our feet while Waipuo calmly found her chair.

Meet the Author

Lan Samantha Chang (b. 1965) grew up in Appleton, Wisconsin, learning about China from her Chinese immigrant parents.

CLOSE READING TOOL

Read and respond to this selection online using the **Close Reading Tool.**

On some nights she sat with us in silence. But on some nights she told us stories, "just to keep up your Chinese," she said.

"In these prairie crickets I often hear the sound of rippling waters, of the Yangtze River," she said. "Granddaughters, you are descended on both sides from people of the water country, near the mouth of the great Chang Jiang, as it is called, where the river is so grand and broad that even on clear days you can scarcely see the other side.

"The Chang Jiang runs four thousand miles, originating in the Himalaya mountains where it crashes, flecked with gold dust, down steep cliffs so **perilous** and remote that few humans have ever seen them. In central China, the river squeezes through deep gorges, then widens in its last thousand miles to the sea. Our ancestors have lived near the mouth of this river, the ever-changing delta, near a city called Nanjing, for more than a thousand years."

"A thousand years," murmured Lily, who was only ten. When she was younger she had sometimes burst into nervous crying at the thought of so many years. Her small insistent fingers grabbed my fingers in the dark.

"Through your mother and I you are descended from a line of great men and women. We have survived countless floods and seasons of ill-fortune because we have the spirit of the river in us. Unlike mountains, we cannot be powdered down or broken apart. Instead, we run together, like raindrops. Our strength and spirit wear down mountains into sand. But even our people must respect the water."

She paused. "When I was young, my own grandmother once told me the story of Wen Zhiqing's daughter. Twelve hundred years ago the civilized parts of China still lay to the north, and the Yangtze valley lay unspoiled. In those days lived an ancestor named Wen Zhiqing, a resourceful man, and proud. He had been fishing for many years with trained cormorants, which you girls of course have never seen. Cormorants are sleek, black birds with long, bending necks which the fishermen fitted with metal rings so the fish they caught could not be swallowed. The birds would perch on the side of the old wooden boat and dive into the river." We had only known blue swimming pools, but we tried to imagine the sudden shock of cold and the plunge, deep into water.

Vocabulary ▶
perilous (per´ ə ləs)
adj. involving peril or risk; dangerous

"Now, Wen Zhiqing had a favorite daughter who was very beautiful and loved the river. She would beg to go out on the boat with him. This daughter was a restless one, never contented with their catch, and often she insisted they stay out until it was almost dark. Even then, she was not satisfied. She had been spoiled by her father, kept protected from the river, so she could not see its danger. To this young woman, the river was as familiar as the sky. It was a bright, broad road stretching out to curious lands. She did not fully understand the river's depths.

"One clear spring evening, as she watched the last bird dive off into the blackening waters, she said, 'If only this catch would bring back something more than another fish!'

"She leaned over the side of the boat and looked at the water. The stars and moon reflected back at her. And it is said that the spirits living underneath the water looked up at her as well. And the spirit of a young man who had drowned in the river many years before saw her lovely face."

We had heard about the ghosts of the drowned, who wait forever in the water for a living person to pull down instead. A faint breeze moved through the mosquito screens and we shivered.

"The cormorant was gone for a very long time," Waipuo said, "so long that the fisherman grew puzzled. Then, suddenly, the bird emerged from the waters, almost invisible in the night. Wen Zhiqing grasped his catch, a very large fish, and guided the boat back to shore. And when Wen reached home, he gutted the fish and discovered, in its stomach, a valuable pearl ring."

"From the man?" said Lily.

"Sshh, she'll tell you."

Waipuo ignored us. "His daughter was delighted that her wish had been fulfilled. What most excited her was the idea of an entire world like this, a world where such a beautiful ring would be only a bauble![1] For part of her had always longed to see faraway things and places. The river had put a spell on her heart. In the evenings she began to sit on the bank, looking at her own reflection in the water. Sometimes she said she saw a handsome young man looking back at her. And her yearning for him filled her heart with sorrow and fear, for she knew that she would soon leave her beloved family.

---

1. **bauble** (bô′ bəl) *n.* trinket.

Vocabulary ▶
forbade (fər bād')
v. commanded not
to do something;
prohibited

"'It's just the moon,' said Wen Zhiqing, but his daughter shook her head. 'There's a kingdom under the water,' she said. 'The prince is asking me to marry him. He sent the ring as an offering to you.' 'Nonsense,' said her father, and he **forbade** her to sit by the water again.

"For a year things went as usual, but the next spring there came a terrible flood that swept away almost everything. In the middle of a torrential rain, the family noticed that the daughter was missing. She had taken advantage of the confusion to hurry to the river and visit her beloved. The family searched for days but they never found her."

Her smoky, rattling voice came to a stop.

"What happened to her?" Lily said.

"It's okay, stupid," I told her. "She was so beautiful that she went to join the kingdom of her beloved. Right?"

"Who knows?" Waipuo said. "They say she was seduced by a water ghost. Or perhaps she lost her mind to desiring."

"What do you mean?" asked Ingrid.

"I'm going inside," Waipuo said, and got out of her chair with a creak. A moment later the light went on in her bedroom window. We knew she stood before the mirror, combing out her long, wavy silver-gray hair, and we imagined that in her youth she too had been beautiful.

Vocabulary ▶
abruptness (ə brupt' nis)
n. curt or gruff quality
in behavior or speech

We sat together without talking. We had gotten used to Waipuo's **abruptness**, her habit of creating a question and leaving without answering it, as if she were disappointed in the question itself. We tried to imagine Wen Zhiqing's daughter. What did she look like? How old was she? Why hadn't anyone remembered her name?

While we weren't watching, the stars had emerged. Their brilliant pinpoints mapped the heavens. They glittered over us, over Waipuo in her room, the house, and the small city we lived in, the great waves of grass that ran for miles around us, the ground beneath as dry and hard as bone.

Close Reading Activities

Read

Comprehension: Key Ideas and Details

1. **(a)** Where does the main story take place?
   (b) Where does the legend take place?
   (c) Distinguish: What details convey the differences between the two settings?

2. **Infer:** What happens to Wen Zhiqing's daughter?

3. **Analyze Cause and Effect:** What effect does the grandmother's story have on her listeners? Cite evidence from the story.

4. **Summarize:** Write a brief, objective summary of the story. Cite story details in your writing.

Text Analysis: Craft and Structure

5. **(a)** What descriptive words does Waipuo use to describe the Yangzte River? **(b) Draw Conclusions:** How do these words reveal Waipuo's attitude toward her homeland?

6. **(a) Interpret:** In what sense is this story two stories in one? Cite details from the text in your answer. **(b) Analyze:** Give two examples where one story interrupts the other. **(c) Evaluate:** Explain what effect the

contrast between the stories has on your appreciation of both.

7. **(a) Analyze:** What traditional storytelling techniques does Waipuo use? **(b) Interpret:** How does she end the story? **(c) Draw Conclusions:** What is her motive in telling this story, and in ending it as she does? In your answer, consider her family's response afterward.

Connections: Integration of Knowledge and Ideas

Discuss
Conduct a **small-group discussion** about the unresolved questions in the story and their relationship to the story's theme.

Research
Lan Samantha Chang writes about Chinese culture and history to better understand her own background. Research elements of Chinese folk tales and legends, including the following:

a. themes

b. connections to Chinese history

c. the ways in which these stories were communicated

Take notes as you perform your research. Then, write a brief **explanation** of the major elements in Chinese legends.

Write
Write an **analytical essay** analyzing what the supernatural elements in the legend add to the main story. Cite details from the story to support your analysis.

 Are yesterday's heroes important today?

The narrator and her sisters live in a new country surrounded by "waves of grass . . . the ground beneath as dry and hard as bone." Why might their grandmother's legends of a river in China matter to them? Explain.

"If everybody was **satisfied** with himself there would be no **heroes**.

—Mark Twain

HEROES AND TRADITIONS

As you read the selections in this section, identify the heroes in each. Think about the reasons people carry stories about such heroes from one generation to the next. The quotation on the facing page will help you start thinking about traditional heroes and their enduring appeal.

◀ **CRITICAL VIEWING** In what way does this photograph illustrate the idea of heroism? What tradition does it show? In what ways might the boy in the photograph benefit from having heroes?

READINGS IN PART 2

ZUNI MYTH
Coyote Steals the Sun and Moon
Richard Erdoes and Alfonso Ortiz (p. 776)

MEXICAN AMERICAN CUENTO • POEM
Chicoria • *from* **The People, Yes**
Rudolfo A. Anaya and José Griego y Maestas • Carl Sandburg (p. 784)

POEMS
from **Out of the Dust**
Karen Hesse (p. 796)

SHORT STORY
An Episode of War
Stephen Crane (p. 808)

CLOSE READING TOOL
Use the **Close Reading Tool** to practice the strategies you learn in this unit.

Elements of the American Folk Tradition

The American folk tradition includes a rich collection of literature, which grew out of the **oral tradition**.

Storytelling and the Oral Tradition
People have always enjoyed telling and listening to stories. Long before reading and writing were invented, societies shared information with the next generation through storytelling. This was the origin of the **oral tradition,** in which stories were passed down over time by word of mouth. Eventually, these stories were collected and written down. American folk literature grew out of this same tradition. Told at festivals, around campfires, and at other gatherings, stories from the oral tradition reflect our culture's richness.

Themes and Cultural Context All good stories have a **theme**—a central message or insight about life. Stories in the oral tradition often express universal themes. **Universal themes** recur regularly in stories from many different cultures and time periods. Examples of universal themes include the power of love and the dangers of greed.

In the American folk tradition, universal themes are expressed from an American perspective, or **cultural context.** The stories are inspired by American history, geography, and beliefs. Set against the rugged landscape of America's past, they often celebrate American **heroes** and **heroines.** Some details in the stories are historically true. Others are based on truth but may be greatly exaggerated. This chart shows techniques that are common to the American folk tradition.

Oral Tradition Storytelling Techniques

Technique	Definitions
Hyperbole	An exaggeration, used for comic effect or to express strong emotion
Understatement	A way of expressing something that treats it as smaller or less serious than it actually is, often used for comic effect
Personification	The technique of giving human characteristics to nonhuman subjects
Dialect	The language and grammar of a particular region or group; used to make dialogue sound realistic and to reflect the cultural background of the story
Idioms	• Expressions that are not meant to be taken literally, such as "It's raining cats and dogs!" • Developed and understood by people of a certain region or group
Informal Speech	Everyday, conversational language; often includes idioms, slang, and dialect

The American Folk Tradition

American folk stories can be divided into different types.

Myths explain the actions of gods or other supernatural forces and the heroes who interact with them. Ancient peoples often used mythology to explain natural phenomena.

Fables are brief stories that often feature animals that act like humans. The main purpose of a fable is to teach an important life lesson, or **moral.**

Trickster tales tell about tricks or pranks and the characters who play them. Trickster characters are typically clever and mischievous.

Tall tales rely on **hyperbole**—exaggeration for comic effect. The heroes of these tales perform impossible feats.

Legends often originate in fact. Through repeated tellings of a factual story, the real-life characters and events in the story become larger than life, and the story becomes a legend.

Epics are long narrative poems about heroes who engage in dangerous journeys, battles, or quests important to the history of a nation or culture.

The American Folk Hero

American folk literature is a living tradition. Over time, new heroes and subjects appear that reflect the manners, customs, sayings, and stories of our changing culture. For example, American folk heroes of the nineteenth century included patriots, soldiers, farmers, and cowboys. A century later, American folk heroes included sports figures, aviators, civil rights leaders, and astronauts. In the American folk tradition, heroes can be real or fictional. However, they all display traits that Americans admire and strive to imitate.

Common Core State Standards

Reading Literature

2. Determine a theme or central idea of a text and analyze its development over the course of the text, including its relationship to the characters, setting, and plot; provide an objective summary of the text.

Common Traits of American Folk Heroes				
adventurous determined	honest loyal	strong humble	courageous resourceful	intelligent creative

Fictional	Based to Some Degree on Fact	Real
Paul Bunyan, lumberjack	Johnny "Appleseed" Chapman, farmer	Sacajawea, Native American guide
Pecos Bill, cowboy	John Henry, African American steelworker	Rosa Parks, African American civil rights activist
Little Sal Fink, known for her powerful scream	Davy Crockett, frontiersman	Roberto Clemente, Latino baseball player

Analyzing Themes in American Stories

Themes in the American folk tradition have a distinctly American point of view.

Themes in American folk stories express ideas about who we are as a people. These stories often present the American landscape as a challenge. Those who triumph over it are considered heroes and heroines.

Social and Cultural Context To recognize the themes in an American folk story, readers should consider the **social and cultural context** of the story—the values and customs of the original tellers of the tale.

America has a rich multicultural heritage shaped by Native Americans, African Americans, Latinos, Europeans, Asians, and others. All of these groups have contributed stories to the national folk literature. While the themes of these stories are distinctly American, they also reflect the cultures of their tellers.

Factors that can influence a storyteller's view of the world, or **social and cultural perspective,** include the historic events of an era. In America, events such as Westward Expansion, slavery, the Civil War, and the Great Depression deeply influenced those who lived through them. American folk stories often capture how Americans responded to the challenges of such events. The stories emphasize universal American themes such as resourcefulness.

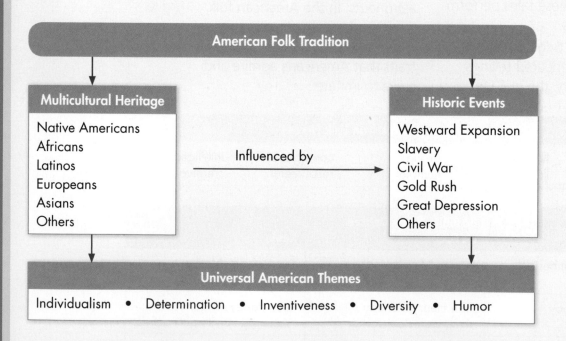

American Folk Tradition

Multicultural Heritage

Native Americans
Africans
Latinos
Europeans
Asians
Others

Influenced by

Historic Events

Westward Expansion
Slavery
Civil War
Gold Rush
Great Depression
Others

Universal American Themes

Individualism • Determination • Inventiveness • Diversity • Humor

As in other literary genres, themes in the American folk tradition are usually developed through details of character, setting, and plot. To determine the theme of a story, read carefully to analyze these details. Think about how the details relate to each other and what underlying message or insight about life they offer.

Character A character is a person, an animal, or an imaginary creature that takes part in the action of a story. In American folk stories, main characters often display remarkable confidence, physical strength, determination, and resourcefulness. These qualities allow them to overcome obstacles, no matter how challenging. The words and actions of these characters, as well as the lessons they learn, help to develop themes such as the value of determination.

Example: Character

Paul Bunyan is an incredibly large, strong, and inventive lumberjack. His deeds illustrate the **theme** that even the greatest challenge can be overcome through hard work and inventiveness.

Setting The setting is the time and place in which the action of a story occurs. American folk stories are often set in real locations. While the places may be real, the details that describe them are often exaggerated to create greater challenges for characters.

Example: Setting

Paul Bunyan's adventures are set in the logging camps of America's North Woods, in real locations such as Wisconsin and Minnesota. Life in the woods offers unique challenges, and when Bunyan overcomes them, his success illustrates **themes** of the power of human beings to tame the wild.

Plot and Conflict Plot is the sequence of events in a story. The plots of many American folk stories, especially legends, are loosely based on real events.

In all stories, the plot is moved forward by the **conflicts,** or struggles, that characters face. In American folk stories, the conflicts are often *external*—they take place between a character and an outside force. Characters may face problems posed by another character, the landscape, economics, or other external obstacles. In some cases, external conflicts may cause characters to deal with *internal* conflicts—struggles within themselves. However, most often the primary conflict in the story is external.

Example: Plot and Conflict

While tales about Paul Bunyan are fictional, the stories often feature activities that actually occurred in logging camps. Paul Bunyan's conflicts reflect the challenges that America's pioneers faced in moving west. These conflicts help to develop **themes** of determination.

Meet the Authors

Richard Erdoes
(1912–2008) was born
in Vienna, Austria, but
in 1940 he moved to the
U.S. to escape Nazi rule.
Erdoes became an author,
a photographer, and an
illustrator. He wrote several
books on Native Americans
and the American West.

Alfonso Ortiz (1939–
1997) was a Tewa Pueblo,
born in New Mexico.
He became a professor
of anthropology at the
University of New Mexico
and a leading expert on
Pueblo culture. He worked
with Erdoes on Native
American story collections.

**Ⓒ Common Core
State Standards**

Reading Literature
2. Determine a theme or central
idea of a text and analyze its
development over the course of the
text; provide an objective summary
of the text.

Language
6 Acquire and use accurately grade-
appropriate general academic and
domain-specific words and phrases;
gather vocabulary knowledge
when considering a word or phrase
important to comprehension or
expression.

? Are yesterday's heroes important today?

Explore the Big Question as you read "Coyote Steals the Sun and
Moon." Take notes on why this myth has enduring appeal.

CLOSE READING FOCUS

Key Ideas and Details: **Summarize**

A **summary** is a short statement that presents the key ideas
of a text. Summarizing helps you identify the most important
information in a passage or work. Follow these steps to summarize:

- Reread the text and write down the main events or ideas.
- Organize your notes. Put the main points in order and cross off
  minor details that are not needed for understanding.
- Restate the major points in as few words as possible. Be sure
  your summary does not include your personal opinions.

Craft and Structure: **Mythology**

A **myth** is a traditional tale presenting the beliefs or customs of
a culture. Many traditional cultures have a **mythology**, or set of
myths. These traditional tales share the following characteristics:

- They explain events in nature or in a people's history.
- They may describe the actions of supernatural beings and
  animals or natural forces that are given human qualities.
- They convey cultural *themes*, or insights into cultural values.

In Greek mythology, for example, the hero Prometheus steals
fire from the god Zeus and gives it to humans. Fire was essential
for cooking, forging weapons, and providing warmth in ancient
Greece. When reading a myth, consider how it reflects the
experiences and values of the storyteller's culture.

Vocabulary

You will find the following words in this myth. Copy them into your
notebook. Explain which ones are nouns, and how you know.

sacred	pestering	lagged
shriveled	pursuit	curiosity

CLOSE READING MODEL

The passage below is from the myth "Coyote Steals the Sun and Moon." The annotations to the right of the passage show ways in which you can use close reading skills to summarize the text and to analyze the elements of myth.

from "Coyote Steals the Sun and Moon"

At last they came to a pueblo, where the Kachinas happened to be dancing.[1] The people invited Eagle and Coyote to sit down and have something to eat while they watched the sacred dances. Seeing the power of the Kachinas, Eagle said, "I believe these are the people who have light."[2]

Coyote, who had been looking all around, pointed out two boxes, one large and one small, that the people opened whenever they wanted light. To produce a lot of light, they opened the lid of the big box, which contained the sun. For less light they opened the small box, which held the moon.[3]

Coyote nudged Eagle. "Friend, did you see that? They have all the light we need in the big box. Let's steal it."

"You always want to steal and rob. I say we should just borrow it."

"They won't lend it to us."

"You may be right," said Eagle. "Let's wait till they finish dancing and then steal it."

After a while the Kachinas went home to sleep, and Eagle scooped up the large box and flew off. Coyote ran along trying to keep up, panting, his tongue hanging out.[4]

Summarize
1 Coyote and Eagle's arrival at the pueblo is a major detail—it explains where the action takes place. The dancing is less important. A summary of this passage should include the first detail, but it might omit the second.

Mythology
2 In this story, Coyote and Eagle are animal characters that have been given human qualities, such as the ability to speak. Myths often feature animals that have been given human characteristics.

Mythology
3 This Native American myth provides an explanation for a natural event. It describes the origin of the sun and the moon.

Summarize
4 A summary of the entire passage, including this last paragraph, might read, "Coyote and Eagle visit a pueblo of the Kachinas. They see the sun and moon in boxes. They steal the box with the sun and run off."

Coyote Steals the Sun and Moon

retold by Richard Erdoes and Alfonso Ortiz

Coyote is a bad hunter who never kills anything. Once he watched Eagle hunting rabbits, catching one after another—more rabbits than he could eat. Coyote thought, "I'll team up with Eagle so I can have enough meat." Coyote is always up to something.

"Friend," Coyote said to Eagle, "we should hunt together. Two can catch more than one."

"Why not?" Eagle said, and so they began to hunt in partnership. Eagle caught many rabbits, but all Coyote caught was some little bugs.

At this time the world was still dark; the sun and moon had not yet been put in the sky. "Friend," Coyote said to Eagle, "no wonder I can't catch anything; I can't see. Do you know where we can get some light?"

"You're right, friend, there should be some light," Eagle said. "I think there's a little toward the west. Let's try and find it."

And so they went looking for the sun and moon. They came to a big river, which Eagle flew over. Coyote swam, and swallowed so much water that he almost drowned. He crawled out with his fur full of mud, and Eagle asked, "Why don't you fly like me?"

"You have wings; I just have hair," Coyote said. "I can't fly without feathers."

At last they came to a pueblo,[1] where the Kachinas happened to be dancing. The people invited Eagle and Coyote to sit down and have something to eat while they watched the sacred dances. Seeing the power of the Kachinas, Eagle said,

Vocabulary ▶
sacred (sā´ krəd) *adj.* considered holy; related to religious ceremonies

---

1. **pueblo** (pweb´ lō) Native American settlement in the southwestern United States.

"I believe these are the people who have light."

Coyote, who had been looking all around, pointed out two boxes, one large and one small, that the people opened whenever they wanted light. To produce a lot of light, they opened the lid of the big box, which contained the sun. For less light they opened the small box, which held the moon.

Coyote nudged Eagle. "Friend, did you see that? They have all the light we need in the big box. Let's steal it."

"You always want to steal and rob. I say we should just borrow it."

"They won't lend it to us."

"You may be right," said Eagle. "Let's wait till they finish dancing and then steal it."

After a while the Kachinas went home to sleep, and Eagle scooped up the large box and flew off. Coyote ran along trying to keep up, panting, his tongue hanging out. Soon he yelled up to Eagle, "Ho, friend, let me carry the box a little way."

"No, no," said Eagle, "you never do anything right."

He flew on, and Coyote ran after him. After a while Coyote shouted again: "Friend, you're my chief, and it's not right for you to carry the box; people will call me lazy. Let me have it."

"No, no, you always mess everything up." And Eagle flew on and Coyote ran along.

So it went for a stretch, and then Coyote started again. "Ho, friend, it isn't right for you to do this. What will people think of you and me?"

"I don't care what people think. I'm going to carry this box."

Again Eagle flew on and again Coyote ran after him. Finally Coyote begged for the fourth time: "Let me carry it. You're the chief, and I'm just Coyote. Let me carry it."

Eagle couldn't stand any more pestering. Also, Coyote had asked him four times, and if someone asks four times, you'd better give him what he wants. Eagle said, "Since you won't let up on me, go ahead and carry the box for a while. But promise not to open it."

"Oh, sure, oh yes, I promise." They went on as before, but now Coyote had the box. Soon Eagle was far ahead, and Coyote

LITERATURE IN CONTEXT

Culture Connection

Kachinas

The Zuni and Hopi are Native American nations of the American Southwest. In both of these cultures, the Kachina dancers serve as links between the earthly world and the spirit world. Every year in colorful ceremonies, dancers perform, wearing masks representing various supernatural beings, or Kachinas.

The dancers play a central role in the religions of both cultures, where the blessings of the powerful spirits are sought every year for a good harvest and good fortune.

Connect to the Literature

What details in the story show that the Kachinas are powerful beings?

◄ **Vocabulary**
pestering (pes′ tər iŋ)
n. constant bothering

Comprehension
What do Coyote and Eagle team up to do?

Mythology
What human trait does
Coyote show here?

Vocabulary ▶
lagged (lagd) *v.*
fell behind

shriveled (shriv´ əld) *v.*
dried up; shrank
and wrinkled

pursuit (pər so͞ot´) *n.*
act of chasing in order
to catch (something)

curiosity (kyo͞or´ ē
äs´ ə tē) *n.* desire to
obtain information

Spiral Review
THEME AND PLOT
What lesson about
bad behavior does the
ending suggest?

lagged behind a hill where Eagle couldn't see him. "I wonder what the light looks like, inside there," he said to himself. "Why shouldn't I take a peek? Probably there's something extra in the box, something good that Eagle wants to keep to himself."

And Coyote opened the lid. Now, not only was the sun inside, but the moon also. Eagle had put them both together, thinking that it would be easier to carry one box than two.

As soon as Coyote opened the lid, the moon escaped, flying high into the sky. At once all the plants **shriveled** up and turned brown. Just as quickly, all the leaves fell off the trees, and it was winter. Trying to catch the moon and put it back in the box, Coyote ran in **pursuit** as it skipped away from him. Meanwhile the sun flew out and rose into the sky. It drifted far away, and the peaches, squashes, and melons shriveled up with cold.

Eagle turned and flew back to see what had delayed Coyote. "You fool! Look what you've done!" he said. "You let the sun and moon escape, and now it's cold." Indeed, it began to snow, and Coyote shivered. "Now your teeth are chattering," Eagle said, "and it's your fault that cold has come into the world."

It's true. If it weren't for Coyote's **curiosity** and mischief making, we wouldn't have winter; we could enjoy summer all the time.

Language Study

Vocabulary Answer each question using a word from the list.

pestering	lagged	shriveled	pursuit	curiosity

1. How would you describe a sheriff chasing a fugitive?

2. Why did the girl ask so many questions?

3. What happened to the garden plants after the first frost?

4. How would you describe an annoying younger child?

5. Why was the bicycle racer sure he would finish last?

WORD STUDY

The **Latin root** *-sacr-*
means "holy." In the
myth "Coyote Steals the
Sun and Moon," Eagle
and Coyote watch the
Kachina people perform
their **sacred**, or holy,
dances.

Word Study

Part A Explain how the **Latin root** *-sacr-* contributes to the meanings of *sacrament* and *consecrate*. Consult a dictionary if needed.

Part B Answer each question. Explain your answers using what you know about the Latin root *-sacr-*.

1. What might you *sacrifice* to do an extracurricular activity?

2. What would you avoid if you considered free time *sacrosanct*?

Close Reading Activities

Literary Analysis

Key Ideas and Details

1. (a) Compare and Contrast: How do Coyote and Eagle differ in their abilities and personalities? Support your answer with story details. **(b) Connect:** How do each character's actions reflect his personality?

2. (a) Analyze: Why do Eagle and Coyote want the Kachinas' box? Include details from the text in your answer. **(b) Infer:** Why does Eagle agree to steal it?

3. Summarize The characters' actions in this myth can be divided into four "scenes," or sections. Use a graphic organizer like the one shown to summarize the important events in each section.

4. Summarize Using your chart, summarize the entire story of "Coyote Steals the Sun and Moon" in as few sentences as possible, leaving out minor details.

Craft and Structure

5. Mythology What element of nature does this myth explain? Cite evidence from the text in your response.

6. Mythology Review the information about mythology on page 774. What characteristics do the main characters in this myth share with characters in other myths? Use examples from the text to support your response.

7. Mythology (a) What does this myth reveal about Zuni culture and beliefs? **(b)** What message, or moral, regarding nature can you infer from the myth? Support your answer with story details.

Integration of Knowledge and Ideas

8. (a) Compare and Contrast: What does this myth share with a scientific theory or explanation? How does it differ from science? Support your comparison with details from the myth.
(b) Generalize: Why might people in a culture that values science, such as modern America, still find this myth appealing?

9. **Are yesterday's heroes important today? (a)** What characters from television or movies can you think of who have qualities in common with Coyote? Explain, supporting your comparison with details from the myth. **(b)** Why might characters of this type appeal to people in diverse cultures?

The Hunt

Summary:

At the Kachinas' Dance

Summary:

Running Away

Summary:

Coyote's Mistake

Summary:

ACADEMIC VOCABULARY

As you write and speak about "Coyote Steals the Sun and Moon," use the words related to traditions and heroes that you explored on page 755 of this textbook.

Conventions: **Basic Sentence Structures**

Sentence structure is defined by the type of clauses in a sentence. The four basic sentence structures are shown below. Independent clauses are shown in boldface. Dependent, or subordinate, clauses (clauses that cannot stand alone as sentences) are underlined.

Sentence Structures	Examples
A **simple sentence** has a single independent clause with at least one subject and verb.	**The cat sleeps on the chair.**
A **compound sentence** consists of two or more independent clauses joined by a comma and a conjunction or by a semicolon.	**The cat sleeps on the chair,** and **the dog sleeps on the floor.**
A **complex sentence** consists of one independent clause and one or more dependent clauses.	**Jack,** who is my cousin, **raises golden retrievers,** which he exhibits at dog shows.
A **compound-complex** sentence consists of two or more independent clauses and one or more dependent clauses.	After she took her exam, **Sue had to pick up her sister,** but **she wanted to finish writing first.**

Practice A

Identify the structure of each of the following sentences.

1. When the world was still dark, Coyote and Eagle went in search of light.

2. Eagle could fly, but Coyote, who did not have feathers or wings, could not.

3. Eagle swooped and scooped up the box.

4. Although he promised not to, Coyote opened the box, and when he did, the sun and moon escaped.

Reading Application Find one example of each of the four basic sentence structures in the myth.

Practice B

Change each item into a compound or a complex sentence, adding words as needed. Identify the structure of each new sentence.

1. Coyote looked around and pointed out a large box and a small box.

2. The Kachinas opened the lid of the box.

3. The moon and the sun flew out of the large box into the sky.

4. Coyote was very curious and mischievous.

Writing Application Write four sentences about the myth using each of the four sentence types.

Writing to Sources

Narrative Text Create your own **myth** to explain a natural phenomenon. Feature the characters Coyote and Eagle from the Zuni myth.

- First, choose a natural feature or event—for example, a rainbow, the seasons, or certain animal behaviors.
- Think of yourself as a storyteller. Entertain your audience with informal elements such as idioms, or colorful turns of phrase, and humor.
- Make sure your myth has a central problem that comes to a reasonable and satisfactory conclusion. The resolution should explain the natural phenomenon you have chosen.
- The characters Coyote and Eagle should speak and act in your myth as they do in the original story.
- Edit your myth to make sure the resolution of the story explains the natural event.

Grammar Application Check your writing to make sure you have used a variety of sentence structures.

Speaking and Listening

Presentation of Ideas With a group, use the Internet and print sources to gather information for an **oral presentation** about "Coyote Steals the Sun and Moon." Look for ways in which history and traditional beliefs influence Zuni life and culture today. Show the connection between what you uncover in your research and specific details from the myth.

Keep these tips in mind while completing the assignment:

- Develop a plan to display information with visuals, such as photographs, charts, maps, and graphs.
- Use appropriate digital tools to create your presentation. For example, you could use multimedia software to create a slideshow of images related to the culture, accompanied by music.
- As you give your presentation, show sensitivity and respect when you discuss another culture's traditions and beliefs.

**Common Core
State Standards**

Writing

3. Write narratives to develop real or imagined experiences or events using effective technique, relevant descriptive details, and well-structured event sequences.

3.b. Use narrative techniques, such as dialogue, pacing, description, and reflection, to develop experiences, events, and/or characters.

3.e. Provide a conclusion that follows from and reflects on the narrated experiences or events.

Speaking and Listening

5. Integrate multimedia and visual displays into presentations to clarify information, strengthen claims and evidence, and add interest.

6. Adapt speech to a variety of contexts and tasks, demonstrating command of formal English when indicated or appropriate.

Meet the Authors

José Griego y Maestas
(b. 1949), an expert
in bilingual education,
and **Rudolfo A. Anaya**
(b. 1937), a celebrated
figure in Latino literature,
share a love of old New
Mexican folk tales, or
cuentos. As partners,
Griego y Maestas finds and
collects the tales, and Anaya
translates them into English.

Carl Sandburg (1878–
1967) was a journalist and
historian as well as a poet
and folklorist. He won two
Pulitzer Prizes, one for a
biography of Abraham
Lincoln and one for poetry.
In the early 1900s, he was
part of a writers' movement
in Chicago, a city that
inspired some of his best-
known poems.

 Are yesterday's heroes important today?

Explore the Big Question as you read "Chicoria" and the excerpt
from *The People, Yes.* Look for details that reflect the values of
specific cultures—as well as details with universal significance.

CLOSE READING FOCUS

Key Ideas and Details: **Summarize**

A **summary** is a short restatement of the main points or events in
a text. Summaries leave out minor details. To summarize a work of
literature, follow these steps:

- Read the text, and then identify the main idea or event.
- Determine additional events or ideas that are important.

When you have identified the main ideas, write your summary.
Consider first organizing ideas in a chart or other graphic organizer.

Craft and Structure: **Oral Tradition**

In the **oral tradition**, storytellers pass on legends, songs, and stories
by word of mouth. The material generally reflects the traditions of
the storytellers' culture. Here are some features of the oral tradition:

- Stories and songs may originally have been told in **dialect**—the
  language of a particular region. Writers who retell these stories
  may imitate the original dialect.
- Stories and songs often contain **idioms**—common expressions
  not meant literally, such as "strictly for the birds."

The use of dialect and idioms affects the tone or "feel" of oral
tradition literature. This literature may also feature repetition and
exaggeration (hyperbole); brave, clever, or strong heroes; and
animal characters acting as humans.

Vocabulary

Copy each of these words from the selections into your notebook.
Which names a type of storm? Explain how you know.

self-confident	cordially	haughty
straddling	cyclone	mutineers

**Common Core
State Standards**

Reading Literature
4. Determine the meaning of
words and phrases as they are used
in a text, including figurative and
connotative meanings; analyze the
impact of specific word choices
on meaning and tone, including
analogies or allusions to other texts.

CLOSE READING MODEL

The first passage below is from "Chicoria." The second passage is from *The People, Yes*. The annotations to the right show ways in which you can use close reading skills to summarize text and to identify elements of oral tradition.

from "Chicoria"

One day one of the big ranch owners asked his workers if there were any poets in New Mexico.

"Of course, we have many fine poets," they replied. "We have old Vilmas, Chicoria, Cinfuegos, to say nothing of the poets of Cebolleta and the Black Poet."

"Well, when you return next season, why don't you bring one of your poets to compete with Gracia. . . ."

When the harvest was done the New Mexicans returned home. The following season when they returned to California they took with them the poet Chicoria. . . .[1]

Summarize

1 The most important idea in this passage is that workers bring the New Mexican poet Chicoria back with them to California to compete with another poet. This main idea should appear in a summary. The rancher's first question and the list of New Mexican poets are less important and should be omitted.

from *The People, Yes*

They have yarns
Of a skyscraper so tall they had to put hinges
On the two top stories so to let the moon go by,
Of one corn crop in Missouri when the roots
5   Went so deep and drew off so much water
The Mississippi riverbed that year was dry,
Of pancakes so thin they only had one side,
Of "a fog so thick we shingled the barn and six
      feet out on the fog,"[2]
Of Pecos Pete straddling a cyclone in Texas and
      riding it to the west coast where "it rained out
      under him, . . ."[3]

Oral Tradition

2 These words are in quotation marks, as if someone were saying them. They also include an idiomatic phrase, "six feet out." A reader can almost "hear" the spoken words being passed along from the storyteller to the writer to the readers.

Oral Tradition

3 The author uses exaggeration to portray a strong and clever character—a characteristic of many tales in the oral tradition.

Chicoria

retold in English
by Rudolfo A. Anaya

adapted in Spanish by
José Griego y Maestas

There were once many big ranches in California, and many New Mexicans went to work there. One day one of the big ranch owners asked his workers if there were any poets in New Mexico.

"Of course, we have many fine poets," they replied. "We have old Vilmas, Chicoria, Cinfuegos, to say nothing of the poets of Cebolleta and the Black Poet."

"Well, when you return next season, why don't you bring one of your poets to compete with Gracia—here none can compare with him!"

When the harvest was done the New Mexicans returned home. The following season when they returned to California they took with them the poet Chicoria, knowing well that in spinning a rhyme or in weaving wit there was no *Californio*[1] who could beat him.

As soon as the rancher found out that the workers had brought Chicoria with them, he sent his servant to invite his good neighbor and friend to come and hear the new poet. Meanwhile, the cooks set about preparing a big meal. When the maids began to dish up the plates of food, Chicoria turned to one of the servers and said, "Ah, my friends, it looks like they are going to feed us well tonight!"

The servant was surprised. "No, my friend," he explained, "the food is for *them*. We don't eat at the master's table. It is not permitted. We eat in the kitchen."

"Well, I'll bet I can sit down and eat with them," Chicoria boasted.

"If you beg or if you ask, perhaps, but if you don't ask they won't invite you," replied the servant.

"I never beg," the New Mexican answered. "The master will invite me of his own accord, and I'll bet you twenty dollars he will!"

Oral Tradition
What ability of Chicoria's could be considered admirable in his culture?

Comprehension
What request did the ranch owner make of the New Mexicans?

---

1. *Californio* (kä′ lē fôr′ nyō) term for any one of the Spanish-speaking colonists who established ranches in California under Spanish and Mexican rule.

◀ **Critical Viewing** What details in this photograph suggest a festive occasion, such as the feast in the story?

Vocabulary ▶
self-confident (self´
kän´ fə dənt) *adj.*
certain of one's ability

cordially (kôr´ jə lē)
adv. warmly

haughty (hôt´ ē) *adj.*
scornfully superior

Oral Tradition
Do you think the teller
of this story is a New
Mexican or a *Californio*?
Why?

Spiral Review
THEME What
possible theme is
suggested by the
conclusion of the story?

Summarize
Would you consider
the winning of the bet
important enough to
include in a summary?
Why or why not?

So they made a twenty-dollar bet and they instructed the serving maid to watch if this **self-confident** New Mexican had to ask the master for a place at the table. Then the maid took Chicoria into the dining room. Chicoria greeted the rancher **cordially**, but the rancher appeared **haughty** and did not invite Chicoria to sit with him and his guest at the table. Instead, he asked that a chair be brought and placed by the wall where Chicoria was to sit. The rich ranchers began to eat without inviting Chicoria.

So it is just as the servant predicted, Chicoria thought. The poor are not invited to share the rich man's food!

Then the master spoke: "Tell us about the country where you live. What are some of the customs of New Mexico?"

"Well, in New Mexico when a family sits down to eat each member uses one spoon for each biteful of food," Chicoria said with a twinkle in his eyes.

The ranchers were amazed that the New Mexicans ate in that manner, but what Chicoria hadn't told them was that each spoon was a piece of tortilla:[2] one fold and it became a spoon with which to scoop up the meal.

"Furthermore," he continued, "our goats are not like yours."

"How are they different?" the rancher asked.

"Here your nannies[3] give birth to two kids, in New Mexico they give birth to three!"

"What a strange thing!" the master said. "But tell us, how can the female nurse three kids?"

"Well, they do it exactly as you're doing it now: While two of them are eating the third one looks on."

The rancher then realized his lack of manners and took Chicoria's hint. He apologized and invited his New Mexico guest to dine at the table. After dinner, Chicoria sang and recited his poetry, putting Gracia to shame. And he won his bet as well.

---

2. **tortilla** (tôr tē´ yə) *n.* thin, round pancake of cornmeal or flour.
3. **nannies** (nan´ ēz) *n.* female goats.

from
The People, Yes

Carl Sandburg

They have yarns[1]
Of a skyscraper so tall they had to put hinges
On the two top stories so to let the moon go by,
Of one corn crop in Missouri when the roots
5 Went so deep and drew off so much water

---

1. **yarns** (yärnz) *n.* tall tales that depend on humor and exaggeration.

▼ **Critical Viewing**
What type of mood
does this illustration
create?

The Mississippi riverbed that year was dry,
Of pancakes so thin they had only one side,
Of "a fog so thick we shingled the barn and six feet out
    on the fog,"
Of Pecos Pete **straddling** a **cyclone** in Texas and riding it
    to the west coast where "it rained out under him,"

10 Of the man who drove a swarm of bees across the Rocky
    Mountains and the Desert "and didn't lose a bee,"
Of a mountain railroad curve where the engineer in his
    cab can touch the caboose and spit in the conductor's eye,
Of the boy who climbed a cornstalk growing so fast he
    would have starved to death if they hadn't shot
    biscuits up to him,
Of the old man's whiskers: "When the wind was with
    him his whiskers arrived a day before he did,"
Of the hen laying a square egg and cackling, "Ouch!"
    and of hens laying eggs with the dates printed on them,

15 Of the ship captain's shadow: it froze to the deck one
    cold winter night,
Of **mutineers** on that same ship put to chipping rust
    with rubber hammers,
Of the sheep counter who was fast and accurate: "I just
    count their feet and divide by four,"
Of the man so tall he must climb a ladder to shave himself,

Vocabulary ▶

straddling (strad′ ′l in)
v. standing or sitting
with a leg on either
side of something

cyclone (sī′ klon′)
n. violent, rotating
windstorm; tornado

mutineers (myo͞ot′
′n irz′) *n.* rebels

Oral Tradition
Does Sandburg's use
of exaggeration and
repetition portray a
country at rest or on
the move? Explain.

Of the runt so teeny-weeny it takes two men and a boy to
    see him,
20 Of mosquitoes: one can kill a dog, two of them a man,
Of a cyclone that sucked cookstoves out of the kitchen,
    up the chimney flue, and on to the next town,
Of the same cyclone picking up wagon-tracks in Nebraska
    and dropping them over in the Dakotas,
Of the hook-and-eye snake unlocking itself into forty
    pieces, each piece two inches long, then in nine seconds
    flat snapping itself together again,
Of the watch swallowed by the cow—when they butchered
    her a year later the watch was running and had the
    correct time,
25 Of horned snakes, hoop snakes that roll themselves
    where they want to go, and rattlesnakes carrying bells
    instead of rattles on their tails,
Of the herd of cattle in California getting lost in a giant
    redwood tree that had hollowed out,
Of the man who killed a snake by putting its tail in its
    mouth so it swallowed itself,
Of railroad trains whizzing along so fast they reach the
    station before the whistle,
Of pigs so thin the farmer had to tie knots in their tails
    to keep them from crawling through the cracks in
    their pens,

Summarize
Would it be essential
to list all of the
characters and animals
in a summary of this
poem? Why or why
not?

Comprehension
What tall tales from
the poem do the
illustrations on pages
788 and 789 show?

BM-17—Paul Bunyan and Babe, his Blue Ox, Bemidji, Minn.

8B-H1052

Critical Viewing ▶
How do the figures shown here capture the spirit of this poem?

Oral Tradition
What characteristics are shared by the folk heroes mentioned at the end of the poem?

30 Of Paul Bunyan's big blue ox, Babe, measuring between
    the eyes forty-two ax-handles and a plug of Star tobacco
    exactly,
    Of John Henry's hammer and the curve of its swing and
    his singing of it as "a rainbow round my shoulder." . . .

Language Study

Vocabulary Use one of the blue words from the list below to complete each analogy.

self-confident   cordially   haughty   straddling   cyclone

1. *Rain* is to *cloudburst* as *wind* is to _____.

2. *Rudely* is to *enemy* as _____ is to *friend*.

3. *Arms* are to *hugging* as *legs* are to _____.

4. *Talkative* is to *silent* as _____ is to *insecure*.

5. *Gentle* is to *rough* as *humble* is to _____.

WORD STUDY

The **suffix -eer** means "one who does (something)." In the excerpt from *The People, Yes,* the narrator describes a group of **mutineers**, or sailors who rebel against their ship's captain.

Word Study

Part A Explain how the **suffix -eer** contributes to the meaning of the words *profiteer* and *rocketeer*. Consult a dictionary if needed.

Part B Answer each question. Use the context of the sentences and what you know about the suffix -eer to explain your answers.

1. Does an *auctioneer* want responses from an audience?

2. Would it be helpful for a *balladeer* to have a pleasant voice?

Close Reading Activities

Literary Analysis

Key Ideas and Details

1. Summarize (a) To help you summarize the plot of "Chicoria," construct a timeline of events. **(b)** Use your timeline to write a brief summary of the plot.

2. Summarize (a) Fill in a cluster diagram like the one shown with descriptions of imagery in the excerpt from *The People, Yes*. **(b)** Summarize the poem by stating the main idea behind the imagery.

Craft and Structure

3. Oral Tradition Review the information about the qualities of the oral tradition on page 782. How is Chicoria both typical and *not* typical of a hero in the oral tradition? Cite textual evidence to support your response.

4. Oral Tradition (a) What features of the oral tradition are contained in lines 8–21 of Sandburg's poem? **(b)** Explain the meanings of *runt* and *teeny-weeny* (line 19) and the tone these words create.

Cluster diagram:

- Pecos Pete straddles a cyclone
- Cattle lost in a redwood tree
- **Main Idea**

Integration of Knowledge and Ideas

5. (a) Draw Conclusions: What does "Chicoria" suggest about the power of words? Cite examples from the text. **(b) Generalize:** What does it suggest about good behavior? **(c) Evaluate:** Might Chicoria's method of teaching people good behavior work in any circumstances, or are there limits? Explain.

6. Synthesize: Sandburg writes about early American folk heroes. List three characters from *The People, Yes,* who have special abilities. Explain why each character's abilities might be valued in a new country, where much of the land is still wild. Support your evaluation with details from the text.

7. Interpret: With a partner, interpret the meaning of the title *The People, Yes.* Support your answer with details from the text. Share your answers with the class.

8. **Are yesterday's heroes important today?** With a small group, discuss the following questions. **(a)** What traits do you think are valued by the cultures that developed these tales? **(b) Evaluate:** Are the heroes of these tales inspirational in today's world?

ACADEMIC VOCABULARY

As you write and speak about "Chicoria" and the excerpt from *The People, Yes,* use the words related to traditions and heroes you explored on page 755 of this textbook.

Conventions: **Commas and Semicolons**

> A **comma (,)** is a punctuation mark that signals a brief pause.
> A **semicolon (;)** may be used to join two independent clauses.

Use a comma . . .	
1) . . . before a conjunction to separate two independent clauses in a compound sentence.	The wind howled, **and** the rain pelted the roof.
2) . . . between items in a series.	Campers **sang songs, told stories, and ate.**
3) . . . between *coordinate adjectives,* adjectives of equal rank whose order may be switched.	The **wet, weary** hikers returned to the cabin. [*No comma*: Two wet hikers returned to the cabin.]
4) . . . after introductory words, phrases, or clauses.	**On the following day,** the sun shone brightly.
5) . . . to set off nonrestrictive, or nonessential, phrases or clauses.	Fish Lake, **which is in Utah,** is lovely. [*No commas*: The lake **where we camp** is lovely.]
Use a semicolon . . .	
1) . . . to join independent clauses not joined by the conjunctions *and, but, or, nor, for, so,* or *yet.*	The car ran out of gas; I called a tow truck.
2) . . . to separate independent clauses joined by adverbs such as *however* and *therefore* or by phrases such as *on the other hand.*	It rained; **however**, I had an umbrella.

Practice A

Identify where commas are needed in each of the following sentences.

1. According to Sandburg's poem folk literature has preserved many tall tales.
2. The long thirsty roots of one corn crop drained the Mississippi River dry.
3. The eggs of some hens were square and the eggs of others had dates on them.
4. Cattle got lost inside a redwood a giant tree.

Reading Application In "Chicoria," find a sentence using comma rule 1 on the chart.

Practice B

Rewrite each sentence, adding a semicolon where it is needed.

1. The New Mexicans went home however, they returned for the next harvest.
2. He sat at the table on the other hand, Chicoria sat in the corner.
3. This tale has many characters it even includes a giant blue ox.
4. The pigs were too thin the farmer had to tie knots in their tails.

Writing Application Use a semicolon in a sentence about *The People, Yes.*

Writing to Sources

Explanatory Text Write a **critical analysis** to explain how language affects the tone, meaning, and mood in folk literature. Use these tips:

- Draw on specific examples from the works you read here. You may add examples from other sources.
- Analyze the literal and figurative meanings of idioms, analogies, metaphors, and similes in the examples. Then, explain how these word choices evoke emotional responses. In "Chicoria," for example, the goat analogy, or comparison, helps readers appreciate Chicoria's cleverness. The analogy may also entertain readers.
- Point out examples of comic techniques, such as the hyperbole, or exaggeration, used in the excerpt from *The People, Yes*.

Grammar Application Check your draft to make sure you used commas correctly, particularly with introductory elements.

Speaking and Listening

Comprehension and Collaboration Working with a group, conduct a **storytelling workshop**. Follow these steps to complete the assignment:

- Choose a folk tale that the class has read, and discuss ways of presenting it.
- Each group member should then make his or her own determinations about the most effective way to interpret the story, including the use of voice and gestures to dramatize the action, the use of props, and the addition of new descriptions.
- Use appropriate language. If there is dialect in the original, performers may choose to translate it for clarity or retain it for faithfulness to the original.
- Group members should take turns retelling the story for the class.
- Audience members should determine the extent to which each retelling is faithful to the original. The audience should also evaluate the choices each performer has made, based on dramatic impact, clarity of meaning, and consistency of approach.

Common Core State Standards

Reading Literature
4. Determine the meaning of words and phrases as they are used in a text, including figurative and connotative meanings; analyze the impact of specific word choices on meaning and tone, including analogies or allusions to other texts.
7. Analyze the extent to which a filmed or live production of a story or drama stays faithful to or departs from the text or script, evaluating the choices made by the director or actors.

Writing
2. Write informative/explanatory texts to examine a topic and convey ideas, concepts, and information through the selection, organization, and analysis of relevant content.
9. Draw evidence from literary or informational texts to support analysis, reflection, and research.

Speaking and Listening
6. Adapt speech to a variety of contexts and tasks, demonstrating command of formal English when indicated or appropriate.

Language
2.a. Use punctuation to indicate a pause or break.

Karen Hesse (b. 1952) shows her imagination and powers of understanding in her vivid characters, who struggle to survive during difficult times in history. Characters in her historical novels include a Russian immigrant in 1919, a woman caught up in the drama of the Civil War, and a boy who stows away on an explorer's ship during the 1700s. "I love research, love dipping into another time and place, and asking questions," Hesse says.

© Common Core State Standards

Reading Literature
1. Cite the textual evidence that most strongly supports an analysis of what the text says explicitly as well as inferences drawn from the text.

Language
4.b. Use common, grade-appropriate Greek or Latin affixes and roots as clues to the meaning of a word (e.g., *precede*, *recede*, *secede*).

? Are yesterday's heroes important today?

Explore the Big Question as you read the three poems from *Out of the Dust*. Take notes on the characters' responses to adversity.

CLOSE READING FOCUS

Key Ideas and Details: **Purpose for Reading**

Focus your attention before you read by setting a **purpose for reading**. You might read for these purposes:

- to learn something new or to find additional information.
- to amuse or to challenge yourself.
- to gain insight into another person's point of view.

An effective way to set and achieve a purpose is to ask questions. As you begin to read, ask yourself what you already know about the topic and what you hope to learn. After reading, ask yourself what you have learned. If you have learned what you set out to, you have achieved your purpose.

Use this technique to set a purpose for reading the excerpt from *Out of the Dust*.

Craft and Structure: **Cultural Context**

The **cultural context** of a literary work is the social and historical environment of the characters, including the historical events through which they live. Understanding these events can give you insight into characters' attitudes and actions.

To understand a work's cultural context, read about the time period. Then, make inferences from textual details to understand how characters respond to the events that you researched.

Vocabulary

Copy these words from the poems into your notebook. Which word is an adjective meaning "full of gratitude or thanks"? How do you know?

feuding	spindly	drought
grateful	sparse	rickety

CLOSE READING MODEL

The passage below is from a poem in *Out of the Dust*. The annotations to the right of the passage show ways in which you can use close reading skills to set a purpose for reading and to analyze the cultural context of a literary work.

from *Out of the Dust*

Daddy is thinking
of taking a loan from Mr. Roosevelt and his men,
to get some new wheat planted
where the winter crop has spindled out and died.[1]
5 Mr. Roosevelt promises
Daddy won't have to pay a dime
till the crop comes in.[2]

Daddy says,
"I can turn the fields over,
10 start again.
It's sure to rain soon.
Wheat's sure to grow."

Ma says, "What if it doesn't?"[3]

Daddy takes off his hat,
15 roughs up his hair,
puts the hat back on.
"Course it'll rain," he says.

Ma says, "Bay,
it hasn't rained enough to grow wheat in
20 three years."[4]

Purpose for Reading

1 In the opening lines of the passage, the poet refers to dead crops. Two purposes for reading further might be to learn what caused the crops to fail and to gain insight into how this crop failure affects the poem's characters.

Cultural Context

2 The poet mentions a promise made by President Roosevelt. Research into Roosevelt's programs would give a reader a better understanding of the poem's cultural context.

Cultural Context

3 The characters are uncertain about whether the crops will grow this year, a reference to a historical event—a crop failure in the 1930s. Background knowledge about the effect of this event would help a reader understand how serious the situation is—and so better understand the characters' reactions.

Purpose for Reading

4 The crops are dead because it has not rained in three years. A reader can now answer the question *What have I learned about the cause of the crop failure?*, achieving a possible purpose for reading.

from
Out of the DUST
Karen Hesse

Purpose for Reading
What is a purpose you could set for reading historical fiction, such as this poem?

Debts

Daddy is thinking
of taking a loan from Mr. Roosevelt and his men,[1]
to get some new wheat planted
where the winter crop has spindled out and died.
5 Mr. Roosevelt promises
Daddy won't have to pay a dime
till the crop comes in.

---

1. **a loan from Mr. Roosevelt and his men** In 1933, President Franklin D. Roosevelt began a series of government programs, called the New Deal, to help Americans suffering from the effects of the Great Depression. Among these programs were government loans to help Dust Bowl farmers.

Daddy says,
"I can turn the fields over,
10 start again.
It's sure to rain soon.
Wheat's sure to grow."

Ma says, "What if it doesn't?"

Daddy takes off his hat,
15 roughs up his hair,
puts the hat back on.
"Course it'll rain," he says.

Ma says, "Bay,
it hasn't rained enough to grow wheat in
20 three years."

Daddy looks like a fight brewing.

He takes that red face of his out to the barn,
to keep from **feuding** with my pregnant ma.

I ask Ma
25 how,
after all this time,
Daddy still believes in rain.

"Well, it rains enough," Ma says,
"now and again,
30 to keep a person hoping.
But even if it didn't
your daddy would have to believe.
It's coming on spring,
and he's a farmer."

March 1934

◄ **Critical Viewing**
Why does a dust storm
like this one pose a
danger to farms and
farmers?

Cultural Context
What does this
conversation indicate
about the effect of
dry weather on farm
families?

◄ **Vocabulary**
feuding (fyo͞od´ iŋ) *v.*
quarreling; fighting

Purpose for Reading
What can you learn
from the poem about
farmers' reactions to the
lack of rainfall in 1934?

Social Studies Connection

The Great Depression

The stock market crashed October 29, 1929—"Black Tuesday"—ushering in the worst economic collapse the United States ever experienced. More than 15 million Americans lost their jobs. The Depression lasted through the early 1940s. Making matters worse, a drought spread through 75 percent of the country during the 1930s, causing devastating dust storms.

BROOKLYN DAILY EAGLE
And Complete Long Island News

LATE NEWS
WALL STREET
1:15 PRICES ★ ★

89th YEAR—No. 295.
★ NEW YORK CITY, THURSDAY, OCTOBER 24, 1929. ★
32 PAGES
THREE CENTS

WALL ST. IN PANIC AS STOCKS CRASH

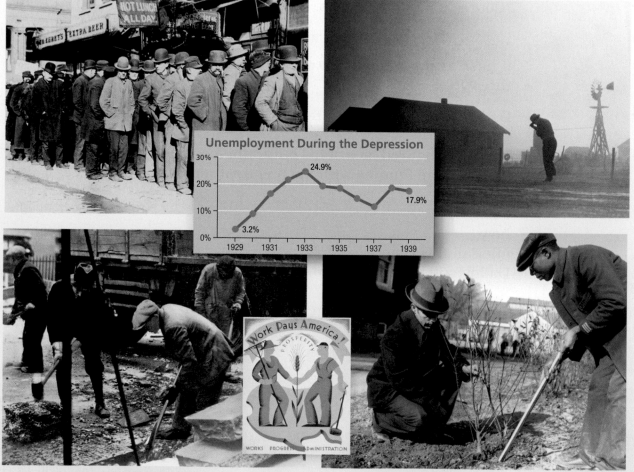

Bread lines were common city sights during ▼ the Depression.

President Franklin D. Roosevelt offered assistance to people in rural areas who were ▼ affected by the drought.

Unemployment During the Depression

3.2% (1929) ... 24.9% (1933) ... 17.9% (1939)

▲ In cities, the WPA (Works Progress Administration) put people to work repairing roads.

▲ Restoring drought-damaged land by planting new trees was another WPA goal.

Connect to the Literature   How could government programs have helped Ma and Daddy?

Fields of Flashing Light

I heard the wind rise,
and stumbled from my bed,
down the stairs,
out the front door,
5   into the yard.
The night sky kept flashing,
lightning danced down on its **spindly** legs.

I sensed it before I knew it was coming.
I heard it,
10   smelled it,
tasted it.
Dust.

While Ma and Daddy slept,
the dust came,
15   tearing up fields where the winter wheat,
set for harvest in June,
stood helpless.

Purpose for Reading
What would you want to know after reading this poem's title?

◀ **Vocabulary**
spindly (spind′ lē)
adj. long and thin

Comprehension
What noise wakes the speaker from her bed?

Vocabulary ▶
drought (drout) *n.*
lack of rain; long
period of dry weather

I watched the plants,
surviving after so much **drought** and so much wind,
20 I watched them fry,
or
flatten,
or blow away,
like bits of cast-off rags.
25 It wasn't until the dust turned toward the house,
like a fired locomotive,
and I fled,
barefoot and breathless, back inside,
it wasn't until the dust
30 hissed against the windows,
until it ratcheted the roof,
that Daddy woke.

Spiral Review
THEME What theme
might the sentence
"You can't stop dust"
suggest?

He ran into the storm,
his overalls half-hooked over his union suit.[2]
35 "Daddy!" I called. "You can't stop dust."

Ma told me to
cover the beds,
push the scatter rugs against the doors,
dampen the rags around the windows.
40 Wiping dust out of everything,
she made coffee and biscuits,
waiting for Daddy to come in.

Cultural Context
What do the
characters' reactions
to the dust storm
tell you about the
emotional effect of
this natural disaster?

Sometime after four,
rubbing low on her back,
45 Ma sank down into a chair at the kitchen table
and covered her face.
Daddy didn't come back for hours,
not
until the temperature dropped so low,
50 it brought snow.

Vocabulary ▶
grateful (grāt´ fəl)
adj. thankful

Ma and I sighed, **grateful**,
staring out at the dirty flakes,
but our relief didn't last.
The wind snatched that snow right off the fields,

---

2. **union suit** type of long underwear, common in the 1930s, that combines a shirt and
leggings in one garment.

55 leaving behind a sea of dust,
waves and
waves and
waves of
dust,
60 rippling across our yard.

Daddy came in,
he sat across from Ma and blew his nose.
Mud streamed out.
He coughed and spit out
65 mud.
If he had cried,
his tears would have been mud too,
but he didn't cry.
And neither did Ma.

March 1934

Migrants

We'll be back when the rain comes,
they say,
pulling away with all they own,
straining the springs of their motor cars.
5 Don't forget us.

And so they go,
fleeing the blowing dust,
fleeing the fields of brown-tipped wheat
barely ankle high,
10 and **sparse** as the hair on a dog's belly.

We'll be back, they say,
pulling away toward Texas,
Arkansas,
where they can rent a farm,
15 pull in enough cash,
maybe start again.

Purpose for Reading
What information does the poem provide about the Dust Bowl that you could not get from a history textbook?

Cultural Context
What economic forces drive away the migrants?

◀ **Vocabulary**
sparse (spärs) *adj.*
thinly spread and small in amount

▶ **Critical Viewing**
What details in this historic photograph indicate that this family is moving?

We'll be back when it rains,
they say,
setting out with their bedsprings and mattresses,
20　their cookstoves and dishes,
their kitchen tables,
and their milk goats
tied to their running boards[3]
in **rickety** cages,
25　setting out for
California,
where even though they say they'll come back,
they just might stay
if what they hear about that place is true.

30　Don't forget us, they say.
But there are so many leaving,
how can I remember them all?

April 1935

Vocabulary ▶
rickety (rik´ it ē) *adj.*
likely to break or
fall because weak

---

3. **running boards** steps, or footboards, that ran along the lower part of each side of a car, as shown in the photograph (p. 801). Running boards were common on cars of the 1930s.

Language Study

Vocabulary The words listed below appear in *Out of the Dust*. For each item, write the vocabulary word that matches the meaning of the pair of synonyms given. Explain why its meaning is similar.

feuding   spindly   drought   sparse   rickety

1. weak, shaky, _____

2. long, thin, _____

3. quarreling, fighting, _____

4. scanty, scattered, _____

5. dryness, aridness, _____

WORD STUDY

The **Latin root -*grat*-**
means "thankful" or
"pleased." In *Out of
the Dust*, characters are
grateful, or thankful,
when a change in the
weather provides a
break from destructive
dust storms.

Word Study

Part A Explain how the **Latin root -*grat*-** contributes to the meanings of *ingrate*, *gratitude*, and *ingratiate*. Consult a dictionary if necessary.

Part B Answer each question. Use the context of the sentences and what you know about the Latin root -*grat*- to explain your answers.

1. Why is *ingratitude* a poor reaction to receiving a gift?

2. Would you *congratulate* someone for doing poorly on an exam?

Close Reading Activities

Literary Analysis

Key Ideas and Details

1. **Purpose for Reading (a)** What purpose did you set for reading the poems? **(b)** What questions did you ask to help you do so?

2. **Purpose for Reading (a)** What details from the poems helped you answer your questions? **(b)** Where could you look to find more information to answer your questions?

3. **Purpose for Reading** One purpose for reading historical fiction is to learn about the problems faced by people who lived in another time and place. What problems did the characters in these poems face? Cite specific details to support your answers.

Craft and Structure

4. **Cultural Context (a)** Explain what each detail from *Out of the Dust* listed in the chart reveals about the poems' cultural context—the living conditions and attitudes of the farmers during the Dust Bowl. **(b)** Choose one of your answers in (a). Cite one additional detail from the text that strongly supports your inference about the poems' cultural context.

5. **Cultural Context (a)** Identify any background knowledge learned in school that helped you understand the poems. **(b)** What sources might you use to learn additional background information about the poems' cultural context?

Integration of Knowledge and Ideas

6. **(a) Compare:** What parallels can you find in the poems between the relentless power of nature and the stubborn determination of people? Cite details from the text. **(b) Draw Conclusions:** Summarize the picture that the poems paint of people's relationship with nature.

7. **Are yesterday's heroes important today? (a)** Do the family members in these poems act in ways that are heroic? Cite specific details from the text to support your response. **(b)** What can we learn by reading about the struggles of Depression-era families like the one in *Out of the Dust*? **(c)** Are those lessons relevant today? Explain.

Detail
1. Dust blew in on the wind and covered the crops.
2. Ma and Daddy do not cry when their wheat crop is destroyed.
3. Daddy decides to plant again, but other families decide to move away.

Cultural Conditions and Attitudes
1.
2.
3.

ACADEMIC VOCABULARY

As you write and speak about the poems from *Out of the Dust*, use the words related to traditions and heroes that you explored on page 755 of this textbook.

Conventions: **Ellipses and Dashes**

An **ellipsis (. . .)** shows an omission from a quoted passage or a pause in speech. A **dash (—)** shows a strong, sudden break in thought or speech.

This chart demonstrates when to use an ellipsis or a dash.

Use an ellipsis . . .	Examples
• . . . to show the reader that you have chosen to omit a word or words from a quoted passage	"The article he wrote about ocean exploration was gripping." ⟶ "The article . . . was gripping."
• . . . to indicate a pause or an interruption in speech	"He warned me, but . . . but I didn't listen."

Use a dash . . .	Examples
• . . . to show the reader that there is a strong, sudden break in thought or speech	"I can't believe—hey, watch your step!—how crowded this store is."
• . . . in place of *in other words, namely,* or *that is* before an explanation	The baker had only one wish—to make the perfect apple pie.
• . . . to set off nonrestrictive elements (modifiers or other elements that are not essential to the meaning of the sentence) when there is a sudden break in thought	The food drive—organized by students—was a great success.

Practice A

Use an ellipsis to omit a portion of each of these quotations without altering the meaning.

1. "In the poem, the girl and her mother are grateful when the snow begins to fall, and they stand staring at the flakes."

2. "The wind comes and, despite what they might have hoped, blows away the snow but leaves the dust."

3. "Apparently, the rain comes, not often enough to grow crops, but often enough to keep them hoping."

Reading Application Find a sentence in *Out of the Dust* in which an ellipsis could be used to indicate a pause in speech.

Practice B

Rewrite each of these sentences, adding a dash or dashes where they are needed.

1. It hasn't rained enough in a long time nearly three years.

2. Ma sank wait, Daddy's still outside!

3. Migrants packed many things dishes, tables, even goats to head west.

4. The speaker senses it coming the dust while her parents are still asleep.

Writing Application Write a five-sentence dialogue about the Dust Bowl, using ellipses and dashes correctly.

Writing to Sources

Explanatory Text Write a brief **research proposal** for a study of how the Dust Bowl affected farmers in the 1930s.

- Identify three specific details from *Out of the Dust* that you would like to investigate, quoting from the poem.

- For each detail, formulate a specific question that you would like answered. In a chart, identify the types of sources that might provide the information you need to answer each question.

- Find at least three sources, including both *primary sources* (firsthand accounts) and *secondary sources* (works by researchers). List these sources in a preliminary bibliography, using an approved format.

- In one paragraph, present and explain your thesis statement, the main idea that you propose exploring through research.

Grammar Application Make sure to use ellipses correctly if you omit any words from material that you quote.

Research and Technology

Build and Present Knowledge *Out of the Dust* is written from the point of view of a young girl, the poem's speaker. Imagine that the speaker's family has decided to move to California after all. Write a **letter** from her point of view to a friend back home. In your letter, describe the family's experience as migrants. Follow these steps:

- Research the experiences of Dust Bowl migrants to California.

- Gather specific textual details about the speaker and her family from the poems in *Out of the Dust*.

- Imagining that you are the speaker, write a letter to a friend whose family has stayed behind in the Midwest.

- Establish context by giving details that describe the speaker's situation. Make sure that the details you give are consistent with the characters and events in the poems. Use vivid sensory details to describe the speaker's experiences on the trip and then upon her arrival.

- Write your letter by hand, and use the proper format for a friendly letter. (See Writing Friendly Letters in the back of this textbook.) Be sure that your letter is neat and legible and uses proper punctuation to indicate pauses and breaks.

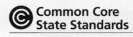

Common Core State Standards

Writing

3. Write narratives to develop real or imagined experiences or events using effective technique, relevant descriptive details, and well-structured event sequences.

3.a. Engage and orient the reader by establishing a context and point of view and introducing a narrator and/or characters; organize an event sequence that unfolds naturally and logically.

3.d. Use precise words and phrases, relevant descriptive details, and sensory language to capture the action and convey experiences and events.

7. Conduct short research projects to answer a question, drawing on several sources and generating additional related, focused questions that allow for multiple avenues of exploration.

Language

2.a Use punctuation (comma, ellipsis, dash) to indicate a pause or break.

2.b Use an ellipsis to indicate an omission.

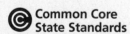

Although **Stephen Crane** (1871–1900) was born years after the Civil War had ended, he was fascinated by the war. He set out to write a book that would change the way people viewed war novels. Crane pored over battlefield maps, reproductions of photographs, and firsthand accounts of the fighting. He may also have spoken with veterans of the war. Crane used his research to craft realistic portraits of the characters in *The Red Badge of Courage*, the novel that made him a household name.

Ⓒ Common Core State Standards

Reading Literature
1. Cite the textual evidence that most strongly supports an analysis of what the text says explicitly as well as inferences drawn from the text.

Language
4.b. Use common, grade-appropriate Greek or Latin affixes and roots as clues to the meaning of a word.

❓ Are yesterday's heroes important today?

Explore the Big Question as you read "An Episode of War." Take notes on what the story shows about the nature of heroism.

CLOSE READING FOCUS

Key Ideas and Details: **Purpose for Reading**

When you set a **purpose for reading**, you determine what your focus will be as you read. Once you have set a purpose, adjust your reading rate to best meet that goal.

- Reading for information: read slowly and carefully. After completing a difficult or important passage, think about what you have read. If necessary, read it again.
- Reading for entertainment: read more quickly. You may reread or linger over certain passages, but studying the text is less important.

Check regularly to make sure you are meeting your purpose. Consult references as needed to better understand the work.

Craft and Structure: **Author's Influences**

An **author's influences** are the cultural and historical factors that affect his or her writing. Take these steps to connect a literary work to its author's heritage, attitudes, and beliefs:

- Read biographical information to learn about an author's important life experiences and cultural background.
- When reading the author's work, note details that show his or her values. Note references to historical events or cultural influences that might have shaped these values.
- Then, make inferences from these details to determine the effect of culture and history on the author's views.

Vocabulary

Copy these words from the short story into your notebook. Which word is an antonym for *respectfully*? How do you know?

winced	audible	compelled
tumultuous	contempt	disdainfully

CLOSE READING MODEL

The passage below is from "An Episode of War." The annotations to the right of the passage show ways in which you can use close reading skills to achieve your purpose for reading and to identify the author's influences.

from "An Episode of War"

As the wounded officer passed from the line of battle, he was enabled to see many things which as a participant in the fight were unknown to him. He saw a general on a black horse gazing over the lines of blue infantry at the green woods which veiled his problems. An aide galloped furiously, dragged his horse suddenly to a halt, saluted, and presented a paper. It was, for a wonder, precisely like a historical painting.[1]

To the rear of the general and his staff a group, composed of a bugler, two or three orderlies, and the bearer of the corps standard,[2] all upon maniacal horses, were working like slaves to hold their ground, preserve their respectful interval, while the shells boomed in the air about them, and caused their chargers to make furious quivering leaps.

A battery, a tumultuous and shining mass, was swirling toward the right. The wild thud of hoofs, the cries of the riders shouting blame and praise, menace and encouragement, and, last, the roar of the wheels, the slant of the glistening guns, brought the lieutenant to an intent pause.[3] The battery swept in curves that stirred the heart;[4] it made halts as dramatic as the crash of a wave on the rocks, and when it fled onward this aggregation of wheels, levers, motors had a beautiful unity,[4] as if it were a missile. The sound of it was a war-chorus that reached into the depths of man's emotions.[4]

Author's Influences

1 The author compares the scene to a historical painting. The author's biographical information explains that he was born after the war. A reader can infer that actual historical paintings may have helped spark his fascination with the Civil War.

Purpose for Reading

2 The author identifies a bugler, a standard bearer, and orderlies. A reader who is unfamiliar with these military roles may decide to consult another source to better understand who it is that the author is choosing to describe.

Purpose for Reading

3 The author provides a lengthy, detailed description of the battery, or troops with cannons. Slowly and carefully rereading a difficult passage such as this one allows a reader to appreciate more fully the author's vivid portrayal of the chaos of war.

Author's Influences

4 The "beautiful" battery "stirred the heart" and "reached into the depths of man's emotions." The author's willingness to see beauty in the machinery of war shows the value machines have in his culture.

AN EPISODE OF WAR

Stephen Crane

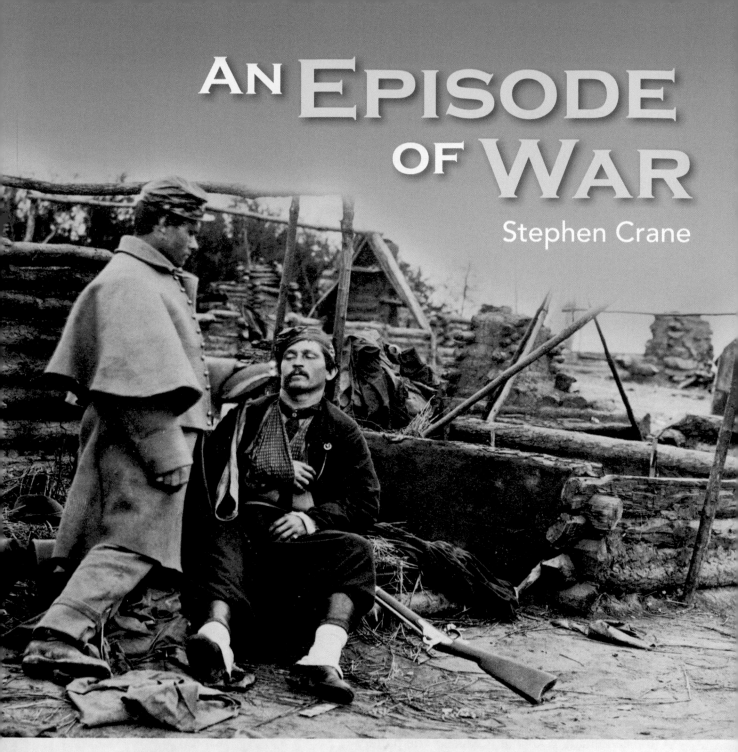

The lieutenant's rubber blanket lay on the ground, and upon it he had poured the company's supply of coffee. Corporals and other representatives of the grimy and hot-throated men who lined the breast-work[1] had come for each squad's portion.

---

1. breast-work *n.* low wall put up quickly as a defense in battle.

The lieutenant was frowning and serious at this task of division. His lips pursed as he drew with his sword various crevices in the heap, until brown squares of coffee, astoundingly equal in size, appeared on the blanket. He was on the verge of a great triumph in mathematics, and the corporals were thronging forward, each to reap a little square, when suddenly the lieutenant cried out and looked quickly at a man near him as if he suspected it was a case of personal assault. The others cried out also when they saw blood upon the lieutenant's sleeve.

He had **winced** like a man stung, swayed dangerously, and then straightened. The sound of his hoarse breathing was plainly **audible**. He looked sadly, mystically, over the breast-work at the green face of a wood, where now were many little puffs of white smoke. During this moment the men about him gazed statuelike and silent, astonished and awed by this catastrophe which happened when catastrophes were not expected—when they had leisure to observe it.

As the lieutenant stared at the wood, they too swung their heads, so that for another instant all hands, still silent, contemplated the distant forest as if their minds were fixed upon the mystery of a bullet's journey.

The officer had, of course, been **compelled** to take his sword into his left hand. He did not hold it by the hilt. He gripped it at the middle of the blade, awkwardly. Turning his eyes from the hostile wood, he looked at the sword as he held it there, and seemed puzzled as to what to do with it, where to put it. In short, this weapon had of a sudden become a strange thing to him. He looked at it in a kind of stupefaction, as if he had been endowed with a trident, a sceptre, or a spade.[2]

Finally he tried to sheathe it. To sheathe a sword held by the left hand, at the middle of the blade, in a

◀ **Vocabulary**
winced (winst) *v.*
shrank or drew back slightly, usually with a grimace, as in pain

audible (ô´ də bəl) *adj.* able to be heard

compelled (kəm peld´) *v.* forced

Comprehension
What happens to the lieutenant while he is distributing coffee?

---

2. **a trident, a sceptre, or a spade** A trident is a three-pronged fishing spear; a sceptre is a decorative ceremonial staff; and a spade is a heavy, flat-bladed digging tool. Any of these three implements would probably be out of place in the lieutenant's hand.

scabbard hung at the left hip, is a feat worthy of a sawdust ring.[3] This wounded officer engaged in a desperate struggle with the sword and the wobbling scabbard, and during the time of it breathed like a wrestler.

But at this instant the men, the spectators, awoke from their stone-like poses and crowded forward sympathetically. The orderly-sergeant took the sword and tenderly placed it in the scabbard. At the time, he leaned nervously backward, and did not allow even his finger to brush the body of the lieutenant. A wound gives strange dignity to him who bears it. Well men shy from his new and terrible majesty. It is as if the wounded man's hand is upon the curtain which hangs before the revelations of all existence—the meaning of ants, potentates,[4] wars, cities, sunshine, snow, a feather dropped from a bird's wing; and the power of it sheds radiance upon a bloody form, and makes the other men understand sometimes that they are little. His comrades look at him with large eyes thoughtfully. Moreover, they fear vaguely that the weight of a finger upon him might send him headlong, precipitate the tragedy, hurl him at once into the dim, grey unknown. And so the orderly-sergeant, while sheathing the sword, leaned nervously backward.

There were others who proffered assistance. One timidly presented his shoulder and asked the lieutenant if he cared to lean upon it, but the latter waved him away mournfully. He wore the look of one who knows he is the victim of a terrible disease and understands his helplessness. He again stared over the breast-work at the forest, and then, turning, went slowly rearward. He held his right wrist tenderly in his left hand as if the wounded arm was made of very brittle glass.

And the men in silence stared at the wood, then at the departing lieutenant; then at the wood, then at the lieutenant.

As the wounded officer passed from the line of battle, he was enabled to see many things which as a participant

Author's Influences
What realistic details in this paragraph suggest the influence of firsthand accounts on the author's writing?

---

3. **sawdust ring** *n.* ring in which circus acts are performed.
4. **potentates** (pōt´ 'n tāts´) *n.* rulers; powerful people.

in the fight were unknown to him. He saw a general on a black horse gazing over the lines of blue infantry at the green woods which veiled his problems. An aide galloped furiously, dragged his horse suddenly to a halt, saluted, and presented a paper. It was, for a wonder, precisely like a historical painting.

To the rear of the general and his staff a group, composed of a bugler, two or three orderlies, and the bearer of the corps standard,[5] all upon maniacal horses, were working like slaves to hold their ground, preserve their respectful interval, while the shells boomed in the air about them, and caused their chargers to make furious quivering leaps.

---

5. **corps** (kôr) **standard** n. flag or banner representing a military unit.

▲ **Critical Viewing**
How does this painting of a Civil War battle capture the confusion of the battlefield?

Comprehension
What does the lieutenant do after he is injured?

Vocabulary ▶
tumultuous (too mul´ choo əs) *adj.* wild; chaotic

Purpose for Reading
For what purpose might you read this story slowly?

▲ **Critical Viewing**
How do Crane's descriptions reflect the influence of Civil War photographs like the one shown here of an 1862 Virginia field hospital?

A battery, a **tumultuous** and shining mass, was swirling toward the right. The wild thud of hoofs, the cries of the riders shouting blame and praise, menace and encouragement, and, last, the roar of the wheels, the slant of the glistening guns, brought the lieutenant to an intent pause. The battery[6] swept in curves that stirred the heart; it made halts as dramatic as the crash of a wave on the rocks, and when it fled onward this aggregation of wheels, levers, motors had a beautiful unity, as if it were a missile. The sound of it was a war-chorus that reached into the depths of man's emotion.

The lieutenant, still holding his arm as if it were of glass, stood watching this battery until all detail of it was lost, save the figures of the riders, which rose and fell and waved lashes over the black mass.

Later, he turned his eyes toward the battle, where the shooting sometimes crackled like bush-fires, sometimes sputtered with exasperating irregularity, and sometimes reverberated like the thunder. He saw the smoke rolling upward and saw crowds of men who ran and cheered, or stood and blazed away at the inscrutable distance.

He came upon some stragglers, and they told him how to find the field hospital. They described its exact location. In fact, these men, no longer having part in the battle, knew more of it than others. They told the performance of every corps, every division, the opinion of every general. The lieutenant, carrying his wounded arm rearward, looked upon them with wonder.

At the roadside a brigade was making coffee and buzzing with talk like a girls' boarding-school. Several officers came

---

6. **battery** (bat´ ər ē) *n.* military unit of men and cannons.

out to him and inquired concerning things of which he knew nothing. One, seeing his arm, began to scold. "Why, man, that's no way to do. You want to fix that thing." He appropriated the lieutenant and the lieutenant's wound. He cut the sleeve and laid bare the arm, every nerve of which softly fluttered under his touch. He bound his handkerchief over the wound, scolding away in the meantime. His tone allowed one to think that he was in the habit of being wounded every day. The lieutenant hung his head, feeling, in this presence, that he did not know how to be correctly wounded. •

The low white tents of the hospital were grouped around an old schoolhouse. There was here a singular commotion. In the foreground two ambulances interlocked wheels in the deep mud. The drivers were tossing the blame of it back and forth, gesticulating and berating,⁷ while from the ambulances, both crammed with wounded, there came an occasional groan. An interminable crowd of bandaged men were coming and going. Great numbers sat under the trees nursing heads or arms or legs. There was a dispute of some kind raging on the steps of the schoolhouse. Sitting with his back against a tree a man with a face as grey as a new army blanket was serenely smoking a corncob pipe. The lieutenant wished to rush forward and inform him that he was dying.

A busy surgeon was passing near the lieutenant. "Good-morning," he said, with a friendly smile. Then he caught sight of the lieutenant's arm, and his face at once changed. "Well, let's have a look at it." He seemed possessed suddenly of a great **contempt** for the lieutenant. This wound evidently placed the latter on a very low social plane. The doctor cried out impatiently, "What mutton-head had tied it up that way anyhow?" The lieutenant answered, "Oh, a man."

When the wound was disclosed the doctor fingered it **disdainfully**. "Humph," he said. "You come along with me and I'll 'tend to you." His voice contained the same scorn as if he were saying: "You will have to go to jail."

The lieutenant had been very meek, but now his face flushed, and he looked into the doctor's eyes. "I guess I won't have it amputated," he said.

"Nonsense, man! Nonsense! Nonsense!" cried the doctor.

Spiral Review
THEME Based on the descriptions of the wounded, what do you think a theme of this story might be?

◄ **Vocabulary**
contempt (kən tempt′) *n.* scorn; disrespect

disdainfully (dis dān′ fə lē) *adv.* scornfully

Comprehension
How was the lieutenant made to feel by the first officer who bandaged his arm?

---

7. **gesticulating** (jes tik′ yoo lāt′ iŋ) **and berating** (bē rāt′ iŋ) *v.* waving arms about wildly and scolding.

"Come along, now. I won't amputate it. Come along. Don't be a baby."

"Let go of me," said the lieutenant, holding back wrathfully, his glance fixed upon the door of the old schoolhouse, as sinister to him as the portals of death.

And this is the story of how the lieutenant lost his arm. When he reached home, his sisters, his mother, his wife, sobbed for a long time at the sight of the flat sleeve. "Oh, well," he said, standing shamefaced amid these tears, "I don't suppose it matters so much as all that."

Purpose for Reading
What insight does the ending give you into attitudes toward wounded soldiers at the time of this story?

Language Study

Vocabulary The italicized words in the sentences below appear in "An Episode of War." Determine whether each item is typically true or typically false. Then, explain your answers.

1. A neat person would feel *compelled* to pick up litter.

2. Someone who gets seasick prefers a *tumultuous* ocean.

3. If a man *winced* while lifting a box, it was probably heavy.

4. People who feel *contempt* for each other make great friends.

5. If I respect someone, I will respond to him or her *disdainfully*.

WORD STUDY
The **Latin root -aud-** means "hear." In this story, a soldier's usually silent breathing becomes **audible**, or able to be heard, as he reacts to receiving a gunshot wound.

Word Study

Part A Explain how the **Latin root -aud-** contributes to the meaning of *auditorium, audio,* and *audition.* Consult a dictionary, if necessary.

Part B Answer each question. Use context and what you know about the Latin root -aud- to explain your answers.

1. What should an *audience* expect to experience at a play?

2. If the music at a concert is *inaudible*, can you enjoy it?

Literary Analysis

Key Ideas and Details

1. **Purpose for Reading (a)** What purpose might you set for reading "An Episode of War"? **(b)** How would this purpose affect your reading rate?

2. **Purpose for Reading (a)** Would this text be an appropriate source to read for information on Civil War leadership? Why or why not? **(b)** For what other research might you consult this work?

3. **(a)** How does the lieutenant react to the doctor's promise not to amputate? **(b) Infer:** Based on his reaction, what can you infer about the frequency of amputations during the Civil War?

Craft and Structure

4. **Author's Influences** Use a chart like the one shown to evaluate the effect of the author's influences on his writing. Refer to the author's biography on page 806 to help you determine his influences. Then, cite specific details from "An Episode of War" that reflect those influences.

5. **Author's Influences** Crane's writing explores the effect of war on the individual soldier. What values are reflected in this approach to writing and in Crane's portrayal of the lieutenant? Find specific passages from the story to support your answer.

Author's Influences
Crane's Interests:
Crane's Research:
Effect on "An Episode of War"
Crane's Interests:
Crane's Research:

Integration of Knowledge and Ideas

6. **Draw Conclusions:** Explain what general view of war Crane's story conveys. In your answer, explain how each of these story details adds to this view:

- what the lieutenant does with his sword after he is wounded
- how his men behave toward him when he is wounded
- the descriptions of the battlefield
- how the doctor behaves toward him
- his family's reaction to his loss, and his response

7. **Are yesterday's heroes important today? (a)** Do the circumstances in which the lieutenant is wounded seem heroic to you? Why or why not? **(b)** Are his reactions to his wounds heroic? Explain. **(c)** Do you think the concept of heroism changes over time? Support your answer with reasons.

ACADEMIC VOCABULARY

As you write and speak about "An Episode of War," use the words related to traditions and heroes that you explored on page 755 of this textbook.

Conventions: **Capitalization**

Capital letters are used at the beginnings of the first words of sentences and for the pronoun *I*. Proper nouns and proper adjectives are also capitalized.

The chart shows examples of how **capitalization** is used.

Capitalize	Examples
the first word in a sentence	The blue jay is a very aggressive bird. Wait! Can you give me back my pen?
the first word in a quotation that is a complete sentence; the first word in a line of dialogue	Einstein said, "Anyone who has never made a mistake has never tried anything new."
the pronoun *I*	After swimming, I felt tired.
proper nouns, including people's names, people's titles when used with as part of their names, place names, and names of organizations	Elsa went sailing down the Hudson River with Ms. Liu and her Girl Scout troop.
proper adjectives, or adjectives formed from proper nouns	Many people of Brazilian background speak the Portuguese language.

Practice A

Identify the capital letter or letters in each sentence. Then, give the reason for each use of capitalization.

1. Southern states such as Georgia and Alabama seceded from the Union.

2. Crane writes, "Finally he tried to sheathe it."

3. The American people were divided during the Civil War.

4. When I go to the library, I will look for other books by Stephen Crane.

Reading Application In "An Episode of War," find examples of two types of capitalization, and explain why each word is capitalized.

Practice B

Rewrite each sentence to correct errors in capitalization. Substitute capital or lowercase letters where appropriate.

1. the Lieutenant approached and said, "captain, a Man has been wounded."

2. soldiers wounded in the civil war did not have the benefit of Modern Medicine.

3. life on the Battlefield was dangerous for soldiers from the north and the South.

4. When the War ended, my fellow soldiers and i felt great relief.

Writing Application Write a paragraph about the American Civil War. In your writing, use each capitalization rule identified in the chart.

Writing to Sources

Argument Write a **persuasive speech** in favor of building a memorial in honor of soldiers who fought in the Civil War.

- Reread "An Episode of War" to find details about the sacrifices that the lieutenant and other soldiers made and the emotions that they and their families experienced as a result.

- Decide what construction of the memorial would accomplish, such as honoring bravery or reminding us of the perils of war.

- Prepare a speech outline divided into an introduction, a body, and a conclusion. Your introduction should grab the listener's attention and provide a preview of your proposal. The body should offer clear reasons for your proposal, supported by relevant evidence from the text. The conclusion should summarize these reasons.

- Draft your speech using a formal tone, avoiding contractions and slang.

- To make the speech more powerful when it is read aloud, add repetition, dramatic pauses, and vivid language.

Grammar Application Check your speech to make sure you have capitalized place names and names of people.

Research and Technology

Build and Present Knowledge Write a **research article** in which you evaluate the accuracy of Crane's portrayal of the Civil War. Follow these instructions to complete the assignment:

- Reread "An Episode of War," taking notes on details that reflect life and conditions during the war, such as details about medical practices or information about military ranks.

- Identify a question that these historical details suggest, such as *How were wounded soldiers treated during the Civil War?*

- Conduct research to answer your question. Use reliable print or online sources and document each relevant fact that you uncover.

- Write an article explaining what your research reveals about the accuracy of Crane's portrayal of the Civil War. Cite specific historical details from the story that are supported or refuted by your research.

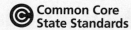 **Common Core State Standards**

Reading Literature
1. Cite the textual evidence that most strongly supports an analysis of what the text says explicitly as well as inferences drawn from the text.

Writing
1. Write arguments to support claims with clear reasons and relevant evidence.
1.a. Introduce claim(s), acknowledge and distinguish the claim(s) from alternate or opposing claims, and organize the reasons and evidence logically.
1.d. Establish and maintain a formal style.
1.e. Provide a concluding statement or section that follows from and supports the argument presented.
2. Write informative/explanatory texts to examine a topic and convey ideas, concepts, and information through the selection, organization, and analysis of relevant content.

Language
2. Demonstrate command of the conventions of standard English capitalization, punctuation, and spelling when writing.

 **Are yesterday's heroes important today?**

Explore the Big Question as you read these texts. Take notes on the ways in which each text brings readers to admire or to appreciate yesterday's heroes.

READING TO COMPARE HEROIC CHARACTERS

Authors Davy Crockett, Carl Sandburg, and Stephen Vincent Benét all write about heroic characters. As you read each text, consider what qualities are portrayed as heroic. After you have read all three texts, compare how each hero overcomes challenges.

"Davy Crockett's Dream"

Davy Crockett (1786–1836) was a genuine frontiersman, but the colorful tall tales in his autobiography helped make him a legend. He joined the fight for Texas independence and was killed at the Battle of the Alamo in 1836.

"Paul Bunyan of the North Woods"

Carl Sandburg (1878–1967) had a lifelong interest in American history and folklore, especially the nation's myths and tall tales. These stories influenced much of his poetry. Sandburg was also a journalist and historian.

"Invocation" from *John Brown's Body*

Stephen Vincent Benét (1898–1943) was a poet, novelist, and short-story writer who often wrote about American history and its heroes. Benét and his wife wrote a collection of poems for young people about characters in American history

• Davy Crockett's Dream
• Paul Bunyan of the North Woods
• Invocation *from* John Brown's Body

Comparing Heroic Characters

**Common Core
State Standards**

Reading Literature

3. Analyze how particular lines of dialogue or incidents in a story or drama propel the action, reveal aspects of a character, or provoke a decision.

9. Analyze how a modern work of fiction draws on themes, patterns of events, or character types from myths, traditional stories, or religious works such as the Bible, including describing how the material is rendered new.

Writing

2. Write informative/explanatory texts to examine a topic and convey ideas, concepts, and information through the selection, organization, and analysis of relevant content.

9. Draw evidence from literary or informational texts to support analysis, reflection, and research.

Heroic Characters Heroic characters are men and women who show great courage and overcome difficult challenges. A hero in a literary work may be real or fictional. Often, the hero in a tall tale or legend is a mixture of both reality and fiction—he or she is a real historical figure whose actions have become so exaggerated that he or she becomes a legend. At the same time that these tales use **exaggeration,** or descriptions that make something seem more than it is, they may also use **understatement,** or descriptions of something as if it were less than it is, for comic effect.

Heroism Across Eras As these selections show, the **theme** of heroism runs across time periods and appears in different literary forms. Carl Sandburg and Stephen Vincent Benét wrote in the period between the world wars—a time when many Americans were looking back fondly at the heroes and values of the western frontier. In contrast, Davy Crockett wrote his own heroic story of the frontier as he lived it—except that he added a few creative touches to fuel his legend.

Heroes and Their Traits "Davy Crockett's Dream" and "Paul Bunyan of the North Woods" portray traditional heroes. The hero of "Invocation" is the American muse, who personifies the American spirit. As you read, look for instances in which the hero overcomes larger-than-life challenges. Identify the heroic traits, such as bravery and endurance, that help the hero to master each challenge. Then, fill in a character web like this one to compare the characters' heroic traits.

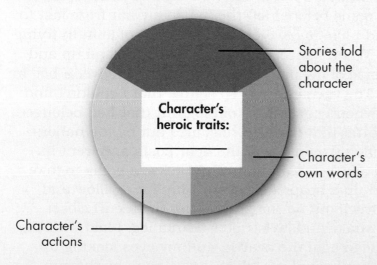

Stories told about the character

Character's heroic traits:
_____

Character's own words

Character's actions

Hero's name: _____

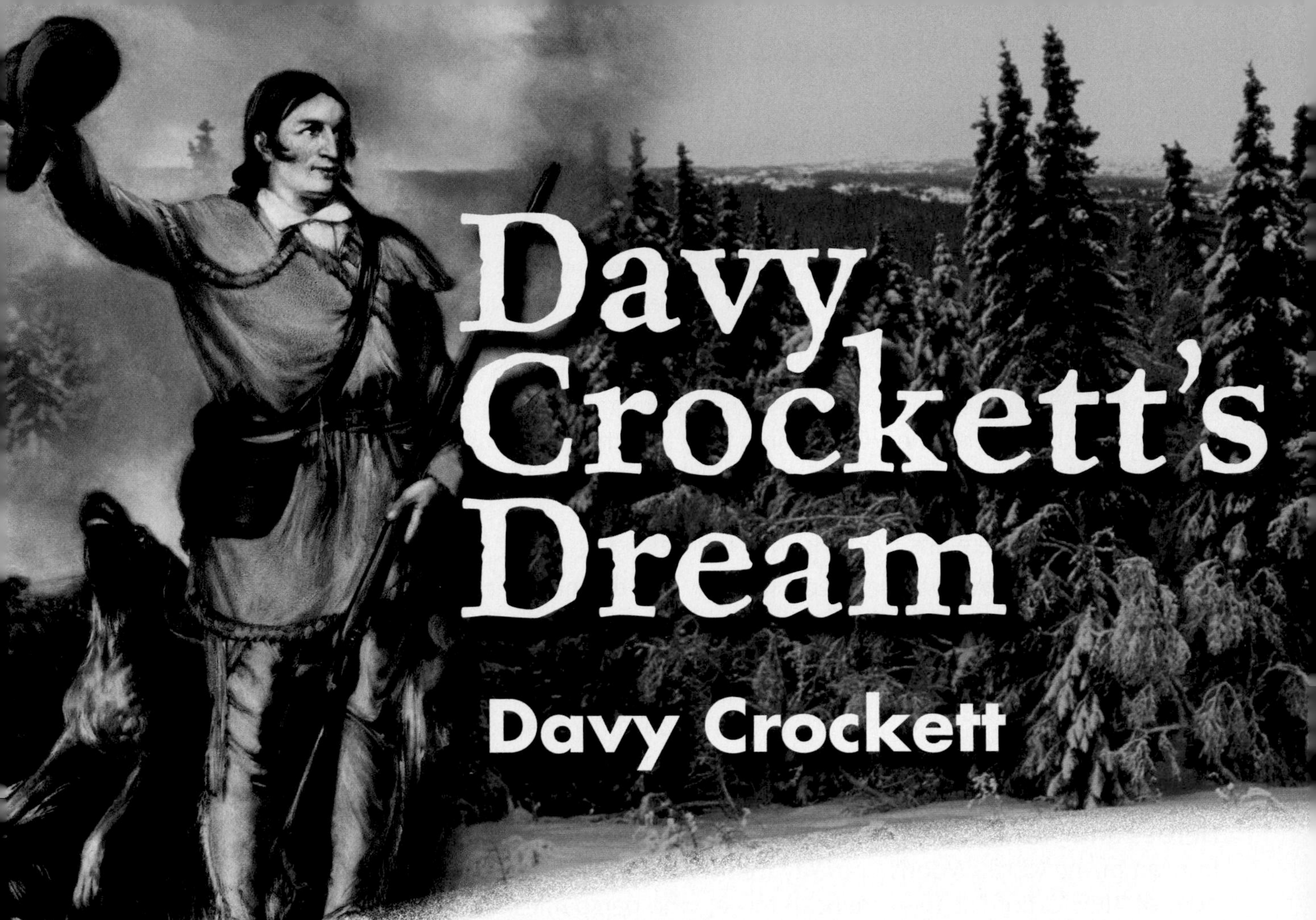

Davy Crockett's Dream

Davy Crockett

One day when it was so cold that I was afeard to open my mouth, lest I should freeze my tongue, I took my little dog named Grizzle and cut out for Salt River Bay to kill something for dinner. I got a good ways from home afore I knowed where I was, and as I had swetted some before I left the house my hat froze fast to my head, and I like to have put my neck out of joint in trying to pull it off. When I sneezed the icicles crackled all up and down the inside of my nose, like when you walk over a bog in winter time. The varmints was so scarce that I couldn't find one, and so when I come to an old log hut that had belonged to some squatter that had ben reformed out by the nabors, I stood my rifle up agin one of the door posts and went in. I **kindled** up a little fire and told Grizzle I was going to take a nap. I piled up a heap of chestnut burs for a pillow and straitened myself out on the ground, for I can curl closer than a rattlesnake and lay straiter than a log. I laid with the back of my head agin the hearth, and my eyes looking up chimney so that I could see when it was noon by the sun, for

Vocabulary ▶
kindled (kind´ əld) v.
built or lit a fire

Heroic Characters
What elements of
comic exaggeration
do you notice here?

Mrs. Crockett was always rantankerous¹ when I staid out over the time. I got to sleep before Grizzle had done warming the eend of his nose, and I had swallowed so much cold wind that it laid hard on my stomach, and as I laid gulping and belching the wind went out of me and roared up chimney like a young whirlwind. So I had a pesky dream, and kinder thought, till I waked up, that I was floating down the Massassippy in a holler tree, and I hadn't room to stir my legs and arms no more than they were withed together with young saplings. While I was there and want able to help myself a feller called Oak Wing that lived about twenty miles off, and that I had give a most almighty licking once, cum and looked in with his blind eye that I had gouged out five years before, and I saw him looking in one end of the hollow log, and he axed me if I wanted to get out. I told him to tie a rope to one of my legs and draw me out as soon as God would let him and as

◀ **Critical Viewing**
Does Davy Crockett, pictured here, look like he might use "a heap of chestnut burs" for a pillow? Explain.

Comprehension
Why does Crockett fall asleep looking up a chimney?

---

1. **rantankerous** (ran taŋ´ kər əs) *adj.* dialect for *cantankerous*, meaning "bad-tempered and quarrelsome."

much sooner as he was a mind to. But he said he wouldn't do it that way, he would ram me out with a pole. So he took a long pole and rammed it down agin my head as if he was ramming home the cattridge in a cannon. This didn't make me budge an inch, but it pounded my head down in between my shoulders till I look'd like a turcle with his head drawn in. This started my temper a trifle, and I ript and swore till the breath boiled out of the end of the log like the steam out of the funnel pipe of a steemboat. Jest then I woke up, and seed my wife pulling my leg, for it was enermost sundown and she had cum arter me. There was a long icicle hanging to her nose, and when she tried to kiss me, she run it right into my eye. I told her my dreem, and sed I would have revenge on Oak Wing for pounding my head. She said it was all a dreem and that Oak was not to blame; but I had a very diffrent idee of the matter. So I went and talked to him, and told him what he had done to me in a dreem, and it was settled that he should make me an apology in his next dreem, and that wood make us square,[2] for I don't like to be run upon when I'm asleep, any more than I do when I'm awake.

Heroic Characters
What examples of exaggeration and understatement can you find in this passage?

---

2. **square** even.

Critical Thinking

1. **Key Ideas and Details: (a)** Why does Davy Crockett head to Salt River Bay? **(b) Infer:** What do the story details suggest about Crockett's style of living?

2. **Key Ideas and Details: (a)** What happens in Davy Crockett's dream, and how does he react? **(b) Analyze Cause and Effect:** How does he actually settle the matter with Oak Wing? **(c) Analyze:** How does this outcome show that this narrative is a "tall tale"?

3. **Craft and Structure: (a)** Dialect is the version of a language found in a particular place. A dialect has its own words and grammatical rules. How does the use of dialect affect the tone of the tale? **(b) Infer:** From the way he tells this tale, how would you describe Davy Crockett?

4. **Integration of Knowledge and Ideas: (a)** Could an adventurer like Crockett become a hero today? Why or why not? **(b)** Do we expect today's heroes to have a sense of humor? Explain. *[Connect to the Big Question: Are yesterday's heroes important today?]*

PAUL BUNYAN
of the North Woods

Carl Sandburg

Who made Paul Bunyan, who gave him birth as a myth, who joked him into life as the Master Lumberjack, who fashioned him forth as an apparition[1] easing the hours of men amid axes and trees, saws and lumber? The people, the bookless people, they made Paul and had him alive long before he got into the books for those who read. He grew up in **shanties**, around the hot stoves of winter, among socks and mittens drying, in the smell of tobacco smoke and the roar of laughter mocking the outside weather. And some of Paul came overseas in wooden bunks below decks in sailing vessels. And some of Paul is old as the hills, young as the alphabet.

---

1. **apparition** (ap´ ə rish´ ən) *n.* sudden or unusual sight.

Critical Viewing ▶
What characteristics in this picture fit Paul Bunyan's role as a legendary hero?

Heroic Characters
What qualities of
Paul Bunyan and
his men does this
anecdote illustrate?

The Pacific Ocean froze over in the winter of the
Blue Snow and Paul Bunyan had long teams
of oxen hauling regular white snow over from
China. This was the winter Paul gave a party
to the Seven Axmen. Paul fixed a granite
floor sunk two hundred feet deep for them
to dance on. Still, it tipped and tilted as
the dance went on. And because the Seven
Axmen refused to take off their hobnailed
boots, the sparks from the nails of their
dancing feet lit up the place so that Paul
didn't light the kerosene lamps. No women
being on the Big Onion river at that time
the Seven Axmen had to dance with each other, the one left
over in each set taking Paul as a partner. The commotion of
the dancing that night brought on an earthquake and the
Big Onion river moved over three counties to the east.

Vocabulary ▶
commotion

(kə mō´ shən) *n.* noisy
movement

One year when it rained from St. Patrick's Day till the Fourth
of July, Paul Bunyan got disgusted because his celebration
on the Fourth was spoiled. He dived into Lake Superior and
swam to where a solid pillar of water was coming down. He
dived under this pillar, swam up into it and climbed with
powerful swimming strokes, was gone about an hour, came
splashing down, and as the rain stopped, he explained,
"I turned the darn thing off." This is told in the Big North
Woods and on the Great Lakes, with many particulars.

Two mosquitoes lighted on one of Paul Bunyan's oxen,
killed it, ate it, cleaned the bones, and sat on a grub
shanty picking their teeth as Paul came along. Paul sent
to Australia for two special bumblebees to kill these
mosquitoes. But the bees and the mosquitoes intermarried;
their children had stingers on both ends. And things kept
getting worse till Paul brought a big boatload of sorghum[2]
up from Louisiana and while all the bee-mosquitoes were
eating at the sweet sorghum he floated them down to the
Gulf of Mexico. They got so fat that it was easy to drown
them all between New Orleans and Galveston.

---

2. **sorghum** (sôr´ gəm) *n.* tropical grasses bearing flowers and seeds, grown for use as
grain or syrup.

Paul logged on the Little Gimlet in Oregon one winter. The cookstove at that camp covered an acre of ground. They fastened the side of a hog on each snowshoe and four men used to skate on the griddle while the cook flipped the pancakes. The eating table was three miles long; elevators carried the cakes to the ends of the table where boys on bicycles rode back and forth on a path down the center of the table dropping the cakes where called for.

Benny, the Little Blue Ox of Paul Bunyan, grew two feet every time Paul looked at him, when a youngster. The barn was gone one morning and they found it on Benny's back; he grew out of it in a night. One night he kept pawing and bellowing for more pancakes, till there were two hundred men at the cook-shanty stove trying to keep him fed. About breakfast time Benny broke loose, tore down the cook shanty, ate all the pancakes piled up for the loggers' breakfast. And after that Benny made his mistake; he ate the red hot stove; and that finished him. This is only one of the hot-stove stories told in the North Woods.

Critical Thinking

1. **Key Ideas and Details: (a)** According to Sandburg, what is the origin of the Paul Bunyan stories? **(b) Interpret:** What does Sandburg mean by saying that "some of Paul is old as the hills, young as the alphabet"?

2. **Key Ideas and Details: (a)** Identify two actions that show that Paul Bunyan is clever as well as strong. **(b) Connect:** How do these qualities relate to the myth of the heroic character?

3. **Key Ideas and Details: (a)** How does Paul Bunyan stop the rain? **(b) Generalize:** What do this anecdote and other details in the selection tell you about life in the Midwest in the early nineteenth century?

4. **Integration of Knowledge and Ideas: (a)** Do you think the Paul Bunyan stories might have been based on a real person? **(b) Hypothesize:** What type of person in today's world might inspire this kind of story?

5. **Integration of Knowledge and Ideas: (a)** Why would a lumberjack have been a hero in frontier America? **(b)** What qualities does Paul Bunyan share with today's heroes? *[Connect to the Big Question: Are yesterday's heroes important today?]*

Invocation

from John Brown's Body

Stephen Vincent Benét

This invocation is the introduction to an **epic**, a
long narrative poem about heroes. Traditionally,
classical writers began an epic by appealing
to the muse of poetry, a goddess who could
provide inspiration. To begin his epic poem
about the Civil War, Benét calls on a different
muse—the spirit of America. He finds that this
muse is hard to get to know because she—like
the country she symbolizes—is so varied and
ever-changing.

American muse, whose strong and diverse heart
So many men have tried to understand
But only made it smaller with their art,
Because you are as various as your land,

5   As mountainous-deep, as flowered with blue rivers,
Thirsty with deserts, buried under snows,
As native as the shape of Navajo quivers.
And native, too, as the sea-voyaged rose.

Swift runner, never captured or **subdued**,
10 Seven-branched elk[1] beside the mountain stream,
That half a hundred hunters have pursued
But never matched their bullets with the dream,

Where the great huntsmen failed, I set my sorry
And mortal snare for your immortal quarry.[2]

15 You are the buffalo-ghost, the broncho-ghost
With dollar-silver in your saddle-horn,
The cowboys riding in from Painted Post,
The Indian arrow in the Indian corn,

And you are the clipped velvet of the lawns
20 Where Shropshire grows from Massachusetts sods,
The grey Maine rocks—and the war-painted dawns
That break above the Garden of the Gods.

The prairie-schooners crawling toward the ore
And the cheap car, parked by the station-door.

25 Where the skyscrapers lift their foggy plumes
Of stranded smoke out of a stony mouth,
You are that high stone and its **arrogant** fumes,
And you are ruined gardens in the South

LITERATURE IN CONTEXT

Cultural Connection

Allusions This poem uses allusions, references to places and events, in order to capture the varied and changeable nature of the American spirit.

- **Navajo quivers** Cases for holding arrows used by Native Americans of the Southwest
- **buffalo-ghost, broncho-ghost** The buffalo and bronco (wild pony), symbols of the western frontier
- **Shropshire** English county known for its green countryside
- **prairie-schooners** Covered wagons used by pioneers moving westward
- **medicine-bag** Small leather bag containing herbs and other sacred objects used by Indian shamans, or healers
- **"Thames and all the rivers of the kings"** England's main river, and those of other Old World powers

◄ **Vocabulary**
subdued (səb do͞od´)
adj. beaten; brought under control

arrogant (ar´ ə gənt)
adj. self-important

Comprehension
What is the speaker trying to understand?

---

1. **seven-branched elk** *n.* large American deer with wide antlers that divide into several branches.
2. **mortal snare for your immortal quarry** The poet is only human and so cannot set a trap (snare) that can catch the muse, who is immortal.

And bleak New England farms, so winter-white
30 Even their roofs look lonely, and the deep,
The middle grainland where the wind of night
Is like all blind earth sighing in her sleep.

A friend, an enemy, a sacred hag[3]
With two tied oceans in her medicine-bag.

35 They tried to fit you with an English song
And clip your speech into the English tale.
But, even from the first, the words went wrong,
The catbird pecked away the nightingale.[4]

The homesick men begot high-cheekboned things
40 Whose wit was whittled with a different sound,
And Thames and all the rivers of the kings
Ran into Mississippi and were drowned . . .

. . . All these you are, and each is partly you,
And none is false, and none is wholly true.

45 So how to see you as you really are,
So how to suck the pure, distillate,[5] stored
Essence of essence from the hidden star
And make it pierce like a riposting[6] sword.

Heroic Characters
How does the imagery
in lines 35–42
emphasize the young
country's break with
its past?

Comprehension
What does the speaker
realize in lines 43–44?

---

3. **hag** (hag) *n.* a witch; also an ugly, old woman.
4. **catbird . . . nightingale** The catbird is an American bird; the nightingale, a European one.
5. **distillate** (dis´ tə lāt´) *adj.* of or like a substance that has been reduced to its purest form, or essence.
6. **riposting** (ri pōst´ iŋ) *adj.* in swordplay, thrusting to counter an opponent's blow.

For, as we hunt you down, you must escape
50 And we pursue a shadow of our own
That can be caught in a magician's cape
But has the flatness of a painted stone.

Never the running stag, the gull at wing,
The pure elixir,[7] the American thing.

55 And yet, at moments when the mind was hot
With something fierier than joy or grief,
When each known spot was an eternal spot
And every leaf was an immortal leaf,

I think that I have seen you, not as one,
60 But clad in diverse semblances and powers,
Always the same, as light falls from the sun,
And always different, as the differing hours. . . .

---

7. **elixir** (i lik´ sər) *n.* a magic potion; or the essential quality of something.

Critical Thinking

1. **Key Ideas and Details: (a)** To whom does Benét address this "Invocation"? **(b) Analyze:** What qualities does he first note about this subject? **(c) Connect:** How does this observation influence the rest of the poem?

2. **Craft and Structure:** Review the background note before the poem, on page 826. **(a)** How does this poem fit the purpose and characteristics of an epic? **(b) Assess:** How does its subject suit an epic treatment?

3. **Integration of Knowledge and Ideas: (a)** In what lines does Benét emphasize conflicts between England and America? **(b) Infer:** Why are those differences important to his vision of America? **(c) Assess:** Does Benét succeed in capturing the American spirit? Why or why not?

4. **Integration of Knowledge and Ideas: (a)** What does Benét find heroic about the American muse? **(b)** Are the many "faces" of this muse still present today? **(c)** What places or figures would you add to Benét's list? *[Connect to the Big Question: Are yesterday's heroes important today?]*

- Davy Crockett's Dream
- Paul Bunyan of the North Woods
- Invocation *from* John Brown's Body

Writing to Sources

Comparing Heroic Characters

1. **Key Ideas and Details: (a)** Identify examples of exaggeration in "Paul Bunyan of the North Woods." **(b)** Why would exaggeration be typical in stories about heroes?

2. **Key Ideas and Details:** What heroic traits does Benét's American muse share with Paul Bunyan and Davy Crockett?

3. **Integration of Knowledge and Ideas: (a)** Complete a chart like the one shown. **(b)** Choose two examples from your chart. Explain how each develops the heroism of the main character.

	Davy Crockett's Dream	Paul Bunyan of the North Woods
Real or Legend?		
Challenges		
Heroic Actions		
Exaggeration		
Tone: Humorous or Serious?		

⏱ Timed Writing

Explanatory Text: Essay

Write an essay comparing how "Davy Crockett's Dream" and "Paul Bunyan of the North Woods" present the theme of American heroism. **(40 minutes)**

5-Minute Planner

1. Read the prompt carefully and completely.

2. Gather your ideas by jotting down answers to these questions:

   - What do these American heroes have in common? How does each reflect the values of a time period?

   - How important are humor and exaggeration in each work?

3. Use the chart above to help you compare Davy Crockett with Paul Bunyan.

4. Reread the prompt, and then draft your essay.

USE ACADEMIC VOCABULARY

As you write, use academic language, such as these words:

cultural

endure

influence

quality

For more information about academic vocabulary, see the Building Academic Vocabulary workshop in the front of your book.

Figurative Language

Common Core State Standards

Language
5. Demonstrate understanding of figurative language, word relationships, and nuances in word meanings.
5.a. Interpret figures of speech in context.

Figurative language is writing that is imaginative and not meant to be taken literally. Figurative language is built on **figures of speech**, which are expressions that use language in a nonliteral or figurative manner. The chart shows some examples.

Type of Figurative Language	Example
Simile: a comparison of two apparently unlike things using *like, as,* or *than*	Her eyes are <u>like</u> diamonds.
Metaphor: a description of one thing as if it were another	You <u>are</u> my sunshine.
Analogy: an extended comparison. An analogy shows how the relationship between one pair of things is like the relationship between another pair.	<u>Juggling</u> is like <u>riding a bicycle</u>. Once you learn how to do it, you never forget.
Personification: giving human characteristics to a nonhuman subject	The <u>willow trees sang</u> a sad song as the wind blew through their branches.
Hyperbole: an intentional (and sometimes outrageous) overstatement, or exaggeration	It is so hot outside that <u>you could fry an egg on the sidewalk.</u>

An **idiom** is a common expression that means something different from the meanings of its individual words, such as "He is always <u>on the go</u>," meaning "He is always busy." The term *idiom* is also often used to refer to commonplace metaphors or similes, such as "He is <u>fishing for a compliment</u>," meaning "He is trying to get someone to praise him." Idioms are usually specific to people in certain regions or groups. Other idioms include these:

have a chip on one's shoulder   resent; hold a grudge
run circles around   win easily against; outshine
a flash in the pan   something or someone who succeeds only briefly

Practice A
Identify the type of figurative language used in each item.

1. This book weighs a ton.
2. Justine is as graceful as a swan when she dances.
3. Aunt Nina's favorite photos are squirreled away in the attic.
4. His smile lights up the room.
5. The waves murmured their sleepy good-nights.
6. My brother is in the doghouse because he broke his curfew.

Practice B

First, identify the figure of speech in each item as an example of simile, metaphor, personification, or hyperbole. Then, explain the meaning of each figure of speech, using its context as a clue.

1. Jamie was as quiet as a mouse, hardly making a sound when she entered the room.
2. Moving quickly from one spot on the ground to another, the tumbleweed danced merrily over the prairie.
3. Jonah's little sister is as cute as a button when she giggles at her own made-up jokes.
4. Tyrone learned to swim like a fish at summer camp, perfectly mastering every stroke.
5. The school collected enough donations to sink a ship.
6. My mother is a whirlwind of activity; she never seems to rest.
7. The water cradled and rocked the young boy as he peacefully floated.
8. Her singing is so pleasant—a soft, sweet breeze that carries a lovely tune.

Activity Write three to five sentences describing an activity that you enjoy. Energize your description with similes, metaphors, personification, or hyperbole. First, create appropriate figures of speech on a note card like the one shown. Use ideas from the note card in your description.

Similes:
Metaphors:
Personification:
Hyperbole:

Comprehension and Collaboration

Working in a small group, create a poster for a school event. Do your best to use one example each of simile, metaphor, personification, and hyperbole in your poster. When the poster is completed, discuss what impact the use of figurative language has on the finished product.

Delivering a Persuasive Speech Using Multimedia

A persuasive multimedia presentation uses visuals, sound, speech, and text to persuade an audience.

Learn the Skills

Use these strategies to complete the activity on p. 835.

Make a claim. Choose a position on your topic. Determine the main claim you will make in support of your position, and sum up that claim in a *thesis statement.* Include your thesis statement in your introduction.

Use primary and secondary sources. Support your claims using facts, as well as firsthand accounts, expert analysis, or observation.

Choose an organization. Use a structure suited to your purpose, such as point-by-point or block method (see p. 276). Use an outline to organize your speech into sections, noting where you will use evidence and examples to support your arguments. Include an introduction, a body, and a conclusion.

Decide which media to use. Focus on matching the media to your purpose. For example, a film or photo can help an audience visualize concepts, music can set the appropriate mood, and a graph can quickly convey a trend.

Integrate media. Use media consistently throughout the presentation rather than using it all at the beginning or end. Try to vary the types of media you include as well. For example, avoid using several photos one after another if there is a better option. Integrate each media piece into the presentation by creating an introduction that explains what it is.

Be prepared. If possible, practice the speech using the equipment. Have a backup plan in case a piece of equipment does not function.

Be dramatic. Use creative language, such as similes and extended comparisons (**analogies**) to make your points. To add persuasive appeal, choose words for their emotional associations (**connotations**), as well as for their literal meanings (**denotations**).

Be clear. When presenting, use transitions, such as *because, next,* or *as a result,* to show connections between ideas.

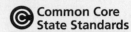 **Common Core State Standards**

Reading Informational Text
7. Evaluate the advantages and disadvantages of using different mediums to present a particular topic or idea.

Speaking and Listening
5. Integrate multimedia and visual displays into presentations to clarify information, strengthen claims and evidence, and add interest.

Language
5.c. Distinguish among the connotations (associations) of words with similar denotations (definitions) (e.g., *bullheaded, willful, firm, persistent, resolute*).

Practice the Skills

Presentation of Knowledge and Ideas Use what you have learned in this workshop to perform the following task.

ACTIVITY: Delivering a Persuasive Presentation

Prepare and deliver a persuasive presentation with multimedia. Follow the steps below:

- Advocate a position on a school- or community-related issue, supporting your position with a well-stated main claim.
- Include similes and analogies.
- Use multimedia (text, graphics, images, and sound).
- Use speaking techniques to deliver your presentation effectively.
- Refer to the Model Outline (below) to help you organize your presentation.

Construct an outline for your presentation similar to the model below. Draft your speech and rehearse with a partner, paying attention to the smooth integration of media. As you present, remember to make eye contact, to use natural gestures, to vary your speaking rate and volume, and to enunciate. Follow language conventions.

Model Outline

My Position

I. **Introduction:**
   A. Introduce my main claim.
   B. Give background, accompanied by multimedia #1: slideshow.

II. **Body of Presentation:**
   A. Discuss supporting example/evidence #1.
   B. Discuss supporting example/evidence #2.
      (Include an analogy to help listeners understand.)
   C. Discuss supporting example/evidence #3.
      i. Present multimedia #2: short video clip.
      ii. Explain implications of clip, using a simile.

III. **Conclusion:**
   Use multimedia, along with a simile or an analogy, to create a strong ending to my persuasive message.

Comprehension and Collaboration At the end of your presentation, elicit and respond to questions from the audience. Ask whether you were successful in advocating for your position.

Write an Argument

Problem-and-Solution Essay

Defining the Form In a **problem-and-solution essay,** a writer identifies a problem and then makes claims about a way to solve it. You might use elements of this type of writing in letters, editorials, and speeches.

Assignment Write an essay in which you identify a problem your school, community, or country faces. Then, make a claim proposing an appealing solution to the problem you describe. Include these elements:

✓ a clearly stated *claim about the problem and proposed solution*

✓ *evidence, examples, and arguments* that support your claims

✓ *support* that answers readers' concerns

✓ a structure that includes an *introduction, body, and conclusion*

✓ a clear and *formal style* with which to present your ideas

To preview the criteria on which your essay may be judged, see the rubric on page 843.

Common Core State Standards

Writing
1. Write arguments to support claims with clear reasons and relevant evidence.
1.d. Establish and maintain a formal style.

FOCUS ON RESEARCH

When you write problem-and-solution essays, you might perform research to

• identify a problem in your school, community, or country.

• devise a solution to the problem you are addressing.

• prove that the solution will be successful with evidence and examples.

Be sure to note all resources you use in your research, and credit those sources in your final drafts. Refer to the Conducting Research workshop in the Introductory Unit for assistance in citing materials.

Prewriting/Planning Strategies

Use a sentence starter. Complete one of these four sentence starters to help you brainstorm for possible topics:

- Our community should fix _____.
- I wish people would _____.
- School would be better if _____.
- I get annoyed when _____.

Write your endings in a cluster diagram like this one, and then choose one of the issues you have raised as your topic.

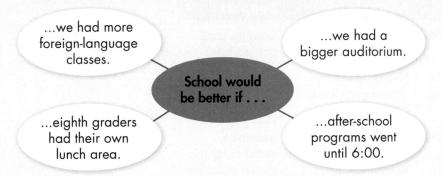

Gather details. Take notes on the problem that you have chosen to address. Decide why the problem needs to be resolved and brainstorm possible solutions. Then, begin your research.

- Consult reliable sources, including library databases and online publications, to gather statistics, facts, and expert opinions on your topic.
- Find schools or communities that have faced a similar problem and find out how it was addressed. Use print or digital school and community newspapers as sources.
- Consider contacting a school or community official who has dealt with a similar problem. Set up a time to speak with him or her and ask whether the solution the school or community settled upon is working.
- Remember to take notes as you gather information.

Consider audience and purpose. Keep your audience in mind as you develop your essay. Ask yourself whether the problem that you are addressing is one that affects your readers. When you are presenting your argument in your essay, be sure to use language that will appeal to your audience.

Drafting Strategies

Choose the most promising ideas that come out of your prewriting and develop them into an essay using the following steps:

Use an appropriate structure. Set up your argument with an introduction that defines and explains the problem. Include a thesis statement that sums up your main claim about the problem and its solution.

Promote your solution. Use the body of your essay to explain and "sell" your solution to readers. Present reasons for your solution and support these reasons with evidence. Some common reasons are listed in this chart.

If a Solution Is...	It Means	Example	Support
economical	It is affordable.	Fluorescent bulbs cost less money.	statistics (cost comparison)
comprehensive	It will solve the entire problem.	Hiring more town workers will keep downtown clean.	statistics and expert opinions
practical	It can be easily carried out.	Community policing is an easy way to prevent crime.	examples, statistics, and expert opinions

Address counterclaims. To strengthen your argument, identify the counterclaims that a reader might make regarding your solution or your evidence. Refute these counterclaims with arguments supported by data and examples.

Use transitions. Transitional words such as *next, then,* and *therefore* will create cohesion and clarify the relationship between your claims, the evidence, and possible counterclaims.

Offer support. Include examples, analogies, statistics, and expert opinions as evidence that your solution makes sense. Focus on relevant details, and include sufficient evidence to show that your solution is likely to be successful. For example, if you are arguing that your after-school program should run later than it does, you might include evidence of the high level of homework completion at schools that have longer after-school programs.

Conclude strongly. End with a conclusion in which you restate why your solution would be effective. Summarize your argument and reaffirm your hope for or confidence in your solution.

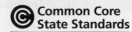

Using Voice in an Argument

Voice is a unique tool a writer can use to communicate ideas and hold an audience's attention. A writer adjusts his or her voice to match his or her message and audience. Writers create voice using sentence length, word choice, and tone.

Choose the right voice. A writer's voice establishes a relationship with readers. An authoritative voice may lead readers to respect or trust the writer. A friendly voice may make them receptive to his or her ideas. Choose the appropriate voice for your problem-and-solution essay by considering your audience and your purpose, as shown in this example.

Audience	Purpose	Appropriate Voice
classmates	to motivate them to participate in my solution	friendly, enthusiastic
adults in the community	to request urgent action	formal, serious, authoritative

Work on tone. Tone, or the writer's attitude toward a subject, is an important part of voice. Word choice is one way a writer creates a tone. Use these questions to help you choose the right words to develop an appropriate tone.

- How do I feel about the problem I am addressing?
- What descriptive words best express my feelings about this problem?

Write your answers to these questions in a chart like the one shown. Choose from the words and phrases in your chart as you draft.

How Do I Feel?	Descriptive Words	
determined	problematic resolved	positive results
outraged	unpardonable fair	immediately responsible

Maintain a consistent voice. Make sure that everything you write contributes to the tone you wish to convey. For example, if you wish to show how strongly you feel about your solution, use decisive words. Eliminate weaker word choices that suggest indecision or ambiguity.

Revising Strategies

Revise to anticipate reader concerns. Be sure to indicate why other solutions would not work as well as yours. Use the chart to address readers' concerns.

If You Claim Your Solution Is...	Question to Answer
economical	Why would a more expensive solution not work better?
comprehensive	What exactly do other solutions not address?
practical	Why are other solutions harder to carry out?

Review the strength of your argument. As you review your draft, circle each major claim in a different color. Make sure that each of these claims supports your overall argument. Then highlight each detail that supports a major claim in the same color that you used to circle the claim. Look at your color-coded essay to evaluate whether some points need additional support. Consider eliminating any details that do not support your argument.

Review transitions. Review the use of transitions in your essay. Each point should flow logically into the next. Make sure that the transitions you use express the connection between ideas that you intend to make. Adjust the wording or add additional transitions where needed.

Model: Revising Transitions

Critics of my solution say it is too expensive;

however,

~~furthermore,~~ ∧they are overlooking the long-term savings.

> The writer replaces a transition with one that better reflects the connection between ideas.

Revise to maintain a formal style. Make sure that your writing remains formal from start to finish. In a problem-and-solution essay, even a friendly voice should be somewhat formal.

- **Formal and authoritative:** It is clear that having a larger auditorium would make home games less problematic.

- **Formal and friendly:** We all know that having a bigger auditorium would make home games easier for everyone.

Common Core State Standards

Writing
1.a. Introduce claim(s), acknowledge and distinguish the claim(s) from alternate or opposing claims, and organize the reasons and evidence logically.

1.b. Support claim(s) with logical reasoning and relevant evidence, using accurate, credible sources and demonstrating an understanding of the topic or text.

1.c. Use words, phrases, and clauses to create cohesion and clarify the relationships among claim(s), counterclaims, reasons, and evidence.

1.d. Establish and maintain a formal style.

Language
1. Demonstrate command of the conventions of standard English grammar and usage when writing or speaking.

Revising to Correct Comparative and Superlative Forms

In addition to their basic, or **positive,** form, most adjectives and adverbs have two forms that are used in making comparisons: the comparative and the superlative.

Identifying Forms Use the **comparative form** to compare two items. Use the **superlative form** to compare three or more items.

- For most one- or two-syllable words, add -*er* to form the comparative: for example, *clearer.* Add -*est* to form the superlative: for example, *clearest.* (For negative comparisons, use *less* or *least: less clear, least clear.*)
- For most adverbs ending in -*ly* and for modifiers of three or more syllables, use *more* (or *less*) to form the comparative: for example, *more beautiful.* Use *most* (or *least*) to form the superlative: for example, *most beautiful.*
- Irregular adjectives and adverbs, however, have unpredictable patterns, as shown in the chart. They must be memorized.

Common Irregular Adjectives and Adverbs

Positive	Comparative	Superlative
bad, badly	worse	worst
good, well	better	best
many, much	more	most
far (distance)	farther	farthest
far (extent)	further	furthest

Fixing Errors To fix faulty use of these forms, take these steps:

1. Determine how many items are being compared.
2. Use the comparative form for two, and use the superlative form for three or more.

   Comparative: Dave did better on the test than Suzie.

   Superlative: Of everyone in the class, Jo did the best.

Grammar in Your Writing
Review your draft. If you find that you have used a comparative or superlative adjective or adverb incorrectly, fix it using the rules above.

My Neighborhood

As I look out my bedroom window, I see the whole neighborhood. I see a lot of things, both good and bad. I see children playing outside on the weekends and after school. I see parades marching through the street during the holidays. I see watchful neighbors keeping an eye on the neighborhood. All of these are great sights, but they get overlooked because of all of the problems in the neighborhood. My neighborhood used to be nice and quiet, but lately it has become worse. Fights are breaking out for no good reason, trash is littering the streets, and kids have nothing to do but hang out on the streets. Something needs to change before it is too late.

The first thing that I would like to change to improve my neighborhood is to make it safer. I want to be able to walk inside a store and not have to wait until a fight is over so I can leave. People have to stop trying to impress others by picking fights with everyone they see. I could feel safer if people were more respectful toward each other.

I also want to change the appearance of my neighborhood. There is trash everywhere. I hate having to clean up after someone else just because they do not know how to put trash into a trash can. I would also like to add some things. People in the neighborhood need a place to play and think. A playground would be a safe place for small children to play. This would be a place where the children would not have to worry about careless drivers or street fights. I would also like to build a community center for teens to have fun, play sports, and be themselves. The center would be a place that helps teens figure out that they can do anything if they put their minds to it. It could be called The Hope Center.

Finally, I would like to change the attitude toward the schools in my neighborhood. Walker Elementary and Ford Road Elementary have math and spelling bees every year, but they do not grab the headlines. Neither school gets positive recognition in the media. Positive attention would help everyone feel better about schools and the work teachers and students do.

My neighborhood is not bad. It just needs a few adjustments like any other neighborhood. So as I look out of my bedroom window, I see what it once was, what it has become, and what it has the potential to be. By committing to local safety and community spaces, we could take important steps toward improvements that can help everyone. I will do everything I can to help improve my neighborhood.

In the introduction, Amnesti clearly states a key claim, defining the problem in a way that conveys a sense of urgency.

She addresses possible solutions in the body of her essay by explaining ideas to improve the quality of life in her neighborhood.

The essay uses the proper conventions of grammar, usage, and mechanics.

Amnesti organizes her essay with a conclusion that summarizes her solution.

Editing and Proofreading

Proofread to correct errors in grammar, spelling, and punctuation.

Focus on spelling homophones. A **homophone** is a word that sounds the same as another word but is spelled differently. People often choose the wrong homophone if they are writing quickly. If you use a computer program to write your essay, you should run a spell-check. Be extra careful with homophones, however. The spell-check will miss mistakes that occur when words such as *there, their,* and *they're* are spelled correctly but used incorrectly.

Spiral Review
Earlier in the unit, you learned about **commas and semicolons** (p. 792) and **capitalization** (p. 816). Review your essay to be sure you have used commas and semicolons correctly and have properly capitalized words.

Publishing and Presenting

Consider one of the following ways to share your writing:

Post your ideas. Post your essay online or on a bulletin board, along with the essays written by other class members.

Implement the solution. If it is possible, carry out the solution you propose in your essay. Then, evaluate how well it worked. Write a summary of the results and post it with your essay.

Reflecting on Your Writing

Writer's Journal Jot down your answer to this question:
What did you learn about the difficulties in solving problems?

Rubric for Self-Assessment

Find evidence that your writing addresses each category. Then, use the rating scale to grade your work.

Criteria	Rating Scale
Purpose/Function Clearly introduces a claim about the problem and proposed solution; provides a concluding section that supports the argument presented	*not very* .... *very* 1 2 3 4
Organization Organizes the reasons and evidence logically; uses words to create cohesion and clarify the relations among claim(s), counterclaims, reasons, and evidence	1 2 3 4
Development of Ideas/Elaboration Supports the claim with logical reasoning and relevant evidence, demonstrating understanding of the topic and addressing opposing claims	1 2 3 4
Language Establishes and maintains an appropriate voice and a formal style	1 2 3 4
Conventions Correctly follows conventions of grammar, spelling, and punctuation, including the correct use of comparative and superlative modifiers	1 2 3 4

SELECTED RESPONSE

I. Reading Literature

Directions: *Read the excerpt from "Brer Possum's Dilemma"*
by Jackie Torrence. Then, answer each question that follows.

**Common Core
State Standards**

RL.8.2; W.8.1.b; L.8.4.a
[For full standards wording, see
the chart in the front of this
book.]

> . . . Brer Snake crawled outa the high grass just as slow as he could,
> stretched 'imself out across the road, rared up, and looked at ol' Brer
> Possum.
>
> Then he hissed. "I've been down there in that ol' hole for a mighty
> long time, and I've gotten a little cold 'cause the sun didn't shine. Do
> you think you could put me in your pocket and git me warm?"
>
> Brer Possum said, "Now you listen here, Brer Snake. I knows you.
> You's mean and evil and lowdown, and if'n I put you in my pocket
> you wouldn't do nothin' but bite me."
>
> Brer Snake hissed.
>
> "Maybe not. Maybe not. Maaaaaaaybe not."
>
> "No sireee, Brer Snake. I knows you. I jist ain't a-goin' to do it."
>
> But jist as Brer Possum was talkin' to Brer Snake, he happened to
> git a real good look at 'im. He was a-layin' there lookin' so <u>pitiful</u>, and
> Brer Possum's great big heart began to feel sorry for ol' Brer Snake.
>
> "All right," said Brer Possum. "You must be cold. So jist this once
> I'm a-goin' to put you in my pocket."
>
> So ol' Brer Snake coiled up jist as little as he could, and Brer
> Possum picked 'im up and put 'im in his pocket.
>
> Brer Snake laid quiet and still—so quiet and still that Brer Possum
> even forgot that he was a-carryin' 'im around. But all of a sudden,
> Brer Snake commenced to crawlin' out, and he turned and faced
> Brer Possum and hissed.
>
> "I'm a-goin' to bite you."
>
> But Brer Possum said, "Now wait a minute. Why are you a-goin'
> to bite me? . . . I got you outa that hole, and I put you in my pocket
> to git you warm. Why are you a-goin' to bite me?"
>
> Brer Snake hissed.
>
> "You knowed I was a snake before you put me in you pocket."
>
> And when you're mindin' your own business and you spot
> trouble, don't never trouble trouble 'til trouble troubles you.

1. **Part A** What type of story from the American **oral tradition** does the passage represent?

   A. myth   C. tall tale
   B. fable   D. epic

   Part B What feature of the story most clearly shows the type of story it is?

   A. The story describes a quest of great national importance.
   B. Brer Possum performs impossible feats of strength.
   C. The story explains how opossums came to be afraid of snakes.
   D. The story teaches a moral lesson and features animal characters that act like humans.

2. Which line best shows the **dialect** in which the passage is written?

   A. "Maybe not. Maybe not. Maaaaaaaybe not."
   B. "I jist ain't a-goin' to do it."
   C. "All right," said Brer Possum.
   D. ". . . I've gotten a little cold 'cause the sun didn't shine."

3. **Part A** What **theme,** or central insight, is the story meant to convey?

   A. It doesn't pay to be generous.
   B. Snakes and opossums are natural enemies.
   C. Do not help others unless it will benefit you.
   D. Avoid putting yourself in a dangerous situation.

   Part B Which detail from the story most clearly conveys its central insight?

   A. "I knows you. You's mean and evil and lowdown."
   B. "[D]on't never trouble trouble 'til trouble troubles you."
   C. "I got you outa that hole, and I put you in my pocket to git warm."
   D. "Brer Possum's great big heart began to feel sorry for ol' Brer Snake."

4. Which phrase from the passage is an example of an **idiom?**

   A. "mindin' your own business"
   B. "put 'im in his pocket"
   C. "crawled outa the high grass"
   D. "looked at ol' Brer Possum."

5. Which detail would it be best to leave out of a **summary** of the story?

   A. The grass by the road is tall.
   B. Brer Possum puts Brer Snake in his pocket.
   C. Brer Snake says he will bite Brer Possum.
   D. Brer Possum takes pity on Brer Snake.

6. How does the story differ from a **legend?**

   A. It emerged out of an oral tradition, whereas legends are written by authors.
   B. It is not based on real people or events, whereas legends usually are.
   C. It contains a central insight about life, whereas legends never do.
   D. It features many lines of dialogue, whereas legends usually feature none.

7. **Vocabulary** Which is the best definition of the underlined word pitiful as it is used in the passage?

   A. compassionate; full of pity
   B. stuck in a hole or pit
   C. tricky; mischievous
   D. deserving of sympathy

⏱ Timed Writing

8. In a brief essay, explain whether Brer Possum is or is not a **heroic character.** Support your argument by comparing or contrasting at least three of Brer Possum's character traits with traits that heroic characters generally share.

GO ON ➡

II. Reading Informational Text

Directions: *Read the passage. Then, answer each question that follows.*

Common Core State Standards

RI.8.1, RI.8.3; L.8.2.a, L.8.3
[For full standards wording, see the chart in the front of this book.]

Ski Jumping at the Olympics

History

Ski jumping originated as a sport in Norway around 1860, when Sondre Norheim soared approximately 98 feet. Since then, jumpers have developed techniques to improve their aerodynamics and greatly increase the distance of their jumps. Now, Olympic ski jumpers can reach past 656 feet—almost seven times the distance of Norheim's first jump!

Technique

Ski jumpers use wide, long skis and wear tight-fitting ski suits. Using their legs for power, they ski down a ramp, accelerating to a speed of about 56 mph at take-off. Then, they snap their skis upward and lean their bodies forward until they are almost parallel with their skis. When they achieve perfect form, skiers almost appear to be in flight.

Ski Jumping Schedule			
Event	**Date**	**Time**	**Place**
Individual Finals	February 17	4:00 pm	Pregalato

1. **Part A** According to the passage, what is the main reason modern ski jumpers can jump farther than nineteenth-century ski jumpers could?

   A. Modern ski jumpers start on longer, steeper ramps.
   B. Nineteenth-century ski suits were extremely heavy.
   C. The legs of modern ski jumpers are seven times as powerful.
   D. Ski jumpers today know better ways to reduce air resistance.

   Part B Which phrase from the passage best supports the answer to part A?

   A. "Ski jumpers use wide, long skis"
   B. "techniques to improve their aerodynamics"
   C. "Using their legs for power, they ski down a ramp, accelerating"
   D. "almost seven times the distance of Norheim's first jump!"

2. Which subhead would be the best choice for a section about how to compete in an Olympic ski jumping event?

   A. Olympic Ski Jumping Rules
   B. Olympic Ski Jumping Records
   C. The First Olympic Games
   D. How Weather Affects Ski Jumpers

III. Writing and Language Conventions

Directions: *Read the passage. Then, answer each question that follows.*

> (1) In the 1800s, many nations dreamed of creating a channel through Central America. (2) ships would then be able to sail directly between the Atlantic ocean and the pacific Ocean. (3) President Theodore Roosevelt was determined to make this dream real. (4) Roosevelt said, "I took the Canal Zone and let Congress debate." (5) The canal cut across an isthmus a narrow strip of land. (6) Although the terrain was challenging, work moved quickly. (7) The first ship passed through the canal locks in 1914. (8) Now, instead of circling the tip of South America to sail between oceans, ships could travel across the new Panama Canal.

1. Which is the best way to combine sentences 6 and 7 using correct **punctuation**?
   - **A.** Although the terrain was challenging, work moved quickly, the first ship passed through the canal locks in 1914.
   - **B.** Although the terrain was challenging, work moved quickly, in fact the first ship passed through the canal locks in 1914.
   - **C.** Although the terrain was challenging, work moved quickly; the first ship passed through the canal locks in 1914.
   - **D.** Although the terrain was challenging, work moved quickly; and the first ship passed through the canal locks in 1914.

2. Which revision corrects the **capitalization** error(s) in sentence 2?
   - **A.** ships would then be able to sail directly between the Atlantic ocean and the Pacific ocean.
   - **B.** Ships would then be able to sail directly between the atlantic ocean and the pacific ocean.
   - **C.** Ships would then be able to sail directly between The Atlantic Ocean And The Pacific Ocean.
   - **D.** Ships would then be able to sail directly between the Atlantic Ocean and the Pacific Ocean.

3. What is the correct way to **punctuate** sentence 5?
   - **A.** The canal cut across an isthmus, a narrow strip of land.
   - **B.** The canal, cut across an isthmus, a narrow strip of land.
   - **C.** The canal cut across, an isthmus a narrow strip of land.
   - **D.** The sentence is correct as is.

4. What is the **sentence structure** of sentence 6?
   - **A.** simple
   - **B.** compound
   - **C.** complex
   - **D.** compound-complex

CONSTRUCTED RESPONSE

 **Common Core State Standards**

RL.8.1, RL.8.2, RL.8.3, RL.8.4, RL.8.9; W.8.1, W.8.2, W.8.7, W.8.9; SL.8.1, SL.8.4; L.8.1, L.8.2
[For full standards wording, see the chart in the front of this book.]

Directions: *Follow the instructions to complete the tasks below as required by your teacher.*

As you work on each task, incorporate both general academic vocabulary and literary terms you learned in Parts 1 and 2 of this unit.

Writing

TASK 1 Literature [RL.8.1; W.8.2]

Analyze Cultural or Historical Context

Write an essay analyzing how the details in a story reveal its cultural or historical context.

- Choose a story from Part 2 of this unit that is clearly connected to a specific cultural or historical context.

- Begin your essay by briefly identifying the story's context.

- Introduce the story's characters and briefly summarize story events.

- Then, give examples of details, such as characters' background, beliefs, roles, circumstances, actions, manner of speaking, and so on, that illustrate the cultural or historical context. Clearly explain the connection of each example to the context.

- Correct any run-on sentences or sentence fragments in your essay.

TASK 2 Literature [RL.8.2; W.8.9; L.8.2]

Compare Themes in Two Works

Write an essay in which you analyze the themes in two works in Part 2 of this unit.

- Select two stories in Part 2 that have identifiable themes.

- In your essay, provide a summary of each story's plot. Explain how the story events you have summarized are connected to the theme, or message, of each story.

- Next, explain the theme's relationship to characters' attitudes and actions and the setting in each story.

- Finally, describe how the two themes are similar and note ways in which they differ. For example, you might explain how one or both stories have universal themes by showing how the same theme occurs in stories from other cultures or time periods.

- As you write, be sure to capitalize characters' names and place names correctly.

TASK 3 Literature [RL.8.4; W.8.1]

Analyze Language and Word Choice

Write an essay in which you analyze the use of dialect, idioms, hyperbole, or understatement in a story or poem in Part 2 of this unit.

Part 1

- Review and evaluate a work from Part 2 of this unit that features dialect, idioms, hyperbole (exaggeration), or understatement.

- As you are reviewing the work, make notes on specific examples of dialect, idioms, hyperbole, or understatement.

- Answer the following questions: What does each example mean? What impact does the use of dialect, idiom, hyperbole, or understatement in the example have on the work's meaning and tone?

Part 2

- Write an essay in which you analyze the overall impact dialect, idiom, hyperbole, or understatement has on the story or poem. State whether or not you think the writer's use of such language is effective, and explain why.

- Review your essay for proper punctuation.

Speaking and Listening

TASK 4 Literature [RL.8.3; SL.8.4; L.8.1]

Present a Speech on a Hero

Present a speech about a hero from one of the texts in Part 2 of this unit.

- Choose a heroic character from one of the texts in Part 2 of this unit.
- Take notes on the traits, qualities, and accomplishments that make this person a hero.
- Identify quotations and descriptions from the text that illustrate the heroic qualities and accomplishments you have identified. Record these examples as evidence to present in your speech.
- Arrange your notes in logical order.
- Present your speech to the class, observing standard English grammar and usage.

TASK 5 Literature [RL.8.9; SL.8.1]

Compare Legends and Retellings

Moderate a group discussion in which you compare Carl Sandburg's presentation of heroes in Part 2 of this unit with the way these heroes are presented in traditional legends.

- As a group, list the heroes mentioned in the excerpt from *The People, Yes*, p. 787, and "Paul Bunyan of the North Woods," p. 823. Then, locate and read examples of more traditional narrative retellings of the legends from which these heroes are drawn.
- Ask participants to compare and contrast the way the heroes are represented in the more traditional retellings with the way that Sandburg represents them.
- Participants should base their responses on evidence from the texts, such as plot events, descriptions, and dialogue.
- Finally, ask participants to judge whether Sandburg's changes improve on or detract from the tales.

Research

TASK 6 Literature [W.8.7, W.8.9]

 ### Are yesterday's heroes important today?

In Part 2 of this unit, you have read literature about heroic figures. Choose a heroic figure from America's past. Conduct a brief research project on the hero. Then, use both the literature you have read and your research to reflect on this unit's Big Question. Follow these guidelines for research:

- Focus your research on one heroic figure.
- Gather information from at least two reliable sources. Your sources may be print or digital.

- Take notes as you investigate the heroic figure.
- Cite your sources.

When you have completed your research, write a response to the Big Question: Are yesterday's heroes important today? Discuss how your initial ideas have changed or been reinforced. Support your response with an example from literature and an example from your research. Be sure to use academic vocabulary words in your response (see p. 755).

"The American war is **over**, but this is far from being the **case** with the American Revolution."

—Benjamin Rush

FREEDOM FIGHTERS

The selections in this unit relate to the Big Question: **Are yesterday's heroes important today?** These heroes include the men and women who have led others in the struggle for human rights and freedoms. The texts that follow include works by or about several important U.S. freedom fighters. As you read, think about their messages, how those messages relate to one another, and how they apply today.

◀ CRITICAL VIEWING The Tuskegee Airmen, including the men pictured here, were the first African Americans permitted to fly as pilots for the United States armed services. Previously, discriminatory policies had excluded African Americans from serving in this role. The Airmen fought with distinction in the Second World War. In what ways does their story illustrate the American fight for freedom?

CLOSE READING TOOL

Use the **Close Reading Tool** to practice the strategies you learn in this unit.

from

THE AMERICAN DREAM

MARTIN LUTHER KING, JR.

Here, Dr. Martin Luther King, Jr., is shown on the occasion of what is perhaps his most famous speech, the "I Have a Dream" speech, delivered August 28, 1963, at the Lincoln Memorial in Washington, D.C.

June 6, 1961

America is essentially a dream,

a dream as yet unfulfilled. It is a dream of a land where men of all races, of all nationalities and of all creeds[1] can live together as brothers. The substance of the dream is expressed in these sublime words, words lifted to cosmic proportions: "We hold these truths to be self-evident, that all men are created equal; that they are endowed by their Creator with certain unalienable rights; that among these are life, liberty, and the pursuit of happiness."[2] This is the dream.

One of the first things we notice in this dream is an amazing universalism. It does not say some men, but it says all men. It does not say all white men, but it says all men, which includes black men. It does not say all Gentiles, but it says all men, which includes Jews. It does not say all Protestants, but it says all men, which includes Catholics.

And there is another thing we see in this dream that ultimately distinguishes democracy and our form of government from all of the totalitarian regimes[3] that emerge in history. It says that each individual has certain basic rights that are neither conferred by nor derived from the state. To discover where they came from it is necessary to move back behind the dim mist of eternity, for they are God-given. Very seldom if ever in the history of the world has a sociopolitical document expressed in such profoundly eloquent and unequivocal language the dignity and the worth of human personality. The American dream reminds us that every man is heir to the legacy of worthiness.

---

1. **creeds** (krēdz) *n.* systems of belief.
2. **"We hold these truths . . . pursuit of happiness."** opening words of the Declaration of Independence, which asserted the American colonies' independence from Great Britain in 1776.
3. **totalitarian** (tō tal´ ə ter´ ē ən) **regimes** (rə zhēmz´) countries in which those in power control every aspect of citizens' lives.

paradoxes ▶
(par´ ə däks´ əz) *n.*
situations that seem
to have contradictory
qualities

Ever since the Founding Fathers of our nation dreamed this noble dream, America has been something of a schizophrenic[4] personality, tragically divided against herself. On the one hand we have proudly professed the principles of democracy, and on the other hand we have sadly practiced the very antithesis of those principles. Indeed slavery and segregation have been strange **paradoxes** in a nation founded on the principle that all men are created equal. This is what the Swedish sociologist, Gunnar Myrdal, referred to as the American dilemma.

But the shape of the world today does not permit us the luxury of an anemic democracy. The price America must pay for the continued exploitation of the Negro and other minority groups is the price of its own destruction. The hour is late; the clock of destiny is ticking out. It is trite, but urgently true, that if America is to remain a first-class nation she can no longer have second-class citizens. Now, more than ever before, America is challenged to bring her noble dream into reality, and those who are working to implement the American dream are the true saviors of democracy.

Now may I suggest some of the things we must do if we are to make the American dream a reality. First I think all of us must develop a world perspective if we are to survive. The American dream will not become a reality **devoid** of the larger dream of a world of brotherhood and peace and good will. The world in which we live is a world of geographical oneness and we are challenged now to make it spiritually one.

devoid ▶
(di void´) *adj.*
completely without

Man's scientific genius and technological ingenuity has dwarfed distance and placed time in chains. Jet planes have compressed into minutes distances that once took days and months to cover. It is not common for a preacher to be quoting Bob Hope, but I think he has aptly described this jet age in which we live. If, on taking off on a nonstop flight from Los Angeles to New York City, you develop hiccups, he said,

---

4. **schizophrenic** (skit´ sə fren´ ik) *adj.* characterized by a fragmented personality and hallucinations, a disorder sometimes known popularly as "split personality."

you will hic in Los Angeles and cup in New York City. That is really *moving*. If you take a flight from Tokyo, Japan, on Sunday morning, you will arrive in Seattle, Washington, on the preceding Saturday night. When your friends meet you at the airport and ask you when you left Tokyo, you will have to say, "I left tomorrow." This is the kind of world in which we live. Now this is a bit humorous but I am trying to laugh a basic fact into all of us: the world in which we live has become a single neighborhood.

Through our scientific genius we have made of this world a neighborhood; now through our moral and spiritual development we must make of it a brotherhood. In a real sense, we must all learn to live together as brothers, or we will all **perish** together as fools. We must come to see that no individual can live alone; no nation can live alone. We must all live together; we must all be concerned about each other.

◀ **perish**
(per´ ish) *v.*
die; be destroyed or wiped out

ABOUT THE AUTHOR

Martin Luther King, Jr.
(1929–1968)

Many people remember Dr. Martin Luther King, Jr., for these lines from a speech in 1963: "I have a dream that my four little children will one day live in a nation where they will not be judged by the color of their skin but by the content of their character."

Born in Atlanta, Georgia, Dr. King came to national attention as a civil rights leader when he led a year-long boycott against the segregated bus system in Montgomery, Alabama, starting in 1955. A long campaign of marches and demonstrations followed, with the aim of bringing down the entire system of segregation. King and his fellow activists faced opposition from segregationist governors, hostile crowds, and unsympathetic police officers. Ultimately, however, King succeeded in getting important reforms passed. He fell victim to assassination on April 4, 1968.

READ

Comprehension

Reread all or part of the text to help you answer the following questions.

1. What point about the origin of human rights does King make?

2. What, according to Gunnar Myrdal, is the American dilemma?

3. What does King say must happen to make the American dream a reality?

Research: Clarify Details Research one unfamiliar detail from the speech. Explain how your findings help you more fully understand the speech.

Summarize Write an objective summary of the speech to clarify your comprehension. Remember to omit your own opinions and judgments.

Language Study

Selection Vocabulary The following passages are from King's speech. Define each boldface word, and use each word in an original sentence.

1. Indeed slavery and segregation have been strange **paradoxes** in a nation. . . .

2. The American dream will not become a reality **devoid** of the larger dream of a world of brotherhood. . . .

3. . . . we must all learn to live together as brothers, or we will all **perish** together as fools.

Diction and Style Study this sentence from the speech, and answer the questions that follow.

> But the shape of the world today does not permit us the luxury of an anemic democracy.

1. (a) What does *anemic* mean, as used here? **(b)** In what technical sense is the word *anemic* often used? **(c)** Why do you think King chose to use this adjective? Consider the word's connotations, or associated feelings and ideas.

2. (a) What does *luxury* mean in this sentence? **(b)** To what group of people might an "anemic democracy" seem like a luxury we cannot afford?

Conventions In this passage, identify the independent clauses that are joined by semicolons. Then, explain how the use of semicolons clarifies the passage's meaning and helps create rhythm in the sentences.

> We must come to see that no individual can live alone; no nation can live alone. We must all live together; we must all be concerned about each other.

Academic Vocabulary

The following words appear in blue in the instructions and questions on the facing page.

observation   **distinguish**   **evidence**

Copy the words into your notebook. For each word, find a related word that is built on the same root (for example, *evaluate/evaluation*). For each pair of related words, write a sentence explaining the relationship between the meanings of the two words.

Literary Analysis

Reread the identified passages. Then, respond to the questions that follow.

> **Focus Passage 1** *(p. 853)*
>
> America is essentially . . . This is the dream.

> **Focus Passage 2** *(p. 855)*
>
> Through our scientific . . . about each other.

Key Ideas and Details

1. What does King mean when he makes the **observation** that "America is essentially a dream, a dream as yet unfulfilled"?

Craft and Structure

2. Analyze: What effect does King's use of repeated words and parallel phrases create in the second paragraph of the speech?

3. Infer: Why do you think King quotes from the Declaration of Independence?

Integration of Knowledge and Ideas

4. Generalize: King says the dream of America is "as yet unfulfilled." Do his words still hold true today? Support your answer with examples.

5. (a) Evaluate: Is the universal brotherhood that King envisions possible? Explain. **(b) Evaluate:** Is it desirable? Explain.

Key Ideas and Details

1. (a) According to King, what effect has "our scientific genius" had on the world? **(b) Infer:** How has that effect led to the need for a worldwide brotherhood?

Craft and Structure

2. Interpret: How does King **distinguish** between a *neighborhood* and a *brotherhood*? Cite details from the text to support your ideas.

3. (a) Interpret: What is King's purpose in writing this passage? **(b) Evaluate:** Does he achieve his purpose? Why or why not?

Integration of Knowledge and Ideas

4. Analyze: What conclusions does King share about the rights of the individual and the power of community? In what way do these two ideas form King's notion of the American dream? Cite **evidence** from the speech to support your response.

Oratory

Oratory is the art of public speaking. Orators such as Dr. King often use **figurative language** such as simile, metaphor, and personification to create memorable, vivid images.

1. (a) What does King mean by "the clock of destiny"? **(b)** What idea does this metaphor reinforce?

2. (a) In what way does King personify "man's scientific genius"? **(b)** How does this use of

personification add a sense of confidence in progress?

3. Freedom Fighters: In what other ways has King used oratorical skills in this speech to promote the cause of freedom?

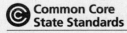

Common Core State Standards

RI.8.1, RI.8.2, RI.8.3, RI.8.4, RI.8.6; L.8.4, L.8.5, L.8.5.b, L.8.5.c
[For full standards wording, see the chart in the front of this book.]

DISCUSS

From Text to Topic **Partner Discussion**

Discuss the following passage with a partner. Take notes during the discussion. Contribute your own ideas, and support them with examples from the text.

> The price America must pay for the continued exploitation of the Negro and other minority groups is the price of its own destruction. The hour is late; the clock of destiny is ticking out. It is trite, but urgently true, that if America is to remain a first-class nation she can no longer have second-class citizens.

QUESTIONS FOR DISCUSSION

1. What link does King make between the ideas of exploitation and destruction?

2. What argument is King making about the importance of freedom for all?

WRITE

Writing to Sources **Informative Text**

Assignment

Write an **informative essay** in which you trace the development of Dr. King's argument in "The American Dream." Cite passages from the text to support your ideas.

Prewriting and Planning Reread the speech carefully, and make an outline of the structure of the text. Examine your outline and identify ways in which King develops his ideas. Then, outline your own essay and plan its organization.

Drafting Begin your draft by introducing your main idea. Then, in the body of your essay, develop your main idea. Cite specific examples from the speech to support the points you make. Include your own evaluations of King's reasoning and evidence. For example, you might consider whether he provides relevant evidence for his claim that technology has turned the world into a neighborhood. Conclude your essay by restating your main idea and sharing your insights.

Revising Reread your essay to ensure that it has a logical flow. If not, rearrange sentences and paragraphs to improve cohesion. Delete unnecessary details, and revise word choices as needed to create a formal tone.

Editing and Proofreading Review any passages you have quoted from King's speech to be sure you have cited them correctly. In addition, make sure that you have used active voice unless passive voice is required (see p. 254).

CONVENTIONS

Review your draft to ensure that whenever you write a sentence with two independent clauses, you have used either a comma and conjunction or a semicolon to join the clauses.

RESEARCH

Research **Investigate the Topic**

Civil Rights Leaders Dr. Martin Luther King, Jr., is regarded as a freedom fighter because of his work during the Civil Rights Movement in the United States. Many other men and women worked alongside Dr. King during that time period, fighting for racial equality and freedom from oppression.

Assignment

Conduct research to find out about other freedom fighters of the 1950s and 1960s, and choose one to conduct further research on. As you conduct research, take clear notes and carefully identify your sources so that you can easily access the information later on. Share your findings in an **informal presentation** for the class.

PREPARATION FOR ESSAY

You may use the results of this research project to support your ideas in the essay you will write at the end of this section.

Gather sources. Locate authoritative print and electronic sources. Primary sources, such as letters, journals, and memoirs, may provide firsthand, detailed information about your subject. You may also want to use secondary sources, such as news reports and magazine articles, which can provide a broader or, in some cases, a more balanced view than some primary sources. Look for sources that feature expert authors and up-to-date information.

Take notes. Take notes on each source, either electronically or on note cards. Use an organized note-taking strategy.

- Avoid plagiarism by using quotation marks around any passage copied directly from the source.

- Record information about your sources so that you can cite them properly.

- Use different cards for each main idea. That way, you can move ideas around easily as you plan your presentation.

Synthesize multiple sources. Assemble information from your sources, and organize it into a cohesive presentation. Use your notes to construct an outline for your presentation. Then, write a brief summary in which you pull together what you have learned.

Present ideas. Review your outline and summary, and practice delivering your presentation. During the presentation, make frequent eye contact with your audience, and speak slowly and clearly. Be ready to answer questions from your audience.

 Common Core State Standards

RI.8.8; W.8.2.a, W.8.2.b, W.8.2.e, W.8.2.f, W.8.7, W.8.8, W.8.9.b; SL.8.1, SL.8.4; L.8.1, L.8.1.b, L.8.2
[For full standards wording, see the chart in the front of this book.]

Runagate Runagate

Robert Hayden

I.

Runs falls rises stumbles on from darkness into darkness
and the darkness thicketed with shapes of terror
and the hunters pursuing and the hounds pursuing
and the night cold and the night long and the river
5   to cross and the jack-muh-lanterns[1] **beckoning** beckoning
and blackness ahead and when shall I reach that somewhere
morning and keep on going and never turn back and keep
    on going
        Runagate[2]
             Runagate
10   Runagate

Many thousands rise and go
many thousands crossing over
            O mythic North
        O star-shaped yonder Bible city

15   Some go weeping and some rejoicing
some in coffins and some in carriages
some in silks and some in **shackles**

        Rise and go or fare you well

No more auction block for me
20   no more driver's lash for me

    If you see my Pompey, 30 yrs of age,
    new breeches, plain stockings, negro shoes;
    if you see my Anna, likely young mulatto
    branded E on the right cheek, R on the left,
25   catch them if you can and notify subscriber.[3]
    Catch them if you can, but it won't be easy.
    They'll dart underground when you try to catch them,
    plunge into quicksand, whirlpools, mazes,
    turn into scorpions when you try to catch them.

◄ **beckoning**
(bek´ ə niŋ) *adj.*
calling; summoning

◄ **shackles**
(shak´ əlz) *n.* metal
bonds used to
restrain prisoners

---

1. **jack-muh-lanterns** (jak´ mə lan´ tərnz) *n.* jack-o'-lanterns, shifting lights seen over a marsh at night.
2. **Runagate** (run´ ə gāt´) *n.* an old term, now outdated, referring to a runaway. Here, it refers to the runaway slaves who escaped to the North from slave states.
3. **subscriber** (səb skrīb´ ər) *n.* here, the person from whom the slave Pompey ran away.

30 And before I'll be a slave
    I'll be buried in my grave

        North star and bonanza gold
        I'm bound for the freedom, freedom-bound
        and oh Susyanna don't you cry for me

35   Runagate

                            Runagate

        II.

Rises from their **anguish** and their power,

                    Harriet Tubman,

                    woman of earth, whipscarred,
40   a summoning, a shining

                    Mean to be free

    And this was the way of it, brethren brethren,
    way we journeyed from Can't to Can.
45 Moon so bright and no place to hide,
    the cry up and the patterollers[4] riding,
    hound dogs belling in bladed air.
    And fear starts a-murbling, Never make it,
    we'll never make it. *Hush that now,*
50 and she's turned upon us, leveled pistol
    glinting in the moonlight:
    Dead folks can't jaybird-talk, she says;
    You keep on going now or die, she says.

    Wanted   Harriet Tubman   alias The General
55 alias Moses   Stealer of Slaves

    In league with Garrison   Alcott   Emerson
    Garrett   Douglass   Thoreau   John Brown[5]

    Armed and known to be Dangerous

    Wanted   Reward   Dead or Alive

60   Tell me, Ezekiel, oh tell me do you see
        mailed Jehovah[6] coming to deliver me?

anguish ▶
(aŋ´ gwish) *n.* great
suffering, as from
worry, grief, or
pain; agony

---

4. patterollers (pa´ tər ōl´ ərz) *n.* dialect for *patrollers,* people who hunt for runaways.
5. Garrison . . . John Brown various abolitionists, or people who were against slavery.
6. Ezekiel (i zē´ kē əl) **. . . Jehovah** (ji hō və) Ezekiel was a Hebrew prophet of the
sixth century B.C.; *Jehovah* is another word for God.

Hoot-owl calling in the ghosted air,
five times calling to the hants[7] in the air.
Shadow of a face in the scary leaves,
65   shadow of a voice in the talking leaves:

   Come ride-a my train

   Oh that train, ghost-story train
   through swamp and savanna movering movering,
   over trestles of dew, through caves of the wish,
70   *Midnight Special on a sabre track movering movering,*
   first stop Mercy and the last Hallelujah.

   Come ride-a my train

   Mean mean mean to be free.

---

7. **hants** (hants) *n.* dialect term for *ghosts*.

ABOUT THE AUTHOR

Robert Hayden (1913–1980)

Robert Hayden grew up in a low-income neighborhood in Detroit, Michigan. Extremely nearsighted and so excluded from activities such as sports, Hayden devoted his time to reading. After graduating from high school, he attended college for a few years on a scholarship. Leaving school, he went to work for the Federal Writers' Project, where he researched African American history. Hayden then earned a graduate degree in English literature and went on to become a professor of English, first at Fisk University in Tennessee and later at the University of Michigan. During his long teaching career, Hayden wrote and published many volumes of poetry. Much of his work centers on the history of slavery and emancipation, but he also addressed political issues, such as the Vietnam War. In 1976, Hayden was appointed as Consultant in Poetry to the Library of Congress, a post now known as "Poet Laureate." Hayden was the first African American to receive this honor.

READ

Comprehension

Reread as needed to answer these questions.

1. What is a "runagate"?
2. What journey is described in this poem?
3. In lines 21 and 23, who are Pompey and Anna?

Research: Clarify Details Research an unfamiliar detail in the poem and explain how your research helps you understand the poem.

Summarize Write an **objective** summary of the poem. Do not include your own opinions.

Language Study

Selection Vocabulary Find a synonym for each boldface word from the poem. Then, explain which word, the original word or the synonym, is a more effective choice for the poem.

1. . . . the river / to cross and the jack-muh-lanterns **beckoning** . . .
2. . . . some in silks and some in **shackles** . . .
3. Rises from their **anguish** and their power . . .

Literary Analysis

Reread the passage identified and answer the questions that follow.

> **Focus Passage** (ll. 19–36, pp. 861–62)
> No more auction block . . . Runagate

Key Ideas and Details

1. **(a)** Who are the two speakers in this section? **(b) Analyze:** What warning does the second speaker give, and to whom is the warning directed?

Craft and Structure

2. **Analyze:** How does the shift in perspective in these lines **intensify** the emotion in the poem?
3. **(a)** Lines 30–31 are from the spiritual "Oh, Freedom." What other song is alluded to in this passage? **(b)** Why might fragments of song spill from the speaker at this time? What effect is created?

Integration of Knowledge and Ideas

4. What insights into fighting for freedom does the poem convey? Cite the text in support.

Forms of Poetry

Two **forms of poetry** are narrative (poetry that tells a story) and lyric (poetry that has a musical quality, using rhyme, repetition, and rhythm to express feelings). Reread the poem. Take notes on **elements** of both narrative and lyric poetry in the poem.

1. **(a)** What elements of narrative poetry are present in the poem? **(b)** How does the narrative hold the reader's interest?
2. **Freedom Fighters: (a)** Identify an example of lyric elements used to capture the emotions of fugitives. **(b)** How do the emotions expressed add to your understanding of these freedom fighters?

DISCUSS • RESEARCH • WRITE

From Text to Topic **Panel Discussion**

Conduct a panel discussion of the following passage. Take notes during the discussion. Contribute your own ideas, and support them with examples from the text.

> And fear starts a-murbling. Never make it,
> we'll never make it. *Hush that now,*
> and she's turned upon us, leveled pistol
> glinting in the moonlight:
> Dead folks can't jaybird-talk, she says;
> You keep on going now or die, she says.

Research **Investigate the Topic**

Underground Railroad "Runagate Runagate" presents a vivid account of the experiences of runaway slaves on the Underground Railroad.

Assignment

Conduct research to find out about the Underground Railroad. Consult multiple online and print sources, making sure that each source is credible and accurate. If possible, interview a professor of history or other historian. Take detailed notes and carefully identify your sources. Then, create visuals based on your research, and share your findings in a **poster presentation** for the class.

Writing to Sources **Narrative**

Parts of "Runagate Runagate" are written from the perspective of an escaping slave, who expresses fear and determination.

Assignment

Write a first-person **narrative** from the perspective of an escaping slave who is using the Underground Railroad. Follow these steps:

- Give your character a unique history and personality.
- Describe the internal and external conflicts faced by your character.
- Relate a series of events leading to a climax, which should be based on or relate to the poem.
- Include a resolution, in which you wrap up the action.

QUESTIONS FOR DISCUSSION

1. What is happening in these lines? What do the italicized words indicate?
2. Why does Tubman take an angry tone with the slaves?
3. What does this passage reveal about the risks associated with seeking freedom?

PREPARATION FOR ESSAY

You may use the results of this research project to support your ideas in the essay you will write at the end of this section.

ACADEMIC VOCABULARY

Academic terms appear in blue on these pages. Use a dictionary to find their definitions. Then, use the words as you speak and write about the text.

ⓒ **Common Core State Standards**

RL.8.1, RL.8.2, RL.8.4; W.8.3, W.8.7, W.8.8; SL.8.1; L.8.4, L.8.6
[For full standards wording, see the chart in the front of this book.]

EMANCIPATION

from Lincoln: A Photobiography

Russell Freedman

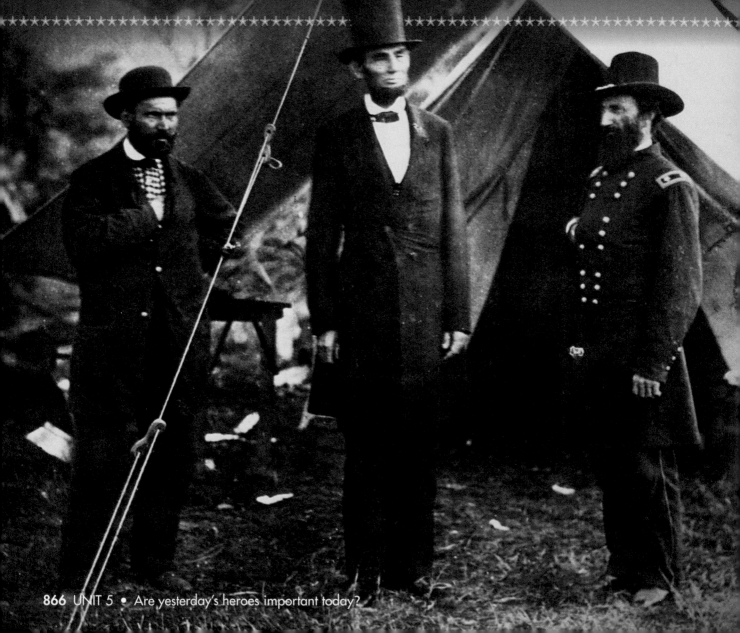

◀ This photograph shows President Abraham Lincoln (center) meeting with Major Allan Pinkerton and General John A. McClernand in October 1862 at the Antietam Creek near Sharpsburg, Maryland, site of the Battle of Antietam.

★★

The toughest decision facing Lincoln[1] . . . was the one he had to make about slavery. Early in the war, he was still willing to leave slavery alone in the South, if only he could restore the Union. Once the rebellion was crushed, slavery would be confined to the Southern states, where it would gradually die out. "We didn't go into the war to put down slavery, but to put the flag back," Lincoln said. "To act differently at this moment would, I have no doubt, not only weaken our cause, but smack of bad faith."

Abolitionists were demanding that the president free the slaves at once, by means of a wartime proclamation. "Teach the rebels and traitors that the price they are to pay for the attempt to abolish this Government must be the abolition of slavery," said Frederick Douglass, the famous black editor and reformer. "Let the war cry be down with treason, and down with slavery, the cause of treason!"

But Lincoln hesitated. He was afraid to **alienate** the large numbers of Northerners who supported the Union but opposed emancipation. And he worried about the loyal, slaveholding border states—Kentucky, Missouri, Maryland, and Delaware—that had refused to join the Confederacy. Lincoln feared that emancipation might drive those states into the arms of the South.

◀ **alienate**
(āl´ yən āt´) v.
make unfriendly

---

1. **Lincoln** Abraham Lincoln (1809–1865), sixteenth president of the United States (1861–1865), and leader of the North during the Civil War.

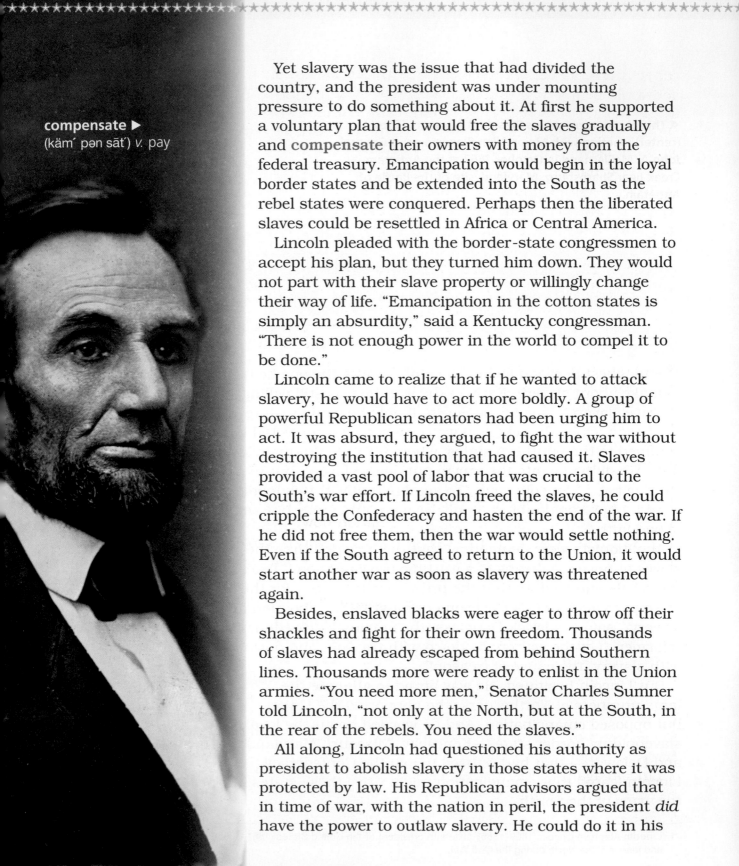

compensate ▶
(käm′ pən sāt′) v. pay

Yet slavery was the issue that had divided the country, and the president was under mounting pressure to do something about it. At first he supported a voluntary plan that would free the slaves gradually and **compensate** their owners with money from the federal treasury. Emancipation would begin in the loyal border states and be extended into the South as the rebel states were conquered. Perhaps then the liberated slaves could be resettled in Africa or Central America.

Lincoln pleaded with the border-state congressmen to accept his plan, but they turned him down. They would not part with their slave property or willingly change their way of life. "Emancipation in the cotton states is simply an absurdity," said a Kentucky congressman. "There is not enough power in the world to compel it to be done."

Lincoln came to realize that if he wanted to attack slavery, he would have to act more boldly. A group of powerful Republican senators had been urging him to act. It was absurd, they argued, to fight the war without destroying the institution that had caused it. Slaves provided a vast pool of labor that was crucial to the South's war effort. If Lincoln freed the slaves, he could cripple the Confederacy and hasten the end of the war. If he did not free them, then the war would settle nothing. Even if the South agreed to return to the Union, it would start another war as soon as slavery was threatened again.

Besides, enslaved blacks were eager to throw off their shackles and fight for their own freedom. Thousands of slaves had already escaped from behind Southern lines. Thousands more were ready to enlist in the Union armies. "You need more men," Senator Charles Sumner told Lincoln, "not only at the North, but at the South, in the rear of the rebels. You need the slaves."

All along, Lincoln had questioned his authority as president to abolish slavery in those states where it was protected by law. His Republican advisors argued that in time of war, with the nation in peril, the president *did* have the power to outlaw slavery. He could do it in his capacity as commander in chief of the armed forces. Such an act would be justified as a necessary war measure, because it would weaken the enemy. If Lincoln really wanted to save the Union, Senator Sumner told him, he must act now. He must wipe out slavery.

The war had become an endless nightmare of bloodshed and bungling generals. Lincoln doubted if the Union could survive without bold and drastic measures. By the summer of 1862, he had worked out a plan that would hold the loyal slave states in the Union, while striking at the enemies of the Union.

On July 22, 1862, he revealed his plan to his cabinet. He had decided, he told them, that emancipation was "a military necessity, absolutely essential to the preservation of the Union." For that reason, he intended to issue a proclamation freeing all the slaves in rebel states that had not returned to the Union by January 1, 1863. The proclamation would be aimed at the Confederate South only. In the loyal border states, he would continue to push for gradual, compensated emancipation.

Some cabinet members warned that the country wasn't ready to accept emancipation. But most of them nodded their approval, and in any case, Lincoln had made up his mind. He did listen to the objection of William H. Seward, his secretary of state. If Lincoln published his proclamation now, Seward argued, when Union armies had just been defeated in Virginia, it would seem like an act of desperation, "the last shriek on our retreat." The president must wait until the Union had won a decisive military victory in the East. Then he could issue his proclamation from a position of strength. Lincoln agreed. For the time being, he filed the document away in his desk.

A month later, in the war's second battle at Bull Run, Union forces commanded by General John Pope suffered another **humiliating** defeat. "We are whipped again," Lincoln moaned. He feared now that the war was lost. Rebel troops under Robert E. Lee were driving north. Early in September, Lee invaded Maryland and advanced toward Pennsylvania.

Lincoln again turned to General George McClellan—Who else do I have? he asked—and ordered him to repel the invasion. The two armies met at Antietam Creek in Maryland on September 17 in the bloodiest single engagement of the

◀ **humiliating**
(hyo͞o mil′ ē āt′ iŋ)
adj. embarrassing

war. Lee was forced to retreat back to Virginia. But McClellan, cautious as ever, held his position and failed to pursue the defeated rebel army. It wasn't the decisive victory Lincoln had hoped for, but it would have to do.

On September 22, Lincoln read the final wording of his Emancipation Proclamation to his cabinet. If the rebels did not return to the Union by January 1, the president would free "thenceforward and forever" all the slaves everywhere in the Confederacy. Emancipation would become a Union war objective. As Union armies smashed their way into rebel territory, they would annihilate slavery once and for all.

The next day, the proclamation was released to the press. Throughout the North, opponents of slavery hailed the measure, and black people rejoiced. Frederick Douglass, the black abolitionist, had criticized Lincoln severely in the past. But he said now: "We shout for joy that we live to record this righteous decree."

When Lincoln delivered his annual message to Congress on December 1, he asked support for his program of military emancipation:

"Fellow citizens, *we* cannot escape history. We of this Congress and this administration, will be remembered in spite of ourselves. . . . In *giving* freedom to the *slave,* we *assure* freedom to the *free*—honorable alike in what we give, and what we preserve."

On New Year's Day, after a fitful night's sleep, Lincoln sat at his White House desk and put the finishing touches on his historic decree. From this day forward, all slaves in the rebel states were "forever free." Blacks who wished to could now enlist in the Union army and sail on Union ships. Several all-black regiments were formed immediately. By the end of the war, more than 180,000 blacks—a majority of them emancipated slaves—had volunteered for the Union forces. They manned military garrisons and served as front-line combat troops in every theatre of the war.

The traditional New Year's reception was held in the White House that morning. Mary appeared at an official gathering for the first time since Willie's death,[2] wearing garlands in her hair and a black shawl about her head.

During the reception, Lincoln slipped away and retired to his office with several cabinet members and other officials for the formal signing of the proclamation. He looked tired. He had been shaking hands all morning, and now his hand trembled as he picked up a gold pen to sign his name.

Ordinarily he signed "A. Lincoln." But today, as he put pen to paper, he carefully wrote out his full name. "If my name ever goes into history," he said then, "it will be for this act."

---

2. **Mary appeared . . . Willie's death** Mary Todd Lincoln was President Lincoln's wife. The couple's son William died in 1862 at age eleven.

ABOUT THE AUTHOR

Russell Freedman (b. 1929)

"I had the good fortune to grow up in a house filled with books and book talk," Russell Freedman has said. His father worked in sales for a large publishing company, and his mother worked in a bookstore. His father's connections introduced him to such well-known writers of the time as John Steinbeck and Margaret Mitchell, who were often guests in the family's home.

One of Freedman's favorite subjects in school was history, an interest that led him to his writing career. The 1961 publication of his book *Teenagers Who Made History* was the spark that led him to quit his advertising job and become a full-time writer. Since then, he has specialized in nonfiction for young people.

Freedman has received many literary awards, the most prestigious being the Newbery Medal in 1988 for *Lincoln: A Photobiography.* It was the first time in 32 years that a nonfiction book had received this prize.

READ

Comprehension

Reread the text as needed to answer these questions.

1. At the beginning of the war, what was Lincoln's primary goal?

2. **(a)** What propelled Lincoln to draft the proclamation? **(b)** How did he time its release?

Research: Clarify Details Research at least one unfamiliar detail from the essay and explain how your research sheds light on the topic.

Summarize Write an objective summary of the text to confirm your comprehension. Do not include opinions and evaluations in your summary.

Language Study

Selection Vocabulary Define each boldface word, and then create a list of related word forms for each.

• He was afraid to **alienate** the large numbers of Northerners. . . .

• . . . free the slaves gradually and **compensate** their owners with money from the federal treasury.

• A month later . . . Union forces . . . suffered another **humiliating** defeat.

Literary Analysis

Reread the identified passage and answer the questions that follow.

> **Focus Passage** *(p. 870)*
> "Fellow citizens . . . every theatre of the war.

Key Ideas and Details

1. **(a) Interpret:** What did Lincoln mean by "In *giving* freedom to the *slave,* we *assure* freedom to the *free*"? **(b) Analyze:** What was one result of freeing the slaves?

Craft and Structure

2. **Draw Conclusions:** Why does the author include the quotation from Lincoln, rather than just paraphrasing its main ideas?

Integration of Knowledge and Ideas

3. **Synthesize:** Does the information in this text change your picture of Lincoln and his motives? Explain, **citing** details from the text in your response.

Word Choice and Tone

An author's **word choice** can help convey **tone**— the author's attitude toward his or her subject.

1. Freedman writes that Lincoln "hesitated" when deciding whether or not to proclaim the slaves emancipated. How would the author's tone have changed if Freedman had used the word *procrastinated* instead? Explain.

2. **Freedom Fighters:** The text describes enslaved blacks as "eager" to "fight for their own freedom." What attitude is revealed by Freedman's word choice?

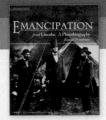

DISCUSS • RESEARCH • WRITE

From Text to Topic **Class Discussion**

Discuss this passage as a class. Take notes during the discussion.
Contribute ideas, supporting them with examples from the text.

> Besides, enslaved blacks were eager to throw off their shackles and
> fight for their own freedom. Thousands of slaves had already escaped
> from behind Southern lines. Thousands more were ready to enlist in
> the Union armies. "You need more men," Senator Charles Sumner
> told Lincoln, "not only at the North, but at the South, in the rear of
> the rebels. You need the slaves."

Research **Investigate the Topic**

The Abolitionists The famous abolitionist Frederick Douglass is
mentioned in this text. Many other abolitionists contributed to the
struggle against slavery. Among them were Harriet Tubman, Sojourner
Truth, John Brown, Dred Scott, and Tunis Campbell.

> ### Assignment
> Conduct research on an abolitionist of your choice. Consult a variety
> of print and online sources, making sure that each one is credible and
> accurate. Take clear notes and carefully identify your sources. Write a
> brief **biographical sketch** based on your findings.

Writing to Sources **Explanatory Text**

An opponent of slavery, Lincoln's secretary of state, William H.
Seward, doubted the power of the Emancipation Proclamation.
Speaking ironically, he said, "We show our sympathy with slavery by
emancipating slaves where we cannot reach them and holding them in
bondage where we can set them free."

> ### Assignment
> Write a brief **analysis** comparing Seward's view of the proclamation
> with Russell Freedman's view of it as a "historic decree."
> - Conduct research as needed to understand Seward's point.
> - In your essay, **develop** your analysis by explaining whether
>   Freedman and Seward disagree about the facts or whether they
>   interpret the same facts differently.

QUESTIONS FOR DISCUSSION

1. Even prior to the Emancipation Proclamation, blacks were ready to fight for the Union. What does this detail reveal about their situation?

2. In what way does Sumner's military strategy also serve to promote freedom?

PREPARATION FOR ESSAY

You may use the results of this research project to support your ideas in the essay you will write at the end of this section.

ACADEMIC VOCABULARY

Academic terms appear in blue on these pages. Use a dictionary to find their definitions. Then use the words as you speak and write about the text.

Common Core State Standards

RI.8.1, RI.8.2, RI.8.4, RI.8.9; W.8.2, W.8.7, W.8.8, W.8.9.b; SL.8.1; L.8.4, L.8.6
[For full standards wording, see the chart in the front of this book.]

Harriet Beecher Stowe[1]

Paul Laurence Dunbar

She told the story, and the whole world wept
    At wrongs and cruelties it had not known
    But for this fearless woman's voice alone.
    She spoke to the consciences that long had slept:
5 Her message, Freedom's clear reveille,[2] swept
    From heedless hovel[3] to **complacent** throne.
    Command and prophecy were in the tone
    And from its sheath the sword of justice leapt.
    Around two peoples swelled a fiery wave,
10   But both came forth **transfigured** from the flame.
Blest be the hand that dared be strong to save,
    And blest be she who in our weakness came—
    Prophet and priestess! At one stroke she gave
    A race to freedom and herself to fame.

complacent ▶
(kəm plā′ sənt) *adj.*
satisfied; self-satisfied,
or smug

transfigured ▶
(trans fig′ yərd) *adj.*
changed; transformed
in a glorious way

1. **Harriet Beecher Stowe** (1811–1896) author of *Uncle Tom's Cabin,*
   a classic antislavery novel.
2. **reveille** (rev′ ə lē) *n.* early morning bugle or drum signal to waken soldiers.
3. **heedless hovel** (hēd′ lis huv′ əl) small, miserable, poorly kept
   dwelling place.

ABOUT THE AUTHOR

Paul Laurence Dunbar (1872–1906)

Paul Laurence Dunbar was the son of former slaves. Encouraged by his
mother, he began writing poetry at an early age. Dunbar was inspired by
Harriet Beecher Stowe's novel *Uncle Tom's Cabin,* and in his own work he
honored people who fought for the rights of African Americans. Over the
course of his life, Dunbar published over ten volumes of poetry, four novels,
and four volumes of short stories.

READ • WRITE

Comprehension

Reread all or part of the text to help you answer the following questions.

1. What does the speaker admire about Harriet Beecher Stowe?

2. According to the speaker, what was the **result** of Stowe's message?

Language Study

Selection Vocabulary Define each boldface word from the poem, and use it in a sentence of your own.

1. From heedless hovel to **complacent** throne

2. But both came forth **transfigured** from the flame

Literary Analysis

Key Ideas and Details

1. Infer: In line 4 of the poem, what are the "consciences that long had slept"?

2. Interpret: What is the meaning of the following lines from the poem: "Around two peoples swelled a fiery wave, / But both came forth transfigured from the flame" (lines 9–10)?

Craft and Structure

3. Analyze: (a) How does the pattern of rhyme (*abba abba cdcdcd*) divide the poem into three sections and reinforce the ideas presented in each? **(b)** In what way does the final section of the poem differ from the first two sections?

Integration of Knowledge and Ideas

4. In what way is Harriet Beecher Stowe a fighter for freedom? Cite details from the poem in your **response**.

Writing to Sources **Informative Text**

Write an essay in which you explore Dunbar's use of imagery and figurative language in the poem. What **overall** effect does Dunbar's word choice create? To what extent does the poem succeed in celebrating Stowe's accomplishment? Be sure to cite details from the text to support the points you make.

Brown
vs.
Board of Education

Walter Dean Myers

There was a time when the meaning of freedom was easily understood. For an African crouched in the darkness of a tossing ship, wrists chained, men with guns standing on the decks above him, freedom was a physical thing, the ability to move away from his captors, to follow the dictates of his own heart, to listen to the voices within him that defined his values and showed him the truth of his own path. The plantation owners wanted to make the Africans feel helpless, inferior. They denied them images of themselves as Africans and told them that they were without beauty. They segregated them and told them they were without value.

Slowly, surely, the meaning of freedom changed to an elusive thing that even the strongest people could not hold in their hands. There were no chains on black wrists, but there were the shadows of chains, stretching for hundreds of years back through time, across black minds.

From the end of the Civil War in 1865 to the early 1950's, many public schools in both the North and South were segregated. Segregation was different in the different sections of the country. In the North most of the schools were segregated *de facto;*[1] that is, the law allowed blacks and whites to go to school together, but they did not actually always attend the same schools. Since a school is generally attended by children living in its neighborhood, wherever there were predominantly African-American neighborhoods there were, "in fact," segregated schools. In many parts of the country, however, and especially in the South, the segregation was *de jure,*[2] meaning that there were laws which forbade blacks to attend the same schools as whites.

◀ **predominantly**
(prē däm´ ə nənt lē)
adv. mainly

The states with segregated schools relied upon the ruling of the Supreme Court in the 1896 *Plessy vs. Ferguson* case for legal justification: Facilities that were "separate but equal" were legal.

In the early 1950's the National Association for the Advancement of Colored People (N.A.A.C.P.) sponsored five

---

1. *de facto* (dē fak´ tō) Latin for "existing in actual fact."
2. *de jure* (dē jo͝or´ ē) Latin for "by right or legal establishment."

▶ Linda Brown (center) is shown in her class at the Monroe School in Topeka, Kansas.

cases that eventually reached the Supreme Court. One of the cases involved the school board of Topeka, Kansas.

Thirteen families sued the Topeka school board, claiming that to segregate the children was harmful to the children and, therefore, a violation of the equal protection clause of the Fourteenth Amendment. The names on the Topeka case were listed in alphabetical order, with the father of seven-year-old Linda Brown listed first.

"I didn't understand why I couldn't go to school with my playmates. I lived in an integrated neighborhood and played with children of all nationalities, but when school started they went to a school only four blocks from my home and I was sent to school across town," she says.

For young Linda the case was one of convenience and of being made to feel different, but for African-American parents it had been a long, hard struggle to get a good education for their children. It was also a struggle waged by lawyers who had worked for years to overcome segregation. The head of the legal team who presented the school cases was Thurgood Marshall.

The city was Baltimore, Maryland, and the year was 1921. Thirteen-year-old Thurgood Marshall struggled to balance the packages he was carrying with one hand while he tried to get his bus fare out of his pocket with the other. It was almost Easter, and the part-time job he had would provide money for flowers for his mother. Suddenly he felt a violent tug at his right arm that spun him around, sending his packages sprawling over the floor of the bus.

"Don't you never push in front of no white lady again!" an angry voice spat in his ear.

Thurgood turned and threw a punch . . . . The man charged into Thurgood, throwing punches that mostly missed, and tried to wrestle the slim boy to the ground. A policeman broke up the fight, grabbing Thurgood with one huge black hand and pushing him against the side of the bus. Within minutes they were in the local courthouse.

Thurgood was not the first of his family to get into a good fight. His father's father had joined the Union Army during the Civil War, taking the names Thorough Good to add to the one name he had in bondage. His grandfather on his mother's side was a man brought from Africa and, according to Marshall's biography, "so ornery that his owner wouldn't sell him out of pity for the people who might buy him, but gave him his freedom instead and told him to clear out of the county."

Thurgood's frequent scrapes earned him a reputation as a young boy who couldn't be trusted to get along with white folks.

His father, Will Marshall, was a steward at the Gibson Island Yacht Club near Baltimore, and his mother, Norma, taught in a segregated school. The elder Marshall felt he could have done more with his life if his education had been better, but there had been few opportunities available for African Americans when he had been a young man. When it was time for the Marshall boys to go to college, he was more than willing to make the sacrifices necessary to send them.

Young people of color from all over the world came to the United States to study at Lincoln University, a predominantly black institution in southeastern Pennsylvania. Here Marshall majored in predentistry, which he found boring, and joined the Debating Club, which he found interesting. By the time he was graduated at the age of twenty-one, he had decided to give up dentistry for the law. Three years later he was graduated, first in his class, from Howard University Law School.

At Howard there was a law professor, Charles Hamilton Houston, who would affect the lives of many African-American lawyers and who would influence the legal aspects of the civil rights movement. Houston was a great teacher, one who demanded that his students be not just good lawyers but great lawyers. If they were going to help their people—and for Houston the only reason for African Americans to become lawyers was to do just that—they would have to have absolute understanding of the law, and be diligent[3] in the preparation of their cases. At the time, Houston was an attorney for the N.A.A.C.P. and fought against discrimination in housing and in jobs.

> Everyone involved understood the significance of the case: that it was much more than whether black children could go to school with white children.

After graduation, Thurgood Marshall began to do some work for the N.A.A.C.P., trying the difficult civil rights cases. He not only knew about the effects of discrimination by reading about it, he was still living it when he was graduated from law school in 1933. In 1936 Marshall began working full-time for the N.A.A.C.P., and in 1940 became its chief counsel.

It was Thurgood Marshall and a battery of N.A.A.C.P. attorneys who began to challenge segregation throughout the country. These men and women were warriors in the cause of freedom for African Americans, taking their battles into courtrooms across the country. They understood the process of American justice and the power of the Constitution.

In *Brown vs. Board of Education of Topeka,* Marshall argued that segregation was a violation of the Fourteenth Amendment—that even if the facilities and all other "tangibles" were equal, which was the heart of the case in *Plessy vs. Ferguson,* a violation still existed. There were intangible[4] factors, he argued, that made the education unequal.

---

3. **diligent** (dil´ ə jənt) *adj.* careful and thorough.
4. **intangible** (in tan´ jə bəl) *adj.* not able to be touched or grasped.

Everyone involved understood the significance of the case: that it was much more than whether black children could go to school with white children. If segregation in the schools was declared unconstitutional, then *all* segregation in public places could be declared unconstitutional.

Southerners who argued against ending school segregation were caught up, as then-Congressman Brooks Hays of Arkansas put it, in "a lifetime of adventures in that gap between law and custom." The law was one thing, but most Southern whites felt just as strongly about their customs as they did the law.

Dr. Kenneth B. Clark, an African-American psychologist, testified for the N.A.A.C.P. He presented clear evidence that the effect of segregation was harmful to African-American children. Describing studies conducted by black and white psychologists over a twenty-year period, he showed that black children felt inferior to white children. In a particularly dramatic study that he had supervised, four dolls, two white and two black, were presented to African-American children. From the responses of the children to the dolls, identical in every way except color, it was clear that the children were rejecting the black dolls. African-American children did not just feel separated from white children, they felt that the separation was based on their inferiority.

Dr. Clark understood fully the principles and ideas of those people who had held Africans in bondage and had tried to make slaves of captives. By isolating people of African descent, by barring them from certain actions or places, they could make them feel inferior. The social scientists who testified at *Brown vs. Board of Education* showed that children who felt inferior also performed poorly.

The Justice Department argued that racial segregation was objectionable to the Eisenhower Administration and hurt our relationships with other nations.

On May 17, 1954, after **deliberating** for nearly a year and a half, the Supreme Court made its ruling. The Court stated that it could not use the intentions of 1868, when the Fourteenth Amendment was passed, as a guide to its ruling, or even those

◀ **deliberating**
(di lib′ ər āt′ in) *v.*
considering carefully

of 1896, when the decision in *Plessy vs. Ferguson* was handed down. Chief Justice Earl Warren wrote:

> We must consider public education in the light of its full development and its present place in American life throughout the nation. We must look instead to the effect of segregation itself on public education.

The Court went on to say that "modern authority" supported the idea that segregation deprived African Americans of equal opportunity. "Modern authority" referred to Dr. Kenneth B. Clark and the weight of evidence that he and the other social scientists had presented.

The high court's decision in *Brown vs. Board of Education* signaled an important change in the struggle for civil rights. It signaled clearly that the legal prohibitions that **oppressed** African Americans would have to fall. Equally important was the idea that the nature of the fight for equality would change. Ibrahima, Cinqué, Nat Turner, and George Latimer

oppressed ▶
(ə prest´) *v.* kept down by unjust power

Thurgood Marshall (center right) is shown being sworn in as a Supreme Court justice. President Lyndon B. Johnson is just left of Marshall.

had struggled for freedom by fighting against their captors or fleeing from them. The 54th had fought for African freedom on the battlefields of the Civil War. Ida B. Wells had fought for equality with her pen. Lewis H. Latimer and Meta Vaux Warrick had tried to earn equality with their work. In *Brown vs. Board of Education* Thurgood Marshall, Kenneth B. Clark, and the lawyers and social scientists, both black and white, who helped them had won for African Americans a victory that would bring them closer to full equality than they had ever been in North America. There would still be legal battles to be won, but the major struggle would be in the hearts and minds of people and "in that gap between law and custom."

In 1967 Thurgood Marshall was appointed by President Lyndon B. Johnson as an associate justice of the U.S. Supreme Court. He retired in 1991.

"I didn't think of my father or the other parents as being heroic at the time," Linda Brown says. "I was only seven. But as I grew older and realized how far-reaching the case was and how it changed the complexion of the history of this country, I was just thrilled that my father and the others here in Topeka were involved."

ABOUT THE AUTHOR

Walter Dean Myers (b. 1937)

Walter Dean Myers was born in West Virginia and raised by foster parents who lived in Harlem, a section of New York City. He began learning to read at a young age. "The public library was my most treasured place," Myers recalls. "I couldn't believe my luck in discovering that what I enjoyed most, reading, was free." Many of his works are set in Harlem and depict the problems and joys of African American teens.

Myers has written more than eighty books for children and young adults. He has received many writing awards, including two Newbery Honors and five Coretta Scott King Awards. "I so love writing," he says. "It is not something that I am doing just for a living; this is something that I love to do."

READ

Comprehension

Reread the text as needed to answer the questions.

1. Why did the families sue the Topeka school board?

2. What was Dr. Kenneth B. Clark's testimony?

3. What was the U.S. Supreme Court's decision in *Brown vs. Board of Education*?

Research: Clarify Details Research an unfamiliar detail from the text. Explain how your findings shed light on an aspect of the essay.

Summarize Write an objective summary of the essay to confirm your comprehension.

Language Study

Selection Vocabulary Define each boldface word below. Then, find a synonym for each word.

1. . . . wherever there were **predominantly** African-American neighborhoods there were, "in fact," segregated schools.

2. On May 17, 1954, after **deliberating** for nearly a year and a half, the Supreme Court made its ruling.

3. . . . the legal prohibitions that **oppressed** African Americans would have to fall.

Literary Analysis

Reread the identified passage and answer the questions that follow.

> **Focus Passage** (pp. 877–78)
>
> From the end . . . she says.

Key Ideas and Details

1. **Compare and Contrast:** How did school segregation differ in the North and the South between 1865 and the early 1950s?

2. What justification for segregation did the Supreme Court give in 1896?

Craft and Structure

3. **Analyze:** Why do you think Myers includes Linda's own words in this passage?

Integration of Knowledge and Ideas

4. **Make a Judgment:** Think about what the text has **revealed**. Can freedom be fully won in court? Explain, citing the text.

Style

Style is the distinctive way an author uses language, created with **elements** such as word choice, imagery, and sentence structure.

1. Reread the first paragraph of the text. **(a)** Identify one striking image. **(b)** Find two instances in which Myers joins an idea with a related idea or restatement, using just a comma.

2. **(a)** Contrast Myers's style in the third paragraph with his style in the first, citing textual details. **(b)** Why has he changed his style? **(c)** Freedom Fighters: How does each style help you understand the struggle for freedom?

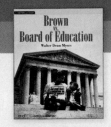

DISCUSS • RESEARCH • WRITE

From Text to Topic **Group Discussion**

Take notes as you discuss this passage with the class. Contribute your own ideas, and support them with examples from the text.

> There was a time when the meaning of freedom was easily understood. For an African crouched in the darkness of a tossing ship, wrists chained, men with guns standing on the decks above him, freedom was a physical thing. . . .
>
> Slowly, surely, the meaning of freedom changed to an elusive thing that even the strongest people could not hold in their hands. There were no chains on black wrists, but there were the shadows of chains. . . .

Research **Investigate the Topic**

Thurgood Marshall's Contributions to Civil Rights Thurgood Marshall had a long career as an **advocate** for civil rights for African Americans, women, children, prisoners, and the homeless.

Assignment

Conduct research to find out about a specific contribution to the Civil Rights Movement made by Thurgood Marshall. Consult a variety of print and online sources, verifying each one for credibility and accuracy. Take clear and detailed notes, and identify your sources. Share your findings in a **multimedia presentation** for the class.

Writing to Sources **Narrative**

Myers's essay opens with a description of Africans being transported by ship across the ocean, enduring extreme suffering. Other ethnic groups reached America in different ways, some driven by need.

Assignment

Write a **narrative** about someone coming to the United States to live, whether willingly or unwillingly. Follow these steps:

- Introduce your characters, setting, and the basic conflict.
- Create a series of events that tell a story with a strong ending.
- Use vivid descriptions of people and places.

QUESTIONS FOR DISCUSSION

1. What two aspects of freedom are explored in this passage?
2. Which type of freedom do you think is harder to attain? Explain.

PREPARATION FOR ESSAY

You may use the results of this research project to support your ideas in the essay at the end of this section.

ACADEMIC VOCABULARY

Academic terms appear in blue on these pages. Use a dictionary to find their definitions. Then, use the words as you speak and write about the text.

 Common Core State Standards

RI.8.1, RI.8.2, RI.8.4; W.8.3, W.8.7, W.8.8; SL.8.1; L.8.4, L.8.6
[For full standards wording, see the chart in the front of this book.]

On Woman's Right to Suffrage

SUSAN B. ANTHONY

1873—Friends and fellow citizens:

I stand before you to-night under indictment for the alleged crime[1] of having voted at the last presidential election, without having a lawful right to vote. It shall be my work this evening to prove to you that in thus voting, I not only committed no crime, but, instead, simply exercised my *citizen's rights*, guaranteed to me and all United States citizens by the National Constitution, beyond the power of any State to deny.

The preamble of the Federal Constitution says:

"We, the people of the United States, in order to form a more perfect union, establish justice, insure *domestic* tranquillity, provide for the common defense, promote the general welfare, and secure the blessings of liberty to ourselves and our posterity, do ordain and establish this Constitution for the United States of America."

It was we, the people; not we, the white male citizens; nor yet we, the male citizens; but we, the whole people, who formed the Union. And we formed it, not to give the blessings of liberty, but to secure them; not to the half of ourselves and the half of our posterity, but to the whole people—women as well as men. And it is a downright **mockery** to talk to women of their enjoyment of the blessings of liberty while they are denied the use of the only means of securing them provided by this democratic-republican government—the ballot.

mockery ▶
(mak´ ər ē) *n.* false, insulting action or statement

---

1. **indictment** (in dīt´ mənt) **for the alleged** (ə lejd´) **crime** in law, a written statement charging a person with supposedly committing a crime.

For any State to make sex a qualification that must ever result in the disfranchisement of one entire half of the people is to pass a bill of attainder, or an *ex post facto* law,[2] and is therefore a violation of the supreme law of the land. By it the blessings of liberty are for ever withheld from women and their female posterity. To them this government has no just powers **derived** from the consent of the governed. To them this government is not a democracy. It is not a republic. It is an odious aristocracy; a hateful oligarchy[3] of sex; the most hateful aristocracy ever established on the face of the globe; an oligarchy of wealth, where the rich govern the poor. An oligarchy of learning, where the educated govern the ignorant, or even an oligarchy of race, where the Saxon[4] rules the African, might be endured; but this oligarchy of sex, which makes father, brothers, husband, sons, the oligarchs over the mother and sisters, the wife and daughters of every household—which ordains all men sovereigns, all women subjects, carries dissension, discord and **rebellion** into every home of the nation.

Webster, Worcester and Bouvier all define a citizen to be a person in the United States, entitled to vote and hold office.

The only question left to be settled now is: Are women persons? And I hardly believe any of our opponents will have the hardihood to say they are not. Being persons, then, women are citizens; and no State has a right to make any law, or to enforce any old law, that shall abridge their privileges or immunities. Hence, every discrimination against women in the constitutions and laws of the several States is to-day null and void, precisely as in every one against negroes.

◀ **derived**
(di rīvd´) *v.* received or taken from a source

◀ **rebellion**
(ri bel´ yən) *n.* open resistance to authority

---

2. **bill of attainder . . . ex post facto law** two practices specifically outlawed by the U.S. Constitution. A bill of attainder declares someone guilty without a trial. An *ex post facto* law applies to acts committed before the law was passed.
3. **aristocracy** (ar´ i stä´ krə sē) . . . **oligarchy** (äl´ i gär´ kē) *Aristocracy* and *oligarchy* are terms for systems of government in which a small group of privileged people govern the rest.
4. **Saxon** (sak´ sən) used here as a term for white Europeans; Anthony is referring to a racist nineteenth-century belief, current even among some abolitionists, that whites were the natural rulers of African Americans.

ABOUT THE AUTHOR

Susan B. Anthony
(1820–1906)

Raised as a Quaker, Susan B. Anthony shared her parents' dislike of slavery and inequality. In fact, the family farm near Rochester, New York, often served as a meeting place for well-known abolitionists, including Frederick Douglass.

At an antislavery conference in 1851, Anthony met Elizabeth Cady Stanton, another activist. The two worked together for many years. After the Civil War, with slavery outlawed, they began to focus more on women's rights. In 1869, Anthony and Stanton founded the National Woman Suffrage Association. Anthony remained in the fight for the vote until she died in her eighties.

Close Reading Activities

READ

Comprehension

Reread the text as needed to answer the questions.

1. For what crime was Anthony indicted?

2. Why does Anthony insist her action was not a crime?

Language Study

Selection Vocabulary Create a word map or graphic that identifies at least one synonym and one antonym for each boldface word from the text. Then, use each boldface word in a sentence.

• And it is a downright **mockery**. . . .

Literary Analysis

Reread the identified passage. Then, respond to the questions that follow.

> **Focus Passage** (p. 887)
> Webster . . . against negroes.

Key Ideas and Details

1. (a) According to Anthony, how do the dictionaries of "Webster, Worcester and Bouvier" define *citizen*? **(b) Analyze:** How does she use this definition to support her position?

Persuasive Techniques

Persuasive techniques are methods used to encourage action or change in others. Reread the speech, and take notes on Anthony's persuasive techniques.

1. (a) Identify an example of repetition in Anthony's speech. **(b)** What point is she **emphasizing** through this repetition?

Research: Clarify Details Choose at least one unfamiliar detail from the speech and briefly research it to clarify meaning.

Summarize Write an objective summary of the text. Do not include your own opinions.

• . . . no just powers **derived** from the consent of the governed.

• . . . this oligarchy . . . carries dissension, discord and **rebellion** into every home of the nation.

2. What is Anthony's conclusion about laws that **discriminate** against women?

Craft and Structure

3. (a) How does Anthony organize the details in the final paragraph of the speech? **(b) Evaluate:** Does this structure help to effectively conclude her argument? Explain.

Integration of Knowledge and Ideas

4. Why does Anthony refer to "negroes" at the end of the passage? What comparison is she making?

2. Freedom Fighters: (a) List two sources Anthony quotes in her speech. **(b)** How does citing these sources lend credibility to her argument for the freedom to vote?

DISCUSS • RESEARCH • WRITE

From Text to Topic **Panel Discussion**

Conduct a panel discussion about the following passage. Take notes during the discussion. Contribute your own ideas, and support them with examples from the text. Evaluate the contributions of others, and encourage classmates to provide more support when needed.

> It was we, the people; not we, the white male citizens; nor yet we, the male citizens; but we, the whole people, who formed the Union. And we formed it, not to give the blessings of liberty, but to secure them; not to the half of ourselves and the half of our posterity, but to the whole people—women as well as men.

Research **Investigate the Topic**

The Women's Movement Susan B. Anthony was an early pioneer in the fight for women's equality in the United States.

Assignment

Conduct research to find out more about the movement for women's suffrage and arguments made against it. Consult online and print sources, including primary sources such as newspaper stories, diaries, journals, and letters. Take notes and carefully identify your sources. Share your findings in an **informal speech** for the class.

Writing to Sources **Argument**

"On Woman's Right to Suffrage" argues for women's right to vote, but it took almost fifty years after Anthony made this speech for that right to be **granted**.

Assignment

Write an **argument** in which you evaluate Anthony's persuasive techniques in the speech. Is her speech effective? Follow these steps:

- Open with a claim indicating whether Anthony's speech is effective.
- Support your claim with relevant details from the text, including references to Anthony's techniques and the evidence she cites.
- Use transitional words and phrases to join your ideas smoothly.
- Provide a conclusion in which you sum up your argument.

QUESTIONS FOR DISCUSSION

1. According to Anthony, who formed the Union, and why did they form it?

2. Identify three contrasts Anthony makes. What point is she making with each?

3. In what way is Anthony a freedom fighter?

PREPARATION FOR ESSAY

You may use the results of this research project to support your ideas in the essay you will write at the end of this section.

ACADEMIC VOCABULARY

Academic terms appear in blue on these pages. Use a dictionary to find their definitions. Then, use the words as you speak and write about the text.

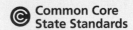 **Common Core State Standards**

RI.8.1, RI.8.2, RI.8.3, RI.8.4, RI.8.5, RI.8.6; W.8.1, W.8.1.a, W.8.1.b, W.8.1.c, W.8.1.e, W.8.7; SL.8.1
[For full standards wording, see the chart in the front of this book.]

from

Address to the Commonwealth Club of San Francisco

Cesar Chavez

November 9, 1984

. . . Today, thousands of farm workers live under savage conditions—beneath trees and amid garbage . . . near tomato fields in San Diego County—tomato fields which use the most modern farm technology.

Vicious rats gnaw on them as they sleep. They walk miles to buy food at inflated prices and they carry in water from irrigation pumps.

Child labor is still common in many farm areas.

As much as 30 percent of Northern California's garlic harvesters are under-aged children. Kids as young as six years old have voted in state-conducted union elections since they qualified as workers.

Some 800,000 under-aged children work with their families harvesting crops across America.

Babies born to migrant workers[1] suffer 25 percent higher infant mortality[2] than the rest of the population.

---

1. **migrant** (mī´ grənt) **workers** farm laborers who move from place to place to harvest seasonal crops.
2. **infant mortality** proportion of children who die before reaching adulthood.

Malnutrition among migrant worker children is 10 times higher than the national rate.

Farm workers' average life expectancy[3] is still 49 years—compared to 73 years for the average American.

All my life, I have been driven by one dream, one goal, one vision: To overthrow a farm labor system in this nation which treats farm workers as if they were not important human beings.

Farm workers are not agricultural **implements**—they are not beasts of burden to be used and discarded.

That dream was born in my youth. It was nurtured in my early days of organizing. It has flourished. It has been attacked.

I'm not very different from anyone else who has ever tried to accomplish something with his life. My motivation comes from my personal life—from watching what my mother and father went through when I was growing up—from what we experienced as migrant farm workers in California.

That dream, that vision grew from my own experience with racism—with hope—with the desire to be treated fairly and to see my people treated as human beings and not as chattel.[4]

It grew from anger and rage—emotions I felt 40 years ago when people of my color were denied the right to see a movie or eat at a restaurant in many parts of California.

It grew from the frustration and humiliation I felt as a boy who couldn't understand how the growers could abuse and **exploit** farm workers when there were so many of us and so few of them.

Later, in the '50s, I experienced a different kind of exploitation. In San Jose, in Los Angeles and in other urban communities, we, the Mexican American people, were dominated by a majority that was Anglo.[5]

I began to realize what other minority people had discovered: That the only answer—the only hope was in organizing.

More of us had to become citizens. We had to register to vote. And people like me had to develop the skills it would take to organize, to educate, to help empower the Chicano[6] people.

◄ **implements**
(im′ plə mənts) *n.* devices used or needed in a given activity; tools; instruments

◄ **exploit**
(ek sploit′) *v.* take advantage of; make profit from the labor of (a person) without giving a just compensation

---

3. **life expectancy** (ek spek′ tən sē) number of years for which a person in a given group will typically live.
4. **chattel** (chat′ 'l) in law, a movable item of personal property; also, a slave.
5. **Anglo** (aŋ′ glō) term for a white person who is of non-Latino descent.
6. **Chicano** (chi kä′ nō) term for a citizen of, or a person living in, the United States who is of Mexican descent. The term entered widespread use during the Chicano Civil Rights Movement of the 1960s and 1970s.

I spent many years—before we founded the union—learning how to work with people.

We experienced some successes in voter registration in politics in battling racial discrimination—successes in an era when Black Americans were just beginning to assert their civil rights and when political awareness among Hispanics was almost non-existent.

But deep in my heart, I knew I could never be happy unless I tried organizing the farm workers. I didn't know if I would succeed. But I had to try.

All Hispanics—urban and rural, young and old—are connected to the farm workers' experience. We had all lived through the fields or our parents had. We shared that common humiliation.

How could we progress as a people, even if we lived in the cities, while the farm workers—men and women of our color—were condemned to a life without pride?

How could we progress as a people while the farm workers—who symbolized our history in this land—were denied self-respect?

How could our people believe that their children could become lawyers and doctors and judges and businesspeople while this shame, this injustice was permitted to continue?

Those who attack our union often say, "It's not really a union. It's something else—a social movement. A civil rights movement. It's something dangerous."

They're half right.

The United Farm Workers[7] is first and foremost a union. A union like any other. A union that either produces for its members on the bread and butter issues or doesn't survive.

But the UFW has always been something more than a union. Although it's never been dangerous if you believe in the Bill of Rights.

The UFW was the beginning! We attacked that historical source of shame and infamy that our people in this country lived with.

We attacked that injustice not by complaining; not by seeking hand-outs; not by becoming soldiers in the War on Poverty.

We organized!

Farm workers acknowledged we had allowed ourselves to become victims in a democratic society—a society where

infamy ▶
(in´ fə mē) *n.* very bad reputation; disgrace; dishonor

---

7. **United Farm Workers** a labor union, or association of workers to protect and benefit its members, made up of American farm workers and founded in part by Cesar Chavez.

majority rule and collective bargaining[8] are supposed to be more than academic theories or political rhetoric.

And by addressing this historical problem, we created confidence in an entire people's ability to create the future.

The UFW's survival—its existence—were not in doubt in my mind when the time began to come—after the union became visible—when Chicanos started entering college in greater numbers—when Hispanics began running for public office in greater numbers—when our people started asserting their rights on a broad range of issues and in many communities across the country.

The union's survival—its very existence—sent out a signal to all Hispanics that we were fighting for our dignity.

That we were challenging and overcoming injustice.

That we were empowering the least educated among us; the poorest among us.

The message was clear: If it could happen in the fields, it could happen anywhere—in the cities, in the courts, in the city councils, in the state legislatures.

I didn't really appreciate it at the time, but the coming of our union signaled the start of great changes among Hispanics that are only now beginning to be seen. . . .

---

8. **collective bargaining** negotiation between workers, acting as a group, and their employers for reaching an agreement on wages, hours, working conditions, and so on.

ABOUT THE AUTHOR

Cesar Chavez (1927–1993)

Cesar Chavez was born on a small family-owned farm in Arizona. The family lost the farm during the Depression, and by age ten Chavez, along with the rest of his family, was working on other people's farms throughout the Southwest. He left school early to earn money for his family and did not attend high school.

While still a teenager, Chavez joined the U.S. Navy and served for two years. He got married in 1948 and settled in California. In 1952, he met an organizer of a barrio-based self-help group. Soon he was a full-time organizer for this group, coordinating voter registration drives and combating discrimination against Chicanos. In 1962, when he could not convince the group to organize the farm workers, he quit and founded the National Farm Workers Association (NFWA) on his own. The NFWA joined with another union to strike against California grape growers in 1965. This merger became the United Farm Workers (UFW).

Chavez spent the rest of his life using nonviolent methods such as marches, boycotts, and even hunger strikes to draw attention to the plight of farm workers.

READ

Comprehension

Reread all or part of the text to help you answer the following questions.

1. According to the text, under what conditions do farm workers live and work?

2. What is Chavez's life goal?

3. What effect does he believe the movement had on his people?

Research: Clarify Details Choose one unfamiliar detail in the speech and conduct research on it. Then, explain how your research clarifies the text.

Summarize Write an objective summary of the speech that is free from opinion.

Language Study

Selection Vocabulary Define each boldface word from the speech and use it in a sentence of your own.

1. Farm workers are not agricultural **implements**. . . .

2. . . . a boy who couldn't understand how the growers could abuse and **exploit** farm workers . . .

3. We attacked that historical source of shame and **infamy**. . . .

Literary Analysis

Reread the identified passage. Then, respond to the questions that follow.

> **Focus Passage** *(p. 891)*
> That dream . . . hope was in organizing.

Key Ideas and Details

1. **Analyze Cause and Effect:** What does Chavez say led him to his life's dream?

2. **Interpret:** What does Chavez mean when he says, "the only hope was in organizing"?

Craft and Structure

3. **Analyze:** The transcript of this speech employs many dashes. **(a)** What do the dashes indicate? **(b)** What effects do the dashes help create?

Integration of Knowledge and Ideas

4. **Synthesize:** In what way is Chavez fighting for freedom? How does Chavez's fight echo the efforts of other freedom fighters?

Claims and Evidence

A valid **claim**, or statement to be proved, must be supported by **evidence**, such as examples, statistics, and **expert** testimony. Reread the speech, and take notes on ways the author supports his claims.

1. **(a)** What basic claim does Chavez make in the beginning of the speech?

(b) What types of evidence support that claim?

2. **Freedom Fighters: (a)** According to Chavez, in what way does the UFW **promote** civil rights? **(b)** What evidence does he give to support this claim?

DISCUSS • RESEARCH • WRITE

From Text to Topic **Partner Discussion**

Take notes as you discuss this passage with a partner. Contribute your own ideas, and support them with examples from the text.

> We attacked that injustice not by complaining; not by seeking hand-outs; not by becoming soldiers in the War on Poverty.
>
> We organized!
>
> Farm workers acknowledged we had allowed ourselves to become victims in a democratic society—a society where majority rule and collective bargaining are supposed to be more than academic theories or political rhetoric.
>
> And by addressing this historical problem, we created confidence in an entire people's ability to create the future.

Research **Investigate the Topic**

The Grape Boycott Beginning in September 1965, Chavez led a boycott against grape growers in California.

Assignment

Conduct research to **investigate** Chavez's campaign for fair treatment of grape workers. Consult online and print sources, including newspaper accounts and interviews if possible. Take clear notes and carefully identify your sources so you can easily access the information later. Record your findings in an **annotated timeline**.

Writing to Sources **Poem**

Cesar Chavez's speech provides insights into the horrific conditions farms workers endured.

Assignment

Write a poem about the farm workers' struggle. Follow these steps:

- Study the speech, and take note of especially vivid descriptions.
- Decide on a poetic form, such as lyric or narrative.
- As you craft your poem, choose words and phrases that bring to life an aspect of the farm workers' lives.
- Consider using rhythm and rhyme to enhance your poem.

QUESTIONS FOR DISCUSSION

1. What strategy did the farm workers put into place to combat injustice?

2. Do you agree that the workers had allowed themselves "to become victims"?

3. How did Chavez's movement help "an entire [people]" win freedom?

PREPARATION FOR ESSAY

You may use the results of this research project to support your ideas in the essay you will write at the end of this section.

ACADEMIC VOCABULARY

Academic terms appear in blue on these pages. Use a dictionary to find their definitions. Then, use the words as you speak and write about the text.

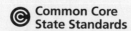

Common Core State Standards

RI.8.1, RI.8.2, RI.8.4; W.8.7, W.8.8; SL.8.1; L.8.6
[For full standards wording, see the chart in the front of this book.]

Nonviolence Tree

Cesar Chavez (1927–1993)
Beginning in 1962, Cesar Chavez leads workers in California, organizing strikes and boycotts to win better wages and living conditions for Mexican Americans and others. In 1968, Chavez fasts for twenty-five days to persuade his followers to keep to the principles of nonviolence. Chavez is a reader of Gandhi.

Martin Luther King, Jr. (1929–1968)
In 1955, Martin Luther King, Jr., leads a bus boycott protesting laws segregating African Americans from whites. His success propels him to the forefront of the Civil Rights Movement. Jailed repeatedly for his beliefs, he helps secure greater rights for African Americans before he is cut down by an assassin. King is a reader of Thoreau and Gandhi.

Chavez's Words *"I am convinced that the truest act of courage, the strongest act of manliness, is to sacrifice ourselves for others in a totally nonviolent struggle for justice. To be a man is to suffer for others."*

King's Words *"[T]he method of nonviolent resistance is the most potent weapon available to oppressed people in their struggle for justice and human dignity."*

Mohandas K. Gandhi (1869–1948)
In 1930, Mohandas K. Gandhi leads the twenty-four-day Salt March to the sea to protest British rule in India. Through peaceful demonstrations, Gandhi helps India become a democracy in 1947. Gandhi is a reader of Thoreau.

Henry David Thoreau (1817–1862)
In 1846, Henry David Thoreau is placed in jail in Concord, Massachusetts, for refusing to pay taxes—his protest against slavery and the war with Mexico. In 1849, Thoreau publishes the essay "On the Duty of Civil Disobedience," declaring that citizens must follow their own conscience.

Gandhi's Words *". . . I discovered, in the earliest stages, that pursuit of Truth did not admit of violence being inflicted on one's opponent, but that he must be weaned from error by patience and sympathy."*

Thoreau's Words *"I cannot for an instant recognize that political organization as my government which is the slave's government also."*

Concepts of Nonviolent Action
Nonviolent action is the pursuit of political change through peaceful means, such as boycotts and protests, meant to resist unjust laws or situations. Often, nonviolent action involves a personal sacrifice that demonstrates a truth or provides an example or a lesson to others.

READ • DISCUSS • RESEARCH

Critical Analysis

Key Ideas and Details

1. (a) What information does this graphic present? **(b)** What is the purpose of the graphic?

Craft and Structure

2. (a) Interpret: Why are the branches arranged as they are, with Thoreau near the roots and Chavez in the upper branches?
(b) Evaluate: What are the advantages and disadvantages of presenting this type of information in a graphic form?

3. (a) Deduce: Why are King and Chavez at roughly the same location on the tree? **(b) Apply:** Based on what you know about the Civil Rights Movement, identify additional individuals or groups that might be included in the branches of this tree.

Integration of Knowledge and Ideas

4. Draw Conclusions: What relationships between power and nonviolence does the text suggest?

From Text to Topic **Class Discussion**

Discuss the graphic and its message with classmates. Use the following discussion questions to focus your conversation.

1. What cause or form of injustice did each leader on the graphic tackle?

2. What do these causes of injustice have in common?

3. What insights into the history of fighting for freedom does the image of the tree help **convey**?

Research **Investigate the Topic**

Henry David Thoreau was a fascinating figure who put forth the idea of **civil** disobedience. Perform research to learn more about Thoreau and his philosophies. Be sure to consult a variety of **valid** sources, both print and digital. Take careful notes as you work. Share your findings and conclusions in a brief **biographical sketch**.

ACADEMIC VOCABULARY

Academic terms appear in blue on these pages. Use a dictionary to find their definitions. Then, use the words as you speak and write about the text.

Common Core State Standards

RI.8.7; W.8.2; SL.8.1, SL.8.2
[For full standards wording, see the chart in the front of this book.]

Speaking and Listening **Group Discussion**

Freedom Fighters and Heroes The texts in this section vary in genre, style, and perspective. However, all of them focus on the common ideal of equality and brotherhood, the different forms of the problems faced in achieving this ideal, and the means by which the dream is translated into reality. The subject of freedom fighters and the heroes who are involved in the struggle is fundamentally related to the Big Question addressed in this unit: **Are yesterday's heroes important today?**

Assignment

Conduct discussions. With a small group of classmates, conduct a discussion about freedom fighters and heroes. Refer to the texts in this section, other texts you have read, and your personal experience and knowledge to support your ideas. Begin your discussion by addressing the following questions:

- What are the obstacles to achieving equality and brotherhood?
- How can these obstacles be overcome?
- What qualities must a person have to fight for freedom?
- Why might society as a whole benefit when the rights of oppressed groups are acknowledged?
- Can the heroes of the past teach us anything about achieving these goals?

Summarize and present your ideas. After you have fully explored the topic, summarize your discussion and present your findings to the class as a whole.

▲ Refer to the selections you read in Part 3 as you complete the activities on this assessment.

Criteria for Success

✓ **Organizes the group effectively**
  Appoint a group leader and a timekeeper. The group leader should present the discussion questions. The timekeeper should make sure the discussion takes no longer than 20 minutes.

✓ **Maintains focus of discussion**
  As a group, stay on topic and avoid straying into other subject areas.

✓ **Involves all participants equally and fully**
  No one person should monopolize the conversation. Rather, everyone should take turns speaking and contributing ideas.

✓ **Follows the rules for collegial discussion**
  As each group member speaks, others should listen carefully. Build on one another's ideas and support viewpoints and opinions with sound reasoning and evidence. Express disagreement respectfully.

USE NEW VOCABULARY

As you speak and share ideas, work to use the vocabulary words you have learned in this unit. The more you use new words, the more you will "own" them.

Writing **Narrative**

Freedom Fighters and Heroes Heroes are necessary in any great struggle that involves danger and high stakes. Some heroes become famous, while others remain unknown. All of us are familiar with heroes, either by hearing about them, observing them, interacting with them, or being one of them ourselves.

Common Core State Standards

W.8.3.a–e; SL.8.1.a–d
[For full standards wording, see the chart in the front of this book.]

> ## Assignment
>
> Write an **autobiographical narrative,** or true story about your own life, in which you discuss your awareness of, experience with, or observation of a heroic freedom fighter. Remember that an effective autobiographical narrative relates a series of events that have significance in the life and personal development of the writer.

Criteria for Success

Purpose/Focus
✓ **Connects specific incidents with larger ideas**
   Make meaningful connections between your experiences and the ideas of heroism and freedom in the texts you have read in this section.

✓ **Clearly conveys the significance of the story**
   Provide a conclusion in which you reflect on your experiences.

Organization
✓ **Sequences events logically**
   Structure your narrative so that individual events build on one another to create a coherent whole. Use transitions to keep the order of events clear.

Development of Ideas/Elaboration
✓ **Supports insights**
   Include both personal examples and details from the texts you have read and the research you have conducted in this section.

✓ **Uses narrative techniques effectively**
   • Consider using dialogue to help develop characters and move the action along.
   • Use pacing, timing your revelation of key details to create a satisfactory resolution or to create effects such as suspense and humor.

Language
✓ **Uses description effectively**
   Use descriptive details to paint word pictures that help readers see settings and characters.

Conventions
✓ **Does not have errors**
   Check your narrative to eliminate errors in grammar, spelling, and punctuation.

WRITE TO EXPLORE

Writing is a way to clarify what you feel and think. Be open to new ideas as you work. Doing so will help ensure that you fully explore the significance of the experiences you narrate.

Writing to Sources **Argument**

Freedom Fighters and Heroes The readings in this section present a range of ideas about freedom fighters and heroes. They raise questions, such as the following, about the meaning of, and the path to, freedom:

- Does it always take a hero to achieve freedom? Why?
- Is freedom from chains enough? Are other types of freedom also essential?
- Does the search for freedom ever end, or are there always new demands?
- What are the different ways to win freedom? Can freedom ever truly be won through force? Through law? Why?
- How can people who are kept powerless find the power to win freedom?
- Do the rest of us benefit when an oppressed group gains freedom? How?

Jot notes as you reflect on these questions. Then, complete this assignment.

Assignment
Argument Write an essay in which you state and defend a claim about what freedom means, whether it can be achieved, and what people must do to achieve it. Clearly present your ideas, and develop and support them with examples and details from the texts.

Prewriting and Planning

Choose texts. Review the texts in this section. Select at least two that will provide strong material to support your argument.

Gather details and craft a working thesis, or claim. Use a chart like the one shown below to develop your claim.

Prepare to answer counterclaims. For each point you plan to make to support your claim, note a possible objection, or counterclaim, to it. Plan to include the strongest of these counterclaims in your essay. Give arguments, supported by evidence, to refute these counterclaims.

Focus Question: How important is it to achieve the ideal of equality?

Text	Passage	Notes
"The American Dream"	[America] is a dream of a land where men of all races . . . can live together as brothers.	The ideal of equality is the principle on which this country was founded.
"Emancipation"	In *giving* freedom to the *slave,* we *assure* freedom to the *free.* . . .	Lincoln acknowledges that emancipation benefits all.
Example Claim: The benefits of equality affect society as a whole.	

INCORPORATE RESEARCH

As you plan your argument, refer to the notes you took as you researched the topic of freedom fighters. Use what you have learned as you develop your argument.

Drafting

Structure your ideas and evidence. Create an informal outline or list of ideas you want to present. Decide where you will include evidence and which evidence you will use to support each point.

Address counterclaims. Strong argumentation takes differing ideas into account and addresses them directly. As you order your ideas, build in sections in which you explain opposing opinions or differing interpretations. Then, write a reasoned, well-supported response to those counterclaims.

Frame and connect ideas. Write an introduction that will grab the reader's attention. Consider beginning with a compelling quotation or a detail. Then, write a strong conclusion that ends your essay with a clear re-statement of your main points. Use words, phrases, and clauses to create cohesion and clarify the relationships among claims, counterclaims, reasons, and evidence.

Revising and Editing

Review content. Make sure that your claim is clearly stated and that you have supported it with convincing evidence from the texts. Underline main ideas in your paper and confirm that each one is supported. Add more proof as needed.

Review style. Check to be sure that you have found the clearest, simplest way to communicate your ideas. Adjust word choice, as necessary, to maintain a formal style.

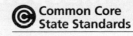

Common Core State Standards

W.8.1.a–e,
W.8.4, W.8.9
[For full standards wording, see the chart in the front of this book.]

CITE RESEARCH SOURCES

Be sure to cite your sources correctly as you finalize your argument. (See the Conducting Research workshop in the front of this book.)

Self-Evaluation Rubric

Use the following criteria to evaluate the effectiveness of your essay.

Criteria	Rating Scale
Purpose/Focus Introduces a precise claim and distinguishes the claim from alternate or opposing claims; provides a concluding section that follows from and supports the argument presented	*not very* .... *very* 1 2 3 4
Organization Organizes the reasons and evidence logically; uses words, phrases, and clauses to create cohesion and clarify the relationships among claims, counterclaims, reasons, and evidence	1 2 3 4
Development of Ideas/Elaboration Supports the claim with logical reasoning and relevant evidence, using accurate, credible sources and demonstrating an understanding of the topic or text	1 2 3 4
Language Establishes and maintains a formal style	1 2 3 4
Conventions Correctly follows conventions of spelling, punctuation, and grammar	1 2 3 4

Titles for Extended Reading

In this unit, you have read a variety of literary works that originated in the oral tradition. Continue to read on your own. Select works that you enjoy, but challenge yourself to explore new writers and works of increasing depth and complexity. The titles suggested below will help you get started.

INFORMATIONAL TEXT

John F. Kennedy
by Howard S. Kaplan

Read about our thirty-fifth president, John F. Kennedy, in this **biography.** Kennedy was an inspirational leader whose promising term in office was cut short by his shocking assassination.

Freedom Walkers
by Russell Freedman
Holiday House, 2006   **EXEMPLAR TEXT ©**

This **historical account** tells the story of the Montgomery Bus Boycott, which gave rise to the U.S. Civil Rights movement. Learn about Rosa Parks, as well as others who fought for justice and equality.

Travels with Charley: In Search of America
by John Steinbeck   **EXEMPLAR TEXT ©**

In this **nonfiction book,** writer John Steinbeck chronicles his journey around the United States with his poodle Charley. This book offers readers a look at 1960s America from the perspective of a curious and perceptive writer.

The Words We Live By: Your Annotated Guide to the Constitution
by Linda R. Monk   **EXEMPLAR TEXT ©**

This **nonfiction book** explains the history and meaning of the U.S. Constitution and its amendments in approachable language, providing a balanced perspective on current constitutional controversies.

LITERATURE

The Adventures of Tom Sawyer
by Mark Twain   **EXEMPLAR TEXT ©**

Read about the escapades of mischievous Tom Sawyer and his best friend, Huck Finn, in this classic nineteenth-century American **novel.**

The American Songbag
Edited by Carl Sandburg
Mariner Books, 1990

Carl Sandburg is best known as a poet, but he was also a collector of American **folk music.** This book includes 290 songs and their lyrics that give voice to many uniquely American experiences.

Cut From the Same Cloth: American Women of Myth, Legend, and Tall Tale
by Robert San Souci

San Souci explores larger-than-life adventures in these often humorous **folk tales** featuring clever, brave, and strong women.

ONLINE TEXT SET

POEM
Ellis Island Joseph Bruchac

LETTER
from **Steinbeck: A Life in Letters**
John Steinbeck

SHORT STORY
Up the Slide Jack London

Preparing to Read Complex Texts

Attentive Reading As you read on your own, ask yourself questions about the text. The questions shown below and others that you ask as you read will help you understand and enjoy literature even more.

When reading texts from the oral tradition, ask yourself…

Comprehension: **Key Ideas and Details**

- From what culture does this text come? What do I know about that culture?
- What type of text am I reading? For example, is it a myth, tall tale, or legend? What characters and events do I expect to find?
- Does the text include the elements I expected? If not, how does it differ from what I expected?
- What elements of the culture do I see in the text? For example, do I notice beliefs or foods that have meaning for the culture?
- Does the text teach a lesson or a moral? If so, is this a valuable lesson? Why or why not?

Text Analysis: **Craft and Structure**

- Who is retelling or presenting this text? Do I think the author has changed the text from the original? If so, how?
- Does the text include characters and tell a story? If so, are the characters and plot interesting?
- What do I notice about the language used in the text? Which aspects seem similar to or different from the language used in modern texts?
- Does the text include symbols? If so, do they have a special meaning in the original culture of the text?

Connections: **Integration of Knowledge and Ideas**

- What does this text teach me about the culture from which it comes?
- What, if anything, does this text teach me about people in general?
- Does this text seem like others I have read or heard? Why or why not?
- Do I know of modern versions of this text? Are they similar to or different from the original?
- If I were researching this culture for a report, would I include passages from this text? If so, what would those passages show?
- Do I enjoy reading this text and others like it? Why or why not?

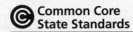

Common Core State Standards

Reading Literature/ Informational Text
10. By the end of the year, read and comprehend literature, including stories, dramas, and poems, and literary nonfiction at the high end of the grades 6–8 text complexity band independently and proficiently.

Resources

Literary Terms

ALLITERATION *Alliteration* is the repetition of initial consonant sounds. Writers use alliteration to draw attention to certain words or ideas, to imitate sounds, and to create musical effects.

ALLUSION An *allusion* is a reference to a well-known person, event, place, literary work, or work of art. Allusions connect literary works to a larger cultural heritage. They allow the writer to express complex ideas without spelling them out. Understanding what a literary work is saying often depends on recognizing its allusions and the meanings they suggest.

ANALOGY An *analogy* makes a comparison between two or more things that are similar in some ways but otherwise unalike.

ANECDOTE An *anecdote* is a brief story about an interesting, amusing, or strange event. Writers tell anecdotes to entertain or to make a point.

ANTAGONIST An *antagonist* is a character or a force in conflict with a main character, or protagonist.

See *Conflict* and *Protagonist.*

ARGUMENT See *Persuasion.*

ATMOSPHERE *Atmosphere,* or *mood,* is the feeling created in the reader by a literary work or passage.

AUTHOR'S INFLUENCES An *author's influences* include his or her heritage, culture, and personal beliefs.

AUTHOR'S STYLE *Style* is an author's typical way of writing. Many factors determine a writer's style, including diction; tone; use of characteristic elements such as figurative language, dialect, rhyme, meter, or rhythmic devices; typical grammatical structures and patterns, typical sentence length, and typical methods of organization. Style comprises every feature of a writer's use of language.

AUTOBIOGRAPHY An *autobiography* is the story of the writer's own life, told by the writer. Autobiographical writing may tell about the person's whole life or only a part of it.

Because autobiographies are about real people and events, they are a form of nonfiction. Most autobiographies are written in the first person.

See *Biography, Nonfiction,* and *Point of View.*

BIOGRAPHY A *biography* is a form of nonfiction in which a writer tells the life story of another person. Most biographies are written about famous or admirable people. Although biographies are nonfiction, the most effective ones share the qualities of good narrative writing.

See *Autobiography* and *Nonfiction.*

CHARACTER A *character* is a person or an animal that takes part in the action of a literary work. The main, or *major,* character is the most important character in a story, poem, or play. A *minor* character is one who takes part in the action but is not the focus of attention.

Characters are sometimes classified as flat or round. A *flat character* is one sided and often stereotypical. A *round character,* on the other hand, is fully developed and exhibits many traits—often both faults and virtues. Characters can also be classified as dynamic or static. A *dynamic character* is one who changes or grows during the course of the work. A *static character* is one who does not change.

See *Characterization, Hero/Heroine,* and *Motive.*

CHARACTERIZATION *Characterization* is the act of creating and developing a character. Authors use two major methods of characterization—*direct* and *indirect.* When using *direct* characterization, a writer states the *character's traits,* or characteristics.

When describing a character *indirectly,* a writer depends on the reader to draw conclusions about the character's traits. Sometimes the writer tells what other participants in the story say and think about the character.

See *Character* and *Motive.*

CHARACTER TRAITS *Character traits* are the qualities, attitudes, and values that a character has or displays—such as dependability, intelligence, selfishness, or stubbornness.

CLIMAX The *climax,* also called the turning point, is the high point in the action of the plot. It is the moment of greatest tension, when the outcome of the plot hangs in the balance.

See *Plot.*

COMEDY A *comedy* is a literary work, especially a play, that is light, often humorous or satirical, and ends happily. Comedies frequently depict ordinary characters faced with temporary difficulties and conflicts. Types of comedy include *romantic comedy,* which involves problems between lovers, and the *comedy of manners,* which satirically challenges social customs of a society.

CONCRETE POEM A *concrete poem* is one with a shape that suggests its subject. The poet arranges the letters, punctuation, and lines to create an image, or picture, on the page.

CONFLICT A *conflict* is a struggle between opposing forces. Conflict is one of the most important elements of stories, novels, and plays because it causes the action. There are two kinds of conflict: external and internal. An *external conflict* is one in which a character struggles against some outside force, such as another person. Another kind of external conflict may occur between a character and some force in nature.

An *internal conflict* takes place within the mind of a character. The character struggles to make a decision, take an action, or overcome a feeling.

See *Plot.*

CONNOTATIONS The *connotation* of a word is the set of ideas associated with it in addition to its explicit meaning. The connotation of a word can be personal, based on individual experiences. More often, cultural connotations—those recognizable by most people in a group—determine a writer's word choices.

See also *Denotation.*

DENOTATION The *denotation* of a word is its dictionary meaning, independent of other associations that the word may have. The denotation of the word *lake,* for example, is "an inland body of water." "Vacation spot" and "place where the fishing is good" are connotations of the word *lake.*

See also *Connotation.*

DESCRIPTION A *description* is a portrait, in words, of a person, place, or object. Descriptive writing uses images that appeal to the five senses—sight, hearing, touch, taste, and smell.

See *Images.*

DEVELOPMENT See *Plot.*

DIALECT *Dialect* is the form of a language spoken by people in a particular region or group. Dialects differ in pronunciation, grammar, and word choice. The English language is divided into many dialects. British English differs from American English.

DIALOGUE A *dialogue* is a conversation between characters. In poems, novels, and short stories, dialogue is usually set off by quotation marks to indicate a speaker's exact words.

In a play, dialogue follows the names of the characters, and no quotation marks are used.

DICTION *Diction* is a writer's or speaker's word choice. Diction is part of a writer's style and may be described as formal or informal, plain or fancy, ordinary or technical, sophisticated or down-to-earth, old-fashioned or modern.

DRAMA A *drama* is a story written to be performed by actors. Although a drama is meant to be performed, one can also read the script, or written version, and imagine the action. The *script* of a drama is made up of dialogue and stage directions. The *dialogue* is the words spoken by the actors. The *stage directions,* usually printed in italics, tell how the actors should look, move, and speak. They also describe the setting, sound effects, and lighting.

Dramas are often divided into parts called *acts.*

The acts are often divided into smaller parts called *scenes.*

DYNAMIC CHARACTER See *Character.*

ESSAY An *essay* is a short nonfiction work about a particular subject. Most essays have a single major focus and a clear introduction, body, and conclusion.

There are many types of essays. An *informal essay* uses casual, conversational language. A *historical essay* gives facts, explanations, and insights about historical events. An *expository essay* explains an idea by breaking it down. A *narrative essay* tells a story about a real-life experience. An *informational essay* explains a process. A *persuasive essay* offers an opinion and supports it.
See *Exposition, Narration,* and *Persuasion.*

EXPOSITION In the plot of a story or a drama, the *exposition,* or introduction, is the part of the work that introduces the characters, setting, and basic situation.

See *Plot.*

EXPLANATORY TEXT *Explanatory text* explains a process or provides directions.

EXPOSITORY WRITING *Expository writing* is writing that explains or informs.

EXTENDED METAPHOR In an *extended metaphor,* as in a regular metaphor, a subject is spoken or written of as though it were something else. However, extended metaphor differs from regular metaphor in that several connected comparisons are made.

See *Metaphor.*

EXTERNAL CONFLICT See *Conflict.*

FABLE A *fable* is a brief story or poem, usually with animal characters, that teaches a lesson, or moral. The moral is usually stated at the end of the fable.

See *Irony* and *Moral.*

FANTASY A *fantasy* is highly imaginative writing that contains elements not found in real life. Examples of fantasy include stories that involve supernatural elements, stories that resemble fairy tales, stories that deal with imaginary places and creatures, and science-fiction stories.

See *Science Fiction.*

FICTION *Fiction* is prose writing that tells about imaginary characters and events. Short stories and novels are works of fiction. Some writers base their fiction on actual events and people, adding invented characters, dialogue, settings, and plots. Other writers rely on imagination alone.

See *Narration, Nonfiction,* and *Prose.*

FIGURATIVE LANGUAGE *Figurative language* is writing or speech that is not meant to be taken literally. The many types of figurative language are known as *figures of speech.* Common figures of speech include metaphor, personification, and simile. Writers use figurative language to state ideas in vivid and imaginative ways.

See *Metaphor, Personification, Simile,* and *Symbol.*

FIGURE OF SPEECH See *Figurative Language.*

FLASHBACK A *flashback* is a scene within a story that interrupts the sequence of events to relate events that occurred in the past.

FLAT CHARACTER See *Character.*

FOLK TALE A *folk tale* is a story composed orally and then passed from person to person by word of mouth. Folk tales originated among people who could neither read nor write. These people entertained one another by telling stories aloud—often dealing with heroes, adventure, magic, or romance. Eventually, modern scholars collected these stories and wrote them down.

See *Fable, Legend, Myth,* and *Oral Tradition.*

FOOT See *Meter.*

FORESHADOWING *Foreshadowing* is the author's use of clues to hint at what might happen later in the story. Writers use foreshadowing to build their readers' expectations and to create suspense.

FREE VERSE *Free verse* is poetry not written in a regular, rhythmical pattern, or meter. The poet is free to write lines of any length or with any number of stresses, or beats. Free verse is therefore less constraining than *metrical verse,* in which every line must have a certain length and a certain number of stresses.

See *Meter.*

GENRE A *genre* is a division or type of literature. Literature is commonly divided into three major genres: poetry, prose, and drama. Each major genre is, in turn, divided into lesser genres, as follows:

1. *Poetry:* lyric poetry, concrete poetry, dramatic poetry, narrative poetry, epic poetry

2. *Prose:* fiction (novels and short stories) and nonfiction (biography, autobiography, letters, essays, and reports)

3. *Drama:* serious drama and tragedy, comic drama, melodrama, and farce

See *Drama, Poetry,* and *Prose.*

HAIKU The *haiku* is a three-line Japanese verse form. The first and third lines of a haiku each have five syllables. The second line has seven syllables. A writer of haiku uses images to create a single, vivid picture, generally of a scene from nature.

HERO/HEROINE A *hero* or *heroine* is a character whose actions are inspiring, or noble. Often heroes and heroines struggle to overcome the obstacles and problems that stand in their way. The term *hero* was originally used only for male characters, while heroic female characters were called *heroines.* It is now acceptable to use *hero* to refer to females as well as to males.

HISTORICAL FICTION In *historical fiction*, real events, places, or people are incorporated into a fictional, or made-up, story.

HUMOR *Humor* is writing intended to evoke laughter or entertain. It can also be used to convey a serious theme.

IMAGERY See *Images*.

IMAGES *Images* are words or phrases that appeal to one or more of the five senses. Writers use images to describe how their subjects look, sound, feel, taste, and smell. Poets often paint images, or word pictures, that appeal to your senses. These pictures help you to experience the poem fully.

INFORMATIVE TEXT *Informative text* provides information on a subject.

INTERNAL CONFLICT See *Conflict*.

IRONY *Irony* is a contradiction between what happens and what is expected. There are three main types of irony. *Situational irony* occurs when something happens that directly contradicts the expectations of the characters or the audience. *Verbal irony* is something contradictory that is said. In *dramatic irony*, the audience is aware of something that the character or speaker is not.

JOURNAL A *journal* is a daily, or periodic, account of events and the writer's thoughts and feelings about those events. Personal journals are not normally written for publication, but sometimes they do get published later with permission from the author or the author's family.

LEGEND A *legend* is a widely told story about the past that may or may not have a foundation in fact. Every culture has legends—its familiar, traditional stories.

See *Folk Tale, Myth,* and *Oral Tradition*.

LETTERS A *letter* is a written communication. In personal letters, the writer shares information and his or her thoughts and feelings with one other person or group. Although letters are not normally written for publication, they sometimes are published with the permission of the author or the author's family.

LIMERICK A *limerick* is a humorous, rhyming, five-line poem with a specific meter and rhyme scheme. Most limericks have three strong stresses in lines 1, 2, and 5 and two strong stresses in lines 3 and 4. Most follow the rhyme scheme *aabba*.

LYRIC POEM A *lyric poem* is a highly musical verse that expresses the observations and feelings of a single speaker. It creates a single, unified impression.

MAIN CHARACTER See *Character*.

MEDIA ACCOUNTS *Media accounts* are reports, explanations, opinions, or descriptions written for television, radio, newspapers, and magazines. While some media accounts report only facts, others include the writer's thoughts and reflections.

METAPHOR A *metaphor* is a figure of speech in which something is described as though it were something else. A metaphor, like a simile, works by pointing out a similarity between two unlike things.

See *Extended Metaphor* and *Simile*.

METER The *meter* of a poem is its rhythmical pattern. This pattern is determined by the number of *stresses,* or beats, in each line. To describe the meter of a poem, read it while emphasizing the beats in each line. Then, mark the stressed and unstressed syllables, as follows:

M̆y fáth | ĕr wás | t̆he fírst | tŏ héar |

As you can see, each strong stress is marked with a slanted line (´) and each unstressed syllable with a horseshoe symbol (˘). The weak and strong stresses are then divided by vertical lines (|) into groups called feet.

MINOR CHARACTER See *Character*.

MOOD See *Atmosphere*.

MORAL A *moral* is a lesson taught by a literary work. A fable usually ends with a moral that is directly stated. A poem, novel, short story, or essay often suggests a moral that is not directly stated. The moral must be drawn by the reader, based on other elements in the work.

See *Fable*.

MOTIVATION See *Motive*.

MOTIVE A *motive* is a reason that explains or partially explains a character's thoughts, feelings, actions, or speech. Writers try to make their characters' motives, or motivations, as clear as possible. If the motives of a main character are not clear, then the character will not be well understood.

Characters are often motivated by needs, such as food and shelter. They are also motivated by feelings, such as fear, love, and pride. Motives may be obvious or hidden.

MYTH A *myth* is a fictional tale that explains the actions of gods or heroes or the origins of elements of nature. Myths are part of the oral tradition. They are composed orally and then passed from generation to generation by word of mouth. Every ancient culture has its own mythology, or collection of myths. Greek and Roman myths are known collectively as *classical mythology.*

See *Oral Tradition.*

NARRATION *Narration* is writing that tells a story. The act of telling a story is also called narration. A story told in fiction, nonfiction, poetry, or even in drama is called a *narrative.*

See *Narrative, Narrative Poem,* and *Narrator.*

NARRATIVE A *narrative* is a story. A narrative can be either fiction or nonfiction. Novels and short stories are types of fictional narratives. Biographies and autobiographies are nonfiction narratives. Poems that tell stories are also narratives.

See *Narration* and *Narrative Poem.*

NARRATIVE POEM A *narrative poem* is a story told in verse. Narrative poems often have all the elements of short stories, including characters, conflict, and plot.

NARRATOR A *narrator* is a speaker or a character who tells a story. The narrator's perspective is the way he or she sees things. A *third-person narrator* is one who stands outside the action and speaks about it. A *first-person narrator* is one who tells a story and participates in its action.

See *Point of View.*

NONFICTION *Nonfiction* is prose writing that presents and explains ideas or that tells about real people, places, objects, or events. Autobiographies, biographies, essays, reports, letters, memos, and newspaper articles are all types of nonfiction.

See *Fiction.*

NOVEL A *novel* is a long work of fiction. Novels contain such elements as characters, plot, conflict, and setting. The writer of novels, or novelist, develops these elements. In addition to its main plot, a novel may contain one or more subplots, or independent, related stories. A novel may also have several themes.

See *Fiction* and *Short Story.*

NOVELLA A *novella* is a fictional work that is longer than a short story but shorter than a novel.

ONOMATOPOEIA *Onomatopoeia* is the use of words that imitate sounds. *Crash, buzz, screech, hiss, neigh, jingle,* and *cluck* are examples of onomatopoeia. *Chickadee, towhee,* and *whippoorwill* are onomatopoeic names of birds.

Onomatopoeia can help put the reader in the action of a poem.

ORAL TRADITION *Oral tradition* is the passing of songs, stories, and poems from generation to generation by word of mouth. Folk songs, folk tales, legends, and myths all come from the oral tradition. No one knows who first created these stories and poems.

See *Folk Tale, Legend,* and *Myth.*

OXYMORON An *oxymoron* (pl. *oxymora*) is a figure of speech that links two opposite or contradictory words, to point out an idea or a situation that seems contradictory or inconsistent but on closer inspection turns out to be somehow true.

PERSONIFICATION *Personification* is a type of figurative language in which a nonhuman subject is given human characteristics.

PERSPECTIVE See *Narrator* and *Point of View.*

PERSUASION *Persuasion* is used in writing or speech that attempts to convince the reader or listener to adopt a particular opinion or course of action. Newspaper editorials and letters to the editor use persuasion. So do advertisements and campaign speeches given by political candidates. An *argument* is a logical way of presenting a belief, conclusion, or stance. A good argument is supported with reasoning and evidence.

See *Essay.*

PLAYWRIGHT A *playwright* is a person who writes plays. William Shakespeare is regarded as the greatest playwright in English literature.

PLOT *Plot* is the sequence of events in a story. In most novels, dramas, short stories, and narrative poems, the plot involves both characters and a central conflict. The plot usually begins with an exposition that introduces the setting, the characters, and the basic situation. This is followed by the *inciting incident,* which introduces the central conflict. The conflict then increases during the *development* until it reaches a high point of interest or suspense, the *climax.* The climax is followed by the *falling action,* or end, of the central conflict. Any events that occur during the *falling action* make up the *resolution* or *denouement.*

Some plots do not have all of these parts. For example, some stories begin with the inciting incident and end with the resolution.

See *Conflict.*

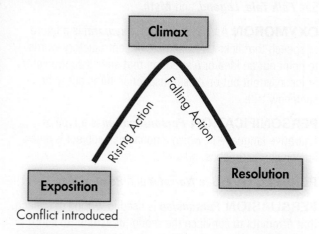

Conflict introduced

POETRY *Poetry* is one of the three major types of literature, the others being prose and drama. Most poems make use of highly concise, musical, and emotionally charged language. Many also make use of imagery, figurative language, and special devices of sound such as rhyme. Major types of poetry include *lyric poetry, narrative poetry,* and *concrete poetry.*

See *Concrete Poem, Genre, Lyric Poem,* and *Narrative Poem.*

POINT OF VIEW *Point of view* is the perspective, or vantage point, from which a story is told. It is either a narrator outside the story or a character in the story. *First-person point of view* is told by a character who uses the first-person pronoun "I."

The two kinds of *third-person point of view,* limited and omniscient, are called "third person" because the narrator uses third-person pronouns such as "he" and "she" to refer to the characters. There is no "I" telling the story.

In stories told from the *omniscient third-person point of view,* the narrator knows and tells about what each character feels and thinks.

In stories told from the *limited third-person point of view,* the narrator relates the inner thoughts and feelings of only one character, and everything is viewed from this character's perspective.

See *Narrator.*

PROBLEM See *Conflict.*

PROSE *Prose* is the ordinary form of written language. Most writing that is not poetry, drama, or song is considered prose. Prose is one of the major genres of literature and occurs in two forms—fiction and nonfiction.

See *Fiction, Genre,* and *Nonfiction.*

PROTAGONIST The *protagonist* is the main character in a literary work. Often, the protagonist is a person, but sometimes it can be an animal or other form of being.

See *Antagonist* and *Character.*

REFRAIN A *refrain* is a regularly repeated line or group of lines in a poem or a song.

REPETITION *Repetition* is the use, more than once, of any element of language—a sound, word, phrase, clause, or sentence. Repetition is used in both prose and poetry.

See *Alliteration, Meter, Plot, Rhyme,* and *Rhyme Scheme.*

RESOLUTION The *resolution* is the outcome of the conflict in a plot.

See *Plot.*

RHYME *Rhyme* is the repetition of sounds at the ends of words. Poets use rhyme to lend a songlike quality to their verses and to emphasize certain words and ideas. Many traditional poems contain *end rhymes,* or rhyming words at the ends of lines.

Another common device is the use of *internal rhymes,* or rhyming words within lines. Internal rhyme also emphasizes the flowing nature of a poem.

See *Rhyme Scheme.*

RHYME SCHEME A *rhyme scheme* is a regular pattern of rhyming words in a poem. To indicate the rhyme scheme of a poem, one uses lowercase letters. Each rhyme is assigned a different letter, as follows in the first stanza of "Dust of Snow," by Robert Frost:

The way a crow	*a*
Shook down on me	*b*
The dust of snow	*a*
From a hemlock tree	*b*

Thus, this stanza has the rhyme scheme *abab.*

RHYTHM *Rhythm* is the pattern of stressed and unstressed syllables in spoken or written language.

See *Meter.*

ROUND CHARACTER See *Character.*

SCENE A *scene* is a section of uninterrupted action in the act of a drama.

See *Drama.*

SCIENCE FICTION *Science fiction* combines elements of fiction and fantasy with scientific fact. Many science-fiction stories are set in the future.

SENSORY LANGUAGE *Sensory language* is writing or speech that appeals to one or more of the five senses.

See *Images.*

SETTING The *setting* of a literary work is the time and place of the action. The setting includes all the details of a place and time—the year, the time of day, even the weather. The place may be a specific country, state, region, community, neighborhood, building, institution, or home. Details such as dialects, clothing, customs, and modes of transportation are often used to establish setting. In most stories, the setting serves as a backdrop—a context in which the characters interact. Setting can also help to create a feeling, or atmosphere.

See *Atmosphere.*

SHORT STORY A *short story* is a brief work of fiction. Like a novel, a short story presents a sequence of events, or plot. The plot usually deals with a central conflict faced by a main character, or protagonist. The events in a short story usually communicate a message about life or human nature. This message, or central idea, is the story's theme.

See *Conflict, Plot,* and *Theme.*

SIMILE A *simile* is a figure of speech that uses *like* or *as* to make a direct comparison between two unlike ideas. Everyday speech often contains similes, such as "pale as a ghost," "good as gold," "spread like wildfire," and "clever as a fox."

SPEAKER The *speaker* is the imaginary voice a poet uses when writing a poem. The speaker is the character who tells the poem. This character, or voice, often is not identified by name. There can be important differences between the poet and the poem's speaker.

See *Narrator.*

STAGE DIRECTIONS *Stage directions* are notes included in a drama to describe how the work is to be performed or staged. Stage directions are usually printed in italics and enclosed within parentheses or brackets. Some stage directions describe the movements, costumes, emotional states, and ways of speaking of the characters.

STAGING *Staging* includes the setting, lighting, costumes, special effects, music, dance, and so on that go into putting on a stage performance of a drama.

See *Drama.*

STANZA A *stanza* is a group of lines of poetry that are usually similar in length and pattern and are separated by spaces. A stanza is like a paragraph of poetry—it states and develops a single main idea.

STATIC CHARACTER See *Character.*

SURPRISE ENDING A *surprise ending* is a conclusion that is unexpected. The reader has certain expectations about the ending based on details in the story. Often, a surprise ending is *foreshadowed,* or subtly hinted at, in the course of the work.

See *Foreshadowing* and *Plot.*

SUSPENSE *Suspense* is a feeling of anxious uncertainty about the outcome of events in a literary work. Writers create suspense by raising questions in the minds of their readers.

SYMBOL A *symbol* is anything that stands for or represents something else. Symbols are common in everyday life. A dove with an olive branch in its beak is a symbol of peace. A blindfolded woman holding a balanced scale is a symbol of justice. A crown is a symbol of a king's or queen's status and authority.

SYMBOLISM *Symbolism* is the use of symbols. Symbolism plays an important role in many different types of literature. It can highlight certain elements the author wishes to emphasize and also add levels of meaning.

THEME The *theme* is a central message, concern, or purpose in a literary work. A theme can usually be expressed as a generalization, or a general statement, about human beings or about life. The theme of a work is not a summary of its plot. The theme is the writer's central idea.

Although a theme may be stated directly in the text, it is more often presented indirectly. When the theme is stated indirectly, or implied, the reader must figure out what the theme is by looking carefully at what the work reveals about people or about life.

TONE The *tone* of a literary work is the writer's attitude toward his or her audience and subject. The tone can often be described by a single adjective, such as *formal* or *informal, serious* or *playful, bitter,* or *ironic.* Factors that contribute to the tone are word choice, sentence structure, line length, rhyme, rhythm, and repetition.

TRAGEDY A *tragedy* is a work of literature, especially a play, that results in a catastrophe for the main character. In ancient Greek drama, the main character is always a significant person—a king or a hero—and the cause of the tragedy is a tragic flaw, or weakness, in his or her character. In modern drama, the main character can be an ordinary person, and the cause of the tragedy can be some evil in society itself. The purpose of tragedy is not only to arouse fear and pity in the audience, but also, in some cases, to convey a sense of the grandeur and nobility of the human spirit.

TURNING POINT See *Climax.*

UNIVERSAL THEME A *universal theme* is a message about life that is expressed regularly in many different cultures and time periods. Folk tales, epics, and romances often address universal themes like the importance of courage, the power of love, or the danger of greed.

WORD CHOICE An author's *word choice*—sometimes referred to as *diction*—is an important factor in creating the tone or mood of a literary work. Authors choose words based on the intended audience and the work's purpose.

Tips for Literature Circles

As you read and study literature, discussions with other readers can help you understand and enjoy what you have read. Use the following tips.

- ## Understand the purpose of your discussion

  Your purpose when you discuss literature is to broaden your understanding of a work by testing your own ideas and hearing the ideas of others. Keep your comments focused on the literature you are discussing. Starting with one focus question will help to keep your discussion on track.

- ## Communicate effectively

  Effective communication requires thinking before speaking. Plan the points that you want to make and decide how you will express them. Organize these points in logical order and use details from the work to support your ideas. Jot down informal notes to help keep your ideas focused.

  Remember to speak clearly, pronouncing words slowly and carefully. Also, listen attentively when others are speaking, and avoid interrupting.

- ## Consider other ideas and interpretations

  A work of literature can generate a wide variety of responses in different readers. Be open to the idea that many interpretations can be valid. To support your own ideas, point to the events, descriptions, characters, or other literary elements in the work that led to your interpretation. To consider someone else's ideas, decide whether details in the work support the interpretation he or she presents. Be sure to convey your criticism of the ideas of others in a respectful and supportive manner.

- ## Ask questions

  Ask questions to clarify your understanding of another reader's ideas. You can also use questions to call attention to possible areas of confusion, to points that are open to debate, or to errors in the speaker's points. To move a discussion forward, summarize and evaluate conclusions reached by the group members.

  When you meet with a group to discuss literature, use a chart like the one shown to analyze the discussion.

Work Being Discussed:	
Focus Question:	
Your Response:	Another Student's Response:
Supporting Evidence:	Supporting Evidence:

Tips for Improving Reading Fluency

When you were younger, you learned to read. Then, you read to expand your experiences or for pure enjoyment. Now, you are expected to read to learn. As you progress in school, you are given more and more material to read. The tips on these pages will help you improve your reading fluency, or your ability to read easily, smoothly, and expressively.

Keeping Your Concentration

One common problem that readers face is the loss of concentration. When you are reading an assignment, you might find yourself rereading the same sentence several times without really understanding it. The first step in changing this behavior is to notice that you do it. Becoming an active, aware reader will help you get the most from your assignments. Practice using these strategies:

- Cover what you have already read with a note card as you go along. Then, you will not be able to reread without noticing that you are doing it.

- Set a purpose for reading beyond just completing the assignment. Then, read actively by pausing to ask yourself questions about the material as you read.

- Use the Reading Strategy instruction and notes that appear with each selection in this textbook.

- Stop reading after a specified period of time (for example, 5 minutes) and summarize what you have read. To help you with this strategy, use the Reading Check questions that appear with each selection in this textbook. Reread to find any answers you do not know.

Reading Phrases

Fluent readers read phrases rather than individual words. Reading this way will speed up your reading and improve your comprehension. Here are some useful ideas:

- Experts recommend rereading as a strategy to increase fluency. Choose a passage of text that is neither too hard nor too easy. Read the same passage aloud several times until you can read it smoothly. When you can read the passage fluently, pick another passage and keep practicing.

- Read aloud into a tape recorder. Then, listen to the recording, noting your accuracy, pacing, and expression. You can also read aloud and share feedback with a partner.

- Use the *Prentice Hall Listening to Literature* audiotapes or CDs to hear the selections read aloud. Read along silently in your textbook, noticing how the reader uses his or her voice and emphasizes certain words and phrases.

Understanding Key Vocabulary

If you do not understand some of the words in an assignment, you may miss out on important concepts. Therefore, it is helpful to keep a dictionary nearby when you are reading. Follow these steps:

- Before you begin reading, scan the text for unfamiliar words or terms. Find out what those words mean before you begin reading.

- Use context—the surrounding words, phrases, and sentences—to help you determine the meanings of unfamiliar words.

- If you are unable to understand the meaning through context, refer to the dictionary.

Paying Attention to Punctuation

When you read, pay attention to punctuation. Commas, periods, exclamation points, semicolons, and colons tell you when to pause or stop. They also indicate relationships between groups of words. When you recognize these relationships you will read with greater understanding and expression. Look at the chart below.

Punctuation Mark	Meaning
comma	brief pause
period	pause at the end of a thought
exclamation point	pause that indicates emphasis
semicolon	pause between related but distinct thoughts
colon	pause before giving explanation or examples

Using the Reading Fluency Checklist

Use the checklist below each time you read a selection in this textbook. In your Language Arts journal or notebook, note which skills you need to work on and chart your progress each week.

Reading Fluency Checklist
☐ Preview the text to check for difficult or unfamiliar words.
☐ Practice reading aloud.
☐ Read according to punctuation.
☐ Break down long sentences into the subject and its meaning.
☐ Read groups of words for meaning rather than reading single words.
☐ Read with expression (change your tone of voice to add meaning to the word).

Reading is a skill that can be improved with practice. The key to improving your fluency is to read. The more you read, the better your reading will become.

Types of Writing

Good writing can be a powerful tool used for many purposes. Writing can allow you to defend something you believe in or show how much you know about a subject. Writing can also help you share what you have experienced, imagined, thought, and felt. The three main types of writing are argument, informative/explanatory, and narrative.

Argument

When you think of the word *argument,* you might think of a disagreement between two people, but an argument is more than that. An argument is a logical way of presenting a belief, conclusion, or stance. A good argument is supported with reasoning and evidence.

Argument writing can be used for many purposes, such as to change a reader's point of view or opinion or to bring about an action or a response from a reader.

There are three main purposes for writing a formal argument:

- to change the reader's mind

- to convince the reader to accept what is written

- to motivate the reader to take action, based on what is written

The following are some types of argument writing:

Advertisements An advertisement is a planned message meant to be seen, heard, or read. It attempts to persuade an audience to buy a product or service, accept an idea, or support a cause. Advertisements may appear in print, online, or in broadcast form.

Several common types of advertisements are public service announcements, billboards, merchandise ads, service ads, and political campaign literature.

Persuasive Essay A persuasive essay presents a position on an issue, urges readers to accept that position, and may encourage a specific action. An effective persuasive essay

- Explores an issue of importance to the writer

- Addresses an issue that is arguable

- Uses facts, examples, statistics, or personal experiences to support a position

- Tries to influence the audience through appeals to the readers' knowledge, experiences, or emotions

- Uses clear organization to present a logical argument

Forms of persuasion include editorials, position papers, persuasive speeches, grant proposals, advertisements, and debates.

Informative/Explanatory

Informative/explanatory writing should rely on facts to inform or explain. Informative/explanatory writing serves some closely related purposes: to increase readers' knowledge of a subject, to help readers better understand a procedure or process, or to provide readers with an enhanced comprehension of a concept. It should also feature a clear introduction, body, and conclusion. The following are some examples of informative/explanatory writing:

Cause-and-Effect Essay A cause-and-effect essay examines the relationship between events, explaining how one event or situation causes another. A successful cause-and-effect essay includes

- A discussion of a cause, event, or condition that produces a specific result

- An explanation of an effect, outcome, or result

- Evidence and examples to support the relationship between cause and effect

- A logical organization that makes the explanation clear

Comparison-and-Contrast Essay A comparison-and-contrast essay analyzes the similarities and differences between or among two or more things. An effective comparison-and-contrast essay

- Identifies a purpose for comparison and contrast

- Identifies similarities and differences between or among two or more things, people, places, or ideas

- Gives factual details about the subjects

- Uses an organizational plan suited to the topic and purpose

Descriptive Writing Descriptive writing creates a vivid picture of a person, place, thing, or event. Most descriptive writing includes

- Sensory details—sights, sounds, smells, tastes, and physical sensations

- Vivid, precise language

- Figurative language or comparisons

- Adjectives and adverbs that paint a word picture

- An organization suited to the subject

Types of descriptive writing include descriptions of ideas, observations, travel brochures, physical descriptions, functional descriptions, remembrances, and character sketches.

Problem-and-Solution Essay A problem-and-solution essay describes a problem and offers one or more solutions to it. It describes a clear set of steps to achieve a result. An effective problem-and-solution essay includes

- A clear statement of the problem, with its causes and effects summarized for the reader

- The most important aspects of the problem

- A proposal for at least one realistic solution

- Facts, statistics, data, or expert testimony to support the solution

- A clear organization that makes the relationship between problem and solution obvious

Research Writing Research writing is based on information gathered from outside sources. A research paper—a focused study of a topic—helps writers explore and connect ideas, make discoveries, and share their findings with an audience. An effective research paper

- Focuses on a specific, narrow topic, which is usually summarized in a thesis statement

- Presents relevant information from a wide variety of sources

- Uses a clear organization that includes an introduction, body, and conclusion

- Includes a bibliography or works-cited list that identifies the sources from which the information was drawn

Other types of writing that depend on accurate and insightful research include multimedia presentations, statistical reports, annotated bibliographies, and experiment journals.

Workplace Writing Workplace writing is probably the format you will use most after you finish school. In general, workplace writing is fact-based and meant to communicate specific information in a structured format. Effective workplace writing

- Communicates information concisely

- Includes details that provide necessary information and anticipate potential questions

- Is error-free and neatly presented

Common types of workplace writing include business letters, memorandums, résumés, forms, and applications.

Narrative

Narrative writing conveys experience, either real or imaginary, and uses time to provide structure. It can be used to inform, instruct, persuade, or entertain. Whenever writers tell a story, they are using narrative writing. Most types of narrative writing share certain elements, such as characters, a setting, a sequence of events, and, often, a theme. The following are some types of narration:

Autobiographical Writing Autobiographical writing tells a true story about an important period, experience, or relationship in the writer's life. Effective autobiographical writing includes

- A series of events that involve the writer as the main character

- Details, thoughts, feelings, and insights from the writer's perspective

- A conflict or an event that affects the writer

- A logical organization that tells the story clearly

- Insights that the writer gained from the experience

Types of autobiographical writing include personal narratives, autobiographical sketches, reflective essays, eyewitness accounts, and memoirs.

Short Story A short story is a brief, creative narrative. Most short stories include

- Details that establish the setting in time and place

- A main character who undergoes a change or learns something during the course of the story

- A conflict or a problem to be introduced, developed, and resolved

- A plot, the series of events that make up the action of the story

- A theme or message about life

Types of short stories include realistic stories, fantasies, historical narratives, mysteries, thrillers, science-fiction stories, and adventure stories.

Writing Friendly Letters

Writing Friendly Letters

A friendly letter is much less formal than a business letter. It is a letter to a friend, a family member, or anyone with whom the writer wants to communicate in a personal, friendly way. Most friendly letters are made up of five parts:

✔ the heading

✔ the salutation, or greeting

✔ the body

✔ the closing

✔ the signature

The purpose of a friendly letter is often one of the following:

✔ to share personal news and feelings

✔ to send or to answer an invitation

✔ to express thanks

Model Friendly Letter

In this friendly letter, Betsy thanks her grandparents for a birthday present and gives them some news about her life.

---

11 Old Farm Road
Topsham, Maine 04011

April 14, 20—

> The **heading** includes the writer's address and the date on which he or she wrote the letter.

Dear Grandma and Grandpa,

Thank you for the sweater you sent me for my birthday. It fits perfectly, and I love the color. I wore my new sweater to the carnival at school last weekend and got lots of compliments.

The weather here has been cool but sunny. Mom thinks that "real" spring will never come. I can't wait until it's warm enough to go swimming.

School is going fairly well. I really like my Social Studies class. We are learning about the U.S. Constitution, and I think it's very interesting. Maybe I will be a lawyer when I grow up.

When are you coming out to visit us? We haven't seen you since Thanksgiving. You can stay in my room when you come. I'll be happy to sleep on the couch. (The TV is in that room!!)

Well, thanks again and hope all is well with you.

> The **body** is the main part of the letter and contains the basic message.

Love,

Betsy

> Some common **closings** for personal letters include "Best wishes," "Love," "Sincerely," and "Yours truly."

Writing Business Letters

Formatting Business Letters

Business letters follow one of several acceptable formats. In **block format,** each part of the letter begins at the left margin. A double space is used between paragraphs. In **modified block format,** the heading and the closing are indented to the center of the page. No matter which format is used, all letters in business format have a heading, an inside address, a salutation or greeting, a body, a closing, and a signature. These parts are shown and annotated on the model business letter below, formatted in modified block style.

Model Business Letter

In this letter, Yolanda Dodson uses modified block format to request information.

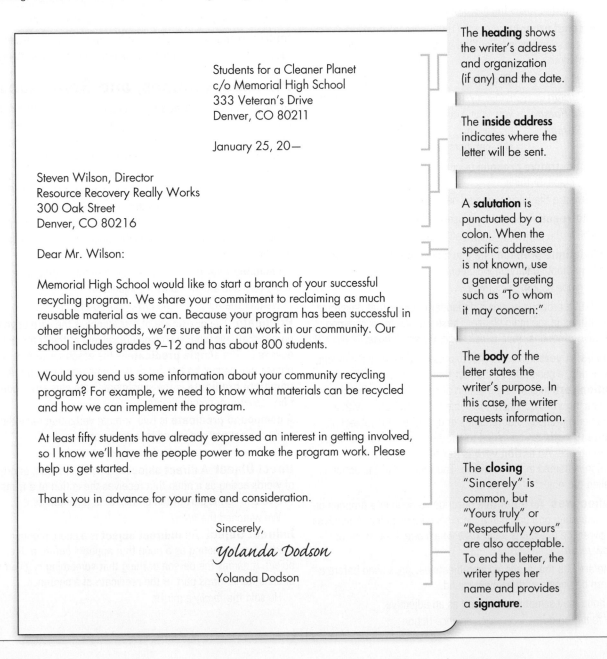

Students for a Cleaner Planet
c/o Memorial High School
333 Veteran's Drive
Denver, CO 80211

January 25, 20—

Steven Wilson, Director
Resource Recovery Really Works
300 Oak Street
Denver, CO 80216

Dear Mr. Wilson:

Memorial High School would like to start a branch of your successful recycling program. We share your commitment to reclaiming as much reusable material as we can. Because your program has been successful in other neighborhoods, we're sure that it can work in our community. Our school includes grades 9–12 and has about 800 students.

Would you send us some information about your community recycling program? For example, we need to know what materials can be recycled and how we can implement the program.

At least fifty students have already expressed an interest in getting involved, so I know we'll have the people power to make the program work. Please help us get started.

Thank you in advance for your time and consideration.

Sincerely,

Yolanda Dodson

Yolanda Dodson

The **heading** shows the writer's address and organization (if any) and the date.

The **inside address** indicates where the letter will be sent.

A **salutation** is punctuated by a colon. When the specific addressee is not known, use a general greeting such as "To whom it may concern:"

The **body** of the letter states the writer's purpose. In this case, the writer requests information.

The **closing** "Sincerely" is common, but "Yours truly" or "Respectfully yours" are also acceptable. To end the letter, the writer types her name and provides a **signature**.

Grammar, Usage, and Mechanics Handbook

Parts of Speech

Nouns A **noun** is the name of a person, place, or thing. A **common noun** names any one of a class of people, places, or things. A **proper noun** names a specific person, place, or thing.

A collective noun is a noun that names a group of individual people or things.

A compound noun is a noun made up of two or more words.

Pronouns A **pronoun** is a word that stands for a noun or for a word that takes the place of a noun.

A **personal pronoun** refers to (1) the person speaking, (2) the person spoken to, or (3) the person, place, or thing spoken about.

	Singular	Plural
First Person	I, me, my, mine	we, us, our, ours
Second Person	you, your, yours	you, your, yours
Third Person	he, him, his, she, her, hers, it, its	they, them, their, theirs

A **demonstrative pronoun** directs attention to a specific person, place, or thing.

These are the juiciest pears I have ever tasted.

An **interrogative pronoun** is used to begin a question.

Who is the author of "Jeremiah's Song"?

An **indefinite pronoun** refers to a person, place, or thing, often without specifying which one.

Everyone bought something.

A relative pronoun begins a dependent clause that describes something in the main clause. These are the most common relative pronouns: *that, which, who, whom, whose.*

Verbs A **verb** is a word that expresses time while showing an action, a condition, or the fact that something exists. An **action verb** indicates the action of someone or something. A **linking verb** connects the subject of a sentence with a noun or a pronoun that renames or describes the subject. A **helping verb** can be added to another verb to make a single verb phrase. An **action verb** is transitive if the receiver of the action is named in the sentence. The receiver of the action is called the object of the verb.

Adjectives An **adjective** describes a noun or a pronoun or gives a noun or a pronoun a more specific meaning. Adjectives answer the questions *what kind, which one, how many,* or *how much.*

The articles *the, a,* and *an* are adjectives. *An* is used before a word beginning with a vowel sound.

A noun may sometimes be used as an adjective.

family home   *science* fiction

Adverbs An **adverb** modifies a verb, an adjective, or another adverb. Adverbs answer the questions *where, when, in what way,* or *to what extent.*

Prepositions A **preposition** relates a noun or a pronoun following it to another word in the sentence.

Conjunctions A **conjunction** connects other words or groups of words. A **coordinating conjunction** connects similar kinds or groups of words. **Correlative conjunctions** are used in pairs to connect similar words or groups of words.

both Grandpa *and* Dad   *neither* they *nor* I

Interjections An **interjection** is a word that expresses feeling or emotion and functions independently of a sentence.

Phrases, Clauses, and Sentences

Sentences A **sentence** is a group of words with two main parts: a complete subject and a complete predicate. Together, these parts express a complete thought. A **fragment** is a group of words that does not express a complete thought.

Subject The **subject** of a sentence is the word or group of words that tells whom or what the sentence is about. The **simple subject** is the essential noun, pronoun, or group of words acting as a noun that cannot be left out of the complete subject. A **complete subject** is the simple subject plus any modifiers.

A **compound subject** is two or more subjects that have the same verb and are joined by a conjunction.

Neither the *horse nor the driver* looked tired.

Predicate The **predicate** of a sentence is the verb or verb phrase that tells what the complete subject of the sentence does or is. The **simple predicate** is the essential verb or verb phrase that cannot be left out of the complete predicate. A **complete predicate** is the simple predicate plus any modifiers, objects, or complements.

A **compound predicate** is two or more verbs that have the same subject and are joined by a conjunction.

She *sneezed and coughed* throughout the trip.

Direct Object A **direct object** is a noun, pronoun, or group of words acting as a noun that receives the action of a transitive verb. It forms part of the predicate of a sentence.

We watched the *liftoff.*

Indirect Object An **indirect object** is a noun, pronoun, or group of words acting as a noun that appears before a direct object. It names the person or thing that something is given to or done for. It forms part of the predicate of a sentence.

He sold the *family* a mirror.

Complement A **complement** is a word or group of words that completes the meaning of the predicate of a sentence. Complements include *object complements* and *subject complements.*

An **object complement** is an adjective or noun that appears with a direct object and describes or renames it.

I called Meg my *friend.*

A **subject complement** is a noun, pronoun, or adjective that appears with a linking verb and tells something about the subject. A subject complement may be a *predicate nominative* or a *predicate adjective.* A **predicate nominative** is a noun or pronoun that appears with a linking verb and renames, identifies, or explains the subject.

Kiglo was the *leader.*

A **predicate adjective** is an adjective that appears with a linking verb and describes the subject of a sentence.

Roko became *tired.*

Sentence Types A **simple sentence** consists of a single independent clause.

A **compound sentence** consists of two or more independent clauses joined by a comma and a coordinating conjunction or by a semicolon.

A **complex sentence** consists of one independent clause and one or more subordinate clauses.

A **compound-complex sentence** consists of two or more independent clauses and one or more subordinate clauses.

A **declarative sentence** states an idea and ends with a period.

An **interrogative sentence** asks a question and ends with a question mark.

An **imperative sentence** gives an order or a direction and ends with either a period or an exclamation mark.

An **exclamatory sentence** conveys a strong emotion and ends with an exclamation mark.

Phrases A **phrase** is a group of words, without a subject and a verb, that functions in a sentence as one part of speech.

A **prepositional phrase** is a group of words that includes a preposition and a noun or a pronoun that is the object of the preposition.

An **adjective phrase** is a prepositional phrase that modifies a noun or a pronoun by telling *what kind* or *which one.*

An **adverb phrase** is a prepositional phrase that modifies a verb, an adjective, or an adverb by pointing out *where, when, in what manner,* or *to what extent.*

An **appositive phrase** is a noun or a pronoun with modifiers, placed next to a noun or a pronoun to add information and details.

A **participial phrase** is a participle modified by an adverb or an adverb phrase or accompanied by an object or a complement. The entire phrase acts as an adjective.

Running at top speed, he soon caught up with them.

An **infinitive phrase** is an infinitive with modifiers, objects, complements, or a subject, all acting together as a single part of speech.

At first I was too busy enjoying my food *to notice how the guests were doing.*

Gerunds A **gerund** is a noun formed from the present participle of a verb by adding *-ing.* Like other nouns, gerunds can be used as subjects, direct objects, predicate nouns, and objects of prepositions.

Gerund Phrases A **gerund phrase** is a gerund with modifiers, objects, or a complement, all acting together as a noun.

Clauses A **clause** is a group of words with its own subject and verb.

An **independent clause** can stand by itself as a complete sentence.

A **dependent,** or **subordinate, clause** has a subject and a verb but cannot stand by itself as a complete sentence; it can only be part of a sentence.

Using Verbs, Pronouns, and Modifiers

Principal Parts A **verb** has four **principal parts:** the *present,* the *present participle,* the *past,* and the *past participle.*

Regular verbs form the past and past participle by adding *-ed* to the present form.

Irregular verbs form the past and past participle by changing form rather than by adding *-ed.*

Verb Tense A **verb tense** tells whether the time of an action or condition is in the past, the present, or the future. Every verb has six tenses: *present, past, future, present perfect, past perfect,* and *future perfect.*

The **present tense** shows actions that happen in the present. The **past tense** shows actions that have already happened. The **future tense** shows actions that will happen. The **present perfect tense** shows actions that begin in the past and continue to the present. The **past perfect tense** shows a past action or condition that ended before another past action. The **future perfect tense** shows a future action or condition that will have ended before another begins.

Pronoun Case The **case** of a pronoun is the form it takes to show its use in a sentence. There are three pronoun cases: *nominative, objective,* and *possessive.*

The **nominative case** is used to name or rename the subject of the sentence. The nominative case pronouns are *I, you, he, she, it, we, you, they.*

The **objective case** is used as the direct object, indirect object, or object of a preposition. The objective case pronouns are *me, you, him, her, it, us, you, them.*

The **possessive case** is used to show ownership. The possessive pronouns are *my, your, his, her, its, our, their, mine, yours, his, hers, its, ours, theirs.*

Subject-Verb Agreement To make a subject and a verb agree, make sure that both are singular or both are plural. Two or more singular subjects joined by *or* or *nor* must have a singular verb. When singular and plural subjects are joined by *or* or *nor*, the verb must agree with the closest subject.

Pronoun-Antecedent Agreement Pronouns must agree with their antecedents in number and gender. Use singular pronouns with singular antecedents and plural pronouns with plural antecedents. Errors can occur when plural pronouns are used to refer to singular antecedents of no specific gender.

Incorrect: Everyone did their best.

Correct: Everyone did his or her best.

The following indefinite pronouns are singular: *anybody, anyone, each, either, everybody, everyone, neither, nobody, no one, one, somebody, someone.*

These indefinite pronouns are plural: *both, few, many, several.*

The following indefinite pronouns may be either singular or plural: *all, any, most, none, some.*

Modifiers The **comparative** and **superlative** degrees of most adjectives and adverbs of one or two syllables can be formed in either of two ways: Use *-er* or *more* to form a comparative degree and *-est* or *most* to form the superlative degree of most one- and two-syllable modifiers. These endings are added to the *positive,* or base, form of the word.

More and *most* can also be used to form the comparative and superlative degrees of most one- and two-syllable modifiers. These words should not be used when the result sounds awkward, as in "A greyhound is *more fast* than a beagle."

Glossary of Common Usage

accept, except: *Accept* is a verb that means "to receive" or "to agree to." *Except* is usually used as a preposition that means "other than" or "leaving out." Do not confuse these two words.

affect, effect: *Affect* is normally a verb meaning "to influence" or "to bring about a change in." *Effect* is usually a noun, meaning "result."

among, between: *Among* is usually used with three or more items. *Between* is generally used with only two items.

bad, badly: Use the predicate adjective *bad* after linking verbs such as *feel, look,* and *seem.* Use *badly* whenever an adverb is required.

beside, besides: *Beside* means "at the side of" or "close to." *Besides* means "in addition to."

can, may: The verb *can* generally refers to the ability to do something. The verb *may* generally refers to permission to do something.

different from, different than: *Different from* is generally preferred over *different than.*

farther, further: Use *farther* when you refer to distance. Use *further* when you mean "to a greater degree or extent" or "additional."

fewer, less: Use *fewer* for things that can be counted. Use *less* for amounts or quantities that cannot be counted.

good, well: Use the predicate adjective *good* after linking verbs such as *feel, look, smell, taste,* and *seem.* Use *well* whenever you need an adverb.

its, it's: The word *its* with no apostrophe is a possessive pronoun. The word *it's* is a contraction for *it is.* Do not confuse the possessive pronoun *its* with the contraction *it's,* standing for "it is" or "it has."

lay, lie: Do not confuse these verbs. *Lay* is a transitive verb meaning "to set or put something down." Its principal parts are *lay, laying, laid, laid. Lie* is an intransitive verb meaning "to recline." Its principal parts are *lie, lying, lay, lain.*

like, as: *Like* is a preposition that usually means "similar to" or "in the same way as." *Like* should always be followed by an object. Do not use *like* before a subject and a verb. Use *as* or *that* instead.

of, have: Do not use *of* in place of *have* after auxiliary verbs like *would, could, should, may, might,* or *must.*

raise, rise: *Raise* is a transitive verb that usually takes a direct object. *Rise* is intransitive and never takes a direct object.

set, sit: *Set* is a transitive verb meaning "to put (something) in a certain place." Its principal parts are *set, setting, set, set. Sit* is an intransitive verb meaning "to be seated." Its principal parts are *sit, sitting, sat, sat.*

than, then: The conjunction *than* is used to connect the two parts of a comparison. Do not confuse *than* with the adverb *then,* which usually refers to time.

that, which, who: Use the relative pronoun *that* to refer to things or people. Use *which* only for things and *who* only for people.

authentic (ô then´ tik) *adj.* genuine; real

authorized (ô´ thər īzd´) *v.* officially approved

aversion (ə vur´ zhən) *n.* intense dislike

awed (ôd) *v.* filled with wonder

B

barren (bar´ ən) *adj.* empty; bare

beckoning (bek´ ə niŋ) *adj.* calling; summoning

beneficial (ben´ ə fish´ əl) *adj.* useful

benefit (ben´ ə fit) 1. *n.* advantage; positive result; 2. *v.* profit (from); receive an advantage

bewildered (bē wil´ dərd) *adj.* hopelessly confused

blackmail (blak´ māl´) *n.* practice of making someone do what one wants by threatening to reveal his or her secrets

bleak (blēk) *adj.* 1. bare and windswept; 2. cold and harsh

bravery (brāv´ ər ē) *n.* courage; quality of facing and dealing with danger instead of running away

brutal (brōōt´ 'l) *adj.* 1. harsh; 2. savage; cruel and unfeeling

buoyed (boid) *v.* lifted up in spirits; encouraged

C

callous (kal´ əs) *adj.* lacking pity or mercy; unfeeling

capable (kā´ pə bəl) *adj.* having or showing a particular ability

capricious (kə prish´ əs) *adj.* tending to change abruptly, without apparent reason

carelessness (ker´ lis nis) *n.* lack of responsibility

cataclysm (kat´ ə kliz´ əm) *n.* sudden, violent event that causes change

categories (kat´ ə gôr´ ez) *n.* classes; types into which things, qualities, and so on can be classified

cause-and-effect (kôz´ ənd ə fekt´) *adj.* showing the relationship between reasons (causes) and results (effects)

challenge (chal´ ənj) *v.* call into question

chaos (kā´ äs´) *n.* extreme confusion or disorder

cite (sīt) *v.* 1. refer to as evidence or as an example; 2. quote

citing (sīt´ iŋ) *v.* referring to as evidence or as an example; quoting

civil (siv´ əl) *adj.* relating to citizens and the government

class (klas) *n.* grouping of people or objects based on common traits

common (käm´ ən) *adj.* 1. ordinary; expected; 2. shared

commotion (kə mō´ shən) *n.* noisy movement

community (kə myōō´ no tō) *n.* unified group within a larger body of people or other living things

compelled (kəm peld´) *v.* forced

compensate (käm´ pən sāt´) *v.* pay

complacent (kəm plā´ sənt) *adj.* satisfied, especially self-satisfied, or smug

compromise (käm´ prə mīz´) 1. *n.* settling of differences in which each side gives up something; 2. *v.* settle

compulsory (kəm pul´ sə rē) *adj.* required

conceivable (kən sēv´ ə bəl) *adj.* imaginable

condemn (kən dem´) *v.* inflict a penalty upon; convict

condition (kən dish´ ən) *n.* state of being

confirmation (kän´ fər mā´ shən) *n.* something that confirms or proves

confronted (kən frunt´ əd) *v.* faced or opposed boldly

connection (kə nek´ shən) *n.* link; tie; relationship

conquistadors (kän kēs´ tə dôrz´) *n.* Spanish conquerors of parts of America in the sixteenth century

consoling (kən sōl´ iŋ) *adj.* comforting

conspicuous (kən spik´ yōō əs) *adj.* noticeable

constructive (kən struk´ tiv) *adj.* leading to improvement

contact (kän´ takt) *n.* 1. touching; 2. communication

contemplation (kän´ təm plā´ shən) *n.* act of thinking about something

contempt (kən tempt´) *n.* scorn; disrespect

contention (kən ten´ shən) *n.* statement that one argues is true or valid

contraction (kən trak´ shən) *n.* act of becoming smaller

contrast (kän´ trast´) *n.* difference (between things being compared)

contrasting (kən trast´ iŋ) *adj.* differing

contribute (kən trib´ yōōt) *v.* add to a common effort

convey (kən vā´) *v.* communicate a message

conviction (kən vik´ shən) *n.* strong belief; certainty

cordially (kôr´ jə lē) *adv.* warmly

courage (kur´ ij) *n.* quality of being fearless; bravery

credible (kred´ ə bəl) *adj.* believable; reliable

criteria (krī tir´ ē ə) *n.* standards by which something can be judged

cultural (kul´ chər əl) *adj.* relating to the customs and beliefs of a group

cunningly (kun´ iŋ lē) *adv.* in a way that is skillfully dishonest

curiosity (kyōōr´ ē äs´ ə tē) *n.* desire to obtain information

cyclone (sī´ klōn´) *n.* violent, rotating windstorm; tornado

D

dabbing (dab´ iŋ) *v.* patting with something soft

debates (dē bāts´) *v.* 1. considers the reasons for and against; 2. argues over a point

deceive (dē sēv´) *v.* cause (someone) to believe what is not true

decision (dē sizh´ ən) *n.* choice; person's determination that he or she will take a certain action

defiance (dē fī´ əns) *n.* refusal to obey authority

deficiency (dē fish´ ən sē) *n.* lack of something that is necessary

degrading (dē grad´ iŋ) *adj.* insulting; dishonorable

deliberating (di lib´ ər āt´ iŋ) *v.* considering carefully

delirious (di lir´ ē əs) *adj.* 1. in a state of extreme mental excitement; 2. restless, confused, and hallucinating, or perceiving imaginary things

demographic (dem´ ə graf´ ik) *adj.* relating to characteristics of a group of people, such as age, gender, education, and so on

denigrate (den´ ə grāt´) *v.* say uncomplimentary things about someone or something

derision (di rizh´ ən) *n.* 1. contempt; 2. statements or actions making fun of someone or something

derived (di rīvd´) *v.* received or taken from a source

descendants (dē sen´ dənts) *n.* children, grandchildren, and continuing generations

desolate (des´ ə lit) *adj.* empty; lonely

deterioration (dē tir´ ē ə rā´ shən) *n.* process of becoming worse

develop (di vel´ əp) *v.* 1. build; expand; 2. make actual

development (di vel´ əp mənt) *n.* 1. event; 2. growth

devoid (di void´) *adj.* completely without

dew (doo) *n.* tiny drops of moisture that condense on cooled objects at night

diplomatic (dip´ lə mat´ ik) *adj.* showing skill in dealing with people

discharged (dis chärjd´) *v.* 1. fired; 2. released

discrepancies (di skrep´ ən sēz) *n.* differences; inconsistencies; cases in which stories, explanations, and so on, do not agree

discriminate (di skrim´ i nāt´) *v.* 1. see the difference between; tell apart; 2. treat unfairly based on particular differences

discrimination (di skrim´ i nā´ shən) *n.* 1. judgment; 2. unfair treatment based on particular differences

disdainfully (dis dān´ fə lē) *adv.* scornfully

disheveled (di shev´ əld) *adj.* rumpled and untidy

disinherit (dis´ in her´ it) *v.* deprive (a person or people) of a right or privilege

dispel (di spel´) *v.* cause (something) to go away

disruption (dis rup´ shən) *n.* disturbance; interruption of the orderly course of events

distinctive (di stiŋk´ tiv) *adj.* unique

distinguish (di stiŋ´ gwish) *v.* 1. see the difference between; tell apart; 2. mark as different; set apart

diverged (dī vurjd´) *v.* branched off

diverts (dī vurts´) *v.* distracts; amuses

divide (də vīd´) *v.* separate

document (däk´ yoo mənt) *n.* printed record

drought (drout) *n.* lack of rain; long period of dry weather

E

elements (el´ ə mənts) *n.* characteristics; essential features; basic parts

eloquent (el´ ə kwənt) *adj.* vividly expressive

embedded (im bed´ əd) *v.* fixed in some surrounding material

emigrated (em´ i grāt´ əd) *v.* left one place to settle in another

emphasize (em´ fə sīz´) *v.* stress; give one idea more importance than others

enchantment (en chant´ mənt) *n.* great delight or pleasure

endure (en door´) *v.* 1. continue; remain; 2. survive difficulties; 3. hold up under

engaged (en gājd´) *adj.* active; personally involved

enhance (en hans´) *v.* improve the quality of

erosion (ē rō´ zhən) *n.* wearing away by action of wind or water

evacuees (ē vak´ yoo ēz´) *n.* people who are removed from a dangerous area

evading (ē vād´ iŋ) *v.* avoiding or escaping from through the use of deceit or cleverness

evaluation (ē val´ yoo ā´ shən) *n.* judgment about something

evidence (ev´ ə dəns) *n.* support; proof

exaggerate (eg zaj´ ər āt´) *v.* speak of something as being greater or more important than it is

exiles (ek´ sīlz´) *n.* people who are forced to live in another country

experience (ek spir´ ē əns) 1. *n.* participation in or passage through an event; 2. *v.* undergo; feel

expert (eks´ pərt) *adj.* of or from someone who is very well-informed about a topic

explanation (eks´ plə nā´ shən) *n.* act or process of making something clear or easy to understand

exploit (ek sploit´) *v.* take advantage of; make profit from the labor of (a person) without giving a just compensation

exploration (eks´ plə rā´ shən) *n.* act or instance of exploring

express (ek spres´) *v.* 1. put into words; 2. represent or show

exquisite (ek skwiz´ it) *adj.* very beautiful

exultantly (eg zult´ 'nt lē) *adv.* triumphantly

exulting (eg zult´ iŋ) *v.* rejoicing

F

factor (fak´ tər) *n.* element that contributes to a condition or situation

fatalist (fāt´ 'l ist) *n.* one who believes that all events are determined by fate and so must be accepted

feedback (fēd´ bak´) *n.* response that helps one strengthen or correct an effort

feuding (fyōōd´ iŋ) *v.* quarreling; fighting, especially if extended over a long period

flatterer (flat´ ər ər) *n.* one who praises insincerely to win approval

forbade (fər bād´) *v.* commanded not to do something; prohibited

forlorn (fôr lôrn´) *adj.* sad and lonely

fugitives (fyōō´ ji tivz´) *n.* people fleeing from danger

G

garbled (gär´ bəld) *adj.* confused; mixed up

generalization (jen´ ər ə li zā´ shən) *n.* broad idea applied to many specific things

genocides (jen´ ə sīdz) *n.* deliberate destructions of groups of people defined by race, culture, religion, or national identity

gesture (jes´ chər) *n.* something said or done to express a feeling

global (glō´ bəl) *adj.* worldwide

granted (grant´ əd) *v.* officially given

grateful (grāt´ fəl) *adj.* thankful

guileless (gīl´ lis) *adj.* not trying to hide anything or trick people; innocent

H

harmonious (här mō´ nē əs) *adj.* combined in a pleasing arrangement

haughty (hôt´ ē) *adj.* scornfully superior

hostile (häs´ təl) *adj.* 1. warlike; 2. unfriendly; 3. antagonistic

humiliating (hyōō mil´ ē āt´ iŋ) *adj.* embarrassing

I

identify (ī den´ tə fī´) *v.* 1. recognize as being; 2. call out as being the thing specified

illogical (i läj´ i kəl) *adj.* using or caused by faulty reasoning

imitate (im´ i tāt´) *v.* copy; follow the example of

immensely (i mens´ lē) *adv.* greatly

immortality (im´ ôr tal´ i tē) *n.* endless life

imperious (im pir´ ē əs) *adj.* overbearing; proud and demanding

impertinently (im purt´ 'n ənt lē) *adv.* disrespectfully

implements (im´ plə mənts) *n.* devices used or needed in a given activity; tools; instruments

imply (im plī´) *v.* 1. hint at; 2. necessarily include or involve

imprint (im print´) *v.* make a lasting mark in or on

inarticulate (in´ är tik´ yōō lit) *adj.* unable to express oneself

incensed (in senst´) *adj.* extremely angry

incentive (in sent´ iv) *n.* something that makes a person take action

incorporate (in kôr´ pə rāt´) *v.* include; add in

individuality (in´ də vij´ ōō al´ ə tē) *n.* characteristics that set a person or thing apart from others

ineffectually (in´ e fek´ chōō ə lē) *adv.* without producing the desired results

inequality (in´ ē kwôl´ ə tē) *n.* state of being unequal in some way, such as in size or social position

inevitable (in ev´ it ə bəl) *adj.* certain to happen

inexplicable (in´ ek splik´ ə bəl) *adj.* impossible to explain

infamy (in´ fə mē) *n.* very bad reputation; disgrace; dishonor

inferior (in fir´ ē ər) *adj.* lower in status or rank

influence (in´ flōō əns) *v.* affect others' views, habits, plans, and so on

inform (in fôrm´) *v.* tell; give information or knowledge

ingratitude (in grat´ i tōōd´) *n.* lack of thankfulness or appreciation

initial (i nish´ əl) *adj.* first

injury (in´ jə rē) *n.* harm or damage to a person

insecurity (in´ si kyōōr´ ə tē) *n.* 1. lack of confidence; self-doubt; 2. unsafe or unstable state

insight (in´ sīt´) *n.* understanding of something's nature

insufferable (in suf´ ə rə bəl) *adj.* unbearable

intellectual (in´ tə lek´ chōō əl) *adj.* relating to the ability to think and understand ideas and information

intensify (in ten´ sə fī´) *v.* strengthen; make more vivid

interact (in´ tər akt´) *v.* 1. change or affect one another; 2. communicate (with)

interactions (in´ tər ak´ shənz) *n.* actions or communications between two or more people or things

intolerant (in täl´ ər ənt) *adj.* not able or willing to accept other people's beliefs and opinions

introspective (in´ trō spek´ tiv) *adj.* thoughtful; inward-looking

intuition (in´ tōō ish´ ən) *n.* ability to sense immediately, without reasoning

invariably (in ver´ ē ə blē) *adv.* all the time; always

investigate (in ves´ tə gāt´) *v.* 1. conduct research into; 2. learn more about

invoke (in vōk´) *v.* 1. call upon for inspiration or support; 2. call forth

irritate (ir´ i tāt´) *v.* anger or annoy

J

jostling (jäs´ əl iŋ) *n.* act of knocking into, often on purpose

judge (juj) *v.* form an opinion about; evaluate

judicious (jōō dish´ əs) *adj.* showing sound judgment; wise

K

kindled (kind´ əld) *v.* built or lit a fire

L

lagged (lagd) *v.* fell behind

lax (laks) *adj.* not strict or exact

legacy (leg´ ə sē) n. something physical or spiritual handed down from an ancestor

liable (lī´ ə bəl) adj. likely

liberators (lib´ ər āt´ ərz) n. persons who set free, especially, those who free a country from an enemy or tyranny

M

maintain (mān tān´) v. keep something going; continue something

malicious (mə lish´ əs) adj. mean; spiteful

meager (mē´ gər) adj. small in amount

meaningful (mē´ niŋ fəl) adj. having significance or purpose

media (mē´ dē ə) n. means of communication, such as newspapers and television, that provide news, entertainment, and so on

methods (meth´ ədz) n. ways of doing something

mislead (mis lēd´) v. cause to form a wrong idea; deceive

misunderstood (mis´ un dər stood´) 1. adj. not appreciated or understood; 2. v. misinterpreted; failed to understand

mockery (mäk´ ər ē) n. false, insulting action or statement

monumental (män´ yoo ment´ 'l) adj. 1. of lasting value or importance, like a monument; 2. massive

morbid (môr´ bid) adj. caused by an unhealthy tendency to focus on the grisly, gruesome, or horrible

motive (mōt´ iv) n. reason for or cause of an action

mutineers (myoot´ 'n irz´) n. rebels

mutinous (myoot´ ən əs) adj. rebellious

N

naïveté (nä ēv tā´) n. state of being simple or childlike

negotiate (ni gō´ shē āt´) v. bargain or deal with another party to reach a settlement

negotiation (ni gō´ shē ā´ shən) n. bargaining; discussion; deal-making

O

objective (əb jek´ tiv) adj. unbiased; from a neutral standpoint

observation (äb´ zər vā´ shən) n. idea or remark based on what one has seen or noticed

omens (ō´ mənz) n. signs of good or bad events that may take place in the future

opinion (ə pin´ yən) n. 1. belief; 2. evaluation

oppose (ə pōz´) v. go against; stand in the way of

opposing (ə pōz´ iŋ) adj. going against one another; fighting or struggling with one another

oppressed (ə prest´) v. kept down by unjust power

orderlies (ôr´ dər lēz) n. hospital attendants

outdated (out dāt´ id) adj. no longer made, used, or in fashion

overall (ō´ vər ôl´) adj. total

overcome (ō´ vər kum´) v. conquer or master, as an opponent, an obstacle, or a setback

P

pageant (paj´ ənt) n. elaborate play

paradoxes (par´ ə däks´ əz) n. situations that seem to have contradictory qualities

passively (pas´ iv lē) adv. without resistance

pattern (pat´ ərn) n. 1. way of doing, acting, and so on that is regular and predictable; 2. repeated design; 3. model

perceive (pər sēv´) v. see; view

percentage (pər sent´ ij) n. part or amount out of every one hundred

perception (pər sep´ shən) n. awareness of something; specifically, awareness of something through the senses

peril (per´ əl) n. danger

perilous (per´ ə ləs) adj. involving peril or risk; dangerous

periscope (per´ ə skōp´) n. tube that rises from a submarine to allow sailors to see objects above the water's surface

perish (per´ ish) v. die; be destroyed or wiped out

persistent (pər sist´ ənt) adj. continuing to happen, especially for longer than is usual or desirable

pervading (pər vād´ iŋ) adj. spreading throughout

pestering (pes´ tər iŋ) n. constant bothering

pollen (päl´ ən) n. powdery grains on seed plants that aid in reproduction

ponderous (pän´ dər əs) adj. very heavy

precise (prē sīs´) adj. 1. exact; 2. definite; clear in meaning

predisposed (prē dis pōzd´) adj. inclined

predominantly (prē däm´ ə nənt lē) adv. mainly

preliminary (prē lim´ ə ner´ ē) adj. introductory; preparatory

presentable (prē zent´ ə bəl) adj. neat enough to be seen by others

primary sources (prī´ mer´ ē sôrs´ iz) n. firsthand accounts, photographs, and other documents of the time

procession (prō sesh´ ən) n. group moving forward, as in a parade

prodigy (präd´ ə jē) n. unusually talented person

promising (präm´ is iŋ) adj. showing potential for future success or excellence

promote (prə mōt´) v. support the growth of (a person or thing)

protruded (prō trood´ əd) v. stuck out

pursuit (pər soot´) n. act of chasing in order to catch (something)

Q

quality (kwäl´ ə tē) n. 1. characteristic; 2. degree of excellence

quantity (kwänt´ ə tē) n. total amount or number

R

radiation (rā´ dē ā´ shən) *n.* rays of energy

radical (rad´ i kəl) *adj.* favoring change in the social structure

ravaged (rav´ ijd) *v.* devastated

reaction (rē ak´ shən) *n.* response to an influence, an action, or a statement

rebellion (ri bel´ yən) *n.* open resistance to authority

recede (ri sēd´) *v.* 1. slope backward; 2. become more distant

recreation (rek´ rē ā´ shən) *n.* activity for the purpose of play or amusement

refugee (ref´ yōō jē´) *n.* person who flees from home or country to seek safety elsewhere

refute (ri fyōōt´) *v.* give evidence to prove a statement false

region (rē´ jən) *n.* geographic area

reinforce (rē´ in fôrs´) *v.* strengthen

relevant (rel´ ə vənt) *adj.* connected to the topic being discussed; related

remote (ri mōt´) *adj.* aloof; cold; distant

represent (rep´ ri zent´) *v.* 1. stand for; 2. speak for

reputation (rep´ yōō tā´ shən) *n.* opinion that others have of a person, whether good or bad

resent (ri zent´) *v.* feel angry out of a sense of unfairness

resolute (rez´ ə lōōt) *adj.* showing a firm purpose

resolved (ri zälvd´) *v.* decided

resources (rē´ sôrs´ iz) *n.* 1. means of accomplishing something; 2. available money or wealth

respond (ri spänd´) *v.* react

response (ri späns´) *n.* answer

result (ri zult´) *n.* end product

reveal (ri vēl´) *v.* uncover; expose; show

revolutionary (rev´ ə lōō´ shə ner´ ē) *adj.* favoring or bringing about sweeping change

rickety (rik´ it ē) *adj.* likely to break or fall because weak

roam (rōm) *v.* go aimlessly; wander

role (rōl) *n.* function or part performed

rut (rut) *n.* groove in the ground

S

sacred (sā´ krəd) *adj.* 1. considered holy; 2. related to religious ceremonies

satisfactory (sat´ is fak´ tə rē) *adj.* adequate; sufficient to meet a requirement

scampering (skam´ pər iŋ) *v.* running quickly

self-confident (self´ kän´ fə dənt) *adj.* certain of one's ability

sensory (sen´ sər ē) *adj.* having to do with the senses

separate 1. (sep´ ə rāt´) *v.* set apart; 2. (sep´ ə rit´) *adj.* not joined or connected

shackles (shak´ əlz) *n.* metal bonds used to restrain prisoners

shanties (shan´ tēz) *n.* roughly built cabins or shacks

shriveled (shriv´ əld) *v.* dried up; shrank and wrinkled

significance (sig nif´ ə kəns) *n.* 1. importance; 2. meaning

singularity (siŋ´ gyə ler´ ə tē) *n.* unique or unusual quality

skeptically (skep´ ti klē) *adv.* with doubt and distrust

software (soft´ wer´) *n.* programs for a computer or computer system

solution (sə lōō´ shən) *n.* 1. way to fix a problem; 2. act of solving a problem or answering a question

somber (säm´ bər) *adj.* dark; gloomy

sources (sôrs´ iz) *n.* 1. origins; 2. people or things, such as books or Web sites, that provide facts, information, evidence, and so on

sparse (spärs) *adj.* thinly spread and small in amount

spindly (spind´ lē) *adj.* long and thin

spineless (spīn´ lis) *adj.* lacking in courage

spite (spīt) *n.* nastiness

stalemate (stāl´ māt´) *n.* standoff; outcome of a conflict when neither side is able to win

statistics (stə tis´ tiks) *n.* numerical facts; numerical data

stealthily (stel´ thə lē) *adv.* in a secret or sly way

straddling (strad´ 'l iŋ) *v.* standing or sitting with a leg on either side of something

strife (strīf) *n.* conflict

subdued (səb dōōd´) *adj.* beaten; brought under control

succumbed (sə kumd´) *v.* gave way; yielded; submitted

suffering (suf´ ər iŋ) 1. *n.* experience of pain or injury; 2. *v.* undergoing an experience, especially a negative one

superficial (sōō´ pər fish´ əl) *adj.* of the surface; without depth; without meaning

support (sə pôrt´) 1. *n.* evidence; 2. *v.* prove

suppressed (sə prest´) *v.* kept back (a cough, laugh, and so on); restrained

symbolize (sim´ bə līz´) *v.* stand for; take the place of and signify an idea

sympathy (sim´ pə thē) *n.* ability to appreciate another person's feelings; compassion; pity

T

tactile (tak´ təl) *adj.* related to the sense of touch

technique (tek nēk´) *n.* particular way of doing something

tenacious (tə nā´ shəs) *adj.* holding on firmly; stubborn

tension (ten´ shən) *n.* nervous, worried, or excited state that makes relaxation impossible

testimonies (tes´ tə mō´ nēz) *n.* statements or declarations made by witnesses

thermal (thur´ məl) *adj.* having to do with heat or temperature

timidly (tim´ id lē) *adv.* in a shy or fearful manner

tolerance (täl´ ər əns) *n.* 1. freedom from prejudice; 2. acceptance of the views of others

tongue (tuŋ) *n.* language

tradition (trə dish´ ən) *n.* custom

transfer (trans´ fər) *n.* sending or taking something or someone from one place to another

transfigured (trans fig´ yərd) *adj.* changed; transformed in a glorious way

trend (trend) *n.* general direction or tendency of events

trepidation (trep´ ə dā´ shən) *n.* fear; anxiety; dread

trivial (triv´ ē əl) *adj.* of little importance

tumultuous (too mul´ choo əs) *adj.* wild; chaotic

U

unanimous (yoo nan´ ə məs) *adj.* in complete agreement

unify (yoo´ nə fī´) *v.* bring together

unseemly (un sēm´ lē) *adj.* inappropriate

urban (ur´ bən) *adj.* related to the city or city life

V

valid (val´ id) *adj.* convincing; true; backed by evidence and sound reasoning

validity (və lid´ ə tē) *n.* quality of being sound and well-grounded in evidence

valuable (val´ yə bəl) *adj.* having worth or importance

vex (veks) *v.* annoy; distress

victorious (vik tôr´ ē əs) *adj.* having won; triumphant

viewpoint (vyoo´ point´) *n.* position regarding an idea or a statement

vigorously (vig´ ər əs lē) *adv.* in an energetic manner

violence (vī´ ə ləns) *n.* physical force causing harm

vulnerable (vul´ nər ə bəl) *adj.* open to attack or injury

W

winced (winst) *v.* shrank or drew back slightly, usually with a grimace, as in pain

wired (wīrd) *adj.* having circuitry designed for performing particular tasks

Y

yearning (yur´ niŋ) *v.* feeling longing for; painfully wanting (something)

Spanish Glossary

El vocabulario académico aparece en **azul.**

A

abruptness / brusquedad *s.* cualidad de tener un comportamiento o forma de hablar brusca o seca

accomplishments / logros *s.* lo que se hace o completa con éxito

account / cuenta *s.* factura por servicios prestados

accumulate / acumular *v.* coleccionar; juntar

accurate / exacto *adj.* 1. cuidadoso; 2. preciso

adjust / ajustar *v.* cambiar para adecuar o adaptarlo

admirably / admirablemente *adv.* de tal manera que se merece ser elogiado

advocate / defensor *s.* que brinda apoyo

affluence / opulencia *s.* riqueza; abundancia

algorithm / algoritmo *s.* conjunto de instrucciones dadas a un computador para que resuelva un problema específico

alienate / enajenar *v.* alejarse de una relación de amistad

anguish / angustia *s.* intranquilidad, ansiedad

annotated / comentado *adj.* que incluye notas explicativas

anonymously / anónimamente *adv.* que no indica el nombre del autor o creador

anticipate / esperar *v.* 1. tener expectativa sobre algo; 2. estar deseando; 3. indicar por adelantado; presagiar

apprehension / aprensión *s.* sentimiento de temor de lo que ocurrirá

argument / argumento *s.* razones que se dan para apoyar algo

argument / discusión *s.* un desacuerdo verbal

aromas / aromas *s.* olores

arrogant / arrogante *adj.* persona engreída e indiferente a otros

artificial intelligence / inteligencia artificial *s.* la capacidad que tienen los computadores para simular el proceso de pensamiento de los seres humanos

aspects / aspectos *s.* 1. formas en las cuales se ve una idea o un problema; 2. elementos

aspirations / aspiraciones *s.* deseos fuertes o ambiciones

assail / asediar *v.* atacar a alguien con argumentos, preguntas, dudas, etc.

assumption / suposición *s.* declaración o idea que se da por verdadera sin tener pruebas

audacity / audacia *s.* gran valor; osadía

audible / audible *adj.* que se puede oír

authentic / auténtico *adj.* genuino; real

authorized / autorizó *v.* que aprobó oficialmente

aversion / aversión *s.* disgusto intenso

awed / sobrecoger *v.* asombrar

B

barren / baldío *adj.* vacío; yermo

beckoning / convocar *v.* llamando

beneficial / beneficioso *adj.* útil

benefit / beneficio *s.* ventaja o resultado positivo

benefit / beneficiar *v.* recibir una ventaja o algo de provecho

bewildered / desconcertado *adj.* completamente confundido

blackmail / chantaje *s.* amenaza de divulgar secretos de una persona, a cambio de dinero

bleak / inhóspito *adj.* desapacible y desértico; frío

bravery / valentía *s.* coraje; cualidad de enfrentar y manejar el peligro en lugar de huir

brutal / brutal *adj.* 1. duro; 2. salvaje; cruel e insensible

buoyed / animado *v.* alentado; impulsado

C

callous / insensible *adj.* que no tiene piedad; que no tiene sentimientos

capable / capaz *adj.* tener o mostrar una habilidad en particular

capricious / caprichoso *adj.* que tiende a cambiar abruptamente, sin razón aparente

carelessness / descuido *s.* falta de responsabilidad

cataclysm / cataclismo *s.* suceso súbito y violento que causa gran cambio

categories / categorías *s.* clases; tipos bajo los que se pueden clasificar cosas, cualidades, etc.

cause-and-effect / causa y efecto *adj.* que muestra la relación entre las razones (causas) y los resultados (efectos)

challenge / desafiar *v.* poner en duda

chaos / caos *s.* confusión extrema o desorden

cite / citar *v.* 1. mencionar algo como evidencia o ejemplo; 2. referirse a

citing / citando *v.* mencionando algo como evidencia o ejemplo; refiriéndose a

civil / civil *adj.* en relación a ciudadanos o al gobierno

class / clase *s.* agrupación de personas u objetos que tienen características en común

common / común *adj.* 1. ordinario; lo esperado; 2. compartido

commotion / conmoción *s.* movimiento ruidoso y desordenado

community / comunidad *s.* grupo específico dentro de una población de mayor tamaño, de personas u otros seres vivientes

compelled / obligó *v.* forzó

compensate / compensar *v.* pagar

complacent / complaciente *adj.* satisfecho, en especial de sí mismo, o creído

compromise / compromiso *s.* solución de las diferencias en la cual ambas partes deben renunciar a algo

compromise / ceder *v.* ponerse de acuerdo; aceptar

compulsory / obligatorio *adj.* requerido

conceivable / concebible *adj.* que se puede imaginar

condemn / condenar *v.* imponer una pena; declarar culpable

condition / condición *s.* estado en que se halla algo o alguien

confirmation / confirmación *s.* algo que confirma o prueba

confronted / enfrentó *v.* se puso frente a frente

connection / conexión *s.* vínculo; atadura; relación

conquistadors / conquistadores *s.* españoles que conquistaron partes de América en el siglo dieciséis

consoling / consolador *adj.* confortador

conspicuous / conspicuo *adj.* notable

constructive / constructivo *adj.* que conduce al progreso

contact / contacto *s.* relación entre dos cosas; comunicación

contemplation / contemplación *s.* acto de pensar en algo o prestarle atención a algo

contempt / desprecio *s.* desdén; irrespeto

contention / disputa *s.* discusión en que uno defiende algo que considera cierto o válido

contraction / contracción *s.* acto de hacerse más pequeño

contrast / contraste *s.* diferencia (entre las cosas que se comparan)

contrasting / contrastando *adj.* diferenciando

contribute / contribuir *v.* aportar a un esfuerzo común

convey / transmitir *v.* comunicar un mensaje

conviction / convicción *s.* creencia fuertemente arraigada; certeza

cordially / cordialmente *adv.* calurosamente

courage / coraje *s.* cualidad de ser temerario; valentía

credible / creíble *adj.* que se puede creer; confiable

criteria / criterio *s.* estándares o pruebas que se usan para juzgar algo

cultural / cultural *adj.* que es pertinente al conjunto de modos de vida y costumbres de un grupo o una comunidad

cunningly / astutamente *adv.* con facilidad para engañar; con ingenio

curiosity / curiosidad *s.* deseo de obtener información

cyclone / ciclón *s.* tormenta de viento rotativa y violenta; tornado

D

dabbing / aplicando con toques suaves *v.* dar golpes ligeros con algo suave

debates / debatir *v.* 1. considerar las razones a favor y en contra; 2. discutir acerca de un punto

deceive / engañar *v.* hacer a alguien creer lo que no es cierto; malinformar

decision / decisión *s.* opción; la determinación que tiene una persona para realizar cierta acción

defiance / desafío *s.* oposición a obedecer la autoridad

deficiency / deficiencia *s.* carencia, o falta, de algo necesario

degrading / denigrante *adj.* insultante; deshonroso; ofensivo

deliberating / deliberar *v.* pensar cuidadosamente

delirious / delirante *adj.* 1. en estado de excitación mental extrema; 2. inquieto, confundido, alucinando o viendo cosas imaginarias

demographic / demográfico *adj.* en relación a las características de un grupo de personas como por ejemplo: la edad, el sexo, educación etc.

denigrate / denigrar *v.* decir cosas poco halagadoras acerca de alguien o algo

derision / escarnio *s.* 1. desprecio; 2. comentarios burlones para reírse o mofarse de alguien o algo

derived / derivado *v.* generado u obtenido de una fuente

descendants / descendientes *s.* hijos, nietos y las generaciones que siguen a una persona

desolate / desolado *adj.* triste; solitario

deterioration / deterioro *s.* proceso por el que algo se daña o empeora

develop / desarrollar *v.* 1. construir; expandir; 2. realizar

development / acontecimiento *s.* suceso

development / crecimiento *s.* evolución

devoid / desprovisto *adj.* que carece completamente

dew / rocío *s.* pequeñas gotas que se forman con el frío de la noche a raíz del vapor en el ambiente

diplomatic / diplomático *adj.* que muestra elegancia y destreza al relacionarse con otras personas

discharged / liberar *v.* eximir a alguien de una obligación; poner en libertad

discrepancies / discrepancias *s.* diferencias; inconsistencias; casos en los cuales las historias, explicaciones y demás no concuerdan

discriminate / discriminar *v.* 1. ver la diferencia entre dos cosas; distinguir; 2. tratar injustamente debido a ciertas diferencias

discrimination / discriminación *s.* 1. opinión; 2. trato injusto debido a ciertas diferencias

disdainfully / desdeñoso *adv.* con indiferencia

disheveled / desaliñado *adj.* desgreñado y desordenado

disinherit / desheredar *v.* privar a las personas de sus derechos como ciudadanos

dispel / disipar *v.* hacer que algo desaparezca

disruption / trastorno *s.* disturbio; interrupción del curso normal de algo

distinctive / distintivo *adj.* único

distinguish / distinguir *v.* 1. ver la diferencia entre dos cosas; diferenciar; 2. marcar como distinto; especificar

diverged / divergir *v.* separarse: tener diferencias

diverts / desvía *v.* distrae; entretiene

divide / dividir *v.* separar

document / documento *s.* registro escrito

drought / sequía *s.* falta de lluvia; periodos largos de clima seco

E

elements / elementos *s.* características; aspectos esenciales; partes básicas

eloquent / elocuente *adj.* que se expresa de manera vívida

embedded / incrustado *v.* adherido a algún material que lo rodea

emigrated / emigró *v.* dejó un sitio para establecerse en otro

emphasize / enfatizar *v.* subrayar; darle mayor importancia a una idea que a otra

enchantment / encanto *s.* sentimiento de fascinación

endure / soportar *v.* 1. continuar; permanecer; 2. sobrevivir ante las dificultades; 3. resistir

engaged / involucrado *adj.* activo; que participa en algo

enhance / mejorar *v.* que pasa a un mejor estado o a una mejor calidad

erosion / erosión *s.* desgaste del terreno a causa del viento o del agua

evacuees / evacuados *s.* personas que se marchan de una zona peligrosa

evading / evadiendo *v.* evitar o escapar usando la audacia y astucia

evaluation / evaluación *s.* juicio acerca de algo

evidence / evidencia *s.* testimonio; pruebas

exaggerate / exagerar *v.* hablar acerca de algo como si fuera más grande o más importante de lo que es

exiles / exiliados *s.* personas que se ven obligadas a vivir en otro país

experience / experiencia *s.* participación o presencia en un suceso

experience / experimentar *v.* padecer; sentir

expert / experto *adj.* alguien que se encuentra bien informado acerca de un tema

explanation / explicación *s.* acto o proceso de aclarar algo o hacerlo más fácil de entender

exploit / explotar *v.* aprovecharse de; obtener ganancias sobre el trabajo de alguien sin darle remuneración

exploration / exploración *s.* acto de explorar

express / expresar *v.* 1. poner en palabras; 2. representar o mostrar

exquisite / exquisito *adj.* muy bello; adorable y delicado

exultantly / de forma exultante *adv.* con gran alegría y satisfacción

exulting / exultar *v.* mostrar gran alegría

F

factor / factor *s.* elemento que contribuye a una condición o situación

fatalist / fatalista *s.* el que cree que todo lo que sucede lo determina el destino

feedback / retroalimentación *s.* una respuesta que ayuda a reforzar o corregir un esfuerzo

feuding / riñendo *v.* disputando; peleando, en especial cuando se extiende por un largo periodo de tiempo

flatterer / adulador *s.* el que prodiga alabanzas interesadas

forbade / prohibió *v.* se le ordenó que no hiciera algo; restringió

forlorn / desolado *adj.* triste y solitario

fugitives / fugitivos *s.* personas que huyen o se esconden

G

garbled / embrollado *adj.* enredado; revuelto

generalization / generalización *s.* idea amplia que se aplica para muchas cosas específicas

genocides / genocidios *s.* exterminación deliberada de grupos de personas definidas por raza, cultura, religión o identidad nacional

gesture / gesto *s.* algo dicho o hecho para expresar un sentimiento

global / global *adj.* mundial

granted / otorgado *v.* entregado oficialmente

grateful / agradecido *adj.* que siente gratitud

guileless / sincero *adj.* sin intención de ocultar algo o engañar a alguien; inocente

H

harmonious / armonioso *adj.* que combina de manera agradable

haughty / arrogante *adj.* altanero

hostile / hostil *adj.* 1. en son de guerra; 2. no amigable; 3. antagónico

humiliating / humillante *adj.* embarazoso

I

identify / identificar *v.* 1. reconocer como tal; 2. señalar como la cosa de la cual se habla

illogical / ilógico *adj.* causado o usado por un razonamiento errado

imitate / imitar *v.* copiar; seguir el ejemplo de algo

immensely / inmensamente *adv.* de gran manera; en gran medida

immortality / inmortalidad *s.* vida eterna

imperious / arrogante *adj.* despótico; orgulloso y exigente

impertinently / de manera impertinente *adv.* con irrespeto

implements / implementos *s.* dispositivos utilizados o necesarios para una determinada actividad; herramientas; instrumentos

imply / implicar *v.* 1. insinuar algo; 2. incluir o involucrar necesariamente

imprint / impresionar *v.* dejar una huella que perdura en algo

inarticulate / inarticulado *adj.* que se expresa con dificultad

incensed / encolerizado *adj.* extremadamente enojado

incentive / incentivo *s.* algo que hace que una persona actúe

incorporate / incorporar *v.* incluir; agregar a

individuality / individualidad *s.* cualidad por la que una persona o cosa se da a conocer o se diferencia de otra

ineffectually / ineficazmente *adv.* sin producir el resultado deseado

inequality / desigualdad *s.* estado de ser desigual en alguna manera, puede ser en tamaño o en posición social

inevitable / inevitable *adj.* que pasará con seguridad

inexplicable / inexplicable *adj.* que no se puede explicar o describir

infamy / infamia *s.* mala fama; desgracia; deshonra

inferior / inferior *adj.* de calidad, nivel o rango más bajos

influence / influenciar *v.* afectar a las demás personas en cuanto a sus puntos de vista, hábitos, planes, etc.

inform / informar *v.* decir; dar información o conocimiento de algo

ingratitude / ingratitud *s.* falta de apreciación

initial / inicial *adj.* primero

injury / lesión *s.* daño o detrimento físico

insecurity / inseguridad *s.* 1. falta de confianza; dudar de uno mismo; 2. estado de sentirse inestable o en peligro

insight / percepción *s.* comprensión de la naturaleza de algo

insufferable / insufrible *adj.* insoportable

intellectual / intelectual *adj.* relacionado con la habilidad de pensar y comprender ideas e información

intensify / intensificar *v.* fortalecer; hacer más vívido

interact / interactuar *v.* 1. cambiar o afectar el uno al otro; 2. comunicarse (con)

interactions / interacciones *s.* acciones o comunicaciones entre dos o más personas o cosas

intolerant / intolerante *adj.* que no es capaz o no está dispuesto a aceptar las opiniones o creencias de los demás

introspective / introspectivo *adj.* que observa internamente; atento

intuition / intuición *s.* habilidad para sentir de inmediato, sin razonamiento

invariably / invariablemente *adv.* constante

investigate / investigar *v.* 1. averiguar sobre un tema; 2. aprender más acerca de algo

invoke / invocar *v.* 1. hacer un llamado a alguien o algo para que sirva como inspiración o apoyo; 2. convocar

irritate / irritar *v.* molestar; fastidiar

J

jostling / empujón *s.* golpe, generalmente intencional

judge / juzgar *v.* formarse una opinión acerca de; evaluar

judicious / sensato *adj.* que demuestra prudencia y honestidad

K

kindled / encender *v.* prender

L

lagged / demorarse *v.* que se retrasa

lax / laxo *adj.* poco estricto o exacto, relajado

legacy / herencia *s.* algo físico o espiritual que se transmite de un ancestro

liable / probable *s.* factible, que puede ocurrir

liberators / libertadores *s.* personas que liberan, en especial aquellos que liberan un país de algún enemigo o tirano

M

maintain / mantener *v.* hacer que algo siga; continuar algo

malicious / malicioso *adj.* de malas intenciones

meager / exiguo *adj.* pequeña cantidad

meaningful / significante *adj.* que tiene importancia o propósito

media / medios de comunicación *s.* medios tales como periódicos y televisión que brindan noticias, entretenimiento, etc.

methods / métodos *s.* formas de hacer algo

mislead / despistar *v.* inducir a creer lo que no es por medio de ideas fingidas; engañar

misunderstood / 1. incomprendido *adj.* que no es apreciado o entendido **2. malinterpretó** *v.* no lo entendió

mockery / burla *s.* farsa; acción o declaración ofensiva o falsa

monumental / monumental *adj.* 1. de una importancia y valor duraderos, como por ejemplo, un monumento; 2. masivo

morbid / mórbido *adj.* causado por una tendencia poco saludable de enfocarse en lo macabro, repelente y horrible

motive / motivo *s.* razón o causa de algún acto

mutineers / amotinadores *s.* rebeldes

mutinous / amotinado *adj.* rebelde

N

naïveté / ingenuidad *s.* sencillez o carácter infantil

negotiate / negociar *v.* tratar con la otra parte para alcanzar un acuerdo

negotiation / negociación *s.* regateo; discusión; acuerdo

O

objective / objetivo *adj.* imparcial; desde un punto de vista neutral

observation / observación *s.* idea o comentario sobre lo que uno ha visto o notado

omens / presagios *s.* señales de sucesos malos o buenos que podrían ocurrir en el futuro

opinion / opinión *s.* 1. creencia; 2. evaluación

oppose / oponer *v.* ir en contra; ser un obstáculo

opposing / opuesto *adj.* que va en contra de algo o alguien; que lucha el uno contra el otro

oppressed / oprimido *v.* dominado por un poder injusto

orderlies / auxiliares *s.* ayudantes de un hospital

outdated / anticuado *adj.* que ya no se fabrica, se usa o está de moda

overall / en total *adj.* en general

overcome / superar *v.* conquistar o vencer a un oponente, un obstáculo o contratiempo

P

pageant / desfile *s.* presentación o espectáculo elaborado

paradoxes / paradojas *s.* situaciones que parecen tener cualidades que se contradicen

passively / pasivamente *adv.* sin resistencia

pattern / patrón *s.* 1. forma de actuar o de hacer algo de manera predecible; 2. diseño repetido; 3. modelo

perceive / percibir *v.* ver; comprender

percentage / porcentaje *s.* parte o cantidad que corresponde proporcionalmente a una parte de cien

perception / percepción *s.* estar consciente de algo; estar consciente de

algo específicamente a través de los sentidos

peril / riesgo *s.* peligro

perilous / riesgoso *adj.* que involucra peligro o riesgo; arriesgado

periscope / periscopio *s.* tubo que sale de un submarino y que permite que los marineros vean los objetos sobre la superficie del agua

perish / perecer *v.* morir; ser destruido o aniquilado

persistent / persistente *adj.* que continúa, especialmente por más tiempo de lo usual o de lo debido

pervading / invasor *adj.* que se extiende por todas partes

pestering / molestia *s.* fastidio constante

pollen / polen *s.* granos en forma de polvo en plantas con semilla y que ayudan a la reproducción

ponderous / ponderoso *adj.* muy pesado

precise / preciso *adj.* 1. exacto; 2. definitivo; claro en significado

predisposed / predispuesto *adj.* de cierta tendencia

predominantly / predominantemente *adv.* principalmente

preliminary / preliminar *adj.* introductorio; preparatorio

presentable / presentable *adj.* lo suficientemente ordenado o limpio para que otros lo vean

primary sources / fuentes primarias *s.* Informes, fotografías y otros documentos de un periodo que dan información de primera mano,

procession / procesión *s.* personas que se movilizan en grupo, como en un desfile

prodigy / prodigio *s.* persona con un talento extraordinario

promising / prometedor *adj.* que muestra potencial de éxito o excelencia en el futuro

promote / promover *v.* apoyar el crecimiento de (una persona o cosa)

protruded / salido *v.* que sobresale

pursuit / persecución *s.* seguimiento con la intención de capturar

Q

quality / calidad *s.* grado de excelencia

quality / cualidad *s.* característica; atributo

quantity / cantidad *s.* número o porción total

R

radiation / radiación *s.* rayos de energía

radical / radical *adj.* que favorece un cambio de la estructura social

ravaged / arruinó *v.* devastó, destruyó

reaction / reacción *s.* respuesta a una influencia, a un acto o a una declaración

rebellion / rebelión *s.* resistencia ante la autoridad

recede / alejarse *v.* 1. inclinarse hacia atrás; 2. incrementar distancia

recreation / recreación *s.* actividad con la finalidad de jugar o divertirse

refugee / refugiado *s.* persona que ha tenido que huir de su país en tiempos difíciles

refute / refutar *v.* dar evidencia que prueba la falsedad de una declaración

region / región *s.* área geográfica

reinforce / reforzar *v.* fortalecer

relevant / relevante *adj.* conectado al tema del que se habla; relacionado

remote / remoto *adj.* apartado; frío; distante

represent / representar *v.* figurar; simbolizar

reputation / reputación *s.* opinión, buena o mala, que otros tienen acerca de una persona

resent / resentir *v.* sentirse bravo o disgustado por una injusticia

resolute / determinado *adj.* que demuestra un propósito fijo

resolved / resolvió *v.* decidió

resources / recursos *s.* 1. medios usados para lograr algo; 2. dinero o riqueza disponibles

respond / responder *v.* reaccionar

response / respuesta *s.* contestación

result / resultado *s.* el producto final

reveal / revelar *v.* descubrir; exponer; mostrar

revolutionary / revolucionario *adj.* que favorece o lleva a un cambio radical

rickety / desvencijado *adj.* con tendencia a romperse o a caerse por debilidad

roam / vagar *v.* andar sin rumbo fijo; merodear

role / papel *s.* parte que se va a representar

rut / surco *s.* hendidura que se hace en la tierra

S

sacred / sagrado *adj.* bendito; relacionado con ceremonias religiosas

satisfactory / satisfactorio *adj.* adecuado; lo suficiente para cumplir con los requisitos

scampering / corretear *v.* correr apresuradamente

self-confident / seguro de sí mismo *adj.* que confía en su propia habilidad

sensory / sensorial *adj.* relativo a los sentidos de la vista, el oído, el gusto, el olfato y el tacto

separate / separar *v.* diferenciar

separate / separado *adj.* que no está unido ni conectado

shackles / grilletes *s.* arco de hierro que se usa para restringir a prisioneros

shanties / barracas *s.* albergue o vivienda rústica construida toscamente

shriveled / marchito *adj.* seco; encogido, arrugado

significance / significado *s.* 1. importancia; 2. sentido

singularity / singularidad *s.* cualidad única o inusual

skeptically / de modo escéptico *adv.* con duda y desconfianza

software / software *s.* programas para computadoras o para sistemas de computadoras

solution / solución *s.* 1. forma de arreglar un problema; 2. acto de resolver un problema o responder a una pregunta

somber / sombrío *adj.* oscuro; lúgubre

sources / fuentes *s.* orígenes

sparse / escaso *adj.* que se distribuye en forma limitada; poca cantidad

spindly / escuálido *adj.* delgado, flaco

spineless / débil *adj.* que carece de coraje

spite / rencor *s.* resentimiento y hostilidad

stalemate / estancamiento *s.* punto muerto; resultado de un conflicto en el cual ninguna de las partes puede ganar

statistics / estadísticas *s.* hechos numéricos; datos numéricos

stealthily / a hurtadillas *adv.* a escondidas o con disimulo

straddling / horcajadas *adv.* con las piernas a cada lado de un objeto

strife / disputa *s.* conflicto

subdued / sometido *adj.* vencido; dominado

succumbed / sucumbió *v.* se entregó; cedió; se sometió

suffering / sufrimiento *s.* sentir dolor o enfermedad

suffering / sufriendo *v.* estar pasando por una experiencia más que todo negativa

superficial / superficial *adj.* de la superficie; sin profundidad; sin significado

support / prueba *s.* evidencia

support / *v.* probar

suppressed / suprimió *v.* reprimió (tos, risa, etc.); contuvo

symbolize / simbolizar *v.* representar; tomar el lugar de y explicar una idea

sympathy / compasión *s.* capacidad para apreciar los sentimientos de otra persona; lástima; piedad

T

tactile / táctil *adj.* relacionado con el sentido del tacto

technique / técnica *s.* forma particular de hacer algo

tenacious / tenaz *adj.* adherido firmemente, con fuerza; terco

tension / tensión *s.* estado nervioso, preocupado o exaltación

testimonies / testimonios *s.* declaraciones hechas por testigos

thermal / térmico *adj.* que tiene que ver con el calor y la temperatura

timidly / tímidamente *adv.* de manera reservada o con inseguridad

tolerance / tolerancia *s.* libertad de prejuicios; aceptación de los puntos de vista de otros

tongue / lengua *s.* idioma

tradition / tradición *s.* costumbre

transfer / transferencia *s.* enviar o llevar a alguien o algo de un lugar a otro

transfigured / transfigurado *adj.* cambiado; transformado en una forma gloriosa

trend / tendencia *s.* dirección general que siguen los sucesos

trepidation / azoramiento *s.* miedo; ansiedad; terror

trivial / trivial *adj.* de poca importancia

tumultuous / tumultuoso *adj.* salvaje; caótico

U

unanimous / unánime *adj.* en acuerdo absoluto

unify / unificar *v.* juntar

unseemly / indecoroso *adj.* inapropiado

urban / urbano *adj.* de la ciudad o relativo a ella

V

valid / válido *adj.* convincente; verdadero; apoyado por evidencia y razonamientos sensatos

validity / validez *s.* cualidad de ser sensato y respaldado con evidencia

valuable / valioso *adj.* que tiene valor o importancia

vex / irritar *v.* molestar; disgustar

victorious / victorioso *adj.* que ha ganado; triunfador

viewpoint / punto de vista *s.* posición ante una idea o aseveración

vigorously / vigorosamente *adv.* de forma enérgica

violcncc / violencia *s.* fuerza física que causa daño

vulnerable / vulnerable *adj.* que está expuesto a ataques o a ser lastimado

W

winced / hizo una mueca de dolor *v.* se encogió o retrocedió ligeramente, usualmente con un gesto como de dolor

wired / equipado con cables *adj.* tener circuitos diseñados para realizar una tarea en particular

Y

yearning / añorar *v.* extrañar; recordar con pena algo o a alguien

Index of Skills

Literary Analysis

Action
rising/falling, 17, 20

Adaptation, comparing to original, 652–653

Alliteration, 363, 364, R1

Allusion, 207, 362, 388, 827, R1

American folk tradition, 770–773
comparing heroic characters, 818–819

Analogy, 207, 362, 415, R1

Anecdote, R1

Antagonist, R1

Appeals, types of persuasive, 236

Argument, lxiv–lxiv, 205, R1
appeals to
authority, 236
emotion, 236
reason, 236
argumentative essay, 236
author's perspective, 310
claims
evaluating, lxiv
evidence and, 740, 894
elements, lxiv
figurative language, 857
main idea and evidence, 334
oratory, 857
rhetorical devices, lxvi, 207, 236
persuasive techniques, lxvi, 236, 888
purposes, lxiv

Argumentative essay, 236

Assonance, 363

Atmosphere, R1

Audience, intended, 246

Author's influences, 806, R1

Author's perspective (point of view), 206, 310

Author's purpose, 205, 744

Author's style, 162, 297, 402, 884, R1

Autobiography, 224, R1

Ballad, 158, 361

Biography, 224, R1

Cause-and-effect organization, 257

Cause-and-effect relationship, 529

Chain of events, 18

Character, 16, 103, 526, 640, 773, 819, R1
comparing from different eras, 102–103
drama, 526
dynamic, 103, R2

flat, 36, R3
folk literature, 773
heroic, 819
history and, 103
main, R4
minor, R4
narrative essay, 208
round, 36
short story, 16
static, 103

Character development, 528

Characterization, 16, 18, R1
direct, 18
indirect, 18

Character's motivation, 16, 528, 596, R4
impact of setting on, 596

Character traits, 16, 36, 819, R1

Chronological order/organization, 18, 257

Claim (assertion)
evaluating, lxiv
evidence and, 740, 894
See also Argument.

Climax, 17, 20, 526, R1

Comedy, 527, R2

Comic relief, 527

Comparison-and-contrast organization, 257

Comparisons, 170

Complex character, 529

Concrete poem, R2

Conflict, 16, 17, 20, 474, 526, 528, 709, 773, R2
drama, 526, 528, 709
folk literature, 773
internal/external, 16, 528, 773, R2

Connotation, 150, 246, 363, 402, R2
poetry, 363, 402

Consonance, 363

Context, social or cultural, 320, 770, 772, 794

Couplet, 360

Cultural context. See Context, social or cultural.

Denotation, 246, 363, R2

Description, 414–415, R2
comparing types of, 414–415

Development, R2

Dialect, 782, R2

Dialogue, 18, 180, 526, 530, 640, R2
drama, 526, 530, 640

short story, 18
TV script, 180

Diary, 716

Diction, 488, R2
See also Word choice.

Direct characterization, 18

Drama, 526–529, R2
analyzing, 528–529
elements/types, 526–527

Dramatic irony, 529, 530

Dramatic poetry, 361

Elegy, 361

End rhyme, 364

Epic, 771

Epic poetry, 361

Essay, R2, 208, 236, 256–257
argumentative, 236
narrative, R2, 208
persuasive, R2
types, R2

Exaggeration, 158, 819
as part of oral tradition, 158

Explanatory nonfiction, 205

Exposition, 17, 20, R2
plot, 17, 20, R2

Extended metaphor, 362, R3

External conflict, 16, 528, 773, R3

External motivation, 596

External rhyme, 364

Evidence, 740, 894
See also Grounds.

Fable, 771, R3

Falling action, 17, 20

Fantasy, R3

Fiction, R3

Figurative language, 362, 376, 832, 857, R3
as element of style, 297
poetry, 362
types, 376, 832

Figurative meaning, 415

First-person point of view, 17, 50

Flashback, 18, R3

Flat character, 36, R3

Folk literature, 770–773
elements of, 770–771
theme, 772–773
See also American folk tradition.

Writing

Applications

Process

Speaking and Listening

Activities

Strategies

Research

Language Conventions

Vocabulary

Assessment

Index of Authors and Titles

The following authors and titles appear in the print and online versions of Pearson Literature.

The following authors and titles appear in the Online Literature Library.

Acknowledgments

Grateful acknowledgment is made to the following for copyrighted material:

Arte Publico Press From *My Own True Name* by Pat Mora. Copyright © 2000 Arte Publico Press-University of Houston. Published by Arte Publico Press. "Baseball" by Lionel G. Garcia from *I Can Hear the Cowbells Ring* (Houston: Arte Publico Press - University of Houston, 1994). Used by permission.

Ashabranner, Brent "Always to Remember: The Vision of Maya Ying Lin" by Brent Ashabranner from *Always to Remember.* Copyright © 1988. Used by permission of Brent Ashabranner.

Associated Press "Tutoring Benefits Seniors' Health, Students' Skills" by David Crary. Copyright © 2010. Used by permission of the Associated Press.

The Bancroft Library, Administrative Offices "Tears of Autumn" from *The Forbidden Stitch: An Asian American Women's Anthology* by Yoshiko Uchida. Copyright © 1989 by Yoshiko Uchida. Used by permission of the Bancroft Library, University of California, Berkeley.

Bantam Doubleday Dell Publishing Group, Inc. "A Wrinkle in Time" by Madeleine L'Engle Franklin from *Dell Publishing.* Copyright © 1962 by Madeleine L'Engle Franklin. All rights reserved.

Berkley Books From *A Small Enough Team to Do the Job* by Andrew Mishkin from *Sojourner.* Copyright © 2003 by Andrew Mishkin.

Black Issues Book Review "Zora Neale Hurston: A Life in Letters, Book Review" by Zakia Carter from *Black Issues Book Review, Nov-Dec 2002;* www.bibookreview.com. Used by permission.

Brandt & Hochman Literary Agents, Inc. "Invocation" from John Brown's Body by Stephen Vincent Benet Copyright © 1927, 1928 by Stephen Vincent Benet. Copyright renewed © 1955 by Rosemary Carr Benet. Any electronic copying or redistribution of the text is expressly forbidden. Used by permission of Brandt & Hochman Literary Agents, Inc.

Curtis Brown London "Who Can Replace a Man" by Brian Aldiss from *Masterpieces: The Best Science Fiction of the Century.* Copyright © 1966 by Brian Aldiss. Reproduced with permission of Curtis Brown Group Ltd, London on behalf of Brian Aldiss.

CBS Rights & Permissions From *Star Trek: The Next Generation,* "The Measure of a Man," #40272-135, 2nd Rev. Final Draft, by Melinda Snodgrass. Copyright © 1999. CBS Studios International.

Charlotte Observer "The Season's Curmudgeon Sees the Light" by Mary C. Curtis *www.charlotte.com.* © Copyright 2004 Knight Ridder. All Rights Reserved. Used by permission.

Cesar Chavez Foundation From "Address to the Commonwealth Club of San Francisco" by Cesar Chavez. Copyright © 1984. Used by permission of the Cesar Chavez Foundation. www.chavezfoundation. org

Child Health Association of Sewickley, Inc. "Thumbprint Cookies" from *Three Rivers Cookbook.* Copyright © Child Health Association of Sewickley, Inc. Used by permission.

Clarion Books, a division of Houghton Mifflin Excerpt from "Emancipation" from *Lincoln: A Photobiography.* Copyright © 1987 by Russell Freedman. Reproduced by permission of Clarion Books, an imprint of Houghton Mifflin Company.

Jonathan Clowes Ltd. "The Adventure of the Speckled Band" from *The Adventure Of The Speckled Band.* Copyright © 1996 Sir Arthur Conan Doyle Copyright Holders. Used with kind permission of Jonathan Clowes Ltd., London, on behalf of Andrea Plunket, the Administrator of the Conan Doyle Copyrights.

Cobblestone Publishing "Julie and the Turing Test" by Linda Formichelli. Copyright © 1997, pp. 28–29 in *Odyssey* magazine, Vol. 6, Iss. 9, Dec97. Carus Publishing.

Ruth Cohen Literary Agency, Inc. "Fox Hunt" by Lensey Namioka, copyright © 1993 from *Join In: Multi-Ethnic Short Stories by Outstanding Writers for Young Adults,* edited by Donald R. Gallo. Used by permission of Lensey Namioka. All rights are reserved by the Author.

Don Congdon Associates, Inc. "The Drummer Boy of Shiloh" by Ray Bradbury published in *Saturday Evening Post April 30, 1960.* Copyright © 1960 by the Curtis Publishing Company, renewed © 1988 by Ray Bradbury.

Copper Canyon Press c/o The Permissions Company "Snake on the Etowah" by David Bottoms from *Armored Hearts: Selected and New Poems.* Copyright © 1995 by David Bottoms. Used by the permission of Copper Canyon Press, www.copppercanyonpress.org. All rights reserved.

Gary N. DaSilva for Neil Simon "The Governess" from *The Good Doctor* © 1974 by Neil Simon. Copyright renewed © 2002 by Neil Simon. Used by permission. CAUTION: Professionals and amateurs are hereby warned that *The Good Doctor* is fully protected under the Berne Convention and the Universal Copyright Convention and is subject to royalty. All rights, including without limitation professional, amateur, motion picture, television, radio, recitation, lecturing, public reading and foreign translation rights, computer media rights and the right of reproduction, and electronic storage or retrieval, in whole or in part and in any form, are strictly reserved and none of these rights can be exercised or used without written permission from the copyright owner. Inquiries for stock and amateur performances should be addressed to Samuel French, Inc., 45 West 25th Street, New York, NY 10010. All other inquiries should be addressed to Gary N. DaSilva, 111 N. Sepulveda Blvd., Suite 250, Manhattan Beach, CA 90266-6850.

Disney-Hyperion Books for Children "Words We Live By: Your Annotated Guide to the Constitution" by Linda R. Monk from *The Stonesong Press.* Copyright © 2003 Linda R. Monk and The Stonesong Press, Inc. All rights reserved.

Doubleday "Table of Contents and Index Page" from *Zora Neale Hurston: A Life In Letters* Carla Kaplan. From *The Diary of a Young Girl: The Definitive Edition* by Anne Frank, edited by Otto H. Frank and Mirjam Pressler. Translated by Susan Massotty. Copyright © 1995 by Doubleday, a division of Random House, Inc. Used by permission of Doubleday, a division of Random House, Inc.

Dramatic Publishing From *Anne Frank & Me* by Cherie Bennett with Jeff Gottesfeld. Copyright © 1997 by Cherie Bennett. Printed in the United States of America. Used by permission. CAUTION: Professionals and amateurs are hereby warned that *Anne Frank & Me,* being fully protected under the copyright Laws of the United States of America, the British Empire, including the Dominion of Canada, and all other countries of the Universal Copyright and Berne Conventions, are subject to royalty. All rights, including professional, amateur, motion picture, recitation, lecturing, public reading, radio and television broadcasting, and the rights of translation into foreign

Forum, SUNY. Copyright © 1985 by Reader's Digest and Robert MacNeil. Used by permission of Robert MacNeil.

Eve Merriam c/o Marian Reiner "Thumbprint" from *A Sky Full of Poems* by Eve Merriam. Copyright © 1964, 1970, 1973, 1986 by Eve Merriam. Used by permission of Marian Reiner.

The Miami Herald Miami Herald Editorial: *Don't Refuse This Deal* from *Miami Herald Online Tuesday, March 29, 2005* http://capefish. blogspot.com/2005/03/miami-herald-editorial-dont-refuse.html. Copyright © 2005 by McClatchy Interactive West. Used by permission of McClatchy Interactive West via Copyright Clearance Center.

N. Scott Momaday "New World" by N. Scott Momaday from *The Gourd Dancers.* Used with the permission of Navarre Scott Momaday.

William Morris Agency "Flowers for Algernon" (short story version edited for this edition) by Daniel Keyes. Copyright © 1959 & 1987 by Daniel Keyes. Expanded story published in paperback by Bantam Books. Used by permission of William Morris Agency, LLC on behalf of the author.

William Morrow & Company, Inc., a division of HarperCollins "The Drum (for Martin Luther King, Jr.)" from *Those Who Ride the Night Winds* by Nikki Giovanni. Copyright © 1983 by Nikki Giovanni. Used by permission of William Morrow & Company, Inc., a division of HarperCollins Publishers, Inc.

Museum of New Mexico Press "Chicoria" by Jose Griego Y Maestas y Rudolfo Anaya from *Cuentos: Tales from the Hispanic Southwest.* Reproduced by permission of Museum of New Mexico Press.

National Public Radio "Profile: World War II veterans who founded the Paralyzed Veterans of America" from *National Public Radio, November 11, 2003.* Copyright © 2005 National Public Radio. Used by permission. All rights reserved.

New College of Florida New College of Florida Work-Study Contract from *http://www.ncf.edu/index.html.* Copyright © 2001-2006 New College of Florida. Used by permission.

Naomi Shihab Nye "Words to Sit in, Like Chairs" by Naomi Shihab Nye from *911: The Book of Help.* "Hamadi" by Naomi Shihab Nye from *America Street.* Used by permission of the author, Naomi Shihab Nye.

Harold Ober Associates, Inc. "Cat!" by Eleanor Farjeon from *Poems For Children.* Copyright © 1938 by Eleanor Farjeon, renewed 1966 by Gervase Farjeon. Used by permission of Harold Ober Associates Incorporated. All rights reserved.

Office of the Governor Arnold Schwarzenegger "Transcript of Governor Arnold Schwarzenegger Signing Legislation Requiring Drivers to Use Hand Free Devices" from *http://gov.ca.gov/index.php?/speech/4116/.* Copyright © 2000-2007 State of California. Used by permission.

Oxford University Press, Inc. "Summary of The Tell-Tale Heart" by James D. Hart from *The Oxford Companion To American Literature.* Copyright © 1983. Used by permission of Oxford University Press, Inc. www.oup.co.uk.

Pantheon Books, a division of Random House Inc. "Coyote Steals the Sun and Moon" by Richard Erdoes and Alfonso Ortiz from *American Indian Myths and Legends,* copyright © 1984 by Richard Erdoes and Alfonso Ortiz. Used by permission of Pantheon Books, a division of Random House, Inc.

Pearson Prentice Hall "Series Circuits and Parallel Circuits" from *Prentice Hall Science Explorer Physical Science.* Copyright © 2005 by Pearson Education, Inc. or its affiliate(s). "The War in Vietnam" from *The American Nation* by Dr. James West Davidson and

Dr. Michael B. Stoff. Copyright © 2003 by Pearson Education, Inc., publishing as Prentice Hall. Used by permission.

Penguin Group (UK), Inc. & Curtis Brown From "The History of the Peloponnesian War" by Thucydides, translated by Rex Warner, with an introduction and notes by M.I. Finley (Penguin Classics 1954, Revised edition 1972). Translation copyright © Rex Warner, 1954. Introduction and Appendices copyright © M.I. Finley, 1972.

Penguin Group (USA), Inc. "Kindertransport" by Diane Samuels from *Plume.* Copyright © Diane Samuels, 1995. All rights reserved.

Perseus Books Group "Vanishing Species" from *Sleeping At The Starlight Motel And Other Adventures On The Way Back Home* by Bailey White. Used by permission of Da Capo Press, a member of Perseus Books Group.

Pew Research Center "The Return of the Multi-Generational Family Household." Copyright © 2010. Used by permission of the Pew Research Center, Social and Demographic Trends Project. http://www.pewsocialtrends.org/2010/03/18/the-return-of-the-multi-generational-family-household/

Placer County Museums Placer County Museum Job Description & Volunteer Application from *http://www.placer.ca.gov.* Copyright © 2006 County of Placer, CA. Used by permission.

Puffin Books From The One Who Watches by Judith Ortiz Cofer from *An Island Like You.* Copyright © Judith Ortiz Cofer 1995.

G.P. Putnam's Sons "Describe Somebody," and "Almost Summer Sky" from *Locomotion* by Jacqueline Woodson, copyright © 2003 by Jacqueline Woodson. Used by permission of G.P. Putnam's Sons, A Division of Penguin Young Readers Group, A Member of Penguin Group (USA) Inc., 345 Hudson Street, New York, NY 10014. All rights reserved. From *Hush* by Jacqueline Woodson. Copyright © 2002 by Jacqueline Woodson. From *Anne Frank and Me* by Cherie Bennett and Jeff Gottesfeld. Copyright © 2001 by Cherie Bennett and Jeff Gottesfeld.

Moumin Manzoor Quazi "Migrant Birds" by Moumin Manzoor Quazi from *Is This Forever, or What? Poems and Paintings from Texas.* Copyright © 2004 by Moumin Manzoor Quazi.

Random House, Inc. From *I Know Why the Caged Bird Sings* by Maya Angelou, copyright © 1969 and renewed © 1997 by Maya Angelou. "Raymond's Run" by Toni Cade Bambara from *Gorilla, My Love.* Copyright © 1971 by Toni Cade Bambara. "Why Leaves Turn Color in the Fall" from *A Natural History of the Senses* by Diane Ackerman. Copyright © 1990 by Diane Ackerman. *The Diary of Anne Frank* by Frances Goodrich and Albert Hackett. Copyright © 1956 by Albert Hackett, Frances Goodrich Hackett and Otto Frank. CAUTION: Professionals and amateurs are hereby warned that *The Diary of Anne Frank,* being fully protected under the copyright Laws of the United States of America, the British Empire, including the Dominion of Canada, and all other countries of the Universal Copyright and Berne Conventions, are subject to royalty. All rights, including professional, amateur, motion picture, recitation, lecturing, public reading, radio and television broadcasting, and the rights of translation into foreign languages, are strictly reserved. All inquiries should be addressed to Random House, Inc. Used by permission of Random House, Inc. "The Blue Stones" by Isak Dinesen from *Winter's Tales.* Copyright © 1942 by Random House, Inc. All rights reserved under International and Pan-American Copyright Conventions.

Marian Reiner, Literary Agent "Concrete Mixers" by Patricia Hubbell from *8 A.M. Shadows.* Copyright © 1965 Patricia Hubbell. Copyright renewed © 1993 Patricia Hubbell. Used by permission of Marian Reiner on behalf of the author.

Vital Speeches of the Day From *Sharing in the American Dream* by Colin Powell from *Vital Speeches, June 1, 1997, V63 N16, P484(2)*. Used by permission of Vital Speeches of the Day.

W. W. Norton & Company, Inc. "Water Names" from *Hunger* by Lan Samantha Chang. Copyright © 1998 by Lan Samantha Chang. Used by permission of W. W. Norton & Company, Inc. (From San by Lan Samantha Chang from *Hunger*. Copyright © 1998 by Lan Samantha Chang.)

Walker & Company "The Baker Heater League" by Patricia and Frederick McKissack from *A Long Hard Journey: The Story of the Pullman Porter*. Copyright © 1989 by Patricia and Frederick McKissack. Used with permission of Walker & Company.

Water Taxi, Inc. Fort Lauderdale Water Taxi™ Map and Schedule from *http://www.watertaxi.com*. Copyright © 2002 - 2007 Water Taxi, Inc. All Rights Reserved. Used by permission.

Western State College of Colorado "Relationships to Place" from "What Is Sense of Place?" by Jennifer E. Cross. Copyright © 2001. Used by permission of the Western State College of Colorado. http://www.western.edu/academics/headwaters/headwaters-conference/archives/cross_headwatersXII.pdf

Richard & Joyce Wolkomir "Sun Suckers and Moon Cursers" by Richard and Joyce Wolkomir. Copyright © 2002 by Richard & Joyce Wolkomir. Used with the authors' permission.

Elie Wiesel From "Remarks on a Visit to Buchenwald" by Elie Wiesel. Copyright © 2009. Elie Wiesel.

Credits

Progressive Image/Corbis; 784 Underwood & Underwood/Corbis; 786 Polina Katritch/Shutterstock; 790 Lake County Museum/CORBIS; 794 Craig Line/AP Images; 796 National Archives and Records Administration; 798 (TL) Library of Congress, (BR) National Archives and Records Administration, (BC) Bettmann/Corbis, 798 (BL) Bettman/Corbis; 798 (CR) Bettmann/Corbis, (TR) Icon Communications/Getty Images; 799 AP Images; 801 Bettmann/Corbis; 814 Katerine Wetzel/The Museum of the Confederacy; 806 Bettmann/Corbis; 808 Art Resource; 811 The Granger Collection, New York; 812 Bettmann/Corbis; 818 (BL) The Granger Collection, New York, (CL) Time Life Pictures/Getty Images, (TL) Burstein Collection/Corbis; 820 Bettmann/CORBIS; 821 Anders Ryman/Corbis; 823 Louella938/Shutterstock; 824 Blank Archives/Getty Images; 825 (TR) iStockphoto, (CR) Patrick Hattori/epa/Corbis; 826 (CL) John Wang/Photodisc/Getty Images, (TC) Andrea Salcioli/ Photodisc/Getty Images, (TL) James Randklev/Photodisc/Getty Images, (TR) Connie Coleman/Getty Images; 828 (Bkgrnd) John Hoffman/Shutterstock, (TR) iStockphoto; 829 (TL) iStockphoto, (TR) iStockPhoto; 850 Bettmann/Corbis; 852 ASSOCIATED PRESS; 853 (TL) Corel Professional Photos CD-ROM™; 855 Time Life Pictures/Getty Images; 860 In Harriet Tubman I Helped Hundreds to Freedom, Elizabeth Catlett, Collection of Hampton University Museum, Hampton, Virginia; 863 Library of Congress; 866 Alexander Graham/Bettmann/Corbis; 868 Corbis; 871 Randy Duchaine/Alamy; 874 (TL) Bettmann/Corbis; 876 Bettmann/Corbis; 878 Carl Iwasaki/Getty Images; 882 Library of Congress; 886 The Granger Collection, New York; 890 Bettmann/Corbis; 893 Najlah Feanny/Corbis.

Staff Credits

Dori Amtmann, Tricia Battipede, Rachel Beckman, Nancy Bolsover, Laura Brancky, Odette Calderon, Pam Carey, Kelly Casanova, Geoff Cassar, Jessica Cohn, Sarah Cunningham. Anthony DeSacia, Kim Doster, Irene Ehrmann, Andy Ekedahl, Sandy Engleman, Samantha Fahy, Janet Fauser, Amy Fleming, Pam Gallo, Mark Gangi, Nicole Gee, Susan Graef, Leslie Griffin, Elaine Goldman, Brian Hawkes, Steve Hernacki, Martha Heller, Amanda House, Rick Hickox, Patricia Isaza, Etta Jacobs, Blair Jones, Jim Kelly, Nathan Kinney, Sarah Kraus, Gregory Lynch, Nancy Mace, Jim McPherson, Charles Morris, Pa Moua, Elizabeth Nielsen, Kim Ortell, Kathleen Pagliaro, Jennie Rakos, Sheila Ramsay, Karen Randazzo, Julianne Regnier, Christopher Richardson, Melissa Schreiner, Hillary Schwei, Jeff Shagawat, Susan Sheehan, Charlene Smith, DeAnn Smith, Sheila Smith, Cynthia Summers, Morgan Taylor, Brian Thomas, Lucia Tirondola, Karen Tully, Merle Uuesoo, Kristen Varina, Jackie Westbrook, Jessica White